"As readers of Scripture we long to know the message of the Bible as a whole. We do not want to miss the forest for the trees. Unfortunately, there are few books that help us to be faithful to the whole counsel of God. What a delight, then, to read Jim Hamilton's book where the story line of the Scriptures is unfolded. Hamilton rightly sees that the glory of God is at the center of the scriptural record, demonstrating with careful attention to the biblical text the supremacy of God in both the Old Testament and the New. Scholars, students, and laypeople will all profit from reading this work, which instructs the mind, enlivens the heart, and summons us to obedience."

Thomas R. Schreiner, James Buchanan Harrison Professor
of New Testament Interpretation,
The Southern Baptist Theological Seminary

"In an era when centers in general no longer hold, Hamilton makes a strong case for the centrality to biblical theology of what C. H. Dodd called the 'two-beat rhythm' of biblical history: salvation through judgment. Hamilton discovers this theme in every book of the Bible and argues that it is the heartbeat of God's ultimate purpose: the publication of his glory. In seeking to do justice to scriptural unity and diversity alike, Hamilton's work represents biblical theology at its best."

Kevin Vanhoozer, Blanchard Professor of Theology,
Wheaton College Graduate School

"Centered on the important themes of salvation and judgment, Hamilton's book models well how a thematic approach toward biblical theology might be applied to the whole of Scripture. It is to be warmly welcomed as an invitation to reflect on biblical truth and an opportunity to dialogue on how the unity of the Old and New Testaments may be articulated best."

T. Desmond Alexander, Senior Lecturer in Biblical Studies
and Director of Postgraduate Studies, Union Theological College

"Who said that the search for a center in biblical theology is a dead end? In this bold and courageous book, which deals with the entire Bible, James Hamilton Jr. dons the mantle of an explorer in search of the holy grail of biblical theology. As he journeys through the Bible, there are many sights in the biblical landscape that will arrest the attention of those who accompany him, including the pivotal revelation of God in Exodus 34:6–7. Hamilton's thoughtful analysis and reflection provide many insights into the biblical text. While you may not agree with all of his conclusions, you won't come back from your journey with him without a greater sense of God's majesty and glory. Rather than being a dead end, this is a gateway into a new world."

Stephen Dempster, Stuart E. Murray Associate Professor
of Religious Studies, Atlantic Baptist University

GOD'S GLORY IN SALVATION THROUGH JUDGMENT

GOD'S GLORY IN SALVATION THROUGH JUDGMENT

A Biblical Theology

JAMES M. HAMILTON JR.

CROSSWAY

WHEATON, ILLINOIS

God's Glory in Salvation through Judgment: A Biblical Theology

Published by Crossway
1300 Crescent Street
Wheaton, Illinois 60187

Cover design: Amy Bristow
Cover photo: The Delivery of Israel—Pharaoh and his hosts overwhelmed in the Red Sea, 1825, by Francis Danby (1793–1861); © Harris Museum and Art Gallery, Preston, Lancashire, UK/The Bridgeman Art Library
Interior Design and Typesetting: Lakeside Design Plus

First printing 2010
Printed in the United States of America

Unless otherwise noted, translations of the biblical text are my own. I have sometimes used the English Standard Version as a base text, altering it somewhat, and always changing "Lord" to "Yahweh."

Hardcover ISBN:	978-1-58134-976-4
PDF ISBN:	978-1-4335-2133-1
Mobipocket ISBN:	978-1-4335-2134-8
ePub ISBN:	978-1-4335-2135-5

Library of Congress Cataloging-in-Publication Data
Hamilton, James M., 1974–
God's glory in salvation through judgment : a biblical theology / James M. Hamilton Jr.
p. cm.
Includes bibliographical references and index.
ISBN 978-1-58134-976-4 (hc)—ISBN 978-1-4335-2133-1 (pdf)—ISBN 978-1-4335-2134-8 (mobipocket)—ISBN 978-1-4335-2135-5 (ePub)
1. Bible—Theology. 2. Salvation—Christianity. 3. Judgment of God. 4. Glory of God—Christianity. I. Title.
BS543.H335 2010
234—dc22
2010021879

Crossway is a publishing ministry of Good News Publishers.

SH 21 20 19 18 17 16 15 14 13 12 11
14 13 12 11 10 9 8 7 6 5 4 3 2

For my mom and dad
who led me to know
the God who is glorified
in salvation through judgment

CONTENTS

Analytical Outline 11

List of Illustrations 21

Acknowledgments 25

A Strategy for Reading This Book 29

Abbreviations 31

1. Can the Center Hold? 37
2. *God's Glory in Salvation through Judgment* in the Torah 67
3. *God's Glory in Salvation through Judgment* in the Prophets 139
4. *God's Glory in Salvation through Judgment* in the Writings 271
5. *God's Glory in Salvation through Judgment* in the Gospels and Acts 355
6. *God's Glory in Salvation through Judgment* in the Letters of the New Testament 443
7. *God's Glory in Salvation through Judgment* in Revelation 541
8. *God's Glory in Salvation through Judgment* and Objections to Its Centrality 553

9. *God's Glory in Salvation through Judgment* in Ministry Today 565

Selected Bibliography 573

General Index 589

Scripture Index 607

ANALYTICAL OUTLINE

Chapter 1. Can the Center Hold?

1 Introduction
2 Do Things Fall Apart? (Is There a Unity in the Bible's Diversity?)
2.1 Finding Our Way in the Widening Gyre: The History and Purpose of Biblical Theology
2.2 How Do We Define the Center of Biblical Theology?
2.3 How Do We Identify the Center of Biblical Theology?
3 Mere Anarchy Is Loosed upon the World: The Plethora of Proposed Centers
4 The World Is Charged with the Grandeur of God: Proposed Centers and the Center
5 "Salvation through Judgment to the Glory of God": What Does This Phrase Mean?
6 Like Shining from Shook Foil

Chapter 2. God's Glory in Salvation through Judgment in the Torah

1 Introduction
1.1 The Story of Torah Book by Book
2 Genesis
2.1 The Heavens Proclaim the Glory of God
2.1.1 The Gods of the Nations
2.1.2 The Purity and Power of the God of the Bible
2.1.3 Gender for the Glory of God
2.1.4 The Primeval Temple
2.2 Paradise Lost
2.3 Blessing and Cursing, Judging and Saving
2.4 The Justice of God: Genesis 3:15

2.5 The Justice of God: Genesis 3:16
2.6 The Justice of God: Genesis 3:17–19
2.7 The Mercy of God: The Seed of the Woman
2.8 The Center of the Theology of Genesis
3 Exodus
3.1 Salvation through Judgment at the Exodus
3.2 From Egypt to Sinai
3.3 At Sinai
3.4 The Glorious Name: Exodus 32–34
3.5 The Center of the Theology of Exodus
4 Leviticus
Excursus: Leviticus 18 and Deuteronomy 30 in Romans 10
4.1 The Center of the Theology of Leviticus
5 Numbers
5.1 The Center of the Theology of Numbers
6 Deuteronomy
6.1 From Sinai to Moab
6.2 Motivation to Obey
6.2.1 Reasons to Obey
6.2.2 Out of the Midst of the Fire
6.2.3 Israel's Heart Problem
6.2.4 Life under Law
6.3 The Covenant Stipulations
6.4 Moses' Last Will and Testament
6.5 The Center of the Theology of Deuteronomy
7 The Center of the Theology of the Torah
8 Appendix: Exodus 34:6–7 in the Law, Prophets, and Writings
8.1 Exodus 34:6–7 in the Law
8.2 Exodus 34:6–7 in the Prophets
8.3 Exodus 34:6–7 in the Writings
8.4 Less Certain Allusions
8.4.1 In the Law
8.4.2 In the Prophets
8.4.3 In the Writings

Chapter 3. God's Glory in Salvation through Judgment in the Prophets

1 Introduction
2 The Former Prophets: Joshua–Kings
2.1 The Former Prophets Book by Book
2.2 Joshua
2.2.1 Crossing Over into the Land
2.2.2 Taking the Land

2.2.3 Dividing the Land
2.2.4 Serving in the Land
2.2.5 The Center of the Theology of Joshua
2.3 Judges
2.3.1 Failure to Complete the Conquest
2.3.2 The Accounts of the Judges
2.3.3 No King, No Restraint
2.3.4 The Center of the Theology of Judges
2.4 Samuel
2.4.1 Samuel
2.4.2 Saul
2.4.3 David
2.4.3.1 Unexpected Salvation
2.4.3.2 No Place to Lay His Head
2.4.3.3 Kingdom and Covenant
2.4.3.4 Sin and Its Consequences
2.4.3.5 The Site of the Temple
2.4.4 The Center of the Theology of Samuel
2.5 Kings
2.5.1 David and His Sons
2.5.2 Solomon, Temple, Idolatry
2.5.3 Divided Kingdom
2.5.4 Judah
2.5.5 The Center of the Theology of Kings
2.6 The Center of the Theology of the Former Prophets
3 The Latter Prophets: Isaiah–Malachi
3.1 The Latter Prophets Book by Book
3.2 Isaiah
3.2.1 Present Sin and Future Hope (Isaiah 1–5)
3.2.2 The Call of Isaiah (Isaiah 6)
3.2.3 The Book of Immanuel: Trust God Not Assyria (Isaiah 7–12)
3.2.4 Oracles against the Nations (Isaiah 13–23)
3.2.5 Isaiah's Apocalypse (Isaiah 24–27)
3.2.6 Assyria, Egypt, and Yahweh (Isaiah 28–35)
3.2.7 The Deliverance of Hezekiah (Isaiah 36–39)
3.2.8 The Incomparable Yahweh (Isaiah 40–48)
3.2.9 The Suffering Servant (Isaiah 49–55)
3.2.10 Future Deliverance (Isaiah 56–66)
3.2.11 The Center of the Theology of Isaiah
3.3 Jeremiah
3.3.1 The Call of Jeremiah (Jeremiah 1)
3.3.2 Early Oracles Calling for Repentance and Announcing Judgment (Jeremiah 2–6)

3.3.3 Increasingly Inevitable Judgment and Jeremiah's "Confessions" (Jeremiah 7–20)
3.3.4 The House of David and the Basket of Figs (Jeremiah 21–24)
3.3.5 Hope beyond Exile (Jeremiah 25–33): Book of Consolation and New Covenant (30–33)
3.3.6 Rejection of Yahweh's Word and Exile (Jeremiah 34–45)
3.3.7 The Oracles against the Nations (Jeremiah 46–51)
3.3.8 Jeremiah's Prophecies Come to Pass (Jeremiah 52)
3.3.9 The Center of the Theology of Jeremiah
3.4 Ezekiel
3.4.1 Salvation through Judgment for God's Glory in Ezekiel
3.4.2 Yahweh Acts for His Own Sake
3.4.3 The Center of the Theology of Ezekiel
3.5 The Book of the Twelve
3.5.1 Hosea
3.5.2 Joel
3.5.3 Amos
3.5.4 Obadiah
3.5.5 Jonah
3.5.6 Micah
3.5.7 Nahum
3.5.8 Habakkuk
3.5.9 Zephaniah
3.5.10 Haggai
3.5.11 Zechariah
3.5.12 Malachi
3.5.13 The Center of the Theology of the Twelve
3.6 The Center of the Theology of the Latter Prophets
4 The Center of the Theology of the Prophets
5 Appendix 1: The Order of the Twelve
6 Appendix 2: All the Earth Filled with the Knowledge of Yahweh's Glory

Chapter 4. God's Glory in Salvation through Judgment in the Writings

1 Introduction
1.1 Wisdom Literature and Biblical Theology
1.2 The Canonical Context of the Writings
2 The Book of Truth: Psalms, Proverbs, Job
2.1 The Book of Truth Book by Book
2.2 Psalms
2.2.1 Book 1, Psalms 1–41
2.2.2 Book 2, Psalms 42–72
2.2.3 Book 3, Psalms 73–89
2.2.4 Book 4, Psalms 90–106

2.2.5 Book 5, Psalms 107–150
2.2.6 The Center of the Theology of Psalms
2.3 Proverbs
2.3.1 Proverbs of Solomon: Parental Teaching to Escape Wicked Men and Wayward Women (Proverbs 1–9)
2.3.2 Proverbs of Solomon: The Way the World Works (Proverbs 10–22:16)
2.3.3 Thirty Sayings of the Wise: How to Relate to Other People (Prov. 22:17–24:22)
2.3.4 More Sayings of the Wise: Justice and Home Economics (Prov. 24:23–34)
2.3.5 Proverbs of Solomon Copied by Hezekiah's Men: The Glory of God and the Glory of Kings (Proverbs 25–29)
2.3.6 The Words of Agur: Humble Descriptions of the World (Proverbs 30)
2.3.7 The Words of King Lemuel: Nobility and the Virtuous Wife (Proverbs 31)
2.3.8 The Center of the Theology of Proverbs
2.4 Job
2.4.1 Yahweh's Challenge to Satan about Job (Job 1–2)
2.4.2 Job's Lament (Job 3)
2.4.3 Job and His Counselors (Job 4–25)
2.4.4 Job Extols God's Majesty (Job 26–31)
2.4.5 Elihu's Speech (Job 32–37)
2.4.6 Yahweh's Response (Job 38–42)
2.6.7 The Center of the Theology of Job
3 The *Megilloth* (Small Scrolls): Song of Songs, Ruth, Lamentations, Ecclesiastes, Esther
3.1 The *Megilloth* Book by Book
3.2 Song of Songs
3.3 Ruth
3.4 Lamentations
3.5 Ecclesiastes
3.5.1 The Riddle of the Numbers
3.5.2 The Messianic Wisdom of a Beautiful Mind
3.5.3 Matching Poems on the "Circle of Life" and "Youth and Old Age" (Eccles. 1:2–11; 11:7–12:8)
3.5.4 What Is Good for Man to Do? (Eccles. 1:12–6:9)
3.5.5 Man's Inability to Understand God's Work (Eccles. 6:10–11:6)
3.5.6 All Has Been Heard: The Conclusion of the Matter (Eccles. 12:9–14)
3.5.7 The Center of the Theology of Ecclesiastes
3.6 Esther

4 Other Sacred Writings: Daniel, Ezra–Nehemiah, Chronicles
4.1 The Other Sacred Writings Book by Book
4.2 Daniel
4.2.1 Daniel Exiled (Daniel 1)
4.2.2 Nebuchadnezzar's Vision: Statue Representing Four Kingdoms (Daniel 2)
4.2.3 Deliverance from the Fiery Furnace (Daniel 3)
4.2.4 Nebuchadnezzar Humbled: Seven Years of Insanity (Daniel 4)
4.2.5 Belshazzar Humbled: Weighed and Found Wanting (Daniel 5)
4.2.6 Deliverance from the Lion's Den (Daniel 6)
4.2.7 Daniel's Visions: Four Kingdoms Represented in Various Ways (Daniel 7–9)
4.2.8 Daniel's Vision of the End of the Exile (Daniel 10–12)
4.2.9 The Center of the Theology of Daniel
4.3 Ezra–Nehemiah
4.4 Chronicles
4.4.1 Genealogies (1 Chronicles 1–9)
4.4.2 Saul (1 Chronicles 10)
4.4.3 David (1 Chronicles 11–29)
4.4.4 Solomon (2 Chronicles 1–9)
4.4.5 Kings of Judah (2 Chronicles 10–36)
4.4.6 The Center of the Theology of Chronicles
5 The Center of the Theology of the Writings
6 The Center of Old Testament Theology
7 Appendix: Old Testament Prayers Appealing to God's Concern for His Own Glory

Chapter 5. God's Glory in Salvation through Judgment in the Gospels and Acts

1 Introduction
2 The Gospels and Acts Book by Book
3 Matthew
3.1 Jesus Relives the History of Israel (Matthew 1–2)
3.2 Call to Kingdom Repentance (Matthew 3–4)
3.3 The Message of the Kingdom (Matthew 5–7)
3.4 Mighty Works That Confirm the Teaching (Matthew 8–9)
3.5 Gathering the Lost Sheep of the House of Israel (Matthew 10)
3.6 Rising Opposition (Matthew 11–12)
3.7 Kingdom Parables (Matthew 13)
3.8 Jesus on Mission (Matthew 14–17)
3.9 Discipleship (Matthew 18)
3.10 Entering Jerusalem (Matthew 19–23)

3.11 The Olivet Discourse (Matthew 24–25)
3.12 Passion, Resurrection, Commission (Matthew 26–28)
3.13 The Center of the Theology of Matthew
4 Mark
4.1 The Baptist and Jesus (Mark 1:1–13)
4.2 Jesus in Galilee (Mark 1:14–8:30)
4.3 Jesus on the Way to Jerusalem (Mark 8:31–10:52)
4.4 Jesus in Jerusalem (Mark 11:1–16:8 [20])
4.5 The Center of the Theology of Mark
5 Luke
5.1 Preparation for Jesus' Ministry (Luke 1–3)
5.2 Temptation and Beginning of Jesus' Public Ministry (Luke 4)
5.3 Ministry in Galilee (Luke 5–9)
5.4 On the Way to Jerusalem (Luke 9:51–19:27)
5.5 In Jerusalem: Arrest, Crucifixion, Resurrection, Commission (Luke 19:28–24:53)
5.6 The Center of the Theology of Luke
6 John
6.1 Prologue (John 1:1–18)
6.2 The Book of Signs (John 1:19–12:50)
6.3 The Book of Glory (John 13–20)
6.4 Epilogue (John 21)
6.5 The Center of the Theology of John
7 Acts
7.1 Witness to the Resurrection in Jerusalem (Acts 1–7)
7.2 Witness to the Resurrection in Judea and Samaria (Acts 8–12)
7.3 Witness to the Resurrection to the Ends of the Earth (Acts 13–28)
7.3.1 Paul's First Journey (Acts 13–14)
7.3.2 The Jerusalem Council (Acts 15)
7.3.3 Paul's Second Journey (Acts 16–18)
7.3.4 Paul's Third Journey (Acts 19–21)
7.3.5 Paul's Captivity and Transfer to Rome (Acts 22–28)
7.4 The Center of the Theology of Acts
8 The Center of the Theology of the Gospels and Acts
9 Appendix: Baptism in the New Testament

Chapter 6. God's Glory in Salvation through Judgment in the Letters of the New Testament

1 Introduction
2 Paul's Letters
2.1 Paul's Letters Book by Book
2.2 Romans

2.2.1 An Overview of the Argument of Romans
2.2.2 God's Glory in Salvation through Judgment in Romans
2.2.2.1 God's Glory in Romans
2.2.2.2 Salvation through Judgment in Romans
2.3 First Corinthians
2.3.1 Schisms (1 Corinthians 1–4)
2.3.2 Sexual Immorality (1 Corinthians 5–7)
2.3.3 Idolatry (1 Corinthians 8–10)
2.3.4 Worship (1 Corinthians 11–14)
2.3.5 Resurrection (1 Corinthians 15)
2.3.6 Travel Plans (1 Corinthians 16)
2.4 Second Corinthians
2.4.1 The Attack on Paul by His Opponents
2.4.2 Paul's Response to the Attack
2.4.3 Salvation through Judgment for God's Glory in Second Corinthians
2.4.3.1 Paul's Gospel
2.4.3.2 Paul's Own Life and Suffering
2.4.3.3 Paul's Ministry and Message
2.4.3.4 Corinthian Repentance and Future Judgment
2.5 Galatians
2.5.1 Deliverance in Christ for God's Glory (Gal. 1:1–5)
2.5.2 The Problem in Galatia (Gal. 1:6–10)
2.5.3 Paul's Gospel from God, Not Man (Gal. 1:11–2:21)
2.5.4 Paul's Gospel Proved by Experience and Scripture (Gal. 3:1–4:11)
2.5.5 Call to Freedom in the Spirit (Gal. 4:12–6:10)
2.5.6 Boasting Only in the Cross (Gal. 6:11–18)
2.6 Ephesians
2.7 Philippians
2.8 Colossians
2.8.1 The Glory of Christ in Colossians
2.8.2 The Colossians "in Christ" by Faith
2.8.3 God Accomplished Salvation through Judgment in the Glorious Christ
2.9 First Thessalonians
2.10 Second Thessalonians
2.11 First Timothy
2.12 Second Timothy
2.13 Titus
2.14 Philemon
2.15 The Center of Paul's Theology

3 Catholic Epistles
3.1 Other Letters Book by Book
3.2 Hebrews
3.2.1 The Glory of God in Christ in the Opening Lines of Hebrews
3.2.2 The Narrative Substructure of Hebrews
3.2.3 Salvation through Judgment for God's Glory in Hebrews
3.3 James
3.4 First Peter
3.4.1 The New Exodus: Praise God and Be Ye Holy (1 Pet. 1:1–2:10)
3.4.2 Submitting and Suffering Sojourners (1 Pet. 2:11–4:11)
3.4.3 Shepherded through Messianic Woes to Glory (1 Pet. 4:12–5:14)
3.5 Second Peter
3.6 First John
3.6.1 The World
3.6.2 Apostates
3.6.3 God Works Salvation in Christ
3.6.4 The Application of Salvation to Worldlings
3.6.5 The New Life
3.7 Second John
3.8 Third John
3.9 Jude
3.10 The Center of the Theology of the Catholic Epistles
4 The Center of the Theology of the New Testament Letters
5 Appendix: Doxologies in the New Testament

Chapter 7. God's Glory in Salvation through Judgment in Revelation
1 Introduction
2 An Overview of the Contents of Revelation
3 The Chiastic Structure of Revelation
4 The New Exodus and Return from Exile in Revelation
5 The Center of the Theology of Revelation
6 The Center of New Testament and Biblical Theology

Chapter 8. God's Glory in Salvation through Judgment and Objections to Its Centrality
1 Introduction
2 Method and Biblical Theology
2.1 Progressive Revelation?
2.2 The Metaphor of a Center?
2.3 Persuasive Definition?
2.4 The Discussion Continues

3 Particular Texts and Biblical Theology
3.1 God's Purpose and the Biblical Authors
3.2 One-Sided Expressions?
3.3 Learning from the Biblical Authors
4 Theology Proper and Biblical Theology
4.1 God's Love and His Pursuit of His Glory
4.2 The Justice of God
4.3 Can There Be More than One Ultimate Purpose?
5 Conclusion

Chapter 9. God's Glory in Salvation through Judgment in Ministry Today
1 Introduction
2 Church Ministry
2.1 Evangelism
2.2 Discipleship
2.3 Corrective Church Discipline
3 Personal Spiritual Discipline
3.1 Bible Reading
3.2 Prayer
4 Conclusion

Selected Bibliography
1 Primary Sources and Translations
2 Concordances, Grammars, and Lexicons
3 Secondary Literature

ILLUSTRATIONS

Figure

2.1	The Camp of Israel	109

Tables

1.1	The Tripartite Shape of the Hebrew Bible	59
1.2	The Books in the Tripartite Order	60
1.3	Narrative Story Line and Poetic Commentary	61
1.4	The Shape of the New Testament	64
2.1	The Story Torah Tells	69
2.2	The Days of Creation	72
2.3	Correspondences between Eden and the Tabernacle and Temple	74
2.4	Imagery from Genesis 3:14–19 in the Old Testament	77
2.5	The Curses of Genesis 3:14–19	80
2.6	Correspondences between Eden and Israel	82
2.7	Curses Answered by Blessings	82
2.8	The Blessing of Abraham in Genesis	83
2.9	Seed Conflict in Genesis	84
2.10	Gender Conflict in Genesis	86
2.11	Terms Common to Genesis 3:17 and 5:29	88
2.12	Be Fruitful and Multiply	90
2.13	The Hardening of Pharaoh's Heart	92
2.14	Pharaoh's False Promises	93
2.15	Yahweh's Intent to Make Himself Known	94
2.16	Deuteronomy's Exposition of the Ten Commandments	128
3.1	The Prophets and the Exile	140
3.2	The Story of the Former Prophets	143
3.3	I Am Yahweh Who Brought You Out	146

3.4 Chiastic Structure in 2 Samuel 21–24 174
3.5 Thematic Chiastic Structure in the Former Prophets 187
3.6 The Years of the Kings and the Prophets 189
3.7 The Story of the Latter Prophets 191
3.8 Oswalt's Chiastic Structure of Isaiah 56–66 210
3.9 Yahweh Acting for His Name before the Nations 226
3.10 Link Words and Thematic Connections at the Beginnings and Ends of the Books of the Twelve 230
3.11 Key Words, Thematic Links, and Similar Phrases and Concepts in the Twelve 232
3.12 Through Judgment to Salvation in Micah 247
3.13 "Burden" Announcement of Destruction in the Book of the Twelve 250
3.14 The Structure of Habakkuk 252
3.15 Dates in Haggai and Zechariah 255
3.16 Eight Visions of the Night in Zechariah 1:7–6:8 258
3.17 Chiastic Structure in Zechariah 7–8 259
3.18 Thematic Chiastic Structure in Zechariah 9–14 261
3.19 The Order of the Twelve in *BHS*, DSS, 8ḤevXIIgr, and LXX 268
4.1 Grant's Arrangement of the Central Section of Book 1 of the Psalms 280
4.2 Zenger's Arrangement of Book 5 of the Psalms (Adapted) 286
4.3 Waltke's Chiasm in Proverbs 1–9 (Adapted) 293
4.4 Job 4–25, The Speeches of Job and His Counselors 302
4.5 Literary Structure of the Song of Songs 307
4.6 The Chiastic Structure of Ecclesiastes 319
4.7 The Chiastic Structure of Daniel 325
4.8 The Kingdoms in Daniel 2 and 7 330
4.9 Old Testament Prayers Appealing to God's Concern for His Own Glory 352
5.1 Major Shifts in Matthew 362
5.2 The Teaching of Jesus in the Gospel of Matthew 363
5.3 The Three Sets of Fourteen in Matthew's Genealogy 364
5.4 Typological Fulfillment in Matthew 1:22–23 365
5.5 Typological Fulfillment in Matthew 2 366
5.6 The Three Passion Predictions in Mark 385
5.7 Parallels between Mark's Disputed Ending and Other New Testament Passages 391
5.8 The Glory of God and Jesus in the Gospel of Luke 393
5.9 Blomberg's Chiasm in Luke–Acts (Adapted) 394

5.10	Gabriel Sent to Zechariah and Mary	394
5.11	Taking the Message to Heart	396
5.12	Predictions, Reminders, and Proofs of the Death and Resurrection in Luke	400
5.13	Prayer in Luke	402
5.14	The Chiasm in John's Prologue	405
5.15	Regeneration and Inability in John	407
5.16	Jesus and the Jewish Festivals in John	409
5.17	"I Am" in John's Gospel	412
5.18	The Spirit's Continuation of the Temple Ministry of Jesus in the Disciples	418
5.19	Programmatic Statements in Acts 1:8 and 9:15	420
5.20	Major Sermons in Acts	420
5.21	The Glory of God and Jesus in Acts	422
5.22	Church Growth in Acts	423
5.23	Peter's Sermon in Acts 3 and the Letter of 1 Peter	426
5.24	Wicked People Killed Jesus, but God Raised Him from the Dead	430
5.25	Jesus, Peter, and Paul in Luke–Acts	432
5.26	God's Sovereignty in Salvation in Acts	434
5.27	Baptism in the New Testament	441
6.1	"In Christ" in Colossians	491
6.2	The Messianic Woes in the Old and New Testaments	493
6.3	Chiastic Structure in Hebrews 1:1–4	516
6.4	Juxtaposition of Speaking and Acting in James	521
6.5	The Glory of God and Christ in 1 Peter	523
6.6	Suffering and Exaltation in 1 Peter	528
6.7	Doxologies in the New Testament	538
7.1	Matching Language Opening the Sections on the Harlot and the Bride	543
7.2	Matching Language Ending the Sections on the Harlot and the Bride	543
7.3	The Chiastic Structure of Revelation	544
7.4	The Exodus Plagues and Revelation's Trumpets	547
7.5	The Exodus Plagues and Revelation's Bowls	547

ACKNOWLEDGMENTS

The words of the Lord are pure words,
like silver refined in a furnace on the ground,
purified seven times. (Ps. 12:6)

The law of the Lord is perfect. (Ps. 19:7)

Forever, O Lord, your word
is firmly fixed in the heavens. (Ps. 119:89)

Oh how I love your law! (Ps. 119: 97)

. . . you have exalted above all things
your name and your word. (Ps. 138:2)

Every word of God proves true. (Prov. 30:5)

Scripture cannot be broken. (John 10:35)

Sanctify them in the truth; your word is truth.
(John 17:17—ESV here and above)

I am overwhelmed by the mercy of God—drenched in it. I did not deserve the parents God gave me, the opportunity to study under talented believing teachers, or the time that has made it possible to study the Bible so that this book could be written. It is all mercy. What a blessing to have the Bible, multiplied by the privilege of studying, teaching, and preaching it.

God showed me favor and gave me the good gift of a wife (Prov. 18:22). What a gift! If I lived a thousand lives, I would want to be married to sweet Jill every time. I could never enumerate all the ways she has been used of the Lord to strengthen, encourage, sustain, and sharpen me as I have worked on this project. She makes happy things happen all the time.

> Behold, children are a heritage from the LORD,
> the fruit of the womb a reward. (Ps. 127:3 ESV)

And I praise God for our reward and heritage. The labor of this project was sweetened by wiffle ball and toy time, sword fights and family walks. May our children know the glorious God who is the subject of this project, and maybe someday they'll even read about him in these pages.

God also mercifully gave church families whose fellowship relieved me from the isolation of writing. I am very grateful to a group of men at Baptist Church of the Redeemer in Houston, Texas, who read the early chapters of this volume, caught many typos, and spurred me on with spirited conversations. I wish to thank Travis Cardwell, Joel Bain, Bill Christen, Billy Newhouse, John Thacker, Joe Rowan, Mike Reed, and Chris Caldwell. Once the Lord moved us from Houston to Louisville, I benefited from another community of people willing to read and offer feedback, along with another church family, at Kenwood Baptist Church. I wish to thank Jim Rairick, Paul Cable, and Josh Philpot, each of whom read portions of this project and pointed out infelicities.

Tom Schreiner has been a constant encouragement and friend. He read some chapters multiple times, and his comments were always valuable. I am privileged to have studied under him. I praise God for the preaching of John Piper, which first pointed me to the center of biblical theology. Thanks are due to Justin Taylor and Thom Notaro at Crossway. Justin encouraged me to pursue the project, and Thom fixed many problems of form and tense. I alone bear responsibility for those that remain. David Reimer and I have never met face to face, but he generously read a portion of the manuscript, as did Stephen Dempster. My thanks to them and to Andy Naselli, who read the whole project and taught me to use Zotero and Microsoft Word.

I am also grateful to the administration of Southwestern Baptist Theological Seminary, specifically President Paige Patterson, Provost Craig Blaising, Dean Denny Autrey, and Chief of Staff Jason Duesing, a dear friend who carefully read and interacted with this material. The Southwestern administration encouraged me with their kind words and generously granted me a sabbatical in the spring of 2007. The staff at Southwestern's Roberts Library in Fort Worth were always helpful in sending resources to me in Houston; special thanks to Kenneth Steffen in this regard. I am grateful to serve now at The Southern Baptist Theological

Seminary, and I would like to thank both the administration and the librarians who have facilitated research in a myriad of ways.

My mom and dad live out Christlikeness as they lay down their lives for the benefit of their children in more ways than I have time to tell. What a blessing to be the child of such parents. I dedicate this book to them, praising God for his mercy.

Louisville, Kentucky
New Year's Day, 2010

A STRATEGY FOR READING THIS BOOK

This is a long book. Many long books sit unread in sad neglect, and I do not want that to happen to this one! Let me invite you to consider a different way to approach the reading of this book. I would be thrilled, of course, for you to plunge right in and go from start to finish. Some will do that (I hope). Others may find this approach more helpful: browse through this book, finding your way to the introductory and concluding paragraphs of chapters and sections of chapters. Dipping into these paragraphs will give you a feel for the book and introduce you to its shape and argument. You can do this as quickly or as slowly as you like, but browsing the whole at one sitting will let you see the forest, which will in turn help you see the trees. Once you have browsed the whole, you will have seen that the body of this study moves book by book through the whole Bible. If you are teaching James tomorrow, you have my permission (as though you need it!) to go directly to the section on James (§3.3) in chapter 6. If you are studying Isaiah this year, feel free to go read that section (§3.2) in chapter 3. If you are in Psalms and Galatians in your daily Bible reading, go to those sections in chapters 4 (§2.2) and 6 (§2.5). The point is that these discussions will benefit you most if you are actually reading the biblical texts under consideration. So I invite you to read the body of this book alongside your reading, your study, your memorization and meditation on the Bible.

One of the most profitable and enjoyable experiences I have had reading a book was when I let Paul House take me on a "guided tour" of the Old Testament. I would read a section of the Old Testament, then read House's discussion of that part of the Bible in his *Old Testament Theology*. Perhaps you have visited a historical site or a museum and checked out an audio tour. As you went from one thing to another, you could enter codes on the device for more or less information about what you were seeing. Looking at some work of art or artifact of history, you could also listen to relevant information that enabled you to understand what was before you. It would be boring to hear that recording if you were not looking at the things being described—unless you knew them so well that you could picture exactly what the narrator was describing. Along these lines, this book is best read with an open Bible—unless you practically have the whole thing memorized. So I encourage you to read this book alongside the Bible, and if you have time for only one and not the other, read the Bible. Its authors were inspired by the Holy Spirit, and God will use it to change your life. My prayer is that this book will help you toward a fuller understanding of the Scriptures.

ABBREVIATIONS

AB	Anchor Bible Commentary
ABD	*Anchor Bible Dictionary*. Edited by David Noel Freedman
ANF	*The Ante-Nicene Fathers*
AOTC	Apollos Old Testament Commentary
BBR	*Bulletin for Biblical Research*
BDAG	Bauer, W., F. W. Danker, W. F. Arndt, and F. W. Gingrich. *Greek-English Lexicon of the New Testament and Other Early Christian Literature*. 3rd ed.
BDB	Brown, F., S. R. Driver, and C. A. Briggs. *A Hebrew and English Lexicon of the Old Testament*
BECNT	Baker Exegetical Commentary on the New Testament
BHS	*Biblia Hebraica Stuttgartensia*. 4th ed.
BST	The Bible Speaks Today
BZAW	Beihefte zur Zeitschrift für die alttestamentliche Wissenschaft
CBQ	*Catholic Biblical Quarterly*
COS	*The Context of Scripture*. Edited by William W. Hallo. 3 vols.
CR:BS	*Currents in Research: Biblical Studies*
CTJ	*Calvin Theological Journal*
CTR	*Criswell Theological Review*
DANE	*Dictionary of the Ancient Near East*. Edited by Piotr Bienkowski and Alan Millard
DJD	Discoveries in the Judaean Desert
DLNTD	*Dictionary of the Later New Testament and Its Development*. Edited by Ralph P. Martin and Peter H. Davids
DOTP	*Dictionary of the Old Testament Pentateuch*. Edited by David W. Baker and T. Desmond Alexander

DPL	*Dictionary of Paul and His Letters*. Edited by Gerald F. Hawthorne, Ralph P. Martin, and Daniel G. Reid
DSS	Dead Sea Scrolls
DSS[SE]	*The Dead Sea Scrolls: Study Edition*. Edited by Florentino García Martínez and Eibert J. C. Tigchelaar. 2 vols.
EBC	*The Expositor's Bible Commentary*. Edited by Frank E. Gaebelein
ET	English Translation
GKC	*Gesenius' Hebrew Grammar*. Edited by E. Kautzsch. Translated by A. E. Cowley
HALOT	*The Hebrew and Aramaic Lexicon of the Old Testament*. Edited by L. Koehler, W. Baumgartner, and J. J. Stamm. 2 vols. Study edition
HR	*A Concordance to the Septuagint and Other Greek Versions of the Old Testament*. Edited by E. Hatch and H. A. Redpath
Int	*Interpretation*
JBL	*Journal of Biblical Literature*
JBMW	*Journal of Biblical Manhood and Womanhood*
JETS	*Journal of the Evangelical Theological Society*
Joüon	Joüon, P. *A Grammar of Biblical Hebrew*. Translated and revised by T. Muraoka. 2 vols.
JSJSup	Supplements to the *Journal for the Study of Judaism*
JSNT	*Journal for the Study of the New Testament*
JSNTSup	*Journal for the Study of the New Testament* Supplement Series
JSOT	*Journal for the Study of the Old Testament*
JSOTSup	*Journal for the Study of the Old Testament* Supplement Series
JTS	*Journal of Theological Studies*
KD	Keil and Delitzsch, *Commentary on the Old Testament*, 10 vols.
LCL	Loeb Classical Library
LNTS	Library of New Testament Studies
LXX	The Greek Translations of the Old Testament. Critical editions where available; otherwise the Rahlfs text is cited.
MT	Masoretic Text: Hebrew text of the Old Testament found in *Biblia Hebraica Stuttgartensia* (*BHS*)
NAC	New American Commentary
NACSBT	New American Commentary Studies in Bible and Theology
NCB	New Century Bible Commentary

NDBT	*New Dictionary of Biblical Theology*. Edited by T. Desmond Alexander and Brian S. Rosner
NETS	New English Translation of the Septuagint
NIBC	New International Biblical Commentary
NICNT	New International Commentary on the New Testament
NICOT	New International Commentary on the Old Testament
NIDOTTE	*New International Dictionary of Old Testament Theology and Exegesis*. Edited by Willem A. VanGemeren. 5 vols.
NIGTC	New International Greek Testament Commentary
NIVApp	NIV Application Commentary
NSBT	New Studies in Biblical Theology
NTS	*New Testament Studies*
OTL	Old Testament Library
RBL	*Review of Biblical Literature*
SBJT	*The Southern Baptist Journal of Theology*
SJT	*Scottish Journal of Theology*
SNTSMS	Society for New Testament Studies Monograph Series
Them	*Themelios*
TJ	*Trinity Journal*
TOTC	Tyndale Old Testament Commentaries
TynBul	*Tyndale Bulletin*
VT	*Vetus Testamentum*
VTSup	Supplements to *Vetus Testamentum*
WBC	Word Biblical Commentary
WTJ	*Westminster Theological Journal*
WUNT	Wissenschaftliche Untersuchungen zum Neuen Testament
ZECNT	Zondervan Exegetical Commentary on the New Testament
ZNW	*Zeitschrift für die neutestamentliche Wissenschaft*

THE SECOND COMING (1919)

William Butler Yeats

Turning and turning in the widening gyre
The falcon cannot hear the falconer;
Things fall apart; the centre cannot hold;
Mere anarchy is loosed upon the world,
The blood-dimmed tide is loosed, and everywhere
The ceremony of innocence is drowned;
The best lack all conviction, while the worst
Are full of passionate intensity.

Surely some revelation is at hand;
Surely the Second Coming is at hand.
The Second Coming! Hardly are those words out
When a vast image out of *Spiritus Mundi*
Troubles my sight; somewhere in sands of the desert
A shape with lion body and the head of a man,
A gaze blank and pitiless as the sun,
Is moving its slow thighs, while all about it
Reel shadows of indignant desert birds.
The darkness drops again; but now I know
That twenty centuries of stony sleep
Were vexed to nightmare by a rocking cradle,
And what rough beast, its hour come round at last,
Slouches towards Bethlehem to be born?

GOD'S GRANDEUR (1877)

Gerard Manley Hopkins

The world is charged with the grandeur of God.
    It will flame out, like shining from shook foil;
    It gathers to a greatness, like the ooze of oil
Crushed. Why do men then now not reck his rod?
Generations have trod, have trod, have trod;
    And all is seared with trade; bleared, smeared with toil;
    And wears man's smudge and shares man's smell: the soil
Is bare now, nor can foot feel, being shod.

And for all this, nature is never spent;
    There lives the dearest freshness deep down things;
    And though the last lights off the black West went
    Oh, morning, at the brown brink eastward, springs—
Because the Holy Ghost over the bent
    World broods with warm breast and with ah! bright wings.

Chapter 1

CAN THE CENTER HOLD?

1. Introduction

William Butler Yeats captured the spirit of Our Time in the opening lines of his poem "The Second Coming":

> Turning and turning in the widening gyre
> The falcon cannot hear the falconer;
> Things fall apart; the centre cannot hold . . .

The image of a world spinning out of control, a world no longer heeding the call of its Master because truth is only "true for you," matches the default settings of our intuitive templates. Biblical scholars and theologians are no exception.[1] Describing theologians since the 1960s, David Wells writes:

> They, too, began not with divine revelation but with human experience, not with God's interpretation of life but with the interpretation that in our self-asserted

[1]For a fascinating example, see the "Afterword" in David J. A. Clines, *The Theme of the Pentateuch*, 2nd ed. (Sheffield: JSOT, 1997), 130–31. Writing twenty years after the first edition was published, Clines states, "Today, since I think that we have moved into a post-modern age, I would be much more careful in speaking of meaning. I would not now be speaking of '*the* meaning' of the Pentateuch nor claiming that 'theme encapsulates the meaning of the work' (p. 24), as if there was only one meaning for the Pentateuch. Nowadays I tend rather to believe that texts do not have meaning in themselves." The page reference in the above quote is to his own book! In terms he uses to describe himself, the postmodern Clines takes exception to statements made by the modern Clines.

> freedom we have devised for ourselves. They rejected the idea that there is any center to the meaning that they sought, any normativity to any one proposal.[2]

Academic practitioners of biblical theology have not transcended the spirit of the age. Walter Brueggemann has written that "in every period of the discipline, the questions, methods, and possibilities in which study is cast arise from the sociointellectual climate in which the work must be done."[3] While I would never assert that everyone who thinks biblical theology has no center has either capitulated to or consciously embraced the spirit of the age, the "sociointellectual climate" corresponds to the view that biblical theology has no center.[4] We are all affected by the temperature of the times. We need not look far to see that the center has not held, and things have fallen apart. As Brueggemann writes, "The new situation in Old Testament theology is reflective of a major breakpoint in Western culture. . . . The breakpoint concerns modes of knowledge that have too innocently yielded certitude."[5]

The purpose of this book, quixotic as it may seem, is to seek to do for biblical theology what Kevin Vanhoozer has done for hermeneutics[6] and David Wells has done for evangelical theology.[7] The goal is not a return to an imaginary golden age but to help people know God. The quest to know God is clarified by diagnosis of the problem (Wells), the vindication of interpretation (Vanhoozer), and, hopefully, a clear presentation of the main point of God's revelation of himself, that is, a clear presentation of the center of biblical theology. I hasten to embrace the humility articulated by Schlatter and recently restated by Schreiner: there is more than one way to pursue biblical theology, and there can be no final, definitive treatment of the subject. Though I am pursuing *the* center, I celebrate the fact that "each of the various approaches and perspectives can cast a different light upon the NT, and in that sense having a number of different approaches is helpful."[8] I hope that even those who are not convinced

---

[2]David Wells, *No Place for Truth, or, Whatever Happened to Evangelical Theology?* (Grand Rapids: Eerdmans, 1993), 66. My capitalization of the phrase "Our Time" above reflects Wells's use of that phrase.

[3]Walter Brueggemann, *Theology of the Old Testament: Testimony, Dispute, Advocacy* (Minneapolis: Fortress, 1997), 11 (italics removed).

[4]For a sampling, see A. J. Köstenberger, "Diversity and Unity in the New Testament," in *Biblical Theology: Retrospect and Prospect*, ed. Scott J. Hafemann (Downers Grove, IL: InterVarsity, 2002), 154; Elmer A. Martens, *Old Testament Theology*, IBR Bibliographies 13 (Grand Rapids: Baker, 1997), 57; C. H. H. Scobie, *The Ways of Our God: An Approach to Biblical Theology* (Grand Rapids: Eerdmans, 2003), 87.

[5]Brueggemann, *Theology of the Old Testament*, 60.

[6]Kevin J. Vanhoozer, *Is There a Meaning in This Text? The Bible, the Reader, and the Morality of Literary Knowledge* (Grand Rapids: Zondervan, 1998).

[7]Wells, *No Place for Truth*; Wells, *God in the Wasteland: The Reality of Truth in a World of Fading Dreams* (Grand Rapids: Eerdmans, 1994); Wells, *Losing Our Virtue: Why the Church Must Recover Its Moral Vision* (Grand Rapids: Eerdmans, 1998).

[8]Thomas R. Schreiner, *New Testament Theology: Magnifying God in Christ* (Grand Rapids: Baker, 2008), 10. Cf. Adolf Schlatter, "The Theology of the New Testament and Dogmatics," in *The Nature of New Testament Theology*, ed. R. Morgan (1909; repr., Naperville, IL: Allenson, 1973), 117.

that I am right about the center for which I argue will nevertheless profit from the perspective articulated here.

Vanhoozer describes his goal as "reinvigorating author-oriented interpretation through a creative retrieval of Reformed theology and speech-act philosophy." The urgency of his task grows out of the recognition that "the fate of hermeneutics and humanity alike stand or fall together."[9] Similarly, Wells writes, "It is not theology alone in which I am interested but theology that is driven by a passion for truth; and it is not evangelicalism alone in which I am interested but evangelicalism as the contemporary vehicle for articulating a historical Protestant orthodoxy."[10] These academic sallies are necessary because, in the words of Machen, "what is today a matter of academic speculation begins tomorrow to move armies and pull down empires."[11] The ramifications ideas have in the wider culture reflect their impact on the church, and as Justin Taylor has noted, "As goes the academy, so goes the church."[12] For Wells, in the providence of God, the upheavals in society "that could portend a very troubled future and perhaps the disintegration of Western civilization" also point to "a moment when, in God's mercy and providence, the Church could be deeply transformed for good."[13]

The transformation the church needs is the kind that results from beholding the glory of God in the face of Christ (2 Cor. 3:18–4:6). This glory of God is a saving and judging glory—an aroma of life to those being saved and death to those perishing (2 Cor. 2:15–16), and this saving and judging glory is at the center of biblical theology. If there is to be a renewal,[14] it will be a renewal that grows out of the blazing center that is the glory of God in the face of Christ. This saving and judging glory, I contend, is the center of biblical theology.

Seeking to exposit the center of biblical theology is necessary because many today question whether the Bible tells a coherent story. There are many who do not embrace the idea of a center for biblical theology and yet maintain that the Bible is coherent,[15] but if the Bible tells a coherent story, it is valid to explore what that story's main point is. That leads us to ask whether the Bible shows us what God's ultimate purpose is. Understanding God's ultimate purpose, even with our limited human capacities, gives us insight into the meaning of all things. We know why things exist because we know the one "for whom and through whom

[9]Vanhoozer, *Is There a Meaning in This Text?* 10, 22.
[10]Wells, *No Place for Truth*, 12.
[11]J. Gresham Machen, "Christianity and Culture," *Princeton Theological Review* 11 (1913): 7. I wish to thank Justin Taylor for drawing my attention to Machen's comment and his essay.
[12]Justin Taylor, "An Introduction to Postconservative Evangelicalism and the Rest of This Book," in Millard J. Erickson, Paul Kjoss Helseth, and Justin Taylor, *Reclaiming the Center* (Wheaton, IL: Crossway, 2004), 31.
[13]Wells, *No Place for Truth*, 91.
[14]See Robert W. Yarbrough's insightful call for a renewal in scholarly interpretation of Scripture, "The Last and Next Christendom: Implications for Interpreting the Bible," *Them* 29 (2003): 30–37, esp. 36–37.
[15]I am grateful for personal correspondence with David Reimer on this point.

are all things" (Heb. 2:10). This knowledge will organize our relationships and priorities, and it is desperately needed in Our Time. Wells writes,

> Whatever else one may say about modernization, one of its principal effects has been to break apart the unity of human understanding and disperse the multitude of interests and undertakings away from the center, in relation to which they have gathered their meaning, pushing them to the edges, where they have no easy relation to one another at all.[16]

Evangelicals have lost the "theological center," and this theological center is the Bible's center. With no center, of course things fall apart. The problem, however, is not that the gravitational center of the Bible's theology cannot hold. The problem is more along the lines of what Yeats described as the falcon not hearing the Falconer. That is to say, if we will listen carefully to the Bible, it will proclaim to us the glory of God. If we do not hear this, the problem is with us, not the Bible. As Schreiner has pointed out, "We could easily fail to see the supremacy of God and the centrality of Christ in the NT precisely because these themes are part of the warp and woof of the NT. Sometimes we fail to see what is most obvious, what is right before our eyes."[17] God means to reveal himself in an astonishing display of his mercy and justice, with the justice highlighting the mercy.[18] Before we can pursue the demonstration of this thesis, however, we must consider several preliminary questions.

2. Do Things Fall Apart? (Is There a Unity in the Bible's Diversity?)

There is much discussion today about the real diversity that exists within the overarching unity of the Bible.[19] In some circles there is also a widespread suspicion that there might be not one orthodoxy or a single theology of the Old and New Testaments but orthodox*ies* and theolog*ies*.[20] Walter Brueggemann asserts that there is "no going back to a singular coherent faith articulation in the text (much as canonical approaches might insist on it)."[21] We cannot go back, but I believe that if we do as Francis Watson proposes and radicalize "the modern theological

[16]Wells, *No Place for Truth*, 7.

[17]Schreiner, *New Testament Theology*, 13.

[18]Cf. Robin Routledge, *Old Testament Theology: A Thematic Approach* (Downers Grove, IL: InterVarsity, 2008), 313: "It is possible to discern a single divine purpose: to reveal God's holiness and glory throughout the earth so that it is acknowledged by all peoples."

[19]For two evangelical discussions, see David Wenham's essay, "Unity and Diversity in the New Testament," in George Eldon Ladd, *A Theology of the New Testament*, rev. and ed. Donald A. Hagner (Grand Rapids: Eerdmans, 1993), 684–719; and Köstenberger, "Diversity and Unity in the New Testament," 144–58.

[20]See, e.g., Erhard S. Gerstenberger, *Theologies of the Old Testament*, trans. John S. Bowden (Minneapolis: Fortress, 2002).

[21]Brueggemann, *Theology of the Old Testament*, xvi. I am not sure how this fits with Brueggemann's assertion on the following page: "Taken all together, these witnesses, different as they are, advocate a Yahweh-version of reality that is strongly in conflict with other versions of reality and other renderings of truth that have been shaped without reference to Yahweh and that determinedly propose a reality and truth that is Yahweh-free" (xvii). It would seem that the trajectory of this statement would tend to a conclusion at odds with the one

and exegetical concern to identify ever more precisely those characteristics that are peculiar to the biblical texts,"[22] we will find ourselves face to face with, as Brueggemann puts it, "a singular coherent faith articulation in the text." At its center, I contend, will be the glory of God in salvation through judgment.

Denny Burk makes the point that scientific study "makes empirically testable predictions" and that theories "can only be tested by attempts to falsify" them.[23] In this book, I am putting forth the theory that the glory of God in salvation through judgment is the center of biblical theology. This theory will be tested against the "grammar" of the biblical evidence, with special attention given to any evidence in the Bible that might falsify it (and see chap. 8, where I discuss objections to the thesis). The remainder of this book will seek to show that this is "a theory that adequately explains a grammatical phenomenon [in this case, the teaching of the whole Bible!] without being falsified by the relevant body of empirical data."[24]

One obstacle facing those committed to the unity of the Bible is a certain disdain some biblical scholars have for systematic theology. A strong desire to avoid the charge that one's prior theological conclusions control one's exegesis, coupled with a vague sense that "belief has a distorting effect on historical inquiry,"[25] leads many to prefer to "let the tensions stand," indefinitely postponing legitimate and necessary theological synthesis.

As the spiral of meaning widens into incoherence for some, we can focus our gaze by beginning with the purpose of biblical theology. Having considered the purpose of biblical theology, we will take up the question of how to define the center of biblical theology and then ask how we identify the center of biblical theology.

2.1 Finding Our Way in the Widening Gyre: The History and Purpose of Biblical Theology

We can think of the practice of biblical theology in two ways. On the one hand, we have the practice of the believing community across the ages. On the other hand, we have a label that describes an academic discipline. Regarding the first, I would argue that biblical theology is as old as Moses. That is, Moses presented a biblical-theological interpretation of the traditions he received regarding Cain and Abel, Isaac and Ishmael, Jacob and Esau, Joseph and his brothers, and his

---

quoted above, but perhaps Brueggemann's commitment to pluralism keeps him from privileging the claims of the Yahweh-version of reality over other versions (cf. 61–64, 93, 95).

[22]Francis Watson, *Text and Truth: Redefining Biblical Theology* (Edinburgh: T&T Clark, 1997), 205.

[23]Denny Burk, *Articular Infinitives in the Greek of the New Testament: On the Exegetical Benefit of Grammatical Precision* (New Testament Monographs 14; Sheffield: Sheffield Phoenix, 2006), 19, quoting Ruth Kempson, *Semantic Theory*, Cambridge Textbooks in Linguistics (Cambridge: Cambridge University Press, 1977), 1.

[24]Burk, *Articular Infinitives*, 20.

[25]Vanhoozer, *Is There a Meaning in This Text?* 23. Vanhoozer is describing Van Harvey's book, *The Historian and the Believer: The Morality of Historical Knowledge and Christian Belief*. For Harvey, "doubt is a virtue; credulity, a vice" (ibid.). Harvey's perspective seems to have been adopted by many evangelical biblical scholars.

own experience with his kinsmen.[26] Joshua then presented a biblical-theological interpretation of Israel's history (Joshua 24), and the same can be said of the rest of the authors of the Prophets and the Writings, the Gospels and Acts, the Epistles and the Apocalypse. The biblical authors used biblical theology to interpret the Scriptures available to them and the events they experienced. For the believing community, the goal of biblical theology is simply to learn this practice of interpretation from the biblical authors so that we can interpret the Bible and life in this world the way they did.

It seems to me, then, that the history of biblical interpretation in the church is a history of more and less success in accurately understanding the interpretive strategies used by the biblical authors. Some figures in the history of the church were more adept at this than others.[27] Some failed miserably, but it seems that a shift happened with the rise of the so-called Enlightenment. Prior to that time, the effort to interpret the Bible the way the biblical authors did was an effort to follow them in typological interpretation, or figural reading of the Bible.[28] Hans Frei has shown how, in view of the rise of historical criticism, figural reading and typological interpretation came to seem "preposterous" and "lost credibility."[29] And this brings us to the second way of thinking about biblical theology, namely, as an academic discipline whose results are measured more by the academy than by the believing community, for as Frei has written, "Figural reading, concerned as it was with the unity of the Bible, found its closest successor in an enterprise called biblical theology, which sought to establish the unity of religious meaning across the gap of historical and cultural differences."[30]

Many recognize that the method of study referred to as biblical theology was marshaled by the Reformers,[31] who wanted to "chasten the church's unbiblical theological speculations."[32] During the Enlightenment, biblical theology came to

[26]For more on what I have in mind here, see my essay, "Was Joseph a Type of the Messiah? Tracing Typological Identification between Joseph, David, and Jesus," *SBJT* 12, no. 4 (2008): 52–77.

[27]See the brilliant biblical theology in Melito of Sardis, *On Pascha and Fragments*, ed. Stuart George Hall (Oxford: Clarendon Press, 1979).

[28]I have suggested the following working definition of typological interpretation: "Typological interpretation is canonical exegesis that observes divinely intended patterns of historical correspondence and escalation in significance in the events, people, or institutions of Israel, and these types are in the redemptive historical stream that flows through the Bible" ("Was Joseph a Type of the Messiah," 53). For brief exposition of this definition, see ibid., 53–54.

[29]Hans W. Frei, *The Eclipse of Biblical Narrative: A Study in Eighteenth and Nineteenth Century Hermeneutics* (New Haven, CT: Yale University Press, 1974), 7.

[30]Ibid., 8.

[31]Scobie points to Irenaeus as an early practitioner of biblical theology (*The Ways of Our God*, 10), yet the methods of biblical theology as we understand them today found wider currency at the time of the Protestant Reformation. For a helpful discussion, see Gerald Bray, "The Church Fathers and Biblical Theology," in *Out of Egypt: Biblical Theology and Biblical Interpretation*, ed. C. Bartholomew et al., Scripture and Hermeneutics 5 (Grand Rapids: Zondervan, 2004), 23–40.

[32]Frank Thielman, *Theology of the New Testament: A Canonical and Synthetic Approach* (Grand Rapids: Zondervan, 2005), 20. Similarly Brueggemann, *Theology of the Old Testament*, 2. Thielman's survey of "The Basic Questions" (19–42) is excellent, and Brueggemann's summary of the history of Old Testament Theology is informative as well (1–60).

be employed by many whose objective was to separate their study of biblical texts from the authority of the Bible and Christian readings of it.[33] Adolf Schlatter called this approach to the Bible's theology a "radical and total polemic against it."[34] Geerhardus Vos is regarded as something of a pioneer by many North American evangelical students of biblical theology. In a sense, Vos salvaged the tool from the damage done to it by the Enlightenment. Vern Poythress suggests that biblical theology had a "checkered history before Vos redefined it."[35]

For Vos, biblical theology was a kind of exegesis that studied "the process of the self-revelation of God deposited in the Bible." Biblical theology is "the study of the actual self-disclosures of God in time and space which lie back of even the first committal to writing of any Biblical document," and it "deals with revelation as a divine activity, not as the finished product of that activity."[36] In the years since Vos wrote, some less conservative scholars—not necessarily following Vos—have pitted "what happened" against "what the text says," and some have suggested that Scripture is merely a record of God's revelation rather than itself being revelation from God.[37] This is probably not what Vos meant to articulate,[38] but because of what has happened since he wrote, his description of biblical theology might be confusing in today's context.

For this reason I would suggest a slightly different description of what biblical theology is and what it should do. Again, there is more than one way to do biblical theology, and this book will not be the final word on the subject. There are insights to be gained from a variety of approaches because the Bible cannot

---

[33]For the history of the discipline, see G. F. Hasel, *Old Testament Theology: Basic Issues in the Current Debate*, 4th ed. (Grand Rapids: Eerdmans, 1991); Hasel, *New Testament Theology: Basic Issues in the Current Debate* (Grand Rapids: Eerdmans, 1978).

[34]Schlatter, "The Theology of the New Testament and Dogmatics," 122.

[35]Vern Sheridan Poythress, "Kinds of Biblical Theology," *WTJ* 70 (2008): 132 (129–42). See especially Geerhardus Vos, *Biblical Theology: Old and New Testaments* (Grand Rapids: Eerdmans, 1948). J. V. Fesko, citing Richard B. Gaffin and Richard Lints, refers to Vos as "the father of Reformed biblical theology" ("On the Antiquity of Biblical Theology," in *Resurrection and Eschatology: Theology in Service of the Church*, ed. Lane G. Tipton and Jeffrey C. Waddington [Phillipsburg, NJ: P&R, 2008], 443).

[36]Vos, *Biblical Theology*, 4–5.

[37]I have in mind here the way that the Baptist General Convention of Texas (BGCT) has preferred the 1963 version of the Baptist Faith and Message over the 2000 version. See the commentary on pages 9–10 of the "1963 and 2000 Baptist Faith and Message Statements: Comparison and Commentary," available online: http://www.bgct.org/TexasBaptists/Document.Doc?&id=610, accessed July 10, 2008. The 1963 version described the Bible as "the record of God's revelation of himself to man," and the 2000 version states that the Bible "is God's revelation of himself to man." The commentary explains that the phrase "'*the record of*' has the effect of centering the revelation of God in God's mighty acts, i.e., in the *events* of salvation history, rather than in the *words* which describe these events. The words of scripture record the faith community's witness to these events, but the self-revelation of God is manifest in the events themselves." This is followed by the assertion that locating the revelation in the words of the Bible rather than in the events exalts the Bible over Christ. Against this, we only know Christ through the Bible's revelation of him. Moreover, the book of Revelation, for instance, claims to be "The Revelation of Jesus Christ" (Rev. 1:1). See further Gregory A. Wills, *Southern Baptist Theological Seminary, 1859–2009* (Oxford: Oxford University Press, 2009), 244–46 passim. Brueggemann is obviously not engaging in this dispute, but I agree with his assertion: "The Bible is a revelation" (*Theology of the Old Testament*, 3).

[38]Poythress notes regarding Vos's *The Pauline Eschatology* and *The Teaching of the Epistle to the Hebrews* that "Vos in these works appears to move past the boundary that he himself earlier put in place in his definition of biblical theology" precisely in that he dealt with the "'finished product,' namely the Pauline corpus and the Letter to the Hebrews" ("Kinds of Biblical Theology," 136).

be exhausted, and its truths are such that looking at them from different angles only increases our appreciation of the book's humble, and yet stunning, beauty. In this study, I will pursue a biblical theology that highlights the central theme of God's glory in salvation through judgment by describing the literary contours of individual books in canonical context with sensitivity to the unfolding metanarrative.[39] In my view this metanarrative presents a unified story with a discernible main point, or center. This study will be canonical: I will interpret the Protestant canon, and the Old Testament will be interpreted in light of the ordering of the books in the Hebrew Bible (see further below). It will be literary: I will seek to interpret books and sections of books in light of their inherent literary features and structures as we have them in the canon.[40]

Interpretation in light of the unfolding metanarrative assumes that the historical and chronological claims in the books be interpreted as they stand. That is, I will assume, for instance, that Deuteronomy was part of the impetus for rather than the product of Josiah's reforms. In doing this, I seek to allow the book to tell its own story instead of imposing onto it an alternative story generated by the modern academy. I would hope that even those who do not believe, as I do, that there was a real Moses who wrote the Pentateuch will nevertheless show themselves liberal enough to grant that the texts do make that claim, and tolerant enough to allow space for interpretations that deviate from critical orthodoxy.[41] Rather than interpreting a disputed scholarly reconstruction, I will interpret the claims the texts make. I believe the texts are true and trustworthy,[42] so Brueggemann's words on Barth's perceived fideism seem relevant:

> It is relatively easy to indict Barth for fideism and theological positivism, and that indictment has been reiterated often. The problem is that there is obviously no legitimate starting point for theological reflection, and one must begin somewhere. The counterindictment is somewhat less obvious and has only more recently been mounted: that *the Cartesian program of autonomous reason, which issued in historical criticism, is also an act of philosophical fideism.*[43]

[39]For a helpful discussion of the Bible as a "nonmodern metanarrative," see Richard Bauckham, "Reading Scripture as a Coherent Story," in *The Art of Reading Scripture*, ed. Ellen F. Davis and Richard B. Hays (Grand Rapids: Eerdmans, 2003), 38–53.

[40]For further thoughts on literary features of texts and biblical theology, see the discussion of the structural features and intertextual connections that the authors used to connect their work to the Bible's big story and encourage their audiences in my essay, "Biblical Theology and Preaching," in *Text-Driven Preaching: God's Word at the Heart of Every Sermon*, ed. Daniel L. Akin, David Allen, and Ned L. Mathews (Nashville: Broadman & Holman, 2010), 193–218.

[41]For an example of intolerance and illiberality that resorts to pejorative slurs and name calling, see Philippe Guillaume, "Review of C. John Collins, *Genesis 1–4: A Linguistic, Literary, and Theological Commentary*," *RBL* 04/2008, available online: http://www.bookreviews.org/pdf/5953_6324.pdf, accessed July 12, 2008.

[42]For my understanding of the nature of the Bible, see my essay, "Still *Sola Scriptura*: An Evangelical View of Scripture," in *The Sacred Text: Excavating the Texts, Exploring the Interpretations, and Engaging the Theologies of the Christian Scriptures*, ed. Michael Bird and Michael Pahl (Piscataway, NJ: Gorgias, 2010), 215–40.

[43]Brueggemann, *Theology of the Old Testament*, 17 (emphasis original). See also Richard B. Hays, "A Herme-

Biblical theology seeks to understand the Bible in its own terms,[44] in its own chronology, as reflected in its canonical form. One of the key tasks of biblical theology is to trace the connections between themes and show the relationships between them.[45] There is an important point of application in connection with this weighing and sorting of scriptural themes: biblical theology is concerned with what the Bible meant for the purpose of understanding what the Bible means. The biblical theologian who writes in the service of the church[46] does so to elucidate the biblical worldview,[47] not merely so that it can be studied but so that it can be adopted.[48] This approach rejects the view that biblical theology is concerned with what the Bible meant, leaving what the Bible means to systematic or dogmatic theology.[49]

To make such a declaration is, in a sense, to plant a flag. Brueggemann explains that

> most scholars who have attempted to work in Old Testament theology since Barth have been double minded . . . . The tension that scholars face is between the epistemological assumptions of modernity that issue in historical criticism and that resist normative statements as fiduciary and potentially authoritarian, and the neoevangelical statement of normative theological claims that are perhaps impositions on the biblical materials. . . . Old Testament scholarship until recently has refused to choose and has sought to have it both ways. This refusal to choose has constituted the great problem for Old Testament theology.[50]

Asserting that what the Bible meant is normative is "fiduciary," but this is not a problem for those of us who are convinced that faith is properly basic.[51] As for "authority," to reassert the claims of the Bible is to assert the Bible's author-

---

neutic of Trust," in *The Conversion of the Imagination: Paul as Interpreter of Israel's Scripture* (Grand Rapids: Eerdmans, 2005), 192 (190–201).

[44]Brueggemann observes that the Reformers "insisted with great passion . . . that their evangelical modes of Bible reading were not imposed but in fact arose from the substance of the biblical text itself" (*Theology of the Old Testament*, 4).

[45]I base this on Thomas R. Schreiner's description of Pauline theology: "The task is not merely to reproduce Paul's thinking on various topics, but to rightly estimate what is most important in his thinking and to set forth the inner connections between the various themes" (*Paul, Apostle of God's Glory in Christ: A Pauline Theology* [Downers Grove, IL: InterVarsity, 2001], 15). See also the helpful description of biblical theology in Paul R. Williamson, *Sealed with an Oath: Covenant in God's Unfolding Purpose*, NSBT (Downers Grove, IL: InterVarsity, 2007), 17.

[46]Cf. Brueggemann, *Theology of the Old Testament*, 26: "The most influential Old Testament interpreters in the twentieth century were admitted and convinced church believers, and they understood their work to be in the service of the church. . . . They intended to serve the preaching of the church."

[47]Cf. Schreiner (*Paul*, 15) again: "The goal in writing a Pauline theology is to unearth Paul's worldview and present it to contemporaries."

[48]See Peter J. Leithart, *A Son to Me: An Exposition of 1 and 2 Samuel* (Moscow, ID: Canon, 2003), 9–23, esp. 22–23.

[49]For the view that biblical theology pursues "what it meant" and leaves "what it means" to dogmatic theology, see K. Stendahl, "Biblical Theology, Contemporary," *The Interpreter's Dictionary of the Bible*, 1:418–32.

[50]Brueggemann, *Theology of the Old Testament*, 19.

[51]See Alvin Plantinga, *Warranted Christian Belief* (New York: Oxford, 2000), and Peter van Inwagen, *God, Knowledge, and Mystery: Essays in Philosophical Theology* (Ithaca: Cornell University Press, 1995), 167.

ity. This is prideful only if we conduct ourselves as though we have invented these claims or are not subject to them ourselves. But we who assert the Bible's authority should be eager to submit humbly to that authority and repent when the Bible indicts us. Placing oneself under the authority of the text in this way would seem to be the best way to avoid "impositions on the biblical materials."[52] This is to make a choice that moves us beyond "the great problem for Old Testament theology."

Thus, the purpose of biblical theology is inductively to understand the canonical form of the Bible's theology as it is progressively revealed in its own literary forms and salvation-historical development, and this sharpens our systematic and dogmatic theology. Biblical theology is always done from some systematic perspective. Rudolf Bultmann's influential *Theology of the New Testament*[53] perfectly illustrates this point: his approach was found by many to be compelling precisely because it presented a holistic *system* that accounted for all the details—of course, the details that did not fit were attributed to a later redactor. But what is at issue here is that Bultmann's *biblical* theology was *systematic*.[54] Similarly, Walther Eichrodt wrote, "We have to undertake a *systematic examination* with objective classification and rational arrangement of the varied material."[55]

Our biblical-theological understanding will line up—implicitly or explicitly—with our systematic conclusions. This cannot be denied, and it should be embraced, with the two disciplines of biblical and systematic theology functioning to further our understanding of God and his word. John Goldingay says, "I want to write on the Old Testament without looking at it through Christian lenses or even New Testament lenses,"[56] but such an approach seems analogous to a botanist examining an acorn in order to predict what will sprout from the seed. How seriously would we take such a botanist professing openness to the idea that the acorn might make potatoes?[57] Botanists know what oak trees are, and Goldingay professes to be a Christian. Rather than trying to transcend our ultimate philosophical and theological conclusions, we should use them to help

---

Brueggemann states that for Barth faith is "a nonnegotiable premise and assumption of all right reading of the Bible and all right faith" (*Theology of the Old Testament*, 17).

[52]See the insightful comments of Bauckham, "Reading Scripture as a Coherent Story," 52–53, and Hays, "A Hermeneutic of Trust," 190–201.

[53]Rudolf Bultmann, *Theology of the New Testament*, trans. Kendrick Grobel, 2 vols. (New York: Scribners, 1955).

[54]So also John Ashton, "History and Theology in New Testament Studies," in *The Nature of New Testament Theology: Essays in Honour of Robert Morgan*, ed. Christopher Rowland and Christopher Tuckett (Oxford: Blackwell, 2006), 3: "Many of his readers might well feel that in his work as a whole theology has the upper hand."

[55]Walther Eichrodt, *Theology of the Old Testament*, trans. J. A. Baker, 2 vols. (Philadelphia: Westminster, 1961, 1967), 1:27 (emphasis his), cf. 28.

[56]John Goldingay, *Old Testament Theology: Israel's Gospel* (Downers Grove, IL: InterVarsity, 2003), 20. Similarly Brueggemann, *Theology of the Old Testament*, 93, 107.

[57]See further the insightful essay by David C. Steinmetz, "Uncovering a Second Narrative: Detective Fiction and the Construction of Historical Method," in Davis and Hays, *The Art of Reading Scripture*, 54–65.

us understand, with constant readiness to submit them to the searchlight of Scripture. We cannot, after all, abstract ourselves from our creatureliness, from our backgrounds and experiences, and from our convictions and beliefs.[58] We have not that ability. If our presuppositions do not help us understand, rather than pretend we do not have them, why not revise or, if necessary, reject them? The great challenge in biblical theology is to hold together everything the Bible says so that nothing is nullified, negated, or neglected. The particular usefulness of biblical theology comes from its inductive approach.

Some today are referring to biblical theology as a "bridge discipline"[59] that connects exegesis and systematic theology, but we can also view biblical theology, systematic theology, and historical theology as equal tools, each of which can be used to sharpen our exegesis and theology.[60] And the reality is that all these methods are used in teaching Christians, which makes them all dogmatic theology. We might not need all these tools for a good reputation in the academy, but we need each of them for the health of the church. As Reventlow says:

> "Biblical theology" is in the widest sense of the term an exegetical, hermeneutical and systematic discipline. . . . For its concern is to present to Christian faith an account of how far and why the *whole* of the Bible, Old Testament and New, has come down to us as Holy Scripture. Biblical scholarship cannot refuse the church an answer to this question.[61]

The purpose of biblical theology, then, is to sharpen our understanding of the theology contained in the Bible itself through an inductive, salvation-historical examination of the Bible's themes and the relationships between those themes in their canonical context and literary form. In this book I am arguing that one theme is central to all others. If one theme is central to all others, how do we define and identify that theme?

2.2 How Do We Define the Center of Biblical Theology?

Reventlow describes the search for the center of biblical theology succinctly as "the attempt to discover a particular concept or central idea as a connecting link between the two Testaments or as their 'centre,' around which a biblical

---

[58]For these reasons, John Barton's proposal to reduce Old Testament theology to a descriptive task that is part of the history of ideas fails (John Barton, "Biblical Theology: An Old Testament Perspective," in *The Nature of New Testament Theology: Essays in Honour of Robert Morgan*, ed. Christopher Rowland and Christopher Tuckett [Oxford: Blackwell, 2006], 21).

[59]Scobie, *The Ways of Our God*, 8.

[60]For the positive value of biblical theology for systematic theology and the "reverse influence of systematic theology on biblical theology," see Poythress, "Kinds of Biblical Theology," 132–34. He writes, "One must get one's framework of assumptions—one's presuppositions—from somewhere. If one does not get them from healthy, biblically grounded systematic theology, one will most likely get them from the spirit of the age, whether that be Enlightenment rationalism or postmodern relativism or historicism" (134; cf. 142).

[61]Henning Graf Reventlow, *Problems of Biblical Theology in the Twentieth Century*, trans. John Bowden (Philadelphia: Fortress, 1986), vii.

theology can be built up."[62] I would suggest that the connecting link between the testaments and the central idea around which we can build a biblical theology is the idea that the texts put forward as God's ultimate purpose. The Bible gives a number of explanations of the actions of God. Sometimes these explanations are presented as statements made by God himself. The center of biblical theology will be the ultimate reason that the Bible gives to explain what God has done. Jonathan Edwards[63] helpfully distinguishes between "subordinate ends" and "ultimate ends."[64] If my ultimate end is to go to work to do my job, there are many subordinate ends that must be accomplished in the pursuit of my ultimate end. Among other things, I get out of bed and get dressed. I make oatmeal in the microwave so that I can eat breakfast to keep from being hungry. I put my key in the car to drive to work. Getting out of bed, putting on clothes, eating breakfast, and driving are all subordinate to the end of doing my job.

When we examine the explanations the Bible gives for why God does what he does, we find clearly stated subordinate and ultimate ends. Though God is beyond our comprehension, we can know him and speak meaningfully about him because he has revealed himself to us in the written and living word. Moreover, God has given his Spirit to teach and lead those who believe. By the Spirit, in faith, we can discern God's subordinate and ultimate ends because the Bible reveals them to us.

If it can be shown that the Bible's description of God's ultimate end produces, informs, organizes, and is exposited by all the other themes in the Bible, and if this can be demonstrated from the Bible's own salvation-historical narrative and in its own terms, then the conclusion will follow that the ultimate end ascribed to God in the Bible is the center of biblical theology.[65] At the conclusion of his treatise concerning *The End for Which God Created the World*, Edwards writes,

---

[62]Ibid., 149. Reventlow characterizes this as one of three different models for regaining a theology of the whole Bible. For a bibliographic summary of proposed centers, see ibid., 154–64.

[63]In defense of allowing Jonathan Edwards to weigh in on a discussion of biblical theology, note William Baird's statement on Edwards in his second volume of his monumental *History of New Testament Research: From Jonathan Edwards to Rudolf Bultmann* (Minneapolis: Fortress, 2003), 10: "Edwards's primary contribution is in the area of biblical theology."

[64]Jonathan Edwards, *The End for Which God Created the World*, in John Piper, *God's Passion for His Glory: Living the Vision of Jonathan Edwards, with the Complete Text of* The End for Which God Created the World (Wheaton, IL: Crossway, 1998), 125. See also Walter Schultz, "Jonathan Edwards's *End of Creation*: An Exposition and Defense," *JETS* 49 (2006): 247–71.

[65]Those who refer to a concept such as "covenant" as the "organizing theological centre . . . around which the entire message of the Old Testament has been constructed, and providing the essential coherence between the Old Testament and the New" are defining the "center of biblical theology" somewhat differently than I do here. The quote is from Williamson, *Sealed with an Oath*, 31. Williamson is discussing Eichrodt's view, and for his own part he sees "covenant simply as *one of* Scripture's major theological themes" (32, emphasis added). See also Brueggemann, *Theology of the Old Testament*, 28: "Eichrodt's program is to explore how all of the variations and developments of Israel's religion can be seen to be in the service of a single conceptual notion, covenant" (italics removed). What I am proposing as the center of biblical theology is the "organizing principle" of biblical theology in the sense that it organizes the thoughts of the biblical authors. Nothing is more important to the biblical authors than God, and from what the texts say of God, nothing is more important to God than his own glory. Therefore, nothing is more important to the biblical authors than the glory of God.

"All that is ever spoken of in the Scripture as an ultimate end of God's works, is included in that one phrase, *the glory of God*; which is the name by which the ultimate end of God's works is most commonly called in Scripture; and seems most aptly to signify the thing."[66]

2.3 How Do We Identify the Center of Biblical Theology?

Many themes have been put forward as the center of biblical theology. Arbitrating between these requires attention to what the Bible tells us about these themes in both their immediate and canonical contexts. The center of biblical theology will be the theme that is prevalent, even pervasive, in all parts of the Bible. This theme will be the demonstrable centerpiece of the theology contained in the Bible itself, because this theme will be what the biblical authors resort to when they give ultimate explanations for why things are the way they are at any point in the Bible's story. Before we consider the various proposed centers, it will be helpful to summarize briefly the metanarrative, or all-encompassing story, the Bible tells.

In broadest terms, the Bible can be summarized in four words: *creation*, *fall*, *redemption*, *restoration*. This sequence functions as an umbrella story encompassing the whole canonical narrative, but it is also repeated countless times on both individual and corporate levels. The whole cosmos is created, is judged when man rebels, is redeemed through Christ's death on the cross, and will be restored when Christ returns, but this also happens to the nation of Israel and to particular individuals. For instance, God's word *creates* Israel as a nation when, having already called Abraham out of Ur, God calls the descendants of Abraham out of Egypt and gives them his law at Sinai. The nation *falls* at Sinai, is *redeemed* by God's mercy, and, in a sense, is *restored* through the second set of stone tablets. This pattern is repeated again and again in the Bible. God's word *creates* David as king of Israel, David *falls* with Bathsheba, he is *redeemed* after coming under the judgment of the prophetic rebuke, and he is *restored* and allowed to continue as king. Within the grand drama that goes from creation to consummation there are many such "plays within the play."

One significant variation on this theme takes shape as Yahweh brings Israel out of Egypt, makes a covenant with them, and gives them the Promised Land, where they sin, they are exiled, and the Old Testament prophets point to a return from exile that will be a new exodus.[67] In significant ways the Gospels interpret the death and resurrection of Jesus in these terms.[68] It is as though his death is the climactic moment of exile, the moment when the temple is destroyed (cf.

[66]Edwards, *The End for Which God Created the World*, 242.
[67]See Roy E. Ciampa, "The History of Redemption," in *Central Themes in Biblical Theology: Mapping Unity in Diversity*, ed. Scott J. Hafemann and Paul R. House (Grand Rapids: Baker, 2007), 254–308.
[68]See N. T. Wright, *Jesus and the Victory of God*, Christian Origins and the Question of God 2 (Minneapolis: Fortress, 1996).

John 2:19), and his resurrection begins the new exodus (cf. Luke 9:31). This story of salvation history is a story of God's glory in salvation through judgment. Those who believe in Jesus have been saved through the salvation through judgment of the exile and restoration he accomplished in his death and resurrection, and we are now sojourning, passing through the wilderness on our way to the Promised Land, looking for that city with foundations, where the Lamb will be the lamp.

At creation Yahweh designed a cosmic theater for his glory. On the cosmic stage God constructed a garden-temple, and he put his image in the temple. The image of God, man, was to extend the borders of the garden-temple by ruling over the earth and subduing it (cf., e.g., Num. 14:21; Hab. 2:14).[69] Describing the commission Adam and Eve received, Beale writes:

> They were to extend the geographical boundaries of the garden until Eden covered the whole earth. . . . The penultimate goal of the Creator was to make creation a liveable place for humans in order that they would achieve the grand aim of glorifying him. . . . God's ultimate goal in creation was to magnify his glory throughout the earth.[70]

Adam and Eve rebelled. They were expelled from the garden-temple. The charge to multiply and fill, rule and subdue, was passed down, however, and eventually a nation, Israel, was given the task. Just as God walked with his image in the garden, he walked with the nation, dwelling in a tabernacle and then a temple, both of which appear to be modeled on the garden.[71]

Just as Adam was to rule and subdue, the nation was to extend its borders until the glory of God covered the land as the waters cover the sea (Num. 14:21; Isa. 11:9; Hab. 2:14), and this would be accomplished as all the kings of the earth bowed the knee to the anointed king of Israel, to whom God said he would give the nations as his inheritance (Ps. 2:1–12). These nations would stream to Zion to learn the law of Yahweh (Isa. 2:1–5). This is the ideal, but just as Adam failed, so the kings of Israel failed. Just as Adam was expelled from the garden, so the nation was expelled from the land. A subtle indication of hope for the future was stated both in the words of judgment at Adam's fall[72] and in those

---

[69]See the texts listed in appendix 2 (§6) to chap. 3, "All the Earth Filled with the Knowledge of Yahweh's Glory." Cf. also G. K. Beale, *The Temple and the Church's Mission: A Biblical Theology of the Dwelling Place of God*, NSBT (Downers Grove, IL: InterVarsity, 2004), 66–80.

[70]Beale, *The Temple and the Church's Mission*, 81–82.

[71]See §2.1.4 in chap. 2 on "The Primeval Temple," with table 2.3: "Correspondences between Eden and the Tabernacle and Temple."

[72]See James M. Hamilton Jr., "The Skull Crushing Seed of the Woman: Inner-Biblical Interpretation of Genesis 3:15," *SBJT* 10, no. 2 (2006): 31–32, and Hamilton, "The Glory of God in Salvation through Judgment: The Centre of Biblical Theology?" *TynBul* 57 (2006): 62.

that accompany Israel's fall. Beyond the exiles from Eden and the land, a new day will dawn.

God never abandoned the purpose of causing his glory to cover the land as the waters cover the sea. Moreover, even though Adam and Israel failed, God's purpose was not thwarted. Mysteriously—in a way that was not revealed until Jesus came—even the failure of Adam and Israel and the judgment that fell on them was part of the outworking of God's purpose.

At long last, the king came with healing in his hands, succeeding where Adam and Israel failed, dying on behalf of his people, rising from the dead in triumph, and building a new temple—not a building but a body of believers (e.g., Eph. 2:19–22; 1 Pet. 2:4–5).[73] This new temple is to be built from people of all nations, but the building of this temple is not the consummation of God's purposes. God's purposes will be realized when all see Jesus coming with the clouds, even those who pierced him, and they will mourn for him as one mourns for an only son, while the redeemed rejoice (Rev. 1:7; Zech. 12:10). He will then ascend the throne and judge the living and the dead (Revelation 19–20), and the dwelling of God will be with men in the new and better Eden, the new creation (Revelation 21–22). God and the Lamb will be the temple (21:22). There will be no need for sun or moon, for the Lamb will be the lamp of God's glory, radiating light aplenty, the centerpiece of praise (21:23–24).

The center of biblical theology is the theme that organizes this metanarrative, the theme out of which all others flow. Having originated from their center, other themes exposit and feed back into it. Many of these other themes have been put forward as central to biblical theology, causing some confusion as to whether the idea of a "center" is even viable. Remarkably, the theme that I am suggesting as *the* center of biblical theology has not received much consideration in this discussion.

3. Mere Anarchy Is Loosed upon the World: The Plethora of Proposed Centers

Scholars have proposed an almost bewildering array of themes each of which contends for the claim to centrality in Old Testament theology, New Testament theology, and biblical theology. These include: God's self-revelation, God as the Lord, the holiness of God, God's steadfast love, the sovereignty of God, God's name, God's rule, God's kingdom, God's presence, God's design, God's election of Israel, the organizing principle of the covenant, promise-fulfillment, the new creation, God himself, and Jesus.[74] The criticisms of these proposals come down

[73]For discussion of the way Jesus constitutes his people as the new temple, see James M. Hamilton Jr., *God's Indwelling Presence: The Holy Spirit in the Old and New Testaments*, NACSBT (Nashville: Broadman & Holman, 2006), 154–60; for the imagery in Paul's letters, 123; for several indications that the church is a new temple in the apostolic Fathers, see 145–46 n. 59.

[74]For documentation of who proposed these centers and where, see Hamilton, "The Glory of God in Salvation through Judgment," 65–70.

to the objection that they are either too broad or too narrow.[75] D. A. Carson, for instance, objecting to the proposal that Jesus is the center of New Testament Theology, writes, "Although at one level that is saying everything at another level it is saying almost nothing."[76] Too general. On the other end, Hasel writes, "Any center of the NT (or the Bible) is not broad, deep, and wide enough to do justice to the whole canonical NT."[77] Too narrow. The validity of these criticisms is attested to by the multiplication of proposals. Unsatisfied scholars continue to search for an adequate center. Joining them, I contend that there is a theme that has not been seriously considered, a theme broad enough to encompass all the data while also being focused enough to help readers of the Bible organize what they find in all the texts they read.

Some conclude that the very fact that so many "centers" have been proposed proves that there is no center. Carson writes: "The pursuit of the center is chimerical. NT theology is so interwoven that one can move from any one topic to any other topic. We will make better progress by pursuing clusters of broadly common themes, which may not be common to all NT books."[78] Andreas Köstenberger concurs: "The quest for a single center of NT theology is misguided and should be replaced with an approach that recognizes several themes as an integrated whole. . . . The search for a single center of the NT should be abandoned. It seems more promising to search for a plurality of integrative motifs."[79] Elmer Martens writes similarly of Old Testament Theology: "One must speak, therefore, of a unity forged via interlocking traditions; the language . . . of trajectories and boundaries rather than 'center.' By the end of the twentieth century, a consensus of sorts emerged questioning the viability of a center."[80] And Charles Scobie writes regarding biblical theology: "It is difficult to understand the obsession with finding one single theme or 'center' for OT or NT theology, and more so for an entire BT. It is widely held today that the quest for a single center has failed. . . . It is the multithematic approach that holds most promise."[81]

In spite of the judgment of these respected scholars, it must be observed that their statements do not seem to have taken into account one theme that has only recently been put forward as the center of biblical theology: the glory of God.[82]

[75]So also Eugene H. Merrill, *Everlasting Dominion: A Theology of the Old Testament* (Nashville: Broadman & Holman, 2006), 20, 27. Merrill's own proposed center is something of a short exposition of Gen. 1:26–28: the sovereign God glorifying himself through man, the agent through whom God will fulfill his purposes (ibid., 27, 647).

[76]D. A. Carson, "New Testament Theology," *DLNTD*, 810.

[77]Hasel, *New Testament Theology*, 164.

[78]Carson, "New Testament Theology," 810.

[79]Köstenberger, "Diversity and Unity in the New Testament," 154.

[80]Martens, *Old Testament Theology*, 57.

[81]Scobie, *The Ways of Our God*, 87.

[82]Virtually everything that John Piper has written argues for the centrality of the glory of God, and Thomas R. Schreiner presents the glory of God in Christ as the center of Paul's theology in *Paul, Apostle of God's Glory in Christ* (Downers Grove, IL: InterVarsity, 2001), 15–35. Bruce Waltke agrees: "The ultimate theological truth that unifies the whole of Scripture is the irruption of the merciful King's rule to his glory" (*An Old Testament*

Whether this theme is broad enough to encompass all other themes will be addressed below. Anticipating the charge that it might be too broad to be useful, I am sharpening the proposal to focus specifically on the glory of God manifested in salvation through judgment. Can the center hold? Is the gravitational force of the glory of God in salvation through judgment sufficient to organize the universe of biblical theology?

4. The World Is Charged with the Grandeur of God: Proposed Centers and the Center

I have suggested that all the Bible's themes flow from, exposit, and feed back into the center of biblical theology. Do other proposed centers relate this way to God's glory in salvation through judgment? Proposed centers in the discussion below are italicized to draw attention to them; otherwise they might be overlooked as they find their proper place in orbit around and in service to the central theme of God's glory in salvation through judgment.

The created realm (*creation*) is a spectacular theater that serves as the cosmic matrix in which God's saving and judging glory can be revealed. God's glory is so grand that no less a stage than the universe—all that is or was and will be, across space and through time—is necessary for the unfolding of this all-encompassing drama. The psalmist sings, "The heavens are recounting the glory of God, and the skies are proclaiming the work of his hands" (Ps. 19:1). Similarly, Paul exclaims, "From him and through him and to him are all things; to him be the glory forever! Amen" (Rom. 11:36). *Creation* is for the glory of God.

If we ask why God reveals himself (*the self-revelation of God*) in creation, we meet with answers in such texts as Numbers 14:21, "The glory of Yahweh will fill the whole earth"; Isaiah 6:3, "The fullness of the whole earth is his glory"; Habakkuk 2:14, "For the earth will be filled with the knowledge of the glory of Yahweh as the waters cover the sea"; Psalm 72:19, "His glory fills the whole earth"; and Revelation 4:11, "You are worthy, our Lord and God, to receive glory and honor and power, because you created all things and because of your will they existed and were created." *The self-revelation of God* is for the glory of God.

The *holiness of God* is an attribute of God that is put on display, particularly when he judges (e.g., Lev. 10:1–3, 10). As such, when God judges he *reveals himself* as a *holy God*. The psalmist urges,

---

Theology: An Exegetical, Canonical, and Thematic Approach [Grand Rapids: Zondervan, 2007], 61, cf. also 144). As this study was in preparation, Schreiner's *New Testament Theology: Magnifying God in Christ* (Grand Rapids: Baker, 2008) appeared, also arguing for the centrality of the glory of God in Christ. Systematic theologians have long recognized the centrality of the glory of God, but in summaries of the discussion of the center of Old Testament, New Testament, Pauline, or biblical theology, the proposal does not appear. See, e.g., H. G. Reventlow, "Theology (Biblical), History of," *ABD*, 6:483–505; Werner E. Lemke, "Theology (OT)," in *ABD*, 6:449–73; Robert Morgan, "Theology (NT)," in *ABD*, 6:473–83; R. P. Martin, "Center of Paul's Theology," in *DPL*, 92–95; Joseph Plevnik, "The Center of Pauline Theology," *CBQ* 51 (1989): 461–78.

> Ascribe to Yahweh the glory of his name;
> worship Yahweh in the splendor of holiness. (Ps. 29:2)

There is a connection here between the *name of Yahweh*[83] and his *holiness*, and both are to result in the worship of Yahweh, which ascribes to him due glory. *The holiness of God* is for the glory of God,[84] and it is most commonly *revealed* in judgment.

Just as the *holiness of God* is often seen in judgment, the *steadfast love* of Yahweh is an attribute of God that is put on display when he works salvation. Just as God's *revelation* of his *holiness* results in his glory, so it is with his *steadfast love*: "Not to us, O Yahweh, not to us, but to *your name* give glory, because of your *steadfast love*, because of your truth" (Ps. 115:1, emphasis added). *The steadfast love of God* is for the glory of God, and it is most commonly *revealed* in *salvation*.

While the *holiness of God* is often seen in judgment, and the *steadfast love* of God is often seen in salvation, it is also true that God *reveals* his *holiness* when he saves, because when he saves he fulfills promises he has made. *Salvation* reveals God's uniqueness and his righteousness (aspects of *holiness*) as he keeps his promises. Judgment and salvation *reveal* God's *holiness*.

Similarly, while God's *steadfast love* is seen in salvation, it is also seen in judgment. When God judges, he enforces standards he himself has set, showing *steadfast love* to himself and the demands of his character. Further, when God judges, he shows *steadfast love* to his people. They are saved from their enemies when he judges those enemies. They are saved from their sins when God judges

[83]It is unfortunate that English translations render *Yahweh* as "the LORD," because the word "LORD" in small caps is a title. This title is not Yahweh's name, even when the letters are put in small caps. The old "Jehovah" might be preferable, but in any case, readers would be helped if they could know Yahweh by name. The practice of replacing *Yahweh* with *Adonai* ("Lord") or some other substitute is as old as the LXX and the DSS, and a significant consideration is that the New Testament seems to follow this practice—citing texts that refer to Yahweh in the Old Testament with the Greek translation's *kyrios*, "Lord." This conveniently allows certain texts from the Old Testament that speak of Yahweh to be applied to Jesus (e.g., Rom. 10:13). The substitution of *Adonai* for *Yahweh*, which led to the translation *kyrios*, apparently does not derive from the command not to take Yahweh's name in vain. Jeffrey Tigay writes, "There is no evidence for the common view that this avoidance of the name was based on the third commandment. Philo and R. Levi think that it is based on Leviticus 24:15–16 . . . . However, this view is rejected in the Talmud" (*Deuteronomy*, JPS Torah Commentary [Philadelphia: Jewish Publication Society, 1996], 431). For discussion of Rabbinic evidence, see Abraham Cohen, *Everyman's Talmud: The Major Teachings of the Rabbinic Sages* (1931; repr., n.p.: BN Publishing, 2008), 25–27. Albert Pietersma ("Kyrios or Tetragram: A Renewed Quest for the Original Septuagint," in *De Septuaginta*, ed. Albert Pietersma and Claude Cox [Mississauga, ON: Benben, 1984], 85–101) shows that in the original translation of the Pentateuch the divine name was rendered *kyrios*, and that its replacement with the tetragram in some manuscripts reflects an "archaizing tendency" (99). See also John William Wevers, "The Rendering of the Tetragram in the Psalter and Pentateuch: A Comparative Study," in *The Old Greek Psalter: Studies in Honor of Albert Pietersma*, ed. Robert J. V. Hiebert, Claude E. Cox, and Peter J. Gentry, JSOTSup 332 (Sheffield: Sheffield Academic, 2001), 21–35. A brief description of Jewish scribal practices can be found in Larry W. Hurtado, *The Earliest Christian Artifacts: Manuscripts and Christian Origins* (Grand Rapids: Eerdmans, 2006), 101–4.

[84]Cf. Robin Routledge, "Is There a Narrative Substructure Underlying the Book of Isaiah?" *TynBul* 55 (2004): 194: "Holiness may be seen as an inward characteristic; it is an essential divine attribute, intimately related to who God is. Glory is the outward manifestation of that holiness: the radiant splendour of the presence of God."

their sins (e.g., Isa. 40:2; Rom. 8:3). And they are saved from self-centered thinking when God's judgment crashes in upon the idolatry of the self and crushes it.

As God enforces the standards he has set and keeps the promises he has made, we see that *promise-fulfillment* serves salvation through judgment. God *promises* to save and judge, and he *fulfills* these *promises* by saving and judging. But again, *promise-fulfillment* is not an end in itself. Salvation and judgment *reveal* God's *steadfast love* and his *holiness*. God *reveals* his *holiness* and his *steadfast love* not as ends themselves, however, but as means to the end of displaying his own glory.

The psalmist describes the way that *holiness* and *steadfast love* are manifestations of God's glory:

> Surely his salvation is near to those who fear him,
> that glory may dwell in our land.
> Steadfast love and truth meet together;
> righteousness and peace kiss each other. (Ps. 85:10–11)

And again,

> Righteousness and judgment are the foundation of your throne;
> steadfast love and truth go before you. (89:15, ET 14)

The *holiness of God*, God's *steadfast love*, and the manifestation of these in *promise-fulfillment* all serve to show the glory of God in salvation through judgment.

The *election of Israel* displays the character of Yahweh. He does not choose the most numerous or the largest and strongest (Deut. 7:7). Rather, he *chooses Israel* in order to establish his *steadfast love* to the weak and lowly. He then enables them to love him and keep his commandments, but he has also chosen them to execute the requiting destruction demanded by his *holiness* against those who hate him (7:9–10). God *elects Israel* to show his *love* by saving them, which entails judgment upon the enemies of the nation—and both Israelites and non-Israelites prove to be enemies of the nation. This shows that the *election of Israel* reveals the *name* of God by affording him an opportunity to *reveal himself* as a *holy God* who shows *steadfast love*. The *election of Israel* demonstrates the glory of God in salvation through judgment.

God's *covenant* with Israel also highlights his glory, as he condescends to reveal his covenant *name* to Moses and Israel (Ex. 3:13–15), a *name* that is later proclaimed by Yahweh himself as he reveals his glory to Moses.[85] As Eichrodt

[85]See the discussion of "The Glorious Name: Exodus 32–34" in chap. 2, §3.4, along with the appendix (§8) to chap. 2, which catalogs Ex. 34:6–7 in the Law, Prophets, and Writings.

recognized, Yahweh's *covenant* with Israel is not an end in itself but serves the greater purpose of forging a relationship with his people,[86] and in this relationship he will make himself known (*God's self-revelation*) as a *holy God* who shows *steadfast love* because of his *covenant*. As Scott Hafemann has written regarding the covenant relationship, "This relationship is the means by which God reveals his glory."[87] God's *covenant* is for his glory, and his glory will be seen in salvation through judgment.

From these considerations of the relationship between other proposed centers and the center proposed here, I submit that these other proposals flow from, exposit, and feed back into the glory of God in salvation through judgment.

5. "Salvation through Judgment to the Glory of God": What Does This Phrase Mean?

What is the glory of God? I would suggest that the glory of God is the weight of the majestic goodness of who God is, and the resulting name, or reputation, that he gains from his revelation of himself as Creator, Sustainer, Judge, and Redeemer, perfect in justice and mercy, loving-kindness and truth.

What is meant by the phrase "salvation through judgment"? As a preview of the argument developed throughout the book, what follows is a brief explanation of what I intend "salvation through judgment" to communicate.

Salvation shows God to be "merciful and gracious, slow to anger, and great in steadfast love and faithfulness, keeping steadfast love for thousands, forgiving iniquity and transgression and sin" (Ex. 34:6b–7a). Ross Wagner rightly states, "These words are invoked repeatedly throughout Israel's sacred writings as a way of characterizing the intimate connection between God's very nature and his commitment to his people."[88] Judgment shows God to be the one "who will by no means clear the guilty, visiting the iniquity of the fathers on the sons and

---

[86]Eichrodt (*Theology of the Old Testament*, 1:41) writes, "The existence of the nation could not become an end in itself. From the start it had to remain subordinate to a higher purpose, an overriding conception, the achievement of the nation's religious destiny." I would suggest that the nation's religious destiny is to rejoice in and thereby glorify God when he saves them through the judgment of both their own sin and the enemies who oppose them. In a statement that clearly subordinates the covenant to God's concern for his own glory, Eichrodt writes, "Israel is to be spared from the judgment of wrath not as a consequence of the indestructibility of the divine *berīt*, but because of God's jealousy for the honour of his Name" (1:60).

[87]Scott J. Hafemann, "The Covenant Relationship," in Hafemann and House, *Central Themes in Biblical Theology*, 30. Hafemann's essay is a thoroughgoing treatment of "the covenant as the integrating concept of Scripture" (24), though he too thinks that "the attempt to isolate [a center] has proved to be too specific to gain a consensus or too general to be of explanatory power" (23). For a trenchant critique of proposals that subsume the various covenants in the Bible under one umbrella "covenant," see Jeffrey J. Niehaus, "An Argument against Theologically Constructed Covenants," *JETS* 50, no. 2 (2007): 259–73. Peter J. Gentry ("Kingdom through Covenant: Humanity as the Divine Image," *SBJT* 12, no. 1 [2008]: 16–42) grants that "Dumbrell may . . . blur the distinction between covenant and covenant renewals, but his definition is based on passages like the treaty in Genesis 21" (18). Gentry also defends Dumbrell's understanding of "cutting a covenant" as a description of the making of a covenant and "confirming/establishing a covenant" as a phrase used to indicate a covenant partner's experience of a promise of a previously initiated covenant (against Williamson, *Sealed with an Oath*, 73).

[88]J. Ross Wagner, *Heralds of the Good News: Isaiah and Paul in Concert in the Letter to the Romans* (Leiden: Brill, 2003), 53.

on the sons of the sons, on the third and on the fourth generations" (Ex. 34:7b; for a catalog of quotations of and allusions to this text, see the appendix to chap. 2, §8, "Exodus 34:6–7 in the Law, Prophets, and Writings"). Thus, salvation and judgment balance one another. The reality of judgment should keep us from thinking of God in purely sentimental terms as though he were a grandfatherly buddy who just lets things go. The reality of salvation should likewise keep us from thinking of God as merely a terrifying, vengeful judge.[89] Those who flee to him will be saved, but those who do not fear him will be judged. Paradoxically, it is the reality of his terrifying judgment that is meant to send us fleeing to him. This matches the "eternal gospel" proclaimed by the angel in Revelation 14:6–7: "Fear God and give him glory, because the hour of his judgment has come, and worship the one who made the heaven and the earth and sea and springs of water."

Salvation always comes through judgment. Salvation for the nation of Israel at the Exodus came through the judgment of Egypt, and this pattern is repeated throughout the Old Testament, becoming paradigmatic even into the New. When God saves his people, he delivers them by bringing judgment on their enemies. This is not limited to Old Testament enemies such as the Philistines. At the cross, the ruler of this world was cast out (John 12:31). At the consummation, Jesus will come to afflict those who afflict his people (2 Thess. 1:6, cf. 6–10).

Salvation for all believers of all ages is made possible by the judgment that falls on Jesus at the cross. The cross allows God to be just and the justifier of the one who has faith in Jesus (Rom. 3:24–26). The cross of Christ, the climactic expression of the glory of God in salvation through judgment, is the turning point of the ages.

Even though members of the old covenant remnant lived before Jesus, saving faith for them was explicit trust in the promises of God. The promises of God began in Genesis 3:15, with the promise of a seed of the woman who would crush the serpent's head.[90] Many of the Old Testament's promises concern an anointed Redeemer, who came to be referred to as the messiah, whom God would raise up to accomplish the salvation of his people. So even though Old Testament saints did not know that the messiah would be named Jesus, grow up in Nazareth, and so forth, in the words of Genesis 3:15 they heard God promise to raise up a man who would save them. Faith came by hearing, and they trusted God to keep his word. They were saved by faith in God's promised messiah.

---

[89]Cf. R. W. L. Moberly, "How May We Speak of God? A Reconsideration of the Nature of Biblical Theology," *TynBul* 53 (2002): 200–202 (177–202). See also Hermann Spieckermann, "God's Steadfast Love: Towards a New Conception of Old Testament Theology," *Biblica* 81 (2000): 305–27.

[90]See Hamilton, "The Skull Crushing Seed of the Woman," and "The Seed of the Woman and the Blessing of Abraham," *TynBul* 58 (2007): 253–73.

Everyone who gets saved is saved through judgment. All who flee to Christ and confess that he is Lord and that God raised him from the dead (Rom. 10:9) do so because they realize their need for a Savior. They realize their need for a Savior because they have become convinced that God is holy, that they are sinful, and that God will judge. In a sense, they feel the force of God's condemning justice. They sense the weight of the wrath that remains upon them (John 3:36), and they recognize that Jesus is their only hope. Thus, historically (in Christ on the cross) and existentially (in their own experience of the wrath of God that makes them feel their need for Christ), believers are saved through judgment.[91]

There is another way in which salvation works itself out in the Bible, chiefly to be seen in the Old Testament Writings and the New Testament Letters. This is the way that announcements and warnings of coming judgment are meant to function to lead people to salvation. The vocalization of the truths of God's justice is meant to cause people to be saved through judgment for the glory of God. The certainty of the justice of God prompts people to seek his mercy, and both sides of this equation glorify God.

All of this reveals God as righteous and merciful, loving and just, holy and forgiving, for his own glory, forever. And his glory is what is best for all concerned.[92]

This section on the way that God's glory in salvation through judgment functions as the center of and organizing principle for biblical theology can be summarized in seven points:

The glory of God in salvation through judgment is

1. God's way of showing his glory and defining his own name (Ex. 33:18–34:7; see the appendix [§8] to chap. 2, "Exodus 34:6–7 in the Law, Prophets, and Writings");
2. the goal of God in redemptive history (e.g., Isa. 66:20–24; Rev. 19:1–8; see the texts in appendix 2 [§6] to chap. 3, "All the Earth Filled with the Knowledge of Yahweh's Glory");
3. the pattern of the Bible's metanarrative—creation, sin, exile, restoration;

[91]As Mark A. Seifrid (*Christ, Our Righteousness: Paul's Theology of Justification*, NSBT [Downers Grove, IL: InterVarsity, 2000], 59) writes, "For Paul, the justification of human beings takes place only through God's triumph and their defeat." In other words, justification takes place by means of salvation through judgment.

[92]Some theologians (particularly those with a strong disdain for Calvinism) allow the philosophical concept of God's "omnibenevolence" to control their reading of the Bible. I think it better to allow the Bible to inform our philosophical concepts. If God wanted to reveal that his controlling attribute is omnibenevolence, surely he would have done so in a statement such as Ex. 33:19, or when he proclaimed his own name to Moses in Ex. 34:6–7. I am not denying God's omnibenevolence. I am, however, insisting that those who submit their theology to the Bible *by definition* must allow the Bible to define this concept for us, and here we look to texts such as Ex. 33:19 and 34:6–7, where we clearly see God setting both his justice and his mercy on display. Biblical theology is in this sense descriptive, not prescriptive. As Denny Burk has written, "We do not dictate *a priori* what should be. We merely analyze what is" (*Articular Infinitives*, 21).

4. the pattern of each major redemptive event in the Bible—fall, flood, exodus, exile from the land, the death and resurrection of Jesus, and the return of Christ;
5. the existential experience of individuals who are convicted of their sin, feel condemnation, trust God for mercy, and join him in seeking the glory of his great name (see the appendix [§7] to chap. 4, table 4.9, "Old Testament Prayers Appealing to God's Concern for His Own Glory");
6. the ground of the Bible's ethical appeals—fear of judgment curbs behavior and keeps people on the path that leads to salvation;
7. the content of the praises of the redeemed (e.g., Exodus 15; Judges 5; Psalm 18; Rev. 11:17–18; see the appendix [§5] to chap. 6, table 6.7, "Doxologies in the New Testament").

6. Like Shining from Shook Foil

It would be impossible to exhaust the Bible's testimony to the glory of God in salvation through judgment. All we need to do is shake the foil, so to speak, and it will gather to a greatness like the ooze of oil.[93] God's glory is like a many-faceted gem, which reflects and refracts light in ever-new, ever-unexpected ways as it is admired. The plan of this book is not to dissect the gem, but selectively to admire it.

As we proceed through the canon in this study, I will follow Stephen Dempster's helpful explanation of the sequence of the books of the Hebrew Bible.[94] On this understanding, the Old Testament falls into three sections (table 1.1): Torah (Law), Neviim (Prophets), and Ketuvim (Writings). This is the way the Old Testament is laid out in the JPS translation of the Old Testament called the Tanak. The word TaNaK is formed from the first letter of each section: *T*orah, *N*eviim, *K*etuvim.

Table 1.1. The Tripartite Shape of the Hebrew Bible

Torah	Law
Neviim	Prophets
Ketuvim	Writings

[93]See the first four lines of Gerard Manley Hopkins's poem, "God's Grandeur," which is presented on the facing page to this introductory chapter.

[94]See Stephen Dempster, *Dominion and Dynasty: A Theology of the Hebrew Bible*, NSBT (Downers Grove, IL: InterVarsity, 2003). Paul House also follows this arrangement of the Old Testament in his *Old Testament Theology* (Downers Grove, IL: InterVarsity, 1998), as does William J. Dumbrell, *The Faith of Israel: A Theological Survey of the Old Testament*, 2nd ed. (Grand Rapids: Baker, 2002).

This is not the only way of approaching the books of the Old Testament (and there is some variation in the arrangement of the books of the Old Testament in the order of the Writings), but this way of looking at the Old Testament seems to match the way Jesus described it in Luke 24:44 when he referred to "the Law of Moses and the Prophets and the Psalms."[95]

The contents of these three sections are slightly different than what might be expected by Christian readers of English translations of the Old Testament, so in table 1.2, the books are listed under their headings. Perhaps the most unexpected features are that the books of Joshua through Kings are referred to as "Prophets," while Daniel is classed with the "Writings." The Prophets actually fall into two parts, the Former Prophets and the Latter Prophets. And the Writings can be divided into three parts, The Book of Truth,[96] the *Megilloth* (small scrolls), and the Other Sacred Writings.[97]

Table 1.2. The Books in the Tripartite Order

Torah
Genesis, Exodus, Leviticus, Numbers, Deuteronomy
Neviim
Former Prophets: Joshua, Judges, Samuel, Kings
Latter Prophets: Isaiah, Jeremiah, Ezekiel, the Book of the Twelve (Hosea, Joel, Amos, Obadiah, Jonah, Micah, Nahum, Habakkuk, Zephaniah, Haggai, Zechariah, Malachi)
Ketuvim
The Book of Truth: Psalms, Proverbs, Job
The Megilloth (Small Scrolls): Song of Songs, Ruth, Lamentations, Ecclesiastes, Esther
Other Sacred Writings: Daniel, Ezra–Nehemiah, Chronicles

Dempster has explored the way that a narrative story line is begun in the Torah and carried through the Former Prophets.[98] This story takes us from Adam to the exile. When we proceed into the Latter Prophets, instead of a continuation of the narrative story line, we find poetic commentary on that story line. Isaiah

[95]See also *Baba Bathra* 14b, the prologue to Sirach, lines 8–10, and 4QMMT, line 10 (4Q397, Frags. 14–21, p. 801 in *DSS*^{SE}). For discussion, see Roger Beckwith, *The Old Testament Canon of the New Testament Church and Its Background in Early Judaism* (Grand Rapids: Eerdmans, 1985), 111–12.

[96]This name appears to be derived from the acronym אמת ("truth") made from the first letter of the three books: Psalms (Hebrew: תהלים, *Tehilim*), Proverbs (Hebrew: משלי, *Mishley*), and Job (Hebrew: איוב, *Ayov*). Cf. Emanuel Tov, *Textual Criticism of the Hebrew Bible* (Minneapolis: Fortress, 1992), 3–4.

[97]I am following the order set forth by Roland Kenneth Harrison, *Introduction to the Old Testament* (Grand Rapids: Eerdmans, 1969; repr., Prince Press, 1999), x–xi.

[98]Dempster, *Dominion and Dynasty*, 45–51.

through Malachi is thus commentary on Genesis through Kings.[99] The poetic commentary continues through the first two-thirds of the Writings, when the narrative story line is resumed in Esther and continued through Chronicles (table 1.3).

Table 1.3. Narrative Story Line and Poetic Commentary

Narrative Story Line
Torah
Genesis, Exodus, Leviticus, Numbers, Deuteronomy
Neviim
Former Prophets: Joshua, Judges, Samuel, Kings
Poetic Commentary
Latter Prophets: Isaiah, Jeremiah, Ezekiel, the Book of the Twelve (Hosea, Joel, Amos, Obadiah, Jonah, Micah, Nahum, Habakkuk, Zephaniah, Haggai, Zechariah, Malachi)
Ketuvim
The Book of Truth: Psalms, Proverbs, Job
The Megilloth (Small Scrolls): Song of Songs, Ruth, Lamentations, Ecclesiastes, Esther
Narrative Story Line
Other Sacred Writings: (Esther) Daniel, Ezra–Nehemiah, Chronicles

Again, approaching the Old Testament this way follows ancient tradition regarding the arrangement of the Old Testament (the prologue to Sirach, lines 8–10; 4QMMT, line 10; Luke 24:44; and *Baba Bathra* 14b). Moreover, Christopher Seitz writes, "In actual fact, the only order that settles down in the history of the Old Testament's reception is the tripartite of the Hebrew order."[100]

In a fascinating essay, David Noel Freedman observes the remarkably balanced amount of material in the major sections of the whole of the Old Testament.[101] The amount of material is based on the number of words, and Emanuel Tov writes, "According to tradition, the Masorah stemmed from the time of Ezra, called a סופר מהיר, 'an expert scribe,' in Ezra 7:6, and the time of the *soferim*

[99]Similarly Rolf Rendtorff, *The Canonical Hebrew Bible: A Theology of the Old Testament*, trans. David E. Orton, Tools for Biblical Study (Leiden: Deo, 2005), 7.

[100]Christopher Seitz, "Canon, Narrative, and the Old Testament's Literal Sense: A Response to John Goldingay, 'Canon and Old Testament Theology,'" *TynBul* 59 (2008): 28 (27–34); cf. also 29: "The convention of modern printed Bibles, with a fourfold order [Law, History, Poetry, Prophecy], is just that: a convention, and it has no known exemplar before the modern period." See also Beckwith, *The Old Testament Canon of the New Testament Church*, 181–234.

[101]David N. Freedman, "The Symmetry of the Hebrew Bible," *Studia Theologica* 46 (1992): 83–108, and Freedman, *The Unity of the Hebrew Bible* (Ann Arbor: University of Michigan Press, 1991). The evidence that Freedman presents excludes the book of Daniel from consideration, but Roger Beckwith presents evidence for an early date for Daniel in "Early Traces of the Book of Daniel," *TynBul* 53 (2002): 75–82. In the numbers I give in the text above, I include Daniel in the Writings. This does not radically alter the total count.

in the generations after him. See *b. Qidd.* 30a: 'The older men were called *soferim* because they counted all the letters in the Torah.'"[102] Freedman finds what he refers to as a "bilateral symmetry" by which he means "that the whole Hebrew Bible is divided into two equal halves, and these in turn are subdivided into relatively equal or proportionate parts."[103] Thus, the Torah and the Former Prophets, the narrative story line, are roughly the same length as the Latter Prophets and the Writings, the poetic commentary and the resumption of the story line:

Torah + Former Prophets = 149,668 words
Latter Prophets + Writings = 155,856 words

Freedman's analysis also finds a roughly chiastic symmetry in the length of these major sections of the Hebrew Bible:

Torah, 79,983 words
  Former Prophets, 69,685 words
  Latter Prophets, 71,852 words
Writings, 84,004 words

This information prompts Freedman to assert:

> It is our contention that such palpable symmetrical patterning cannot be the result of random forces; the canonical collection we know as the Hebrew Bible could not have been achieved by the process advocated by most scholars, i.e., gradual accretion over a long period of time. . . . The collection as we know it (with modifications . . .) must be the product of one person, or of a very small group, working at one time, in one place, to achieve the results visible in the entire structure of the Hebrew Bible.[104]

On the basis of this information, which Stephen Dempster has referred to as "an extraordinary fact,"[105] Freedman concludes, "We attribute the conception and execution to the Scribe Ezra and Governor Nehemiah, who may have worked partly in tandem, but also in sequence, with Ezra responsible chiefly for the conception and Nehemiah for the execution and completion of the project."[106]

---

[102]Tov, *Textual Criticism of the Hebrew Bible*, 72. Tov also observes that "More extensive than the lists in biblical manuscripts are the lists at the ends of books in the second Rabbinic Bible . . . , which were culled from various sources by the editor of that edition. . . . This final Masorah of the second Rabbinic Bible counts the number of letters, words, and verses in the different books of the Bible" (74). Cf. also Beckwith, *The Old Testament Canon of the New Testament Church*, 161: "In the Babylonian Talmud, we are told that 'the early scholars were called *sopherim* (scribes) because they used to count (*saphar*) all the letters of the Law.'"
[103]Freedman, "The Symmetry of the Hebrew Bible," 83.
[104]Ibid., 83–84.
[105]Stephen Dempster has used Freedman's analysis constructively in "An 'Extraordinary Fact': *Torah and Temple* and the Contours of the Hebrew Canon: Parts 1 and 2," *TynBul* 48 (1997): 23–56; 191–218.
[106]Freedman, "The Symmetry of the Hebrew Bible," 105.

If Ezra and Nehemiah did organize the Old Testament in the way that Freedman suggests, it would not seem too much to imagine that they understood their work to communicate a coherent message with a main or central theme.[107]

The argument that the Bible's theology does have a center is strengthened by this evidence that a "canonicler" arranged the books of the Old Testament and presented them in their canonical form, presumably under the inspiration of the Holy Spirit.[108] The idea that the Bible's theology has a center is not, however, dependent upon this way of accounting for the Old Testament canon.

I am convinced that God's revelation of his saving and judging glory to the earliest biblical author on record, Moses, had a decisive influence on the progress of revelation as it unfolded. More will be said about this in the discussion of the book of Exodus in chapter 2 (§3),[109] but introducing this consideration here is warranted because it is so decisive for my argument. Yahweh declared his own name to Moses when Moses asked to see his glory (Ex. 33:18–34:8). Can there have been a greater influence on Moses' understanding of Yahweh than that event? In short, Yahweh announced himself to Moses as a merciful and forgiving God who upholds justice (34:6–7). Moses quickly bowed low and worshiped (34:8). What I am arguing is that when Yahweh declared his name to Moses (33:19), showed him his glory (33:18), and caused all his goodness to pass before him (33:19), he defined himself as a saving and judging God, a God who saves through judgment. Yahweh's steadfast love and refusal to clear the guilty, then, are intrinsic to his identity and inform everything he does. Yahweh's declaration of his name, which announces both his reputation and his character, profoundly influenced Moses, whose writings in turn profoundly influenced every other biblical author.[110] I hope to show that the saving and judging glory of God dominated the implicit assumptions of the biblical authors, that it was the gravitational lodestone that held together the stories they told, the songs they sang, and the instructions they gave. Indeed, the glory of God in salvation through judgment is the center of biblical theology.

Returning to the way the biblical canon will be approached in this study, Dempster further observes that the New Testament can be seen to have a similar shape in that it begins with the narrative story line of Jesus and the early church in the Gospels and Acts, continues with commentary on the story line in the Letters, and concludes with a resumption of the narrative story line in

---

[107]Freedman offers his assessment of "the purpose of the author/editor" and the Old Testament's "pervasive unity" in *The Unity of the Hebrew Bible*, 39, 98.

[108]For the use of the term "canonicler," see John H. Sailhamer, *Introduction to Old Testament Theology: A Canonical Approach* (Grand Rapids: Zondervan, 1995), 240.

[109]See esp. chap. 2, §3.4, "The Glorious Name: Exodus 32–34."

[110]See the appendix to chap. 2 (§8), "Exodus 34:6–7 in the Law, Prophets, and Writings."

the Apocalypse (Revelation).[111] Viewed this way (see table 1.4), the Bible is seen to be a unified metanarrative that begins at creation and ends with the consummation of all things.

Table 1.4. The Shape of the New Testament

Narrative Storyline
Gospels and Acts
Commentary
Letters
Narrative Storyline
Revelation

This metanarrative is, of course, composed of individual books, written by many different human authors who were guided by the divine author. A word is in order on how these individual books will be treated in the following study, for, as Paul Hoskins has noted, "Two common pitfalls accompanying studies in OT and NT theology are insufficient care in interpreting biblical texts in their contexts and focusing attention upon certain passages while failing to integrate others."[112] This book intends to cover the whole Bible, treating every text in context and integrating all the Bible's teaching (especially parts that might appear to be in conflict with my thesis), but this book cannot be a full commentary on every verse of the Bible.

Structuring what follows according to its canonical form identifies this study with the "canonical approach" to biblical theology.[113] For the most part, each chapter that follows will begin with an overview of the biblical books covered in

[111]Dempster, *Dominion and Dynasty*, 232–34. Dempster also engages in a canonical exercise in biblical theology that treats the Bible along these divisions in his essay, "The Servant of the Lord" in *Central Themes in Biblical Theology*, 128–78.

[112]Paul M. Hoskins, *Jesus as the Fulfillment of the Temple in the Gospel of John*, Paternoster Biblical Monographs (Waynesboro, GA: Paternoster, 2006), 9 n. 37.

[113]Elmer Martens identifies six different ways of approaching biblical theology: (1) structured (Eichrodt); (2) diachronic (von Rad); (3) lexicographic (P. F. Ellis); (4) thematic (Bright); (5) canonical (Childs, Rendtorff, House, Dumbrell, Dempster, Sailhamer); and (6) narrative (Goldingay) (Elmer Martens, "Old Testament Theology Since Walter C. Kaiser, Jr.," *JETS* 50 [2007]: 674–78 [673–91]). It should be noted that several who approach biblical theology from a "canonical" perspective are also very "literary" in their approach, which means that they also do "narrative theology." I am pursuing biblical theology canonically, with sensitivity to literary features of the text, and assuming the reliability of the historical claims of the canonical text. Daniel J. Treier has presented a "fivefold typology of ways to relate" biblical theology to "theological interpretation of Scripture," and it seems to me that most evangelical biblical theologians would see themselves as occupying *both* Treier's second and fourth categories—believing biblical theology that is *both* historical (category two) and literary (category four). Treier understands himself and "theological interpretation of Scripture" to be in the third category. Treier concedes that D. A. Carson, his example of someone who belongs in category two with its historical emphasis, has balanced his approach with more literary sensitivity, which Treier says belongs to category four (Daniel J. Treier, "Biblical Theology and/or Theological Interpretation of Scripture?" *SJT* 61 [2008]: 16–31; the note on Carson is on p. 26, n. 24). Perhaps it would be more accurate to say that a historical emphasis prevailed among evangelicals in the twentieth century, with more and more attention being given to literary/narrative features near the end of the millennium and at the beginning of the twenty-first century.

the chapter: their story, themes, and particular way of showing forth the glory of God in salvation through judgment. After the overview, each book will be discussed in more depth, and most will be examined according to the literary structure inherent to the book itself. I am seeking to show how the glory of God in salvation through judgment is communicated in the parts and the wholes of the biblical books in an effort to preempt the charge that I have foisted this center onto the material. So the treatment will seek to attend to canonical and literary features, but in some cases, Genesis, for instance, my discussion will be more thematic. I make this choice for a book like Genesis because the ten *toledoths* that appear to structure the book (Gen. 2:4; 5:1; 6:9; 10:1; 11:10, 27; 25:12, 19; 36:1, 9; 37:2) are well known and often discussed,[114] and so it seems to me that there is a place for discussing the contents of Genesis according to themes growing out of Genesis 3 and 12 in an effort to showcase the center of the theology of Genesis. Drawing attention to these themes in Genesis will also point out key features of the stage on which the rest of the Bible's drama will be enacted.

There will surely be a main theme of this overarching story. Seeking to discover this theme is a legitimate enterprise, for as Dempster writes, "If it is the case that the Hebrew canon is also a Text with a definite beginning, middle, ending and plot, then the task of discovering a fundamental theme becomes not an exercise in futility but an imperative of responsible hermeneutics."[115] Similarly, Elmer Martens states that "Biblical theology is an attempt to get to the theological heart of the Bible."[116]

The New Testament authors present their accounts as the completion of the story begun in the Old Testament, and the Old Testament itself creates the expectations realized in the New Testament. The two are to be read together, and this book will follow, in its general outline, the structure of the Old and New Testaments that has been briefly discussed above. As the story unfolds, the central theme of the theology contained in the Bible itself will flame out like shining from shook foil, and the dearest freshness deep down in these rich soils will be the glory of God in salvation through judgment.

---

[114]See, e.g., Richard Schultz, "What Is 'Canonical' About a Canonical Biblical Theology? Genesis as a Case Study of Recent Old Testament Proposals," in *Biblical Theology: Retrospect and Prospect*, ed. Scott J. Hafemann (Downers Grove, IL: InterVarsity, 2002), 83–99.

[115]Dempster, *Dominion and Dynasty*, 43. Dempster helpfully explores the theme of dominion and dynasty, geography and genealogy in the Old Testament, tracing the interrelationships of the promises of the land and the deliverer. In my view, this twin theme serves the central theme of God's glory in salvation through judgment, as the one whose dynasty is traced is the one who will be God's agent of both salvation and judgment, and the restoration to the land will be salvation for God's people and judgment on their enemies. Dominion and dynasty display the glory of God in salvation through judgment.

[116]Martens, "Old Testament Theology Since Walter C. Kaiser, Jr.," 680 n. 37, citing his own essay, "Tackling Old Testament Theology," *JETS* 20 (1977): 123.

Chapter 2

God's Glory in Salvation through Judgment IN THE TORAH

And there were gardens bright with sinuous rills,
Where blossomed many an incense-bearing tree;
And here were forests ancient as the hills,
Enfolding sunny spots of greenery.

—Samuel Taylor Coleridge, "Kubla Khan"

1. Introduction

The Torah is a story of the glory of God in salvation through judgment. The main character is Yahweh, God of Israel, and the five books of the Pentateuch narrate the beginnings of the stately pleasure dome that he decreed. The world is created, the image bearers rebel, judgment and mercy are shown them, and a covenant is eventually initiated with Abraham through which the nations will be blessed. According to Torah, the world was brought into being by the word of Yahweh, exists as the effulgence of his overflowing goodness, and experiences both justice and mercy from its Maker. A brief overview of the story line of the Pentateuch, presented book by book, will prepare us to see how the glory of God in salvation through judgment is central to the theology of each book of the Torah.

1.1 The Story of Torah Book by Book

Genesis, the book of beginnings, tells us where we came from: God made us and all things. It tells us how everything was made: God spoke and it was. The genealogies hint at when these things took place, and the whole scene is set in Eden. The sinless condition in the pristine garden with uninhibited access to God's presence is soon lost. Adam and Eve are banished from the garden. They are judged, with promises of mercy folded into the judgment. Mankind becomes increasingly wicked, until God de-creates the world with a flood (just as the waters were separated that the dry land might appear, so now the dry land has been overwhelmed by the waters), saving Noah and his family through the judgment. The descendants of Noah in Shinar move to build their own tower into heaven, and God judges this effort by confusing human language. God then promises to bless Abraham and all the world through him. These blessings of Genesis 12 correspond to the curses of Genesis 3 in significant ways, and the rest of Genesis traces the passing down of the blessing to Isaac, Jacob, and Joseph, with Judah also figuring prominently in the narrative.

Exodus briefly recounts the fulfillment of part of God's promise—that the descendants of Abraham would be numerous—before recounting the way that Yahweh made a great name for himself by saving Israel through the judgment of Egypt: mighty hand and outstretched arm, forcing the world's superpower to bend the knee, getting glory over Pharaoh, whom he raised up for this very thing. After the judgment of Egypt, the narrative moves to the judgment of the stiff-necked people Yahweh chose for himself. Then at Sinai, just as Yahweh spoke creation into existence, he speaks Israel into existence, fulfilling another part of the promise to Abraham by making his descendants a great nation. Woven into the instructions for the building of the tabernacle, which is something of a new Eden, is another instance of salvation through judgment: Yahweh judges Israel's sin with the calf, saves them through the judgment, and announces that his goodness, which is his glory, is bound up in the meaning of his saving and judging name. He is free to show mercy and compassion to whomever he pleases.

Leviticus continues with Israel at Sinai, the nation learning how to live with a holy God. Yahweh takes up residence in the tabernacle, which requires that he be surrounded with holiness, and outside the holiness is cleanness. The camp of Israel must be clean. Outside the camp is the unclean realm. If the holy, Yahweh, comes into contact with anything unclean, death results. Israel can be made unclean in two ways: contact with the dead and transgression of Yahweh's commands. Israel can be made clean one way: by offering the prescribed sacrifices and following the clear instructions for cleansing. High-handed sin is the sin of casting off the covenant by refusing to repent and follow the instructions given in order to be cleansed. The Levitical system operates only by faith: Israel must believe that Yahweh really is in the tabernacle, that he really is holy, that sin and uncleanness really do make it dangerous to be near Yahweh, and that the prescribed sacrifice really will atone for sin. All of this must be taken on faith. All of it proclaims the blazing glory of Yahweh, who judges sin and justly punishes transgression, but who also mercifully provides a way for Israel to enjoy his presence.

Numbers opens with a census at Sinai, describing the people of Israel as a military host encamped around the tabernacle. From Sinai the people march on to the land, but they bog down in the wilderness because of their rebellions against the covenant Lord. At each point Yahweh saves the people through judgment. Some Israelites die when Yahweh judges, but the nation is preserved through these outbreaks of his holiness. The oracles of Balaam allude to the blessing of Abraham and bind it fast to the promises of a coming king of Israel. Another census is taken upon the death of the wilderness generation, and Israel comes right up to the border of the Promised Land.

Deuteronomy pulses out the heartbeat of the Old Testament. Bringing together all that has gone before, and setting the standard by which all that comes after will be judged, Deuteronomy prepares the nation for the next aspect of the fulfillment of the promise to Abraham: the conquest of the land. The nation's history is briefly reviewed, they are given every reason to love Yahweh and keep his commands, and the clear choice between life and death, obedience and disobedience, blessing and cursing, is set before them. Yahweh spoke to them out of the midst of the fire, he saved them by a mighty hand and outstretched arm, and he will execute justice and show mercy in accordance with his testimonies, statutes, judgments, and laws. The laws in Deuteronomy elaborate upon and exposit the Ten Commandments, and the book closes with blessings and curses, poetry and promises, the departure of Moses and the investiture of Joshua.

The major movements of the Torah might be summarized as shown in table 2.1.

Table 2.1. The Story Torah Tells

Genesis 1–11	Creation, fall, flood, Babel
Genesis 12–50	The fathers: Abraham, Isaac, Jacob, and Joseph
Exodus 1–15	The exodus from Egypt
Exodus 16–18	Judgment and mercy in the wilderness
Exodus 19:1–Numbers 10:10	The giving of the law at Sinai
Numbers 10:11–36:13	Death of the wilderness generation
Deuteronomy	Sinai commands applied to life in the land

With this preview of the Pentateuch before us, we can examine more closely the glory of God in salvation through judgment as the central and controlling theme both of the Torah as a whole and of each of its constituent parts. We move forward to examine each book in turn.

2. Genesis

2.1 The Heavens Proclaim the Glory of God

Genesis opens with the proclamation that God made all things by his spoken word. Contrasting what Genesis says with other accounts of the origin of all things will help us see more clearly how Genesis 1 and 2 proclaim the glory of God.[1] When compared with other ancient creation accounts, the Genesis narrative is remarkable for its presentation of the purity and power of Yahweh.

2.1.1 The Gods of the Nations

We will briefly consider Babylonian, Egyptian, and Greek creation myths. The noteworthy feature of these accounts, for this discussion, is the ungodliness of the gods.

In the Babylonian *Enuma Elish* (ca. 1400–1100 BC), "Primeval Absu was their progenitor, And matrix-Tiamat was she who bore them all."[2] From other gods Marduk is eventually born. There is conflict in the pantheon, and Marduk does battle with Tiamat, whom he kills, and having triumphed over "the demonic horde," he "crushed her skull." This done, "he split her in two . . . . Half of her he set up and made as a cover, heaven" (*COS*, 1:398). With the other half he makes the earth, builds Babylon as "the abode of [his] pleasure," and makes humans from the blood of the vanquished god Qingu (*COS*, 1:400–401).

According to ancient Egyptian texts (ca. 1300–1100 BC),[3] the god Shu is the atmosphere, who stands on Geb, the earth, and with upraised arms holds up Nut, the sky.[4] One of these texts reads, "I am the *ba* of Shu, the self-evolving god: it is in the body of the self-evolving god that I have evolved" (*COS*, 1:8). Other texts "describe the birth of Shu through the combined metaphors of masturbation and spitting."[5] Everything apparently derives from Atum, "the sum of all the forces and elements of the created world,"[6] who claims, "I am

---

[1]G. K. Beale outlines five ways the Old Testament can be seen to relate to parallel accounts in ancient Near Eastern mythology: (1) the Old Testament engages in polemic against these ideas; (2) the Old Testament reflects general revelation recounted by pagan and biblical authors; (3) the Old Testament and its parallels reflect a common ancient tradition; (4) the Old Testament uses ancient Near Eastern concepts in productive ways; and (5) the biblical writers unconsciously absorbed the ancient Near Eastern worldview (G. K. Beale, "Myth, History, and Inspiration: A Review Article of *Inspiration and Incarnation* by Peter Enns," *JETS* 49 [2006], 289–90 [287–312]). Justin Martyr attributes mythological parallels to the Bible, particularly where prophecies of Jesus are concerned, to demonic attempts to keep people from believing the Bible ("First Apology," chap. 54, in *ANF*, 1:181). While I do not agree with Walther Eichrodt (*Theology of the Old Testament*, trans. J. A. Baker, 2 vols. [Philadelphia: Westminster, 1961, 1967], 1:25) in his assertion that "no presentation of OT theology can properly be made without constant reference to its connections with the whole world of Near Eastern religion," in what follows I draw attention to some other accounts of things the Bible records to highlight the way the biblical narratives portray the superiority of Yahweh to the deities described in other texts.

[2]"Epic of Creation (1.111) (*Enuma Elish*)," trans. Benjamin R. Foster, in *The Context of Scripture: Canonical Compositions from the Biblical World* (hereafter COS), ed. William W. Hallo, 3 vols. (Boston: Brill, 2003), 1:391.

[3]These texts were captions to images on ceilings in tombs or spells inscribed on coffins.

[4]See "From Coffin Texts Spell 76 (1.6)," trans. James P. Allen, in *COS*, 1:10 n. 4.

[5]Introductory note, *COS*, 1:11.

[6]*COS*, 1:9 n. 12.

the one who acted as husband with my fist: I copulated with my hand, I let fall into my own mouth, I sneezed Shu and spat Tefnut" (*COS*, 1:14). James Allen comments on these lines, "Atum's semen is envisioned as falling into his mouth, from which it is 'sneezed' and 'spat' to produce the two gods."[7] Atum thus disgustingly generates Shu and Tefnut, who is associated with the natural order of the universe. Shu (atmosphere) and Tefnut (order) then give birth to Geb (earth) and Nut (sky).[8]

Hesiod's "Theogony" (ca. 700 BC?) is a major source of what we know of Greek mythology. According to Hesiod's poetry, "Verily at the first Chaos came to be." Next comes Gaia (Earth), then "dim Tartarus in the depth," followed by Eros (Desire), "who unnerves the limbs and overcomes the mind and wise counsels of all gods and all men within them." No explanation is given as to the origin of Chaos, Gaia, Tartarus, or Eros. Chaos produces Erebus (Darkness) and Nyx (Night). Nyx conceives from union in love with Erebus and bears Aither (Brightness) and Hemera (Day). Next Gaia brings forth Ouranos (Heaven), then Ourea (Mountains), Nymphs, and Pontos (Sea)—all apart from "sweet union of love." Gaia then "lay with" Ouranos, thereby giving birth to twelve Titans, among whom is Cronos (Time). On this explanation of all things, "mother earth," Gaia, spontaneously appears. We are not told whence she comes. She then brings forth "father sky," Ouranos, parthenogenically; they mate, and "father time," Cronos, is among their offspring. Ouranos knows that one of his children will overthrow him, so he seeks to confine them within Gaia. Cronos overcomes his father, Ouranos, by castrating him.[9] In this violent account, the Time-Space universe is personified, and while a cause-effect explanation of the sequence of the beginning of all things is given, there is no first mover, no ultimate purpose, which leaves the big questions unanswered. The Roman poet Hyginus (64 BC to AD 17) tells a story that has Cura (Persephone) molding man from clayey mud (*Fabulae*, 220). Other myths say that Prometheus fashioned man from clay.

2.1.2 The Purity and Power of the God of the Bible

Seen against the backdrop of these perverse and brutal accounts, Genesis presents Yahweh in sovereign, dignified majesty speaking the universe into existence. No conflict and no sexual perversion is to be found in Genesis 1.[10] Yahweh needs no rival gods out of which he makes either the world or human beings. Instead, Yahweh does as he pleases, bringing creation into existence by his powerful word (Rom. 4:17; Heb. 11:3). The description of creation is orderly: key phrases

---

[7]*COS*, 1:14 n. 7.

[8]E. C. Lucas, "Cosmology," *DOTP*, 134.

[9]Hesiod, *The Homeric Hymns and Homerica*, trans. Hugh G. Evelyn-White, LCL 57 (Cambridge, MA: Harvard University Press, 1914), 87–89.

[10]Similarly Rolf Rendtorff, *The Canonical Hebrew Bible: A Theology of the Old Testament*, trans. David E. Orton, Tools for Biblical Study (Leiden: Deo, 2005), 13–14.

are repeated with a regular but uneven rhythm, such as "and God said," "and it was so," "and God called," "and there was evening and there was morning," "and God saw that it was good." These give the account an epic beauty, a simple elegance of style matched to the grandeur described.

The process of creation is presented as two sets of three days followed by rest—not from weariness but because work is done—on the seventh (see table 2.2). On the first three days, God as it were prepares the canvas: (1) light and darkness, named day and night; (2) expanse separating waters above and below, named heaven; (3) gathered waters and dry land with vegetation, named earth and sea. Then on the next three days the canvas is adorned by the Master: (4) sun, moon, and stars are the lights to separate day from night; (5) the waters below swarm with living creatures and the heaven above is filled with birds; (6) the dry land is filled with beasts and creation is crowned with the image of God: man.[11] The result is that "God saw all that he had made, and behold, it was very good. And there was evening and there was morning, the sixth day" (Gen. 1:31). In contrast to Babylonian, Egyptian, and Greek gods, Yahweh is a God in whom there is no guile, the Father of lights with whom there is no variation or shifting shadow (James 1:17).

Table 2.2. The Days of Creation

No Longer Formless	No Longer Void
Day 1. Light and darkness, named day and night	Day 4. Sun, moon, and stars are the lights to separate day from night.
Day 2. Expanse separating waters above and below, named heaven	Day 5. The waters below swarm with living creatures and the heaven above is filled with birds.
Day 3. Gathered waters and dry land with vegetation, named earth and sea	Day 6. The dry land is filled with beasts and creation is crowned with the image of God: man.
Day 7. Rest	

2.1.3 Gender for the Glory of God

The description of the creation of woman in Genesis 2 can also be compared to an account of the creation of woman in Greek mythology. In his poem "Works and Days," Hesiod presents the creation of woman as a punishment against both Prometheus and man. Prometheus had stolen fire from Zeus, who was unwilling to give it to men himself, so Zeus punished Prometheus and man by making woman. Hesiod presents Zeus announcing to Prometheus, "You are glad that you have outwitted me and stolen fire—a great plague to you yourself

[11]For an insightful analysis of Gen. 1:26–28, see Peter J. Gentry, "Kingdom through Covenant: Humanity as the Divine Image," *SBJT* 12, no. 1 (2008): 16–42.

and to men that shall be. But I will give men as the price for fire an evil thing in which they may all be glad of heart while they embrace their own destruction." Zeus then bade Hephaestus to "make haste and mix earth and water and to put in it the voice and strength of human kind, and fashion a sweet lovely maiden-shape . . . . And he charged Hermes the guide, the Slayer of Argus, to put in her a shameless mind and a deceitful nature."[12]

Comparing the Bible with such an account highlights the benevolence of the only true and living God, who creates a helper for man because it is not good for him to be alone (Gen. 2:20). The woman is not a curse on the man but his helper—the man is created to work and keep the garden (2:15), and the woman is made to help the man (2:18).[13]

When set next to other ancient accounts of the creation of the world and humanity, the Genesis account is aglow with the power, goodness, purity, and uniqueness of the God revealed in the Bible. He is responsible for all that is, and all that is, is good. Genesis 1 and 2 show God to be glorious indeed. Not only is the God of the Bible unsullied by the brutality and perversity of other ancient accounts of the origin of all things, but he is also presented as building for himself a cosmic temple. In this cosmic temple, he places his image, whose task is to fill the earth and subdue it such that the glory of Yahweh covers the land as the waters cover the sea (see the texts in appendix 2 [§6] to chap. 3, "All the Earth Filled with the Knowledge of Yahweh's Glory").

2.1.4 The Primeval Temple

The description of the garden of Eden is echoed in the descriptions of the tabernacle and the temple, leading to the conclusion that Genesis 2 presents creation as a cosmic temple, a holy dwelling place of God.[14] The charge to Adam to fill the earth and subdue it (Gen. 1:28) is a priestly charge to expand the borders of Eden so that God's habitable dwelling will be the whole earth. Thus, the glory of Yahweh will cover the earth as the waters cover the sea (Num. 14:21; Isa. 6:3; 11:9; Hab. 2:14).[15] The language used to describe Adam's "working and keeping" the garden (Gen. 2:15) is used elsewhere in the Pentateuch to describe the priests' "working and keeping" the tabernacle. And this language is used for no other purpose.[16] The significant tree in the midst of the garden

---

[12]Hesiod, *The Homeric Hymns and Homerica*, 7.

[13]For my take on Paul's interpretation of what Genesis 1–3 has to say about gender roles, see James M. Hamilton Jr., "What Women Can Do in Ministry: Full Participation within Biblical Boundaries," in *Women, Ministry and the Gospel*, ed. Mark Husbands and Timothy Larsen (Downers Grove, IL: InterVarsity, 2007), 48–49 (32–52).

[14]See J. H. Walton, "Creation," in *DOTP*, 164–65 (155–68); similarly William J. Dumbrell, *The Faith of Israel: A Theological Survey of the Old Testament*, 2nd ed. (Grand Rapids: Baker, 2002), 19–20.

[15]See G. K. Beale, *The Temple and the Church's Mission: A Biblical Theology of the Dwelling Place of God*, NSBT (Downers Grove, IL: InterVarsity, 2004), 81–167.

[16]Gordon J. Wenham observes that "the only other passages in the Pentateuch where these verbs [עבד, "serve/work"; and שמר, "keep/guard"] are used together are to be found in Num. 3:7–8, 8:26, 18:5–6, of the Levites'

is matched by the lampstand, with its branches and almond blossoms, in the tabernacle. The cherubim woven into the wall hangings and overshadowing the ark are reminiscent of the bearer of the flaming sword, guarding the entrance to the garden. Alexander, Beale, and others have suggested that the tabernacle and temple were likely conceived as "microcosms"—buildings that depicted the universe.[17] Table 2.3 summarizes observations made by Gordon Wenham, Greg Beale, and others.[18]

Table 2.3. Correspondences between Eden and the Tabernacle and Temple

Correspondences	Eden	Tabernacle/Temple
God walking among his people	Gen. 3:8	Lev. 26:11–13; Deut. 23:14; 2 Sam. 7:6–7
Holy tree/blooming lampstand	Gen. 2:9	Ex. 25:31–40; 1 Chron. 28:15
Gold and precious stones	Gen. 2:11–12	Ex. 25:7, 11, etc.
Entered from the east	Gen. 3:24	Num. 3:38
Guarded by cherubim	Gen. 3:24	Ex. 25:10–22; 26:1; 1 Kings 7:29
Food/bread	Gen. 2:9	Ex. 25:30; 1 Kings 7:48
Priest who "works and keeps"	Gen. 2:15	Num. 3:7–8; 8:26; 18:5–6
Rivers flowing out	Gen. 2:10–14	Ezek. 47:1; Joel 3:18; Zech. 14:8

The implication of these parallels is that God put man in a place where man was to know, serve, and worship God, a place where God was present. God is known, served, worshiped, and present in his temple, the cosmos. And both Beale and Alexander state the upshot of the imagery. Beale writes, "This understanding of the temple as a small model of the entire cosmos is part of a larger perspective in which the temple pointed forward to a huge worldwide sanctuary in which God's presence would dwell in every part of the cosmos."[19] Alexander agrees: "Linked to both Eden and the cosmos, the tabernacle, as a model, conveys the idea that the whole earth is to become God's dwelling place."[20]

duties in guarding and ministering in the sanctuary. If Eden is seen then as an ideal sanctuary, then perhaps Adam should be described as an archetypal Levite" ("Sanctuary Symbolism in the Garden of Eden Story," in *I Studied Inscriptions from before the Flood*, ed. R. S. Hess and D. T. Tsumara [Winona Lake, IN: Eisenbrauns, 1994], 401).

[17]See T. Desmond Alexander, *From Eden to the New Jerusalem: Exploring God's Plan for Life on Earth* (Nottingham England: InterVarsity, 2008), 37–42, and Beale, *The Temple and the Church's Mission*, 32–38, 45–47, 48–50, and the literature they cite.

[18]Wenham, "Sanctuary Symbolism in the Garden of Eden Story," 399–404; Beale, *The Temple and the Church's Mission*, 66–99. See also T. Desmond Alexander, *From Paradise to the Promised Land: An Introduction to the Main Themes of the Pentateuch* (Grand Rapids: Baker, 1995), 21; J. H. Walton, "Creation," in *DOTP*, 161, 165 (155–68); Walton, "Eden, Garden of," in *DOTP*, 202–7; Walton, "Flood," in *DOTP*, 316–17 (315–26); R. E. Averbeck, "Tabernacle," in *DOTP*, 816–18 (807–27); Jon D. Levenson, *Sinai and Zion: An Entry into the Jewish Bible* (San Francisco: Harper and Row, 1985), 131–33.

[19]Beale, *The Temple and the Church's Mission*, 48.

[20]Alexander, *From Eden to the New Jerusalem*, 41–42.

2.2 Paradise Lost

Adam fails to keep the realm of God's dwelling pure, allowing an unclean serpent to enter the garden.[21] The serpent subverts the created order by tempting the woman rather than the man,[22] and his attack is an assault on the goodness of God (Gen. 3:1–5). Eve falls to the temptation, Adam transgresses, and the man and woman immediately experience alienation from one another and God (Gen. 2:25; 3:6–8).

This account can again be compared with Hesiod's account of how evil was unleashed in the world, though we must note that whereas in Genesis human sin defiles a pristine creation, in Hesiod the world is hardly holy prior to the opening of Pandora's "box." In his poem "Works and Days," Hesiod tells us that the woman is named Pandora, "because all they who dwelt on Olympus gave each a gift, a plague to men who eat bread."[23] Hesiod claims that prior to this, "men lived on earth remote and free from ills and hard toil and heavy sicknesses." He does not explain how men could have been that way, given the corruption and violence of the gods one sees when considering his account of the origin of all things. Moreover, these gods are anything but benevolent toward mankind. Hesiod has a significant problem of good, which he fails to notice. Pandora is given a jar (mistranslated "box"), and this jar is commonly taken as a symbol for the woman's womb, purportedly because a jar is similar in shape to the womb.[24] Hesiod tells us:

> The woman took off the great lid of the jar with her hands and scattered all these and her thought caused sorrow and mischief to men. Only Hope remained there in an unbreakable home within under the rim of the great jar, and did not fly out at the door; for ere that, the lid of the jar stopped her, by the will of Aegis-holding Zeus who gathers the clouds.[25]

If Pandora's jar is indeed a symbol of the womb, then it would appear that the trouble that comes upon humanity comes through the offspring of the woman. The other side of this is that hope is also to be found in the womb of the woman.

In the Genesis account, God is presented not as taking vengeance upon man by giving him woman, but as a kind and just God who gives man a needed

---

[21]Beale, *The Temple and the Church's Mission*, 87. This is an interpretive judgment that the text does not explicitly describe. Bruce K. Waltke (*An Old Testament Theology: An Exegetical, Canonical, and Thematic Approach* [Grand Rapids: Zondervan, 2007], 259) writes, "Adam, like the Aaronic priesthood, fails to keep the garden sacrosanct. Ironically, by his not driving Satan from the garden, Adam was expelled by Satan."

[22]See Thomas R. Schreiner, "An Interpretation of 1 Timothy 2:9–15: A Dialogue with Scholarship," in *Women in the Church*, ed. Andreas J. Köstenberger and Thomas R. Schreiner, 2nd ed. (Grand Rapids: Baker, 2005), 115.

[23]"Pandora" is a combination of the Greek words for "all" (*pan*) and "gift" (*dora*).

[24]I first encountered this suggestion from Elizabeth Vandiver's Teaching Company lecture series on "Classical Mythology."

[25]Hesiod, *Homeric Hymns and Homerica*, 9.

companion. God commands Adam not to eat from the tree of the knowledge of good and evil. God provides free access to all other trees and communicates the consequences of transgression: death (Gen. 2:16–17). It is God's world, and he has the right to make the rules. There is nothing unfair or deceptive about this command, nor is keeping it beyond Adam's physical ability. After the man and the woman transgress the command, God takes the initiative. As God justly keeps his word to Adam, justice is laden with mercy. Indeed, the justice of God sets the scene for unlooked-for displays of mercy.

God does not owe kindness. He does not even owe patience. He has every right to implement the promised punishment with no questions asked. But instead of putting Adam and Eve to death on the spot, he invites Adam to explain by asking the simple but profound question: "Where are you?" (Gen. 3:9).

After drawing out the facts, revealing along the way that Adam and Eve are unwilling to take responsibility for what they have done (Gen. 3:10–13), God announces his judgment, folding mercy into the middle. Different judgments fall on the three transgressors, but only the serpent is absolutely condemned. The serpent becomes the most cursed animal: he will go on his belly, and dust will be his food (3:14). Moreover, there will be enmity between the serpent and the woman and between their respective seeds. The seed of the woman will crush the serpent's head, and the serpent will strike the heel of the seed of the woman (3:15). The serpent will be in constant conflict with the woman and her seed. The word "seed" can refer to either the single or the collective seed of the woman.[26] The serpent, agent of uncleanness who instigated transgression, will be ultimately defeated when the seed of the woman crushes his head. This points to the final defeat of evil,[27] and it is here that salvation first comes through judgment.

The serpent will strike the heel of the seed of the woman. Judgment. The seed of the woman will crush the head of the serpent. Salvation. Later texts interpret this to mean that the seed of the woman will stomp on the head of the serpent (Pss. 58:4, 6, 10; 91:13; 108:13; Rom. 16:20).[28] As table 2.4 indicates, this

---

[26]Jack Collins, "A Syntactical Note (Genesis 3:15): Is the Woman's Seed Singular or Plural?" *TynBul* 48 (1997), 139–48. Collins argues that when used with singular pronominal suffixes and verbs, the term can be understood as a singular rather than as a collective plural. This is similar to English, where the term *seed* can refer to one seed or to a bag of seed, depending upon other contextual indicators. *Contra* John Ashton ("History and Theology in New Testament Studies," in *The Nature of New Testament Theology: Essays in Honour of Robert Morgan*, ed. Christopher Rowland and Christopher Tuckett [Oxford: Blackwell, 2006], 6), who mistakenly asserts, "The Hebrew word translated as *sperma never* has a singular reference: when used of a human individual it *always* refers to his descendants in their entirety." The use of the term in 1 Sam. 1:11 is commonly translated as a singular "child." Cf. *HALOT* s.v. זרע, 282–83; and BDB s.v. זרע states this, "specif. of a *particular child* (son)" (282, 4.d). See further below.

[27]Paul R. House, *Old Testament Theology* (Downers Grove, IL: InterVarsity, 1998), 65.

[28]See James M. Hamilton Jr., "The Skull Crushing Seed of the Woman: Inner-Biblical Interpretation of Genesis 3:15," *SBJT* 10, no. 2 (2006): 30–54. Similarly John H. Sailhamer, *The Pentateuch as Narrative: A Biblical-Theological Commentary* (Grand Rapids: Zondervan, 1992), 107–8.

announcement of judgment on the serpent provides fundamental imagery that is reused and interpreted throughout the rest of the Old Testament.[29]

Table 2.4. Imagery from Genesis 3:14–19 in the Old Testament

	Broken Heads	Broken Enemies	Trampled Enemies	Enemies Lick Dust	Stricken Serpents
Law	Num. 24:17	Ex. 15:6; Num. 24:8			
Prophets	Judg. 4:21; 5:26; 9:53; 1 Sam. 17:49; Isa. 1:4–5; 7:8–9; 28:3; Jer. 23:19; 30:23; Hab. 3:13	1 Sam. 2:10; 2 Sam. 22:39, 43; Isa. 14:25; Jer. 13:14; 23:29; 48:4; 51:20–23	Josh. 10:24; 2 Sam. 22:39/ Ps. 18:39 (ET 38); Isa. 63:3, 6; Mal. 3:20–21 (ET 4:2–3); Zech. 10:5	Isa. 49:23; Mic. 7:17	Isa. 27:1; 51:9
Writings	Pss. 68:22–24 (ET 21–23); 74:12–14; 110:6	Pss. 2:9; 72:4; 89:24 (ET 23); 137:9; Dan. 2:34–35; Job 34:22–25	Pss. 44:5; 60:14 (ET 12); 108:14 (ET 13); 91:11–13	Ps. 72:9	Pss. 58:5–7, 11 (ET 4–6, 10); 74:12–14; 89:11 (ET 10); (cf. Ps. 44:19); Job 26:12–13; 40:25–41:26

Often interpreters have failed to see these interpretations of Genesis 3:14–19 that resonate through the Old Testament because they have approached biblical theology the way a computer might compile a subject index for a book. As *The Chicago Manual of Style* puts it, "A computer can search, record, and alphabetize terms and can arrange numbers far more efficiently than a person. But it cannot distinguish between a term and a concept or between a relevant and an irrelevant statement. At best it can generate a concordance."[30] Too much biblical theology has fallen prey to the word-study fallacy and has failed to see that themes can be developed with synonymous terms. Charles Halton has shown that "ancient writers felt no compulsion to provide direct links with their allusions . . . . Instead, they borrowed imagery and fused it with their own rhetorical purposes."[31] I would suggest that this is exactly what has happened in the Old Testament with Genesis 3:15.

As salvation comes through judgment, readers of Genesis are given key insight into the nature of God. The promise that the serpent's head will be crushed comes leavened in the statement of judgment against the serpent. It is

[29]*Pace* Rendtorff, *The Canonical Hebrew Bible*, 15: "This narrative . . . is quite isolated within the Hebrew Bible itself. 'No prophet, psalm, or narrator makes any recognizable reference to the story of the fall' (von Rad 1972, 74)."
[30]*The Chicago Manual of Style*, 15th ed. (Chicago: University of Chicago Press, 2003), 757, §18.4.
[31]Charles Halton, "Allusions to the Stream of Tradition in the Neo-Assyrian Oracles," *Ancient Near Eastern Studies* 46 (2009): 58.

important to note that had there been no transgression, there would have been no judgment. Had there been no judgment, there could be no mercy. It would not be needed.

The justice of God is put on display as he judges the serpent. The mercy of God is demonstrated as he announces—from no compulsion or constraint—a future salvation that humanity has neither merited nor requested. God freely declares that the seed of the woman will crush the head of the seed of the serpent, and in this salvation that comes through judgment—judgment that results from the human transgression and promises final justice on the evil of the serpent—comes the first picture of free mercy in the Bible. Adam and Eve are responsible for their actions. They are guilty. They deserve death. God does not owe them mercy, and they have only sought to avoid justice by shifting blame (Gen. 3:10–13). They are not seeking God; they are hiding from him (3:8). They do not ask for mercy; they do not take responsibility for what they have done. Even if they ask for mercy, God is under no obligation to grant it.

This mercy, then, arises only from God. This is not something that humans deserve, not even in part. Of his own goodness, displaying his own intrinsic character, God announces that the woman will have seed—which means that the promised punishment of death will not be immediately enacted on the physical bodies of the human couple. Not only will their physical lives continue, but they will have seed: offspring. Not only will they have seed, but their seed will triumph over the snake. Salvation comes through judgment, and God makes known his character in justice and mercy. His justice is as exacting as his mercy is surprising.

Justice does fall. The actions of the human couple—hiding themselves from one another (Gen. 3:7) and from God (3:8)—show that the penalty is felt as soon as the deed is done.[32] Adam, at the moment of his sin, brings death into the world. Death is alienation from the life of God. Death truly removes the couple from the freedom and innocence and lack of shame and fear that is found only in perfect obedience. The moment they sin, Adam and Eve are removed from that realm of life, and in the opening of their eyes (3:7), they find themselves in the realm of death. This spiritual reality is made a physical reality when they are banished from the garden of Eden (3:23–24). But even here there is mercy: they will not have access to the tree of life, whereby they might live forever in a fallen state. God gives the gift of physical death (3:22; 5:5).

[32]In his novel, *Crime and Punishment*, Fyodor Dostoevsky depicts the way that judgment for sin is built into the nature of things. Neither trial nor announced penalty is necessary for human beings to feel the horrible consequences of their actions. Crimes result in punishment, even if the criminal avoids capture. Sin makes humans miserable.

Justice falls not only in the spiritual death that will eventuate in physical death; the man and the woman also have their God-ordained roles made more difficult. Adam and Eve were commissioned to be fruitful and multiply (Gen. 1:28). This is made doubly difficult in that the woman will have pain in childbearing (3:16a) and want to rule her husband,[33] with the result that he will rule over her with more force than necessary (3:16b). It is here in the curse on the woman that we find ourselves face to face with the first feminism. The woman was made to help the man (2:18), and before the rebellion they experienced shameless intimacy (2:23–25). After sin, God announces that the woman will now want to rule over her husband. So the command to be fruitful and multiply is made difficult by the intensified pain in childbearing and the relational strain between the man and the woman. This is judgment.

Salvation comes through judgment, however, for the promise is that the seed of the woman will crush the head of the serpent. So through the judgment of pain and relational difficulty, the conquering seed will nevertheless come. The coming of the deliverer points to the overcoming of both labor pains and relational difficulties. Salvation comes through judgment.

Adam was commissioned to work and keep the garden. Having cursed the serpent and promised pain and strife to the woman, Yahweh announces to Adam that the ground is cursed because of his sin (Gen. 3:17). His labor will be painful and sweaty, and the cursed land will bear thorns and thistles for him. Then, dust that he is, to dust he shall return (3:17–19).

The curses can thus be grouped under three headings: (1) enmity between the seed of the serpent and the seed of the woman, (2) difficulty in childbearing and male-female relations, and (3) problems with the land (see table 2.5).

These curses are major themes in the book of Genesis, and they are answered in the blessing of Abraham. Before we turn to that, however, there is more salvation through judgment to see in Genesis 3. In the announcement of judgment, Adam and Eve hear that they will have seed, and he (note the masculine singular pronoun) will crush the head of the serpent. It is apparently on the basis of this hope that Adam names his wife Eve, "because she was the mother of all living" (Gen. 3:20).[34] Adam and Eve are judged, and in the judgment they hear a word of promise, which, as Eve's name indicates, Adam believes.[35]

Adam and Eve are saved through judgment—judgment against their own transgression. They recognize that they deserve to die: they feel the force of condemnation and seek to hide from God. There is no place to hide. After God

[33]Her "desire" will be for her husband. The verbal parallel with Gen. 4:7 shows that just as sin's "desire" is to master Cain, so also the woman's "desire" is to control her husband as sin would control Cain.

[34]Note the similarity between the Hebrew word for "living," (חַי, with the feminine form, חַיָּה) and Eve's name (חַוָּה).

[35]Gerhard von Rad, *Genesis: A Commentary*, OTL (Philadelphia: Fortress, 1976), 96; Stephen G. Dempster, *Dominion and Dynasty: A Theology of the Hebrew Bible*, NSBT (Downers Grove, IL: InterVarsity, 2003), 68.

Table 2.5. The Curses of Genesis 3:14–19

Recipient of the Curse	Wording of the Curse	Import of the Curse
Serpent	• Go on his belly • Eat dust • Enmity between the seeds • Crushed head	There will be enmity between Satan and the singular Seed of the Woman, and there will also be enmity between the collective seed of the woman (the people of God) and the collective seed of the serpent (those who refuse to honor God as God and give thanks to him). The seed of the woman will triumph over the seed of the serpent.
Woman	• Pain in childbearing • Desire for husband • He will rule over her.	New difficulty enters into childbearing, which includes the possibility of barrenness, the lack of the ability to bear children, as well as the possibility that a woman might die during or after childbirth. The conflict between the man and the woman also points to relational strain that will give rise to all sorts of perversions of God's original good intention.
Man	• The ground cursed • Labor more difficult • Return to dust	The land will no longer cooperate with man in his efforts at cultivation, and eventually man's body will return to the dust from which he was taken: he will die.

speaks the curses, Adam and Eve know that their only hope is what God says will be. God speaks the hope of salvation into being. Adam and Eve's only hope of salvation is the judgment that God promises will fall on the snake through their seed.

2.3 Blessing and Cursing, Judging and Saving

A ten-member genealogy in Genesis 5 traces the line of descent from Adam to Noah, and then another ten-member genealogy in Genesis 11 traces the line of descent from Noah's son Shem to Abraham.[36] Abraham is then blessed by God in Genesis 12. The content of the blessings in Genesis 12:1–3 matches the content of the curses in Genesis 3:14–19.[37] Against Sailhamer's suggestion that "the narratives of Genesis 12–50 show little relation to Genesis 1–11,"[38] I will argue here that the narratives of Genesis 12–50 are thick with the blessings of Genesis 12 overcoming the curses of Genesis 3.

Sarah is barren (Gen. 11:30), which is an outworking of the difficulty God added to childbearing in Genesis 3:16. God promises that this barrenness will be overcome when he announces to Abraham that he will be a great nation

[36]Cf. T. Desmond Alexander, "Genealogies, Seed and the Compositional Unity of Genesis," *TynBul* 44 (1993): 255–70.

[37]For a more technical version of the argument that follows, see James M. Hamilton Jr., "The Seed of the Woman and the Blessing of Abraham," *TynBul* 58 (2007): 253–73.

[38]John H. Sailhamer, *The Meaning of the Pentateuch: Revelation, Composition and Interpretation* (Downers Grove, IL: InterVarsity, 2009), 301.

(12:2). So in spite of Sarah's barrenness, and in spite of the relational difficulties (3:16 again) she and Abraham will face (see, e.g., 16:1–5), God will grant them seed (12:7). The genealogies that connect Abraham to Adam show that the seed of Abraham is the seed of the woman. Yahweh declares to Abraham that it is through Isaac that his seed will be named (Gen. 15:4; 17:19). Isaac is the seed of the woman, the seed of Abraham whose birth overcomes the curse of Genesis 3:16.

Before we ever get to the blessing of Abraham, however, the conflict between the seed of the serpent and the seed of the woman first manifests itself when Cain kills Abel.[39] Cain thus shows himself to be seed of the serpent (see John 8:44; 1 John 3:8–15).[40] When the Lord promises to bless Abraham, and when he declares that all the families of the earth will be blessed in Abraham (Gen. 12:3), he is promising victory to the seed of the woman over the seed of the serpent.

Abraham will have a great name and be a blessing (Gen. 12:2). This will find its ultimate fulfillment when the seed of Abraham crushes the head of the serpent so that all the families of the earth can be blessed in Abraham and in his seed (22:18; 26:4; Gal. 3:14).

In the initial blessing of Abraham, the Lord promises to make him a great nation (Gen. 12:2). This not only points to triumph over the curse on the genders but also implies land. The land promise is then made explicit in Genesis 12:7, when "the Lord appeared to Abram and said, 'To your seed I will give this land.'" As the story of the Pentateuch unfolds, the Promised Land almost becomes a new Eden. The Lord will walk among his people in the land, just as he walked in the garden (Gen. 3:8; Lev. 26:11–12; Deut. 23:15, ET 14).[41] Like the fertile garden of Eden, the Promised Land will flow with milk and honey. On the way to the Promised Land, the camp of Israel is even described in Edenic terms.[42] Table 2.6 sets forth several points of contact between the description of Eden in Genesis 2:8–10 and the description of the camp of Israel in Numbers 24:5–6.

---

[39]Rightly, T. D. Alexander, *The Servant King: The Bible's Portrait of the Messiah* (Leicester: Inter-Varsity, 1998), 18: "Within the overall context of Genesis the 'seed of the woman' refers to those who are righteous, whereas the 'seed of the serpent' denotes those who are wicked."

[40]See the discussions in chap. 6, §3.6.1–5. One of the criteria for discerning echoes set forth by Richard B. Hays (*The Conversion of the Imagination: Paul as Interpreter of Scripture* [Grand Rapids: Eerdmans, 2005], 34–45) entails historical plausibility—would contemporaries have understood the text this way? And another of Hays's criteria looks at the history of interpretation—has the text been read this way in the history of interpretation? Jesus appears to have had Cain's murder of Abel in view when he referred to the Devil being a murderer from the beginning (John 8:44), and John understands this to mean that Cain was "of the evil one," as opposed to those who have God's "seed" in them (1 John 3:8–15). The text has also been read this way throughout history, as evidenced in the poem *Beowulf*, where the monster Grendel is described as a "demon" of Cain's clan (lines 100–110), and Grendel's mother is called "hell-bride," the poet saying that "from Cain there sprang misbegotten spirits, among them Grendel, the banished and accursed" (lines 1258–70).

[41]Wenham, "Sanctuary Symbolism in the Garden of Eden Story," 400–401.

[42]John Sailhamer, "Creation, Genesis 1–11, and the Canon," *BBR* 10 (2000): 97 (89–106).

Table 2.6. Correspondences between Eden and Israel

Genesis 2:8–10	Numbers 24:6
Yahweh	Yahweh
Planted	Planted
Garden	Gardens
River	River
Tree(s)	Trees

The promise of seed to Abraham guarantees that the cursed difficulty in childbirth and conflict between the genders will be overcome. The conflict between the seed of the serpent and the seed of the woman will also be resolved by the seed of Abraham, in whom all the nations will be blessed. And the curse on the land is answered by the promise of land, where the collective seed of Abraham will become a great nation.[43]

Yahweh judges in Genesis 3, and in Genesis 12 he promises to save. The curses of Genesis 3 are matched point for point in the blessing of Abraham, as seen in table 2.7.[44]

Table 2.7. Curses Answered by Blessings

Curses	Blessings
Seed conflict (3:15)	All the families of the earth will be blessed in you (12:3; 22:18; 26:4).
Gender conflict (3:16)	I will make you a great nation (barren Sarah shall have a seed) (11:30; 12:2; 17:16).
Land conflict (3:17–19)	To your offspring, a great nation, I will give this land (12:1–2, 7).

2.4 The Justice of God: Genesis 3:15

The seed conflict that runs through Genesis and into the rest of the Bible takes both an individual and a collective shape. The individuals in the line of promise are seed of the woman, and at points an individual seed of the woman is opposed by an individual seed of the serpent. There are also instances where the collective seed of the woman, the righteous remnant, is opposed by the collective seed of the serpent. We will begin with the individuals before looking at the groups.

Eve speaks of Seth as "another seed instead of Abel, for Cain killed him" (Gen. 4:25), indicating that she sees Abel as a possible fulfillment of the one promised in Genesis 3:15. The genealogies that take us to Abraham have been

[43]See Hamilton, "The Seed of the Woman and the Blessing of Abraham."

[44]Similarly Michael Fishbane, *Biblical Interpretation in Ancient Israel* (Oxford: Clarendon, 1985), 372–73: "It cannot fail to strike one that these three blessings [land, seed, and earthly blessing] are, in fact, a typological reversal of the primordial curses in Eden."

noted, and the blessings of Abraham are successively transmitted to Isaac, to Jacob, and to Joseph's younger son Ephraim[45] (see the references for each in table 2.8), though "Judah prevailed . . . and the prince came from him" (1 Chron. 5:2; cf. Gen. 49:8–12). These individuals are regarded as the seed of the woman, and Abel, Isaac, Jacob, and Joseph are directly opposed by individuals who are seed of the serpent.

Table 2.8. The Blessing of Abraham in Genesis

Abraham	12:1–3, 7; 13:15–16; 15:5, 18; 17:1–9; 18:18; 22:17–18
Isaac	17:19; (cf. 24:60); 26:2–5, 24
Jacob	25:23; 27:27–29; 28:2–4, 13–15; 32:12, 28–29; 35:9–12; 46:2–4
Ephraim	48:14–20 (cf. 1 Chron. 5:2; Ps. 78:67–69)

The conflict between Cain and Abel has been noted above. When Jesus said that Satan was "a murderer from the beginning" (John 8:44), he was almost certainly referring to Cain killing Abel. Then John speaks of the "children of the devil" who are "like Cain, who was of the evil one and murdered his brother" (1 John 3:10, 12).

Ishmael also shows himself to be seed of the serpent as he mocks[46] the seed of the woman, Isaac (Gen. 21:8–9). This is to be expected from the "wild donkey of a man" whose "hand is against everyone" with "everyone's hand against him" (16:12).

Esau reveals himself to be seed of the serpent by despising his birthright (Gen. 25:34). Then Isaac pronounces over him what looks like a curse (27:39–40). Esau hates Jacob, the seed of the woman, loved by his mother, and wants to kill him (27:41).[47]

Cain killed Abel. Esau wanted to kill Jacob. And Joseph's brothers hated him and wanted to kill him (Gen. 37:4–5, 18–19).

The seed conflict is worked out on the individual level in the instances just seen, and there are also instances of collective seed conflict in Genesis (see table 2.9). Abraham goes to war to rescue Lot (Gen. 14:14–16) and has harsh words for the king of Sodom (14:22–24). He also comes into conflict with Abimelech and his servants, who are Philistines (21:22–34). Isaac, too, is troubled by the Philistines (26:14–16). The defiling of Dinah results in the slaughter of Shechem

[45]See further Alexander, *From Eden to the New Jerusalem*, 42, and his essay cited in 42 n. 62.

[46]As an example of an early interpretation that may reflect an understanding of this wider seed conflict, see *t. Sotah* 6.6, "R. Ishmael says, 'The word *playing*, refers only to bloodshed'" (citing 2 Sam. 2:14–16). I owe this reference to Richard H. Bell, *The Irrevocable Call of God: An Inquiry into Paul's Theology of Israel*, WUNT 184 (Tübingen: Mohr Siebeck, 2005), 176 n. 90.

[47]Note that having stated that "the children of the promise are counted as seed," Paul discusses God's choice of Isaac rather than Ishmael and Jacob rather than Esau (Rom. 9:8–13). The implication seems to be that Paul regards Isaac and Jacob as "seed" (Rom. 9:7–8, 29).

(34:1–29), which causes Jacob some concern (34:30). In an ironic twist, the children of Israel, Joseph's brothers, at least for a time, fill the role of the seed of the serpent as they hate Joseph (37:4–5) and entertain the notion of killing him (37:18).

Table 2.9. Seed Conflict in Genesis

Reference	Seed of the Serpent	Seed of the Woman
		Individual
4:1–16	Cain	Abel
21:8–9	Ishmael	Isaac
27:41	Esau	Jacob
37:1–28	Sons of Israel	Joseph
		Collective
12:10–20	Pharaoh and Egypt	Abraham and Sarah
14:13–24	Kings of the world (Sodom)	Abraham and his men, Lot, Melchizedek
21:22–34	Abimelech and the Philistines	Abraham and his people
26:14–16	Abimelech and the Philistines	Isaac and his people
34:1–29	The men of Shechem	Simeon, Levi, and Israel (Dinah)
37–44	Sons of Israel	Joseph

These individual and corporate enmities are outworkings of the justice of God announced in Genesis 3:15. In the symbolic world Genesis gives its readers, people are either seed of the serpent, on the side of the snake in the garden, or seed of the woman, on the side of God and trusting in his promises.

There is also mercy in some of these instances, as when Abraham and Abimelech make a covenant (Gen. 21:27) and when Joseph is reconciled to his brothers (45:1–15). Genesis teaches that God is faithful, and God kept his promise to put enmity between the seed of the woman and the seed of the serpent. Paul acknowledges the collective nature of the enmity between the serpent and the seed of the woman when he says that God will crush Satan beneath the feet of the Roman Christians (Rom. 16:20). Evidently, Paul understands God's purposes, articulated in the garden, as being accomplished through the church. Paul also knows that at some points references to the "seed" are references to *the* seed of the woman, as evidenced by his words in Galatians 3:16, "It does not say, 'And to your seeds,' as to many, but as to one, 'And to your seed,' who is messiah." Similarly, in the Apocalypse, John shows the dragon thwarted in his efforts against the singular seed of the woman (Rev. 12:13–16), only to make war on the collective seed of the woman (12:17).

2.5 *The Justice of God: Genesis 3:16*

All that God owes to the world is justice, and Genesis shows God visiting upon the world the justice promised in Genesis 3. Difficulty in childbearing can be seen in the barrenness of Sarah (Gen. 11:30), Rebekah (25:21), and Rachel (30:1, 22). The barrenness of these women often generates marital disharmony (e.g., 16:5; 30:1–2), and there are many other instances of conflict between the genders (see table 2.10). Abraham's action of using Sarah as a human shield is hardly noble manhood (12:10–20; 20:1–13), nor does Abraham honor Hagar's femininity (16:3–4, 6). Gender relations are so perverted in Sodom and Gomorrah that the men of Sodom wish to "know" males instead of females (19:5). Lot's offer of his daughters is outrageous (19:8), as is their later treatment of him, with the wretched consequence that he becomes the incestuous father of his own grandsons (19:30–38).

We see a partial reversal of gender conflict in the account of the seed of Abraham, Isaac, who loves his wife (Gen. 24:67). But like Abraham, he passes her off as his sister to protect himself (26:6–11). The sad circumstances of Jacob's marriage to two women, one of whom is hated (29:31), the other bitter at her barrenness (30:1), are vivid pictures of the gender trouble resulting from the curse. A most vicious example of this gender conflict is given in the account of the rape of Dinah (34:2), and then there is the shameful treatment of Tamar (38:6–14) by Judah (38:15–18). Potiphar's wife makes illicit advances on Joseph (39:7, 10–18), and her lies are plausible enough outside Eden (39:19–20). All of this grows out of the curse on gender relations in Genesis 3:16.

Some of these instances are direct examples of women seizing the initiative with negative results: Sarah recommends that Abraham go in to Hagar; Lot's daughters plot to conceive by their father; Tamar puts herself in Judah's path dressed like a harlot; Potiphar's wife seeks to seduce Joseph. This is the way that God said things would be in Genesis 3:16, and the narrative bears out the truthfulness of God's word. God's justice is worked thoroughly through all of human life, so that Paul can confidently assert that those who marry will have trouble (1 Cor. 7:28).

2.6 *The Justice of God: Genesis 3:17–19*

God said to Adam that the ground was cursed because of his sin (Gen. 3:17), and the cursed ground tragically receives the blood of Abel (4:11). The cursed land is then deluged with waters that prevail on the earth (7:19), resulting in the death of all flesh (7:21). Everything on the dry land dies (7:22).

The land is not only defiled with dead bodies but also afflicted with famines. A famine causes Abraham to go to Egypt (Gen. 12:10). Isaac is also confronted with famine (26:1), as is Jacob (41:54; 42:1–5). God faithfully administers the

Table 2.10. Gender Conflict in Genesis

Usurping Women "Your desire will be for your husband."	Sarah's plan for the seed to come through Hagar (16:1–4)
	Lot's daughters' plan to preserve the lineage of their father (19:30–38)
	Rachel's magic mandrakes (30:14)
	Leah's buying Jacob with mandrakes (30:16)
	Tamar's trap for Judah (38:14)
Marital Disharmony	Sarah's dispute with Abraham (16:5)
	Rachel's dispute with Jacob (30:1–2)
Husbands Abusing Their Wives "He will rule over you."	Abraham's use of Sarah for his own protection, twice (12:10–20; 20:1–13)
	Isaac's use of Rebekah for his own protection (26:6–11)
	Hatred of Leah (29:31)
Death in Childbearing "I will multiply your pain in childbirth."	Rachel's death while birthing Benjamin (35:16–20)
Barrenness "In pain you will bring forth children."	Sarah (11:30)
	Rebekah (25:21)
	Rachel (30:1, 22)
Sexual Dysfunction	Abraham and Hagar (16:3–4)
	Men of Sodom (19:5)
	Lot and his daughters (19:8, 30–38)
	The rape of Dinah (34:2)
	Reuben and his father's woman (35:22)
	Onan and Tamar (38:8–9)
	Judah and Tamar (38:11–18)
	Potiphar's wife (39:7–18)

justice he promised, and the patriarchs of Israel face famine on a cursed land made unclean by corpses.

2.7 The Mercy of God: The Seed of the Woman

Justice is not God's final word, however, and it does not appear to be his ultimate purpose. But justice does provide a backdrop for the display of mercy. Without justice, mercy has no meaning. Significantly, the reversal of the curses of Genesis 3:14–19 is related to the seed of the woman at every point. The difficulty between the seeds will end when the seed of the woman crushes the head of the serpent. The difficulties in childbirth and between the genders must be overcome for the seed of the woman to be born. And, the curse on the land is answered by the promise of land to the seed: "To your seed I will give this land" (Gen. 12:7).

Relational difficulties are continually overcome: the Lord gives Abraham and Isaac their wives back after they forfeit them through the sister fib. Isaac loves Rebekah (Gen. 24:67), and Jacob loves Rachel (29:18). In spite of the way Judah and Tamar come together, God blesses the children of their union (Gen. 38:27–30; Ruth 4:18–22).

Difficulty in childbearing is also conquered as barren women bear children: Isaac is born of Sarah (Gen. 21:1). Jacob and Esau are born to Rebekah (25:21). Joseph and Benjamin are born to Rachel (30:22).

It is God who has cursed childbearing and gender relations, and it is God who makes possible and preserves these marriages, as seen when Yahweh answers the prayer of Abraham's servant and leads him straight to Rebekah (Genesis 24). It is God who opens wombs. Once again, the only thing that God owes to humanity is justice. When Abraham twice forfeits his wife to protect himself, God is under no obligation to restore Sarah to him, but God will keep his promise in spite of the Patriarch's wife-forfeiting ploy.[48] Nor is God under any obligation to reverse the curse on childbearing and speak life into a dead womb. God mercifully gives hope to those who have none, and he mercifully maintains the descent of the seed of the woman.

God was not obligated to bless Abraham, for he "served other gods" beyond the Euphrates (Josh. 24:2). By blessing Abraham, God put mercy on display against the wider backdrop of his justice. Justice is God's keeping his word and displaying his righteous character. Mercy is God's freely pardoning and blessing those who deserve justice. Justice reveals who God is and accentuates the gratuitous splendor of his mercy.

Yahweh delivers Sarah from Pharaoh (Gen. 17:17) and protects her from Abimelech (20:3, 6–7). Yahweh visits Sarah with the result that she conceives (21:1). Yahweh leads Abraham's servant to Rebekah (24:12, 14, 21, 26–27, 44, 48). Yahweh grants Isaac's prayer that Rebekah would conceive (25:21). Yahweh providentially protects Rebekah from Abimelech (26:8–9). Yahweh opens Leah's womb (29:31), and then Rachel's (30:22). Yahweh redeems the situation between Judah and Tamar, giving Perez and Zerah (38:1–30).

Yahweh also delivers the seed of the woman from the seed of the serpent. Cain killed Abel, but Abel was accepted by God (Gen. 4:4). Ishmael mocked Isaac, but through Isaac Abraham's seed was named.

We are given an important picture, too, when God commands Abraham to sacrifice Isaac. The child of promise, beloved of his father, is to be slain on Mount Moriah.

---

[48]Bell (*The Irrevocable Call of God*, 128–29) points out that "in contrast to this Rabbinic view [that Abraham, Isaac, and Jacob merited God's favor], the Patriarchs in Genesis are generally not portrayed as righteous. . . . The power of these Patriarchal narratives lies in the fact that despite their shortcomings, God chose Abraham, Isaac and Jacob. Later Judaism, however, was to whitewash them."

Abraham believes that both he and his child will return from the mount of sacrifice (the verb for returning in Gen. 22:5 is plural), and Abraham believes that God will provide for himself the lamb for a burnt offering (22:8). However Abraham expects this to be accomplished (cf. Heb. 11:17–19), he intends to sacrifice Isaac (Gen. 22:10), when at the last moment God provides a ram to be sacrificed *instead of* Isaac (22:13). Isaac is saved through the judgment that falls on the ram. God is then glorified for his mercy (see 22:14).

In spite of (and through) the wickedness of Rebekah, Jacob is spared from Esau. Then later, though Joseph's brothers mean evil against him, God means their actions for good (Gen. 50:20).

From the beginning, those who hoped in God were looking for God to reverse the curses through the promised seed of the woman. Eve indicated this first in her response to the birth of Cain (Gen. 4:1), then in her response to the birth of Seth (4:25). When Noah is born, his father gives him a name related to the word *rest*, and speaks of Noah giving "relief from our work and from the painful toil of our hands because of the land which Yahweh cursed" (5:29). The language used here corresponds almost exactly to the language of the curse on the land in Genesis 3:17 (see table 2.11), and the only other place (in addition to Gen. 3:17 and 5:29) in the Old Testament that the word for "painful toil" (עצבון) is used is in the curse on childbirth in Genesis 3:16. Lamech is presented as making a statement reflecting his hope that the seed of the woman will reverse the curse on the land (5:29).[49]

Table 2.11. Terms Common to Genesis 3:17 and 5:29

Genesis 3:17	Genesis 5:29
Cursed land	(Relief from) cursed land
Painful toil	(Relief from) painful toil

From what the narrative tells us, Lamech's hopes that the birth of Noah portends the reversal of the curse can only be based on what God said in Genesis 3:15. These hopes are later augmented in God's promise of land to Abraham (12:7).

In spite of the curse on the land, God blesses the fields and flocks of Abraham (Gen. 12:16; 13:6; 21:22; 24:35), Isaac (26:12–14), and Jacob (31:5–9; 33:11). And then, through unexpected turns of events, the whole earth is blessed in the seed of Abraham, as Joseph provides food in the famine (41:57).

In all these instances, salvation comes through judgment to the glory of God. The curse on the land highlights both the blessing of the fields and flocks of the patriarchs and Joseph's provision of food for the world. The curse on childbear-

[49]Similarly Fishbane, *Biblical Interpretation in Ancient Israel*, 372.

ing makes precious the mercy of God in giving seed to barren women. Then God saves the seed of the woman by judging those who are against his people, the seed of the serpent. God shows himself to be just to the seed of the serpent and merciful to the seed of the woman.

2.8 The Center of the Theology of Genesis

In Genesis, creation displays the glory of God. The crown of God's creation rebels against God's just command, and God justly announces curses against the serpent, upon childbearing and male-female relations, and upon the land and man's work. All is not lost, however, for God reveals himself to be merciful as well as just. Having orchestrated a realm in which his justice is put on display, Yahweh surprises the condemned with the wonder of free mercy. He announces that a seed of the woman will come, which means that death is at least postponed, and there are hints that it might even be overcome (see Enoch, Gen. 5:24). The promise of seed means that the curses on male-female relations are not insuperable and that the pain in childbearing does not altogether prevent procreation. Not only is there the hope of the new life of a child, but this seed will also crush the head of the serpent. He will defeat evil, which implies that he will open the way to a renewed Eden where men find rest from painful labor in the very presence of God (4:26; 5:29).[50]

God's mercy often comes folded into his justice. For instance, when Sodom is about to be visited with God's just wrath, God mercifully delivers Lot. Lot, however, does not seem to want to be delivered: "And he lingered, and the men seized his hand, and the hand of his wife, and the hand of his two daughters, with the mercy of Yahweh upon him, and they brought him and caused him to rest outside the city" (Gen. 19:16). Lot finds the mercy of Yahweh irresistible—those angels have delivered him against his will. Yahweh is mighty to save, whether the saved desire his salvation or not. The fire that rains down on Sodom makes the overcoming deliverance Yahweh works for Lot all the more precious.

God confirmed his promised mercy when he declared to Abraham that his seed would overcome the curses, and then the promises to Abraham were passed to Isaac, then to Jacob. Genesis closes with promises of a king from the line of Judah, in the splendor of Joseph reigning over Egypt, pattern of the coming seed of the woman, seed of Abraham, in whom all the nations of the earth have been blessed. Salvation comes through judgment, setting forth the grandeur of the glory of God.

---

[50]Cf. Dumbrell, *The Faith of Israel*, 31: "The rest of the Pentateuch focuses on . . . how the paradise of Eden might be realized in and through Israel."

3. Exodus

Exodus continues the story of God glorifying himself in salvation through judgment as the promises to Abraham continue to find fulfillment against the backdrop of the curses. God promised to make Abraham a great nation (Gen. 12:2), and the seventy people who went down to Egypt are described in Exodus 1:7 in terms of the original commission to Adam to be fruitful and multiply (Gen. 1:28). They have been fruitful and have multiplied, in spite of opposition from Pharaoh (Ex. 1:7, 12). The commission to be fruitful and multiply was not only given to Adam and Eve but also passed to Noah and his sons (Gen. 8:17; 9:1, 7). God's promise to multiply Abraham (22:17) links Abraham and his line with God's original charge to Adam, and these connections are made with the children of Abraham right down to the exodus generation (see table 2.12). Isaac asserts that Yahweh has enabled him to be fruitful (26:22), and when he passes the blessing of Abraham to Jacob, he prays that God will make him fruitful and multiply him (28:3–4). When Jacob returns to the land, God himself commands him to be fruitful and multiply (35:11), an incident Jacob recounts before blessing Ephraim and Manasseh, the sons of Joseph (48:4).

Table 2.12. Be Fruitful and Multiply

Adam	Gen. 1:28
Noah and sons	Gen. 8:17; 9:1, 7
Abraham	Gen. 17:6; 22:17
Isaac	Gen. 26:22, 24
Jacob	Gen. 28:3–4; 35:11
Joseph's sons	Gen. 48:4, 16
Israel	Gen. 47:27; Ex. 1:7, 12

Thus, the Old Testament establishes the universal significance of Israel in God's purposes by showing that the nation of Israel has inherited God's charge to Adam to be fruitful and multiply. The wickedness of Adam's descendants resulted in the flood, and God charged Noah with the same task he had given Adam. The wickedness of Noah's descendants resulted in the confusion of language at Babel, and the task given to Adam and Noah passed to Abraham and his seed. Thus, the statement that "the people of Israel were fruitful and increased greatly; they multiplied and grew exceedingly strong, so that the land was filled with them" (Ex. 1:7) connects Israel to Adam and foregrounds the cosmic significance of what God is doing in Israel.

God is keeping the promise he made to Abraham to make him into a great nation, and this in spite of the new king in Egypt who does not know about

Joseph. The king of Egypt, serpent on his crown,[51] is of his father the Devil, who was a murderer from the beginning. This seed of the serpent commands the Hebrew midwives to murder the male seed of the woman (Ex. 1:15–17), and when that fails, he orders his people to throw the newborn Hebrew boys into the river (1:22). Through the wicked opposition of the seed of the serpent, Providence places one particular seed of the woman in Pharaoh's own house (2:1–10). Pharaoh's best efforts are thus overcome, and Yahweh's ability to orchestrate the deliverance of Moses condemns the seed of the serpent to the coming confrontation.

3.1 Salvation through Judgment at the Exodus

God delivers Israel from Egypt so that they will know that he is Yahweh (Ex. 6:7). He judges Egypt so that the Egyptians will know that he is Yahweh (7:4–5). He protects Israel from the plagues that fall on Egypt so that Pharaoh will know that he is Yahweh (8:20–22). He explains to Pharaoh:

> For this time I will send all my plagues on you yourself, and on your servants and your people, so that you may know that there is none like me in all the earth. For by now I could have put out my hand and struck you and your people with pestilence, and you would have been cut off from the earth. But for this purpose I have raised you up, to show you my power, so that my name may be proclaimed in all the earth. (9:14–16)

God wants Pharaoh to know that there is no one else like God (9:14). He wants Pharaoh to see his power (9:16a). He wants all the earth to know his name, to hear the tale of his saving and judging glory (9:16b). Yahweh declares to Pharaoh that he intends to be known, to be glorified in his salvation of Israel through the judgment of Egypt.

Yahweh also wants Israel to pass this experience of his glory on to coming generations (Ex. 10:2). However offensive these things may be to modern sensibilities, the earth belongs to Yahweh (9:29). He raises Pharaoh up (9:16), hardens his heart (4:21, see table 2.13),[52] and slays the firstborn of Egypt (11:4–5). Yahweh does these things in order to save Israel through the judgment of her oppressors.

---

[51]Cf. Susan Wise Bauer, *The History of the Ancient World* (New York: Norton, 2007), 24.

[52]See also Deut. 2:30: "And Sihon the king of Heshbon was not willing to allow us to cross over by him, for Yahweh your God hardened his spirit and made his heart obstinate, that he might give him into your hand, as he is this day"; and Josh. 11:20: "For it was from Yahweh to harden their hearts to meet Israel in battle, in order to cause them to be devoted to destruction without mercy, even in order to wipe them out, just as Yahweh commanded Moses."

Table 2.13. The Hardening of Pharaoh's Heart

Yahweh's Declaration: I will harden Pharaoh's heart.	References Back to Yahweh's Declaration: Pharaoh's heart was hardened *as Yahweh had said.*	Pharaoh's *Heart* as the Grammatical Subject: Pharaoh's heart was hardened.	*Pharaoh* as the Grammatical Subject: Pharaoh hardened his heart.	*Yahweh* as the Grammatical Subject: Yahweh hardened (or will harden) the heart of Pharaoh.
4:21				4:21
7:3				7:3
	7:13	7:13		
		7:14		
	7:22	7:22		
	8:11 (ET 15)		8:11 (ET 15)	
	8:15 (ET 19)	8:15 (ET 19)		
			8:28 (ET 32)	
		9:7		
				9:12
			9:34	
		9:35		
				10:1
				10:20
				10:27
				11:10
14:4				14:4
		14:5		
				14:8
				14:17

It is sometimes suggested that Yahweh hardens Pharaoh's heart only *after* Pharaoh hardens his own heart.[53] But as table 2.13 shows, Yahweh twice announces to Moses that he will harden Pharaoh's heart, and then there are two references to Pharaoh's heart being hardened "as Yahweh said" before we read that Pharaoh hardened his own heart. Pharaoh is clearly responsible for his own choices, but Yahweh announces to him that he has raised him up in order to show his power (Ex. 9:16). Further, Yahweh takes responsibility for the hardening of Pharaoh (10:1). Paul recognizes the astonishing implications of these statements, and he addresses the objections that this might raise about God's justice (Rom. 9:14–18) and human responsibility (9:19–23). Paul's answers to these objections will be examined later in this study (see chap. 6, §2.2.1). At

[53]E.g., A. E. Steinmann, "Hardness of Heart," in *DOTP*, 383.

this point it is imperative that we see that Yahweh clearly declares *why* Pharaoh is being treated in this way:

> Then Yahweh said to Moses, "Go in to Pharaoh, for I have hardened his heart and the heart of his servants, that I may show these signs of mine among them, and that you may tell in the hearing of your son and of your grandson how I have dealt harshly with the Egyptians and what signs I have done among them, that you may know that I am Yahweh." (Ex. 10:1–2)

Yahweh states that he has hardened Pharaoh's heart *so that* he can display his signs *so that* Israel can pass the story down *so that* they might know him as he is, Yahweh.

On several occasions Pharaoh takes steps toward acknowledging Yahweh's lordship, even indicating that he might let some of the people go. But each time, his heart is hardened anew. These instances demonstrate that Pharaoh is unable to let the people go, and that even when he confesses his own sin and Yahweh's righteousness (e.g., Ex. 9:27) or makes promises to let the people go (e.g., 8:8), it is Yahweh's word that stands. Yahweh has declared that he will harden Pharaoh's heart (4:21; 7:3), and it is this, not Pharaoh's false promises, that will come to pass (see table 2.14).

Table 2.14. Pharaoh's False Promises

Pharaoh Promises to Let the People Go	Hardened Heart, Broken Promise, as Yahweh Said
8:8	8:15
8:28	8:32
9:27–28	9:35–10:1
10:16–17	10:20
10:24	10:27
12:31–32	14:4–5, 8, 17

This matter of the hardening of Pharaoh is not some arcane, peripheral theological question. Again and again through the Exodus narrative the hardening of Pharaoh is linked to Yahweh's revelation of himself. Yahweh makes himself known by hardening Pharaoh so that he can demonstrate his power through the plagues against Egypt.

This point is also made through what seems to be Yahweh's response to Pharaoh's question, "Who is Yahweh?" (Ex. 5:2). Again and again Yahweh asserts, "I am Yahweh!" and at several points this assertion is introduced by the declaration, "You shall know."[54] Yahweh tells Israel that they will know that he is Yahweh (6:7), and he tells Egypt (7:5) and Pharaoh (e.g., 9:29) the same thing. At several points Yahweh tells Pharaoh that he will know that there is none like Yahweh (8:10; 9:14). The repeated assertions that people will *know* that "I am Yahweh" demonstrate that Yahweh is purposefully revealing his own identity. These events are not happening by accident. Yahweh has engineered them to make himself known (table 2.15).

Table 2.15. Yahweh's Intent to Make Himself Known

Recipients of the Revelation	"You Shall Know" (ידע)		"I Am Yahweh" (אני יהוה)
Moses			(4:11)
Moses			6:2
Israel			6:6
Israel	6:7		6:7
Israel			6:8
Moses			6:29
Egyptians	7:5		7:5
Pharaoh	7:17		7:17
Pharaoh	8:10	(none like Yahweh)	
Pharaoh	8:22		8:22
Pharaoh	9:14	("none like me")	
Pharaoh	9:29	("the earth is Yahweh's")	
Israel	10:2		10:2
Pharaoh	11:7	(Yahweh distinguishes between Israel and Egypt)	
Egyptians	14:4		14:4
Egyptians	14:18		14:18
Israel			15:26

Following Yahweh's announcement to Moses, "I Am who I Am" (Ex. 3:14),[55] the story of Yahweh hardening Pharaoh's heart so that he can deliver Israel from

[54]God often announces that the purpose of what he has done is "so that you will know that I am Yahweh." The texts in which Yahweh declares that people or other things will *know that I am Yahweh* (and related expressions) that occur in the early chapters of Exodus appear in table 2.15. For all the texts in the Old Testament in which these declarations are made, see Ex. 6:7; 7:5, 17; 8:18 (ET 22); 10:2; 14:4, 18; 16:12; 29:46; 31:13; Deut. 29:5; 1 Kings 20:13, 28; Isa. 45:3; 49:23, 26; 60:16; Jer. 9:23 (ET 24); 24:7; Ezek. 5:13; 6:7, 10, 13, 14; 7:4, 9, 27; 11:10, 12; 12:15, 16, 20; 13:14, 21, 23; 14:8; 15:7; 16:62; 17:21, 24; 20:12, 20, 38, 42, 44; 21:4 (ET 20:48), 10 (ET 5); 22:16, 22; 24:27; 25:5, 7, 11, 17; 26:6, 14; 28:22, 23, 26; 29:6, 9, 21; 30:8, 19, 25, 26; 32:15; 33:29; 34:27, 30; 35:4, 9, 12, 15; 36:11, 23, 36, 38; 37:6, 13, 14, 28; 38:23; 39:6, 7, 22, 28; Joel 4:17 (ET 3:17).

[55]See Randall J. Pannell, "I *Would* Be Who *I* Would Be! A Proposal for Reading Exodus 3:11–14," *BBR* 16 (2006): 351–53, who argues that either one or both occurrences of אהיה should be understood as cohortatives, such that Yahweh is declaring, "*No one controls me but me!*" (353, emphasis original). Israel is to hear and obey Yahweh, not seek "to appease, placate, influence, or control him" (ibid.).

Egypt through a series of crushing judgments against the gods of Egypt (12:12) shows who Yahweh is by recounting what he says and what he does. In all this, Yahweh's ultimate commitment is to make known his name: "I am Yahweh" (see the references in table 2.15). He wants his name to be proclaimed in all the earth: "But for this purpose I have raised you up, to show you my power, so that my name may be proclaimed in all the earth" (9:16). He wants to get glory for himself: "And I will harden Pharaoh's heart, and he will pursue them, and I will get glory over Pharaoh and all his host, and the Egyptians shall know that I am Yahweh" (14:4, similarly 14:17). Yahweh accomplishes this purpose by showing justice to Egypt and mercy to Israel.

But is what Yahweh does to Pharaoh just? From the perspective of the biblical authors, all human creatures owe their Creator thanks and praise (e.g., Rom. 1:21). No human creatures successfully give God the glory and thanks due him (3:23). Therefore all human creatures stand under God's condemnation. The severity of the judgment meted out matches the unspeakable evil of refusing to honor God as God and render him thanks. He does not owe mercy. The only thing he owes is justice, and the gravity of the heinousness of disregarding the infinite worth and beneficence of God calls for punishment that fits the crime. If God does not visit a just punishment, it shows that he has as little regard for himself as the creatures who have refused to honor him as God and give thanks to him. God shows his own great worth by visiting due justice against Egypt, and he shows his love by mercying Israel.

But is this mercy just? If Israel is also guilty, how can God maintain justice if he shows them mercy? Just as a principle of substitution was set forth in the provision of a ram in place of Isaac in Genesis 22, the blood on the doorposts at Passover teaches an important lesson. Judgment falls on the Passover lamb, and thereby the firstborn of Israel are saved. As Alexander puts it, "The sacrifice of the animal atones for the sin of the people, the blood smeared on the doorposts purifies those within, and the eating of the sacrificial meat consecrates those who consume it."[56] Where the doorpost is not covered by the blood of the lamb, the firstborn dies (Ex. 12:1–13). Those Israelites who believe that Yahweh will keep his word save their firstborn sons through the judgment that falls on the Passover lamb. This salvation through judgment is by faith—they have to believe what Yahweh has spoken, and believe it enough to slay the lamb and smear the blood.

In addition to the ten plagues that culminate in the death of the Egyptian firstborn, Yahweh destroys the Egyptian army in the Red Sea. In Egypt, Israel has

[56] Alexander, *From Paradise to the Promised Land*, 78. He goes on to write: "By linking the crucifixion of Jesus to the Passover, the NT church drew attention to the redemptive nature of Jesus' death. Like the original sacrifice, his death atoned for the sin of the people, his blood purified and cleansed, and his body sanctified those who ate it at the Lord's Supper" (80).

been saved through the judgment of the plagues.[57] On the way out of the land of Egypt, Israel is saved through the waters of judgment that engulf Pharaoh's army, just as Noah was saved through the waters of judgment that engulfed all living things (Gen. 7:21–23). Yahweh's intentions—to show his power, make known his name, and exalt himself over Pharaoh—are realized when he delivers Israel. Israel sings a song of praise extolling Yahweh's might (Ex. 15:1–18),[58] and Yahweh's fame resounds through the nations so that Rahab says, "The fear of Yahweh has fallen upon" the inhabitants of Jericho (Josh. 2:9–10). Even the Philistines, years later,[59] know of the mighty deeds of Yahweh against Egypt (1 Sam. 4:7–8; 6:6).

3.2 From Egypt to Sinai

The Exodus narrative repeatedly states that Yahweh delivered Israel from Egypt so that they could serve him in the wilderness by sacrificing to him.[60] Yahweh will be their God, and Israel will be his people (Ex. 6:7). Once they are in the wilderness, however, rather than serving and sacrificing, Israel grumbles because they do not have water (15:24; again at 17:2), because they do not have bread, and because they do not have meat (16:2–3). Yahweh sweetens the water for the people (15:25), announces "I am Yahweh" (15:26), announces "you shall know that Yahweh has brought you out of the land of Egypt" (16:6), and then appears in glory (16:10), again asserting "you shall know that I am Yahweh" (16:12). The first instance is referred to as a test (15:25)—Israel is to trust Yahweh on the basis of all they have seen (Exodus 1–14), and they are to keep his word (15:26). The second time the people grumble, Yahweh responds with another test, to see if the people will follow his instructions regarding the seventh day (16:4–5). The people disobey by gathering more than they need (16:19–20) and by gathering food on the seventh day (16:27). Yahweh rebukes them (16:28–29), and as a result they obey him and rest (16:30). Obeying Yahweh's instructions, the people eat manna for forty years (16:35). By disciplining his children, Yahweh enables them

[57] God had promised Abraham, "I will bring judgment on the nation that they serve" (Gen. 15:14, cf. 13–16). And then God said to Moses, "I will redeem you with an outstretched arm and with great acts of judgment" (Ex. 6:6).

[58] Norbert Lohfink ("The Song of Victory at the Red Sea," in *The Inerrancy of Scripture and Other Essays*, trans. R. A. Wilson [Berkeley: Bibal, 1992; reprint of *The Christian Meaning of the Old Testament*, 1968], 67–86) argues that the repetition of the pattern in Ex. 15:8–11 (narrow passage through waters on right and left to deliverance) in 15:12–17 (narrow passage through nations on right and left to deliverance) indicates that "in its literal meaning, the song of Moses already was composed in such a way that later saving acts of Yahweh could be introduced and read into its account of history, reduced as it was to a few basic images. Its very structure already assumed its typological application" (84). He suggests that the entrance into the land under Joshua, "the passage of Israel over the Jordan," is presented as "a second Exodus from Egypt," and that "the prophets expected that Yahweh would repeat his act of salvation at the exodus" (ibid.). Lohfink also identifies "the passage of Christ through his death to resurrection" and Christian baptism as legitimate typological fulfillments (85). I wish to thank Professor Peter J. Gentry for drawing my attention to Lohfink's essay.

[59] The Bible indicates that the Exodus took place in 1446 BC (1 Kings 6:1), and the battle with the Philistines at Aphek (1 Sam. 4:1) probably took place ca. 1104 BC (for this chronology, see Eugene H. Merrill, *Kingdom of Priests: A History of Old Testament Israel* [Grand Rapids: Baker, 1987, 1996], 149).

[60] See, e.g., Ex. 3:12; 5:3, 17; 7:16; 8:1, 8, 20, 27; 9:1, 13; 10:3, 7, 11.

to follow his instructions and receive his provision. Through judgment (rebuke) on their disobedience, salvation—in the form of daily provision—comes.

There is more complaining, and Yahweh again provides water for the people at Massah and Meribah (Ex. 17:1–7). Yahweh tells Moses, "Behold, I will stand before you there on the rock at Horeb, and you shall strike the rock, and water shall come out of it, and the people will drink" (17:6). As Psalm 78 sings these events (Ps. 78:15–20), the psalmist may interpret the rock that was struck as Yahweh himself: "They remembered that God was their rock" (78:35).[61] If we have here a picture of Yahweh standing before the rock, Moses striking the rock, and Yahweh being identified with the rock, with the result that water flows out that the people might drink, then it would seem that Yahweh is being struck so that the people might drink. Through the striking of their Lord, the people receive the water of life. Such an interpretation might inform those places in the Gospel of John where Jesus indicates that he will provide living water for his people, and then, when he is struck, blood and water flow from his side (John 4:10–14; 7:37–39; 19:34).

When Amalek fights against Israel in Exodus 17:8–13, we have another instance of the seed of the serpent opposing the seed of the woman. Yahweh announces that he will destroy the Amalekites (17:14), and Moses builds an altar named "Yahweh is my banner" (17:15–16).

Moses recounts to his father-in-law, the priest of Midian, all that Yahweh did for Israel (Ex. 18:1–8). In response to this, Jethro the Gentile priest of Midian rejoices, blesses Yahweh, confesses, "Now I know that Yahweh is greater than all gods," and offers sacrifices to the God of Israel (18:9–12). The salvation through judgment that Yahweh accomplished in Egypt wins him praise from those of other nations.

3.3 At Sinai

Everything narrated from Exodus 19 through Numbers 10 takes place at Mount Sinai. Exodus 19–24 recounts Israel's experience of the laws given by Yahweh himself at Sinai. Chapters 25–31 move to instructions for the tabernacle, the incident of the golden calf is described in chapters 32–34, and that is followed by the construction of the tabernacle in chapters 35–40. Exodus concludes with Yahweh taking up residence in the tabernacle as his glory cloud is seen to cover the tabernacle and fill it. As we will see below, there are significant differences between the appearance of Yahweh in glory in Exodus 19, prior to the giving

[61]Following G. K. Beale, "Did Jesus and the Apostles Preach the Right Doctrine from the Wrong Texts? Revisiting the Debate Seventeen Years Later in the Light of Peter Enns' Book, *Inspiration and Incarnation*," *Them* 32 (2006): 33–34 (18–43). Beale suggests that Paul read the passage this way (1 Cor. 10:4), as does E. Earle Ellis, *Christ and the Future in New Testament History* (Leiden: Brill, 2001), 91.

of the law, and his appearance in glory in Exodus 40, with the law given and the tabernacle built.

When Yahweh reveals himself to Israel in Exodus 19, he has delivered them from Egypt, but the terms of the relationship between Yahweh and Israel have not been set. Yahweh comes as one known but unknown, imposing and unpredictable, and the awestruck Israelites are undone by his overwhelming glory.

Yahweh sets the terms for Moses: if Israel will obey him and keep his covenant, they will be his "treasured possession among all peoples," for all the earth belongs to him (Ex. 19:5). Moreover, as Adam was a priest, so Israel will be a "kingdom of priests and a holy nation" (19:6). The people state that they will do everything Yahweh has spoken, and Yahweh announces that he will come in a thick cloud, that the people may hear him speak and believe what Moses says (19:7–9).

The people are then instructed to wash and consecrate themselves for their meeting with Yahweh, which will take place "on the third day" (Ex. 19:10–15).[62] On the third day, Yahweh descends on Mount Sinai. The heaven thunders. The lightning flashes. The earth quakes. The shofar blast is long and loud. It is as though the elements and the dimensions are strained and would crack under the burden of the weight of the glory of God. The people, naturally, tremble (19:16). Moses positions them at the foot of the mountain—which they must not touch lest they die (19:12–13)—that they might meet their God (19:17).

The mountain smokes, and Yahweh descends in fire (Ex. 19:18). Yahweh tells Moses to go warn the people not to break through to gawk at Yahweh, lest they die, and to instruct the priests who will draw near to consecrate themselves, "lest Yahweh break out against them" (19:21–22). Moses protests that this has already been done (19:22). With two abrupt imperatives Yahweh responds, "Go! Get down!" (19:24). Moses obeys (19:25).

---

[62]Rather than interpret the text as it now stands, John Sailhamer looks "behind" the text of Exodus 19 and reconstructs an event that "should have happened" but never did. He writes, "According to this narrative, there is an expectation that the people are eventually, in three days, to go up the mountain with Moses, and there they were to meet with God on the mountain" (Sailhamer, *The Meaning of the Pentateuch*, 383). Sailhamer then alleges, "When they refused, they became subject to stricter requirements . . ." (384). But this is not at all what the text as it stands communicates. Ex. 19:12 states that boundaries are to be put around the mountain because anyone who touches it must be put to death. Then 19:13 states that anyone who touches the mountain will be stoned, and, against Sailhamer (381–82 with notes), in this context the most natural reading of the phrase in 19:13, יעלו בהר, is "they shall come up to the mountain" (ESV), where they will hear Yahweh dictate the Ten Commandments, as Exodus 20 shows him doing. In my view the text as it now stands gives no evidence of Sailhamer's reconstruction, wherein "God's original intention to meet with the people on the mountain . . . was fundamentally altered by the people's fear of approaching God. . . . In their fear, the people traded a personal, face-to-face relationship with God for a priesthood" (392). Sailhamer only gets to this conclusion by examining what he describes as "important biblical-theological questions that lie behind the present shape of the Sinai narrative" (389), which is odd in view of his insistence elsewhere in the volume on interpreting the text as it stands rather than interpreting the events behind the text (100–49, esp. 103). In my view he should follow his own statement and cease giving "attention . . . to the historical reconstruction of biblical (OT) events at the expense of the meaning embodied in biblical narratives" (103, cf. 604).

And then, that most frightful moment: thunder roaring, sky flashing, mountain quaking, smoke shrouding, shofar blaring, fire blazing, people trembling, Yahweh speaks the ten words. He is, as Eichrodt described him, "the jealous God, who will admit no derogation from his majesty."[63]

Yahweh is the most significant thing about the Ten Commandments.[64] When he gives voice to the inauguration of this covenant, the first thing he does is announce his own identity: "I am Yahweh your God, who brought you out of the land of Egypt, out of the house of slavery" (Ex. 20:2).[65] No gods before him. No carved images of him. No misuse of his name. No work on the day he hallowed and blessed. These first four commandments obviously pertain to Yahweh, but perhaps the centrality of Yahweh to the last six commandments is less apparent—on the surface, anyway. These commands come with Yahweh's authority. They reflect the way that he has created the world. They are to be obeyed because he has spoken them, because he created this world by his word, because this world is made to work according to his word (cf. James 2:11). Fathers and mothers are to be honored because God is a Father to his people, and God is to be honored (Ex. 4:22–23; Eph. 3:14–15).[66] No murder because God alone gives life (Deut. 32:39), and people are in God's image (Gen. 1:27; 9:6).[67] No adultery because God made man male and female, that the two might become one flesh (Gen. 2:23–24; Matt. 19:4–5). No theft because God makes poor and rich (1 Sam. 2:7). No false witness because God does not lie (Num. 23:19). No coveting because God alone is to satisfy, and at his right hand there are pleasures evermore (Ps. 16:11). The authority and majesty and identity of Yahweh are central to all ten of the commandments, and "moral action is inseparably bound up with the worship of God."[68]

In response to what they see and hear—thunder and lightning, shofar and smoke—the people ask Moses to intercede for them: "You speak with us and we will hear, but let not God speak with us lest we die" (Ex. 20:15–16, ET 18–19). Yahweh then gives to Moses a representative set of laws in Exodus 21–23,[69] along with the promise that an Angel bearing Yahweh's name will go with Israel

[63]Eichrodt, *Theology of the Old Testament*, 1:44.

[64]Describing George Mendenhall's suggestion about the Decalogue in *Law and Covenant*, Walter Brueggemann (*Theology of the Old Testament: Testimony, Dispute, Advocacy* [Minneapolis: Fortress, 1997], 25) writes, "The absolute power of Yahweh thus deabsolutizes every other claim and pretension to power, and so makes Israel a most peculiar phenomenon in the world of Canaanite religion."

[65]Note the parallel with another covenant text, Gen. 15:7, "I am Yahweh, who brought you out of Ur of the Chaldeans . . ." (see table 3.3 below). Fishbane (*Biblical Interpretation in Ancient Israel*, 376) suggests that the language of Gen. 15:7 and Ex. 20:2 has been matched because "the narrator wished to establish a typological nexus between the two events."

[66]Alexander (*From Paradise to the Promised Land*, 85) writes regarding this commandment, "In all likelihood parents were envisaged as representing God to their children."

[67]Ibid.

[68]Eichrodt, *Theology of the Old Testament*, 1:76.

[69]For a helpful discussion, see Russell Fuller, "Exodus 21:22–23: The Miscarriage Interpretation and the Personhood of the Fetus," *JETS* 37 (1994): 169–84.

(23:20–21). Yahweh's commands come from his own personal authority, and his presence is the motivating factor for all obedience. Israel will live before Yahweh, and transgression will be a direct affront to his holiness. This makes the fear of Yahweh central to obedience: "Moses said to the people, 'Do not fear, for God has come to test you, that the fear of him might be before you, that you might not sin'" (20:17, ET 20).

Moses and Aaron, Nadab and Abihu, and seventy elders of Israel are then summoned to draw near to worship Yahweh (Ex. 24:1–2). Moses reports Yahweh's words to the people, and they agree to do all he has commanded (24:3). The text then tells us something that much modern scholarship allegorizes[70] into a fictional narrative having to do with symbolic nonentities that undermines the text's claim to be an authoritative revelation of God. This fictional narrative has as its main characters "the Jahwist," "the Elohist," "the Deuteronomist," and "the Priest," but the text makes the simple claim, "Moses wrote all the words of Yahweh" (24:4).[71]

Having offered burnt offerings and sacrificed peace offerings, Moses reads the book of the covenant to the people, the people again promise to obey, and then Moses sprinkles blood from the sacrifices on the people (Ex. 24:5–8). The covenant is inaugurated with blood. Judgment falls on the sacrificial animals in place of the people, and just as blood covered the doorposts on the night of the Passover, blood covers those entering into this covenant with Yahweh. Since the sacrificial victim is slain, their penalty is paid, and they are covered by the blood of the substitute. Through the judgment they are saved. And this clears the way for the manifestation of God's glory. Moses and Aaron, Nadab and Abihu, and the seventy elders go up the mountain, behold God, and partake of a covenant meal (24:9–11). Moses then ascends the mountain with Joshua, and the cloud of Yahweh's glory covers the mountain, as the waters cover the sea, for six days (24:13–16). The people of Israel, too, behold the glory, and it looks to them like a consuming fire on the mountaintop (24:17).

Yahweh then gives Moses instructions for building the tabernacle (Exodus 25–31). Yahweh announces the purpose of this tabernacle, "that I may dwell

[70]I owe the insight that "scientific" historical critical research is in many ways allegorical—in that it imports into the text a fanciful story not in any way suggested by the text for the "spiritual" benefit of the interpreter (in this case, liberating the interpreter from the claim the text has on the interpreter if it is the word of God)—to Peter J. Leithart, *A Son to Me: An Exposition of 1 and 2 Samuel* (Moscow, ID: Canon, 2003), 20–23. Cf. also O. Palmer Robertson, *The Christ of the Prophets* (Phillipsburg, NJ: P&R, 2004), 32–33: "The historical Moses along with his prophetic ministry . . . has been turned into a ghost, while some unknown person designated as the Deuteronomist, along with his Deuteronomistic school, has risen to unparalleled heights of glory. . . . In the end, Scripture itself offers a more convincing testimony."

[71]For other references to what Moses wrote, see Deut. 31:9, 24; 33:4; and the rest of the Bible refers again and again to the Torah of Moses or of Yahweh (Josh. 1:7; 8:31; 23:6–8; 1 Kings 2:3; 2 Kings 14:6; 17:37; Hos. 8:12; Dan. 9:11, 13; Ezra 3:2; 1 Chron. 16:40; 2 Chron. 17:9; 23:18; 31:3; 35:26). See the helpful "Canonical Synthesis: God's Word and Moses" in House, *Old Testament Theology*, 194–95. Cf. also Roger Beckwith, *The Old Testament Canon of the New Testament Church and Its Background in Early Judaism* (Grand Rapids: Eerdmans, 1985), 65, 93 n. 10, and 247.

among them" (25:8). The significance of Yahweh's presence among Israel cannot be overstated. Yahweh's presence is the distinguishing characteristic of Israel. His presence demands their holiness and gives rise to the particular shape of the Mosaic covenant. All of it is informed by the simple fact that Yahweh dwells in their midst, and all of it reveals his saving and judging glory.

Like the shadow of the dome of pleasure floating midway on the waves,[72] the tabernacle is constructed as a movement back toward Eden. As a command was given in the garden, the testimony given to Moses goes into the ark of the covenant (Ex. 25:16). As cherubim with flaming sword guard the way to Eden, cherubim of gold are stationed over the mercy seat (25:17–21). As Yahweh met with Adam and Eve in the garden, so Yahweh will meet with Moses from above the mercy seat (25:22). As there was abundant food in the garden, there is showbread on the table (25:30). As there were sacred trees in the garden, there is a lampstand with branches and bowls shaped like almond blossoms in the tabernacle (25:31–40). As the image of God, Adam, was placed in the garden, so also Aaron and his sons minister as priests in the tabernacle (28:1–3). Unlike the situation in the garden, where no sin offerings were necessary, when Aaron and his sons are consecrated as priests, a bull must be offered as a sin offering (29:14). As Adam faced death for transgression, so Aaron and his sons must follow Yahweh's instructions lest they die (28:35, 43). The tabernacle will be sanctified by the very glory of Yahweh (29:43). Yahweh will dwell among Israel and be their God (29:45). And they will know that he is Yahweh, their God, who brought them up from the land of Egypt that he might dwell among them. And these declarations are punctuated with words of weight: "I am Yahweh their God!" (29:46).

All of this is to be done according to the pattern shown to Moses on the mountain (Ex. 25:9, 40; 26:30; 27:8), and Yahweh has filled the artisans with the spirit of wisdom for the work (28:3), giving the Spirit of God to Bezalel and Oholiab (31:1–6). The instructions for the building of the tabernacle are given in Exodus 25–31, and then it is actually built in chapters 35–40. Chapters 32–34 recount an episode in which Yahweh proclaims his saving and judging name.

3.4 The Glorious Name: Exodus 32–34

While Yahweh is revealing, instructing, and enabling, the people are busy forgetting, departing, and sinning. They have been redeemed from Egypt that they might serve Yahweh in the wilderness. They agreed to do everything he said when he spoke to them from the mountain, but these commitments are soon forgotten.

When the people see the delay of the prophet, Moses, they approach the priest, Aaron, who at their bidding fashions for them "gods" that will go before them (Ex. 32:1). Yahweh was a man of war (15:3) who reigned (15:18) at the Exodus,

[72]This wording comes from the poem cited at the beginning and end of this chapter, Samuel Taylor Coleridge's "Kubla Kahn."

but the people have rejected him from being king over them.[73] They have thus placed other gods before Yahweh, the first thing he told them not to do. When they celebrate these "gods,"[74] they proclaim a "feast to Yahweh" (32:5). This seems to indicate that the worship of the calf Aaron fashioned has been added onto the worship due Yahweh alone. They have thus made carved images for themselves, the second thing Yahweh told them not to do.

In response to this, Yahweh distances himself from the nation, describing them as Moses' people whom he, Moses, brought out of Egypt (Ex. 32:7). Yahweh brought them out of Egypt (20:1) to be his people (6:7), but in response to their idolatry Yahweh is prepared to destroy them (32:9–10). Significantly, Yahweh threatens to do for Moses what he earlier promised to do for Abraham, saying, "I will make you a great nation" (32:10; cf. Gen. 12:2).

Moses understands the implications of such a declaration. If Yahweh does not follow through on his promise to Abraham, how can Moses be sure that Yahweh will follow through on the promise to him, either? Moses pleads with Yahweh, asking him why his wrath is hot against his, Yahweh's, people, whom he, Yahweh, brought up from Egypt (Ex. 32:11). From there, Moses appeals to Yahweh's concern for what the Egyptians will think.[75] If Yahweh destroys the people, the Egyptians will conclude that Yahweh took Israel out of Egypt with the evil intent of harming, killing, and consuming them (32:12). Moses appeals to Yahweh that he remember the promises made to Abraham, Isaac, and Israel, and he quotes Yahweh's promises back to him (32:13). "And Yahweh relented concerning the evil which he spoke to do to his people" (32:14).[76]

This episode shows Moses appealing to Yahweh on the very basis of what earlier narratives have shown to be Yahweh's controlling concerns. Yahweh has acted to make known his matchless name by showing his steadfast love to the

[73]I have phrased this to draw out the typological correspondence to what will happen later when Israel refuses to heed the warnings of the prophet Samuel and rejects Yahweh from being king over them, asking instead for a king like all the nations (2 Samuel 8). As Israel does with the golden calf, when they follow Saul they follow an image, a person impressive in appearance, who eventually sets up an image in his own honor (1 Sam. 15:12).

[74]The Hebrew is plural, which is normal for references to Yahweh, but the verbal form in Ex. 32:4 is also plural, and verbal forms used to indicate what Yahweh does are usually singular (so also GKC, §145i). The Greek translation picks up on this and renders these items in the plural, whereas English translations are divided (the ESV correctly has "gods"). See John William Wevers, ed., *Exodus*, Septuaginta Vetus Testamentum Graecum 2 (Göttingen: Vandenhoeck and Ruprecht, 1991).

[75]See the appendix (§7) to chap. 4, table 4.9, "Old Testament Prayers Appealing to God's Concern for His Own Glory."

[76]It is interesting to compare Yahweh with Zeus at this point. There is a moment in Homer's *Iliad* when as Achilles chases Hector around the walls of Troy, Zeus remembers the many sacrifices Hector has burned to him, and he calls the gods to take counsel whether they should save Hector from death. Athene objects because Hector is "doomed long since by fate" (Homer, *The Iliad: Books 13–24*, ed. William F. Wyatt, trans. A. T. Murray, 2nd ed., LCL 171 [Cambridge, MA: Harvard University Press, 1999], 465, 22.175–81). Though Zeus would like to save Hector from Achilles, Fate has decreed that pious Hector die at Achilles' hand. Zeus cannot overcome what Fate has decreed. By contrast, the Old Testament shows that Yahweh is unbound by fate and free to change his mind. For further discussion of these issues, see Bruce A. Ware's two books, *God's Lesser Glory: The Diminished God of Open Theism* (Wheaton, IL: Crossway, 2000), and *God's Greater Glory: The Exalted God of Scripture and the Christian Faith* (Wheaton, IL: Crossway, 2004).

children of Abraham and simultaneously showing his unparalleled power and justice by judging Egypt. Yahweh could justly destroy the nation of Israel and start over with Moses, and this might even fulfill the promise to Abraham, since Moses himself descends from Abraham. But when Moses appeals to Yahweh's concern for his reputation in Egypt, to his commitment to the people, and to the promises to Abraham, Isaac, and Jacob, Yahweh shows mercy. This underscores Yahweh's supreme concern for his own glory.

Like Adam, the garden priest who shifted blame when confronted with his disobedience, Aaron, the national priest shifts the blame when Moses confronts him (Ex. 32:22–24). Just as Adam the priest failed to restrain Eve from sinning, then followed her into it, so Aaron the priest fails to restrain Israel from sin, then follows them into it (32:1–4, 25). This means war.

Moses summons all on Yahweh's side to himself, and because of the great worth of Yahweh, they go through the camp and kill brothers, friends, and neighbors. Three thousand fall in Israel that day (Ex. 32:26–28). Through this judgment, salvation comes. Moses understands what Yahweh's holiness requires, and he offers himself as a sacrifice of atonement for Israel: telling Israel he is going up to Yahweh to seek to make atonement for their sin (32:30) and confessing the sin of the people to Yahweh (32:31), he offers himself to be blotted out of Yahweh's book if the people cannot be forgiven (32:32). Yahweh responds with both justice and mercy. The justice comes in his immediate answer (32:33–35), and the mercy comes when, at Moses' insistence, Yahweh agrees to continue with his stiff-necked, obstinate people (33:1–17).

Before the tabernacle is built, the tent where Moses encounters Yahweh's presence is outside the camp (Ex. 33:7). Yahweh only enters the camp once his holy dwelling is fully prepared and the camp is made clean by his statutes.

Once Moses is assured that Yahweh will go with the people, just as he earlier expressed Yahweh's own priorities in his petition that Yahweh not destroy the people (Ex. 32:11–13), so now he expresses Yahweh's own priorities in asking to see Yahweh's glory (33:18). As we have seen, God often announces that the purpose of what he has done is "so that you will know that I am Yahweh."[77] When God says this, he is declaring that he wants people to know his *name*. He wants them to know him as he is. The clearest indication of what this means is found in Exodus 33:18–34:7. Responding to Moses' request to see his *glory*, Yahweh says, "I will make all my *goodness* pass before you, and I will *proclaim my name*, 'Yahweh,' before you," (33:19a, emphasis added). Note that when Moses asks to see God's *glory*, God responds that he will show him his *goodness* and

[77]The texts in which Yahweh declares that people or other things will *know that I am Yahweh* (and related expressions) that occur in the early chapters of Exodus appear in table 2.15 above. For all the texts in the Old Testament in which these declarations are made, see n. 54 above.

proclaim his *name*. This means that God's glory is seen in his goodness, and the proclamation of his name reveals Yahweh's goodness, which is his glory.

Yahweh then adds, "And I will be gracious to whom I will be gracious, and I will mercy whom I will mercy" (Ex. 33:19b). These words declare that Yahweh is not obligated to do what Moses has asked. Yahweh chooses when and to whom he will reveal his glorious goodness.

When Yahweh reveals his goodness to Moses, showing him his glory and proclaiming his name, we read,

> And Yahweh passed before him and proclaimed, "Yahweh, Yahweh, a God merciful and gracious, slow to anger, and great in steadfast love and faithfulness, keeping steadfast love for thousands, forgiving iniquity and transgression and sin, but who will by no means clear the guilty, visiting the iniquity of the fathers on the sons and on the sons of the sons, to the third and the fourth generations." (Ex. 34:6–7)

In this revelation of the glory of Yahweh, Yahweh makes known his character by proclaiming his name. Yahweh's goodness is first explained in the declaration that he is merciful and gracious. This mercy and grace is shown in the way that Yahweh is patient, loves with steadfast extravagance, and forgives. The declaration that he does not give the guilty a free pass also explains Yahweh's goodness. He is just, and he punishes iniquity for generations. In this declaration of his name, Yahweh announces his mercy and his justice: this is his glory, and this glory of Yahweh is reflected all through the Old and New Testaments.[78]

Yahweh's declaration of his name in Exodus 34, which is the revelation of his glory, informs the places in the Bible before and after this incident where Yahweh states his intention of making known to people that he is Yahweh. To know that he is Yahweh is to know that he is merciful and gracious, not clearing the guilty but punishing iniquity. To know that he is Yahweh is to know his name, his character. To know that he is Yahweh is to know his goodness—goodness that upholds what is right. If he does not uphold what is right, he is not good. If he does not keep his word, he is not faithful and cannot be trusted. Yahweh's righteousness, therefore, is an essential component of his love. An unrighteous, unfaithful god is not a loving god but a scary, unpredictable horror in the likeness of the ancient Near Eastern deities or the gods of the Greco-Roman pantheon. But Yahweh is righteous, faithful, and loving. Even when his holiness demands

[78]See the appendix (§8) to this chapter, which catalogs Ex. 34:6–7 in the Law, Prophets, and Writings. Cf. also Hermann Spieckermann ("God's Steadfast Love: Towards a New Conception of Old Testament Theology," *Biblica* 81 [2000]: 311 n. 9), who writes of Ex. 34:6–7: "The formula of grace occurs in Joel 2,13; Jonah 4,2; Ps 86,15; 103,8; 145,8; Neh 9,17; references of the enlarged formula or references presupposing the enlarged formula are to be found in Exod 34,6–7; 20,5–6=Deut 5,9–10; 7,9–10; allusions to the formula can often be assumed but not always be proved, cf. Deut 4,31; Exod 33,19; Num 14,18; Isa 48,9; 54,7–8; 63,7; Jer 15,15; 32,18; Mic 7,18; Nah 1,2–3; Ps 78,38; 86,5; 99,8; 111,4 belonging together with 112,4; 116,5; Dan 9,4; Neh 1,5; 9,31–32; 2 Chr 30,9; Sir 2,11; 5,4–7 et al." For allusions in the New Testament, see John 1:17 and James 5:11.

the death of transgressors, this is an expression of his goodness and love as it upholds his faithfulness and shows him trustworthy.

The Bible has established that mankind is set on sin (Gen. 6:5; 8:21), so all deserve to be punished. But God is also pleased to show mercy, which he is not obligated to give to anyone. He mercies whomever he pleases (Ex. 33:19b). To pardon the guilty unjustly would not be loving to those whom the guilty offended, and in this age of the weightless god we do not recognize that the person most offended by sin is God.[79] We can also understand this on analogy with human relationships: if a judge fails to sentence a convicted murderer, the rights of the wronged are not upheld, and those who survive the murdered person probably do not feel that the judge has been loving. In this scenario, the judge has not been loving. He has only been unjust. But God's mercy is not unjust.

When God mercifully pardons, he upholds his own righteous standard. He satisfies the wrath he justly feels when he has been offended. In the old covenant God's righteous standard was upheld through the Levitical system of sacrificial, substitutionary atonement,[80] but even this was looking forward to the cross. Paul says God demonstrated his righteousness when he put Jesus forward as a propitiatory sacrifice, explaining that this demonstration of righteousness was necessary because God had previously passed over sins (Rom. 3:24–26). Yahweh's perfect goodness is displayed in the balance between justice and mercy, which he works together to display his unique character: "Steadfast love and truth have met together, righteousness and peace have kissed each other" (Ps. 85:10). Yahweh judges the substitute so that the one for whom the sacrifice is made can be saved—mercifully and justly saved. When God causes people to know that he is Yahweh, he shows them his glory in salvation through judgment.

Moses' response to such a revelation is natural and right: "And Moses quickly bowed his head toward the earth and worshiped" (Ex. 34:8). Yahweh's revelation of his just and merciful character wins him glory. Yahweh then declares that he will reveal more of his own greatness to elicit more praise for himself: "And he said, 'Behold, I am cutting a covenant; before all your people I will do marvels, such as have not been created in all the earth or in any nation. And all the people in the midst of whom you are shall see the work of Yahweh, for it is a fearful thing that I will do with you'" (34:10).

---

[79]See David F. Wells, "The Weightlessness of God," in *God in the Wasteland: The Reality of Truth in a World of Fading Dreams* (Grand Rapids: Eerdmans, 1994), 88–117.

[80]For helpful discussions, see the essays in Roger T. Beckwith and Martin J. Selman, eds., *Sacrifice in the Bible* (Grand Rapids: Baker, 1995); David Peterson, ed., *Where Wrath and Mercy Meet: Proclaiming the Atonement Today* (Carlisle, PA: Paternoster, 2001); Steve Jeffery, Michael Ovey, and Andrew Sach, *Pierced for Our Transgressions: Rediscovering the Glory of Penal Substitution* (Wheaton, IL: Crossway, 2007), esp. 42–50, 214–15, and 226–28; and Frank S. Thielman, "The Atonement," in *Central Themes in Biblical Theology: Mapping Unity in Diversity*, ed. Scott J. Hafemann and Paul R. House (Grand Rapids: Baker, 2007), 105–6 (102–27).

Yahweh then stirs the hearts of the people to provide the material for the building of the tabernacle (Ex. 35:21–22), so much that the people are told not to give any more (36:4–7). The tabernacle is then constructed, and Israel's scrupulous obedience is punctuated by almost twenty statements that Israel built the tabernacle "as Yahweh had commanded Moses" (39:1, 5, 6, 21, 26, 29, 31, 32, 42, 43; 40:16, 19, 21, 23, 25, 26, 27, 29, 32).

Disobedience is judged, and through the judgment the people are disciplined to obey. This marked obedience in building the tabernacle is followed by Yahweh's taking up residence among the people, stiff-necked (Ex. 34:9) though they be:

> And the cloud covered the tent of meeting, and the glory of Yahweh filled the tabernacle. And Moses was not able to enter the tent of meeting because the cloud settled on it, and the glory of Yahweh filled the tabernacle. In all their journeys, when the cloud lifted up from over the tabernacle, the sons of Israel would set out. But if the cloud did not lift up, then they did not set out till the day that it lifted up. For the cloud of Yahweh was on the tabernacle by day, and fire was in it by night, in the sight of all the house of Israel in all their journeys. (40:34–38)

Israel is saved through judgment, and the tabernacle, with its implements of sacrifice, makes it possible for the glorious Yahweh to take up residence—no longer outside the camp (cf. 33:7), but in their midst. Salvation comes through judgment and leads to the experience of the glory of God, a glory so overwhelming that it dictates the movements of those who perceive it. Israel has constructed the tabernacle "as Yahweh had commanded Moses." Thus, in obedience to Yahweh's word, they have built a microcosm—a symbolic picture of the cosmos on a reduced scale. The tabernacle symbolically depicts the world that God has made, and when his people obey him, God does for the tabernacle what he will do for the world: he fills it with his glory. The filling of the tabernacle with the glory of Yahweh is a proleptic enactment of the earth being filled with the glory of Yahweh. This is why the world exists.

3.5 The Center of the Theology of Exodus

The book of Exodus is very clear in its presentation of Yahweh's intentions. He intends to save Israel through the judgment of Egypt, and he intends this judgment on Egypt to be severe. He intends to humble Pharaoh and his people. He intends to force them to recognize that he, not their gods, is Lord. He wants Egypt, Israel, and all the earth to know that he is Yahweh. And they will know that he is simultaneously just and merciful, so much so that the finite mind can scarcely perceive the glory of the justice and the mercy as they intermingle and radiate with the blinding splendor of the one they reveal. Yahweh glorifies himself at the exodus by saving Israel through the judgment of Egypt.

Genesis leads readers to expect Yahweh's defeat of evil to be accomplished through a seed of the woman, seed of Abraham, seed of Jacob, and perhaps seed of Joseph or Judah.[81] Unexpectedly, however, the seed of the woman in the book of Exodus is raised up from the house of Levi (Ex. 2:1). This sets an important pattern, as the one who leads Israel to deliverance is from the tribe of the priests and serves as a prophet.[82] Moreover, he is raised in the royal house of Egypt. In a sense, the seed of the woman through whom the seed of the serpent is crushed in the book of Exodus, bringing salvation for the people of God through the judgment of their enemies and putting the glory of God on display, is a prophet, a priest, and a king.[83]

Once the exodus was accomplished, Yahweh took Israel out in the wilderness to make himself known to them. All along it was stated that once out of Egypt, Israel would serve Yahweh in the wilderness. His self-revelation to them at Sinai, trumpet blast, thick darkness, earthquake, lightning, and fire on the mountain, overwhelmed them with the awareness of his frightful greatness. This was meant to discipline them, that they might serve him in fear and holiness, which was meant to keep them from sin. Sin would be disregarding Yahweh to pursue their own course, reflecting gross ingratitude and brazen boldness against their covenant Lord. When the people did not honor Yahweh as God and give thanks to him, Yahweh judged their sin, and through the judgment, he saved them from themselves even as thousands died. With the revelation of the tabernacle, and with its construction, salvation again comes through judgment as Yahweh takes up residence among Israel, glory filling the tent. In the book of Exodus, all things find their place with relationship to the central revelation of the glory of Yahweh in salvation through judgment.

4. Leviticus

Israel has learned that no one can dwell with the consuming fire, no one can dwell with the everlasting burning (cf. Isa. 33:14). Freed from bondage to the Egyptians, only the remnant within the nation has been freed from bondage to sin.[84] At Sinai God creates a covenant with Israel designed to allow the holy God to dwell among the sinful people, and Leviticus sets forth the terms of the covenant as it relates to sacrifice, the status of clean and unclean, and daily life.

[81]See the pregnant references to the "stone" and the "shepherd" who comes from Joseph (Gen. 49:24). It seems to have become clear later that Judah was chosen over Joseph as the line from which the king would come—see the reference to Joseph being "rejected" in Ps. 78:67–68 and the explanation in 1 Chron. 5:2, "Though Judah prevailed among his brothers and the prince came from him, yet the birthright was to Joseph."

[82]Cf. Dumbrell, *The Faith of Israel*, 34.

[83]Similarly Sailhamer, *The Meaning of the Pentateuch*, 236: "In the Pentateuch the Messiah is a prophetic priest-king modeled after Moses who will reign over God's kingdom, bring salvation to Israel and the nations, and fulfill God's covenants."

[84]This statement reflects my view that old covenant believers were regenerate, though not indwelt—the tabernacle and temple were indwelt, not believers. See further James M. Hamilton Jr., *God's Indwelling Presence: The Holy Spirit in the Old and New Testaments*, NACSBT (Nashville: Broadman & Holman, 2006).

Leviticus 1–7 relates the laws on the sacrifices. Chapters 8–10 describe the institution of the priesthood. Chapters 11–16 deal with uncleanness and its treatment. Chapters 17–24 then give prescriptions for practical holiness.[85] Just as Yahweh is the most significant thing about the Ten Commandments, he is the most significant thing about the Levitical cult.

The governing reality is that Yahweh dwells in the Holy of Holies in the tabernacle. Everything near him is holy, and outside what is holy is what is clean. Outside the clean realm is the unclean realm of the dead. If the Holy One comes into contact with anything unclean, death results. Yahweh's glory is thus bound up in his otherness, his holiness, and if he is to be with Israel, they too must be separated from all that is unclean, lest they die. These regulations are a judgment—it was not this way before sin entered the world—but through the judgment of these regulations, and through the judgment of death that is visited upon the numerous sacrificial beasts, the people of Israel are saved and enabled to remain in the presence of their glorious God.

In Exodus, God's instructions to Moses regarding the making of the tabernacle are recounted, and the tabernacle is something of a new garden of Eden.[86] God will walk among Israel just as he walked with Adam and Eve (Gen. 3:8; Lev. 26:11–13). These texts present an arrangement whereby God will dwell among the nation in the tabernacle. God teaches Israel how they must live if he is to remain among them. The instructions in Exodus, Leviticus, and Numbers address specific details but do not give an overview explanation of the Levitical cult. The rationale of the sacrifices is not fully explained.[87] From the details, however, a fairly clear picture can be deduced.

The key ideas are these: Yahweh is going to reside in the Holy of Holies, enthroned above the cherubim, with the ark as his footstool (Ps. 132:7–8). Yahweh is holy (Lev. 11:44; 19:2). Again, when the holiness of Yahweh comes into contact with anything unclean, death results (see the account of Nadab and Abihu and the resulting instructions in Lev. 10:1–11).[88] Therefore, the camp of Israel must be clean.

The camp of Israel is built on the idea that there are degrees of holiness surrounding Yahweh. The closer one gets to Yahweh, the more sacred the space becomes.[89] He dwells in the Most Holy Place. Only the high priest can enter the Most Holy Place, and only once a year. Outside the Holy of Holies is the holy place, which only the priests can enter. Moses and Aaron and his sons camp in front of the tabernacle to

---

[85]Gordon J. Wenham, *The Book of Leviticus*, NICOT (Grand Rapids: Eerdmans, 1979), 4.
[86]See table 2.3, "Correspondences between Eden and the Tabernacle and Temple," and the literature cited in n. 18 above.
[87]Cf. Gordon Wenham, "The Theology of Old Testament Sacrifice," in Beckwith and Selman, *Sacrifice in the Bible*, 77.
[88]Wenham, *The Book of Leviticus*, 26.
[89]Dumbrell, *The Faith of Israel*, 48.

Figure 2.1. The Camp of Israel

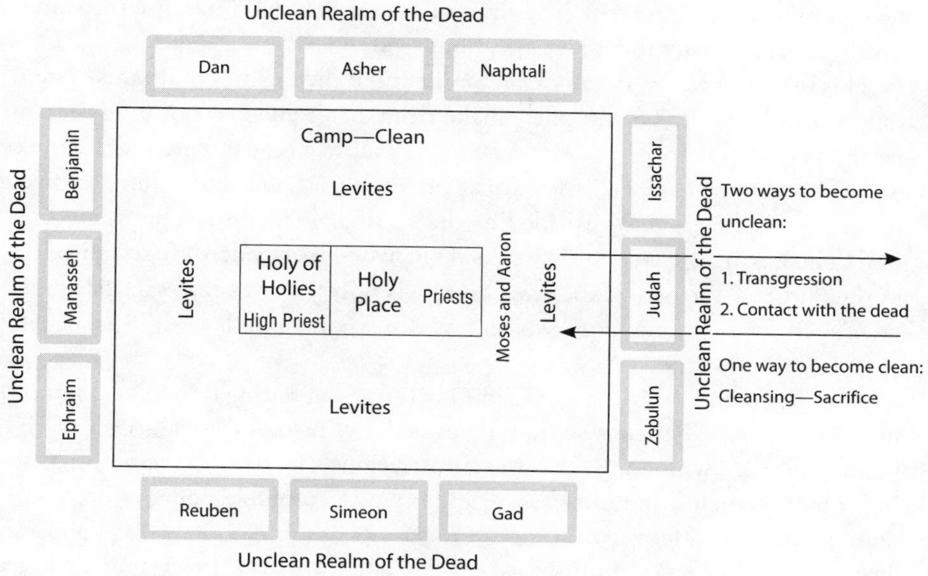

the east, guarding the sanctuary for the protection of the people of Israel. Unauthorized people who draw near are put to death (Num. 3:38). Encamped around the tabernacle are the Levites, who act as a buffer for the rest of the people "so that there may be no wrath on the congregation of the people of Israel" (Num. 1:53). The twelve tribes of Israel are then camped around the tabernacle (Num. 2:1–31). Outside the camp is the unclean realm of the dead (see fig. 2.1).[90]

There are two ways to become unclean: contact with the dead and transgression. There is one way to be cleansed and thereby reenter the camp without danger: sacrifice.[91] Contact with the dead includes contact with blood or other bodily discharges, which explains, for instance, why women are unclean after childbirth (Leviticus 12). Lepers are always unclean because they are constantly exposed to deadness on their skin (Leviticus 13, esp. 13:45–46).

Transgressions are either intentional or unintentional (cf. Lev. 4:2; Num. 15:27–31). The fact that a transgression is deliberately chosen or even premeditated does not make it necessarily "intentional" or "high handed." In the Levitical system, high-handed sin is unrepentant sin. Sin is "intentional" when the sinner refuses to repent of the sin and offer the prescribed sacrifices (cf. Ps. 7:13, ET 12).[92] The sinner is throwing off the covenant. He or she does not believe the

[90] Wenham, *The Book of Leviticus*, 25–26.

[91] Ibid., 23, 56. See also Alexander's treatment, *From Paradise to the Promised Land*, 112–19.

[92] So also Jacob Milgrom, *Leviticus*, A Continental Commentary (Minneapolis: Fortress, 2004), 46, cf. 49, 58, 72–73. It seems that this understanding can fit with Kiuchi's proposal that "*hata'* ["sin"] means to 'hide oneself'" (Nobuyoshi Kiuchi, *Leviticus*, AOTC [Downers Grove, IL: InterVarsity, 2007], 36–37).

claims of the Bible—that God dwells among the people, that he is holy, and that he will punish transgression. The sinner does not fear God because the sinner does not believe what the Bible says about God.

This brings us to a very important point about the Levitical cult: this system only works by faith. The prophets make clear that Yahweh is not interested in perfunctory obedience. In their statements that Yahweh desires mercy not sacrifice (e.g., Hos. 6:6; Mic. 6:6–8), they are not rejecting sacrifice but calling for lives that show that the mercy provided by the sacrificial system has been internalized. The Levitical system only works if the worshiper believes that Yahweh is in the midst of the people, believes that he is holy, believes that sacrifice must be offered for cleansing, and lives in a way that corresponds with these beliefs (e.g., Lev. 15:31; 22:9).

The meaning of Leviticus 18:5 in its Old Testament setting is to be understood in this context: "The one who does them shall live by them" means that (1) the holiness of God will not break out against the unclean and kill them if they do the commandments and offer sacrifices, and (2) acceptable doing of the commandments and offering of sacrifices requires faith in God and his promises. The Levitical system is a faith-based system, not a works-based system, and the experience of Enoch (Gen. 5:24) shows that walking with God gives the word *life* connotations that go beyond the threescore and ten. Doing the commandments by faith in order to live results in life now and hereafter.

All of this glorifies God by highlighting his holiness and his authority. As Gordon Wenham notes, "God's demand to be holy, to keep the commandments and so on was recalled in every sacrifice."[93] God's presence among Israel is so significant that the elaborate rituals and requirements are a small thing compared to the weight of the one who resides in their midst. As noted above, the elaborate system is also a judgment. Whereas Adam and Eve needed none of these prescriptions regarding cleanliness, sin, and sacrifice in Eden, the system is a judgment on Israel's sin because only through this system can God dwell among people east of the garden. As Kiuchi puts it, "Holiness is what the first man and woman had before the fall, and . . . the various rules in Leviticus aim to lead the Israelites, as it were, back to this existential condition."[94] Thus, even as the system of sacrifices is a judgment brought on by sin, House is correct that "the sacrifices in Leviticus 1–7 are based on God's mercy, grace, and kindness. God willingly forgives those who do not have any intrinsic merit of their own."[95]

The substitution seen in both the sacrifice of the ram in place of Isaac and the Passover lamb in place of the firstborn of Israel is also reiterated in the Levitical system. Wenham writes, "In some degree substitution seems to form part of the

[93]Wenham, "Theology of Old Testament Sacrifice," 84.
[94]Kiuchi, *Leviticus*, 29.
[95]House, *Old Testament Theology*, 127.

theology of all the sacrifices."[96] The worshiper places his hand on the head of the sacrificial animal (e.g., Lev. 1:4). The description of the Day of Atonement ritual in Leviticus 16 adds that when the high priest places his hands on the head of the animal, he is to confess the sins of the people over the animal (16:21), and this seems to make explicit what is implicit elsewhere. As Wenham writes, "In sacrifice it appears that the worshipper identifies himself with the animal he offers. What he does to the animal, he does symbolically to himself. The death of the animal portrays the death of himself."[97] The substitute is judged on behalf of the worshiper. The transfer of guilt from the worshiper to the sacrificial beast, and then the death of the beast, cleanses the worshiper of sin. The blood of the beast atones for the soul of the worshiper (Lev. 17:11). Kiuchi writes, "The offerer is viewed as the object of the Lord's wrath to varying degrees, and the offerings symbolize the offerer appeasing the Lord's wrath."[98] The worshipers are saved by faith through the judgment that falls on the sacrifice. God is glorified in salvation through judgment.

Excursus: Leviticus 18 and Deuteronomy 30 in Romans 10

The Levitical system was not intended as a ladder for Israel to use in her climb to heaven. Rather, it was the means whereby God dwelt among the sinful nation without killing them, and the system also separated Israel from the nations (Lev. 20:24). Two texts in the New Testament could give the impression that the Levitical system is works based,[99] but when we understand the salvation-historical perspective of Romans 10 and Galatians 3, we see that Paul is not claiming that Moses taught Israel to earn their salvation by works of the law.[100]

Paul writes in Romans 10:5–8:

> For Moses writes about the righteousness that is from the law, "the man who does them shall live by them." But the righteousness from faith speaks thus: "Do not say in your heart, 'Who will ascend into heaven?'" (that is, to bring Christ down) "or 'Who will descend into the abyss?'" (that is, to bring Christ up from the dead).

---

[96]Wenham, *The Book of Leviticus*, 111.

[97]Wenham, "Theology of Old Testament Sacrifice," 77.

[98]Kiuchi, *Leviticus*, 47.

[99]Thus, Mark A. Seifrid (*Christ, Our Righteousness*, NSBT [Downers Grove, IL: InterVarsity, 2000], 105) writes, "When Paul rejects the saving value of the 'works of the law' in Galatians and Romans, he does so with full recognition that he is dealing not merely with a misreading of the law, but with the law itself. The law is a 'law of works,' which demands deeds of obedience in order to obtain the offer of life (Rom. 3:27; cf. 10:5; Gal. 3:12). The misuse of the law lies in the refusal to confess the reality of sin and guilt which it exposes, a refusal which entails seeking to be justified before God by the 'works' which lie with our power (Rom. 3:20)." If Seifrid is describing the attempt to find salvation by means of the law *only* now that Christ has come, I agree with him. But I do not think this is the way the law was intended to function for the remnant of old covenant Israel before the coming of Christ.

[100]Here I will only discuss Romans 10. I have discussed Gal. 3:10–14 along these lines in "The One Who Does Them Shall Live By Them: Leviticus 18:5 in Galatians 3:12," *Gospel Witness*, August 2005, 10–14. See also in chap. 6 below, §2.2.1 and §2.5.4. For a stellar discussion of the law in biblical theology, see Thomas R. Schreiner, "The Commands of God," in *Central Themes in Biblical Theology: Mapping Unity in Diversity*, ed. Scott J. Hafemann and Paul R. House (Grand Rapids: Baker, 2007), 66–101.

> But what does it say? "The word is near you, in your mouth and in your heart" (that is, the word of faith which we proclaim).

One could get the impression that in Romans 10:5 Paul is claiming that Moses taught that righteousness from the law is based on works—doing the commandments—whereas in 10:6 the righteousness from faith is based on trust. One major problem with such a conclusion would be that it overlooks the salvation-historical contribution of Romans 10:4, which says, "Christ is the end of the law for righteousness to everyone who believes." This statement has many profound implications, but one of them is that now that Christ has come, the time during which the Levitical system was operational has ended: "Christ is the end of the law."[101] Now that Christ has come and the law has ended, anyone who seeks to establish his own righteousness apart from Christ must do so through perfect obedience to the law since no other sacrifice for sin is available.[102]

We must also observe that whereas Paul refers to Leviticus 18:5 in Romans 10:5 ("the man who does them shall live by them") to illustrate "the righteousness that is from the law," he then quotes statements from Deuteronomy 30:11–14, interspersed with christological applications, to illustrate "the righteousness from faith." It would be very strange for Paul to quote Moses' words in Leviticus 18 to point to law-based righteousness, followed by quotations of Moses' words in Deuteronomy 30 to point to faith-based righteousness. Paul is not saying that when Moses wrote Leviticus 18 he was a legalist, but then when he wrote Deuteronomy 30 he was teaching justification by faith! The key point is that "Christ is the end of the law for righteousness" (Rom. 10:4). Now that Christ has brought an end to the law, no sacrifice remains for sin (see Heb. 10:26), and so anyone who refuses to trust Christ must attain to God's standard of righteousness through perfect obedience to the law.[103]

The context of Deuteronomy 30 is also instructive for our understanding of Paul's argument. To briefly anticipate the discussion of Deuteronomy below, Moses had just stated in Deuteronomy 29:3 (ET 4), "To this day, Yahweh has not given to you a heart to know and eyes to see and ears to hear," which means that whereas God has given them everything they need for life and godliness, he has not changed them on the volitional level. God gave Israel commandments that would allow him to walk among them (Deut. 23:14) and give them long life in the land (5:16). These commandments were not beyond the physical abilities of

---

[101]Bell (*The Irrevocable Call of God*, 42) writes, "The law comes to an end not because of its failure but rather because the law has a time-limited function to condemn until the revelation of Christ (Gal. 3.15–4.7). . . . The law in fact continues to condemn those who do not believe in Christ even after the Christ event." See also N. T. Wright, *The Climax of the Covenant: Christ and the Law in Pauline Theology* (Minneapolis: Fortress, 1992), 241: "The Torah . . . was a good thing whose job is done."

[102]So also Schreiner, "The Commands of God," 87.

[103]Similarly ibid., 80, 88–89.

the Israelites, and this is the point of the statements in Deuteronomy 30:11–14. The Israelites do not have to accomplish superhuman feats to get God's instructions; "the word is very near you, in your mouth and in your heart to do it" (30:14). Deuteronomy 30:11–14 teaches that the word is in their hearts in that it is available to them, but Deuteronomy 29:3 (ET 4) states that the word is not in their hearts such that they want to do it. They have the physical ability to do everything they are required to do (30:11–14). They do not want to do what they are required to do (29:3, ET 4).

Thus, in its own salvation-historical context, Leviticus 18:5 refers to living by doing the commandments *by faith*. Not doing them in order to earn salvation by works, but doing them on the basis of the belief that Yahweh has given them. Yahweh resides in the midst of the people, and the commandments are the means whereby the people may remain in God's presence.[104] This word to which Israel has access in Deuteronomy 30 benefits them only if they believe it. So the fact that Paul sets these two texts against one another in Romans 10:5–8 leads to the conclusion that Paul is quoting Leviticus 18:5 not as it applied in Moses' day but as it applies to Paul's own Jewish contemporaries who "have a zeal for God, but not according to knowledge" (Rom. 10:2). They are "ignorant of the righteousness that comes from God" and are "seeking to establish their own" (10:3). They do not believe that "Christ is the end of the law for righteousness to everyone who believes" (10:4), and so if they are to be righteous, they have two options: either they can obey the law perfectly (which they cannot actually accomplish), or they can repent and confess Jesus as Lord (10:9–10). Paul is not dealing with what Leviticus 18:5 meant prior to the coming of Christ. Paul is dealing with what Leviticus 18:5 means for those who are not submitted to the righteousness of God that has now been revealed in Christ (Rom. 10:3; cf. 3:21–22).[105]

Those who refuse to believe in Jesus and cling to the Levitical system no longer have sacrifices to offer for their sins and uncleanness. If they are to be saved by the Levitical system now that they have rejected faith in Christ, they must keep the law perfectly, stumbling at no point (cf. Gal. 5:2–3; James 2:10). Paul teaches this in Romans 10 in the hope that the crushing judgment of the righteous requirement

[104]To my thinking, this is a more satisfying explanation than Sailhamer's suggestion that "the Pentateuch is an attempt to contrast the lives of two individuals, Abraham and Moses. Abraham, who lived before the Law . . . , is portrayed as one who kept the law, whereas Moses, who lived under the Law . . . , is portrayed as one who died in the wilderness because he did not believe. If such a contrast between faith and works is a part of the compositional strategy of the book, then we may rightfully conclude that part of the Pentateuch's purpose was to show not merely the way of faith, but also the weakness of the Law" (*The Pentateuch as Narrative*, 61–62). It seems to me that such a reading not only fails to recognize the need for faith if the law is to be kept but also unduly emphasizes Moses' failure in striking the rock to the exclusion of his clear knowledge of and faith in God—he is described as a man of faith in Heb. 11:23–28.

[105]Similarly Guy Waters, *The End of Deuteronomy in the Epistles of Paul*, WUNT 2.221 (Tübingen: Mohr Siebeck, 2006), 181: "Paul, then, has been directed to Deut. 30:12–14 by very concrete and immediate concerns."

of the law will be brought home to his kinsmen according to the flesh, so that for the glory of God they might be saved through being condemned.

4.1 The Center of the Theology of Leviticus

Yahweh is holy. His holiness tolerates neither sin nor uncleanness. Kiuchi suggests that the notion of uncleanness is based on what happened with the serpent in Genesis 3.[106] The regulations set forth in Leviticus are a judgment, and they make it possible for people to substitute animals of sacrifice that will be judged in their place, that they might be saved. Genesis gives rise to the expectation of a seed of the woman who will accomplish salvation for Israel through the judgment of their enemies. Exodus typologically shows Moses doing these very things as Yahweh's agent. And Leviticus adds that Israel herself is sinful and must seek atonement for sin through substitutionary sacrifice that appeases the wrath of God. Thus may Yahweh justly show mercy. The penal substitutionary sacrifices are demanded by the very glory of God. If they are not offered, God cannot keep his word and show mercy. In Leviticus, God is glorified in salvation through judgment.

5. Numbers

The book of Numbers opens one month after what is recounted at the end of Exodus (cf. Num. 1:1; Ex. 40:17), and the first ten chapters of Numbers are set at Sinai, with the cloud lifting and the people setting out in Numbers 10:11–12. There is a census taken in Numbers 1, and another in Numbers 26. Between these two a generation dies in the wilderness. After the second, no Israelite deaths are recorded in the book of Numbers. After the census in Numbers 1, chapters 2–11 order the camp of Israel for its march on Canaan. Numbers 12–25, however, recount Israel's wickedness in the wilderness. After the exodus generation dies, the generation that will enter the land is numbered in chapter 26. In chapters 27–36, the camp of Israel is again ordered for a march on Canaan. Through judgment on one generation, the next gets an opportunity to enter and take the land.

The numbering of the people in Numbers 1 sets the stage for what amounts to a continuation of Leviticus in Numbers.[107] Before the first chapter ends, we read that the Levites are to encamp around, carry, and guard the tabernacle and its furnishings (Num. 1:47–54). Non-Levites draw near on pain of death (1:51).[108] East of the tabernacle are encamped the tribes of Judah (significantly listed first), Issachar, and Zebulun (2:1–9). On the south are Reuben, Simeon, and Gad (2:10–16). To the west are Ephraim, Manasseh, and Benjamin (2:18–24). And on the north are Dan, Asher, and Naphtali (2:25–31). The tribes are encamped by

[106]Kiuchi, *Leviticus*, 29, 39.

[107]Sailhamer (*The Pentateuch as Narrative*, 369) writes, "Traditionally, Numbers has been treated as an independent book. As is the case with the other books of the Pentateuch, Numbers is not really a separate book but only a section of a larger work." He describes Leviticus in similar terms (323).

[108]Philip J. Budd, *Numbers*, WBC (Waco, TX: Word, 1984), 18.

their standards, they are numbered, and the order of march is assigned. The use of military terminology befits the coming conquest. The tribes thus encamped around the tabernacle complete the picture of the concentric rings radiating out from Yahweh: Holy of Holies, holy place, courts of the tabernacle, Moses and Aaron with his sons at the entrance, Levites encamped around the tabernacle, tribes of Israel encamped around the Levites.

The Levites are to serve Aaron and his sons, the priests (Num. 3:1–9), and again, non-Levites who draw near face death (3:10). The Levites are substituted for the firstborn of Israel (3:11–13), Yahweh asserting that they shall be his own, punctuating his claim with the assertion, "I am Yahweh" (3:13). Israel's time at Sinai is rounded out with more regulations (Numbers 4–9), before the people set out at Yahweh's command (10:11–13).

Moses' triumphant words when the ark sets out and comes to rest point to the glory of Yahweh that will be demonstrated in the deliverance of Israel that will come through Yahweh's judgment of her enemies: "And when the ark set out, Moses would say, 'Arise, O Yahweh, and let your enemies be scattered, and let those who hate you flee before you.' And when it rested, he would say, 'Return, O Yahweh, to the ten thousand thousands of Israel'" (Num. 10:35–36).

The continual presence of Yahweh in the pillar of fire and cloud leads and protects, but it also observes and condemns. Dumbrell observes, "The glory-cloud is God's manifested presence, serving both to save and to judge Israel during this wilderness period."[109] None of Israel's complaints escapes Yahweh's notice: the grumbling is heard and judged. In Egypt Yahweh saved Israel through judgment on her Egyptian oppressors. In the wilderness, Yahweh saves Israel through (and from) his judgment on her sinfulness.

There are unspecified complaints that provoke Yahweh's anger (Num. 11:1–2), complaints about what Yahweh has not provided—meat and fish, leeks and onions (11:4–5)—complaints about what he has provided—manna (11:6)—and Yahweh's anger blazes out (11:10). Yahweh's reaction to these complaints is based on the fact that Israel owes Yahweh gratitude for the liberation and provision she enjoys. Rather than gratitude, the people indict Yahweh, who, in their eyes, has given them what is not good, manna, and not given them what is good, meat and melons, cucumbers and garlic. This rejection of what Yahweh has given and the concomitant suggestion that better things should have been provided is diagnosed as despising Yahweh (11:20). Moses cries out to Yahweh for help (11:10–15), and Yahweh says that he will give the Spirit to seventy men who will help Moses (11:16–17).

The complaints come not only from the people; even Aaron and Miriam speak against Moses, and they too are saved through judgment (Num. 12:1–16).[110] There

[109]Dumbrell, *The Faith of Israel*, 53.

[110]On the significant statements made in this account concerning Moses as a prophet, see Robertson, *The Christ of the Prophets*, 31–44.

is more trouble from people in leadership when the spies come back with their bad report (Numbers 13). The glory of Yahweh appears to the people (14:10), and the people's fear of the inhabitants of the land is diagnosed as a rejection of Yahweh and a refusal to believe him (14:11). Yahweh has announced that he will bring the people into the land, and their fear of the descendants of Anak (14:33) shows that they do not fear the one who made the giants. As he did when Israel made the golden calf, Yahweh again states that he will destroy Israel and make a greater and mightier nation from Moses (14:12). Again Moses appeals to Yahweh's concern for his reputation among the Egyptians (14:13) and to how that reputation will spread (14:14),[111] and Moses quotes Yahweh's own declaration of his name back to him:

> And now, please let the power of the Lord be great, just as you said, saying, "Yahweh is slow to anger and great in steadfast love, forgiving iniquity and transgression, but he will by no means clear the guilty, visiting the iniquity of the fathers on the sons, to the third and the fourth generations." Please pardon the iniquity of this people, according to the greatness of your steadfast love, just as you have forgiven this people, from Egypt until now. (14:17–19)

Yahweh has declared that he will show his power (e.g., Ex. 9:16), and Moses appeals for him to show his power in Numbers 14:17. In Exodus 34:6–7,[112] Yahweh announced himself to be all the things Moses quotes back to him in Numbers 14:18, and in petitioning this way Moses is calling for Yahweh to show his greatness by being justly merciful, asking for pardon according to Yahweh's great mercy, which Yahweh has consistently shown to Israel (14:19).

Yahweh grants Moses' request, saying, "I have pardoned, according to your word" (Num. 14:20), and he then goes on to affirm that this pardoning will not keep him from accomplishing his ultimate purpose: "But truly, as I live, all the earth will be filled with the glory of Yahweh" (14:21). This is an explicit declaration of what has been implicit all along, which is that Yahweh's glory will cover the land as the waters cover the sea.[113] It also becomes explicit at this point that Yahweh's demonstrations of mercy will neither detract from his justice nor keep him from his purpose, and the next words explain how. Mercy will be shown, but it will be a mercy that comes through judgment. Israel will not be wiped out—mercy—but the generation that came out of Egypt will die in the wilderness—judgment (14:22–23, 29).

[111] See the appendix (§7) to chap. 4, table 4.9, "Old Testament Prayers Appealing to God's Concern for His Own Glory."

[112] See the appendix (§8) to this chapter, which catalogs Ex. 34:6–7 in the Law, Prophets, and Writings.

[113] See appendix 2 (§6) to chap. 3, "All the Earth Filled with the Knowledge of Yahweh's Glory."

The leadership again rebels when 250 chiefs of Israel join with Korah against Moses and Aaron (Num. 16:1–3). Moses declares that theirs is a gathering together against Yahweh (16:11). The glory of Yahweh appears to the congregation (16:19), and Moses and Aaron intercede for Israel (16:20–22). The earth splits and swallows the rebels (16:31–33), a fire consumes 250 men offering incense (16:35), and thus is the word of Moses confirmed that these men despised Yahweh (16:30). Remarkably, the congregation grumbles against Moses and Aaron the next day (16:41)! Again the glory of Yahweh appears to judge the nation, and again Moses and Aaron intercede on behalf of the people (16:42–50). Aaron's staff buds to show that Yahweh chose him and to stop the grumbling (Numbers 17). Aaron, his sons, and the Levites are to work and keep the tabernacle, "that there may never again be wrath on the people of Israel" (18:5–6).

The point being made in all these episodes is that Israel is in the presence of Yahweh, and they owe him praise and thanks for what he has done and how he has provided. Grumbling about circumstances, the kind of food, or who is in charge directly attacks the one who sovereignly orchestrated the circumstances, chose *this* food not *that*, and appointed the leaders who are in place. Grumbling against Yahweh suggests that what he has brought to pass is not good, or that his choices were not wise, or that he will not be able to do what he has said, or that he has not been faithful to his promises. Yahweh responds to suggestions that he is not faithful, able, wise, and good—which are at the heart of unbelief—with wrathful indignation. He is a consuming fire—even with Moses.

Numbers 20 is a bleak chapter: Miriam dies, the people need water, Moses strikes the rock, Edom refuses to let Israel pass, then Aaron dies. After Miriam's death (20:1) the people again assemble against Moses and Aaron because there is no water (20:2–5). The glory of Yahweh again appears, and Yahweh tells Moses to speak to the rock that it may yield water (20:6–8).

Yahweh said to speak to it. Moses decides to strike it (Num. 20:11). Water comes forth, but Yahweh holds Moses and Aaron accountable for not believing him so as to hallow him before the eyes of the sons of Israel (20:12). There is a direct connection between believing Yahweh, obeying him, and upholding him as holy. The person who refuses to obey Yahweh's word exalts himself over the expressed will of Yahweh. Judgment falls: Moses will not take the people into the land (20:12). But there is also mercy: the water comes from the rock. And there is glory: for though the people quarreled with Yahweh, "he was hallowed among them" (20:13).

The importance of obeying Yahweh's word is seen in the judgment against Moses, and the same is brought into focus when the people are saved from fiery serpents. After they again speak against God and Moses (Num. 21:5), Yahweh sends fiery serpents whose bite is deadly (21:6)—judgment. The people urge Moses to seek mercy from Yahweh, which he does (21:7). Yahweh instructs Moses to make a bronze serpent and set it on a pole, and all who look to it will live when they see it (21:8–9). The narrative teaches that it is not those who rely on their own understanding who find salvation, but those who believe what Yahweh says. Yahweh is again glorified in this salvation through judgment.

Having defeated Sihon and Og (Num. 21:21–35), Israel arrives on the plains of Moab (22:1), and Balak summons Balaam to curse Israel (22:2–6). Readers of the Torah know that Yahweh promised Abraham that he would bless those who blessed him and curse those who cursed him, and so Balaam's prospects are not bright. Try as he might, he simply cannot curse Israel. So, in the darkened wisdom of those who know not God, Balaam keeps trying. His first oracle seems to reflect an awareness of the promise to Abraham (Gen. 12:3). Balaam acknowledges the difficulty of cursing those whom God has not cursed, denouncing those whom God has not denounced (Num. 23:8). The promise of innumerable descendants to Abraham (Gen. 13:16) is also echoed in Balaam's first oracle (Num. 23:10). God's faithfulness to the promises to Abraham is implicitly affirmed in Balaam's second try, as he asserts that God is not going to lie or fail to fulfill what he has said (23:19). Balaam is then forced to confess that he cannot overcome Yahweh so as to revoke his blessing (23:20). He goes on to celebrate Yahweh's bringing Israel out of Egypt (23:22), saying that there is no magic that can stand against what Yahweh has done (23:23). The second and third oracles are concluded with words reminiscent of Jacob's blessing on Judah (23:24; 24:9; cf. Gen. 49:9). Balak dismisses Balaam in frustration, but this elicits yet another blessing on Israel, ancestral voices prophesying war, speaking of a scepter and a star that will arise out of Jacob to crush the head of the seed of the serpent (Num. 24:17; see table 2.4).[114]

Balaam fails in his attempt to curse Israel, so instead he incites Israel to wicked idolatry (Num. 31:15–16; 25:1–2). As House observes, "Balak now realizes that Israel can be stopped only if the people stop worshiping Yahweh."[115] Yahweh responds in wrath (25:3), calling for a killing purge (25:4–5). The zeal of Phinehas for Yahweh's name is yet another example of deliverance—the atonement Phinehas makes (25:13)—coming through judgment as Phinehas spears the flagrant idolaters (25:6–8). These events are followed by the new census in Numbers 26, and the nation is prepared for the taking of the land in the remaining chapters of Numbers (27–36).

---

[114]For the argument that Numbers 24 weaves together lines of promise from Genesis 3, 12, 27, and 49, see Hamilton, "The Seed of the Woman and the Blessing of Abraham." See also Sailhamer, *The Pentateuch as Narrative*, 408–09.

[115]House, *Old Testament Theology*, 164.

5.1 The Center of the Theology of Numbers

In the wilderness Yahweh judges Israel's sin, and after judgment falls on a whole generation, the nation arrives on the plains of Moab. Judgment even falls on Moses, who is not permitted to enter the Promised Land because he failed to uphold Yahweh as holy in the eyes of Israel. These judgments fall, but Israel is saved through them. Yahweh judges. Rebels die. Indeed, a generation perishes in the wilderness, but because of the steadfast love of the Lord the nation is not consumed (Lam. 3:22, MT, ESV mg.). Through these judgments Yahweh's justice shines forth with a severe and painful brightness, but through them all Yahweh mercifully perseveres with his persnickety people.

Yahweh even turns an attempt of a pagan prophet to curse his people into an opportunity to remind them of his promises. Not only does Yahweh reiterate his promises; he weaves several lines of promise together. Numbers 24:17 refers to a "scepter" and "star" that will arise out of Jacob and "crush the forehead" of Moab. The head crushing alludes to Genesis 3:15, and the "scepter" is reminiscent of the "scepter" that will not depart from Judah (Gen. 49:10). The many references throughout Numbers 22–24 to the impossibility of reversing Yahweh's blessing on Israel reminds readers of the blessing of Abraham (Gen. 12:1–3). Thus, the Balaam oracles connect the seed of the woman to the blessing of Abraham and the promise of a king from Judah who will judge the enemies of Israel.

In Numbers, then, Israel is saved through the judgments that fall on them, and the promise of the conquering seed of the woman is reaffirmed. Because of Yahweh's mercy, Israel continues to enjoy his presence, protection, and provision. In Numbers, the salvation of Israel comes through Yahweh's judgment of their wickedness, seen chiefly in the generation of corpses that fall in the wilderness. Through exacting justice Israel is mercifully brought to the border of the Promised Land that the land might be filled with the glory of Yahweh.

6. Deuteronomy

The first mention of loving God in the Bible came in Exodus 20:6, which referred to "those who love" Yahweh and keep his commandments. But the idea of loving God is not elaborated upon until Deuteronomy.[116] In Leviticus, Israel is urged to obey Yahweh's commands on the basis of his identity, the assertion "I am Yahweh" often prefacing or following his commands.[117] In Numbers, the God

---

[116]Alexander points out that "love in Deuteronomy is never presented as something emotional . . . . True love will demonstrate itself in perfect obedience" (*From Paradise to the Promised Land*, 167). Similarly Eichrodt (*Theology of the Old Testament*, 1:93–94), who describes legalism as a perversion of Deuteronomy's call for Israel to love God by obeying him.

[117]See Lev. 11:44–45; 18:2, 4, 5, 6, 21, 30; 19:3, 4, 10, 12, 14, 16, 18, 25, 28, 30, 31, 32, 34, etc.

who is a consuming fire purges the wickedness of his people in the wilderness. In Deuteronomy, Moses prepares the people to enter the land.[118]

The first three chapters of Deuteronomy review Israel's history from Sinai to the plains of Moab. Deuteronomy 4–11 then seeks to motivate Israel to keep the law. Chapters 12–28 set forth the stipulations of the covenant, and in chapters 29–34 Moses gives his last will and testament.[119] As Peter Vogt writes, "At the heart of the Deuteronomic world view is the supremacy of Yahweh. One of the primary goals of the book is to inculcate a sense of total loyalty to him."[120]

6.1 From Sinai to Moab

Forty years have passed since the exodus from Egypt (Deut. 1:3). Deuteronomy describes its own contents as Moses' attempt to explain the Torah (1:5).[121] It is important to recognize that the historical review on which Moses takes the people in Deuteronomy 1–3 has the intention of *motivating* Israel to obey Yahweh.[122] Moses recounts Israel's history that they might learn from their past.

Reviewing the departure from Sinai (Deut. 1:5–8), the appointment of leaders to help Moses (1:9–18),[123] and what happened with the spies sent from Kadesh-barnea (1:19–28) gives Moses an opportunity to tell the new generation what he said at that time:

> And I said to you, "Do not tremble, and do not be afraid of them! Yahweh your God is the one who goes before you. He will fight for you, as in all that he did with you in Egypt before your eyes, and in the wilderness which you saw, where

---

[118]Cf. Peter T. Vogt, *Deuteronomic Theology and the Significance of* Torah*: A Reappraisal* (Winona Lake, IN: Eisenbrauns, 2006), 108: "Their relationship with Yahweh will change upon their entry into the promised land. . . . Deuteronomy, then, addresses the people at a crucial turning point in the way in which they live out their lives as the people of Yahweh." Similarly J. Gary Millar (*Now Choose Life: Theology and Ethics in Deuteronomy*, NSBT [Downers Grove, IL: InterVarsity, 1998], 145) describes Deuteronomy 12–26 as "a new application of the revelation at Horeb . . . for the new situation which Israel is about to face in Canaan."

[119]This description of the contents of Deuteronomy is based on the content of the chapters, and it roughly corresponds to the following statements: "These are the words that Moses spoke to all Israel" (1:1); "This is the Torah that Moses put before the sons of Israel" (4:44); "This is the commandment, the statutes and the judgments, which Yahweh your God commanded to teach you" (6:1); "These are the statutes and the judgments that you shall keep to do in the land" (12:1); "These are the words of the covenant which Yahweh commanded Moses to cut with the sons of Israel in the land of Moab, besides the covenant which he cut with them at Horeb" (28:69, ET 29:1); "This is the blessing with which Moses, the man of God, blessed the sons of Israel before his death" (33:1). See the excellent discussion of the various ways to describe the structure of Deuteronomy—and how these influence one's reading—in Vogt, *Deuteronomic Theology*, 15–31.

[120]Vogt, *Deuteronomic Theology*, 227.

[121]Jeffrey H. Tigay (*Deuteronomy*, JPS Torah Commentary [Philadelphia: Jewish Publication Society, 1996], 3) notes a chiasm in Deut. 1:1–5 (I have modified his description of the verses):

1:1, Beyond the Jordan

    1:2, Eleven days journey from Sinai to Kadesh-barnea (cf. Deut. 1:19–2:1)

        1:3, First day, eleventh month, fortieth year, Moses gives Deuteronomy

    1:4, Defeat of Sihon and Og (cf. Deut. 2:24–3:11)

1:5, Beyond the Jordan

[122]Millar (*Now Choose Life*, 70): "This is not simply a history lesson."

[123]Vogt points to the way this passage stresses the supremacy of Yahweh, "since it is his judgment that must be carried out by the judges" (*Deuteronomic Theology*, 112).

> Yahweh your God carried you just as a man carries his son, in all the way which you walked until you came to this place." (1:29–31)

Moses recounts Israel's history so that he can remind Israel of both the way that Yahweh has worked on their behalf and the wrong response of the generation that fell in the wilderness: "But in this matter you did not believe in Yahweh your God" (1:32).[124] The recounting of these events from Numbers 10–13 affords Moses the opportunity to teach Israel who Yahweh is on the basis of what he has said and done. These events angered Yahweh, and he swore that the evil generation would not inherit the land—Caleb and Joshua excepted (Deut. 1:36, 38). The generation entering the land is also warned not to presume on Yahweh's grace, for when the wilderness generation tried to repent and obey Yahweh's command to go up and take the land, the Lord did not go up with them, their enemies defeated them, and Yahweh did not hear their prayers (1:41–45). Moses reminds Israel of the judgment that fell on the wilderness generation that they might learn from the mistakes of their predecessors and be saved through the judgment that fell on them.

Yahweh's authority to give Israel the land he has promised is stressed when he tells them not to contend with those whose land he is not giving them: the people of Esau in Seir (Deut. 2:1–8), Moab (2:8–13), and, once the wilderness generation has perished (2:14–16), Ammon (2:17–23). The narrative thus demonstrates that Yahweh is Lord of all lands. He has allotted Israel's portion to them. This should make Israel confident as they cross into the portion allotted to them by Yahweh, the Lord of all.

Moses recounts how Yahweh commanded Israel to rise and cross the Valley of Arnon, how he announced that he, Yahweh, had given Sihon, king of Heshbon, into Israel's hand, and how he promised to put the dread and fear of Israel on all the peoples under heaven, making them tremble when they heard the report of Israel (Deut. 2:24–25).

Just as Yahweh hardened Pharaoh at the exodus, so he hardened Sihon at the beginning of the conquest (Deut. 2:30). As surely as Yahweh brought Israel out of Egypt, he will bring them into the land he has promised them. Both divine sovereignty and human responsibility are affirmed here: Sihon, literally, "was not willing" to allow Israel to pass. He is responsible for his unwillingness. But there is something behind his unwillingness: Yahweh hardened him. Yahweh's hardening does not remove Sihon's responsibility for his unwillingness.

There is also divine sovereignty and human responsibility in the taking of Sihon's land. In Deuteronomy 2:31, Yahweh announces that he has given Sihon

[124]Cf. ibid., 228: "That Deuteronomy, like some ANE political treaties, includes a historical prologue in which Yahweh's generous actions on behalf of Israel are recounted further highlights the supremacy of Yahweh. He has shown himself willing and able to act on Israel's behalf in the past."

over to Israel—divine sovereignty. But it is also true that Israel must take possession and occupy his land—human responsibility. Similarly in 2:33, Moses relates, "And Yahweh our God gave him over to us, and we struck him and his sons and all his people." Yahweh did the giving; Israel did the striking.

The striking and hardening of Sihon is reminiscent of the exodus. And the striking of Og, king of Bashan, reminds readers of the report of the spies (Num. 13:28), because Og was a giant (Deut. 3:1–11). Neither Pharaoh nor giants can keep Yahweh's people from the land he is giving them.[125] Moses presses home the historical lesson in Deuteronomy 3:21–22: "And I commanded Joshua at that time saying, 'Your eyes have seen all that Yahweh your God did to these two kings; thus Yahweh will do to all the kingdoms into which you are crossing. Do not fear them, because Yahweh your God, he is the one who fights for you!'"

The rejected repentance of the wilderness generation (Deut. 1:41–45) teaches Israel to obey the first time Yahweh commands, and Moses' failed attempt to gain permission to enter the land (3:23–28) functions the same way. Yahweh has shown mercy in response to Moses' prayers in the past, but he is not obligated to mercy anyone. With respect to entering the land, Yahweh does not show mercy to Moses, even though he appeals to Yahweh's incomparable greatness (3:24). There is a measure of mercy, though, for while the judgment that Moses not enter the land is upheld, he is allowed to go up to the top of Mount Pisgah and greet it from afar (3:27; cf. Heb. 11:13–16).

6.2 Motivation to Obey

Before the exposition of the law in Deuteronomy 12–28, Moses seeks to motivate Israel to do the law in chapters 4–11.

6.2.1 Reasons to Obey

In Deuteronomy 4 Israel is urged to obey because of the way Yahweh judged their disobedience at Baal Peor (4:1–4), because of the good effects and matchless quality of the laws Yahweh has given (4:5–8), because of their frightful experience of Yahweh at Sinai (4:9–24), because of what Yahweh will do to them if they disobey (4:25–31), and because of the unique love Yahweh has shown them (4:32–40). Yahweh has dealt with them the way he has so that they might know him. Yahweh wants them to know that he is God, that there is no other (4:35, 39), and therefore they should obey (4:40). As Vogt notes, "The emphasis is on Israel's unique experience of Yahweh's nearness and their status as recipients of *Torah*. . . . It is through *Torah* that Yahweh's nearness is experienced by Israel."[126] It would be difficult to imagine a more compelling case for love-driven law keeping than the one made by Moses in Deuteronomy 4.

---

[125]Cf. Millar, *Now Choose Life*, 53.
[126]Vogt, *Deuteronomic Theology*, 129.

6.2.2 Out of the Midst of the Fire

The experience of Yahweh at Sinai is recounted in Deuteronomy 5. Yahweh spoke to Israel "face to face at the mountain, from the midst of the fire" (Deut. 5:4). Moses stood between Yahweh and the people (5:5), and Yahweh announced his identity (5:6), then spoke the Ten Commandments (5:7–18, ET 7–21). Again, the most significant thing about the Ten Commandments is Yahweh himself.[127] Moses reviews how the people confessed that they had seen Yahweh's "glory and greatness" (5:21, ET 24), expressed fear that continual exposure to Yahweh would consume them (5:22, ET 25), and asked Moses to go hear everything Yahweh had to say and report back to them, promising obedience (5:24, ET 27).

6.2.3 Israel's Heart Problem

Yahweh agrees to this arrangement (Deut. 5:25, ET 28), and his response to the willingness of the people to obey (5:26, ET 29) picks up a key theme in biblical theology. Readers of the Bible see that something is wrong with the human heart as early as Genesis 6:5, where Yahweh, who knows the hearts of all men, sees that "every inclination of the reckonings of [man's] heart is only evil all the time." Knowing this, Yahweh responds to Israel's professed willingness to obey with the words, "Who will give that their hearts might be like this, to fear me and to keep all my commandments always?" (Deut. 5:26, ET 29).[128] Later in the canon, Yahweh will answer the question "who will give" through Ezekiel's promise that Yahweh will give a new heart to his people (Ezek. 36:26; cf. Jer. 32:39). The theme of the heart problem in Deuteronomy is addressed almost

[127]In ibid., 159, Vogt writes, "In Deut 5:1–6:9 the supremacy of Yahweh as creator of the people of God is stressed and demands for total loyalty are made"; and again (227), "The supremacy of Yahweh is also evident in the fact that it is Yahweh who commands. He dictates the terms of the covenant relationship between himself and Israel." Cf. also Millar, *Now Choose Life*, 105: "The biblical laws are theocentric in essence and expression."

[128]Modern English translations all take the phrase מִי־יִתֵּן as an idiom to mean something like, "Oh that their hearts would be this way," and in their defense, the phrase does appear to function as an idiom meaning "would that it were" elsewhere (see, e.g., Ex. 16:3; 2 Sam. 19:1; cf. also Bruce K. Waltke and M. O'Connor, *An Introduction to Biblical Hebrew Syntax* [Winona Lake, IN: Eisenbrauns, 1990], 680, §40.2.2d). But the earliest translations appear to have understood the phrase more literally. The Greek translation reads, τίς δώσει ("who will give?" See John William Wevers, ed., *Deuteronomium*, 2nd ed., Septuaginta Vetus Testamentum Graecum 3 [Göttingen: Vandenhoeck and Ruprecht, 2006]), and the Vulgate has "quis det" ("who gives?" See Robertus Weber et al., ed., *Biblia sacra: Iuxta Vulgatam versionem*, 4th ed. [Stuttgart: Deutsche Bibelgesellschaft, 1994]). On this phrase, Joüon (§163d) writes, "In some cases the sense *to give* etc. is fully retained, whilst in other cases it is weakened or even lost." He cites Num. 11:29 as an instance where "give" is retained, but takes Deut. 5:26 as "an optative formula" meaning, "Oh that they had kept this attitude!" The analysis in GKC, §151a–d is similar, and cf. *HALOT*, 733. Because Yahweh's own promise to give Israel a new heart (Ezek. 36:26; cf. Jer. 32:39) looks like a direct answer to this question, it seems as though Yahweh is provoking thought by saying in Deut. 5:26 (ET 29), "Who will give that their hearts might be like this," only to answer later by saying, "I will!" as Ezekiel and Jeremiah promise that Yahweh will give his people new hearts. Even in Deuteronomy Yahweh later promises to circumcise the people's hearts (Deut. 30:6). As a side note on translation, the more one moves toward the "dynamic equivalent" end of the translation spectrum, the more one sacrifices these kinds of intertextual connections. There is no word for "mind" in Hebrew, but some English translations render the Hebrew word "heart" as "mind" when they think "mind" is in view. Rendering "heart" as "mind" in Deut. 5:29, however, obscures intertextual connections. Perhaps this is simply more evidence for the absolute necessity of learning the biblical languages.

immediately after this, when Moses tells the Israelites, "And these words which I command you today shall be upon your hearts" (Deut. 6:4). Later in the canon, apparently in response to Israel's inability to keep these words on their hearts, Yahweh promises through Jeremiah that he, Yahweh, will write the Torah on the hearts of his people (Jer. 31:33).

The heart problem comes up again in Deuteronomy 10:16, when Moses calls on Israel, "Circumcise the foreskin of your heart and stiffen your neck no more." The second phrase exposits the first—the call to circumcise one's heart is a call to cease resisting the authority of Yahweh. But this is something that Israel cannot do to herself, which Moses recognizes in Deuteronomy 29:3 (ET 4), "To this day, Yahweh has not given to you a heart to know and eyes to see and ears to hear."[129] Yahweh alone can remedy this problem: "Yahweh your God will circumcise your heart and the heart of your seed to love Yahweh your God with all your heart and with all your soul, that you may live" (Deut. 30:6).[130] Deuteronomy 30:6 makes plain that the circumcision of the heart enables one to love Yahweh.

We saw above in Deuteronomy 10:16 that the circumcision of the heart would make Israel willing to submit to Yahweh's authority ("stiffen your neck no more"). This indicates that heart circumcision equips people with a volitional ability to love and submit to Yahweh, a reality that seems to have been recognized by Jeremiah, who wrote, "To whom shall I speak and testify, that they may hear? Behold, they are uncircumcised of ears, and they are not able to listen. Behold, the word of Yahweh is for reproach to them; they do not delight in it" (Jer. 6:10). Those who do not have circumcised ears *are not able* to listen, but they do hear—enough for the word to be a reproach to them. In other words, they hear the word physically, but "they do not delight in it." They cannot hear it in the sense that they do not perceive its beauty: it is a reproach to them (cf. 1 Cor. 2:14). These observations lead me to the conclusion that the ability provided by *heart circumcision* is equivalent to the ability provided by the *new birth*.[131]

---

[129]Tigay suggests that this verse should be rendered, "But the LORD did not give you a mind to understand . . . until today," going on to say that the other translation "implies that even now Israel lacks the capacity to understand its experiences properly. If that were Moses' meaning, his appeal that Israel observe the covenant would be hopeless" (*Deuteronomy*, 275). Neither the ancient Greek (cf. Wevers, *Deuteronomium*) nor modern English translations follow Tigay in this understanding, and Paul does not seem to have read Deut. 29:3 (ET 4) the way Tigay does. Paul combines words from Deut. 29:3 (ET 4), Isa. 6:9–10, and 29:10 in Rom. 11:8 to say, "Just as it has been written, 'God gave them a spirit of stupor, eyes not to see and ears not to hear, until this very day.'" In the wider context of Romans 11, Paul seems to understand Deuteronomy and Isaiah to be pointing to an eschatological renewal of Israel, while Deuteronomy is most naturally taken to indicate that the people do not have the heart necessary to obey.

[130]Millar (*Now Choose Life*, 179) writes, "Deuteronomic theology ultimately rests on the conviction that human nature is deeply flawed, and can be transformed only by God. This basic conviction underwrites all the ethical teaching of the book."

[131]See further Hamilton, *God's Indwelling Presence*.

The verse that immediately precedes Deuteronomy 30:6, where Yahweh promises to circumcise the hearts of his people, indicates that this will happen after the nation is exiled. When Yahweh brings the people back from all the places he has scattered them for breaking the covenant (30:5), then he will circumcise their hearts (30:6).

This means that Deuteronomy 30:6, Jeremiah 32:29, and Ezekiel 36:26 all point to a day in the future. Nevertheless, there is evidence that there were people under the old covenant who did delight in the law of the Lord (see Psalm 119), which indicates that there has always been "a remnant according to the election of grace" (cf. Rom. 11:5).

6.2.4 Life under Law

A new direction is opened up when Moses begins to appeal to love as a motivation for obedience in his address to the nation on the plains of Moab. Again and again Moses urges Israel to love Yahweh and obey his commands.[132] When we stop to ask whether anyone would *love* one of the fearsome deities described in other ancient Near Eastern texts, whether any Greek or Roman would *love* Zeus or any other member of the pantheon, we see that while those other deities are imagined as awe inspiring, terrifying, even grand, there is none like Yahweh. What other god actually *loves* his people and instructs them to love him?

Obedience to Yahweh will result in blessing (Deut. 6:1–3), and Israel is to love Yahweh alone, with his word on their hearts (6:4–6).[133] Having the word on the heart is to issue in teaching it to the children in and through daily routines (6:7). The Torah is to guide Israel's actions and function as the grid through which they view the world: "And you shall bind them as a sign on your hand, and they shall be as frontlets between your eyes" (6:8). The Torah is to adorn their homes (6:9).

When they enjoy the prosperity of the Promised Land, Israel's adherence to Torah will show their devotion to him (Deut. 6:10–13). If they go after other gods, Yahweh will destroy them (6:14–15). The terms are clearly set, and the warning of possible judgment is to lead them to salvation. They should not put Yahweh to the test, since they have seen his faithfulness to his word in the past (6:16–19). They are to remember their history (6:20–24), and their obedience to the law will produce a Phinehas-like righteousness (6:25; cf. 9:4–6).

Yahweh chose Israel because they were unimpressive (Deut. 7:6–7), because he loves them and will keep the oath he swore to their fathers (7:8).[134] Therefore

---

[132]Deut. 5:10; 6:5; 7:9; 10:12; 11:1, 13, 22; 13:3; 19:9; 30:6, 16, 20.

[133]On the Shema, see Waltke and O'Connor, *Hebrew Syntax*, 135, §8.4.2g.

[134]For a discussion of the point that Israel did not choose God, but God chose Israel, see David Novak, *The Election of Israel: The Idea of the Chosen People* (New York: Cambridge University Press, 1995).

they are to know Yahweh, who is everything he declared himself to be in Exodus 34:6–7, which is alluded to in Deuteronomy 7:9–10.[135] Faithfulness to Yahweh is the path to blessing and triumph (7:11–16). Israel is not to fear any of the peoples they will face in the land because Yahweh is with them (7:17–26).

This section of Deuteronomy seeks to motivate Israel to obey the Torah, and the strategy employed in chapters 8 through 10 is to remind Israel of their history of disobedience. Yahweh humbled Israel in the wilderness to know their hearts (Deut. 8:2). He sustained them with manna, something they did not anticipate, to teach them to rely upon his word (8:3). As a father disciplines his son, so Yahweh disciplined Israel in the desert (8:5). The land promised to them is an Edenic place of brooks and streams, milk and honey (8:7–9).[136] Israel is to bless Yahweh for this land (8:10). They are not to forget the way Yahweh saved them through the judgment he wrought against Egypt (8:11–14), nor are they to forget the way he saved them through his judgment on their wickedness, judgments of fiery serpents and thirsty ground where there was no water (8:15–16). If they exalt themselves in their own thinking and do not remember Yahweh, then just as Yahweh is judging the nations of the land, he will judge them (8:17–20). This threat of judgment is meant to preserve them in salvation.

Moses calls on Israel to know that Yahweh is a consuming fire who will destroy Israel's most intimidating enemies (Deut. 9:1–3), and the Israelites are to know that God is judging the wicked nations he is driving out before them (9:4–5). Israel is not receiving the land because they are righteous; they are stubborn (9:6). They are to remember the way they provoked Yahweh from Egypt to Moab (9:7). The incident with the golden calf at Sinai is recounted (9:8–21), as are Israel's other rebellions (9:22–24). When Moses narrates the way he interceded for Israel (9:25–29), we see again that he appealed to Yahweh on the basis of Yahweh's character: Yahweh must be faithful to the promises he made to Abraham, Isaac, and Jacob (9:27); he must protect his reputation in Egypt (9:28); and he must hold fast his heritage, the people he redeemed through his mighty acts (9:26, 29).[137]

After rehearsing God's mercy in the second set of tablets (Deut. 10:1–5, 10–11), the death of Aaron (10:6), the journey (10:7), and the setting apart of the tribe of Levi (10:8–9), the call to obedience to Torah culminates in one of the most beautiful passages in the Bible: Deuteronomy 10:12–22.

What Yahweh requires of Israel is summarized in Deuteronomy 10:12–13. They are to walk in his ways, love him, and serve him with all they are, and the

[135]See the appendix (§8) to this chapter, which catalogs Ex. 34:6–7 in the Law, Prophets, and Writings.

[136]Dumbrell, *The Faith of Israel*, 20, 58, 64; Millar, *Now Choose Life*, 55.

[137]See the appendix (§7) to chap. 4, table 4.9, "Old Testament Prayers Appealing to God's Concern for His Own Glory."

way they are to do this is by keeping the commandments and statutes Moses is giving them for their good. Verse 14 asserts Yahweh's authority to make these demands: "Behold, to Yahweh your God belong the heavens of the heavens, the earth and all that is in it" (10:14). Yahweh is the Lord of all, and he has chosen Israel "above all the peoples" (10:15). On the basis of this, their unique position in Yahweh's cosmic purposes, Israel is called to circumcise their hearts and stiffen their necks no more (10:16), "for Yahweh your God, he is God of gods and Lord of lords, the great, mighty, and fearsome God, who shows no partiality and takes no bribes" (10:17). Knowing Yahweh as the one who does justice for the orphan and the widow, who loves and provides for the sojourner, should prompt Israel to do likewise (10:18–19). Israel is to fear Yahweh, serve him, cleave to him, and swear by his name (10:20). Yahweh is to be the central reality of their existence. He is to be the most relevant thing in their lives. He is their praise, their God, who has done magnificent and fearsome things for them, making a small tribe into a myriad of people (10:21–22).

Israel is called to love Yahweh (Deut. 11:1), consider what he did in Egypt (11:2–7), and obey the good law in the good land that they might enjoy the good life (11:8–15). If they follow other gods, they will perish (11:16–17). As in Deuteronomy 6:6–9, Israel is urged to put these words Moses is giving them on their hearts, in their souls, on their hands, before their eyes. They are constantly to discuss them, adorn their homes with obedience to them, and enjoy the way that Yahweh will keep his promises (11:18–25). Before moving to the stipulations themselves, Moses makes clear what is at stake. He sets before Israel the consequence and the reward, the blessing and the curse. Blessing will follow obedience as cursing will follow disobedience. Therefore, Israel should obey (11:26–32).

6.3 The Covenant Stipulations

Yahweh is the supreme reality in the universe, and in Deuteronomy 12–26 he sets forth the stipulations to the covenant between himself and Israel. They will be blessed beyond anything they can imagine if they obey but frightfully cursed if they do not. The promise of the curse is meant to motivate obedience. Israel is to be saved through the promise of judgment for the glory of Yahweh. If they are not, they will be judged, and there will be a salvation that will come through the judgment of the exile, as Deuteronomy 4:25–31 and 30:1–10 indicate. In between are the laws by which Israel is to live.

There is a sense in which everything that follows the recital of the Ten Commandments in chapter 5 serves to exposit those ten words. Broadly speaking, all of Deuteronomy 6–25 can be understood as a development of the Ten Commandments, as table 2.16 shows.[138]

---

[138]There is some variety in the way scholars divide and group the material, and there are some items that do not fit. In general, however, viewing the material this way seems legitimate. See Millar (*Now Choose Life*, 107–8),

Table 2.16. Deuteronomy's Exposition of the Ten Commandments

Commandment	Chapters in Deuteronomy and Exposition
1. No other gods	6–11, love and worship Yahweh
2. No idols	12–13, central sanctuary and false gods
3. Name	13–14, holiness to Yahweh
4. Sabbath	14–16, periodic duties
5. Parents	16–18, authority: judge, king, priest, and prophet
6. Murder	19–22, life and law
7. Adultery	22–23, regulations on sexuality
8. Theft	23–25, property
9. False testimony	24–25, truthfulness
10. Coveting	25, unselfish levirate marriage

Yahweh is to be dearer to Israel than the convenience of worshiping where they please (Deuteronomy 12).[139] Anyone who seeks to lead Israel away from Yahweh through false prophecy—be that person brother, son, daughter, wife of one's bosom or soul-mate friend—the person is to be stoned to death (Deuteronomy 13). Israel is to be distinct, set apart to Yahweh, and this will be reflected in what they do with their hair, their food, their money, and their calendar (Deuteronomy 14–15). They are to worship Yahweh as he has prescribed and no other way, appearing before him three times a year at the place he chooses to set his name (Deuteronomy 16–17). Israel's leaders, judges, kings, priests, and prophets, serve at Yahweh's pleasure and according to his instructions (Deut. 16:18–18:22).[140] Yahweh gives Israel cities of refuge (Deuteronomy 19), instructions for warfare (Deuteronomy 20–21), instructions concerning human sexuality (Deuteronomy 22), regulations for keeping the camp clean (Deuteronomy 23), laws for marriage and divorce (Deuteronomy 24), instructions for levirate marriage (Deuteronomy 25), instructions for tithes and offerings (Deuteronomy 26), and many other things. Peter Vogt states, "At the core of Deuteronomy is a theology of the supremacy of Yahweh, expressed in the life of Israel through adherence to *Torah*."[141]

Adherence to these laws will result in Yahweh's protection and blessing. Transgression of them results in judgment. An intimate acquaintance with the laws of the Torah is assumed by later narrators of the Old Testament. The Torah is the standard by which later narratives measure, whether they say that is what they

who discusses the seminal proposals of S. A. Kaufman and G. Braulik.

[139]As Millar (*Now Choose Life*, 103) writes regarding Deut. 12:1–5, "The primary motive for going to the place is not simply conformity in worship, but to meet with Yahweh himself."

[140]Vogt (*Deuteronomic Theology*, 226) writes, "This section of Deuteronomy, then, highlights what I believe is at the heart of the Deuteronomic program. The supremacy of Yahweh is firmly established, because it is he who gives *Torah*, commands its obedience, enforces its terms, and chooses king and prophet."

[141]Ibid., 5–6.

are doing or not. The intellectual furniture of the Old Testament worldview is built and arranged by the laws of Torah, revealed by Yahweh.

Deuteronomy 27–28 recounts the blessings and cursings that attend the Torah. If Israel breaks the covenant, they will be exiled from the land, scattered among all nations (Deut. 28:64). Moses is remarkably explicit about Yahweh's emotions in this: "And it shall be that just as Yahweh rejoiced over you, to cause good for you and to multiply you, so Yahweh will rejoice over you to consume you and destroy you and pull you up from the land where you are entering there to possess it" (28:63). Once again, the intention of this frightful announcement of the pleasure Yahweh will take in doing justice is to promote obedience.

6.4 Moses' Last Will and Testament

After all that was said to motivate obedience in Deuteronomy 4–11, and after the gracious giving of the Torah in Deuteronomy 12–26, obedience would seem to be a reasonable consequence. Reason alone, however, does not govern the human heart. Sin never makes sense. In order to obey, one must have a circumcised heart. Circumcision of the heart, however, is not something one does to oneself. One must be given what one needs by Yahweh himself, and Moses declares to Israel that Yahweh has not given them the kind of heart they need (Deut. 29:3, ET 4).

Moses reminds Israel of what Yahweh has done for them (Deut. 29:4–8, ET 5–9), informs them that they are entering into sworn covenant with Yahweh (29:9–14, ET 10–15), and reminds them of how they lived in Egypt and the idols they have seen on the way to the land (29:15–16, ET 16–17). From there Moses warns Israel against apostasy and declares to them that Yahweh will bring on them "all the curses written in this book" (29:19, ET 20; cf. 29:17–19, ET 18–20).

As Moses commences to tell Israel what will happen *if* they break the covenant, it is almost as though he is prophesying what will happen *when* they break the covenant (Deut. 29:20–27, ET 21–28). Noteworthy here is the way that Moses describes the glory Yahweh will get from other nations when he judges Israel. The other nations will ask why Yahweh has destroyed his land, what has caused "the burning of this great wrath" (29:23, ET 24). The answer will be that Israel broke the covenant and worshiped gods not allotted to them (29:24–25, ET 25–26). "And Yahweh's anger burned against this land to bring upon it all the curses written in this book; and Yahweh uprooted them from the land in anger and in fury and in great wrath, and he cast them to another land as it is this day" (29:27, ET 28). Other nations will understand that Yahweh is holy when he judges Israel. They will, as this text shows, confess the righteous judgment of Yahweh against covenant-breaking Israel when he sends them into exile.

Remarkably, Deuteronomy 29:28 (ET 29) seems to acknowledge both the mysterious purposes of Yahweh with which the people are being confronted and the opportunity to avoid the fate being promised to them if they disobey. I take the reference to "the secret things" that "belong to Yahweh our God" in the first half of Deuteronomy 29:28 (ET 29) to refer to Yahweh's sovereign plan in which Israel will experience everything Moses is describing; this will become clearer in the first verse of chapter 30. The rest of Deuteronomy 29:28 (ET 29), however, states that the things that are revealed belong to Israel and the children of Israel that they may obey the law. In other words, the prophecy of what will happen if/when Israel transgresses the covenant is given in order to motivate Israel to keep the covenant.

It is not as though Israel has no chance. They are receiving fair warning. It is not as though they are robots. They will choose what they want. It is not as though they are being asked to do something that is beyond human capacity. The word is near them, in their mouths and hearts so they can do it (Deut. 30:14). But they will not do it. They do not have the heart to do it (29:3, ET 4). In spite of all the history of what Yahweh has done for them (Deuteronomy 1–3), in spite of all of Moses' rhetorical brilliance in seeking to motivate them to keep the law (Deuteronomy 4–11), in spite of the straightforward revelation of what it is they are to do (Deuteronomy 12–28), Israel will break the covenant. Yahweh knows this (31:16–21), and because Yahweh warns him of it, Moses knows it too (31:27–29).

But there is hope beyond the judgment. And here it seems that Yahweh's secret things are the reasons he has—reasons only he knows—for working history such that he will get glory in salvation through judgment. We read in Deuteronomy 30:1–3,

> And it shall be when all these things come upon you, the blessing and the curse, which I have set before you and you return to your heart among all the nations where Yahweh your God has driven you, and you return to Yahweh your God, and you listen to his voice according to all that I am commanding you today, you and your sons, with all your heart and with all your soul, then Yahweh will return your captivity and have mercy on you, and he will turn and gather you from all the people where Yahweh your God scattered you.

Here the warning of punishment described in chapter 29 is treated as a prophecy, and Moses declares that after exile will come restoration to the land. This, however, will be a supernatural return, for the exiles will be gathered from the end of heaven (30:4), Israel will be more prosperous and more numerous than ever (30:5), and Yahweh himself will circumcise their hearts (30:6a). As a result of Yahweh's heart-circumcising work, the people will love Yahweh and live (30:6b). Through the judgment will come salvation.

Israel has a genuine choice between life and death, blessing and curse (Deut. 30:11–18), and heaven and earth are witness to the covenant between Yahweh and his people (30:19). Israel is urged to choose life, to love Yahweh, to cleave fast to him (30:19–20). They have a real choice, but their "chooser" will always select sin because Yahweh has not given them the heart they need (29:3, ET 4). But they will make their choice, and they will be judged for the rightness or wrongness of the choice they make. The fact that Yahweh promises to change their chooser by circumcising their hearts does not remove their responsibility for the choice they will make. Nor does it make Yahweh unjust if he chooses not to change their chooser, or if he chooses only to change the choosers of those he chooses. People are responsible. And Yahweh is sovereign.

Yahweh will go before Israel (Deut. 31:3), with them never to leave nor forsake (31:6). Joshua is charged to be strong and courageous (31:7–8, 14, 23). Yahweh appears in a pillar of cloud and prophesies that Israel will whore after other gods and break his covenant (31:16). He declares that he will be angry, forsake them, and hide his face, and that evil will come upon them (31:17–18). He instructs Moses to teach a song to Israel as a witness against them (31:19).

The song of Moses calls heaven and earth to witness (Deut. 32:1) and proclaims the name of Yahweh (32:3). Yahweh is the Rock who is faithful, just, perfect, and upright (32:4), but the people have dealt corruptly against him (32:5). Yahweh's love to Israel is recounted (32:6–14), as are the abominations with which Israel repaid his kindness (32:15–18). Yahweh will judge Israel, and part of the judgment is the promise to provoke Israel to jealousy by those who are no people (32:21, cf. 19–26). Yahweh's concern for his own reputation, and his concern that Israel's enemies not boast over him, will prompt him to mercy (32:27). Israel will be saved through judgment for the glory of God. Israel's folly is announced, the folly of failing to respond appropriately to Yahweh (32:28–33). Like the secret things that belong to Yahweh (29:28, ET 29), this too is stored up with Yahweh, sealed in his storehouse (32:34). Vengeance is Yahweh's, the foot of those who disregard him will slide in due time (32:35), and Yahweh will judge his people and be satisfied against his servants (32:36). He will taunt the folly of worshiping other gods (32:37–38), and he declares that he alone is God—none beside him; he kills and makes alive, wounds and heals, and none can deliver from his hand (32:39).

Yahweh raises his hand and swears that he will judge (Deut. 32:40–42), but after the promise of judgment is a promise to avenge the blood of his children and atone for their land (32:43). Through the judgment comes salvation. All of this is a warning from Moses to Israel (32:46). Through this word—and the fear of Yahweh it engenders—they will live long in the land they are crossing the Jordan to possess.

Yahweh then commands Moses to go up on Mount Nebo and die because he acted unfaithfully against Yahweh and did not treat Yahweh as holy (Deut. 32:48–51). The death of Moses functions as a seal on all that he has announced to Israel. Yahweh will keep his word, and Moses' own death outside the land is proof of it.[142] Israel is to understand that Moses died outside the land because he did not believe Yahweh's word and treat Yahweh as holy, and they should learn from his death. Their salvation is to come through the judgment that falls on Moses.

Moses blesses the twelve tribes of Israel (Deuteronomy 33), ascends Mount Nebo, sees the land, and dies (34:1–5). Yahweh buries him (34:6), Israel mourns him (34:8), and though Joshua is full of the spirit of wisdom because Moses laid his hands on him (34:9), no prophet like Moses has arisen when the closing words of Deuteronomy are put down (34:10–12).[143]

6.5 The Center of the Theology of Deuteronomy

Yahweh's glory is the central reality of Deuteronomy. It is Yahweh who has saved Israel through the judgment of their enemies (Deuteronomy 1–3). It is ultimately Yahweh whose compelling existence is to motivate obedience (Deuteronomy 4) to the law he revealed when Israel heard his voice out of the midst of the fire on the mountaintop (Deuteronomy 5). It is Yahweh that Israel is to love (Deuteronomy 6–11), Yahweh Israel is to serve (Deuteronomy 12–28), and it is Yahweh who must give them the heart they need (29:3, ET 4; 30:6). Yahweh has the secret things to himself (29:28, ET 29), laid up with him, sealed in his storehouses (32:34). Israel will break Yahweh's covenant (30:1; 31:16–32:42), but Yahweh will restore them through the judgment he visits upon them (30:2–10; 32:43). There is none like Yahweh, God of Jeshurun (33:26), who is glorified in salvation through judgment in the manifestation of his justice and his mercy.

7. The Center of the Theology of the Torah

From the garden to the plains of Moab, the Torah proclaims the glory of God in salvation through judgment. Yahweh speaks the world with a word, and it

[142]So also Millar, *Now Choose Life*, 178.

[143]See the helpful discussion of the prophet like Moses in Deut. 18:15–20 and 34:10–12 in Robertson, *The Christ of the Prophets*, 59–65. John Sailhamer understands Deut. 34:10 to mean, "A prophet like Moses *never did* arise in Israel," and concludes, "Clearly, the author who made this statement knows about the entire line of prophets who followed Moses" (Sailhamer, *The Meaning of the Pentateuch*, 31, emphasis added). I agree with Sailhamer that Deut. 34:10 sheds light on the prophecy in 18:15–18, but it does not exclude the *office* of prophet as he claims (18). Nor, in my judgment, does the content of Deut. 34:10 demand that the author of the statement be aware of every prophet who arose in Israel's history. It seems that the phrase in question, ולא־קם נביא עוד בישראל כמשה, could just as well be interpreted to mean, "And a prophet like Moses has not arisen yet in Israel," which leaves open the possibility that the one making the statement might not be at the end of the line of prophets. Sailhamer's rendering is possible, but it is not the only way the text can be taken.

is. When his word is broken, the creation itself is subjected to futility. In the judgment, though, comes a hint of a future salvation. Some few hold to that hint, and the hints and promises grow, waiting for the day when the seed of the woman arises to crush the head of the serpent and his seed. Sailhamer proposes that "the big idea of the Pentateuch is 'the importance of living by faith.'"[144] I agree that the Pentateuch teaches its audience to live by faith, but I think this stops one step short of the center of its theology. The faith the Pentateuch teaches is faith in a God who is just and merciful, and it is not faith that is ultimate but God's glory in the salvation through judgment he will accomplish.

The Torah gives the truth about the real world. It furnishes the framework through which life is to be read. All experience is to be interpreted in light of Torah. The central reality of this all-interpreting word is the one who proclaims his own name, putting his goodness on display, showing his glory to Moses, defining himself as patient, steadfast in love, merciful, unconstrained, exacting in justice and thorough in its execution (Ex. 34:6–7).

The Torah is a story of the glory of God in salvation through judgment. He will save his people by judging their enemies, and he will judge the sin of his people, saving them through the purifying judgment of exile. When he triumphs over the enemies of his people, he will be glorified for his matchless might. When he saves his people from their own wicked hearts, he will be glorified because he is mighty to save. No force in the wicked hearts of people, no power in heaven or earth, will keep him from winning for himself a people for his name. At the center of the theology of the Torah is the truth that God will be glorified in salvation through judgment.

> *. . . And all who heard should see them there,*
> *And all should cry, Beware! Beware!*
> *His flashing eyes, his floating hair!*
> *Weave a circle round him thrice,*
> *And close your eyes with holy dread . . .*
>
> —Samuel Taylor Coleridge, "Kubla Khan"

8. Appendix: Exodus 34:6–7 in the Law, Prophets, and Writings

This list of verses (all texts here ESV) tracing the influence of Exodus 34:6–7 is "font coded," meaning that corresponding elements are all placed in a similar kind of font. Here is a key from the constituent thoughts of Exodus 34:6–7:

Bold	references to "Yahweh God": **The LORD, THE LORD, a God**
Grey	Yahweh passing before

[144]Sailhamer, *The Meaning of the Pentateuch*, 22.

Italics	Yahweh as *merciful and gracious, slow to anger, and abounding in steadfast love and faithfulness*
Helvetica	Yahweh's steadfast love for thousands
small caps	Yahweh as forgiving iniquity and transgression and sin
Underlining	Yahweh who will by no means clear the guilty
ALL CAPS	Yahweh VISITING THE INIQUITY OF THE FATHERS ON THE CHILDREN AND THE CHILDREN'S CHILDREN, TO THE THIRD AND THE FOURTH GENERATION

8.1 Exodus 34:6–7 in the Law

> You shall not bow down to them or serve them, for I **the Lord your God** am a jealous God, VISITING THE INIQUITY OF THE FATHERS ON THE CHILDREN TO THE THIRD AND THE FOURTH GENERATION of those who hate me, but showing steadfast love to thousands of those who love me and keep my commandments. "You shall not take the name of the Lord your God in vain, for the Lord will not hold him guiltless who takes his name in vain." (Ex. 20:5–7)

> **The Lord** passed before him and proclaimed, "**The Lord, the Lord, a God** *merciful and gracious, slow to anger, and abounding in steadfast love and faithfulness*, keeping steadfast love for thousands, forgiving iniquity and transgression and sin, but who will by no means clear the guilty, VISITING THE INIQUITY OF THE FATHERS ON THE CHILDREN AND THE CHILDREN'S CHILDREN, TO THE THIRD AND THE FOURTH GENERATION." (Ex. 34:6–7)

> **The Lord** is *slow to anger and abounding in steadfast love*, forgiving iniquity and transgression, but he will by no means clear the guilty, VISITING THE INIQUITY OF THE FATHERS ON THE CHILDREN, TO THE THIRD AND THE FOURTH GENERATION. (Num. 14:18)

> You shall not bow down to them or serve them; for I **the Lord your God** am a jealous God, VISITING THE INIQUITY OF THE FATHERS ON THE CHILDREN TO THE THIRD AND FOURTH GENERATION of those who hate me, but showing steadfast love to thousands of those who love me and keep my commandments. "You shall not take the name of the Lord your God in vain, for the Lord will not hold him guiltless who takes his name in vain." (Deut. 5:9–11)

> Know therefore that **the Lord your God** is God, the faithful God who keeps covenant and steadfast love with those who love him and keep his commandments, to a thousand generations, and repays to their face those who hate him, by destroying them. He will not be slack with one who hates him. He will repay him to his face. (Deut. 7:9–10)

8.2 Exodus 34:6–7 in the Prophets

I will recount the *steadfast love* of **the LORD**,
the praises of **the LORD**,
according to all that **the LORD** has granted us,
and the great goodness to the house of Israel
that he has granted them according to his *compassion*,
according to the *abundance of his steadfast love*. (Isa. 63:7)

You show steadfast love to thousands, but you REPAY THE GUILT OF FATHERS TO THEIR CHILDREN AFTER THEM, O great and mighty **God**, whose name is **the LORD** of hosts. (Jer. 32:18)

And I will betroth you to me forever. I will betroth you to me in righteousness and in justice, in steadfast love and in *mercy*. I will betroth you to me in faithfulness. And you shall know **the LORD**. (Hos. 2:19–20)

". . . and rend your hearts and not your garments."
Return to **the LORD your God**,
for he is gracious and merciful,
slow to anger, and abounding in steadfast love;
and he relents over disaster. (Joel 2:13)

And he prayed to the LORD and said, **"O LORD**, is not this what I said when I was yet in my country? That is why I made haste to flee to Tarshish; for I knew that you are a *gracious God and merciful, slow to anger and abounding in steadfast love*, and relenting from disaster." (Jonah 4:2)

Who is a **God** like you, PARDONING INIQUITY
and passing over TRANSGRESSION
for the remnant of his inheritance?
He does not retain his anger forever,
because he delights in *steadfast love*. (Mic. 7:18)

The LORD is a jealous and avenging **God**;
the LORD is avenging and wrathful;
the LORD takes vengeance on his adversaries
and keeps wrath for his enemies.
The LORD is *slow to anger* and great in power,
and **the LORD** <u>will by no means clear the guilty</u>.
His way is in whirlwind and storm,
and the clouds are the dust of his feet. (Nah. 1:2–3)

8.3 Exodus 34:6–7 in the Writings

But you, O Lord, are **a God** *merciful and gracious,*
slow to anger and abounding in steadfast love and faithfulness.
(Ps. 86:15)

The Lord is *merciful and gracious,*
slow to anger and abounding in steadfast love. (Ps. 103:8)

He has caused his wondrous works to be remembered;
the Lord is *gracious and merciful.* (Ps. 111:4)

The Lord is *gracious and merciful,*
slow to anger and abounding in steadfast love. (Ps. 145:8)

But you are **a God** ready to forgive, *gracious and merciful, slow to anger and abounding in steadfast love*, and did not forsake them. (Neh. 9:17)

Nevertheless, in your great mercies you did not make an end of them or forsake them, for you are a *gracious and merciful* **God.**

Now, therefore, our **God**, the great, the mighty, and the awesome **God**, who keeps covenant and *steadfast love*, let not all the hardship seem little to you that has come upon us, upon our kings, our princes, our priests, our prophets, our fathers, and all your people, since the time of the kings of Assyria until this day. (Neh. 9:31–32)

For if you return to **the Lord**, your brothers and your children will find compassion with their captors and return to this land. For **the Lord your God** is *gracious and merciful* and will not turn away his face from you, if you return to him. (2 Chron. 30:9)

8.4 Less Certain Allusions

8.4.1 In the Law

And he said, "I will make all my goodness pass before you and will proclaim before you my name '**The Lord.**' And I will be *gracious* to whom I will be *gracious*, and will show *mercy* on whom I will show *mercy*." (Ex. 33:19)

For **the Lord your God** is a *merciful* **God.** He will not leave you or destroy you or forget the covenant with your fathers that he swore to them. (Deut. 4:31)

8.4.2 In the Prophets

For my name's sake I defer my anger,
for the sake of my praise I restrain it for you,
that I may not cut you off. (Isa. 48:9)

"For a brief moment I deserted you,
but with great *compassion* I will gather you.
In overflowing anger for a moment
I hid my face from you,
but with everlasting *love* I will have *compassion* on you,"
says the LORD, your Redeemer. (Isa. 54:7–8)

O LORD, you know;
remember me and VISIT me,
and take vengeance for me on my persecutors.
In *your forbearance* take me not away;
know that for your sake I bear reproach. (Jer. 15:15)

8.4.3 In the Writings

Yet he, *being compassionate*,
atoned for their iniquity
and did not destroy them;
he restrained his anger often
and did not stir up all his wrath. (Ps. 78:38)

For you, O Lord, are good and forgiving,
abounding in steadfast love to all who call upon you.
(Ps. 86:5; cf. also 106:7, 45)

O LORD our God, you answered them;
you were a FORGIVING **God** to them,
but an avenger of their wrongdoings. (Ps. 99:8)

Light dawns in the darkness for the upright;
he is gracious, merciful, and righteous. (Ps. 112:4)

Gracious is **the LORD**, and righteous;
our **God** is *merciful*. (Ps. 116:5)

I prayed to the **LORD** my **God** and made confession, saying, "O Lord, the great and awesome **God**, who keeps covenant and *steadfast love* with those who love him and keep his commandments . . ." (Dan. 9:4)

And I said, "**O LORD God** of heaven, the great and awesome **God** who keeps covenant and *steadfast love* with those who love him and keep his commandments . . ." (Neh. 1:5)

DELIVER US

Our enemy, our captor is no pharaoh on the Nile
Our toil is neither mud nor brick nor sand
Our ankles bear no calluses from chains, yet Lord, we're bound
Imprisoned here, we dwell in our own land

Our sins they are more numerous than all the lambs we slay
These shackles they were made with our own hands . . .

Deliver us, deliver us
Oh Yahweh, hear our cry
And gather us beneath your wings tonight

—Andrew Peterson, from the album
"Behold the Lamb of God," used by permission

Chapter 3

God's Glory in Salvation through Judgment IN THE PROPHETS

1. Introduction

The three sections of the Old Testament (Law, Prophets, and Writings) each begin with an emphasis on the power of the word of God.[1] At the beginning of the Torah, Genesis opens with God speaking the world into being, each new aspect of creation ignited by the explosive phrase "and God said" (Gen. 1:3, 6, 9, 11, 14, 20, 24, 26, 28, 29). In Joshua, the first book of the Prophets, Yahweh charges Moses' replacement, for whom the book is named, not to let the Torah depart from his mouth. He is to meditate on it day and night, to keep and do it all, that he may be "prosperous and successful" (Josh. 1:8). These words are echoed in the first lines of the first book of the Writings, where Psalm 1 pronounces a blessing on the man who meditates on the Torah of Yahweh day and night (Ps. 1:2), promising that whatever he does will "prosper" (1:3). The Torah opens with Yahweh speaking, and the Prophets and the Writings begin by pointing to the necessity of meditating on Yahweh's words day and night.

The Lord's word is his standard of *judgment*, and reliance upon that word leads to *salvation*. The Prophets and the Writings advocate the way of prosperity (Josh. 1:8; Ps. 1:3), but that path does not wind its way toward the economic wisdom of the day. It is the path of constant meditation on the word of Yahweh.

[1]Stephen Dempster, *Dominion and Dynasty: A Theology of the Hebrew Bible*, NSBT (Downers Grove, IL: InterVarsity, 2003), 33.

He is *honored* when his people keep his word, and the primacy of his word is emphasized at the beginning of each major section of the Old Testament. That word has an overarching message. The thesis of this chapter is that if the Bible were likened to a multisyllabic term, its controlling syllable would be the glory of God in salvation through judgment. This chapter will seek to show from the Prophets how the accent on this syllable controls the pronunciation and meaning of the word of God.

The section of the Old Testament referred to as the Prophets falls into two parts, the Former Prophets and the Latter Prophets. The Former Prophets, Joshua through Kings, present the narrative story line that continues the plot begun in the Pentateuch. This plot begins with the conquest of the land and ends with the exile from it. Most of the Latter Prophets, Isaiah through Zephaniah, provide poetic commentary on events narrated in the Former Prophets, particularly 1–2 Kings.[2] At the end of 2 Kings the nation goes into exile, and the narrative story line later resumes in the Writings with Esther–Chronicles. The remaining Latter Prophets—Haggai, Zechariah, and Malachi—address the post-exilic situation described in Esther–Chronicles.

Table 3.1. The Prophets and the Exile

In the Land	In Exile	Returning to the Land
	Narrative Story Line	
Joshua–Kings 1406 BC–586 BC	Esther–Daniel 586 BC–516 BC	Ezra, Nehemiah, Chronicles 539 BC–ca. 400 BC(?)
	Poetic Commentary	
Isaiah–Zephaniah	Ezekiel	Haggai, Zechariah, Malachi

The theological center of the Prophets is the glory of God in salvation through judgment. The macro-level story is one that narrates Israel entering the land, visiting Yahweh's justice on the wicked inhabitants of the land only to do evil themselves in the eyes of Yahweh, being judged and delivered through a series of chastisements, and ultimately suffering the climactic judgment of exile from the land. Through the judgment of the exile, however, comes a purging that leads to salvation. Yahweh glorifies himself in his justice and his steadfast mercy. The stories and oracles that tell this overarching story will be discussed in two groups below, first the Former Prophets, then the commentary thereon in the Latter Prophets.

[2]So also Rolf Rendtorff, *The Canonical Hebrew Bible: A Theology of the Old Testament*, trans. David E. Orton, Tools for Biblical Study (Leiden: Deo, 2005), 7.

2. The Former Prophets: Joshua–Kings

The wilderness generation perished outside the land, and through that judgment a new generation prepares to enter the land. With the wicked purged from their midst, once they cross the Jordan, God's people take the land through the judgment they visit upon the enemies of God. Then, just as a Pharaoh arose who did not know Joseph, a generation of Israelites arises who do not know Yahweh and Joshua (Judg. 2:7, 10). Once Joshua and his elders die, the nation enters the period of the judges. Yahweh uses other nations to judge Israel's sin, and then he raises up deliverers, who save Israel by visiting justice upon her oppressors. The period of the judges ends when Israel rejects Yahweh from being king over them and asks for a king like all the nations, which is exactly what they get in Saul. Once Saul comes under judgment, the Lord mercifully raises up David to shepherd his people. David's sin with Bathsheba points the nation in the direction of exile. Solomon builds the temple, but David's sinful infidelity is exaggerated by Solomon, whose many wives turn his heart away from Yahweh. The kingdom is rent asunder after Solomon's death, and Yahweh's patience and mercy are displayed throughout the nation's slow march toward the purging punishment of the exile.

2.1 The Former Prophets Book by Book

In the book of Joshua, Moses' appointed successor leads the people into the Promised Land. Israel takes the land (Joshua 1–11), then apportions it to the twelve tribes (12–24). The book of Joshua shows much of what was announced in Torah, particularly in Deuteronomy, being fulfilled, while the stage is cleared of Canaanites for the drama of Israel's life in the land. The nature of the conquest—the inhabitants of Canaan being placed entirely under the ban—forcefully communicates the glory of God in salvation through judgment. The total destruction of the inhabitants of the land is just only if the deity who calls for such a measure is worthy of all honor. If Yahweh's worth is not so great that those who reject him have committed a crime that cries out for infinite justice, then the zero-tolerance policy against the people of the land is a brutal, unjust, egomaniacal atrocity.[3] But Yahweh's policies are not like those of mere men, whose importance does not warrant the slaughter of their opponents. Nor is this a kind of immature self-centered phase that Yahweh eventually grows out of when he decides to be nice and send his Son, Jesus. Rather, the ban on the Canaanites heralds the infinite majesty of the justice of Yahweh, whose holiness demands perfect loyalty, whose worth is such that anything less than absolute allegiance defiles unto death. The conquest of Canaan enacts the glory of God's justice against those who look to worthless things to be for them what only God

[3]So John J. Collins, *Encounters with Biblical Theology* (Minneapolis: Fortress, 2005), 5: "The testimony about the conquest of Canaan by divine command runs afoul of modern sensibilities about the morality of genocide. No one in modern pluralist society can live in a world that is shaped by the Bible."

can be for them. This justice against the inhabitants of Canaan is intended to deliver Israel from the deleterious influence of idolaters and give them the land that has been promised. Yahweh commissioned Adam and Eve to "fill the earth and subdue it" (Gen. 1:28), and in Joshua 18:1, the sons of Israel assemble in Shiloh and "the land was subdued before them."[4]

Judges takes up the story, and whereas Joshua succeeded Moses, no one succeeds Joshua. Moreover, the music of Joshua had some scattered notes in a dark, foreboding, minor key. These tones stated that not all the land was conquered, nor were all its inhabitants put to the ban. In Judges it is as though the music has been transposed into this frightful minor key as the statements in Joshua about the remaining people of the land are stacked up in summary form in Judges 1. If Adam was undone by one unclean serpent, the presence of so many unclean seed of the serpent bodes ill for the seed of the woman. The minor key melody of Judges sounds the glory of the justice of Jehovah, who does not spare the rod with Israel, his unfaithful son. Yahweh's fatherly chastisement of his wayward child makes meaningful the mercy he shows his people when they cry out to him. Judges depicts a progressive deterioration of the situation in Israel, but near the end a new note begins to be sounded. This new note is reminiscent of tones heard earlier in the grand symphonic poem of Israel's Scriptures. It recalls the promise to Abraham that he would sire kings (Gen. 17:6) and to Judah that he would hold the ruler's staff (Gen. 49:9–11). This note is rich and layered with Balaam's words of a scepter and star that would arise in Israel (Num. 24:17). And this is no haphazard note; it finds its place in the music with the elegance of mathematical precision—ordered as it is by the Mosaic instructions regarding Israel's king (Deut. 17:14–20). This note sounds that in those days there was no king in Israel, and when this note of explanation is joined to the melodic song of Judges, the listener is haunted by the hope of the ravishing beauty of what might be.

That beauty is approximated in the story of Samuel, but not in the way the world expects. God judges all human pride and presumption based on worldly estimations of beauty, and he hears the humble who cry to him. The proud are consumed in the flames of God's justice, and God raises the weak and lowly up to defeat his enemies. Hannah's rival provokes her, but God hears Hannah's prayer, opens her womb, and gives her what she "asks"[5] for, Samuel. Hannah dedicates Samuel to the service of Yahweh at Shiloh, where the proud sons of Eli are abusing the people. The Lord judges them and establishes Samuel as the prophet of his word. In Samuel's declining years, the people exchange Yahweh for Saul, a tall proud king like the kings of the nations, but, ironically, Saul's concern for *himself* and *his* kingdom robs him of the freedom to pursue God's

[4]The verb כבשׁ ("subdue") is used in both Gen. 1:28 and Josh. 18:1 with reference to the ארץ ("land").
[5]Throughout Samuel there are many plays on the Hebrew verb שׁאל, "ask," and Saul's name, שׁאול.

kingdom with reckless abandon—he has to protect himself. Whereas mighty Saul should fight Goliath, David shows a disregard for himself that comes from supreme concern for the honor of the name, the reputation, of Yahweh. Thus, David slays Goliath for God's glory. As the story unfolds, proud Saul is brought low, and humble David is exalted. Once exalted, David falls grievously. God is just against David's sin. The key difference between Saul and David is that David repented of his sin, and he received mercy through God's justice. Part of God's justice is the revolt of proud Absalom, but in the midst of David's pain over the death of Absalom is the mercy of his return to Jerusalem and continuance as king. In Samuel God glorifies himself in the salvation through judgment that comes through the raising up of the reliant and the putting down of the proud. This glorifies God because the proud rob God of the glory he alone deserves, while the reliant declare their need for the all-sufficient, all-powerful one, and this reliance honors and pleases the Lord.

First and Second Kings begin with the scion of David, Solomon, and trace out the story of national decline. Solomon reigns in a new garden as a new Adam and builds a new dwelling of God in the temple. But the messianic splendor of Solomon makes his inability to resist foreign women and their gods all the more tragic. Ten tribes are torn from the Davidic house and given to Jeroboam, who invents his own religion and makes the northern kingdom of Israel sin. The kings of the north fail to turn from the sin of Jeroboam, and God's justice falls when the Assyrians demolish the northern kingdom of Israel. Fitful faithfulness shown by Judah's kings delays her exile, but only for so long. Through the crushing judgment of the exile, all that Israel is tempted to trust is pulverized, and a remnant is thereby saved to praise the God who keeps his promises.

Table 3.2. The Story of the Former Prophets

Joshua 1–11	Taking the land
Joshua 12–24	Dividing the land
Judges 1–2	Military and religious failure
Judges 3–16	The judges (6–8, Gideon; 11–12, Jephthah; 13–16, Samson)
Judges 17–21	No king: no restraint
1 Samuel 1–8	Samuel, the last judge
1 Samuel 9–15	King Saul
1 Samuel 16—2 Samuel—1 Kings 1–2	King David
1 Kings 2–11	King Solomon
1 Kings 12—2 Kings 17	Divided kingdom and destruction of the north (1 Kings 17—2 Kings 13, Elijah and Elisha)
2 Kings 18–25	Judah and exile

2.2 *Joshua*

Joshua 1–5 describes the "crossing over" (עבר) into the land, chapters 6–12 then relate the "taking" (לקח) of the land, followed by the "apportioning" (חלק) of the land in chapters 13–21, and the book concludes with a call to "serve" (עבד) in the land in chapters 22–24.[6]

2.2.1 *Crossing Over into the Land*

As the people prepare to enter the land, Yahweh commissions Joshua (Joshua 1), the spies are helped by Rahab in Jericho (Joshua 2), and the nation miraculously crosses the Jordan in a way that recalls the parting of the Red Sea, celebrating Yahweh's wonders with twelve memorial stones (Joshua 3–4). Yahweh's glory radiates through these narratives. The nation is then circumcised, Passover is celebrated, and just as Yahweh appeared to Moses to initiate the exodus, the commander of the hosts of Yahweh appears to Joshua, who like Moses is commanded to remove his sandals because the ground is made holy by the presence of God (Joshua 5). These narratives demonstrate that what was true of Genesis through Deuteronomy will continue to be true of Joshua: Yahweh is the central reality of the universe. Creation displays his glory. The calling of Abraham shows that he is perfectly compelling. The transformation of the patriarchs from scoundrels to saints shows his patient power. His mercy and might are then seen as he pries the lowly loose from the iron fist of the Pharaoh in Egypt. His holiness and authority are seen in the laws of Leviticus and the chastenings of Numbers. And Deuteronomy lifts up this glorious God that Israel might trust him. Yahweh is the most significant reality of Torah, as seen in the narratives describing creation, the patriarchs, the exodus, and the law, and Yahweh will be the most significant reality in the Prophets, as seen in these narratives of the conquest of the land (Joshua).[7]

The book of Joshua presents Yahweh speaking to Joshua after the death of Moses (Josh. 1:1–9). In this speech Yahweh himself commands Joshua to lead Israel now that Moses is dead (1:2), and he announces that he will now fulfill the promise to Abraham by giving Israel all the ground on which the soles of their

---

[6]Dempster, *Dominion and Dynasty*, 126–27, and Tremper Longman III and Raymond B. Dillard, *An Introduction to the Old Testament*, 2nd ed. (Grand Rapids: Zondervan, 2006), 129, both citing H. J. Koorevaar, *De opbouw van hed boek Jozua* (Heverlee: Centrum voor Bijbelse Vorming Belgie, 1990), and noting the discussion of Koorevaar's work in J. G. McConville, *Grace in the End: A Study in Deuteronomic Theology* (Grand Rapids: Zondervan, 1993), 101–2. Joshua can thus be understood according to the following thematic chiasm (note the matching Hebrew consonants in the inner and outer pieces of the chiasm):

Chaps. 1–5, עבר, Crossing into the land
  Chaps. 6–12, לקח, Taking the land
  Chaps. 13–21, חלק, Dividing the land
Chaps. 22–24, עבד, Serving in the land

[7]So also Paul R. House, *Old Testament Theology* (Downers Grove, IL: InterVarsity, 1998), 203: "No issue in the conquest matters more than the glorification of the Creator before the peoples of the earth."

feet tread (1:3; cf. Gen. 13:18; Deut. 11:24). The opening of Joshua is connected to the end of Deuteronomy through verbal and thematic links with Deuteronomy 31:1–8, and especially through the command in Joshua 1:6–9 to be strong and courageous because Yahweh is with him (cf. Deut. 31:6).[8] These connections show forth the theme of Yahweh's faithfulness to his word, but his faithfulness to his word is part of a yet greater theme: Yahweh's presence and the knowledge of his unassailable might are to give Joshua and Israel confidence even if they seem like grasshoppers in their own eyes (cf. Num. 13:33). Moreover, the call to courage announces that Yahweh's worth is such that it would be better to perish fighting for him than to quail before his enemies. If Yahweh is not worth more than even life itself, this call to courage is cruel and dangerous.[9] But these narratives are written from the perspective that there is none like Yahweh, that his holiness will be vindicated against the idolaters of Canaan, and that his mercy will be shown as Israel inhabits the land. Yahweh is the most significant reality of Joshua 1, and his presence with Joshua (cf. 1:5, 9, 17) guarantees Israel's success—if they are careful to do his word.

Preparing to enter the land, Joshua sends two men to spy it out, and the greatness of Yahweh is declared to the Israelite spies by the Canaanite harlot Rahab. Yahweh promised to Moses that he would put the dread and fear of Israel on all the inhabitants of the land (Deut. 2:25), and Rahab, an inhabitant of Jericho, declares that he has done so:

> I know that Yahweh has given to you the land, and that the terror of you has fallen on us, and that all the inhabitants of the land have melted because of you. For we have heard how Yahweh dried up the waters of the Red Sea from before you when you came out of Egypt, and what you did to the two kings of the Amorites who were across the Jordan, to Sihon and to Og, whom you put under the ban. And we heard, and our hearts dissolved, and no more spirit rose in the men before you because Yahweh your God, he is God in the heavens above and on the earth below! (Josh. 2:9–11)

The terror Israel provokes does not result from the might of her army, the multitude of her men, the strategic genius of her generals, or the overwhelming superiority

[8]Bruce K. Waltke (*An Old Testament Theology: An Exegetical, Canonical, and Thematic Approach* [Grand Rapids: Zondervan, 2007], 57) writes that "Joshua 1 is a pastiche of Deuteronomy."

[9]Cf. G. K. Chesterton, *Orthodoxy* (1908; repr., Colorado Springs: Waterbrook, 2001), 136–37 (chap. 6): "Courage is almost a contradiction in terms. It means a strong desire to live taking the form of a readiness to die. . . . The paradox is the whole principle of courage; even of quite earthly or brutal courage. A man cut off by the sea may save his life if he will risk it on the precipice. He can only get away from death by continually stepping within an inch of it. A soldier surrounded by enemies, if he is to cut his way out, needs to combine a strong desire for living with a strange carelessness about dying. He must not merely cling to life, for then he will be a coward, and he will not escape. He must not merely wait for death, for then he will be a suicide, and will not escape. He must seek his life in a spirit of furious indifference to it; he must desire life like water and yet drink death like wine."

of her technology (and it does not appear that they employed a market strategist, either). The terror of Israel results from the report of what Yahweh did in Egypt and the fact that he is God in heaven and on earth. This report has brought all that Rahab trusts under judgment: it stands condemned before Yahweh's overwhelming greatness. And through this judgment she is saved by and for his glory.

This passage has been described as "thoroughly Deuteronomistic in language and theology,"[10] but it is perhaps more accurate to say that it reflects the Bible's relentless emphasis on the center of its theology.[11] What Rahab describes the inhabitants of Jericho feeling is a fulfillment of something promised in Deuteronomy (Deut. 2:25), but her words also recount events that were narrated in Exodus (Red Sea crossing, Exodus 14) and Numbers (Sihon and Og defeated, Numbers 21). Those who overemphasize "deuteronomic" theology run the risk of neglecting the way that the theology of Deuteronomy is consonant with the theology of the rest of the Torah. For instance, Yahweh declared to Pharaoh that it was his intention to cause his name to be proclaimed in all the earth (Ex. 9:16), and this is fulfilled when the Israelites have the mighty deeds of Yahweh extolled to them by the Canaanite prostitute.

Yahweh brought the world into being by the word of his power (Genesis 1), and by that word he summoned Abraham from Ur (Gen. 12:1; cf. 15:7) and Israel from Egypt (Ex. 20:1) (table 3.3).

Table 3.3. I Am Yahweh Who Brought You Out

Genesis 15:7	Exodus 20:1
"And he said to him, 'I am Yahweh, who brought you out of Ur of the Chaldees.'"	"And God spoke all these words, saying, 'I am Yahweh your God, who brought you out of the land of Egypt.'"

[10]Leonard J. Greenspoon, "Rahab (Person)," in *ABD*, 5:611. I am not a little sympathetic with Jeffrey J. Niehaus (*Ancient Near Eastern Themes in Biblical Theology* [Grand Rapids: Kregel, 2008], 30 n. 53), who writes, "There is no such thing as a 'Deuteronomistic History.'" See also Ronald E. Clements, "A Royal Privilege: Dining in the Presence of the Great King (2 Kings 25.27–30)," in *Reflection and Refraction: Studies in Biblical Historiography in Honour of A. Graeme Auld*, ed. Robert Rezetko, Timothy H. Lim, and W. Brian Aucker, VTSup (Boston: Brill, 2007), 50–51: "I have elsewhere expressed the view that, to follow Martin Noth in labeling this the Deuteronomistic History, is to give this narrative a misleading title. In company with Graeme Auld, I remain convinced that the title should be dropped as drawing too much attention to a feature which cannot have been primary in respect of its composition."

[11]In her trenchant reassessment of "an inherited paradigm of deuteronomistic interpretation known as the Name Theology," Sandra L. Richter notes that "in contradistinction to Noth's view of a single thesis within the DH [Deuteronomistic History] of 'unrelieved and irreversible doom,' Cross claims that through his history [the historian] accommodated the themes of judgment *and* grace" (Sandra L. Richter, *The Deuteronomistic History and the Name Theology: lešakkēn šemô šām in the Bible and the Ancient Near East*, BZAW [New York: Walter de Gruyter, 2002], 1–3). Moreover, Richter argues regarding the phrase *lešakkēn šemô šām* (which she would translate "to place his name there") that "this particular . . . idiom [was chosen] in order to emphasize the sovereignty and fame of YHWH by right of conquest. . . . The king has captured this new territory; he has claimed it as his own. Let the people be subject, let them bring tribute, and let them always remember that it is he who has defeated their foes and it is he to whom allegiance is due" (217). In other words, the main theme of the "DH" is that Yahweh has saved his people through the judgment of their enemies for the glory of his name.

In the same way, Yahweh is about to take Israel into the land. They go by his mighty word, on the power of his promises. The spies confidently report back to Joshua, "Yahweh has given into our hands the whole land; indeed, all the inhabitants of the land have melted because of us" (Josh. 2:24). The judgment of Canaan, declared by a Canaanite, gives confidence to Israel. The most significant thing about the account of the spies in Joshua 2 is the reputation of Yahweh, that is, the esteem in which he is held—in a word, his glory. Not only is Yahweh glorious, but Israel will give more glory to Yahweh if they trust the report of the spies (cf. Rom. 4:20–21).

Joshua announces to the people that Yahweh will do wonders in their midst (Josh. 3:5), and he does just that when he causes the waters of the Jordan River to pile up in a heap such that Israel crosses over on dry ground (3:13–17). Significantly, Joshua states, "By this you shall know that the living God is in your midst, and he will surely dispossess from before you the Canaanites, the Hittites, the Hivites, the Perizzites, the Girgashites, the Amorites, and the Jebusites" (3:10). The wonder of Yahweh's stopping the waters of the Jordan is to inspire Israel to believe that he will indeed keep his word. They are to *know* his presence among them, and more specifically, they are to know that Yahweh is going to give them the Promised Land through the defeat of Canaan: their salvation will come through the judgment of the Canaanites and their gods for the glory of Yahweh.[12]

The display of Yahweh's power in Israel's crossing of the Jordan is marked with twelve memorial stones to this mighty act of Yahweh (Josh. 4:1–9). These twelve stones will help the Israelites pass down the story of Yahweh's power when the children ask what they are (4:6, 21), and there is an explicit comparison to what Yahweh did at the Red Sea (4:23).[13] Joshua announces that Yahweh has dried up the Jordan River "in order that all the peoples of the land might know the hand of Yahweh, that it is mighty, that you might fear Yahweh your God

[12]For the argument that "the crossing of the Jordan is best read as a blatant polemic against Baal . . . . intended to extol Yahweh as *the* Lord of the earth, not Baal," with the upshot being that "Israel's living God is present in the midst of his people and victorious over Baal," see J. Michael Thigpen, "Lord of All the Earth: Yahweh and Baal in Joshua 3," *TJ* 27 (2006): 245, 254.

[13]Michael Fishbane (*Biblical Interpretation in Ancient Israel* [Oxford: Clarendon, 1985], 352, 358–60 [350–79]) cites this comparison as an instance of the kinds of inner-biblical references that form the basis of the typological interpretation endorsed by the Bible itself. Typology highlights historical correspondence between divinely intended patterns of events and the escalation in the significance of those events as they recur. For an excellent discussion of typology, see Paul M. Hoskins, *Jesus as the Fulfillment of the Temple in the Gospel of John*, Paternoster Biblical Monographs (Waynesboro, GA: Paternoster, 2006), esp. 18–32. For some of the ways that Joshua "prefigures" Jesus, see R. S. Hess, "Joshua," in *NDBT*, 171. For my attempts at typological interpretation, see "The Virgin Will Conceive: Typological Fulfillment in Matthew 1:18–23," in *Built upon the Rock: Studies in Matthew*, ed. John Nolland and Dan Gurtner (Grand Rapids: Eerdmans, 2007), 228–47; my Julius Brown Gay Lecture, "The Typology of David's Rise to Power: Messianic Patterns in the Book of Samuel," available online in audio: http://www.sbts.edu/media/audio/JBGay/20080313hamilton.mp3, or text format: http://jimhamilton.files.wordpress.com/2008/03/the_typology_of_davids_rise_to_power2008-03-101.doc, and "Was Joseph a Type of the Messiah: Tracing Typological Identification between Joseph, David, and Jesus," *SBJT* 12, no. 4 (2008): 52–77.

always" (4:24). Israel is to fear Yahweh; the peoples of the land are to know his power. They hear the news, and their hearts melt (5:1). Yahweh exalts himself by saving his people and causing their enemies to fear the coming judgment.

On their way to the salvation of taking the land, Israel passes through a judgment of sorts when Yahweh commands the uncircumcised conquest generation to be circumcised (Josh. 5:2–8), and there is a reminder/warning of the generation that fell under judgment in the wilderness (5:6). Through the judgment of circumcision, the reproach of Egypt is rolled away (5:9). This recalls the circumcision of the sons of Moses that took place before the exodus from Egypt (Ex. 4:24–26). Yet another connection is made to the exodus from Egypt when Joshua encounters the captain of the host of Yahweh (Josh. 5:13–15). Just as Moses drew near and inspected the burning bush, Joshua draws near the man with the drawn sword (5:13). Just as Moses was instructed to remove his sandals because of the holy ground, so Joshua is told to remove his (5:15). These historical correspondences connect the beginnings of the triumphant exodus to the beginnings of what is hereby guaranteed to be the triumphant conquest. There might be an escalation of significance in that whereas Moses was resistant to what Yahweh commanded him to do and is not said to have worshiped, Joshua not only does not question and object, as Moses did, but he worships (5:14).[14]

This man with the drawn sword stands to the east of the land, at its entrance, creating an intriguing connection between the land Israel is crossing over to possess, and the land from which Adam and Eve were expelled.[15] The way to Eden was guarded at the east by a cherubim with a flaming sword (Gen. 3:24). Similarly, Balaam likened the camp of Israel to a garden planted by Yahweh (Num. 24:6), and as he made his way to their camp, he met the angel of Yahweh, who had a drawn sword in his hand (Num. 22:22–35). With Yahweh in their midst, Israel has recaptured something of the Edenic experience. As they cross into the land, Israel moves in the direction of the reversal of the curse.[16]

The typological connections between the exodus and conquest set forth in Joshua 4:23, where the crossing of the sea is compared to the crossing of the river, and 5:13–16, where, like Moses, Joshua unshods his feet on holy ground,

[14]The fact that elsewhere in the Bible angelic beings do not allow themselves to be worshiped (e.g., Rev. 19:10) might hint at the identity of this commander of Yahweh's hosts. On the other hand, Andrew Chester discusses several Jewish texts that seem to describe figures other than God receiving worship (*Messiah and Exaltation*, WUNT 207 [Tübingen: Mohr Siebeck, 2007], 109–15).

[15]This connection was brought to my attention by Matt Perman's unpublished piece, "Science, the Bible, and the Promised Land: An Analysis of John Sailhamer's *Genesis Unbound*," available online: http://www.geocities.com/Athens/Delphi/8449/genesis.html, accessed November 2007. Stephen Dempster also sees a connection between the angel barring the way to Eden and the angel Joshua encounters (*Dominion and Dynasty*, 128).

[16]Dempster, *Dominion and Dynasty*, 127: "The land itself is positively viewed as a new Eden." Richter (*The Deuteronomistic History and the Name Theology*, 11) writes, "The paradise that was Eden, the paradise that is the Holy of Holies, and the coming paradise which the prophets envision are all characterized by this single concept: YHWH is present."

join with other features in the text[17] to indicate that Yahweh's goal at the conquest is the same goal he had at the exodus. There he wanted all to *know that he is Yahweh*. He pursued his glory—the proclamation of his name—by saving Israel through the judgment of Egypt. At the conquest, Yahweh causes the inhabitants of the land to *know that he is God* (2:9–11), he makes Israel *know that he is among them* (3:10), and he makes the peoples of the land *know his might* (4:24). Just as Yahweh hardened the heart of Pharaoh to accomplish his purpose at the exodus, so he hardens the hearts of the kings of the land at the conquest (11:18, 20).[18] Just as Yahweh demonstrated his glory at the exodus by saving Israel through the judgment of Egypt, he demonstrates his glory at the conquest by saving Israel through the judgment of the peoples of the land.

If one follows the inner logic of the theology of the Bible, the destruction of the peoples of the land is not unjust. Because of their wickedness (Deut. 9:5), Yahweh commands Israel to place them under the ban lest their idolatry be contagious (20:16–18). Just as Yahweh making himself known was the most significant thing about the destruction of Egypt, so also the demonstration of Yahweh's holiness is the most significant thing about the ban on the Canaanites.[19] The conquest will be seen as a brutal, uncivilized, merciless atrocity only if we reject what the first five chapters of Joshua proclaim: that Yahweh is glorifying himself in the salvation of Israel wrought through the judgment they visit on the peoples of the land. Yahweh is showing astonishing mercy to Israel, and he is not clearing the guilty of the land (cf. Ex. 34:6–7).

2.2.2 Taking the Land

The account of the taking of the land continues to highlight God's glory in mercy and justice. Israel takes Jericho (Joshua 6), Ai (chaps. 7–8), Gibeon (chap. 9), southern Canaan (chap. 10), and northern Canaan (chap. 11), and then the Lord's victories through Moses and Joshua are summarized (chap. 12). Mercy comes to unexpected people like the harlot Rahab (chap. 6), repentant Israel (chap. 8), and even deceptive Gibeon (chap. 9). The absolute justice visited against the Canaanites and the Israelite clan of Achan brings mercy into stark relief.

Just as Yahweh alone saved Israel from Egypt, with no help from the Israelites, so also Yahweh initiates the conquest of the land. Yahweh puts the fear of Israel on the peoples, and he gives Israel what is surely one of the most counterintuitive strategies for taking a walled city ever attempted. The plan? They are to march

---

[17]Waltke draws attention to the crossing of waters (Jordan and Red Sea), the striking of fear into enemies, the initiation of circumcision, and the celebration of Passover as actions common to Moses and Joshua (*An Old Testament Theology*, 518 n. 22).

[18]Similarly Patrick D. Miller, "The Story of the First Commandment: Joshua," in *The Way of the Lord: Essays in Old Testament Theology* (Grand Rapids: Eerdmans, 2007), 83–84; and Rendtorff, *The Canonical Hebrew Bible*, 99.

[19]Cf. Miller, "The Story of the First Commandment: Joshua," 85: "The ban . . . is rooted totally in the First Commandment."

around the walls of Jericho (Josh. 6:1–5). That's it. Brilliant! This plan makes no sense to the wisdom of the world. Rather, it looks like folly and weakness. Israel is to trust Yahweh even if they cannot see how he will accomplish his plan, and even if his declaration of how he *will* do so does not make sense to them. And Yahweh brings down the walls (6:20). Having chosen the weak things of the world, Israel (Deut. 7:7–8), Yahweh gives victory over Jericho such that Israel has no grounds for boasting of their power or wisdom. It is only by faith that Joshua engages in this strategy (Josh. 6:6–16), and by trusting the word of Yahweh rather than his own understanding (cf. Prov. 3:5–6), Joshua glorifies Yahweh by depending upon him.

Yahweh did not choose the greatest nation on earth; he chose the fewest, Israel (Deut. 7:7). And when he is pleased to show mercy to an inhabitant of Jericho, he does not choose the most virtuous or noble of the citizenry; he chooses Rahab, a harlot (cf. Josh. 6:17, 22–23, 25). No one in Jericho deserves to live. None of them has honored Yahweh as God or given thanks to him (cf. Rom. 1:21). Yet Yahweh is pleased to show kindness, and as he declared to Moses that he would show mercy to whomever he pleased (Ex. 33:19), he chooses to show mercy to one whose unworthiness underscores the riches of his grace. Thus is the free, unconstrained mercy of God displayed in all its glory, and the burning of all Jericho makes the salvation of Rahab and her family more heavy with the weight of the glory of God.

Achan, however, sins in Jericho, taking "devoted things" for himself (Josh. 7:1). In response, Yahweh visits judgment on Israel at the hand of the Canaanites (7:2–5). When Yahweh dried the waters of the Jordan, the hearts of the people of the land melted (5:1). When the anger of Yahweh burns against Israel because of Achan's sin (7:1), the hearts of the men of Israel melt (7:5).

This episode demonstrates that Yahweh's righteousness is not limited by his commitment to Israel. His commitment to them does not cause him to show an unjust favoritism toward his chosen people. When they sin he punishes them, showing the glory of his justice. Through the judgment of the defeat at Ai, however, Israel is delivered because they are thereby prompted to purge the evil from their midst. In a crisis of faith brought on by this defeat, Joshua petitions Yahweh on the same basis that Moses did: "And what will you do for your great name?" (Josh. 7:9, cf. the appendix [§7] to chap. 4, table 4.9, "Old Testament Prayers Appealing to God's Concern for His Own Glory"). Yahweh explains, "I will be with you no more, unless you destroy the devoted things from among you" (7:12). The transgressor is identified, "And all Israel stoned him with stones. They burned them with fire and stoned them with stones. . . . Then Yahweh turned from his burning anger" (7:25–26).[20]

[20]The switch from the singular "stoned him" to the plurals "burned them . . . stoned them" is in the Hebrew and seems to reflect the primary responsibility of Achan with its consequences for his family. Similarly Robert G. Boling and G. Ernest Wright, *Joshua*, AB (Garden City: Doubleday, 1982), 228.

We must not too easily pass over this. A man received the death penalty, and his family died with him, because he plundered a cloak from Shinar along with some silver and gold (Josh. 7:21). It is only the majesty of Yahweh that makes this just. For this to be just, the greatness of Yahweh must be such that trusting in what one can see, rather than what Yahweh has said, is a crime that warrants the forfeiture of life. The ancient Israelites were not a barbaric, bloodthirsty people, but Yahweh is a God whose holiness is a consuming fire. Achan himself gives "glory to God" and "praise to him" and confesses his sin against Yahweh (7:19–20). Israel is saved from Yahweh's wrath through the judgment that falls on Achan. Yahweh is shown to be just and merciful, and the awful demands of holiness thunder transcendent greatness.

Through the judgment on Achan, Israel places Ai under the ban (Josh. 8:1–29). Israel then engages in the covenant-confirming ceremony prescribed at the end of Deuteronomy (Josh. 8:30–35). In their reading "all the words of the Torah, the blessing and the curse" (8:34), salvation through judgment is enacted upon the people as the promises of God's judgment, announced in the curses, come as a means of salvation. The people are to be motivated by the promised curses to trust and obey and enjoy the blessing of Yahweh's saving glory.

Remarkably, even the Gibeonite Gentiles experience the glory of God in salvation through judgment. As other nations gather together against Yahweh and his anointed, Joshua (9:1–2; cf. Deut. 34:9; Ps. 2:1–3), the Gibeonites recognize their inability to stand against Israel and her God and deceive Israel into making a covenant of peace. When they come to Joshua, though what they say in the first part of Joshua 9:9 is not true—they have *not* come from a very great distance—what they say in the rest of the verse is: "Your servants have come because of the name of Yahweh your God, for we have heard a report of him and all that he did in Egypt." The Gibeonites have heard what Yahweh did to Egypt, and they have also heard that Yahweh "commanded his servant Moses . . . to destroy all the inhabitants of the land," so they "feared greatly" for their lives (9:24). Yahweh's greatness brings condemnation on everything the Gibeonites have trusted, and through that they desperately seek salvation. Israel fails to seek Yahweh (9:14), and Joshua makes peace with them (9:15). The fear of Yahweh and the fear that Israel will destroy them provokes the Gibeonites to subject themselves to Israel. Having learned of their deception, Joshua curses them and makes them servants (9:23). This is judgment, but through the judgment they keep their lives. Moreover, these Gentiles who are saved through judgment become servants of the house and altar of Yahweh (9:23, 27). As with Rahab, the overwhelming glory of Yahweh forces those who feel the coming condemnation to risk all they have to seek mercy.

The report of what has happened causes the inhabitants of the land more fear (Josh. 10:1–2). The nations again gather, this time to fight Gibeon (10:3–5). The Gibeonites cry out to Joshua for salvation (10:6), and Yahweh tells Joshua not to fear because he has already given the enemy into his hand (10:8). Yahweh routs the enemy (10:10), casts down hailstones from heaven to kill the enemy (10:11), and makes the sun stand still for approximately a whole day (10:12–14). Through these judgments, Yahweh's power and justice are displayed, Gibeon is saved, and the captains of Israel make their enemies a footstool for their feet (10:24; cf. Ps. 110:1). Again and again, Yahweh fights for Israel and delivers their enemies into their hands (Josh. 10:28–43).[21] After a final spasm of resistance (11:1–5) and Yahweh's telling Joshua not to fear and delivering the enemies into Israel's hand (11:6–15), the announcement comes that Joshua "took" (לקח) all the land (11:16–23).

2.2.3 Dividing the Land

Once the land is taken, it is apportioned (חלק) to the tribes (Joshua 13–22). As noted above, scattered through this section of Joshua are a series of notes in an ominous minor key. These dark elements of the music give a sense of foreboding to the conquest of the land, and the unease created by these features is realized in the book of Judges. The notes in the minor key to which I refer are the statements that Israel has not fully driven out the Geshurites or the Maacathites (13:13), the Jebusites (15:63),[22] or the Canaanites in Gezer (16:10), and a series of Canaanite cities remain in the allotment to Manasseh (17:11–13). Near the time of his death (23:14), Joshua warns Israel about the polluting influence of these wicked people (23:7, 12).

Just as Adam was tempted in Eden by the serpent, so Israel will be tempted in the land by these seed of the serpent, the remnants of the peoples of the land. As for what Yahweh swore to Israel, he has faithfully given them all the land he promised (Josh. 21:41, ET 43). Moreover, just as Yahweh rested on the seventh day (Gen. 2:2–3), in fulfillment of Lamech's hope that Noah might give rest from the cursed land (Gen. 5:29), "Yahweh gave rest to them on every side, according to all he swore to their fathers" (Josh. 21:42a, ET 44). It is almost as though Israel has another chance at Eden. And this salvation comes through the judgment of their enemies: "Not a man stood before them from all their enemies; Yahweh gave all their enemies into their hand" (21:42b, ET 44). "Not a word fell from

[21] Accordingly, Walter C. Kaiser Jr. (*The Promise Plan of God: A Biblical Theology of the Old and New Testaments* [Grand Rapids: Zondervan, 2008], 101) refers to these battles as "Yahweh's wars."

[22] Two observations can be made regarding Josh. 15:63, "But the Jebusites, the inhabitants of Jerusalem, the people of Judah could not drive out, so the Jebusites dwell with the people of Judah at Jerusalem to this day" (ESV). On the one hand, this seems to have been written before David drove the Jebusites out of Jerusalem (see 2 Sam. 5:6–10, ca. 1010 BC), and on the other hand, the statement "to this day" in Josh. 15:63 was not altered/edited after that conquest.

every good word that Yahweh spoke to the house of Israel. The whole came to pass" (21:43, ET 45). Yahweh glorifies himself in the judgment of the Canaanites, through which he takes Israel into the land he promised them.

2.2.4 Serving in the Land

Joshua 22 demonstrates Israel's zeal for Yahweh's glory. Then in chapter 23 Joshua summons the elders and leaders of the people (23:2) and proclaims Yahweh's mighty acts to them (23:3), assuring them that Yahweh will continue to fight for them (23:5). Joshua passes on to these leaders the charge Yahweh gave to him in the opening of the book, to be strong and live on Torah (23:6). He urges them to cling to Yahweh and love him (23:8, 11), otherwise they face judgment (23:13).

Joshua then summons all the people to Shechem and gives them a lesson in biblical theology before his death (Joshua 24). Joshua addresses Israel as a prophet, beginning with the words, "Thus says Yahweh, God of Israel" (23:2). Joshua's authoritative, prophetic lesson in biblical theology begins with the assertion that Yahweh showed mercy to Abraham. Abraham did not earn God's favor, for he was an idolater before Yahweh took him to Canaan (24:2–3).[23] Joshua then recounts what Yahweh did for Israel, from the giving of Isaac to Abraham to the giving of the Promised Land (24:3–13), then he calls Israel to devote themselves to Yahweh (24:14–15). The people declare that they will serve Yahweh alone (24:16–18), and then Joshua tells them something that is both surprising and consonant with the Torah: "And Joshua said to the people, 'You are not able to serve Yahweh, for he is a holy God, he is a jealous God, he will not forgive your transgressions and your sins'" (24:19).

This is surprising because Joshua calls the people to serve Yahweh, they agree to do so, and then he tells them they are unable to do so. It is consonant with Torah because this is precisely what Moses did when he called Israel to choose life (Deut. 30:11–14), having just told them they had not the heart to do so (29:3, ET 4). Just as the people insisted that they would keep the Ten Commandments (Deut. 5:24–27), prompting Yahweh to indicate that they lacked the heart to do so (5:28–29), so the people assure Joshua that they will serve Yahweh (Josh. 24:21). It is almost as though this moment of covenant commitment at the end of Joshua's life is a replay of what happened at Sinai,[24] and Israel's asseveration makes them witnesses against themselves (24:22).[25] Israel serves Yahweh all the

---

[23]So also Scott J. Hafemann, "The Covenant Relationship," in *Central Themes in Biblical Theology: Mapping Unity in Diversity*, ed. Scott J. Hafemann and Paul R. House (Grand Rapids: Baker, 2007), 42.

[24]Miller ("The Story of the First Commandment: Joshua," 90) writes, "Covenantal renewal will always be an appropriation of the fundamental claim of the Primary Commandment."

[25]Dempster states, "The capacity Israel lacks is a heart that will keep Torah" (*Dominion and Dynasty*, 130). Waltke (*An Old Testament Theology*, 533) writes, "Ironically, their confession of fidelity is at the same time a confession of their infidelity. They trust themselves, not *I AM*, to keep faith. . . . The book of Joshua implicitly

days of Joshua, and all the days of the elders who outlive him (24:31). Just as Joseph requested, Israel buries his bones in the land (Gen. 50:24–25; Ex. 13:19; Heb. 11:22). Joshua thus ends with indications of God honoring Joseph's faith while pointing to a day when Israel will be unwilling, and thereby unable, to serve Yahweh.

2.2.5 The Center of the Theology of Joshua

Israel crossed into the land in obedience to and by the power of the word of God. They took the land by humble reliance on the word of God, even when that word called them to do what appeared to be ineffective—march around Jericho. Yahweh gave Israel the land through the judgment of its inhabitants, and Israel apportioned the land to her tribes. Joshua then called Israel to serve Yahweh alone. Yahweh glorified himself by keeping his promise to give Israel the land, and he glorified himself by bringing justice against the wickedness of its inhabitants. Insofar as the salvation that came to Israel, her rest in the land, came by the mighty hand of Yahweh judging the wicked inhabitants of the land, the book of Joshua is a story of God's glory in salvation through judgment; and the ending of the book points beyond itself to more of the same.

2.3 Judges

The book of Judges begins the story of the way Israel was unable to serve Yahweh in the Land of Promise, the new Eden. Judges opens with a summary of the political and theological aspects of Israel's failure to complete the conquest (1:1–3:6), and then follow the accounts of the judges (3:7–16:31). The book is concluded with two vignettes that demonstrate that with no king the nation has no restraint (17:1–21:25).[26]

2.3.1 Failure to Complete the Conquest

In spite of the success of Judah (Judg. 1:1–19), Canaanites remain in the land (1:21, 27–36), and Israel fails to do as God commanded regarding the inhabitants of Canaan. As a result, the angel of Yahweh announces that judgment is coming on their disobedience (2:1–3). Just as the land brought forth thorns and thistles for Adam, the inhabitants of the land and their gods become thorns and snares to Israel (2:3). Israel enters into a cycle of sin, judgment, salvation, and more sin (summarized in 2:11–3:6).

Everything seen in the Old Testament to this point—Yahweh's creation and preservation of the world (Genesis 1–11), his purpose of filling the earth with his glory (Num. 14:21), his mercy to Israel's patriarchs (Genesis 12–50), his redemption of Israel from Egypt (Exodus 1–15; Judg. 2:1), the covenant he

looks forward to the need for a new covenant even as the book of Deuteronomy explicitly prophesies a new covenant after exile."

[26]For a chiastic arrangement of the book, see Waltke, *An Old Testament Theology*, 592–93.

made with them at Sinai (Exodus 19–Leviticus; Judg. 2:1), and the blessings and curses invoked upon entry into the land (Leviticus 26; Deuteronomy 28; Josh. 8:30–35)[27]—informs the statement in Judges 2:11 that the people did evil in Yahweh's eyes. Yahweh responds to Israel's idolatry with righteous indignation: "They provoked Yahweh to anger" (Judg. 2:12). Yahweh's response is not an out-of-control emotional outburst that is somehow beneath a deity. Rather, his anger is faithfulness to his word. He sells Israel into the hands of their enemies because if he does not do so, he will be as faithless as they have been (2:14–15; cf. Deut. 31:16–21). Yahweh keeps his word and establishes the glory of his justice. God is true, and every man a liar (cf. Rom. 3:4).

Judges 2:16–19 seems to anticipate the refrain in Judges 17–21 (17:4; 18:1; 19:1; 21:25). Yahweh would mercifully raise up a judge to deliver Israel (2:16), but then Israel would not listen to the judge (2:17). Then when the judge died, Israel would become more corrupt than the previous generations (2:19). This is connected to the refrain about there being no king in Israel because it shows that if Israel's sin is to be restrained, some authority greater than that of a temporary judge is needed. Nevertheless, Yahweh's judgment of Israel provides the context for his salvation of them. The deliverer becomes the agent of Yahweh's salvation for Israel. The judges save Israel by defeating their oppressors: salvation for Israel comes through judgment against her own sin administered by her oppressors, and then through the judgment the judges visit on those who oppressed her. This cycle shows that Yahweh is righteous and judges Israel for her iniquity. It also shows that Yahweh is faithful to the promises he has made and able to deliver Israel when they turn to him (2:18). The book of Judges glorifies Yahweh in salvation through judgment.

2.3.2 *The Accounts of the Judges*

God's glorious justice, which is followed by his merciful salvation, is the story told through these accounts of Othniel (Judg. 3:7–11), Ehud (3:12–30), Shamgar (3:31), Deborah (4:1–5:31), Gideon (6:1–8:35), Abimelech (not a judge, 9:1–57), Tola (10:1–2), Jair (10:3–4), Jephthah (10:6–12:7), Ibzan (12:8–9), Elon (12:11–12), Abdon (12:13–15), and Samson (13:1–16:31).[28]

A clear pattern marks the accounts of Othniel, Ehud, Deborah, Gideon, Jephthah, and Samson. The pattern begins with a statement that Israel did evil in the eyes of Yahweh (Judg. 3:7, 12; 4:1; 6:1; 10:6; 13:1). It continues with

[27]For a discussion of allusions to Joshua in the prologue (1:1–2:5) and epilogue (chaps. 17–21) of Judges, see Gregory T. K. Wong, *Compositional Strategy of the Book of Judges: An Inductive, Rhetorical Study*, VTSup (Boston: Brill, 2006), 47–74. For "Deuteronomic Theology in the Book of Judges," see McConville, *Grace in the End*, 103–110.

[28]Wong (*Compositional Strategy in the Book of Judges*, 241) suggests that the minor judges have been included because "the author/redactor aimed at presenting twelve judges in order to represent all the tribes of Israel" and that they have been arranged "to reflect the same south-to-north geographic trajectory introduced in the prologue of the book in Judges 1."

Yahweh's response: he sold them into the hand of an enemy, strengthened an enemy against Israel, or gave them into an enemy's hand (3:8, 12; 4:2; 6:1; 10:7; 13:1). In Deuteronomy the people were promised that if they turned to the Lord when they came under discipline, he would show them mercy (Deut. 4:29; 30:2; 32:36). When the people come under discipline in Judges, they cry out to Yahweh—at first (Judg. 3:9, 15; 4:3; 6:6–7; 10:10–16). The people do not cry to Yahweh in the account of Samson, which seems to indicate that the nation is getting progressively worse.[29] Yahweh hears the cries and raises up a deliverer, a judge, to save Israel (3:9, 15; 4:4–9; 10:10–16), but after Jephthah there is no notice given that the people have cried out to the Lord. In some cases the angel of Yahweh calls the judge (6:11–12) or announces his coming birth (13:3–22). In several instances, the Spirit of Yahweh is upon, clothes, stirs, or rushes upon the judge (3:10; 6:34; 13:25; 14:6, 19; 15:14).[30] Once the judge delivers Israel, significantly, the land has "rest" (3:11, 30; 5:31; 8:30). This rest enjoyed by the land resonates with God's rest upon the completion of his work—shades of Eden. The fact that Jephthah and Samson do not give the land rest points again to the worsening of Israel's state.

Yahweh establishes the glory of his justice when he keeps his word and disciplines Israel, and he then establishes the glory of his mercy not only by remaining faithful to the promises he has made to unworthy Israel, but also in the way that he chooses to deliver Israel. These judges who deliver Israel are unlikely, unexpected, surprising conquerors. Ehud is a left-handed "son of the right hand," that is, a Benjaminite[31] (Judg. 3:15). Shamgar appears to have been a Gentile[32] and uses an unconventional weapon, an oxgoad (3:31). A woman, Jael, shows herself to be seed of the woman when she crushes the head of the seed of the serpent (4:21; 5:26).[33] Gideon is hiding from the enemy (6:11), doubts what the angel proclaims to him (6:13), objects that he is from a weak clan and the least in his father's house (6:15), and then asks for signs (6:17–21). When he does obey Yahweh, he does so at night for fear of his family and neighbors (6:27). Whatever we conclude about the famed story of the men whom Gideon takes

[29]Waltke sees a shift in the character of the judges in the account of Gideon from better to worse (*An Old Testament Theology*, 601). Wong traces deterioration through the judges' decreasing faith in Yahweh (*Compositional Strategy in the Book of Judges*, 158–65), through the increasing prominence of the judges' self-interest (165–76), through the decreasing participation of the tribes in military campaigns (176–78), through increasing harshness against fellow Israelites (178–80), and through Yahweh's increasing frustration with Israel (181–85).

[30]House (*Old Testament Theology*, 220) makes the interesting observation, "Even Spirit-empowered judges like Jephthah . . . and Samson . . . are unable to be faithful to the covenant themselves." For a discussion of the Spirit in the Old Testament, see James M. Hamilton Jr., *God's Indwelling Presence: The Holy Spirit in the Old and New Testaments*, NACSBT (Nashville: Broadman & Holman, 2006), chap. 3; and for a chart that classifies all 389 occurrences of "s/Spirit" in the Old Testament, see James M. Hamilton Jr., "God with Men in the Torah," *WTJ* 65 (2003): 131–33.

[31]See the discussion in Wong, *Compositional Strategy in the Book of Judges*, 113–20.

[32]See the discussion in Daniel I. Block, *Judges, Ruth*, NAC (Nashville: Broadman & Holman, 1999), 172–75.

[33]See James M. Hamilton Jr., "The Skull Crushing Seed of the Woman: Inner-Biblical Interpretation of Genesis 3:15," *SBJT* 10, no. 2 (2006): 30–54.

to the river to drink, when some lap like dogs and others kneel to drink,[34] the point is that Yahweh is making Gideon's army smaller so that he will get more glory when this little force of three hundred (7:8) overcomes those as numerous as the sand by the sea (7:12). Yahweh declares that Gideon has too many people with him (7:2, 4). And the battle strategy is not about the readiness or alertness of the men with Gideon but about their willingness to do what Yahweh says, even though, as a battle strategy, what Yahweh says to do sounds like folly and weakness: they are to blow their trumpets, shout, smash their pots, and lift up their torches (7:16–21). They triumph not because they are alert but because Yahweh causes the men of the enemy to fight each other (7:22). This passage is most emphatically not about alert Israelites. Rather, it is about Yahweh's ability to overcome the wisdom and power of the world with the folly and weakness of obedience.

As the son of a prostitute, Jepthah is an unlikely hero (Judg. 11:1). And as he breaks every one of his Nazarite vows, Samson shows that the only reason Yahweh continues to use him to defeat his enemies and save his people is that Yahweh is a God merciful and gracious, slow to anger and abounding in steadfast loving-kindness.[35] These accounts of the judges resound with the glory of God as his mercy is highlighted by his justice.

2.3.3 No King, No Restraint

The refrain at the end of Judges is that there was no king in Israel, and as a result everyone did what was right in his own eyes (17:6; 18:1; 19:1; 21:25).[36] This creates the impression that Israel's king was to restrain the evil of the people by enforcing the law of Yahweh, just as Deuteronomy 17:18–20 stipulates. As Dempster puts it, "Israel is in need of lasting kingship instead of a temporary judge."[37]

The lack of restraint in Israel is illustrated by two stories that show how the sins of several judges have gone to seed. Gideon's idolatry (Judges 8) is matched and exceeded by Micah's (Judges 17–18); Samson's violation of Nazirite regulations

---

[34]Josephus suggests that this resulted in Gideon taking the most fearful of the army into battle that God might receive credit for the victory (*Ant*. 5.215–17). C. F. Keil, on the other hand, thinks that Gideon took the most brave into battle, but agrees that the point was that God would get all the glory for the victory (*Judges*, in KD, 2:248–49).

[35]Charles Halton demonstrates that there is a pun in the Samson account where the ESV describes how Samson "entertained" the Philistines in Judg. 16:25–27; a closely related Hebrew verb has the meaning "crush," so that there is a play on the connection between the sounds of these two Hebrew verbs as Samson entertains/crushes the Philistines when he brings down their temple upon them. See further Charles Halton, "Samson's Last Laugh: The *Ś/ŠḤQ* Pun in Judges 16:25–27," *JBL* 128 (2009): 61–64.

[36]Eugene H. Merrill (*Everlasting Dominion: A Theology of the Old Testament* [Nashville: Broadman & Holman, 2006], 423–24) observes that these stories at the end of Judges "have a Bethlehem connection, suggesting that they had a theological role to play in anticipation of the Davidic monarchy."

[37]Dempster, *Dominion and Dynasty*, 133. Similarly T. D. Alexander, *The Servant King: The Bible's Portrait of the Messiah* (Leicester: Inter-Varsity, 1998), 47. *Pace* William J. Dumbrell, *The Faith of Israel: A Theological Survey of the Old Testament*, 2nd ed. (Grand Rapids: Baker, 2002), 79–80, who suggests that Judges reflects an "antimonarchical stance."

(Judges 13–16) is matched and exceeded by the Levite's violation of Levitical regulations (Judges 17–18); Samson's doing what is right in his own eyes when he takes a wife (14:1–7) is matched and exceeded by the Danites' doing what is right in their own eyes when they take an inheritance (18:1–31); Samson's wooing and abandoning his wife (15:1–8) is matched and exceeded by the Levite's wooing and abandoning his concubine (19:1–20:7); Ehud the Benjaminite's left-handed use of deception (3:12–30) is perverted and exceeded by the left-handed Benjaminites who defend Gibeah's wickedness (20:12–16); Gideon and Jephthah's harsh treatment of their fellow Israelites (8:7–19; 12:1–6) is matched and exceeded by Israel's harsh treatment of Benjamin (20:29–48); and Jephthah's rash oath that results in the loss of his virgin daughter (11:29–40) is matched and exceeded by Israel's rash oath that results in the forced "marriages" of six hundred virgins in Israel to the men who remain from the ban on Benjamin (21:1–25).[38]

2.3.4 The Center of the Theology of Judges

Gregory Wong writes, "If one is to sum up the author's portrayal of this period of Israel's history with a single phrase, it would be 'progressive deterioration.'"[39] We can go one step further and ask, why was it necessary to show this progressive deterioration in Israel? The author seems to be tracing the nation's decline in order to demonstrate the justice of God's punishment of Israel's sin, and the horror of the flagrant sinfulness of Israel makes Yahweh's patient mercy shine all the more brightly. In short, the author of Judges is showing the glory of Yahweh in salvation through judgment.

2.4 Samuel

The narrative of Samuel[40] focuses on the three major figures in the story: Samuel, Saul, and David. Samuel is the last judge of Israel (1 Samuel 1–8), who anoints Israel's first king, Saul (1 Samuel 9–15). Saul is followed by David (1 Samuel 16—2 Samuel 24). This narrative is bound together by three poems, one at the beginning (1 Sam. 2:1–10), one in the middle (2 Sam. 1:19–27), and one at the end (2 Sam. 22:1–23:7). Reversal is the rhyme and rhythm of these poems: the mighty, handsome, seemingly impressive people of the world (such as Peninnah, Saul, Goliath, and Absalom) are exposed as bankrupt, while the small, weak, infertile, and unimpressive (such as Hannah, Samuel, Jonathan, and David) are exalted (see 1 Sam. 2:1–10). In Samuel, the important distinctions between the worldly strong and the worldly weak are that those who are weak in the world's eyes rely on Yahweh and repent of their sin. Not so with those

[38]These statements are based on Wong's lengthy argument for each of these seven correspondences (Wong, *Compositional Strategy in the Book of Judges*, 83–135).
[39]Ibid., 249.
[40]Waltke notes that the division of the Hebrew book of Samuel into two books did not happen until the fifteenth century AD (*An Old Testament Theology*, 624 n. 2). The Greek translation treats the books of Samuel and Kings as 1–4 Reigns (or Kingdoms).

who are impressive in worldly terms. Yahweh judges them, therefore, and their death shows that no matter how strong they may be in the world's eyes, those who seek their own kingdom rather than Yahweh's meet bitter ends: "How the mighty have fallen!" (see 2 Sam. 1:19–27). Through the judgment of the proud and strong Yahweh vindicates the humble and weak who, by relying on him, testify to his greatness: "Yahweh is my rock" (see 2 Sam. 22:1–23:7). Thus, Yahweh is glorified in salvation through judgment in the book of Samuel. This can be seen in the accounts of Samuel, Saul, and David.

2.4.1 Samuel

Preparing the context in which salvation will come through judgment, the account of Samuel includes his barren mother's prayer for his birth (1 Samuel 1) and her hymn of praise when her prayer is answered (2:1–11). We read of Eli's sons of Belial, the curse on their house (2:12–36), and Yahweh calling Samuel into his service (3:1–21). Samuel is not mentioned in the account of the capture and return of the ark (4:1–7:2), but after twenty years (7:2) his faithful ministry leads to repentance and deliverance for Israel (7:3–17). In response to the people's request for a king, Samuel prophesies about the king's wicked ways (8:1–22).

The first poem in Samuel (1 Sam. 2:1–10) sets the theological trajectory for the book of Samuel,[41] and this trajectory is one of salvation through judgment for God's glory. The poem is prefaced by the story of how God closed the womb of Samuel's mother, Hannah (1:5). Her rival grievously provokes her (1:6), but when Yahweh opens her womb (1:19–20), Hannah sings, "My heart rejoices in Yahweh; my horn is exalted in Yahweh; my mouth is wide against my enemies, because I am glad in your salvation" (2:1). The birth of the child represents Yahweh's vindication of his faithful servant, Hannah, against her enemy, Peninnah (1:2, 6). This vindication results in Hannah deriding her enemy (2:1), extolling the uniqueness of Yahweh (2:2), warning her enemy against pride (2:3), and explaining the way that Yahweh reverses fortunes: "The bows of the mighty are shattered, and those who stumbled gird on strength; the full hire themselves out for bread, and those who hungered have ceased to hunger; the barren has given birth to seven, and the one with many children is feeble" (2:4–5). This praise comes to Yahweh precisely because he has shut the mouth of the one boasting over Hannah. Hannah is praising Yahweh for saving her through the judgment of Peninnah, and salvation through judgment for God's glory will be the story of Samuel.

Hannah continues to praise Yahweh's power with the words, "Yahweh kills and makes alive; he brings down to Sheol and raises up" (2:6). Just as it is wrong to imagine oneself as somehow superior to others, and then to conclude that this

[41]So also Dumbrell, *The Faith of Israel*, 82.

superiority accounts for one's military might, physical strength, sufficient food, or fertile womb (blessings mentioned in 2:4–5), so it is wrong to assume that one has *life* by one's own power (2:6). Yahweh determines who lives and who dies. This theme of God's sovereignty over life and death will be seen in the death of Eli's sons (2:25; 4:11), the death of the men of Beth-shemesh who look upon the ark (6:19–20), the sudden death of Nabal when Yahweh strikes him (25:38), the certainty of Saul's prophesied death (26:10; 28:19; 30:4), Yahweh's striking of Uzzah (2 Sam. 6:7), and the many who die as a result of David's sin (24:15). Yahweh judges all human pride and presumption. First Samuel 2:6 teaches that Yahweh's just judgment when people die makes even life itself a mercy, and this is especially true for sinners.

Samuel's mother continues to sing of reversals, which continue to introduce the contents of the book of Samuel: "Yahweh dispossesses[42] and makes rich; he lays low and exalts. He raises the poor from the dust; from the ash heap he lifts up the needy to sit with princes, and a throne of glory he causes them to inherit, for to Yahweh are the pillars of the earth, and he has set upon them the world" (1 Sam. 2:7–8). Through the birth of her children, Hannah has been raised up and Peninnah put down (1 Samuel 1–2). Eli's sons, who bully those who come to worship Yahweh (2:12–17), are killed; meanwhile the little child Samuel is raised up and his word comes to all Israel (2:21, 34–35; 3:19–4:1). When the Philistines capture the ark, they think they have overcome Yahweh, but in the morning their god Dagon is prostrate before the ark (5:1–3), and the next morning Dagon is broken before Yahweh (5:4). Then the "conquered" ark goes on a victory romp through Philistine territory (5:6–6:1).[43] Saul, so impressive in the eyes of the world, is replaced by David, whose own father did not expect him to be king—not even bothering to summon him from the fields when Samuel came to anoint one of his sons as king. Little David brings down mighty Goliath. And Absalom, with his fifty runners, his impressive chariot, his political savvy (2 Sam. 15:1–6), and even the revered counsel of Ahithophel (15:31; 16:23), comes to nothing when he tries to steal the very kingdom of God. These reversals—where the proud are brought low and the humble exalted—exalt the God who of his own free

[42]The participle מוריש is typically rendered "makes poor" here, but the verb ירש has strong connotations of "taking possession" or "dispossessing," and the verb is often used to describe Israel taking the land of Canaan. According to *HALOT* (442), the translation "make poor" is dependant upon the reading מריש (from the verb רוש). This would fit the context, but there is no indication that the Hebrew read מריש rather than מוריש. The waw is present in "A Reconstruction of the Song of Hannah" in F. M. Cross et al., *Qumran Cave 4.XXI: 1–2 Samuel*, DJD 17 (Oxford: Clarendon, 2005), 37–38, cf. 30–31. (But only one word of 1 Sam. 2:7 is visible from 4QSam[a], so this waw is merely part of the editor's reconstruction and not based on what is visible in the scroll, though the reconstruction is probably based on measurements that would indicate how many letters might fit in the text that has been lost.) There is not yet a critical edition of the Greek translation of Samuel, but the Rahlfs text has πτωχίζει, "make poor." Perhaps the translator had a text that lacked the waw in the verb, reading מריש instead of מוריש, or perhaps his translation of מוריש was influenced by the conceptual parallelism with "make rich." According to HR, this is the only instance of πτωχίζω in the Greek translations of the Old Testament.

[43]Peter J. Leithart, *A Son to Me: An Exposition of 1 and 2 Samuel* (Moscow, ID: Canon, 2003), 59.

mercy saves the weak who rely on his power to overcome those strong in their own strength.[44]

The next words of Hannah's poem make explicit the salvation through judgment for those who glorify Yahweh: "He will keep the feet of his faithful ones, and the wicked will be made silent in darkness, for not by strength will a man prevail" (1 Sam. 2:9). The reference to Yahweh guarding the feet of the faithful could allude to the statement that the serpent would strike the heel of the seed of the woman (Gen. 3:15; cf. Ps. 91:12–13; Matt. 4:6; Luke 4:10–11).

The wicked will be judged, the faithful will be preserved, and this will not come through the might of men but by the power of God: "As for Yahweh, those who contend with him will be shattered; he will thunder in the heavens against them. Yahweh judges the ends of the earth, and he will give strength to his king, and he will exalt the horn of his anointed" (1 Sam. 2:10). Aside from prefiguring the way that Yahweh thunders against the Philistines (see 7:10), this text makes an important statement about *how* Yahweh will accomplish salvation through judgment. The concluding phrases of 1 Samuel 2:10 equate Yahweh's *king* with Yahweh's *anointed*.[45] Moreover, the strengthening of the king seems to be explained in the statement that the anointed's horn—a reference to military power—will be exalted. And this reference to the military might of Israel under the anointed king explains the idea that "Yahweh will judge the ends of the earth," which is itself elaborating on the idea that the adversaries of Yahweh will be shattered. This shattering has overtones of broken heads (Gen. 3:15), and it appears that Yahweh's judgment of the ends of the earth will come through the defeat of his enemies by means of the victorious rise of his anointed king to military power. This text points to the expansion of the borders of Israel through the conquest of rival kingdoms, and the expanding of Israel will mean that Yahweh's glory is

[44]As noted above, there is not yet a critical edition of the Greek translation of Samuel, but the insertion of a passage very much like Jer. 9:22–23 (ET 23–24) into the Greek translation of 1 Sam. 2:10 (there are slight differences in wording in the Greek of 1 Sam. 2:10 and Jer. 9:23–24) captures the message of Hannah's song: "The Lord will make his adversary weak; the Lord is holy. Let not the clever boast in his cleverness, and let not let [*sic*] the wealthy boast in his wealth, but let him who boasts boast in this: to understand and know the Lord and to execute justice and righteousness in the midst of the land" (1 Sam. 2:10a, NETS). Cf. the NETS translation of Jer. 9:23–24, and Joseph Ziegler, ed., *Ieremias, Baruch, Threni, Epistula Ieremiae*, 3rd ed., Septuaginta Vetus Testamentum Graecum 15 (Göttingen: Vandenhoeck and Ruprecht, 2006). 4QSam[a] witnesses to a longer reading in 1 Sam. 2:10, but it does not match the LXX precisely. For brief discussion see P. Kyle McCarter Jr., *1 Samuel: A New Translation with Introduction, Notes and Commentary*, AB (Garden City: Doubleday, 1980), 67–71, and now Cross et al., *Qumran Cave 4.XXI: 1–2 Samuel*, 32–33, 37, where it is noted that the addition's "prosodic pattern differs from that of the body of Hannah's Song . . ." (37). If this addition is an interpretive statement added by the translator, it matches the theology of Hannah's song quite well. Klein's statement (Ralph W. Klein, *1 Samuel*, WBC [Waco, TX: Word, 1983], 13) that the differences between LXX 1 Sam. 2:10 and Jer. 9:23–24 mean that "we must conclude that the Hebrew copy of Samuel used by the LXX translator had already been glossed" does not leave room for other possibilities: for instance, the translator could be (a) working from memory, (b) providing his own rendering of Jer. 9:22–23 into Greek, or (c) paraphrasing from memory, from Hebrew, or even from a Greek translation of Jer. 9 (cf. Natalio Fernández Marcos, *The Septuagint in Context: Introduction to the Greek Versions of the Bible* [Boston: Brill, 2000], 56).

[45]This is worth noting because Deuteronomy 17 does not mention the king being anointed, while priests are to be anointed (e.g., Ex. 28:41). See also Judg. 9:8.

spreading over the dry land. This spreading of the knowledge of the greatness and goodness of Yahweh comes through the judgment and defeat of the opposition. All of this leads to the conclusion that Hannah's poem prepares the audience of Samuel to expect the glory of Yahweh in salvation through judgment to be brought about by Yahweh's anointed king.

Meanwhile, Eli's sons Hophni and Phineas are sons of Belial, wicked priests (1 Sam. 2:12–17) whom Yahweh promises to judge (2:27–36; 3:11–14). In a shocking statement, the author of Samuel relates that when their father rebuked them, "they would not listen to the voice of their father, for it was the will of Yahweh to put them to death" (2:25). This states Yahweh's desire to show judgment against these priests who have intimidated his people (cf. 2:13–16). It seems that in referring to them as "sons of Belial," the author of Samuel has designated them with a phrase that means "seed of the serpent."[46]

When we compare Eli's reaction to the prophecy of coming judgment (1 Sam. 3:10–18a) to the reactions of Moses and Joshua, we learn something important about the announcement of judgment as it relates to prayer. When Yahweh announced to Moses his intention to destroy Israel, Moses appealed for mercy on the basis of God's concern for his own glory (Ex. 32:11–14). When Israel was defeated before her enemies, Joshua made the same appeal (Josh. 7:6–9). But when Samuel announces to Eli that God intends to keep his promise to kill his sons (cf. 1 Sam. 2:34 with 3:12–13), unlike Moses and Joshua, Eli resigns himself and his sons to judgment with the words: "He is Yahweh. Let him do what seems good to him" (1 Sam. 3:18).

Yahweh announces judgment in order to bring about repentance (see Jer. 18:1–11). Yahweh has ordained that the sons of Eli will die (1 Sam. 2:25), but this does not remove Eli's responsibility to rebuke and restrain his sons (3:13). And Eli's sons are responsible for their failure to repent. They have had fair warning that Yahweh would judge, and they have refused to repent. Yahweh sovereignly ordained what would take place, and Eli and his sons have chosen their path. This is the mystery of divine sovereignty and human responsibility.[47] We cannot deny either side of this equation. God is sovereign. People are responsible. In the face of these realities, we should not resign ourselves to a fatalistic acceptance of judgment, as Eli does, but cry out to Yahweh, who is free and mighty to save, as Moses and Joshua did. Yahweh honors those who honor him, and those who despise him meet judgment (2:30). Those who do not want to fall into the

[46]Pseudepigraphic texts (e.g., *Mart. Isa.* 1:8, 2:4; 4:2; *Jub.* 1:20; 15:33; 20:1) and texts from Qumran (CD 16:5; 1QM 13:11) understand Belial to be "the angel of wickedness." Many more texts from Qumran and the Pseudepigrapha could be cited; see T. J. Lewis, "Belial," *ABD*, 1:655–56. See also David Toshio Tsumura, *The First Book of Samuel*, NICOT (Grand Rapids: Eerdmans, 2007), 122–24, 154–55. Tsumura interprets "the Daughter of Beliyaal" in 1 Sam. 1:16 as a reference to "the Queen of the underworld" (124).

[47]Cf. D. A. Carson, *Divine Sovereignty and Human Responsibility: Biblical Perspectives in Tension* (Grand Rapids: Baker, 1994; repr., Eugene, OR: Wipf and Stock, 2002), 15, 225 n. 16.

doom of Eli and his sons are taught—through the judgment that falls on Eli's house—to repent and pray like Moses and Joshua for the honor of Yahweh. Salvation comes through judgment, and when his people rely upon him, Yahweh is honored as the one who is free to change his mind.

Yahweh accomplishes his purpose when the Philistines defeat Israel in battle. They kill Hophni and Phineas and capture the ark of the covenant (1 Sam. 4:11). The Philistines think they have overcome Yahweh since they have overcome Israel, so they set up the symbol of Yahweh's presence, the ark, as a household servant in the temple of Dagon, placing it next to the image of Dagon (5:2). If Yahweh is defeated when the ark is captured, it is a defeat like the one that will take place at Golgotha.[48] The Philistines awake to find Dagon on his face before the "defeated" Yahweh (5:3). It is worse the next day; Dagon's head and *hands* are cut off (5:4), while Yahweh's *hand* is heavy against Ashdod (5:6), Gath (5:8–9), and Ekron (5:10–11). The defeat of Israel in battle was Yahweh's judgment against the wicked sons of Eli, and the severity of the penalty was felt in loss of the ark—the very symbol of God's presence. Through this judgment upon Israel, however, Yahweh accomplishes judgment upon his enemies as the mere presence of the ark among them forces them to recognize that they cannot overcome him. Through these judgments, Yahweh disciplines Israel and defeats the Philistines, who are forced to "give glory to the God of Israel" (6:5). Moreover, the Philistines are eager to send the ark on its way back to Israel. Yahweh glorifies himself in salvation through judgment. Later, Yahweh again exalts himself by saving repentant Israel through judgment upon the Philistines when he thunders against them in 1 Samuel 7:3–17 (7:10).

In spite of the way that Yahweh delivered Israel and reigned as king over them, the people of Israel reject Yahweh in their appeal for a king (1 Sam. 8:7). It was prophesied that Israel would have a king (e.g., Gen. 17:6; 49:9–11; Num. 24:7, 17; Deut. 17:14–20), so the desire for a king is not itself evil.[49] The evil lies in the fact that rather than desiring a human king through whom Yahweh will exercise his power and authority, the people reject Yahweh (1 Sam. 8:7; cf. Judg. 8:23). Yahweh knows the heart, and his analysis of human motivation is declared to and through the prophet Samuel. Just as their ancestors did, the people commit idolatry by trusting in something other than Yahweh (8:8). Rather than being a kingdom of priests (Ex. 19:6) they want to be "like all the nations" (1 Sam. 8:5, 20). Samuel's warning about the ways of the king is an announcement of judgment (8:10–18),[50] and he promises the people that when they cry out because of

[48]Leithart, *A Son to Me*, 57.

[49]Similarly P. E. Satterthwaite, "Samuel," in *NDBT*, 179.

[50]Yahweh instructs Samuel to warn the people about the "ways of the king" (1 Sam. 8:9 ESV), and the Hebrew term rendered "ways" is משפט, which can also mean "judgment." The term is used again in 8:11 as Samuel begins to describe the way the king will "take" the people's sons (8:11), he will "take" their daughters (8:13), he will "take" their fields (8:14), he will "take" their grain (8:15), he will "take" their male and female servants

the king, Yahweh will not answer (8:18). The people do not respond rightly to this warning of judgment and insist on having a king (8:19). King Saul, then, comes as a judgment against Israel (8:20–22). Mercifully, and in the mystery of his sovereign providence, Yahweh nevertheless uses the "judgment" of Saul to save his people (1 Samuel 11), and then through the judgment of Saul he raises up David to shepherd them (1 Samuel 13–16).

2.4.2 Saul

Some suggest that the account of Saul is "organized in a positive-to-negative fashion, beginning with the good stories about Saul . . . followed by stories about Saul's failures and rejection by God."[51] But it seems that the "gift" of Saul is a judgment on Israel for rejecting Yahweh, and it also seems that even in the earlier stories Saul is cast in an extremely negative light. From start to finish, Saul is a negative foil for David.

Saul the son of Kish is tall and handsome, and there is none better than he in Israel (1 Sam. 9:2). But he is no replacement for Yahweh and proves to be a failure. The failures to come are hinted at when Saul fails to find his father's donkeys (9:1–5). Israel has forsaken Yahweh for a man who cannot find his father's donkeys. Then Saul's unnamed servant proves to be more resourceful than he is. This servant suggests that they seek the man of God (9:6), and when Saul objects that they have nothing to present to the man of God (9:7), the servant—not Saul—has brought money along while Saul has nothing (9:8). Both in the idea and in its execution the servant is more resourceful than Saul.

As Saul and his servant make their way to Samuel (1 Sam. 9:9–14), the narrator recounts what Yahweh revealed to Samuel the previous day (9:15). This information confirms the interpretation of the concluding statements of Hannah's song offered above (see comments above on 1 Sam. 2:10). Yahweh says to Samuel:

> "At this time tomorrow I will send to you a man from the land of Benjamin, and you will anoint him as prince over my people Israel. He will save my people from the hand of the Philistines, for I have seen my people, for their cry has come to me." When Samuel saw Saul, Yahweh told him, "Behold, the man of whom I spoke to you. This one will restrain my people." (9:16–17)

Two observations here: First, in the canonical context of Samuel, the fact that Saul is from Benjamin bodes ill for him in light of the indications that the promised king is to be from Judah (cf. Gen. 49:8–12). Second, as noted with reference to 1 Samuel 2:10, a strong connection is established between *anointing*, becoming

(8:16), and he will "take" the tenth of their flocks (8:17). This warning of the "ways" of the "taking" that the king will do is a warning of "judgment" for rejecting Yahweh.

[51]David A. Dorsey, *The Literary Structure of the Old Testament: A Commentary on Genesis—Malachi* (Grand Rapids: Baker, 1999), 130.

king, and *delivering* Israel by *defeating* their enemies; and the mention that the king will *restrain* the people seems to answer the lack of restraint, with the refrain that there was no king, seen at the end of the book of Judges.[52]

The narrative is arranged such that Israel's cry for a king in 1 Samuel 8 is immediately answered by the introduction of Saul in chapter 9, and the mention of Yahweh seeing the people and hearing their cry in 9:16 points back to their appeal for a king. This context colors our understanding of Saul's initial encounter with Samuel. They meet (9:18), Samuel declares that he will feast with Saul (9:19), he tells Saul where the lost donkeys are—apparently before Saul mentions them—and then in the second half of verse 20 Samuel makes a statement that must be understood in the context of Israel's desire for a king: "And for whom is all the desire of Israel,[53] is it not for you and for all the house of your father?" (9:20). Saul's question in response—"Am I not a Benjaminite, from the smallest of the tribes of Israel, and my family the smallest of all the families of the tribes of Benjamin? And why do you speak to me like this?" (9:21)—indicates that he understands Samuel to be hinting that he will be king. Perhaps this reply also suggests surprise that the king will be chosen from the tribe of Benjamin rather than Judah. Samuel then sets a banquet before Saul, giving him the best portion among the invited guests (9:22–24). As Saul prepares to go his way, Samuel declares to him "the word of God" (9:27).

Before Samuel declares the word of God to Saul, he anoints him, kisses him, then says, "Has not Yahweh anointed you over his inheritance as prince?" (1 Sam. 10:1). The ESV adopts a note, attested in the LXX but not found in the MT (cf. ESV 10:1b), indicating that what Samuel says in 10:2–8 is "the sign to you that the Lord anointed you over his inheritance as ruler" (10:1b LXX). The "word of God" that Samuel declares to Saul, then, consists of the announcement that Yahweh has anointed him—via the prophet—as prince, and this is then validated by the three signs given in 10:2–8: (1) when Saul leaves Samuel he will meet men with a message from his father (10:2); (2) he will then meet three men who will give him

[52]This verb is also used to refer to an "imprisoning" kind of restraint, which might point back to Samuel's statements about the ways the king will oppress Israel (cf. 1 Sam. 8:10–18), but Saul does positively restrain the people when he keeps them from eating meat with the blood (14:31–35). For the important trajectory 1 Samuel 9:16–17 sets for kingship in Israel, see my essay, "The Typology of David's Rise to Power: Messianic Patterns in the Book of Samuel."

[53]This rendering of the phrase understands the noun חמדת as referring to what Israel feels—desire for a king (so also HCSB, KJV, NAB, NET, NIV, NLT), rather than as a reference to objects that people desire, "desirable things" (so LXX, ESV, NASB, NJB, RSV). It seems to me that the context of Israel's desiring a king is determinative for understanding the statement, but even if this word refers to "beautiful things" or "desirable things," it can be understood to indicate that Samuel is inviting Saul to recognize that he is the king who will possess the choicest things in Israel. The fact that חמדת is used in the singular here is not determinative because a plural form never appears, and the singular seems to refer to more than one thing elsewhere (cf., e.g., Isa. 2:16; Ezek. 26:12; Dan. 11:8). This term is often used to refer to objects of desire, but it is also used with reference to the lack of remorse (i.e., desire that he continue) people felt at the death of King Jehoram in 2 Chron. 21:20. Cf. A. Even-Shoshan, ed., *A New Concordance of the Old Testament* (Jerusalem: Kiryat Sefer, 1997), 377; BDB, 326; *HALOT*, 325.

two loaves of bread (10:3–4); and (3) Saul will then meet a troop of prophets, the Spirit will rush upon him, and he will prophesy with them (10:5–6).

These signs are evidently given to Saul to verify Samuel's word that Yahweh has anointed him. Samuel then says to Saul, "And it shall be, when these signs come to you, do all that your hand finds, for God is with you" (1 Sam. 10:7). Samuel's words about waiting seven days in 10:8 seem to point to exactly what he has in mind, for the reference to Saul's waiting seven days prepares the way for the occasion on which Saul will fail to wait the appointed time (13:8–14).

We then read, "And it came about, as he turned his shoulder to go from Samuel, that God overturned his heart" (1 Sam. 10:9a). This language of the heart being overturned appears several other places in the Old Testament,[54] but this is not the language used to indicate that someone has been enabled to hear Yahweh and obey him.[55] Yahweh has "turned" Saul into "another man" (10:6), but from what Saul does after this it does not appear that Saul has had his heart circumcised, that is, been regenerated. The signs that Samuel has given to Saul, however, are immediately confirmed: "And all these signs came on that day" (10:9b).

The confirmation of the signs should seal for Saul the reality that Yahweh has anointed him as the prince over his people. Curiously, however, Saul does not mention to his inquiring uncle what Samuel said to him about the kingdom (10:16), and then it gets worse. Samuel summons the people, and Saul is chosen king by lot, but he is nowhere to be found (10:17–21). Yahweh reveals that Saul is hiding among the baggage (10:22). When the prophet of Yahweh has declared "the word of God" to Saul, given him three confirming signs—all of which came to pass, and when the lots have fallen to him, hiding among the baggage is not humility.[56] It is not humble to hide from what God has appointed one to do. Rather, Saul's hiding among the baggage should be interpreted in view of the word Samuel declared and the signs he gave. In this light, Saul's hiding of himself looks more like cowardice and refusal to do what Yahweh has said than it looks like humility. After these events, Saul returns home to Gibeah (10:26), and in the canonical context the mention of Gibeah recalls the putrid smell of the events that took place there in Judges (cf. Judges 19–20). Moreover, Saul refuses to act against those who speak against him (1 Sam. 10:27).

Yahweh is merciful and saves even when his people reject him as king (1 Sam. 8:7; 10:19), and even through the judgment of Saul Israel is delivered from her enemies (11:1–11; 14:31, 47; 15:1–9). Victory in battle, however, does not nec-

[54]For the verb הפך, "turn, overturn, change," used with reference to the לב, "heart," see Ex. 14:5; Hos. 11:8; Ps. 105:25; and Lam. 1:20. None of these passages has to do with a kind of "new birth/conversion." Thus, the phrase does not seem to be used to describe that kind of change. R. B. Chisholm, "הפך," in *NIDOTTE*, 1:1050 connects this to Saul's ability to prophesy "in an ecstatic manner."

[55]This is usually referred to by means of a "circumcision" metaphor, whether of the heart (e.g., Deut. 30:6) or of the ears (e.g., Jer. 6:10).

[56]*Pace* Leithart, *A Son to Me*, 76.

essarily constitute a positive story about Saul's kingship. McCarter notes that there "is widely recognized" similarity between Saul's deliverance of Jabesh Gilead (11:1–11) and the accounts of the major judges.[57] Perhaps the narrator styles this account such that it corresponds to the accounts of the judges in order to make the point that Israel does not need a king, for it is still Yahweh who sends his Spirit (the language of 1 Sam. 11:6 matches Judg. 13:6, 19, and 15:14 exactly) and empowers the victorious deliverer.[58] We might also note that Samson, whom this language recalls, was empowered by Yahweh in spite of his faithless behavior. Further, the way that Saul summons the tribes to battle—cutting a yoke of oxen to pieces and sending them out with a threat—does not convey positive connotations (cf. Judg. 19:29, where the concubine is cut into twelve pieces and sent throughout Israel, another reminder of the stench at the end of Judges). After the battle, some want to enact justice against those who spoke against Saul (1 Sam. 11:12; cf. 10:27), but Saul, unlike Yahweh, has no interest in justice (11:13).[59]

It seems that virtually everything about Saul's kingship is negative, and this would explain Samuel's harsh tone against the people in 1 Samuel 12. As Joshua did (Joshua 24), Samuel provides a lesson in biblical theology for the people of Israel as he summarizes Yahweh's redemption of Israel, the ways they forgot him, the ways he judged them, and then their rejection of him (1 Sam. 12:6–12). This leads to a call to fear Yahweh and obey him (12:13–15), which is backed up by Yahweh thundering from heaven and sending rain at Samuel's request (12:16–18). The people recognize that they deserve God's judgment and plead with Samuel to pray for them (12:18). Samuel assures them that "Yahweh will not forsake his people on account of his great name" (12:22). Yahweh's reputation is at stake in Israel, and he will act on behalf of his great name. First Samuel 12:22 portrays the prophet understanding what is ultimate in Yahweh's motivations—his own name. The author of Samuel endorses this theology by choosing to include this account of what the prophet Samuel said.

But things get worse before they get better. Saul does not trust Yahweh when Samuel appears to delay, and Yahweh seeks a king according to his own heart (13:1–14). In contrast to Saul, Jonathan relies upon the Lord and boldly goes into battle declaring that "nothing can hinder the Lord from saving by many or by few" (14:6 ESV). Saul would not put sons of Belial who spoke against him to death (10:27; 11:13), but he is ready to put Jonathan to death for tasting honey (14:24–30, 36–44). Saul places a curse on anyone who eats before *he*, Saul, is

---

[57] McCarter, *1 Samuel*, 205–206.

[58] Cf. David G. Firth, "'Play It Again, Sam': The Poetics of Narrative Repetition in 1 Samuel 1–7, *TynBul* 56, no. 2 (2005): 15.

[59] It is noteworthy that whereas David will forgive his enemies, such as Shimei, the narrator takes pains to recount Shimei's repentance (see 2 Sam. 19:18–23). There is no indication in 1 Samuel 11 that the enemies of Saul have repented.

avenged on *his* enemies (14:24; and cf. the monument Saul builds for himself, 15:12). Saul's concern seems to be for his own name, and the result of his silly curse is the limitation of Israel's success (14:30) and the extension of Israel's sin (14:31–33). The people rightly object and save Jonathan from Saul's unjust wrath (14:45). In the salvation of Jonathan, there is rejection, a judgment, of Saul's foolish curse.

When Saul refuses to carry out the ban against the Amelakites (1 Sam. 15:1–9), the word of Yahweh comes to Samuel: Saul is rejected (15:10–35, esp. 15:23, 26).[60] This sets the stage for Yahweh to seek a king "after his own heart" (13:14). Earlier it was stated that there was none better (טוב) than Saul in Israel (9:2), but now Yahweh tears the kingdom from Saul and gives it to one who is better (טוב) than he (15:28). The narrative reorients the audience's understanding of the word "better": there was none *better* than Saul in terms of physical stature; but David is *better* than Saul because he lives for God's name rather than his own. Through this judgment on Saul, salvation comes as David is anointed king.

2.4.3 David

David enjoys initial success when he slays Goliath, but then Saul chases him from his home. In the wilderness, David shows himself to be a model of nobility and restraint. Eventually Saul dies, and the narratives vindicate David of any culpability in the deaths of Saul, Abner, and Ish-bosheth. The kingdom is united around David, and Yahweh makes astonishing promises to him. Yahweh begins to cover the dry land with his glory as the territory of David begins to expand. But then the terrible incident with Bathsheba unleashes judgment upon David's house. David repents of his sin, but the prophetic word that the sword will never depart from his house rings true. This begins to work its way out when Amnon rapes Tamar. In response, Absalom murders Amnon. Absalom does not repent, and David does not do justice against him. Then when Absalom is brought back to Jerusalem, he instigates a coup that ends in his death. All of this is judgment on David for his sin with Bathsheba, but Yahweh remains merciful. David returns to Jerusalem, sings Yahweh's praise, and buys the land on which the temple will be built. The glory of Yahweh is rightly psalmed at the conclusion of Samuel in response to the manifestation of God's glory in salvation through judgment.[61]

2.4.3.1 Unexpected Salvation. Jesse's smallest, youngest son, David, is anointed king (1 Sam. 16:1–12) and the Spirit comes upon him (16:11–13). Judgment on

---

[60]Saul's protestation that he wants to "worship" in 1 Sam. 15:30 has more to do with the desire he communicates to Samuel earlier in the verse in the words, "honor me now before the elders of my people," than it has to do with genuine repentance and a desire to worship Yahweh. Cf. David J. Reimer, "Stories of Forgiveness: Narrative Ethics and the Old Testament," in Rezetko, Lim, and Aucker, *Reflection and Refraction*, 374.

[61]There is some overlap between the next two sections and the longer discussion in my essay, "The Typology of David's Rise to Power."

Saul results in the anointing of David, and then David, the seed of the woman, smites Goliath, the seed of the serpent, on the head to deliver Israel (17:49).[62] David was provoked to fight Goliath because he "defied the armies of the living God" (17:36). David trusts that Yahweh will deliver him (17:37). David tells Goliath:

> I come against you *in the name of Yahweh of hosts*, the God of the armies of Israel, whom you have defied. This day Yahweh will deliver you into my hand, and I will strike you down and cut off your head. And I will give the dead bodies of the host of the Philistines this day to the birds of the air and to the wild beasts of the earth, *that all the earth may know that there is a God in Israel*, and that all this assembly may know that Yahweh saves not with sword and spear. For the battle is Yahweh's, and he will give you into our hand. (17:45–47, emphasis added)

As he challenges Goliath with these words, it is clear that David relies on Yahweh, not his own boyish might (17:47). Moreover, David is defending not his own reputation but Yahweh's, whom Goliath has defied (17:45). David is not concerned with the reputation he will gain, but he wants all to know that there is a God in Israel (17:46). Through the judgment on Saul comes salvation by David through judgment on the Philistine champion for the glory of God.

Saul's reward for exalting himself rather than Yahweh is the loss of the loyalty of his own children: Jonathan embraces God's declared intentions and enters into a covenant with David (1 Sam. 18:3–4), and Michal, whom Saul seeks to use as a snare for David (18:21), loves David and helps him escape (18:20; 19:11–17). God's justice thus comes home to Saul, and Yahweh, who does not save with sword and spear, makes all the spears Saul throws at David come to nothing but Saul's own ruin.

2.4.3.2 No Place to Lay His Head. Saul wickedly pursues David, "but God did not give him into his hand" (1 Sam. 23:14). Yahweh does put Saul into David's hand (24:10), and David refuses to lift his hand against Saul because Saul is Yahweh's anointed (24:10). Yahweh brings justice against Saul by Saul's own hand (31:4). God's justice is visited when Saul takes his own life, but though his death is God's justice, Saul remains responsible for what he has done. After Saul's death David's kingdom is established (2 Samuel 2, 5).

As David flees Saul, he eats holy bread (1 Sam. 21:1–6) and acquires Goliath's sword (21:8–9). He then has a close encounter when he flees to, of all places, Gath, Goliath's hometown (21:10–15). To add to David's own problems, a band of people with problems gathers to him: people in distress, people in debt, and

[62] Cf. Dempster, *Dominion and Dynasty*, 140.

all who are bitter in soul take David as their captain (22:2). The weak and foolish things of the world, the things that are not impressive, will be the people led by David to experience a resurrection of righteousness in Israel. God's judgment will bring Saul and those who exalt themselves low, and his mercy will exalt David and those like him who are trusting in Yahweh.

Saul's concern for his own name is so great that his hatred of Yahweh's anointed, David, leads him to murder Yahweh's priests (1 Sam. 22:6–19). Remarkably, when David hears of this, he takes responsibility for something for which he is clearly not responsible—the death of these priests (22:20–22). These narratives establish many points of typological contact between David and Jesus.[63] Not only does David take responsibility for sin he has not committed, but a city he has saved is ready to hand him over to Saul (23:1–13). On the way to the establishment of the kingdom, while living among the Philistines (1 Sam. 27:1–6), David works to complete the conquest as he puts non-Israelite "inhabitants of the land from of old" under the ban (1 Sam. 27:8–12).

Then simultaneous events of salvation through judgment take place when the nation is delivered from Saul, who falls in battle, as David is delivering Ziklag through the judgment he visits upon those who have raided it. Saul visits the witch of Endor and is surprised to have Samuel tell him that he will die on the morrow (1 Samuel 28). The means of Saul's death become immediately apparent as the next chapter shows the Philistines massing for battle (1 Samuel 29). While they are gathering, they send David back to Ziklag (29:4).[64] When David comes to Ziklag on the third day after the Philistine-Israeli battle in which Saul and Jonathan perish, he finds it burned and the inhabitants—including David's wives—captured (30:1–5). The people with David are ready to stone him, but he strengthens himself in God and leads the people to kill the Amalekite raiders and recapture the women and children (30:6–29). Having taken captivity captive, David sends gifts to Israel (30:26–31). So as David is glorifying God by relying upon him and bringing salvation to Israel through the judgment of the Amalekites, God is glorifying himself by delivering Israel from wicked king Saul through the justice visited when Saul takes his own life (1 Samuel 31).

2.4.3.3 Kingdom and Covenant. Second Samuel opens with David's lament for Saul and Jonathan (2 Sam. 1:17–27). This is the second of three key poems in the book of Samuel, and this middle poem matches the first one that Hannah sang in 1 Samuel 2:1–10. Hannah's song celebrated the way the Lord raises up the needy and puts down the proud. The song at the opening of 2 Samuel, David's lament for Saul and Jonathan, is the noble reaction of a needy one who has been raised

[63]See further my essay, "The Typology of David's Rise to Power: Messianic Patterns in the Book of Samuel."
[64]See Yael Shemesh, "David in the Service of King Achish of Gath: Renegade to His People or a Fifth Column in the Philistine Army?" *VT* 57 (2007): 73–90.

up, to the death of proud Saul, who has been put down. The reversal promised in Hannah's song is honored and commemorated in David's lament.

David is anointed king over Judah (2 Sam. 2:1–7), but then Abner and Ish-bosheth wickedly rebel against Yahweh's anointed. With no word from the Lord and no prophetic anointing of Ish-bosheth, Abner nevertheless makes him king (2:8–11). It seems that his name has been altered from Ish-baal (see 1 Chron. 8:33) to Ish-bosheth, which means "man of shame," and shameful it is to set oneself up as rival king to Yahweh's anointed. Abner's actions result in war (2 Sam. 2:12–3:6), but then Ish-bosheth accuses Abner of an indiscretion (3:7–8), in response to which Abner promises to "accomplish for David what Yahweh has sworn to him" (3:9). Abner's experience of the treachery of those who oppose Yahweh (judgment) forces him to join those pursuing what he knows Yahweh intends to do (salvation). The judgment of the wicked saves Abner. But not for long. Abner is soon murdered by Joab (3:26–30). Then Ish-bosheth is also murdered (4:1–8). The death of an opposing general and a rival claimant to the throne (judgment) mark David's ascension to the throne (salvation), but David has nothing to do with these murders. Indeed, David rebukes Joab and punishes Ish-bosheth's killers (3:31–39; 4:9–12).

Through the judgment that falls on Abner and Ish-bosheth, David becomes king over Israel and Judah (2 Sam. 5:1–5). He then takes Jerusalem from the Jebusites (5:6–9); Yahweh's presence with him makes him greater and greater (5:10); and in the strength of Yahweh he defeats the Philistines (5:17–25). David transports the ark into Jerusalem[65] (6:1–23), and Yahweh gives him rest (7:1).

This rest that David experiences has Edenic connotations, as do the references to Yahweh's "moving about" among the people in 2 Samuel 7:6–7.[66] David's rest, mentioned in 7:1, appears to trigger the desire to build the temple, mentioned in 7:2.[67] This is significant because it connects David's understanding of his role in God's purposes with Adam's role in God's purposes. Adam's responsibility is to "subdue the earth," which appears to refer to the expansion of the borders of the cosmic temple of Eden to cause the glory of God to cover the dry land as the realm in which God dwells expands. David's desire to build a temple in

[65]For God's glory in salvation through judgment against Uzzah, see the discussion of the parallel passage in Chronicles in chap. 4, §4.4.3.

[66]The same Hebrew verb in the same stem is used to describe Yahweh walking in the garden in the cool of the day in Gen. 3:8 (cf. Lev. 26:11–12; Deut. 23:14).

[67]Niehaus (*Ancient Near Eastern Themes in Biblical Theology*, 30) argues that "a shared theological structure of ideas existed in the ancient Near East, a structure that finds its most complete and true form in the Old and New Testaments. The basic structure of ideas is this: A god works through a man (a royal or prophetic figure, often styled a shepherd) to wage war against the god's enemies and thereby advance his kingdom. The royal or prophetic protagonist is in a covenant with the god, as are the god's people. The god establishes a temple among his people . . . because he wants to dwell among them. This can mean the founding (or choice) of a city, as well as a temple location. The ultimate purpose is to bring into the god's kingdom those who were not part of it." We can add that the Bible presents an ultimate purpose beyond God's bringing those outside his kingdom into it: namely, that they glorify him for who he is.

2 Samuel 7:2 seems to point to his desire to establish the place where God will cause his name to dwell, a place referred to often in Deuteronomy. David also seems to have set himself to the Adamic task of expanding the borders of the new Eden, the land of Israel (2 Samuel 8–10).[68]

Yahweh does not permit David to build the house, and instead promises to build David's house (2 Sam. 7:4–17). David's response to Yahweh's astonishing promises in 2 Samuel 7 is instructive. David recognizes that what Yahweh has promised to him is mercy:

> And what more can David say to you? For you know your servant, O Lord Yahweh! Because of your promise, and according to your own heart, you have brought about all this greatness . . . . Therefore you are great, O Lord Yahweh. For there is none like you, and there is no God besides you, according to all that we have heard with our ears. (2 Sam. 7:20–22)

David states in verse 21 that the reason Yahweh has blessed him is "because of your promise," probably referring to God's promise to Abraham, and "according to your own heart," meaning that Yahweh has done what he chose to do, not what he was obligated to do. It also seems that "according to your own heart" refers to the way that Yahweh brings down the proud while exalting the humble (1 Sam. 2:1–10), using the weak to thwart the strong.[69] God is pleased to use the weak and foolish to accomplish his purposes, thereby condemning the strong and proud. David's emphasis on the Lord's mercy is also reminiscent of Yahweh's statement to Moses that he shows mercy and compassion to whomever he pleases (Ex. 33:19). The author of Samuel presents David as recognizing why Yahweh has done what he has done, and the purpose given is that Yahweh might make a great name for himself (2 Sam. 7:23), a name that will be magnified forever (7:26). Yahweh mercifully promises to build David a house (7:1–16), and David recognizes that Yahweh's self-revelation is mercy (7:18–29, esp. 27), which means that the revelation of Yahweh's merciful character, his name, has evoked praise from David.[70]

David's praise for Yahweh furthers the theme of the glory of God in salvation through judgment, for it is David's understanding of the uniqueness of Yahweh

[68]See further Peter J. Gentry, "Rethinking the 'Sure Mercies of David' in Isaiah 55:3," *WTJ* 69 (2007): 282–88.

[69]This idea should probably inform the statement in 1 Sam. 13:14 that Yahweh sought a man "according to his own heart." Thus, it is not David's heart but Yahweh's purpose that is in view. David confesses in 2 Sam. 7:21 that Yahweh has acted "according to his own heart," meaning according to his own purpose, and the Hebrew expression is the same in the two texts. I think this fits with the citation in Acts 13:22, which can also be read to mean God chose David according to his own purpose. Another instance of this expression in Samuel is when Jonathan is told to act "according to your own heart," meaning according to his stated intentions, in 1 Sam. 14:7.

[70]For the idea that the temple is built for Yahweh's name in the sense of his *reputation* as opposed to the notion of "Name Theology" as understood by proponents of the Deuteronomistic History (where Yahweh himself is not in the temple, but his Name, which is something of a hypostasis, is there), see Richter, *The Deuteronomistic History and the Name Theology*, 69–75.

(2 Sam. 7:22) that sends him out to subjugate the nations to Yahweh. The next chapter shows that while David does not build the temple, he does pursue the task of taking the nations as his inheritance (cf. Ps. 2:8). David defeats the Philistines to the southwest (2 Sam. 8:1), Moab and Edom to the southeast (8:2, 13–14), and Zobah and Syria to the north (8:3–8). Hamath hears and sends tribute to David (8:9–10), and David dedicates the spoil of these victories to Yahweh for the future building of the temple (8:11–12). Twice in chapter 8 the narrator states that Yahweh "gave victory to David wherever he went" (8:6, 14 ESV).[71] David then shows kindness to Mephibosheth (2 Samuel 9) and conquers Ammon and Syria (2 Samuel 10).[72]

David has risen to power. The Lord has finally delivered him from Saul and all his enemies, promising him a lasting dynasty. On the strength of those promises, David has begun to subdue the nations round about, acting as God's representative who delivers the people of God by visiting justice on their enemies. And then something happens that serves as a warning to all who enjoy prosperity and blessing.

2.4.3.4 Sin and Its Consequences. David has been raised up as a new Adam in a new Eden, and tragically he falls prey to a new temptation that sets the nation on a path to a new exile from the place where God dwells. David despises the word of Yahweh (2 Sam. 12:9) by the way he treats Uriah and Bathsheba (11:1–27). Yahweh promises David through Nathan, "The sword will never depart from your house" (12:10), and "I will raise up evil against you out of your own house. And I will take your wives . . . and give them to your neighbor, and he shall lie with your wives in the sight of this sun" (12:11). Nathan also promises that the child will die (12:14).

The rest of 2 Samuel glorifies Yahweh by showing him faithful to these promises. Even with David Yahweh plays no favorites. His justice is as exact with his chosen and anointed king as it is with anyone else. The child dies (12:18), and the sword is raised up against David from within his own house: David's son Amnon rapes his half sister Tamar (2 Sam. 13:14). David does not do what the law would seem to require—either stone Amnon or require him to marry Tamar, never to divorce her (cf. Deut. 22:25–29). So Absalom, Tamar's brother, kills Amnon (2 Sam. 13:28–29). For this, Absalom deserves to die (Ex. 21:12; Lev. 24:17; Num. 35:30; Deut. 19:11–13). When Absalom returns to Jerusalem, he steals the hearts of the people (2 Sam. 15:6), and David must flee when Absalom

[71]The phrase "gave victory" is the ESV rendering of the hiphil forms of the verb ישׁע, "save"; so also HCSB, NIV, while the NASB renders this "helped," and the NKJV has "preserved."

[72]Many interpreters see the two lists of court officials (2 Sam. 8:15–18; 20:23–26) as marking the end of two sections. I recognize the appeal of this division, but it seems to me that chapters 9–10 fit better with what goes before than with the sin and its consequences that follow in chapters 11–20.

seizes the kingdom (15:10–14). David leaves ten concubines in Jerusalem (15:16), whom Absalom "went in to . . . in the sight of all Israel" (16:22). Absalom is an agent of God's justice against David, but at the same time Absalom is a rebel against Yahweh's anointed king. Absalom dies (18:14–15). David is then faced with civil war (20:1–2), but this is soon resolved. God's justice has been severe against David. He has been saved through it, but in many ways his life has been made miserable by God's justice against his sins.

Yahweh is merciful, but he is not indulgent toward sin. He is loving and patient, but he is not unjust. David suffers the just consequences of his sin, but he confesses his sin, repents, and worships the Lord (2 Sam. 12:13, 16, 20). Through the judgment, David's sin has been addressed, and his repentance and reliance upon Yahweh results in mercy. God is glorified in salvation through judgment.

2.4.3.5 The Site of the Temple. The final chapters of Samuel form a widely acknowledged chiasm (see table 3.4).

Table 3.4. Chiastic Structure in 2 Samuel 21–24

21:1–14, The Lord's wrath
  21:15–22, David's mighty men
    22:1–23:7, David's praise and last words
  23:8–39, David's mighty men
24:1–25, The Lord's wrath

This literary structure highlights David's praise of Yahweh in the central section, and it also draws attention to the matching sets of mighty men and the Lord's wrath in the two famine stories. I would suggest that reading the two stories of God's wrath against Israel in light of one another allows them to be mutually interpretive of one another.

In the first story of God's wrath on Israel (2 Sam. 21:1–14), David goes to Yahweh to determine the cause of the famine (21:1), and then he goes to the Gibeonites to determine its remedy (21:2–3). The Gibeonites call for the death of seven men from Saul's house (21:4–6). It seems significant that the text attributes God's mercy in lifting the famine not to the justice visited upon these descendants of Saul but to the "plea for the land" (21:14, cf. NASB "entreaty," NIV "prayer").[73] When we compare this with the second story of famine, when the prophet sets the various options before David, David's response in 24:14 is perhaps influenced by his experience with the severe vengeance demanded by

[73]Similarly Frank Thielman, "The Atonement," in Hafemann and House, *Central Themes in Biblical Theology*, 105.

the Gibeonites: "Let us fall into the hand of Yahweh, for his mercy is great, but into the hand of man let me not fall!" In both accounts of God's wrath on Israel, the justice God visits against the nation brings them back to himself. They are saved through his judgment.

The accounts of David's mighty men (2 Sam. 21:15–22; 23:8–39) show the triumph of those who rely on Yahweh and seek to advance Yahweh's kingdom, and this is also a main theme of the third and final poem of Samuel. Hannah's poem at the beginning of Samuel announced the reversals that would be seen throughout the book. David's lament for Saul in the middle of the book marked the story's most significant reversal—Saul made low and David exalted. And the third and final poem, in 2 Samuel 22 (cf. Psalm 18), shows Yahweh's humble, reliant servant, David, crying out for help (2 Sam. 22:1–7). Yahweh is then depicted as a divine warrior, rising to help the one who cries to him (22:8–16). And then the recipient of Yahweh's help sings the deliverance of Yahweh (22:17–46), concluding with praise in response to the way that Yahweh has saved him through the judgment of his enemies (22:47–51). Yahweh's king is mighty *because he relies on Yahweh*, which glorifies Yahweh, who saves his people through the judgment of their enemies.

The book of Samuel ends by setting up the story of the building of the temple as David acquires the threshing floor of Araunah (2 Samuel 24). In this remarkable passage, "the anger of Yahweh was kindled against Israel, and he incited David against them, saying 'Go, number Israel and Judah'" (2 Sam. 24:1). In the parallel account in 1 Chronicles 21:1 we read, "Then Satan stood against Israel and incited David to number Israel." The Chronicler appears to have interpreted 2 Samuel 24:1 to mean that Yahweh used Satan to accomplish his purpose as he did with Job. Yahweh did not tempt David to sin (cf. James 1:13), Satan did, but not apart from God's ultimate purposes (cf. Rev. 17:17). In this instance, Yahweh uses Satan to set up a situation in which he will display his justice and his mercy. The numbering of the people originates in Yahweh's purpose to discipline Israel, but David is responsible for his actions, especially since he rejects Joab's attempt to deter him (2 Sam. 24:3–4).[74] David recognizes that he has sinned and pleads with Yahweh to take away his iniquity (24:10). The word of Yahweh's justice comes through the prophet Gad (24:11–13). Yahweh will be just and punish David's sin, but in choosing his punishment David says, "Let us fall into the hand of Yahweh, for his mercy is great; but let me not fall into the hand of man" (24:14). David knows that Yahweh is going to punish him justly, but he also knows that Yahweh is merciful. Seventy thousand die from Dan to Beersheba (24:15), but then Yahweh relents as the angel stretches out his hand

[74]See Carson's discussion, *Divine Sovereignty and Human Responsibility*, 11–12, 224.

toward Jerusalem (24:16). In this account, as in all of Samuel, Yahweh's majestic holiness is displayed in terrifying justice that highlights his tender mercy.

2.4.4 The Center of the Theology of Samuel

The story of 1 and 2 Samuel is an account of the glory of Yahweh in salvation through judgment. Through the judgment that falls on the wicked sons of Eli, on the nation that rejected the Lord, and on the proud king like the nations, salvation is brought through King David. David rises as a new Adam in a new Eden. Reigning from Zion, he begins to pursue the task of spreading the knowledge of the glory of God. Doing so means bringing God's justice on surrounding nations, and through the judgment of conquest, those nations experience deliverance from their false gods and are introduced to the law of the one true God. The narrative is designed, however, to show that what was true of Adam is also true of David. Not very much time passes, in terms of narrative space, in the pursuit of the program of spreading God's glory before the new Adam in the new Eden has a new fall. David's sin with Bathsheba is the nation's first step in the direction of exile, and his transgression sets the trajectory of trespass that leads straight to Babylon. God's justice is visited as David's sons exaggerate his sins. David committed adultery and murder. The adultery is aggravated by Amnon's rape of Tamar, and the murder by Absalom's treacherous fratricide in the murder of Amnon, a recapitulation of what took place with Cain and Abel. Through this justice, however, mercy comes, as it is the wife of Uriah who gives birth to the one named Jedidiah (2 Sam. 12:25), "beloved of Yahweh," Solomon. The story of Samuel is a story of God being glorified in salvation that comes through judgment.

2.5 Kings

Like Samuel, Kings was originally one book.[75] As Iain Provan has written, "The primary theological theme in Kings is Israel's God as the true and only God."[76] The one true God of Israel reveals himself in Kings as the God who keeps his promises—promises to save and promises to judge. The story of God's glory in salvation through judgment in Kings begins with David still on the throne but near death. David passes the kingdom to Solomon, who brings judgment on David's enemies (1 Kings 1–2). It is almost as though Solomon purges the land of serpents. Solomon receives a divine gift of wisdom to reign righteously, builds the temple, then has his heart turned away by his many wives (1 Kings 3–11). The kingdom is split after Solomon, and the slow march toward exile, in

[75]Mordechai Cogan (*1 Kings*, AB [New York: Doubleday, 2001], 84) writes, "Not until the printing of the *Bomberg Rabbinic Bible* (Venice, 1517) was the division into two books introduced into Jewish tradition. . . . Within Greek tradition, Samuel and Kings were considered a continuous work, and they were divided into the four books of 'Kingdoms.'"

[76]I. W. Provan, "Kings," in *NDBT*, 183.

spite of the efforts of Elijah and Elisha, arrives at the destruction of the northern kingdom of Israel (1 Kings 12—2 Kings 17). Judah continues in the land, experiences revival, but then reverts to wickedness and is exiled from the land (2 Kings 18–25).[77] God glorifies himself by keeping his promises to his people in Kings. He preserves the line of David, and he also visits justice against sin. At the beginning of Kings, Israel is in the land, her wisest king ruling and building the temple. At the end of Kings, God's justice has been visited, the people are in exile, and the temple has been destroyed. God has kept his promises, and in his freedom he has judged his wayward people. Kings nevertheless ends with hope for the future, hope that through the judgment of the exile salvation might come for the glory of God.

2.5.1 David and His Sons

The account of the tumultuous circumstances of Solomon's becoming king includes three different tellings of Adonijah's subversive feast (1 Kings 1:9–10, 18–19, 25–26). These three reports of what Adonijah does are matched by three announcements of the anointing of Solomon (1:32–35, 38–40, 43–46). The rejection of Adonijah (judgment) is coordinate with the enthronement of Solomon (salvation—Solomon's life is at stake), and this results in glory for Yahweh: "And the king [David] bowed himself on the bed and the king also said, 'Blessed be Yahweh, the God of Israel, who has granted one to sit on my throne this day, my own eyes seeing it'" (1:47–48). David's final words to Solomon (2:2–4) recall the Mosaic instructions for Israel's king (Deut. 17:14–20), echo the charge Joshua received (Josh. 1:6–9), allude to the promises made to David (2 Sam. 7:12–16), and are reminiscent of the description of the blessed man in Psalm 1.

The book of Kings shows that though Yahweh brought judgment upon Israel, he nevertheless remained faithful to the promises he made to them. David is presented as interpreting Yahweh's promises to him (2 Samuel 7) when he tells Solomon that he is to walk in Yahweh's ways "as written in the Torah of Moses" (1 Kings 2:3; cf. Deut. 17:14–20) "that Yahweh may establish his word which he spoke concerning me, saying, 'If your sons keep their ways to walk before me

[77]The discussion here will follow the breakdown of the material just articulated (1 Kings 1–2, David; 1 Kings 3–11, Solomon; 1 Kings 12—2 Kings 17, divided kingdom; 2 Kings 18–25, Judah), but both George Savran ("1 and 2 Kings," in *The Literary Guide to the Bible*, ed. R. Alter and F. Kermode [Cambridge, MA: Harvard University Press, 1987], 148) and Bruce Waltke (*An Old Testament Theology*, 693, 704) offer the following chiastic arrangement of 1–2 Kings:

- A Solomon/united monarchy, 1 Kings 1:1–11:25
  - B Jeroboam/Rehoboam; division of kingdom, 1 Kings 11:26–14:31
    - C Kings of Judah/Israel, 1 Kings 15:1–16:22
      - D Omride dynasty, 1 Kings 16:23—2 Kings 12
    - C′ Kings of Judah/Israel, 2 Kings 13–16
  - B′ Fall of northern kingdom, 2 Kings 17
- A′ Kingdom of Judah, 2 Kings 18–25

in truth with their whole heart and their whole soul,' saying, 'there shall not be cut off for you a man from the throne of Israel'" (1 Kings 2:4).[78] Throughout the book of Kings, the kings of Israel are evaluated as to whether they walk in the way of David and whether their hearts are whole toward Yahweh. Paul House puts his finger on a significant contrast between David and his sons: "Of all the personal flaws David exhibits and all the problems he encounters, none is a result of idolatry."[79]

David's final instructions to Solomon are also instructions regarding judgment. Judgment is due to Joab and Shimei (1 Kings 2:5–6, 8–9), and mixed into the middle is the loyalty Solomon must show to Barzillai the Gileadite (2:7).

2.5.2 Solomon, Temple, Idolatry

Solomon's establishment as king of Israel amounts to the saving of his life and the life of his mother (cf. 1 Kings 1:12). In the early days of Solomon's reign judgment falls upon Adonijah (2:25), Joab (2:28–34), and Shimei (2:36–46). Adonijah's crafty solicitation of help from Bathsheba (2:13–25) is like the serpent's temptation of Eve (Gen. 3:1–7). Rather than openly attacking the man in charge, both the serpent and Adonijah approach a beloved female. Both the serpent and Adonijah seek to subvert God's kingdom and rule. Both the serpent and Adonijah are able to persuade the beloved female. Eve ate the fruit, and Bathsheba takes the insidious request to Solomon (1 Kings 2:17–20). Here, however, is where the typological correspondence between Adam and Solomon takes a decisive turn: Adam ate the fruit with no objection, but though Solomon has sworn not to refuse his mother (2:19), he does so, recognizing that Adonijah is seeking to gain for himself the kingdom (2:22). Adam ate the fruit and was expelled from the garden-temple, barred from the tree of life in the garden of God. Adam let the serpent live and was expelled from the dwelling of God. Solomon, by contrast, puts Adonijah to death (2:23–25) and goes on to build the temple, establishing the presence of God among Israel and making the land the realm of life.[80] Salvation for Solomon comes through judgment on Adonijah, and the glory of God inhabits the temple.

Solomon is also saved through judgment against the nations as the land is subdued and he exercises "dominion over all the region west of the Euphrates from Tiphsah to Gaza, over all the kings west of the Euphrates. And he had peace on all sides around him" (1 Kings 5:4, ET 4:24; cf. 5:1, ET 4:21). As Solomon reigns in messianic grandeur, every man under his own vine and fig tree (5:5, ET 4:25),

[78]For helpful discussion of the expectations that attend David and his seed being in a Father-son relationship with Yahweh, see Gentry, "Rethinking the 'Sure Mercies of David' in Isaiah 55:3," 282–86.
[79]House, *Old Testament Theology*, 251.
[80]Cf. Richter, *The Deuteronomistic History and the Name Theology*, 55: "It is possible to speak of the deity's entire land-holdings by means of speaking of the critical center of them, the temple. This is particularly evident in Ex. 15:17 in which the promised land is spoken of as the 'sanctuary which your hands have established.'"

he images God in Adamic proportions. Like Adam he exercises dominion over the created order: as Adam named the animals, Solomon "spoke of trees . . . of animals, of birds, of creeping things, and of fish" (5:13, ET 4:33; cf. Gen. 1:26; 2:20). Solomon's blessed messianic peace glorifies God, who gave him wisdom and breadth of mind (5:9, ET 4:29), blessing him with all he asked for and more (3:9–13). Yahweh's glory shines in salvation through judgment in the triumph of Israel over her enemies and the Solomonic splendor she enjoyed. Even Hiram the Gentile blesses Yahweh because of Solomon (5:21, ET 5:7).

Solomon is thus depicted as a new Adam who overcomes the temptation of the serpentine Adonijah and takes up the task of ruling over the earth and subduing it, extending the realm of Yahweh's dominion that the glory of the Lord might cover the dry land as the waters cover the sea.[81] This task he pursues particularly through the building of the temple (1 Kings 6–7). Once built, the temple is crowned with the glory of Yahweh's presence: "A cloud filled the house of Yahweh, so that the priests could not stand to minister because of the cloud, for the glory of Yahweh filled the house of Yahweh" (1 Kings 8:10–11). Solomon then blesses Yahweh for keeping his promises (8:15–21), extols Yahweh's uniqueness (8:23), and calls on Yahweh to hear prayer for his own glory: "Hear in heaven your dwelling place . . . in order that all the peoples of the earth may know your name and fear you, as do your people Israel, and that they may know that this house that I have built is called by your name" (8:43).[82] After he blesses Yahweh again (8:56–58), Solomon prays that his petition will be heard so "that all the peoples of the earth may know that Yahweh is God; there is no other" (8:60). As Solomon offers sacrifices (8:5, 62–63) and stands "before the altar," he almost functions as a priest[83] (and cf. 2 Sam. 8:18, "David's sons were priests," ESV).[84] Moreover, he is interceding for the people (1 Kings 8:22–60) in prophetic terms (note the prayers prophesying Israel's sin, exile, and redemption in 8:46–53). Solomon thus stands as a new Adam, filling the roles of prophet, priest, and king.

Even the Queen of Sheba blesses Yahweh because of the fame of Solomon (1 Kings 10:1, 9). And then things go bad. Just as David was faithful and honorable when he was dodging Saul's spears and fleeing from cave to cave, so Solomon appears to have been faithful while occupied with the grand task of temple building. Just as David sinned with Bathsheba when he was established as

[81]See appendix 2 (§6) to this chapter, "All the Earth Filled with the Knowledge of Yahweh's Glory."

[82]On the point that in 1 Kings 8 there are not competing ideas—an older tradition of Yahweh himself being in the temple, which is "corrected" by the Deuteronomic idea that only Yahweh's "name" is in the temple, see Richter, *The Deuteronomistic History and the Name Theology*, 76–90. She writes, "As we discussed regarding 2 Samuel 7, the particular 'name' idiom . . . reflects the establishing of a memorial in order to perpetuate a reputation" (79).

[83]So also Dumbrell, *The Faith of Israel*, 92.

[84]For discussion, see Eugene H. Merrill, "Royal Priesthood: An Old Testament Motif," *Bibliotheca Sacra* 150 (1993): 50–61, esp. 60–61.

king and enjoyed a certain amount of rest, so Solomon, once the temple and his palaces are built, multiplies wives who turn his heart away. Solomon conquered the temptation that came from Adonijah through Bathsheba, but his palace becomes infested with the seed of the serpent—hundreds of foreign wives—and Solomon, like Adam and David before him, falls.[85]

2.5.3 Divided Kingdom

After Solomon's death, his son Rehoboam reigns in his place. Whereas Israel was explicitly commanded not to intermarry with the people of the land (Deut. 7:3–4), when Rehoboam comes to the throne, the nation receives a king whose mother was an Ammonitess (1 Kings 14:21, 31). This observation raises a significant point in the interpretation of these narratives: the narrative records events from a perspective that assumes the teaching of Torah.[86] While the perspective of Torah is assumed, transgressions of Torah are generally not explicitly noted. In order to understand Kings, however, readers must be aware of the terms of the covenant in order to see the justification for the visitation of the curses of the covenant. It seems that what the author of Kings has chosen to include is largely informed by the teaching of Torah, such that while the law of the king in Deuteronomy 17:14–20 is not overtly mentioned, 1 Kings 10:14–11:8 shows Solomon breaking these laws point for point (horses, wives, excessive silver and gold, disregard for the Torah he was to copy and keep).

Yahweh judges Solomon for his sin: the rending of the kingdom from the house of David is something that comes from the Lord (1 Kings 12:15, 22–24). Ten tribes in the north follow Jeroboam as their king.

In overt defiance of Yahweh's law, Jeroboam invents his own, self-made religion (1 Kings 12:28–33). He does this to keep the northern tribes from traveling regularly to Jerusalem, lest their hearts revert to the house of David (12:26–27). Jeroboam places his desire to keep the kingdom over fidelity to the one who made him king (cf. 11:29–39). Not only does Jeroboam desire his kingdom more than he desires to please Yahweh, but he desires his kingdom more than he cares for the faithfulness of Yahweh's people. This is the meaning of the damning refrain that repeatedly declares that Jeroboam made the people of Israel commit sin (e.g., 1 Kings 14:16; 15:25–26, 30, 34; 16:2; 2 Kings 13:2; 15:28, etc.).

The dramatic account in 1 Kings 13 serves as an illustration of the state of the whole nation. Israel received a clear word from Yahweh in the Torah. The

---

[85]This is a point of speculation, but I nevertheless put it forward: if the Jewish tradition that Solomon wrote Ecclesiastes *in his old age* is correct, that document would appear to indicate that Solomon repented of his idolatry and committed himself to fearing Yahweh and keeping his commandments. Cf. Duane A. Garrett, *Proverbs, Ecclesiastes, Song of Songs*, NAC (Nashville: Broadman, 1993), 277–79.

[86]In this usage of the term "Torah" I am not necessarily limiting its referent to the Pentateuch. The Pentateuch would be prominent, but it seems to me that the author of Kings assumes as much as has been revealed of the Old Testament at the time that he writes. Cf. Clements, "A Royal Privilege," 54.

man of God who denounces Jeroboam's altar also received a clear word. He was to denounce Jeroboam's altar, eat no bread, drink no water, nor return by the way he came (13:9). He obeys, but he is accosted by an old prophet, who lies to him and leads him to do exactly what he has been commanded not to do (13:10–19). Just as Jeroboam makes up his own religion with his own priests, his own sacrifices, his own symbols, his own appointed feasts (12:28–33), so also the old prophet makes up his own "revelation" from Yahweh (13:18). Just as the man of God who denounces the altar of Jeroboam should not listen to the old prophet who is lying to him, so also Israel should not follow Jeroboam into the worship of lies. Just as the man of God who denounces Jeroboam's altar is torn by a lion (13:23–25), Israel's true prophets announce that she will be torn by a lion, Yahweh (Hos. 5:14; Joel 3:16; Amos 1:2). The Lion of the Tribe of Judah will judge them that he might save them. First Kings 13:33–34 connects what happens between the man of God and the old prophet to the sin of Jeroboam, forming an *inclusio* with the description of Jeroboam's homemade religion in 12:28–33 and stating that because they refuse to turn from sin, Jeroboam's dynasty will be destroyed (13:34).

The narrative of the divided kingdom not only is marked by self-made religion but also has self-made kings, as the northern kingdom experiences assassinations and conspiracies that cause dynasty after dynasty to fall.[87] The houses of Jeroboam, Baasha, and Ahab all fall under the same curse (1 Kings 14:11; 16:4; 21:24). The Lord preserves his remnant, seven thousand who have not bowed to Baal (19:18), and the means of this preservation is, in part, the ministry of the prophets Elijah and Elisha.[88]

The Lord gives programmatic instructions to Elijah when he tells him to anoint Hazael over Syria, Jehu over Israel, and Elisha in his own place (1 Kings 19:15–16). The statement "The one who escapes from the sword of Hazael shall Jehu put to death, and the one who escapes from the sword of Jehu shall Elisha put to death" (19:17 ESV) makes clear that these three are appointed for judgment on the northern kingdom. Through this judgment, however, Yahweh also works salvation, for it is the next verse in which he declares that he will preserve his remnant that will not bow to Baal (19:18).

The judgment that falls in these narratives comes because Jeroboam "provoked Yahweh God of Israel" (1 Kings 15:30), as did Baasha (16:2, 7, 13), Omri (16:26), Ahab (16:33; 21:22), and Ahaziah (22:53). Idolatry is provocation because it gives what is due to Yahweh, worship, to those who are not worthy of worship. Not

[87]Cf. the poetic commentary on this in Hos. 8:4, "They made kings, but not through me. They set up princes, but I knew it not. With their silver and gold they made idols for their own destruction" (ESV).

[88]See the intriguing presentation concluding that "perhaps in Elisha we are also witnessing a transitional figure, a royal—and perhaps even a priestly—prophet," in W. Brian Aucker, "A Prophet in King's Clothes: Kingly and Divine Re-presentation in 2 Kings 4 and 5," in Rezetko, Lim, and Aucker, *Reflection and Refraction*, 25. For a brief but stimulating discussion of typology in Kings, see Provan, "Kings," in *NDBT*, 187–88.

only does this deny Yahweh the glory due his name, but idolatry also corrupts and destroys those who engage in it.[89] Yahweh is thus provoked because of his supreme love for himself and because of his concern for what is good for his people. Idolatry corrupts and destroys lives, and Yahweh is too righteous to be so unconcerned that he does not discipline. The discipline is meant to lead to salvation. And the salvation through judgment in these narratives has the same end we have seen elsewhere: that people may know Yahweh (cf. 18:21, 36–37; 20:13, 28). Those who know Yahweh glorify him.

Yahweh's patience and mercy are almost beyond belief. Ahab is repeatedly said to have done more evil than all who were before him (1 Kings 16:33; 21:25), and yet he repents in response to Elijah's rebuke (21:20–27). Astonishingly, the Lord defers the calamity due to Ahab's house to the days of his sons in response to Ahab's repentance (21:28–29). Justice will be done, but there is mercy in the delay of justice. Nor is this unfair to Ahab's sons; they will get their just deserts.

God's glory in judgment is seen not only in military defeat. God is glorious, and his laws teach the way of life. Those who do not walk in the way of life find their lives ruined, and that ruination takes shape in all manner of alienation and misery. The sins of the fathers are visited upon their descendants (Ex. 34:7), and the son of Jeroboam dies (1 Kings 14:17). There is mercy in his death, though, because unlike the rest of Jeroboam's house he will not be eaten by dogs or birds (14:11–13).

Whereas Israel was to annihilate the peoples of the land and rely on Yahweh alone, even the good King Asa of Judah, when threatened by Baasha of Israel, cries out for help to the king of Syria (1 Kings 15:16–19)! Not only has Asa not relied upon Yahweh, but he is at war with other Israelites. Not only is he at war with other Israelites, but he forms an alliance with non-Israelites against Israelites (15:20–21). This is not an isolated instance of what would have been unthinkable to Joshua's generation. Failure to trust in and obey Yahweh brings about Yahweh's justice, and Yahweh's justice comes in surprising and appropriate ways.

Kings provides a study in contrast between the ways the kings of Israel provoke Yahweh to wrath over against the ways Yahweh provides mercy and salvation to those who fear and honor him. A famine comes at the word of Elijah (1 Kings 17:1), but the Lord provides for Elijah (17:2–7) and for the widow of Zarephath (17:8–16). The author of Kings seems to be making the point that those who rely on the human power of other nations will be judged, while those who rely on Yahweh will be saved and provided for against all odds.

The children of the wicked die, but Elijah raises up the dead son of the widow of Zarephath (1 Kings 17:17–23). The woman acknowledges the truth of Elijah's

[89]For this theme, see G. K. Beale, *We Become What We Worship: A Biblical Theology of Idolatry* (Downers Grove, IL: InterVarsity, 2008).

word (17:24), something the wicked queen in Israel, Jezebel, will not do (cf. 19:2). The prophets of Baal can accomplish nothing (18:23–29), but Yahweh can and does answer prayer (18:30–38). Significantly, the prayer of Elijah is similar to the prayers of Moses, Joshua, David, and Solomon, all of whom prayed for Yahweh to be concerned for his own reputation and glorify himself (Ex. 32:12; Num. 14:13–19; Josh. 7:9; 2 Sam. 7:26; 1 Kings 8:43, 60).[90] Elijah prays, "O Yahweh, God of Abraham, Isaac, and Israel, let it be known today that you are God in Israel and I am your servant. . . . Answer me, O Yahweh! Answer me that this people may know that you are Yahweh, the God . . ." (1 Kings 18:36–37). The faithful in the Old Testament consistently pray for God to glorify himself, and God consistently answers these prayers. In this instance with Elijah, the fire falls in response to Elijah's prayer and the people cry, "Yahweh, he is the God! Yahweh, he is the God!" (18:38–39). God glorifies himself by answering Elijah's prayer, and then Elijah calls for judgment on the prophets of Baal. They are seized, taken to the Brook Kishon, and executed (18:40). Salvation comes through judgment for the glory of God.

Those who do not trust Yahweh do not honor him, and Yahweh's judgment is to orchestrate events such that those who refuse to honor him suffer the loss of all things (cf. Deut. 28:15–68). The narrative of Kings demonstrates this in the futility of the wretched lives of the sinful kings. By contrast, those who trust the word of God manifested through the prophet Elisha have bad water made sweet (2 Kings 2:19–22; cf. Ex. 15:22–25). Those who mock the prophet of God are mauled by bears (2 Kings 2:23–24; cf. Hos. 13:8; Amos 5:19), but Jehoshaphat seeks the Lord through the prophet and is delivered (2 Kings 3:11–25).

The Lord is able to meet the needs of his people: a widow is provided with miraculous oil that her debts might be paid (2 Kings 4:1–7). The dead are raised by the mercy of God through the prophet's intercession (4:14–37). The death in the pot of poisoned stew is restored to sustaining nutrition by the prophet's intercession (4:38–41), and twenty loaves of barley feed one hundred men and leftovers remain (4:42–44). If the people will trust Yahweh, they will be saved by his power for his glory. The cleansing of Naaman the leper illustrates the humility necessary to submit to the prophetic word (5:1–19). Naaman initially refuses to do something so lowly as wash in the dirty waters of Jordan (5:12), but once he humbles himself and is cleansed, he confesses that "there is no God in all the earth except in Israel" (5:15).[91] This matches the question provoked by the faithlessness of the Israelites: "Where is Yahweh, the God of Elijah?!" (2:14;

[90] See further the appendix (§7) to chap. 4, table 4.9, "Old Testament Prayers Appealing to God's Concern for His Own Glory."

[91] On Naaman taking two mule-loads of earth to Syria and asking pardon for bowing in the house of Rimmon (2 Kings 5:17–19), Paul House observes (1) that Naaman has asked not for permission to worship Rimmon but only for pardon when he must perform duties related to his position, (2) that Naaman has stated his opinion of Rimmon and declared that he will worship only Yahweh, and (3) that with the loads of dirt Naaman appar-

cf. 3:11); and it is synonymous with Elisha's declaration that Naaman should come to him to "know that there is a prophet in Israel" (5:8). Yahweh's presence is mediated by the prophetic word, and one's response to that word determines whether one will be saved or judged.

A flood of images washes over the audience of Kings: Elisha's servant Gehazi is made leprous because he values Naaman's treasures more than walking with God in integrity (2 Kings 5:20–27); an axe head floats for those who cry out to the Lord and believe the prophetic word (6:1–6); unseen horses and chariots of fire protect Elisha from the seen army of Syria (6:8–17); kindness shown to captured enemies overcomes their hostility (6:18–23); the true prophet Elisha is blamed for the wretched desperation of the besieged city (6:24–33), but he is vindicated and his prophecy fulfilled when the Lord drives away the Syrian army and lepers find their camp deserted (7:1–20); the Shunammite woman appears before the king to petition for her land just when Gehazi tells the king how Elisha raised her son from the dead (8:1–6); at Elisha's word Ben-hadad, king of Syria, recovers and Hazael becomes king of Syria (8:7–15); King Jehoram does what is evil in the eyes of Yahweh and loses territory (8:16–24); Elisha anoints Jehu king over Israel, and Jehu promptly kills the reigning kings of Israel and Judah (8:25–9:29); Jehu then slays Jezebel (9:30–37), Ahab's seventy sons (10:1–11), Ahaziah's relatives (10:12–14), all who remained to Ahab (10:15–17), and all the worshipers of Baal (10:18–28), fulfilling the word of the Lord spoken by Elijah (10:10, 17); Jehu does not turn from Jeroboam's sin and the Lord cuts off parts of Israel (10:28–36); Ahaziah's mother Athaliah murders all the royal family[92]—except Joash, who escapes—and makes herself queen until Jehoida the priest installs Joash and brings justice against Athaliah (11:1–21); Joash (a.k.a. Jehoash) does what is right and repairs the temple (12:1–21); Jehoahaz does evil, comes under judgment, repents, and finds mercy (13:1–9); Elisha, the father of his people, the chariots of Israel and its horsemen, prophesies victory over Syria, dies, and when a dead man is placed in his tomb, Elisha's bones give him life (13:14–25);[93] Amaziah is a good king in Judah, but he is killed in civil war with Israel (14:1–22); a string of relatively short accounts of kings (14:23–15:38) precedes a longer account of Ahaz's apostasy (16:1–20); then the northern kingdom of Israel is captured by Assyria (17:1–6); a programmatic explanation of Israel's idolatry, rejection of Yahweh's prophets, and refusal to believe Yahweh follows (17:7–23);

---

ently intends to create sacred space to Yahweh in Syria (*1, 2 Kings*, NAC [Nashville: Broadman & Holman, 1995], 274).

[92]Dempster (*Dominion and Dynasty*, 152) draws attention to the similarity between this and Pharaoh's command to murder the male children of Israel. He comments, "This represents a struggle going back to the garden of Eden (Gen. 3:15)."

[93]Commenting on 2 Kings 13:20–21, where the dead man placed in Elisha's tomb is restored to life, Paul House (*1, 2 Kings*, 308) writes, "Elijah has gone to heaven without dying; Elisha has kept giving Israel life after he has died."

Assyria resettles the land of Israel with foreigners, and Yahweh sends lions among them—it is as though his holiness is breaking out against these unclean Gentiles (17:24–26); the Assyrians send a priest of Yahweh, but the nations resettled in the land continue in their idolatry (17:27–41).

This flood of images functions like a cloud of witnesses. They testify to the truth of God's word. They testify to the futility of relying upon anything other than Yahweh. They testify that Yahweh faithfully judges those who reject his word, and they testify that Yahweh saves those who trust his word and rely on him for deliverance. These witnesses give their testimony to the glory of God in salvation through judgment.

2.5.4 Judah

With the northern kingdom of Israel gone, the narrative of Kings continues its testimony to the glory of Yahweh in his righteousness and power to save. When Hezekiah is threatened by the Assyrians (2 Kings 18–19), he calls on the Lord in the same way that Elijah, Solomon, David, Joshua, and Moses did: appealing to Yahweh's concern for his great name.[94] Hezekiah extols Yahweh as God, sole Maker of heaven and earth (19:15), and then he prays that Yahweh would hear how Sennacherib has reproached him (19:16) and calls on Yahweh to deliver Judah from his hand "that all the kingdoms of the earth may know that you, Yahweh, are God alone" (19:19). Yahweh declares his glory in mind-elevating terms through the prophet Isaiah (19:20–34), concluding with the declaration, "For I will defend this city to save it for my own sake and for the sake of my servant David" (19:34). Hezekiah appeals to God's concern for his glory, and God answers for his own sake. Then the angel of Yahweh kills 185,000 in the Assyrian camp, Sennacherib goes home, and he is murdered by his own sons while worshiping in the temple of his god (19:35–37). Nisroch, Sennacherib's god, cannot defend his subjects, even in his own temple. Yahweh, by contrast, is able to defend his people. It is as though the stories of the kings are all given to establish the points made in this episode. Other nations and their gods are not to be looked to for deliverance, no matter how impressive they seem. Yahweh alone is to be trusted and called upon, no matter how impossible the situation may seem. When Yahweh's people rely upon him alone, he gets glory as they testify to his unique reliability, and he gets glory when he saves his people by judging their enemies. Yahweh shows his glory in salvation through judgment.

Yahweh adds fifteen years to Hezekiah's life, again declaring that he will defend Jerusalem for his own sake and for the sake of David (2 Kings 20:6; cf. 1–6), and then Hezekiah's son Manasseh comes to the throne. Manasseh does much evil and provokes Yahweh to anger (21:6; cf. 1–9), and Yahweh declares that he will bring

[94]See the appendix (§7) to chap. 4, table 4.9, "Old Testament Prayers Appealing to God's Concern for His Own Glory."

evil (translated "disaster"[95]) upon Jerusalem and Judah (21:12, 15, cf. 10–15). The evil of Manasseh is checked by the reforms of his grandson Josiah, who repairs the temple (22:5) and reforms the nation in accord with the rediscovered "Scroll of the Torah" (22:8–11; 22:14–23:14). In the process of the reforms, which includes destroying Jeroboam's altar at Bethel and burning the bones in the tombs on that mountain in fulfillment of the word the man of God proclaimed in 1 Kings 13 (2 Kings 22:15–16), Josiah finds the tomb of that man of God (22:17–18). This account demonstrates the fulfillment of that man of God's prophecy against Jeroboam's altar, and, if the suggestion that 1 Kings 13 is a picture of the nation as a whole is correct, the fulfillment of the word of the man of God reaffirms that God will also keep the promises he has made to the nation.

In spite of the fact that there is no king like Josiah, before or after him (2 Kings 23:25), Yahweh does not turn from the wrath aroused by Manasseh's provocations (23:26). The remaining lines of 2 Kings are like the "Dream of the Witch's Sabbath" in the fifth movement of Berlioz's *Symphonie fantastique*. Judah goes into exile. Judgment has fallen. John Barton writes:

> The whole Deuteronomistic History might similarly be regarded as a confession of national sin, and this is true whether it sees nothing beyond the disaster, as Noth thought, or holds out a hope for restoration, as argued by von Rad and Wolff. In telling the story of how Israel left Egypt for Canaan, but once there behaved in such a way that those who were not exiled to Babylon returned to Egypt (thus nullifying the exodus), the History expresses the conviction that Israel is a sinful people and deserves the punishment it has received from the hands of God.[96]

The people have been exiled from the land because Yahweh has kept the covenant he made with them at Sinai. As Eichrodt states, "All that survives the destruction of state and Temple is the God who is jealous for the honour of his Name."[97]

2.5.5 *The Center of the Theology of Kings*

Kings teaches the reliability of Yahweh's word, showing that those who reject that word are judged, while those who rely on it are saved. Yahweh is depicted in incomparable majesty. He reigns in the midst of his people from the temple Solomon built for him, and in the face of his holiness, before his very eyes, Israel and Judah provoke him to wrath. Yahweh shows astonishing mercy by forgiving those who repent and delivering those who call on him, but his judgment falls. He is faithful to his word, to truth, to the covenant he made. Then through the

[95] Cf. *HALOT*, 1262: "The distinction between the groups [of usage] subdivided below is often subjective and the transition from one to the other is fluid. The basic meaning . . . is probably 'that which is harmful.'"
[96] John Barton, "Historiography and Theodicy in the Old Testament," in Rezetko, Lim, and Aucker, *Reflection and Refraction*, 30. Similarly Dumbrell, *The Faith of Israel*, 104.
[97] Walther Eichrodt, *Theology of the Old Testament*, trans. J. A. Baker, 2 vols. (Philadelphia: Westminster, 1961, 1967), 1:60.

judgment, salvation comes. In exile, the captive king of Judah receives favor (2 Kings 25:27–30).[98] Perhaps the favor shown to Jehoiachin hints at the influence of Daniel in the Babylonian court. Perhaps it hints at the favor that will be shown in the decree that ends the book of Chronicles and opens the book of Ezra. It seems to point to a salvation that will come through judgment for the glory of the Lord Yahweh.

2.6 *The Center of the Theology of the Former Prophets*

Thematically speaking, there is a kind of chiastic arrangement of the Former Prophets, Joshua through Kings (see table 3.5):

Table 3.5. Thematic Chiastic Structure in the Former Prophets

Joshua—Obedience and conquest of the land

  Judges—No king and rampant wickedness

  Samuel—King Saul and King David

Kings—Disobedience and exile from the land[99]

In Joshua, the nation of Israel relied upon Yahweh and obeyed his word, even as he called them to do things that defied human wisdom, and they destroyed the nations of the land. In Kings, the nation of Israel relied upon human wisdom and other gods, and they were destroyed by other nations. In Judges, there was no king in Israel, and everyone did what was right in his own eyes. In Samuel, the people asked for a king like all the nations, and the Lord gave them Saul as a judgment because they had rejected Yahweh as their king. Then Yahweh mercifully raised up David and promised him an eternal dynasty, but David fell. David's sins were exaggerated in the sins of his sons: adultery to rape; murder to fratricide; several wives to hundreds of them. Yet God's promise remained. Those who believed the promise did so because everything else they trusted had been crushed under the weight of the curse narrated in Genesis 3. They were saved

[98]See especially Provan, "Kings," in *NDBT*, 185–87. For a discussion of 2 Kings 25:27–30 from a different perspective, see Clements, "A Royal Privilege," 49–66.

[99]The suggestion that these books are arranged intentionally to correspond to one another in this way would appear to be supported by David Noel Freedman's observation that the Former Prophets match each other in terms of word count: Joshua has 10,051 words; Judges has 9,885; Samuel has 24,301, and Kings has 25,421. Freedman then observes that when the totals are added according to a chiastic arrangement,

Joshua, 10,051 words

  Judges, 9,885 words

  Samuel, 24,301 words

Kings, 25,421 words

the total word count from adding the two outer books of the collection, Joshua and Kings, comes to 35,472, which is very close to the total word count from the two inner books of the collection, Judges and Samuel: 34,186. See David N. Freedman, "The Symmetry of the Hebrew Bible," Studia Theologica 46 (1992): 99–100 (83–108).

through judgment to glorify God. Those who believed the promise held out hope that God would deliver them by bringing judgment against their enemies. Those who did not believe the promise joined those enemies and placed themselves under God's judgment. The exile itself was a judgment on those who trusted in things other than Yahweh, and through that judgment Yahweh brought people to the salvation that comes only by trusting in him alone.

3. The Latter Prophets: Isaiah–Malachi

The latter prophets consist of three long books—Isaiah, Jeremiah, and Ezekiel—and a fourth that consists of twelve shorter books.[100] This Book of the Twelve is only a bit shorter than the three longer prophecies.[101] Earlier prophets in Israel's history, such as Elijah and Elisha, along with others named in the Former Prophets, did not leave written prophecies like the ones found among the Latter Prophets of the Old Testament.

The written prophecies in this section of the Old Testament all proclaim the glory of God in salvation through judgment. They provide commentary on the events recounted in the Former Prophets,[102] asserting that the people have put themselves under the curses of the covenant God made with them, and holding out hope that if the people will repent, God will delight to show them mercy. Yahweh will save them through the verbal condemnation of the prophet and spare them the physical condemnation of national destruction if they will repent. His glorious justice and surprising mercy continue to summon forth his praise, and the prophets match the beauty of the Psalms as they hymn the glory of God.

Considered in terms of their chronology (see table 3.6), Amos and Hosea seem to have come on the scene first (ca. 760s BC), with Amos prophesying in

[100]Russell E. Fuller observes regarding 4QXII^{g}, "The Book of the Twelve was considered a single book at Qumran, and the scribe appears to have left one full line blank between the individual Prophets" (Eugene Ulrich et al., *Qumran Cave 4.X: The Prophets*, DJD 15 [Oxford: Clarendon, 1997], 274). The Greek Minor Prophets Scroll from Naḥal Ḥever was either one long scroll containing the Twelve or two or even three "sister scrolls"; see Emanuel Tov with the collaboration of R. A. Kraft and a contribution by P. J. Parsons, *The Greek Minor Prophets Scroll from Naḥal Ḥever (8HevXIIgr)*, DJD 8 (Oxford: Clarendon, 1990), 9, 14.

[101]Freedman gives the word counts as follows: Jeremiah, 21,835 words; the Twelve, 14,355; Isaiah, 16,932; Ezekiel, 18,730. He again suggests a chiastic pattern, with the arrangement:

Jeremiah, 21,835
  Isaiah, 16,932
  Ezekiel, 18,730
The Twelve, 14,355

Freedman is followed in this analysis by Dempster, who places Jeremiah first in his discussion of the prophets (*Dominion and Dynasty*, 50–51). Once again, adding the word counts from the first and last, Jeremiah and the Twelve, yields a total of 36,190 words, which again matches the total from adding the inner two books, Isaiah and Ezekiel, almost exactly: 35,662 (Freedman, "The Symmetry of the Hebrew Bible," 99–100). I am attracted to this analysis, but my discussion here departs from it by treating Isaiah first. See further Roger Beckwith, *The Old Testament Canon of the New Testament Church and Its Background in Early Judaism* (Grand Rapids: Eerdmans, 1985), 206, 209, 450–51.

[102]House, *Old Testament Theology*, 273. Cf. Dempster, *Dominion and Dynasty*, 159.

the north. Hosea, Micah, and Isaiah seem to have ministered through the same period of Israel's history (ca. 740–680), and they may have known one another personally. The land of Israel is not a large place, geographically speaking. Amos, Hosea, Micah, and Isaiah prophesied around the time of the destruction of the northern kingdom by Assyria (721 BC). Nahum was perhaps next to appear (between 660 and 612 BC), and then Habakkuk, Zephaniah, and Jeremiah (ca. 640–570 BC).[103] Again it is possible that these men were personally acquainted

Table 3.6. The Years of the Kings and the Prophets

Prophet	King(s)	Years of the Kings[1]
Isaiah	Uzziah	792–740
	Jotham	750–731
	Ahaz	735–715
	Hezekiah	729–686
Jeremiah	Josiah	640–609
	Jehoiakim	608–598
	Zedekiah	597–586
Ezekiel	Jehoiachin	598–97
Hosea	Uzziah	792–740
	Jotham	750–731
	Ahaz	735–715
	Hezekiah	729–686
	Jeroboam II	793–753
Joel		
Amos	Uzziah	792–740
	Jeroboam II	793–753
Obadiah		
Jonah	(2 Kings 14:25, Jeroboam II)	793–753
Micah	Jotham	750–731
	Ahaz	735–715
	Hezekiah	729–686
Nahum		(ca. 650)
Habakkuk		(ca. 640–615)
Zephaniah	Josiah	640–609
Haggai		520
Zechariah		520
Malachi		

[1]The dates in this table follow those found in Eugene H. Merrill, *Kingdom of Priests: A History of Old Testament Israel* (Grand Rapids: Baker, 1987), 320.

[103]Cf. House, *Old Testament Theology*, 306: "In the canon Jeremiah paves the way for ideas in the Twelve. In history these individuals influenced Jeremiah."

as they prophesied in the years leading up to the crisis of the destruction of Jerusalem and the temple and the exile to Babylon (586 BC). Ezekiel was active at the time of and during the exile; he might have known Jeremiah, and he names Daniel (Ezek. 14:14, 20), whose book is grouped with the Old Testament Writings. As Stephen Dempster has written, "The Latter Prophets provide commentary on the grand narrative from creation to exile, showing the just judgment and gracious mercy of God."[104]

3.1 *The Latter Prophets Book by Book*

The prophecy of Isaiah presents a strong case that the glory of God in salvation through judgment is the center of biblical theology. His book[105] declares that the curses of Deuteronomy will indeed fall on the people. They will be exiled, but through the exile and the ministry of the servant of Yahweh, the people's sins will be taken away, and through the judgment will come an eschatological salvation for God's people so saturated with the glory of God that mere words cannot bear the weight of the tremendous majesty.

Jeremiah initially calls the people to repentance, but it becomes increasingly clear in his day that judgment will not be averted: the people accustomed to evil cannot learn to do good. Once judgment is certain, through Jeremiah Yahweh commands the people to capitulate to Babylon and look for the day, seventy years hence, when Yahweh promises to bring his people home. Once Yahweh has completed his judgment against Judah, Jeremiah prophesies judgment against the nations. The fall of Jerusalem attests to Jeremiah's status as a true prophet, who declares that after Yahweh glorifies himself in judgment (exile) he will glorify himself in salvation (return).

Ezekiel tastes the judgment of exile, and by the river Chebar he sees the glory of Yahweh. He is commissioned to prophesy and to act out signs that point to the destruction of both Jerusalem and the land. And then Ichabod: he beholds the glory depart. This judgment of Yahweh abandoning his temple is followed by announcements of doom to Israel and Judah, followed by announcements of doom to the nations. But through the judgment salvation comes to Yahweh's glory. Ezekiel prophesies a new day when the people will have new hearts and when Yahweh will reside in a new temple, with the nation led by a new David. Moreover, Yahweh declares that he does all this for his own sake, not Israel's. That is, Yahweh acts for his own glory.

[104] Dempster, *Dominion and Dynasty*, 191.

[105] See G. K. Beale, "A Specific Problem Confronting the Authority of the Bible: Should the New Testament's Claim That the Prophet 'Isaiah' Wrote the Whole Book of Isaiah Be Taken at Face Value?" in Lane G. Tipton and Jeffrey C. Waddington, *Resurrection and Eschatology: Theology in Service of the Church* (Phillipsburg, NJ: P&R, 2008), 135–76. Beale's answer is yes. See now G. K. Beale, *The Erosion of Inerrancy in Evangelicalism: Responding to New Challenges to Biblical Authority* (Wheaton, IL: Crossway, 2008), 123–59.

The twelve Minor Prophets individually move through judgment to salvation for Yahweh's glory, but this movement can also be detected when we consider the Twelve as a unit. Broadly speaking, in Hosea through Micah the covenant sin of Israel is denounced. Then the coming punishment, judgment, is declared in Nahum through Zephaniah. And through judgment salvation comes as the restoration to the land and the glorious future for which Israel still longs come into view in Haggai through Malachi.[106]

Table 3.7. The Story of the Latter Prophets

Isaiah	After the judgment of the exile, Yahweh will return to Zion in glory, and a shoot from the stump of Jesse will reign in Edenic splendor.
Jeremiah	After the judgment of the exile, Yahweh will make a new covenant with his people, and a righteous branch from David will be called "Yahweh is our righteousness."
Ezekiel	After the judgment of the exile, Yahweh will inhabit his eschatological temple, and "my servant David shall be king over them."
The Twelve	Hosea–Micah: Denunciation of covenant and cosmic sin Nahum–Zephaniah: Announcement of covenant and cosmic punishment Haggai–Malachi: Announcement of covenant and cosmic restoration

3.2 Isaiah

The book of Isaiah opens with five chapters that address the nation's present sin and future hope, followed by what appears to be Isaiah's account of his own call to be a prophet in Isaiah 6. The nation is then urged to trust Yahweh rather than Assyria in chapters 7–12, and these passages have such significant things to say about the coming Davidic king that they have been dubbed "The Book of Immanuel." Isaiah then gives a series of oracles against foreign nations in chapters 13–23, and these are followed by an apocalyptic vision of the triumph of Yahweh over evil in Isaiah 24–27. Warnings of judgment for those who trust Assyria and Egypt are followed by declarations that Yahweh is glorious in power to save in Isaiah 28–35, and then the deliverance of Hezekiah from an Assyrian threat is narrated in Isaiah 36–39.[107] Isaiah 40–48 opens with an announcement of comfort for God's people: Isaiah comforts by declaring the incomparable glory and utter uniqueness of Yahweh. In Isaiah 49–55 the nation is given a picture of the suffering servant who will bear the sins of the people, and then in Isaiah 55–66 the prophet heralds the future deliverance of God's people. Each of these sections will be broadly considered. In some ways passing through Isaiah like this can be compared to a one-day visit to the Louvre. A lifetime could be spent

[106]Adapted from Paul R. House, *The Unity of the Twelve*, JSOTSup (Sheffield: Almond, 1990), 72. See also House, *Old Testament Theology*, 348.

[107]Joseph Blenkinsopp (*Isaiah 1–39*, AB [New York: Doubleday, 2000], 82) refers to this breakdown of the chapters as the way Isaiah 1–39 is typically divided.

in each room, but wandering through Isaiah to get an impression of the whole, one cannot help seeing the majesty of the glory that Yahweh demonstrates as he judges in order to save, giving meaning to mercy. Barry Webb writes that Isaiah "is a book about demolition and reconstruction, judgment and salvation. And the order is significant: paradoxically, salvation emerges out of judgment and is possible only because of it."[108]

3.2.1 Present Sin and Future Hope (Isaiah 1–5)

Isaiah summons the witnesses to the covenant between Yahweh and his people, the heavens and the earth (Deut. 4:26; 32:1), to hear Yahweh's case (Isa. 1:2) against the nation that has forsaken and despised the Holy One of Israel (1:4). This is the root issue that gives rise to the other symptoms of evil in Israel: they are doing the opposite of worshiping Yahweh and cleaving to him. Yahweh offers a purifying cleansing (1:18), declares that he will avenge himself (1:24), and promises that he will thereby smelt away the dross in Israel (1:25) and restore good leadership for the nation (1:26). Zion will be justly redeemed, and those who repent will be saved in righteousness (1:27), but the sinful who persist in forsaking Yahweh will be consumed (1:28). In short, salvation will come through judgment for the glory of God.[109]

This glory will take the form of Jerusalem being exalted as the capital of the globe, the nations streaming to Zion to learn Yahweh's law, Yahweh initiating justice that brings true and lasting peace, and people compulsively seeking to honor Yahweh by obeying his law and walking in his light (Isa. 2:1–5). In addition to this, Isaiah 4:2–6 describes a beautiful and glorious "branch of Yahweh" (4:2, see further below on Isa. 11:1).[110] Those recorded for life in Jerusalem (4:3) will survive and remain and be holy, for Yahweh will have washed the filth of his people by a Spirit of judgment and purifying burning (4:4). The canopy over

[108]Barry G. Webb, *The Message of Isaiah: On Eagles' Wings*, The Bible Speaks Today (Downers Grove, IL: InterVarsity, 1997), 31. I wish to thank Andy Naselli for bringing this quotation to my attention.

[109]Cf. Karen H. Jobes and Moisés Silva, *Invitation to the Septuagint* (Grand Rapids: Baker, 2000), 94–95: "The peculiar preference for the word *doxa* in Septuagint Isaiah has led scholars to conclude that 'glory' is one of the central characteristics of God for the translator of that book." Emanuel Tov writes, "for a prominence of δόξα in [the LXX] (against [MT]) see Exod 15:1–18; Isa 11:3; 30:27; 33:17; 40:6; 52:14; 53:2" (*Textual Criticism of the Hebrew Bible* [Minneapolis: Fortress, 1992], 127). For a fascinating recent discussion of the Greek translation of Isaiah, see Ronald L. Troxel, *LXX-Isaiah as Translation and Interpretation: The Strategies of the Translator of the Septuagint Isaiah*, JSJSup (Boston: Brill, 2008), and on the "glory" and "salvation" themes in LXX-Isaiah, Troxel writes, "They are not themes brought into the book from the outside, but were essential elements of the book that the translator appropriated as leitmotifs in his interpretation of the whole" (132).

[110]J. Alec Motyer (*Isaiah*, TOTC [Downers Grove, IL: InterVarsity, 1999], 59) writes, "'Branch' is a messianic title (Je. 23:5; 33:15; Zc. 3:8; 6:12), and the view taken here is that Isaiah 4:2 marks its earliest occurrence." Cf. Brevard S. Childs, *Isaiah*, OTL (Louisville: Westminster John Knox, 2001), 36: "Once the term 'branch' had become a technical term for the Messiah in later prophetic literature, it is difficult to imagine this earlier, non-technical usage not accumulating a richer connotation than perhaps originally intended." In my view the development to which Childs points is possible within the book of Isaiah itself because of the way that Isaiah 4 would be read with Isaiah 11. Though the terms used in the two texts are different (see below), the two terms partake of the same imagery and would have been mutually interpretive.

the glory may point to a wedding (4:5),[111] and Yahweh will provide "a booth for shade by day from the heat, and for a refuge and a shelter from the storm and rain" (4:6 ESV).

Isaiah seeks to provoke his audience to long for what he announces in this vision by proclaiming to them the certainty of the justice of God against their sin.[112] He seeks to compel repentance by announcing "the terror of Yahweh" and "the splendor of his majesty" as he comes to bring low the haughty, "and Yahweh alone will be exalted in that day" (Isa. 2:10–11; cf. 2:17, 19, 21). Isaiah's contemporaries who have forsaken Yahweh and disregard his active presence among them as they sin are not thinking on these realities when they glory in such things as the twenty-one items of adornment Isaiah rails against in 3:18–23. As Vos wrote, "Beauty, irreligiously esteemed, infringes upon the glory of Jehovah."[113] Irreligiously esteemed beauty has ruined the vineyard Yahweh cultivated, with the result that it has produced stinking, worthless grapes (5:1–7), and Yahweh mercifully sends Isaiah to warn his people of the woes coming upon them (5:8–30). The likening of Israel to a vineyard presents the nation in Edenic terms, reinforcing the idea we have seen elsewhere in our study that the purposes God carried forward in the nation of Israel were the purposes he set out to achieve when he placed man in the garden. The announcement of the woes that follow condemns the wickedness of the people, and this condemnation is intended to bring them to the place of salvation: a place of repentance and resolve to exalt Yahweh alone.[114] If they do not repent, they will be exiled from Yahweh's vineyard just as Adam was exiled from Eden.

3.2.2 The Call of Isaiah (Isaiah 6)

After the six woes announced in Isaiah 5, Isaiah sees the exalted Lord surrounded by seraphim declaring his holiness, the antiphonal call resounding that "the fullness of the whole earth is his glory" (Isa. 6:3).[115] Their powerful voices shake the foundations of the thresholds of the temple (6:4), and Isaiah proclaims a seventh woe against himself (6:5). Isaiah has been announcing Yahweh's glory and greatness (cf., e.g., 3:8; 5:16, 24), and yet even he is overwhelmed by the king, Yahweh Sabaoth. This passage is not only about Yahweh's glory, however; it is also about salvation through judgment. Isaiah not only pronounces a woe upon himself; he states that he is a man of unclean lips among a people of unclean lips

[111] So Motyer, *Isaiah*, 60, citing Ps. 19:6 and Joel 2:16.
[112] Similarly John N. Oswalt, "The Book of Isaiah: A Short Course on Biblical Theology," *CTJ* 39 (2004): 62.
[113] Geerhardus Vos, *Biblical Theology: Old and New Testaments* (Grand Rapids: Eerdmans, 1948), 281.
[114] Dumbrell (*The Faith of Israel*, 107) writes, "The prophetic ministry was most normally associated, up to the exile at least, with impending judgment. But their message was actually a saving message. For unless the sin of Israel was so deeply ingrained that it could not be eradicated, the threat of judgment was an implicit invitation to repentance."
[115] See the discussion of "The Glory of God in the Book of Isaiah" in Robin Routledge, "Is There a Narrative Substructure Underlying the Book of Isaiah?" *TynBul* 55 (2004): 194–95.

(6:5), and then one of the seraphim flies to him, holding a burning coal from the altar in tongs, which he touches to Isaiah's mouth and proclaims, "Behold, this has touched your lips; your guilt is taken away, and your sin atoned for" (6:6–7 ESV). Yahweh's holiness exposes Isaiah's sin, and after he realizes and confesses his sin, through the purging of the burning coal from the altar, Isaiah's guilt is removed. Glory—judgment—salvation.

After Isaiah is called (Isa. 6:8), in a mystifying passage he is commissioned to harden the hearts of the people (6:9–10). When he asks how long, he is told that it will be until the land is devastated and the people are exiled (6:11–12). And then even the remnant, which will be like the stump of a tree that has been felled, will be burned.[116] But there is hope. The holy seed is in that stump (6:13). Through the judgment of the exile, the shoot will sprout from that holy seed to bring salvation (cf. 11:1), Jerusalem will be exalted (2:1–5), and the glory of God will cover Mount Zion (4:5). In view of the kinds of claims sometimes made about different sections of the book, it seems worth pointing out that the eschatological promises in Isaiah 1–39 are no less extravagant than those in Isaiah 40–66.

3.2.3 The Book of Immanuel: Trust God Not Assyria (Isaiah 7–12)

In response to a conspiracy between Syria and the northern kingdom of Israel, Yahweh sends Isaiah to meet Ahaz to encourage him to trust Yahweh (Isa. 7:1–9). Through Isaiah Yahweh declares that the conspiracy will come to nothing, but Ahaz will stand only by faith (7:4, 7–9). We know from the near context (e.g., 7:17) and from 2 Kings 16:5–9 that Ahaz was tempted to trust Assyria, rather than Yahweh, and that he gave in to that temptation (2 Kings 16:10–18). Yahweh invites Ahaz to ask for a remarkable sign (Isa. 7:10–11). Ahaz refuses to do so (7:13), and the Lord gives the sign of Immanuel (7:14). The next verses speak of the land whose two kings Ahaz dreads, Syria and Ephraim, being deserted before this prophesied boy knows how to refuse evil and choose good (7:16), and these verses speak of the boy eating curds and honey when he knows how to refuse evil and choose good (7:15). This context indicates that Isaiah is referring to a particular virgin *of his own time* who will give birth and name her child Immanuel in 7:14.[117] The name Immanuel, "God with us," asserts that the child is a sign of God's presence with his people. Thus, this child's birth in the near future will guarantee to Ahaz that Syria and Ephraim will be "broken" (7:8). The threat

[116]For a canonical synthesis dealing with the king and the remnant, see House, *Old Testament Theology*, 280–81.

[117]For a more detailed discussion of this passage, see my essay, "The Virgin Will Conceive: Typological Fulfillment in Matthew 1:18–23," 228–47. Thomas R. Schreiner (*New Testament Theology: Magnifying God in Christ* [Grand Rapids: Baker, 2008], 71–73) interprets Isaiah 7 as I do (and as far as I can tell we arrived at our conclusions independently of one another, but Schreiner's influence on my thinking is so extensive that I might have forgotten learning this view from him). See also the discussion of Matthew 1:22–23 in chap. 5, §3.1, with tables 5.4 and 5.5.

from Syria and Ephraim will be ended by the Assyrian onslaught, which will also sweep into Judah (8:8). The Assyrian horde will depopulate the land, such that there will be an abundance of food for the child Immanuel (7:15–25). For these reasons, Ahaz should not fear Syria and Ephraim but should trust Yahweh rather than Assyria. This sign is basically reiterated in Isaiah 8 with the birth of Isaiah's child, Maher-shalal-hashbaz (8:1–10), who may be the child promised in 7:14 in view of Isaiah's declaration that he and his children are "signs and portents in Israel from Yahweh of hosts" (8:18).

If the northern kingdom is going to be overcome by Assyria (cf. Isa. 8:4), the Assyrian devastation is likely the cause of the darkness, gloom, and thick darkness predicted in 8:22. The turning of this darkness to dawn in the "latter time" (8:23, ET 9:1) points beyond the devastation of the northern kingdom to the nation's restoration.[118] The dawning of the light is described as though it is taking place (8:23–9:1, ET 9:1–2); the nation is described as being multiplied as it was just before the exodus (9:2, ET 3; cf. the use of "multiplied," רבה in both Isa. 9:2, ET 3, and Ex. 1:7); and the enemies are described as being defeated as they were "on the day of Midian" (Isa. 9:3, ET 4), which recalls Gideon's small band of three hundred defeating the Midianites (Judges 7). These intertextual references indicate that the restoration of the nation after the judgment brought by Assyria will correspond to the ways the Lord delivered his people at the exodus and at other significant points in the nation's history. The new exodus will typologically correspond to the old exodus (though note that the exodus is not the only saving event mentioned).

Thus, Isaiah 8:22 describes the coming darkness of exile, then 8:23–9:1 (ET 9:1–2) points to the dawn that comes after the night of destruction that fell on the northern tribes, and the rays of light in the breaking of this dawn shine with the defeat of the nation's enemies, recalling triumphs at the exodus and in the land in 9:2–4 (ET 3–5). This prophecy of exile and restoration, judgment followed by salvation (which entails judgment on enemies), is followed by the prophecy of a child who will be king in Isaiah 9:5–6 (ET 6–7):

> For a child is born to us, a son is given to us; and the government shall be upon his shoulder, and his name shall be called Wonderful Counselor, Mighty God, Everlasting Father, Prince of Peace. Of the increase of his government and of peace there will be no end, on the throne of David and over his kingdom, to establish it and to uphold it, in justice and in righteousness from now and unto the age. The zeal of Yahweh of hosts will do this.

[118]Matthew seems to understand Jesus as initiating the fulfillment of this restoration. See the citation of Isa. 8:23–9:1 (ET 9:1–2) in Matt. 4:12–16. See chap. 5, §3.2.

The word "for" (כִּי) indicates that the salvation of the nation through its triumph over her enemies will come through the agency of this child, who will be a Davidic king, and who is described with exalted titles, including Mighty God![119] The salvation that arrives when the Everlasting Father who is the Prince of Peace reigns will come through judgment, however, and that judgment is what Isaiah announces in 9:7–10:4 (ET 9:8–10:4). The announcements of the devastation that will manifest Yahweh's wrath (9:19) in this section are punctuated by the refrain, "For all this his anger has not turned away, and his hand is stretched out still" (9:11, ET 12; 9:16, ET 17; 9:20, ET 21; 10:4).

Lest anyone think that Assyria is righteous or that her defeat of Israel signifies the defeat of Yahweh, Isaiah describes the concursus of Yahweh's righteous will with the wicked intentions of the Assyrians in Isaiah 10:5–15. The Assyrians have their own arrogant purposes (Isa. 10:7–11), and Yahweh's sovereignty is such that they choose to accomplish what he has planned. Assyria is the axe with which Yahweh will hew down the rotted tree of Israel (10:5–6, 12–15). As with the programmatic declaration in Isaiah 6:11–13 (stump, holy seed in the stump), so in Isaiah 10:16–34 a remnant will remain when the tree of Israel is cut down with the axe of Assyria (10:19). This remnant will rely on Yahweh, not Assyria (10:20–23).

And then the stump will sprout with its holy seed: "A shoot will come forth from the stem of Jesse, and a branch from his roots will bear fruit" (Isa. 11:1). Different terms are used to describe the branch in Isaiah 4:2 and 11:1 (צמח, "sprouting," 4:2;[120] חטר, "rod/shoot," and נצר, "branch," 11:1), but both texts speak of fruit, and it is likely that the different words describing the new plant-like growth are merely stylistic variants, all pointing to the same reality: the upspringing of the Davidic king described in Isaiah 11:1–5. The Spirit, modified by seven descriptors, is upon the king (11:2), who delights in the fear of Yahweh (11:3), judging truly (11:4), righteously defending the poor, and smiting the wicked (11:5). He will be faithful (11:5). The reign of this king will be accompanied by dramatic alterations in the nature of things: predators will no longer be feared by their prey, as wolves, leopards, lions, and bears will dwell with lambs, goats,

[119]John N. Oswalt (*The Book of Isaiah: Chapters 1–39*, NICNT [Grand Rapids: Eerdmans, 1986], 246) insists that "such extravagant titling was not normal for Israelite kings," but Blenkinsopp suggests the translation "Hero Warrior" (*Isaiah 1–39*, 246, cf. 250). Isa. 9:6 is not cited in the New Testament as a proof text for the deity of the messiah (appendix IV of NA[27], "Loci Citati Vel Allegati," lists only Luke 1:32 next to Isa. 9:6, but the correspondences in wording do not constitute a citation). Nor does it seem that those who heralded Jesus as the messiah were necessarily expecting the messiah to be God incarnate. The deity of Jesus seems to have surprised his followers—see their reaction when he calms the storm in Mark 4:35–41. The "Son of God" language has these overtones, but it can be explained as referring to a human ruler who rules the way God would, growing out of 2 Sam. 7:14 (cf. the peacemakers who are called "sons of God" in Matt. 5:9). It may be that in Isa. 9:6 we have an instance of *sensus plenior*, Isaiah speaking better than he knows (for biblical recognition of *sensus plenior*, see John 11:51–52).

[120]For a full study of the term צמח that comes to conclusions of which I am not entirely persuaded, see Wolter H. Rose, *Zemah and Zerubbabel: Messianic Expectations in the Early Postexilic Period*, JSOTSup (Sheffield: Sheffield Academic, 2000), 91–120. Cf. Chester, *Messiah and Exaltation*, 199, 204, 330.

cows, and oxen, led by a little child, and the predators will graze with cows and eat straw like oxen (11:6–7). This altered state of affairs looks almost Edenic, and then a statement is made that indicates that the curse of Genesis 3:15 will have been removed: "The nursing child shall play over the hole of the cobra, and the weaned child shall put his hand on the adder's den" (Isa. 11:8). This is a picturesque way of declaring that after the judgment on God's people, through which they are brought to salvation, there will be no more enmity between the seed of the serpent and the seed of the woman. And it culminates with God accomplishing his purpose, stated in language that recalls the song of the seraphim (6:3b; cf. Num. 14:21), "for the earth will be full of the knowledge of Yahweh, as the waters cover the sea" (Isa. 11:9b).[121] As the weight of the waters rests on the ocean floor, so the glory of Yahweh will rest on the dry land, and all nations shall be gathered together, united in the worship of Yahweh. As the Red Sea was parted and the Jordan River stopped, Yahweh will lead his people "over the River" (11:15 ESV), and "there will be a highway from Assyria for the remnant that remains of his people, as there was for Israel when they came up from the land of Egypt" (11:16). The regathering of the people from the exile will typologically correspond to the exodus from Egypt.

The whole first section of Isaiah, from the indictment in chapter 1 to the woes in chapter 5, from Isaiah's commission to harden the people until they go into exile to the announcement of the glorious salvation that will be wrought through the judgment Assyria brings, all of this issues in the praise due to Yahweh, rendered in Isaiah 12. The refrain that Yahweh's anger was not turned away and his hand still stretched out (Isa. 9:11, ET 12; 9:16, ET 17; 9:20, ET 21; 10:4) gives way to the gratitude expressed when Isaiah declares, "You will say in that day: 'I will give thanks to you, O Yahweh, for though you were angry with me, *your anger turned away*, that you might comfort me'" (Isa. 12:1, emphasis added).

3.2.4 Oracles against the Nations (Isaiah 13–23)

Isaiah 1–11 declares that God's people will face the judgment of exile, through which they will be saved to enjoy the reign of a righteous and triumphant king who will lead them to defeat their enemies, and all this results in a renewal of Edenic conditions. This spells doom for the rival kingdoms of the world. Interestingly, Isaiah 13–23 opens with an oracle not against Assyria but against Babylon—the nation that would later defeat Assyria (Isa. 13:1).[122] Then in the oracle against Babylon, the Medes are mentioned (13:17), and it was a united Medo-Persian force that took Babylon in 539 BC (see also Jer. 51:11, 28). Just as the future salvation of Israel is compared to past salvation events in Israel's

[121]See appendix 2 (§6) to this chapter, "All the Earth Filled with the Knowledge of Yahweh's Glory."
[122]Assyria is named in Isa. 14:25, which seems to come at the end of the ongoing oracle against Babylon (cf. 14:4).

history, so the promised destruction of Babylon is likened to the destruction of Sodom and Gomorrah (Isa. 13:19).

From the broader stage the focus shifts to the nearby powers of Philistia (Isa. 14:28–32), Moab (15:1–16:14), and Damascus (17:1–14). Ethiopia and Egypt are addressed (18:1–19:25), and Isaiah makes himself a sign against Egypt and Ethiopia, going naked and barefoot for three years to demonstrate what Assyria will do to them (20:1–6). There are oracles against "the wilderness of the sea" (21:1–17), against the "valley of vision" (22:1–25), and against Tyre (23:1–18). The Lord's judgment is against all nations. His justice will be the universal standard.

3.2.5 Isaiah's Apocalypse (Isaiah 24–27)

Universal judgment is followed by universal, cosmic salvation. Isaiah 24 opens with 13 verses declaring the all-consuming wrath of God. In response to this, Isaiah 24:14–16 announces:

> They lift up their voices; they sing for joy; over the majesty of Yahweh they shout from the west. Therefore in the east give glory to Yahweh; in the coastlands of the sea, give glory to the name of Yahweh, the God of Israel. From the ends of the earth we hear songs of praise, of glory to the Righteous One.

After this praise for Yahweh, which seems to have been prompted by the display of his justice, Isaiah continues at the end of verse 16, "But I say, 'I waste away, I waste away. Woe is me! For the traitors have betrayed, with betrayal the traitors have betrayed.'" This sudden shift seems to return from the worship in response to the apocalyptic demonstration of God's justice to Isaiah's immediate present, wherein his own generation stands under God's judgment. That judgment is then graphically depicted in 24:17–23, with the earth splitting and shaking (Isa. 24:19), Yahweh reigning on Mount Zion, "and his glory will be before his elders" (24:23; cf. Rev. 4:4).

Again the glory of God's justice is immediately followed by worship, as Isaiah praises Yahweh, who accomplishes his ancient plans (Isa. 25:1), wins glory from strong peoples (25:3), shelters the poor and needy (25:4), humbles the proud (25:5), prepares a feast for all peoples (25:6), swallows up death and wipes away tears (25:7–8), and tramples his enemies in the dust (25:9–12). Once again, the salvation for which Yahweh is praised is a salvation that comes through the justice he visits on his opponents. The song of praise for this salvation through judgment resonates through Isaiah 26, and the opening words of chapter 27 seem to reach back to the beginning of all the trouble. Yahweh "with his hard and great and strong sword will punish Leviathan the fleeing serpent, Leviathan the twisting serpent, and he will slay the dragon that is in the sea" (Isa. 27:1). This judgment on the serpent (cf. 51:9) alludes to the promised crushing of the serpent's head (Gen. 3:15).[123] The sea, leviathan, and the dragon are symbols of evil. Naturally, Yahweh's triumph over the great beast of evil in the sea is followed by another vineyard song (cf. Isa. 5:1–7), but this time the vineyard is pleasant because Yahweh is its keeper (27:2). The thorns and briers that are reminiscent of the curse on the ground (Gen. 3:17–19) will be gone (Isa. 27:4), indicating that this vineyard is untouched by the curse after Yahweh's triumph. When Yahweh saves by slaying the dragon (27:1), the great trumpet, announcing the Year of Jubilee, will sound and the lost will be drawn from Assyria and Egypt to worship Yahweh on his holy mount in Jerusalem (27:13; cf. Lev. 25:8–12; Isa. 61:1–4).

3.2.6 Assyria, Egypt, and Yahweh (Isaiah 28–35)

This section of Isaiah moves from woes on north (Isa. 28:1–29) and south (29:1–24) because of Assyria, to a woe on those who trust Egypt (30:1–31:9), and then shifts to the glory of Yahweh (32:1–20). The woe in 33:1[124] addresses the agent of destruction to whom Yahweh says, "When you have ceased to destroy, you will be destroyed" (33:1). The nations are summoned to see Yahweh's justice against the destroyer in Isaiah 34, and the rejoicing over the salvation through judgment he achieves is detailed in Isaiah 35. The argument not to trust in Assyria is based on the fact that Yahweh is using Assyria to bring judgment on those who do not trust him (Isa. 28:1–29:24). Isaiah's attention then turns to the impulse to rely on Egypt to defend Israel against Assyria (30:1–31:9). Then follow four chapters (Isaiah 32–35) that declare Yahweh's glory and the marvelous salvation he will achieve.

Isaiah 28 returns to the threat that Assyria poses to the northern kingdom. Ephraim, the north, is promised that Yahweh will overcome their proud rebellion against him (28:1–4), and the result of his triumph will be that he, Yahweh, will be the "crown of glory" and "diadem of beauty" to the remnant (28:5). Because prophet and priest are drunk with strong drink rather than love for Yahweh (28:7–9), Yahweh will speak to them "by people of strange lips and with a foreign tongue" (28:11). This apparently means that Yahweh will no longer speak to his people through a prophet, whom they can understand, but will instead speak to them by the Assyrians, whom they cannot understand.

The leaders of the people who rule in Jerusalem appear to have scoffed at Isaiah's predictions of coming doom (Isa. 28:14), and Isaiah exposes their reliance upon human wisdom and human alliances, rather than Yahweh, as "a covenant with death" and an agreement with Sheol. Indeed, they have made lies their

[123]See Dempster, *Dominion and Dynasty*, 182 and n. 22. Cf. Elain A. Phillips, "Serpent Intertexts: Tantalizing Twists in the Tales," *BBR* 10 (2000): 233–45.

[124]Note the use of הוֹי in Isa. 28:1; 29:1, 15; 30:1; 31:1; 33:1. Most translations render this "woe" in these cases, but cf. BDB, 222: "expressing usually dissatisfaction and pain, Ah, Alas; Ha (not distinctly *Woe!* which is אוֹי)." Blenkinsopp (*Isaiah 1–39*, 380) nevertheless refers to these as "woe-sayings."

refuge and taken shelter in falsehood (28:15). In response, Yahweh declares that he has laid a foundation in Zion, a tested, precious cornerstone, and whoever believes will not be anxious (28:16). Since this cornerstone in Zion is presented as an antidote to "scoffers, who rule . . . in Jerusalem" (28:14), it appears to be a reference to what Yahweh has established, that is, made to be a cornerstone of a sure foundation (28:16). Yahweh has established the house of David in Zion. Thus, it would appear that the themes from the Book of Immanuel (Isaiah 7–12), as well as the statements about the royal Davidic deliverer made in Isaiah 16:5 and 19:20 (cf. 22:22–25), are resumed by these words about the cornerstone in Zion (28:16).

Having asserted that Yahweh will judge in righteousness and annul the covenants with death and Sheol (Isa. 28:17–18, cf. 15), Isaiah describes the coming judgment in terms of an overwhelming scourge (28:18b), which recalls earlier descriptions of the coming of the Assyrians (cf. the use of שׁטף, "overflow," in 8:8; 10:22; 28:2, 15, 17, 18). The overflowing Assyrian onrush through the land is then described in terms of Yahweh rising up to judge Israel as he judged their enemies in the past: "For Yahweh will rise up as on Mount Perazim; as in the Valley of Gibeon he will be roused; to do his deed—strange is his deed!—and to work his work—alien is his work!" (Isa. 28:21; cf. 2 Sam. 5:20; Josh. 10:10–14). Judgment, as the references to Yahweh's judgment of Israel's enemies show, is not a strange or alien deed for Yahweh. What is strange and alien is for Yahweh to do this to Israel.

As announced in Isaiah's commission, however, salvation for Israel will come after this judgment.[125] This salvation is depicted with imagery that communicates the opposite of what Isaiah was commissioned to do. He was sent to close ears, blind eyes, and make hearts dull (Isa. 6:9–10). The announcement that Jerusalem will be visited by God's justice (29:1–10) is accompanied by the declaration that "the vision of all this has become to you like the words of a book that is sealed" (29:11 ESV). Yahweh's judgments against Israel will be "wonderful" (29:14). None can hide (29:15). Yahweh is the potter, his creation the clay (29:16). But in "a little while" Lebanon will bloom, and "in that day the deaf shall hear the words of a book, and out of their gloom and darkness the eyes of the blind shall see" (29:18). This seems to point beyond the exile announced in Isaiah 6, and the reference to seeing out of "gloom and darkness" recalls the day that dawns after the gloom of exile in Isaiah 9. Through judgment comes salvation, and it once again results in glory for God: "The meek shall obtain fresh joy in Yahweh, and the poor among mankind shall exult in the Holy One of Israel" (29:19; cf. 29:23).

[125]So also J. J. M. Roberts ("Isaiah in Old Testament Theology," *Int* 36 [1982]: 138): "Out of this judgment would arise a purged and glorified city of God, a new Jerusalem."

The denunciation of those who trust in Egypt (Isa. 30:1–31:9)[126] is followed by the declaration that "a king will reign in righteousness" (32:1). Once again, the curse of blinded eyes, closed ears, and hearts that do not understand is reversed (32:3–4). The city will be forsaken (32:14) "until the Spirit is poured upon us from on high, and the wilderness becomes a fruitful field, and the fruitful field is deemed a forest" (32:15; cf. 29:17). There seems to be a connection made here between the reversing of the blinded eyes, closed ears, and dull hearts on the one hand, and the eschatological outpouring of the Spirit on the other. As with many texts in the prophets, the return from exile is depicted in eschatological splendor.

As in Isaiah 10, where Yahweh promised to judge Assyria after using them to judge Israel, so in Isaiah 33 Yahweh promises destruction to the destroyer (Isa. 33:1). None can dwell with the consuming fire of the everlasting burnings of Yahweh (33:14).

3.2.7 The Deliverance of Hezekiah (Isaiah 36–39)

Isaiah 36–39 parallels 2 Kings 18–20 (see the discussion earlier in this chapter in §2.5.4). It is worth pointing out that Hezekiah's trust in Yahweh and willingness to heed the prophet Isaiah present a stark contrast to the way that Ahaz trusted in Assyria and rejected Isaiah's message.[127] Attention is drawn to this contrast between Ahaz and Hezekiah by the notation of the location, "the conduit of the upper pool on the highway to the Washer's Field" (Isa. 7:3; 36:2 ESV); by the prophetic command, "Do not be afraid" (7:4; 37:6); and by the offer of a sign (7:11; 37:30).[128] Once again, Yahweh judges Judah's self-sufficiency with the Assyrian threat, and through that judgment they are saved by Yahweh's glorious power. The salvation accomplished by Yahweh is wrought through the judgment of Assyria, the rod Yahweh has used to discipline his people (cf. Isa. 10:5–19).

3.2.8 The Incomparable Yahweh (Isaiah 40–48)

Great books make great readers,[129] and exposure to lofty thoughts is a challenging and inspiring experience. Loftier thoughts than Isaiah's, recorded in chapters 40–66 of his prophecy, are scarcely to be found. In these chapters Isaiah draws out the implications of what it means for Yahweh to be the one true God, Maker of heaven and earth, and his expression of these ideas is piercing and transforming. Making one's way through these chapters is like climbing a

[126] Note how Isa. 30:18 brings together Yahweh's intention to "exalt himself" with the ideas of Yahweh being a "God of justice" and being "gracious" and showing "mercy": "Therefore Yahweh waits to be gracious to you, and therefore he exalts himself to show mercy to you. For Yahweh is a God of justice; blessed are all those who wait for him."

[127] So also Dumbrell, *The Faith of Israel*, 114–15.

[128] Cf. Blenkinsopp, *Isaiah 1–39*, 459.

[129] Robert Littlejohn and Charles T. Evans, *Wisdom and Eloquence: A Christian Paradigm for Classical Learning* (Wheaton, IL: Crossway, 2006), 97.

mountain: the experience is demanding and exhausting as the air thins, while the breathtaking beauty of the glory of God shines like clear Colorado sky.

In Isaiah 40–66, Isaiah prophesies of the coming return from exile. The opening announcement of comfort and pardon (40:1–2) is followed by a cry to prepare the way of Yahweh, whose glory will be revealed, for his mouth has spoken (40:3–5). The end of the first section, Isaiah 40–48, matches the opening announcement of return with a call to go out from Babylon (48:20–22). The end of the next unit, Isaiah 49–55, is also concluded with an announcement of the way the name of Yahweh will be made great when the people "go out with joy" and are "led forth in peace," singing as the mountains and hills break forth while the trees clap their hands and the thorn is replaced by cypress and myrtle (55:12–13; cf. 40:4). Within these bookends, Isaiah 40–55 is also bracketed by proclamations of the eternality and effectiveness of Yahweh's word (40:6–8; 55:10–11).[130]

Isaiah 40 opens with Yahweh's call to speak comfort "to Jerusalem's heart . . . that her warfare is complete, that her iniquity is pardoned, that she has received from Yahweh's hand double for all her sins" (Isa. 40:1–2). The tender mercy spoken to Jerusalem's heart comes after the judgment of her sins. This judgment was announced at the end of the previous chapter, when Isaiah declared that the treasures of the kingdom and some of Hezekiah's sons would be taken to Babylon (39:5–8). As Isaiah prophesies of the exile and return before it happens, his proclamation prepares the remnant for what they face. They are assured that Yahweh is not being defeated but bringing justice, and that after the justice will come the mercy. Through this "the glory of Yahweh will be revealed, and all flesh will see it together" (40:5). Israel can believe what Isaiah proclaims, for unlike grass and flesh, the word of Yahweh will stand forever (40:6–8).

It is important to stress that the comfort Isaiah speaks to Jerusalem's heart (Isa. 40:1–2) is related to the way that is being prepared in the wilderness (40:3). This way is not merely the path Israel will trod in her return to the land. The way prepared is "the way of Yahweh . . . a highway for our God" (40:3). This is the good news to be proclaimed by Zion and Jerusalem: "Behold your God!" (40:9), which introduces an important consideration related to the return from exile. The physical return to the land that began in 539 BC may end the exile from the land begun in 721 and carried through 586, but until Yahweh returns to Zion in glory, the exile from Eden begun in Genesis 3 continues. Isaiah's prophecy seems to present the physical return from exile to the land as coterminous with

[130]I owe these observations to Joseph Blenkinsopp, *Isaiah 40–55*, AB (New York: Doubleday, 2002), 59. Much as I would like to find Antti Laato's proposed chiasm compelling ("The Composition of Isaiah 40–55," *JBL* 109 [1990]: 207–28), I do not think his extremely detailed proposal works. For instance, Isaiah 40:3–8 is not similar enough to 42:14–17. Moreover, if Isaiah intended to structure chapters 40–55 chiastically, a compelling argument for that intended chiasm would need to encompass all of chapters 40–55, rather than only covering 40–53, as Laato's does. Still, it seems that Isaiah structured chapters 40–55 as a unit, and there may be a convincing chiastic structure to this material.

the return of Yahweh to Zion in glory (cf. Isa. 2:1–4; 4:2–6). Later prophecies will clarify that there will be an interval of time between these events.[131]

Though Isaiah's contemporaries might not see Yahweh return to Zion, those with ears to hear "see" him as they hear Isaiah proclaim his greatness. Isaiah comforts the people by showing them their God. In calling Zion and Jerusalem to announce the "good news" (Isa. 40:9) of Yahweh's return in saving and judging glory (40:10–11), Isaiah summons Israel to the vocation for which Yahweh initially redeemed them from Egypt (Ex. 19:6).[132]

Having urged them to behold their God (Isa. 40:9), Isaiah declares to his audience the massive greatness of Yahweh, whose magnitude is such that oceans are measured by the palm of his hand and the mountains can be placed on his scales (40:12). The nations are a drop in the bucket (40:15); indeed, they are regarded as nothing (40:17). Yahweh's wisdom is such that he needs no counselors, and this reality also points to his absolute self-referential freedom—he footnotes no one on his insights or plans (40:13–14; 41:28).

Isaiah 40–48 celebrates the uniqueness of Yahweh as the Creator. Isaiah asks, "To whom will you liken God? Or what likeness will you compare to him?" (Isa. 40:18, 25; cf. 46:5). The first instance of this question is followed with observations on the way that idols are made by those who worship them (40:19–20). This is followed by a poetic description of Yahweh stretching out the heavens as a curtain (40:21). The second instance of the question, to whom can God be compared? (40:25) is followed by the invitation to gaze on the stars that Yahweh made and calls by name (40:26).[133] There is a stark contrast between Yahweh, the Maker, and the idols, which are made. The folly of worshiping and relying upon what one has made rather than one's Maker will be pressed home again and again in these passages. Idolatry is condemned through the force of Isaiah's logic, and those who are convinced by that logic are brought to salvation—trusting in Yahweh alone—through the condemnation of idolatry.

The folly of sin and the absurd worthlessness of idolatry often have a blinding, mind-numbing affect upon those participating in them. The implications and consequences of sin and idolatry are ignored as people enjoy what Hebrews 11:25 calls "the fleeting pleasures of sin." Through Isaiah, Yahweh mercifully exposes the true nature of idolatry, tracing out the process by which an idol is shaped and adorned (Isa. 40:18–20); showing that it cannot hold itself up but must be soldered and pegged so that it will not totter (41:5–7); daring the idol to reveal

[131]See, for instance, the prophecies in Zechariah, delivered after the physical return to the land and pointing to a future return of Yahweh to Zion (see §3.5.11 in this chapter, below), and the four kingdoms and seventy weeks prophesied in Daniel (see in chap. 4, §4.2 with table 4.8, "The Kingdoms in Daniel 2 and 7").

[132]Cf. Routledge, "Is There a Narrative Substructure Underlying the Book of Isaiah?" 190.

[133]The imagery of the heavens as a tent curtain confirms what G. K. Beale argues regarding the created world being described as a cosmic temple in *The Temple and the Church's Mission: A Biblical Theology of the Dwelling Place of God*, NSBT (Downers Grove, IL: InterVarsity, 2004).

the future (41:22), which would prove its deity (41:23a); inviting the idol to do good or evil (41:23b); pressing the conclusion that the idol is nothing, the idol's work is nothing, and those who choose the idol make themselves an abomination (41:24, cf. 29).[134] Idolaters do not process the upshot of these realities, and Isaiah in 44:9–20 and 46:6–7 repeats this merciful exercise of showing idolaters what they themselves do to produce their objects of worship. These passages invite Isaiah's audience to consider their ways and live in reality. Exposing the processes of idol making deflates the attraction of the evil and reveals that only the living and true God is worthy of worship and trust. These carved and decorated blocks of wood are, in Isaiah's words and in reality, worthless and nothing (41:24, 29).[135]

Unlike the idol, which was made by its worshipers, Yahweh alone is the Creator of all things (Isa. 40:22, 26; 41:20; 42:5; 44:24; 45:18; 48:13). Nor should anyone think that while Yahweh made what is good, some dark Zoroastrian power is responsible for the other side of things. Isaiah declares with astonishing boldness:

> I am Yahweh and there is no other;
> besides me there is no God.
> I will gird you, though you have not known me,
> that they may know from the rising of the sun to the place of its setting
> that there is none besides me.
> I am Yahweh and there is no other;
> shaping light and creating darkness,
> making peace and creating evil [ובורא רע];[136]
> I am Yahweh, the one who does all these. (45:5–7)

---

[134]There seems to be a chiastic arrangement in Isaiah 41:

41:2–4, Yahweh announces that he is raising up one from the east.
  41:5–7, The coastlands respond by crafting an idol.
    41:8–20, Yahweh assures Israel that he will save them.
  41:21–24, The idols are invited to declare the future or do good or evil.
41:25–29, Yahweh announces that he has raised up one from the north.

[135]Perhaps if Isaiah were prophesying today, he would indict the cult of the female body, worshiped by men gawking at pornography and by women giving themselves to eating disorders in attempts to attain the perceived ideal. Perhaps Isaiah would invite men to consider that there is really nothing they can do with pictures or videos that will ultimately satisfy them, and perhaps he would remind them that these are pictures of real people (who will age) with real souls—someone's daughter, granddaughter, sister, friend—people who will stand before the real God. Perhaps he would invite women to recognize that the look they hope to achieve has not given the women that have that look the fulfillment and glamour advertised in the images. The miserable lives of these stars and starlets are on display on magazine racks in grocery stores everywhere. Like Paul, Isaiah urges his audience to worship the Creator rather than the created. Only in worshiping God will we find satisfaction, fulfillment, and lasting joy.

[136]This phrase, ובורא רע, is typically translated "create disaster/calamity." However we render רע ("bad/evil"), there is no escaping the conclusion that it pertains to what is unpleasant—things no one wants to experience. We see this from the statement of its opposite, שלום, "peace," which is often a holistic description of the good life. It is also worth pointing out that the verb ברא, "create," is the same term used in Gen. 1:1, and only Yahweh is the subject of this verb in the Old Testament.

Yahweh is the only God. This makes him responsible for all that is. He is not evil. He never does evil. He is altogether holy, righteous, and good. Evil's existence, however, was no accident. Evil does not thwart Yahweh's plan, and it was not brought into existence by Satan. Moreover, the use of the verb ברא, "create," indicates that evil actually is something (against the idea that it should be thought of as merely the absence of good). Probably none of us would write Isaiah 45:7. Perhaps Isaiah did so only because he was inspired to do so (cf. Isa. 6:9–10; 63:17). Isaiah 45:7 teaches that God is absolutely sovereign over all that is. This should not trouble us with questions about God's goodness. We know he is good. He showed his goodness to Moses when he revealed himself as a saving and judging God (Ex. 33:18–34:7). Rather than being troubling, the teaching of Isaiah 45:7, that Yahweh created evil—that is what the text says—is a comfort, because it tells us, as hymned in "God Moves in a Mysterious Way," that behind the frowning providence God hides a smiling face. God has good purposes that are not thwarted but accomplished by evil. Apart from this, hope could be challenged. But if God is even sovereign over evil, hope can be affirmed with full-throated, unabashed resolution. God will be glorified by all that is, even if we do not yet understand how everything will come together.

Yahweh is the first and the last (Isa. 41:5; 43:10, 13; 44:6; 48:12). He declares the future (42:9; 43:9; 44:7; 45:11, 21; 46:10; 48:3–8). Because Isaiah's argument against the idols leans so heavily on Yahweh's ability to declare the future and the inability of the idols to do so (cf. 41:22), this conclusion must inevitably follow: if Yahweh cannot declare the future, he is no better than the idols. But this is not Isaiah's view. Isaiah is convinced of Yahweh's claim to be the only God (44:8; 45:6, 18, 21–22; 46:9). Yahweh will defend Israel and enable them to conquer (41:8–20; 42:6; 46:4, 12–13). Israel's current woes are Yahweh's justice against their covenant infidelity (42:24–25), but Yahweh will be the one who saves them after the judgment (43:1–28). This pattern of an announcement of salvation immediately following an explanation of Yahweh's just judgment can also be seen in Isaiah 45:16, a statement of judgment, followed by 45:17, a statement of salvation. Israel has weighed Yahweh down with her sins (43:24). They have sinned like their first father (43:27), but Yahweh, the only Savior (41:28; 43:11), blots out their transgressions and redeems them (44:22).

The next section of Isaiah, chapters 49–55 (cf. 52:13–53:12), will clarify the role of Yahweh's enigmatic servant (41:8–9; 42:1–4, 19; 43:10; 44:1, 21; 45:4) in this process of Yahweh's redemption. In the current section, Isaiah 40–48, the servant takes on the blindness and deafness Isaiah was commissioned to produce (cf. 6:9–10; 42:18–19), and this seems to open the way for Israel to experience the alleviation of blindness and deafness (cf. 42:7, 16, 23; 43:8; cf. 44:18).

Yahweh will bring his people back from the exile he promised to inflict when he commissioned Isaiah in 6:11–13 (Isa. 43:5–6, 14–20; 48:20–21). Ministering from about 740 BC to perhaps the 680s, Isaiah prophesies of the Persian king, Cyrus, who will conquer Babylon in 539 BC. Yahweh identifies Cyrus as his servant who will send his people home (41:2–4, 25–29;[137] 44:28–45:13; 46:11; 48:15). Bel and Nebo, false gods who do not carry (cf. 40:31) but must be carried (46:1), will themselves go into exile (46:2). Babylon will be judged (47:1–15; 48:14).

When Israel is delivered, foreign nations will recognize Yahweh as the only God (Isa. 45:14). In this way the renewal of Israel will be hope and light for the nations (42:6). Yahweh saves his people from idolatry through the judgment of exile, and then he saves them through the judgment of their captors. He will not give his glory to another (42:8; 48:11). When Israel conquers her enemies (42:14–15), she will "rejoice in Yahweh and glory in the Holy One of Israel" (41:16). Yahweh's praise will come from the ends of the earth (42:10–13). He formed his people for himself that they would declare his praise (43:21). The justified will glory in Yahweh (45:25).

If Yahweh is the only true God, the only Creator, who is responsible for all that is, if he declares that he will not share his glory with others, and if history culminates in Yahweh being glorified, then it is difficult to avoid the conclusion that Yahweh has worked to bring about a situation that results in glory for himself. Indeed, Isaiah celebrates Yahweh's intention: Yahweh has acted for the sake of his own righteousness (Isa. 42:21). He has created his people for his own glory (43:7). Yahweh has blotted out the transgressions of his people "for my own sake" (43:25). He has "glorified himself" (44:23). He has acted so that he will be known as Yahweh (45:3, 6). He swears by himself that every knee will bow and every tongue swear allegiance (45:23). He asserts that he defers his wrath on Israel "for my name's sake," restraining it "for my praise" (48:9), declaring with repetitious insistence, "for my own sake, for my own sake I will act, for how can my name be profaned? And my glory to another I will not give" (48:11).

It is righteous only for Yahweh to act for his own sake, for his own glory, because he alone is the first and the last, the only Creator, the only Redeemer, the only one who can declare the future. He judges to vindicate his holiness. He saves to display his mercy. He glorifies himself. "For Yahweh is our judge; Yahweh is our lawgiver; Yahweh is our king; he will save us" (Isa. 33:22).

3.2.9 The Suffering Servant (Isaiah 49–55)

In Isaiah 49–55 the focus shifts from the matchless greatness of Yahweh to his servant, who will be glorified (Isa. 52:13). Yahweh announces that he himself will be glorified in his servant (49:3), whom he formed to bring Jacob and Israel back

[137] I follow John N. Oswalt (*The Book of Isaiah: Chapters 40–66*, NICOT (Grand Rapids: Eerdmans, 1998), 81, 103) in identifying both the "one from the east" (41:2) and the "one from the north" (41:25) as Cyrus.

to himself—and the servant says that he will be glorious in Yahweh's eyes and that God will be his strength (49:5). Yahweh then declares that bringing Jacob and Israel back through his servant is "too small": "I will also give you as a light to the nations, to be my salvation to the end of the earth" (49:6). Through the servant (note the singular pronouns in 49:8) the captives will be released (49:9), sheltered and led (49:10) on the highways (49:11) even from north and south and the land of Sinim (49:12; ESV, "Syene"), and the heavens and earth will break forth in singing because Yahweh has *comforted* his people (49:13; cf. 40:1). Yahweh will not forget his people (49:14–26). He has inscribed them on the palms of his hands (49:16). When the enemies of his people lick the dust—judgment (cf. Gen. 3:14)—his people will know that he is Yahweh—salvation and glory (Isa. 49:23). All flesh will know that he is Yahweh, Savior and Redeemer to his people, the mighty one of Jacob (49:26).

After Yahweh's questions, which seem to contrast his ability to save with the inability of those on whom Israel has relied (Isa. 50:1–3), it appears that Yahweh's servant begins to describe what Yahweh has done for him. Yahweh has given the servant a tongue to speak and ears to hear (50:4–5), and this enables the servant to bear reproach: "I gave my back to those who strike, and my cheeks to those who pull out the beard; I hid not my face from disgrace and spitting" (50:6). The servant is able to do this because Yahweh helps and justifies him, making it so that none can condemn him (50:7–9). Then in Isaiah 50:10, Isaiah asks his contemporaries who among them fears Yahweh and obeys the servant. He who would do so is exhorted to "trust in the name of Yahweh and rely upon his God" (50:10). Those who do not do so face torment (50:11). From Isaiah 50, it appears that the servant, who glorifies Yahweh (49:3), through whom Yahweh will turn Israel and the nations to himself (49:6), is one who will obediently (50:4–5) bear reproach and rejection (50:6), trusting Yahweh for vindication and help (50:7–9). Meanwhile Isaiah encourages his audience to "obey the voice" of Yahweh's servant (50:10) or face torment (50:11). This is reminiscent of the promised prophet like Moses, whose word Yahweh will enforce, promising to punish any who do not obey him (Deut. 18:15–19).

I have argued elsewhere that the promises to Abraham in Genesis 12:1–3 answer the curses of Genesis 3:14–19, pointing to Yahweh's intention to overcome those curses by blessing Abraham and reopening the way to Eden.[138] Isaiah 51 seems to support this interpretation as Isaiah reminds his audience of the way Yahweh blessed Abraham (Isa. 51:1–2) and then promises that when he comforts Zion, "he will make her wilderness like Eden, and her desert like the garden of Yahweh" (51:3).

[138]See James M. Hamilton Jr., "The Seed of the Woman and the Blessing of Abraham," *TynBul* 58 (2007): 253–73.

When Yahweh refurbishes Zion, what was prophesied in Isaiah 2:1–5 will be realized. This can be seen from the way that Isaiah 51:4–6 matches Isaiah 2:1–5. Law goes forth from Yahweh to establish justice (Isa. 51:4). Yahweh judges the people (51:5). And his salvation and glory stand forever in the new earth.

This is the vision of the future that Isaiah calls his contemporaries to embrace. Yahweh commanded Israel to have his law on their hearts (Deut. 6:6), and Isaiah addresses God's people as those in whose hearts is Yahweh's law: he calls them not to fear reproaches from men, who will perish with the years, for Yahweh's salvation and righteousness stand forever (Isa. 51:7–8).

After celebrating the way Yahweh delivered Israel in the past (Isa. 51:9–16),[139] Isaiah calls Israel to recognize that they have tasted the cup of the fury of his wrath (51:17). Drinking this cup has made them drunk (51:18–21), but God's people will no longer drink from it. It will be given to their enemies (51:22–23). Israel will be saved through drinking the cup of judgment, and then Israel will be saved when her enemies drink the cup of judgment. Salvation will come through judgment for the glory of Yahweh.

Isaiah 52 calls Zion to awaken and adorn herself and shake off the bonds of captivity from her neck (Isa. 52:1–2), for Yahweh will redeem Zion just as he redeemed his people from Egypt (52:3–10)—by the might of his arm (52:10) for the glory of his name (52:5b–6). Interestingly, just before the servant passage in Isaiah 52:13–53:12, Isaiah 52:11–12 calls Israel to go out, to depart from captivity, to experience the new exodus. Unlike the first exodus, they will not go out in haste; but like the first exodus, Yahweh will go before them and be their rear guard (52:12). The juxtaposition of these passages connects the sin-bearing work of the servant in Isaiah 53 to the new exodus, the return from exile, the return to Eden, in Isaiah 52.

The servant accomplishes salvation through judgment for God's glory in a way that baffles the world.[140] The servant will be exalted and lifted up (Isa. 52:13), but not in a worldly way. The disfigurement of the servant will be astonishing (52:14), but through this, many nations will be sprinkled (52:15). The servant's work will shut the mouths of kings, and it causes Isaiah to ask who has believed his report (52:15–53:1). The description of the servant as a tender shoot, a root out of dry ground (53:2a), connects this servant to the king who will spring up from Jesse's roots (Isa. 11:1). And yet he is not a king impressive by human standards of measurement. He is not beautiful but despised (53:2b–3a), not glad but grieving (53:3b), not accepted but rejected and shunned (53:3c).

---

[139] See Fishbane's comments on typology, *Biblical Interpretation in Ancient Israel*, 354–55.

[140] See Oswalt's discussion, "The Book of Isaiah: A Short Course on Biblical Theology," 65–66. Cf. also John H. Walton, "The Imagery of the Substitute King Ritual in Isaiah's Fourth Servant Song," *JBL* 122 (2003): 734–43.

In all this, the servant bears the griefs and sorrows of the people, who esteem him stricken, smitten, and afflicted (Isa. 53:4). This estimation is false, however, for the truth is that he is wounded for the transgression of the people, pierced for their iniquities. His chastisement results in their peace, and the stripes he receives result in their healing (53:5). The people have strayed like sheep, and Yahweh puts their iniquity on the servant (53:6), who goes like a lamb to slaughter through oppression and affliction (53:7). He is cut off for their transgression, his grave is with the wicked, and yet he is with the rich at his death; he does no violence and tells no lies (53:8–9). It pleases Yahweh to crush him. He makes his soul a sin offering. The pleasure of Yahweh prospers in his hand (53:10). This must mean that Yahweh's justice against the people is satisfied through the servant's vicarious, substitutionary sacrifice. And this sacrifice is penal. He is cut off for their transgression. Through judgment he accomplishes salvation, bearing the sins of others and achieving their justification, making intercession for them (53:11–12). Through the judgment that falls on the servant, salvation comes for the people.[141] The connection between the servant's work (52:13–53:12) and the return from exile (cf. 52:11–12) informs the announcement in Isaiah 40:2 that the iniquity of the people is pardoned because they have received from Yahweh's hand—vicariously through the punishment of the servant who satisfies Yahweh—double for all their sins.

Through judgment salvation comes for God's glory. The opening statement of the next chapter, Isaiah 54:1, calls the barren to sing! The tent will be enlarged (54:2–3) because shame has been taken away and Yahweh will husband his people (54:5). His everlasting kindness will make his wrath seem little, and his mercy will make the hiding of his face seem momentary (54:7–8).

Isaiah 55 summons the people to satisfy themselves on Yahweh, to incline to the prophetic word and thereby find life and enjoy the blessings of the Davidic covenant (Isa. 55:1–3). The Davidic king will rule the nations because Yahweh has glorified him as the leader of his people (55:4–5). Peter Gentry connects this to "the Servant King in Isa 53 whose offering of himself as an *'āšām* and whose resurrection enable him to bring to fulfillment the promises of Yahweh in the Davidic Covenant and is at the same time the basis for the New or Everlasting Covenant."[142] Through the judgment on the servant in Isaiah 49–55, Yahweh brings his people to salvation for his own glory. The fact that this glory is so unexpected by the world, so little esteemed by those who measure by human

[141]Cf. Routledge, "Is There a Narrative Substructure Underlying the Book of Isaiah?" 199–200.

[142]Gentry, "Rethinking the 'Sure Mercies of David' in Isaiah 55:3," 301. See also the discussion of Isa. 55:1–5 as an interpretation of Psalm 89 in Knut M. Heim, "The (God-)Forsaken King of Psalm 89: A Historical and Intertextual Enquiry," in *King and Messiah in Israel and the Ancient Near East*, ed. John Day, JSOTSup (Sheffield: Sheffield Academic, 1998), 306–14.

standards, so difficult to recognize, augments the glory of the wisdom that Yahweh displays in saving through judgment.

3.2.10 Future Deliverance (Isaiah 56–66)

If the nation's immediate future is decreed[143]—as Yahweh announces the exile and return through his prophet Isaiah—how should Isaiah's own generation respond? That is the question Isaiah answers in chapters 56–66. Isaiah opens this portion of his prophecy with the declaration, "Thus says Yahweh: 'Keep justice and do righteousness, for my salvation is about to come and my righteousness to be revealed'" (Isa. 56:1). The certainty of Yahweh's sovereign plan summons his people to responsibility. Their quality of life will improve if they respond in faith to Isaiah and seek Yahweh's glory. As will be seen in the accounts of Daniel, Yahweh blesses his people in exile such that those who honor him are honored, even if they never return to the land. There is something worse than exile: continuing in rebellious rejection of Yahweh. Those who drink from the waters, who buy wine and milk without money and without price (Isa. 55:1), satisfying their souls on the richest of fare (55:2), that is, Yahweh himself, find blessing even if they are not native to Israel, even if they are a eunuch (cf. Isa. 56:3–8).

John Oswalt proposes[144] a chiastic arrangement of Isaiah 56–66 (see table 3.8).

Table 3.8. Oswalt's Chiastic Structure of Isaiah 56–66

55:1–8, Foreign worshipers

  56:9–59:15a, Ethical righteousness

    59:15b–21, Divine warrior

      60–62, Eschatological hope

    63:1–6, Divine warrior

  63:7–66:17, Ethical righteousness

66:18–24, Foreign worshipers

Through Isaiah, Yahweh roundly condemns idolatry and unrighteousness, offering the way to salvation—the way of trusting Yahweh and heeding Isaiah's word. The concluding chapters of Isaiah are rich with the life that will accompany trust in Yahweh, the power of the divine warrior to save and judge, and the worship Yahweh's redeemed will render to him. He saves through judgment to the glory of his name.

[143]See Joseph Jensen, "Yahweh's Plan in Isaiah and in the Rest of the Old Testament," *CBQ* 48 (1986): 443–55.
[144]Oswalt, *The Book of Isaiah: 40–66*, 465.

3.2.11 The Center of the Theology of Isaiah

Yahweh's glory covers Isaiah's New Jerusalem (Isaiah 2, 4).[145] Yahweh's glory will be seen in the rollback of the curses, when the nursing child plays by the hole of the cobra (Isaiah 11). Yahweh's glory is shown when he slays the dragon in the sea (Isaiah 27), when he makes the desert a new Eden (Isaiah 35, 51), and when he returns to Zion (Isaiah 40) because the servant has been crushed for the people's iniquities (Isaiah 53). And after the sacrifice in Bozrah (Isaiah 34), when his robe is spattered with blood from the judgment of his enemies (Isaiah 63), Yahweh's people will gather to worship him. They will worship him for the mercy he has shown them by saving them, and they will worship him for the justice they see displayed in the undying worm and the unquenched flame (Isaiah 66). The center of Isaiah's theology is the glory of God in salvation through judgment.[146]

3.3 Jeremiah

Jeremiah narrates his call to serve as a prophet (Jeremiah 1), and from there he begins to announce the coming judgment and calls the people to repentance (Jeremiah 2–6). In Jeremiah 7–20 judgment looks increasingly inevitable. Jeremiah is pained (Jeremiah's "confessions") by the awful sin of the people that is exposed by the radiating light of Yahweh's glory. When the judgment becomes unavoidable, Jeremiah is shown that the nation should surrender to Babylon (Jeremiah 21–24). In chapters 25–33 the exile is prophesied, but these chapters also promise hope beyond exile, especially in Jeremiah 30–33 (the "Book of Consolation"). These promises of hope show that Jeremiah's prophecy matches the argument of this book: God will be glorified in salvation through judgment.[147] In Jeremiah,

---

[145]Dumbrell (*The Faith of Israel*, 108) states, "If the book is read as a unit, one overarching theme may be seen to unite the whole: Yahweh's interest in and devotion to the city of Jerusalem." But throughout Isaiah it is clear that Jerusalem is not an end in itself. Isaiah explicitly declares that the New Jerusalem will be a display of Yahweh's glory, achieved through the demonstration of his just wrath and loving mercy. As Routledge writes, "The main concern of the book as a whole is the revelation of God's glory to the world. This approach recognizes the importance of God's dealings with Israel, but sees them as a means to an end: an end that involves the nations recognizing God's glory . . . . The pilgrimage of the nations in Isaiah 2:2–4 is not primarily about the exaltation of Zion. Zion is exalted, but only so that the nations may be drawn to the God who has made his dwelling there" ("Is There a Narrative Substructure Underlying the Book of Isaiah?" 203).

[146]Cf. the assessment of John Oswalt ("The Book of Isaiah: A Short Course on Biblical Theology," 67): "I agree with the late Gerhard Hasel when he said that the center of Old Testament theology, and indeed, of biblical theology, is God [citing G. F. Hasel, *Old Testament Theology: Basic Issues in the Current Debate*, 4th ed. (Grand Rapids: Eerdmans, 1991), 168–71]. . . . Before the Israelites needed to know deliverance, they needed to know the Deliverer. Thus, throughout the Bible, the cause of deliverance is the self-revelation of God." Roberts's conclusion ("Isaiah in Old Testament Theology," 131) is similar: "If there is any one concept central to the whole Book of Isaiah, it is the vision of Yahweh as the Holy One of Israel." My proposal is in basic agreement with the conclusion of Roberts, Hasel, and Oswalt, but seeks to sharpen it into a more precise and yet still comprehensive statement.

[147]Cf. Jack R. Lundbom, *Jeremiah 1–20*, AB (New York: Doubleday, 1999), 141: "Ideas about Yahweh, Yahweh's word, the covenant, judgment, and salvation have their embodiment in rhetoric, i.e., in metaphors, argument, and ironic comment, in lyric poetry and impassioned preaching . . . ." Lundbom later (148) writes, "While sin and judgment form the bulk of Jeremiah's preaching, interwoven throughout are messages of grace and salvation, where 'salvation' is understood to mean primarily deliverance from one's enemies. . . . Jeremiah prayed for his salvation (17:14–18), and when doubts gave way to belief and the crisis had passed, he expressed profound gratitude to Yahweh (20:11–13)." Jeremiah's gratitude glorifies the one who saves through judgment.

through the judgment of the exile, the people will be redeemed. In Jeremiah 34–45 the people decisively reject Yahweh's word, justifying the exile. Yahweh's land has been defiled by the idolatry of the people, and the holiness of his glory is vindicated by the exile. The happiness of the salvation promised when the exile is over will be the enjoyment of Yahweh's glory, when they will be his people and he will be their God (Jer. 7:23; 11:4; 24:7; 30:22; 31:1, 33; 32:38). The narrative of the fall of Jerusalem is both painful and purging: through the chastening comes the cleansing. As is typical in the Latter Prophets, once Yahweh has judged his people, he judges those he has used to discipline them: thus Jeremiah's oracles against the nations in chapters 46–51.[148] Chapter 52 punctuates Jeremiah's prophecy by retelling (cf. 39:1–10) the fall of Jerusalem, validating Jeremiah's prophecies. What he prophesied came to pass, and the end of his prophecy reiterates this story to make that point. Like 2 Kings, Jeremiah ends on the hopeful note of the kindness shown to Jehoiachin in Babylon (52:31–34).[149]

The opening chapter of Jeremiah, and the first section, chapters 2–6, are programmatic for the whole book. Accordingly, they will receive the fullest treatment here. For the other sections of the book, space limitations permit only summaries of major themes.

3.3.1 The Call of Jeremiah (Jeremiah 1)

Jeremiah opens by identifying himself and his times. The word of Yahweh came to him, Son of Hilkiah,[150] of the priests in Anathoth, in the thirteenth year of Josiah's reign, 627 BC, until the end of the eleventh year of Zedekiah, when

[148]In the LXX the oracles against the nations, Jeremiah 46–51, follow Jer. 25:13, and the Greek text of the whole book has been estimated as between one-eighth (J. A. Thompson, *The Book of Jeremiah*, NICOT [Grand Rapids: Eerdmans, 1980], 117) and one-sixth shorter than the Masoretic Text (Natalio Fernández Marcos, *The Septuagint in Context: Introduction to the Greek Version of the Bible* [Boston: Brill, 2000], 81). David Reimer places it at one-seventh, citing the statistic of 3,097 words of the MT lacking in LXX (David J. Reimer, *The Oracles Against Babylon in Jeremiah 50–51: A Horror Among the Nations* [San Francisco: Mellen Research University Press, 1993], 108). For a chart of the discrepancies in verse numbering between English texts and the Rahlfs text, see appendix D in Jobes and Silva, *Invitation to the Septuagint*, 329–31. Reimer (*The Oracles Against Babylon*, 293) provides a table that compares the editions of Ziegler and Rahlfs to the MT. Marcos writes, "Jeremiah-LXX reflects a first, shorter edition of Jeremiah, which is earlier than the second enlarged edition transmitted by the Masoretic text" (81), and Peter J. Gentry observes, "The biographical notes in the book of Jeremiah clearly indicate that the work was rewritten several times. The book was sent to the exiles in Babylon, but Jeremiah himself migrated to Egypt. This history in itself suggests that perhaps the version in Egypt is not the canonical version" ("The Septuagint and the Text of the Old Testament," *BBR* 16 [2006]: 217 [193–218], and see the extensive bibliography of studies on the Greek text of Jeremiah, 217–18 n. 66).

[149]This way of breaking down the chapters of Jeremiah is adapted from the outline of the book in Gordon McConville, "Jeremiah, Theology of," *NIDOTTE*, 4:757. For another discussion of the structure of Jeremiah, which seems to be followed by Thompson in his NICOT volume, see John Bright, "The Book of Jeremiah: Its Structure, Its Problems, and their Significance for the Interpreter," *Int* 9 (1955): 262–67.

[150]This could be the Hilkiah who found the book of the Torah (2 Kings 22:8), but if that is the same Hilkiah as the one in the genealogy in 1 Chron. 6:13, Jeremiah is not listed after him there. It could be that Jeremiah was not the eldest son. C. F. Keil ("Jeremiah," in KD, 8:25) notes that Clement of Alexandria, Jerome, and "some Rabbins" identified Jeremiah's father as the one who found the Torah, but Keil rejects the identification because Hilkiah is a common name, and the high priest would have lived in Jerusalem rather than Anathoth. The proximity of Anathoth to Jerusalem, two miles, would seem to allow for the possibility, but we cannot be certain. If Jeremiah's father was the high priest who found the Torah, it would fit with Jeremiah's many points of contact with Deuteronomy, his access to the kings of Judah, and his powerful friends (cf. 26:24).

Jerusalem was taken into exile in 586 BC (Jer. 1:1–3). The last event Jeremiah narrates is the elevation of Jehoiachin in Babylon in 561 BC (52:31–34).[151] Yahweh revealed to Jeremiah that he knew him before he formed him in the womb, and that he sanctified him to be a prophet to the nations before he was born (1:5). Such a declaration highlights God's sovereign foreknowledge of and control over history.

After Jeremiah's protests about his tender age (Jer. 1:6), Yahweh promises to be with Jeremiah, touches his mouth, and then puts his words in Jeremiah's mouth (1:8–9).[152] That Yahweh puts his word in Jeremiah's mouth means that Yahweh will accomplish his purposes through Jeremiah: "to pluck up and to break down, to destroy and to overthrow, to build and to plant" (1:10).[153] The plucking up, breaking down, destroying, and overthrowing precede the building and the planting. Salvation will come through judgment. Yahweh will use Jeremiah himself to judge his people, and through the judgment he will save them.

Yahweh reveals that he is watching over his word to perform it (Jer. 1:11–12), and then shows Jeremiah a boiling pot facing away from the north, about to pour down on his people (1:13–15). The word Yahweh is going to perform is the troth he pledged in the covenant curses of Leviticus 26 and Deuteronomy 28. He will do this because his people have forsaken him and have worshiped idols (Jer. 1:16). The theme of forsaking Yahweh is significant in Jeremiah,[154] pointing as it does to the root issue of sin: not trusting, enjoying, and worshiping Yahweh, which is to say, not glorifying him.

Anticipating the reception Jeremiah faces, Yahweh tells Jeremiah not to be dismayed by the people, lest he be dismayed by Yahweh, because Yahweh is setting Jeremiah among the people like a fortified city, an iron pillar, bronze walls, against them and their leaders (Jer. 1:17–18). Jeremiah will face opposition, "'but they will not prevail over you, for I am with you,' an utterance of Yahweh, 'to deliver you'" (1:19; cf. 1:8). The judgment Jeremiah will proclaim will stand among the people like an unyielding fortress, and Yahweh's word will prevail.

[151]Thompson (*The Book of Jeremiah*, 10–11) suggests that Jeremiah would have been 16 to 18 years old when his ministry began (cf. 1:6–7), which would mean that by 561 he would be in his 80s. Lundbom (*Jeremiah 1–20*, 107) suggests Jeremiah was 12 or 13 when he was called, born ca. 640 BC. Some have suggested that Jeremiah was born in the thirteenth year of Josiah (for bibliography see Thompson, *The Book of Jeremiah*, 10 n. 1), but that is not the most natural reading of the text. For a chart of "Dated Material in Jeremiah," see Dillard and Longman, *An Introduction to the Old Testament*, 341. For external (from Babylonian records, Lachish Ostraca, and Bullae) and internal (from historical settings, "mistakes," and literary criticism) evidence that in Jeremiah "the gap between event and text is not impossibly large," see David J. Reimer, "Jeremiah Before the Exile?" in *In Search of Pre-exilic Israel*, JSOTSup, ed. John Day (New York: T&T Clark, 2004), 207–24.

[152]Cf. Isaiah's recognition of his unclean lips, the touching of his lips with the coal from the altar, and the commission that followed (Isa. 6:5–10).

[153]This language and imagery recurs throughout Jeremiah's prophecy: cf. Jer. 12:17; 18:7; 24:6; 31:28, 40.

[154]See Jer. 1:16; 2:13, 17, 19; 5:7, 19; 15:6; 16:11; 17:13; 19:4; cf. 22:9. This theme is not limited to the usage of עזב, "forsake," as נטשׁ, "forsake," is also used (e.g., 15:6). There are many related ideas, as well, such as the people going far from Yahweh (2:5), turning their backs to Yahweh, not their faces (2:27), and so forth.

3.3.2 Early Oracles Calling for Repentance and Announcing Judgment (Jeremiah 2–6)

The precise structure of the book of Jeremiah is difficult to ascertain, but it seems that the formula "and the word of Yahweh came to me saying" in 2:1 marks the beginning of a new section.[155] The conclusion of this section seems to be signaled by the similarity between 6:27–30 and 1:17–19. In 6:27–30 Yahweh again tells Jeremiah that he set him among the people as a fortress (6:27); again bronze and iron are referenced—but this time they refer to the people rather than Jeremiah (6:28); and again the people's opposition to Jeremiah will not prevail, for Yahweh has rejected them (6:30).[156]

In keeping with the idea that the Latter Prophets provide an explanatory commentary on the narrative story line of the Torah and the Former Prophets, these chapters of Jeremiah depict the exodus from Egypt and the covenant at Sinai as a wedding between Yahweh and his virgin bride, Israel (Jer. 2:2; cf. Hos. 2:17–18, ET 15–16).[157] While a virgin bride's memories of the glory of the wedding day would keep her faithful to her husband, Israel has forgotten Yahweh "days without number" (Jer. 2:32). Jeremiah calls the people to repent of their spiritual adultery.[158] The horror of covenant infidelity, forsaking Yahweh and turning to idols (1:16), should be recognized by the fruit it will bear: Jeremiah prophesies that it will lead to the unwanted pregnancy that gives birth to exile. Yahweh asks what wrong was found in him by Israel's fathers to prompt them to trade him in for idols (2:4–5). The problem is not on his side, however: the people did not seek him who redeemed them (2:6), and they defiled the good land he gave (2:7). Therefore, Yahweh brings charges (ריב) against the people (2:9; cf. Hos. 2:4, ET 2).

With a rhetorical question reminiscent of Moses (cf. Deut. 4:32–40), Jeremiah invites his audience to search the east and the west (coasts of Cyprus to the west, Kedar to the east) "and see if there has been such a thing. Has a nation changed its gods, and they are not gods! But my people have changed their glory for what

[155]For similar formulas that may mark new sections, or sections within sections, see Jer. 7:1; 11:1; 14:1; 17:19; 18:1; 21:1; 25:1; 27:1; 30:1; 32:1; 33:1. In chapter 33 and following the formula seems to recur more frequently, and so it may be less significant: 33:19, 23; 24:1, 8, 12; 35:1, 12; 36:1, etc.

[156]For a similar juxtaposition of these ideas that may mark the end of one sub-section and the beginning of another, see Jer. 15:20–21; 16:1.

[157]It is interesting to observe how freely the prophets move between the metaphors used to describe Yahweh's relationship with his people. For instance, immediately following the wedding imagery in Jer. 2:20, where Israel is depicted as a harlot, Jeremiah describes Yahweh planting Israel as a choice vine in 2:21 (cf. Ps. 128:3). Similarly, in language that seems to recall Yahweh announcing to Pharaoh that Israel is his firstborn son, Jeremiah says in 3:19 that the people will call Yahweh "My Father" (3:19), and this is immediately followed in 3:20 by language of a wife cheating on her husband. The various metaphors all capture and communicate different aspects of Yahweh's relationship with his people. For a discussion of "The Forms and Imagery of Jeremiah 50–51" that ranges widely through Jeremiah and the rest of the Hebrew Bible, see Reimer, *The Oracles Against Babylon*, 159–243.

[158]Lundbom (*Jeremiah 1–20*, 142) writes, "Jeremiah's preaching betrays indebtedness to the northern prophet Hosea."

does not profit" (Jer. 2:10–11). The situation in Jeremiah's day is even more dire than it was in Isaiah's, so when, like Isaiah (cf. Isa. 1:2), Jeremiah calls a witness to the covenant to testify against Israel, the heavens are invoked with a horrified cry: "'Be astonished at this, O heavens; bristle and be desolate,' an utterance of Yahweh, 'for my people have committed two evils: they have forsaken me, the fountain of living water, to hew for themselves cisterns, broken cisterns that are not able to hold water'" (Jer. 2:12; cf. Deut. 4:26; 30:19; 32:1).

Rather than trust Yahweh, Israel has relied upon Egypt and Assyria (Jer. 2:18, 36).[159] Reliance upon these nations is like refusing an ever-flowing spring of fresh water in favor of a broken cistern that does not hold water (2:13; cf. 17:13). Trying to drink from that cistern, which only collects runoff water and cannot hold what it collects, makes Israel seem like a beaten and broken slave (2:14–17). Jeremiah does not let his audience forget the main problem: they have forsaken Yahweh (2:19). They cannot wash themselves clean (2:22), nor can they deny their idolatry (2:23). They are like a camel or a donkey in heat, resolutely pursuing lovers (2:23–25). Israel is caught, and their gods cannot deliver (2:26–28).

The implications of Israel's spiritual adultery are rigorously pursued in Jeremiah 3–4. Having vividly described Israel's whoring ways (Jer. 3:1–10), Yahweh calls his people to repentance (3:11–13), promising to take them back, provide shepherds after his own heart, and make Jerusalem his throne (3:14–17). Jeremiah teaches Israel to acknowledge their sin (3:13) and provides them with appropriate words to say: a confession of trust in Yahweh and a denunciation of the futility of idolatry (3:22–25).[160]

Yahweh promises to take his people back if they repent (Jer. 4:1–2), even though a husband forgiving his wife in such circumstances would pollute the land (3:1). Adding to the tragedy of Israel's refusal to repent is the indication that if Israel repents and swears "'as Yahweh lives,' in truth, in justice, and in righteousness, the nations will bless themselves in him, and in him they will glory" (4:2). The reference to the nations' blessing themselves in Yahweh indicates that the promises to Abraham would be realized (cf. Gen. 12:3) if Israel would repent and glorify Yahweh. The nations could enjoy Yahweh through Israel's restoration, but Israel still needs to do what Moses commanded in Deuteronomy 10:16, circumcise their hearts (Jer. 4:4).

The coming fierce anger of Yahweh (Jer. 4:4, 8) calls for a trumpet blast of alarm (4:5). The threatened destruction (4:5–9) leads Jeremiah to accuse Yahweh

[159] J. G. McConville (*Judgment and Promise: An Interpretation of the Book of Jeremiah* [Winona Lake, IN: Eisenbrauns, 1993], 29–33) discusses the complexity of the use of "Israel" and "Judah" in Jeremiah 2 and concludes that the two together represent historic Israel, of which only Judah remains, and the fate of the north is recalled for the benefit of Judah. He also suggests that Assyria is something of a cipher for Babylon.

[160] Thompson (*The Book of Jeremiah*, 208–9) says that this could be either a record of repentance or a rhetorical modeling of repentance. Charles L. Feinberg ("Jeremiah," in *EBC*, 6:403–404) takes it as a record of repentance.

of deceiving the people by offering mercy if they repent (4:10). In fact, that is what the people are getting—mercy—even in Jeremiah's accusation! Such an accusation forcibly communicates the certainty of the coming judgment in the face of unlikely repentance. People will repent only if they become convinced of the certainty of coming judgment, so convinced that they cease to presume on Yahweh's mercy and "ask for the ancient paths" (6:16). If Jeremiah's audience were to repent, they would be saved precisely through the announcement of coming judgment, a judgment that would avenge Yahweh's glory.

Jeremiah describes the severity of the judgment to come in four statements set up by the phrase "I looked" (ראיתי) in 4:23–26. Jeremiah speaks of the plundered land (ארץ) after Yahweh has destroyed it in terms of damage done to tents and curtains (4:20). The most important dwelling that will be affected is Yahweh's, and when the judgment is visited, the temple will be destroyed. The temple functions as a microcosm, a symbolic depiction of the world, which explains why Jeremiah says that he sees the earth (ארץ) "without form and void" (תהו ובהו, 4:23; cf. Gen. 1:2; Isa. 34:11). Through Yahweh's purging judgment, the land will be returned to the "formless and void," uninhabited and unproductive state it was in before Yahweh began to create.[161] Like the judgment of the flood, which was a kind of de-creation, so the judgment of exile will be a kind of de-creation. When the people are exiled and the temple is destroyed, it is as though the world is being torn down. And as there was no light before Yahweh called it into being (Gen. 1:3), so Jeremiah sees that the heavens have no light (Jer. 4:23). Mountains and hills tremble (4:24), there are no humans and the birds have fled (4:25), and the fruitful land is made a wilderness (4:26). Such are the remains of the world "from the presence of Yahweh, from before his fierce anger" (4:26).

Jeremiah 5:1 seems reminiscent of the way Abraham bargained with God to get the guarantee that if ten righteous men could be found in Sodom, the city would not be consumed (Gen. 18:22–33). Here, however, only one man who does justice and seeks truth would win Yahweh's pardon (Jer. 5:1). Repentance, however, looks increasingly unlikely.[162] Yahweh repeatedly asks, "'Shall I not punish them for these things?' an utterance of Yahweh, 'and shall I not avenge myself on a nation such as this?'" (Jer. 5:9, 29; 9:9).[163] Yahweh declares that his word will be like fire in Jeremiah's mouth, and the people will be like wood, devoured by the word of judgment (5:14). And yet he will not make a complete end (5:18).

---

[161]For "uninhabited and unproductive," see C. John Collins, *Genesis 1–4: A Linguistic, Literary, and Theological Commentary* (Phillipsburg, NJ: P&R, 2006), 44–45 n. 15, citing David Tsumara, *The Earth and the Waters in Genesis 1 and 2: A Linguistic Investigation* (Sheffield: Sheffield Academic, 1989), 41–43.

[162]Cf. McConville, *Judgment and Promise*, 39–40.

[163]McConville writes, "Often there is a contrast between Israel/Judah, the *'am* (people) of YHWH, and the other *goyim*, familiar in other Old Testament literature." The reference to Yahweh's people as a *goy* in 5:9, 29; 9:9 is then taken to "imply that Judah is a *goy* like any other" (ibid., 46).

Isaiah was commissioned to close eyes and ears, to dull hearts until the exile came (Isa. 6:9–11). Jeremiah recognizes that the people have eyes but cannot see, ears but cannot hear (Jer. 5:21). Yahweh's word is a reproach to them, and they take no delight in it because their ears are uncircumcised, and they are unable to incline to Yahweh's word (6:10). This is only augmented by the problem of false prophets and priests promising peace when there is no peace (6:14). Yahweh has placed Jeremiah among the people as a fortress precisely to show their stubborn refusal to repent (6:27–29; cf. 1:18–19). Their refusal to repent leads to Yahweh's rejection (6:30).

3.3.3 Increasingly Inevitable Judgment and Jeremiah's "Confessions" (Jeremiah 7–20)

In this section the problem that God's people have comes fully into view—they are disabled by sin (cf. Jer. 2:22). With their uncircumcised ears (6:10), they have uncircumcised hearts (9:25, ET 26; cf. 4:4). The people are fully responsible for the failure to worship and the concomitant aberrant behavior that Jeremiah denounces, and yet he can also declare, "I know, O Yahweh, that the way of man is not in himself, that it is not in man who walks to direct his steps" (10:23). Mysteriously, people are responsible even if they do not direct their own steps. The people, who are accustomed to doing evil, can no more do good than an Ethiopian can change his skin or a leopard its spots (13:23). Judah's sin is written with an iron stylus, engraved on the tablets of their hearts with the point of a diamond (17:1). And, Jeremiah says plainly,

> The heart is deceitful above all things,
>   and desperately sick;
>   who can understand it? (17:9 ESV)[164]

Jeremiah, therefore, faces a people disabled by sin. Yahweh proclaims to him, "So you shall speak all these words to them, but they will not listen to you. You shall call to them, but they will not answer you" (Jer. 7:27 ESV; cf. Isa. 6:9–10). Jeremiah declares, "Your words were found, and I ate them, and your words became to me a joy and the delight of my heart, for your name is called over me, O Yahweh, God of hosts" (Jer. 15:16). This sounds like an allusion to the finding of the Torah in 2 Kings 22, but the people do not share Jeremiah's enthusiasm. Instead, they "rejected the word of Yahweh" (Jer. 8:9), forsaking the Torah (9:12, ET 13). Yahweh's command to Jeremiah not to pray for the people is a shocking development (7:16; 11:14; 14:11), and he, Yahweh, even announces that Moses and Samuel could not move him to mercy (15:1). The situation is so bad that

---

[164]For a similar summary of Jeremiah's teaching, see Dempster, *Dominion and Dynasty*, 163–64.

Jeremiah is commanded not to marry because wives and children will be killed by the coming army (16:1–4). The people are so rebellious that there are threats on Jeremiah's life (11:18–19; 18:18). In response to one of these Jeremiah prays an imprecation against his opponents (11:20), and Yahweh promises to answer (11:21–23).

In spite of all this, Jeremiah does appeal to Yahweh's concern for his own glory in 14:7–9 and 20–22 (see the appendix [§7] to chap. 4, table 4.9, "Old Testament Prayers Appealing to God's Concern for His Own Glory"). Jeremiah explicitly calls on Yahweh to act for his own name's sake (14:7, 21).[165] Unlike other instances when he relents or saves in response to such appeals, this time Yahweh will act for his name by judging his people. McConville writes, "Judah's God, who fought for her ancestors, is now set against her in a reversal of the holy war, the only possible outcome being the 'death' of exile."[166] While repentance is still held out as a possibility (17:24–26; 18:5–11), the real hope lies in what comes through and after the judgment of exile.[167] Like Isaiah, Jeremiah proclaims a new exodus (Jer. 16:14–21; cf. 3:16–18). Interestingly, Yahweh likens the regathering of his people to the work of fishermen who will fish out his people (16:16; cf. Matt. 4:19). Salvation comes through judgment, and Jeremiah's paean to Yahweh's glory as contrasted with the worthlessness of the idols is Isaianic in the power and beauty of its celebration of Yahweh's glory (Jer. 10:6–16). Those who know him boast in him alone (9:22–23, ET 23–24).

3.3.4 The House of David and the Basket of Figs (Jeremiah 21–24)

Jeremiah 21–24 begins and ends with references to Zedekiah (Jer. 21:1; 24:8).[168] In contrast to the way that Jeremiah later writes to the exiles in Babylon (29:11), Yahweh declares regarding Jerusalem, "I have set my face against this city for harm and not for good" (21:10). The Davidic house is in view in these chapters (21:1, 3, 7, 11–12; 22:1–7, 11, 18, 24, 28–30; 24:1, 8). Hope will not come from the present line of kings (cf. esp. 22:30).[169] Instead, hope is fixed on the future, when Yahweh regathers the flock he drove away and sets up shepherds over them (23:3–4; cf. 3:15). Yahweh declares that after the judgment he "will raise up for David a righteous Branch, and he shall reign as king and deal wisely, and shall

---

[165]McConville (*Judgment and Promise*, 68) observes that Jeremiah is "cast . . . in a kind of 'servant' role," wherein he "images" Yahweh to the people. McConville concludes, "There is an incarnational aspect to this role, by which he embodies both the experience of the people and that of YHWH, yet without ever ceasing to be an individual personality" (76; similarly Dumbrell, *The Faith of Israel*, 139). Dempster (*Dominion and Dynasty*, 160) observes that Jeremiah is "patterned after the prophet like Moses envisioned in Deuteronomy 18, as God's words are directly placed in his mouth (Deut. 18:18; Jer. 1:7, 9)."

[166]McConville, *Judgment and Promise*, 75.

[167]There is far more of this in Jeremiah than can be discussed here. For instance, Dumbrell writes of Jer. 18:1–17, "The passage is a clear picture of salvation beyond judgment" (*The Faith of Israel*, 141).

[168]I owe this observation to McConville, *Judgment and Promise*, 55. We can also observe that 21:1 and 25:1 have the formula, "The word that came to Jeremiah."

[169]Ibid., 56–57.

execute justice and righteousness in the land. In his days Judah will be saved, and Israel will dwell securely. And this is the name by which he will be called: Yahweh our righteousness" (23:5–6). The regathering of the people will eclipse the exodus as the major saving event of God's people (23:7–8). Through the judgment of exile comes salvation in that great new exodus when a new David will reign, and in the judging, the saving, and the righteous ruling of the new David, Yahweh's glory shines.

In Jeremiah 24 Yahweh shows Jeremiah a basket of figs, some ripe and some rotten (Jer. 24:1–2). The good figs are the exiles to Babylon, who will be built and planted, not pulled down or plucked up (24:4–6). Moreover, Yahweh declares, "I will give them a heart to know me, that I am Yahweh, and they shall be my people and I will be their God" (24:7). The rotten figs, by contrast, are those who try to resist Babylon and face destruction (24:8–10).

3.3.5 Hope beyond Exile (Jeremiah 25–33): Book of Consolation and New Covenant (30–33)

Yahweh's wrath will be so glorious that those who behold it will be astonished (Jer. 25:9, 11), but his people will serve Babylon for only seventy years (25:11). Yahweh declares through the prophet, in 605 BC (25:1), that after seventy years he will punish Babylon (25:12). Babylon falls to the Medes and the Persians in 539 BC (cf. Dan. 5:30–6:1, ET 5:30–31).[170] Jeremiah is given the cup of Yahweh's wrath to make all nations—including Judah—drink (Jer. 25:15–29). Yahweh goes out like a lion to judge (25:30–38). It is interesting that in the final form of the text of Jeremiah, an oracle from the beginning of Jehoiakim's reign (609–608 BC) in Jeremiah 26 comes after the oracle from the fourth year of his reign in Jeremiah 25. Chronologically, the "perhaps" held out in 26:3—perhaps Israel will repent and Yahweh will show mercy (26:1–3)—and the promise that if they will amend their ways, Yahweh will relent (26:12–13) came before the announcement of the seventy years for Babylon, the cup of Yahweh's wrath, and the going forth of Yahweh like a lion in Jeremiah 25. Canonically, the present arrangement of the chapters holds out hope to the audience of the final form of the book that if those who hear the announcement of judgment will repent, Yahweh might show mercy (cf. 18:5–10).[171]

---

[170]For the fascinating tale of how Cyrus took Babylon, see Herodotus *Histories* 1:189–91. The relationship between Cyrus and Darius is difficult to sort out. Some hold that Cyrus the Persian installed Darius the Mede as viceroy (so Gleason L. Archer Jr., *A Survey of Old Testament Introduction*, rev. ed. [Chicago: Moody, 1974], 392–94), while others take Dan. 6:28 to indicate that Cyrus is Darius (e.g., David W. Baker, "Further Examples of *Waw Explicativum*," *VT* 30 [1980]: 129–36).

[171]For an intriguing essay that catalogs and classifies the "perhaps" and "who knows?" texts in the Old Testament, see David J. Reimer, "An Overlooked Term in Old Testament Theology—Perhaps," in *Covenant as Context: Essays in Honour of E. W. Nicholson*, ed. A. D. H. Mayes and R. B. Salters (Oxford: Oxford University Press, 2003), 325–46.

Jeremiah again faces a death threat (Jer. 26:8), but the princes and the people stand up for him against the accusations of the priests and prophets (26:16), and the elders defend him from the example of Micah of Moresheth (26:17–19). The issue of the yoke of Babylon is prominent in Jeremiah 27–28. Yahweh summons the nations to take the yoke of the king of Babylon on their necks (27:1–11), referring to Nebuchadnezzar as "my servant" (27:6). Jeremiah calls Zedekiah and the priests to serve Nebuchadnezzar and live (27:12, 17). This leads to Jeremiah's confrontation with Hananiah, who proclaims that Yahweh has broken the yoke of Babylon (28:1–11). Yahweh reveals to Jeremiah that Hananiah's action has only made things worse (28:12–16), and Hananiah is dead before the year is out (28:17).

Jeremiah's letter to those in exile (Jer. 29:1–32) assures them that Yahweh will save them when Babylon's seventy years are complete (29:10). At that point they will do as Moses instructed: seek Yahweh with all their hearts (Deut. 4:29), find him, and be restored to the land (Jer. 29:11–14).[172]

That restoration to the land is the dominant thought in Jeremiah 30–33. The yoke will be broken (Jer. 30:8) and David will be king (30:9). Yahweh has loved his people with an everlasting love (31:2, ET 3). He will satisfy them with his goodness (31:13, ET 14). As Yahweh plucks up, breaks down, throws down, destroys, and afflicts them, so he will build and plant them (31:28). This will be replete with a new covenant not like the old (31:30, ET 31). Yahweh will write the Torah on their hearts (31:32, ET 33),[173] they will all know him, and their sins will be forgiven (31:33, ET 34).[174]

These promises are so certain that Yahweh sends Jeremiah to buy land because, though they face the exile (Jer. 32:1–5), he will bring the people back as he has promised (32:6–15). This prompts Jeremiah to pray a biblical-theological confession (32:16–23) celebrating Yahweh's power in creation (32:17), his loving-kindness to thousands and repayment of the iniquity of the wicked to their children (32:18),[175] his wisdom (32:19), his making a name for himself in the signs and wonders in Egypt (32:20), his bringing his people out with a strong hand and an outstretched arm (32:21), and his giving them the land (32:22); and Jeremiah laments the disobedience of the people in the land (32:23). Jeremiah's prayer concludes with an exclamation that he is buying land that is being given into the hands of the Chaldeans (32:24–25), prompting Yahweh to rehearse his own greatness and righteousness in giving the land to the Chaldeans because the people provoked him to wrath (32:26–35), but he also promises to bring them back from exile (32:36–44).

[172]David Reimer also draws attention to points of contact between Deut. 4:29–30 and Jer. 50:4–5 (*The Oracles Against Babylon*, 187).

[173]Dempster points out the conceptual similarity between the law written on the heart and the heart circumcision referred to in Jer. 4:4; 9:24–25 (ET 25–26) (*Dominion and Dynasty*, 166).

[174]See the helpful discussion in Dumbrell, *The Faith of Israel*, 144–47.

[175]See the appendix (§8) to chap. 2, which catalogs Ex. 34:6–7 in the Law, Prophets, and Writings.

Yahweh will cleanse Judah by slaying those who oppose the Chaldeans (Jer. 33:1–5). He will bring purified exiles back to be "a name of joy, a praise and a glory before all the nations of the earth who shall hear of all the good that I do for them. They shall fear and tremble because of all the good and all the prosperity I provide for it" (33:9, cf. 6–13). Salvation will come through judgment for God's glory. That this will be accomplished through the agency of an anointed king who descends from David can be seen from the repetition of the promises to David from 23:5–6 in 33:15–16. Moreover, while none of Coniah's descendants will sit on the throne of David (22:24–30),[176] David will not lack a man on the throne of Israel (33:17). The covenant with David will not be broken (33:19–26).

3.3.6 Rejection of Yahweh's Word and Exile (Jeremiah 34–45)

The rejection of Yahweh's word is prominent in all of Jeremiah, but particularly so in Jeremiah 34–37: Judah will be judged for not keeping Yahweh's commands regarding Hebrew slaves (Jeremiah 34), the Rechabites have been more faithful to the commands of their father than God's people have been to his (Jeremiah 35), and Jehoiakim king of Judah has gone so far as to burn Jeremiah's prophecy (Jeremiah 36). Then Zedekiah imprisons the prophet Jeremiah (Jeremiah 37), but though he allows Jeremiah to suffer in awful conditions, he is not so bold as to put him to death (Jeremiah 38).

Jeremiah 39–45 tells the sad tale of the fall of Jerusalem and the cowardly flight of her king (Jeremiah 39). As Rendtorff writes, "The possibility of repentance and thus of obviation of disaster had been offered to Israel, but it did not take up the offer."[177] The wickedness of those remaining in the land is displayed in the record of the aftermath of the exile, with the murder of Gedaliah and the disobedient return to Egypt, reversing the exile (Jeremiah 40–44). Yahweh, however, remains faithful to those, such as Baruch, who keep his word (Jeremiah 45). These chapters of Jeremiah demonstrate Yahweh's righteousness in judgment, and they confirm the need for the salvation that Yahweh has promised to work. Only he can circumcise the heart, and his people clearly need him to do so.

3.3.7 The Oracles against the Nations (Jeremiah 46–51)

Yahweh has used the nations to bring justice against his people. That task accomplished, he brings justice against the nations: Egypt (Jeremiah 46), Philistia (Jeremiah 47), Moab (Jeremiah 48), the Ammonites (49:1–6), Edom (49:7–22), Damascus (49:23–27), Kedar and Hazor (49:28–33), Elam (49:34–39), and Babylon (Jeremiah 51–52). As with other oracles against Babylon, the Medes are mentioned as the instrument Yahweh will use to judge them (51:11, 28; cf. Isa.

---

[176]See the brief, but suggestive, comments on this in Reimer, "Jeremiah Before the Exile?" 217–18.
[177]Rendtorff, *The Canonical Hebrew Bible*, 225.

13:17). Yahweh brings salvation through judgment, and the salvation of his people after exile will come through the justice he does against their oppressors. This comes into focus when we consider what David Reimer observes in Jeremiah 50–51: "Language typical of Jeremiah and used prominently for pronouncing judgment against Judah has been reapplied to Babylon."[178]

3.3.8 Jeremiah's Prophecies Come to Pass (Jeremiah 52)

A prophet is known to be true or false by the simple criterion of whether his prophecies come to pass (cf. Deut. 18:21–22). Jeremiah 52 serves as a punctuation mark vindicating Jeremiah's prophetic ministry. This shows Jeremiah to be a true prophet, one to whom Israel should listen (Deut. 18:15–19). Jeremiah proclaimed that Yahweh would save his people through the judgment of exile, and throughout it is clear that the judgment comes to vindicate Yahweh's glory, which has been despised. Similarly, the salvation will display Yahweh's steadfast loving-kindness and faithfulness and enable his people to enjoy his glory.

3.3.9 The Center of the Theology of Jeremiah

In Jeremiah, Israel and Judah are seen to be spiritually enslaved to the folly of sin. Their hearts and ears are uncircumcised, so they reject Yahweh's word and persecute his prophet. Instead of drinking from the fountain of living water, enjoying the love of their faithful Father, celebrating the glory of their marriage to the covenant Lord, and knowing their God, they have turned to broken cisterns, sold themselves to be abused slaves, committed adultery, and entrusted themselves to idols that cannot deliver. Jeremiah announces that all this has provoked Yahweh to righteous wrath, and that he will vindicate his holiness by bringing the nations to judge his people. After the judgment, however, he will again save them. The glory of the future, new covenant salvation promised after the judgment will shine with the goodness and satisfaction only Yahweh can produce, and this salvation will come through the judgment of the enemies of God's people.[179] In Jeremiah, salvation comes through judgment for Yahweh's glory.[180]

3.4 Ezekiel

The book of Ezekiel is dominated by the glory of God. Opening with Ezekiel's description of "the appearance of the likeness of the glory of Yahweh" (Ezek. 1:28), the drama is driven by the departure of the glory of Yahweh from the temple

---

[178]Reimer, *The Oracles Against Babylon*, 185. Reimer also describes the way that Jer. 50:18–20 "juxtaposes Israel's restoration and Babylon's judgment" (189).

[179]Cf. Reimer, *The Oracles Against Babylon*, 243: "The oracles against foreign nations are not outbursts of xenophobia; rather they attest to the prophets' belief that Yahweh was sovereign over other nations just as he was over Israel and Judah. This is in line with other theological strands in the Hebrew Bible."

[180]Cf. Dumbrell, *The Faith of Israel*, 150: "In effect, the proclamation of a new Israel . . . a new covenant, and thus a new age for the people of God is the book's message." But again, the new Israel and the new covenant and the new age are not ends in themselves in Jeremiah but rather the matrix in which God's glory will be more fully seen, more fully enjoyed, and more fully praised.

in chapters 8–11, which is answered by the vision of the return of the glory of Yahweh (43:5) to the eschatological temple in chapters 40–48. The major reality of the prophecy of Ezekiel is Yahweh in his indescribable glory.[181]

The book opens with Ezekiel's call (Ezekiel 1–3), followed by his announcement of doom to Israel and Judah (4–24), doom to the nations (25–32), and hope rising from the east after judgment (33–48). Ezekiel's prophecy is punctuated some sixty-eight times by Yahweh's own declaration of what will ensue when he acts: "You/They shall know that I am Yahweh!"[182] The Lord intends to make himself known by his actions. And he will be known in his majesty, righteousness, holiness, integrity, and mercy, and ultimately, in his commitment to his own glory.

Rather than move through each section of Ezekiel as we have done with Isaiah and Jeremiah, here I will present a wide-angle summary of the theme of salvation through judgment to the glory of God in Ezekiel. From there we will briefly consider Yahweh's specific declarations in Ezekiel that he "acts for his own sake."

3.4.1 Salvation through Judgment for God's Glory in Ezekiel

Ezekiel has been taken from the land before the destruction of Jerusalem in 586 BC.[183] He is suffering the judgment of exile. Driven out of the land by Yahweh's wrath, he and his countrymen find themselves in the Gentile realm of the dead. But there in 593 BC, by the river Chebar, Yahweh visits the prophet Ezekiel (Ezek. 1:1–2:8). Ezekiel receives a scroll to eat, and lamentations and mourning and woe are written inside and out on this scroll (2:9–3:2). The temple has not yet been destroyed, but Ezekiel is commissioned to announce that it will not withstand the Babylonians. Even as Ezekiel, in Babylon, is commissioned to announce the devastation of the place Yahweh chose to set his name, he hears behind him "a great rumbling sound, 'Blessed is the glory of Yahweh from his place!'" (3:12). This shows that Yahweh is not praised only from the temple in Jerusalem, as he is apparently blessed from his heavenly dwelling even among the Chaldeans.[184] Yahweh's glory and the praise rightly due him shine on through the destruction of Jerusalem.

---

[181]Commenting on Ezekiel's opening vision, Daniel I. Block (*The Book of Ezekiel: Chapters 1–24*, NICOT [Grand Rapids: Eerdmans, 1997], 89–90) describes the problems in morphology, grammar, style, and substance in Ezekiel's description and concludes, "Although Ezekiel is fully conscious, he is at a loss for words that will report the vision adequately."

[182]Ezek. 5:13; 6:7, 10, 13, 14; 7:4, 9, 27; 11:10, 12; 12:15, 16, 20; 13:14, 21, 23; 14:8; 15:7; 16:62; 17:21, 24; 20:12, 20, 38, 42, 44; 21:4 (ET 20:48), 10 (ET 5); 22:16, 22; 24:27; 25:5, 7, 11, 17; 26:6, 14; 28:22, 23, 26; 29:6, 9, 21; 30:8, 19, 25, 26; 32:15; 33:29; 34:27, 30; 35:4, 9, 12, 15; 36:11, 23, 36, 38; 37:6, 13, 14, 28; 38:23; 39:6, 7, 22, 28.

[183]For a chart of "Chronological Notes in Ezekiel," see Dillard and Longman, *An Introduction to the Old Testament*, 357, and another presentation of the material is given in John W. Wevers, *Ezekiel*, NCB (London: Oliphants, 1969), 2.

[184]Similarly Walther Zimmerli, "The Message of the Prophet Ezekiel," in *The Fiery Throne: The Prophets and Old Testament Theology* (Minneapolis: Fortress, 2003), 80.

By commissioning Ezekiel as a prophet, Yahweh once again establishes the responsibility humans bear for their choices. Ezekiel is a watchmen (Ezek. 3:17), and in response to his proclamation the wicked should repent and the righteous persevere (3:19, 21). Ezekiel's audience is responsible for their reaction to his message. And yet it is Yahweh who sends his angel through Jerusalem to put a tav (ת), which in the script of the time appears to have been a cross-shaped mark, on the foreheads of those who sigh and groan over the abominations done in Jerusalem (9:4).[185] This mark, like the blood of the lamb on the doorpost at the first Passover, preserves those who bear it from the visitation of the angel of death.[186] For Ezekiel's part, his responsibility is simply to warn the righteous and the wicked. If Ezekiel warns them, he is not responsible for their reactions (3:19, 21). If he does not warn them, their blood is on his head (3:18, 20).

Yahweh's people have crushed him by their adulterous hearts (Ezek. 6:9). So the assurance they have had on the basis of Yahweh's covenant with Israel, his ownership of the land, his residence in Jerusalem, and his covenant with David[187] has been undermined by their infidelity. They have broken the covenant, and he is coming in judgment (e.g., 5:8; 6:3–5). Through the judgment will come salvation: "Then your survivors will remember me among the nations where they were taken captive . . . and they will loathe themselves for the evils they did and for all their abominations" (6:9). The judgment of the exile brings about the realization of their own wretchedness, and this recognition gives way to the knowledge of God: "And they shall know that I am Yahweh; I did not speak in vain that I would do this evil to them" (6:10).

In 592 BC Ezekiel is transported by the Spirit in visions of God to Jerusalem (Ezek. 8:1–3). The initial judgments on the city do not prompt repentance, and there is gross abomination in the temple (8:7–10). The elders of Israel burn incense to their idols, thinking that Yahweh has forsaken the land and does not see them (8:11–12). The women weep for Tammuz[188] (8:13–14), and in the temple of Yahweh people gather to worship the sun (8:15–16). As briefly described above, the Lord seals his own with the cross-shaped tav, while his fury is poured out on the rest (9:1–11). Ezekiel then beholds the same glory he saw in his inaugural vision (1:4–28) exiting the temple (10:1–22). God's intention in giving such visions to Ezekiel is to prompt repentance from idolatry and to encourage his

---

[185]See the discussion in Oskar Skarsaune, *In the Shadow of the Temple: Jewish Influences on Early Christianity* (Downers Grove, IL: InterVarsity, 2002), 370–71, citing Origen *Selecta in Ezechielem* 9. Cf. the "Table of Alphabets" that follows the table of contents in GKC, or the comparative chart of Semitic fonts available online here: http://www.bibleplaces.com/fonts/Paleo-Hebrew_Fonts_Chart,_by_Kris_Udd.pdf, accessed July 21, 2008.

[186]Cf. the way the sealing of God's servants functions in Rev. 7:2–3, and the beast's attempt to counterfeit it in Rev. 13:16–18. Cf. also CD 19.9–13; *Pss. Sol.* 15:6–9. Tertullian (*Against Marcion* 3.22) writes: "Now the Greek letter *Tau* and our own letter T is the very form of the cross, which He predicted would be the sign on our foreheads in the true Catholic Jerusalem." I take Tertullian to be referring to Revelation 7 here (quoted from *ANF*, 3:340–41).

[187]Block (*The Book of Ezekiel: 1–24*, 8) presents these as the four pillars of Israel's house of pride.

[188]See Jeremy Black, "Dumuzi (Tammuz)," in *DANE*, 96–97.

people to trust in him, not the temple. This is clear from Yahweh's announcements that people will know him as Yahweh through these judgments (11:10, 12), and from his statement that he will be a sanctuary for his people in exile (11:16). The people love the temple rather than Yahweh, and so Yahweh mercifully judges them by destroying the temple, ultimately so that he can give them himself. Through judgment comes salvation to God's glory. Moreover, Yahweh promises that after the judgment of exile, he will gather his scattered people and give them the land of Israel (11:17); he will give them one heart and a new spirit, removing the heart of stone and replacing it with a heart of flesh (11:19). As a result, the people will keep the law, "and they shall be my people, and I will be their God" (11:20).[189] God judges that he might save, and that his people might know him as God.

Ezekiel has announced destruction to the city and land (Ezekiel 4–7) and to the temple (8–11), and in chapters 12–24 he earnestly warns Israel of coming woe. He enacts the flight of the people from the city, predicting before the destruction of 586 what will take place then (12:1–14; cf. Jer. 39:2–7 and 2 Kings 25:4–7). Yahweh twice announces that this is for people to know him as Yahweh (Ezek. 12:15–16). Ezekiel denounces the false prophets who assure the people of peace (12:21–14:11), and he announces that not even the presence of Noah, Daniel, and Job would keep Yahweh from destroying the land (14:12–21). There will be a remnant, however, that will be comforted concerning the evils brought on Jerusalem (14:22), and they will know that what Yahweh has done is just (14:23). Through judgment comes salvation to the glory of God.

The prophecy of Ezekiel the priest (1:3) often refers to Leviticus.[190] For instance, there are allusions to the Leviticus 18:5 statement that the one who does the law will live by it (Ezek. 18:9; 20:11, 13, 21), as well as to the Leviticus 10:10 need to distinguish between the holy and the unholy, the clean and the unclean (Ezek. 22:26; 44:23). In at least one place Ezekiel also takes up the concept of atonement set forth in Leviticus. Yahweh announces that he will establish an everlasting covenant with his people (Ezek. 16:60), that his people will be ashamed of their ways (16:61) and know that he is Yahweh (16:62), and these blessings will come, Yahweh says, "when I make atonement for you, for all that you have done, an utterance of the Lord Yahweh" (16:63). Yahweh will show mercy, but the mercy he shows will not be unjust. Rather, it will be based on an atonement that he himself will provide for his people.

[189]For discussion of regeneration (new heart) and the indwelling of the Spirit under the old and new covenants, see my study, *God's Indwelling Presence*.

[190]See further T. J. Betts, *Ezekiel the Priest: A Custodian of Tora*, Studies in Biblical Literature (New York: Peter Lang, 2005), and the examples cited in M. A. Lyons, "Marking Innerbiblical Allusion in the Book of Ezekiel," *Biblica* 88 (2007): 245–50.

3.4.2 Yahweh Acts for His Own Sake

Much more could be said regarding Ezekiel's announcements of Yahweh's righteousness and the mercy that comes through and after judgment, but this treatment cannot be exhaustive. We turn our attention to a sampling of statements in Ezekiel that present us with God's ultimate intentions and priorities. These intentions are the organizing feature of this prophecy of God's glorious presence among the exilic community (Ezekiel 1), leaving the temple in judgment (8–11), and returning to a rebuilt temple (40–48).

Why does God bring judgment on Israel? God himself answers the question and makes clear the connection between his reputation—alluded to in the references to his name, which is synonymous with his glory—and the behavior of the Israelites. This happens three times in chapter 20 alone (see table 3.9).

Table 3.9. Yahweh Acting for His Name before the Nations

	Ezekiel 20:9	Ezekiel 20:14	Ezekiel 20:22
What Yahweh did	"But I acted	"But I acted	"But I withheld my hand and acted
Why Yahweh did it	for the sake of my name, that it should not be profaned	for the sake of my name, that it should not be profaned	for the sake of my name, that it should not be profaned
Who saw	in the sight of the nations among whom they lived, in whose sight I made myself known to them in bringing them out of the land of Egypt" (ESV).	in the sight of the nations, in whose sight I had brought them out" (ESV).	in the sight of the nations, in whose sight I had brought them out" (ESV).

Later in the same chapter Yahweh announces that he will reveal his holiness to Israel after he restores them: "As a pleasing aroma I will accept you, when I bring you out from the peoples and gather you out of the countries where you have been scattered. And I will manifest my holiness among you in the sight of the nations" (Ezek. 20:41 ESV).

Just a few verses later God's holiness is seen to prompt the Israelites to loathe themselves for their evil deeds (Ezek. 20:43). Experiencing true beauty prompts them to feel revulsion for the cheap imitations with which they have been idolatrously satisfied. This judgment of their sin results in the true knowledge of God, and God acts for his name in showing them mercy: "'And you shall know that I am Yahweh, when I deal with you for my name's sake, not according to your evil ways, nor according to your corrupt deeds, O house of Israel,' an utterance of the Lord Yahweh" (20:44).

The manifestation of God's holiness results from him acting for his own sake, that he might be known. This holds not only for Israel but for other nations, such as Sidon: "And say, 'Thus says the Lord Yahweh: "Behold, I am against you, O Sidon, and I will be glorified in your midst. And they shall know that I am Yahweh when I execute judgments in her and am sanctified in her"'" (Ezek. 28:22). Lest Israel come to the mistaken conclusion that they are more important to Yahweh than upholding righteousness, and lest they think that his love and justice are somehow in conflict, Ezekiel declares to Israel the true reason that Yahweh will restore the wayward nation:

> But I had concern for my holy name, which the house of Israel had profaned among the nations to which they came. Therefore say to the house of Israel, "Thus says the Lord Yahweh: 'It is not for your sake, O house of Israel, that I am about to act, but for the sake of my holy name, which you have profaned among the nations to which you came. And I will make my great name holy, which has been profaned among the nations, and which you have profaned among them. And the nations will know that I am Yahweh,' an utterance of the Lord Yahweh, 'when I am made holy through you before their eyes.'" (36:21–23)

Yahweh's holiness is strongly linked to his reputation, his name. The point that Yahweh is showing mercy to Israel neither for what they have done nor for what he feels for them is so important as to be restated: "'It is not for your sake that I will act,' an utterance of the Lord Yahweh; 'let that be known to you. Be ashamed and confounded for your ways, O house of Israel'" (36:32). Yahweh is acting for the sake of his name. He is neither clearing the guilty nor forsaking steadfast, forgiving love (cf. Ex. 34:6–7). In acting for the sake of his name—the name he declared to Moses when he revealed his glory (Ex. 33:18–19; 34:6–7)—Yahweh is making known his own character.[191] He is manifesting righteousness in his own supreme regard for himself. This manifestation of holiness is intended to prompt Israel to feel shame and repent. If they do so, they will be saved through judgment to the glory of God.

Even the enemies of Israel ultimately serve Yahweh's purpose in allowing him to demonstrate his holiness as he reveals his glory:

> You will come up against my people Israel, like a cloud covering the land. In the latter days I will bring you against my land, that the nations may know me, when through you, O Gog, I vindicate my holiness before their eyes. . . . So I will show my greatness and my holiness and make myself known in the eyes of many nations. Then they will know that I am Yahweh. (Ezek. 38:16, 23 ESV adapted)

[191]Rendtorff connects this to God's faithfulness to his promise with the words, "If God wants to stay God, then he must remain God for Israel" (*The Canonical Hebrew Bible*, 255).

And after the judgment there will come a day when Yahweh will be truly known, his glory rightly regarded, and his name no longer profaned: "And my holy name I will make known in the midst of my people Israel, and I will not let my holy name be profaned anymore. And the nations shall know that I am Yahweh, the Holy One in Israel" (39:7 ESV adapted). The defeat of his enemies affords Yahweh the opportunity to show his great power in the revelation of his glory: "'All the people of the land will bury them, and it will bring them renown on the day that I show my glory,' an utterance of the Lord Yahweh" (39:13). These judgments make Yahweh known, and having finished judgment, Yahweh will have thereby redeemed Israel, vindicated his own righteousness, and then he will take up residence in his temple:

> And I will set my glory among the nations, and all the nations shall see my judgment that I have executed, and my hand that I have laid on them. . . .
>
> Therefore thus says the Lord Yahweh: Now I will restore the fortunes of Jacob and have mercy on the whole house of Israel, and I will be jealous for my holy name . . . when I have brought them back from the peoples and gathered them from their enemies' lands, and through them have vindicated my holiness in the sight of many nations. (39:21, 25, 27 ESV adapted)

The intricate description of the eschatological temple in Ezekiel 40–48 has the major function of bringing glory to Yahweh. The character and glory of God in all his saving and judging majesty will be so manifest in this new temple that Ezekiel's prophecy concludes with the words, "And the name of the city from that day is, 'Yahweh is there!'" (48:35).

3.4.3 The Center of the Theology of Ezekiel

The center of Ezekiel's theology is the glory of God in salvation through judgment as Yahweh acts for the sake of his name, saving to show mercy and judging to show holiness, that all might know that he is Yahweh. Zimmerli has it right:

> The judgment makes known Yahweh's nature. But here it becomes clear that full knowledge of Yahweh's nature can only be reached when the desire to save is seen behind the act of judgment. Or, stated more precisely, when one knows Yahweh himself, both in his judging and in his rising up in majesty, which contains within itself both the blessing of his holiness and his utter faithfulness to the work that he has begun. For this is the center around which all of Ezekiel's words revolve: Yahweh's glory is revealed in Israel, and beyond Israel to all the world.[192]

Ezekiel's message complements Jeremiah's in significant ways. Jeremiah sends a letter to the exiles in Babylon, promising them good and not harm from the Lord

[192] Zimmerli, "The Word of God in the Book of Ezekiel," in *The Fiery Throne*, 106.

(Jeremiah 29), and at the same time Jeremiah admonishes those who remain in the land to submit to the king of Babylon (Jeremiah 27). Ezekiel's prophecy opens *in Babylon*, where Ezekiel receives a vision of the indescribable glory of God (Ezekiel 1). Jeremiah's famous "temple sermon" (Jeremiah 7) warns the people not to trust in the temple, as though it were a guarantee that Yahweh would not judge them. Ezekiel sees the glory of Yahweh leave the temple (Ezekiel 8–11). Jeremiah prophesies a new covenant (Jeremiah 31), and Ezekiel prophesies a new heart (Ezekiel 36) and a new temple (Ezekiel 40–48) in which Yahweh will reside. And both Jeremiah and Ezekiel promise a day when a new David will reign (e.g., Jer. 23:5; Ezek. 37:24)[193] after Yahweh has saved his people through the judgment of exile. And Ezekiel is as explicit as Isaiah on the point that Yahweh means to glorify himself in the judging and the saving, the sending out and bringing back. As Dumbrell puts it, "If Israel is to have a future, Yahweh himself will bring about a new beginning, with himself at the center."[194] In Ezekiel, Yahweh is glorified in salvation through judgment.

3.5 The Book of the Twelve

Hosea identifies Israel's idolatry as spiritual adultery. Joel connects a locust plague to the curses of the covenant Yahweh made with Israel. Amos calls Israel to seek Yahweh, the roaring lion, and live. Obadiah denounces Edom for violence to Jacob. Jonah sees Nineveh repent in response to the proclamation of coming judgment. Micah beholds the mountains melt when Yahweh treads on them to judge and save. Nahum prophesies the fall of Nineveh. Habakkuk questions Yahweh, and trusts him, regarding the judgment Babylon brings against Israel, then experiences. Zephaniah proclaims that those who seek Yahweh will be hidden on the day of his wrath and delivered, and that he will sing over them. Haggai calls the people to rebuild the temple. Zechariah declares it will be rebuilt not by might or by power but by the Spirit of Yahweh. Malachi assures Israel of Yahweh's love and points to the day when Elijah will prepare the way for Yahweh to be glorified in a decisive act of salvation through judgment.

The order of the Twelve seems to reflect an intentional arrangement that resulted in these twelve prophets' being read together as a single book[195] (see appendix 1 [§5] to this chapter, which lists the order of the Twelve in *BHS,* the DSS, 8ḤevXIIgr, and the LXX). This intentional arrangement can be seen from the way that key words found at the end of one book often recur at the beginning of the next.[196] Where there

---

[193]*Pace* Dumbrell, who sees a "diminished role assigned to David and to kingship generally in this book" (*The Faith of Israel*, 170).

[194]Ibid.

[195]Cf. *Sirach* 49:10, "May the bones of the twelve prophets revive from where they lie, for they comforted the people of Jacob and delivered them with confident hope" (RSV). Paul L. Redditt helpfully summarizes the ancient evidence, citing Sirach, manuscript evidence from Qumran, Josephus (*Ag. Ap.* 1.8), *2 Esdras* 14:44–45, and the Babylonian Talmud ("The Formation of the Book of the Twelve: A Review of Research," in Paul L. Redditt and Aaron Schart, eds., *Thematic Threads in the Book of the Twelve*, BZAW [New York: Walter de Gruyter, 2003], 1).

[196]Cf. Aaron Schart, "Reconstructing the Redaction History of the Twelve Prophets," (citing F. Delitzsch, "Wann weissagte Obadja?" *Zeitschrift für die gesammte Lutherische Theologie und Kirche* 12 [1851]: 92–93) in *Reading*

are not key words, there are sometimes thematic links, such as the way that Nahum, who prophesies the destruction of Assyria, is followed by Habakkuk, who prophesies the destruction of Babylon. These connections are traced in table 3.10.

Table 3.10. Link Words and Thematic Connections at the Beginnings and Ends of the Books of the Twelve

Ending	Link Words or Thematic Connections	Beginning
Hosea 14:8 (ET 7)	•inhabitants •wine •vine	Joel 1:2 1:5 1:7
Joel 3:16	•Yahweh roars from Zion. •The judgment of Joel 4 (ET 3) is carried out in Amos 1:3–2:16.	Amos 1:2 1:3–2:16
Amos 9:12	•Edom	Obadiah 1:1
Obadiah 1:1 1:11 1:12–14	•messenger to the nations, "rise" •cast lots •Edom positions itself to rejoice over Judah's destruction, and Jonah positions himself to rejoice over Nineveh's destruction.	Jonah 1:2, 6 1:7 4:5
Jonah 4:2	•Exodus 34:6–7	Micah 7:18–19
Micah 7:18–19	•Exodus 34:6–7	Nahum 1:2–3
Nahum 3:7, 18	•prophecy of the destruction of Nineveh/Assyria, which destroyed the northern kingdom of Israel, followed by a prophecy of the destruction of Babylon, which will destroy the southern kingdom of Judah	Habakkuk 1:6
Habakkuk 2:20	•keep silent before Yahweh	Zephaniah 1:7
Zephaniah 3:20	•time (brought back, gathered)	Haggai1:2, 4
Haggai 2:20	•dates: Haggai, Dec. 18, 520; Zechariah, Oct./Nov. 520 •key figures: Joshua and Zerubbabel	Zechariah 1:1
Zechariah 4:6–7; 14:20–21	•Zechariah prophesies that the temple will be rebuilt in Jerusalem, while Malachi announces that Edom will never be rebuilt.	Malachi 1:4

The nature of this evidence does not point, in my view, either to intense editorial activity or, necessarily, to literary dependence between the prophets.[197] Some

and Hearing the Book of the Twelve, ed. J. D. Nogalski and M. A. Sweeney, SBL Symposium Series (Atlanta: SBL, 2000), 35: "F. Delitzsch noted that the ending of one writing and the beginning of the adjacent one often share significant vocabulary. The following instances were considered significant: Hos 14:2 // Joel 2:12; Joel 4:16 // Amos 1:2; Amos 9:12 // Obad 19; Obad 1 // Jonah (as a messenger to the nations); Jonah 4:2 // Mic 7:18–19 // Nah 1:2–3; Nah 1:1 // Hab 1:1 (משׂא); Hab 2:20 // Zeph 1:7."

[197]See my review of Paul-Gerhard Schwesig, *Die Rolle der Tag-JHWHs-Dichtungen im Dodekapropheton*, BZAW 366 (Berlin/New York: Walter de Gruyter, 2006) in *BBR* 19 (2009): 104–5. Cf. Richard Coggins, "Interbiblical Quotations in Joel," in *After the Exile: Essays in Honor of Rex Mason*, ed. John Barton and David J. Reimer (Macon, GA: Mercer, 1996), 81.

of these link words are not terribly significant, and there is no connection to the end of Jonah at the beginning of Micah—the connection noted in table 3.10 is from the end of Micah's prophecy. In other cases there are no link words at all, such as between Nahum and Habakkuk or between Zechariah and Malachi, and the connections between these books noted in table 3.10 are thematic rather than lexical.[198] In my view, then, any editorial activity that resulted in the arrangement of these prophecies appears to have dealt with the documents as they stood rather than to have altered them to tie them together.[199] Whoever put the Twelve into the order we find them in the MT (Ezra?) appears to have proceeded by working with what he had before him rather than inserting material that would establish a clear connection between the end of one prophecy and the beginning of the next.[200]

The kinds of links we find at the seams of the Twelve and in the body of the books appear to point to these twelve prophets addressing similar themes from similar perspectives. As one reads through the Twelve together, similar images recur, and, as Andrew Chester has noted, once the Old Testament texts are placed side by side in the canon, a sort of composite picture naturally emerges.[201] For a composite picture of the key words and thematic connections related to warnings, judgments, and promises of salvation in the Twelve, see table 3.11.[202]

The information reflected in tables 3.10 and 3.11 supports the idea that the prophets were aware of one another, with earlier prophets influencing the language and imagery of those who came later. All the prophets indicted Israel on the basis of the terms of the Mosaic covenant. Because the covenant had been broken, the prophets called Israel to repentance. When the people did not repent, the prophets declared that the covenant curses would fall: the people would be exiled from the land just as Adam was exiled from Eden. But the prophets also announced hope for the future. The exile and return have a scriptural basis: Moses prophesied these very things (Deut. 4:25–31; 29:18–30:10). The judgment on Israel and Judah would be a purging judgment, and once Yahweh had purged his people, just as he had judged Egypt, he would judge their enemies. Just as Sinai had been shaken when the covenant was made, once more he would shake the heavens and earth. Just as he had restored the people to the Land of Promise

[198]For attempts to establish connections between Zechariah and Malachi by reaching past Zechariah 9–14 to Zechariah 8, see James Nogalski, *Literary Precursors to the Book of the Twelve*, BZAW (New York: Walter de Gruyter, 1993), 53–56.

[199]For helpful bibliography on studies of these issues, see the "Introduction" by Aaron Schart and Paul Redditt in *Thematic Threads in the Book of the Twelve*, ix–x and notes 2 and 3. See also the works cited in Redditt's contribution to the volume, "The Formation of the Book of the Twelve: A Review of Research," 1–26.

[200]Cf. James Nogalski, *Literary Precursors to the Book of the Twelve*, BZAW (New York: Walter de Gruyter, 1993), 57: "The translators [LXX, Vulgate, and Syriac] exhibit no cognizance of these [link/*stich*] words as a unifying technique in the compilation of the Book of the Twelve. . . . One may further speculate reasonably that the translators were *unaware* of these catchword connections, and thus made no effort to accentuate them."

[201]Chester, *Messiah and Exaltation*, 279–80.

[202]A similar set of themes, though not set out in table form, is identified by Paul R. House, "Endings as New Beginnings: Returning to the Lord, the Day of the Lord, and Renewal in the Book of the Twelve," in Redditt and Schart, *Thematic Threads in the Book of the Twelve*, see especially the conclusion, 337–38.

Table 3.11. Key Words, Thematic Links, and Similar Phrases and Concepts in the Twelve

Warnings
Burden: Nah. 1:1; Hab. 1:1; Zech. 9:1; 12:1; Mal. 1:1
The burden of the word of the Lord: Zech. 9:1; 12:1; Mal. 1:1
Day of the Lord:[1] Joel 1:15; 2:1, 11; 3:4 (ET 2:31); 4:14 (ET 3:14); Amos 5:18, 20; Obad. 1:15; Zeph. 1:7, 14–16; (Zech. 14:1); Mal. 3:23 (ET 4:5)
Great and dreadful day of the Lord: Joel 3:4 (MT 3:4); Mal. 4:5
Day of darkness: Joel 2:2; 3:4 (ET 2:31); Amos 4:13; 5:8, 18; 8:9; Zeph. 1:15
Harlot's wages: Hos. 2:14 (ET 12); 9:1; Mic. 1:7
Yahweh a roaring lion: Hos. 5:14; 11:10; 13:7–8; Joel 3:16; Amos 1:2; 3:8
Command/call to repent/return: Hos. 6:1; 12:7 (ET 6); 14:2–3; Joel 2:12–13; Jonah 3:8; Zech. 1:3–4; Mal. 3:7
Contention (ריב): Hos. 4:1; Mic. 6:2; Hab. 1:3
Who knows (whether Yahweh will relent)? Joel 2:14; Jonah 3:9
Perhaps (Yahweh will relent): Amos 5:15; Jonah 1:6; Zeph. 2:3
Retribution on your own head: Joel 4:4, 7 (ET 3:4, 7); Obad. 1:15
"For it is an evil time": Amos 5:13; Mic. 2:3
Judgments
Not my people: Hos. 1:8; Amos 9:7
Do not prophesy: Amos 7:16; 8:11; Mic. 2:6; 3:6
Gather all nations: Joel 4:2 (ET 3:2); Zech. 14:2
Locusts: Joel 1:4; 2:25; Amos 4:9; 7:1; Nahum 3:15–17
Earthquake: Joel 2:10; 4:16 (ET 3:16); Amos 1:1; Nah. 1:5; Hag. 2:6–7, 21; Zech. 14:5
The earthquake: Amos 1:1; Zech. 14:5
Mountains melt/shake: Mic. 1:3–4; Nah. 1:5; Hab. 3:5–6, 10; Zech. 14:4
All faces gather pallor: Joel 2:6; Nah. 2:10
Who can stand? Joel 2:11; Nah. 1:6; Mal. 3:2
Firstborn: Mic. 6:7; Zech. 12:10
Promises of Salvation
King/messiah: Hos. 1:11; 3:5; 10:15 (11:1); 13:10; Amos 9:11–15; Mic. 2:13; Hab. 3:13; Hag. 2:23
Sit under vine and fig tree: Mic. 4:4; Zech. 3:10; (1 Kings 4:25)
Vines and fig trees: Hos. 2:14 (ET 12); Joel 1:7, 12; 2:22; Mic. 4:4; Hab. 3:17; Hag. 2:19; Zech. 3:10
For Yahweh has spoken: Joel 3:8; Obad. 1:18
On Mount Zion there shall be deliverance: Joel 3:5 (ET 2:32); Obad. 1:17
Brand from the burning: Amos 4:11; Zech. 3:2
Yahweh dwells in Zion/Zion established: Joel 4:17; Obad. 1:17; Mic. 4:1–2, 7; Zeph. 3:8; Zech. 6:1; 8:3
Mountains drip new wine and hills flow with (milk): Joel 4:18 (3:18); Amos 9:13

[1]Specifically mentioned in Isa. 13:6, 9; Ezek. 13:5; Joel 1:15; 2:1, 11; 3:4; 4:14; Amos 5:18, 20; Obad. 15; Mal. 3:23; cf. also Isa. 2:12; Ezek. 30:3; Zech. 14:1; Isa. 34:8; Jer. 46:10; Isa. 22:5; Lam. 1:12; 2:22. A. Joseph Everson, "The Canonical Location of Habakkuk," in *Thematic Threads in the Book of the Twelve*, 167, holds that day of Yahweh "rhetoric and imagery provide a fundamental unifying theme" in the Twelve (so also David L. Petersen, "A Book of the Twelve?" in *Reading and Hearing the Book of the Twelve*, ed. J. D. Nogalski and M. A. Sweeney, SBL Symposium Series [Atlanta: SBL, 2000], 10). This supports my thesis because "day of the Lord" rhetoric and imagery refers to the climactic display of God's glory in salvation through judgment.

after the sojourn in Egypt, he would bring them back from exile. Just as the people had taken the land, they would once again conquer their enemies, and a new David would rule in Jerusalem. In this way Yahweh would fill the dry land with his glory as the waters fill the seas.

Yahweh displays his glory in the righteous standard by which the prophets measure Israel, in the justice he brings against them when they fall short, and in the mercy he shows when he saves them. The Twelve highlight the glory of God by stressing that Yahweh is his people's Savior (Hos. 13:4, 9; Amos 2:9–11; Jonah 2:9; Mic. 7:7), and the salvation he works comes by no mortal machination but by his power alone (Hos. 1:7; Zech. 4:6). The salvation Yahweh will achieve is one that will result in his glory filling the earth,[203] emanating out from the rebuilt temple (Hab. 2:14; 3:3; Hag. 1:8; 2:7, 9; Zech. 2:5; 6:13). He calls for the temple to be rebuilt so that he will be glorified (Hag. 1:8). Those Yahweh redeems will respond by worshiping him, rejoicing in him, and singing his praise (Hos. 2:15; Joel 2:23, 27; Jonah 2:9; Hab. 3:17–19; Zeph. 2:11; 3:14–15; Zech. 2:10; 9;9). Yahweh indicts his people because they do not know him (Hos. 4:1; 5:4; 8:14; Jonah 4:2; Mic. 4:12), and he points to a day when they will know him (Hos. 2:20; 6:3, 6; 8:2; 13:4; Joel 2:27; 4:17, ET 3:17; Mic. 6:5; 7:18–19). Yahweh will do this for himself (Hos. 2:23), and he has sworn by himself and by his holiness that he will bring it to pass (Amos 4:2; 6:8). The people do not confess him or call upon him (Hos. 7:7, 14), but they will (Hos. 2:23; Joel 3:5, ET 2:32; Jonah 1:6, 13, 16; 2:1–2, 7; 2:5–9; Zeph. 3:9; Zech. 13:9). They do not fear him (Hos. 10:3; Mal. 3:5), but they will (Hos. 3:5; Jonah 1:9, 16; Hab. 2:20; 3:16; Zeph. 1:7; Hag. 1:12; Zech. 2:12; Mal. 1:14; 2:5; 3:16; 4:2). They will seek Yahweh (Hos. 5:15; 7:10; 10:12; Zech. 8:21–22; Mal. 3:1). They do not exalt Yahweh (Hos. 11:7), but he will be exalted (Mal. 1:5). He holds responsible those who do not show him due honor (Mal. 1:6). He asserts that he is Yahweh, that he is God (Hos. 11:9; 12:9; 13:4; Joel 2:27; Zech. 10:6; Mal. 3:6). He indicts the people for defiling his holy name (Amos 2:7), and he asserts the worth of his name (Hos. 12:5; Joel 2:26; Amos 4:13; 5:8; 9:6; Mic. 4:5; 5:4; Zeph. 3:9; Zech. 10:12; 14:9; Mal. 1:6, 11; 2:2, 5; 3:16; 4:2). Yahweh's mighty acts are extolled in the Twelve, displaying his glory (Hos. 11:10–11; 13:7; Joel 2:21; 4:16, ET 3:16; Amos 1:2; 3:8; 4:13; 5:8–9; 9:5–6, 12; Obadiah; Jonah 1:9, 14; Mic. 1:3–4; 2:12–13; 4:1–5:15; 7:10–17; Nah. 1:2–8; Hab. 3:14–15; Zech. 9:14–17; 14:3–4).

The central theological idea in the Book of the Twelve is the glory of Yahweh in salvation through judgment. Judgment primarily refers to the judgment of God's people through exile, and once that judgment is complete, it falls on the exilers. Salvation takes the form of the return to the land so that Yahweh's purpose of filling the earth with his glory, emanating out from the temple in Jerusalem,

[203] See appendix 2 (§6) to this chapter, "All the Earth Filled with the Knowledge of Yahweh's Glory."

might be realized. As noted above, Paul House[204] suggests that the Book of the Twelve has a plot that moves from sin to punishment to restoration:

- Hosea–Micah (first six of the Twelve): Sin, covenant and cosmic
- Nahum, Habakkuk, Zephaniah: Punishment, covenant and cosmic
- Haggai, Zechariah, Malachi: Restoration, covenant and cosmic

We move to the glory of God in salvation through judgment in each book of the Twelve.

3.5.1 Hosea

Yahweh initiated a marriage-like covenant with Israel at Sinai.[205] As they stood on the threshold of the Promised Land, Israel was commanded not to raise their eyes to the gods allotted to other nations (Deut. 4:19). They were a people for Yahweh's own possession (4:20). They were promised that Yahweh would give them rain and grass on the fields for their flocks (11:14–15), and they were warned that if they served other gods, Yahweh would shut up the heavens and withhold the rain, with the result that the land would bear no fruit (11:16–17). Rain and fruitful land were basic to human survival in the ancient world. Relying on Yahweh to provide rain to make the grass grow for the flocks to have pasturage was the equivalent of our relying on Yahweh today to sustain the economic forces that make modern jobs possible. Depending on Yahweh for rain is the logical antecedent of depending upon him for daily bread.

Israel's neighbors did not rely on Yahweh to provide the necessary stuff of day-to-day existence. They worshiped Baal, of whom Gerald Mattingly writes, "Throughout the ancient Near East, Baal was viewed as a storm-god and was associated with clouds, thunder, lightning and rain. Among the peoples who practised agriculture in relatively dry climates, he was understood as a god of fertility."[206] There seems to have been some connection between the worship of Baal and "sacred prostitution."[207] Human sexual activity in the worship of Baal was somehow connected to Baal's bringing rain on the land.[208] Several statements in Hosea indicate that the people of Israel were following their neighbors

[204]House, *The Unity of the Twelve*, 72. For brief discussion and pointers to other proposals, see David L. Petersen, "A Book of the Twelve?" in Nogalski and Sweeney, *Reading and Hearing the Book of the Twelve*, 8–9; Schart, "Reconstructing the Redaction History of the Twelve Prophets," 38–41.
[205]Dumbrell, *The Faith of Israel*, 174.
[206]Gerald L. Mattingly, "Baal," in *DANE*, 42.
[207]Anthony Green and Jeremy Black, "Prostitution and Ritual Sex," in *DANE*, 235–36.
[208]Several scholars cite Herodotus *Hist.* 1.199 as ancient testimony to ritual prostitution in Babylon. Judith M. Hadley objects that what Herodotus claims is "not supported by contemporary evidence" ("Baal," in *NIDOTTE*, 4:426). For a primer on the discussion from the perspective that the biblical texts do not support the alleged sacred prostitution in Israel, see Mayer Gruber's review of Stephanie Lynn Budin, *The Myth of Sacred Prostitution in Antiquity*, in *RBL* (March 2009): http://www.bookreviews.org/pdf/6566_7109.pdf. In defense of the reliability of the primary sources (which indicate that ritual prostitution did happen in antiquity), see Jay Smith's devastating review of Budin's book in a forthcoming issue of *JETS*.

in relying on Baal and participating in these defiling practices (see, e.g., Hos. 4:13, 14, 15, 18; 9:1; 13:1–2).

Through Hosea, Yahweh exposes this reliance on Baal for what it really is: spiritual adultery. As Ortlund puts it, "If Yahweh is the husband of his people, then their lapses from faithfulness to him may properly be regarded as the moral equivalent to whoredom."[209] Yahweh commands Hosea to take for himself a wife of harlotries, because the land of Israel has committed harlotry against Yahweh (1:2). The analogy between Hosea's marriage and Yahweh's relationship with Israel is the subject of Hosea 1–3, and then Hosea 4–14 addresses the behavior that has been figuratively depicted as adultery in the first three chapters.[210] Dumbrell notes that Hosea depicts "the normal prophetic presentation of salvation through judgment."[211] Bostrom observes that salvation through judgment is built into the very structure of the book: "In the first three chapters each group of judgment oracles is followed by the promise of a future era of obedience and re-established relationship with God (1:10–2:1; 2:14–23; 3:5). This redactional arrangement is evident also in the other two sections of the book (11:10–11; 14:5–9)."[212] Similarly, Brueggemann writes, "In the world of YHWH's rule *judgment* comes in historical processes, but judgment is penultimate and leaves open *postjudgment well-being*."[213] As elsewhere, in the Twelve, salvation through judgment displays Yahweh's glory.

After the birth of Hosea's children and the attendant promises of salvation through judgment in chapter 1, charges are brought against Mother Israel in chapter 2. The mother of the children of Israel mistakenly thinks that her lovers have given her bread and water, wool and linen, oil and drink, but the reality is that these gifts have come from Yahweh (Hos. 2:7, ET 5). In response, Yahweh announces that he will hedge up her way with thorns, build a wall blocking her paths, and make sure that she can neither catch nor find her lovers (2:6–7). Frustrated, Mother Israel will decide to return to her first husband (2:7). The judgments of the barred path will force Israel back to Yahweh. He is kindly leading her to repentance (cf. Rom. 2:4).

Hosea 2:4–9 (ET 2–7) is, in a sense, recapitulated in 2:10–17 (ET 8–15). Yahweh takes so seriously the honor and gratitude due him for the gifts he has given that because Israel neither honors him as the all-sufficient God nor gives

[209]Raymond C. Ortlund Jr., *God's Unfaithful Wife: A Biblical Theology of Spiritual Adultery*, NSBT (Downers Grove, IL: InterVarsity, 1996), 8.

[210]Similarly Dumbrell, *The Faith of Israel*, 174. House writes, "One could take Hosea 1–3, affix it to virtually any of the other eleven books and have an introduction to the prophetic genre that explains the purpose of the book. . . . How does Hosea 4–14 operate in the Twelve? These chapters unfold the constant disregard of the Sinai covenant by Israel, Yahweh's anger at this outrage, God's unwillingness to cast off his 'child,' and the solution to the whole problem, salvation through judgment" (*The Unity of the Twelve*, 75).

[211]Dumbrell, *The Faith of Israel*, 172.

[212]N. E. L. Bostrom, "Hosea," in *NDBT*, 237.

[213]Walter Brueggemann, *An Introduction to the Old Testament: The Canon and Christian Imagination* (Louisville: Westminster John Knox, 2003), 213.

thanks to him, he will take away the gifts he has given. No one can deliver Israel from his hand (Hos. 2:10–12, ET 8–10). Yahweh will put a stop to her feast days, new moons, and Sabbaths (2:13, ET 11), destroy the vines and fig trees she considers wages from her lovers (2:14, ET 12), and punish her for going after them and forgetting Yahweh (2:15, ET 13). Just as the judgment of the barred path prompts Mother Israel to return to her first husband in 2:9 (ET 7), Yahweh states in 2:16–17 (ET 14–15):

> Therefore behold, I will allure her, and I will lead her to the wilderness. And I will speak to her heart, and I will give to her her vineyards from there, and the valley of Achor as the door of hope. And she will answer there as in the days of her youth, even as the day when she came up from the land of Egypt!

The whoring wife will be brought back—through judgment—to respond the way she answered on her wedding day (cf. Ex. 20:19; Deut. 5:27). Yahweh continues in Hosea 2:18–19 (ET 16–17): "And it shall be on that day, declares Yahweh, you will call me 'My husband,' and you will no longer call me 'My Baal.' For I will remove from her mouth the names of the Baals, and they shall no longer remember their names." The phrase "on that day" often points to a time of eschatological renewal, and features to be noted in the next verse also point Hosea's audience to a glorious future. In this verse (2:19, ET 17), Yahweh states that his people will no longer be confused as to his identity. They will no longer wrongly associate him with Baal but will rightly understand who their husband is. When they correctly identify him—and probably also we are to understand that the people will no longer mistakenly attribute the good gifts they enjoy to the Baals (cf. 2:10, 14, ET 8, 12)—Yahweh will be glorified as he receives due regard. His people will understand reality because of his intervention—he will remove the names of the Baals from their mouths.

In Hosea 2:20 (ET 18) Yahweh declares that "on that day" he will "cut a covenant for them with the beasts of the field, and with the birds of the heavens and the creeping things of the ground. Then bow and sword and battle I will break from the ground; and I will make you lie down in safety." Mark Rooker notes, "The animals listed in this verse occur in the same order as in Gen 1:30. . . . The reference to the animals from Gen 1:30 in the restoration passage of Hos 2:18 [20] is thus a re-creation accomplished by God under the provisions He promised to Israel in the new covenant."[214] In addition to the overtones of Eden in the order of the created beings, we find here concepts that are synonymous with other texts, such as Isaiah 2 and 11, which point to Israel's glorious future. In both

[214]Mark F. Rooker, "The Old Testament in the Book of Hosea," *CTR* 7, no. 1 (1993): 52. H. W. Wolff states that here we have the first reference to the new covenant in the Old Testament (*Hosea*, Hermeneia [Minneapolis: Fortress, 1974], 51).

Hosea 2 and Isaiah 2 we read of an end of warfare (Isa. 2:4; Hos. 2:20, ET 18), and in both Hosea 2 and Isaiah 11 we read that the people will lie down in safety, fearing no danger (Isa. 11:6–8; Hos. 2:20, ET 18; cf. Isa. 14:30; Ps. 4:9, ET 8).[215] These statements indicate that Yahweh's judgment will purge Mother Israel of her penchant for her lovers, return her to the fidelity of her wedding day, and on that day a new covenant will be cut, replete with eschatological blessings.

The covenant will be like a renewed marriage, and Yahweh proclaims that on that day he will promise to marry his people:

> I will betroth you to me forever;
> and I will betroth you to me
> in righteousness and in justice
> and in loving-kindness and in mercy;
> and I will betroth you to me in faithfulness;
> and you shall know Yahweh. (Hos. 2:21–22, ET 19–20)

The manner in which Yahweh will betroth his people to himself matches his own declaration of his name in Exodus 34:6–7. The righteousness and justice is balanced by the loving-kindness and mercy. Yahweh is both just and forgiving, and Israel will know him in his faithfulness to himself. The overtones of the use of the word "know" in the Bible (Adam "knew" his wife; Joseph did not "know" Mary until she had borne a son) should not be missed in this declaration of betrothal. Not that we are to conceive of something so foul as what Yeats described in "Leda and the Swan," but that the intimacy and purity of the one flesh union of the faithfully married is analogous to the intimacy and love between The Lover and the beloved. And this Lover purifies his harlot bride and cleanses her for himself through a purging judgment. Through judgment comes salvation, and the salvation is here depicted in the most intimate and beautiful terms known to mankind. Hosea 2:23–24 (ET 21–22) seems to reflect the expectations of the fertility cult, with Yahweh declaring that he will do what the people vainly relied upon Baal to accomplish: Yahweh will answer the heavens, which will answer the earth, probably with rain, and the earth will then answer with grain, with grapes for new wine, and with olives for oil. Indeed, Yahweh himself will sow his people, multiplying them according to promise. The names of Hosea's children are now reversed, as those who have not received mercy are mercied, those who are not Yahweh's people become his people, and he will be their God (2:23–25, ET 21–23). Again, through judgment salvation comes, and in it all Yahweh shows his glory.

[215]Similarly Eugene H. Maly, "Messianism in Osee," *CBQ* 19 (1957): 221.

Hosea 3 seems to move from the eschatological future to the days until that future. Hosea is to show love for a woman who is loved by another, just as Yahweh loves his people who look to other gods (3:1). This will continue for many days until, "Afterward the sons of Israel shall return and seek Yahweh their God and David their king. And they shall be in dread of Yahweh and of his goodness in the latter days" (3:5). This reference to Yahweh's "goodness" may very well look back to Exodus 33:19, where in response to Moses' request to see Yahweh's glory, Yahweh said he would cause his "goodness" to pass before Moses. Yahweh then proclaimed his goodness to Moses in much the same language with which he says he will betroth himself to Israel in Hosea 2:21–22 (ET, 19–20).

The remainder of Hosea's prophecy addresses the spiritual adultery of Israel in less figurative language: they swear, lie, kill, steal, and commit adultery (4:2), disregarding the Ten Commandments. Because of this, judgment will fall (4:3–10). Yahweh will be a lion that tears the people so that none can rescue them (5:14) until they confess their sins and seek his face (5:15; cf. 3:5). They will say, "Come, and let us return to Yahweh, for he has torn but he will heal us; he struck but he will bind us up. He will give us life after two days; on the third day he will raise us that we may live before him" (6:1–2). The "tearing" of the lion is probably a figurative way of saying that Yahweh will exile Israel. When he drives them from the land, they will enter the realm of the dead. They will die as a nation. Through the judgment of Yahweh's tearing like a lion comes the salvation of Yahweh raising as from the dead. As Maly puts it, the "renovation is accomplished through suffering. The punishment Israel would endure is not merely the rod of anger of a vindictive God; it is the necessary passageway to purification."[216] And this leads to the true knowledge of Yahweh, wherein he is rightly regarded, rightly esteemed, honored as God, known in faithfulness: "And let us know, let us press on to know Yahweh! As the dawn is established, so is his going forth; and he will come as the rain to us, like the spring rain watering the earth" (6:3).

Yahweh is glorified in salvation through judgment in Hosea, and Hosea calls his contemporaries to be like their covenant Lord in righteousness and mercy: "Sow for yourselves in righteousness; reap loving-kindness. Break up your fallow ground, for it is time to seek Yahweh, until he comes and rains righteousness on you" (Hos. 10:12). Even when Bethel is destroyed and her king cut off (10:15), Israel is exhorted to remember the exodus from Egypt (11:1–11).[217] The dead will be raised (cf. 5:14–6:3). The remembrance of the exodus is to remind Israel that Yahweh will bear with his wayward people, just as he did in the wilderness, and though he judges them, he will save them through the judgment, revealing

[216]Ibid., 224–25.

[217]For the view that the use of Hos. 11:1 in Matt. 2:15 is an instance of typological fulfillment, see chap. 5, §3.1 with table 5.4. Cf. Hamilton, "'The Virgin Will Conceive': Typological Fulfillment in Matthew 1:18–23." So also Schreiner, *New Testament Theology*, 73–74.

his justice and his mercy and getting glory for his name. Like Psalm 1, the book of Hosea sets before its audience two paths. The path of the wise is to know Yahweh, recognize that his ways are right, and walk in them, but the path of transgressors is to stumble on these ways (Hos. 14:9).[218] Hosea's closing words offer a way to be saved through the promised judgment; those who heed the prophetic word will fear Yahweh's judgment and find life and mercy in his good ways, to the glory of God alone.

3.5.2 Joel

John Barton has written, "Joel is a complex book, about which we do not possess enough information to come to firm conclusions."[219] Despite the interpretive difficulties in the book, it can nevertheless be demonstrated that the center of Joel's theology is the glory of God in salvation through judgment.[220] It appears that a locust plague (Joel 1) has prompted Joel to prophesy of an army from the north that will come to judge God's people (2:1–11).[221] Through judgment comes salvation: when the judgment induces repentance (whether in the near or long-term future), the people will turn to Yahweh with all their hearts (2:12–17), and he will make the land fruitful and defeat their enemies (2:18–27), pour out his Spirit on all flesh (3:1–5, ET 2:28–32), bring back the exiles (4:1–3, ET 3:1–3), judge the nations (4:4–14, ET 3:4–14), and inhabit Jerusalem in glory (4:15–21, ET 3:15–21).

The book of Joel must be read in light of both its near context in the Twelve and the wider context of the canon. Thus, Israel was warned in Deuteronomy 28 that if they were not careful to observe all of Yahweh's commands (28:15), among the other curses that would befall them was this: "You shall go out to the field with much seed, but you will gather only a little, because the locust will consume it" (28:38). Joel sees a locust plague (1:1–20) and prophesies an army from the north (2:1–11). This matches the movement of Deuteronomy 28, where the locust plague announced in verse 38 gives way to Yahweh's judging

[218] Jan Joosten's analysis ("Exegesis in the Septuagint Version of Hosea," in *Intertextuality in Ugarit and Israel*, ed. Johannes C. de Moor, Oudtestamentische Studiën [Boston: Brill, 1998], 62–85) indicates that the translator of Hosea understood the significance of the divine word in Hosea and respected it: "The thesis of this paper has been that the exegesis within the Septuagint should be studied in the framework of the translational process. Translation and interpretation are of one piece: 'creaming off' the exegesis while disregarding the other characteristics of the version will lead to a false picture. . . . Apart from the at times striking divergences due—as it seems to us—to a misreading or erroneous analysis of the Hebrew, LXX Hosea engages in contextual exegesis and occasionally in the decoding of figures of speech; both of these steps belong to the task of the translator as strictly defined and no version of a text of any length can do without them. Beyond these there is nothing, except the implicit testimony to the guiding principle: to trust the inspired text" (85).

[219] John Barton, *Joel and Obadiah*, OTL (Louisville: Westminster John Knox, 2001), 3.

[220] John Strazicich's subtitle to his "Structural Analysis of the Book of Joel" makes this point: "Yahweh's Character Revealed in Judgment and Salvation in Zion at the Coming Day of the Lord 1:2–4:21," in *Joel's Use of Scripture and the Scripture's Use of Joel: Appropriation and Resignification in Second Temple Judaism and Early Christianity*, Biblical Interpretation Series (Boston: Brill, 2007), 40.

[221] Similarly Dumbrell, *The Faith of Israel*, 186.

Israel with a human army in Deuteronomy 28:49–68.[222] Yahweh summons his people to repentance (Joel 2:12), in response to which Joel urges his contemporaries to rend their hearts, not their garments.[223] Because Yahweh is everything he declared to Moses in Exodus 34:6–7, merciful and gracious, slow to anger and abounding in loving-kindness, relenting from doing harm (Joel 2:13, see the appendix [§8] to chap. 2, which catalogs Ex. 34:6–7 in the Law, Prophets, and Writings), "Who knows," asks Joel, "perhaps he will turn and relent and leave a blessing behind him" (2:14). Joel then confidently asserts that if Israel will indeed repent earnestly and appeal to God's own concern for his reputation among the nations (2:15–17), "Yahweh will be zealous for his land and will have pity on his people" (2:18). The rest of the book prophesies a glorious salvation for Yahweh's people.

This salvation for Israel comes through judgment upon them. Joel does not name the sins of his people,[224] but both the overtones of Deuteronomy 28 and the book's context among the Twelve point toward this national disaster as a judgment of God. As Paul House notes, Joel "urges repentance as the key to renewal and argues that only the penitent will receive restoration."[225] Salvation comes through judgment, and the devastating nature of the day of Yahweh (Joel 1:15; 2:1–2, 11) highlights his awesome power. Yahweh is not glorified in the demonstration of wrath alone, however, for even the mention that he might relent (2:13) recognizes that he is a God who shows mercy. Moreover, Joel urges his contemporaries to appeal to Yahweh's concern for his reputation among the nations the same way that Moses and others did (see the appendix [§7] to chap. 4, table 4.9, "Old Testament Prayers Appealing to God's Concern for His Own Glory"). Having called the people to rend their hearts, not their garments (2:13), Joel calls on the priests to say, "Spare your people, O Yahweh, and do not give your heritage over to reproach, by the nations ruling over them. Why should they say among the peoples, 'Where is their God?'" (2:17). God is glorified in his justice and his mercy, and Joel recognizes God's own concern for his reputation among the nations.

God is glorified as Israel is saved when they repent after experiencing judgment, and God is also glorified as he saves Israel through the judgment against their enemies: the northern army (2:20), all nations (4:2, ET 3:2), Tyre, Sidon, and Philistia (4:4, ET 3:4), Egypt and Edom (4:19, ET 3:19). The enemies of God's people will experience his judgment (4:2, 12, ET 3:2, 12); Yahweh will roar against

[222]Duane A. Garrett, *Hosea, Joel*, NAC (Nashville: Broadman & Holman, 1997), 298–300.
[223]Cf. Strazicich, *Joel's Use of Scripture*, 57: "The prayer of Solomon lays out the prescription for dealing with national calamities, such as a drought, locust infestations, and the enemy threat, with the call for prayers and repentance to be made at the temple (1 Kings 8:22–52). Joel's message closely follows this . . . prescription."
[224]Cf. Barton, *Joel and Obadiah*, 19: "There is no denunciation of national sin, indeed no comment on 'ethical' matters at all, but a conviction that the way to deal with national distress is to call a solemn fast."
[225]House, *Old Testament Theology*, 355.

them (4:16, ET 3:16). Through this, salvation will come for Yahweh's people, for whom the years the locusts ate will be restored (2:25), on whom the Spirit will be poured out (3:1–5, ET 2:28–32), whose captives will be brought home (4:1, ET 3:1), whose weak will be made strong (4:10, ET 3:10), who will be sheltered by Yahweh when he roars (4:16, ET 3:16), whose mountains will drip with new wine, with brooks flooded with water and a fountain flowing from the temple of Yahweh (4:18, ET 3:18), and who will be acquitted of their guilt (4:21, ET 3:21). As Garrett puts it, "Joel addressed the problems facing his own generation and saw in those problems theological parallels to eschatological events."[226] The people will be saved when they repent in response to the judgment that comes upon them, and then they will be saved through the judgment of their enemies. Barton writes of "a familiar pattern in the Old Testament: national disaster is seen as the action of YHWH against the people, but YHWH is ready to reverse the disaster and to grant new life in response to a wholehearted 'turning' to God in prayer and lamentation."[227] This will result in what Yahweh himself declares: "And you shall know that I am Yahweh your God, dwelling on Zion, my holy Mountain, and Jerusalem shall be holy" (4:17, ET 3:17). The holiness of Jerusalem does have ethical implications for God's people, for as Barton notes, "Knowing the secret of the future that God is about to implement can challenge the hearers to radical obedience, in preparation for taking part in the glories of the age to come."[228] For this future to be realized, however, God's people must know him in his justice and his mercy, and Joel proclaims that they will know that he is Yahweh (4:17, ET 3:17) when he saves them through judgment for his own glory, acquitting them of guilt and dwelling in Zion (4:21, ET 3:21).

3.5.3 Amos

Yahweh roars from Zion in the prophecy of Amos, and the king's roar causes shepherds to mourn and mountaintops to wither (1:2) in the days of Uzziah of Judah (ca. 792–740 BC) and Jeroboam of Israel (ca. 793–753) (1:1). Amos recounts what Yahweh will do for three sins and for four against Damascus, Gaza, Tyre, Edom, Ammon, Moab, Judah, and Israel (1:3–2:16). In its literary context, this judgment in Amos 1–2 "carries out the judgment in Joel 4 [ET 3]."[229] In chapters 3–6, Amos summons Israel to "Hear!" (3:1, 13; 4:1; 5:1), before calling down "Woe!" upon them (5:18; 6:1). Chapters 7–9 of Amos are structured around five visions (7:1, 4, 7; 8:1; 9:1)[230] and close with a hymn of praise to the triumph of

---

[226]Garrett, *Hosea, Joel*, 286.
[227]Barton, *Joel and Obadiah*, 32.
[228]Ibid., 28.
[229]House, *The Unity of the Twelve*, 10, noting that the suggestion was put forward by H. W. Wolff.
[230]Amos 7:1, 4 and 8:1 all begin with the formula, "Thus the Lord Yahweh showed me: behold . . ." Slightly different formulas are employed in Amos 7:7 ("Thus he showed me: behold the Lord . . .") and 9:1 ("I saw the Lord").

God in the day of salvation.[231] The book thus moves from the holiness of Yahweh, presumed in his roaring and defiled by the sins Amos denounces (Amos 1–2), to the justice of Yahweh in judging these sins (Amos 3–6), and on to more judgment (Amos 7–9) through which comes the restoration of David's fallen booth (Amos 9:11–15): salvation through judgment for God's glory.

Gary Smith suggests that the oracles against the nations who are not in covenant with Yahweh respond to the transgression of "international standards set forth in interstate treaties, written laws that regulate acceptable social behavior in the ancient Near East (cf. Barton), and the laws of conscience that make every person accountable for his or her actions (cf. Rom 1:18–20; 2:12–15)."[232] Judah, on the other hand, has "rejected the Torah of Yahweh, and his statutes they have not kept" (Amos 2:4). Israel's transgressions are also explicit violations of the Mosaic law (cf., e.g., Amos 2:7 with Lev. 18:8, 15). Yahweh denounces the manifest evil of what Israel has done "to profane my holy name" (Amos 2:7). The roaring of the Lion points to his zeal for his holiness (for lion imagery in Amos, see 1:2; 3:4, 8; 5:19; for Yahweh's holiness, see 2:7; 4:2). The covenant Lord's insistence on his rights may also be seen in his assertions of what he did for Israel at the conquest (2:9), at the exodus (2:10), and when he raised up Nazirites and prophets for Israel (2:11). Yahweh's people responded to his good gifts by giving the Nazirites wine and commanding prophets not to prophesy (2:12). Justice will be done against these violations of the covenant, and even the most courageous will flee naked (2:13–16).

There are several indications in Amos that the northern kingdom of Israel faces exile (3:12; 5:5, 27; 6:7; 7:11; 9:4). Five times in Amos 4 the announcement comes that Yahweh gave partial judgments to Israel such as famine (4:6), drought (4:8), locusts (4:9; cf. Joel 1:2–4), plagues like those of Egypt (Amos 4:10), even overthrow like Sodom and Gomorrah (4:11), and after each announcement of Yahweh's justice he declares, "Yet you did not return to me" (4:6, 8, 9, 10, 11). These judgments are clearly intended to produce repentance, but because they do not, Yahweh announces[233] that his people will see him in all his splendid fullness:

> Therefore thus I will do to you, O Israel, because I will do this to you,
> prepare to meet your God, O Israel!
> For behold, the one who forms mountains
> and creates the wind

[231]For an alternative approach to structuring the book, see Duane A. Garrett, *Amos: A Handbook on the Hebrew Text*, Baylor Handbook on the Hebrew Bible (Waco, TX: Baylor University Press, 2008), 4.

[232]Gary V. Smith, "Amos: Theology of," in *NIDOTTE*, 4:374.

[233]I am reading this passage as though Yahweh is presented as the speaker in both verses 12 and 13, the participles in verse 13 continuing the first person verbs of verse 12. Thus, Amos 4:12–13 is analogous to Ex. 34:6–7, where Yahweh announces his own name. It could be that Amos is speaking in verse 13. For discussion of critical issues such as "sources" of and relationships between the "fragments" in Amos 4:13; 5:8–9; and 9:5–6, see Francis I. Andersen and David Noel Freedman, *Amos*, AB (New York: Doubleday, 1989), 453–55, 486–90.

and declares to man what is his thought,
making dawn of darkness,
and making his way on the high places of the land,
Yahweh, God of hosts, is his name. (4:12–13)

Yahweh will come in majestic glory to judge the unrepentant. Amos caps several significant exclamations of Yahweh's splendor with the assertion "Yahweh . . . is his name." These are found in Amos 4:13, 5:8 (cf. 5:27), and 9:6.

Amos twice calls his contemporaries to "seek Yahweh and live" (5:6; cf. 5:4; Isa. 55:3). The prophet holds out a life that is more than merely physical for his old covenant contemporaries, indicating that those who seek Yahweh can experience a spiritual life that is at least akin to regeneration. As noted above, elsewhere the Old and New Testaments describe this in terms of heart circumcision (cf. Jer. 6:10; Rom. 2:29; Col. 2:11–13).[234]

If Israel will seek Yahweh according to his instructions, they will live (cf. Lev. 18:5). But if they do not trust Yahweh enough to believe what he has spoken, he will break out against them like a fire, consuming them in his holiness (Amos 5:6). Seeking to inspire faith in Yahweh, Amos announces the unique greatness of the Creator God:

The one who makes the Pleiades and Orion,
and turning the shadow of death into morning,
and he causes the day to darken into night;
the one who called to the waters of the sea,
and poured them upon the face of the earth:
Yahweh is his name,
Who causes destruction to flash upon the strong,
and destruction he will bring upon the fortress. (5:8–9)

Because Yahweh is the alone Creator (4:13; 5:8), he is sovereign over all that has been made. This is demonstrated when he overwhelms the defenses of those who oppose him.

Israel has not repented, however, so there will be no Passover like there was in Egypt. Instead of passing over, Yahweh will pass through Israel (Amos 5:17; 7:8; 8:2).[235] Like Joel, Amos announces the coming day of Yahweh (5:18, 20; cf. 8:9). This announcement is followed by a call for Israel to repent. Should they respond, they would be saved through judgment. Yahweh's desire is for his people to be what he created them to be: his image and likeness. This means that he wants them to worship him and rule as he rules, with supreme regard for his

[234]See further *God's Indwelling Presence*.
[235]Schwesig, *Die Rolle der Tag-JHWHs-Dichtungen im Dodekapropheton*, 14.

glory and honor. Thus, Amos calls Israel to "let justice roll down like water, and righteousness like an ever flowing wadi" (5:24). Mirroring Yahweh's justice and righteousness displays his glory. Moreover, Israel was called to be like Yahweh and "hate evil, love good, and establish justice in the gate" (5:15a). Doing so would be a repudiation of the way the nation has been conducting itself; indeed, it would be repentance. If Israel will repent, "Perhaps Yahweh, God of hosts, will be gracious to the remnant of Joseph" (5:15b). Like Joel (2:13) and Jonah (3:9), Amos proclaims that though Yahweh owes only justice, he might show mercy to those who repent.

Yahweh's own absolute commitment to himself requires that due regard be paid to him and informs his hatred of sin: "The Lord Yahweh has sworn by his own soul, declares Yahweh, God of hosts, 'I loathe the pride of Jacob, and his citadels I hate; so I will deliver up the city and all its fullness'" (Amos 6:8). Pride is offensive to Yahweh because it takes credit due him alone, and thus he swears by his own soul to humble those who exalt themselves.

Yahweh shows himself to be a God who not only punishes iniquity, transgression, and sin, but is also abounding in loving-kindness in Amos. In response to his first two visions, Amos cries out, "O Lord Yahweh, please pardon, who[236] will raise Jacob, for he is small? Yahweh relented concerning this. 'This shall not be,' says Yahweh" (7:2–3). This exchange after the first vision is repeated almost verbatim after the second vision in Amos 7:5–6. The visions reveal the coming judgments of locusts and fire, prompting Amos to cry out to Yahweh for mercy, and when Yahweh grants Amos's requests, he has saved through judgment. This display of mercy demonstrates that Yahweh is more tender, loving, forgiving, and merciful than human tongue can tell.

As in Amos 4:13 (cf. 5:8), in 9:5–6 Amos appears to present Yahweh declaring his own name.[237] Having warned that he will bring judgment upon Israel in verses 1–4, Yahweh asserts his own power beginning in the last words of verse 4:

> I will set my eyes upon them for evil and not for good,
> even the Lord Yahweh of hosts,
> the one who touches the earth and it melts,
> and all who dwell on it mourn;

[236]This is usually rendered, "Oh, that Jacob may stand" (NKJV) or "How can Jacob stand?" (ESV, NASB). I am taking the interrogative pronoun מִי to mean "who." Bruce K. Waltke and M. O'Connor, *An Introduction to Biblical Hebrew Syntax* (Winona Lake, IN: Eisenbrauns, 1990), §18.2d (320 n. 10) write, "The sense of *mî yāqûm ya'ăqōb* in Amos 7:2, 5 is not clear; the usual rendering is 'How can Jacob stand?', but more apt may be 'Who is Jacob that he can stand?'" The rendering I offer above seems preferable to me. Cf. GKC, §37a, §137a–b, and for other ways it can be used, §137c. See also Joüon, §144.

[237]Yahweh is presented as speaking in the first person in 9:4 and 9:7, so it seems that the participles in verses 5–6 should be read as elaborations upon the first-person utterances of verse 4. This can be contrasted with 5:8–9, where the last clear indication that Yahweh is speaking in the first person is in verse 4. The first-person statements are probably continued in verse 5, but the third-person statements in verse 6 seem to be Amos's comments, which continue in verses 7–9 and following.

and all of it shall rise as the Nile and subside like the Nile of Egypt.
The one who builds in the heavens his upper chambers,
and his vaults on the earth he established;
the one who calls to waters of the sea,
and he poured them upon the face of the earth:
Yahweh is his name. (9:4b–6)

Yahweh announces that he will not show favoritism to the children of Israel, whom he likens to the people of Ethiopia, the Philistines, and the Syrians (9:7). He will destroy the sinful kingdom (9:8), but the destruction will be a sifting (9:9), the sinners will die, and then Yahweh will restore the fallen booth of David (9:11). On that day the Gentiles who are called by Yahweh's name will belong to David's kingdom (9:12), the land shall know Edenic prosperity (9:13), the captives will come home (9:14), and Yahweh will plant them in their land never to be pulled up (9:15). In Amos, salvation comes through judgment by and for the glory of God.

3.5.4 Obadiah

Salvation through judgment for God's glory is fast and furious in Obadiah. Threats are made against Edom (1:1–9). After the announcement of coming judgment, the reasons for the coming judgment are stated (1:10–14). The reasons for judgment on Edom are followed by the proclamation of the nearness of the day of the Lord against all nations (1:15–16), accompanied by the promise of salvation to Yahweh's people (1:17–21).[238]

Edom is denounced for pride (Obad. 1:3). Their mountain stronghold will not protect them from Yahweh's justice (1:3–4), which will be so destructive that no gleanings will be left (1:5–6), and none of their allies will help (1:7). Both the wise and the mighty will be overcome (1:8–9). The wise will be made foolish, the strong weak, and the proud brought low.

The judgment against Edom announced in Obadiah 1:1–9 comes for crimes against Israel (1:10–14). Edom has done violence against their kinsmen, the people of Jacob (1:10). When Israel was taken into captivity, Edom not only did not come to Israel's aid (1:11–13), but it seems they captured escaping Israelites and returned them to their conquerors (1:14). This setting seems to place the oracle of Obadiah after the capture of Jerusalem in 586 BC, though there is not enough information for a conclusive decision. We can be certain, however, that Obadiah believes that the sins of Edom against Israel will be judged.

Obadiah then segues into reprisal against the nations in 1:15–16. The day of the Lord will come against all the nations who opposed God's people. Through the judgment on Edom and the nations, however, salvation will come to God's

[238] Cf. Schwesig, *Die Rolle der Tag-JHWHs-Dichtungen im Dodekapropheton*, 287.

people (1:17–21).[239] Mount Zion will be delivered and holy (1:17). Jacob will bring fires of judgment against the house of Esau (1:18), and Israel will possess the lands round about (1:19–20). The kingdom shall belong to Yahweh (1:21). The message of Obadiah is that Edom—and the nations—will be judged, and through that judgment Israel will be saved, while Yahweh is glorified for his justice and mercy.

3.5.5 Jonah

The book of Jonah is about God's glory in salvation through judgment,[240] and in some ways it is a microcosm of the whole history of Israel.[241] Yahweh commissions Jonah (cf. 2 Kings 14:25–27) to announce judgment to Nineveh, where dwell the enemies of God's people. Rather than going to Nineveh, the prophet goes in the opposite direction to "flee . . . from the presence of Yahweh" (Jonah 1:3). Yahweh judges the prophet, bringing him to "the belly of Sheol" (2:3) for "three days and three nights" (1:17). Under the judgment of Yahweh, Jonah calls out to Yahweh for deliverance (2:2) and confesses that Yahweh "brought up my life from the pit" (2:6). "Salvation belongs to Yahweh!" (2:9), and this salvation comes to Jonah through judgment.

Yahweh sends Jonah to Nineveh a second time (Jonah 3:2), and this time Jonah goes and announces that Yahweh's judgment is about to fall. Like the sailors in Jonah 1, who experienced the storm of Yahweh's wrath against Jonah, heard Jonah's prophetic word, heeded it, and were delivered (1:3–16), the Ninevites experience the storm of Yahweh's wrath in Jonah's announcement, heed the prophetic word, and are shown mercy (3:3–10). Like the nation of Israel as a whole, Jonah is a somewhat reluctant "light to the nations," and he pursued his calling only after the resurrection that followed the death of three days and nights in the belly of the great fish.

Having seen Yahweh's mercy to Nineveh, Jonah is hardly pleased. He asserts that he fled to Tarshish precisely because he knew Yahweh would be gracious and merciful, slow to anger and abounding in steadfast love (cf. Ex. 34:7, and see the appendix [§8] to chap. 2, which catalogs Ex. 34:6–7 in the Law, Prophets, and Writings). He then pouts, and Yahweh mercifully communicates his righteous concern, which extends even to Nineveh (Jonah 4:3–11). That this episode is recorded with such honesty seems to indicate that Jonah later realized how petty his behavior had been and communicated it for the benefit of others. Here

[239] Similarly Elizabeth Achtemeier, *Minor Prophets I*, NIBC (Peabody, MA: Hendrickson, 1996), 240: "On the day of the Lord, God will destroy Edom and exalt the people Israel, who will then reign secure from Mt. Zion."
[240] See Bryan D. Estelle, *Salvation through Judgment and Mercy: The Gospel According to Jonah*, The Gospel According to the Old Testament (Phillipsburg: P&R, 2005).
[241] See the fascinating and thorough study of Jonah's many links with other Old Testament texts in Katharine J. Dell, "Reinventing the Wheel: The Shaping of the Book of Jonah," in Barton and Reimer, *After the Exile*, 85–101.

too, through the striking of the plant and the exposure of his churlish disregard for Ninevite souls, Jonah was brought through the judgment of his attitude to salvation. This salvation takes the form of rejoicing in Yahweh's inclination to relent and show mercy.

Like Jonah, Israel must be brought through judgment to salvation, and salvation opens up into the reconciliation of the nations for God's glory. Commissioned as a kingdom of priests (Ex. 19:6) to walk in the way of Yahweh's Torah, Israel walked instead in the way of Canaan. This is the spiritual equivalent of being commanded to go to Nineveh only to flee to Tarshish. Just as Jonah undergoes a death and resurrection of sorts before obeying and going to Nineveh, so the nation will go through a death and resurrection of sorts when they are exiled to the realm of death and then restored to life in the land of Yahweh's presence, at which point Jerusalem will indeed become a light to the nations, shining with the very glory of Yahweh as nations stream to Jerusalem to learn his ways (Isaiah 2; Micah 4).

3.5.6 Micah

Micah's prophecy seems to be organized around calls to "hear" (1:2; 3:1; 6:1),[242] and within these calls there appears to be a movement from judgment to salvation (see table 3.12).

Table 3.12. Through Judgment to Salvation in Micah

Judgment	Salvation
1:2b–2:11	2:12–13
3:1–12	4–5
6:1–7:6	7:7–20

Among the various proposals for structuring Micah, this movement from a section on judgment into a section on salvation seems most compelling.[243] Anderson and Freedman write:

> The book begins with an outpouring of God's energies into the world. The destruction is global and total. But not final. God's mercy does not arrest his justice—it operates beyond judgment. His wrath does not quench his love; his compassion does not cancel his anger. . . . It is possible to restore relationships because God himself takes up the task of salvation. . . . The way to this end is through the

[242]House, *The Unity of the Twelve*, 85. "Hear" (שׁמעו) also occurs in Mic. 3:9 and 6:2, but 3:9a is almost a verbatim quotation of 3:1a and continues the address to "Jacob" and "the house of Israel" regarding "justice" begun there, and 6:2 is continuing 6:1.

[243]For a brief survey of different proposed outlines of Micah, see House, *Old Testament Theology*, 369.

> earthquake and fire of judgment. The city must become a heap of rubble before it can be splendidly rebuilt.[244]

Whereas Isaiah and Jeremiah called the heavens and earth to witness against Israel, Micah announces that Yahweh himself will be a witness against Israel and Judah (Mic. 1:2), and he describes Yahweh's coming in theophanic glory (1:3). When he treads on the high places, where the idols have been worshiped,

> the mountains will melt under him,
>   and the valleys will split open,
> like wax before the fire,
>   like waters poured down a steep place. (1:4 ESV)

According to Micah, when Yahweh comes in judgment, the created order will dissolve before him, "for the transgression of Jacob and for the sins of the house of Israel." In view of the idolatrous calves set up in the northern kingdom, it is no surprise that Micah identifies "the transgression of Jacob" as Samaria, but the identification of "the high place of Judah" as Jerusalem is a stunning announcement, a harbinger of exile (1:5 ESV).

Micah declares that judgment is coming from Yahweh, and in language reminiscent of David's lament over Saul and Jonathan (2 Sam. 1:20), Micah cries, "Tell it not in Gath" (Mic. 1:10). The only difference between 2 Samuel 1:20 and Micah 1:10 is in word order. Thus, Micah quotes a phrase well known from a previous defeat of Israel—indeed, a phrase reminiscent of the death of Israel's first king—to warn of the judgment that will fall in the near future. Exile will be like death, like Saul's suicide. Yahweh will demonstrate his righteousness when he judges Israel, but Micah does not want the Philistines to celebrate as though their gods have triumphed over Yahweh (cf. 1 Sam. 31:9, where they carried "the good news to the house of their idols").

Micah is not only concerned for Yahweh's reputation among the nations, reflected in his plea that Israel's bad news not be reported as good news for the nations; he is also concerned for Yahweh's reputation in Israel. Thus, in 2:1–2 he seems to describe Ahab's wicked seizure of Naboth's vineyard (cf. 1 Kings 21:2–19). The outright mention of Ahab in Micah 6:16 strengthens these connections. Because of such injustices, the wicked family faces judgment (Mic. 2:3–5). Anyone tempted to think that the coming judgment is unwarranted needs only to be reminded of the nation's history to be convinced that Yahweh is just to judge Israel. Yahweh is just to judge not only because of wicked kings. The

[244]Francis I. Anderson and David Noel Freedman, *Micah*, AB (New York: Doubleday, 2000), 28–29.

people have urged the prophets not to preach and have accepted lying prophets (2:6–11).

Through the judgment comes salvation. The imagery of the gathering of the remnant in Micah 2:12 presupposes exile, and the king in 2:13, who breaks through and leads the people out, who is identified with Yahweh, assumes that there will be a new exodus, a new return to the land. Through judgment comes salvation when Yahweh leads his people home by the agency of his king.

Following the next call to "hear" (Mic. 3:1; cf. 1:2), Micah indicts Israel's rulers for injustice (3:1–3, 9–11). Judgment is Yahweh's righteous response to Israel's abusive leadership (3:4–7, 12), and Micah is filled with the Spirit of Yahweh, and with justice and power to call sin what it is (3:8). Again, salvation comes through judgment. "In the latter days," Micah proclaims, Israel will experience what Isaiah promised in Isaiah 2:1–5 (Mic. 4:1–5). Yahweh will gather his lame, afflicted exiles (4:6–7), and give victory to Israel (4:8–13).

Micah promises a ruler who will come from Bethlehem (Mic. 5:1, ET 2), and remarkably this statement is preceded by a statement about the "judge of Israel" being struck on the cheek (Mic. 4:14, ET 5:1). Micah states:

> He shall give them up until the time when she who is in labor has given birth; then the rest of his brothers shall return to the people of Israel. And he shall stand and shepherd his flock in the strength of Yahweh, in the majesty of the name of Yahweh his God, and they shall dwell secure, for now he shall be great to the ends of the earth. And he shall be their peace (5:2–4a, ET 3–5a).

This remarkable prophecy seems to indicate that God will "give them up" until the birth of the ruler, "whose origin is from of old, from ancient days" (5:1, ET 2), is born (5:2, ET 3). This would seem to point to the dawning of the restoration of God's people at the birth of this promised ruler, and it seems likely that when he cited Micah 5:1 (ET 2), Matthew had the broader context of this prophecy in view (cf. Matt. 2:5–6).[245] Until then, judgment. After judgment, Israel will defeat Assyria (Mic. 5:4–5, ET 5–6), and the remnant of Israel will be delivered from idolatry by Yahweh himself (5:6–14, ET 7–15).

Micah's third call to "hear" (Mic. 6:1; cf. 1:2; 3:1) summons the mountains and the foundations of the earth to hear (6:1–2) Yahweh's case against his people (6:1–7:6). Yahweh delivered them from Egypt, provided Moses, Aaron, and Miriam as leaders (6:3–4), and overcame Balak and Balaam, and Micah calls them to remember so that they may "know the righteousnesses[246] of Yah-

[245]See G. K. Beale, ed., *The Right Doctrine from the Wrong Texts? Essays on the Use of the Old Testament in the New* (Grand Rapids: Baker, 1994), esp. pt. 4, "Did the New Testament Authors Respect the Context of the Old Testament Text? Affirmative Arguments," 167–276, essays by Dodd, Sundberg, Marshall, Beale, and Seccombe.

[246]The ESV renders "righteousnesses" (צדקות) as "saving acts."

weh" (6:5). The people do not do what Yahweh requires, which is for them to do justice, love mercy, and walk humbly with him (6:8), and so the voice of Yahweh announces judgment (6:9–16). Micah pronounces a woe on himself because of the detailed wickedness of Israel (7:1–6), but he resolves to wait for Yahweh (7:7). Micah warns his enemies not to rejoice over his fall, for he will surely rise, and Yahweh will be his light (7:8). When Yahweh satisfies his just indignation against the people's sin, he will turn, plead their case, and vindicate them (7:9). As Dumbrell puts it, "Micah believes in a restoration beyond judgment."[247] The enemy will be trampled down (7:10). Through judgment comes salvation, and then the glory of Yahweh will shine in the building of walls and extending of boundaries, in the serpent licking the dust (cf. Gen. 3:14), and in the people trembling before him (Mic. 7:11–17). Micah plays on his name ("who is like you" מִיכָה, 1:1), asking, "Who is a God like you [מִי־אֵל כָּמוֹךָ]" and alluding to Yahweh's declaration of his name in Exodus 34:6–7 in the words, "pardoning iniquity and passing over transgression . . . because he delights in steadfast love" (Mic. 7:18, and see the appendix [§8] to chap. 2, which catalogs Ex. 34:6–7 in the Law, Prophets, and Writings). Having thus exalted Yahweh, Micah declares that Yahweh will show compassion to his people, trample their enemies underfoot (cf. Gen. 3:15), forgive the sin of his people, and keep his promises to Abraham (Mic. 7:19–20). In Micah, there is no God like Yahweh, who is glorified in the judgment of his people that results in their salvation.

3.5.7 Nahum

In Jonah Nineveh was shown mercy, but Nahum's "burden against Nineveh" (1:1 NKJV) announces that Yahweh will at last avenge himself on Nineveh. This word "burden" appears as a heading five times in the Book of the Twelve (Nah. 1:1; Hab. 1:1; Zech. 9:1; 12:1; Mal. 1:1), and in each case the "burden" seems to be the announcement of the destruction of the enemies of the people of God (see table 3.13).

Table 3.13. "Burden" Announcement of Destruction in the Book of the Twelve

Nahum 1:1	Destruction of Nineveh
Habakkuk 1:1	Destruction of Babylon
Zechariah 9:1	Destruction of Damascus, Hamath, Tyre and Sidon, and Philistia
Zechariah 12:1	Destruction of those who besiege Judah
Malachi 1:1	Destruction of Edom

[247]Dumbrell, *The Faith of Israel*, 209.

This use of "burden/oracle" to introduce a promise of destructive judgment in the Twelve also matches its use in Isaiah's oracles against the nations (cf. Isa. 13:1; 14:28; 15:1; 17:1; 19:1; 21:1, 11, 13; 22:1; 23:1; cf. 30:6).

Yahweh's jealous justice roars with fury through the forty-seven verses of Nahum. The second verse of the prophecy describes Yahweh as jealous, avenging, and wrathful, and the third links this to Yahweh's declaration of his name in Exodus 34:6–7: "Yahweh is slow to anger and great in power, and Yahweh will by no means clear the guilty" (Nah. 1:3, and see the appendix [§8] to chap. 2, which catalogs Ex. 34:6–7 in the Law, Prophets, and Writings).[248] Yahweh comes "in whirlwind and storm, and the clouds are the dust of his feet" (Nah. 1:3b). In Micah the mountains melted when Yahweh stood on them, and in Nahum seas and rivers are made dry at his rebuke (1:4), then the mountains quake and hills melt (1:5). No one can stand before Yahweh (1:6), but in all the focus on judgment, there is salvation too: "Yahweh is good, a stronghold in the day of trouble; he knows those who take refuge in him" (1:7).

The announcement of Nineveh's destruction calls forth a quotation of Isaiah 52:7:

> Behold, upon the mountains, the feet of him
> who brings good news,
> who publishes peace! (Nah. 2:1, ET 1:15 ESV)

The good news here results from the salvation of God's people established by the judgment of their enemies. Jacob and Israel have been plundered, but Nahum announces that Yahweh will restore majesty to them through the destruction of Nineveh (2:3, ET 2).

The severity of the judgment on Nineveh is communicated as Nahum twice relates, "'Behold, I am against you,' an utterance of Yahweh of hosts" (Nah. 2:14, ET 13; 3:5).[249] Yahweh will shatter his enemies, and those who hear the good news will rejoice over the destruction of the evildoers (3:19).[250] In Nahum, salvation comes through the judgment of Nineveh, demonstrating the glory of Yahweh.

---

[248]For a brief summary of the difficulties of the half acrostic in Nahum 1:2–8, see Wilfred G. E. Watson, *Classical Hebrew Poetry: A Guide to Its Techniques* (1984; repr., New York: T&T Clark, 2005), 192, 199; and Ralph Smith, *Micah-Malachi*, WBC (Waco, TX: Word, 1984), 65.

[249]See further Simon Sherwin, "'I Am Against You': Yahweh's Judgment on the Nations and Its Ancient Near Eastern Context," *TynBul* 54, no. 2 (2003): 149–60. He notes that this phrase also occurs in Jer. 50:31 and 51:25.

[250]Smith (*Micah-Malachi*, 68) quotes Watts on the point that Assyria is a symbol of "the ultimate supernatural evil that frustrates and suppresses the purposes and people of God."

3.5.8 *Habakkuk*

In Habakkuk the prophet poses a question, Yahweh replies, and the reply prompts a second question. Yahweh's reply to this second question then prompts a psalm of trust from the prophet.[251] This can be laid out as seen in table 3.14.

Table 3.14. The Structure of Habakkuk

The Prophet's Questions	Yahweh's Replies
1:2–4	1:5–11
1:12–2:1	2:2–20
The Prophet's Psalm, 3:1–19	

Significantly for our purposes, Habakkuk's questions and Yahweh's replies are mainly concerned with judgment and salvation. Habakkuk asks why Yahweh does not do justice against Israel's sin (Hab. 1:2–4). Yahweh replies that he is raising up Babylon to judge Israel (1:12–2:1). Habakkuk is appalled by this reply: how can Yahweh use a nation more wicked than Israel to devour his people (1:12–2:1)? Yahweh replies that the righteous will live by faith (2:4), even if it appears that the vision God has revealed is not coming to pass (2:2–3). Once Yahweh has used Babylon to judge Israel, he will judge Babylon (2:5–13), and Yahweh's purpose will not be thwarted: "For the earth will be filled with the knowledge of the glory of Yahweh, as the waters cover the sea" (2:14).[252] Yahweh will be glorified when he does justice on Israel and Babylon, and then Habakkuk psalms a plea for Yahweh to remember mercy (3:1–19; cf. 3:2). In this prayer, Habakkuk asserts that he will do what Yahweh calls the righteous to do in 2:4,[253] namely, he will trust Yahweh and rejoice in him even if it seems that Yahweh's promises of a prosperous land—blossoming fig trees, fruit on the vines, flocks in the folds, herds in the stalls—are not seen (3:17–19). Habakkuk is undone by the judgment declared against Israel (3:16a), but he will wait for the judgment promised against those who will exile them (3:16b). Through this judgment on their enemies, Israel will be saved, and Yahweh will be glorified in his justice and his mercy. Moreover, the faith of those who believe that Yahweh will do this, in spite of the fact that they do not see evidence of it, glorifies Yahweh as a God who is worthy of trust.

Habakkuk proclaims that Yahweh is in his holy temple, all the earth should be silent before him (2:20), and all the earth will be filled with the glory of Yahweh (2:14). Habakkuk's psalm of praise rehearses Yahweh's past acts of salvation through judgment in order to assure his audience that they can trust Yahweh, in

[251]For a more detailed outline, see Francis I. Anderson, *Habakkuk*, AB (New York: Doubleday, 2001), 15.
[252]See appendix 2 (§6) to this chapter, "All the Earth Filled with the Knowledge of Yahweh's Glory."
[253]Similarly Dumbrell, *The Faith of Israel*, 220.

spite of the faith-threatening nature of their circumstances. Habakkuk sings Yahweh's reliability by rehearsing Yahweh's mighty deeds at the exodus and conquest: when Yahweh appeared to Israel, "his glory covered the heavens, and his praise filled the earth" (3:3). Yahweh brought the plagues (3:5) and made mountains tremble (3:6, 10). He afflicted Cushan and Midian (3:7), and he defeated the seas and the rivers, allowing Israel to pass through on dry land (3:8–9). Habakkuk describes Yahweh in terms reminiscent of Genesis 3:15—he "trampled the nations" when he "marched" out "for the salvation" of his "anointed," and he "crushed the head from the house of the wicked, laying bare from tail to neck" (Hab. 3:12–13).[254] Through the judgment of the enemy, the crushing of the head of the seed of the serpent, Yahweh saves his people. And the description of the epic conquest glorifies the might of the God who saves through judgment, upholding justice and remembering mercy. In Habakkuk, Yahweh is glorified in salvation through judgment.

3.5.9 Zephaniah

Zephaniah proclaims the great day of Yahweh, the day he will be glorified when he judges in order to save. After identifying himself and his times (Zeph. 1:1), Zephaniah announces that God will de-create what he has made because of Judah's idolatry (1:2–6).[255] He then makes clear that this moment of de-creation is the day of Yahweh, a day when he will justly punish evildoers (1:7–18). The announcement of coming judgment, however, provides an opportunity to respond in repentance (2:1–3). Those who repent might be hidden on the day of wrath (2:3). The day of Yahweh threatens not only sinners in Zion but also the nations (2:4–3:7). Sweeney writes, "Judgment against Israel and Judah would be followed by universal judgment against the nations at large prior to universal restoration and recognition of YHWH as the sovereign G-d of all the earth."[256] Thus Zephaniah prophesies against the Philistines (2:4–7), Moab and Ammon (2:8–11), Ethiopia (2:12), Assyria (2:13–15), and Jerusalem (3:1–7). The judgment of the day of the Lord will be transnational, but it will not be merely retributive. Zephaniah 3:8–13 shows that salvation will come through this judgment: after the fire of Yahweh's wrath in 3:8 will come a day that reverses the confusion of the languages at Babel (Genesis 11) in Zephaniah 3:9.[257] The "pure speech" Yahweh gives to the peoples after judgment is for "all of them to call on the name of Yahweh" (3:9). Yahweh's worshipers will be gathered from "beyond the rivers of Ethiopia" (3:10), the proud will be removed from the midst of his people (3:11),

[254]Smith (*Micah-Malachi*, 116) writes, "'Your Anointed' probably refers to the Davidic king in Jerusalem. 'From tail to neck' (v 13) appears to be a reference to the enemy in the form of a dragon."
[255]Cf. Adele Berlin, *Zephaniah*, AB (New York: Doubleday, 1994), 13–14, and cf. p. 83 for the suggestion that the created order breaks down when Israel's worship is misused or corrupted.
[256]Marvin A. Sweeney, "Zephaniah: A Paradigm for the Study of the Prophetic Books," *CR:BS* 7 (1999): 119.
[257]Berlin, *Zephaniah*, 14.

and those he leaves will be humble, seeking refuge in Yahweh's name, doing no injustice and speaking no lies, fearing nothing (3:12–13). Zephaniah summons the daughter of Zion to sing and shout (3:14) because Yahweh has taken away her judgments and her enemies (3:15). She should not fear or be weak because Yahweh is in her midst:

> . . . a mighty one who will save;
> he will rejoice over you with gladness;
> he will quiet you by his love;
> he will exult over you with loud singing. (3:17 ESV)

Yahweh then declares that he will gather the exiles, judge the oppressors, and make his people a display of his glory (3:18–20). In Zephaniah, Yahweh is glorified in salvation that comes through judgment.

3.5.10 Haggai

Considered from a historical perspective, the final three books of the Twelve were written after the exile. This means that at one level the day of the Lord that the earlier prophets announced has come to pass, though at another level it awaits the great day of God's final visitation. The destruction of Jerusalem and temple by the Babylonians typifies the future day of the Lord. As Adam was exiled from Eden, Israel and Judah were exiled from the land of Israel. The story line of the Former Prophets ends with the people in exile and favor shown to Jehoiachin. That story line will be carried forward in the Writings, in the books of Esther, Daniel, Ezra–Nehemiah, and Chronicles. The prophecies of Haggai and Zechariah are situated historically after the events narrated in Chronicles and Daniel and before those recounted in Esther and Ezra–Nehemiah. The canonical position of Haggai, Zechariah, and Malachi is thus determined by concerns for genre and literary connections (thus its place in the Twelve) rather than chronology (which would locate it with other post-exilic books).

Considered from a literary perspective, then, these final three books of the Twelve obviously partake of the same genre as the other books of both the Twelve and the Latter Prophets. The prophet Haggai opens with a historical marker—one of several—that alerts readers to what has taken place, and the historical markers in Haggai and Zechariah show that they ministered at the same time (see table 3.15). Byron Curtis has demonstrated that the forms in which the dates are given match those used by Jeremiah to mark the fall of the temple so that the dates in Haggai and Zechariah herald the end of Jeremiah's seventy years: "In this dated framework, in imitation of and counterbalance to the date forms of Jeremiah that memorialized the temple's loss, we find the returned community's eschatological and imminent expectation of the end of seventy years' chastisement."[258]

Table 3.15. Dates in Haggai and Zechariah

Aug. 29, 520	Haggai exhorts the people to rebuild the temple (Hag. 1:1).
Sept. 21, 520	The people obey Haggai and work (Hag. 1:14–15).
Oct. 17, 520	Haggai promises greater glory for the rebuilt temple (Hag. 2:1–9).
Oct./Nov. 520	Zechariah makes first proclamation (Zech. 1:1–6).
Dec. 18, 520	Haggai promises blessing for the defiled people (Hag. 2:10, 18).
Dec. 18, 520	Haggai says Zerubbabel will be Yahweh's signet ring (Hag. 2:20–23).
Feb. 15, 519	Zechariah has night visions (Zech. 1:7–6:8).
Dec. 7, 518	Zechariah calls the people to do justice and mercy (Zech. 7:1–14).

Haggai exhorts the people to rebuild the temple (Hag. 1:1–11). The people obey, led by Zerubbabel and Joshua (1:12–15). Yahweh promises to fill the rebuilt temple with greater glory (2:1–9). Though the people are defiled, Yahweh promises to bless them (2:10–19). Yahweh will shake heavens and earth, overthrow kingdoms, and make Zerubbabel his signet ring (2:20–23).

Judgment has fallen in the exile, and now the people are back in the land. Salvation through judgment for God's glory, however, continues: Haggai indicts the people for paneling their own houses while Yahweh's house lies in ruins (Hag. 1:4). Yahweh has condemned their selfishness, making their efforts unsatisfying (1:5–6), and through this judgment he saves them to know that he is central to satisfaction. Richard Taylor observes that "the task that lay before them [rebuilding the temple] was a test of whether they would put God first in their lives."[259] And this is for Yahweh's glory, in line with the purpose he began to pursue when he set out to make the world.

The heavens and the earth are the stage on which Yahweh will display beauty, truth, and goodness, and that beauty, truth, and goodness are his glory. Adam was charged to rule over the earth and subdue it, which seems to mean that he was to expand the borders of Eden until the place where Yahweh's glory was known by his image bearers covered the dry land as the waters cover the sea. Adam rebelled, sought to be like God himself, and was expelled from the garden. The Lord then chose Abraham, and he promised land to him and his seed. Then the Lord brought the seed of Abraham into the Promised Land, and it was as though a new Adam, the people of Israel, were given a new Eden, whose

[258]Byron G. Curtis, *Up the Steep and Stony Road: The Book of Zechariah in Social Location Trajectory Analysis*, Academia Biblica (Atlanta: Society of Biblical Literature, 2006), 112, see the wider discussion, 92–113.
[259]Richard A. Taylor and E. Ray Clendenen, *Haggai, Malachi*, NAC (Nashville: Broadman & Holman, 2004), 25.

boundaries they were to extend. As Israel subdued the nations round about, the land in which Yahweh's word was law, the land where Yahweh dwelled among his people, would grow. Here again, Yahweh's purpose was to cover the dry lands with his glory, and so he invited the messiah, king of Israel, to ask of him, and he would make the nations his inheritance (Ps. 2:8). Like Adam, Israel sinned. Like Adam, Israel was expelled from the land. As with Adam, Yahweh means to save through judgment. The exile displays Yahweh's justice, and the return is lavish mercy.

Yahweh makes clear to these who have returned from exile that the charge he gave to Adam, which was later given to Israel, is now their charge: they are to build the temple, Yahweh says, "that I may be pleased with it and that I may be glorified" (Hag. 1:8). Yahweh calls the people through Haggai to reestablish the focal point of his glory on earth, the temple. Once they accomplish this task, they are to begin to pursue the task of ruling over the earth and subduing it, that the glory of Yahweh might cover the dry lands as the waters cover the sea.

Earlier prophets in Israel's history likened the promised return from exile to the exodus from Egypt and the conquest of the land, and Haggai does the same. Observing that the rebuilt second temple is as nothing in comparison with the temple's former glory (Hag. 2:3), Yahweh announces that he is with the people "according to the covenant that I made with you when you came out of Egypt" (2:4–5 ESV). When the people were delivered from Egypt, they plundered the Egyptians. Yahweh provided for them in the wilderness, and when they arrived at Sinai, Yahweh shook the heavens and the earth when he came down on the mountain, spoke the ten words, gave the instructions for the building of the tabernacle, and then took up residence in the tent, which was overlaid with the gold the people took from Egypt. Haggai has just referenced Yahweh's presence with the people at the exodus, the covenant he made with them, and the pillar of fire and cloud of Yahweh's presence among them in 2:4–5, and he goes on to announce:

> For thus says Yahweh of hosts, "Yet once more in a little while, and I will shake the heavens and the earth, the sea and the dry land; and I will shake all the nations, and the desire of all the nations will come, and I will fill this house with glory," says Yahweh of hosts. "The silver is mine and the gold is mine," an utterance of Yahweh of hosts. "The latter glory of this house will be greater than the former," says Yahweh of hosts, "and in this place I will give peace," an utterance of Yahweh of hosts. (2:6–9)

The reference to another shaking of the heavens and the earth seems to point back to the theophany at Sinai, where the covenant with Israel was inaugurated, and at the same time forward to a new covenant, promised by Jeremiah and others.

The reference to "the desire of all the nations" in Haggai 2:7 (חמדת כל־הגוים) is reminiscent of Samuel's words when he said to Saul, "And for whom is all the desire of Israel" (ולמי כל־חמדת ישראל, 1 Sam. 9:20). The echo of 1 Samuel 9:20 in Haggai 2:7 seems to indicate that the desire of all nations that Haggai says will come is a king who will bring righteousness and peace to the world.[260] The claim that Yahweh lays on the silver and the gold in Haggai 2:8 seems to refer to the way that he funded the building of the first temple with Egyptian gold and the second with Persian. Later in the chapter, the seed of the Davidic house, Zerubbabel, is told that he will be Yahweh's signet ring (Hag. 2:23).[261] Preceding this is another reference to the shaking of the heavens and earth (2:21), and a promise that chariots, horses, and riders will be overthrown, with soldiers turning their swords against their brothers (2:22). The shaking of the heavens recalls the Sinai theophany; the discomfiting of chariots and the overthrow of horse and rider recalls Yahweh's casting the Egyptian army into the Red Sea (Ex. 15:1); and the turning of a man's sword against his brother recalls the way Yahweh set the swords of the Midianites against their companions (Judg. 7:22). The new exodus and the return from exile will be replete with a new covenant, a new David, and a new conquest of the land, in which a new temple will be built, typologically fulfilling what these narratives prefigured. From the focal point in Zion, Yahweh's glory will begin to spread. Yahweh will be glorified in salvation through judgment.

3.5.11 Zechariah

Zechariah came alongside Haggai and prophesied with him (see table 3.15, above). The book of Zechariah seems to be structured by the historical markers at 1:1, 1:7, and 7:1, along with the two "burdens," one beginning at 9:1 and the other at 12:1.[262]

The first date given (Zech. 1:1) marks Zechariah's opening summons to the people: repent (1:1–6). The second date given (1:7) stands at the head of eight night visions, all of which assure the people that the temple will be rebuilt in the purified land (1:7–6:8), and after this the high priest is typologically identified as "the man whose name is the Branch" and crowned king (6:9–15).[263] The third date given (7:1) is followed by a question about how the post-exilic community should conduct itself, and Zechariah's reply redirects attention to the real issues at hand

[260] *Pace* Mark J. Boda, "Figuring the Future: The Prophets and Messiah," in *The Messiah in the Old and New Testaments*, ed. Stanley E. Porter (Grand Rapids: Eerdmans, 2007), 52, who writes regarding Hag. 2:6–9, "Although the early church did find in this pericope a reference to a future messianic figure ('the Desired One'), identified as Jesus, this view has no foundation in the original text." The royal connotations in the echo of 1 Sam. 9:20 provide a "foundation in the original text."

[261] Cf. Merrill, *Everlasting Dominion*, 558.

[262] So also Barry G. Webb, *The Message of Zechariah*, BST (Downers Grove, IL: InterVarsity, 2003), 31 n. 46.

[263] Cf. Zech. 3:8, where the declaration to Joshua that he and his companions "are men of portent" is followed by the assertion, "I am bringing my servant the Branch."

(7:4–8:23). Then follow the two "burdens" concerned with the salvation through judgment Yahweh will accomplish for Jerusalem (9:1–11:17; 12:1–14:21).

Zechariah's opening call to repentance (Zech. 1:1–6) invites those who have returned to the land to return to Yahweh, with the promise that he will return to them (1:3). With Haggai, Zechariah calls the people to rebuild the temple, and Yahweh's promise to return to the people anticipates nothing less than the realization of Isaiah's promise that Yahweh would return to Zion (Isa. 40:1–11) to take up residence in the rebuilt temple. After the judgment of exile is salvation, restoration to the land, where Yahweh's glory will shine forth from Jerusalem, the city on the hill (cf. Zech. 1:13–17).

Zechariah's eight visions (Zech. 1:7–6:8), which apparently all came on the single night of February 15, 519 BC, are all concerned with Yahweh's return to the rebuilt temple in the cleansed land.[264] Barry Webb has shown that the eight night visions of Zechariah have a chiastic structure (see table 3.16).[265]

Table 3.16. Eight Visions of the Night in Zechariah 1:7–6:8

1:7–17, Comfort for Zion: four horses scout territory

  2:1–4 (ET 1:18–21), Craftsmen overcome horns

    2:5–17 (ET 2:1–13), Restoration celebrated

      3:1–10, Joshua the high priest

      4:1–14, Zerubbabel the governor

    5:1–4, The flying scroll: commandments

  5:5–11, Removal of wickedness

6:1–8, Four chariots conquer

The four horsemen scouting the territory in the first vision (Zech. 1:7–17) are matched by the four conquering chariots of the last vision (6:1–8). Yahweh sends his horsemen out to patrol the land, and then his charioteers take it. The craftsmen who overcome the horns of the second vision symbolize the way that those who rebuild the temple overcome the opposition facing them (2:1–4).[266] Just as the opposing army, symbolized by the horns, is overcome, the ethics of the opposition are overcome in the symbolic removal of wickedness to the land of Shinar in the second-to-last vision (5:5–11). The reference to Shinar resurfaces the reality that two kingdoms are at war—two seeds, two powers. At this point in salvation history the kingdom of God is advancing through the work done on a humble temple in Jerusalem. The celebration of restoration in the third vision

[264]Webb, *Zechariah*, 66, 105–106.
[265]Ibid., 106. I have modified Webb's presentation of this structure slightly.
[266]Following ibid., 74–79. By contrast, Curtis (*Up the Steep and Stony Road*, 133–34) takes the craftsmen as a symbol of Persia, which overcame those who scattered Judah, Israel, and Jerusalem. Webb's view is more satisfying as it unites all the visions in relationship to the rebuilding of the temple.

(2:5–17) corresponds to the renewal of the law's jurisdiction in the third-to-last vision (5:1–4). And in the center of the chiasm are the two sons of oil: the cleansed high priest Joshua (3:1–10) and the temple building Zerubbabel (4:1–14).[267]

These night visions portray Yahweh as surveying the land and conquering it, empowering his people to cleanse the land of wickedness, and celebrating the restoration of the land and upholding the law; and with all this Yahweh provides a cleansed priest and an effective ruler. This pattern of events is reminiscent of the people entering the land under an earlier Joshua's leadership: just as Israel put the Canaanites under the ban, so also woman wickedness was removed; just as the people affirmed the covenant with Moses, so also the flying scroll roams the land; just as the scion of David would later build the temple, so also will Zerubbabel.

In the same way that Psalm 110 portrays the Davidic king as a priest, Zechariah 6:9–15 portrays the crowning of Joshua the high priest as king and his ruling on the throne. This symbolic action seems to point forward to a day when Israel will have a priest-king who will "build the temple of Yahweh, and he will lift up splendor" (Zech. 6:13). His name is "Branch," and he will "branch out" (6:12). When this happens, "those who are far off will come and build the temple of Yahweh" (6:15). Zechariah's crowning of Joshua the high priest, then, seems to be a symbolic action that points forward to a day when a similar pattern of events will typologically fulfill what is depicted in the crowning of the high priest, the temple builder whom the nations will serve as king in Jerusalem.

Just as the first six chapters of Zechariah have a chiastic structure (see table 3.16), chapters 7–8 of Zechariah also appear to have a chiastic structure (see table 3.17).[268]

Table 3.17. Chiastic Structure in Zechariah 7–8

- 7:1–3, Delegation to pray before Yahweh: shall we continue?
  - 7:4–7, The fast
    - 7:8–10, Call to righteous behavior
      - 7:11–14, Refusal to obey and exile
        - 8:1–6, Yahweh's zeal for Zion
      - 8:7–15, Regathering and restoration
    - 8:16–17, Call to righteous behavior
  - 8:18–19, The fast
- 8:20–23, Delegation to pray before Yahweh: let us continue!

[267]So also Curtis, *Up the Steep and Stony Road*, 137. He notes that Kline takes the trees as anointers, Boda as Haggai and Zechariah, and Rose as heavenly beings (137 n. 22).

[268]This chiastic structure was arrived at before I came across the proposals of Chisholm and Butterworth summarized in Curtis, *Up the Steep and Stony Road*, 150. I think this analysis better captures the content and message of the passage.

In what follows we will consider the corresponding sections of this chiasm—the first and last element, the second and second to last, and so forth.

The people of Bethel have sent a delegation "to entreat the favor of Yahweh" (Zech. 7:2), inquiring as to whether they should continue to "weep and abstain in the fifth month" (7:3).[269] At the end of this section, Zechariah prophesies that "many peoples and strong nations" will come to seek Yahweh and "to entreat the favor of Yahweh" (8:22). As Isaiah (2:3) and Micah (4:2) indicated, Gentiles will seek to learn Yahweh's ways from his people (Zech. 8:23).

Zechariah questions whether the people have been fasting for Yahweh or for themselves (7:4–7), and he points to a day when the fasts will be "seasons of joy" (8:19 ESV). Zechariah's two sections on righteous behavior correspond to one another (7:8–10 and 8:16–17), as do the sections on the way Yahweh "scattered them with a whirlwind" (7:11–14) but will "bring them to dwell in the midst of Jerusalem" (8:7–14).

At the center of this chiasm is Yahweh's declaration of his jealousy for Zion (Zech. 8:2). He announces his return to Zion, which will be called the faithful city, the mount of Yahweh of hosts, the holy mountain (8:3). Yahweh's presence will bring long and joyful life to the people (8:4–5). If the announcement is incredible to Zechariah's audience, it is not so to Yahweh (8:6).

Zechariah 1–6, then, assures the people that the temple will be built by the power of God's Spirit (Zech. 4:6), while Zechariah 7–8 announces that Yahweh is zealous for Zion, calls the people to righteous behavior, and assures them that fasting will be joy. Rather than give a straight yes or no to the question of whether they should fast (7:1–3), Zechariah addresses the motives for fasting (7:4–7; 8:18–19) and the behavior that is in keeping with fasting (7:8–10; 8:16–17); he describes the justice that fell on wickedness in the past (7:11–14) and the mercies that Yahweh will show his people (8:7–14) because of his strong love for them (8:1–6). The question of whether the fast should continue gives the prophet an occasion to rebuke the sinfulness and self-centeredness of the people and redirect their attention to Yahweh's redemptive historical purposes. Just as the story line of redemptive history went through the judgment of exile to the salvation of the new exodus and return to the land, so the personal experience of Zechariah's contemporaries goes through Zechariah's condemnation of their shortsightedness to the saving power of the message that God will ensure the rebuilding of the temple (Zechariah 1–6); he is zealous for Zion (Zechariah 7–8), and all this

[269]Zechariah's reference to seventy years in his reply (7:5) seems to indicate that the weeping and abstaining, i.e., fasting, in view was for the temple, which was destroyed in the fifth month (2 Kings 25:8). So also the seventh month Zechariah mentions in 7:5 probably alludes to the murder of Gedaliah (2 Kings 25:25; Jer. 41:1–3).

sets on display the one who will be "a wall of fire around . . . and the glory in her midst" (2:9, ET 5).[270]

The rest of Zechariah's prophecy describes the way that Yahweh will return to Zion. This consists of two sections, 9:1–11:17 and 12:1–14:21, each opening with the words, "The burden of the word of Yahweh."[271] These chapters seem to present Yahweh's climactic victory in a "kaleidoscopic and recursive" fashion,[272] and the contents of these chapters have matching elements that form a chiasm that can be depicted as in table 3.18.

Table 3.18. Thematic Chiastic Structure in Zechariah 9–14

A 9:1–17: Yahweh conquers and converts the nations (Syria, Tyre and Sidon, and Philistia); the king comes; and Yahweh leads Israel (Ephraim) and Judah into battle for victory.

B 10:1–12: Yahweh provides rain, punishes bad leaders and provides good ones, and strengthens Judah and Israel (Ephraim), bringing them back from exile and increasing them as their enemies (Egypt and Assyria) are defeated.

C 11:1–17: Enacted parable: Yahweh, the Good Shepherd, rejected by his people, bought out for thirty pieces of silver, breaks his covenant with Israel, divides the nation, and raises up a foolish shepherd.

C′ 12:1–14: Yahweh brings victory and is struck.

B′ 13:1–9: Yahweh purifies the land, and the shepherd is struck.

A′ 14:1–21: Yahweh brings victory, and Jerusalem becomes the Holy of Holies.

If we analyze Zechariah 9–14 along the lines of this chiasm, the following observations can be made: In the first and the last sections, A (Zech. 9:1–17) and A′ (14:1–21), Yahweh brings decisive victory to Jerusalem. In the second and second-to-last sections, B (10:1–12) and B′ (13:1–9), Yahweh cleanses the land. In the two central sections, C (11:1–17) and C′ (12:1–14), Yahweh, the Good Shepherd, is rejected by his people, slain. Somehow these events at the center of the chiasm (C and C′) result in the cleansing of the land in the second and second-to-last sections of the chiasm (B and B′) and lead to the triumph of Yahweh on Mount Zion in the first and last (A and A′) sections.

---

[270]Byron Curtis (*Up the Steep and Stony Road*, 133) notes that Yahweh as a wall of fire around and the glory in Zion's midst is "reminiscent both of Elisha's vision at Dothan (2 Kings 6:17) and of Exodus-Sinai traditions (Ex. 14:20; 40:38)."

[271]For a full study of the structure of Zechariah 9–14, see Paul Lamarche, *Zacharie IX-XIV: Structure littéraire et messianisme* (Paris: Gabalda, 1961). He presents these chapters as being structured in a w-shaped chiasm. My independent analysis presented above is not altogether unlike Lamarche's, but mine is less detailed. Looking at Lamarche's w-shaped chiasm prompted me to compare my analysis to his, at which point I noticed that my analysis could also result in a w-shaped chiasm, and in thinking on that, I arrived at the chiasm presented here.

[272]I owe this phrase, "kaleidoscopic and recursive," to a stimulating conversation with Professor Peter Gentry.

Zechariah 9–14 seems to consist of two cycles of prophecies that address the same topic: the way that Yahweh will glorify himself by saving Israel through the judgment of her enemies. The main ideas in the two cycles of prophecies are as follows:[273]

1. Yahweh will do battle against his enemies and secure decisive victory against them and their idols, plundering them (Zech. 9:1–5, 10, 14–16; 10:2, 11–12; 11:1–3; 12:2–9; 13:2; 14:1–9, 12–16).
2. Yahweh empowers Ephraim/Israel and Judah to fight (9:13, 15; 10:6–7; 12:6, 8; 14).
3. Some of the enemies will be converted and transformed through Yahweh's victory over them—they will be saved through judgment (9:6–7; 14:16–19).
4. Yahweh will take up his post to defend his temple from future attack, inhabiting Jerusalem, making it the Holy of Holies (9:8; 12:8; 14:20–21).
5. Yahweh will bring his people home from exile (9:12–13; 10:6, 8, 10; 12:6; 14:10–11).
6. The king/good shepherd returns to Zion (9:9–10);[274] Yahweh provides righteous leadership for his people (10:4); the people reject the Good Shepherd (Yahweh) and buy him out for thirty pieces of silver (11:4–14); Yahweh is pierced (12:10); Yahweh awakens the sword against his shepherd, his companion (13:7).[275]
7. Yahweh pours out a spirit of grace that causes those who struck him to mourn as one mourns for an only son (12:10–14); a fountain opens to cleanse God's people from sin, living water from Jerusalem (13:1; 14:8); a purifying judgment of fire causes those refined like gold and silver to call on Yahweh's name and confess Yahweh as their God (13:9).
8. Yahweh judges the worthless shepherds (10:3; 11:15–17).
9. Yahweh provides for the fertility of the land and the people (9:17–10:1, 7, 9–10).
10. Yahweh's people rejoice in and worship him (9:9, 17; 10:7, 12; 13:9; 14:16–19).

[273]Cf. the similar but not identical list of ten themes in Zechariah 9–14, which Curtis refers to as an "anthology" in *Up the Steep and Stony Road*, 163–64.

[274]Richard L. Schultz ("The Ties That Bind: Intertextuality, the Identification of Verbal Parallels, and Reading Strategies in the Book of the Twelve," in Redditt and Schart, *Thematic Threads in the Book of the Twelve*, 36–37) argues that Yahweh's return to Zion in Zech. 2:10 is verbally, conceptually, and contextually paralleled by the king's coming to Zion in Zech. 9:9–10.

[275]See the interesting attempts to relate these statements in Zechariah to information in Nehemiah and Chronicles, in Curtis, *Up the Steep and Stony Road*, 202–6, 220–21.

We can see from this list of intermingled themes in these chapters that judgment falls on all parties—on the nations, on Yahweh's people, who are refined like gold or silver is refined by fire—and judgment even falls on Yahweh himself as he, the shepherd, is rejected by the people and stricken, and Yahweh wakes the sword against his companion, the shepherd who stands next to him. Through these judgments, salvation comes: Israel is liberated by the judgment of her enemies, and the fountain of cleansing in Zechariah 13:1 seems to result from the striking of Yahweh in 12:10. As Curtis puts it, "The purified remnant shall be joined by the remnant of the nations in worshiping Yahweh (14:16), in a land purged of all evil, holy through and through."[276] These mysteries will await further revelation, but we can affirm that Zechariah teaches that Yahweh will be glorified in a salvation that comes through judgment as he returns to Zion, there to dwell in splendor, enjoyed by those who worship him.

3.5.12 Malachi

Malachi was probably written between 480 and 450 BC. The people have returned to the land and rebuilt the temple, and soon the walls of Jerusalem will stand as well. But Isaiah promised that the desert would bloom, Jeremiah described a new covenant, Ezekiel spoke of a temple from which waters would flow, and the earlier installments of the Twelve have affirmed these things. Malachi addresses the questions of his generation with "the burden of the word of Yahweh to Israel" (Mal. 1:1). The book of Malachi seems to be structured by the refrain "But you say, 'How have we . . . ?'" (1:2, 6–7; 2:17; 3:7–8, 13).[277] If we take the assertions Yahweh makes to prompt these responses from Israel as the subject of these sections, the book can be summarized through 3:15 as follows:[278]

1:1	Heading
1:2–5	I have loved you.
1:6–2:16	You despise my name and defile me.
2:17–3:5	You weary Yahweh with your words, but he will come with purifying judgment.
3:6–12	Return with tithes and offerings.
3:13–15	Your words were harsh against me.

The last refrain "But you say, 'How have we . . . ?'" appears in 3:13, so the remainder of the book must be outlined according to the content of the sections:

[276]Ibid., 280.
[277]The Hebrew in these instances is ואמרתם ("and you say") followed by some variation of במה ("in what").
[278]This outline is independent of but close to the "thematic outline" in Andrew E. Hill, *Malachi*, AB (New: York: Doubleday, 1998), xxxv. For a review of several proposals regarding the structure of Malachi and his own, see Clendenen's discussion in Taylor and Clendenen, *Haggai, Malachi*, 227–31.

3:16–18	The book of remembrance for those who fear Yahweh
3:19–24 (ET 4:1–6)	The day of Yahweh

I am arguing that the center of biblical theology is the glory of God in salvation through judgment, with the judgment serving to highlight the mercy, as mercy and justice display the God who announces his name, his goodness, and his glory, expositing the balance between his compassionate loving-kindness and his refusal to clear the guilty (Ex. 34:6–7).[279] This is exactly what we see in the way the book of Malachi opens with encouragement for Israel from the doctrine of election.

Malachi asserts Yahweh's love for his people (Mal. 1:2–5), anticipating their question, "How have you loved us?" (1:2). The people are back in the land, but Jerusalem is hardly the capital of the globe. The nations are not streaming to Zion. There is no Davidide on the throne. Where is Yahweh's love?[280] And Malachi points his contemporaries to the justice they deserve—the justice that will be visited on a nation that Yahweh did not choose, Edom. The fact that Jacob and Esau were brothers highlights the reality that there was no prior ethnic distinction between Israel, descendants of Jacob, and Edom, descendants of Esau (1:2). Jacob and Esau were twin sons of Isaac, son of Abraham, heirs to the promises of God. Yahweh declares through Malachi, "And I loved Jacob and Esau I hated" (1:2–3; cf. Deut. 7:6–8). Malachi then sets before Israel the way that Yahweh has destroyed Edom never to be rebuilt (Mal. 1:3–4). This information is presented to Israel in order to highlight Yahweh's commitment to rebuilding Israel, even if it seems slow in coming. Israel is to compare the way that Yahweh has treated them with the way that he has treated Edom; they are to realize that they do not deserve Yahweh's love more than Edom did; and they are to be assured of Yahweh's love for them. This is a love they have not earned. This is a love that is mercy. This is a special love that not all have received. This love should make them feel what is true: that they are Yahweh's special possession, even if what they see with their eyes seems unimpressive. Malachi tells them that they will see what happens to Edom, and they will know that Yahweh is great beyond the borders of Israel (1:5). Yahweh is glorified precisely because the justice he visits upon Edom highlights the mercy he shows to Israel.

Yahweh then indicts Israel for failing to show him the honor he deserves, and this indictment highlights Yahweh's concern for his glory (Mal. 1:6–2:16). Yahweh

[279]Hill (*Malachi*, 46–47) sees "the person and presence of God as the organizing tenet for OT/HB theology," and he states, "I concur with those who view Malachi as primarily a theology of Yahweh." In agreement with this, again, I believe that the thesis that God is the center of biblical theology can be sharpened to the assertion that all else serves to exposit or display his glory in salvation through judgment.

[280]Cf. Clendenen's remarks (Taylor and Clendenen, *Haggai, Malachi*, 231) about the "skepticism and cynicism concerning God's plan for their future."

wants his people to know that he has set his special love on them, and he wants their experience of that love to transform their lives so that they glorify him. This they do not do, and so Yahweh asks his people why they do not honor him as their Father and Master (1:6). Malachi explains how the actions of the priests despise the name of Yahweh (1:7–2:9), and he shows how the people of Judah profane the covenant (2:10–16). As he explains how the behavior of priests and people defame Yahweh, Yahweh makes an assertion similar to that found in Habakkuk 2:14, where he declared that he would accomplish his purpose of filling the earth with his glory as the waters cover the sea. We read in Malachi 1:11,

> "For from the rising of the sun to the place of its setting
> my name shall be great among the nations;
> and in every place incense and a pure offering shall be offered to my
> name,
> for my name shall be great among the nations,"
> says Yahweh of hosts.

Just a few verses later Yahweh asserts, "For I am a great King . . . and my name is feared among the nations" (Mal. 1:14). Yahweh summons the priests "to give glory to my name" (2:2) in a way that corresponds to the covenant Yahweh made with Levi (2:4–6).

Having indicted the sins of people and priests, sins that trample on his glory, Yahweh describes the purifying judgment he will bring against Israel (Mal. 2:17–3:5). The people are summoned to repentance (3:6–12), and Yahweh exposes the way that faithless talk is harsh against him (3:13–15).

Malachi appears to have seen a revival in response to his prophecy (3:16–18), and the book ends with a call to remember the Torah of Moses and watch for the coming of Elijah the prophet before "the great and dreadful day of Yahweh" (3:19–24, ET 4:1–6). Here at the end of the history of the revelation God gave to Israel, the recipients of the oracles of God are exhorted to heed Moses and the Prophets.

Paul House writes of Malachi:

> The prophecy effectively summarizes major segments of the Twelve. The emphasis on love and divorce remind the reader of Hosea. The admonitions of the priests echo Joel and Zechariah. The stressing of Yahweh's day of punishment links the book with Amos, Zephaniah, etc. Malachi's conclusion ties together the Haggai–Zechariah–Malachi corpus by claiming that all facets of restoration will indeed take place.[281]

[281] House, *The Unity of the Twelve*, 108.

3.5.13 The Center of the Theology of the Twelve

The twelve Minor Prophets present salvation through judgment for God's glory from a variety of perspectives applied to many situations.[282] Hosea is a living parable of the loving Husband redeeming the harlot wife, who is saved through the tearing of the lion, after which she is raised up on the third day to know Yahweh. Joel sees a locust plague and warns of the day of the Lord, after which the years the locusts have eaten in judgment will be restored when Yahweh dwells in glory on Mount Zion, and the mountains drip new wine (pointing to the abundant vineyards lush with grapes), while the hills flow with milk (pointing to strong, healthy flocks of goats and herds of cattle). Amos indicts the nations, then Israel and Judah also, for three sins and four, as the lion roars in judgment; but after judgment the fallen booth of David will be raised up, for Yahweh is his name (4:13; 5:9, 27; 9:6). Obadiah sees Judah judged, and he promises judgment against Edom on the day Yahweh saves his people. Jonah, the sailors, and the Ninevites are all saved through judgment—the sailors through the storm, Jonah through the fish, the Ninevites through the prophetic word, then Jonah again through the experience with the plant and the worm. Micah's name glorifies Yahweh, as it is a short form of the great question, "Who is like Yahweh our God?" and his prophecy alternates between oracles of judgment and promises of salvation, each oracle of judgment giving way to promised salvation.

Whereas Obadiah promises judgment on Edom, in Nahum judgment is promised to Nineveh, and through the judgment of the superpower, Yahweh will be glorified through the deliverance of his lowly people. Habakkuk teaches that the superpower that replaced Assyria, Babylon, will be used against Judah as Assyria was against Israel, and just as Yahweh judged wicked Assyria, so he will judge wicked Babylon. Through the judgment the righteous will live by faith. Zephaniah proclaims the coming day of Yahweh when, having saved his people through judgment, Yahweh will sing over them.

Haggai and Zechariah encourage the people to rebuild the temple after their return from exile, and they point to the day when Yahweh will return to Zion. Malachi calls his contemporaries to see Yahweh's mercy to them by contrasting the way they have been treated with the way nonelect Esau was treated, and Malachi calls the people to honor Yahweh and heed the Law and the Prophets as they await the great day.

3.6 The Center of the Theology of the Latter Prophets

Each of the prophets responds distinctively to the way they apprehend the glory of God in salvation through judgment. These responses are obviously affected

[282] Similarly Francis Watson, *Paul and the Hermeneutics of Faith* (New York: T&T Clark, 2004), 138: "The Book of the Twelve marks the intersection between a past dominated by the divine judgment and a future characterized by the hope of salvation."

by the differing individual backgrounds of the prophets, the differing settings, and the differing ways in which Yahweh reveals himself. Isaiah sees the king in glory and praises his incomparability, boldly calling his contemporaries out of idolatry. The nation's grievous provocation of Yahweh causes Jeremiah to weep over the perverse and persistent wickedness of the people. Jeremiah laments the profanation of Yahweh's glory, he laments that Israel chooses worthless idols over their covenant Lord, and he laments that because of Israel's failure the nations do not enjoy the blessings of Abraham. Ezekiel the priest is at a loss to describe the appearance of the likeness of Yahweh's glory, which he sees abandon the defiled temple, but that judgment gives way to a new temple that Yahweh will indwell. When the voice of the Twelve is added to Isaiah, Jeremiah, and Ezekiel, a four-part harmony emerges: a hauntingly mournful lament of sin and failure that resolves into a song of hope for the future. The sin will be judged, showing the justice of Yahweh, who is mighty to save and merciful to restore. Through the judgment comes the salvation, and the mercy and the justice highlight the one whose glory is past all praise.

4. The Center of the Theology of the Prophets

The story line of the prophets is straightforward. The people of Israel enter the land promised them by God. In doing so, they are like a new Adam in a new Eden. Their task is to rule over the earth and subdue it, but they fare no better than Adam did. The initial conquest under Joshua is subverted by the Canaanization of Israel in Judges, and then the nation rejects Yahweh for a king like all the other nations. Having removed Saul, Yahweh mercifully raises up David and promises that his seed will rule. Solomon builds the temple, but then he worships the gods of his many wives. The nation is rent asunder. Israel falls to Assyria, Judah to Babylon.

Along the way, Isaiah, Jeremiah, Ezekiel, and the Twelve call the kings, priests, and people to repentance. They also prophesy that Yahweh will redeem his people after the exile. Just as he brought his people out of Egypt, he will bring them back from all the lands in which he scattered them. Just as he shook heaven and earth at Sinai, he will once again shake heavens and earth, and once again enter into covenant with Israel, and the people will know Yahweh. He will return to Zion to be a wall of fire around Jerusalem and the glory in its midst. The nations will stream to worship him at his rebuilt temple, and a new David will reign over all the earth in peace, righteousness, and justice. Yahweh's glory will cover the dry land as the waters cover the sea. From the rising of the sun to the place of its setting he will be worshiped. Through the judgment of exile, Yahweh will purge his people, bring them to final salvation, and his glory will be the centerpiece of praise, as it is the center of biblical theology.

5. Appendix 1: The Order of the Twelve

Table 3.19. The Order of the Twelve in *BHS*, DSS, 8ḤevXIIgr, and LXX

BHS	4QXII^{a}	4QXII^{b}	4QXII^{c}	4QXII^{d}	4QXII^{e}	4QXII^{f}	4QXII^{g}	8ḤevXIIgr	LXX
Hos.			Hos.	Hos.			Hos.		Hos.
Joel			Joel				Joel		Amos
Amos			Amos				Amos		Mic.
Obad.							Obad.		Joel
Jonah						Jonah	Jonah	Jonah	Obad.
Mic.						Mic.	Mic.	Mic.	Jonah
Nah.							Nah.	Nah.	Nah.
Hab.							Hab.	Hab.	Hab.
Zeph.		Zeph.	Zeph.				Zeph.	Zeph.	Zeph.
Hag.		Hag.			Hag.			[Hag.]	Hag.
Zech.	Zech.				Zech.		Zech.	Zech.[1]	Zech.
Mal.	Mal.		Mal.						Mal.
	Jonah[2]								

[1]Emanuel Tov, with the collaboration of R. A. Kraft and a contribution by P. J. Parsons, *The Greek Minor Prophets Scroll from NaḤal Ḥever (8ḤevXIIgr)*, DJD VIII (Oxford: Clarendon, 1990).

[2]The evidence that Jonah follows Malachi is hardly overwhelming, given the fragmentary nature of the surviving scroll, and see 4QXII$^{f\ and\ g}$; cf. Eugene Ulrich et al., *Qumran Cave 4.X: The Prophets*, DJD 15 (Oxford: Clarendon, 1997).

6. Appendix 2: All the Earth Filled with the Knowledge of Yahweh's Glory

This list of verses (all texts here ESV) is "font coded" according to the following elements:

Bold	**glory/knowledge of**
Underlining	all/whole earth
Italics	*full/filled with*

But truly, as I live, and as all the earth shall be *filled* with **the glory of the LORD** . . . (Num. 14:21)

And one called to another and said:

"Holy, holy, holy is the LORD of hosts;
the whole earth is *full* of **his glory**!" (Isa. 6:3)

They shall not hurt or destroy
  in all my holy mountain;
for the earth shall be *full* of **the knowledge of the LORD**
  as the waters cover the sea. (Isa. 11:9)

For the earth will be *filled*

with **the knowledge of the glory of the LORD**
as the waters cover the sea. (Hab. 2:14)

Blessed be his glorious name forever;
may the whole earth be *filled* with **his glory!**
Amen and Amen! (Ps. 72:19)

Chapter 4

God's Glory in Salvation through Judgment IN THE WRITINGS

The seas will dry and the mountains turn to dust, but his glory will not pass.

—Henryk Sienkiewicz, *Quo Vadis*

1. Introduction

The Torah (Genesis through Deuteronomy) tells the true story of the world, from the beginning of all things to the moment when Israel is about to enter the land. The Former Prophets (Joshua through Kings) sing the saga of Israel from the conquest of the land to their exile from it. The poetic commentary on these events begins in the Latter Prophets (Isaiah through Zephaniah) and continues through the first part of the Writings (Psalms through Ecclesiastes). The story line is then resumed in the Writings and carried into the post-exilic period (Esther through Chronicles, with poetic commentary in later psalms and in the post-exilic prophets). The books that make up the section of the Old Testament referred to as the Writings have their own genres and emphases, but their inclusion in the canon indicates that they were understood to complement rather than contradict the message of the Law and the Prophets.[1] This chapter will seek to demonstrate that the Writings have the same theological center as the Law and the Prophets: the glory of God in salvation through judgment.

[1]See M. J. Selman, "Chronicles," in *NDBT*, 191.

As noted in chapter 1, the Old Testament books described as the Writings can be divided into three sections: the Book of Truth (Psalms, Proverbs, and Job), the *Megilloth* (small scrolls: Song of Songs, Ruth, Lamentations, Ecclesiastes, and Esther), and the Other Sacred Writings (Daniel, Ezra–Nehemiah, and Chronicles).[2] After briefly addressing the question of the relationship between the Wisdom Literature (Job, Proverbs, Song of Songs, Ecclesiastes) and biblical theology, this chapter will seek to show the gravitational force of the center of biblical theology in the Book of Truth, the *Megilloth*, and the Other Writings.

1.1 Wisdom Literature and Biblical Theology

One of the chief complaints raised against various attempts to describe the Bible's theology has been that the Wisdom Literature is often neglected. Duane Garrett writes:

> Old Testament theologians have stumbled at the point of integrating wisdom literature into the rest of the Old Testament. Theological themes that seem promising as unifying threads for the rest of the Old Testament are found to be cut short where Proverbs and Ecclesiastes are concerned. No single "center" proposed for the Old Testament has shown itself to be able to incorporate all the texts, genres, and motifs of the Old Testament.[3]

It seems that this is largely because books such as Proverbs are not usually interpreted with primary reference to their canonical context.[4] The fear of God so prominent in Proverbs and Ecclesiastes is informed by the holiness of Yahweh that breaks out against transgressors such as Nadab and Abihu (Leviticus 10). The voice of wisdom that cries out from these books is not spouting philosophical speculation on right and wrong; it is the song of a holy siren, wooing readers to return to the Law (Torah) and the Prophets. For instance, Proverbs 29:18 proclaims, "Where there is no vision [חזון] the people are let loose, but as for the one who keeps the law [תורה], blessed is he." The word rendered "vision" is a term often used to describe the visions of the prophets.[5] Proverbs 29:18 appears to be

---

[2]This is the order of the books as they appear in modern Hebrew Bibles (slightly different from the order in *BHS*). For the various other arrangements, see Roger Beckwith, *The Old Testament Canon of the New Testament Church and Its Background in Early Judaism* (Grand Rapids: Eerdmans, 1985), appendix 2, "The Order of the Prophets and Hagiographa in the Jewish Tradition," 449–68.

[3]Duane A. Garrett, *Proverbs, Ecclesiastes, Song of Songs*, NAC (Nashville: Broadman & Holman, 1993), 55. See also John Goldingay, "The 'Salvation History' Perspective and the 'Wisdom' Perspective within the Context of Biblical Theology," *Evangelical Quarterly* 51, no. 4 (1979), 194–207.

[4]See, for example, John J. Collins, *Encounters with Biblical Theology* (Minneapolis: Fortress, 2005), chap. 9, "Proverbial Wisdom and the Yahwist Vision," 105–16. The winds are changing, however, and more interpreters are reading with reference to canonical context. See, for instance, Tremper Longman III, "Reading Wisdom Canonically," in *Canon and Biblical Interpretation*, ed. C. G. Bartholomew et al., Scripture and Hermeneutics Series 7 (Grand Rapids: Zondervan, 2006), 352–73. Going beyond Longman is Ryan P. O'Dowd, "Wisdom as Canonical Imagination: Pleasant Words for Tremper Longman," in *Canon and Biblical Interpretation*, 374–92.

[5]E.g., Isa. 1:1; Jer. 14:14; 23:16; Lam. 2:9; Dan. 8:1; Hos. 12:11; Obad. 1:1; Nah. 1:1; Hab. 2:2, 3.

describing the blessed restraining power of the Law and the Prophets.[6] Disregarding the visions of the prophets is like walking blindly toward a precipice, but the danger is not an abstract fall from an impersonal height. Rather, the danger lies in defiling the holy God by transgressing his boundaries. Yahweh is a God of justice, and "the ways of a man are before the eyes of Yahweh, and all his paths he observes" (Prov. 5:21). The fear of judgment leads to salvation.[7]

The blessedness of keeping Torah ("as for the one who keeps the Torah, blessed is he," Prov. 29:18) is described with surprising creativity and poignancy throughout Proverbs. The one who obeys Proverbs will not be enticed by *murderers* and *thieves* who *covet* the possessions of others (1:9–19, esp. 11, 13, 19). He will be delivered from the *adulteress* (2:16). He will *honor his father and mother* (1:8; 10:1). He will not *bear false witness* (6:16–19). He will not profane the *name* of Yahweh (18:10; 30:9, italics here highlighting correspondence to the Ten Commandments). Often Proverbs describes the psychological stability, contentment, and joy that accompany obedience to the Torah. And all of this is informed by the injunction to know God in all one's ways (3:6). Proverbs sets forth the benefits of obedience and the consequences of transgression, and the reference point for right and wrong is Yahweh.[8] The knowledge of God's righteousness produces fear, which leads to hatred of evil (8:13) and blessing. The Lord is in sovereign control of all these things, bringing about his purposes: "Yahweh made everything for its own purpose, even the wicked for the day of evil" (16:4).

In order to understand the Writings, and the Wisdom Literature contained in them, we must read these books in their canonical context. Holding that the Writings have the same main theme as the Law and the Prophets entails grasping the threads and discerning from the feel of the fibers that they are indeed made of the same stuff. To show this, the next section will isolate some strands of the Torah. When we feel the Torah's texture in conjunction with that of the Writings, we will know from experience that though the weave may have a different pattern, the fiber is the same.

1.2 The Canonical Context of the Writings

Genesis introduces readers to the glory of God in salvation through judgment: salvation for the seed of the woman will come through the judgment of the serpent and his seed. God then reveals himself at the Exodus by saving Israel

[6] I wish to thank Professor Peter Gentry for this insight, which he brought to my attention in personal correspondence.

[7] In 2 Tim. 3:15 Paul reminds Timothy of the "sacred writings"—surely a reference to the Old Testament—which, he says, make people "wise unto salvation." Even though "Wisdom Literature" was probably not a technical term referring to these particular books for Paul, the reference to wisdom in this statement would seem to allude to those Old Testament books thick with instruction on how to live wisely.

[8] Similarly Craig G. Bartholomew, "A God for Life and Not Just for Christmas! The Revelation of God in the Old Testament Wisdom Literature," in *The Trustworthiness of God: Perspectives on the Nature of Scripture*, ed. Paul Helm and Carl R. Trueman (Grand Rapids: Eerdmans, 2002), 45.

through the judgment of Egypt, and then he declares his glory to Moses (Ex. 33:18–19). Yahweh is a saving and judging God (34:6–7). Leviticus describes the sacrificial cult of Israel, whereby the faithful remnant will be saved through the judgment that falls on the sacrifices. Numbers recounts various manifestations of the glory of God in salvation through judgment (e.g., Num. 14:11–24), and then Deuteronomy sets the terms for life in the land.

In many ways, Deuteronomy is the heart of the Old Testament. What comes before it leads up to this climactic moment of entering the land, and what comes after it is judged by the standards set in Deuteronomy. This is relevant to our consideration of books such as Proverbs because important instructions are given in Deuteronomy about parents teaching Torah to their children and the king writing out his own copy and keeping the Torah.

We read in Deuteronomy 6:6–8:

> And these words that I command you today shall be on your heart. You shall teach them diligently to your sons, and shall talk of them when you sit in your house, and when you walk by the way, and when you lie down, and when you rise. You shall bind them as a sign on your hand, and they shall be as frontlets between your eyes.

Israelite parents were to make sure that their children knew the law. As Solomon, in obedience to Deuteronomy 6, instructs his son, he restates the language of Deuteronomy 6:6–8 in Proverbs 6:20–22: "My son, keep your father's commandment, and forsake not your mother's torah. Bind them on your heart always; tie them around your neck. When you walk, they will lead you; when you lie down, they will watch over you; and when you wake, they will talk with you."[9] Moreover, Israel's king had a responsibility to know the law and enforce it in Israel. Deuteronomy 17:18–19 says of the king:

> And when he sits on the throne of his kingdom, he shall write for himself in a scroll a copy of this law, in the presence of the Levitical priests. And it shall be with him, and he shall read in it all the days of his life, that he may learn to fear Yahweh his God by keeping all the words of this law and these statutes and doing them.

Israel enters the land (Joshua) and needs a king (Judges); then the book of Samuel recounts the rise of David. As we turn to the Book of Truth in the Writings, Psalms presents us with a king whose delight is in the Torah (Ps. 1:2). In

[9]Commonalities between the two passages include the following: Moses tells parents to instruct their "sons," and Solomon addresses his "son" and tells him to keep his father's commandment and forsake not his mother's Torah. Moses tells Israel that what he is commanding is to be on their hearts, and Solomon tells his son to bind his commandment on his heart. Moses commands Israel to talk of the commandment when they sit, walk, lie down, and rise, and Solomon tells his son that the commandment will lead him when he walks (like the frontlets Moses says they will be), watch over him when he lies down, and talk to him when he rises.

Proverbs, King Solomon teaches Torah to his son.[10] The Torah's familiar fiber is felt in these lines from the Writings.

2. The Book of Truth: Psalms, Proverbs, Job

2.1 The Book of Truth Book by Book

The Book of Psalms falls into five books, each ending with a doxology. By attending to the superscriptions, we can see that these five books tell a story. Book 1 focuses on David's rise to power through affliction. Book 2 sings of David's reign down to the time of Solomon. Book 3 then reflects the time of Solomon to the exile from the land. Book 4 consists of exilic reflections on Yahweh's past deliverance of Israel. Then book 5 looks beyond exile and hopes for Yahweh's future deliverance of his people through the agency of the Davidic king, who is seated at Yahweh's right hand until he puts all his enemies under his feet. This is a story of salvation through judgment to Yahweh's glory: through the judgment of Saul, David is delivered to reign over Israel, and then he sings Yahweh's praise. Through the judgment of exile, the nation will be saved and restored to the land to worship their God. In addition to the broad angle story, there are many instances of salvation through judgment in particular psalms, such as when David is saved through the judgment of his sin to sing Yahweh's praise in Psalm 51, or when he teaches the same message in Psalm 32. Disobedience to Torah is condemned, while the blessing of having God's revelation is celebrated with abandon. Opposition to the Lord's anointed will result in judgment, while allegiance to him guarantees deliverance. The book of Psalms celebrates the glory of God in salvation through judgment.

In Proverbs we see the son of David, king of Israel obeying the exhortation in Deuteronomy 17 that kings were to know the Torah and live by it all their days. Moreover, Solomon is obeying Deuteronomy 6 and instructing his son in the ways that Torah applies to all of life. He admonishes his son to fear and trust Yahweh, and by announcing judgment on evil ways of life, he seeks to bring his son through judgment to salvation so that the glory of God will be reflected in his life.

Yahweh challenges Satan to recognize the integrity of Job. Satan takes up the challenge and ruins Job's life. Job begins to live out a pattern familiar in the Psalms and in the stories of Jacob, Moses, and David. This pattern involves the rejection and persecution of a righteous man and includes false accusations and wrong conclusions drawn from what appears to be God's rejection of the righteous one. The logic of Job's worthless counselors is simple: God is righteous and punishes the wicked; Job is being punished; therefore Job must be wicked.

[10]See Katharine J. Dell, "The King in the Wisdom Literature," in *King and Messiah in Israel and the Ancient Near East*, ed. John Day, JSOTSup (Sheffield: Sheffield Academic, 1998), 163–86.

Job maintains that though his righteousness is not like God's, he has conducted himself in integrity. He hopes for a mediator between himself and God, and he resolutely trusts God to vindicate him—even if it must await his resurrection ("though he slay me . . . yet in my flesh will I see God"). Suddenly Job is saved through judgment as the glory of God is manifested: Yahweh rejects Satan's false charges once Job has been tried, condemns the false theology of the worthless counselors, and even judges Job's presumption. And through these judgments, which are largely accomplished through the manifestation of Yahweh's glory at the end of the book, Job is vindicated and restored. In the book of Job, God is glorified in salvation through judgment.

2.2 Psalms

The Psalms of the Hebrew Bible are not to be read as abstract poetic installments in the world's literary register. Rather, the Psalms are to be read in light of the story the Old Testament tells.[11] The more detailed superscriptions invite readers of the Psalter to compare the psalm at hand to the Old Testament narrative referenced by the superscription.[12] Often this locates a psalm at a specific point in the Old Testament narrative, and the psalm functions as commentary on the narrative.[13] In the face of a tendency to neglect "the forgotten God," James Luther Mays reminds us that "the Psalms themselves . . . contain more direct

[11]For a summary of several canonical readings of the Psalms, see Gordon Wenham, "Towards a Canonical Reading of the Psalms," in Bartholomew et al., *Canon and Biblical Interpretation*, 333–51.

[12]In defense of interpreting the Psalms in light of their superscriptions, I would observe that we have no manuscript evidence that indicates that these superscriptions do not belong to the canonical form of the Psalter. If they are part of the canon, and all the manuscript evidence we have (DSS, MT, LXX, etc.) indicates that they are, they should inform our interpretation of the Psalms. Disregarding them is, in my view, as dangerous as disregarding the salutations in Paul's letters. If it matters that Paul was writing occasional letters to particular churches or individuals, then it also matters that the Psalms bear superscriptions. We do not know who was involved in the arrangement of the Psalter as we now find it in the canon. In order for the believing remnant to accept the work and recognize the final form of the Psalter as canonical, they must have regarded those who did this work as having been inspired by the Holy Spirit. I doubt very much that the believing remnant would have allowed someone who did not have prophetic status, i.e., someone whom they did not recognize as being inspired by the Spirit of God, to alter anything in the Holy Scriptures. Perhaps Ezra and Nehemiah were involved in the final edition of the Psalter, but we do not know. In my view, the high regard for writings that were recognized as being inspired by the Spirit would have permitted only the mildest forms of editorial or "redactional" adjustments. It seems to me that the major work of whoever brought out the final form of the book of Psalms was in the arrangement and placement of the individual psalms. I find Roger Beckwith's argument that "the eccentric Psalms MSS from Qumran are probably liturgical adaptations" to be compelling (see Roger T. Beckwith, "The Early History of the Psalter," *TynBul* 46 [1995]: 1–27, quote from p. 1). For a description of the Psalms manuscripts among the Dead Sea Scrolls, see Dwight D. Swanson, "Qumran and the Psalms," in *Interpreting the Psalms: Issues and Approaches*, ed. David Firth and Philip S. Johnston (Downers Grove, IL: InterVarsity, 2005), 247–61. Against Swanson's assertion of "the pluriformity of the biblical texts into the first century CE" (258) is the evidence that Pietersma describes as the "interlinearity" of the Greek translation, i.e., the close ties between the Hebrew original and the Greek translation (see on this Albert Pietersma, "Septuagintal Exegesis and the Superscriptions of the Greek Psalter," in *The Book of Psalms: Composition and Reception*, ed. Peter W. Flint and Patrick D. Miller [Leiden: Brill, 2005], 443–75). If the text were in flux, would we expect such a high degree of literalness in the Greek translation? The best way to gain an appreciation for how close the translation is to the Hebrew is simply to compare the Greek translation to the Hebrew word by word, line by line.

[13]This happens in the Targum of Psalm 81, where the reference to Joseph is exposited with material from Genesis, see Timothy M. Edwards, "The Targum of Psalms," in Firth and Johnston, *Interpreting the Psalms*, 287–293 (279–94).

statements about God than any other book in the two testaments of the Christian canon. . . . The works of God and the attributes of God are the constant agenda of the Psalms."[14] And the centerpiece of this agenda is the way that God shows his righteousness and power in judgment, through which he also demonstrates mercy and love in salvation. In the Psalms, this often comes through the agency of the anointed king of Israel, the messiah,[15] and it always results in the praise of God, the ubiquitous "hallelujah"—praise Yahweh.

The Psalms are presented as five books: book 1, Psalms 1–41; book 2, Psalms 42–72; book 3, Psalms 73–89; book 4, Psalms 90–106; book 5, Psalms 107–50.[16] Exciting work is being done on the story told in the movement through these five books.[17] Gordon Wenham writes:

> The first two Davidic collections [the first two books of Psalms, 1–41 and 42–72] cover episodes from David's life, though not in chronological order. But the great hopes for David's descendants expressed in Psalm 72 were apparently shattered by the fall of Jerusalem and the monarchy, events alluded to in many psalms of book 3, and most explicitly in Psalm 89.
>
> However, books 4 and 5 respond to Psalm 89's lament with the call to trust in the LORD's rule not in human rulers . . . . Kleer holds that in the fourth and fifth books of the Psalter, the Davidic psalms must be understood as the psalms of a future David.[18]

This discussion of the Psalter will seek to trace out the implicit story line that seems to be reflected in the arrangement of the Psalms, the titles that accompany them, and some of the relationships between individual psalms. Some preliminary observations on the superscriptions in the Psalter and the arrangement of the psalms will put us in position to follow the story.

Only book 5 of the Psalter contains more psalms than book 1: book 1 has forty-one psalms and book 5 has forty-four. This is significant because of the heavily Davidic nature of book 1. Thirty-eight of book 1's forty-one psalms have a superscription that names David; the remaining three psalms (Psalms 1,

---

[14] James Luther Mays, "The God Who Reigns: The Book of Psalms," in *The Forgotten God: Perspectives in Biblical Theology*, ed. A. Andrew Das and Frank J. Matera (Louisville: Westminster John Knox, 2002), 29–30.

[15] Similarly ibid., 36–37.

[16] For helpful discussion, see Paul R. House, *Old Testament Theology*, (Downers Grove, IL: InterVarsity, 1998), 405–6. See also Gerald H. Wilson, "The Use of Royal Psalms at the 'Seams' of the Hebrew Psalter," *JSOT* 35 (1986): 85–94; James Luther Mays, "The Place of the Torah-Psalms in the Psalter," *JBL* 106 (1987): 3–12.

[17] My thoughts have been stimulated by and are heavily indebted to the Julius Brown Gay lectures given by Gordon Wenham at Southern Seminary in 2006. The audio for these lectures is available online at http://www.sbts.edu/resources/category/lectures/jb-gay/, accessed December 31, 2009. For a summary of research through 1991, see David M. Howard Jr., "Editorial Activity in the Psalter: A State-of-the-Field Survey," in *The Shape and Shaping of the Psalter*, ed. J. Clinton McCann, JSOTSup (Sheffield: JSOT, 1993), 52–70; and David M. Howard Jr., "The Psalms and Current Study," in Firth and Johnston, *Interpreting the Psalms*, 23–27.

[18] Wenham, "Towards a Canonical Reading of the Psalms," 343. Wenham is summarizing the views of Martin Kleer, *Der liebliche Sänger der Psalmen Israels* (Bodenheim: Philo, 1996).

2, and 10) have no superscriptions at all. David is also prominent in book 2, where his name occurs in the superscriptions of eighteen of book 2's thirty-one psalms.[19] The final psalm of book 2, Psalm 72, is addressed "To Solomon," and it concludes with the notice, "The prayers of David, the son of Jesse, are ended" (Ps. 72:20).[20]

Some superscriptions contain information alluding to events in Old Testament narratives, but these are largely confined to books 1 and 2 (see the superscriptions to Psalms 3, 7, 9 NKJV, 18, 30, and 34 in book 1, and in book 2 see Psalms 51, 52, 54, 56, 57, 59, 60, and 63). There is no historical information in the superscriptions in book 3, while three psalms in book 4 contain what appear to be statements about when the song was to be sung ("for the day of the Sabbath" in Psalm 92; "for thanksgiving" in Psalm 100; and "when he faints and before Yahweh pours out his complaint" in Psalm 102). The only historical notice in book 5 is found in the superscription to Psalm 142.

These observations on the superscriptions give the impression that books 1 and 2 provide poetic commentary on the life of David down to the transition to Solomon. The despair over the end of the Davidic line at the end of book 3 in Psalm 89 indicates that the seventeen psalms of book 3 sing the story of Solomon to exile, with Psalms 74 and 79 reflecting the violation of the temple (see Pss. 74:3–8; 79:1).[21]

Only two names are mentioned in the superscriptions to the seventeen psalms in book 4: Moses in Psalm 90, and David in Psalms 101 and 103. Psalm 102 mentions "the one who is afflicted" in its superscription, and situated between the mention of David in 101 and 103, this recalls David's affliction. The psalms of book 4 seem to respond to the exile at the end of book 3 by pointing back to Moses, celebrating the fact that Yahweh reigns, remembering David's path through affliction to exaltation, and recalling Yahweh's past faithfulness to Israel.[22] All this serves to inspire hope that through the judgment of the exile, Yahweh might again save his people for his own glory.

[19]The other thirteen are as follows: eight Psalms mention the sons of Korah (42–49), one mentions Asaph (50), Psalms 66, 67, and 71 name no names, and 72 mentions Solomon. Though these psalms do not name David, the people named in their superscriptions—the sons of Korah and Asaph—are associated with his reign in 1 Chron. 6:31–39, and then he passes the torch to Solomon in Psalm 72.

[20]For a text-critical study of the additional superscriptions that mention David in the Greek translation of the Psalms, see Albert Pietersma, "David in the Greek Psalms," *VT* 30 (1980): 213–26. These additions to the superscriptions do not warrant speaking of an "LXX-type" Psalter in distinction from the "MT-type" Psalter, as Swanson does. They will not bear the weight Swanson places upon them (see Swanson, "Qumran and the Psalms," 258–59).

[21]Similarly Erich Zenger, "Zion as Mother of the Nations in Psalm 87," in Norbert Lohfink and Erich Zenger, *The God of Israel and the Nations: Studies in Isaiah and the Psalms*, trans. Everett R. Kalin (Collegeville, MN: Liturgical, 2000), 159: "In this 'Messianic' Psalter, on the one hand, there is a meditative review of Israel's . . . experiences with its historic monarchy: from David (Psalms 3ff.) through Solomon (Psalm 72 is a prayer of the aged David for his son Solomon) to the end of the monarchy in the year 587 (Psalm 89)."

[22]Cf. Gerald H. Wilson, "The Structure of the Psalter," in Firth and Johnston, *Interpreting the Psalms*, 229–240.

This hoped-for salvation appears to be what is celebrated in the forty-four psalms of book 5. Psalms 108–10 have Davidic superscriptions, and Psalm 110 sings the triumph of what appears to be a new David, one who will arise after the exile seen in book 3 and the period of waiting endured through book 4. In book 5 this new David sees Yahweh crush the head of his enemy (מחץ ראש, 110:6). The response to the victory of the new David can be seen in the "hallelujah!" superscriptions to Psalms 111–13, and the praises continue through Psalm 118. Interestingly, in Psalm 118 the king enters the gates (118:19–26), then in Psalm 119 he extols the blessing of the Torah. The Songs of Ascent that follow in Psalms 120–34 appear to herald the return from exile made possible by the triumph of the new David. A "hallelujah" follows in Psalm 135, and Yahweh's enduring steadfast love is the refrain of Psalm 136. Psalm 137 blesses the one who will rise to crush the heads of the seed of the serpent (137:8–9), and then Psalms 138–45 all mention David in their superscriptions as the new David leads a chorus of praise to Yahweh, which culminates in hallelujahs! Psalms 146–50 each begin with that happy word. If this reading of the story line of the Psalms is correct, it has profound implications for understanding not only the book of Psalms but also what the Psalms reflect of Old Testament theology, as well as the interpretation of the Psalms seen in the New Testament.[23]

The Psalms, then, recount the history of Israel from David to the exile, and then they look beyond the exile to the new David who will arise and lead the people back to the land. The story of Israel's past and the expressions of hope for her future are centered on the glory of God in salvation through judgment. Yahweh's praise is obviously central in the Psalter. He is praised as he judges Israel, and through that judgment Israel looks beyond exile to future salvation. That future salvation will come when Yahweh visits justice on the enemies of Israel (e.g., Psalms 110, 137). The glory of God in salvation through judgment, accomplished by Yahweh's agent, Israel's messiah, is the center of the theology of the Psalter. What follows cannot be an exhaustive analysis of every psalm, but some of the detail from this broad-brush summary can be sketched in to substantiate the picture that has been traced out to this point.

2.2.1 Book 1, Psalms 1–41

Jamie Grant has put forth a significant thesis with respect to what we can learn from the way that individual psalms are arranged within the Psalter as a whole.

[23]For a study of the use of the Psalms in the Gospels and Acts, see Dale A. Brueggemann, "The Evangelists and the Psalms," in Firth and Johnston, *Interpreting the Psalms*, 263–78. Brueggemann's understanding of the typological interpretation of the Psalms in the New Testament fits very well with the approach to the Psalms I am advocating here.

> One of the redactional emphases of the Book of Psalms is the juxtaposition of kingship and torah psalms alongside one another, in an attempt to reflect the theology of the Kingship Law [Deut. 17:14–20] in the Psalter's final form. The purpose of this redaction was two-fold: (1) to shape the reader's understanding of the eschatological king, expected in the period of the closure of the Psalter; and (2) to encourage the type of devotion to Yahweh amongst the readers and hearers of the psalms, which the Kingship Law expected of the king. Eschatological hope in a monarch who will be the true "keeper" of the torah of Yahweh in accordance with the Deuteronomic Law of the King, and a piety based in the keeping of that torah are the joint foci of this redaction.[24]

Grant argues that Psalms 1 and 2 introduce these twin points, with Psalm 1 focusing on the Torah and Psalm 2 on the messiah. He then suggests that book 1 of the Psalms is arranged such that this twin emphasis is reinforced in Psalms 18–21, at the heart of Psalms 1–41. He proposes that book 1 has been arranged as follows:[25]

Psalms 1–14
    Psalms 15–24
Psalms 25–41

The central section of book 1, Psalms 15–24, is itself structured to highlight the Torah and the messiah. The arrangement can be depicted as seen in table 4.1.[26]

Table 4.1. Grant's Arrangement of the Central Section of Book 1 of the Psalms

Psalm 15, Entry psalm
    Psalm 16, Comfort
        Psalm 17, Lament
            Psalm 18, Kingship
                Psalm 19, Torah
            Psalms 20–21, Kingship
        Psalm 22, Lament
    Psalm 23, Comfort
Psalm 24, Entry psalm

[24]Jamie A. Grant, *The King as Exemplar: The Function of Deuteronomy's Kingship Law in the Shaping of the Book of Psalms*, SBL Academia Biblica (Atlanta: SBL, 2004), 9.
[25]Ibid., 239.
[26]Ibid., 11, 73–74.

When we combine Grant's observations on the arrangement of the psalms in book 1 with their heavily Davidic character, it does seem that the program advocated is that of a messianic king who will enforce the Torah. But the psalms recognize that there is no switch that can be flipped to create an idyllic society in Israel where a Davidide reigns in accordance with the law of Moses. The challenges to be overcome are internal and external. At the internal level, personal ambitions and sins must be subjected to Yahweh's intentions. At the external level, enemies must be defeated.

A major focus of books 1 and 2 of the Psalms is the overcoming of these external and internal challenges to the messiah living out the Torah himself and enforcing it in Israel. If we take our cues from the historical notices in the superscriptions, the challenges in book 1 focus on the problem of the messiah's external enemies: in Psalm 3 the enemy is Absalom, in Psalm 7 it is Cush, in Psalm 18 it is Saul and all others, and in Psalm 34 it is Abimelech. These challenges continue in book 2, but here it is almost as though the external challenges are resumed only after internal failure. The first historical note in a superscription in book 2 sets Psalm 51 as David's response to his sin with Bathsheba. Then the enemies come rushing at David: Doeg the Edomite in Psalm 52; the treacherous Ziphites in Psalm 54; the Philistines in Psalm 56; Saul again in Psalms 57, 59, and seemingly also 63.[27]

Thus, books 1 and 2 of the Psalms reflect Israel's King David pursuing a society that conforms to Yahweh's Torah *through struggle*. The king must lead his people through the challenges brought on by their own sin and posed by their enemies to the Edenic society of life under Torah. If he succeeds, their adherence to Torah will be for their own good to Yahweh's glory, and they will get to this salvation through judgment. Their sins and their enemies must be judged and defeated, and through that judgment they will attain salvation to Yahweh's glory.

The king in the Psalms is the blessed man who delights in the Torah (Psalm 1), proclaiming the decree of Yahweh that all the kings of the earth will be subjected to him (Psalm 2). These first two psalms function as a lens through which the rest of the Psalter is to be read.[28] The Psalms sing the glory of God as his justice and salvation are accomplished through his messiah. Mays also notes the way

---

[27]We know from 1–2 Samuel that in terms of historical sequence, David was first opposed by Saul, then later by Absalom as a judgment on his sin with Bathsheba. Saul and Absalom are similar in certain respects, such as their physical attractiveness and ability to win the confidence, unduly, of Israel. I would suggest that whoever put the Psalter into its final form (Ezra?) has reversed the order, presenting David first opposed by Absalom (Psalm 3), then later by Saul, in order to forge a link between David's enemies, as though they are all the same. This might have given rise to what Roger Beckwith describes as "homiletical identification," seen in rabbinical haggadah where "different characters from Scripture who are linked by similarity of name or of other characteristics are often said to be the same person, and this in the face of the plainest evidence to the contrary" (*Old Testament Canon of the New Testament Church*, 217; see the whole discussion, 217–20, with notes 86–93 on 232–33).

[28]Grant, *The King as Exemplar*, 10, 41–70, 230–31; John H. Walton, "Psalms: A Cantata about the Davidic Covenant," *JETS* 34 (1991): 23.

that Psalms 1 and 2 set up "the polarity of the wicked and righteous, and the polarity of Zion and messiah and people of God versus the nations."[29]

Some scholars have suggested that the book of Psalms is to be viewed as the prayer book of Israel's anointed king, that is, her messiah.[30] Taking such a perspective leads us to understand Psalm 1, which extols the blessedness of the man who delights in the Torah of Yahweh, as claiming that delight in the Torah is crucial for righteous kingship. This forges a strong link with the instructions for the king in Deuteronomy 17.[31]

The Psalter is announcing that blessedness is in not merely keeping the Torah but delighting in it (Ps. 1:2). The deliverance from the path of the wicked that results from day and night study of the Torah (1:1–2) has its converse, however. While the righteous will experience Edenic prosperity, as a blooming tree by a flowing stream (1:3), the wicked will be blown away like chaff (1:5) and will not stand in the judgment (1:4). Yahweh, who knows the way of the righteous (1:6), will do what he has said. Salvation comes through the threat of judgment.

From this starting point, Psalm 2 proclaims the decree of Yahweh that the messiah has been installed as king in Zion (Ps. 2:5–7). Accompanying this announcement is a promise from Yahweh to the king messiah: at his request, in spite of their raging (2:1–4), the nations will be his inheritance, the ends of the earth his possession (2:8).[32]

Reading these psalms as commentary on the Old Testament narrative story line brings several things into focus. Yahweh promised David that he would build him a sure house (2 Sam. 7:11), that David's seed would establish his kingdom (7:12) and build the temple, and that Yahweh would make his throne endure forever (7:13). Indeed, Yahweh promised to be a Father to David's seed, and David's seed would be a son to him (7:14). Psalm 2 is exulting in these promises, as Psalm 2:7 asserts, "I will proclaim the decree of Yahweh: he said to me, 'You are my son; as for me, today I have begotten you.'"

When Psalm 2:9 proclaims to the messiah, "You will smash them with a rod [שֵׁבֶט] of iron, as vessels of the potter you will shatter them," two images from

[29]James L. Mays, "The Question of Context in Psalm Interpretation," in McCann, *The Shape and Shaping of the Psalter*, 16.

[30]Cf. Richard B. Hays, "Christ Prays the Psalms: Israel's Psalter as Matrix of Early Christology," in *The Conversion of the Imagination: Paul as Interpreter of Israel's Scripture* (Grand Rapids: Eerdmans, 2005), 101–18; Bruce Waltke, "A Canonical Process Approach to the Psalms," in *Tradition and Testament* (Chicago: Moody, 1981), 3–18; and Waltke, "Psalms: Theology of," in *NIDOTTE*, 4:1111. On the other side of the issue, S. E. Gillingham writes, "I believe that it is difficult to propose that any Messianic interpretation was intended, both in the earliest stages of the composition of individual psalms and in the later stages of the assemblying of the Psalter as a whole" ("The Messiah in the Psalms: A Question of Reception History and the Psalter," in Day, *King and Messiah in Israel and the Ancient Near East*, 209 [209–37]).

[31]Cf. Grant's argument that "the Law of the King [Deut. 17:14–20] has been used as an intellectual construct to shape and nuance the psalmic presentation of kingship" (*The King as Exemplar*, 2).

[32]See the discussion of "The Messianic Kingdom" in Craig A. Blaising and Darrell L. Bock, *Progressive Dispensationalism* (Wheaton, IL: Victor, 1993), 217–18.

Genesis are brought together. On the one hand, Psalm 2:9 employs the same Hebrew term used to describe the "scepter" that will not depart from Judah in Genesis 49:10 (שבט). On the other hand, though the idea that the enemies will be "smashed" and "shattered" in Psalm 2:9 does not employ the same verb that describes the crushing of the serpent's head in Genesis 3:15, the imagery is the same.[33]

Psalm 2 glories in the judgment that Yahweh's anointed will visit upon those who "gather together" against him and his messiah (2:1–2). This shows Yahweh's greatness over his enemies, for none can overthrow him. The psalm also sings the greatness of God in the salvation that comes to those aligned with him and his messiah as those who would threaten them are shattered. God is thus glorified in salvation through judgment.

The combination of Psalms 1 and 2 provides the perspective from which the rest of the Psalter is to be interpreted. When Psalm 3 presents David crying out to God as he flees from Absalom, David's confident appeal for help is based on both Yahweh's decree, announced in Psalm 2, and his power seen in the narratives of the Law and the Prophets. David trusts that Yahweh is the shield about him (Ps. 3:4, ET 3; cf. Gen. 15:1) because of the decree proclaimed in Psalm 2:4–9. David delights in the word of God (Ps. 1:2), specifically in the promises made to him (2:4–9 and 2 Samuel 7), and he calls on Yahweh to rise and break the teeth of the wicked (Ps. 3:8, ET 7), which is yet another variation on the imagery of the broken head of the serpent from Genesis 3:15.

Through the rest of book 1 the details of this picture are supplied. The afflictions faced by the messiah, David, are the sufferings through which he will enter his glory. Psalm 16:10–11 seems to declare that Yahweh's power is such that he can even deliver his messiah from death, and such a reading fits with the way the passage is interpreted in the New Testament (cf. Acts 2:24–31; 13:35). Though the afflictions make it seem that God has forsaken him, the dawn will break (cf. Psalm 22 and its superscription). Through judgment salvation will come for Yahweh's glory.

2.2.2 Book 2, Psalms 42–72

The first eight psalms of book 2, Psalms 42–49, are "of the Sons of Korah." We read elsewhere that

> these are the men whom David put in charge of the service of song in the house of Yahweh after the ark rested there. They ministered with song before the tabernacle of

[33]See James M. Hamilton Jr., "The Skull Crushing Seed of the Woman: Inner-Biblical Interpretation of Genesis 3:15," *SBJT* 10, no. 2 (2006): 30–54. Cf. Charles Halton, "Allusions to the Stream of Tradition in the Neo-Assyrian Oracles," *Ancient Near Eastern Studies* 46 (2009): 50–61.

> the tent of meeting until Solomon built the house of Yahweh in Jerusalem . . . . These are the men who served and their sons. . . . son of Korah. (1 Chron. 6:31–33, 37)

Reading these superscriptions in light of the historical narrative, then, would place these psalms after the events of 2 Samuel 6, which describes David bringing the ark into Jerusalem. Psalm 50 mentions Asaph, who is also mentioned in 1 Chronicles 6:39. These psalms would thus appear to accompany the exciting events in 2 Samuel 7–10. Based on Yahweh's promises (2 Samuel 7), David's power was growing as he conquered nations and extended Israel's borders in every direction (2 Samuel 8–10).

The superscription to Psalm 51 links it to David's tragic sin with Bathsheba and Nathan's confrontation of David (2 Samuel 11–12). Fittingly, Psalm 52 returns David to affliction and opposition, just as the judgments on David's sins are recounted in 2 Samuel 13–20. The treachery lamented in Psalm 55:13–15 (ET 12–14), 21–22 (ET 20–21) matches the actions of Absalom and Ahithophel in 2 Samuel 15–17. Those traitors met the fate of all those who set themselves against Yahweh and his messiah (cf. Ps. 55:23–24, ET 22–23).

The Psalms that follow (Psalms 56–64) present David (named in the superscriptions) praising God through every difficulty. Then it seems that salvation has come through these judgments when we arrive at the unafflicted praises celebrating the God who hears prayer (65:3, ET 2), does awesome deeds (66:5), and neither rejects prayer nor removes steadfast love (66:20). Psalm 67 reflects God's universal purpose to cover the dry lands with his glory, and Psalm 68 extols him as the one who will arise to judge all his enemies, through which salvation will come for his people to his glory. Praise and trust through affliction and opposition continue in Psalms 69–71.

The superscription at the beginning of Psalm 72, "Of Solomon," and the last verse of the psalm, "The prayers of David, the son of Jesse, are ended" (72:20), indicate that this is one of David's final prayers for Solomon. He prays that the king will be just and the land fruitful (72:1–3), that the king will crush the oppressor and his enemies lick the dust (72:4, 9; cf. Gen. 3:14–15); and he prays that the dominion of the Davidic messiah will stretch from sea to sea, "from the River to the ends of the earth" (Ps. 72:8; cf. Zech. 9:10), as his name endures forever and people are blessed in him and "all nations call him blessed" (Ps. 72:17; cf. Gen. 12:3). This remarkable prayer weaves together the definitive triumph of the seed of the woman over the seed of the serpent with Yahweh's purpose to cover the dry lands with his glory and bless all nations through the seed of Abraham.[34] In book 2 of the Psalter, salvation comes through judgment

[34]See appendix 2 (§6) to chap. 3, "All the Earth Filled with the Knowledge of Yahweh's Glory."

to the glory of Yahweh through the agency of the messiah, son of David, king in Jerusalem.

2.2.3 Book 3, Psalms 73–89

The combination of the Psalm 72 superscription "Of Solomon" and its concluding notice that the prayers of David are ended (72:20) gives the impression that when we begin book 3 of the Psalter, we have moved from the era of David's reign to that of his son. It seems, then, that Psalms 73–89 are concerned with Solomon and those who followed him down to the destruction of Jerusalem in 586 BC. The destruction of Jerusalem and the fall of the house of David are lamented in Psalm 89 (Ps. 89:39–52, ET 38–51).

In book 3 of the Psalter expressions of the hope of the world are intermingled with anticipations of judgment day. The world's last and only hope is Yahweh and his program, which is for the wicked to be judged (Psalms 73, 75, 82); Yahweh to be known from his temple in Zion (Psalms 77, 84), while his mighty deeds of old are rehearsed (Psalm 78); and his people saved through the judgment of their enemies (Psalms 80, 83), in response to which they sing his praise (Psalm 81).

Alongside these pious expressions of what Yahweh will accomplish through king messiah we find ominous statements of the people's sin and its covenant consequences. The juxtaposition of psalms of hope (e.g., Psalm 73) with psalms that seem to speak in the present tense of the destruction of the temple (Psalms 74 and 79) draws readers into Israel's inexorable march toward exile. The fitful faithfulness of the few could not keep judgment from falling. Again and again in book 3 we find psalms that deal with the destruction of the temple and the nation (Psalms 74, 79, 83, 88, 89).

Even in the midst of these psalms that speak of the horrifying destruction of the temple in Jerusalem, we see salvation through judgment for Yahweh's glory. Like Moses and others in Israel's history, the psalmist appeals to Yahweh on the basis of Yahweh's concern for his own glory (Ps. 79:9; see table 4.9 appended to this chapter [§7], "Old Testament Prayers Appealing to God's Concern for His Own Glory"). The psalmist does not want God's name reviled (74:10), so he appeals to his former salvation through judgment when he broke the heads of the sea monsters and crushed the heads of Leviathan (74:13–14; cf. 89:11, ET 10).

Through the judgment of exile salvation will yet come for the people of God (Ps. 80:4, ET 3, 8, ET 7, 20, ET 19). When Yahweh saves his people through the judgment of their enemies, those who are defeated will know that he alone is most high over all the earth (83:15–19, ET 14–18). Mercy and truth will meet, righteousness and peace will kiss each other (85:11, ET 10). All nations will worship God for the salvation he works through judgment (Psalm 86), and foreigners will be regarded as having been born in Zion (Psalm 87).[35]

Before the glory of God in salvation can be experienced, judgment must fall. Heman the Ezrahite laments the casting away and wrath (Psalm 88). Ethan the Ezrahite then sings of Yahweh's covenant with David (89:4–5, ET 3–4, 20–38, ET 19–37),[36] but of the fall of his house (89:39–50, ET 38–49). The salvation that will come through the judgment of the exile will be like resurrection from the dead (80:15–19, ET 14–18), and hoping in Yahweh's power the psalmist calls on Yahweh to remember (89:51–52, ET 50–51).

At the end of book 3 judgment has fallen, but hope has not died. The call on Yahweh to "remember" (Ps. 89:51, ET 50) and the hope that the "anointed" might no more be mocked (89:52, ET 51) testify against those who think that the decisive end has come upon the house of David. Because Yahweh reigns, as will be affirmed in Psalms 93–100, the Psalter will again sing the triumphs of a coming David (cf. Psalm 110).

2.2.4 Book 4, Psalms 90–106

Book 4 of the Psalms seems to be an expression of faith in exile. That is, though the walls are breached and the crown is in the dust (Ps. 89:40–41, ET 39–40), yet the faithful trust in Yahweh. The opening statement of this trust is a return to Moses in Psalm 90, which bears the superscription, "A prayer of Moses, the man of God." Erich Zenger writes:

> Psalm Book IV has a Moses dimension that distinguishes it from the other psalm books. As the first psalm in the composition Psalm 90 begins with the creation of the world and of humanity described in Genesis (Ps 90:3 alludes to Gen 3:19), and Psalm 106 as the last psalm recapitulates the conquest and life in the land, with the latter being evaluated under the perspective of Deut 7:1–5, 16; 29:26; 31:17; 32:17. To that extent the composition Psalms 90–106 is Pentateuch-oriented, that is, Moses-oriented. Moreover, Moses is named seven times in the collection! (90 [title, MT 1]; 99:6; 103:7; 105:26; 106:16, 23, 31), while he is mentioned elsewhere in the Psalter only a single time (77:20 [21]).[37]

There are thematic links between Psalms 90 and 91 (cf., e.g., Pss. 90:1 and 91:9), and the last words of Psalm 92 allude to Deuteronomy 32 (cf. Ps. 92:15 and Deut. 32:4).[38] This brackets Psalms 90–92 with Mosaic material.

[35]Cf. Zenger, "Zion as Mother of the Nations in Psalm 87," 159–60.
[36]See Knut M. Heim, "The (God-)Forsaken King of Psalm 89: A Historical and Intertextual Enquiry," in Day, *King and Messiah in Israel and the Ancient Near East*, 301: "Psalm 89 is a highly artistic piece of poetry. It may go *beyond* its source text [2 Sam. 7], but it does not go *against* it."
[37]Erich Zenger, "The God of Israel's Reign over the World (Psalms 90–106)," in Lohfink and Zenger, *The God of Israel and the Nations*, 165.
[38]Ibid., 167–68.

Psalms 93–100 then declare that Yahweh reigns. David Howard has shown that these Psalms are "all concerned with YHWH's kingship in one way or another."[39] After the pointer back to Moses (Psalms 90–92) and the strong affirmation that Yahweh reigns (Psalms 93–100), David reappears in the superscription of Psalm 101. In a dark moment Psalm 89:50 (ET 49) asks, "Lord, where is your steadfast love of old, which by your faithfulness you swore to David?" And Psalm 101:1 answers, "I will sing of steadfast love and justice; to you, O Yahweh, I will make music." Through judgment the hope of salvation returns to Yahweh's glory. It is still only a hope, however, as Psalm 102 is "a prayer of one afflicted, when he is faint and pours out his complaint before Yahweh."

Hope grows stronger as the psalm "Of David" numbered 103 sings of Yahweh who forgives and heals (Ps. 103:3) and quotes Exodus 34:6–7 (Ps. 103:8). These hopes for what will come after exile through judgment are then fed in Psalms 104–6. Future hope is here built on the foundation of what God has done in history from creation (104:2–30) through the covenant with Abraham, Isaac, and Jacob (105:7–11) to Joseph (105:16–25), then Moses and the exodus from Egypt (105:26–45), through which Yahweh saved his people "for his name's sake, that he might make known his mighty power" (106:8) at the Red Sea (106:9–12). Future hope is squarely placed on Yahweh's history of glorifying himself in salvation through judgment when the people rebelled against Moses (106:13–27), at Baal Peor (106:28–31), at Meribah (106:32–33), at the conquest (106:34–39), and through the time of the judges (106:40–46).

The point of application for the exiles is that Yahweh always "remembered his covenant, and relented according to the abundance of his steadfast love" (Ps. 106:45). And thus the psalmist pleads, "Save us, O Yahweh our God, and gather us from among the nations, that we may give thanks to your holy name and glory in your praise" (106:47). Thus book 4 ends with a review of the ways that Yahweh has shown his glory in salvation through judgment; and with the people under judgment, the cry is that he might bring them through it once again to salvation for his glory.

2.2.5 Book 5, Psalms 107–150

The cry for Yahweh to gather his people from among the nations that concludes book 4 is answered by the proleptic affirmation that opens book 5: "Let the redeemed of Yahweh say so, whom he has redeemed from trouble and gathered in from the lands, from the east and from the west, from the north and from the south" (Ps. 107:2–3). With this opening reason to give thanks to Yahweh (107:1), book 5 opens by speaking of the return from exile as though it has already taken place. This seems to be the perspective of faith. Psalms 107–50 present the

[39]David M. Howard Jr., *The Structure of Psalms 93–100*, Biblical and Judaic Studies from the University of California, San Diego (Winona Lake, IN: Eisenbrauns, 1997), 183.

eschatological triumph of Yahweh through the conquering Davidic king, who decisively brings about the salvation that comes to Israel through the exile by means of judgment upon the enemies of Israel. Thus the new exodus and the return from exile begin through the agency of the messiah. For Yahweh's glory, the messiah brings salvation through judgment.

The arrangement of the fifth book of the Psalms can be depicted as shown in table 4.2.[40]

Table 4.2. Zenger's Arrangement of Book 5 of the Psalms (Adapted)

Psalms 107, 108–10 (royal), 111–12 (acrostic)
David, eschatological and messianic

Psalms 113–18
exodus, Passover

Psalm 119 (Acrostic)
Torah, Weeks

Psalms 120–37
Zion, Booths

Psalms 138–44 (royal), 145 (acrostic)
David, eschatological and messianic

As he trusts Yahweh, Israel's anointed king will be Yahweh's agent of judgment upon the enemies of the people of God, the corollary of which is that he is also the agent of salvation for the people of God.[41] The psalms that have David as their subject reflect this basic perspective. Psalm 137 envisions salvation through judgment for God's glory in vibrant colors tinged with Genesis 3:15, blessing the one who will arise to crush the seed of the serpent, visiting the judgment of God on the enemies of God and simultaneously delivering God's people (Ps. 137:8–9). The language of these imprecatory psalms is harsh (dashed heads against rock, broken teeth, etc.), but it is justly fierce,

[40]Adapted from Erich Zenger, "The Composition and Theology of the Fifth Book of Psalms, Psalms 107–145," *JSOT* 80 (1998): 98. Zenger suggests that book 5 of the Psalter functions as a "spiritual pilgrimage to Zion" as the faithful recite and meditate on these psalms, which he suggests have been arranged according to "the three great feasts of the Jewish calendar." Thus, those contemplating these psalms reencounter the exodus and the origin of the nation in 113–18, the giving of the law at Sinai in 119, and the entry into the Promised Land in 120–36 (ibid., 100–101). Cf. the similar proposal put forward by Jinkyu Kim, "The Strategic Arrangement of Royal Psalms in Books IV–V," *WTJ* 20 (2008): 143–57.
[41]Cf. House, *Old Testament Theology*, 423.

corresponding to the depth of wickedness displayed by those who would join the serpent against God.[42]

All this saving and judging, along with all else sung in the Psalms, redounds to God's glory. Both the righteous praise and the indignant denunciation of evil in the Psalms show that those who take refuge in Yahweh also take his priorities.[43] In the Psalter, everything culminates in the praise of Yahweh, who acts for the glory of his own name. Yahweh will lead his king in paths of righteousness "on account of his name" (Ps. 23:3). Yahweh is called upon to pardon guilt for his name's sake (25:11). The Rock and Fortress, he is called upon to lead and guide for his name's sake (31:4, ET 3). Yahweh, God of salvation, is called upon to help for the glory of his name, to deliver and provide atonement for the sins of his people for the glory of his name, for the sake of his name (79:9). The cry for mercy comes to Yahweh for his own name's sake (109:21). These texts show appeals to Yahweh to be merciful, to forgive, to deliver, and to lead his people for his own glory (see table 4.9 appended to this chapter [§7], "Old Testament Prayers Appealing to God's Concern for His Own Glory").

Yahweh's acting for his own glory allows him to reveal the wonder of his character, and this is what those who love him long to see. David's great desire is to dwell in the house of Yahweh, gazing on the beauty of Yahweh in his temple (27:4). The beauty of Yahweh evokes praise, with which the Psalter brims. Indeed, praise is built into its very structure: each of the Psalter's five books concludes with a benediction glorifying God (41:14, ET 13; 72:19; 89:53, ET 52; 106:48; 150:1–6).

2.2.6 The Center of the Theology of Psalms

The main theme coursing through these five books is the glory of God seen in the deliverance of the righteous who meditate on the Torah, as described in Psalm 1, and kiss the Son, as described in Psalm 2.[44] This salvation is realized as the righteous call on Yahweh for deliverance from their enemies (e.g., Ps. 59:2, ET 1), and it takes the form of Yahweh coming in theophanic glory to deliver those who take refuge in him (18:8–16, ET 7–15). The fact that the righteous must take refuge in Yahweh and call on him to act highlights the fact that Yahweh's power is made perfect in the weaknesses, afflictions, and needs of those

[42] *Contra* the perspective articulated by Gerald Wilson, who writes, "This is not to say, however, that the psalms and Psalter endorse all the very human attitudes and emotions expressed by the psalmists, including the vicious vengeance anticipated in the imprecatory psalms" ("Psalms and Psalter: Paradigm for Biblical Theology," in *Biblical Theology: Retrospect and Prospect*, ed. Scott J. Hafemann [Downers Grove, IL: InterVarsity: 2002], 102). Appeals for and celebrations of God's judgment in the Psalms are not "less than Christian" (p. 101), as any reader of the book of Revelation can see. In fact, descriptions of the horrifying terror of the coming judgment are merciful warnings that invite the wicked to repent, and they glorify the God who will demonstrate his wrath and make known his power (Rom. 9:22).

[43] The scene in Canto VIII of *The Inferno* where Virgil commends Dante for berating a soul being tormented in hell (lines 31–54) indicates that Dante understood this aspect of the Bible's theology.

[44] *Pace* Wilson, who writes, "There is no clear center of the Psalter" ("Psalms and Psalter," 109).

who trust in him. Salvation for the righteous is judgment against the enemies of God and his people (e.g., 7:7–9, ET 6–8; 79:1–13). The psalmist calls on the sons of God to ascribe to Yahweh the glory due his name, to worship him in the splendor of holiness (29:1–2; 96:9). In the Psalms, God is glorified in salvation through judgment. As Gerald Wilson writes:

> The concluding *hallel* psalms (Pss 146–50) provide a conclusion to the whole Psalter in response to the final verse of Psalm 145:21: "My mouth will speak the praise of YHWH, and let all flesh bless his holy name forever and ever" [Wilson's trans.]. The effect of this concluding praise is to affirm that the final word of the Psalter is one of praise. . . . Thus it is appropriate that the final Hebrew title for the Book of Psalms is *tehillim*, "praises," not as a way of denying the reality and validity of lament but as a way of affirming the ultimate end of the "way YHWH knows" (Ps 1:6).[45]

The center of the Psalter is the glory of Yahweh. This glory will be manifested as Yahweh shows his righteousness against his people's sin, and through that judgment he delivers them to trust him. Having triumphed over unrighteousness and delivered his people from their own wickedness, Yahweh is glorified as his people rely upon him alone. Yahweh then triumphs over the enemies of his people, and through the judgment that falls on the wicked his people are saved. They respond by glorifying Yahweh. The glory of God in salvation through judgment is the center of the theology of Psalms. It is the experience of the individual psalmist, and it is the experience of the nation of Israel. Yahweh shows justice and mercy, and his people praise him.

2.3 Proverbs

The book of Proverbs results from Solomon's obedience to Deuteronomy 6, filtered through his obedience to Deuteronomy 17, as he creatively teaches the Torah to his son.[46] Proverbs shows that life in the fear of God leads to shalom; rebellion leads to misery. Even in the details of life as basic as boundary stones and balances, God is glorified in salvation through judgment as his mercy and justice are displayed.

Proverbs opens with the words, "The proverbs of Solomon, son of David, king of Israel" (Prov. 1:1). Then again in Proverbs 10:1 we find the heading, "The proverbs of Solomon," and it is remarkable that Proverbs 10:1–22:16 contains 375 lines (which correspond to the modern verse numbers), and 375 is the

[45]Ibid., 105.

[46]Most interpretations of Proverbs do not read Deuteronomy 6 and 17 as the impetus for Proverbs as I am here. It seems to me that the dichotomizing tendency of critical scholarship works like a reverse magnetic force, preventing these kinds of connections, while the broader context of ancient Near Eastern parallels can easily distract interpreters from the nearer context of the Old Testament canon. See, e.g., James L. Crenshaw, "The Wisdom Literature," in *The Hebrew Bible and Its Modern Interpreters*, ed. Douglas A. Knight and Gene M. Tucker (Atlanta: Scholars, 1985), 369–77, and Michael V. Fox, *Proverbs 1–9*, AB (New York: Doubleday, 2000).

numerical value, in Hebrew, of the name "Solomon."[47] The "thirty sayings of the wise" (22:20) follow in Proverbs 22:17–24:22, with more "sayings of the wise" in 24:23–34. The final Solomonic heading is found in Proverbs 25:1: "These also are proverbs of Solomon which the men of Hezekiah king of Judah copied." These features of the book all connect the majority of the book of Proverbs to King Solomon.[48] The final two headings are in Proverbs 30:1, "The words of Agur son of Jakeh," and in 31:1, "The words of King Lemuel." These headings will serve to structure this discussion.

Solomon and the others involved in the compilation of the book of Proverbs are doing what all good teachers do: communicating the great truths of the tradition (which in this case stems from the Pentateuch, and chiefly Deuteronomy) in new, surprising, and memorable ways. Proverbs has affinities with other ancient Near Eastern wisdom literature, but the theological content of the book is synonymous with the theological content of the Pentateuch, and especially Deuteronomy. Israel's king was responsible to know the law, enforce the law, and teach the law (Deuteronomy 17)—especially to his own children (Deuteronomy 6). Thus, many times in Proverbs we encounter phrases such as, "Hear, my son."[49] It would seem that as Solomon had been blessed by God with a wise and discerning heart (1 Kings 3:12), making him the wisest man on earth (4:29–31), he exercised his wisdom in the composition of three thousand proverbs (4:32) in obedience to Deuteronomy's instructions for fathers (Deut. 6:4–9) and kings (17:18–20).

The discrepancy between the ideal picture in Proverbs and the accounts of Solomon's life and the behavior of his sons in Kings provokes hope for an anointed king of Israel who will live out the wisdom Solomon articulated. Nevertheless, the wisdom taught in Proverbs is a fear of God that results precisely from the knowledge that God is watching and that he will judge. Through fear of judgment, then, Proverbs commends a path that does not lead to destruction, a way of life that reflects Yahweh's glory. Thus, the teaching of Proverbs produces a life that corresponds to the knowledge that Yahweh will be glorified in salvation through judgment.

2.3.1 Proverbs of Solomon: Parental Teaching to Escape Wicked Men and Wayward Women (Proverbs 1–9)

The introduction to the book of Proverbs in 1:1–7 explains the book's purpose. The Proverbs of Solomon seek to instruct people in righteousness (1:3), and the righteousness in view is in accord with what we read of righteousness

---

[47] William J. Dumbrell, *The Faith of Israel: A Theological Survey of the Old Testament*, 2nd ed. (Grand Rapids: Baker, 2002), 263.

[48] Cf. Bruce K. Waltke, "Proverbs: Theology of," in *NIDOTTE*, 4:1082: "Denial of Solomonic authorship is based on the academic skepticism inherited from the historical criticism of the last century, not on *any* scientific data." For the other perspective, which is no less dogmatic, see Fox, *Proverbs 1–9*, 6: "In fact, the Solomonic ascription is untenable . . . ."

[49] E.g., Prov. 1:8, 10, 15; 2:1; 3:1, 11; 4:1, 20; 5:1; 6:1, 20; 7:1; 10:1; 13:1; 15:20; 19:13, 26, 27; 23:15, 19, 24, 26; 24:13, 21; 27:11; 28:7; 31:2.

elsewhere in the Old Testament. Among others, Dennis Olson has suggested that the body of Deuteronomy 12–26 "largely follows the sequence of the ten commandments."[50] Just as Deuteronomy 12–26 can be seen as an exposition of the Ten Commandments, Proverbs serves as an exposition of the Ten Commandments.[51] Solomon is teaching the Torah to his son and, by extension, to his people. Paul House rightly states, "It is as if the fear of the Lord summarizes the first four commands and inspires the keeping of the last six."[52]

Fearing Yahweh is the beginning of knowledge (Prov. 1:7). The converse of this is that those who suppress the truth of God are on a path that leads away from sanity (see Rom. 1:18–32, esp. 22, 28). Fearing Yahweh is the beginning of wisdom, and knowing God gives insight (Prov. 9:10) because when God is rightly esteemed, other things take their proper place in one's priorities, emotions, and reckonings.[53] God came down on Mount Sinai in thundercloud, lightning, and fire; he spoke the Ten Commandments; and Moses said to the people of Israel, "Do not fear, for God has come to test you, that the fear of him may be before you, that you may not sin" (Ex. 20:20). The experience was so overwhelming that the Israelites feared that if God continued to speak directly to them, they would die (Deut. 5:26). They were reminded again and again of this terrifying experience of the awful majesty of God in Deuteronomy: "Yahweh spoke to you out of the midst of the fire" (4:12); "Yahweh spoke to you at Horeb out of the midst of the fire" (4:15); "Yahweh your God is a consuming fire" (4:24); "Did any people ever hear the voice of a god speaking out of the midst of the fire, as you have heard, and still live?" (4:33); "You heard his words out of the midst of the fire" (4:36).[54]

The way that Moses applied Israel's perception of the terror of God in Exodus 20:20 was also the way the reminders of the experience functioned in Deuteronomy. Israel was to be conscious of the holy dread, the consuming fire, the sovereign Lord, and their fear of him was to motivate obedience to him ("that you may not sin," Ex. 20:20). Moses urged Israel, "Take care, lest you forget . . . . For Yahweh your God is a consuming fire, a jealous God" (Deut. 4:23–24). The reason that the fear of Yahweh motivates obedience is that Yahweh calls people to account for breaking his commandments. The curses outlined in Leviticus 26 and Deuteronomy 28 promised destruction if the people disobeyed, and these curses were meant to make Israel want to

[50]Dennis T. Olson, *Deuteronomy and the Death of Moses: A Theological Reading*, Overtures to Biblical Theology (Minneapolis: Fortress: 1994), 3.

[51]For instance, Israel was commanded not to steal, murder, or covet the possessions of others (Ex. 20:13, 15, 17; Deut. 5:17, 19, 21). Knowing that naïve people find themselves in the wrong places, with the wrong people, doing the wrong things, Solomon admonishes his son in Prov. 1:8–19 to resist the enticements of sinners (1:10), who invite others to participate in murder (1:12) and theft (1:13). Those who are greedy are in fact self-destructive (1:19). Prov. 1:8–19 is a specific, situational application of three of the Ten Commandments.

[52]House, *Old Testament Theology*, 444.

[53]Similarly Dumbrell, *The Faith of Israel*, 267.

[54]See also Deut. 4:11; 5:4, 22, 24, 25, 26; 9:3, 10, 15; 10:4; 18:16.

obey to avoid God's wrath. Israel was also encouraged to obey out of love for Yahweh (Deut. 6:4–5; 10:12–13), but they got fair warning that life would not be pleasant if they transgressed.

Like Exodus and Deuteronomy, Proverbs tells its audience that the fear of Yahweh is a guardrail that keeps travelers from going over the precipice to destruction. This message is communicated in carefully crafted, pithy, memorable bits. The obedience Yahweh desires is not a perfunctory outward show. He wants people to be motivated to obey by their awareness of the kind of God he is. Thus Proverbs says, "The fear of Yahweh is the beginning of knowledge; fools despise wisdom and instruction" (Prov. 1:7). Only a fool would plunge headlong into disobedience in view of the fact that Yahweh is a consuming fire, "For the eyes of Yahweh are in every place, observing the wicked and the good" (15:3). The beginning of wisdom is to recognize that God will bring people to judgment, and the wise will be led to salvation through the fear of that judgment. This point is important enough to be repeated with a slight variation: "The fear of Yahweh is the beginning of wisdom, and the knowledge of the Holy One is insight" (9:10).

After the introductory seven verses of the book, the rest of Proverbs 1–9 has a chiastic structure (see table 4.3).[55]

Table 4.3. Waltke's Chiasm in Proverbs 1–9 (Adapted)

- A 1:8–19, Two invitations: from the father and from sinners
  - B 1:20–33, Wisdom crying aloud in the street
    - C 2:1–22, Father's warnings: devious men and the forbidden woman
      - D 3:1–4:27, Father's command to heed parental teaching
        - 3:1–21, Parental instruction
          - 3:27–35, Dealing with neighbors
        - 4:1–27, Parental instruction
      - D′ 5:1–6:35, Father's command to be faithful in marriage
        - 5:1–23, Flee the forbidden woman and enjoy your wife
          - 6:1–19, Three mistakes: security for a neighbor, sloth, and thuggery
        - 6:20–35, Avoid adultery
    - C′ 7:1–27, Father's warning: the fool who flirts with the forbidden woman
  - B′ 8:1–36, Wisdom crying aloud in the street
- A′ 9:1–18, Two invitations: from Lady Wisdom and Madame Folly

[55]Adapted from Bruce K. Waltke, *The Book of Proverbs: Chapters 1–15*, NICOT (Grand Rapids: Eerdmans, 2004), 12.

From this overview of the structure it can be seen that Proverbs 1–9 focuses on (1) exhorting a young man to listen to his parents as they warn him against (2) devious men and their foolish ways and (3) the lure of sexual immorality with a forbidden woman. This parental teaching calls young men to be saved through judgment for the glory of God.

The parental instruction announces the judgment that devious men who pursue foolish ways will meet with destruction:

> These men lie in wait for their own blood;
> they set an ambush for their own lives. (Prov. 1:18 ESV)

Wisdom is personified as crying out in the streets, and her verdict is that

> the simple are killed by their turning away;
> and the complacency of fools destroys them. (1:32 ESV)

The father teaches his son (2:1) that "none who go to [the forbidden woman, 2:16] come back, nor do they regain the paths of life" (2:19), and as for devious men, "the wicked will be cut off from the land, and the treacherous will be rooted out of it" (2:22). These judgments come from Yahweh himself: "for the devious person is an abomination to Yahweh . . . . Yahweh's curse is on the house of the wicked" (3:32–33). The father teaches his son that the forbidden woman is

> . . . bitter as wormwood,
> sharp as a two-edged sword.
> Her feet go down to death;
> her steps follow the path to Sheol. (5:4–5 ESV)

Those who go to the forbidden woman will not escape judgment because "a man's ways are before the eyes of Yahweh, and he ponders all his paths" (5:21). The father warns his son against putting up security for a neighbor (6:1–5), sloth (6:6–11), and thuggery (6:12–19). Yahweh hates the practices of the wicked (6:16). Inexorable is the judgment against adulterers (6:27–35). The fool who flirts with the forbidden woman (7:5–9) will pay: "for many a victim has she laid low, and all her slain are a mighty throng. Her house is the way to Sheol, going down to the chambers of death" (7:26–27). Wisdom should not be neglected but be taught by parents (1:8; 2:1; 3:1, 21; 4:1, 11, 20; 5:1, 7; 6:1, 20; 7:1, 24). She is personified as crying aloud in the street (1:20–21, 24; 8:1–3; 9:3). Even Yahweh delighted in wisdom as he created the world (8:30, cf. 22–31; 3:19–20). "He who fails to find [wisdom] injures himself; all who hate [wisdom] love death" (8:36). He who heeds the call of folly, personified as a lewd madame, rather than the call of Lady Wisdom, will think that "'stolen water is sweet, and bread eaten in secret is pleasant.' But he does not know that the dead are there, that her guests are in the depths of Sheol" (9:17–18). Judgment on the foolish actions of deceitful men and on sexual immorality with the forbidden woman is announced *to deliver* those who are simple from destruction. Solomon means to save his son through the fear of God's judgment.

The salvation that Solomon offers his son is the path to everything that people seek to attain by consorting with devious men and forbidden women. The book of Proverbs exists "to give prudence to the simple" (Prov. 1:4), which is to say, to keep the simple from the judgment the book announces against wickedness. The beginning of this deliverance from judgment is the fear of Yahweh (1:7). The next step is to heed one's parents (1:8), and from there, if one answers the call of Lady Wisdom, she promises, "I will pour out my spirit to you" (1:23). The benefits of wisdom are not merely physical. It is as though those who are delivered through judgment regain something of the Edenic experience of the presence of Yahweh. "He is a shield to those who walk in integrity, guarding the paths of justice and watching over the way of his saints" (2:7–8). Those whom wisdom (2:10) delivers "from men of perverted speech" (2:12) and "from the forbidden woman" (2:16) "will walk in the way of the good and keep to the paths of the righteous. For the upright will inhabit the land, and those with integrity will remain in it" (2:20–21). Being saved from folly through the judgment announced against it will yield a long, peaceful life (3:2), as well as "favor and good success in the sight of God and man" (3:4).

The way of wisdom is not some recipe for the good life that has no reference to knowing and trusting God. The fear of Yahweh is its beginning (Prov. 1:7), and he is to be wholeheartedly trusted and known throughout one's ways (3:5–6). The way of wisdom is the path of embracing Yahweh's fatherly discipline (3:11–12), and this path leads to incomparable blessings, better treasures than gold, silver, and precious stones (3:14–15). Wisdom holds long life, wealth, and honor (3:16). Pleasantness and peace mark her paths, and

> She is a tree of life to those who lay hold of her;
> those who hold her fast are called blessed. (3:18 ESV)

The way of wisdom is the way to enjoy God's presence, as if one walked with him in the cool of the day in the garden of Eden.

Solomon's instruction for his son "will be life for [his] soul and adornment for [his] neck" (Prov. 3:22). Yahweh "blesses the dwelling of the righteous" (3:33). Yahweh founded the earth by wisdom (3:19), and those who would live by wisdom must fear Yahweh (1:7; 8:13; 9:10) and trust him (3:5–6). This means that those who walk in wisdom's ways declare that Yahweh is more trustworthy than the offerings made by other paths to joy. Those who walk in wisdom's ways declare that Yahweh is just, and that he is inescapable (cf. 5:21). Thus, Proverbs tells us who will shine with the glory of Yahweh: those who are delivered from deviant behavior and wicked women through the announcement of the certain judgment that will fall on the wicked. In contrast to the path that leads to destruction, "the path of the righteous is like the light of dawn, which shines brighter and brighter until full day" (4:18).

The one who is delivered from the allure of the wayward woman (Prov. 5:1–14) to enjoy the wife of his youth (5:15–19) is saved through judgment by the teaching of Proverbs, and the happiness of his marital bliss shines for the glory of Yahweh. The same is true of wise financial dealings (6:1–5), disciplined labor and good stewardship (6:6–11), and the rejection of deceptive scheming (6:12–19). Yahweh's glory shines in the world he made by wisdom (8:22–31), and Yahweh's glory shines in the lives of those who live by wisdom (8:4–21, 32–35). Proverbs 9 closes this first section of the book with the invitations from Lady Wisdom and Madame Folly. In this section of the book, Solomon seeks to save his son through the judgment wisdom announces against folly, and the one who is saved through that judgment lives out the glory of Yahweh.

2.3.2 Proverbs of Solomon: The Way the World Works (Proverbs 10–22:16)

Proverbs 10–15 continues to teach that God is glorified in salvation through judgment, largely through the use of antithetical proverbs. Proverbs 16:1–22:16 treats the tension between divine sovereignty and human responsibility, speaking also to kings and other noble figures.[56] These sections can be summarized by means of illustrations drawn from each.

Both the antithetical nature of the statements in Proverbs 10–15 and the glory of Yahweh in salvation through judgment can be seen in Proverbs 10:29, "The way of Yahweh is a stronghold to the blameless, but destruction to evildoers." Yahweh's justice will be a comfort and a refuge to those who embrace the wisdom mercifully revealed in Proverbs. But that same justice guarantees the destruction of those who refuse the mercy offered in wisdom's call. Yahweh sets his character on display in people's lives as he renders to them according to their works. This can be seen in how wise and foolish sons respond to their parents (Prov. 10:1, 5), how the wicked and the righteous accumulate wealth (10:2, 4), how the righteous are blessed while the wicked rot away in violence (10:6–7), and how the lifestyles of the righteous and the wicked bear fruit (10:9–12). Crucial considerations throughout are how people respond to the commandments (10:8), which determines whether Yahweh satisfies one's desires or thwarts one's

[56] Cf. ibid., 15–21.

cravings (10:3). The judgment announced on wickedness functions to produce wise young men who seek Yahweh's glory. Yahweh glorifies himself in salvation through judgment.

Another antithetical announcement of judgment that is meant to lead to salvation for Yahweh's glory comes in Proverbs 11:21 (ESV):

> Be assured, an evil person will not go unpunished,
> but the offspring of the righteous will be delivered.

And again in 12:2: "A good man obtains favor from Yahweh, but a man of evil devices he condemns." Those who fear Yahweh are brought through the fear of his judgment to salvation, while those who are foolish show contempt for Yahweh: "Whoever walks in uprightness fears Yahweh, but he who is devious in his ways despises him" (14:2). We see a clear statement that the exposure of the judgment that will fall on evildoers is meant to deliver people from that judgment—to take them through judgment to salvation—in Proverbs 14:27: "The fear of Yahweh is a fountain of life, that one may turn away from the snares of death." Through the announced judgment, the simple are to be made wise unto salvation for Yahweh's glory. The antithetical statements in Proverbs 10–15 bring Solomon's son through judgment to salvation for the glory of God.

The teaching in Proverbs 16:1–22:16 seems held together by three concerns: first, the burden of this section concerns the responsibility to live wisely; second, with this focus on human responsibility, there is a repeated assertion of God's sovereignty over all aspects of human life; and third, in keeping with the idea that Solomon is teaching his son the Torah in Proverbs, there are a number of statements that relate to kings and how they should reign. The central idea that God glorifies himself in salvation through judgment permeates this threefold concern of Proverbs 16:1–22:16.

Salvation through judgment for God's glory manifests itself in this section of Proverbs as judgment on wickedness is announced and righteous behavior is commended. The arrogant are an abomination to Yahweh and will be punished (Prov. 16:5). Those who mock the poor insult their Maker and will be punished (17:5). Those who cheat with weights and measures are an abomination to Yahweh (20:10, 23). The righteous one will throw the wicked down in ruin (21:12).

As these judgments on wickedness are taught, saving wisdom is commended: "By steadfast love and faithfulness iniquity is atoned for, and by the fear of Yahweh one turns away from evil" (Prov. 16:6). One must believe what Yahweh has revealed in the judgments on evildoing and trust him as one pursues righteousness: "Blessed is he who trusts in Yahweh" (16:20). Yahweh's name is a strong tower where the righteous find safety (18:10). Those who fear Yahweh will be satisfied and live (19:23; 22:4). Their trust and their fear of Yahweh result in their experience of the good life, and they bring glory to him. Those who fear the Lord and trust him are saved through judgment for his glory.

As elsewhere in the Old Testament, Israel's king is presented as the agent through whom Yahweh will accomplish salvation through judgment. This is especially clear in Proverbs 16:10–15, where the king renders judgment (16:10; cf. 20:8, 26), has his throne established by righteousness (16:12; cf. 17:7), delights in righteousness (16:13), and sends the messenger of death when his wrath is aroused (16:14; cf. 20:2); and the light of his face is like God's own favor (16:15; cf. 19:12).

All the salvation through judgment described in Proverbs is accomplished under Yahweh's sovereign hand as he seeks to demonstrate his glory. Thus, wisdom recognizes Yahweh's control over the evil, on whom he will demonstrate his justice, and the good, to whom he has shown mercy. Consider the following Proverbs:

- 16:4: "Yahweh has made everything for its purpose, even the wicked for the day of trouble."
- 16:9: "The heart of man plans his way, but Yahweh establishes his steps."
- 16:33: "The lot is cast into the lap, but its every decision is from Yahweh."
- 19:14: "House and wealth are inherited from fathers, but a prudent wife is from Yahweh."
- 19:21: "Many are the plans in the mind of a man, but it is the purpose of Yahweh that will stand."
- 20:24: "A man's steps are from Yahweh; how then can man understand his way?"
- 21:1: "The king's heart is a stream of water in the hand of Yahweh; he turns it wherever he will."
- 21:30–31: "No wisdom, no understanding, no counsel can avail against Yahweh. The horse is made ready for the day of battle, but victory belongs to Yahweh."

Proverbs 10:1–22:16 teaches that Yahweh is glorified in salvation through judgment. Through antithetical statements Solomon teaches his son in chapters 10–15 that wickedness will be judged, and through that judgment he means to lead his son to enjoy the good life for God's glory. Then in 16:1–22:16 Solomon juxtaposes God's sovereignty over all that is with man's responsibility to be wise and live righteously. Folly will be judged and wisdom rewarded, as the crown prince is instructed in how he should carry out his duties as Yahweh's vice-regent who will glorify God by enacting salvation through judgment in Israel.

2.3.3 Thirty Sayings of the Wise: How to Relate to Other People (Prov. 22:17–24:22)

The thirty sayings of the wise in this section of Proverbs are to be studied that Solomon's sons might trust in Yahweh (Prov. 22:19). Through judgment on false dealings with others, these sayings bring the young man to salvation for God's glory by instructing him in how to relate to others. It seems that every potential relationship is addressed in these thirty sayings: from the poor (22:22–23), to the skillful (22:29), to the king (23:1–3), to one's own children (23:13–14), to one's parents (23:22–25), to wicked women (22:26–28), to one's enemies (24:17–18), to many others not mentioned. The one who heeds these instructions fears Yahweh (24:21).

2.3.4 More Sayings of the Wise: Justice and Home Economics (Prov. 24:23–34)

The additional sayings of the wise in this section of Proverbs focus on judging justly (24:24–26) and diligence (24:27). This twofold focus is then repeated with an admonition against being a false witness at court (24:28–29) and observations on the field of the one who lacks diligence (24:30–34). Skillful living results from these judgments announced against wickedness and folly, and through the judgment young men are delivered to live for Yahweh's glory.

2.3.5 Proverbs of Solomon Copied by Hezekiah's Men: The Glory of God and the Glory of Kings (Proverbs 25–29)

Solomon's proverbs copied by the men of Hezekiah (Prov. 25:1) begin with an assertion that connects the Wisdom Literature to the center of biblical theology: "It is the glory of God to conceal things, but the glory of kings is to search things out." Solomon apparently understands the mysteries of life about which he writes in Proverbs and Ecclesiastes to be ways that God has demonstrated his glory in the world. God has shown his glory by hiding these unsearchable riddles all through life. King Solomon exposes the glory of God in the mysteries and reflects that glory himself as he traces the outlines of what God has concealed. Solomon's efforts to search out what God has hidden draw attention to God's glory and in turn reflect it in the king's glory.

These chapters of Proverbs explore the conduct of the wise and the way the world works. Wisdom is seen in these chapters to be something that God has hidden. It is not what the human mind would expect it to be. Only by understanding Yahweh and his character can wisdom begin to be comprehended. As Proverbs 28:5 puts it, "Evil men do not understand justice, but those who seek Yahweh understand it completely." Yahweh is the central reality in the universe, and seeking to understand life apart from him is folly. Those who know Yahweh understand life.

As an example of this reality, we can consider the notions of justice and mercy. Apart from the knowledge of Yahweh, the human mind expects justice to be done, and there is only a category for mercy if justice ceases to be. Those who know Yahweh, however, understand that Yahweh's mercy is as free as his justice is exacting. Thus, though it might not make sense to human logic, those who know Yahweh comprehend Proverbs 28:13: "Whoever conceals his transgressions will not prosper, but he who confesses and forsakes them will obtain mercy."

Similarly, to the human mind there is a path to wealth that makes perfect sense. But those who know Yahweh understand that "a greedy man stirs up strife, but the one who trusts in Yahweh will be enriched" (Prov. 28:25). The path to wealth is the path of trusting Yahweh, not the path of greed. Human ways of thinking are confounded, and as the judgment comes down regarding the limits of human knowledge, the simple are mysteriously led, trusting Yahweh, through judgment to salvation and Yahweh's glory.

2.3.6 The Words of Agur: Humble Descriptions of the World (Proverbs 30)

An unknown, possibly non-Israelite, man named Agur continues the exploration of what God has hidden in Proverbs 30. God's transcendent glory is recognized (30:3), and there is a remarkable challenge to declare the name of God's son if it is known (30:4). Noteworthy, too, is the affirmation that "every word of God proves true" (30:5). The humility expressed in Proverbs 30 seems to reflect the exhausting experience (cf. 30:1) of foolishly exalting oneself (30:32), and through the frustration, the judgment, of that course of life, this Agur is brought to wisdom. Through judgment he is saved to fear and worship God.

2.3.7 The Words of King Lemuel: Nobility and the Virtuous Wife (Proverbs 31)

Proverbs 31 contains the reflections of King Lemuel (31:1), who was apparently not an Israelite king—at least he is not mentioned anywhere else in the Old Testament. This chapter is a fitting conclusion to the book of Proverbs, and in itself it affirms the center of biblical theology. After a final warning against wayward women, strong drink, and injustice (31:2–9), it is almost as though the book concludes with a return to Eden in the meditation on the virtuous wife in Proverbs 31:10–31.

2.3.8 The Center of the Theology of Proverbs

Through the judgments announced against the company of evil men, against the folly of sexual immorality, and against wicked and deceitful practices that undermine one's integrity, the book of Proverbs seeks to deliver the simple son of Solomon to a life of wisdom. Wise man that he will become through the fear of Yahweh and through trusting what Yahweh has revealed in the Law and the Prophets, this son of Solomon will arrive at the end of Proverbs to find this exotic

King Lemuel preparing him to reign in God's stead and enjoy a virtuous wife, a helpmeet suitable for Israel's king. The beauty of this virtuous bride reflects the glory of God, and the harmony between her and her husband and children (31:28–31) is achieved through the judgments announced against every evil way. Proverbs teaches that God is glorified in salvation through judgment.

2.4 Job

The Psalms assert that Yahweh will reign through his anointed messiah, to whom all the kings of the earth will be subject. The Proverbs teach that obedience to the Torah is the path to life and blessedness. While some psalms wrestle with the reality that the wicked sometimes prosper while the righteous are afflicted (e.g., Psalms 44, 73), this conundrum receives extended treatment in the book of Job. The reality that sometimes life does not follow the pattern described in Proverbs is explored in the book of Job, which teaches the proper response to the apparent failure of God to be glorified in salvation through judgment: we must watch, wait, and speak what is right (Job 1:22; 2:10; 42:7). Job teaches that if God is not immediately glorified in salvation through judgment, the afflicted should, like Job, wait and trust that one day they will be vindicated (cf. James 5:11). We have not all the evidence, and we know not all God's purposes. As Robert Fyall puts it, "The man of faith has to live with crushing questions."[57]

2.4.1 Yahweh's Challenge to Satan about Job (Job 1–2)

The opening of Job shows God issuing a challenge to Satan regarding Job (Job 1:7–12; 2:1–6). Yahweh appears intent on demonstrating his power to keep Job faithful to himself, regardless of what it might cost Job to prove this point to Satan. Yahweh is going to show his glory by saving Job through all the judgments that fall upon him as Satan's accusations are condemned.

2.4.2 Job's Lament (Job 3)

The Bible depicts real people in real life and in real pain. Job's response to the unspeakable tragedies that strike him is to curse the day of his birth (Job 3:1–10) and to ask why he lived (3:11–19). He goes on to ask why life continues at all (3:20–26). He is lamenting in severe pain, but he is not sinning with his lips (2:10) or charging God with wrong (1:22; cf. 42:7–8).

2.4.3 Job and His Counselors (Job 4–25)

There is a clear pattern in Job 4–25. Job's friends speak in the same order twice, and each speech from a counselor is followed by a response by Job. They start into a third cycle of speeches, but only the first two of the friends speak

---

[57]Robert S. Fyall, *Now My Eyes Have Seen You: Images of Creation and Evil in the Book of Job*, NSBT (Downers Grove, IL: InterVarsity, 2002), 37.

before Job enters into a longer discussion in chapters 26–31, and Zophar never gives his third speech. The dialogues fall out as seen in table 4.4.

Table 4.4. Job 4–25, The Speeches of Job and His Counselors

Job 4–14		Job 15–21		Job 22–25	
4–5	Eliphaz's 1st speech	15	Eliphaz's 2nd speech	22	Eliphaz's 3rd speech
6–7	Job's response	16–17	Job's response	23–24	Job's response
8	Bildad's 1st speech	18	Bildad's 2nd speech	25	Bildad's 3rd speech
9–10	Job's response	19	Job's response		
11	Zophar's 1st speech	20	Zophar's 2nd speech		
12–14	Job's response	21	Job's response		

Job's friends are not caricatures. Their arguments are not presented as those of straw men. They make real attempts to understand and explain what has happened to Job, and at points they make true statements. It seems, however, that the true statements made by Job's counselors do not arise from and are not couched within a biblical worldview. The truth claims of Job's friends are made from a different religious framework than the one Job embraces. Theirs is a mental universe in which a strict equation between justice and retribution exists, with no room for mercy, no room for mystery, and no room for Yahweh, who shows his glory in *both* justice *and* mercy.

Eliphaz's first speech asks whether man can be right before God (Job 4:7, 17). Job insists that his righteousness stands (6:29–30). Bildad asserts that God is just and judges justly (8:3–6, 20). At this point the complexity of Job's position begins to manifest itself. Job will repeatedly assert his integrity (e.g., 9:21), but at the same time he asks, "How can a man be in the right before God" (9:2 ESV). Job intends to seek mercy (9:15). Job's pain, his recognition of his finitude and God's absolute righteousness, and his sense that there is a place for mercy all seem to lead him to a growing awareness that what he needs is a mediator between himself and God. The first instance of this is a recognition that he does not have this mediator he needs (9:32–35). Zophar's first speech amounts to a demand that Job repent (11:14). Job extols the majesty of God and asserts that he will trust God even if God slays him (13:15).

Eliphaz's second speech asserts that Job is condemned by his own mouth (Job 15:6). Job seems to have grown in understanding. Whereas before he recognized a need for a mediator he did not have (9:32–35), now he knows that his witness is in heaven (16:19, cf. 21). Bildad rebukes Job by asserting that the wicked are punished (16:2–3, 5–21). Job seems to take yet another step of faith and understanding when he asserts that his redeemer lives (19:25), and he also indicates his belief that he, Job, will be raised from the dead (19:26). While his counselors look only for impersonal justice to be visited on Job, Job acknowledges his sin, offers sacrifice, looks for a mediator between himself and God, and trusts God in spite of all that has happened to him. Thus, Job embraces the religion seen elsewhere in the Old and New Testaments, but his counselors have a theology that is to be expected from human reason and man-made religion. Zophar reinforces this with his speech on the just punishment of the wicked (20:5, 29). Job responds to this argument by pointing out that sometimes the wicked prosper (21:7).

Eliphaz's third speech argues that Job is guilty (Job 22:5–9). Job argues against the religion of his counselors by maintaining, in chapter 23, that God is hidden and, in chapter 24, that people are wicked. Bildad then asks how man can be righteous before God (25:4).

From his dialogues with his counselors, it appears that Job is looking for God to be glorified in salvation through judgment. Job seeks a judgment that will uphold God's righteousness and a salvation that will be somehow achieved by a mediator and demonstrate God's mercy. When this is accomplished, God will be seen as more glorious than his counselors can imagine.

2.4.4 Job Extols God's Majesty (Job 26–31)

In the midst of blinding pain, Job knows God and sings his praise in Job 26–31. Job clings to what he knows of God as a just and merciful Savior. God has triumphed over the serpent (Job 26:13; cf. Gen. 3:15). The fear of the Lord is wisdom (28:28). Job has fled evil, refusing to look on a woman with lust, because he knows that God sees all his ways (31:1–4). Job seems to be aware of the fall narrative in Genesis 3 (Job 31:33, 38–40).

2.4.5 Elihu's Speech (Job 32–37)

Enter the mysterious Elihu. Remarkably, Elihu states, "Behold, I am as your mouth to God" (Job 33:6), and he seeks to justify Job (33:32). Elihu's words in Job 36:4,

> For truly my words are not false;
> one who is perfect in knowledge is with you, (ESV)

can be read as though he is an arrogant young man, or as though he is the mediator Job seeks. For our purposes here we can simply observe that Elihu glorifies God who is both merciful and just (34:10–11; 35:6–7; 36:5–10; 37:22–24). It is also interesting to observe that this one who celebrates God's saving and judging glory is not rebuked as Job's other counselors are (42:7–10).

2.4.6 Yahweh's Response (Job 38–42)

Yahweh answers Job (Job 38–42). He does not take up Job's questions one by one, but instead gives Job something far better: himself. Answering Job out of the whirlwind (38:1), Yahweh shows Job his greatness by calling attention to the heavens, the earth, and the sea (38:4–38). From the created realm, Yahweh moves on to show Job the animal kingdom (38:39–39:30). Job is silenced (40:4–5). Yahweh continues by revealing his justice to Job (40:6–14). Yahweh made Behemoth (40:15–24), and he makes Leviathan do his bidding (41:1–34).

Leviathan seems to symbolize the great evil power in the place of the deep, from which evil comes. Viewed this way, there is a kind of *inclusio* in the book of Job: the whole book is bracketed by Yahweh's enticing Satan to do his bidding at the beginning, and by his putting a hook in Leviathan's nose at the end. This indicates that Yahweh has orchestrated all the events described in the book of Job, and the clear implication is that Yahweh's purpose is to put the glory of his justice and his mercy on display as he saves Job through the judgment of both Satan the accuser and Job's accusing counselors.

Yahweh's revelation of himself is a mercy to Job. And in this mercy, Yahweh has also condemned Job's impertinence. Job is satisfied (Job 42:1–6). Yahweh rebukes Job's counselors (42:7–8), who repent and offer sacrifice as Yahweh commanded (42:9). They too are saved through judgment. Through all the judgments that came upon Job, and thereby through the condemnation of Satan's accusations, Job is restored (42:10–17) and enjoys the very glory of God himself.

2.6.7 *The Center of the Theology of Job*

We can best approach the theology of Job by a review of the narrative: Job's life is shattered. His children are dead. His wife abandons him. His friends insist that he suffers because of his sin. Throughout, Job does not charge God with wrong (1:22) or sin with his lips (2:10). Job is not insisting that he is sinless—he offers sacrifices (1:5)—but in the interchanges he is objecting to the conclusions of his friends. Moreover, Job dares to ask for a hearing before God (13:15). Job even recognizes his need for a mediator between himself and God (9:32–35; 16:18–21; 19:25). Commenting on Job 19:25 ("Yet I know that my Vindicator lives and that in the end he will stand upon the dust"), Fyall writes, "It seems if we take the concept of canon seriously, we cannot but think of the advocacy of Christ here and see this as one of the Old Testament intimations of the light that was to come into the world."[58]

At long last, God answers Job by appearing to him out of the whirlwind (Job 38:1). Chapters 38–41 reveal the awful majesty of God himself, and God's terrible glory causes Job to put his hand over his mouth (40:4). In spite of all his pain, Job is satisfied—not by the restoration of his health and property, but by the revelation of God. He says, "I know that you can do anything, and that no purpose of yours can be thwarted. . . . I had heard you by the hearing of the

[58]Ibid., 49; the translation of Job 19:25 is also Fyall's (44).

ear, but now my eyes have seen you. Therefore I retract and repent in dust and ashes" (42:2, 6).

In calling for a hearing before God and recognizing his need for a mediator, Job is looking for vindication as he clings to biblical faith. Though the reader is aware of what has taken place between God and Satan in the heavenly court, Job does not have access to this information. The book of Job teaches the mysterious, hidden nature of the justice and mercy of God. We must trust what we cannot see. Job gets the vindication he desires when Yahweh declares that he has spoken what is right (42:7), but this vindication comes only after the purifying condemnation of his ignorance and presumption in chapters 38–41.[59] Job's vindication is accompanied by the rejection of Satan's accusations and the false conclusions of his friends, and through the condemnation of their ignorance the friends too might be saved (42:7–9). Job experiences the glory of God in a salvation that comes through judgment, and that is the central message of the book that bears his name.

3. The *Megilloth* (Small Scrolls): Song of Songs, Ruth, Lamentations, Ecclesiastes, Esther

3.1 The Megilloth *Book by Book*

The Song of Songs sings of the Davidic king who overcomes the alienation and distance between himself and his ideal bride to enjoy one flesh intimacy in a lush garden and in Zion. The Song hints at the renewal of Edenic bliss as Israel's anointed king, her messiah, overcomes the effects of the curse. God's glory in marital intimacy and joy are seen as the restoration comes through the judgment of banishment from Eden and the cursed difficulty between man and wife.

The book of Ruth depicts an effect of the curse on the land, a famine that results in a family from Bethlehem leaving the Land of Promise for the plains of Moab. Against Mosaic prescription, Israelite sons marry Moabite women, and in God's mysterious mercy Ruth the Moabitess is received into the community when widowed Naomi returns to the land. Though Perez was conceived of Judah and Tamar on the way to the threshing floor, Boaz's faithful dealing with Ruth at the threshing floor reverses the failure of his ancestor. The selfish actions of the kinsman redeemer nearer than Boaz recall the failures of Judah's sons, and Boaz takes Ruth to be his lawfully wedded wife. Yahweh overcomes the curse on childbearing that left Ruth with no children through ten years of marriage, condemning that curse as he has overcome the curse on the ground by visiting his people to give food after famine. As Yahweh reverses these outworkings of the curses on land and gender relations, he is also sustaining the line of descent from which the seed of the woman will arise to crush the head of the serpent.

[59] Cf. ibid., 53.

Through judgment salvation comes: Yahweh gives conception to Ruth; Boaz fathers Obed, who fathers Jesse, through whom David comes. Yahweh's glory shines in salvation through judgment in the book of Ruth.

The acrostic poems of Lamentations bewail the destruction of Jerusalem. In the first acrostic poem, Lady Zion, princess of the provinces, widowed and ruined, sighs her lamentation. In the second, Yahweh, the man of war, throws down his enemies—his own people! The perspective of the third poem is that of the man who has seen affliction, and it is almost as though this individual dies, only to rise from the dead at the remembrance of Yahweh's new morning mercy. The fourth poem sings the unexpected reversals that show God's glorious justice to the nations as he does what they would not have believed: visits his holy wrath on his chosen people. Through this judgment comes the certainty of Lamentations 5 that Yahweh will judge the enemies of his people and restore his own to himself, renewing them to enjoy his glory again.

Ecclesiastes comes to us as messianic wisdom. Written by the son of David, king in Jerusalem, the preacher teaches the circularity and vanity of life without God. This judgment is meant to lead the simple to salvation as they cease to live for anything but God. The positive message of the book is that while a godless pursuit of pleasure, wisdom, and toil are a grasping for the wind, the gift of God is the ability to eat, drink, and enjoy one's labor. Further, while people are ultimately unable to know fully what is best at all times, and while they cannot know the future, yet they can enjoy the gift of God—to eat, drink, and enjoy their labor in the fear of God and in obedience to his commands. In this way Ecclesiastes condemns vanity, and through that judgment those who learn from the messianic sage are delivered to live for God's glory, fearing God and enjoying his goodness.

In Esther the seed of the serpent, Haman, who descends from those Saul should have put under the ban, is at enmity with the seed of the woman, Mordecai, an exiled Jew whose only defense is an orphan girl he has taken into his care. Out of the mouths of babes and infants Yahweh establishes strength (cf. Ps. 8:3, ET 2). He uses the weak to bring down the strong. In God's providence Mordecai and Esther, like Joseph before them, are Jews raised to prominence in a foreign court. In a surprising reversal, against all expectation Haman is hanged on the gallows he has built for Mordecai, and Esther secures for the Jews the right to defend themselves. The seed of the woman crushes the serpent's head. Judged for covenant infidelity in exile, the Jewish people are saved through the judgment of their enemies for God's glory.

3.2 Song of Songs

The most sublime Song opens with the words, "The Song of Songs, which is Solomon's" (1:1), and then Solomon is named in the text six more times (1:5;

3:7, 9, 11; 8:11, 12). The son of David, heir to the promises of 2 Samuel 7, is then referred to as "king" five times in the Song (1:4, 12; 3:9, 11; 7:5; cf. 6:12). The Song is set in Jerusalem (1:5; 2:7; 3:5, 10; 5:8, 16; 6:4; 8:4), with reference also to Zion (3:11). In addition to the city of David, some of the scenes in the Song are set in the king's garden (2:12–13; 4:16–5:1; 6:2, 11). The Song sings of the ideal Israelite man—son of David, king in Jerusalem, "radiant and ruddy, distinguished among ten thousand" (5:10)—with his ideal wife (1:8; 4:7, 12; 6:8–9), and the two of them are reversing the effects of the fall as they recapture the intimacy of marriage in a lush garden. I would suggest that the literary structure of the Song can be depicted as shown in table 4.5.

Table 4.5. Literary Structure of the Song of Songs

1–2, Opening dialogues
- 3:1–6, Bride's dream?
  - 3:6–11, The beloved praises Solomon's arrival
    - 4:1–15, Solomon praises his beloved
      - 4:16–5:1, Consummation
- 5:2–8, Bride's dream?
  - 5:9–6:3, The beloved praises Solomon
    - 6:4–10, Solomon praises his beloved
      - 6:11–13, Back in the garden

7:1–8:14, Closing dialogues

Adam and Eve were naked with no shame (Gen. 2:25), but after they sinned, their alienation from one another led to their covering themselves (3:7) and evading blame, Adam by passing it to the woman, and the woman by passing it to the serpent (3:12–13). This culminated in the curse, in which God said to the woman, "Your desire [תשוקתך] will be for your husband, and he shall rule over you" (3:16).

The Song of Solomon shows the Solomonic king, who is seed of the woman, seed of Abraham, seed of Judah, seed of David, overcoming the alienation of the fall and renewing the intimacy of Eden.[60] One of the main features of the Song is the persistence of alienation between the man and the woman. This alienation is a result of the judgment announced in Genesis 3:16. The intimacy

[60]For a fuller development of these ideas, see my article, "The Messianic Music of the Song of Songs: A Non-Allegorical Interpretation," *WTJ* 68 (2006): 331–45. For a similar perspective, see Iain D. Campbell, "The Song of David's Son: Interpreting the Song of Solomon in the Light of the Davidic Covenant," *WTJ* 62 (2000): 17–32. I am grateful that Chad Knudson alerted me to this essay. F. Delitzsch also understood the Song as typical but not allegorical, seeing Solomon as a type of the one greater than Solomon, *Proverbs, Ecclesiastes, Song of Solomon*, in KD, 6:vii, 499–500.

lost at the fall (judgment) is renewed (salvation), and the beauty of God's intention is celebrated (glory). The king and his beloved are separated by the woman's insecurity about her appearance (Song 1:6), and the man overcomes this with his complimentary words (1:8–10). In response, the beloved exults in the glory of the relationship (1:12–14), which is compounded by the king's celebratory delight (1:15) and more of her own (1:16–2:1). Then the couple is separated by a wall (2:9), by distance (3:1–3), and by her unwillingness (5:2–3). In each case the separation is overcome, and it is usually at the king's initiative (an exception being 3:4, in which the female finds her beloved). The king bounds over the hills to woo his beloved into the springtime of love (2:8–17), he comes up from the wilderness arrayed in wedding splendor (3:6–11), and he puts myrrh on the lock (5:5).

His efforts toward the renewal of the intimacy lost at the fall culminate in the bride's statement in 7:10, "I am my beloved's, and his desire [תשוקתו] is for me." The use of this term "desire" in Genesis 3:16 was noted above. Yahweh cursed the woman with "desire" for her husband, which meant that she would inappropriately seek to take the initiative in the relationship. The Song sings the righting of reversed desire. The one who desires is the man, and it is he who takes proper initiative in the relationship. Overcoming the judgment of the curse on gender relations, the man and the woman find reconciliation and intimacy. Through the cursed land they travel to gardens, vineyards, and places of springtime fertility, renewing the intimacy of Eden. The joy of verdant fields, flocks, and fellow heirs in the grace of life redounds in the Song to the glory of God. The seed of the woman, son of David, king in Jerusalem, has overcome the curse and taken his loving wife to a lush garden. Here is an inspiring beauty. Through the judgment comes salvation to the praise of the good Creator.

3.3 Ruth

After Adam and Eve transgressed the commandment, Yahweh promised the serpent that the seed of the woman would crush his head, he promised the woman that childbearing would be painful, and he cursed the land (Gen. 3:15–17). These themes are prominent in Ruth, and as the triumphant seed of the woman crushing the head of the serpent points to salvation through judgment in Genesis 3:15, so the birth of a male child at the end of Ruth portends deliverance.[61]

The book opens with an outworking of the curse on the ground (Gen. 3:17): there is famine in the land (Ruth 1:1). This drives a family from Bethlehem into exile.[62] Driven out of the Edenic Promised Land, the Bethlehemites are afflicted with difficulties akin to those promised in Genesis 3:16—not merely

[61]House, *Old Testament Theology*, 455: "It describes the eventual joyous vindication of the faithful."
[62]Stephen G. Dempster, *Dominion and Dynasty: A Theology of the Hebrew Bible*, NSBT (Downers Grove, IL: InterVarsity, 2003), 191.

that childbearing is painful, but that it does not happen for ten years, and then the husbands die (1:2–5).

Yahweh visits the land (Ruth 1:6), and the afflicted widow Naomi returns with her widowed daughter-in-law, Ruth. The narrator relates that Ruth "happened" to find herself in Boaz's field (2:3). God is seen to be providentially directing these events, for Boaz "happens" to be a kinsman redeemer to Naomi's family (2:20).[63]

Yahweh does not owe mercy to Ruth the Moabitess; in fact, no Moabite was to enter the assembly of Yahweh to the tenth generation! (Deut. 23:3–4). As the events of the book of Ruth are guided by Yahweh's sovereign hand, he is showing mercy to Ruth: mercy she does not deserve, mercy she does not expect, mercy on which she has no claim, mercy that could have been directed to some other family in response to Naomi's claim that Yahweh has dealt bitterly with her (Ruth 1:20–21).

Ironically, in spite of what Naomi thinks, while the lack of children and the curse on the land indeed spring from the curses of Genesis 3, Yahweh is working even these difficulties together for good.[64] Through these judgments (the famine on the land that results in expulsion from the Edenic Land of Promise, which leads to the acquisition of Moabite wives, followed by the death of husbands and sons) Yahweh is preparing the way for Boaz and Ruth to be wed.

Boaz descends from Judah, from whom the scepter shall not depart (Gen. 49:10). And this Boaz takes to himself a Gentile bride, to whom Yahweh gives conception (Ruth 4:13). This reverses the curse on gender relations in Genesis 3:16 and moves in the direction of the blessing of all the nations through Abraham and his seed (Gen. 12:3).[65] The seed of the (Moabite) woman, Obed, fathers Jesse, who fathers David (4:21). From the strands of seemingly disparate and mundane events—a famine that leads to exile, ten years of barrenness, bereavement, the persistence of a Moabite girl, the field in which she happens to glean—Yahweh has woven a magnificent tapestry of mercy. The cloth of this tapestry is canonical fabric.[66] Boaz arrives as an unexpected redeemer from the line of Judah who righteously takes a Gentile bride through whom the seed is raised up. Salvation has come through the various judgments, and God's surprising providence wins him praise.[67]

[63]Cf. Timothy H. Lim, "The Book of Ruth and Its Literary Voice," in *Reflection and Refraction: Studies in Biblical Historiography in Honour of A. Graeme Auld*, ed. Robert Rezetko, Timothy H. Lim, and W. Brian Aucker, VTSup (Boston: Brill, 2007), 282.

[64]Barry G. Webb, *Five Festal Garments: Christian Reflections on the Song of Songs, Ruth, Lamentations, Ecclesiastes, and Esther*, NSBT (Downers Grove, IL: InterVarsity, 2000), 53, 57.

[65]Similarly Kirsten Nielsen, *Ruth*, OTL (Louisville: Westminster John Knox, 1997), 33.

[66]House, *Old Testament Theology*, 462: "It is hard to imagine a book so short doing more to maintain the faith of the whole canon."

[67]Philip R. Davies suggests that books such as Ruth and Esther were written "largely for pleasure" (*Scribes and Schools: The Canonization of the Hebrew Scriptures*, Library of Ancient Israel [Louisville: Westminster John Knox, 1998], 142). There is no doubt that these books are highly enjoyable, but they are enjoyable because they

3.4 Lamentations

Lamentations presents a poetic response to the destruction of Jerusalem. Barry Webb summarizes both the structure of Lamentations and what that structure accomplishes:

> Each of the five chapters contains one poem of twenty-two verses, except for chapter 3, which has sixty-six. The reason is that each of the poems is based, in one way or another, on the Hebrew alphabet with its twenty-two consonants. . . . The acrostic form of the poems has the effect of giving grief a shape which is itself a kind of resolution. . . . The acrostic form . . . allow[s] the grief to be fully expressed, and yet at the same time sets limits to it.[68]

Lamentations finds its setting only in the context of the wider canon: "The historical narratives of 2 Kings 25 and Jeremiah 52 give the facts; the five poems of Lamentations capture the emotions."[69] The first chapter of Lamentations bewails the ruin of Lady Zion. The city is personified and depicted as a degraded widow (Lam. 1:1) with "none to comfort her" (1:2, 9, 17, 21). In fulfillment of the curse announced in Deuteronomy 28:44, Israel's enemies have become the head, with the implication that Israel is the tail (Lam. 1:5; cf. Deut. 28:13, "Yahweh will make you the head and not the tail"). Just as Isaiah promised, the Lord has come in judgment and trod the wicked in the winepress of his wrath (Lam. 1:15; cf. Isa. 63:2–3). Weeping without comfort (Lam. 1:16–17), still Zion makes the good confession, "Yahweh, he is righteous, for I rebelled . . ." (1:18). The judgments promised in the Law and the Prophets have been fulfilled because Israel has rebelled against Yahweh's word (1:18). In these judgments, Yahweh has displayed his holiness in that he is utterly devoted to his own character, which sets him apart from everything else in existence. The other side of this coin is that Yahweh simultaneously displays his love for himself as he chooses to keep his word and demonstrate his justice rather than give Israel a pass. By upholding justice, Yahweh shows his love. By loving himself, Yahweh does justice. His commitment to his own love and justice takes precedence over his affection for Israel.

The point of view in Lamentations 2 is not that of widow Zion. The poet distances himself somewhat from the pain of the people to describe the actions of Yahweh against Israel. This steadfastly precludes the notion that Yahweh has been overcome by the gods of the nations that routed Israel and asserts instead that it is Yahweh who has used the nations to discipline his wayward people. Yahweh's love for his own holiness is seen to outrank his commitment to Israel;

present typological history that has profound theological ramifications. The enjoyment to be found in these books is not mere literary "entertainment" but knowing the God they reveal.

[68] Webb, *Five Festal Garments*, 60–61.

[69] J. R. Soza, "Lamentations," in *NDBT*, 227.

the poet describes him casting down the beauty of Israel from heaven to earth and not remembering his footstool (Lam. 2:1). Perhaps recalling the way that Yahweh preferred to uphold his holiness rather than allow Adam and Eve to defile Eden in their sinful state, "he did violence to his booth like the garden, he destroyed his meeting place" (2:6). He spurned his altar, abandoned the sanctuary, and broke down the walls of Zion, and the gates sank into the ground (2:7–9). As the nations triumph over Zion (2:16), again the poet makes the good confession: "Yahweh has done what he purposed; he has carried out his word which he commanded from ancient days" (2:17).

In spite of the judgment that has been visited, the poet clings to hope. This hope is reflected in the prayers for mercy that we see in Lamentations 1–2 (1:9, 11, 20–22; 2:20–22). Several of these prayers cry out, "See, O Yahweh . . . ! [ראה יהוה]" (1:9, 11, 20; 2:20), and in 1:11 and 2:20 the cry is "See, O Yahweh, and consider! [ראה יהוה והביטה]." The prophets announced that Yahweh would use a foreign nation to discipline his people, but the rod of discipline in Yahweh's hand—the wicked foreign nation—would also receive its due punishment (e.g., Isa. 10:5–19; Hab. 1:5–2:20). On this basis, the poet pleads, "You have brought the day you announced; now let them be as I am. Let all their evil come before you, and deal with them as you have dealt with me" (Lam. 2:21c–22b). This prayer later modulates into an assertion of Yahweh's certain justice against the enemies of his people in 3:55–66. The poet of Lamentations recognizes that Yahweh has been faithful to his word, and on the basis of his word Yahweh has judged Israel. Yahweh's faithfulness encourages the poet to cry out to Yahweh to continue to be faithful to his word by judging the enemies of Israel.

In Lamentations 1 the poet has mourned the bereavement of Lady Zion, in chapter 2 he has declared Yahweh's mighty overthrow of Zion, and in chapter 3 the poet speaks of the fall of Jerusalem in the first person singular: "I am the man who has seen affliction." Chapter 1 describes the devastation of Zion in terms that would befit the affliction and bereavement of a noble lady. Chapter 2 describes Yahweh as a righteous Judge punishing the sin of Israel. In chapter 3 the poet speaks as though the judgments of Yahweh have been visited against his own body (Lam. 3:1–20).

Hope dawns in Lamentations 3:21. In the midst of the blackest darkness, the poet sings:

> But this I bring back to my heart,
>   and therefore I have hope:
> the loving kindnesses of Yahweh never cease;
>   his mercies never come to an end;
> they are new every morning;
>   great is your faithfulness.

"My portion is Yahweh," says my soul,
 "therefore I will hope in him."
Yahweh is good to those who wait for him,
 to the soul who seeks him.
It is good that one should wait quietly
 for the salvation of Yahweh. (Lam. 3:21–26 ESV adapted)

With priests and prophets slain in the temple, with women having eaten their own children (2:20), even still, the steadfast love, the mercy, and the faithfulness of Yahweh inspire hope. There is no God but Yahweh. He has not failed to protect Israel. He has justly punished her transgression, and this the poet affirms with the words, "Who is this who speaks and it comes to pass? The Lord, did he not command? Does it not come from the mouth of the Most High, the evil and the good?" (3:37–38). If Yahweh is the only God, there is not some other power who might be ordaining what comes to pass. The woe that has come upon Jerusalem represents not some other deity's triumph over Yahweh but his covenantal discipline of his people.[70] Even this sparks hope. Again the poet confesses the righteousness of Yahweh against Israel's sin (3:39–42), and again the poet hopes that Yahweh will see the plight of his people (3:50).

The first half of Lamentations 4 explores how the judgment of Yahweh has taken things from one extreme to the other: gold has become dim and precious stones are scattered in the street (Lam. 4:1); precious sons have become worthless as clay pots (4:2); tender mothers behave cruelly to their young (4:3–4); those accustomed to fine things embrace dust and ashes in the street (4:5); the extended punishment of Zion is worse than the sudden overthrow of Sodom (4:6); glorious Nazirites have become sullied and emaciated (4:7–8); death by the sword is preferred to surviving only to starve (4:9); compassionate mothers have cannibalized their own children (4:10).

Could it be worse? Could people suffer greater humiliation? Could there be further dehumanization? These judgments are in direct proportion to the greatness of Yahweh, whose glory has been defiled by Israel's wickedness.

The connection between the humiliation of Zion for her sin and the exaltation of Yahweh's righteousness is established in the second half of Lamentations 4, where the poet explains that by punishing Israel Yahweh vindicates his holiness in the eyes of the nations. Restating the ferocity of Yahweh's wrath against Zion, the poet asserts, "They would not have believed—the kings of the earth and all the inhabitants of the world—that the enemy and adversary could enter in the gates of Jerusalem" (Lam. 4:12). Yahweh judges Jerusalem to show the nations that he supremely loves his holiness, and his character will not be altered by his affection for his people.

[70]See Webb, *Five Festal Garments*, 64–65.

With the punishment of Israel accomplished (Lam. 4:22), the poet calls on Yahweh's mercy (5:1–22). The poet of Lamentations has throughout asserted the glory of Yahweh's righteousness in the justice done to Israel, and through the judgment he expects salvation to come for Yahweh's glory. In keeping with the prophecy of Moses regarding Israel's future (Deut. 4:25–31), the poet calls on Yahweh to turn his people back to himself that they might be restored and renewed (Lam. 5:21). The concluding statement (5:22) assumes that God has not rejected his people, and it calls on him to be faithful to his promises to restore Israel after judgment.

Lamentations bewails the awful but just wrath of God. The unimaginable horrors of the judgment that has fallen, mothers eating their own children, virgin daughters raped (Lam. 5:11), choice young men strung up by their hands (5:12), demand the recognition that God must be worthy of infinite glory to exact such punishment. The glimmers of hope in the midst of the pain arise from the certainty of the mercy of Yahweh, mercy that is new every morning (3:23). Yahweh's sovereign power in the display of his justice, and his faithful, steadfast love, reveal his glory. In Lamentations, God is glorified in salvation through judgment, for Yahweh reigns forever, and his throne endures to all generations (Lam. 5:19).

3.5 *Ecclesiastes*

Addison G. Wright has unlocked the riddle of the literary structure of Ecclesiastes, and this discussion adapts and applies his work.[71] Understanding the book's literary structure allows one to see the positive message of Ecclesiastes. At the center of the theology of that positive message is the notion that God is glorified in salvation through judgment.

3.5.1 The Riddle of the Numbers

Ecclesiastes contains exactly 222 poetic verses, and the verse numbering we find in the book today is in basic agreement with these poetic lines. The book divides evenly into two halves of 111 verses. There are 111 verses from Ecclesiastes 1:1 to 6:9, and another 111 from Ecclesiastes 6:10 to 12:14. This structure is neither accidental nor artificial. It reflects the work of a beautiful mind. The number 111 is not insignificant. The numerical value of the consonants in the book's key word,

---

[71]Addison G. Wright, "The Riddle of the Sphinx: The Structure of the Book of Qoheleth," *CBQ* 30 (1968): 313–34; Wright, "The Riddle of the Sphinx Revisited: Numerical Patterns in the Book of Qoheleth," *CBQ* 42 (1980): 38–51; and Wright, "Additional Numerical Patterns in Qoheleth," *CBQ* 45 (1983): 32–43. In my view Tremper Longman III (*The Book of Ecclesiastes*, NICOT [Grand Rapids: Eerdmans, 1998], 21 n. 76) unconvincingly sets aside Wright's proposal. I also find Wright's proposal more compelling than that of Stephan de Jong, "A Book on Labour: The Structuring Principles and the Main Theme of the Book of Qohelet," *JSOT* 54 (1992): 107–16. De Jong argues that the book's main theme is labor. As will be seen below, I would add to this that godless labor is condemned so that people can enjoy the deliverance of enjoying their work, which is God's gift, and in this salvation through judgment God will be glorified.

הבל, "vanity/meaningless," is thirty-seven.[72] Thirty-seven multiplied by three is 111. This term occurs three times in the singular in Ecclesiastes 1:2, as though it is a hint for the audience to triple the word's numerical value, and it occurs exactly thirty-seven times in the book, surely another hint at the significance of these numbers for the book's structure.[73] The three instances of the term in 1:2 and the thirty-seven instances of it through the book confirm that the book has been structured on the numerical value of הבל: thirty-seven, tripled to equal 111, matching the two halves of the book, each 111 verses long.[74]

3.5.2 *The Messianic Wisdom of a Beautiful Mind*

Several features of the book add up to the almost unavoidable conclusion that Ecclesiastes was written by Solomon. The author identifies himself as "the son of David, king in Jerusalem" (Eccles. 1:1, 12), asserts that he gained more wisdom than all who came before him (1:16), and points to his building projects and amassed wealth to prove that he excelled all who were before him in Jerusalem (2:4–9). Either Solomon is the author of the book of Ecclesiastes, or someone is deceptively trying to convince the book's audience that Solomon wrote it.[75] As it seems to be historically implausible that the Israelites would have either accepted a forgery or been duped on such an important point, the most plausible explanation is that Ecclesiastes was indeed written by Solomon, whom the Old Testament elsewhere shows to have been the recipient of a gift of divine wisdom from Yahweh (1 Kings 3:4–14; 4:29–34). Solomonic authorship

---

[72]The Old Greek (LXX) translator rendered הבל with the term ματαιότης, while Aquila, Theodotion, and Symmachus employed ἀτμός or ἀτμίς instead. For the evidence, see Phillip Samuel Marshall, "A Critical Edition of the Hexaplaric Fragments of Ecclesiastes" (PhD diss., Louisville: The Southern Baptist Theological Seminary, 2007), 32–35.

[73]If we include the textually suspect instance in Eccles. 9:9, the total number of times the term occurs in the book is thirty-eight. On the basis of this internal evidence, it seems to me that the ESV and the NASB are right to leave it out of their translations, while the HCSB, NIV, and the NKJV are wrong to include it.

[74]Cf. Wright, "The Riddle of the Sphinx Revisited," 47: "The conclusion is ineluctable that the units which we call verses are original to the book, that the author and editor were counting them and constructing the text on numerical patterns and that Qoheleth announced his patterns in the inclusion in 1:2 and 12:8."

[75]I base this assertion on the progression from 1:1, "The words of the Preacher . . . ," to 1:2, ". . . says the Preacher . . . ," to 1:12, "I the Preacher . . ." The switch back to the third person at 12:9, ". . . the Preacher also taught . . ." is like the third person reference at 1:1, but then there is a switch back to the first person at 12:12, "My son, beware . . ." In view of the numerical precision of the book's 222 verses, the most natural conclusion is that the whole book comes from one author who has referred to himself in the third person in some places. If these third person references did come from an editor, in order for the book's numerical precision to be achieved it would seem that the mind behind the book's literary structure must have given detailed oversight to this editorial work so that his design would not be violated. In view of this strict limitation of his freedom, the activity of this hypothetical editor seems hardly worth discussing. Thus, either Solomon was the king, the son of David, who described himself as the preacher and wrote this book of Ecclesiastes, or someone else sought to lead the audience to that conclusion. Unless historical information comes to light on some king in Israel who better fits the description found in Ecclesiastes, and unless it can be shown that the first audience of Ecclesiastes would have thought of this hypothetical king rather than Solomon, if someone other than Solomon wrote Ecclesiastes, it would seem that he intended to deceive his audience. When we consider the book's place in the canon, it does not seem likely that those who recognized Ecclesiastes as canonical would have been deceived, nor would they have recognized a book they knew to be deceptive. Rightly Garrett, *Proverbs, Ecclesiastes, Song of Songs*, 262–64. For a different perspective, see Michael A. Eaton, *Ecclesiastes*, TOTC (Downers Grove, IL: InterVarsity, 1983), 22–24; Tremper Longman III and Raymond B. Dillard, *An Introduction to the Old Testament*, 2nd ed. (Grand Rapids: Zondervan, 2006), 281–82.

of Ecclesiastes is significant because it means that the author of this book was the anointed king of Israel. In this sense, the author of Ecclesiastes was Israel's messiah. Ecclesiastes, then, is messianic wisdom, and by means of this messianic wisdom Solomon means to "shepherd" his people Israel (cf. 12:11). The attribution of the book to the seed of David (cf. 2 Samuel 7) in Ecclesiastes 1:1 and the reference to the "shepherd" in 12:11 mean that the teaching of Ecclesiastes is bracketed by these statements that present the book as messianic instruction.[76]

3.5.3 Matching Poems on the "Circle of Life" and "Youth and Old Age" (Eccles. 1:2–11; 11:7–12:8)

Immediately following the attribution of the book to the son of David is a poem on the circularity of life in Ecclesiastes 1:2–11. Immediately preceding the concluding statement in 12:9–14 is a poem on youth and old age in 11:7–12:8.

These two poems are in their own ways words of judgment meant to lead to salvation for God's glory. The pronouncement of the vanity of the circularity of life in the first (Eccles. 1:2–11) prompts reflection on what is meaningful. So also the poem on youth and old age in the second (11:7–12:8). Young men should enjoy themselves, but only in a way that recognizes that God is going to judge what they enjoy (11:9). And the vivid description of aging and dying (12:2–7), judgments in themselves, motivates the call to "remember also your Creator in the days of your youth" (12:1 ESV). The preacher seeks to deliver his audience through the condemnation of their vanity and the things they will regret as they age and die. Through judgment he wants to save them to enjoy God's glory.[77]

Between the opening (Eccles. 1:1) and closing (12:9–14) and the two poems (1:2–11 and 11:7–12:8) we find two main bodies of teaching. The first, 1:12–6:9, examines what is good for man to do. The second, 6:10–11:6, teaches man's inability to understand God's work. Each section uses punctuating phrases to

---

[76]Nicholas Perrin's essay "Messianism in the Narrative Frame of Ecclesiastes?" *Revue Biblique* 108 (2001): 37–60 drew my attention to these connections, but in my view he has seriously misunderstood the relationship between Ecclesiastes and later messianic wisdom. Perrin seems to think that Ecclesiastes comes from the same milieu as *Psalms of Solomon* (cf. 42–43). It seems far more plausible to me that Ecclesiastes generated the later concepts seen in texts such as *Psalms of Solomon*. Perrin writes, "Significant thematic connections exist between Eccl 1:1 and other messianic descriptions of the period, particularly as found in the *Psalms of Solomon*" (38). He goes on to state that "even if C. F. Whitley overstates his case in assigning Ecclesiastes to a date of 152–145 BCE, he may be not more than decades off the mark. Most likely, however, the body of this book was written in the second half of the third century, the later Ptolemaic era" (39). These assertions seem difficult to maintain in light of the historical evidence from Qumran, where we have manuscript evidence on Ecclesiastes, and from the Greek translations of the Old Testament, which include Ecclesiastes. The editors of *The Dead Sea Scrolls Bible* write, "4QQoh[a] is among the oldest manuscripts at Qumran, dating from about 175–150 BCE" (*The Dead Sea Scrolls Bible*, trans. and ed. Martin Abegg Jr., Peter Flint, and Eugene Ulrich [San Francisco: HarperSanFrancisco, 1999], 619). For a study of the text history of LXX Ecclesiastes, see Peter J. Gentry, "'The Role of the "Three" in the Text History of the Septuagint': II. Aspects of Interdependence of the Old Greek and the Three in Ecclesiastes," *Aramaic Studies* 4 (2006): 153–92.

[77]Similarly Eaton, *Ecclesiastes*, 48: "The Preacher wishes to deliver us from a rosy-coloured, self-confident godless life. . . . He wishes to drive us to see that God is there . . . and that only such an outlook makes life coherent and fulfilling."

mark the end of sections within these two main bodies of teaching. We will consider them each in turn.

3.5.4 What Is Good for Man to Do? (Eccles. 1:12–6:9)

The punctuating phrase in Ecclesiastes 1:12–6:9 is the verdict that a thing is "a striving after wind." There is a double introduction in 1:12–18. Both units conclude with a proverb (1:15, 18), and the phrase "striving after wind" immediately precedes these two proverbs (1:14, 17). Both of these statements highlight man's finitude and affliction.

Wright seems to be correct that Solomon's chief concern in this first main section of the book is stated in Ecclesiastes 2:3b, "till I might see what was good for the children of man to do under heaven during the few days of their life" (ESV).[78] This statement comes in the introduction to the preacher's description of his testing of himself with pleasure (Eccles. 2:1–11). Having described the lengths to which he went to gratify himself, he concludes that "all was vanity and a striving after wind" (2:11).

Having tested pleasure, the preacher turns to consider wisdom (Eccles. 2:12–17). Here too he concludes that "all is vanity and a striving after wind" (2:17).

It shortly becomes clear that pleasure and wisdom *apart from the pleasure of God* are "vanity and grasping for the wind." This reality comes into view as Solomon devotes the remainder of this part of his book to four sections on the results of toil.[79] These four sections are each concluded with the verdict that what has been considered is "vanity and a striving after wind" (Eccles. 2:26; 4:4–6, 16; 6:9). There are two short sections and two long sections, and they alternate, short, long, short, long. The first short section (2:18–26) treats the problem that the fruit of one's toil will be left to another. The second section (3:1–4:6), a long one, explores the question of timing. There is a time for everything, and as one toils away at life, it is difficult to hit on the right time to act. The third section is short (4:7–16), and here the preacher discusses the problems of solitary toil. It is not good for the man to be alone (Gen. 2:18). The last section of the first half of the book is again long (Eccles. 4:17–6:9, ET 5:1–6:9), and here the problem of having and enjoying the fruits of one's toil is considered.[80]

As the verdict that all this is "vanity and a striving after wind" is reiterated at the end of each of these four sections, the preacher does give a positive answer to the question of what is good for man to do (Eccles. 2:3b). Three times Solomon states that there is nothing "better"—and "better" in Hebrew is simply a comparative usage of the word "good," for which goodness Solomon is

[78]Wright, "The Riddle of the Sphinx Revisited," 38.
[79]See the many noun and verb forms of עמל, "toil/labor" in this section: 2:18 (2x), 19 (2x), 20 (2x), 21 (2x), 22, 24; 3:9, 13; 4:4, 6, 8 (2x), 9; 5:14 (ET 15), 15 (ET 16), 17 (2x, ET 18), 18 (ET 19); 6:7.
[80]Wright, "The Riddle of the Sphinx," 320–29.

searching—than for man to eat and drink and enjoy his labor, which is a gift of God (the ESV is cited in the following texts, and I have italicized the statements common to each text):

> There is *nothing better* for a person than that he should *eat and drink* and *find enjoyment in his toil*. This also, I saw, is *from the hand of God*, for *apart from him who can eat or who can have enjoyment*? (2:24–25)

> I perceived that there is *nothing better* for them than to be joyful and to do good as long as they live; also that everyone should *eat and drink* and *take pleasure in all his toil*—this is *God's gift* to man. (3:12–13; cf. also 3:22)

> Behold, what I have seen to be *good* and fitting is to *eat and drink* and *find enjoyment in all the toil* with which one toils under the sun the few days of his life that *God has given him*, for this is *his lot*. Everyone also to whom *God has given* wealth and possessions and *power to enjoy them*, and to accept *his lot* and *rejoice in his toil—this is the gift of God*. (5:18–19)

These positive statements clarify that the preacher is teaching his people how to deal with the frustrations of life outside Eden. In the pain and sorrow of this world, "What is crooked cannot be made straight, and what is lacking cannot be counted" (Eccles. 1:15). Increasing wisdom only increases pain (1:18), and all is vanity and a striving after the wind. In response to these realities, people should enjoy what they have. They should eat and drink and enjoy their work. The ability to do so is the gift of God. God does not give everyone this ability to enjoy provisions and labors (2:26; 6:2).

Through the judgment of discontentment and unrealistic expectations, the preacher delivers his audience to enjoy what God has given them.

3.5.5 Man's Inability to Understand God's Work (Eccles. 6:10–11:6)

Two questions dominate the discussion in the second main body of the preacher's teaching, and these two questions are both asked in Ecclesiastes 6:12: "For who knows what is good for man while he lives the few days of his vain life, which he passes like a shadow? For who can tell man what will be after him under the sun?"

The first question, "who knows what is good for man?" is explored in Ecclesiastes 7:1–8:17 (cf. the statements in 7:14, 24, 28–29 about what can or cannot be found). Just as punctuating phrases closed the sections in the first half of the book, punctuating phrases close these two main sections in its second half. In this case the punctuating phrase is a threefold repetition of the idea that the work of God is past all finding out (8:17). The exact wording of these three phrases is structured in an A-B-A pattern as follows:

A ". . . man is not able to find out . . ."

B ". . . he will not find . . ."

A′ ". . . not able to find out . . ."

While this section clearly stresses humanity's inability to find the good in the mysterious working of God, the positive conclusion seen in the first half of the book is restated: "And I commend joy, because there is *nothing better* for man under the sun but to *eat and drink* and *be joyful*, for this will go with him *in his toil* through the days of his life that *God has given* him under the sun" (Eccles. 8:15, emphasis added). Once again we see the book's positive stress: in the face of human inability to comprehend life's mysteries and pains, God gives men the ability to eat and drink and enjoy their labor.

The second question in Ecclesiastes 6:12, "who can tell man what will be after him?" is exposited in 9:1–11:6 (cf. the statements about what cannot be known in 9:1, 5, 10, 12; 10:14, 15; 11:2). Once again there is a threefold repetition of the punctuating phrase of this section in 11:5–6, and once again there is an A-B-A pattern in the statements of what cannot be known:

A "Just as there is not in you the knowing what . . ."

B "thus you will not know . . ."

A′ "because there is not in you the knowing whether . . ."

Again, while this section stresses humanity's inability to attain full and future knowledge, the book's positive conclusion is reinforced:

> Go, *eat* your bread *in joy*, and *drink* your wine *with a merry heart*, for *God* has already approved what you do. . . . *Enjoy life* with the wife whom you love, all the days of your vain life that *he has given* you under the sun, because *that is your portion in life and in your toil* at which you toil under the sun. (Eccles. 9:7, 9 ESV, emphasis added)

It would seem that Ecclesiastes is teaching that in the midst of the limitations that God has placed on human ability and knowledge, he has nevertheless given to those in whom he delights (2:26) the ability to enjoy their eating and drinking and laboring.[81] The preacher seeks to deliver his audience to this happiness through his judgment on vain pursuits. Ecclesiastes teaches people to be saved through judgment for God's glory.

[81]While I do not quote him directly, this whole section is deeply indebted to Addison G. Wright's three essays cited above.

3.5.6 All Has Been Heard: The Conclusion of the Matter (Eccles. 12:9–14)

Working backward from the last statement made in this section, my argument is that the preacher is seeking to be the agent of salvation through judgment for those who will heed his teaching. Ecclesiastes 12:14 announces that God will judge. The knowledge of this judgment is intended to ground the saving exercise of wisdom commended in 12:13: "Fear God and keep his commandments." The final word to "my son" in 12:12 reinforces the impression that Solomon is obeying Deuteronomy 6 and 17 (see, earlier in this chapter, §1.2 and §2.3). Verse 11 announces that this book is intended to function like a goad, pricking the conscience with the knowledge of coming judgment so that salvation might be experienced. Moreover, it is the shepherd who uses this goad, and as the agent of Yahweh, the messiah who does the instructing is Yahweh's agent of salvation through judgment. The preacher's hard work on the book is hinted at in 12:10, his pondering and setting wisdom in order in 12:9.

The salvation through judgment for God's glory taught in Ecclesiastes can thus be seen to have a chiastic shape (see table 4.6).

Table 4.6. The Chiastic Structure of Ecclesiastes

1:1: The messianic wisdom of the son of David

  1:2–11: The circularity of life

    1:12–6:9: Pleasure, wisdom, and toil are a grasping for wind, but the gift of God is to eat, drink, and enjoy your labor.

    6:10–11:6: Man is unable to understand God's work by finding what is good or knowing what will be, but the gift of God is to eat, drink, and enjoy your labor.

  11:7–12:8: Youth and old age

12:9–14: The messianic wisdom of the one shepherd: fear God and keep his commandments.

3.5.7 The Center of the Theology of Ecclesiastes

The message of Ecclesiastes is that Yahweh is behind the puzzling questions of life, accomplishing his purposes through its enigmas: "Whatever God does endures forever; nothing can be added to it, nor anything taken from it. God has done it, so that people fear before him" (Eccles. 3:14; cf. 2:26). God has appointed a time for all things (3:1–8), and people will be satisfied only when they accept the lot assigned to them by God: "Behold, what I have seen to be good and fitting is to eat and drink and find enjoyment in all the toil with which one toils under the sun the few days of his life that God has given him, for this is his lot" (5:18, cf. 19–20). There is inscrutable mystery in what God has done,[82] which should prompt people to humility (4:16–5:1, ET 5:1–2), silence (5:2, ET 3), integrity (5:3, ET 4), holiness (5:4–5, ET 5–6), and the fear of God (5:6, ET 7).[83]

Those who do not fear God will not be satisfied by anything (6:1–6). Apart from the awareness that God will bring all to judgment (11:9), which is remembrance of the Creator (12:1), there is no satisfaction to be found in wisdom (1:17), construction projects (2:4), gardens (2:5), irrigation (2:6), slaves (2:7), treasures, entertainers, concubines (2:8), toil (2:18–23), oppressions, death, skill (4:1–4), solitude (4:7–8), unmerited exaltation to kingship (4:13–16), or money (5:9–16, ET 10–17). According to the one whose wisdom surpasses all in Jerusalem before him (1:16), the son of David (1:1), who is shepherd king in Jerusalem (1:1; 12:11), the "end of the matter" is to "fear God and keep his commandments, for this is the whole duty of man. For God will bring every deed into judgment, with every secret thing, whether good or evil" (12:13–14; cf. 3:17). Like Proverbs, Ecclesiastes is a Solomonic attempt to obey Deuteronomy 6 and 17.

Ecclesiastes announces the vanity of the pursuit of pleasure divorced from the knowledge of God. Life is vain unless one lives for God. This is a condemnation, a judgment, of godless living. People who do not fear God and live for him are condemned to vain lives, and along with this the audience of Ecclesiastes is taught that God will bring all things to final judgment (3:17; 12:14). Satisfaction under the sun and salvation at the final judgment depend upon fearing God and obeying his commandments (12:13). Salvation comes to those who heed the announcement of present vanity and coming judgment. Further, by showing the centrality of God in all of life, asserting that only in knowing God will any human have shalom, Solomon teaches the massive significance of God for human life.[84] This glorifies God in salvation through judgment.

3.6 Esther

To this point in the Writings, we have enjoyed poetic commentary on the narrative story line that began in Genesis and continued through Kings (ca. 586 BC). When we arrive at Esther, we resume the narrative story line, which continues through Daniel (ca. 605–530 BC), Ezra–Nehemiah (ca. 458–434 BC), and Chronicles. As we resume the story in Esther, Israel is in exile with some of the

---

[82]Eccles. 7:13–14, "Consider the work of God: who can make straight what he has made crooked? In the day of prosperity be joyful, and in the day of adversity consider: God has made the one as well as the other, so that man may not find out anything that will be after him." Cf. 8:17; 11:5.

[83]Compare the similar conclusion of C. L. Seow, *Ecclesiastes*, AB (New York: Doubleday, 1997), 59–60: "This is why Qohelet says that everything is *hebel*. He does not mean that everything is meaningless or insignificant, but that everything is beyond human apprehension and comprehension." So also Bartholomew, "A God for Life," 52.

[84]Note also the connections Garrett (*Proverbs, Ecclesiastes, Song of Songs*, 278–79) draws between Ecclesiastes and Genesis 1–3: in Ecclesiastes humanity is subjected to toil and condemned to death; God is absent, and the loss of his presence results from the fall; the word rendered "meaningless" may be a play on Abel's name, as both are written הבל; and Ecclesiastes reflects on what has become of man, אדם, and how then he should now live.

people trickling back to the land. The events described in Esther (ca. 483–474 BC) are set in Persia.

When we commence our reading of Esther, we find the Torah's true story functioning as the controlling framework for the events that are being described.[85] The truth of Torah not only affects Israel, but holds sway everywhere. For instance, in spite of all the wealth and splendor of a fabulous 180-day feast (Est. 1:3–4), capped off by another seven-day feast (1:5), the king of Persia cannot escape the curses announced in Genesis 3:14–19.[86] When Ahasuerus summons Vashti, she rejects his request (Est. 1:12), as a result of which he banishes her from his presence (1:19). Vashti's desire is for her husband, but he rules over her (Gen. 3:16). Vashti's rebellion sets off a desperate counsel among the king's advisors. They seek to quell an anticipated outbreak of female insubordination, but apart from God's grace there is no stopping human evil. Ahasuerus's attempt to overcome the curse only fulfills the other side of it, as his reaction to his wife's insubordination is excessively harsh and compounds his own sinful culpability. This is not the way back to Edenic harmony between man and wife. Through the outworking of this judgment, however, God is secretly working salvation, for it is through the judgment played out between Vashti and Ahasuerus that the seed of the woman, Esther, rises to crush the head of the seed of the serpent, Haman.[87] God's ways are past finding out. Though he is never explicitly named, in the book of Esther, God is glorified in salvation through judgment.

This way of viewing the book of Esther allows us to regard Esther's willingness to go to Ahasuerus's bed not as an act of "questionable morality,"[88] but as one that actually works to overcome the curse of Genesis 3:16. Moreover, we do not read that Esther volunteers for a beauty pageant but that she "was taken" (Est. 2:8).[89] It seems her choice is either to obey Mordecai and submit to the authorities or resist and be shamed and ruined. Faced with these circumstances, she behaves obediently and submissively (note her obedience to Mordecai, 2:20; 4:13–5:3). Unlike Vashti, who conducts herself like a cursed woman, Esther behaves like a woman in whom the curse has been reversed. It seems to be precisely her submissive femininity—expressed in the note that she did exactly as

[85]The apocalyptic imagery in the Greek translations of the book seems to reflect this perspective. See the additions to Esther 1:1d–j (in NETS, A:4–10, dream, thunder, earthquake, dragons, cry to God, a great river of deliverance, cf. Rev. 12:1–6; 13–17) and the interpretation in additions to Esther 10:3a–i (in NETS, F:1–9, the river is Esther; the dragons are Haman and Mordecai).

[86]The author of Esther seems far more interested in recounting God's secret work on behalf of his people from the perspective of the Bible's view of the world than in being "primarily concerned with telling an interesting and lively story which would provide the 'historical' basis for the festival of Purim" (so Carey A. Moore, *Esther*, AB [Garden City: Doubleday, 1971], liii). Moreover, the author of Esther presents Purim as the result of what happens in his narrative rather than his narrative as the result of Purim.

[87]Dempster, *Dominion and Dynasty*, 223.

[88]As Webb interprets it, *Five Festal Garments*, 120.

[89]This also weighs against Peter J. Leithart's suggestion that Mordecai puts Esther forward and tells her to conceal her identity from a desire to gain power (*A House for My Name: A Survey of the Old Testament* [Moscow, ID: Canon, 2000], 226).

she was advised (Est. 2:15)—that wins the king's favor. In contrast to Vashti's refusal to submit, Esther's feminine virtue in submitting to the desires of her husband so powerfully affects the king that he makes her queen, gives a great feast and many generous gifts, and remits taxes (2:17–18). Esther overcomes the curse of Genesis 3:16 by submitting to the desires of her husband-king, and as a result the curses are also reversed in Ahasuerus. Instead of abusively ruling he becomes the beneficent protector not only of Esther but also of all her people (Esther 7–8). The circumstances may not be ideal, but this is a broken world, a world that God has judged (Rom. 8:20), in which God is glorified as he works salvation through those who lay down their lives on behalf of others (cf. Est. 4:16, "if I perish, I perish").

Another charge has been leveled against the conduct of Esther and Mordecai, to the effect that "when they finally have the power to do so, they act with a vindictiveness and cruelty that are not far removed from those of Haman himself."[90] This conclusion fails to see the crushing of the serpent's head in the defeat of the enemies of Israel. This is not vindictiveness and cruelty. It is just judgment for the greatest crime in the universe: refusing to honor God and give thanks to him and making war on his people.[91] The center of the theology of Esther is that God glorifies himself by saving his people through the judgment visited upon their enemies. He is worthy of all praise.

4. Other Sacred Writings: Daniel, Ezra–Nehemiah, Chronicles

The primary history of Genesis through Kings began in a garden, from which Adam was exiled. Eventually the nation of Israel came on the stage as a new "son of God," a sort of "new Adam" with a chance to dwell in God's presence and serve him. Like Adam, Israel was exiled from the "new Eden" of the Promised Land.

Having worked through the Torah and the Former Prophets in this primary history, we surveyed the Latter Prophets, which begin the poetic commentary on the primary history. The basic message of Isaiah through the Twelve is that Israel has broken the covenant God made with them at Sinai. God will be just and keep his word, and the promised curse is that Israel will go into exile. In keeping with what Moses prophesied, however (e.g., Deut. 4:25–31), in exile Israel will seek Yahweh. Through the judgment of exile, Yahweh will save his people with a new exodus and a return from exile. The future will be magnificent: it holds a new exodus, a new covenant, a new David, and a return from exile to dwell in God's presence in a new Eden.

[90]Webb, *Five Festal Garments*, 129.

[91]*Contra* the appeal to self defense and a "wish-fulfilling message of traditional narrative" that arises from the "folktale quality of the work" (so Susan Niditch, "Legends of Wise Heroes and Heroines," in *The Hebrew Bible and Its Modern Interpreters*, ed. Douglas A. Knight and Gene M. Tucker [Atlanta: Scholars, 1985], 450).

As I have interpreted the Psalms, the Psalter tells the same story sung in the Latter Prophets. The Psalms trace the line of David down to exile (Psalms 1–89), reflect on Yahweh's promises and the Torah of Moses in exile (Psalms 90–106), and look for restoration (Psalms 107–50) led by a new David who will sit at God's right hand with all his enemies under his feet (Psalm 110). As we come now to the book of Daniel, we return to historical narrative.[92] The poetic commentary has come to an end, and these other books narrate Israel's experience in exile and on the way back to the land.

Daniel, Ezra–Nehemiah, and Chronicles are fully aware of the prophecies announced by Isaiah, Jeremiah, Ezekiel, and the Twelve. These prophecies often presented the new exodus and return from exile as though the return to the land would also mean the return from the exile from Eden. Isaiah 11 is a good example of this, with its promise that the enmity between seed of woman and seed of serpent (Gen. 3:15) will be rolled back and the nursing child will play by the hole of the cobra (Isa. 11:8). Reading Isaiah, one could conclude that when Cyrus restores the people to the land (Isa. 44:28–45:1), they will also be restored to Eden (cf. Isa. 51:3).

One of the tensions developed in Daniel–Chronicles is a kind of Old Testament "inaugurated eschatology." These books show key aspects of the new-exodus and return-from-exile prophecies being realized—such as Isaiah's prophecy of Cyrus and Jeremiah's prophecy of seventy years for Babylon. And yet it is also revealed to Daniel that there will be seventy weeks of years before all things are consummated. The nation returns from one exile but not the other. That is, the people returned to the land but not to Eden. They are "already" back in the land, but they have "not yet" seen the desert bloom, Jerusalem exalted over every other mountain, and the nations streaming to Zion.

These books maintain, however, that the "not yet" prophecies will be realized. As the authors of these books re-present key aspects of the promises to David (1 Chronicles 17) and retell the narrative of Solomon's building the temple, they are reaffirming the program: God will raise up a seed of David who will rule from the restored temple, and God's glory will radiate out from Jerusalem to cover the dry lands as the waters cover the sea.

4.1 The Other Sacred Writings Book by Book

In the book of Daniel, judgment has fallen on exiled Israelites. After displaying his holiness and justice in the judgment of his people, Yahweh will show his mercy and love in their salvation, which will entail the judgment of their enemies. So in Daniel a huge statue that symbolizes the kingdoms of the world is crushed.

---

[92]See Beckwith's argument that Daniel's place in the canon is due to its being treated as historical narrative (*Old Testament Canon of the New Testament Church*, 138–39).

A mighty king goes crazy until he acknowledges the Most High. Another king is weighed in the scales and found wanting. Then the beast that symbolizes the culmination of evil empires is killed. Judgment falls on the enemies of God, and through judgment God's people are saved from the fiery furnace and the lion's den. When they rise, they will shine like the sky's brightness, like the glory of God. The glory of God in salvation through judgment is the center of the theology of Daniel.

Ezra–Nehemiah carries the history of Israel forward. Redeemed from Egypt, through sea and sands, the nation of Israel stood on the plains of Moab and heard Moses promise curses for disobedience. Through the Jordan, with Canaanites conquered, the nation of Israel did everything they could to bring those curses down on their own heads. They succeeded. Yahweh drove them from the land. Then the rest of what Moses prophesied was realized. He had told them that in exile they would seek Yahweh and find him when they sought him with all their hearts. Yahweh would restore them to the land. And he did. The story of Ezra and Nehemiah[93] is the story of the inauguration of restoration that comes through judgment. Israel was judged and exiled. Then Yahweh judged her enemies, and through those judgments returned his people to the land. Ezra the scribe seeks to rebuild the people spiritually by teaching them the law. Having faithfully proclaimed the word since his return in 458 BC, he is joined by Nehemiah in 445 BC. Nehemiah leads the people to rebuild the wall, and then revival breaks out. For God's glory, the people recommit themselves to the law and the covenant. Though their return to failure in the form of mixed marriages—something drastic not seen to this point in the story—indicates that they need yet more help from Yahweh, salvation comes through judgment for Yahweh's glory.

The books of 1–2 Chronicles summarize the story and give an inspired interpretation of it. At the end of the canon the Chronicler goes all the way back to the beginning and retells the whole story. What he chooses to include reaffirms God's promises to David and the significance of the temple as the place from which God's glory will begin to spread. In this narrative it is the weak and outnumbered who rely on Yahweh and are delivered. From Adam to exile to the decree that those who desire may return to the land, the Chronicler is the first to write a comprehensive theology of the Old Testament. He tells it as it is: a tale of the glory of God in salvation through judgment.

[93]Cf. H. G. M. Williamson, *Ezra, Nehemiah*, WBC (Waco, TX: Word, 1985), xxi: "The separation between Ezra and Nehemiah, first attested by Origen (. . . though with acknowledgement that in Hebrew tradition they are reckoned as one) and then by Jerome in the Vulgate (. . . he too acknowledges their unity in Hebrew tradition) . . . was adopted into Jewish tradition only in the Middle Ages, being attested first in the early printed editions of the Hebrew Bible."

4.2 Daniel

There seems to be a chiastic structure to the book of Daniel. A chiasm is widely recognized for chapters 2–7,[94] and building on this I would propose that the whole book can be seen to have been so structured. The widely acknowledged chiasm needs to be adjusted so that chapters 7–9 are set across from chapter 2. This is not a difficult point to establish since the visions in Daniel 8–9 are concerned with the same future events dealt with in the visions of Daniel 2 and 7. With this, Daniel's own exile to Babylon, described in chapter 1, is matched by the vision he has in Daniel 10–12, which is concerned with the ultimate return from exile.[95] The book of Daniel, then, can be seen to fall into the chiastic structure shown in table 4.7.

Table 4.7. The Chiastic Structure of Daniel

- 1, Daniel exiled
  - 2, Nebuchadnezzar's vision (statue representing four kingdoms)
    - 3, Deliverance from the fiery furnace
      - 4, Nebuchadnezzar humbled (seven years of insanity)
      - 5, Belshazzar humbled (weighed and found wanting)
    - 6, Deliverance from the lion's den
  - 7–9, Daniel's visions (four kingdoms represented in various ways)
- 10–12, Daniel's vision of the end of the exile

The discussion that follows will be informed by this understanding of the book's literary structure, but before we look more closely at each section of the book, some observations on the book's structure will help us to appreciate the way this literary arrangement highlights the center of the book's theology: the glory of God in salvation through judgment.

We have seen elsewhere in this volume how the exile was announced by both Moses and the prophets. Daniel begins with the exile from the land and ends with new information about the end of the exile. Significantly, the end of the exile is presented in Daniel 10–12 in eschatological and apocalyptic terms. Through the judgment of the exile will come the salvation of the eschatological return from exile.

[94]Joyce G. Baldwin, "Daniel: Theology of," in *NIDOTTE*, 4:499–505; Shemaryahu Talmon, "Ezra and Nehemiah," in *The Literary Guide to the Bible*, ed. R. Alter and F. Kermode (Cambridge, MA: Harvard University Press, 1987), 343–56.

[95]Daniel 11 is largely concerned with the events leading up to the actions of Antiochus Epiphanes, but in my view he is presented in this chapter as a type of a final opponent of God and his people. For this reason Daniel 12 presents the end of all things following the persecution and affliction wrought by Antiochus. Given what Jesus says about a future abomination of desolation (e.g., Matt. 24:15), it seems that he is presented as interpreting what Daniel shows Antiochus doing (Dan. 11:31) as typological of the end.

Within the outer frame of the chiasm—the exile in chapter 1 and the return from exile in chapters 10–12—Daniel prophesies about the various kingdoms that will be raised up on the world stage before the people of God receive their kingdom. These prophecies accompany Nebuchadnezzar's vision of a statue representing four kingdoms in Daniel 2 and the visions Daniel has of the beasts and horns that also represent four kingdoms in Daniel 7–9. These matching sets of visions end the same way: the final earthly kingdom will be judged, and through the judgment of their enemies the people of God will be saved, they will receive their kingdom, and God's glory will shine.

Proleptic proof that God will save his people through the judgment of their enemies is given in the matching accounts of deliverance in Daniel 3 and 6. In chapter 3 God saves the three young men through the fiery furnace, and in chapter 6 he saves Daniel through the lion's den. These are anticipatory evidences that God will overcome those opposed to his purposes, delivering his people through the judgment of their enemies.

The whole book of Daniel centers on two instances of Yahweh's judgment of his enemies: the humbling of Nebuchadnezzar through his insanity in Daniel 4, and the humbling of Belshazzar through the handwriting on the wall in Daniel 5. Belshazzar's fall means that those who will restore Israel to the land have come to power. At the center of the book of Daniel these two arrogant kings are brought low (Daniel 4–5). Working out from there, these accounts of the judgment of the wicked are preceded and followed by accounts of Yahweh saving those faithful to him (Daniel 3, 6). Before and after that are prophecies that relate to the time that will pass before the end of the exile (Daniel 2, 7–9), and the book opens with descriptions of the exile and closes with prophecies of its end (Daniel 1, 10–12).

Through all of this the clear message of Daniel is that Yahweh is glorified in salvation through judgment. Yahweh will be glorified as this story plays itself out: he saves his people through the judgment of their enemies when the exile comes to an end just as he said it would. Yahweh will be glorified as he saves his people through the judgment of their enemies. Like the statue crushed by the small stone in Daniel 2, those opposed to God's purposes will crumble. Through the salvation that comes through such judgment, Yahweh's glory will be revealed.

4.2.1 Daniel Exiled (Daniel 1)

The exilic narrative story line is continued in Daniel. From the perspective of the book of Daniel, the exile is God's judgment on Israel because of their sin (Dan. 1:2; 9:7). Through the judgment of the exile, however, the book of Daniel testifies that God is preserving a remnant. Among the members of this remnant are Daniel, Hananiah, Mishael, and Azariah (1:6). God gives Daniel favor in the eyes of his captor (1:9), and to these four young men God gives understanding of visions and dreams (1:17) and tenfold superiority versus the magicians and enchanters of Babylon (1:20).

4.2.2 Nebuchadnezzar's Vision: Statue Representing Four Kingdoms (Daniel 2)

Nebuchadnezzar king of Babylon may have triumphed over Israel, but this does not mean he has thwarted Yahweh's purpose. Nebuchadnezzar is not the sovereign Lord of the universe. Yahweh is. Nebuchadnezzar's limitations are seen in his inability to understand his dreams. We might also note the reality that we humans are unable to control what we dream. King Nebuchadnezzar has a troubling dream (Dan. 2:1–3), and he is ready to kill his wise men because they cannot interpret it (2:12–13). With their lives in danger, Daniel and his companions seek mercy from God, the one who can reveal secrets (2:17). When God reveals the dream and its interpretation to Daniel, he and his friends are delivered. In response, Daniel blesses God (2:19–23).

Daniel's blessing highlights God's wisdom and power: "May the name of God be blessed from age to age, because wisdom and might are his" (Dan. 2:20). God's power is then exposited as Daniel speaks of God's control over times and kings (2:21a), and then God's wisdom is exposited as Daniel blesses God as the one who gives wisdom to the wise, revealing deep secrets (2:21b–22). Daniel closes the blessing by thanking God for answering his prayer and revealing the king's dream to him (2:23). Daniel is swift to declare to the king that the ability to know the dream comes from God, not his own superior wisdom (2:30).

Daniel reveals Nebuchadnezzar's dream to him, in which a stone is cut out—not by human hand—and the stone strikes a mighty statue. The statue, representing the successive world powers, crumbles, and the stone grows into a great mountain that fills the whole earth (Dan. 2:31–35).[96] When he interprets the dream, Daniel explains that God's kingdom will smash the other kingdoms to pieces—salvation for God's people will come through the judgment of the powers of the world (2:36–45). God's kingdom will never be destroyed. It cannot be overcome. The dream reveals the incomparable greatness of God, for he alone is able to sustain an everlasting kingdom (2:44).

The mighty statue is brought down by a small stone, reminding readers of the mighty Goliath, felled by a small stone, and shading the narrative in Daniel with a Davidic hue.[97] Moreover, the smashing of these kingdoms may employ imagery that grows out of the reference to the crushing of the serpent's head in Genesis 3:15. And the promise that God's kingdom will never be destroyed

---

[96]G. K. Beale connects the kingdom that "fills the whole earth" to God's charge to Adam to "fill the earth" in Gen. 1:26, 28 (*The Temple and the Church's Mission*, NSBT [Downers Grove, IL: InterVarsity, 2004], 144).
[97]Dempster, *Dominion and Dynasty*, 214.

recalls God's promise to David to establish his seed on the throne forever (2 Sam. 7:12–16).

The narrative proclaims that Yahweh is Lord not merely in Israel; his sovereignty extends to other nations—even the nations that conquered Israel. Yahweh has given Nebuchadnezzar his kingdom (Dan. 2:37–38).

4.2.3 Deliverance from the Fiery Furnace (Daniel 3)

Nebuchadnezzar acknowledges Daniel's God as the God of gods (Dan. 2:47), but he nevertheless builds an image for all to worship (3:1–6). Everyone worships the image except the faithful Jews (3:7–12), and for their faithfulness they are cast into the flaming furnace. The world regards the evil of idolatry as goodness and the goodness of devotion to Yahweh as evil. Through this judgment, however, God saves his people and judges their adversaries: those who escorted the Hebrew men to the furnace are consumed by the flames of judgment (3:22). In the furnace, the three Hebrews are joined by one who is "like the son of God" (3:25). The flames have no power over these who are faithful to Yahweh (3:27). Death is defied as Yahweh saves his people through the judgment of their captors' vain attempt to enforce idolatry. Nebuchadnezzar's gods have no power over Yahweh's people, and the king confesses, "There is no other God who is able to deliver like this" (3:29).

4.2.4 Nebuchadnezzar Humbled: Seven Years of Insanity (Daniel 4)

Nebuchadnezzar acknowledges the work of the Most High God on his behalf, confessing that God's kingdom is everlasting (Dan. 3:31–33, ET 4:1–3), but Nebuchadnezzar must still be taught that "the Most High is the ruler in the kingdom of men, and to whom he pleases he gives it. And the lowest of men he raises up over it" (4:14, ET 17).[98] In spite of his prior experiences with Yahweh, Nebuchadnezzar congratulates himself, saying, "Is this not Babylon the great, which I myself built for a royal house in the might of my power and for the honor of my majesty?" (4:27, ET 30). These arrogant words are still in his mouth when judgment is announced from heaven (4:28, ET 31). He must learn that "the Most High is the ruler in the kingdom of men, and to whom he pleases he gives it" (4:29, ET 32). The repetition of this statement that Yahweh rules and gives authority to whom he pleases (4:14, ET 17; 4:22, ET 25; 4:29, ET 32; cf. 4:23, ET 26) underscores Yahweh's righteous insistence that he be regarded as Lord of all.

---

[98]For a list of references to God as the Most High in Jewish Literature from 250 BC to AD 150, see Richard Bauckham, "The 'Most High' God and the Nature of Early Jewish Monotheism," in *Israel's God and Rebecca's Children: Christology and Community in Early Judaism and Christianity: Essays in Honor of Larry W. Hurtado and Alan F. Segal*, ed. David B. Capes et al. (Waco, TX: Baylor University Press, 2007), 51–53. In my judgment Bauckham is wrong to include Daniel in this literature. It is more probable that Daniel pioneered the apocalyptic genre, with Zechariah, and was a generating influence on many of these references.

It is insane to refuse to acknowledge Yahweh as the sovereign ruler of the affairs of men, and for arrogating lordship to himself, Nebuchadnezzar is punished with a period of insanity. When his reason returns to him, he appears to have been delivered (at least from insanity) through the judgment he experienced. Nebuchadnezzar is brought to recognize that Yahweh possesses everlasting dominion and an enduring kingdom (Dan. 4:31, ET 34). He confesses that Yahweh acts according to his own will; that the inhabitants of the earth are as nothing; that none can restrain Yahweh's hand or question what he has done (4:32, ET 35). Nebuchadnezzar praises, extols, and honors the king of heaven, confessing that all his ways are truth and justice, and that he has the power to humble the proud (4:34, ET 37). Nebuchadnezzar is delivered through judgment, and as a result he glorifies God.

4.2.5 Belshazzar Humbled: Weighed and Found Wanting (Daniel 5)

Daniel 4 closes with Nebuchadnezzar praising the one true and living God, but Daniel 5 opens with Belshazzar praising the gods of gold and silver, bronze and iron, wood and stone—with the help of the vessels taken from the temple in Jerusalem (5:1–4). This is met with the handwriting on the wall (5:5), which causes the king's knees to knock together (5:6). Daniel is brought before Belshazzar, and he proclaims God's sovereign grant of the kingdom to Belshazzar's father Nebuchadnezzar (5:18). Daniel repeats again the statement that Nebuchadnezzar learned that "the Most High is the ruler in the kingdom of men, and to whom he pleases he sets over it" (5:21; cf. 4:14, ET 17, 22, ET 25, 29, ET 32), then rebukes Belshazzar for not humbling himself (5:22) but exalting himself against the Lord of heaven, using Yahweh's vessels to praise the gods of silver and gold, bronze and iron, wood and stone, and refusing to glorify the God who holds his breath and ways (5:23). Then comes the judgment, which is revealed in the handwriting on the wall: God has brought an end to his kingdom (5:26); Belshazzar has been weighed in the balances and found wanting (5:27); his kingdom will be given to the Medes and the Persians (5:28); and that very night he is slain (5:30). Yahweh takes his glory very seriously.

4.2.6 Deliverance from the Lion's Den (Daniel 6)

Daniel 6 recounts the episode of Daniel being unjustly cast into the den of lions. As with the men cast into the fiery furnace, Daniel's piety is punished as a capital crime. King Darius expresses hope that Daniel's God will deliver him (6:17, ET 16), but the stone is sealed over Daniel's sure death (6:18, ET 17). God reverses the unjust judgment, however, and the king comes in the morning asking Daniel whether his God has indeed been able to deliver him (6:21, ET 20). Daniel announces that God has shut the mouths of the lions; Daniel has not been harmed at all (6:23–24, ET 22–23). When the stone is rolled away, it is almost as though Daniel has been raised from the dead. The wicked schemers are judged as their plans are foiled, Daniel is saved through God's rejection of their plan, and then the wicked are cast into the den of lions and devoured (6:25, ET 24). In response, Darius announces the everlasting kingdom and dominion of Daniel's God, heralding his wondrous deliverance of Daniel (6:26–28, ET 25–27). God is glorified as Daniel is saved through judgment.

Nebuchadnezzar king of Babylon and Darius the Mede both confess the everlasting kingdom of Yahweh. Both these kings are led to this confession through Yahweh's judgment against them. Salvation comes through judgment to the glory of God.

4.2.7 Daniel's Visions: Four Kingdoms Represented in Various Ways (Daniel 7–9)

After Nebuchadnezzar's dreams and visions in chapters 2 and 4, Daniel himself has dreams and visions in chapters 7 and 8. What is remarkable about these visions is the way that they cover the period of time from Daniel's own day down to the time when messiah Jesus comes and inaugurates his kingdom. The kingdoms represented by beasts in Daniel's dream in chapter 7 match the different materials of the statue in Nebuchadnezzar's dream in chapter 2 (see table 4.8).

Table 4.8. The Kingdoms in Daniel 2 and 7

Daniel 2 Statue	Daniel 7 Beasts	Kingdom	Years
Head of gold	Lion with wings of an eagle	Babylon	605–539
Chest and arms of silver	Bear	Medo-Persia	539–330
Middle and thighs of bronze	Leopard with wings of a birds	Greece	330–63
Legs of iron, feet of clay	Beast with Iron Teeth	Rome	63–

After this succession of kingdoms, one like a son of man approaches the Ancient of Days and receives an everlasting dominion (Dan. 7:1–14). The seating of the court, opening of the books, slaying of the beast, and the removal of dominion from prior kingdoms all point to judgment upon the kingdoms of the world (7:10–12). It is through this judgment that salvation—in the form of a kingdom that will never end—comes to the "holy ones of the Most High" (7:18, 27). Their kingdom is the one given to the one like a son of man (7:13), and glory is also given to him (7:14).

The Daniel 7 vision depicts God being glorified through the coming of the kingdom of the one like a son of man, and the kingdom comes as salvation for his people and as judgment upon the world forces ranged against them. These assertions also hold true of the "vision for the time of the end" (Dan. 8:17). This vision in Daniel 8 concerns itself with the third kingdom of Greece, as Gabriel explains to Daniel (8:16, 20–21), and the goat portends the rise of Alexander the Great (8:5–8a, 21).[99] The four horns that replace the single great horn correspond to the four men who ruled Greece after Alexander's death (8:8b, 22; cf. the four heads of the leopard in 7:6). The little horn that comes from them points to the rise of Antiochus Epiphanes (8:9–12, 23–26), who typifies the Antichrist.

The main function of these visions is to comfort the people of God with the knowledge that God is in sovereign control of what will take place; indeed, he is directing events to their intended outcome.[100] These events will lead to judgment on their enemies, through which their own deliverance will come. The knowledge that God has the future mapped out and can reveal it is to give his people high thoughts of him. This reassures those whose beleaguered lives might tempt them to think that their God has been overcome. God has not been overcome; each added piece of evidence that things look dark for his people heightens the drama and deepens the meaning of his certain triumph.

In chapter 9, Daniel studies and understands earlier parts of the Bible and then lives out what they prophesy. Daniel discerns from Jeremiah that the desolations of Jerusalem will last seventy years (Jer. 25:12; Dan. 9:2). Evidently realizing that approximately seventy years have passed, Daniel sets his face to the Lord God in order to pray and confess sin (Dan. 9:3–19). When Solomon prayed at the dedication of the temple, he asked that God would hear and forgive when his people were exiled, repented, and returned to the Lord (1 Kings 8:46–53). Solomon's prayer grew out of earlier revelation, as does Daniel's, for texts such as Leviticus 26:14–45 (esp. 33, 40, 42) and Deuteronomy 4:25–31 refer to the time when, driven into exile by Yahweh's righteousness, the people repent of sin, seek Yahweh, and find mercy. Solomon called on Yahweh to hear and forgive when the people found themselves in these circumstances (1 Kings 8:49–50), and his appeal was based on Yahweh's prior promise to do just that (Lev. 26:40–42; Deut. 4:29–31). Daniel lives out Solomon's prayer, which was based on Mosaic prophecy.

Throughout his prayer of confession and repentance (Dan. 9:4–6), Daniel affirms Yahweh's faithfulness, mercy, and righteousness (9:4, 7, 9, 14). The exile is viewed as a confirmation of Yahweh's word (9:12), which took place "just as it was written in the Torah of Moses" (9:13).

On what basis, then, can Daniel appeal to Yahweh to forgive? Israel is receiving just punishment according to Yahweh's word, and there is a sense in which

[99]Josephus (*Ant.* 11.336–37 [LCL 326, bks. 9–11, 477]) writes that when Alexander arrived in the land of Israel, the priests went out to meet him, "and, when the book of Daniel was shown to him, in which he had declared that one of the Greeks would destroy the empire of the Persians, he believed himself to be the one indicated; and in his joy he dismissed the multitude for the time being, but on the following day he summoned them again and told them to ask for any gifts which they might desire."

[100]Similarly John J. Collins, *Daniel*, Hermeneia (Minneapolis: Fortress, 1993), 61.

it would be unjust of him to forgive. To go against his own word would make him as unrighteous as Israel has been.

For this reason, Daniel prays, "O Lord, according to all your righteousnesses, please turn your face and your fury from your city, Jerusalem, the holy mountain" (9:16). Daniel wants God to forgive, not in a way that would make God unrighteous, but in a way that accords with his righteousness. The Levitical sacrificial system indicates that God can give forgiveness while maintaining his just standard,[101] and there are some indications that the punishment of the exile establishes God's justice (e.g., Isa. 40:2). Daniel's appeal moves from concern for God's righteousness to God's own concern for himself: "And now hear, our God, the prayer of your servant and his pleas for mercy, and shine your face on your desolate sanctuary for the sake of my Lord" (Dan. 9:17). Daniel bases his appeal on God's own concern to display his mercy and power: "Not because of our righteousnesses are we causing our pleas for favor to fall before you, but because of your great mercies" (9:18b).

The nature of this appeal for mercy acknowledges that God could justly deny these requests. Daniel is not demanding from God something that God owes. What people deserve is not called mercy. Daniel's prayer culminates with fervent cries based on God's concern for his own glory: "O Lord hear; O Lord forgive; O Lord listen and act; do not delay! For your own sake, my God, because your name is called over your city and over your people" (Dan. 9:19). Daniel petitions God to act righteously by showing mercy to Israel and delivering them from their enemies and oppressors, and the ground of Daniel's appeal is God's own concern for his glory, his name. God's glory is at stake in Jerusalem, and Daniel wants Jerusalem restored because he loves God's glory.

God answers Daniel's prayer by sending Gabriel to him (Dan. 9:21), and what Gabriel reveals to Daniel concerns the same period of time that was foretold by Nebuchadnezzar's statue in Daniel 2 and the four beasts of Daniel 7. The seventy years prophesied by Jeremiah (Dan. 9:2) give way to the seventy weeks decreed for Israel (9:24). These "weeks" are periods of seven years. Seven times seventy is 490. So seventy weeks of years refers to 490 years. Israel celebrated a Jubilee every 49 years, so this is a tenfold Jubilee. Gabriel tells Daniel that this is the period of time "decreed about your people and your holy city, to finish the transgression, to put an end to sin, and to atone for iniquity, to bring in everlasting righteousness, to seal both vision and prophet, and to anoint a most holy place" (9:24 ESV). It seems, then, that at the end of this period of time, all will be accomplished. Sin will be ended, iniquity atoned for, everlasting righteousness brought in, and the

[101]See David Peterson, "Atonement in the Old Testament," in *Where Wrath and Mercy Meet: Proclaiming the Atonement Today*, ed. David Peterson (Carlisle, PA: Paternoster, 2001), 1–25.

Most Holy Place anointed. The exile will be over, and one might suggest that the way to Eden—the enjoyment of God's presence—will be reopened.

Then Gabriel tells Daniel more about this period of time, saying in 9:25, "Know and understand that from the going out of the word to restore and rebuild Jerusalem until messiah the prince, seven weeks and sixty two weeks. The street and the trench will be restored and rebuilt, even in times of distress." In this rendering I have not followed the Masoretic accentuation on the point of the placement of the athnach. Following the Masoretes in their placement of the athnach yields the rendering of the ESV, which I will place below the rendering of the NASB for easy comparison:

- NASB: "Until Messiah the Prince there will be seven weeks and sixty-two weeks."
- ESV: "An anointed one, a prince, there shall be seven weeks. Then for sixty-two weeks"

The ESV follows the Masoretic accentuation and divides the seven weeks from the sixty-two weeks. The HCSB, NASB, NET, NIV, and NJB, along with Theodotion's Greek translation,[102] join the seven weeks and the sixty-two weeks. I am mainly persuaded to reject the Masoretic placement of the athnach here[103] because doing so yields a reading that fits with what we see elsewhere in Daniel. That is, putting the seven weeks with the sixty-two weeks yields a period of sixty-nine weeks, 483 years. If we take the statement in Daniel 9:25 that "from the going out of the word to restore and rebuild Jerusalem" refers to the sending of Nehemiah to Jerusalem in 445 BC, the 483-year period of time takes us down to the time of Jesus' public ministry.[104] This fits with what we see elsewhere in Daniel 2 and 7:

- Daniel 2: The statue represents four kingdoms; a small stone crushes the statue (kingdoms of the world); and the God of heaven sets up his kingdom.
- Daniel 7: Four beasts represent four kingdoms; the final beast is destroyed; and one like a son of man approaches the Ancient of Days to receive a kingdom and everlasting dominion.

---

[102]It was Theodotion's translation of Daniel that was embraced by the early church.

[103]It is perhaps worth pointing out that while the Masoretic tradition is ancient and reliable, the vowels and accents were not original to the text. The Masoretes added vowels and accents through the Middle Ages. I embrace the Chicago Statement on Biblical Inerrancy, which takes the view that the original authors were inspired by the Spirit, making what they wrote inerrant. On this understanding, only the consonantal text would be regarded as inspired by the Holy Spirit.

[104]Harold W. Hoehner (*Chronological Aspects of the Life of Christ* [Grand Rapids: Zondervan, 1978], 115–39) argues that once we account for necessary calendrical adjustments (such as calculating by 360-day years and accounting for leap years), the sixty-ninth week ended on the day that Jesus triumphantly entered Jerusalem on a colt, the foal of a donkey.

- Daniel 9: A 483-year period is prophesied from the rebuilding of the city (Nehemiah in 445 BC) to the coming of messiah the prince.

This reading is also confirmed by what we find in Daniel 9:26a: "And after the sixty-two weeks the messiah will be cut off and have nothing." I take this to mean that after the sixty-two weeks that follow the seven weeks—after the 483 years have passed—"the messiah will be cut off and have nothing." In my view this predicts the crucifixion of Jesus the messiah, where salvation was accomplished through judgment.[105]

We will return to what Daniel says regarding that seventieth week when we consider the book of Revelation. Consider the contribution that Daniel makes to Old Testament prophecy:

- Moses prophesied the history of Israel to the exile and beyond.
- Isaiah prophesied Yahweh's use of Cyrus to accomplish his purposes.
- Jeremiah prophesied seventy years for Babylon.
- And Daniel prophesied repeatedly (Daniel 2, 7, 8, 9) the period of time between his own day and the coming of messiah Jesus.

Through his prophets, Yahweh announces that he will save through judgment, then shows his glory when he keeps his word, proving his predictions.

4.2.8 Daniel's Vision of the End of the Exile (Daniel 10–12)

The final chapters of Daniel constitute a unit that reveals to Daniel "what is inscribed in the book of truth" (Dan. 10:21 ESV). This concerns what will take place from Daniel's own day down to the end of history and beyond into the resurrection (12:2–3). Daniel 10 sets up the revelation of the future that will be given in Daniel 11–12.

Daniel 10 describes Daniel's overwhelming encounter with what appear to be two heavenly beings (cf. Dan. 10:5, 16). The "one having the appearance of a man" (10:18 ESV) tells Daniel that he will make known to him "what is inscribed in the book of truth" (10:21 ESV). This appears to begin when he says in Daniel 11:2, "And now I will show you the truth" (ESV). The period of time prophesied in Daniel 2, 7, 8, and 9 is again prophesied in Daniel 11:2–45 as the future kings of Persia and Greece are described in detail. In the midst of these difficulties, "the people who know their God shall stand firm and take action. And the wise among the people shall make many understand" (Dan. 11:32b–33a ESV).

As we move through the passage, we find several indications that there is an appointed end of all things (citations below from the ESV):

---

[105]Cf. Dempster, *Dominion and Dynasty*, 218–19, and Eugene H. Merrill, *Everlasting Dominion: A Theology of the Old Testament* (Nashville: Broadman & Holman, 2006), 549.

- Daniel 11:27: ". . . for the end is yet to be at the time appointed."
- Daniel 11:29: "At the time appointed . . ."
- Daniel 11:35: ". . . for it still awaits the appointed time."

In Daniel 11:36 it seems that Antiochus Epiphanes typifies the Antichrist. Then the appointed time of the end seems to come in Daniel 11:40, "At the time of the end . . ." Once again Daniel describes the end of the enemy of God's people (11:45), and after a great "time of trouble" through judgment, "at that time your people shall be delivered, everyone whose name shall be found written in the book" (12:1). Then there will be a resurrection to everlasting life or to everlasting contempt (12:2),[106] and the wise will shine with God's glory (12:3).

Daniel is told to seal the book "until the time of the end" (Dan. 12:4, 9), and he learns that all things will be consummated "when the shattering of the power of the holy people comes to an end" (12:8). Through judgment they will be saved for God's glory.

4.2.9 The Center of the Theology of Daniel

Daniel and Zechariah are seminal forces that give rise to other apocalyptic literature. Prominent features of this literature include interaction with a heavenly being who interprets visions for the human visionary, symbolic imagery, and disclosure of what will happen at the end of all things.[107] The symbolic imagery and the heavenly interpreter both serve the end of disclosing the real meaning of history and how God will bring all things to their proper consummation. That proper consummation is the manifestation of God's glory when he saves his people through the judgment of their enemies, having already saved them through the judgment of their own sinfulness. Both in Daniel and in apocalyptic literature more broadly, the center of the theology at work is the glory of God in salvation through judgment.

4.3 Ezra–Nehemiah

Daniel's prayer for God to act at the end of Jeremiah's seventy years is fulfilled in Ezra 1:1, but this is not the only prophecy that finds its fulfillment. Isaiah announced, "Thus says Yahweh, your Redeemer, and the one who formed you from the womb, I am Yahweh, the one who makes all . . . the one who says to Cyrus, 'My shepherd,' and he will complete all my pleasure, saying of Jerusalem, 'She shall be built, and the temple established'" (Isa. 44:24, 28). This prophecy makes the words of Ezra 1:1–2 lovely to those who wait for Yahweh to do what he has promised:

---

[106]Cf. Daniel P. Bailey, "The Intertextual Relationship of Daniel 12:2 and Isaiah 26:19: Evidence from Qumran and the Greek Versions," *TynBul* 51 (2000): 305: "The language of 'awakening' from the sleep of death in Daniel 12:2 is apparently borrowed directly from Isaiah 26:19."

[107]Cf. Ernest Lucas, *Daniel*, AOTC (Downers Grove, IL: InterVarsity, 2002), 310.

> And in the first year of Cyrus, king of Persia, to fulfill the word of Yahweh from the mouth of Jeremiah, Yahweh roused the spirit of Cyrus, king of Persia, and he made a proclamation in all his kingdom and in writing, saying, "Thus says Cyrus, king of Persia: All the kingdoms of the earth Yahweh the God of the heavens gave to me. And he appointed me to build for him a house in Jerusalem which is in Judah."

This text in Ezra may set a precedent for New Testament texts such as Mark 1:2–3, where prophecies from multiple prophets are cited but only attributed to one of them. So here, Ezra 1:1–2 clearly fulfills the Isaiah prophecy concerning Cyrus, but only Jeremiah is mentioned. Jeremiah followed Isaiah, and it seems that Jeremiah's prophecies concerning the limit of Babylon's power and the restoration of Israel to her land are in view (e.g., Jer. 25:11–12; 29:10–14).

Yahweh's power extends to the Persian king, Cyrus. Indeed, "A channel of water is the heart of the king in the hand of Yahweh; he inclines it to whatever he pleases" (Prov. 21:1). Yahweh judged his people for their covenant-breaking sins by sending them into exile. Long before the exile, however, Yahweh's prophet Isaiah announced that Yahweh would use Cyrus to rebuild his temple. Then at the exile Yahweh's prophet Jeremiah announced that Yahweh would punish Babylon after seventy years. The seventy years pass. Yahweh's prophet, Daniel, understands Jeremiah and begins to confess his sin and the sins of the people and earnestly seek Yahweh. And Yahweh stirs the heart of King Cyrus, who funds both the return of Yahweh's people to their land and the rebuilding of Yahweh's temple.

Yahweh has judged his people, but through the judgment he saves them as they return to the land chastened and purified. Yahweh judges Cyrus in that Cyrus's purposes are subordinated to Yahweh's, but through the judgment Cyrus may come to know Yahweh—he is depicted using the covenant name (cf. Isa. 45:4–5).[108] At any rate, it is through conforming Cyrus's desire to his own will that Yahweh works restoration for his own people. There is a mysterious concursus here:[109] Yahweh works such that Cyrus comes to desire and choose what Yahweh has ordained and prophesied will take place. Cyrus does what he wants, but his wanting is molded and shaped by forces he can neither control nor discern. He chooses what he desires, but Yahweh has stirred his heart to fulfill what Isaiah and Jeremiah predicted, for which also Daniel prayed.

[108]But Lee I. Levine notes, "Comparative data demonstrate that such phenomena are not exceptional: Cyrus presented himself as a servant of Marduk to the Babylonians, of the God of Israel to the Judaeans, and as a pharaoh to the Egyptians" (*Jerusalem: Portrait of the City in the Second Temple Period (538 B.C.E.–70 C.E.)* [Philadelphia: Jewish Publication Society, 2002], 8–9).

[109]See the discussion of "The Problem of Double Agency" in Michael Horton, *Covenant and Eschatology: The Divine Drama* (Louisville: Westminster John Knox, 2002), 85–92.

The articles taken from Yahweh's house in Jerusalem are freely returned to the Israelites as they return to Jerusalem (Ezra 1:7; cf. Dan. 5:2–3). Yahweh has condemned the effort to plunder his house, and as at the exodus from Egypt, his people are enriched by their captors when they leave for the Promised Land.

There is opposition to the returnees in both Ezra and Nehemiah (e.g., Ezra 4:4; Neh. 4:1–3). The rebuilding of both temple and wall points to God's restoration of his people by triumphing over their enemies. Both successful building projects result in praise for Yahweh as temple worship is resumed (Ezra 6:14–17; cf. 3:10–13) and two choirs sing God's praise at the rebuilding of the walls (Neh. 12:31–43).[110] In fact, as these projects get underway, God is praised at every point: when the foundation of the temple is laid (Ezra 3:10–11); when Artaxerxes sends Ezra to teach the law[111] (7:27–28); when Ezra's traveling party arrives safely in Jerusalem (8:31); when Nehemiah rebukes those who extort others in the community (Neh. 5:13); when Ezra opens the book of the law to the people (Neh. 8:5–6, 12; 9:3–38); and when the walls are rebuilt (12:31–47).

Salvation through judgment for God's glory is a staple feature of the prayers of Ezra and Nehemiah. Ezra acknowledges that God's judgment was just against Israel (Ezra 9:5–7), but that after judgment Yahweh has given grace to the remnant (9:8). This remnant survives because Yahweh shows them mercy and does not forsake them (9:9). The deliverance has come through the judgment, and the judgment was less than what was deserved (9:13). Yahweh's justice and his mercy win him the praise of "those who tremble at the commandment of our God" (10:3; cf. 9:4). They confess, "O Yahweh, God of Israel, you are righteous, for we remain a remnant as it is this day. Behold us before you in our guilt, because none can stand before you because of this" (9:15). This remnant sees God's holiness, feels the condemning power of his righteousness, and through this judgment is saved (cf. 10:1–44).

In the prayers of Nehemiah, we see him calling on God to let his kingdom come through the rebuilding of the walls (Neh. 1:3–11). Nehemiah prays that God would judge the God-dishonoring designs of his enemies, which judgment would simultaneously deliver the people of God from threats (3:36–37, ET 4:4–5). It is Nehemiah's concern for God's glory that prompts him to pray for God to be just rather than merciful to Sanballat and Tobiah (3:37, ET 4:5; 6:14; cf. 13:29). Nehemiah wants God's name to be hallowed—so he cleanses the temple (13:7–9); he wants God's kingdom to come—so he rebuilds the wall (6:15); he wants God's will to be done—so he zealously pursues the purity of the

[110]See further Peter J. Gentry, "Nehemiah 12: Restoring the City of God or How to Preach a List of Names," *SBJT* 9, no. 3 (2005): 28–37.

[111]For Ezra's role as "editor" of the Old Testament, see Russell T. Fuller, "Ezra: The Teacher of God's Word and Agent of Revival," *SBJT* 9, no. 3 (2005): 52–61. Similarly David Noel Freedman, "The Symmetry of the Hebrew Bible," *Studia Theologica* 46 (1992): 105, quoted in chap. 1, above n. 106.

people according to the law (cf. 13:23–31). These realities show that Nehemiah's calls for God to remember him for good (5:19; 13:14, 22, 31) are not expressions of self-interest but calls for God to show mercy (see esp. 13:22) by saving him through the judgment of his enemies.

God's glory inspires the people as Nehemiah encourages them to "remember the Lord, great and dreadful, and fight for your brothers, your sons, your daughters, your wives, and your houses" (4:8, ET 14). God brings the plan of the enemies to nothing (4:9, ET 15), and Nehemiah exhorts the people to believe that God will fight for them (4:14, ET 20).

The point of returning to Jerusalem to rebuild wall and temple is not nationalistic pride but zeal for God's glory. Nehemiah is not seeking his own advancement, in spite of what his enemies allege (6:5–9). Nehemiah and Ezra seek to remove reproach from Israel out of concern for God's glory (Ezra 8:22, 31; Neh. 2:17–18). When the enemies of God's people heard of what had been done and saw the work of God, "they fell exceedingly in their own eyes" (6:16). God's glory puts the proud in their proper place.

Nehemiah 9 gives us a biblical theology of the history of Israel, and it is instructive that God is glorified—blessed—for his work in creation (9:5–6), for the election of and covenant with Abram (9:7–8), and for mercifully delivering Israel from Egypt (9:9–12). And here it is noteworthy that they say to Yahweh regarding the Exodus, "And you made for yourself a name, as it is this day" (9:10)—Yahweh brought glory to himself. They bless him for giving the law through Moses at Sinai (9:13–14), for providing for the people and showing mercy to them in the wilderness (9:15–17), for showing manifold mercy after the golden calf and through the forty years (9:18–21), for giving them the land (9:22), for keeping the promise to Abraham to multiply them as the stars of heaven (9:23), for the mercy shown through the period of the judges (9:28), for God's patience in sending the prophets (9:30), and for his mercy in not utterly consuming the people (9:31–32). And all this culminates in the confession that Yahweh has been just and faithful in all that has come upon Israel (9:33) because they neither kept the law nor served Yahweh (9:34–35). Now that the people have returned to the land, having been restored through the judgment of exile, they glorify God, seeking his mercy as they enter into covenant[112] with him (9:32–10:1, ET 9:32–38).

As they recount the return to the land, Ezra and Nehemiah not only describe instances of salvation through judgment for Yahweh's glory in their own day, but they also show the continuance of the theme in the wide-angle story of Israel.

[112]Levine (*Jerusalem*, 30) rightly notes the similarity between this incident and the reforms under Josiah, where we also read that the people entered into covenant with Yahweh (2 Chron. 34:31). Similar covenants are made under Ezra (Ezra 10:3), Asa (2 Chron. 15:12), Jehoida as he restores Joash to the kingship (23:16), and Hezekiah (29:10).

Israel was judged when driven from the land, and through that judgment they are restored to the land by Yahweh's power. The Old Testament's story of salvation through judgment sees the first intimations of salvation after judgment in Ezra–Nehemiah. The foundation has been laid for the inauguration of the kingdom that will be described in the New Testament.[113] The glory of God in salvation through judgment is the center of the theology of Ezra and Nehemiah.

4.4 Chronicles

The Chronicler passes over David's sin with Bathsheba and Solomon's sin with his foreign wives not because he is producing revisionist history but because his purpose is different from that of the authors of Samuel and Kings. The authors of Samuel and Kings are, among other things, justifying God's wrath on Israel, which culminates in exile. They are showing how Israel deserved to be cast out of the land. The Chronicler's purpose is different because he writes after the exile has taken place. One of the major issues facing the remnant that returned is whether God would continue his program with Israel. Has the nation sinned so severely that God has cast them off entirely?[114] Or, will God resume his purpose to cover the dry lands with his glory? Will he install a new Davidide on the throne in Jerusalem, see to it that a new temple is built on Zion, and transform the hearts of the sons of Israel such that they will keep Torah, all with the result that Yahweh's glory will radiate out from the temple and the peoples round about be brought to worship him and serve the king of Israel? I submit that by rehearsing God's promises to David (1 Chronicles 17) and by retelling the story of Solomon's building the temple (2 Chronicles 2–7) the Chronicler is asserting his faith that God will resume his purposes through Israel. The temple will be built. A new David will reign. Yahweh will cover the dry lands with his glory. The Chronicler writes to rekindle Israel's hope and faith that God will keep his word to them, and the many stories of the weak and outnumbered being delivered when they rely on Yahweh show the remnant that returned how to seek Yahweh's glory in their own victories.

4.4.1 Genealogies (1 Chronicles 1–9)

In a sense, the Chronicler caps off the Old Testament with his own biblical theology of the Old Testament.[115] The nine chapters of names present a full but

---

[113]See the important essay by J. G. McConville, "Ezra–Nehemiah and the Fulfillment of Prophecy," *VT* 36 (1986): 205–24, where he argues that the accounts express dissatisfaction with the situation of the returnees, arising from evidence (such as the mixed marriages) that the full salvation proclaimed by the prophets has not been realized. McConville also shows, however, that there are allusions to Isaiah and Jeremiah that point to a continuing hope for that salvation to come.

[114]Cf. Lam. 5:21–22 (ESV): "Restore us to yourself . . . unless you have utterly rejected us, and you remain exceedingly angry with us."

[115]Similarly Joseph Blenkinsopp, *Ezra–Nehemiah*, OTL (Philadelphia: Westminster, 1988), 37. Blenkinsopp argues that the Chronicler is responsible for Chronicles and Ezra–Nehemiah, as does Jacob M. Myers, *1 Chronicles*, AB (Garden City: Doubleday, 1965), xviii.

concise summary of the Old Testament that goes from Adam to the exile.[116] The impetus to compile genealogies and preserve "ancient words" (1 Chron. 4:22) springs from the promises made to Israel. Promises are made about a coming seed of the woman, so the descendants of the woman are carefully tracked and recorded. These genealogies in 1 Chronicles 1–9 bear witness to the hope that God will raise up the individual seed of the woman who will deliver the collective seed of the woman through judgment on the head of the serpent and his seed. The making of a genealogy is an act of faith. And faith testifies that one believes that God will do what he has said, which gives him glory (Rom. 4:20).

4.4.2 Saul (1 Chronicles 10)

One chapter is given to Saul (1 Chronicles 10), recounting his defeat on Mount Gilboa. First Chronicles 10 testifies to the concursus of divine sovereignty and human responsibility as we are told that Saul kills himself (1 Chron. 10:4) and that Yahweh kills Saul (10:14). The unfaithfulness for which Saul is judged is stated in 1 Chronicles 10:13, and following the statement that Yahweh kills him in verse 14 is the announcement that after killing Saul, Yahweh turns the kingdom over to David. Salvation, in the form of David's rise to the throne, comes through the judgment of Saul. And no one does more for the praise and worship of Yahweh in Israel than David (see, e.g., 1 Chron. 23:2–32).[117] Salvation comes through judgment for the glory of God.

4.4.3 David (1 Chronicles 11–29)

As David becomes king, salvation comes through judgment not only in the form of judgment on Saul with the result that David rules; it also comes as David brings salvation to the people of God through judgment on their Gentile enemies. David defeats the Jebusites to take Zion (1 Chron. 11:4–5), and his success is ascribed to the fact that Yahweh is with him (11:9). David and Eleazar the mighty man strike the Philistines, with the result that Yahweh saves Israel from the Philistines with a great salvation (11:13–14).[118] Acknowledging Yahweh's role in these events ascribes due glory to him as his agent of salvation, King David, brings judgment on those gathered together against the Lord and his anointed.

---

[116]House, *Old Testament Theology*, 523.

[117]For discussion, see Peter J. Leithart, *From Silence to Song: The Davidic Liturgical Revolution* (Moscow, ID: Canon, 2003), and Allen P. Ross, *Recalling the Hope of Glory: Biblical Worship from the Garden to the New Creation* (Grand Rapids: Kregel, 2006), 253–61.

[118]We see divine sovereignty and human responsibility again in 1 Chron. 11:13–14. We read that Eleazar, one of the mighty men, "was with David at Pasdammim. And the Philistines were gathered there for battle. The portion of the field was full of barley, and the people fled from before the Philistines. But they took their stand in the midst of the portion of the field, and they defended it, and they struck the Philistines. And Yahweh saved with a great salvation" (1 Chron. 11:13–14). David and Eleazar struck the Philistines; Yahweh brought about a great victory. Both assertions are true; it is rationalistic and unbiblical to reject one in favor of the other.

As David is gaining strength in Israel, we read that some from Benjamin (Saul's tribe) and Judah gather to David while he is still in the stronghold (1 Chron. 12:17, ET 16). Not knowing whether these have come to fight him or to join him, David calls on God to "see . . . and judge" if they have come to betray him (12:18, ET 17). The Spirit then clothes Amasai, captain of the group gathering to David, and he professes loyalty to David and blesses him and his men with shalom "because your God helps you" (12:19, ET 18).

Salvation through judgment for God's glory can be seen when David defeats the Philistines. David says that "God broke through my enemies by my hand as a breakthrough of water" (1 Chron. 14:11). David is the agent of God's judgment against the Philistines, which is salvation for Israel, and the gods the Philistines leave behind as they flee are "burned with fire" (14:12). The defeat of the Philistines is Yahweh's triumph over their false gods.

Salvation comes through judgment for Israel, too, as judgment purifies their worship. Yahweh judges David's disregard for the Torah as he attempts to bring the ark into Jerusalem. The Philistines returned the ark to Israel on a cart (1 Sam. 6:7–12). Rather than consult Torah, David follows the example of the Philistines and loads the ark onto a cart (2 Sam. 6:3; 1 Chron. 13:7). Yahweh prefers the explicit instructions he gave for the transport of the ark, which is to be carried on poles so that the holy things will not be touched. Yahweh gave these instructions "lest they die" (see Num. 4:6–7, 15, 19–20).

Yahweh keeps his word. If he did not, who could trust him? When Uzzah touches the ark, Yahweh's wrath burns against Uzzah, and he strikes him dead (2 Sam. 6:7; 1 Chron. 13:10). David is initially angry, confused, and afraid, unsure that it is possible to live with such a God (2 Sam. 6:8–9; 1 Chron. 13:11–12). It would not be possible, save for God's revelation of himself and his astonishing mercy. David learns this through the judgment on Uzzah. When they attempt to bring the ark into Jerusalem the second time, David has evidently studied the Torah, for he announces that only the Levites may carry the ark, since God chose them to do so (1 Chron. 15:2), he explains that Yahweh's wrath broke out because they did not seek him according to the statute (15:13), and the narrator tells us that "the sons of the Levites carried the ark of God just as Moses commanded, according to the word of Yahweh, on their shoulders with the poles" (15:15).

Israel is saved through the judgment against Uzzah—God could have struck down everyone present for disregarding his instructions about how the ark was to be transported, but only Uzzah died. David is forced back to the Torah, recognizing that Yahweh's holiness mandates that he be approached according to his commandments. This account teaches the people of God that they are to conduct themselves according to God's commands rather than the example of the Philistines.

Israel is seeking to worship God when Uzzah is struck dead (2 Sam. 6:5; 1 Chron. 13:8), but God rejects the worship that comes from those who are disregarding his instructions. Through the judgment, Israel is made wise to worship Yahweh in accordance with the commands of Moses (1 Chron. 15:15). The assembly of Levites thus sing with the voice of joy and the sound of the trumpet (15:16–24). God even helps the Levites (15:26), as David dances in his linen ephod, a priestly king (15:27–29).[119]

On the day the ark enters Jerusalem, David gives a psalm of blessing and thanksgiving to Asaph (1 Chron. 16:1–7). The psalm summons Israel to worship Yahweh (16:8–13), recounts Yahweh's faithfulness to Abraham, Isaac, and Jacob (16:14–22), exults in the "good news of his salvation" and exhorts all the families of the peoples to ascribe due glory to Yahweh (16:23–30), summoning heaven to rejoice, earth to be glad, and sea to roar, "for he is coming to judge the earth" (16:33). This announcement of coming judgment is followed by a celebration of Yahweh's mercy, which endures forever (16:34). This mercy prompts the call to "say, 'Save us, O God of our salvation, and gather us, deliver us from the nations, to give thanks to your holy name, to glory in your praise. Blessed be Yahweh, God of Israel, from everlasting to everlasting!' And all the people said, 'Amen!' and praised Yahweh" (16:35–36).[120] In this narrative the returned exiles are instructed as to how they should pray—praising Yahweh and calling him to bring the rest of their kinsmen home—and David's example of trusting Yahweh and praising him is held up for them to emulate. Believing audiences of these texts still benefit from the way these narratives celebrate the glory God displays as he saves those who trust him and judges his enemies.

4.4.4 Solomon (2 Chronicles 1–9)

The Chronicler's account of Solomon highlights God's mercy in exalting him to kingship (2 Chron. 1:1, 8), revealing himself to him (1:7), and giving him wisdom, knowledge, riches, wealth, and honor (1:11–12). Solomon does not fit himself out to be king; Yahweh raises him up and equips him.

With Solomon established as king, the focus shifts to the way that Solomon honors God by building the temple. Yahweh's anointed king is a temple builder, as David's desire to build and Solomon's building program demonstrate.[121] In this, they are following the pattern of Moses, builder of the tabernacle. Solomon's

[119]Cf. the discussion of "The King as Priest after the Order of Melchizedek" in John Day's essay, "The Canaanite Inheritance of the Israelite Monarchy," in *King and Messiah in Israel and the Ancient Near East*, 73–75, and see Deborah W. Rooke's essay in the same volume, "Kingship as Priesthood: The Relationship between the High Priesthood and the Monarchy," 187–208.

[120]For God's covenant with David, see chap. 3, §2.4.3.3. Cf. also H. G. M. Williamson, "The Dynastic Oracle in the Books of Chronicles," in *Isac Leo Seligman Volume*, ed. Alexander Rofé and Yair Zakovitch, vol. 3 (Jerusalem: E. Rubinstein, 1983), 305–18.

[121]Beale notes "the close relation of temple building and complete sovereign rest as a result of defeating all enemies" (*The Temple and the Church's Mission*, 63).

temple is "for the name of Yahweh" (2 Chron. 1:18, ET 2:1; 2:3, ET 4), who deserves a great temple "because our God is greater than all the gods" (2:4, ET 5). Solomon recognizes that this task is beyond human capability, asking, "Who is able to build for him a temple, since the heavens and the heavens of heavens cannot contain him?" (2:5, ET 6).

Solomon's desire to build the temple elicits praise and blessings for Yahweh from the Gentile Hiram, king of Tyre (2 Chron. 2:10–11, ET 11–12). The program is being affirmed, and the nations are depicted as being drawn to Yahweh because of the greatness of the Davidic king who builds a splendid temple. This narrative calls the returned remnant to see that Yahweh is still pursuing the same agenda. He will cover the dry lands with his glory, and he will use Israel to do it. The elaborate descriptions of the temple and its contents redound to Yahweh's praise (2 Chronicles 3–4).[122] While Yahweh is being praised and thanked at the dedication of the temple, his glory fills the house as a cloud so that the priests cannot continue their service (5:13–14). This means what the filling of the tabernacle with Yahweh's glory meant. Yahweh will do in the cosmos what he has done in the microcosm: fill it with his glory. Twice before Solomon's prayer it is stated that the temple was filled with the glory of Yahweh (5:13, 14), and then three times after Solomon's prayer, in 2 Chronicles 7:1, 2, and 3. The first filling of the temple with the glory of Yahweh seems to evoke a worshipful prayer from Solomon, and

> when Solomon finished praying, the fire came down from heaven and consumed the burnt offering and the sacrifices; and the glory of Yahweh filled the temple. And the priests were not able to go into the temple of Yahweh because the glory of Yahweh filled the temple of Yahweh. And all the sons of Israel, seeing the falling of the fire and the glory of Yahweh over the temple, bowed their faces to the ground on the pavement, and they worshiped and praised Yahweh because he is good, because his mercy endures forever. (2 Chron. 7:1–3)

Solomon's prayer begins with praise for Yahweh (2 Chron. 6:1–15), followed by a petition that Yahweh would keep the promises made to David (6:16–17). The recognition of Yahweh's transcendence (6:18) is then followed by petitions that Yahweh would save through judgment. When individual Israelites sin (6:22), when the nation is defeated because of its sin (6:24), when there is no rain because they have sinned (6:26), when there is famine in the land (6:28), Solomon appeals to Yahweh to hear Israel's realization that she is under judgment: "When they know, each one, his plague and his sorrow, and he spreads his hands to this

[122]Ross notes, "The place of worship, after all, reflects not only the priorities and procedures of the worshippers who assemble there but also the value they place on the holy God they worship" (*Recalling the Hope of Glory*, 249).

temple, then hear from heaven, your dwelling place, and forgive" (6:29–30). Knowing the plague and sorrow that result from sin amounts to realizing God's just judgment, and through that judgment those who seek mercy from Yahweh find forgiveness. Solomon prays that God will forgive under such circumstances, "in order that they may fear you" (6:31). Solomon's prayer assumes the truth of Proverbs 28:13, "The one who hides his sins will not prosper, but the one who confesses and forsakes them will be mercied."

Solomon calls on Yahweh to forgive the penitent, and when sinners seek forgiveness, believing Yahweh to be both just and merciful, they are made righteous:

> If a man sins against his neighbor and is made to take an oath and comes and swears his oath before your altar in this house, then hear from heaven and act and judge your servants, repaying the guilty by bringing his way on his own head, and making righteous the righteous by rewarding him according to his righteousness. (2 Chron. 6:22–23)

The "righteous" here are not those who do no sin, but those who confess their sin (cf. 6:29). Solomon will note later in his prayer that "there is no one who does not sin" (6:36), but after sinning, "when they return to their hearts . . . and repent and seek your favor . . . saying, 'we have sinned and done wrong and acted wickedly'" (6:37), Solomon asks God to forgive (6:39). In this prayer Solomon is articulating the justification of sinners by faith. Through judgment, people come to see their guilt before Yahweh. Realizing this, believing that God is just and punishes the guilty, people recognize that their only hope is mercy, for which they appeal. Having done so, Yahweh reveals himself to be both just and merciful, and he forgives the penitent, justifying those who righteously recognize their unrighteousness and appeal to him for mercy. We cannot overstate the significance of this for Old Testament theology: the Chronicler is presenting Solomon as a model Israelite. He is teaching how to be saved in the Old Testament, and as in the New, the way of salvation is justification by faith, which upholds the mercy and the justice of the glorious God. The Old Testament teaches that people are declared righteous by God through faith.

Yahweh judges the wicked and saves the righteous. Solomon anticipates the result of Yahweh's displays of justice and mercy in judging the wicked and saving the righteous, knowing that this will gain him glory among the nations:

> And also, when a foreigner, who is not of your people Israel, comes from a far country for the sake of your great name and your mighty hand and your outstretched arm, when he comes and prays toward this house, hear from heaven your dwelling place and do according to all for which the foreigner calls to you, in order that all the peoples of the earth may know your name and fear you, as do your people

> Israel, and that they may know that this house that I have built is called by your name. (6:32–33)

Solomon understands that God's revelation of his glory, his name, will draw the nations, and he calls on Yahweh to show mercy and hear the prayers of foreigners that they might know his glory. Second Chronicles 9 recounts that the Queen of Sheba was drawn by the wisdom of Solomon to bless and glorify the Lord Yahweh (9:5–8) who gave Solomon wisdom (9:23).

4.4.5 Kings of Judah (2 Chronicles 10–36)

The remainder of Chronicles follows the kings of Judah down to the exile. Many years of the reigns of these kings are silently passed over, while key episodes are highlighted as the Chronicler teaches his post-exilic community. The Chronicler wants his audience to have supreme confidence in Yahweh, who works a sovereign concursus between his own purposes and the wickedness of the kings of Israel and Judah (cf. 2 Chron. 10:15; 11:4; 25:20).

Whatever difficulties the audience of Chronicles may be facing, from the Chronicler they learn that Yahweh is able to save by many or by few (1 Sam. 14:6). Even if his people are vastly outnumbered, Yahweh can deliver them by judging their enemies in battle. He will do this if his people cry out to him for help, relying on him rather than other nations.

After a prophetic warning of coming judgment, Rehoboam and the leaders of Israel humble themselves in response to the threat from Shishak king of Egypt. As a result, God does not destroy Israel, though he does make them serve Shishak so that they will know how much better it is to serve Yahweh (2 Chron. 12:5–8). Yahweh is glorified through this (partial) salvation that comes through the announcement of judgment.

Abijah goes out with four hundred thousand against Jeroboam, who has eight hundred thousand. Abijah announces that Yahweh gave dominion to David (2 Chron. 13:5) and that Jeroboam is a rebel (13:6) accompanied by sons of Belial (13:7) worshiping golden calves (13:8). But Judah has not forsaken Yahweh, and God is with Abijah's warriors (13:10–12). As Abijah is speaking, Jeroboam ambushes him and his forces (13:13), but Judah cries out to Yahweh. Though vastly outnumbered, Judah is delivered as God strikes Jeroboam and Israel before Abijah and Judah (13:14–17). The Chronicler notes that Judah was delivered "because they relied on Yahweh" (13:18). Then "Yahweh struck [Jeroboam] and he died" (13:20).

This pattern of Yahweh's delivering his people by judging their enemies when his people call on him is repeated in 2 Chronicles 14, when Zerah the Ethiopian comes with his one million men and three hundred chariots (14:9) against Asa and his five hundred and eighty thousand (14:8). Asa cries out to Yahweh, stating that he and his men go out in Yahweh's name, proclaiming to Yahweh his own unique status as God (14:11). In response, Yahweh strikes the Ethiopians (14:12–13), and the fear of Yahweh comes upon them (14:14).

Asa's righteous response is paralleled by an unrighteous one: when Baasha king of Israel comes against him, rather than rely on Yahweh he relies on the king of Syria (2 Chron. 16:1–6). When Hanani the seer rebukes him for this, Asa imprisons Hanani and oppresses the people (16:7–10), but Hanani testifies that "Yahweh's eyes go quickly in all the land, that he may show himself strong with those whose hearts are complete toward him" (16:9). Through this record of Asa's actions, the audience of Chronicles learns that even if wickedness prevails in the short term, those who lift high Yahweh's name will be remembered (as is Hanani), and wicked deeds (like Asa's) are exposed for what they are.

Yahweh helps Jehoshaphat when he is surrounded in battle and cries out to God (2 Chron. 18:31). And more emphatically, when the Moabites and Ammonites come up to battle against Jehoshaphat (20:1), he confesses Yahweh's power and sovereignty (20:5–8), and asserts that Yahweh will hear their cries and save (20:9), and that this salvation will entail judgment on their enemies (20:12). The Spirit comes upon Jahaziel (20:14), who proclaims that the battle is God's (20:15), that Israel will not need to fight—they only need to stand still and see Yahweh's salvation (20:17). Jehoshaphat and his people worship Yahweh in response to this (20:18–19), and Jehoshaphat exhorts the people to believe in Yahweh and his prophets (20:20). Jehoshaphat then appoints those "singing to Yahweh and praising the beauty of holiness, as they go out before the armed force, and saying, 'Praise Yahweh, for his mercy endures forever!'" (20:21). As they praise Yahweh, he ambushes the Ammonites and Moabites, and they slay one another (20:22–23). Judah arrives to find dead bodies (20:24), which they plunder (20:25), and they bless Yahweh (20:26). Yahweh saves his people by judging their enemies, and for this they praise him. It would be hard to come away from these narratives doubting Yahweh's ability to save by many or by few.

God also helps Uzziah against the Philistines (2 Chron. 26:7), and when Sennacherib, king of Assyria, encamps in Judah against Hezekiah, Hezekiah assures the people that "there are more with us than with him. With him is the arm of flesh, but with us is Yahweh our God, to help us and to fight our battles!" (32:7–8). In spite of Sennacherib's taunts (32:9–12), in spite of his claim that no other god has delivered from him and Yahweh will not be able to either (32:13–16), in spite of his letters reviling Yahweh (32:17–19),

> Hezekiah the king and Isaiah the prophet, son of Amoz, prayed and cried out to heaven for help. And Yahweh sent an angel and cut down every mighty man of valor and prince and leader in the camp of the king of Assyria. And he returned with shame on his face to his land. And he went into the temple of his god, and

> some who came from his loins cut him down there with the sword. And Yahweh saved Hezekiah and the inhabitants of Jerusalem from the hand of Sennacherib king of Assyria. (32:20–22)

Yahweh saves Hezekiah through judgment on Sennacherib, and Yahweh gets the glory.

Perhaps the most remarkable instance of salvation through judgment in Chronicles comes when we read of Manasseh, who is bound in bronze fetters and carried off to Babylon (2 Chron. 33:11). In affliction there, he prays to Yahweh, humbles himself, is heard, and is restored to Jerusalem, "And Manasseh knew that Yahweh, he is the God" (33:12–13).

This pattern of God's saving those who cry out to him through judgment is also seen when kings are sick: Asa was severely diseased in his feet, but he sought the physicians rather than Yahweh (2 Chron. 16:12). Hezekiah, by contrast, prays to Yahweh when he becomes ill and is given a sign and healed (32:24). The judgment of sickness is one through which deliverance can come, if the afflicted honor Yahweh by relying upon him.

Key indicators as to righteousness or wickedness include the theme of "seeking Yahweh," a theme also illustrated by those who do not seek him. Both בקשׁ and דרשׁ are used to communicate this motif: the Levites abandon Jeroboam to seek Yahweh in Jerusalem (2 Chron. 11:14–16). Rehoboam does evil because he does not prepare his heart to seek Yahweh (12:14). Asa commands Judah to seek Yahweh (14:3, ET 4; cf. 14:6, ET 7; 15:2, 4, 12–13, 15), but then Asa does not seek Yahweh when his feet are diseased (16:12). Jehoshaphat does not seek Baals but the God of his father (17:3–4; cf. 18:4, 7; 19:3; 20:3–4; 22:9). Uzziah seeks God in the days of Zechariah (26:5). Hezekiah seeks his God (31:21). Josiah seeks the God of his father David even while he is young (34:3; cf. 34:21, 26).[123] From their history, the audience of Chronicles learns that Yahweh saves those who seek him by repenting of their sin.

Moreover, attentive readers of Chronicles learn that Yahweh not only saves the repentant and judges their enemies, but is also sovereign over who repents. There is mystery here, but we need not draw the circle of mystery more widely than the Chronicler does. The Chronicler unblushingly asserts that great reform took place quickly under Hezekiah because "God had prepared the people" (2 Chron. 29:36). Similarly, when Hezekiah sent runners through the land to call people to return to Yahweh by keeping the Passover, while those in Ephraim,

[123]Some significant contributions to this theme earlier in Chronicles include the following: Saul sought a medium instead of Yahweh (1 Chron. 10:13–14). David desires to seek God through the ark (13:3), and realizes that Uzzah died because God was not sought on the proper method of transporting the ark (15:13). After the ark is brought to Jerusalem, David exhorts those who seek Yahweh to rejoice and seek his strength (16:10–11). David commands the leaders of Israel to help Solomon, seek Yahweh, and build the temple (22:19). See also Ezra 6:21; 7:10; 8:22

Manasseh, and Zebulun mocked the runners (30:10), "the hand of God was on Judah to give to them one heart to do the commandment of the king and the leaders at the word of Yahweh" (30:12). These texts indicate that people repent because of the work of God in preparing them and uniting their hearts (cf. Ps. 86:11, "Teach me your way, O Yahweh, I will walk in your truth; unite my heart to fear your name").

The other side of what we have just seen is that Yahweh is also sovereign over those who do not repent. When the people of Israel ask Rehoboam to lighten their yoke, "The king did not listen to the people, because it was a turn of events from God, in order that Yahweh might fulfill his word which he spoke by the hand of Ahijah the Shilonite to Jeroboam son of Nebat" (2 Chron. 10:15). Then when Rehoboam wants to reunite the kingdom by force, Yahweh sends his word through Shemaiah the man of God saying, "Thus says Yahweh, you shall not go up, and you shall not fight with your brothers. Return, each man to his house, for this thing is from me" (11:4). Rehoboam is responsible for speaking harshly to the people and not listening to them, which is politically disastrous. But at the same time, the division of the kingdom is from Yahweh. Yahweh does not do the evil; Rehoboam does. Rehoboam's evil, however, is "a turn of events from God" (10:15).

Another contribution to this theme of Yahweh's sovereignty over the good and evil actions of people is found in the account of Jehoshaphat's joining with Ahab to fight the Syrians at Ramoth Gilead.[124] Jehoshaphat insists on seeking Yahweh through a true prophet (2 Chron. 18:4, 6), but Ahab hates the true prophet Micaiah "because he never prophecies good concerning me but always evil" (18:7). Ahab's false prophets tell him what he wants to hear (18:10–11), and initially Micaiah does the same (18:13–14).[125] Ahab enjoins him to speak truly, however, and Micaiah prophesies that he saw Israel scattered like sheep without a shepherd (18:16). After Ahab's virtual "I told you so" to Jehoshaphat (18:17), Micaiah declares:

> Therefore hear the word of Yahweh: I saw Yahweh, sitting on his throne, and all the host of the heavens standing on his right and on his left. And Yahweh said, "Who will entice Ahab, king of Israel, that he might go up and fall in Ramoth Gilead?" And this one spoke saying this, and that one saying that. And a spirit came out and stood before Yahweh and said, "I will entice him." And Yahweh said to him, "In what way?" And he said, "I will go out and I will be a spirit of falsehood in the

[124]For the argument that this alliance results in an ambivalent portrayal of Jehoshaphat by the Chronicler, see Steven L. Mckenzie, "The Trouble with King Jehoshaphat," in Rezetko, Lim, and Aucker, *Reflection and Refraction*, 299–314.

[125]See the excellent discussion in P. J. Williams, "Lying Spirits Sent by God? The Case of Micaiah's Prophecy," in *The Trustworthiness of God: Perspectives on the Nature of Scripture*, ed. Paul Helm and Carl R. Trueman (Grand Rapids: Eerdmans, 2002), 60–63.

> mouth of all his prophets." And he said, "You shall entice and also prevail. Go and do thus." And now, behold, Yahweh has given a spirit of falsehood in the mouth of these, your prophets, and Yahweh has decreed evil concerning you. (18:18–22)

After a confrontation between Micaiah and the false prophets, Ahab, disguising himself to protect his life, goes into battle. "And a man drew a bow innocently, and he struck the king of Israel between the joints of the body armor. . . . And he died at the going down of the sun" (2 Chron. 18:33–34). In this episode, Yahweh "decrees evil" (דבר . . . רעה, 18:22) concerning Ahab, but Yahweh does not sin. He orchestrates to have Ahab enticed to go out to battle, but he does not tempt Ahab to sin. Moreover, in giving Ahab the true word from Micaiah, Yahweh gives him fair warning and a last chance to repent. Yahweh sovereignly coordinates Ahab's location, down to the joints of his body armor, with the trajectory of an arrow shot with no intention of killing the king of Israel.

4.4.6 The Center of the Theology of Chronicles

Yahweh's actions in the narratives of Chronicles indicate that he does not do everything he possibly can in all circumstances to save every individual human being.[126] It seems, rather, that Yahweh does everything he can to demonstrate his justice and his mercy, to make known his name, his goodness, his character. The way that Yahweh defines his goodness and character may not match human expectations. Yahweh sends a lying spirit in the mouths of Ahab's prophets. And yet, the whole point of Micaiah's revelation of what has taken place in the heavenly court is to prompt Ahab's repentance. As Williams concludes, "The narrative asserts that God is utterly sovereign and still utterly truthful in what he says."[127] Perhaps Paul had instances such as this in mind when he wrote of those who perish because they refuse to love the truth: "On account of this God sends to them a strong delusion, so that they may believe what is false, in order that all who do not believe the truth but take pleasure in unrighteousness may be judged" (2 Thess. 2:10–12). The conclusion that God wants to demonstrate justice by judging the wicked, and its corollary, that he therefore does not seek to lead them to repentance but gives them over to their desires (cf. Rom. 1:24, 26, 28), is inescapable. The only thing distinguishing the condemned from the redeemed is the mere mercy of God.

In all this, Yahweh is seen to be the majestic Lord who saves and judges according to what he revealed by Moses and the Prophets. The kings who hear judgment announced by a prophet and repent are saved through judgment, and they respond to Yahweh's mercy by praising him. On the other hand, those who refuse to repent are justly condemned. God is glorified in these individual

[126] See also 2 Chron. 22:7; 25:16, 20.
[127] Williams, "Lying Spirits Sent by God?" 66.

episodes of salvation through judgment, and on a wider scale, Chronicles closes with the climactic judgment of exile, but not without reference to the salvation that comes through the judgment. This salvation is announced in the decree of Cyrus (2 Chron. 36:22–23, see above in §4.3 on Ezra–Nehemiah).[128] The author of Chronicles gives his original audience, the remnant that returned from exile, and his broader audience, the people of God who have received his work as Scripture, exactly what they need: the truth about the character of their God. The center of the theology of Chronicles is the glory of God in salvation through judgment.

5. The Center of the Theology of the Writings

The Writings of the Old Testament teach the message of the Pentateuch under the banner of the fear of God. Much of this material provides poetic commentary on the historical narratives in the Former Prophets. Life in the land will be blessed for those who delight in the Torah and kiss the anointed king, in whose hearts are the highways to Zion. The universe will function for them under the fear of Yahweh, but the curse hangs over those who disregard this wisdom. Those who do not worship will find that their lives are meaningless, and sometimes it even seems that way to those who do worship. Life is to be enjoyed as the commandments are kept. Job teaches those who do not see God's justice to speak what is right while they wait for Yahweh to come with redemption.

The compelling Song of the mystery of harmonious human relationships mesmerizes and woos people to the way of life. The way is straight, the gate narrow, and the path difficult at points, but the strains of the music of the Song of Songs awaken joy and hope in the hearts of weary travelers. They climb on, kept from the precipice by the fear of God, convinced that God will keep his promises, seeking to live the beauty of the music they have heard.

Ruth presents a pattern where exile from the land is answered by restoration to it with a resumption of the genealogy of the seed of the woman. There is hope for the seed of the woman who comes with healing in his wings. Lamentations allows the depth of anguish at sin and its consequences to be explored within the limits of the acrostic form. All the fullness of God's wrath is experienced, but not without a greater purpose.

Daniel points to the greater purpose, and though the full revelation is sealed for the end (Dan. 12:4, 9), what is made known announces God's victory over evil. Anticipations of this victory come with the rebuilding of the temple and the wall in Ezra and Nehemiah. And Chronicles teaches the outcome of the rejection of the message of the Torah and the Prophets: exile. It is God's holiness that has

[128] John H. Sailhamer makes important observations on the differences between the accounts of Cyrus's decree in Ezra and in 2 Chronicles ("Biblical Theology and the Composition of the Hebrew Bible," in Hafemann, *Biblical Theology: Retrospect and Prospect*, 35).

been defiled, his name that has been profaned, and it is his faithfulness to his word that is displayed when Israel is finally cast out of his presence. The long history of disobedience only highlights the loving-kindness of the Lord, which clothes justice with faithfulness, patience, and mercy, without which trust and hope are impossible. The story does not end with judgment. Judgment serves as the backdrop, and through it salvation comes as mercy shines against it. The center of the theology of the Writings is the glory of God in salvation through judgment.

6. The Center of Old Testament Theology

The story told by the Old Testament is that of the glory of God, who reveals himself to be both merciful and just, righteous and forgiving. The story began in the garden, where our first father was judged and shown mercy. It continued with God's choice of and promise to Abraham, his deliverance of Israel from Egypt, and his long patience with the wayward nation. God's justice finally fell when the nation was exiled, and all the cruelty of the destruction of Israel and Judah points to the incalculable worth of the God who would exact such punishment.

The Old Testament is a forward-looking book.[129] It ends with the demonstration of God's faithfulness to the promises he has made to his people. It also ends with the frank acknowledgment that not all the promises have been realized, and those with eyes of faith strain to glimpse their fulfillment. God's faithfulness comes through judgment. There is a sense in which John Barton is correct: "It is little exaggeration to say that theodicy is the central theme of the Old Testament—the attempt to show that God is just in his dealings with his people and that whatever ill happens to them, they have deserved it. Even promise normally arises out of a prior conviction of just judgment."[130] The theodicy presented in the Old Testament is the argument that God will be glorified in salvation through judgment.

The Law, Prophets, and Writings show Yahweh's love to be longer than their sin, higher and deeper and able to forgive it. The sinful people do not exhaust the kindness of Yahweh, who frees his people from their captors and causes their oppressors to finance both the exodus from Egypt and the return to the land after the Babylonian captivity, along with the rebuilding of the temple and later the wall; and he gives them hope to watch for the one who will be enthroned in Zion on his holy hill.

[129]For the view that the ending of Chronicles looks forward with messianic hope, see John H. Sailhamer, "The Messiah and the Hebrew Bible," *JETS* 44 (2001), 12, and Dempster, *Dominion and Dynasty*, 225.
[130]John Barton, "Historiography and Theodicy in the Old Testament," in Rezetko, Lim, and Aucker, *Reflection and Refraction*, 33.

The story of the Old Testament is a story that leads its readers to think high thoughts of the Lord Yahweh, to glorify him. And the reason we are led to glorify him is that we see his justice and his mercy, which he makes to kiss each other (Ps. 85:11, ET 10). When the story continues with the coming of the baptizing prophet, there will be more salvation that comes through more judgment, and this will only lead to more praise for the one who is worthy.

7. Appendix

Table 4.9. Old Testament Prayers Appealing to God's Concern for His Own Glory

Text[1]	Person Praying	Appeal to God's Glory	Request Made
Ex. 32:12 (cf. Deut. 9:25–29)	Moses	"Why should the Egyptians say, 'With evil intent did he bring them out, to kill them . . .'?"	That God would forgive after the incident with the golden calf
Num. 14:13–19	Moses	"The Egyptians will hear of it . . . . the nations . . . will say, 'It is because Yahweh was not able . . .'"	That God would pardon iniquity and forgive
Josh. 7:9	Joshua	"What will you do for your great name?"	That God would give victory over Ai
2 Sam. 7:26	David	"And your name will be magnified forever."	For God to do as he has promised to David
1 Kings 8:43	Solomon	". . . in order that all the peoples of the earth may know your name and fear you."	That God would hear foreigners who pray at the temple
1 Kings 8:60	Solomon	". . . that all the peoples of the earth may know that Yahweh is God; there is no other."	That God would maintain the cause of Solomon and Israel
1 Kings 18:36–37	Elijah	"Let it be known this day that you are God in Israel . . . . that this people may know that you, O Yahweh, are God."	That God might consume the burnt offering in the contest with the priests of Baal
2 Kings 19:19	Hezekiah	". . . that all the kingdoms of the earth may know that you alone are Yahweh" (adapted).	Deliverance from Sennacherib king of Assyria
Isa. 37:20	Hezekiah	". . . that all the kingdoms of the earth may know that you alone are Yahweh."	Deliverance from Sennacherib king of Assyria
Jer. 14:7	Jeremiah	"for your name's sake"	"Though our iniquities testify against us, act, O Yahweh."
Jer. 14:21	Jeremiah	"for your name's sake"	"Do not spurn us."
Ps. 25:11	"Of David"	"For your name's sake"	Pardon of guilt
Ps. 31:4 (ET 3)	"A Psalm of David"	"for your name's sake"	Leading and guidance
Ps. 79:9	"A Psalm of Asaph"	"for the glory of your name . . . for your name's sake"	Help and deliverance

Text[1]	Person Praying	Appeal to God's Glory	Request Made
Ps. 109:21	"A Psalm of David"	"for your name's sake"	Deliverance
Dan. 9:16–19	Daniel	". . . for your own sake . . . . because of your great mercy . . . . for your own sake . . . because your city and your people are called by your name."	For God to have mercy on the exiles and restore them
1 Chron. 17:19, 21, 24	David	". . . and your name will be established and magnified forever."	For God to do as he has promised to David
2 Chron. 6:32–33	Solomon	". . . in order that all the peoples of the earth may know your name and fear you."	For prayer to be heard at the temple
2 Chron. 14:11	Asa	"Let not man prevail against you."	Deliverance from Zerah the Ethiopian
2 Chron. 20:9	Jehoshaphat	". . . your name is in this house."	Deliverance from Moab and Ammon

[1]All texts here are from the ESV, with the divine name adapted as "Yahweh."

Chapter 5

God's Glory in Salvation through Judgment

IN THE GOSPELS AND ACTS

After many trials, he was destined to face the end of his days in this mortal world; as was the dragon, for all his long leasehold on the treasure [159] . . . . The war-king threw his whole strength behind a sword-stroke and connected with the skull [181]. . . . Once again the king gathered his strength and drew a stabbing knife he carried on his belt, sharpened for battle. He struck it deep into the dragon's flank. Beowulf dealt it a deadly wound. . . . but now, for the king, this would be the last of his many labours and triumphs in the world. . . . Beowulf discovered deadly poison suppurating inside him . . . [183].

—*Beowulf,* trans. Seamus Heaney

1. Introduction

Biblical theology seeks to explain the worldview behind the statements we now find in the Bible. Biblical theology attempts to elucidate the metanarrative embraced by the biblical authors.[1] I am arguing in this book not only that the biblical authors were consistent with one another in terms of their mutual adoption of an overarching explanation of the world, but also that this story of the whole world, which the biblical authors all believed, has a theological center. I think the evidence indicates that the various biblical authors agreed on what that center is. The word "center" communicates the metaphorical idea that this theme holds all others in orbit and shines on them as the sun shines on the planets

[1]That worldview is built with stones from the Old Testament quarry, so I could not disagree more with John Ashton's assertion, "NT theologians do not need to be OT theologians also" (John Ashton, "History and Theology in New Testament Studies," in *The Nature of New Testament Theology: Essays in Honour of Robert Morgan*, ed. Christopher Rowland and Christopher Tuckett [Oxford: Blackwell, 2006], 6).

in its solar system, thereby giving them light, life, gravity, order, and purpose. Now that we have worked through the Old Testament, here at the threshold of the New it will serve our purposes to summarize what we have seen of the story so far and preview the ways the New Testament will develop the plot.

The setting for the world's true story is the cosmos God made. In this cosmos he intends to be known and worshiped by his image and likeness. In that sense, the world God made is a cosmic temple. Within the cosmic temple God planted a garden, and it appears that the image and likeness of God was charged to expand the borders of that garden until the glory of the Lord covered the dry land as the waters covered the sea.[2] But the image and likeness failed, rebelled, and was exiled from God's presence in the garden. Adam and Eve left the realm of life with a promise, however, that one of their descendants would end the exile through a decisive, though painful, triumph over the serpent (see table 2.4).

The line of descent was traced through Noah to Abram, to whom God made promises (Gen. 12:1–3) that answered the curses (3:14–19; see table 2.7). The promises to Abraham were passed through Isaac to Jacob, and Joseph was sold as a slave in Egypt to prepare for the incubation of Israel there (cf. Ps. 105:17; see table 2.8). When the time of fulfillment arrived (cf. Gen. 15:13–14), God raised up Moses, visited judgment on Egypt, and through the plagues, culminating in the Passover, Israel made her exodus from Egypt, was baptized into Moses in the Red Sea, and ate bread from heaven and drank water from the spiritual Rock, the hope of the coming messiah (1 Cor. 10:1–4; Heb. 11:26). Israel went out to Mount Sinai, where the nation entered into a marriage covenant with Yahweh, only to commit spiritual adultery; but thanks to the mediatorial intervention of Moses, they built the tabernacle and God took up residence in their midst.

Under Joshua, Israel entered the Promised Land, passing by the angel with the flashing sword and through the waters of Jordan to conquer the Canaanites and enjoy God's presence in a new Eden. Like Adam in the first Eden, the nation failed, rebelled, and was exiled from God's presence. Remarkably, Isaiah the prophet was commissioned to harden the hearts of God's people, to close eyes and ears, and when he asked how long, he was told that his ministry was to continue until exile (Isa. 6:8–13). This passage is strategically quoted in all four Gospels and at the end of the book of Acts.

Like Adam and Eve, Israel went into exile, with prophets promising a new exodus and a return from exile. The new exodus pointed forward to a new redemption from slavery, a new decisive judgment of the enemies of God through which he would save his people (see table 3.11). The promises of the return from exile pointed not merely to a return to and conquest of Canaan land, however, but also to a new experience of Eden in Canaan. Isaiah 11, for instance, describes

[2] See appendix 2 (§6) to chap. 3, "All the Earth Filled with the Knowledge of Yahweh's Glory."

life in the land under the new David using pre-fall Edenic imagery that points beyond the curses to a transformed reality in a new heavens and new earth (cf. Isa. 65:17). Isaiah also heralds the return of Yahweh to Zion in Isaiah 40:3, and all four Gospels quote this text to explain the role of John the Baptist in preparing the way for Jesus. After Isaiah prophesied these things, the nation of Israel was exiled.

At this point we must note that when Israel's prophets announced the new exodus and the return from exile, they were not merely dealing with the exile from the land connected to the destruction of the temple in 586 BC. At a deeper level they were prophesying the end of the exile from Eden narrated in Genesis 3.[3] This is significant because God kept promises to Israel when the decree was issued in 539 BC, allowing exiles to return to the land. The promises kept included the seventy years for Babylon (cf. Jer. 25:12; Zech. 1:12; Dan. 9:2) and the fulfilling of Yahweh's purpose by Cyrus, his servant who did not know him (Isa. 44:28–45:4).[4] These promises were kept when a remnant of the nation physically returned from exile, but other new-exodus and return-from-exile promises were yet to be fulfilled. So Israel was back in the land, but the desert was yet to bloom like the garden of Eden; the enemies of God and his people were yet to be defeated once and for all; the child was yet to play by the hole of the cobra; the Spirit was yet to be poured out on all flesh; the new and greater David was yet to sit on the throne of his father; and the new heavens and new earth were yet to be filled with the glory of Yahweh as the waters cover the sea.[5]

Just as Joseph had been sent to Egypt ahead of the people, so also Daniel was sent into exile before others. The presentation of Daniel's role in the Babylonian and Medo-Persian courts is intentionally reminiscent of Joseph,[6] and I would suggest that the story of Daniel fits the typological pattern of the story of Joseph so that readers will see similarities in the roles Joseph and Daniel played in salvation history. The role that Joseph played with relationship to the

[3]For the notion that expulsion from Eden was the first "exile," I am indebted to Stephen G. Dempster, *Dominion and Dynasty: A Theology of the Hebrew Bible*, NSBT (Downers Grove, IL: InterVarsity, 2003), 67. I think this way of formulating the issues clarifies what N. T. Wright has argued (e.g., *The New Testament and the People of God*, Christian Origins and the Question of God 1 [Minneapolis: Fortress, 1992], 268–72), and I believe it stands up against the critique of Wright's argument for the ongoing exile in Steven M. Bryan, *Jesus and Israel's Traditions of Judgment and Restoration*, SNTSMS (Cambridge: Cambridge University Press, 2002), 12–20. For Dempster's take on Wright and Bryan, see *Dominion and Dynasty*, 219 n. 7. To be clear, I am arguing that the end of the exile, the restoration prophesied by the Old Testament prophets, points to the return to the land *as* a return to Eden. Return to the land was realized. Return to Eden was not. Thus, the New Testament claims that the new exodus and return from exile were inaugurated in Jesus, to be consummated when he returns. See also the discussion of Old Testament "inaugurated eschatology" in chap. 4, §4.

[4]Bryan (*Jesus and Israel's Traditions of Judgment and Restoration*, 16 n. 39) drew my attention to J. G. McConville, "Ezra–Nehemiah and the Fulfillment of Prophecy," *VT* 36 (1986), 205–24.

[5]See appendix 2 (§6) to chap. 3, "All the Earth Filled with the Knowledge of Yahweh's Glory." On the "already–not yet" "overlap of the ages" in the New Testament, see Thomas R. Schreiner, *New Testament Theology: Magnifying God in Christ* (Grand Rapids: Baker, 2008), 25–26, 41–79.

[6]See especially Jan-Wim Wesselius, "The Literary Nature of the Book of Daniel and the Linguistic Character of Its Aramaic," *Aramaic Studies* 3 (2005): 241–83.

deliverer, Moses, and the exodus he led, appears to be similar to the role that Daniel played with relationship to the Son of Man, the messiah, and the new exodus he would lead. Both Joseph and Daniel rose to prominence in foreign courts. Both preceded the deliverer and pointed forward to him. Joseph preceded the one who would lead the exodus from Egypt; Daniel preceded the one who would lead the new and greater exodus and return from exile.

As noted in chapter 1, the Old Testament canon is structured so that the historical narrative in Genesis–Kings is complemented by the poetic commentary in the Prophets and the first part of the Writings. The latter parts of the Writings then resume the historical story line, with a dose of apocalyptic expectation (see tables 1.1–1.3). The structure of the New Testament canon is similar. The historical narrative in the Gospels–Acts is complemented by the explanatory commentary found in the New Testament letters. Then the historical story line is continued in the apocalyptic prophecy of Revelation (see table 1.4).

When the curtain rises on the continuation of the Old Testament's story in the Gospels and Acts, the nation is in the land. So in that sense they have experienced a physical return from exile. They still expect, however, the new exodus and the return from the exile from Eden. With these ideas in mind, we can consider the use made in the Gospels and Acts of passages such as Isaiah 40:3 and 6:9–10.

The Baptist comes quoting Isaiah 40:3 precisely because he is looking for the new exodus that will give way to the return from the exile from Eden. Each of the Gospels strategically quotes Isaiah 6:9–10 to explain Israel's rejection of her messiah, Jesus, because the hardening of Israel unto exile has not yet reached its fulfillment.

The New Testament presents two decisive moments of salvation through judgment that are the climactic fulfillments of the new exodus and return from the exile from Eden. These two moments are the cross and the apocalyptic consummation of all things. The Gospels treat the death of Jesus on the cross as the new exodus. And at the same time the book of Revelation depicts the apocalyptic judgments of the trumpets and bowls as typological fulfillments of the plagues on Egypt (see tables 7.4 and 7.5), judgments through which the people of God are saved.[7] At the end of Revelation, the return from the exile from Eden finally happens as the New Jerusalem, the bride of the Lamb, descends from heaven and the glory of God covers the land as the waters cover the sea.

Between the new exodus at the cross and the return from the exile from Eden at the consummation of all things, the gospel must be preached to all nations, and then the end will come (Matt. 24:14). The disciples will be witnesses of Jesus to the ends of the earth (Acts 1:8), and they will be a light to the nations

[7]Cf. N. T. Wright, *Jesus and the Victory of God*, Christian Origins and the Question of God 2 (Minneapolis: Fortress Press, 1996), 218: "The creation itself will experience its exodus, its return from exile, consequent upon the resurrection of the Messiah and his people."

(13:47). Meanwhile, the hardening of Israel described in Isaiah 6:9–10, quoted to explain their rejection of Jesus in the Gospels, remains, as stated in Acts 28:25–27, so that the good news of God's salvation will be sent to the Gentiles (28:28).[8] Paul explains in Romans 11:25–27 that when the full number of the Gentiles has come in, the end of the exile from Eden will come.

Until that time comes, Christians are like Israel in the wilderness sojourning toward the Promised Land. Believers have been redeemed, bought with a price (e.g., 1 Cor. 6:20), just as Israel was redeemed from slavery in Egypt. As Israel was delivered at Passover, so Christ the Passover Lamb has been slain (5:7). As Israel was baptized into Moses and ate spiritual food and drink, so Christians are baptized into Christ and partake of the Lord's Supper (10:1–6). As Israel went out to Sinai and received the law and the tabernacle, so Christians are under the law of Christ (9:21) and are themselves the temple of the Spirit (3:16; 6:19). The new covenant has been inaugurated through the new exodus accomplished by Jesus the messiah in Jerusalem (cf. Luke 9:31).

The center of this story, this cosmic metanarrative, is the glory of God in salvation through judgment. God built the cosmos so that he could display his glorious justice and mercy. He intends to be known.[9] He upheld justice and promised mercy when Adam sinned in the garden, and he hardened Israel to display justice that would make mercy precious. To this point in this volume I have argued that the Old Testament authors are in agreement on both the story line and its center, and we now pursue the case with the authors of the New Testament.[10]

2. The Gospels and Acts Book by Book

Matthew's genealogy and narratives of the early life of Jesus establish connections between Jesus and the story of Israel at both prophetic and typological levels. He is shown to be the seed of David prophesied in 2 Samuel 7, and he typologically relives the history of Israel through the nature of his birth, the exile to and sojourn in Egypt, and the mini-exodus therefrom. As Israel went through

[8]Cf. Mark A. Seifrid, *Christ, Our Righteousness: Paul's Theology of Justification*, NSBT (Downers Grove, IL: InterVarsity, 2000), 25: "According to Paul, a new exile has begun in Israel's unbelief which will be ended only at the Messiah's return." I am grateful for the ways in which David W. Pao (*Acts and the Isaianic New Exodus*, WUNT 2.130 [Tübingen: Mohr Siebeck, 2000; repr., Grand Rapids: Baker, 2002], 91–110) stimulated my thinking regarding the use of Isaiah in Acts, and while we agree that Luke has strategically cited Isaiah, the nuances of my interpretation do not follow his at every point.

[9]See the chapter on "The Centrality of God in New Testament Theology," in Schreiner, *New Testament Theology*, 119–67.

[10]What Simon Gathercole (*The Preexistent Son: Recovering the Christologies of Matthew, Mark, and Luke* [Grand Rapids: Eerdmans, 2006], 17) says of his method can be applied here as well: "This book is a study of the . . . Gospels in the sense that it is an analysis of the Gospels as they stand. It pays little attention to questions of tradition history, sources, and the relationship between the canonical Gospels and *Thomas* or the elusive 'Q.' . . . Similarly, it is not a study of the historical Jesus: we are interested almost exclusively in the interpretation of the *Greek* texts of the Gospels as they would have been understood by their earliest readers, and questions of Aramaic originals have little place here." See also the discussion of "The Historical Jesus and the Gospels" in E. Earle Ellis, *Christ and the Future in New Testament History* (Boston: Brill, 2000), 3–19.

the sea, Jesus passes through the waters of baptism, overcomes temptation in the wilderness, ascends the mountain to teach God's word, and then conquers the land. But like all of Israel's prophets, and like David, he faces opposition from within Israel. In spite of the moral authority of his teaching, in spite of the mighty power of his healings, in spite of his ability to defeat the arguments against him, faithless Israel opposes him. The cleansing of the temple by Jesus and the two references to his destroying the temple and raising it after three days hint at the meaning of Jesus' death. The exile is coming to fulfillment. As Jesus is crucified, the temple is destroyed. He drinks the whole cup of judgment, and through the cross salvation comes. Raised from the dead, he commissions his disciples to cover the dry lands with his glory by making disciples of all nations. The center of the theology of Matthew is the glory of God in salvation through judgment.

The Gospel according to Mark opens with Jesus as an adult, striding across the shores of Galilee, amazing and frightening all who behold him, larger than life, for the kingdom has come. He brings salvation through judgment in his teaching, which glorifies God by authoritatively explaining God's word. He brings salvation through judgment in his ability to cast out demons, which glorifies God, whose servant has bound the strong man and is plundering his house. He brings salvation through judgment in his healings, which glorifies God, whose king comes with healing in his hands to reverse the effects of the curse. He brings salvation through judgment as he condemns worldly wisdom and worldly ways of getting ahead, which glorifies God as the one who makes the first last and the last first, the one whose greatness is such that it is worth losing one's life to gain entrance to his kingdom, the one whose king is so worthy that people should take up the cross to follow him. Jesus brings salvation through judgment in his death and resurrection, which glorifies God by upholding justice and making mercy possible for those whose faith will save them.

Luke writes as though the Old Testament narratives are receiving their next installment. It is as though the story told in 1 and 2 Samuel is being continued. As there, so here: the mighty are thrown down, judged, and through that the weak and lowly are exalted, saved. Baby Jesus is born into Caesar's empire. Through the judgment that falls on the king of the Jews, the evil empire, of which Caesar's is only a type, is thrown down. Along the way to this recapitulation of the humbling of Pharaoh and the exaltation of Moses, who himself went through the waters as a babe, Jesus has scathing words for the religious people, while tax collectors and sinners, widows and demonized women, all and sundry low and despised, find forgiveness when they humble themselves, repent of their sins, and go to Jesus in faith. Their wicked ways have been condemned, and through that judgment they are purged and brought to salvation. The exodus Jesus accomplishes in Jerusalem enables him to proclaim forgiveness to those who have the cosmic drama of God's glory in salvation through judgment enacted on the small stages of their lives.

John's prologue gives insight into the creation narrative, showing the role of Jesus the Word, through whom God made the world. The prologue also presents the major themes of the Gospel as the Baptist testifies that the new exodus and return from exile are beginning, the incarnation of the Word being presented as the coming of a new tabernacle. Everything hinges on the rejection or reception of Jesus. Jesus typologically fulfills the temple and its feasts, and along the way he presents himself as the I Am: Bread of Life; Light of the World; door for the sheep; Good Shepherd; resurrection and life; way, truth, and life; giver of living water; Bridegroom. He prepares the disciples for his death, which is both the moment when salvation comes through judgment and the moment when Father and the Son are glorified. Having replaced the temple as the place of God's presence on earth, he puts an end to temple sacrifice when he finishes the work the Father gave him to do on the cross. Raised from the dead, Jesus commissions his disciples, making them the new temple of the Spirit where sin can be forgiven. Their large haul of fish points forward to the ministry they will have.

Luke's narrative of the Acts done in Jesus' name first shows Jesus presenting himself alive by many proofs, then instructing his disciples. They reconstitute themselves as twelve, then Jesus gives them the Spirit. Baptized in the Spirit, the disciples announce salvation through judgment for God's glory in the death and resurrection of Jesus. They hold their contemporaries responsible for the death of Jesus, even as they affirm God's sovereignty over it. The word makes progress in Jerusalem as the enemies of the gospel find all their efforts judged and thwarted, and through that judgment God's people are delivered. Through persecution the gospel advances from Jerusalem to Judea and Samaria. Peter sees the Spirit fall on Gentiles at the home of Cornelius apart from circumcision, and all attempts to smuggle the requirements of the law into prerequisites for church membership are condemned. Salvation by grace through faith is upheld through the rejection of the demands of the circumcision party. As Paul takes the gospel to the uttermost parts of the earth, paganism is exposed as powerless, Roman officials are shown to be unjust, and Jewish opposition to the gospel is seen to be vain. God triumphs and shows his glory in the upholding of justice and mercy. Those who repent and believe the gospel are brought through judgment to salvation to praise God.

3. Matthew

The Gospel according to Matthew[11] presents Jesus as the typological fulfillment of Israel's story. Just as Jonah lived out a sort of enacted history of Israel (see the discussion of Jonah in chap. 3, §3.5.5), so also Jesus will relive Israel's history, except that Jesus does it right. Jesus embodies salvation through judgment. His death on the cross is the judgment through which salvation comes, and along with that, his healings, teachings, and controversies enact both judgment and salvation, glorifying God and showing his disciples the way to salvation by announcing judgment against the way to condemnation. Matthew is about the glory of God in salvation through judgment.[12]

There are two major turning points in the narrative of Matthew's Gospel, at Matthew 4:17 and 16:21 (table 5.1). In both places Matthew employs the same phrase to highlight the shift in direction: "From that time Jesus began . . ." At Matthew 4:17 Jesus goes public, and at 16:21 he begins to announce that he will go to Jerusalem to be crucified and raised on the third day. This means that what precedes Matthew 4:17 sets up Jesus' public ministry. Then all the material between 4:17 and 16:21 presents that public ministry. After 16:21, everything tends toward Jerusalem, cross, and empty tomb.

Table 5.1. Major Shifts in Matthew

Beginning of Jesus' Public Call to Repentance	Beginning of Jesus' Preparation of the Disciples for His Death and Resurrection
Matthew 4:17: "From that time Jesus began to preach, saying, 'Repent, for the kingdom of heaven is at hand'" (ESV).	Matthew 16:21: "From that time Jesus began to show his disciples that he must go to Jerusalem and suffer many things from the elders and chief priests and scribes, and be killed, and on the third day be raised" (ESV).

In addition to these two major shifts in direction at Matthew 4:17 and 16:21, Matthew marks off five major discourses of Jesus by putting a concluding note at the end of each.[13] These are set forth in table 5.2.

Jesus relives the history of Israel (Matthew 1–2), then the Baptist prepares the way by calling Israel to repentance, a call that Jesus himself takes up (Matthew 3–4). The teaching of the Sermon on the Mount (Matthew 5–7) is validated

[11]For a nice summary of the evidence favoring Matthean authorship, see Mark L. Strauss, *Four Portraits, One Jesus: An Introduction to Jesus and the Gospels* (Grand Rapids: Zondervan, 2007), 252–53. For a rejection of the only evidence we possess to arrive at the conclusion that Matthew was not the Gospel's author, making no alternative suggestion as to who wrote the Gospel, see John Nolland, *The Gospel of Matthew: A Commentary on the Greek Text*, NIGTC (Grand Rapids: Eerdmans, 2005), 2–4.

[12]Cf. Strauss, *Four Portraits, One Jesus*, 214, who states that the "central theme" of Matthew is that "Jesus is the Jewish Messiah who brings salvation history to its climax, saving his people from their sins" (cf. also 245). Amen. And Jesus does this through judgment to God's glory.

[13]See further David R. Bauer, *The Structure of Matthew's Gospel: A Study in Literary Design*, JSNTSup (Sheffield: Almond, 1989).

Table 5.2. The Teaching of Jesus in the Gospel of Matthew

Chap(s).	Teaching	Concluding Note
5–7	Sermon on the Mount	7:28, "when Jesus finished these sayings"
10	Sending of the Twelve	11:1, "When Jesus had finished instructing his twelve disciples"
13	Parables	13:53, "when Jesus had finished these parables"
18	Discipleship	19:1, "when Jesus had finished these sayings"
24–25	Eschatological discourse	26:1, "When Jesus had finished all these sayings"[1]

[1]Michael Knowles, *Jeremiah in Matthew's Gospel: The Rejected-Prophet Motif in Matthean Redaction*, JSNTSup (Sheffield: Sheffield Academic, 1993), 240, draws attention to the similarity between Matt. 26:1 and the Greek translation of the concluding statement in Deut. 31:24 (cf. also 32:44–45). He sees this as contributing to "Moses typology" in Matthew (237–41).v

by mighty works (Matthew 8–9). Jesus then sends his disciples to gather the lost sheep of the house of Israel (Matthew 10), and opposition to Jesus begins to mount (Matthew 11–12). The parables communicate in a guarded way the surprising paradoxes and absolute value of the kingdom (Matthew 13), and then an extended section shows Jesus on mission: healing, providing, disputing, and transfigured in glory on the mountain (Matthew 14–17). Jesus teaches his disciples how to deal with sin in the community (Matthew 18), and then he enters Jerusalem (Matthew 19–23), where he predicts the destruction of the temple and describes the time of the end, calling his disciples to be ready (Matthew 24–25). Then he is betrayed, crucified, and raised from the dead (Matthew 26–28).

3.1 Jesus Relives the History of Israel (Matthew 1–2)

Matthew has learned from the Chronicler. His Gospel opens the same way Chronicles opens, with a genealogy, and his genealogy opens with the phrase used in the Greek translation to render key "toledoth" formulas ("these are the generations of . . .") in Genesis (cf. Gen. 2:4; 5:2). The purpose of Matthew's genealogy (Matt. 1:1–17) is the same as the purpose of those in Chronicles. By means of the genealogy, Matthew reaches back and grabs key threads from the Law, Prophets, and Writings, weaves them together, and readies his audience for the continuation of the story begun in the Old Testament.[14]

Matthew's genealogy begins with Abraham, recalling the promises God made to Abraham, promises that pointed to the reversal of the curses.[15] From there the genealogy shouts "David!" Fourteen is the numerical value of the Hebrew consonants in David's name, so in its arrangement—three sets of fourteen

[14]See the similar conclusions, arrived at independently, in Joel Kennedy, *The Recapitulation of Israel: Use of Israel's History in Matthew 1:1–4:11*, WUNT 2.257 (Tübingen: Mohr Siebeck, 2008), 25–102.

[15]See James M. Hamilton Jr., "The Seed of the Woman and the Blessing of Abraham," *TynBul* 58 (2007): 253–73.

names—the genealogy points to the realization of God's promises to David (see table 5.3).[16] This genealogy also serves as a quick summary of the entirety of the Old Testament.[17]

Table 5.3. The Three Sets of Fourteen in Matthew's Genealogy[1]

"From Abraham to David"	"From David to Exile"	"From Exile to Messiah"
1. Abraham	1. David	1. Jechoniah
2. Isaac	2. Solomon	2. Shealtiel
3. Jacob	3. Rehoboam	3. Zerubbabel
4. Judah	4. Abijah	4. Abiud
5. Perez	5. Asaph	5. Eliakim
6. Hezron	6. Jehoshaphat	6. Azor
7. Ram	7. Joram	7. Zadok
8. Amminadab	8. Uzziah	8. Achim
9. Nahshon	9. Jotham	9. Eliud
10. Salmon	10. Ahaz	10. Eleazar
11. Boaz	11. Hezekiah	11. Matthan
12. Obed	12. Manasseh	12. Jacob
13. Jesse	13. Amos	13. Joseph
14. David	14. Josiah	14. Jesus

[1]In this presentation, 14 in the first is David, and 1 in the second is David, following the "headings" Matthew gives in 1:17. If we start with Solomon as 1 in the second list, we must count Jechoniah as 14 on the second and 1 on the third in order to have fourteen names on the third list. For a different account of the three sets of fourteen, see Nolland, *The Gospel of Matthew*, 86.

Having taken his audience through the long story of Israel in his carefully arranged list of names, Matthew next presents Jesus as recapitulating the history of Israel. Matthew accomplishes this by showing Jesus as the typological fulfillment of the history of Israel.[18] Matthew identifies the events he relates of the early life of Jesus as "fulfilling" four texts in Matthew 1–2: Isaiah 7:14 in Matthew 1:22–23, Hosea 11:1 in Matthew 2:15, Jeremiah 31:15 in Matthew 2:17–18, and no identifiable text in Matthew 2:23.[19] When we examine each of these Old Testament texts, we find that none of them is a prediction of the distant future. In each case the text that Matthew cites relates directly to the historical situation the prophet was addressing in his own day. From this we see

[16]See further the comments on gematria, which finds meaning in the numerical value of consonants, in Larry W. Hurtado, *The Earliest Christian Artifacts: Manuscripts and Christian Origins* (Grand Rapids: Eerdmans, 2006), 115–19.

[17]So also Nolland, *The Gospel of Matthew*, 34.

[18]See further James M. Hamilton Jr., "The Virgin Will Conceive: Typological Fulfillment in Matthew 1:18–23," in *Built upon the Rock: Studies in Matthew*, ed. John Nolland and Dan Gurtner (Grand Rapids: Eerdmans, 2007), 228–47, and Schreiner, *New Testament Theology*, 71–73.

[19]Matthew also quotes Mic. 5:1 (ET 2) in Matt. 2:5–6, but he does not use "fulfillment" language to introduce that quotation.

that the kind of "fulfillment" that Matthew is claiming is not predictive but typological. In other words, Matthew is not claiming that these Old Testament prophets looked ahead and foretold that these events would happen to the messiah. Rather, he is claiming that these events that happen to the messiah fulfill the pattern of events seen in the Old Testament texts he cites.

Typological interpretation attends to historical correspondence and escalation. Real events that took place in history are seen to match in sequence and import, and as we progress from a type to fulfillment, we find an increase in significance. The typological fulfillment of Isaiah 7:14 in Matthew 1:22–23 can be depicted as shown in table 5.4.

Table 5.4. Typological Fulfillment in Matthew 1:22–23

	Historical Correspondence		
Points of Contact	**Isa. 7:14**	**Matt. 1:22–23**	**Escalation**
Wicked king	Ahab	Herod	Ahab is Jewish, but does not believe. Herod is not even Jewish, and he is not only disbelieving, but is seeking to kill the messiah.
National threat	Syria and Ephraim	Rome	Ahab, the rightful king, rules. Herod is not the rightful king, and rightful kings have not ruled since the exile.
Promise of deliverance	"It shall not stand" (Isa. 7:7).	"He will save" (Matt. 1:21).	Isaiah is promising national deliverance for Israel (Judah); Jesus brings forgiveness of sins.
Sign of guarantee	"The young woman/virgin will conceive" (Isa. 7:14).	"She will bear a son" (Matt. 1:21).	Whereas all indications are that the child born in Isaiah's day (cf. Isa. 7:15–16) was conceived through natural intercourse, Matthew testifies that Joseph did not "know" Mary until after Jesus was born (Matt. 1:25).
Confident name	"Immanuel"	"Immanuel," God with us	The child born in Isaiah's day (cf. Isa. 7:15–16) evidently receives this name as a testimony that God will protect his people by his presence with them. Jesus, by contrast, receives this name because he is God.

We find similar points of historical correspondence and escalation in Matthew's fulfillment claims in Matthew 2 (see table 5.5).[20]

What does typological fulfillment have to do with salvation through judgment for God's glory? The first prophet Matthew cites, Isaiah, was commissioned to harden Israel's hearts "until cities lie waste without inhabitant" (Isa. 6:11, cf. 9–13), that is, until exile. The second prophet Matthew cites, Hosea, mentioned the exodus from Egypt (Hos. 11:1–4) in a context where he said that the north-

[20]Similarly Nolland, *The Gospel of Matthew*, 34, and Schreiner, *New Testament Theology*, 73–76.

Table 5.5. Typological Fulfillment in Matthew 2

Points of Contact	Historical Correspondence		Escalation
	Hos. 11:1–2	**Matt. 2:15**	
God's son	Nation of Israel (Hos. 11:1)	Jesus is representative of Israel (Matt. 2:15).	Jesus is the Son of God as the representative and fulfillment of Israel, whom God called his son (cf. Ex. 4:22–23).
Summoned out of Egypt	Nation of Israel at the exodus (Hos. 11:1)	Jesus is summoned from Egypt after Herod's death (Matt. 2:13–15).	The exodus of Jesus from Egypt has implications for the salvation of mankind that exceed those of Israel's exodus.
Trials in the wilderness	Israel rebelled when tempted in the wilderness (Hos. 11:2).	Jesus resists temptation in the wilderness (Matt. 4:1–11).	Jesus succeeds where Israel failed.
	Jer. 31:15	**Matt. 2:16–17**	
Rachel weeping for her children	Jeremiah depicts Rachel as a symbolic matriarch of Israel weeping over the coming exile (Jer. 31:15).	Matthew depicts a similar moment when Herod slaughters the infants of Bethlehem (Matt. 2:16–17).	Because of the heightened significance of the coming of Jesus, resistance to God's purposes is more evil than ever before. Moreover, the weeping in Jeremiah's day accompanied the exile, which is fulfilled in the death of Jesus.
Hope	"There is hope for your future, declares the Lord" (Jer. 31:17).	Herod kills the children of Bethlehem, but Jesus escapes to Egypt (Matt. 2:14).	Jesus lives to bring a salvation that fulfills everything hoped for in the return from exile.
	OT "Branch"	**Matt. 2:23**	
Branch	No OT text prophesies, "He shall be called a Nazarene," but several texts point to a "branch" (Heb. *netser*, which is possibly behind the name Nazareth).	Jesus comes as the promised shoot of Jesse, the righteous branch.	Jesus comes as the fulfillment of everything promised in texts such as Isaiah 11, Jeremiah 23, and Zechariah 6 (which identified Joshua the high priest in Zechariah's day as "the man whose name is Branch" Zech. 6:12).

ern kingdom would not go to Egypt but would be exiled by Assyria (11:5–6). The mention of the exodus from Egypt in the context of the destruction of the north by Assyria hints at a new exodus after exile. The third prophet Matthew cites, Jeremiah, spoke of Rachel weeping at the slaughter of the children of Israel when Babylon exiled them from the land (cf. Jer. 31:2, 10, 16).[21] It seems, then, that Matthew claims these passages are fulfilled in the events of the early

[21] Michael Knowles (*Jeremiah in Matthew's Gospel: The Rejected Prophet Motif in Matthaean Redaction* [Sheffield: JSOTSup, 1993], 52) is right that Matthew sees "a correspondence between the suffering of the children of Israel in Exile . . . and the suffering of the children of Israel under Herod" but wrong that Matthew has connected the two by "ignoring altogether the original context of the passage."

life of Jesus because the exile is coming to its completion. The prophets pointed beyond the judgment of exile to a future day of salvation, and a central feature of the shining glory of God that would come through and after judgment was the raising up of a new Davidic king, a branch (cf. Isaiah 11; Jer. 23:5; Ezek. 37:24; Hos. 3:5; Amos 9:11; Mic. 5:1–3, ET 2–4). Matthew claims that these hopes are fulfilled in Jesus.

According to Matthew, the exile is coming to its end, fulfilled in Jesus, and the salvation that comes through judgment begins to dawn with his appearance. Matthew presents Jesus as the fulfillment of the salvation through judgment for God's glory revealed in the Prophets.

3.2 Call to Kingdom Repentance (Matthew 3–4)

The recapitulation of Israel's history and its fulfillment continues. Malachi promised a new Elijah before the coming of the great and dreadful day of the Lord (Mal. 4:5).[22] Isaiah prophesied of one who would herald the end of the exile and the return of Yahweh to Zion (Isa. 40:3). Matthew identifies John as the voice in the wilderness ("For this is the one spoken through the prophet Isaiah," Matt. 3:3), and later Jesus identifies John as the Elijah who was to come (Matt. 11:10, 14). The Baptist is the typological fulfillment of the expected Elijah-forerunner, even being clothed like Elijah (Matt. 3:4; cf. 2 Kings 1:8).

The Baptist is preparing the way, and the way he is preparing is that of a typological fulfillment of the new conquest of the land that will follow the new exodus at the return from exile. Naturally, he is bivouacked at the Jordan River, where his baptism with water for repentance (Matt. 3:11) enacts the fulfillment of Yahweh's promise to cleanse his people with clean water when he brings them back (Ezek. 36:25). He celebrates the superiority of Jesus to himself, and he announces that Jesus will save through judgment when he uses his winnowing fork to clear his threshing floor, gathering his wheat into his barn and burning the chaff with unquenchable fire (Matt. 3:11–12). In Jesus God is glorified in salvation through judgment, fulfilling the Old Testament prophecies and typological patterns.[23]

While the seed of the serpent, the brood of vipers denounced by John (Matt. 3:7), are warned of the wrath to come, the seed of the woman, Jesus of Nazareth, fulfills all righteousness as heaven opens, the Spirit descends, and the Father speaks his approval (3:13–17). As Jesus is baptized in the water, the descent

[22]For the expectation of Elijah in other Jewish literature, see Emil Schürer, *The History of the Jewish People in the Age of Jesus Christ (175 B.C.–A.D. 135)*, ed. Geza Vermes, Fergus Millar, and Matthew Black (Edinburgh: T&T Clark, 1973), 515–16.

[23]Cf. George Eldon Ladd, *A Theology of the New Testament*, rev. ed. (Grand Rapids: Eerdmans, 1993), 35: "John's announcement of the Kingdom anticipated the fulfillment of Old Testament expectation in a twofold direction. God is to act in his kingly power for the salvation of the righteous and the judgment of the wicked—the two central themes that run throughout the Old Testament."

and ascent of his immersion (which is what the word *baptism* means) points to another baptism, a judgment through which salvation will come.[24]

But having passed through the waters of Jordan, he is lead by the Spirit into the wilderness. It is as though he has been brought up from Egypt (Matt. 2:15) to the wilderness where Israel failed, but here the star predicted in the midst of Israel's failures (Num. 24:17; cf. Matt. 2:2, 9–10) triumphs where the nation was defeated. Citing Scripture to shield himself from Satan's fiery darts, Jesus shows himself to be the king who lives out what Deuteronomy 17 sought to inculcate. He shows himself to be the blessed man of Psalm 1. Condemning the serpent, he calls for the Lord to be worshiped (Matt. 4:10).[25]

Salvation through judgment for God's glory is seen in the overarching story of the end of the exile and the new exodus that Jesus will accomplish, and in the events and incidents along the way. So once John is arrested, Jesus repairs to Capernaum (Matt. 4:13), and to explain the significance of this, Matthew again quotes (4:14–16) an Isaianic text that pointed to the dawn that would break after the gloom of exile, Isaiah 8:23–9:1 (ET 9:1–2). Matthew is claiming that Jesus fulfills the expectations for the deepest darkness of the exile, and now morning has begun to break as the day that will bring God's glory (in the salvation that comes through the judgment) begins to dawn.

Then one of Matthew's key structural markers in his Gospel (Matt. 4:17; cf. 16:21) announces Jesus' call that people repent because of the nearness of the kingdom. The exile is coming to an end. The light is beginning to break. Therefore, people should repent and experience the joy of the new exodus. In keeping with this, Jesus calls his disciples to be those who will gather the scattered exiles. In Jeremiah 16:13 Yahweh announced his intention to throw Israel out of the land. He went on to promise that a day would come when the new exodus would eclipse the old (Jer. 16:14–15). He also announced that he would gather many *fishermen*, who would fish his people out (16:16).[26] This promise in Jeremiah *that fishers of men would regather the people from exile* informs Jesus' telling Peter and Andrew that he would make them "fishers of men" (Matt. 4:19).

The exile is being fulfilled. Preparations are being made for the new exodus and the return from exile.[27] Satan is losing his grip on the world as Jesus comes

---

[24]Cf. Douglas J. Moo, *The Old Testament in the Gospel Passion Narratives* (Sheffield: Almond, 1983), 120–21.

[25]Gathercole (*The Preexistent Son*, 69 n. 83) notes the relationship between this assertion and the many statements in the Gospels that Jesus was "worshiped" (cf. 69–70).

[26]Knowles (*Jeremiah in Matthew's Gospel*, 194–97) does not consider the contextual relationship of Jer. 16:16 to 16:14–15, and thus takes "the metaphors of fishing and hunting [to] convey a sense of divine judgment." The near and broad contexts firmly locate Jer. 16:16 as an assertion regarding the regathering of the people at the return from exile.

[27]In support of the idea that Matthew presents Jesus working out a new exodus are the indications that Jesus fulfills Moses typology. On this see Dale C. Allison Jr., "The Embodiment of God's Will: Jesus in Matthew," in *Seeking the Identity of Jesus: A Pilgrimage*, ed. Beverly Roberts Gaventa and Richard B. Hays (Grand Rapids: Eerdmans, 2008), esp. 119–21, summarizing Allison, *The New Moses: A Matthean Typology* (Minneapolis:

reversing the curses and pushing back the effects of sin and evil on the land, healing, exorcising, crushing the serpent's head (Matt. 4:23–25). And this salvation through judgment results in the spreading of his fame (4:24).

3.3 The Message of the Kingdom (Matthew 5–7)

The seed of the woman, born of a virgin to save his people from their sins, comes up from Egypt, passes through the waters, faces down temptation in the wilderness, gathers his fishermen, then ascends the mountain to give his people a new word from God. The new David is a new Moses who leads a new exodus for a new Israel replete with a new Sinai, all pointing toward the new covenant.

Through the judgment of exile salvation begins to dawn. John Nolland writes, "The Matthean beatitudes in 5:3–10 have as their background the sufferings of the Exile. Their good news is that for those who have learned the lesson of the Exile the time of painful loss and deprivation will now come to an end, and God's people will be fully restored."[28] Those blessed to live in the way Jesus describes "will inherit the earth" (Matt. 5:5), and the word rendered "earth" here could just as well be translated "land."

The salvation Jesus offers, which itself comes through the judgment of exile, will also come through messianic woes.[29] Jesus calls his followers to rejoice and be glad when they are persecuted because of him (Matt. 5:11–12). They are salt and light, and their good deeds are to shine for the Father's glory (5:13–16). The followers of Jesus are to do good through all the purging judgments they face until the kingdom for which they strive comes, and in their persevering and receiving of the kingdom God's glory will shine.

Reliving the story of Israel and teaching the true meaning of the law of Moses, as he does in the "antitheses" (Matt. 5:21–48), Jesus is not abolishing but fulfilling the Law and the Prophets (5:17–20). The Law and the Prophets pointed forward to a prophet like Moses (Deut. 18:15–18) who would mediate a new covenant (Jer. 31:31–34). Jesus announces himself as the fulfillment of these expectations.

There is a common thread that runs through the body of the Sermon on the Mount: in his teaching on murder (Matt. 5:21–26), adultery (5:27–30), divorce (5:31–32), oaths (5:33–37), retaliation (5:38–42), enemies (5:43–48), alms (6:1–4),

---

Fortress, 1993). For the expectation of the "gathering of the dispersed" in other Jewish literature, see Schürer, *The History of the Jewish People*, 530–31.

[28]Nolland, *The Gospel of Matthew*, 37.

[29]For a catalog of references to the "messianic woes," see table 6.2, below. Cf. also Schürer, *The History of the Jewish People*, 514, where in his discussion of messianism he describes "the final ordeal and confusion" as follows: "Reference to the last things is almost always accompanied by the notion, recurring in various forms, that a period of special distress and affliction must precede the dawn of salvation. It was of course reasonable to suppose that the way to happiness should lie through affliction. This is also explicitly predicted in the Old Testament (Hos. 13:13; Dan. 12:1 and elsewhere). In rabbinic teaching, the doctrine therefore developed of the חבלי המשיח, the birth pangs of the Messiah which must precede his appearance (the expression is from Hos. 13:13; cf. Mt. 24:8 . . . Mk. 13:8 . . .)."

prayer (6:5–15), fasting (6:16–18), treasuring (6:19–24), trusting (6:25–34), judging (7:1–6), and beseeching (7:7–11), Jesus is condemning the false way in order to bring people to the way of truth. He means to save his disciples through the judgment he pronounces on external obedience. The assertion that he came to fulfill the law in Matthew 5:17 is matched by the summary of his teaching in the golden rule in 7:12, "for this is the Law and the Prophets." In the Sermon on the Mount Jesus seeks to produce people who live out God's glory, going through the narrow gate (7:13–14), rejecting false teachers (7:15–20), being delivered from final judgment (7:21–23) by his explanation of the outcome of the two ways (7:24–27). Those who build their lives on the teaching of Jesus experience salvation through the exposure of unsound thinking that his teaching accomplishes.

3.4 Mighty Works That Confirm the Teaching (Matthew 8–9)

The mighty works in Matthew 8–9 are tied to the authoritative teaching in chapters 5–7 by the repetition of Matthew 4:23 in Matthew 9:35. This indicates that Matthew intended to bracket the teaching and the mighty works, tying the two units of material together. The mighty works in Matthew 8–9 validate the authoritative teaching (cf. Matt. 7:28–29) in Matthew 5–7.

These mighty works enact salvation through judgment for God's glory. Jesus not only resists Satan's temptations (Matt. 4:1–11) and exposes Satanic misperceptions about the kind of obedience that pleases God (Matthew 5–7), but he also pushes back the domain of darkness in the lives of people (Matthew 8–9).

Jesus exercises his authority (cf. Matt. 9:6) over all the brokenness in the world as a result of sin: he heals leprosy, restoring a man to a clean state (8:1–4), heals a servant at a distance (8:5–13), casts out demons and unclean spirits (8:14–17, 28–34),[30] calms the sea (8:23–27), forgives sins (9:1–8), raises the dead and heals long-term suffering (9:18–26), and gives sight to the blind (9:27–31) and speech to the mute (9:32–34). Hereby Jesus is condemning the work of darkness. Reversing its judgments, he annuls its power and repeals its verdicts. Jesus is saving by rendering judgment on the effects of the curse.

How can Jesus repeal the effects of the curse on sin? Matthew ties the healing ministry of Jesus to his suffering and death on the cross by quoting Isaiah 53:4 in Matthew 8:17. Jesus is able to raise the dead, forgive sin, cleanse the unclean, heal the sick, and cast out demons precisely because of what he will do on the cross.[31] To establish this point, having narrated healings and exorcisms, Matthew explains that Jesus does these things "in order that he might fulfill what was

[30]See the argument that "the exorcisms signify the reduction and destruction of Satan's kingdom, as God's kingdom breaks into the world," in Craig A. Evans, "Inaugurating the Kingdom of God and Defeating the Kingdom of Satan," *BBR* 15 (2005): 49–75.

[31]So also Schreiner, *New Testament Theology*, 266.

spoken by Isaiah the prophet saying, 'he took our weaknesses, and our diseases he bore'" (Matt. 8:17).

Jesus saves through judgment, and what results is glory for him and God: his disciples marvel (Matt. 8:27); the crowds are afraid and glorify God (9:7); the reports are broadcasted (9:26) as his fame spreads (9:31) and the crowds marvel (9:33). Jesus comes bringing salvation through judgment for God's glory, calling sinners to himself (9:9–13). There is also an implicit condemnation of those who are unwilling to sacrifice all to follow him (8:18–22), those who ask him to leave (8:34), who allege that he blasphemes (9:3) or that his power is demonic (9:34).

Hosea prophesied that after exile Yahweh would woo his faithless bride into the wilderness and betroth her to himself anew (Hos. 2:14–20). Jesus comes announcing himself as the Bridegroom, offering the new wine of the new covenant (Matt. 9:14–17).[32] The new covenant wine is for those saved through judgment for God's glory.

3.5 Gathering the Lost Sheep of the House of Israel (Matthew 10)

To prosecute the return from exile, Jesus sends out the fishermen he has gathered to find "the lost sheep of the house of Israel" (Matt. 10:6). Having given them authority to do what he has done as they proclaim the coming of the kingdom (10:1, 7–8), Jesus apparently means to gather the remnant within Israel. He has warned of false teachers who are wolves in sheep's clothing (7:15), and he sends his disciples out as sheep among wolves (10:16). He knows that there will not be a universal reception of his message. As his people are persecuted and killed for the sake of his name (10:18, 22), they testify to his supreme worth. No human power can save from hell, so the followers of Jesus glorify God when they fear only the one "who is able to destroy both soul and body in hell" (10:28). Enabled by this clear word to overcome every human fear and stand against any human power, they are saved, and those martyred declare God's glory. The followers of Jesus also declare the supreme worth of God and his messiah as they leave home to announce his kingdom, thereby showing their devotion to Christ to be greater than their devotion to father, mother, son, or daughter (10:32, 37). This demonstration condemns the idolatry of exalting human relationships over one's obligation to God. Through the judgment salvation comes and God is glorified.

The word about taking up the cross to follow Jesus probably sounded like a call to risk Roman retribution when Jesus spoke it (Matt. 10:38). In the context of Matthew's Gospel, this word calls the followers of Jesus to lay down their lives

---

[32]Commenting on the parallel episode in Mark's Gospel, Peter G. Bolt (*The Cross from a Distance: Atonement in Mark's Gospel*, NSBT [Downers Grove, IL: InterVarsity, 2004], 25) writes, "God's salvation beyond judgment was pictured in terms of Israel once again enjoying the fruit of the land, including the blessings of wine (Hos. 2:22)."

by faith for others in obedience to God, just as Jesus did. Herein is the paradox that condemns all selfishness, and through that judgment comes the salvation of living for others to God's glory by faith: "The one who finds his life will lose it, and the one who loses his life on account of me will find it" (10:39).

3.6 Rising Opposition (Matthew 11–12)

The many parallels between John and Jesus hint that they will meet similar opposition.[33] Matthew has already noted John's imprisonment (Matt. 4:12), and so the message John sends to Jesus from prison (11:2–6) prompts Jesus to make observations on John's role (11:7–15) and on the absurdity of the rejection of both John and Jesus himself (11:16–19). Jesus pronounces woe on those who have rejected him (11:20–24), and this functions to warn the audience of Matthew's Gospel not to bring that woe on themselves. They are to be saved through the announcement of judgment. Similarly, when Jesus praises God for the way that he hides and reveals according to his own good pleasure (11:25–27), the audience of the Gospel hears of the privilege that is theirs in having access to this information.[34] Fittingly, Jesus then calls them to come and find rest for their souls (11:28–30). The easy yoke and the light burden of rest in the Land of Promise reverberates with the statements in the Old Testament of when Israel enjoyed rest in the land. Jesus is bringing an end to exile through all the tribulations and rejections he is enduring.

When the Pharisees confront Jesus (Matt. 12:1–2), he condemns them with his logic. He asserts that he is fulfilling the typological pattern of what David and the priests did (12:3–6);[35] he asserts that he is greater than the temple (12:6); and if that were not enough to state his glory, he claims to be Lord of the Sabbath (12:8). This claim is validated by his right choice of doing good on the Sabbath and his demonstration of power in healing the man with the withered hand (12:9–13). The Pharisees choose condemnation for themselves by conspiring to destroy him (12:14). Jesus continues to bring salvation through judgment as he heals (12:15, 22), and God is glorified as people are amazed (12:23). The logic of Jesus carries the force of truth as he shows that the kingdom of God has come (12:28), he threatens those who blaspheme the Spirit (12:31–32), and he denounces his enemies as a brood of vipers, seed of the serpent (12:34). Again

[33]For a list of ten parallels and the suggestion that Matthew is using them to "foreshadow his passion narrative," see Allison, "The Embodiment of God's Will," 124–25.

[34]Cf. Gathercole, *The Preexistent Son*, 52, who highlights "Jesus' intimacy with the Father in his knowledge of heavenly secrets" to demonstrate the transcendence of Jesus.

[35]For Davidic typology, see my Julius Brown Gay Lecture delivered at Southern Seminary on March 13, 2008, "The Typology of David's Rise to Power: Messianic Patterns in the Book of Samuel"; cf. also Knowles, *Jeremiah in Matthew's Gospel*, 233–37.

he interprets the Old Testament typologically, asserting his superiority over both Jonah and Solomon (12:38–42).[36]

3.7 Kingdom Parables (Matthew 13)

Jesus enacts the hiding and revealing for which he praised the Father (Matt. 11:25–27), living out his own description of the way he reveals the Father to anyone he pleases (11:27) as he teaches in parables. These parables also enact the glory of God in salvation through judgment as they bring the work of Isaiah to its fulfillment. Isaiah hardened hearts until exile (Isa. 6:9–13), and Jesus fulfills this ministry by telling the parables. Matthew quotes Isaiah to make that point (Matt. 13:14–15).[37] The exile is coming to its end in Jesus, but he will fulfill Isaiah's ministry until it is complete. Jesus will judge and save, and God's glory will be seen by eyes blessed to see (13:16).

God's glory is demonstrated as the supreme value of his kingdom is highlighted while the value of other things is condemned—and through the condemnation those who hear are led to salvation, and they shine like the sun with the glory of God (Matt. 13:43). Jesus has the ability to reveal things hidden from the foundation of the world (13:35). The seed of the serpent (13:38) may hide among the seed of the woman, but they will be judged (13:42). The kingdom is so valuable that it is worth selling all one has to gain it (13:44–46).

3.8 Jesus on Mission (Matthew 14–17)

Herod's death-dealing feast communicates its own injustice and condemnation as the Baptist is cruelly murdered (Matt. 14:1–12). Jesus, by contrast, heals the multitudes then holds a feast of his own (14:13–21). He goes where he pleases, walking on water if it gets in his way (14:22–25). The disciples are terrified (14:26), but Jesus tells them not to fear (14:27). Then his disciples worship him and confess that he is truly the Son of God (14:33). Jesus exposes and condemns the false, lip-service worship of the Pharisees and scribes (15:1–20), and then he is honored by the Canaanite woman who seeks mercy from the Son of David (15:21–25). She will not be put off, and he recognizes her faith and grants her petition (15:26–28).

Again Jesus heals. Again crowds marvel. And again they glorify God for the works of Jesus (Matt. 15:29–31).

When Jesus asks his disciples how the people identify him, the audience of Matthew's Gospel comes to a crucial turning point in the narrative. A new Elijah was predicted in the Old Testament (Mal. 4:5), and this would perhaps explain

---

[36]Cf. Moo, *The Old Testament in the Gospel Passion Narratives*, 333–34; Knowles, *Jeremiah in Matthew's Gospel*, 241–43. See also Wright, *Jesus and the Victory of God*, 535.

[37]Cf. Douglas S. McComiskey, "Exile and the Purpose of Jesus' Parables (Mark 4:10–12; Matt 13:10–17; Luke 8:9–10)," *JETS* 51 (2008), 59: "The contention of this article is that, contrary to the standard approaches to Jesus' purpose statement, Jesus adopts a meaning for Isa 6:9–10 virtually identical to the original meaning in Isaiah."

why some identify Jesus with Elijah. But no Old Testament text indicates that a new Jeremiah will arise, nor is there any indication of a new John the Baptist. Why, then, would the crowds identify Jesus with Jeremiah or John the Baptist (Matt. 16:13–14)? I submit that this identification reflects a typologically generated expectation for a new suffering prophet. What Jeremiah, Elijah, and the Baptist have in common is that they were all genuine prophets who were rejected and persecuted by the people to whom God sent them.[38] Peter's answer goes in a different direction. It has been revealed to him (cf. Matt. 11:25–27) that Jesus is the messiah, the Son of the living God (16:16). Having affirmed that Peter's answer is correct, Jesus then seems to affirm what the crowds have discerned when he asserts that, like the suffering prophets who preceded him, he will go to Jerusalem and suffer (16:21). Peter will have none of this, apparently embracing the conquering messiah but rejecting the suffering servant (16:22).[39] Jesus rebukes Satan and tells Peter that in this he is setting his mind on the things of man rather than the things of God (16:23). Through judgment salvation will come to God's glory. Jesus will go to Jerusalem and suffer.

And through the judgment on Satan's kingdom the kingdom of God will be built. On the apostolic foundation and the confession that Jesus is the Christ, Jesus will build his church.[40] The gates of hell will not hold people against the onslaught of the kingdom of heaven.[41] They will not stand. Jesus will build his church. He judges Satan and his kingdom, and through that judgment he saves his people. In this triumph the glory of God shines.

Jesus calls the one who would follow him to take up the cross, deny himself, and lose his life to gain his soul (Matt. 16:24–26). When Jesus comes with his angels in the glory of his Father to repay each for what he has done (16:27), this bargain will have been well made. Until that day those who trust that he will do as he says glorify him.

Six days after these events (Matt. 17:1) Jesus is transfigured before Peter, James, and John and converses with Moses and Elijah (17:2–4). The one who fulfills the Law (Moses) and the Prophets (Elijah) is then acknowledged by the presence of a shining cloud, from which the voice announces him as the well-pleasing beloved

---

[38]Similarly Knowles, *Jeremiah in Matthew's Gospel*, 90–92. Cf. also Craig L. Blomberg, "Matthew," in *Commentary on the New Testament Use of the Old Testament*, ed. G. K. Beale and D. A. Carson (Grand Rapids: Baker, 2007), 10.

[39]For discussion of references to "The Suffering Messiah" in other early Jewish literature, see Schürer, *The History of the Jewish People*, 547–49.

[40]For a concise summary of the discussion regarding the "rock" in Matt. 16:18, see Strauss, *Four Portraits, One Jesus*, 244. I would argue that Paul has interpreted this incident in a way that understands Peter as the first among equals when he refers to the apostles as the "foundation," with Christ as the cornerstone, in Eph. 2:20.

[41]For the kingdom of heaven in Matthew, see Jonathan T. Pennington, *Heaven and Earth in the Gospel of Matthew* (Leiden: Brill, 2007), summarized in Pennington, "The Kingdom of Heaven in the Gospel of Matthew," *SBJT* 12, no. 1 (2008): 44–51. See also Pennington, "Heaven, Earth, and a New Genesis: Theological Cosmology in Matthew," in *Cosmology and New Testament Theology*, ed. Jonathan T. Pennington and Sean M. McDonough, LNTS (New York: T&T Clark, 2008), 28–44.

Son, the one to whom all should listen (17:5). This is a tacit identification of Jesus as the prophet like Moses (Deut. 18:15–18). These things are not to be publicized, Jesus says, until he is raised from the dead (Matt. 17:9; cf. 16:21; 17:23). Through judgment Jesus will accomplish salvation for God's glory, and when he is vindicated by the resurrection, his own glory will be proclaimed to the nations.

3.9 Discipleship (Matthew 18)

Matthew 18 presents Jesus addressing his followers regarding sin. Followers of Jesus will heed his instructions, and this is a central aspect of their discipleship. Jesus calls his followers to childlike humility (Matt. 18:1–4), then states that it would be better to be drowned in the sea, dragged to its depths by a millstone, than to cause one of his little ones to sin (18:5–6). Jesus means this threat of judgment to deliver his followers from temptation, and the same can be said for the radical action he calls them to take against temptation—better to lose a hand, foot, or eye than to use it for sin (18:7–9). The followers of Jesus have angels in the Father's presence, and the Father will not allow any of his straying sheep to be lost (18:10–14). It seems that the means God uses to bring back his straying sheep are outlined in Matthew 18:15–20. Jesus instructs his followers to call sinners to repentance individually, and if they will not repent, to take one or two others and repeat the call to repentance. If there is still no repentance, the church as a whole is to be brought into the process, with all the members of the church uniting as one to call the unrepentant home. Those who persist in unrepentance are to be treated as a Gentile or a tax collector, and from the use of these terms elsewhere in Matthew it is clear that this means they are no longer considered members of the believing remnant (cf. 5:46–47).

Peter's question that follows seems to address those who repeatedly sin and repeatedly repent (Matt. 18:21). Jesus offers a surprising mercy that apparently has no bounds other than those illustrated in the parable of the unmerciful servant, which he tells in response to Peter's question (18:23–35). The parable seems to mean that the only way to limit the mercy one receives from God is to refuse to extend that mercy to others (cf. 6:14–15).

Throughout the discourse in Matthew 18 on sin and discipleship, sin is clearly judged, and the possibility of mercy is held out for those who will repent of sin and trust in God. In this God's glory shines in justice and mercy, which is another way to say that he is glorified in salvation through judgment.

3.10 Entering Jerusalem (Matthew 19–23)

As Jesus interacts with the Pharisees on divorce, his remarks condemn their hardness of heart and call them to the path of deliverance (Matt. 19:1–12). He welcomes children (19:13–15), and he seeks to condemn the self-righteousness of the man who thinks he has kept the commandments (19:16–22). He then promises his disciples that those who have sacrificed for the sake of his name will receive a great inheritance (19:23–30, esp. 29).

The parable of the laborers in the vineyard condemns human standards of measurement (Matt. 20:1–15), affirms God's freedom to show mercy (20:15), and drives home the point that the last shall be first and the first last—the parable is framed by two assertions of that truth (19:30; 20:16). These paradoxical truths are also seen in the counterintuitive announcement that Jesus continues to make: he is going to Jerusalem to be crucified and raised on the third day (20:17–19). He will save by being judged. Worldliness is condemned again as the mother of the sons of Zebedee asks for a privileged place for her sons (20:20–25), and Jesus asserts that those who would be great must serve (20:26). Those who would be first must make themselves the servants of others (20:27), in keeping with the way that the Son of Man himself "came not to be served but to serve and to give his life as a ransom for many" (20:28).[42] Then Jesus gives sight to the blind who recognize him as the Son of David and cry out for mercy (20:29–34). It is as though sight comes through the condemnation of earthly standards of reckoning. Salvation comes through judgment, and God's glory is seen.

Judgment will fall on Jerusalem precisely because her leadership and the majority of her people have not been like the blind men crying out to the Son of David for mercy.[43] Matthew 21 presents the judgment on Jerusalem from several angles. Jesus humbly enters Jerusalem on a donkey (Matt. 21:1–11). He then cleanses the temple, an act of purging judgment (21:12–13). The blind and lame are healed, but the Pharisees see and are blind, seeking proof of Jesus' credentials. In response, Jesus quotes Psalm 8:3 (ET 2) on the praise that comes from babes and infants (Matt. 21:14–17). Jesus saves the weak and childlike even as he condemns the strong and proud.

Faithless Israel is like the fig tree that Jesus curses (Matt. 21:18–20), and it seems that his word about the disciples' removing the mountain into the sea by faith points to the removal of temple mount (21:21–22). Though Jerusalem has been blessed with the ministries of John the Baptist and Jesus, they have not believed but instead accuse, like their father the Devil (21:23–27). The parable of the two sons means that repentant sinners do God's will, while smug religious leadership agrees to serve but does not (21:28–32). The lease is up. As depicted in the parable of the wicked tenants, the Lord has come seeking fruit, like Jesus inspecting the fig tree, and the beloved son is the stone the builders rejected

---

[42]For the connections between Matt. 20:28/Mark 10:45 and Isaiah 53, see Moo, *The Old Testament in the Gospel Passion Narratives*, 122–27.

[43]Cf. Wesley G. Olmstead, *Matthew's Trilogy of Parables: The Nation, the Nations and the Reader in Matthew 21.28–22.14*, SNTSMS (New York: Cambridge University Press, 2003), 161–62: "Matthew's narrative portrait of Jesus' encounter with Israel suggests that he did not intend the judgment that this trilogy declares to be restricted to the Jewish leadership. Instead, the nation itself is indicted. 'This generation' is guilty of rejecting God's climactic appeal. . . . Israel's marginalised are consistently portrayed in a favourable light."

(21:33–42). Judgment falls: the kingdom will be taken from the tenants and given to those who produce its fruits (21:43–44). All Jewish leadership—whether chief priests or Pharisees—know that Jesus speaks against them (21:45–46).

Faithless Israel has become like guests invited to a wedding they do not wish to attend (Matt. 22:1–14). Both Pharisees (22:15–22) and Sadducees (22:23–33) seek to trap Jesus, but they are silenced, and people marvel at Jesus (22:22, 33). Jesus knows the inner meaning of the Law and the Prophets—love for God and neighbor (22:34–40). Mysteriously, he is both David's son and David's Lord (22:41–45). His wisdom is unanswerable, and none dare continue to question him (22:45–46). The hick carpenter from Nazareth shuts their mouths and condemns their unbelief, and as he triumphs over them, his glory is made known.

Jesus then goes on the offensive against the scribes and Pharisees, pronouncing seven woes against them (Matt. 23:1–36). The final woe identifies them with all those in Israel's history who have murdered and opposed the prophets. From Abel to Zechariah, all the blood of the righteous will come on them as they typologically fulfill this pattern in the murder of Jesus (23:29–36).[44] They are the wicked tenants who think to kill the son and take his inheritance (21:38).[45] They are seed of the serpent, a brood of vipers (23:33). Their house (the temple?) is desolate, and they will not see Jesus again until they bless him as he comes in the name of the Lord (23:37–39). Somehow, through the judgments Jesus announces against them, salvation will apparently come even for the people of Israel. As Olmstead puts it, Matthew "dares to hope for the day when many of Israel's sons and daughters will yet embrace Israel's Messiah (23.39), and in that hope engages in a continued mission to her."[46]

3.11 The Olivet Discourse (Matthew 24–25)

As the cross looms large on the horizon, Jesus predicts the destruction of the temple (Matt. 24:1–2). In response, his disciples ask him when these things will take place, what the sign of his coming will be, and when the age to come will dawn (24:3). Jesus explains that there will be birth pains until the gospel has gone through the whole world (24:4–14). When the full number of the Gentiles has come in (cf. Rom. 11:25), the events of the end will begin. Matthew presents Jesus interpreting Daniel's prophecies of the abomination of desolation (Matt. 24:15; cf. Dan. 9:27; 11:31; 12:11) ushering in a time of tribulation (Matt. 24:21, 29). A vicious time of persecution (24:15–28) seems to precede the coming of the Son of Man in glory, like lightning from east to west (24:27). When the tribulation

---

[44]Cf. Olmstead, *Matthew's Trilogy of Parables*, 162: "Israel . . . has re-enacted her tragic history of repudiating Yahweh's servants . . . . This rebellion is a climactic re-enactment, bringing Israel's sins to full measure and eliciting the decisive judgement of her God."

[45]See further my essay, "Was Joseph a Type of the Messiah? Tracing Typological Identification between Joseph, David, and Jesus," *SBJT* 12, no. 4 (2008): 52–77.

[46]Olmstead, *Matthew's Trilogy of Parables*, 163.

is over, apocalyptic darkening of sun and moon with falling stars and shaking heavens will be followed by the coming of the Son of Man "on the clouds of heaven with power and great glory" (24:29–30). He will gather his elect (24:31). Salvation will come through judgment.[47]

Through the judgments of the time of tribulation, salvation will come. Through the judgment of the false christs and false prophets (Matt. 24:24), salvation will come. And through the announcement of these judgments before they happen, Jesus means to save his disciples and Matthew means to teach his audience. Jesus urges his disciples to learn the lesson of the fig tree (24:32–35).[48] Because the judgments are coming, his followers should be ready, as Noah was (24:36–39).[49] Because Jesus will come when he is not expected (24:40–44), his followers should be faithful and wise servants who will be found doing what he commanded them to do (24:45–47). Threats of judgment give urgency to Jesus' call to be faithful—again, he means to save through the threat of judgment (24:48–51). Readiness is stressed through the parable of the ten virgins (25:1–13) and the parable of the talents (25:14–30), and the sheep who will inherit the kingdom will be serving Jesus by doing good for Jesus' brothers—members of his church (25:31–40). The goats will not serve the church, and they will be judged (25:41–46). The Son of Man will come in his glory with all his angels and sit on his glorious throne (25:31), the hosts will be gathered before him, and he will judge (25:32). Salvation will come through judgment, and the glory of Christ will be more impressive than words can tell.

3.12 Passion, Resurrection, Commission (Matthew 26–28)

The end of the exile, like the exodus, came through a Passover celebration. As Jesus celebrates the Passover with his followers, he gives them a new meal and a new cup, and in the cup is the blood of the new covenant (Matt. 26:26–28). As the new exodus takes place, like the first exodus, the new one comes with a covenant. Like the first exodus it comes through the slaughter of a lamb, whose blood covers the people. The blood of the lamb on the lintel is typologically

[47]Discussing the interpretation of the "Son of Man" from Dan. 7:13 in early Judaism, Gathercole quotes Collins and Slater on four agreed-upon points about the Son of Man in *1 Enoch* and *4 Ezra*, one of which is that this figure will be "instrumental in the judgment and destruction of the wicked" (Gathercole, *The Preexistent Son*, 268–69).

[48]For a typological understanding of the statement of Jesus that "this generation will not pass away until all these things take place" (Matt. 24:34 ESV), see Evald Lövestam, *Jesus and "This Generation": A New Testament Study*, trans. Moira Linnarud, Coniectanea Biblica (Stockholm: Almqvist and Wiksell, 1995), esp. 81–87. Lövestam examines the treatment of the "generation of the flood" and the "generation of the wilderness" in early Judaism and finds that the references to "this generation" in the Synoptic Gospels point to the conclusion that "it is primarily the typology of the [generation] of the Flood which is in focus, as the Flood was looked on as the first end of the world, which typologically foretells the last one" (85). Moreover, the words of Jesus call "this generation" to repent while comforting those who believe and urging them to be prepared (86).

[49]Cf. Knowles, *Jeremiah in Matthew's Gospel*, 243: "Both Noah and the coming Son of man are (not unlike Jonah and Jesus) figures who represent the promise of salvation in the midst of a great and sudden judgment."

fulfilled in the blood of Jesus, "which is poured out for many for forgiveness of sins" (26:28).

After all the judgment that Jesus has been announcing, what takes place is something of a shock. Yes, he has predicted that he will go to Jerusalem to die (Matt. 16:21; 17:22–23; 20:17–19), but he has also announced woe on the scribes and Pharisees and predicted the destruction of the temple (Matthew 23–24). Though he could appeal to the Father for legions of angels (26:53), the hour has come for the Scriptures to be fulfilled (26:54–56). As if to highlight the connections between the death of Jesus and the exile, the words John records Jesus saying when he cleansed the temple—about the temple being destroyed and raised after three days (John 2:19)—resurface at Jesus' trial (Matt. 26:61). The death of Jesus is something of a typological fulfillment of the destruction of the temple. Through judgment salvation comes, then glory, as the Son of Man will take his seat at the right hand of power and come on the clouds of heaven (26:64).

In fulfillment of the Scriptures (Matt. 27:9), Jesus is slain. Again the word about the temple being destroyed and rebuilt is hurled at him on the cross (27:40). Apocalyptic darkness covers the land (27:45). The curtain of the temple is rent,[50] as the earth shakes and the rocks split (27:51). Just as Ezekiel prophesied about the dry bones coming to life at the end of the exile (Ezek. 37:1–14), tombs are opened and saints are raised from the dead (Matt. 27:52–53). The exile is over. The new exodus has begun. No more will the people of God speak of the day when the Lord brought them out of Egypt. Instead, their focus will be on the time when Jesus the temple was destroyed and rose on the third day, and through the judgment their salvation came for God's glory (cf. Jer. 16:14–21).

The last defense against evil holds. Jesus breaks the back of evil, and he rolls back the power of death. Just as he said, once the temple, his body, is destroyed, he rises on the third day. Through judgment comes salvation, and his followers worship him, even through doubt (Matt. 28:17). Because of his triumph, he has all authority in heaven and on earth (28:18). On this basis he commissions his followers to carry forward the task of covering the dry lands with Yahweh's glory as the waters cover the seas by making disciples of all nations,[51] baptizing them in the triune name,[52] and teaching them all he has commanded. He promises to

---

[50]See Daniel M. Gurtner, *The Torn Veil: Matthew's Exposition of the Death of Jesus*, SNTSMS (New York: Cambridge University Press, 2007), esp. 199–201.

[51]Rightly Olmstead, *Matthew's Trilogy of Parables*, 163: Jesus is "rescinding his earlier prohibition of mission outside of Israel (10.5–6, cf. 15.24)." Olmstead also sees an allusion to the promises to Abraham in Gen. 12:1–3 in Matt. 28:16–20 (163–64).

[52]Cf. Gathercole, *The Preexistent Son*, 73: "The order Father-Son-Spirit in Matt. 28.19 is not incidental; rather, it is born out of the early Christian thinking that the Father has authority over the Son, who in turn has authority over the Spirit."

be with his people to the end of the age (28:19–20), building his church just as he said (16:18).[53]

3.13 The Center of the Theology of Matthew

I. Howard Marshall writes, "As in all the Gospels the center of Matthew's theology is Jesus."[54] I agree with this but think that sharpening it in the following ways makes it more helpful: the Gospel of Matthew shows the fulfillment of the exile in the death of Jesus, and through that judgment salvation comes for God's people to God's glory. Jonathan Pennington has written, "The kingdom is the central message of Jesus' teaching. Moreover, a good argument can be made that the same is true for the rest of the Scriptures, Old and New."[55] I think this stops one step short and can be helpfully sharpened with Schreiner's observation: "The coming of the kingdom that Jesus proclaimed designated something new, a time when God's enemies would be demonstrably defeated and the righteous would be visibly blessed."[56] So the kingdom will come in salvation through judgment, and the purpose of the kingdom is the enjoyment of God's glory under the rule of his king. In Matthew the kingdom comes as a result of the new exodus and the return from exile that Jesus accomplishes—in short, in the salvation through judgment accomplished by the messiah for the glory of God.[57] In addition to this metanarrative of God's glory in salvation through judgment, Matthew also shows an ethical dimension to God's glory in salvation through judgment, as the people of Jesus are instructed regarding the way of life that will glorify God. Much of this instruction comes through the condemnation of worldliness and selfishness and faithlessness, and through that judgment the disciples of Jesus are brought to salvation and life for God's glory. The center of Matthew's theology is the glory of God in salvation through judgment, supremely manifested in the cross of Christ. As Jesus warns many times in Matthew, there will be another moment of salvation through judgment when the Son of Man comes in power and glory on the clouds of heaven with all his holy ones.

4. Mark

Matthew opens with a genealogy and narratives of the early life of Jesus. Luke begins with the parents of the Baptist, narrates the birth of Jesus, then also has a genealogy. John begins with a prologue that starts "in the beginning" (John

[53]Cf. Michael F. Bird, *Jesus and the Origins of the Gentile Mission*, LNTS (New York: T&T Clark, 2007), 176: "Jesus appropriated the role of Israel and the temple and its universal function for himself and his disciples who would be to the world what Israel and the temple refused to be: a light to the nations."

[54]I. Howard Marshall, *New Testament Theology: Many Witnesses, One Gospel* (Downers Grove, IL: InterVarsity, 2004), 111. Cf. his statement of Matthew's "main theme" (125).

[55]Pennington, "The Kingdom of Heaven in the Gospel of Matthew," 44.

[56]Schreiner, *New Testament Theology*, 53–54. Cf. also 62: "On the day of judgment and salvation the kingdom will be consummated."

[57]Cf. Ellis, *Christ and the Future in New Testament History*, xi.

1:1), setting the coming of Jesus in the context of cosmic history. In comparison with the other Gospels, Mark seems to plunge right into the salvation-historical significance of the Baptist and Jesus (Mark 1:1–13).[58] Mark "immediately" begins his account of the public ministry of Jesus in Galilee (1:14–8:30). As in Matthew, so in Mark: Peter's confession (Mark 8:27–30) marks a turning point from ministry in Galilee to Jesus predicting his suffering and vindication and moving toward Jerusalem (Mark 8:31–10:52). Then Jesus triumphantly enters Jerusalem, where after controversies and teachings, he is betrayed, crucified, and raised from the dead (Mark 11:1–16:8). Like Matthew, Mark presents Jesus as the culmination of the long story of salvation through judgment for God's glory that began in the garden and culminates in Jesus. Jesus is the end of the judgment of exile, and the judgment is completed in his death on the cross. The new exodus begins in his resurrection, and from that follows the inauguration of the return from exile. Mark presents Jesus as the embodiment of salvation through judgment for God's glory.

4.1 The Baptist and Jesus (Mark 1:1–13)

The features in Matthew that herald the end of the exile in the coming of Jesus are also present in Mark, which opens with the announcement of the Baptist's role as the fulfillment of the forerunning messenger prophesied by Malachi (Mal. 3:1) and the voice crying in the wilderness prophesied by Isaiah (Isa. 40:3).[59] The prophets indicated that the new exodus and return from exile would be accompanied by an outpouring of the Holy Spirit (e.g., Isa. 32:15; Ezek. 36:27; 37:14; Joel 3:1–5, ET 2:28–32), and the Baptist prophesies that Jesus will baptize in the Holy Spirit (Mark 1:8). The Gospel of Mark declares that through the judgment of exile salvation is coming in Jesus the messiah for the glory of God.[60]

4.2 Jesus in Galilee (Mark 1:14–8:30)

The most remarkable feature of Mark's fast moving narrative is its central character, Jesus.[61] And perhaps the most remarkable thing about Jesus in Mark is his apparent audacity.[62] With a certainty that is almost incomprehensible today,

---

[58]See the argument that the superscriptions of the Gospels "were not secondary additions but part of the Gospels as originally circulated" and that "the Gospels did not first circulate anonymously . . ." in Martin Hengel, *The Four Gospels and the One Gospel of Jesus Christ: An Investigation of the Collection and Origin of the Canonical Gospels*, trans. John Bowden (Harrisburg, PA: Trinity Press International, 2000), 50–56.

[59]See further Rikki E. Watts, *Isaiah's New Exodus in Mark*, WUNT 2.88 (Tübingen: Mohr Siebeck, 1997; repr., Grand Rapids: Baker, 2000), 53–121.

[60]So also Wright, *Jesus and the Victory of God*, 160.

[61]For discussion of the titles of Jesus used in Mark, see Marshall, *New Testament Theology*, 81–85.

[62]Cf. Watts, *Isaiah's New Exodus in Mark*, 138–39: "Mark's presentation of Jesus' understanding of his exorcisms, his accounts of Jesus' healings of the blind, deaf-mute, and lame, of Jesus' pardoning of sins, and of the miraculous feedings appear to be cast in an Isaianic N[ew] E[xodus] perspective. It is interesting, therefore, that several scholars have regarded the miracles reported in, for example, 4:35–5:43, 6:34–44, 45–52; 7:32–37; and 8:1–10 as epiphanic [citing Kertelge, Achtemeier, and Dibelius]. Such powerful 'self-manifestations' are entirely in keeping with the proposal that Mark presents Jesus as the inaugurator of the Isaianic promises whereby Yahweh himself comes to deliver as he 'makes bare his arm' (cf. Isa 40:3, 10; 51:9; 52:10; 53:1; 59:16ff; 63:5)."

Jesus announces that the kingdom of God has come and tells people they should therefore repent and believe (Mark 1:15). He calls men to leave livelihoods and families, and to fish out the exiles with him (1:16–20). He teaches with authority (1:22), commanding unclean spirits (1:25), who obey (1:26)! People are amazed (1:27), and his fame spreads (1:28).

Jesus heals and casts out demons (Mark 1:29–34);[63] he cleanses a leper at will (1:40–44). In these actions he overturns the condemnation of sin and reverses its sentence. This is salvation through judgment—judgment on the judgment itself. The news of the glory of Jesus is such that he cannot openly enter towns (1:45).

Jesus preaches and teaches (Mark 1:39; 2:2, 13), and perhaps the most audacious thing that he does is forgive sin (2:5).[64] He backs this up, though, with a healing that demonstrates his authority to do so (2:10).[65] Amazement follows, and all glorify God (2:12).

Jesus has the temerity to eat with tax collectors and sinners (Mark 2:16). When asked why his disciples do not fast, he unblushingly asserts that he is the Bridegroom (2:19–20). When questioned about what his disciples do on the Sabbath (2:25–26), he compares himself to David,[66] then has the chutzpah to declare himself Lord of the Sabbath (2:28).[67] When he faces down the Pharisees and heals the man with the withered hand on the Sabbath (3:1–5), they take counsel with the Herodians as to how they might destroy him (3:6).

Who would take it upon themselves to ascend a mountain, appoint twelve companions, name them apostles, send them out to preach, and give them authority to cast out demons? Jesus does just this (Mark 3:13–19). Not surprisingly, his family thinks him crazy (3:20–21), while the scribes from Jerusalem say that he himself is the one who is possessed by a demon (3:22). Jesus then has the impudence to imply that he is a strong man who has bound Satan and is plundering his goods (3:23–27), to assert that those who blaspheme the Holy Spirit—by which he claims to act—will not be forgiven (3:28–30), and to disown his family in favor of those who do the will of God (3:31–35).

Jesus has the nerve to claim that those who follow him have been given the secret of the kingdom of God (Mark 4:11), while those who do not understand the parables are experiencing the fulfillment of Isaiah 6:9–10. Mark presents this fulfillment of Isaiah to the same end that Matthew did, to contribute to

[63]Gathercole makes the observation that the way the demons recognize Jesus demonstrates that "Jesus has heavenly identity throughout his ministry, and not only when he receives moments of prophetic inspiration. . . . It is clearly as heavenly beings that they identify who Jesus is" (*The Preexistent Son*, 53).

[64]Cf. ibid., 57–61.

[65]See the discussion of the "authority" of the Son of Man derived from Daniel 7 in Simon Gathercole, "The Son of Man in Mark's Gospel," *Expository Times* 115, no. 11 (2004): 366–72, esp. 369.

[66]For more on this, see my Julius Brown Gay Lecture delivered at Southern Seminary on March 13, 2008, "The Typology of David's Rise to Power: Messianic Patterns in the Book of Samuel."

[67]See Gathercole, *The Preexistent Son*, 244–45, 250–52 on the use of "Lord" in Mark.

the theme of the realization of the exile in Jesus. Hear the boldness of these parables Jesus tells! He asserts that those who receive his word and act on it are good soil, while anyone who rejects his word is bad soil (Mark 4:13–20). He claims that this little kingdom he is proclaiming, with these nobodies from Galilee, is going to become the largest tree in the garden, with the birds nesting in its shade (4:30–32), and in saying this he clearly recalls the greatness of King Nebuchadnezzar (cf. Dan. 4:10–12, 20–22).

The dauntless speech of Jesus is not limited to the words he speaks to people. Awaking to find himself in a boat being tossed by a stormy sea, Jesus presumes to rebuke the wind and sea, commanding it to be still and at peace (Mark 4:39; cf. Ps. 107:23–30). He cannot be bothered with the little detail that most carpenters from places like Nazareth do not give orders to the winds and the waves. The marvel of those following him is what we would expect (Mark 4:40).[68]

Having dismissed a legion of demons from a man who would have frightened any other mortal, Jesus has the cheek to tell that man, "Go home to your friends and tell them how much the Lord has done for you, and how he has had mercy on you" (Mark 5:19 ESV). The man does so, with the result that everyone marvels (5:20). A troubled father comes to Jesus, desperate to see his daughter made well (5:21–23). Jesus brazenly feeds the man's feverish hopes and goes with him. On the way, Jesus is touched by a woman whose malady is beyond the help of many physicians, and he is not ashamed to tell her that her faith has made her well (5:25–34). Meanwhile the man receives word that his daughter has died, and rather than comfort him Jesus recklessly tells the man not to fear but believe (5:35–36). Not surprisingly, the mourners mock him for his optimism (5:37–40). The only thing that makes the behavior remotely acceptable is the fact that he raises that little girl from the dead (5:41–43) and heals that woman who has touched him (5:29).

It is as G. K. Chesterton wrote:

> Instead of looking at books and pictures about the New Testament I looked at the New Testament. There I found an account, not in the least of a person with his hair parted in the middle or his hands clasped in appeal, but of an extraordinary being with lips of thunder and acts of lurid decision, flinging down tables, casting out devils, passing with the wild secrecy of the wind from mountain isolation to a sort of dreadful demagogy; a being who often acted like an angry god—and always like a god. Christ had even a literary style of his own, not to be found, I think, elsewhere; it consists of an almost furious use of the *a fortiori*. His "how

[68]Cf. Frank Thielman, *Theology of the New Testament: A Canonical and Synthetic Approach* (Grand Rapids: Zondervan, 2005), 63: "The disciples know that the stilling of raging storms is the business of Yahweh (Ps. 65:7; 89:9; 107:28–30), and their question implies the unthinkable—that when they are in the presence of Jesus, they are in the presence of God himself."

> much more" is piled one upon another like castle upon castle in the clouds. The diction used *about* Christ has been, and perhaps wisely, sweet and submissive. But the diction used by Christ is quite curiously gigantesque; it is full of camels leaping through needles and mountains hurled into the sea. Morally it is equally terrific; he called himself a sword of slaughter, and told men to buy swords if they sold their coats for them. That he used other even wilder words on the side of non-resistance greatly increases the mystery; but it also, if anything, rather increases the violence. We cannot even explain it by calling such a being insane; for insanity is usually along one consistent channel. The maniac is generally a monomaniac. Here we must remember the difficult definition of Christianity already given; Christianity is a superhuman paradox whereby two opposite passions may blaze beside each other. The one explanation of the Gospel language that does explain it, is that it is the survey of one who from some supernatural height beholds some more startling synthesis.[69]

That synthesis is not seen by those in Jesus' hometown, so when he goes there, they are astonished and offended by him (Mark 6:1–6). Jesus sends out the disciples to drive out demons, and wonder of wonders, his disciples not only do that but also heal many sick (6:7–13). Herod slays the Baptist (6:14–29), and Jesus feeds the multitude (6:30–43). Then Jesus goes marching by his disciples, walking on the water and, of all things, tells them not to be afraid (6:45–52; cf. Job 9:8).[70] Who could heed such an admonition with him acting like that? Even those who touch the fringe of his garment are healed (Mark 6:53–56).

Then Jesus looks the religious people, the Pharisees, in the face and calls them hypocrites when they question him. And if that were not enough, he charges them with nullifying God's commands by means of their human traditions (Mark 7:1–13). Expecting his simple assertions to inform what everyone thinks about the clean and unclean, he even declares all foods clean (7:14–23).

From a distance he drives a demon from a woman's daughter (Mark 7:24–30). His command gives hearing and speech to a deaf man with a speech impediment (7:31–35). Not surprisingly, people vigorously announce the deeds of Jesus and are more astonished at him than tongues could tell (7:36–37).

Jesus is not afraid to try and feed four thousand people with seven loaves and a few small fish, supernaturally pulling it off (Mark 8:1–10). He refuses the Pharisees when they seek a sign (8:11–12),[71] and he warns the disciples against

---

[69]G. K. Chesterton, *Orthodoxy* (1908; repr., Colorado Springs: Waterbrook, 2001), 221–22 (chap. 9).

[70]Cf. Gathercole, *The Preexistent Son*, 64: ". . . Jesus' mastery of the sea points very strongly to a close identification of him with Yahweh in the OT" (following discussion of Job 9:8) (63).

[71]Bryan writes that "when asked to support such language [evoking Israel's awaited restoration] with a manifestation of divine power modeled after the wondrous epiphanies of the Exodus and Conquest, [Jesus] flatly refused, offering instead the sign of the Son of man—the sign of approaching and unavoidable judgment" (*Jesus and*

their leaven (8:13–21). As the disciples fail to understand, Jesus does a miracle that seems to symbolize the way that they partially see the significance of who he is and what he is doing. A blind man comes to be healed—imagine Jesus feeding the hopes of people in such a condition—and Jesus spits in his eyes. The man looks and sees people who look like trees. Then Jesus lays his hands on the man's eyes, enabling him to see clearly (8:22–26). No daring hopes does Jesus dash.

As will be seen from the cycle of three passion predictions, three failures on the part of the disciples, and three teachings of Jesus on discipleship (see table 5.6), the disciples are like the blind man, partially seeing. Three times in Mark 8–10 Jesus predicts his death, the disciples fail to understand or to respond appropriately, and he then teaches them about discipleship.[72]

Table 5.6. The Three Passion Predictions in Mark[1]

Announcement of Jesus' Death	Failure on the Part of the Disciples	Jesus Teaches on Discipleship
8:31: He will "suffer . . . be rejected . . . be killed . . . after three days rise again."	8:32: Peter rebukes Jesus.	8:33–9:1: Take up the cross.
9:30–31: He will "be delivered . . . . killed, after three days he will rise."	9:32: "They did not understand the saying, and were afraid to ask him."	9:33–50: "If anyone would be first he must be last . . . and servant . . . . Whoever receives one such child in my name receives me . . . . the one who is not against us is for us . . . . millstone . . . . cut it off. . . . tear it out."
10:33–34: He will "be delivered . . . . kill[ed] . . . . after three days he will rise"	10:35–37: "Grant us to sit, one at your right hand and one at your left, in your glory."	10:38–45: "Whoever would be great among you must be your servant . . . first . . . must be slave . . . . the Son of Man came not to be served but to serve, and to give his life as a ransom for many."

[1]Texts are from the ESV.

The disciples see clearly enough for Peter to confess that Jesus is the messiah (Mark 8:29), but it is as though they see trees walking (cf. 8:24). They do not understand what kind of messiah Jesus is.

Before we move to the next section of Mark's Gospel, we should connect the dots between the impudent audacity of Jesus and the glory of God in salvation

Israel's Traditions of Judgment and Restoration, 45). As is evident from this chapter, I think the texts show that Jesus has not refused, but rather that he offers his death and resurrection as the new exodus and conquest.

[72]See the important discussion of Isaiah's "servant songs" in relation to the passion predictions in Moo, *The Old Testament in the Gospel Passion Narratives*, 86–97.

through judgment. Jesus has shown the world its bankruptcy so that the world might feel its need for the bailout he provides. He has condemned the world in order to save it. His teaching with authority exposes and condemns the failures of human tradition. His healing the sick and raising the dead judges and triumphs over the effects of sin and the outworkings of the curse in the world. Casting out demons, he reveals that he has entered the home of the strong man, bound him, weighed him in the scales, and found him wanting, and he is now plundering his possessions. Jesus brings salvation through judgment, and in response his fame spreads, the people marvel, and everyone glorifies God. Mark does not use the formulation, but it is clear that the centerpiece of the theology of his Gospel is that Jesus is bringing in the kingdom by conquering all other kingdoms. He is glorifying God in salvation achieved through judgment.

There is a paradoxical element, too, in all this audacious behavior of Jesus: he asserts himself in the most shameless ways and combines that with commands not to make known what he has done (cf. Mark 1:25, 34, 44; 3:12; 4:10–12, 34; 5:43; 7:17, 24, 36; 8:26, 30; 9:9, 30). This is not from any fear or sense of impropriety, but appears rather to stem from his awareness that he must complete a certain course. To keep the tension from escalating to the point of open confrontation, he orders people and demons not to make him known.[73]

4.3 Jesus on the Way to Jerusalem (Mark 8:31–10:52)

Having gone about condemning all the principalities and powers and Pharisees and Herods, saving those they lifted no finger to help, Jesus responds to Peter's confession with the announcement that he will bring salvation by undergoing judgment himself, in his own person. He will be killed and rise after three days (Mark 8:31). When Peter rebukes him, Jesus has the audacity to set all human wisdom on its head, declaring that anyone who seeks to save his life will lose it, while anyone who loses his life "*for my sake and the gospel's* will save it" (8:35, emphasis added, cf. 32–34). Not only does Jesus overturn all human expectation regarding the way the world works, but he makes himself and his message the nonnegotiable element of the equation.

Jesus calls those who would follow him to take up their cross (Mark 8:34)—they are to do as a crucified man does when forced to carry his own cross to the place of execution. The decision to follow Jesus is the decision one makes when one recognizes that this is a one-way trip to the place of the skull. The

[73]See the discussion of The "Messianic Secret" in Robert H. Stein, *Mark*, BECNT (Grand Rapids: Baker, 2008), 23–26. Stein holds that Mark uses this theme to show that "Jesus was not put to death because he was a political revolutionary" and "as a literary device to highlight the greatness and glory of Jesus and his identity. Jesus is too great to be hidden" (25). Ladd comments, "They wanted a king to deliver them from Rome, not a savior to redeem them from their sins. . . . Had Jesus publicly proclaimed himself to be the Messiah, that proclamation would have been received by the people as a rallying call to rebellion against Rome" (*A Theology of the New Testament*, 138).

one who seeks to save his life by refusing to follow Jesus and shoulder the means of his own execution will not survive. The one willing to stare death in the face *for the sake of Jesus and his message* will gain life (8:35). The Greek phrase Mark uses to represent the words of Jesus,[74] "for my sake [ἕνεκεν ἐμοῦ]," is the same phrase used in the Greek translation of Isaiah 48:11, "For my sake [ἕνεκεν ἐμοῦ] I will act for you, because my name is profaned and my glory I will not give to another."[75] Jesus speaks of himself in the same language that God uses to speak of himself, and this is not an isolated instance in the Synoptic Gospels (see also Matt. 5:11; 10:18, 39; 16:25; Mark 10:29; 13:9; Luke 9:24).

In Isaiah 48:11 Yahweh acts for his own sake. In Mark 8:35 Jesus demands that his followers act for his sake. This is powerful evidence of "early high Christology." It also brings a certain tension that I hope has been rising as I have described the actions of Jesus in Mark: does Jesus have the right to conduct himself with divine audacity or does he not? However the audience of Mark's Gospel might answer that question, Mark's answer is clear. Narrating the story of Jesus in the way that he does everywhere assumes that Jesus has the requisite authority to take the prerogatives he does. To answer the question in the negative and conclude that Jesus does not have the right to act this way is nothing less than a repudiation of the earliest and most reliable primary source data in our possession. When scholars make such moves, they subtly shift the genre of their own writing from history to fiction, for if we do not rely on the sources for our information, we are relying on some other source that we have invented from our own imaginings.

What Jesus goes on to say gives a glimpse into why taking up one's cross to follow him to Golgotha might be the right choice. In Mark 8:36–37 Jesus speaks of gaining the whole world but losing one's soul, which makes clear that he assumes that there is something beyond this world and this life worth losing everything in this world and this life to gain. In other words, Jesus is not simply saying that he is going to Jerusalem to lead a rebellion against Rome, and that anyone who wants to go with him needs to be prepared for crucifixion if the cause fails. Jesus is not asserting his confidence that the cause against Rome will not fail when he says that those who seek to save their lives—by not going along—will lose them because when he overcomes Rome, he will visit those who have not fought with him. No, Jesus is saying something much larger. He is not merely saying that one's allegiance to him determines one's earthly destiny; he is claiming, with a

---

[74]I put it this way simply because I do not know whether Jesus spoke Aramaic, in which case the words of Jesus have been translated.
[75]Here I have rendered the Greek text of Isa. 48:11.

divine audacity, that one's allegiance to him determines the fate of one's soul. Thus he declares in Mark 8:38, "For whoever is ashamed of me and my words in this adulterous and sinful generation, the Son of Man will also be ashamed of him, when he comes in the glory of his Father with the holy angels."

Jesus is going to come with a host of heavenly beings and crush the kingdoms of the earth, and through that great judgment salvation will come for those who have risked all for his cause. Jesus promises to come "in the glory of his Father" (Mark 8:38). Jesus is making a proleptic announcement of judgment in order to bring about salvation. He refers to this coming to motivate anyone who thinks it is not worth it to risk a cross to follow him. Jesus seeks to accomplish salvation through the announcement of judgment for the glory of God.

Anticipating that glorious appearance, and grounding the call to take up the cross, Mark recounts how Jesus is gloriously transfigured and converses with Elijah and Moses, symbolic of the Old Testament Law and Prophets (Mark 9:1–5).[76] Naturally Peter is terrified, and then the glory cloud overshadows them, and from the cloud the Father affirms Jesus, to whom they should listen (9:6–7).

Jesus foretells how he will suffer and rise from the dead (Mark 9:9–13), shows offense at any doubt regarding his ability to heal (9:23), and continues to teach that he will be killed and raised on the third day (9:30–32). The contrast between the willingness of Jesus to be last and the desire of the disciples to be first is starkly portrayed (9:33–37); then Jesus affirms his priority as he commends the one casting out demons in his name (9:38–41).

Jesus renders judgment on disputes about divorce (Mark 10:1–12), on low views of children (10:13–16), and on a worldly preference for wealth over him and his kingdom (10:17–31). Amazing and frightening his followers, he leads the way to Jerusalem announcing his imminent demise and claiming that after three days he will rise (10:32–34). Those who seek greatness in his kingdom (10:35–45) must look for it where he has placed it: in serving others, "for even the Son of Man did not come to be served but to serve and to give his life as a ransom for many" (10:45).[77] Through judgment salvation will

[76]Noting the way the transfiguration (Mark 9:2–8) anticipates the future glory that Jesus has just announced (8:38–9:1) takes nothing away from Gathercole's argument (*The Preexistent Son*, 50) that "the transfiguration is not merely proleptic of the resurrection or parousia in the future, but [Jesus' shining heavenly identity] is also already present just as his identity as Son of God [announced at Jesus' baptism] is already a present reality."

[77]See the discussion of the "ransom" in Bolt, *The Cross from a Distance*, 71–75. He argues that "the concept of ransom is associated with both the original exodus and the servant's new exodus, and the servant's death is clearly a substitionary, exclusive place-taking exchange. In accordance with Isaiah 53, the Son of Man will give his life as a ransom for many" (72–73). The ransom was from sin (73–73), enabling Jesus to plunder the strong man (74), while ransoming also from death and from God's wrath (74–75). See also the sections discussing Daniel 7, "Jesus Dies as the Son of Man," and Isaiah 53, "Jesus Dies as Isaiah's Suffering Servant," in Thielman, *Theology of the New Testament*, 68–71, 71–74.

come for God's glory, and Jesus will serve "the many" by taking their judgment in order to ransom them.[78] The final episode on the way to Jerusalem seems to point the way into the group referred to as "the many" whom Jesus will ransom: blind Bartimaeus cries out for the Son of David to show him mercy, and Jesus tells him that his faith has saved him (10:46–52). Those who would be ransomed must acknowledge the identity of Jesus ("Son of David," 10:47–48), recognize they have no claim on him and seek his mercy ("show mercy to me!" 10:47–48), and trust him to do what none else can, making requests as far reaching as that of a blind man asking for sight ("your faith has saved you," 10:52).[79] Sight comes through the judgment of blindness, through the judgment of one's own ability to restore one's sight, through the judgment of the source of blindness in a world broken by sin. Through judgment salvation comes to God's glory.

4.4 Jesus in Jerusalem (Mark 11:1–16:8 [20])

Jesus barnstorms Jerusalem. With shouts of Hosanna, the crowds bless the one coming in the name of the Lord (Mark 11:1–11). The fruitless fig tree symbolizes the state of things in the temple (11:12–14). Jesus curses the fig tree (11:14) and cleanses the temple (11:15–19), and the withered fig tree points to what will become of the temple and its establishment (11:20–21). Again Jesus makes the comment about those who have faith removing the mountain into the sea, and again it seems that the replacement of temple mount by the believing community seems to be in view (11:22–25).[80]

Those who oppose him cannot answer him (Mark 11:27–33), and Jesus tells the parable of the wicked tenants against them (12:1–12). He renders judgment against them (cf. 12:9), and it will be "marvelous in our eyes" (12:11). When they try to trap him with the tax question, they marvel at his judicious reply (12:13–17). Then Jesus silences the Sadducees by his reply to their levirate marriage–resurrection dilemma (12:18–27), silences all questioners with his verdict on the greatest commandment (12:28–34), then delightfully confounds the crowds by asking how David's Lord could be his son (12:35–37). He presumes to assert that hypocritical scribes will receive "greater condemnation" (12:38–40) and speaks as though he knows who has put more into the offering box than others (12:41–44).

The audacity continues: Jesus declares that the temple will be destroyed, that many will claim to be him, that his message will be carried to all nations, and that his followers will be hated for the sake of his name (Mark 13:2, 6, 10, 12). Interpreting Daniel, Jesus warns of an abomination of desolation

---

[78]See especially Gathercole, "The Son of Man in Mark's Gospel," 370–71.
[79]So also Bolt, *The Cross from a Distance*, 75: "Bartimaeus is often recognized as the model disciple."
[80]Watts (*Isaiah's New Exodus in Mark*, 332–37) takes this view and responds to the objections of various scholars.

and a great tribulation, then his apocalyptic coming (13:14–27). Through the judgment of that time of tribulation salvation will come when the Son of Man comes in power and glory to gather his elect and defeat his enemies (13:19, 26–27).[81]

The conspiracy is introduced (Mark 14:1–2), the Lord is anointed (14:3–9), the traitor is found (14:10–11), the Passover is eaten (14:12–16), the Scriptures are fulfilled, and the traitor's judgment is announced (14:17–21). Fittingly, the new exodus, like the first, is inaugurated by a Passover meal.[82] At that meal Jesus redirects its symbolic elements.[83] The unleavened bread that symbolized a hasty departure from Egypt will henceforth symbolize his pure body, broken on behalf of his people. The cup, likely the third cup that symbolized redemption, will henceforth symbolize his blood, "poured out for many" (14:22–24). Through the judgment that will fall in the breaking of his body and shedding of his blood, salvation will come, and Jesus will next drink of the fruit of the vine in the kingdom of God (14:25).

Jesus fulfills Zechariah's words in that he is the shepherd, and when he is stricken the sheep scatter (Mark 14:26–31).[84] He submits to the Father's will and takes the cup (14:32–42).[85] The Scriptures are fulfilled as Jesus is betrayed by a friend (14:43–50). Like Matthew, Mark surfaces the words of Jesus that connect his death to the symbolic moment of exile in the destruction of the temple at the trial (14:58) and on the cross (15:29).

Jesus acknowledges his identity as the messiah, Son of God, king of the Jews (Mark 14:62; 15:2).[86] Simon Gathercole notes the salvation-through-judgment-resulting-in-glory paradigm in the Son of Man statements in Mark: "The narrative pattern which holds the Son of Man sayings together is: *the authoritative Son of Man revealed—the authority of the Son of Man rejected—the authority of the Son of Man vindicated*."[87] Symbolically, Barabbas deserves to die and Jesus does not. Jesus dies in place of Barabbas (15:6–15). Judgment falls, and with the heavens dark (15:33) the curtain of the temple is torn (15:38). The way into God's presence is open. Salvation has come through judgment for the glory of God. Then judgment is rendered on the false verdict that condemned Jesus to

[81]On Mark 13, Wright states, "It is the story of the real return from exile; the story, once more, of YHWH returning to judge and save" (*Jesus and the Victory of God*, 359).
[82]Cf. Watts, *Isaiah's New Exodus in Mark*, 365.
[83]Similarly Bolt, *The Cross from a Distance*, 104–6; Wright, *Jesus and the Victory of God*, 557.
[84]For the citations of Zech. 9:9–10; 11:12–13; 12:10; and 13:7 in the passion narratives, see Moo, *The Old Testament in the Gospel Passion Narratives*, 173–224.
[85]Cf. Bolt, *The Cross from a Distance*, 67: "The image of the cup, too, is a well established Old Testament symbol of God's wrath."
[86]Gathercole writes, "The heavenly preexistence of Christ, then, does not diminish the importance of his death, but rather is part of the reason for the scandalous paradox of that death" (*The Preexistent Son*, 292).
[87]Gathercole, "The Son of Man in Mark's Gospel," 372.

death—it is reversed, annulled—and Jesus is raised from the dead (16:1–8).[88] The "decisive victory over evil" has been won.[89]

4.5 The Center of the Theology of Mark

In Jesus salvation comes through judgment for God's glory. In his ministry in Galilee Jesus condemns false sources of authority, upstages ineffectual sources of healing, judges the unclean spirits and demons, and shows the folly of the world's wisdom.[90] Through his teachings, healings, and mighty acts, Jesus judges in order to save. Then on the way to Jerusalem Jesus teaches explicitly that what looks like the way down is in reality the way up. In Jerusalem he brings salvation through judgment in his ransoming death, and symbolically the long story of salvation through judgment in Israel's exile is resolved by means of the new exodus and return from exile that Jesus inaugurates in his body and blood. The center of Mark's theology is the glory of God in salvation through judgment.[91]

Mark Strauss writes, "Jesus' central message in Mark concerns the coming of the kingdom of God (1:15)."[92] True enough, but the kingdom serves the greater purpose of God's glory. Moreover, once again we can focus this centrality of the kingdom by observing that this is a kingdom whose coming will be through the judgment of all other kingdoms, and its inauguration spells salvation, with the manifold display of justice and mercy glorifying God.[93] Robert H. Stein writes,

---

[88]The weight of evidence seems to be against the originality of Mark 16:9–20, and table 5.7 shows how the material there is found elsewhere in the New Testament:

Table 5.7. Parallels between Mark's Disputed Ending and Other New Testament Passages

Mark 16:9	Luke 8:2
Mark 16:10	John 20:11–18
Mark 16:11	Luke 24:11, 14; Matt. 28:17b
Mark 16:12–13	Luke 24:13–35; John 20:19, 26
Mark 16:14	Luke 24:41
Mark 16:15–16	Matt. 28:18–20
Mark 16:16	John 3:17–18; cf. 1 Pet. 3:21; Titus 3:5
Mark 16:17–18	John 14:12
Mark 16:17	Mark 9:37; Acts 2:3–4; 10:46; 19:6; 1 Cor. 12:28; Eph. 6:10–18
Mark 16:18	Acts 28:3–4; James 5:13–16; cf. Luke 10:19
Mark 16:19	Luke 24:50–53; Acts 1:2, 11, 22; Acts 7:55–56; Rom. 8:34; Eph. 1:20; Col. 3:1; 1 Tim. 3:16; Heb. 1:3; 8:1; 10:12; 12:2; 1 Pet. 3:22; Rev. 3:21
Mark 16:20	Acts 2–28; Heb. 2:3–4

For discussion of this difficult issue, see the essays by Daniel B. Wallace, Maurice Robinson, Keith Elliott, David Alan Black, and Darrell Bock in David Alan Black, ed., *Perspectives on the Ending of Mark: 4 Views* (Nashville: Broadman & Holman, 2008).

[89]Wright, *Jesus and the Victory of God*, 607.

[90]As Watts puts it, "In a word, Mark is 1 Corinthians 1:18–25 writ large" (*Isaiah's New Exodus in Mark*, 383).

[91]Cf. Michael F. Bird, "Tearing the Heavens and Shaking the Heavenlies: Mark's Cosmology in Its Apocalyptic Context," in *Cosmology and New Testament Theology*, 45–59, esp. 58–59.

[92]Strauss, *Four Portraits, One Jesus*, 199. Similarly Marshall, *New Testament Theology*, 78: "The kingdom of God is the main theological theme in the teaching of Jesus."

[93]Rightly Brian J. Vickers, "Mark's Good News of the Kingdom of God," *SBJT* 8, no. 3 (2004): 12: "For Jews living in first century Israel, with hippodromes and arenas scattered throughout the land and in Jerusalem, Roman standards flying in prominent places, Roman crosses at times lining the roads, Roman soldiers in barracks in the Temple precinct, and with a Roman governor living secure in his palace in Jerusalem, the coming of the 'Kingdom'

"The central and dominating theme of Mark is christological in nature."[94] From my analysis above, it should be clear that I agree with this and would only add the following: the nature of the christological truth that Mark communicates centers on Jesus' role as God's definitive agent of salvation through judgment for God's glory. Jesus not only brings salvation through judgment for God's glory, but he experiences it in himself in his death and resurrection.

5. Luke

Matthew's five great discourses of Jesus make the first Gospel reminiscent of the five books of Moses. Rikki Watts has suggested that "Isaiah's schematic of the N[ew] E[xodus] from 'the nations,' along the 'Way,' to 'Jerusalem' provides the paradigm" for the structure of Mark's Gospel, which moves from Galilee (Mark 1:1–8:26) on the Way (8:27–10:52) to Jerusalem (11:1–16:8).[95] If Matthew reminds readers of the Pentateuch and Mark is Isaianic, the Gospel according to Luke[96] bears a striking resemblance to the narratives in Samuel.[97]

Like Samuel, Luke opens with a godly priest and a remarkable birth. As in Samuel, the seed of promise (David in Samuel, Jesus in Luke) is raised up through difficulty, suffers, and in the end is vindicated.[98] Like Samuel, Luke pursues his story across two volumes, with the first tracing the rise of the king, and the second showing him enthroned and reigning. Like Samuel, Luke–Acts is a story of reversals, with the small and weak exalted while the proud and strong are brought low. As in Samuel, the center of the theology of Luke's Gospel is the glory of God in salvation through judgment.[99]

Jesus brings salvation as he heals, teaches, conquers, and dies, and this salvation comes through judgment as he defeats his enemy and pronounces condemnation

---

meant deliverance. God would deliver his people as he promised. Their enemies will be destroyed, God will visit his people in a decisive way and Israel will be restored and exalted with God as her King. The 'Kingdom of God' may have meant more than that, but it certainly did not mean less." Similarly Ladd, *A Theology of the New Testament*, 86: "The meaning of God's Kingdom is both salvation and judgment."

[94]Stein, *Mark*, 21. Similarly Marshall, *New Testament Theology*, 77: "Mark's theme is the Messiah and Son of God who proclaims the kingdom and acts it out in ways that express who he is" (cf. also 91).

[95]Watts, *Isaiah's New Exodus in Mark*, 123.

[96]Cf. E. Earle Ellis, *The Gospel of Luke*, rev. ed., NCB (Grand Rapids: Eerdmans, 1974), 53: "The balance of probabilities favours the view that Luke was a hellenistic Jew. This leaves open the possibility that Luke is the Lucius (Paul's cousin?) mentioned in Rom. 16:21. Like Silas and Silvanus, Luke and Lucius were alternate forms of the same name" (citing Cadbury and Ramsay).

[97]Cf. C. Kavin Rowe, *Early Narrative Christology: The Lord in the Gospel of Luke* (Berlin: Walter de Gruyter, 2006; repr., Grand Rapids: Baker, 2009), 32: "Nils Dahl suggested Luke's intention was to 'write the continuation of the biblical history'" (citing Nils A. Dahl, "The Story of Abraham in Luke-Acts," in *Studies in Luke-Acts*, ed. Leander Keck and J. Louis Martyn [Philadelphia: Fortress, 1966], 153).

[98]See further my Julius Brown Gay Lecture, "The Typology of David's Rise to Power: Messianic Patterns in the Book of Samuel," and "Was Joseph a Type of the Messiah?"

[99]Marshall (*New Testament Theology*, 152) writes, "The main theme [of Luke] is the coming of the Savior who brings salvation to the needy." Cf. Strauss, *Four Portraits, One Jesus*, 260, who states that the central theme of Luke-Acts is that "God's end-times salvation predicted by the prophets has arrived through the coming of Jesus the Messiah, the Savior of the world, and this salvation is now going forth to the whole world." Once again, I would only add that this salvation comes through judgment (the judgment that falls on Jesus, and the judgment that will be visited on the enemies of God's people), and the justice and the mercy manifest God's glory.

on those allied with Satan, who falls from heaven like lightning. The glory of God and Jesus are expressed in a number of different ways in the Gospel of Luke, and table 5.8 seeks to account for this variety and to note where these expressions are found.[100]

Table 5.8. The Glory of God and Jesus in the Gospel of Luke

Blessing God or Jesus	1:64, 68; 2:28; 8:16; 13:35; 19:38; 24:53
Thanking God or Jesus	2:38; 17:16; 22:17, 19
Rejoicing in God or Jesus	1:14, 47, 58; 10:21; 13:17; 15:6, 9–10; 19:6, 37
Praising God or Jesus	2:13, 20; 17:15, 18; 18:43; 19:37; 23:47
Worship of God or Jesus	2:37; 24:52
Fear or fearing God or Jesus	1:12, 29, 65; 2:9; 5:10, 26; 7:16; 8:25, 35; 12:5; 23:40; 24:37
In God's or Jesus' name or for his sake	9:24, 48, 49; 10:17; 11:2; (12:8–9); (18:29); 21:8, 12, 17; 24:47
Glory or majesty of God or Jesus, glorifying God or Jesus, God or Jesus being glorified or magnified	1:46; 2:9, 14, 19, 20, 32; 4:15; 5:25, 26; 7:16; 9:26, 29, 31, 32, 34, 43; 13:13; 18:43; 19:38; 22:69; 24:26
Wonder, amazement, marveling, or being astonished at God or Jesus	2:18, 47, 48; 4:22, 32, 36; 5:9, 26; 8:25, 56; 11:14; 20:26; 24:12
Spreading report of Jesus	2:18; 4:14, 23, 37; 5:15; 7:17; 8:39; 10:1
Mercy of God or Jesus	1:50, 54, 58, 72, 78; 5:36; 7:13; 17:13; 18:13, 38, 39
Falling before Jesus	5:8, 12; 8:28; 17:16
God and Jesus conceal or reveal (cf. Prov. 25:2)	(2:50); 8:10; 9:45; 10:21–22; 18:34; 24:16, 31, 32, 45
Glory of Jesus at his coming	12:40; 13:35; 17:24, 30; 18:8; 19:38; 21:27; 21:34–36

The discussion here will be structured according to the following understanding of Lucan literary structure: Luke's opening narratives present parallel accounts of the births of John and Jesus, moving then to the Baptist's preparation of the way (Luke 1–3). Having overcome temptation (Luke 4), Jesus ministers in Galilee (Luke 5–9). Jesus then sets his face toward Jerusalem and slowly makes his way there (Luke 9:51–19:27). Jesus triumphantly enters Jerusalem, where he is betrayed, arrested, crucified, and raised (Luke 19:28–24:53).

Luke's two-volume work can be seen to have a broadly chiastic structure as seen in table 5.9.[101]

[100]This catalog of various ways that God's glory is communicated in Luke's Gospel demonstrates again that biblical theology is more than mere word studies of selected terms.

[101]I have adapted this chiasm from Craig L. Blomberg, *Jesus and the Gospels: An Introduction and Survey* (Nashville: Broadman & Holman, 1997), 142–43, who cites Kenneth Wolfe, "The Chiastic Structure of Luke-Acts and Some Implications for Worship," *Southwestern Journal of Theology* 22 (1980): 60–71.

Table 5.9. Blomberg's Chiasm in Luke–Acts (Adapted)

Jesus in relationship to the Roman Empire
  Jesus in Galilee
    Jesus in Samaria and Judea
      Jesus in Jerusalem
        Resurrection and ascension (Luke 24–Acts 1)
      Witnesses in Jerusalem
    Witnesses in Judea and Samaria
  Witnesses to the ends of the earth
Paul in relationship to the Roman Empire

5.1 Preparation for Jesus' Ministry (Luke 1–3)

Luke's prologue (Luke 1:1–4) declares that the purpose of the Gospel is to give a believer, Theophilus, certainty concerning the things he has been taught (1:4).[102] This certainty is meant to arise from Luke's "orderly account" (1:3). Based on my study of the narrative, I take this reference to orderliness to refer to the way that Luke has juxtaposed mutually interpretive episodes.

An early instance of this careful arrangement can be seen in the parallels between the births of John and Jesus (see table 5.10), and these parallels highlight the superiority of Jesus to John.

Table 5.10. Gabriel Sent to Zechariah and Mary

	To Zechariah, Luke 1:13	To Mary, Luke 1:30–31
1.	"Do not be afraid, Zechariah"	"Do not be afraid, Mary"
2.	"for your prayer has been heard"	"for you have found favor with God"
3.	"your wife Elizabeth will bear you a son"	"you will conceive in your womb and bear a son"
4.	"you shall call his name John" (ESV)	"you shall call his name Jesus" (ESV)

John's own greatness only increases the stature of Jesus as Luke presents it. Gabriel tells Zechariah, the Baptist's father, that John "will be great before the Lord," will conduct himself as a Nazirite (another connection to Samuel), will be filled with the Spirit (Luke 1:15), and will play the part of the Elijah who is to come (1:16–17). The part that John will play in the outworking of salvation history is second in significance only to one.

Gabriel tells Mary that Jesus also "will be great" (Luke 1:32, same terms as 1:15), but from there it goes through the roof: in fulfillment of 2 Samuel 7:14, Jesus "will be called Son of the Most High, and the Lord God will give to him

[102]Cf. Thielman, *Theology of the New Testament*, 111 and n. 1.

the throne of his father David, and he will reign over the house of Jacob forever, and of his kingdom there will be no end" (Luke 1:32–33).

These two birth narratives are introduced with the words, "And it came about in the days of Herod, king of Judea" (Luke 1:5), so the coming of the Davidic king and his kingdom implies the end of Herod's kingdom. Salvation will come through judgment for God's glory as the little people who are faithful are exalted while the Herods of the world are brought low.

Hannah was a barren woman whose womb the Lord opened (1 Sam. 1:5–6, 19–20). Mary is a virgin to whom the Lord has given conception (Luke 1:34–38). Like Hannah's song (2 Sam. 2:1–10), Mary's paean of praise celebrates the God who saves the weak and humble by visiting justice against prideful oppressors (Luke 1:46–55). By the strength of his arm the Lord scatters the proud and dethrones the mighty, exalting the humble, satisfying the hungry, sending the rich away empty (1:51–53). The Lord does this in *mercy* (1:54), in accordance with the promise to Abraham and his seed (1:55).

The long wait is finally drawing to its close. The darkest hours of the night have passed. The birth pangs at their strongest, longing and yearning too full to be spoken, John is born (Luke 1:57). Through the judgment felt in the curse of Genesis 3:16, salvation dawns. Hope begins to be realized. Ordained praise comes from the babe's mouth at the miracle baby's birth. Zechariah's silence is lifted (Luke 1:20, 64), as salvation comes through judgment, and he employs his loosened tongue to bless God (1:64, 68–79). His blessing of God is based on his conviction that God has visited his people to redeem them by raising up a horn of salvation from the line of David (1:68–69). Hereby God is keeping his promise to *save his people from their enemies*—and that salvation is going to come through the judgment of those enemies (1:70–71). This will be a demonstration of Yahweh's *mercy* to Israel, even as he keeps covenant with them (1:72), fulfilling his promise to Abraham (1:73) so that his people can worship him (1:74–75). This salvation includes deliverance from the oppression of their enemies (1:74) *and* the forgiveness of sins (1:77). The sun is rising from on high, and, recalling Isaiah 9, the light is shining on those sitting in the darkness of the shadow of death (1:78–79).[103]

In a key juxtaposition, next to the description of the reigning Caesar and all his pompous registrations and officials, Luke sets the description of the birth of the world's king and Savior (Luke 2:1–20). Caesar has his Quirinius; Jesus has the lowly shepherds. The humble will be exalted and the lofty brought low, and the former will come through the latter. Caesar has his legions. What has the peasant child? Only the heavenly host announcing glory to God at his birth.

[103]See Simon J. Gathercole, "The Heavenly ἀνατολή," *JTS* 56 (2005): 471–88, summarized in Gathercole, *The Preexistent Son*, 238–42.

Rome claims to bring peace, but those who know sing the peace this child's birth means for those with whom God is pleased (2:14).

Luke wants his message to be taken to heart and pondered, and he commends this behavior by noting how it was modeled for his audience (table 5.11).

Table 5.11. Taking the Message to Heart

1:66	"And all who heard them laid them up in their hearts" (ESV).
2:19	"But Mary treasured up all these things, pondering them in her heart" (ESV).
2:51	"And his mother treasured up all these things in her heart" (ESV).

As the parents of Jesus do all that is required by the law of Moses (Luke 2:22–24, 27, 39), they encounter two elderly members of the remnant, Simeon and Anna. They have the same hope that Luke describes in two synonymous phrases: Simeon awaits "the consolation of Israel" (2:25); Anna is with those waiting for "the redemption of Jerusalem" (2:38). He blesses God (2:28), and she worships and gives thanks (2:37–38), because both hope for the salvation that will come through judgment when, in Simeon's words, the child appointed for the fall and rise of many in Israel does his work (2:34).[104] These narratives of the circumstances surrounding the births of John and Jesus are saturated with the glory of God in salvation through judgment.

Luke also depicts salvation through judgment happening in the proclamation of the Baptist. In response to John's call to repentance, announcement of the second exodus and return from exile, and warning of the wrath to come (Luke 3:1–9), crowds, tax collectors, and soldiers are saved through the warnings of judgment (3:10–17).

Luke then works backward from the thirty-year-old Jesus through his genealogy all the way to Adam (Luke 3:23–38). Ending the genealogy with Adam allows Luke to introduce another key juxtaposition: the genealogy ends with Adam, the son of God (3:38), who, accompanied by his wife, was tempted by Satan in the garden of Eden.[105]

5.2 Temptation and Beginning of Jesus' Public Ministry (Luke 4)

Unlike Adam, who was in the garden of Eden, Jesus is in the wilderness (Luke 4:1). Unlike Adam, who was with his wife, Jesus is alone. Unlike Adam, who had all the trees of the garden for food, Jesus eats nothing for forty days (4:2).

[104]Ellis (*The Gospel of Luke*, 72) writes, "According to some Jewish tradition the prophetic gift ceased at the close of the Old Testament period, but its presence or revival was generally expected in the messianic times (cf. 1 Mac. 14:41; Jos. *c. Apion*. I,41; *Ta*. 8a . . .)." This could inform Luke's presentation of Mary, Elizabeth, Zechariah, Simeon, and Anna prophesying in the first two chapters of his gospel.

[105]Ellis notes, "Elsewhere Adam is viewed as a type of Messiah, the one who restores the Paradise that Adam lost. See on 23:43; cf. Rom. 5:12ff.; 1 C. 15:45; Heb. 2:6ff." (*The Gospel of Luke*, 93).

Like Adam, Jesus is tempted by the Devil (4:2). Unlike Adam, Jesus trusts God's word and conquers (4:3–13). Salvation comes through judgment for God's glory. Judgment fell on Adam for his sin, and Jesus brings judgment on Satan by resisting his temptations. The steadfastness of Jesus exposes the lies of Satan, judging and condemning them, and God's faithfulness to his promises and ability to provide what Satan never could are celebrated by Jesus. Thus God is glorified in salvation through judgment as Jesus resists temptation.

Then Jesus goes home to Nazareth, where having identified himself as Isaiah's anointed servant of Yahweh (Luke 4:16–21), he draws typological parallels between himself and Elijah and Elisha (4:24–27). This is not what the people in the synagogue want to hear (4:22–23), so they try to kill him (4:28–29). Their verdict will not stand, and by avoiding it Jesus judges their rejection of God's will (4:30). Luke then validates the claims that Jesus has made by showing him teaching with authority, casting out demons, building a reputation, and rebuking sickness (4:31–41).[106] Jesus has set out to preach the good news of God's kingdom (4:42–44), and that good news celebrates the glory of God in salvation through judgment.

5.3 *Ministry in Galilee (Luke 5–9)*

No doubt many, along with Simeon and Anna, are looking for the eschatological promises of the prophets to dawn. Their hopes are surely piqued by the Baptist and his ministry. Like Peter and the others who have fished all night (Luke 5:5), they may feel that all their efforts have brought meager results. Then Jesus gets in the boat, gives the word to let down the nets, and there is a miraculous haul (5:4–6). This demonstration of majesty convicts Peter of his sin (5:8),[107] and the judgment astonishes people, glorifying God. Then Jesus applies the spiritual truth of what he has physically done in the assertion, "From now on you will be catching men" (5:10). The miraculous catch of fish points to the fishing out of the exiles prophesied by Jeremiah (Jer. 16:16). However past attempts at national reformation may have failed, Jesus comes with portents of success. Those he calls leave everything to follow him (Luke 5:11).

The portents of success are bolstered by the cleansed leper (Luke 5:12–14), the growing crowd and spreading report (5:15), and the evident piety and humility of Jesus in prayer (5:16). Return from exile means forgiveness of sin (cf. Isa. 40:2), and this gives a wider significance to the forgiveness Jesus announces (Luke 5:17–24). Not only does he announce forgiveness; he does mighty works—such as making the lame walk—that authenticate the announcement (5:24). The

[106]Cf. ibid., 100: "According to Jewish tradition demonic power was to be crushed in the messianic age (see on 11:22; cf. *SBK* IV, 527; *Test. Zebulun* 9:8)." Cf. also ibid., 101, "The 'rebuking' seems to personify an impersonal evil, but it may rather reflect the conviction that behind all sickness is the working of Satan."
[107]Cf. Gathercole, *The Preexistent Son*, 75.

infirmity and the sin that caused it have been judged and nullified, the enemies who oppose Jesus have their mouths shut, and in response to the salvation that comes through judgment those who see redemption glorify God (5:25–26). Jesus is so compelling that he calls a tax collector right out of his money-grubbing booth (5:27). The sick and the sinful are summoned home, while the religious grumble (5:27–32).

There is no fasting among the disciples of Jesus because he is the Bridegroom who has come for the wedding, the new covenant that will accompany the end of the exile and the inauguration of the new exodus (Luke 5:33–39). Jesus is the new David, typologically fulfilling David's role, but greater—so great, he is even Lord of the Sabbath (6:1–5). His doing good on the Sabbath by restoring a man's hand seems to hint at the new creation that Jesus will bring, but his opponents prefer the old wine (5:36–39) and respond to the new life he gives on the Sabbath by planting the seeds of the plot to kill Jesus (6:6–11).

The selection of the Twelve (Luke 6:12–16) in the orderly context of these other indications of the dawning of the new exodus and return from exile recalls the martial arrangement of the twelve tribes in the wilderness. Then Jesus, as Moses had done, gives God's word to those who have been freed by his power (6:17–49). The international implications of this new exile and new covenant are perhaps hinted at in the healing of the servant of the Roman centurion (7:1–10, cf. 9, "not even in Israel have I found such faith"). The Jews see Jesus and reject him, while the Gentiles hear of him and receive him.[108] The raising from the dead of the widow's son at Nain recalls Elijah's mighty acts,[109] and resurrection from the dead signals return from exile (cf. Ezek. 37:11–14). Jesus condemns death, reverses it, and in response to the salvation he brings through that judgment, everyone glorifies God (Luke 7:15–17).

The Baptist has announced that the one coming after himself will baptize with the Holy Spirit and fire, judging and saving, clearing the chaff and gathering the wheat (Luke 3:16–17). In the absence of the eschatological outpouring of the Spirit and the purging flames of judgment, the Baptist asks whether Jesus is the one expected (7:18–19).[110] Luke presents Jesus responding with reports of the kinds of restorative ministry promised by Isaiah (7:22). From there Jesus denounces those who have rejected both the Baptist and himself (7:23–34). Wisdom cries out in the street (Prov. 1:20), and the wise recognize wisdom (Luke 7:35). These words imply that those who embrace wisdom will embrace Jesus. The following episode, in which the sinful woman of the city wets Jesus' feet with her tears and wipes them with her hair while Simon, the disapproving Pharisee, looks on and

[108] Cf. Ellis, *The Gospel of Luke*, 117.
[109] The phrase "and gave him to his mother" in Luke 7:15 exactly matches the wording of the Greek translation of 1 Kings 17:23.
[110] Cf. Ellis, *The Gospel of Luke*, 119.

draws unwise conclusions (7:36–50), demonstrates that those who are aware of their own sinfulness will love Jesus, who forgives sin (7:41–50).

Those who recognize their sin and embrace the message of Jesus are saved by faith (Luke 7:50). Those who reject the message of the Baptist have not declared God just but have rejected for themselves God's purpose (7:29–30). Wisdom does not justify them but condemns them (7:35).[111] People from all levels of society embrace the message of the kingdom proclaimed by Jesus, men such as the Twelve, and women too, from the formerly demon possessed to the wife of Herod's steward (8:1–3). The secrets of the kingdom are revealed in the parables Jesus tells (8:4–15). Those who hear the word of God proclaimed by Jesus and do it are the members of his family (8:21). Every other source of truth has been judged and condemned, and through that judgment they are saved by faith in what he proclaims. By contrast, even the members of his literal family will be rejected if they do not embrace God's word (8:19–20).

Jesus calms wild winds (Luke 8:22–25) and wild men (8:26–39), and in both instances he triumphs over what appears to be out of control and wins praise for himself (8:25, 39). Earle Ellis correctly notes, "Messiah opposes the demonic powers at work in man and in nature in order to redeem man-in-nature, man as a totality and as part of the created cosmos."[112]

Having healed the woman with the flow of blood and raised the daughter of Jairus (Luke 8:40–56), Jesus sends out the disciples (9:1–6). Luke narrates the Baptist's death (9:7–9), the return of the disciples (9:10), and the feeding of the five thousand (9:11–17), before coming to a decisive turning point in the narrative.

As in Matthew and Mark, so in Luke: at the account of Jesus' asking the disciples who the crowds say he is, the narrative begins to turn a corner. In response to Peter's correct confession, Jesus makes the first of several statements in Luke regarding his death and resurrection. These are listed in table 5.12.

What this means for the thesis of this book must be underscored: the death and resurrection of Jesus of Nazareth is the definitive moment when the glory of God is displayed in salvation through judgment. The death and resurrection of Jesus is the climactic moment at the end of all four canonical Gospels: Matthew, Mark, Luke, and John. And the moment when Jesus first begins to announce that he will go to Jerusalem to be crucified and raised is a decisive turning point in the first three of these: Matthew, Mark, and Luke. Thus the claim can be made that at the level of narrative structure, Matthew, Mark, and Luke all pivot on

---

[111]Cf. Gathercole, *The Preexistent Son*, 204: "Wisdom's works are in fact manifest in *both* John *and* Jesus, as they announce the kingdom." See further Gathercole, "The Justification of Wisdom (Matt 11.19b/Luke 7.35)," *NTS* 49 (2003): 476–88.

[112]Ellis, *The Gospel of Luke*, 129.

Table 5.12. Predictions, Reminders, and Proofs of the Death and Resurrection in Luke[1]

9:22	"The Son of Man must suffer many things and be rejected . . . and be killed, and on the third day be raised."
9:44	"The Son of Man is about to be delivered into the hands of men."
12:50	"I have a baptism to be baptized with."
13:32–33	"I cast out demons and perform cures today and tomorrow, and the third day I finish my course. . . . for it cannot be that a prophet should perish away from Jerusalem."
17:25	"But first he must suffer many things and be rejected by this generation."
18:32–33	"He will be delivered over to the Gentiles and will be mocked and shamefully treated and spit upon. And after flogging him, they will kill him, and on the third day he will rise."
24:6–7	"Remember how he told you, while he was still in Galilee, that the Son of Man must be delivered into the hands of sinful men and be crucified and on the third day rise."
24:25–26	". . . slow of heart to believe all that the prophets have spoken! Was it not necessary that the Christ should suffer these things and enter into his glory?"
24:46	"Thus it is written, that the Christ should suffer and on the third day rise from the dead."

[1]All texts here are from the ESV.

and drive toward the demonstration of the glory of God in salvation through judgment in the death and resurrection of Jesus.

This is the center of the theology of these Gospels. The cross of Jesus upholds the justice and the mercy of God, glorifying him. The kingdom dawns only because of the death and resurrection of Jesus, because of this definitive display of God's glory in salvation through judgment. The end of the exile, new exodus, new covenant, and return from exile are all inaugurated by the death and resurrection of Jesus. God's righteousness is supremely demonstrated, and his mercy is made known. Christ has died. Christ is risen. Christ will come again.

The glory of this coming (Luke 9:26) grounds the call to deny oneself and take up the cross (9:23), to lose one's life for Christ's sake (9:24), to lose the whole world but not lose one's soul (9:25), to reject any shame that might be heaped on those who cling to Christ (9:26). In Luke's narrative, all this is validated by the foretaste of the future glory of Christ, in which he has promised to come (9:26), seen at the transfiguration (9:27–36). The narrative's logic urges that those who hear of such glory must *believe* what they do not see—that Jesus will indeed come in such glory. This faith must then inform those faced with the choice between the world and Christ. God states his position on the question, declaring that Jesus is his Son, his chosen one, to whom all should listen (9:35). This identifies Jesus as the prophet like Moses.[113] Moreover, at the transfiguration Moses and Elijah, the Law and the Prophets, are discussing with Jesus the "exodus" he is about to

[113]Cf. the Greek translation of Deut. 18:15 and Luke 9:35.

accomplish in Jerusalem (9:31). Luke is presenting God, Moses, and Elijah as identifying Jesus as the way of salvation. One will either side with them or choose destruction. Luke makes no bones about the fact that Jesus is at war, rebuking unclean spirits and astonishing all with his display of God's majesty (9:37–43).

A remarkably comforting theme surfaces in the midst of the marveling (Luke 9:43) and the insistence on the looming cross (9:44). Luke introduces the idea that even as Jesus announces these truths, they remain concealed: "But they were not understanding this word and it was concealed from them, that they might not perceive it, and they were afraid to ask him concerning this word" (9:45; cf. also 2:50; 8:10; 9:45; 10:21–22; 18:34; 24:16, 31–32, 45). This is comforting to anyone who reads the Old Testament and finds it difficult to know for certain how the story will play out. This is comforting to anyone who recognizes how natural it would be for the disciples to expect a conquering rather than a suffering messiah. This is comforting for anyone who embraces the perspectives articulated by those whose minds Jesus will open (the apostles and authors of the New Testament), that they might understand the Scriptures (Luke 24:45), because we know that those who reject the "open-minded" interpretations of the authors of the New Testament writings are operating under the same constraints that the formerly "closed minded" experienced before Jesus revealed the truth to them. What he does for them he can do for others.

Two incidents that relate to things being done in the name of Jesus portend the many things done in his name[114] in Acts (Luke 9:46–48, 49–50; cf. Acts 2:38; 3:6, 16 (2x); 4:7, 10, 12, 17, 18, 30; 5:28, 40, 41; 8:12, 16; 9:14, 15, 16, 21, 27–28; 10:43, 48; 15:17; 16:18; 19:5, 13, 17; 21:13; 22:16). Then Jesus sets his face to go to Jerusalem. This portion of the Gospel of Luke is thick with the center of Luke's theology, which is that Jesus has come as the messiah, who is the supreme agent of God for the manifestation of his glory in salvation through judgment.

5.4 On the Way to Jerusalem (Luke 9:51–19:27)

The high degree of overlap between Matthew, Mark, and Luke allows for some summary at this point, lest the discussion grow unnecessarily repetitive. Summarizing in this way does not minimize unique emphases of Luke's Gospel, such as his heavy interest in prayer (see table 5.13) or his strategic use of the title *Lord* for Jesus.[115] Within the scope and purposes of the argument of this book, such summary can function to demonstrate the thesis of this book and allow us to move forward.

---

[114]See the discussion of this feature of Synoptic christology in Gathercole, *The Preexistent Son*, 65–68, concluding on 76: "The Synoptic Gospels all use the formula 'in the name of Jesus' in such a way that it stands in for the OT formula 'in the name of Yahweh.'"

[115]On this see further Rowe's study of "the Lord in the Gospel of Luke," *Early Narrative Christology*. Also, more briefly, Gathercole, *The Preexistent Son*, 247–48.

Table 5.13. Prayer in Luke

Text	Nature of the Prayer
1:10	Multitude prays at the hour of incense.
1:13	Gabriel tells Zechariah his prayer has been answered.
1:46–55	Mary blesses God in a psalm-like prayer.
1:67–79	Zechariah blesses God, prophesying a psalm-like prayer.
2:13	A multitude of the heavenly host praises God.
2:20	The shepherds praise and glorify God.
2:28–32	Simeon blesses God.
2:37–38	Anna continually prays in the temple and gives thanks to God when she meets Jesus.
3:21	Jesus is praying as the heavens are opened at his baptism.
5:16	Jesus withdraws to lonely places to pray.
5:33	The disciples of John and the Pharisees fast and pray often.
6:12	Jesus spends all night in prayer the night before he chooses the Twelve.
6:28	Jesus teaches the crowd to pray for those who abuse them.
9:18	Jesus is praying alone before asking who the crowds say he is.
9:28–36	Jesus goes up on the mountain to pray and is transfigured.
10:2	Jesus teaches the seventy-two to pray that the Lord of the harvest will send out laborers.
10:21–22	Jesus praises God in the Holy Spirit for concealing and revealing.
11:1–4	Jesus is praying and teaches the disciples to pray.
11:5–13	Jesus teaches the disciples to persist in prayer and assures them the Father will give the Holy Spirit.
18:1	Jesus tells the parable of the unjust judge to teach his disciples always to pray and not lose heart.
18:9–14	Jesus tells the parable of the Pharisee and the tax collector, both praying in the temple, and addresses it to those who trust in themselves.
19:46	Jesus says that the temple is to be a house of prayer.
20:47	Jesus warns against the scribes who make long prayers for show.
21:36	Jesus warns his hearers to pray for strength to escape the things that will take place at the end and to stand before the Son of Man.
22:32	Jesus tells Peter that he has prayed for him.
22:40	Jesus tells his disciples to pray that they not enter into temptation.
22:41	Jesus prays about the cup.
22:44	Jesus prays more earnestly.
22:45–46	Jesus rises from prayer, finds the disciples sleeping, and tells them to pray that they not enter into temptation.

In this section of Luke's Gospel we see more judgment on the wicked, most prominently when Jesus announces that he has seen Satan fall like lightning (Luke 10:18).[116] He has given his disciples authority to tread on serpents and scorpions and all the enemy's power (10:19). Jesus brings salvation through the judgment

[116]For the view that Jesus saw an eschatological vision of the end-time fall of Satan, see Simon Gathercole, "Jesus' Eschatological Vision of the Fall of Satan: Luke 10.18 Reconsidered," *ZNW* 94 (2003): 143–63.

he accomplishes on the ruler of the forces of darkness (see also the binding of the strong man in 11:14–23). In his teaching, Jesus also brings judgment on those who think in worldly, foolish ways, such as in the parable of the rich fool whose soul is required as he plans to build bigger barns (12:13–21). Through judgment on the forces of darkness and on the ways of thinking that align with those forces, Jesus intends to save people, delivering them to true thoughts that glorify God. Jesus sets out to accomplish salvation through judgment for God's glory, as we see in Luke's recitation of all that Jesus began to do and teach (cf. Acts 1:1).

Jesus has come[117] casting the fire on earth of which the Baptist spoke (Luke 12:49). And he himself will go through the baptismal waters of God's judgment (12:50).[118] Those who repent of their sins in response to his condemning announcement of judgment (e.g., 13:1–9), those who humble themselves (14:11), confess their unworthiness (15:17–19, 21), cry out for mercy (17:13; 18:13, 37, 39), and believe in a way that compels them to act accordingly (11:28; 17:19; 18:8, 42), will be saved by faith through judgment for God's glory. Indeed, this salvation by faith through judgment puts the enemies of God and Christ to shame while the believing rejoice at the mighty acts of God (cf. 13:17).

5.5 *In Jerusalem: Arrest, Crucifixion, Resurrection, Commission (Luke 19:28–24:53)*

Once again this section can be quickly summarized: Jesus enters Jerusalem to the praise of God (Luke 19:37–40). He shows genuine compassion for Jerusalem (19:41–44), but upholds justice and visits judgment by cleansing the temple (19:45–48). The parable of the wicked tenants promises that those who fall on the stone the builders have rejected will be crushed by it (20:9–18). The wisdom of Jesus silences opposition (20:19–26, 27–40). Jesus describes the history of the future, which will culminate in his triumphant appearing, rendering judgment and accomplishing redemption (21:5–36).[119]

On the eve of the "exodus" he will accomplish in Jerusalem (Luke 9:31), Jesus redirects the Passover meal and makes it a celebration of the "new covenant" in his blood (22:14–20).[120] The death and resurrection of Jesus are the new exodus that eclipses the exodus from Egypt as the definitive moment of God's glorifying

---

[117]For the argument that the "I have come" sayings of Jesus constitute the strongest evidence of his preexistence in the Synoptic Gospels, see Gathercole, *The Preexistent Son*, 83–189.

[118]Cf. Moo, *The Old Testament in the Gospel Passion Narratives*, 117: "The 'fire' in Lk. 12:49 is almost certainly a reference to the eschatological judgment. In light of the parallelism present in both verses, it is necessary to define the baptismal metaphor in such a way that its reference is closely associated with Jesus' experience of God's wrath and the inbreaking of the eschatological judgment. That this reference is to the death of Jesus can scarcely be doubted."

[119]Ellis writes, "Like Jesus, Luke sets no chronological deadlines and apparently places the parousia after the fulfilment of 'the times of the Gentiles,' that is, after the completion of the Gentile mission, which in Luke's day was only beginning" (*Christ and the Future in New Testament History*, 122).

[120]For connections to Isaiah 53, see Moo, *The Old Testament in the Gospel Passion Narratives*, 127–32, and see the quotation of Isa. 53:12 in Luke 22:37, which Moo also discusses, ibid., 132–38.

himself in salvation through judgment. Just as the Passover meal was a regular celebration of God's glory in salvation through judgment, so the Lord's Supper replaces the Passover as the commemoration of God's deliverance of his people through the judgment of their enemies.

Having fulfilled the Scriptures by going to the cross (Luke 22:37), Jesus rises from the dead (22:6). Through the judgment he experienced on the cross, Jesus brings salvation, and those who hear the report marvel (24:12). Jesus then explains Moses and the Prophets and all the Scriptures to the two on the road to Emmaus (24:13–17). And if we want to know how he interpreted the Scriptures, we need only examine the way that the Scriptures are interpreted in Luke–Acts and the rest of the New Testament.[121] Those two men have their eyes opened (Luke 24:31; cf. 24:16). Then Jesus opens the minds of his disciples (24:44–46), and Luke closes his Gospel in a way that prepares readers for the continuation of his story in the book of Acts (Luke 24:47–53).

5.6 *The Center of the Theology of Luke*

In the Gospel according to Luke, Jesus is the one who comes as the new David to accomplish the new exodus and inaugurate the new covenant through the definitive display of the glory of God in salvation through judgment at the cross. As Satan falls from heaven like lightning, those joined with him against the Lord and his anointed are defeated. All their arguments and objections are shown to be mush. Jesus upholds the truth and righteousness and holiness of God's justice, establishing his covenant and redeeming with perfect equity. Balancing this is the display of mercy, love, steadfast loyalty, and kindness in the Father's plan and the willingness of Jesus to die for his people. This salvation that is achieved as judgment falls on Jesus opens the way for sins to be forgiven, and this forgiveness is so glorious that it should be proclaimed to all the nations. Those who humble themselves and pray to the Lord will find that their faith has saved them, they will go in peace, and they will have been saved through judgment to live for the kingdom Jesus brings. As Schreiner rightly notes, "To live for the sake of the kingdom is simply another way of saying that human beings live for God's sake—for his glory."[122] The Gospels are about the glory of God in Christ, as Wright has it:

> The portrait of Jesus . . . suggests, not a terrifying God from whose immediate embodied presence we would shrink, but one whose glory is strangely revealed in the welcome and the warning, the symbol and the story, the threat to the Temple, the celebration in the upper room, and the dark night at noon on Calvary.[123]

[121]See E. Earle Ellis, "Jesus' Use of the Old Testament and the Genesis of New Testament Theology," in *Christ and the Future in New Testament History*, 20–37.
[122]Schreiner, *New Testament Theology*, 123.
[123]Wright, *Jesus and the Victory of God*, 662.

6. John

The temple dominated ancient Jerusalem, which has been likened to a temple with a small city around it.[124] The temple and its festivals are likewise prominent in the Gospel of John, which has Jesus in Jerusalem at the temple all through the narrative rather than, as in Matthew, Mark, and Luke, only at the end. The majesty and profundity of the Fourth Gospel are such that approaching it is like drawing near to the Holy of Holies. The glory of God pervades the Fourth Gospel, and it is most clearly seen in the demonstration of God's justice and mercy when Jesus is glorified on the cross. Leading up to that climactic moment, Jesus typologically fulfills the temple and its ministries, fulfills Old Testament expectation for a good shepherd, declares his unity with the Father, and sends his disciples as the Father sent him. The Gospel consists of a prologue (John 1:1–18), a Book of Signs (1:19–12:50), a Book of Glory (chaps. 13–20), and an epilogue (chap. 21).[125] The Bible is more to be admired than the Louvre Museum, and the Gospel of John is perhaps its *Mona Lisa*. John's theology centers on the glory of God in salvation through judgment.

6.1 Prologue (John 1:1–18)

Small words and short sentences are often the most profound uttered, and thus it is in John's prologue. John introduces his Gospel with brief but suggestive statements that are masterfully presented in chiastic shape (table 5.14).

Table 5.14. The Chiasm in John's Prologue

1:1–5, The deity of the Creator Word, life and light unconquerable
  1:6–8, The Baptist came as a witness.
    1:9, The shining of the true light
      1:10–11, Unknown by the world, rejected by his own
      1:12–13, Received by those born of God
    1:14, We saw the glory of the tabernacled Word.
  1:15, The Baptist bore witness.
1:16–18, From his fullness, grace, law, and truth, God makes God known.

The glory of the life of the light-shining, world-making Word is heralded in this chiasm, which hinges on salvation and judgment. The first five verses of John's Gospel present themselves as on par with Torah by means of the clear

[124] One gets this impression from the model of ancient Jerusalem in the modern city and from artistic depictions of it, see for instance, "Jerusalem in the Time of Jesus," in *The ESV Study Bible* (Wheaton, IL: Crossway, 2008), 1878–79.

[125] For a comprehensive account, see now Andreas J. Köstenberger, *A Theology of John's Gospel and Letters: The Word, the Christ, the Son of God*, Biblical Theology of the New Testament (Grand Rapids: Zondervan, 2009).

allusion to the opening of Genesis. They then add to the revelation given there by declaring that Jesus is the Word through whom God made the world. He was with God in the beginning, without whom nothing is, in whom is life and light beyond comprehension or compeer.[126]

The opening of John's prologue is matched by its closing verses (John 1:16–18), where the allusion to Genesis in John 1:1 is matched by the salvation-historical placement of the revelation that comes through Jesus in the statement in 1:17 that "the law was given through Moses, grace and truth came through Jesus the messiah." The deity of the Word announced in John 1:1–2 is also matched by the statement in 1:18 that "the unique God, who is in the bosom of the Father, has made him known."[127]

In John's prologue the Baptist bears twofold witness to this glorious Word (1:6–8, 15). The statement in 1:9 that the true light shines on every man is matched by the testimony, "we saw his glory," in 1:14. And in the midst of these descriptions of God's glory in the tabernacled, enfleshed Word to which the Baptist testifies, we find a dual statement of judgment and salvation.

The judgment is not enacted but described in the mention of the world that does not know its Maker and of his own who did not receive him (John 1:10–11). To understand how the theme of the rejection of Jesus is introduced here, we must observe the way that John's prologue introduces his major themes. Jesus as life is introduced in 1:4 and returned to in, for example, 5:25–29 and 11:25–26. Jesus as light is introduced in 1:4–5 and returned to in, for instance, John 3:19–21 and 8:12. These themes emanate out of the glory heralded in John 1:14 and returned to in 2:11, and often thereafter (e.g., 7:39; 8:54; 11:4; 12:16, 23; 13:31, 32; 16:14; 17:1, 5, 10). And thus also it is with the theme of the rejection of Jesus. This theme will be resumed in John when the Gospel declares, for instance, that the wrath of God remains on those who do not believe in Jesus (3:36), that those who have done evil will rise to judgment (5:29), and that those who oppose Jesus are seed of the serpent, of their father the Devil (8:44).

Similarly, the theme of salvation is introduced with the mention of those who receive Jesus, those who are born of God, in John 1:12–13.[128] John returns to the theme of the new birth in 3:1–12, and the life given by the Spirit is announced

[126]The verb rendered "overcome" in John 1:5 can mean both "overcome" and "understand," and it seems that John intends both meanings.

[127]See Marianne Meye Thompson's thorough essay, "Jesus: 'The One Who Sees God,'" in *Israel's God and Rebecca's Children: Christology and Community in Early Judaism and Christianity*, ed. David B. Capes et al. (Waco, TX: Baylor University Press, 2007), 215–26.

[128]For further comments on John 1:12–13, see my essay, "The Church Militant and Her Warfare: We Are Not Another Interest Group," *SBJT* 11, no. 4 (2007): 73. *Contra* Marshall, *New Testament Theology*, 493, who thinks that "God responds to human faith by conferring the new birth on believers." John 1:12–13 is clear that the birth from God in 1:13 explains the ability some have to receive Jesus in 1:12. Cf. John 3:3–8, where apart from the new birth people are unable to *see* and *enter* the kingdom.

also in 6:63. The regenerating power of the new birth is the answer to human inability, as can be seen in the texts in table 5.15.

Table 5.15. Regeneration and Inability in John

New Birth/Regeneration	Human Inability (apart from the Spirit's work in the new birth)
"Born . . . of God" (1:13)	The world did not receive him; his own did not know him (1:10–11).
"Born again" (3:3, 5, 6, 7, 8)	One is not able to see or enter the kingdom (3:3, 5)
"It is the Spirit who gives life" (6:63).	No one is able to come to Jesus (6:44, 65).
	Who is able to accept this teaching (6:60)?
	"The flesh is of no avail" (6:63).
	They were not able to hear Jesus' word (8:43).
	They were not able to believe (12:39).
	The world is not able to receive the Spirit (14:17).

The Gospel of John clearly teaches that the new birth gives people an *ability* that they did not otherwise have. This new ability enables those who are born again to perceive the glory of Jesus and believe in him.[129] The guarantee of life to those who entrust themselves to Jesus is a common theme, too (e.g., John 5:24; 6:40; 8:51, etc.).

This prologue—so full of glory, salvation, and judgment—introduces the Gospel written "that you may believe that Jesus is the messiah, the Son of God, and that believing you may have life in his name" (John 20:31). John's Gospel, then, is a story of the salvation through judgment for God's glory accomplished by Jesus the messiah. And this story is told so that people will be saved through its proleptic announcement of judgment on those who do not believe in Jesus, through its promise of salvation to those who do believe in Jesus, and through the persuasion that comes by the description of the manifest glory of Jesus in these pages. John's Gospel is about the glory of God in salvation through judgment in Jesus the messiah.

6.2 The Book of Signs (John 1:19–12:50)

The Fourth Gospel opens with the Baptist announcing that the salvation through the judgment of the exile is beginning to dawn. He himself is the voice in the wilderness, preparing the way for the return of Yahweh to Zion (John 1:23). He is baptizing with water (1:25), in fulfillment of the total cleansing Yahweh promised at the return from exile (Ezek. 36:25). After him comes the one who

[129]See further James M. Hamilton Jr., *God's Indwelling Presence: The Holy Spirit in the Old and New Testaments*, NACSTB (Nashville: Broadman & Holman, 2006), 58–59, 127–43.

will baptize in the Holy Spirit (John 1:33), in fulfillment of the promise in the prophets of an eschatological outpouring of the Spirit (e.g., Isa. 32:15; Ezek. 36:27; Joel 3:1–5, ET 2:28–32). John's first chapter also sounds the notes of messianic expectation, mentioning the messiah (John 1:20, 41), the Prophet (1:21), the Elijah who prepares the way (1:21, 25), the Rabbi and Teacher (1:38), the one of whom Moses and the Prophets wrote (1:45), the king of Israel (1:49), and the Son of Man (1:51). The Baptist is clearly the one who prepares the way, though he is not literally Elijah (1:21), he fulfills the prophecy, and Jesus is the king messiah who will pour out the Spirit in fulfillment of eschatological expectation.

Not only does this first chapter of John's Gospel identify Jesus as the messiah through whom salvation comes after exile, but it also begins to point to the way that salvation will come through the judgment that will fall on the messiah. Thus the Baptist identifies Jesus as the Lamb of God who takes away the sin of the world (John 1:29, 36). Recalling such texts as Isaiah 53, Zechariah 12:10, 13:7, and Daniel 9:26, John begins to point to the way that the eschatological promises of the return from exile will be realized through the judgment that will fall on the messiah himself. The messiah himself will be judged, and through that judgment will come salvation. As John's Gospel unfolds, the notes sounded in this first chapter are developed and exposited.

Before the development and exposition, however, we find more pointers forward at a wedding. Old Testament prophets such as Hosea (Hos. 2:16–20) and Jeremiah (Jer. 3:1, 12) spoke of Israel's eschatological future in terms of a new wedding between God and his people, resulting in a new covenant (Jer. 31:31–34). In John 2 Jesus attends a wedding and the wine runs out (John 2:3). When Jesus addresses the situation, he gives instruction for stone water jars used "for the cleansing rites of the Jews" (2:6) to be filled with water (2:7). He then orders the water to be drawn, and it has become wine (2:8–9). John explains that this is the first sign done by Jesus, that in it he manifests his glory, and that in response his disciples believe in him. The filling up of the jars used in Old Testament purification rites seems to symbolize the fulfillment of the time in which such things would be done,[130] and out of that fulfillment Jesus brings something as superior as wine to water, the best of wine, no less (2:10). The message seems to be that the fullness of time has come, and something new is about to be brought forth.

This message is reinforced by the following episode at Passover in John 2:13–25. The Jewish feasts play a significant role in the Gospel of John, and John presents Jesus as the typological fulfillment of these festivals (see table 5.16).[131]

---

[130]Similarly Ladd, *A Theology of the New Testament*, 267.

[131]See Paul M. Hoskins, *Jesus as the Fulfillment of the Temple in the Gospel of John*, Paternoster Biblical Monographs (Waynesboro, GA: Paternoster, 2006). Similarly Strauss, *Four Portraits, One Jesus*, 314, and Helen K.

Table 5.16. Jesus and the Jewish Festivals in John

Passover	2:13, 23	Jesus: temple and Lamb
Unnamed (possibly Tabernacles)	5:1	Jesus: Bread of Life
Passover	6:4	Jesus: provides in the wilderness
Tabernacles (Booths)	7:2	Jesus: living water and Light of the World
Dedication (Hanukkah)	10:22	Jesus: Good Shepherd
Passover	11:55; 12:1	Jesus: Resurrection (new exodus) and Life

The first instance of festival fulfillment in John's Gospel brings together Passover and exile themes, promising also the resurrection of the body of Jesus. At the Passover (John 2:13), Jesus cleanses the temple of the beasts of sacrifice (2:14–16). As if to remind readers that Jesus himself is the Lamb of God who takes away the sin of the world (1:29), John notes that Jesus' disciples later remember Psalm 69:9 and see it fulfilled in Jesus: "Zeal for your house will consume me" (John 2:17). Jesus' zeal for God's house will take him to his death. In the temple, there is a surface reference to Jesus' concern for the temple. There appears also to be a deeper reference, however, to the new temple, the people of God, for ultimately Jesus goes to the cross for God's people, in whom he will take up residence by his Spirit, making them the temple. When the Jews demand a sign, Jesus says, "Destroy this temple and in three days I will raise it" (2:19). The Jews see only the surface-level reference to the physical temple (2:20), but Jesus speaks of the temple of his body (2:21). This reference to the destruction of the temple brings into the Passover context an exile overtone. Jesus speaks of his death in terms of the destruction of the temple because he is the fulfillment of the temple. His death is the destruction of the temple because his death is the darkest moment of exile. Forsaken by the Father, he will pass through judgment to bring about salvation as he is raised on the third day. John indicates that the disciples understand and believe these things once Jesus has been raised from the dead (2:22). This passage, then, presents Jesus as the typological fulfillment of the Passover. He drives out the sacrificial animals because he will be the fulfillment of the Levitical sacrificial system. Simultaneously, he is the fulfillment of the exile because his death is the destruction of the temple. Wright provides an insightful summary of the symbolic import of the ministry of Jesus:

> Healing, forgiveness, renewal, the twelve, the new family and its new defining characteristics, open commensality, the promise of blessing for the Gentiles, feasts replacing fasts, the destruction and rebuilding of the Temple: all declared, in the powerful language of symbol, that Israel's exile was over, that Jesus was himself

Bond, "Discarding the Seamless Robe: The High Priesthood of Jesus in John's Gospel," in Capes et al., *Israel's God and Rebecca's Children*, 190–91.

> in some way responsible for this new state of affairs, and that all that the Temple had stood for was now available through Jesus and his movement.[132]

The return-from-exile themes continue in John 3 as Jesus tells Nicodemus of his need to be born of water and spirit in terms reminiscent of Ezekiel 36:25–27. The Spirit blows like the wind (John 3:8), giving life just as the wind Ezekiel prophesied gave life to the dry bones in the valley (Ezek. 37:1–14). The new life Jesus offers comes as a result of a new birth, and it comes by the power of the Spirit to those who look to the typological fulfillment of the uplifted bronze serpent (John 3:14; cf. Num. 21:9). This comparison of the lifted-up Jesus to the uplifted snake in the wilderness recalls the events of the exodus and wilderness wanderings, and adds a new-exodus dimension to the return-from-exile themes in what Jesus says to Nicodemus.

Those who believe in Jesus will be saved (John 3:16–17). They will experience the return from exile and the new exodus. Those who do not believe in Jesus will be damned (3:18). Jesus is the light, the emanation of God's glory (cf. 1:9, 14). He is the point of division in humanity. Those in whom God has worked go to him (3:21), while those who do wickedness flee the light of his presence (3:19–20). Salvation through judgment for God's glory is realized in Jesus.

As with the wedding in John 2, marriage overtones color the narrative in John 3 as the Baptist testifies that Jesus is the Bridegroom (John 3:29). This identification of Jesus as the Bridegroom immediately precedes the account of his meeting the unwed, immoral Samaritan woman at Jacob's well in John 4.

Taking nothing away from the historical reality of the events John records in this conversation Jesus has with the Samaritan woman in John 4, or from what Jesus says about his flesh being the Bread of Life in John 6, it seems that John presents these events such that they have a deeper symbolic resonance. Jesus will wed himself to the (largely) Gentile church, which will feast on his body and blood.

The power of Jesus and the significance of faith are reinforced in the second sign Jesus does (John 4:46–54). The official believes and obeys the remarkable command of Jesus to go (4:50), and before he reaches home, he hears that his son was healed at the hour Jesus said he would live (4:53).

In Jerusalem at an unnamed feast (John 5:1), Jesus heals a man on the Sabbath and makes himself equal with God (5:2–19). Responding to his critics, he explains that the Father has given judgment to the Son because the Father seeks the Son's honor (5:22–23). The Father wants to see Jesus glorified, so he grants him the right to judge. Those who do not honor Jesus do not honor

[132]Wright, *Jesus and the Victory of God*, 436.

the Father (5:23). Those who believe Jesus are delivered from judgment (5:25). Salvation through judgment for the honor of the Father and the Son comes through Jesus.

It is almost painful to try to summarize the ways that John's theology centers on God's glory in salvation through judgment. So much is passed over without comment. I say nothing, for instance, of the offer of living water Jesus makes to the Samaritan woman—an offer that shows how parched are other ways to satisfy thirst (John 4:10–14), and so much could be said about the discourse of Jesus that John presents in 5:19–47. These words could be memorized, meditated upon, and exposited for a lifetime. For the purposes of the argument being advanced here, I simply observe that Jesus has much to say about the judgment he will execute (5:27, 29, 30), much to say about those who testify to the rightness of his cause (the Father, 5:31–32, 37–38; John, 5:33–35; the works Jesus does, 5:36; the Scriptures, 5:39; and Moses, 5:45–46), and about the salvation he offers (5:26, 29). Their testimony condemns those who oppose Jesus. The problem with his opponents is that they prefer the glory of man to the glory of God (5:44; cf. 12:43).

Having fed the multitude (John 6:1–15) and walked on the water (6:16–21), Jesus identifies himself as the typological fulfillment of the manna in the wilderness (6:32–33). Just as the children of Israel were sustained by the bread from heaven as they sojourned toward the Promised Land, so the followers of Jesus will be sustained by the bread of heaven, as they trust in Jesus (6:29, 35, 40, 47), eating his flesh and drinking his blood (6:51, 53–57) until he raises them up on the last day (6:39, 40, 44, 54) for everlasting life (6:47, 50, 58) in the new and better Promised Land. This offensive message is spoken in words that are spirit and life, and only the Spirit gives life (6:63). Only those drawn to Jesus by the Spirit (6:44, 65), those given to him by the Father (6:37, 39), can receive this message.

John 7 and 8 seem united on the theme of Jesus' response to those seeking his life at the Feast of Tabernacles (see John 7:1, 19, 20, 25, 30, 32, 44; 8:20, 37, 40, 44, 59).[133] The world hates Jesus because he exposes its evil (7:7; 8:34, 43, 45, 47), condemning it. Their efforts against him will come to nothing because Jesus' time has not yet come (7:6, 8, 30; 8:20). In their opposition to him, they show themselves to be seed of the serpent, of their father the Devil (8:19, 23, 38, 44). But as the source of living water (7:37–39) and the Light of the World (8:12), Jesus is the fulfillment of the Feast of Tabernacles. Moreover, Jesus is the I Am, as the texts in table 5.17 show.

[133]This assumes that John 7:53–8:11 rightly has double brackets around it, as in the ESV, indicating that most scholars do not believe it to be part of John's original Gospel.

Table 5.17. "I Am" in John's Gospel

Absolute "I Am" Statements	6:20; 8:24, 28, 58; 18:5
Metaphorical "I Am" Statements	
1. I am the bread of life.	6:35, 48, 51
2. I am the light of the world.	8:12 = 9:5
3. I am the gate for the sheep.	10:7 = 9
4. I am the good shepherd.	10:11 = 14
5. I am the resurrection and the life.	11:25
6. I am the way, the truth, and the life.	14:6
7. I am the vine.	15:1

Announcing judgment on his seed-of-the-serpent enemies, he also announces that he will be "lifted up" (John 8:28), that is, killed, and that those who believe in him will be saved through the judgment that falls upon him (8:24, 28, 52). Jesus is seeking the glory of God (7:18; 8:29, 54), which will be manifested in this salvation through judgment.

Jesus feeds the multitude (John 6:1–14) then declares himself the Bread of Life (6:35, 48, 51). Having declared himself the Light of the World (8:12; cf. 9:5), he then heals a man born blind (9:1–7). Later he will declare himself the resurrection and life (11:25) before raising Lazarus from the dead (11:43–44).

Jesus declares that the man was born blind so that the works of God might be displayed in him (John 9:3). When Jesus heals him, the Jews demand, ironically, that the man give glory to God, while they allege that Jesus is a sinner (9:24). The blind man now sees, and the Pharisees are blind (9:40). Since they claim to see, Jesus announces that their guilt remains (9:41). God's glory is displayed in his saving the blind man and consigning those who refuse to acknowledge the glory of God in Christ to guilt.

Ezekiel 37 describes the return from exile (37:14) in terms of resurrection from the dead (37:1–13), then goes on to speak of David, the Lord's shepherd who will be king over his people (37:24; cf. 34:23–24). In John 10 Jesus explains how he is the Good Shepherd, while the nation has been afflicted with bad shepherds (cf. Ezek. 34:1–10). Then in John 11, Jesus raises Lazarus from the dead. The return from exile is dawning. Judgment is reaching its appointed fulfillment. The new exodus will soon begin. The sickness and death of Lazarus are for the glory of God in Christ (John 11:4), and so it is with the exile, new exodus, and return from exile being carried out in the life of Jesus. Those who believe will not die (11:26); indeed, they will see the glory of God (11:40).

Jesus, the Good Shepherd (cf. John 10), enters Jerusalem on a donkey in fulfillment of Psalm 118 (in LXX 117, John 12:13[134]) and Zechariah 9:9 (John 12:14–15). Zechariah 11 contains an enacted parable about a shepherd of the flock who, in Zechariah 13:7, was struck. What follows in John's Gospel will fulfill those aspects of Zechariah as well, and John 12 sets the stage for the glorification of Jesus at the cross, where salvation comes through judgment for the glory of God.

In fact, John 12 connects Zechariah's struck shepherd to Isaiah's suffering servant, with the result that the first half of John's Gospel concludes by focusing on the fulfillment of these lines of promise in Jesus the messiah. The temple is about to be destroyed, this destruction reenacting the exile. The new exodus is about to take place, and the voice in the wilderness has prepared the way for the return from exile. The way to that eschatological salvation goes through the judgment that will fall on the messiah, and that moment of judgment bringing salvation is all about the glory of God in Christ.

The connection between Zechariah and Isaiah is established by the reference to the glorification (ἐδοξάσθη) of Jesus in John 12:16, immediately following the quotation of Zechariah 9:9 in John 12:15, the moment of "glorification" being the cross. The idea that the cross is where Jesus is glorified is based squarely on the references to the servant being "lifted up [ὑψωθήσεται]" and "glorified [δοξασθήσεται]" in Isaiah 52:13 (LXX). Isaiah 52:15 speaks of the nations and those who have not heard being made aware of and benefiting from the servant's work, and John 12:20–23 depicts the coming of "some Greeks" to see Jesus as a decisive turning point. In response to their coming, Jesus says, "The hour has come for the Son of Man to be glorified [δοξασθῇ]" (John 12:23). Neither the Hebrew nor the Greek translation of Isaiah 52:13–53:12 describes the servant as the "son of man," so it seems that Jesus has interpreted the Old Testament to mean that the "Son of Man" from Daniel 7:13 is the "servant" who will be glorified not only as Daniel 7 describes but also as Isaiah 53 does.

The glorification spoken of in John 12:23 is clearly the cross, for in John 12:24 Jesus speaks of the grain of wheat that falls into the earth, dies, and bears fruit, and in 12:25 he speaks of losing life. John 12:27 records Jesus

[134]The statement "even the King of Israel" at the end of John 12:13 does not come from Ps. 118:25–26 (LXX 117:25–26), but it is rightly placed in quotes in English translations because the phrase appears to be drawn from Zeph. 3:15 (so the marginal reference in NA[27]). Zeph. 3:15 celebrates the king's presence when Israel is redeemed, and the king seems to be identified with the Lord. The only other instances of the phrase "King of Israel" (βασιλεὺς Ἰσραηλ) in the Greek translations of the prophets are in Isa. 7:1, which is narrating the events of that chapter, and Hos. 10:15–11:1. This instance of the phrase in Hos. 10:15–11:1 would appear to be relevant to John's purposes. The context in Hos. 10:15–11:1 appears to refer to the king of Israel being "cast out" when the nation is exiled, and then comes the statement that God called Israel out of Egypt (quoted in Matt. 2:15). If John is alluding to Hos. 10:15–11:1, this would further establish the connections between the death and resurrection of Jesus and the exile, new exodus, and return from exile.

saying that his soul is troubled because the "hour" of his glorification has come. He is troubled not at the prospect of resurrection and returning to the Father in heaven but at what he must go through to get there. Then, decisively moving toward the cross, he says in 12:28, "'Father, glorify your name.' Then a voice came from heaven, 'I have glorified it and I will glorify it again.'" This text clearly presents Jesus and the Father speaking of the cross as a moment when not only Jesus will be glorified but the Father also. Jesus and the Father are joined together to glorify one another at the cross. The cross will be the moment when the world is judged and the archenemy defeated, as Jesus says in John 12:31, "Now is the judgment of this world, now the ruler of this world will be cast out." The sins of the world will be exposed and condemned by the cross of Christ, Satan will be conquered, and Jesus and the Father will be glorified. Salvation comes through judgment for God's glory.[135]

The lifting up of Isaiah's servant for the benefit of the world (Isa. 52:13, 15) is restated as Jesus says in John 12:32, "And I, if I am lifted up [ὑψωθῶ] from the earth, I will draw all men to myself." As if to guard against the idea that the lifting up of Jesus refers to anything other than the cross, John notes, "Now he said this signifying what kind of death he was about to die" (12:33).

The crowd that responds in John 12:34 seems to be struggling to understand Jesus' interpretation of the Old Testament. They have categories for a conquering messiah (Psalm 2), a heavenly son of man receiving a kingdom (Dan. 7:13), and a suffering servant (Isaiah 53), but as Jesus announces that he will fulfill all these expectations, the crowd responds as though taught by (many) modern Old Testament scholars: "Then the crowd answered him, 'We have heard from the Law that the messiah remains forever, and how are you saying that it is necessary for the Son of Man to be lifted up? Who is this Son of Man?" Jesus cryptically replies that he is the light and urges the crowd to believe what he says, that they might be sons of light (John 12:35–36).

John then states that Jesus did his signs "that the word of the prophet Isaiah might be fulfilled" (John 12:37–38), and John quotes Isaiah 53:1, no doubt to invoke the whole context of Isaiah 52:13–53:12. Then John states in 12:39, "On account of this they were not able to believe, because again Isaiah said . . . ," and here John quotes Isaiah 6:10 (John 12:40). Remarkably, John's next words in 12:41 are, "Isaiah said *these things* [pl.] because he saw

[135]Cf. Schreiner, *New Testament Theology*, 93: "Jesus' intention in coming into the world was to save it, but those who refused to believe in him were thereby judged, and so he came to judge in a secondary but not a primary sense. . . . Jesus' death spells salvation for the world, but it is also the case that Jesus by his death judges the world and evicts its ruler (John 12:31)."

his glory, and he spoke concerning him." The apostle John here asserts that in Isaiah 6 and Isaiah 53 the prophet Isaiah saw the glory of Jesus.[136]

In Isaiah 6, the prophet Isaiah was commissioned to harden Israel until the exile was complete (cf. Isa. 6:11–13). In John 12:39–40 the apostle John declares that the crowd of Israelites cannot believe Jesus because of what was stated in Isaiah 6:10. This appears to mean that the exile will be fulfilled in Jesus. Moreover, the quotation of Isaiah 53:1 immediately before the quotation of Isaiah 6:10 explains how the exile will be fulfilled. God's wrath on Israel in the judgment of exile will be realized as the representative of Israel, her king, experiences full separation from God; forsaken by God on the cross, the Lamb of God (John 1:29; cf. Isa. 53:7) will bear the sins of his people (Isa. 53:4). Those afraid of the consequences of believing in him prefer the glory of man to the glory of God (John 12:42–43; cf. 5:44).

6.3 The Book of Glory (John 13–20)

The yearly Passovers in John 2, 6, and 11 in John 1–12 show the events of Jesus' ministry unfolding over the course of several years, and the feast in John 5 might be yet another Passover. By contrast, the events in John 13–20 focus in on the night Jesus is betrayed (John 13–18:27[137]), the crucifixion (18:28–19:42), and the day of the resurrection (20:1–29).

Jesus washes the disciples feet (John 13:1–11), then instructs them on serving one another (13:12–17). He explains that Psalm 41:9 will be fulfilled, and one who eats his bread will lift his heel against him (John 13:18). This indicates that Jesus is teaching his disciples not only that he will typologically fulfill the pattern of events experienced by the nation at the exile, but also that he will typologically fulfill the pattern of events David experienced in having a trusted companion become a traitor. Jesus gives a morsel of bread to Judas (13:26), who then leaves to accomplish his awful task (13:27–30).

---

[136]For discussion of the role of Daniel 7, Isaiah 53, and Isaiah 6 in all four Gospels, see Thielman, *Theology of the New Testament*, 186–90.

[137]John 13–17 may be chiastically arranged as follows:

13:1–35, Jesus washes the disciples' feet.
  13:36–38, Prediction of Peter's denial
    14:1–14, Jesus is leaving but the disciples can trust God.
      14:15–26, Promise of the Paraclete
        14:27–31, Peace from Jesus, trouble from the ruler of the world
          15:1–17, Abide in Jesus.
        15:18–16:4, Rejection from the world, help from the Spirit
      16:5–15, Promise of the Paraclete
    16:16–28, Jesus is leaving, but they will see him again.
  16:29–33, Prediction of disciples' abandoning Jesus
17:1–26, Jesus prays for the disciples.

John then focuses his audience on the cross and its outworking in the Christian life. What Jesus is about to accomplish on the cross will glorify God in salvation through judgment, and it will pattern Christian living. Jesus is about to lay down his life to love others and glorify God on the cross, and that is the way he urges his disciples to show that they belong to him. Thus, when Judas is gone, Jesus declares, "Now is the Son of Man glorified, and God is glorified in him. If God is glorified in him, God will also glorify himself in him,[138] and he will glorify him immediately" (John 13:32–32).

At this point we can reflect on the ways that God and Christ will be glorified in the cross. God will be glorified in mercy and justice. His justice will be seen in the outpouring of his wrath to uphold truth and establish his righteousness. His mercy will be seen in the fact that the substitutionary death of Jesus makes it possible for God righteously to extend forgiveness to those who believe. God's love and justice, then, are put on display at the cross.

Christ also is glorified, as his unique ability to absorb God's wrath without remainder is displayed. Jesus exhaustively receives the wrath of God. His greatness is seen both in his ability to satisfy the demands of God's justice and in his own righteousness whereby he is a sinless sacrifice.

Moreover, the love of the Son for the Father's honor is displayed as Jesus obediently goes to the cross. The love of the Father for the Son is displayed as the Father honors the Son for his greatness. The love of both Father and Son for sinners is displayed by the enormous length to which each goes to establish salvation.

The cross uniquely displays that both Jesus and the Father are committed to justice and mercy, even unto death. The cross displays that Jesus and the Father are unique—holy—in their devotion to righteousness, to mercy, and to one another. The cross displays the all-conquering love of Father and Son for rebels who will repent and believe in Jesus. Such a sacrifice to save sinners!

The God-honoring, righteousness-upholding, others-benefiting, self-sacrificial way that Jesus loves his disciples is the way he then calls them to love one another in the "new commandment" of John 13:34–35. This is a love that upholds the righteousness of God while extending unmerited kindness and mercy to others at the expense of oneself. The display of this kind of love, then, cannot but show forth the priority of God, emphasizing his glory. The new-commandment love that Jesus enjoins on his disciples, like the cross where he supremely manifests

[138]This phrase in John 13:32, καὶ ὁ θεὸς δοξάσει αὐτὸν ἐν αὐτῷ, is usually translated "God will also glorify him in himself" (ESV, KJV, NASB, NIV, NKJV, NRSV, RSV). This treats the dative αὐτῷ as the reflexive element, "himself." As I have translated the phrase, I am treating the accusative αὐτόν as the reflexive element since John employs αὐτόν as a reflexive in John 2:24, Ἰησοῦς οὐκ ἐπίστευεν αὐτὸν αὐτοῖς ("Jesus was not entrusting *himself* to them" [emphasis added]). Cf. E. A. Abbott, *Johannine Grammar* (London: Black, 1906), 279, §2374: "Αὐτός . . . John uses it always to mean 'himself.'"

that love, centers on the display of God's glory in justice and in mercy, justice highlighting the gracious, free character of the mercy.

To enable them to love others in this way, Jesus calls his disciples to trust him and sets their eyes on the reward he promises at his return (John 14:1–4). In response to questions from Thomas and in dialogue with Philip, Jesus teaches on the unity between himself and the Father (14:5–11). The Father and the Son will be glorified by what the disciples do (14:12–31).

Jesus is the true vine (cf. Isa. 5:1–11; 6:13; 11:1; 53:2). The disciples must remain in him as a branch stays connected to its vine (John 15:1–6). For the disciples to abide in Jesus, his words must abide in them (15:7). Thus will the Father be glorified in them (15:8). They are to glorify the Father by abiding in the love with which Jesus has loved them (15:9). Doing this means keeping the new commandment (cf. 13:34), which means loving others as he has loved them (15:10, 12–17). In this they will find true joy—as they find their own happiness in benefitting others at their own expense (15:11). The world will treat them as it has treated Jesus (15:18–25), and even here the righteousness of God will shine in relief against the unrighteousness of wicked men.

Jesus promises the Holy Spirit's help for the disciples to testify when they are persecuted (John 15:26–27), and what he has told them will function to keep them faithful when trouble comes upon them (16:1–4). When the Spirit comes, he will enable the disciples to understand and explain what they have learned from Jesus. As the disciples proclaim the truth of Jesus by the power of the Spirit, through them the Spirit will glorify Jesus and convict the world of sin, righteousness, and judgment (16:5–15). In the rest of John 16 Jesus prepares his disciples for his coming death, assuring them that he has overcome the world (16:33).

As Jesus prays in John 17, two concerns predominate. He asks the Father to glorify him that he might glorify the Father (17:1, 4–5), and he asks the Father to secure the disciples such that they will be kept in the name of the Father to experience the glory of Jesus (17:6, 10–13, 17, 22, 24, 26). He prays not only for his disciples, but also for the disciples who will believe through their testimony (17:20). He wants them to be unified in love (17:11, 21–23, 26) and sanctified by the word (17:8, 14, 17, 19). This will result in the world knowing the truth about Jesus (17:21, 23), that others might be given to Jesus out of the world (17:6, 9). Jesus prays that the disciples will live out the salvation that comes through judgment for God's glory. In their lives, they will love each other, condemning by their deeds all selfishness, injustice, and God-dishonoring behavior. They will live this way as the Father keeps them, and as they keep the word of Jesus. The mercy they receive will be drenched with God's glory. The world will be condemned. Those kept by the Father in his name, sanctified by the true word in answer to Jesus' prayer, those given to Jesus by the Father, they will be saved. And God's glory will be displayed.

Jesus is impressive even as he allows himself to be arrested,[139] and John reminds his audience that one man is dying for the people (John 18:1–14; cf. 18:14 and 11:50). The high priest has no answer to the righteousness of Jesus (18:19–24). Jesus is righteous, but he is treated unjustly (18:28–38). Jesus will be crucified in place of Barabbas, who is clearly guilty (18:39–40), and this substitution is a picture of the way Jesus dies on behalf of the people (18:14).

Jesus dies as the Passover Lamb and as the suffering Davidic servant (John 19:36–37; cf. Ex. 12:46; Num. 9:12; Ps. 34:20; Zech. 12:10). His death inaugurates the new exodus, and he is with a rich man in his death (John 19:38–42; cf. Isa. 53:9).

Through judgment comes salvation, and on the first day of the week Jesus rises from the dead (John 20:1–10). He appears to Mary (20:11–18), commissions the disciples as the new temple (20:19–23),[140] and convinces Thomas that he is Lord and God (20:24–29). John wrote that people might believe and have life (20:30–31).

6.4 Epilogue (John 21)

The epilogue depicts a marvelous catch of fish, perhaps pointing to the way the disciples will catch men (John 21:1–14).[141] Then Jesus reinstates Peter (21:15–23). John testifies truly (21:24–25).

6.5 The Center of the Theology of John

As with the Gospels of Matthew, Mark, and Luke, the center of the theology of the Gospel of John is the glory of God in salvation through judgment.[142] In John, Jesus comes as the typological fulfillment of both the temple and the suffering servant. He fulfills Israel's festivals and sacrificial system precisely *through* his

[139]On which, see Schreiner, *New Testament Theology*, 253.

[140]See my argument in Hamilton, *God's Indwelling Presence*, 143–60, which can be summarized as follows:

Table 5.18. The Spirit's Continuation of the Temple Ministry of Jesus in the Disciples

Temple Ministry	The Temple	Jesus	Disciples
Dwelling of God	God dwells in the temple (Deut. 12:5 etc.).	Jesus replaces the temple as the locus of God's presence (John 1:14, 32–33, 51; 2:19–21 etc.).	The disciples receive the Spirit once Jesus puts an end to sacrifice (John 7:39; 14:17; 16:7; 20:22).
Place of sacrifice	Sacrifices are to be made at the temple (Deut. 12:6–14 etc.).	Jesus lays down his life for his people, putting an end to temple sacrifice (John 10:11, 17–18; 11:49–52; 19:30).	Now that the final sacrifice has been offered, forgiveness is administered through the church (John 20:23).

[141]See Richard Bauckham's fascinating study, "The 153 Fish and the Unity of the Fourth Gospel," in *The Testimony of the Beloved Disciple: Narrative, History, and Theology in the Gospel of John* (Grand Rapids: Baker, 2007), 271–84.

[142]I find this formulation more compelling than Marshall's (*New Testament Theology*, 525, cf. 512): "The main theme of the Gospel is to present Jesus as the Messiah and Son of God who came into the world to reveal the truth and to die so that all people might have the opportunity to receive life through believing in him." This language of "opportunity" reflects Marshall's Wesleyan and Methodist commitments more than it does the actual teaching of John's Gospel.

fulfillment of the role of the new suffering Davidic servant. The first twelve chapters of the Gospel set the stage for the work of the sin-bearing Davidic servant to be understood as the fulfillment of the exile when the "temple" is destroyed as the servant dies on the cross. John 12, 13, and 17 lay the groundwork for the cross to be understood as the moment when God and Christ are glorified and glorify one another, for at the cross love and truth meet, righteousness and peace kiss each other (cf. Ps. 85:11, ET 10). In the Upper Room Discourse Jesus teaches his disciples to love one another as he has loved them, and he is so lovingly committed to the truth that he sacrificed himself to make mercy possible for others. Jesus prays in John 17 that the Father will glorify him, that his disciples will see his glory and thereby unite in loving one another the way he has loved them. This is a love that shows forth God's glory in justice and in mercy. The love of Jesus upholds justice and extends mercy. Through the judgment that falls on Jesus, salvation comes. That judgment is depicted in such a way that the death of Jesus is to be interpreted in light of the cosmic story (cf. John 1:1), and within that, in terms of the history of Israel ("destroy this temple"), so that in the death and resurrection of Jesus the exile is completed, and the new exodus and return from exile begin. Salvation has come through judgment for God's glory.[143]

7. Acts

How could a crucified man be the messiah?[144] Is that what the Old Testament promised? Is that what will bring in God's kingdom? These questions inform Luke's second volume, especially his presentation of the way the followers of Jesus quote the Old Testament to explain the crucifixion and resurrection to which they were witnesses. The book of Acts has two programmatic statements that structure the volume, and both have to do with proclamation (table 5.19). In the first, Acts 1:8, Jesus tells his disciples that they will be his witnesses in Jerusalem, Judea and Samaria, and to the ends of the earth.[145] Acts then shows the witness borne in Jerusalem in chapters 1–7, in Judea and Samaria in chapters 8–12, and to the ends of the known world in chapters 13–28. Then in Acts 9:15 Paul is to be told that he will carry the name of the Lord before Gentiles, kings, and Israelites. The remainder of the book shows Paul doing just this.

---

[143]Thus "salvation through judgment for God's glory" better captures the center of John's theology than Mark Strauss's proposal of John's "central theme," which is that "Jesus is the divine Son of God who reveals the Father, providing eternal life to all who believe in him" (*Four Portraits, One Jesus*, 298). Cf. Wright, *Jesus and the Victory of God*, 473–74.

[144]Cf. Wright, *Jesus and the Victory of God*, 544: "When Jesus was crucified, the general impression in Jerusalem that day must have been that he was one more in a long line of would-be, but failed, Messiahs."

[145]David W. Pao (*Acts and the Isaianic New Exodus*, 91–92) notes that "The text of Isaiah is also behind this programmatic statement" in Acts 1:8, where the phrase "to the ends of the earth (ἕως ἐσχάτου τῆς γῆς)" matches the Greek translation of the last phrase of Isa. 49:6.

Table 5.19. Programmatic Statements in Acts 1:8 and 9:15

Programmatic Text	Region Named	Narrative of Ministry There
	Jerusalem	Acts 1–7
Acts 1:8	Judea and Samaria	Acts 8–12
	To the ends of the earth	Acts 13–28
Programmatic Text	**People Named**	**Narrative of Ministry to Them**
	Gentiles	Acts 13–14, 16–20, 27–28
Acts 9:15	Kings	Acts 24–26
	Israel	Acts 15, 21–23, 28

At the center of Luke's theology in the book of Acts is God's glory in salvation through judgment.[146] He communicates this theology through the words and deeds done in Jesus' name[147] by the witnesses to the resurrection. The preaching of the disciples of Jesus in Acts is organized according to major speeches in table 5.20.

Table 5.20. Major Sermons in Acts

Speaker	Text	Audience	Content
	2:14–26	Jews in Jerusalem	Resurrection and giving of the Spirit fulfill the OT
Peter	3:11–26	Jews in Jerusalem	Lame man healed in Jesus' name, therefore repent and believe
	10:34–43	Cornelius's household	Synoptic Gospel pattern
Stephen	7:1–53	Jews in Jerusalem	Typology: God's appointed leader rejected by wicked Israelites
	13:16–47	Synagogue in Pisidian Antioch	God raised up Jesus, the seed of David
	17:22–31	Greeks in Athens	There is one true God who is calling all to repentance.
Paul	20:18–35	Elders of the church in Ephesus	Shepherd the flock, for wolves will arise from among you.
	22:1–21	Jews in Jerusalem	Paul's conversion
	24:10–21	Felix and his court	Paul's defense
	26:1–29	Agrippa and his court	Paul's life, conversion, and a call to repentance

I suggested above that the book of Luke corresponds in some ways to the book of Samuel. It might even be said that Luke–Acts has certain structural similarities

[146]In addition to the present discussion, see my essay, "The Center of Biblical Theology in Acts: Deliverance and Damnation Display the Divine," *Them* 33, no. 3 (2008): 34–47.

[147]See Acts 2:38; 3:6, 16 (2x); 4:7, 10, 12, 17, 18, 30; 5:28, 40, 41; 8:12, 16; 9:14, 15, 16, 21, 27, 28; 10:43, 48; 15:17; 16:18; 19:5, 13, 17; 21:13; 22:16.

with 1–2 Samuel.[148] The king of Israel dies at the end of both 1 Samuel and the Gospel of Luke, and the king of Israel ascends the throne and builds the kingdom of God in both 2 Samuel and the book of Acts. Second Samuel opens with Saul dead, and David avenges and laments Saul and Jonathan (2 Samuel 1), and is anointed over Judah (2 Samuel 2). A war with Israel ensues that finally sees David anointed over Israel and Judah (2 Samuel 3–5). Uzzah is struck dead (2 Samuel 6), then God promises to build David's house (2 Samuel 7), and David expands the kingdom (2 Samuel 8–10). Then he sins with Bathsheba (2 Samuel 11) and repents (2 Samuel 12), and the rest of the book relates how David triumphed through the suffering brought on by his sin (2 Samuel 13–24).

Just as David killed the Amelakite and lamented Saul and Jonathan in 2 Samuel 1, in the book of Acts, after Jesus gives instructions and ascends to heaven (Acts 1:1–11), the apostles quote Scripture about the death of Judas and seek the Lord about his replacement (1:12–26). As David was anointed king over Judah and then entered into conflict with Israel in 2 Samuel 2–4, the Spirit is poured out on the apostles on the day of Pentecost (Acts 2:1–12), they have great success with three thousand converts (2:14–47), and they heal the man at the beautiful gate (3:1–26), only to find themselves at war with the Jewish religious establishment in Acts 4–5. At the end of Acts 5 they are rejoicing and freely preaching Jesus. Just as Uzzah was struck dead once David was enthroned (2 Samuel 6), Ananias and Sapphira are struck dead (Acts 5:1–11). Just as David's kingdom was granted and grew in 2 Samuel 7–10, so the church enjoys remarkable growth in Acts 6–12. David sinned with Bathsheba, repented, and triumphed through suffering and judgment. Similarly, in Acts, Saul (Paul) sins by persecuting the church (Acts 7–8), and he repents when he is confronted by Jesus (Acts 9). David was told by Nathan that the sword would never depart from his house (2 Sam. 12:7), and Paul is shown how much he will suffer for the name of the Lord (Acts 9:16). Like David suffering through the events related in 2 Samuel 13–24, Paul triumphs through suffering as he takes the gospel to the ends of the earth in Acts 13–28.

As with the first volume, so with the second: Luke expresses the glory of God and Christ in a variety of ways, as table 5.21 shows.[149]

---

[148]Cf. Brian S. Rosner, "Acts and Biblical History," in *The Book of Acts in Its Ancient Literary Setting*, ed. Bruce W. Winter and Andrew D. Clarke, The Book of Acts in Its First Century Setting 1 (Grand Rapids: Eerdmans, 1993), 65–82, esp. 82: "Acts is reminiscent of the books of Samuel and Kings and of Chronicles which reflect upon sacred history for the benefit of their respective communities."

[149]This table does not include indirect ascriptions to God and Christ in Acts, such as the statements that people feared God (2:43; 5:5, 11; 9:31), God's assertions that he will display wonders (4:30; 5:12; 14:3), all the references to the "name of Jesus" noted above, and the many statements of scriptural fulfillment, which show that God has kept his word.

Table 5.21. The Glory of God and Jesus in Acts

Glory to God
"We hear them speaking the magnificent deeds of God." 2:11, of those filled with the Spirit on the day of Pentecost
"praising God" 2:47, in a summary description of the early church
"All were glorifying God for what had happened, for the man was more than forty years old." 4:21–22, healing of the lame man in 3:1–10
"the God of glory" 7:2, at the beginning of Stephen's speech
"He saw the glory of God and Jesus standing at the right hand of God." 7:55–56, Stephen as he is martyred
"speaking in tongues and declaring the greatness of God" 10:46, of those filled with the Spirit at Cornelius's home
"And they glorified God saying, so then also to the Gentiles God has granted repentance unto life." 11:18, Spirit poured out at Cornelius's home
"And immediately the angel of the Lord struck him because he did not give the glory to God." 12:23, Herod's death
"The Gentiles were rejoicing and glorifying the word of the Lord." 13:48, at Pisidian Antioch in response to the gospel coming to them
"They were glorifying God." 21:20, the brothers in Jerusalem hearing Paul's report
Jesus Glorified/Exalted/Magnified
"having been exalted to the right hand of God" 2:33, Peter speaking of Jesus in his Pentecost sermon
"God made him both Lord and messiah, this Jesus whom you crucified." 2:36, Peter speaking of Jesus in his Pentecost sermon
"The God of our fathers glorified his servant Jesus." 3:13, Peter preaching after the healing of the lame man
"God exalted him to his right hand as Champion and Savior." 5:31, Peter and the apostles before the Sanhedrin
". . . rejoicing . . . that they were counted worthy to be dishonored for the name." 5:41, the apostles after being beaten, their reaction clearly glorifying Jesus
"And it came about that there was much joy in that city." 8:8, joy over Phillip's proclamation of Christ (cf. 8:4–7)
"He was going on his way rejoicing." 8:39, the Ethiopian eunuch rejoicing in "the good news about Jesus" (8:35)
"And the name of Jesus was magnified." 19:17, when people hear of the demonic response to the seven sons of Sceva
"I could not see from the glory of that light." 22:11, the glory of Jesus when he appeared to Paul on the road to Damascus

The display of the glory of God and Christ that saturates the book of Acts is centered on the salvation that comes through judgment.[150] This salvation through judgment is manifested in two primary ways. The first is the proclamation of the redemption accomplished through the death and resurrection of Jesus. The second is the preservation and growth of the church through the judgment that falls on her enemies. For the "progress reports" on the advance of the gospel in Acts, see table 5.22.

Table 5.22. Church Growth in Acts

Text[1]	Reference to Growth	Text	Reference to Growth
1:15	"The company of persons was in all about 120."	11:24	"A great many people were added to the Lord."
2:41	"There were added that day about three thousand souls."	12:24	"But the word of God increased and multiplied."
2:47	"And the Lord added to their number day by day those who were being saved."	13:48	"As many as were appointed to eternal life believed."
4:4	"Many . . . believed, and the number of the men came to about five thousand."	14:1	"A great number of both Jews and Greeks believed."
5:14	"More than ever believers were added to the Lord, multitudes of both men and women."	16:5	"So the churches were strengthened in the faith, and they increased in numbers daily."
6:1	"The disciples were increasing in number."	17:4	"Some of them were persuaded and joined . . . as did a great many of the devout Greeks and not a few of the leading women."
6:7	"The number of the disciples multiplied greatly . . . and a great many of the priests became obedient to the faith."	17:12	"Many of them . . . believed, with not a few Greek women."
9:31	"The church . . . multiplied."	17:34	"Some men joined him and believed."
9:35	"All the residents of Lydda and Sharon . . . turned to the Lord."	18:8	"Crispus . . . his entire household. . . . And many of the Corinthians hearing . . . believed."
9:42	"Many believed in the Lord."	21:20	"You see . . . how many thousands there are among the Jews . . . who have believed."
11:21	"A great number . . . believed."	28:24	"Some were convinced."

[1]All texts are from the ESV.

[150]Cf. Schreiner, *New Testament Theology*, 128: "The heart of NT theology is the work of God in Christ in saving his people, and such saving work brings praise, honor, and glory to God."

In both cases, however, God is manifesting his glory in a display of justice that highlights his mercy. God is being glorified in salvation through judgment. The following discussion will be structured by the book's programmatic statements.

7.1 Witness to the Resurrection in Jerusalem (Acts 1–7)

Acts 1 sets the stage for the day of Pentecost, which is described in Acts 2. Acts 3–4 then largely focuses on the healing of a lame man at the temple gate and the conflicts engendered by it with the religious leadership. Acts 5 tells of the death of Ananias and Sapphira, before again showing the apostles in conflict with the Jewish religious establishment. Acts 6 introduces the deacons and Stephen, and Acts 7 largely consists of his speech. Stephen's speech provides an exposition of several themes sounded in earlier chapters. Along the way Luke provides several summary statements of the way things were going for the early church (cf. Acts 1:12–14; 2:42–47; 4:31–35; 5:12–16; 6:7). Flowing out of the central theme of God's glory in salvation through judgment in Acts are three main ways in which this theme is established. First there is the announcement that God has fulfilled the Scriptures in the death and resurrection of Jesus. Second there is the announcement of judgment on the sinners who crucified Jesus, and because of the resurrection, they can repent and find forgiveness. They can be saved through judgment because God has accomplished salvation through judgment. Third there is the gathering opposition to the early church, which culminates in the death of Stephen. Acts 1–3 focuses on the death and resurrection of Jesus and the call to repentance; then the focus shifts to the gathering opposition in Acts 4–7.

Crucifixion hardly looks like proof of God's approval. In fact, crucifixion looks like God's disapproval. Crucifixion looks like proof that Jesus was not the messiah, but such considerations are outweighed and overcome by resurrection. Thus, after suffering, Jesus presents himself alive by many proofs to his disciples (Acts 1:3), and thus they understand themselves to be witnesses of the resurrection (1:22).

The disciples must give the answer of the resurrection to the question of the crucifixion, and they must answer another question raised by common Old Testament expectation. It is a question they themselves have. Luke shows the disciples posing this question to Jesus in Acts 1:6 when they ask if he will now restore the kingdom to Israel. Jesus answers that it is not for them to know the Father's fixed times and seasons, but they will be empowered by the Spirit to bear witness to him (1:7–8). Then as Luke describes the ascent of Jesus to heaven, he depicts an event that provides the answer to the question posed by the disciples. Luke notes in Acts 1:9 that "while they were looking, he was taken up and a cloud received him." Then heavenly figures in white robes (1:10) tell them that "this Jesus who has been taken up from you into heaven, thus he will come—in the way you saw him going into heaven" (1:11). Jesus is taken up and the cloud receives him, and he will come on the clouds of heaven. What the angel says, as well as the way Luke describes the scene, amounts to an unmistakable allusion to Daniel 7:13. After the one like a son of man comes with the clouds of heaven in Daniel 7:13, he receives everlasting dominion and a kingdom never to be destroyed (7:14). The reader who comes to the book of Acts from the Gospels will have seen this text quoted by Jesus there (Matt. 26:64; Mark 14:62; cf. Luke 22:68–68). Picking up on the way that Jesus apparently has interpreted the Old Testament, Luke recounts the ascension to answer the disciples' question about when Jesus will restore the kingdom to Israel. He will do so at his return, when he comes just as he went—with the clouds of heaven. It is worth observing that both the book of Daniel and the book of Revelation depict that moment as a consummate display of the glory of God in salvation through judgment (cf. Dan. 7:26–27; 9:27; 12:1–3; Rev. 19:11–21; cf. also 2 Thess. 1:5–10).

Judas's end prefigures the outcome of those who reject and oppose Jesus and his kingdom (Acts 1:16–20). The enemies of the messiah and his people will be judged, and salvation will be accomplished through all their counterplotting and opposition (cf. Acts 2:23–24; 4:27–28).

The day of Pentecost (Acts 2:1–4) temporarily reverses the judgment that fell at Babel (Genesis 11) and points to the day when all nations will speak with one voice in praise of "the mighty acts of God" in Christ (Acts 2:5–11). Peter explains this by quoting the prophet Joel (Acts 2:16–21). The prophecy of the outpouring of the Spirit in the eschatological days of the messiah is realized on the day of Pentecost.

Luke depicts the flow of events on that day as follows: Peter begins by explaining the event that has just taken place (Acts 2:1–12) as the eschatological outpouring of the Spirit, quoting Joel and claiming fulfillment (2:14–21). From the explanation of the event he moves back to the oxymoronic idea of the crucified messiah. He claims the messiah has been attested by God (2:22), asserts that the crucifixion was God's definite plan, upholds human responsibility for wicked actions (2:23), and testifies to the resurrection (2:24).[151] Peter then seeks to prove, by quoting and explaining Psalm 16:8–11, that the definite plan of God was for the messiah to suffer and then enter his glory (cf. Luke 24:26). Luke presents Peter's claim that David prophesied (Acts 2:30a) on the basis of the promises God made to him in 2 Samuel 7 (Acts 2:30b) concerning the resurrection of Jesus (2:31a), to whom alone the comment in Psalm 16 about the holy one not seeing corruption can apply (Acts 2:29, 31b). The assertion of Jesus' resurrection in

[151]See my essay, "The Center of Biblical Theology in Acts," 38–41, discussing Acts 2:23–24; 3:15; 4:10; 5:30; 10:39–40; 13:28–30, each of which juxtaposes human responsibility for the crucifixion with the assertion that God raised Jesus. In each of these contexts we also find forgiveness offered to those who repent and then those who are forgiven glorify God. Salvation comes through judgment for God's glory. The wicked are condemned, they repent, and then they praise. Through the judgment they are saved.

Acts 2:24 is supported through the citation and explanation of Psalm 16, and then the resurrection is restated in Acts 2:32.

Peter then argues that Jesus has indeed ascended to the Father and poured out the Spirit, as prophesied, and that he has fulfilled Psalm 110 and taken his seat at the Father's right hand, where he will be until the Father makes his enemies his footstool (Acts 2:34–35). The argument is punctuated with the call for Israel to recognize that God has made Jesus, whom they have crucified, Lord and Christ (2:36). The announcement that they have crucified Jesus condemns them—they are pierced to the heart (2:37). Peter calls them to repent and be baptized for forgiveness (2:38), and three thousand do so and are saved (2:40) through the judgment that has been announced (2:41). Because God judged Jesus at the cross, those who repent and believe in Jesus can be saved through the announcement of judgment. They devote themselves to the apostles' teaching (2:42) and praise God (2:47).

This announcement of salvation through judgment for God's glory is repeated in Acts 3 after Peter and John heal the lame man in Jesus' name (Acts 3:1–10). Peter again indicts the crowd for denying and crucifying Jesus, announcing again that God reversed their verdict by raising Jesus from the dead (3:14–15). Salvation is available in Jesus' name (3:16; 4:12), which glorifies him. Once again Peter argues that what has taken place in Jesus was prophesied in the Old Testament (3:21–24). There are several correspondences between Peter's sermon in Acts 3 and the letter of 1 Peter, as can be seen in table 5.23:

Table 5.23. Peter's Sermon in Acts 3 and the Letter of 1 Peter

Text[1]	Statement	Similar Statement	Text
Acts 3:16	"the faith that is through Jesus"	"who through him are believers in God"	1 Pet. 1:21
Acts 3:18, 21	"what God foretold by the mouth of all the prophets, that his Christ would suffer . . . until the time for restoring all things"	"the prophets . . . prophesied . . . the Spirit of Christ . . . predicted the sufferings of Christ and the subsequent glories"	1 Pet. 1:10–12
Acts 3:20	"the Christ appointed for you"	"He was foreknown before the foundation of the world"	1 Pet. 1:20

[1]All texts here are from the ESV.

In Acts 4 the Jewish religious leadership begins to make war on God (cf. Acts 5:39). Their opposition will be thwarted as God judges them, and through the judgment he brings upon them God will carry out his purpose to save. This will glorify him. The leadership arrests Peter and John and calls them to account (Acts 4:1–7). God fills Peter with the Holy Spirit, and he declares that God raised

Jesus, whom they crucified, from the dead, announcing that salvation is possible only in Jesus' name (4:8–12). The authorities try to command Peter and John to stop preaching in Jesus' name, but the apostles declare that they will obey God rather than men (4:13–20). Meanwhile, people are praising God for the mighty act the apostles have done in Jesus' name (4:21).

In his speech to the Jewish authorities Peter declares that Jesus was the rejected stone that became the cornerstone (Acts 4:11; cf. Ps. 118:22). Upon their release, the apostles join the early church in a prayer that confesses that Psalm 2:1–2 was fulfilled in the conspiracy against Jesus (Acts 4:23–28). They call on God to give them boldness to speak (4:29) and to do more signs and wonders in Jesus' name (4:30). Luke notes the answer to their prayer for boldness right away (4:31), and the mighty works follow shortly (5:12–16).

Opposition, however, arises from within and continues from without. The opposition from within comes from the sinfulness of Christians. This is seen first in the selfishness of Ananias and Sapphira (Acts 5:1–2), then in the racial and linguistic tensions between Hebrews and Hellenists (Acts 6:1). God preserves the church through judgment and wins praise for himself. He strikes Ananias and Sapphira dead (5:3–10). The church fears God (5:11) and prospers (5:12–16). In the case of the widows, the apostles address the need by ordaining servants (6:2–6), and the gospel continues to spread (6:7).

The opposition from without takes the form of persecution from the high priest and his religious party, the Sadducees (Acts 5:17–18), and also from the synagogue of the Freedmen (6:9). Hauled before the Sanhedrin again, Peter asserts that the Christians will obey God rather than men (5:29). Again he charges humans with responsibility for Jesus' death and states that God raised Jesus (5:30). And again he holds out the possibility of repentance and forgiveness (5:31). When the authorities have them beaten, the power of God is seen in the fact that the apostles are counted worthy to suffer for the name of Jesus (5:41).

The speech of Stephen answers the three charges that the synagogue of the Freedmen have leveled against him: speaking against Moses and God (Acts 6:11); speaking against the temple (6:13–14); and speaking against the law (6:13–14). Stephen responds to each charge, and the most explosive part of his response, the part that gets him killed, is his response to the charges about Moses and the Law.[152]

Stephen implicitly attacks the sacrosanctity of the temple by noting that God appeared to Abraham in Mesopotamia (Acts 7:2), that Joseph was in Egypt and the people multiplied there (7:9, 17), that Moses was born in Egypt and met God at Sinai (7:20, 30), and that God declared the place of the burning bush holy ground (7:33). Adding to the fact that God met the fathers outside the

[152]This section assumes the argument I made in "Was Joseph a Type of the Messiah?" 52–77.

land, Stephen quotes Amos 5:25–27 (LXX) where the prophet charged Israel with idolatry in the wilderness—though they had the tabernacle—and promised exile to Babylon. The argument that the temple does not guarantee God's favor and protection climaxes when Stephen alludes to the words of Solomon, the temple builder himself (Acts 7:47–48; cf. 1 Kings 8:27), and quotes Isaiah the prophet on the point that the Most High does not dwell in houses made by human hands (Acts 7:48–50; cf. Isa. 66:1–2). The charge itself, that Jesus would destroy the temple (Acts 6:14), hints at a misunderstanding of the way Jesus did just that when he fulfilled the exile in his death and began the new exodus and return from exile in his resurrection. This misunderstanding was also thrown at Jesus in his trial and while he was on the cross (cf. John 2:17–21; Matt. 26:61; 27:40; Mark 14:58; 15:29). Luke's presentation of Stephen's views on the temple indicates that he shares the views of his sometime travel companion, who sees churches and Christians as the temple of the Holy Spirit (cf. 1 Cor. 3:16; 6:19). Paul's view on that point is itself likely based on the teaching of Jesus (cf. John 2:17–22; 14:15–17; 16:7; 20:21–23).[153]

Stephen's response to the first charge, of speaking against Moses and God (Acts 6:11), and the third charge, of speaking against the law and teaching that Jesus would change the customs Moses delivered (6:14), is the part that, I would suggest, got him killed. The lynchpin for this part of Stephen's address is found in his final statements, where he says in Acts 7:51–53:

> Stiff-necked and uncircumcised in hearts and ears! You always resist the Holy Spirit; as your fathers did so do you. Which of the prophets did your fathers not persecute? And they killed those who announced the coming of the Righteous One, whose betrayers and murderers you have now become. You who received the Law as ordinances of angels, and you have not kept it!

Notice the connection here between the failure to keep the law (Acts 7:53) and the persecution of the prophets and the murder of the one they announced (7:52). Moreover, this rejection of the Law and the Prophets defines their resistance of the Spirit (7:51).

Luke presents Stephen as giving two examples of rejected and persecuted prophets: Joseph and Moses. Both these men were prophets.[154] In both cases they were marked out by God. God was with Joseph and gave him favor before Pharaoh (Acts 7:9–10), and Moses was beautiful in God's sight (7:20). Both men were initially opposed by their kinsmen. Joseph's brothers envied him and sold him into Egypt (7:9). Moses was asked who made him ruler and judge (7:27,

[153]See Hamilton, *God's Indwelling Presence*, 44.

[154]Cf. Joseph's ability to interpret dreams and Pharaoh's recognition that he had the Spirit (Gen. 41:38); and for Moses, see Num. 12:1–8.

cf. 23–29). After an interval of time, both men brought deliverance for God's people. Joseph's brothers came to him in Egypt for food (7:12–15). Moses led the people out of Egypt (7:36). Stephen then points out that Moses said that God would raise up a prophet like him (Moses, 7:37; cf. 3:22), and this quotation of Deuteronomy 18:15–18 is preceded and followed by references to the rejection of Moses (Acts 7:35, 39).

Stephen's argument, then, is that his contemporaries have treated Jesus the way their fathers treated Joseph, Moses, and the prophets. Neither Joseph nor Moses was slain by Israelites, so Stephen's words that "they killed those who announced the coming of the Righteous One" probably allude to those whom Jesus referenced in Luke 11:49–51. There Jesus said:

> The wisdom of God said, "I will send them prophets and apostles, and some of them they will kill and persecute, that the blood of all the prophets that has been shed from the foundation of the world might be sought from this generation, from the blood of Abel to the blood of Zechariah who perished between the altar and the temple." Yes, I say to you, it will be sought from this generation. (Luke 11:49–51)

So it seems that Luke presents Stephen arguing the same way that Jesus argued. In this case, the argument is that Joseph, Moses, the prophets, and Jesus stand on one side, and against them are the wicked Israelites. Jesus and Stephen identify themselves with the martyrs and their opponents with the murderers.

This is typological identification, and it fits with Jesus' statement that those who believe Moses will believe him, for Moses wrote about him (John 5:46). It also fits with Luke's presentation of Jesus' opening the minds of his disciples (Luke 24:25–27, 44–46). Thus, Stephen's response to the charges of (1) speaking against Moses and God, and (2) teaching that Jesus would change the customs of Moses (Acts 6:13–14) is twofold. First, those making the charge about the law do not understand the law. The law typologically foreshadows Christ as the rejected prophet; thus those who reject him are also typologically foreshadowed by those who rejected Joseph, Moses, and the prophets (cf. Acts 17:2–3). If they understood the law, they would see that the law testifies to Jesus as the messiah (John 5:39, 44). Second, those making the charge about Moses do not understand Moses, who wrote that God would raise up a prophet like him (Deut. 18:15–18; Acts 7:37). The "likeness" in view has to do with the fulfillment of the typological pattern seen in Joseph, Moses, and the prophets. These figures were designated by God, were rejected by God's people, and then delivered God's people.

This pattern is fulfilled in Jesus, and it is a pattern of salvation that comes through judgment for God's glory. God judged Joseph's brothers (Gen. 42:21–22;

44:16), exalted Joseph (e.g., 45:9), and through judgment brought the brothers to repentance (44:16, 18–34; 50:15–18), and all along what they meant for evil he meant for good (50:20). So also with Moses: though Israel had rejected him (Ex. 2:14), God exalted Moses (e.g., Ex. 4:16), judged Israel when they grumbled against him (e.g., Num. 14:1–23), through judgment brought them into the Promised Land (e.g., Deut. 2:16), and made his glory known (e.g., Ex. 14:4; 34:6–7; Num. 14:21).

Stephen's opponents get it, and they act in accord with the typological pattern being described. They kill him (Acts 7:54–60). This is no doubt part of Luke's point. The followers of Jesus are being treated just as Jesus was (cf. John 15:18–25). Just as Joseph interceded for his brothers before Pharaoh (Gen. 47:1–2) and Moses interceded with God for Israel (e.g., Ex. 32:11–14, 31–34; Num. 14:13–20), so Jesus interceded for those who denied him and put him to death (Luke 22:32; 23:34), and Stephen follows his Master in the same (Acts 7:60).

Everything in these first seven chapters of Acts centers on the glory of God in salvation through judgment. God's glory is seen in justice and mercy. The church glorifies God for the mercy he has shown to them through the judgment that fell on Christ. The church announces this judgment on Christ, and it also declares that judgment awaits those who acted wickedly in putting him to death. God judged that wicked judgment by raising Jesus from the dead. The church's consistent proclamation of these truths can be seen in table 5.24.

Table 5.24. Wicked People Killed Jesus, but God Raised Him from the Dead

People Responsible for the Death of Jesus	God Raised Jesus from the Dead
The messiah would suffer at the hands of men (Luke 9:22; 18:33; 24:7, 26, 46) . . .	and rise from the dead on the third day (Luke 9:22; 18:33; 24:7, 26, 46).
You killed him (Acts 2:23) . . .	God raised him (Acts 2:24).
And you killed the Champion of life (3:15) . . .	whom God raised from the dead, of which we are witnesses (3:15).
Jesus the messiah of Nazareth, whom you crucified (4:10),	whom God raised from the dead (4:10).
. . . whom you put to death (5:30) . . .	The God of our Fathers raised Jesus (5:30) . . .
. . . whom also they killed, having hung him upon a tree (10:39) . . .	this one God raised on the third day (10:40).
They asked Pilate for him to be put to death (13:28) . . .	but God raised him from the dead (13:30).

Through this announcement of judgment the church holds out the possibility of forgiveness for those who will repent.[155] The church is announcing salvation through judgment, and God is glorified as those who repent glorify him, as those who oppose him are judged and shown to be wicked, and as his purposes prevail.[156]

7.2 Witness to the Resurrection in Judea and Samaria (Acts 8–12)

Saul's persecution scatters the church (Acts 8:1–4). Philip preaches in Samaria (8:5–25) then to the Ethiopian eunuch (8:26–40). Saul is converted (9:1–31), then Peter heals (9:32–35), raises the dead (9:36–43), and takes the gospel to the house of Cornelius (10:1–48). What Peter has done has to be explained in Jerusalem (11:1–18), and in Antioch the church is thriving (11:19–30).[157] Herod kills James (12:1–5), but he cannot hold Peter (12:6–19), nor can he maintain his own life (12:20–25).

As we see from what happens to Saul and Herod, those who oppose God face one of two futures, but both include judgment. Through judgment Saul (Paul) is converted and experiences salvation. Herod, on the other hand, is judged, and he becomes a testimony to God's justice and power. Both he and Paul glorify God, Paul being a display of God's mercy.

The incident at Samaria shows the triumph of the gospel over racial pride and division. The apostles come from Jerusalem and the Samaritans receive the Spirit, with the result that there will be no Samaritan Christianity as there has been Samaritan Judaism. Racial exclusion is judged, and through that judgment salvation comes to the Samaritans.[158]

Philip proclaims Isaiah 53 to the Ethiopian eunuch, a passage that prophesies the salvation through judgment Jesus fulfilled on the cross.[159] The message is not only for the Jews but also for the Gentiles, as is demonstrated when Peter pioneers

---

[155]In the quotations below references to *repentance* and *the forgiveness of sins* are italicized: "'Thus it has been written that the Messiah should suffer and rise from the dead . . . and for *repentance* unto *forgiveness of sins* to be proclaimed in his name to all the nations" (Luke 24:46–47—this forgiveness is not announced in Luke until after the resurrection). "And Peter said to them, *'Repent!'* He said, 'And each one of you must be baptized in the name of Jesus the Messiah *for the forgiveness of your sins* and you will receive the gift of the Holy Spirit" (Acts 2:38). "*Repent*, then, and turn so *that your sins might be wiped away*" (3:19). "And there is no *salvation* in any other, for there is no other name under heaven given among men in which it is necessary for us *to be saved*" (4:12). "God exalted this one as Champion and Savior to his right hand to grant *repentance* to Israel and *forgiveness of sins*" (5:31)."In this one all the prophets bear witness that everyone who believes in him receives *forgiveness of sins* through his name" (10:43). "Therefore let it be known to you, men, brothers, that through this one *forgiveness of sins* is proclaimed to you" (13:38).

[156]Note the references to the progress of the word in Acts 6:7, "And the word of God continued to increase . . ."; 12:24, "But the word of God increased and multiplied"; 13:49, "And the word of the Lord was spreading throughout the whole region"; 19:20, "So the word of the Lord continued to increase and prevail mightily."

[157]Irina Levinskaya (*The Book of Acts in Its Diaspora Setting*, The Book of Acts in Its First Century Setting 5 [Grand Rapids: Eerdmans, 1996], 127–35) discusses evidence on the Jewish community in Antioch.

[158]See further my essay, "Rushing Wind and Organ Music: Toward Luke's Theology of the Spirit in Acts," *Reformed Theological Review* 65, no. 1 (2006): 15–33, also available as appendix 3 in *God's Indwelling Presence*, 183–203.

[159]See further "The Center of Biblical Theology in Acts," 43–45.

the gospel to the Gentiles. Their inclusion in the church apart from circumcision is so significant that the story will be told three times in Acts (chaps. 10, 11, and 15). The witnesses to the resurrection testify in Jerusalem (Acts 1–7), then Samaria (Acts 8), and once Peter takes the gospel to the Gentiles (Acts 10–11), the stage is set for Paul to go to the nations with the good news of God's glory in salvation through judgment in Christ.

7.3 Witness to the Resurrection to the Ends of the Earth (Acts 13–28)

Peter's ministry is highlighted in the first half of Luke's account in Acts, and in the second half the focus switches to Paul. There is essential continuity between the two in word and deed, as both continue the ministry of Jesus. Representative examples can be seen in table 5.25.

Table 5.25. Jesus, Peter, and Paul in Luke–Acts

Type of Ministry	Jesus	Peter	Paul
Preaching that the OT is fulfilled in messiah Jesus	Luke 4, 24	Acts 2–3	Acts 13, 17
Casting out unclean spirits	Luke 4:31–37	Acts 5:16	Acts 16:16–18
Healing the lame	Luke 6:6–11	Acts 3:1–10	Acts 14:8–10
Raising the dead	Luke 7:11–17	Acts 9:36–43	Acts 20:7–12
Healing by an unknown touch, a shadow, or cloths	Luke 8:42–48	Acts 5:15	Acts 19:11–12

Luke shows that Paul is preaching the same message of salvation through judgment to God's glory as Jesus and Peter preached. Paul quotes the same passages from the Old Testament that Peter quoted and offers the same explanations of them. Psalm 2 was quoted in the prayer after Peter and John were released in Acts 4:25–26, and Paul quotes this text in his sermon at Pisidian Antioch (Acts 13:33). So also with Psalm 16, which Peter quoted and explained in his sermon on the day of Pentecost (Acts 2:24–32); Paul too quotes and explains it just as Peter did (Acts 13:35–37).

This section of Acts shows the progress of the gospel to the uttermost parts of the known world.[160] Luke seems to have organized the material according to the geographical realities related to Paul's various trips. Paul goes on four missionary journeys in Acts 13–28: three in which he is free, and a fourth when he is arrested and taken through Caesarea Philippi to Rome. The first three

[160]For studies of cultural and social issues, the provinces to which the gospel was taken, the "asiarchs" and "politarchs," and the "we" passages, see David W. J. Gill and Conrad Gempf, eds., *The Book of Acts in Its Graeco-Roman Setting*, The Book of Acts in Its First Century Setting 2 (Grand Rapids: Eerdmans, 1994).

journeys seem to begin in Antioch and end in Jerusalem.[161] Here we will highlight the centrality of God's glory in salvation through judgment in Paul's first journey (Acts 13–14), the Jerusalem Council (Acts 15), Paul's second journey (Acts 16–18), Paul's third journey (Acts 19–21), and Paul's captivity and transfer to Rome (Acts 22–28).

7.3.1 Paul's First Journey (Acts 13–14)

Once sent out, by the power of the Holy Spirit Paul pronounces judgment on Elymas the magician—denouncing him as a "son of the devil" (i.e., seed of the serpent)—and the hand of the Lord blinds him (Acts 13:9–11). Through the judgment visited on Elymas, the proconsul believes, and his amazement glorifies God: "Then the proconsul, having seen what happened, believed, being astonished by the teaching of the Lord" (13:12).[162]

Paul's sermon in Pisidian Antioch concludes with the announcement that salvation is available through the judgment that fell on Jesus (Acts 13:29–30, 37). Further, Paul states that Jesus can justify people whereas the law of Moses cannot (13:38–39). The rendering of this verdict on what is possible through obedience to the law is intended to draw people to Christ. The proclamation of judgment against those who would justify themselves by the law is meant to lead to salvation. Paul then warns his hearers not to be those on whom God exercises justice (13:40–41). Again, the announcement of judgment against those who reject the gospel is meant to lead to salvation. The Gentiles rejoice and glorify the word of the Lord when the message comes to them (13:40).

The book of Acts is clear that God appoints people to eternal life. The text does not say that those who believe are appointed to eternal life, but rather that "as many as were appointed to eternal life believed" (Acts 13:48). Acts is clear that God is sovereign in salvation, and table 5.26 seeks to capture the various ways Luke communicates this.

As more Jews and Greeks in Iconium believe (Acts 14:1), Jewish opposition to the gospel mounts (13:45–46, 50; 14:2, 4–5). This opposition will be crushed by God's judgment, even as they try to crush Paul with stones (14:19). Between the mounting of the opposition and the attempt to stone Paul, Luke recounts an incident that exposes the bankruptcy of the Greco-Roman pantheon (14:8–18). Remarkably, indeed miraculously, after being stoned Paul does not even need a day off. He gets up the next day and goes to the next place to preach the gospel (14:20). Those who enter life will do so through refining experiences of tribulation, as Paul tells the churches on the way home: "Through many tribulations

---

[161] Journey 1: Antioch (Acts 13:1–4), Jerusalem (15:2); journey 2: Antioch (15:35–36), Jerusalem (18:22); journey 3: Antioch (18:22–23), Jerusalem (21:17).

[162] Cf. Pao, *Acts and the Isaianic New Exodus*, 202.

Table 5.26. God's Sovereignty in Salvation in Acts[1]

God Ordained the Cross	God Calls, Adds, and Appoints to Eternal Life	God Gives Faith and Repentance, and Cleanses and Opens Hearts
2:23: "Jesus, delivered up according to the definite plan and foreknowledge of God . . ."	2:39: ". . . everyone whom the Lord our God calls to himself."	3:16: "The faith that is through Jesus . . ."
3:18: "What God foretold by the mouth of all the prophets, that his Christ would suffer, he thus fulfilled."	2:41: "There were added that day . . ."	5:31: "God exalted him . . . to give repentance to Israel."
4:27–28: "There were gathered together . . . Herod and Pontius Pilate, along with the Gentiles and the people of Israel, to do whatever your hand and your plan had predestined to take place."	2:47: "The Lord added to their number . . ."	11:18: "To the Gentiles also God has granted repentance that leads to life."
	5:14: "Believers were added to the Lord . . ."	15:8–9: "God . . . having cleansed their hearts by faith."
	11:24: "People were added to the Lord."	16:14: "The Lord opened her heart to pay attention to what was said by Paul."
	13:48: "As many as were appointed to eternal life believed."	18:27: ". . . those who through grace had believed."

[1]All texts here are from the ESV.

we must enter into the kingdom of God" (14:22). Commending the churches to the Lord (14:23), Paul and Barnabas return to Antioch to declare the mighty acts of God (14:27).

7.3.2 The Jerusalem Council (Acts 15)

Like the concluding statements of Paul's sermon at Pisidian Antioch, where salvation comes through the judgment pronounced on justification by law (Acts 13:38–39), the Jerusalem Council pronounces judgment against the law-keeping requirement of circumcision.[163] Through this judgment on the requirement of the law for justification and acceptance, salvation by grace through faith is upheld (15:9, 11).

7.3.3 Paul's Second Journey (Acts 16–18)

The truth sometimes appears contradictory, but only at a superficial level. Thus it is with Paul's circumcision of Timothy (Acts 16:1–5). Timothy is circumcised not so that he will be justified, but so that Paul can take him to do evangelism

[163]See the interesting study by Richard Bauckham, "James and the Jerusalem Church," in *The Book of Acts in Its Palestinian Setting*, The Book of Acts in Its First Century Setting 4 (Grand Rapids: Eerdmans, 1995), 415–80.

among Jews (16:3). Judgment is pronounced on an evil spirit in a slave girl (16:18), through which she is delivered. The Romans react to the loss of their source of profit by opposing Paul and the gospel (16:19–24). God condemns this opposition to the gospel, and the very jailer keeping Paul and Silas is converted (16:25–34). The jailer and those who believe with him in his household rejoice in God (16:34). They have been saved through God's triumph over the attempts to thwart the spread of the gospel.

Luke shows that Christianity is not a political threat to the Roman Empire in the incident recounted in Acts 16:35–40, and the point is made again in the incident at Corinth recounted in 18:12–17. The Christians are not pursuing the overthrow of a worldly government. Rather, they are obeying God and only disobey human authorities when those human authorities forbid obedience to God (cf. 4:19–20; 5:29). The rabble-rousing opponents of the gospel, meanwhile, are trumping up charges about how the Christians have been turning the world upside down, acting against Caesar's decrees, and claiming that there is another king, Jesus (17:7). The trial before Gallio gives the lie to these charges (18:12–17). Given the way the Jews professed their loyalty to Rome against Jesus ("We have no king but Caesar!" John 19:15), we can be sure that if the charges shouted by the mob against Paul in Acts 17:7 were true, the Jews would have used those charges against him. Again and again, however, the narrative demonstrates that all charges against Paul and the Christians—whether made by Jews or by pagans—are groundless.[164]

N. T. Wright suggests, "When the Paul of Acts is on trial in 17.7 for overthrowing the laws of Caesar by saying that there is 'another king, namely Jesus,' we see what I take to be an authentic memory of the typical impression made by his gospel preaching."[165] But Paul is not on trial in Acts 17. Rather, a mob (Acts 17:5) is blustering out false charges. If Wright were correct about this being an "authentic memory of the typical impression made by his gospel preaching," surely witnesses of such preaching would be brought forward when Paul is on trial. Instead, Paul can explicitly declare before the Roman governor Festus, ". . . nor against Caesar have I committed any offense" (25:8 ESV). Then he asserts that if he has done wrong and deserves to die, he is not seeking to escape justice (25:11). These are not the words of a man who has been out challenging Caesar only to deny the same when called to account. If that were the way of things, when the Jews lay out their case against Paul, they would need no favors from Festus (25:1–10). Festus would not tell Agrippa that the dispute is over the law and the resurrection of Jesus (25:19). He would not find Paul innocent, but have definite charges to send with Paul to Caesar

[164]Cf. Acts 16:35–40; 17:8–9; 18:12–17; 19:35–41; 22:25–29; 23:29; 24:22–27; 25:9, 11, 26–27; 26:32.
[165]N. T. Wright, *Paul: In Fresh Perspective* (Minneapolis: Fortress, 2006), 70.

(25:25–27), and Agrippa would not be telling Festus that Paul could be set free but for his appeal to Caesar (26:32). According to Luke, the Christians are not out trying to subvert the Roman Empire, but their opponents are falsely charging them of doing just that. Luke's narrative only depicts Paul and the other Christians obeying the authorities, subverting the claims falsely made against them.[166]

In Athens Paul warns of the day of judgment (Acts 17:31), and through that announcement of judgment some believe and are saved (17:32–34). In Corinth the Lord tells Paul in a dream that no one will harm him because he has many to be saved in the city (18:10).

7.3.4 Paul's Third Journey (Acts 19–21)

In Ephesus the episode with the disciples of John pronounces judgment on any attempt to maintain Old Testament religion apart from faith in the one to whom the Old Testament prophets pointed, Jesus (Acts 19:1–10). Judgment is rendered on magic and superstition, with the result that the superstitious are trounced, magic books are burned, and the name of Jesus is extolled as the word of the Lord prevails (19:11–20; cf. 19:17, 19, 20). A riot ensues in Ephesus when the little trinket-gods cannot defend themselves, but once again Luke shows that those fomenting social unrest are the opponents of Christianity rather than the Christians themselves (19:21–41).

In Troas Paul raises Eutychus from the dead and celebrates the Lord's Supper with the church (Acts 20:7–12). On the way home to Jerusalem he bids farewell to the elders of the church in Ephesus (20:17–38). Paul spent considerable time in Ephesus (cf. 19:10), and the church received not only this significant address in Acts 20 but also his letter to the church in Ephesus. Tradition holds that the apostle John later ministered there, making it likely that the churches in and around Ephesus received the letters of John, and Jesus addressed the church in Ephesus in Revelation 2:1–7. Jesus obtained the church through his blood (Acts 20:28), which condemns pride and self-centeredness (20:19, 35). Through the judgment that fell on Jesus, and through the judgment of human wickedness, salvation is possible for those who repent and believe in Jesus (20:21) by the power of this gospel of God's grace (20:27). To God and the word of his grace Paul commends the church in Ephesus (20:32), and God is glorified in salvation

[166]This contextual understanding of the statements in Acts 17:7 subverts N. T. Wright's suggestion that "whatever we may think about the portrait of Paul in Acts, the letters confirm that not only he but a good many other Christians . . . believed it their business to travel around the known world telling people that there was 'another king, this Jesus'" (N. T. Wright, *The New Testament and the People of God*, Christian Origins and the Question of God 1 [Minneapolis: Fortress, 1992], 361, cf. also 374–75). On the contrary, Luke does not indicate that Paul thinks this is his business, but rather shows that the opponents of Christianity make this *false charge* to agitate against Christians. See also Denny Burk, "Is Paul's Gospel Counterimperial? Evaluating the Prospects of the 'Fresh Perspective' for Evangelical Theology," *JETS* 51 (2008): 309–37.

through judgment. The mutual love between Paul and the church displays the beauty of God's purposes (20:36–38).

Paul is "constrained by the Spirit" to go to Jerusalem (Acts 20:22 ESV), and this does not contradict the fact that in Cyprus the disciples tell Paul "through the Spirit" not to go to Jerusalem (21:4). The reason this is not contradictory is that, in what follows, Luke makes plain that Paul and the church have received the same message from the Spirit: that in Jerusalem Paul will face imprisonment and afflictions (20:23; 21:11). The difference is not in the information received from the Spirit but in the reactions to that information. Paul's reaction is to assert that his life does not matter to himself, because his desire is to finish the course and the ministry Jesus gave to him (20:24). The people in Cyprus respond to the prophecy of Agabus by urging Paul not to go to Jerusalem (21:12), but when Paul declares his readiness to be imprisoned and even die for Jesus' name (21:13), they commit themselves to God's will (21:14). What happens to Paul matches what Agabus prophesied in a way that is typical of the fulfillment of biblical prophecies.[167]

When Paul meets with James in Jerusalem, James proposes a plan designed to take away roadblocks to Jewish evangelism (Acts 21:17–26). This plan involves Paul engaging in Jewish piety with four other Christians who have taken a vow (21:23–24). We do not have enough information here to know the extent to which the first generation of Jewish Christians continued to practice Judaism, but James does reaffirm the decisions of the Jerusalem Council (21:25), which demonstrates that whatever their involvement in Judaism, they maintain the view that salvation is by grace through faith. Nor does Paul compromise himself by engaging in these purification rites, for Luke shows him taking and keeping vows earlier in Acts (18:18), and Paul himself declares elsewhere that for the sake of evangelizing those under the law he is willing to be under the law, though he is not himself under the law (1 Cor. 9:20).[168]

In the temple, Paul is arrested, and for the rest of the book of Acts he is in Roman custody.[169]

---

[167]Compare the prophecy of the death of Ahab and its fulfillment (1 Kings 21:19, 24; 22:34–37) to the prophecy of the handing over of Paul and its fulfillment (Acts 21:11, 27–36). Grudem claims that the details of the prophecy regarding Paul do not match what actually happened to Paul (Wayne Grudem, *The Gift of Prophecy in the New Testament and Today*, rev. ed. [Wheaton, IL: Crossway, 2000], 77–83), but the prophecy about Paul matches what happened to him as closely as the prophecy about Ahab matches what happened to him, and the author of Kings clearly sees what happened to Ahab as the fulfillment of the prophecy (1 Kings 22:37).

[168]See also Paul's letter to the Galatians, and the discussion of that letter in chap. 6 below. Early Christians do not appear to have understood Paul and James to be tolerating (or advocating) a mix of Christianity and Judaism. Ignatius says to the Magnesians, "It is utterly absurd to profess Jesus Christ and to practice Judaism. For Christianity did not believe in Judaism, but Judaism in Christianity, in which every tongue believed and was brought together to God" (Ignatius *Magn.* 10:3, translation from Michael W. Holmes, ed., *The Apostolic Fathers: Greek Texts and English Translations*, 3rd ed. [Grand Rapids: Baker, 2007], 209).

[169]For a stimulating discussion of the realities of Paul's situation, see Brian Rapske, *The Book of Acts and Paul in Roman Custody*, The Book of Acts in Its First Century Setting 3 (Grand Rapids: Eerdmans, 1994).

7.3.5 Paul's Captivity and Transfer to Rome (Acts 22–28)

Paul asks for and receives permission to address the mob that has nearly torn him to bits. The Roman captors at hand, Paul recounts his testimony of being saved through judgment for God's glory on the road to Damascus (Acts 22:1–21). The crowd listens until Paul mentions his commission to the Gentiles, which sends them into a fury (22:22–23). The Roman tribune first wants to beat Paul to find out what he has done, but ceases the plan when Paul divulges his Roman citizenship (22:24–29). Instead he takes Paul before the Jewish Sanhedrin, where Paul declares that he is on trial for proclaiming the fulfillment of Old Testament expectation. The Pharisees on the Sanhedrin, believing the Old Testament, rise to his defense (23:1–10). Jesus appears to Paul in a vision to strengthen and encourage him, telling him that he must testify in Rome also (23:11). Then a conspiracy forces the removal of Paul from Jerusalem (23:12–35).

The Jews who oppose Paul are shown by Luke to be trumping up false charges (Acts 24:1–21), and the Roman governor Felix is shown to be a self-serving bribe seeker (24:22–27). Paul proclaims God's justice to him, hoping to lead him to salvation through judgment, but Felix, though scared, avoids the issue (24:25). When Festus replaces Felix, he shows himself no more concerned with justice than Felix, and Paul, knowing that he must testify in Rome (23:11), appeals to Caesar (25:1–12).

Paul then defends himself before King Agrippa (Acts 25:13–26:32), where again Paul testifies of the way he was saved through judgment for God's glory on the Damascus road (26:12–18). Then he declares how in Christ God has wrought salvation through judgment for his glory in fulfillment of the Old Testament (26:22–23). Just as Pilate and Herod have declared Jesus innocent (Luke 23:13–16), Agrippa declares Paul innocent (Acts 26:32). Remarkably, Felix, Festus, and Agrippa are united in their inability to implement justice. They provide a stark contrast with God, who upholds both justice and mercy.

When Paul is shipped to Rome, the rejection of his good counsel (Acts 27:10–11) bears the fruit of injury and loss (27:21), but God promises deliverance to Paul and those with him (27:23–26). By adhering to Paul's words (27:31, 33–36), through the shipwreck all reach shore safely (27:27–44). Paul is unharmed from the bite of a poisonous snake (28:1–6) and heals the father of the island's chief and many others (28:7–10). And so they come to Rome (28:14, cf. 11–16), where Paul proclaims the glory of God in salvation through judgment (28:17–31).

7.4 The Center of the Theology of Acts

The book of Acts bears explicit and implicit testimony to the triumph of God over idolatry. The implicit testimony I have in mind comes in the form of the names that appear in the account. These names make clear that the Greco-Roman gods and heroes are thought to be honored by their namesakes, but they cannot help or hold the allegiance of those with their names: Aeneas is paralyzed but Jesus heals him through Peter (Acts 9:34). Zeus and Hermes are dismissed by Paul as vain things (14:12, 15). Apollo(s) is mighty in the Scriptures and is taught the way of God more accurately (18:24–28). The son of Pyrrhus is a companion of Paul (20:4). This implicit testimony is reinforced by the explicit calls for pagans to turn from idols to the living God (e.g., 14:15; 17:29–31). These calls judge the gods as worthless, and through that judgment those who repent are saved to the glory of God.

The glory of God in salvation through judgment is also repeatedly seen in Acts as the death and resurrection of Jesus is announced again and again. Judgment fell on Jesus, and through that judgment salvation is available. Judgment is announced on sinful humans, and those who are led by that judgment to repentance will be saved. The opposition to Christianity is also judged and thwarted, and through the judgment of their enemies the followers of the way are delivered to the glory of God. The center of the theology of Acts is the glory of God in salvation through judgment.[170]

8. The Center of the Theology of the Gospels and Acts

The four Gospels all proclaim that salvation has come through the judgment that fell on Jesus. This has individual, community, and cosmic expressions. Jesus triumphs over the cosmic principalities and powers as he casts out demons, then makes a public display of them at the cross. He judges the powers of darkness, casting them out, and through the judgment of the spiritual forces of evil in heavenly places he saves his people. Simultaneously, Jesus himself comes under the judgment of God. Having recapitulated Israel's history and typologically fulfilled it, he saves his people by undergoing judgment. Salvation then comes through that judgment as God raises Jesus from the dead, accomplishing salvation through judgment for all who trust in Jesus. God is glorified by this as the power of God in Christ is seen to be superior to all powers in heaven and on earth.

The cosmic dimension of the glory of God in salvation through judgment comes also through the renewal of creation that Jesus teaches and enacts in his mighty works. He is able to calm storms, provide food, give living water, curse fig trees that do not bear, and point to the day when the desert will bloom. In all this Jesus is pronouncing judgment on the results of sin in the world. By this judgment, and by means of his finishing the work the Father

[170] Thielman (*Theology of the New Testament*, 113–14) suggests that "salvation history" is Luke's "organizing principle." It will be obvious from my discussion above that I would only add to this that the originating purpose of, energizing force in, and final aim for salvation history is the glory of God in salvation through judgment.

gave him to do, he will bring about salvation for the created order in the renewal of all things.

The glory of God in salvation through judgment finds expression also in the birth and growth of the early Christian community. It is impossible to discuss this apart from the glory of God in salvation through judgment at the individual level, for communities are composed of individuals. These individuals come under personal judgment as a result of which they perceive their own condemnation. Through this, they are compelled to repent, and because of the death and resurrection of Jesus, when they repent they are saved. Saved individuals are then baptized, which is itself a picture of salvation through judgment. Through the experience of going into the water, they are buried with Christ, united with him in the judgment he experienced. Coming up out of the water, they are raised with Christ, united with him in the salvation through judgment of resurrection life (see the appendix to this chapter, table 5.27). Through these individual experiences of salvation through judgment, a community of believers is formed. This community of believers loves one another as Jesus has loved them, and in doing so they live out God's glory in justice and mercy as they relate to one another and to outsiders. The community also experiences opposition, and that opposition is judged. Through the judgment that falls on the enemies of God and his people, the community, the congregation, the church is delivered and thrives for God's glory.

In Christ, in the cosmos, in individual lives, and in the church, the glory of God in salvation through judgment is the center of the theology of the Gospels and Acts.

9. Appendix

Table 5.27 references all uses of baptism language in the New Testament. It thus takes into account both verbal (*baptize*) and noun (*baptism, Baptist*) forms.

Table 5.27. Baptism in the New Testament

Baptized in water or Jordan River	Matt. 3:6, 11, 13, 14, 16; 21:25; Mark 1:4, 5, 8, 9; 11:30; Luke 3:3, 7, 12, 16, 21; 7:29, 30; 20:4; John 1:25, 26, 28, 31; 3:22, 23, 26; 10:40; Acts 1:5, 22; 2:38; 8:36, 38; 10:37, 47; 11:16; 13:24; 18:25; 19:3, 4; Rom. 6:4; Col. 2:12
Baptized in/with/ by the Holy Spirit	Matt. 3:11; Mark 1:8; Luke 3:16; John 1:33; Acts 1:5; 11:16
Baptized into Moses	1 Cor. 10:2
The cross as a baptism	Mark 10:38, 39; Luke 12:50; Rom. 6:3, 4
The baptism of new believers	Matt. 28:19; Mark 16:16; John 4:1, 2; Acts 2:41; 8:12, 13, 16, 38, 9:18; 10:47, 48; 16:15, 33; 18:8; 19:5; 22:16; Rom. 6:3; 1 Cor. 1:13, 14, 15, 16, 17; 12:13; 15:29; Gal. 3:27; Eph. 4:5; Col. 2:12; Heb. 6:2; 1 Pet. 3:21
Baptized for ritual cleansings	Mark 7:4; Luke 11:38; Heb. 9:10
John's title (the one who baptizes)	Matt. 3:1; 11:11, 12; 14:2, 8; 16:14; 17:13; Mark 6:14, 24, 25; 8:28; Luke 7:20, 33; 9:19

Chapter 6

God's Glory in Salvation through Judgment

IN THE LETTERS OF THE NEW TESTAMENT

> *. . . what an upheaval of the universe it will be, when everything in heaven and earth blends in one hymn of praise and everything that lives and has lived cries aloud: "Thou art just, O Lord, for Thy ways are revealed" . . . . Then, of course, the crown of knowledge will be reached and all will be made clear.*
>
> —Fyodor Dostoevsky, *The Brothers Karamazov*[1]

1. Introduction

Canonically speaking, the New Testament letters play a role similar to that of the "poetic commentary" that begins in the Latter Prophets and continues into the Writings of the Old Testament. Both Testaments open with narrative (Torah, Gospels and Acts), then both Testaments continue with a form of "commentary" on the narrative. The first portion of this "commentary" in the New Testament is the collection of thirteen letters from the arch-persecutor who was transformed into an apostle. He was saved through judgment: everything he stood for was condemned when Christ appeared to him in glory on the road to Damascus, and through that condemnation he was saved to proclaim the good news of God's glory in Christ.[2] The second portion of the New Testament's

[1]Fyodor Dostoevsky, *The Brothers Karamazov*, trans. Constance Garnett (New York: Modern Library, 1996), 271 (bk. 5, chap. 4). The lines in this quote are spoken by Ivan, who is wrestling with and, at this point in the novel, rejecting this theodicy. Dostoevsky, however, is presenting Ivan as a rebel (the chapter is entitled "Rebellion"), and Ivan later in the speech asserts, "I would rather remain with my unavenged suffering and unsatisfied indignation, *even if I were wrong*" (272, emphasis original).

[2]See the way that so much of Paul's theology is traced to this encounter, which can be seen as "the origin of

"commentary" comprises another eight letters. These eight come from the one anonymous author of the letter to the Hebrews along with Peter, James (son of Joseph not Zebedee), John, and Jude.

The events described in the Old Testament unfolded across thousands of years, and the books of the Old Testament were produced across a millennium, from Moses in the 1400s BC to Ezra–Nehemiah in the 400s BC. The events described in the New Testament, by contrast, unfolded across only one century, from circumstances leading up to the birth of Jesus somewhere between 6 and 4 BC to the exile of John to Patmos late in the first century AD (ca. AD 95). The books of the New Testament, meanwhile, were produced at various points between the resurrection of Jesus and the mid-to-late AD 90s.

The New Testament gives every indication that the authors of its books knew one another, and strong ancient tradition indicates that many ministered in the same churches.[3] The Gospel according to Matthew was likely written in Antioch,[4] and it was from Antioch that Paul and Barnabas were sent out in Acts 13. The Gospel according to Mark probably reflects Peter's preaching and was written by the same man who traveled with Paul and Barnabas for part of that journey, and who was later associated with Paul (Col. 4:10; 2 Tim. 4:11). The Gospel according to Luke was also written by one who traveled with Paul, and since he was likely with Paul on the return trips to Antioch, it would seem probable that Matthew, Mark, and Luke crossed paths in Antioch. Surely the burden of proof would be on those who think that Luke and Matthew were unknown to one another personally.[5] The Gospel according to John was written by one with whom Paul had fellowship in Jerusalem (Gal. 2:9), and who later ministered in Ephesus, where Paul had spent considerable time. We do not know who wrote Hebrews, but given his call for Christians to meet together (Heb. 10:24–25), he could have known the others (cf. also Heb. 2:3). Paul indicates that he met James in Jerusalem (Gal. 1:19), and however later interpreters may have struggled to see that the two men preached the same message, Paul claims that James gave him the right hand of fellowship (Gal. 2:9). The actual evidence indicates that Paul was on good terms with James throughout his years of ministry (1 Cor. 15:7; Acts 21:17–26). Likewise, there is no evidence of disharmony between Paul and Peter (Gal. 1:18). Peter refers to Paul as a "brother," and calls Paul's letters Scripture (2 Pet. 3:15–16)! Jude calls himself the brother of James (Jude 1:1), so we know

Paul's gospel," in Seyoon Kim, *Paul and the New Perspective: Second Thoughts on the Origin of Paul's Gospel* (Grand Rapids: Eerdmans, 2002).

[3]As witnessed to in the writings of the New Testament and in Eusebius, *Ecclesiastical History*, trans. K. Lake and J. E. L. Oulton, 2 vols., LCL (Cambridge, MA: Harvard University Press, 1932).

[4]D. A. Carson and Douglas J. Moo, *An Introduction to the New Testament*, 2nd ed. (Grand Rapids: Zondervan, 2005), 151–52.

[5]I am not here directly engaging the so-called Synoptic problem, but given the interlinked nature of the early church, I think it highly unlikely that Matthew and Luke did not know one another. Cf. Richard Bauckham, ed., *The Gospels for All Christians: Rethinking the Gospel Audiences* (Grand Rapids: Eerdmans, 1998).

that they knew one another, and thus Jude probably knew others associated with James, including John, Peter, Paul, and others in Christian circles.[6]

The point to be observed here is so significant that I risk belaboring it. All the evidence we have indicates that several of these men had particularly strong, even *volatile*, personalities. Peter's passion is often evident in Gospel narratives. John and his brother once asked Jesus whether they should call down fire from heaven to consume their adversaries (Luke 9:54). Jesus called them sons of thunder (Mark 3:17). James the brother of Jesus pronounced woes on the rich that display no little boldness (James 5:1–6). Paul disputed with Barnabas—Barnabas!—so violently that they parted company (Acts 15:36–39), at least for a time. He was not afraid to stand publicly against Peter (Gal. 2:11), and at points in his letters to the Galatians and the Corinthians, it is fair to say that he is incensed.[7] Does it not seem historically plausible, then, that if these men were truly opposed to one another at any point—if at any point there was a real disagreement between them—we would have direct accounts of the confrontations and would see repercussions of the fallouts?

Instead, what we have in the writings of the New Testament indicates that the authors of these documents and their associates were not only familiar with each other but united in the task of the Great Commission (Matt. 28:18–20).[8] This does not mean there were no disagreements, but I would posit that the texts record the most significant disagreements: Paul and Barnabas separated, but Paul's later words about Mark indicate that reconciliation happened. Similarly, Paul confronted Peter, but Peter evidently repented and agreed with Paul. The authors of the New Testament had their own personalities and perspectives, but for all the vaunted "diversity" in New Testament theology, what seems most remarkable about these writings is the universal acceptance of so many hard-edged, particularistic, simple-yet-complex, perfectly balancing notions.[9] There

[6]See the suggestion put forward by E. Earle Ellis "that our New Testament is the product of four apostolic missions: *Jacobean* [James], *Johannine*, *Pauline* and *Petrine*. . . . The leaders of the missions appear in Gal 2 and in the book of Acts as cooperating and allied apostles commissioned by Jesus Christ . . ." (E. Earle Ellis, *Christ and the Future in New Testament History* [Boston: Brill, 2000], 235; see also E. Earle Ellis, *The Making of the New Testament Documents* [Boston: Brill, 1999], 32–47).

[7]G. B. Caird's statement, "The whole tenor of the New Testament is opposed to dogmatism and authoritarianism," is everywhere contradicted by the actual assertions made by the authors of the New Testament (G. B. Caird, *New Testament Theology*, ed. L. D. Hurst [Oxford: Clarendon, 1994], 8). See, e.g., 1 Cor. 15:35–36.

[8]These observations about early Christianity are historically plausible and based squarely on primary source data. Often what passes for "historical critical" scholarship is neither historical nor critical, but rather a rejection of primary source material in the pursuit of historical reconstructions that are not plausible. See, for example, the discussion of F. C. Bauer in Stephen Neill and Tom Wright, *The Interpretation of the New Testament, 1861–1986*, 2nd ed. (Oxford: Oxford University Press, 1988), 20–30. See also "Historical-Literary Criticism—After Two Hundred Years," in E. Earle Ellis, *History and Interpretation in New Testament Perspective*, Biblical Interpretation Series (Boston: Brill, 2001), 1–16; and "Appendix VI: Ferdinand Christian Bauer and His School," in Ellis, *The Making of the New Testament Documents*, 435–45.

[9]*Pace*, e.g., Bart D. Ehrman, *The Orthodox Corruption of Scripture: The Effect of Early Christological Controversies on the Text of the New Testament* (New York: Oxford University Press, 1993), 8–9; and Bart D. Ehrman, *Misquoting Jesus: The Story Behind Who Changed the Bible and Why* (New York: HarperSanFrancisco, 2005), 166–67, 212.

is no indication that unstated disagreements have been passed over in silence. If Paul had disagreed with James's letter, would he not have anathematized it (cf. Gal. 1:8–9)? Would it have been possible to whitewash such a rupture? Is it possible that Paul was not aware of James's letter? Given the interlinked early Christian community,[10] would someone not have shown it to him? If they had thought themselves to be in real disagreement with each other, is it not likely that there would be some historical evidence of such a disagreement, and would both of their writings have been recognized by the early Christians as canonical? On this question, there have always been exceptional people, like Luther, who have rejected one in favor of the other, but across space and through time the great tradition has had little difficulty accepting both Paul and James and understanding them to have taught a message that is harmonious, not discordant.

Scholars sometimes speak of "contradictions" between the authors of the New Testament, but they cannot really point to contradictions. A real contradiction could be claimed if in the face of John's assertion that those who know Jesus keep his commands (1 John 2:3), Paul countered that those who know Jesus live no differently than those who do not know him. But this is manifestly not what Paul says. He may say it differently than John, using vice lists and referring to the fruit of the Spirit and such, but even when he speaks of the ways Christians fail to keep the commands of Jesus, he speaks of it in terms of doing what is hated and not doing what is wanted (Rom. 7:13–15). John is arguably teaching the same thing in his words on confessing sin (1 John 1:8–10). These examples could be multiplied,[11] but the point is that those who would claim contradictions should bring out real contradictions. Instead they play references to the Son of Man off the references to the messiah, subtly insinuating disagreements where there are none.[12]

Again, what is remarkable about the New Testament is the high degree of agreement about what are—to Roman or Jewish (or worldly) minds—bizarre ideas. The authors of the New Testament all agree that Jesus is Israel's hoped-for messiah, in spite of the fact that he was crucified.[13] They agree that with the resurrection of Jesus the future has broken into the present.[14] They agree that Jesus is God, in

[10]Note that in Romans 16 Paul greets many Christians in a church he had not yet visited.

[11]A real contradiction, for instance, would be if one gospel had the voice from heaven say, "This is my beloved son," while another had the voice from heaven say, "This is *not* my beloved son." It is no contradiction for one gospel to say "You are my beloved son" and another to have "this is my beloved son." The two accounts are saying the same thing in a way that was acceptable in the ancient world before tape recorders and video cameras.

[12]For nuanced discussion of these two titles and interaction with the secondary literature, see Thomas R. Schreiner, *New Testament Theology: Magnifying God in Christ* (Grand Rapids: Baker, 2008), 197–232.

[13]Cf. Michael J. Gorman, *Apostle of the Crucified Lord: A Theological Introduction to Paul and His Letters* (Grand Rapids: Eerdmans, 2004), 99: "This fixation on a 'dead criminal' or even a dead Messiah sounds narrow, if not morbid."

[14]See the lucid grammatical discussion of the disciples' earlier confusion about the resurrection from the dead at the end of the age in Mark 9:10, in Denny Burk, *Articular Infinitives in the Greek of the New Testament: On the Exegetical Benefit of Grammatical Precision*, New Testament Monographs 14 (Sheffield: Sheffield Phoenix Press, 2006), 133–34; here Burk agrees with and quotes N. T. Wright, *The Resurrection of the Son of God*,

spite of their strong Jewish monotheism.[15] They agree that the Spirit is God, and they agree in their differentiation of Jesus from the Spirit and the Father. They agree that the eschaton has dawned and will be consummated at Jesus' return, in spite of the unexpected nature of the concept. In other words, they hold to a tension between what has already happened and what has not yet been realized.[16] The authors of the New Testament agree that justification is by faith apart from works. They agree that God is sovereign, but also that humans are responsible for their actions. They agree that humans must be born again, made alive, regenerated. They agree that the new covenant has been inaugurated. And the burden of this chapter is to show that the center of the theology reflected in the letters of the New Testament is the glory of God in salvation through judgment.

2. Paul's Letters

Paul's letters are occasional, logical, and dense. This discussion cannot be a full-scale treatment of Paul's theology, nor will it engage every dispute in Pauline studies.[17] My objective here is to show that the glory of God in salvation through judgment is the center of Paul's theology.[18] This theme animated his astonishing perseverance through shipwreck and stoning, through all-night preaching and careful argumentation in writing as he pursued the great task of making disciples of Jesus. As we think on the center of Paul's theology, we must keep in mind that Paul wrote neither for the ancient equivalent of annual SBL meetings nor for the reviews that would appear in academic journals. Paul wrote so that people would know God by faith in Christ and the power of the Spirit.[19]

Christian Origins and the Question of God 3 (Minneapolis: Fortress, 2003), 415, on the future resurrection being brought into the present in Jesus.

[15]Larry W. Hurtado (*Lord Jesus Christ: Devotion to Jesus in Earliest Christianity* [Grand Rapids: Eerdmans, 2003], 31) writes, "The incorporation of Christ into the devotional pattern of early Christian groups has no real analogy in the Jewish tradition of the period."

[16]On inaugurated eschatology in Paul's letters, see Schreiner, *New Testament Theology*, 97–103.

[17]This is not the place for wider discussions of disputed questions in Pauline theology, such as the massive debate over Paul and the law. For my summary of N. T. Wright's reliance on E. P. Sanders, Friedrich Avemarie's demonstration that Sanders's treatment of rabbinic materials is not satisfying, Mark Adam Elliott's demonstration that Sanders has not accurately accounted for the treatment of election and remnant theology in the Qumran and Pseudepigraphic literature, and the conflict between Wright's claims and what Paul himself said, see James M. Hamilton Jr., "N. T. Wright and Saul's Moral Bootstraps: Newer Light on 'The New Perspective'" 25 (2004): 139–55. Cf. Friedrich Avemarie, *Tora und Leben: Untersuchungen zur Heilsbedeutung der Tora in der frühen rabbinischen Literatur*, Texte und Studien zum Antiken Judentum (Tübingen: J.C.B. Mohr, 1996), summarized in Friedrich Avemarie, "Erwählung und Vergeltung," *NTS* 45 (1999): 108–26, and Mark Adam Elliott, *The Survivors of Israel: A Reconsideration of the Theology of Pre-Christian Judaism* (Grand Rapids: Eerdmans, 2000). See also Simon Gathercole, *Where Is Boasting? Early Jewish Soteriology and Paul's Response in Romans 1–5* (Grand Rapids: Eerdmans, 2002).

[18]For Schreiner's discussion of the center of Paul's theology, with which I am in agreement, see Thomas R. Schreiner, *Paul, Apostle of God's Glory in Christ: A Pauline Theology* (Downers Grove, IL: InterVarsity, 2001), 16–35. See also Joel White's discussion of how "God created the cosmos in order to bring glory to himself" in "Paul's Cosmology: The Witness of Romans, 1 and 2 Corinthians, and Galatians," in *Cosmology and New Testament Theology*, ed. Jonathan T. Pennington and Sean M. McDonough, LNTS (New York: T&T Clark, 2008), 95.

[19]For Paul as an apostle of Jesus Christ on mission, see Schreiner, *Paul*, 37–102; Robert L. Plummer, *Paul's Understanding of the Church's Mission: Did the Apostle Paul Expect the Early Christian Communities to Evangelize?*

2.1 Paul's Letters Book by Book

One of the most remarkable features of the thirteen letters of Paul in the New Testament is the stability of Paul's theological positions, which are so flexibly applied to a wide variety of situations and circumstances. In Romans Paul proclaims his gospel to a church he has not visited, and it is perhaps his most theoretical theological statement (but note the specific points of application in Romans 5–8, 11, and 12–15). In 1 Corinthians he applies the same gospel he proclaims in Romans to specific problems in the Corinthian church's life, answering direct questions they have posed. In 2 Corinthians the power of God in weakness is heralded against an ongoing problem with a worldly perspective in the Corinthian church, and in Galatians Paul shows how the gospel cannot be mixed with works of the law. Ephesians celebrates the glory of God in the church. Philippians celebrates life as Christ and death as gain, in conformity to the one who made himself nothing and obeyed unto death. Colossians holds up the glory of Jesus to woo the church from human traditions, philosophy, and empty deceit. Paul's first letter to the Thessalonians features the way Christians imitate Jesus in joyful reception of the word of God in much affliction. In 2 Thessalonians Paul assures the church that Jesus will come in glory to save them and judge their enemies. Paul's first letter to Timothy calls him to silence false teaching and preach the true gospel that produces orderly, God-honoring relationships. In his second letter to Timothy Paul encourages Timothy to join him in suffering for the gospel in the strength of grace given before the ages began. Paul encourages Titus to appoint elders who will teach sound doctrine and refute false teachers, and he calls Philemon to live out the gospel by receiving Onesimus as a brother.

The gospel that Paul brings to bear on these many situations and problems is the good news of the salvation God has wrought through the death and resurrection of Jesus, which the Spirit applies to those who believe by grace through faith in Jesus. Jesus has come under the judgment of God, and through judgment he brought salvation and was raised from the dead. Having propitiated God's wrath and established God's justice (Rom. 3:25–26), the death and resurrection of Jesus vindicate God and simultaneously judge wicked humans and the enemy powers of darkness in heavenly places.[20] Saving through the judgment of Jesus, God has simultaneously brought salvation through the judgment of sinful humans and Satan's powers. God's power and justice are displayed, and

---

Paternoster Biblical Monographs (Waynesboro, GA: Paternoster, 2006); Eckhard Schnabel, *Early Christian Mission*, 2 vols. (Downers Grove, IL: InterVarsity, 2004), esp. vol. 2, subtitled *Paul and the Early Church*.

[20]Cf. Mark A. Seifrid, "Paul's Use of Righteousness Language Against Its Hellenistic Background," in *Justification and Variegated Nomism: A Fresh Appraisal of Paul and Second Temple Judaism*, vol. 2, *The Paradoxes of Paul*, ed. D. A. Carson, Peter T. O'Brien, and Mark A. Seifrid (Grand Rapids: Baker, 2004), 41: "The triumph of one party obviously brings the defeat of the other. The 'justification of God' has the condemnation of his enemies as its counterpart."

that display serves to magnify the mercy and love of God. God will be all in all (1 Cor. 15:28). As David Wells has written, "Paul stressed this point emphatically. God was the center from which his thought arose and to which it was always returning, for it was in God that Paul found the ultimate meaning of life, the reality of grace, and the wonder of boundless glory."[21]

2.2 Romans

Paul's letter to the Romans begins with justification by faith (Romans 1–4) and moves from there to the life that flows out of justification by faith (Romans 5–8). Paul then takes up the question of Israel's election in light of her rejection of Jesus as the messiah (Romans 9–11). Having plumbed the depths of it, Paul teaches the church in Rome the ethical implications of God's mercy (Romans 12–15) and closes the letter with a chapter of greetings (Romans 16). From beginning to end, with everything in between, Romans is about the glory of God in salvation through judgment.[22] This discussion will first trace through the argument of Romans before circling back to focus in on some ways Paul's argument reveals the centrality of the glory of God in salvation through judgment in his theology.

2.2.1 An Overview of the Argument of Romans

The first four chapters of Romans are largely concerned with the righteousness of God[23] in justification by faith. Paul opens his letter to the Romans with his most expansive salutation (Rom. 1:1–7), then explains why he wants to come to Rome (1:8–15). He states the theme of the letter—the righteousness of God revealed in the gospel (1:16–17)—and launches into an argument that everyone stands guilty before God (1:18–3:20).[24] This sets up an exposition of the glory of God in salvation through judgment at the cross (3:21–26), from which Paul concludes that human boasting is altogether excluded. God is the God of both Jew and Gentile, and in this gospel the law is upheld (3:27–31). Paul then moves to an explanation of how one comes to be justified, insisting that it is by faith, not by works (4:1–25).[25]

---

[21]David F. Wells, *God in the Wasteland: The Reality of Truth in a World of Fading Dreams* (Grand Rapids: Eerdmans, 1994), 121.

[22]Cf. Thomas R. Schreiner, *Romans*, BECNT (Grand Rapids: Baker, 1998), 23: "I have endeavored to show inductively in my exegesis of the letter that God's glory is indeed ultimate."

[23]See the helpful discussion of God's righteousness in John Piper, *The Future of Justification: A Response to N. T. Wright* (Wheaton, IL: Crossway, 2007), 62–71. Piper defines God's righteousness as his "unwavering commitment to act for the sake of his glory" (68 passim). See also Mark A. Seifrid, "Righteousness Language in the Hebrew Scriptures and in Early Judaism," in *Justification and Variegated Nomism: A Fresh Appraisal of Paul and Second Temple Judaism*, vol. 1, *The Complexities of Second Temple Judaism*, ed. D. A. Carson, Peter T. O'Brien, and Mark A. Seifrid (Grand Rapids: Baker, 2001), 415–42, who argues that God's righteousness belongs more to creational thought than to covenant faithfulness.

[24]See the discussion in Gathercole, *Where Is Boasting?* 197–215.

[25]Rightly ibid., 250–51: "Paul locates justification and forgiveness purely in divine decision on the basis of faith rather than attributing any role to obedience. God's declarative act of justification can be seen to be both an act

Chapters 5–8 of Romans are focused on the kind of life lived by those who are justified by faith. Justification by faith results in hope for the past, present, and future (Rom. 5:1–11), hope based on the way that the obedience of Jesus overcomes the condemnation resulting from Adam's sin: Jesus is the second Adam, of whom the first Adam was a type (5:12–21). Paul then refutes three false conclusions that could be drawn from what he has taught in the first five chapters of this world-changing letter: he contends that (1) Christians should not remain in sin so that grace might abound (6:1–14); (2) Christians should not sin because they are under grace, not law (6:15–7:6); and (3) the law is not sin but holy, righteous, and good (7:7–12). Paul shows that the law did not become sin for him; rather, sin was exacerbated by the law (7:13–25), but there is no condemnation for those in messiah Jesus who fulfill the law by the power of the Spirit (8:1–11). The Spirit gives assurance to believers of their adoption as children of God (8:12–17). This makes the sufferings of the present time unworthy of comparison to the glory that will be revealed to them (8:18–25).[26] The Spirit intercedes for believers, whom God has predestined for glorification (8:26–30), and nothing can overcome God so as to undo justification, condemn believers, or otherwise separate them from messiah Jesus (8:31–38).

In Romans 9–11, Paul shows that God's word has not failed (9:6), even though Israel's rejection of the messiah has resulted in their being separated from the love of God (cf. 8:35, 39). Paul grieves that Israel is lost (9:1–5), but then asserts that Israel's rejection of Jesus as the messiah does not mean that God's word has failed, because the promise is for the elect (9:6–13). Election does not make God unrighteous, because God does not owe mercy but distributes it as he pleases (9:14–18). Election does not nullify human responsibility, and humans are in no position to question their Maker. God shows wrath to magnify his mercy on elect Jews and Gentiles (9:19–29).[27] In Romans 9:30–10:4, Paul shows that Gentiles are righteous by faith, but Jews stumbled over the stumbling stone, because messiah is the goal of the law for righteousness to all who believe. The righteousness of faith trusts the finished work of God in Christ (10:5–13).[28] Faith comes from hearing, and hearing through the word of messiah (10:14–21). As for the fact that Israel has rejected Jesus, God has not forsaken his people but has elected according to grace (11:1–6). The elect have obtained salvation, and

of creation, where righteousness is positively counted to the one who believes, but also an act of forgiveness, where sin is *not* reckoned but covered."

[26]Joel White ("Paul's Cosmology," 99) refers to the way that God intends to impart "his own glory to humanity (cf. Rom 8.18, 21) and thereby [multiply] it (cf. Rom 8.28–30)."

[27]This analysis is based on my own attempt to trace the argument of Romans, which confirms the conclusions demonstrated in the full study by John Piper, *The Justification of God: An Exegetical and Theological Study of Romans 9:1–23*, 2nd ed. (Grand Rapids: Baker, 1993). J. Ross Wagner, *Heralds of the Good News: Isaiah and Paul in Concert in the Letter to the Romans*, Supplements to Novum Testamentum (Boston: Brill, 2003), 75–78, fails to grasp the argument Paul makes here.

[28]See the discussion of this passage in the "Excursus: Leviticus 18 and Deuteronomy 30 in Romans 10" in chap. 2, §4, above.

the rest have been hardened (11:7–10). Yet Israel has not stumbled so as to fall (11:11–24). Remarkably, Israel has been hardened for the full number of the Gentiles to come in. Once that has happened, Israel will be saved (11:25–32).[29] In response to these truths, Paul proclaims that all glory belongs to God because all things are from him, through him, and to him (11:33–36).

Paul has exposited the mercy of God in Romans 1–11, and on the basis of God's mercy he urges believers to offer their bodies as living sacrifices, not conforming to the world but being transformed by the renewal of their minds (Rom. 12:1–2). Paul then tells them how to do this: by rightly esteeming their place in the body according to the gifts given to them (12:3–8), loving without hypocrisy (12:9–13), blessing those who persecute them (12:14–21), submitting to the authority over them (13:1–6), fulfilling the law by love (13:7–10), and being ready for the coming of Jesus (13:11–14). The transformation of renewed minds offering bodies as living sacrifices (12:1–2) also entails Jew and Gentile accepting each other in the church (14:1–15:13). This will affect how they view meat offered to idols and sacred days (14:1–6); they are to live for Christ, who is Lord of all (14:7–12), not judging but loving one another and living by faith (14:13–23), the strong seeking what is good for the weak as the messiah sought what was good for them (15:1–6), with Jew and Gentile welcoming each other (15:7–13). Paul concludes the body of the letter by detailing his rationale in writing (15:14–16), boasting in what Christ has worked in him (15:17–21), relating his travel plans (15:22–29),[30] presenting his prayer requests and blessing the church (15:30–33), and greeting the members of the church (16:1–23), including a warning against false teachers (16:17–20). Then Paul sings the glory of God in Christ in a doxology that punctuates what may be the most important book ever written (16:25–27).

2.2.2 *God's Glory in Salvation through Judgment in Romans*

The entire argument of Romans is shot through with the glory of God in salvation through judgment. This discussion does not need to be exhaustive to demonstrate the ways in which the center of Paul's theology is reflected in Romans. Here we will first summarize the pervasive glory of God in Romans. From there we will consider the way salvation through judgment is built into the structure of Paul's argument and appears in the salutation (Rom. 1:1–7), in the letter's thematic statement (1:16–17), in Paul's statement of "the innermost

---

[29]Rightly Mark A. Seifrid, *Christ, Our Righteousness: Paul's Theology of Justification*, NSBT (Downers Grove, IL: InterVarsity, 2000), 168: "Paul sees the Deuteronomic sequence of apostasy, exile and return in Israel's present rejection of Jesus as Messiah and its salvation at his appearing." For discussion of Richard H. Bell, *The Irrevocable Call of God: An Inquiry into Paul's Theology of Israel*, WUNT 184 (Tübingen: Mohr Siebeck, 2005), see my review in *BBR* 18 (2008): 161–64.

[30]Cf. the claim that Paul went "to the end of the west" (i.e., Spain) in *1 Clem.* 5:7.

meaning of the cross" (3:21–26),[31] in a classic passage on living the Christian life (6:1–14), in Paul's statement of God's purpose in election (9:22–23; 11:32–36), and in his call for the church at Rome to be on guard against false teachers (16:17–20). Though not an exhaustive look at salvation through judgment in Romans, this will demonstrate the significance of the center of Paul's thought in every section of his argument.

2.2.2.1 God's Glory in Romans. Paul articulates praise and thanks to God or explicitly mentions God's or Christ's glory in almost every chapter of Romans (the exceptions are chaps. 10 and 13): Paul's goal is for the nations to obey for the sake of Christ's name (Rom. 1:5). The primal sin is the refusal to honor and thank God (1:21), and the problem with the Jews is that they have dishonored God and caused his name to be blasphemed among the nations (2:24). All fall short of God's glory (3:23). Abraham's faith glorified God (4:20), and believers hope for the manifestation of God's glory (5:2). Jesus was raised by the glory of the Father (6:2), and Paul thanks God for salvation (7:25). Christ has been glorified, and those who suffer with him will be glorified with him (8:17); for he is "God over all, blessed forever" (9:5 ESV; see also 9:23). Paul ascribes glory to God forever (11:36) and urges Christians to live worshipfully (12:1), honoring the Lord (14:6–9). Christ became a servant so the Gentiles would glorify God for his mercy (15:8–9), and Paul closes the letter by ascribing glory to God through Christ forever (16:27).

2.2.2.2 Salvation through Judgment in Romans. Not only is Romans suffused with God's own concern for himself, but the manifestation of God's glory in salvation through judgment is the central and controlling reality of the letter's inner logic. The structure of the argument of the first four chapters moves through judgment to salvation, as all humanity is placed under condemnation so that all humanity will be seen to stand in need of the gospel (Rom. 1:18–4:25; cf. also 11:32). In addition to this, from the salutation forward at key junctures in every section of the letter we see salvation through judgment for God's glory.

Salutation. Paul evokes the narrative of the Old Testament in his salutation (Rom. 1:1–7), stating that God's good news (1:1) was promised by the prophets in the Scriptures (1:2; cf. Isa. 52:7; Nah. 1:15). This gospel concerns God's Son, descended from David (Rom. 1:3), vindicated by the resurrection (1:4). Paul will elaborate on the need for the resurrection in coming chapters, but here we note that Paul opens with the declaration of Jesus as Son of God in power by the resur-

[31] C. E. B. Cranfield, *A Critical and Exegetical Commentary on the Epistle to the Romans: Introduction and Commentary on Romans I-VIII*, International Critical Commentary (Edinburgh: T&T Clark, 1975), 213.

rection.[32] Paul here celebrates the victory that came through judgment, for behind the resurrection stands the cross.[33] As noted above, Paul has been given grace and apostleship, that Christ's name might be exalted as the nations obey by faith (1:5). Salvation came through the judgment of Jesus for the sake of his name.

Thematic Statement. Romans 1:16–17 is widely recognized as Paul's thesis statement in Romans. For the purposes of this study, I would observe that Paul speaks of the gospel as God's power for salvation (Rom. 1:16), then describes the righteousness of God being revealed in the gospel (1:17). From the way that Paul goes on to explain this gospel in Romans 1:18–3:26, it seems that the revelation of God's righteousness and his wrath against sin (1:18–3:20) provokes the need for the revelation of his righteousness at the cross (3:21–26), whereby those who believe are justified; though ungodly, they are counted righteous (4:5). Through the revelation of God's righteous wrath against sin (1:18), the whole world stands condemned (3:19–20), and God reveals his righteousness in the justification he accomplishes by the propitiating sacrifice of the death of Christ on the cross (3:24–25). This is the good news that is the power of God unto salvation.[34] God's power is communicated in the revelation of his righteousness in the gospel, and it is a power that condemns the sinner so that the sinner might recognize his need for a Savior, trust the Savior, and be saved by faith. In this gospel God's righteousness is revealed by faith from start to finish (Rom. 1:17),[35] and this good news is a message of salvation through judgment for God's glory.

The Gospel. Paul argues that both pagan Gentiles (Rom. 1:18–32) and Jews (2:1–3:18) stand condemned under the law (3:19), and that no human being will be justified by works (3:20). All are sinners (3:23), with the result that all need justification as a gift of grace. This gift is available because of the redemption made in Christ (3:24). How did God make this gift of grace possible? He put Christ forward as a propitiating sacrifice (3:25). The death of Jesus on the cross satisfied the wrath of God against sin and accomplished redemption (3:24–25). This upholds God's justice and righteousness, and Paul states three times in

[32]The prominence of these messianic themes in Rom. 1:1–4 contradicts Chester's suggestion that "Paul appears to say almost nothing . . . that is distinctively messianic, or that reflects the full force of the fact that the Messiah has come and the messianic age should have arrived" (Andrew Chester, *Messiah and Exaltation: Jewish Messianic and Visionary Traditions and New Testament Christology*, WUNT 207 [Tübingen: Mohr Siebeck, 2007], 383), nor does it appear that Chester has grasped Paul's understanding of inaugurated eschatology.

[33]Cf. Seifrid, "Paul's Use of Righteousness Language," 44: "Salvation presupposes that judgment has been meted out."

[34]Mark A. Seifrid, "Unrighteous by Faith: Apostolic Proclamation in Romans 1:18–3:20," in Carson, O'Brien, and Seifrid, *The Paradoxes of Paul*, 107, writes, "In much the same way that Romans 1:16–17 contains *in nuce* the whole theology of the letter, Paul's argument is in a sense complete at Romans 3:26. . . . Paul does not proceed by the addition of new topics but by elaboration and expansion of what he has said from the start."

[35]Schreiner takes the phrase in question, ἐκ πίστεως εἰς πίστιν, to mean "by faith from first to last" (*Romans*, 76). For the suggestion that the phrase indicates the progress of the gospel, particularly its advance among Gentiles, see John W. Taylor, "From Faith to Faith: Romans 1.17 in the Light of Greek Idiom," *NTS* 50 (2004): 337–48.

Romans 3:25–26 that God put Christ forward to demonstrate his righteousness.[36] God demonstrated his righteousness because passing over sins previously committed could cause his justice to be questioned (3:26). Cranfield calls this passage "the centre and heart of the whole of Rom 1.16b–15.13," and notes that here "Paul's concern [is] with something even more important than men's being made aware of God's righteousness, namely, God's being righteous."[37] Because God demonstrated his righteousness in the present (3:26a), God can justify the ungodly and maintain his justice (3:26b; 4:5). The demonstration of the righteousness of God through Christ's death on the cross legitimates God as the one who justly shows mercy (cf. Isa. 1:27). Salvation comes through judgment, and the fact that the judgment is a demonstration of God's righteousness shows that God put Christ forward as a sacrifice of propitiation to show his character as a just and merciful God.[38]

Christian Life. Paul's comments on why Christians are not to continue in sin in Romans 6:1–14 apply the reality that they have been saved through judgment for God's glory to the process of growth in behavioral holiness. Christians cannot live in sin because they are dead to sin (Rom. 6:2). They died this death when they were buried with Christ in baptism (6:3), and from that death they were raised to walk in newness of life (6:4). The old self was crucified (6:6), setting those killed free from sin (6:7), so Christians should reckon themselves dead to sin and alive to God in Christ (6:11). This does nothing less than apply to their behavioral patterns the fact that they have passed through judgment. And it is by and for God's glory: Christ was raised by the Father's glory (6:4), and Paul thanks God for the transformation that has happened in believers (6:17).

Israel and Election. In Romans 9:22–23 Paul explains why God has shown mercy to some and hardened others (cf. Rom. 9:18). Paul has answered the objection to election that it makes God unjust (9:14–18), and on the heels of his assertion that God shows mercy and hardens as he pleases (9:18), Paul addresses the objection that election would seem to remove human responsibility and make it so that God should not judge people because they have only done what he willed (9:19). Paul's first assertion is that people are not in position to evaluate God (9:20–21), and from there Paul posits his understanding of God's purposes in Romans 9:22–23. English translations (cf. ESV, NASB, NIV, etc.) present what Paul says in Romans 9:22–23 in the form of a question, and this matches the punctuation of the NA[27]: "What if God, desiring to show his wrath and to make known his power, has endured with much patience vessels of wrath prepared for

[36]Cf. Brian Vickers, *Jesus' Blood and Righteousness: Paul's Theology of Imputation* (Wheaton, IL: Crossway, 2006), 100: "In the Old Testament texts, the idea is that justice cannot be suspended or brushed aside, that guilt must be punished, and that right must be upheld. All these criteria are met in the substitutionary death of Christ."

[37]Cranfield, *Romans*, 1:199, 209.

[38]See the full discussion of Rom. 3:25–26 in Piper, *The Justification of God*, 135–50.

destruction, in order to make known the riches of his glory for vessels of mercy, which he has prepared beforehand for glory?" (9:22 ESV). In Romans 9:22 Paul states that God patiently endures vessels of wrath that are being prepared for destruction, desiring to demonstrate his wrath and make known his power. God wants to demonstrate his righteous indignation against injustice, transgression, iniquity, and sin. God wants to demonstrate his power to uphold the truth, to defeat those who defame his name and glory, and to establish righteousness. Wanting to do these things, God patiently endures the vessels of wrath who are being "prepared for destruction" (9:22),[39] which indicates that Paul believes they will be judged. God will demonstrate wrath and make known his power on the day he visits judgment upon the vessels of wrath. This will not be a mere abstract demonstration of justice, however; its purpose is to highlight the glory of God's mercy, as Paul explains in Romans 9:23. There Paul states that God has borne with the vessels of wrath *in order to make known the wealth of his glory upon vessels of mercy which he prepared for glory*.[40] The vessels of wrath are endured so that the vessels of mercy will see the wealth of God's glory. What Paul says about the rich display of God's glory in mercy in Romans 9:22–23 matches the display of God's glory made to Moses (cf. Ex. 33:18) when God showed Moses his goodness (33:19; note that Paul quotes 33:19b in Rom. 9:15) and proclaimed his name in Exodus 34:6–7. There God declared himself to be a forgiving God who does not clear the guilty; that is, he is a God who upholds justice and extends mercy. Piper's conclusion stands:

> God's glory and his name consist fundamentally in his propensity to show mercy and his sovereign freedom in its distribution. Or to put it more precisely, *it is the glory of God in his essential nature mainly to dispense mercy (but also wrath, Ex 34:7) on whomever he pleases apart from any constraint originating outside his own will. This is the essence of what it means to be God. This is his name.*[41]

So also in Romans 9:22–23, the vessels of mercy see the wealth of God's glory when God demonstrates his wrath and makes known his power on the vessels of wrath, and when they recognize that the only difference between the vessels of wrath and themselves is the mere mercy of God. They see God's judgment. They feel the awful force of it. They know they deserve it too. In view of God's justice, the wonder of mercy melts them. The wealth of God's glory on the vessels of mercy is the display of the justice and mercy of God. Through the judgment of the vessels of wrath, the vessels of mercy understand what salvation and mercy

[39]Daniel B. Wallace, *Greek Grammar beyond the Basics: An Exegetical Syntax of the New Testament* (Grand Rapids: Zondervan, 1996), 417–18.
[40]Cf. Piper, *The Justification of God*, 186–89, 217–20.
[41]Ibid., 88–89; see the whole chapter on Ex. 33:19 in its Old Testament context, 75–89.

are, and through the judgment of Jesus on the cross, they know that they have been shown a just mercy. Paul asserts that God has shut both Jews and Gentiles up in sin so that Jews and Gentiles will know what mercy is (Rom. 11:32). Little wonder that Paul then exclaims:

> Oh, the depth of the riches and wisdom and knowledge of God! How unsearchable are his judgments and how inscrutable his ways!
>
> "For who has known the mind of the Lord,
> or who has been his counselor?"
> "Or who has given a gift to him
> that he might be repaid?"
>
> For from him and through him and to him are all things. To him be glory forever. Amen. (Rom. 11:33–36 ESV)[42]

The Church's Vigilance. In response to God's mercy, Paul calls the church to live transformed lives as living sacrifices (Romans 12–15). As he concludes the letter to the Romans, in the midst of his many greetings, which show a man as intensely interested in real people as he is in the high truths of deep theology, Paul warns the church to be on the watch against those who cause divisions by departing from the truth he has taught them (16:17). He speaks of them in 16:18 in the same way that he speaks elsewhere of those who do not take up the cross and follow Christ (cf. Rom. 16:18 and Phil. 3:18–19; 1 Tim. 4:1–2; 2 Tim. 3:2–6, etc.). Paul reformulates the teaching of Jesus that his followers are to be wise as serpents, innocent as doves (Matt. 10:16), as he calls the Roman believers to be wise as to the good, innocent as to the evil (Rom. 16:19).[43] Then he promises them that God is going to save them through the judgment of their enemies: "Now the God of peace will crush Satan under your feet with rapidity" (16:20). Here Paul sees the false teachers who reject the gospel as the seed of the serpent, just as he elsewhere asserts that they follow deceitful spirits and doctrines of demons (1 Tim. 4:1). He also sees believers as the seed of the woman by virtue of their union with Christ by faith (cf. Gal. 3:16, 26–29). In the ongoing conflict between the seed of the serpent and the seed of the woman (cf. Gen. 3:15; Rev. 12:1–17), God delivers his people through the judgment of their enemies (cf. Psalm 58, esp. 58:4–6, 10). This judgment is ultimately based on Christ's triumph over the Evil One and his forces at the cross (cf. Col. 2:15), which was

[42]See Andrew David Naselli, "Paul's Use of Isaiah 40:13 and Job 41:3a (Eng. 41:11a) in Romans 11:34–35" (PhD diss., Trinity Evangelical Divinity School, 2010).
[43]For an argument that Paul knew Jesus traditions now in the Gospels, see David Wenham, *Paul: Follower of Jesus or Founder of Christianity?* (Grand Rapids: Eerdmans, 1995). See also Seyoon Kim's essay, "The Jesus Tradition in Paul," in *Paul and the New Perspective*, 259–90.

anticipated by Jesus' ability to bind the strong man and plunder his house as he did exorcisms and healings. Paul now tells the church in Rome that as they guard the gospel and reject false teaching, God will be crushing the serpent under their feet through the advance of the saving and judging proclamation of Christ crucified and risen. God is glorified in salvation through judgment, as Paul declares in his closing doxology:

> Now to him who is able to strengthen you according to my gospel and the preaching of Jesus Christ, according to the revelation of the mystery that was kept secret for long ages but has now been disclosed and through the prophetic writings has been made known to all nations, according to the command of the eternal God, to bring about the obedience of faith—to the only wise God be glory forevermore through Jesus Christ! Amen. (Rom. 16:25–27 ESV)

2.3 First Corinthians

In God's remarkable providence, the various occasions that prompted Paul's letters have given us documents that address all aspects of life with the gospel. Romans is generally recognized as the most "systematic" presentation of Paul's gospel. As the letters are now ordered in the New Testament, the reader moves from the very full presentation of the gospel in Romans to the application of that gospel to a myriad of life issues in 1 Corinthians.[44] In 1 Corinthians Paul is responding to reports he has received (1:11; 5:1; 11:18; 15:12) and questions the Corinthians have sent to him (7:1, 25; 8:1; 12:1; 16:1, 12). Paul first applies the gospel to the schisms in the church in Corinth (1 Corinthians 1–4), and from there he addresses sexual immorality (1 Corinthians 5–7) and idolatry (1 Corinthians 8–10) before turning to the church's conduct when it gathers for worship (1 Corinthians 11–14). Paul then corrects mistaken notions about the resurrection (1 Corinthians 15) and closes the letter by preparing the church for his coming (1 Corinthians 16). In each section of the letter Paul confronts Corinthian error with Christian gospel.[45] At every step Paul is condemning Corinthian transgressions and errors, and through these judgments he means to bring his readers to salvation for God's glory.

2.3.1 Schisms (1 Corinthians 1–4)

Paul teaches in 1 Corinthians 1–4 that God has outmatched worldly power through the weakness of the cross, perplexing human wisdom with its folly.[46]

---

[44]First Corinthians was written sometime between AD 53 and 56, and Romans was likely written in the spring of AD 57. Historically considered, the letters were not composed to complement one another. Canonically considered, we find a full explication of the gospel in Romans and the application of the gospel to life in 1 Corinthians.
[45]So also Gordon D. Fee, "Toward a Theology of 1 Corinthians," in *Pauline Theology, Volume II: 1 and 2 Corinthians*, ed. David M. Hay (Minneapolis: Fortress, 1993), 38–40.
[46]See especially D. A. Carson, *The Cross and Christian Ministry: An Exposition of Passages from 1 Corinthians* (Grand Rapids: Baker, 1993).

God has triumphed through what the world thinks is weakness and folly (1:25), and he has chosen those who are not impressive by worldly standards (1:26–28). This means that no human being can boast about his own understanding or power (1:29), and there is no place for Christians to exalt themselves by identifying with their favorite teacher (1:12–13; 3:4–9). The gospel means that all people are helpless before God, that Christ is everything to believers (1:30), and that humans have nothing that they have not received (4:7). The only thing to boast in is the Lord (1:31), and when everyone thinks this way, the church will be unified (1:10).

These chapters of 1 Corinthians, then, condemn worldly standards of evaluation so that members of the Corinthian church will be delivered from the wisdom that God will destroy (1:19). Through this judgment on worldly wisdom, Paul wants the Corinthians to know the wonders of the gospel, which no one expected (2:7–13).[47] God will catch the wise in their craftiness (3:19), judging their proud speculations. Meanwhile those who follow the apostles will suffer and then be exalted (4:9–16). God's glory is shown in the display of apostolic weakness (4:9–13), and Paul wants the Corinthians to imitate him so that God's glory will be seen in their weakness (4:16). By passing judgment against human strength and wisdom, Paul seeks to deliver the Corinthians to the glory of the cross, the glory of God's weakness and folly that is stronger and wiser than men (1:18–25).

2.3.2 Sexual Immorality (1 Corinthians 5–7)

Paul's teaching on the gospel in 1 Corinthians 1–4 is meant to deliver the Corinthians from worldly estimations of the relative worth of people, and the implications of Paul's gospel are applied to sexual ethics in 1 Corinthians 5–7. The Corinthians should judge the man who has his father's wife so that this man can be saved from damnable behavior (5:1–13, esp. 5:4). This call to practice church discipline is based on the fact that Christ the Passover Lamb has been sacrificed (5:7). Judgment has fallen on Jesus, and therefore the Corinthians are to pursue purity now that they have been saved through that judgment (5:6–8).

By condemning the lawsuits they bring against one another, Paul seeks to deliver the church from the reproach such contentions bring on the church (1 Cor. 6:1–11). Once again the ground of Paul's appeal is the fact that they have been justified in the name of Jesus and set apart through his cleansing work by the Holy Spirit (6:11).

Evidently some of the Corinthian Christians are visiting prostitutes (1 Cor. 6:15), and again Paul calls them to purity because they have been bought by the

[47]Jay E. Smith, "1 Corinthians," in *The Bible Knowledge Word Study: Acts–Ephesians*, ed. Darrell L. Bock (Colorado Springs: Victor, 2006), 218.

blood of Christ (6:20). Paul seeks to deliver the Corinthians through the judgment he renders on their attempt to justify such behavior (6:12–20).[48]

Having dealt with the sexual misbehavior of the Corinthians, Paul turns to answer questions from the church regarding the proper context for sexual relations in marriage (1 Cor. 7:1–40).[49] Yet again the basis of Paul's appeal that the church live in appropriate ways is the gospel: the fact that they have been bought with a price (7:23). Through judgment they have been saved for God's glory.

2.3.3 Idolatry (1 Corinthians 8–10)

When Paul addresses the questions the Corinthians have about food offered to idols, his judgment is that idols are nothing and there is only one true and living God, with his Son the Lord Jesus (1 Cor. 8:4–6). This means that there is nothing inherently wrong with eating food that has been offered to an idol (8:7–8), yet the Corinthians should take care not to cause those with weaker consciences to stumble (8:7–13). The strong have a right to eat, but they should sacrifice their rights for the benefit of others. Paul offers himself as an example of one who has surrendered rights that he has—to be paid for ministry (9:18) or take a believing wife (9:5)—in order to benefit others (9:1–27). Paul then warns the Corinthians not to be presumptuous because they have been baptized and partake of the Lord's Supper (10:1–13), for that will not protect them against the consequences of idolatry (10:14–22). Paul apparently does not want the Corinthians to participate in idolatrous feasts in the temples of idols (10:20–21), but as long as they are not causing another to stumble, they can eat and drink to the glory of God without asking questions as to where the food was purchased (10:23–33).[50]

Through the condemnation of idolatry and by passing judgment on an attitude that would disregard others, Paul seeks to deliver the Corinthians to gospel life for the glory of God (1 Cor. 10:31). He models this gospel life for them by laying down his rights and privileges to serve others, and he calls the Corinthians to follow him in this as he follows Christ (11:1).

2.3.4 Worship (1 Corinthians 11–14)

Paul condemns the abuse of gender roles in the gathered worship of the Corinthian church because he wants their embrace of gender roles to reflect

---

[48]See Denny Burk, "Discerning Corinthian Slogans through Paul's Use of the Diatribe in 1 Corinthians 6:12–20," *BBR* 18 (2008): 99–121; and Jay E. Smith, "The Roots of a Libertine Slogan in 1 Corinthians 6:18," *JTS* 59 (2008): 63–95.

[49]Cf. the early Christian statement on marital morality and pro-life commitment in *Diogn.* 5:6–7: "They marry like everyone else, and have children, but they do not expose their offspring. They share their food but not their wives" (Michael W. Holmes, ed., *The Apostolic Fathers: Greek Texts and English Translations*, 3rd ed. [Grand Rapids: Baker, 2007], 703).

[50]See the valuable discussion of this text in Smith, "1 Corinthians."

God's glory (esp. 1 Cor. 11:7; cf. 11:2–16).[51] The headship of Christ is at stake in the way that the Corinthians embrace their gender roles (11:3).[52]

Paul then turns to the failures of the church when they partake of the Lord's Supper (1 Cor. 11:17–34).[53] Whereas the Lord's Supper celebrates the way that Jesus gave himself for others (11:23–26), the selfish behavior of the Corinthians (11:18, 21, 33) means that they are not celebrating the gospel, not living out the gospel, and indeed, not partaking of the Lord's Supper (11:20). It is the self-giving of Jesus that condemns their behavior (11:23–26), and Paul calls them to live this out as they celebrate the Lord's death, or else stay home (11:22, 34).[54] Those who do not heed Paul's words are not approved (11:19). Paul means to judge the behavior of the Corinthians by rehearsing what Christ has done for them, and through that judgment he seeks to save them, that they might proclaim the gospel (11:26).

Paul's concern in his discussion of the Corinthians' use of spiritual gifts (1 Corinthians 12–14) is again to condemn their worldly assessment of the relative worth and importance of different gifts (cf. 12:21–26). Paul exhorts the Corinthians to the more excellent way of love (13:1–13), and he calls them to use their gifts for the upbuilding of the body (14:3–5). Paul wants the Corinthians to live out the gospel when they gather for worship. This means they are to lay down their lives and embrace the gender roles given to them, set aside their own concerns and serve others in the Lord's Supper, and use their spiritual gifts to build others up in love. To deliver the Corinthians to this display of God's glory, Paul judges and condemns their worldly and selfish behavior. Through this judgment he means to deliver them to Christlikeness for the glory of God.

2.3.5 Resurrection (1 Corinthians 15)

Whatever the nuances of the view the Corinthians had adopted regarding the resurrection, and however it might or might not have influenced the other issues Paul has addressed to this point in the letter,[55] of this we can be sure: Paul condemns their mistaken perspective, and through that judgment he means to bring them to salvation for God's glory. Paul restates the gospel and the proof

---

[51]See Thomas R. Schreiner, "Head Coverings, Prophecies and the Trinity: 1 Corinthians 11:2–16," in *Recovering Biblical Manhood and Womanhood: A Response to Evangelical Feminism*, ed. John Piper and Wayne Grudem (Wheaton, IL: Crossway, 1991), 124–39, 485–87; and Schreiner, "'Praying and Prophesying in the Assemblies: I Corinthians 11:2–16' (Ch 8) by Gordon D. Fee," *JBMW* 10 (2005): 17–21. See also James M. Hamilton Jr., "What Women Can Do in Ministry: Full Participation within Biblical Boundaries," in *Women, Ministry and the Gospel: Exploring New Paradigms* (Downers Grove, IL: InterVarsity, 2007), 32–52; and Hamilton, "Gender Roles and the Glory of God: A Sermon on 1 Corinthians 11:2–12," *JBMW* 9 (2004): 35–39.

[52]On headship, see the definitive studies in Wayne Grudem, *Evangelical Feminism and Biblical Truth: An Analysis of More Than 100 Disputed Questions* (Sisters, OR: Multnomah, 2004), 201–11, 544–51, 552–99.

[53]For further discussion, see James M. Hamilton Jr., "The Lord's Supper in Paul: An Identity Shaping Proclamation of the Gospel," in *The Lord's Supper*, ed. Thomas R. Schreiner and Matt Crawford, NACSBT (Nashville: Broadman & Holman, forthcoming).

[54]Schreiner, *New Testament Theology*, 733.

[55]For discussion of these issues, see Wright, *The Resurrection of the Son of God*, 278–361.

of the resurrection (1 Cor. 15:1–11), articulates the implications of there being no resurrection (15:12–19), rejects these implications because Christ has been raised (15:20–28),[56] and makes plain the ethical consequences of mistaken ideas (15:29–34, esp. 33, cf. 58). Paul then exposits the nature of the resurrection (15:35–49) and summarizes what the Corinthians can expect about the future (15:50–58). He judges and condemns false notions about the resurrection and through that seeks to deliver the Corinthians for the glory of God.

2.3.6 Travel Plans (1 Corinthians 16)

The proof that the Corinthians have been saved through judgment will be seen by the way they give of their money for the benefit of others, living out the gospel in financial terms (1 Cor. 16:1–4). Paul also instructs them to show forth God's glory in the way they receive Timothy (16:5–11), Apollos (16:12), and the leaders among them (16:13–18).

Throughout 1 Corinthians, Paul reminds the members of the Corinthian church of the way that God has saved them through judgment. On the basis of this salvation through judgment, Paul renders judgments on their misbehavior and mistaken ideas in order to enable them to live out the gospel for the glory of God.

2.4 Second Corinthians

In the letter we know as 2 Corinthians,[57] Paul explains his travel plans and his ministry (chaps. 1–7), calls those who have repented of sin and embraced Paul and his gospel to give (chaps. 8–9), and entreats the unrepentant who have not embraced Paul and his gospel to examine themselves to see whether they are in the faith (chaps. 10–13).[58] The glory of God in salvation through judgment is seen in 2 Corinthians as Paul returns to a theme he discussed in 1 Corinthians 1–4: the way that God shows his power through weakness. The paradoxical demonstration of God's power through Paul's weakness judges and condemns the worldly strength and wisdom of Paul's opponents in Corinth. We will begin with a summary of the indications in 2 Corinthians that Paul has been attacked by those teaching a different gospel (cf. 2 Cor. 11:4), then consider Paul's response

[56]Cf. Joel White, "Paul's Cosmology," 106: "In the final act of Paul's cosmological narrative, Christ, to whom the entire cosmos and all its inhabitants have sworn their fealty, will subject himself to God, 'so that God may be all in all' (1 Cor. 15.28). With that, God's purpose in creation, to bring glory to himself, will have been utterly and incontestably fulfilled."

[57]In 1 Cor. 5:9 Paul refers to a letter he previously wrote to the Corinthians, which would indicate that 1 Corinthians is at least his second letter to the church in Corinth. Then in 2 Cor. 2:3–4 Paul describes an anguished letter that appears to have been written between what we call 1 and 2 Corinthians. Thus, 1 and 2 Corinthians might be the second and fourth letters that Paul wrote to the church in Corinth, though there could have been other letters not referenced and not preserved.

[58]Adapted from the outline in Scott J. Hafemann, *2 Corinthians*, NIVApp (Grand Rapids: Zondervan, 2000), 37–39.

to the attack. This will put us in position to look more closely at key statements of the glory of God in salvation through judgment in 2 Corinthians.

2.4.1 The Attack on Paul by His Opponents

In order to understand how the saving and judging glory of God is presented in 2 Corinthians, it is necessary to glean what we can about Paul's opponents. Paul's comments give us some insight into the situation.[59] Some in Corinth have evidently questioned Paul's sincerity (2 Cor. 1:12), suggesting perhaps that he made plans according to the flesh and then vacillated (1:12, 17). Moreover, the correspondence between how Paul comports himself in person and how he does in his letters has been called into question (1:13; 10:1, 9–11), and apparently some have alleged that Paul has "commended himself" to the Corinthians in an illegitimate manner (3:1; 4:2; 5:12; 6:4; 7:11; 10:12, 18; 12:11). Perhaps those who have made such suggestions have presented letters of recommendation to the Corinthians, letters that, they point out, Paul lacks (3:1). Paul's opponents may have also suggested that Paul is inferior to Moses, prompting Paul to argue that his new covenant ministry is superior to the ministry of Moses under the old covenant (3:7–13). Paul refers to those who peddle the word of God, doing disgraceful, underhanded things, tampering with God's word (2:17; 4:2). Perhaps this is how he views his opponents in Corinth. Given the way that Paul interprets the outcome of his ministry as it relates to people rejecting the gospel (2:14–15; 4:3–4), his opponents may have suggested that if Paul would employ different methods, he might have more success. The underhandedness of his opponents also explains why Paul details his own experience of tribulation and—in the world's eyes—shameful treatment (4:7–12, 16–18; 6:4–10; 11:16–33). Paul uses this as evidence of his own authenticity, but according to the insinuations of his opponents, these facts mount an impressive case that, considered "according to the flesh" (cf. 1:17; 5:12, 16; 10:2–3, 12), Paul is neither an impressive speaker nor a successful evangelist (since so many reject his message). In sum, they argue, he cannot be trusted because he does not come when he says he will. He lacks authenticating documentation from the authorities, letters of recommendation (3:1), and he has been treated so shamefully that anyone who associates with him will be discredited by their identification with such a notorious loser.

2.4.2 Paul's Response to the Attack

Paul's basic response to the way he has been attacked in Corinth is a celebration of his own weakness because in it God's power is displayed. This means that

[59]See the discussion of the occasional nature of Paul's letters and "mirror reading" in Thomas R. Schreiner, *Interpreting the Pauline Epistles*, Guides to New Testament Exegesis (Grand Rapids: Baker, 1990), 41–50; and for observations similar to the ones made here, with a summary of scholarly proposals as to the identity of the opponents, see John B. Polhill, *Paul and His Letters* (Nashville: Broadman & Holman, 1999), 261–63.

those who follow Paul do so because of God's power in the gospel, not because Paul is impressive by worldly standards.

This paragraph will summarize Paul's response to the situation in Corinth, and following paragraphs will move through the letter in more detail. Having blessed God who comforts the afflicted (2 Cor. 1:3–11), Paul defends his sincerity with an explanation of his travel plans and harsh letter (1:12–2:13). From there he describes his ministry in terms of a Christlike triumph in defeat—Paul, Christ's opponent, was defeated, and is being led as a conquered slave: defeated he conquers (2:14–17).[60] Just as Jesus conquered through what looked like a defeat, so Paul is the aroma of Christ even as he is treated shamefully by the world powers. Paul then explains his new covenant ministry (3:1–7:16). He seems to address the repentant in Corinth with a word on the gospel and giving (8:1–9:15), followed by an appeal to the unrepentant to test themselves to see if they are in the faith (10:1–13:13). Paul closes the letter with the Trinitarian grace (13:14).

Characteristically, Paul opens by blessing God (2 Cor. 1:3; cf. Rom. 1:25; 2 Cor. 11:31; Eph. 1:3; 1 Tim. 6:15–16, and see the appendix to this chapter [§5], table 6.7, "Doxologies in the New Testament"). The unexpected nature of the blessing gets at the heart of this letter: Paul is blessing God for the way that God comforts the afflicted. Indeed, God purposes to comfort the afflicted so that they might comfort others (2 Cor. 1:4), and he purposes to afflict his people so that they rely on him rather than themselves (1:9). Here we see the main theme of 2 Corinthians: the demonstration of the power of God in the weakness and affliction of Paul. This demonstrates God's sufficiency rather than Paul's (glorifying God), condemns the self-sufficiency of Paul's opponents in Corinth (judging them), and promises salvation for those who, like Paul, rely on God, who raises the dead (salvation). Paul sees his own experience of this salvation through judgment for God's glory as patterned after the experience of Jesus, through the judgment of whom God accomplished salvation for his own glory.

Paul's blessing of God, who comforts the afflicted (2 Cor. 1:3–11), responds directly to the situation that has developed in the Corinthian church. Because of the way they have been led to question his sincerity (1:12–14), Paul seeks to dispel any misinformation that might be circulating about why he did not go to Corinth when he said he would (1:15–24). Paul's opponents in Corinth, those who preach "another Jesus" and who impart "a different Spirit" and "a different gospel" (11:4), whom Paul identifies as servants of Satan (11:14–15), have apparently suggested that Paul cannot be trusted because he did not come when he said he would. Paul explains that rather than going to Corinth and causing them pain, he sent them a harsh letter (2:1–4), and from Paul's encouragement

[60]For discussion of the Roman triumphal procession and Paul's use of the imagery, see Scott J. Hafemann, *Suffering and Ministry in the Spirit: Paul's Defense of His Ministry in II Corinthians 2:14–3:3* (Grand Rapids: Eerdmans, 1990), 16–34.

to the church to forgive a repentant sinner (2:5–11), it seems that this harsh letter had its intended affect—someone in the church repented and Paul is now exhorting the church to forgive him and welcome him back into the church, saved through judgment. Paul elaborates further on his sincerity by discussing the unrest he felt as a result of his concern for the Corinthian church, an unrest that prevented him from taking ministry opportunities and propelled him to Macedonia (2:12–13).

In 2 Corinthians 2:14–17 Paul explains the nature of his ministry to the Corinthians, and it is a ministry that displays the glory of God in salvation that comes through judgment. Paul's opponents in Corinth have perhaps objected to his divisive gospel, which offends many and causes him much suffering. Perhaps it has been suggested that if Paul were not so emphatic about sin and so exclusive in his presentation of the gospel, more people would respond to his message. Paul replies that he is a conquered slave being led in triumph by the victorious Christ (2:14). Just as the triumphator would parade conquered enemies in a triumphal parade, so Christ, who conquered his enemy, Paul, on the road to Damascus, is now leading Paul in triumph (cf. 1 Cor. 4:9). Paul was saved through judgment, showing forth the glory of the one who took him captive.[61] Just as Christ was divisive, so also Paul's ministry, as he is being paraded about, perfumes the world with the aroma of Christ (2 Cor. 2:15). This aroma is the fragrance of death to death among those who are perishing, and life to life among those who are being saved (2:15–16).[62] Paul acknowledges that there are many peddlers of God's word, but he asserts that he speaks in sincerity (2:17). The fragrance of the true knowledge of Christ is judgment to those who are perishing, salvation to those who are being saved. Through Paul, the glory of God is known, and this glory is seen in salvation that comes through judgment.

Paul's description of the two responses to his sincere ministry in 2 Corinthians 2:14–17 can be seen as a conclusion of 1:3–2:13, and this sincere new covenant ministry will be exposited from 3:1 to the end of the letter. Paul argues that the greater glory of his new covenant ministry eclipses the glory of the ministry of Moses (3:1–18), and he explains that he is encouraged in the midst of his weakness because his weakness displays God's power (4:1–18). Paul grounds his encouragement in his theological perspective: he has courage based on his knowledge of what the death and resurrection of Jesus mean for life now and on the day of judgment (5:1–21). Paul then appeals to the Corinthians that they not receive the grace of God in vain. Paul's appeal takes the form of commending himself as a genuine servant of God (attested by his sufferings) and calling

[61]Cf. ibid., 31: "The role of those thus 'led in triumph' was to reveal the glory and might of the victor."
[62]Hafemann argues that the imagery shifts from the Roman triumph to "the OT cultic backdrop of the 'sacrificial aroma'" when Paul describes himself in 2 Cor. 2:14–16 as the "fragrance" and "aroma" of Christ (*Suffering and Ministry in the Spirit*, 37–44, 45).

the Corinthians to reject the false teachers (6:1–18). Paul urges the Corinthians to accept him (7:1–7), explains God's purposes in his harsh letter (7:8–12), and describes the way God comforted and rejoiced him (7:13–16). Based on the salvation through judgment for his glory that God accomplished in Jesus (esp. 5:21; 13:4), Paul is living out a ministry that enacts judgment on worldliness so that through that judgment people will be saved (2:14–17). Paul's suffering simultaneously authenticates his gospel and condemns the false gospel his opponents teach (2:17; 11:30; 12:9, 11).

That Paul moves from such a thorough and spirited defense of himself and his ministry in 2 Corinthians 1–7 to an appeal for financial support in 2 Corinthians 8–9 shows his confidence in the way that God will work by the Spirit in what he has written in 2 Corinthians 1–7. Paul knows that there is a strong contingent in the Corinthian church that either has repented or will repent in response to the first section of his letter. In his appeal that the Corinthians give to the relief of the saints (2 Cor. 8:4), Paul applies the gospel to giving. The basis of his appeal is their knowledge of the grace of Jesus, who was rich but became poor for the sake of those who would become rich through his poverty (8:9). This has motivated the impoverished churches of Macedonia to generosity in the midst of affliction (8:1–5), which in turn grounds Paul's sending of Titus to the Corinthians so that he can collect the monetary demonstration of their genuine love (8:6–8). For the glory of God, and to defend against the accusations of opponents, Paul pursues a blameless course with the funds, entrusting the mission to several faithful coworkers (8:16–24).[63] Paul confidently sends them (9:1–4) because Christians are to give, trusting God and for God's glory (9:5–15).

From the change in direction at 2 Corinthians 10:1, it seems that just as Paul knows of a contingent in the church that is sure to repent, he knows of some who will need more encouragement to repent. Paul explains the divine power of his unworldly warfare (10:1–6), calls the Corinthians to see through rumors to what is really the case (10:7–11), and explains that the approved are not those who boast in themselves but those whom the Lord commends, who boast in the Lord (10:12–18).

The problem in Corinth is then explicitly addressed: there is a false gospel (2 Cor. 11:1–4) being preached by false apostles whom Paul opposes (11:5–15). In response to their worldly message and worldly assessment of Paul, he boasts in his weakness (11:16–33), describes his vision (12:1–6) and thorn (12:7–10), reminds the Corinthians that he has neither burdened nor taken advantage of them (12:11–18), and explains that he speaks in God's sight for their upbuilding and fears only their ungodliness (12:19–21).

[63]For a chart listing "36 co-workers under 9 designations," see Ellis, *History and Interpretation in New Testament Perspective*, 85.

Paul concludes the letter by calling the Corinthians to examine themselves in light of the power God has shown through the weakness of both Jesus and Paul (2 Cor. 13:1–5). The message is clear: through the weakness of Jesus, the worldly strength peddled by the "super-apostles" (12:11) is condemned as God's power is shown. This same salvation through judgment is demonstrated in the suffering and weakness of Paul, in which God's power is displayed. The Corinthians, then, are to embrace their weakness, which condemns both what they can do in demonstration of worldly greatness and what those who proclaim a different Jesus value. Through judgment they will be saved for God's glory.

2.4.3 Salvation through Judgment for God's Glory in Second Corinthians

The centerpiece of Paul's theology, the glory of God in salvation through judgment, finds expression in a variety of ways in 2 Corinthians. It is at the heart of the gospel of the crucified and risen Lord. It is experienced in Paul's own life, particularly in his suffering. It is the nature of his new covenant ministry and binds together his message. The Corinthians, too, experience it as they repent, and the prospect of future judgment is held out to make repentance complete.

2.4.3.1 Paul's Gospel. Paul's theology centers on the cross, where justice and mercy met in an unparalleled display of God's glory. The love of Christ that controls Paul is the love that Christ expressed when he died for all, with the result that all died (2 Cor. 5:14). Christ loved people in this way so that others would live for him, not themselves, and love others the way that he loved them (5:15). Through the judgment of Jesus, believers are saved from selfishness, lovelessness, and the wrath of God that will be visited on such sin. This is made clear in 2 Corinthians 5:21, where Paul states that God made Christ to be sin for our sake, so that in Christ we might become the righteousness of God. In the near context, 5:19b, Paul states that as God reconciles the world to himself in Christ, he does not count their trespasses against them and imputes Christ's righteousness to them.[64] When we put together what Paul says in this passage, we see the salvation God has accomplished through the judgment of Jesus: three times in 5:14–15 Paul states that Christ died for all; then he speaks of trespasses not being counted against the world in 5:19, before saying in 5:21, "The one who did not know sin he made to be sin for our sake." God can show mercy to the world and not count their trespasses against them precisely because God made Christ sin on our behalf and then Christ died for our sake (5:14–15, 19, 21). Salvation comes through the judgment of Christ, and those who respond

[64]Cf. Piper, *The Future of Justification*, 174–80.

to the appeal God makes through the ambassadors for Christ (5:20) become the righteousness of God in Christ (5:21).[65]

Paul also indicates in this passage that the death and resurrection of Jesus are to be understood as the fulfillment of what was prophesied in the Old Testament. As he spoke of the glorious eschatological future that would come through and after the judgment of exile, Isaiah prophesied of a new creation (Isa. 65:17; 66:22). Ezekiel identified the return from exile and the glorious eschatological restoration with resurrection from the dead (Ezek. 37:13–14). Paul sees the inauguration of the fulfillment of these prophecies in the resurrection of Jesus (2 Cor. 5:15), which makes those who are in Christ new creations (5:17). The imagery that Paul employs in 2 Corinthians 6:14–7:1 fits with this picture, as the church is spoken of as a new dwelling place of God by the Spirit, a new temple. The new exodus and return from exile have been typologically fulfilled in Christ's death and resurrection (5:15), inaugurating a new creation (5:17), and the church's new sojourn in the wilderness is replete with a new covenant (2 Corinthians 3), while the church itself is the new tabernacle, indwelt by the Spirit (2 Cor. 6:14–7:1). The glory of God that will be consummated in the future has broken into the present age as a result of the salvation that has come through the judgment of Jesus.[66]

2.4.3.2 Paul's Own Life and Suffering. Paul's self-confidence and self-reliance were judged and condemned; he thought he was going to die (2 Cor. 1:8–9). But that was to make him rely on God, not himself, for God is able to raise the dead (1:9–10).[67] Paul was saved through judgment, and his reliance on God glorifies God as many give thanks to God for the way he is working in Paul (1:11). Because of God's grace to him, Paul glorifies God by boasting in his weakness, in which God's power is displayed (12:9–10).

Paul understands himself to be filling up the messianic woes (see table 6.2 below) as he shares in the sufferings of the messiah (2 Cor. 1:5). Like Christ's suffering, which benefits others, so also Paul's suffering is for the benefit of others (1:4–6), and for this Paul blesses God (1:3). It is as though Paul understands his suffering as a participation in the judgment of Jesus for the benefit of others:

---

[65]Schreiner (*Paul*, 201–2) writes: "Believers are declared to be righteous before God as the divine judge because Jesus, as the sinless one, bore their sins. God's righteousness, therefore, consists both of his judgment and salvation. He saves those who put their faith in Jesus, and he judges his Son at the cross. . . . All human beings have sinned and therefore stand before the divine judge as condemned. Nevertheless, because of the cross of Christ, God both saves and judges at the cross. . . . It should be added that God himself sent his Son to satisfy his wrath, and so righteousness is rooted in God's love." See also the important discussion of 2 Cor. 5:21 in Vickers, *Jesus' Blood and Righteousness*, 159–90.

[66]For other expressions of God's glory in salvation through the judgment of Christ on the cross, see 2 Cor. 8:9; 13:3–4.

[67]Cf. Hafemann, *Suffering and Ministry in the Spirit*, 65: "Paul's suffering provides the *occasion* for the manifestation of God's power/glory as the one who rescues the apostle from his suffering, but also ensures that the power thus displayed is recognized to be God's alone."

". . . always carrying in the body the death of Jesus . . . . always being given over to death for Jesus' sake . . . . So death is at work in us" (4:10a, 11a, 12a ESV). This threefold expression of the way that Paul experiences the messianic woes, participating in the death of Jesus as he suffers for the gospel, is accompanied by a threefold expression of the benefits of the salvation that comes through the judgment in which Paul participates: ". . . so that the life of Jesus may also be manifested in our bodies. . . . so that the life of Jesus also may be manifested in our mortal flesh. . . . life in you" (4:10b, 11b, 12b ESV). The salvation that comes through the judgment that Paul experiences as he participates in Christ's sufferings will result in glory for God: Paul is confident of future resurrection and knows he will experience the presence of Jesus (4:14); his ministry for others increases thanksgiving to God's glory (4:15); and through all the afflictions, Paul knows that the future holds "an eternal weight of glory beyond all comparison" (4:17 ESV).

2.4.3.3 Paul's Ministry and Message. In 2 Corinthians 2:14–17 we see that God's glory in salvation through judgment is central to Paul's understanding of both what has happened to him and the effects of his ministry. Paul understands himself to have been conquered, and the result of Christ's conquest of Paul is the spread of the fragrance of the knowledge of Christ (2:14). This fragrance is the mercy and justice of God: to those being saved it is a fragrance from life to life, while to those perishing it is a fragrance from death to death (2:15–16). God's mercy and justice are made known as God has saved Paul through judgment.[68]

This pattern of salvation through judgment to God's glory is not only Paul's experience, but it is the dynamic of the relationship between the old and new covenants. The old covenant is a ministry of death (2 Cor. 3:7), as the letter kills (3:6). This death comes as a result of the condemnation brought by the law of Moses (3:9), which sets the stage for the life-giving Spirit to do his work (3:6). The message of the new covenant gives life to those killed by the law. Through judgment they are saved, and as they behold the glory of Christ, they are transformed into his image (3:18). This is a ministry of God's mercy (4:1), and God saves by making known his glory in the face of Christ (4:6).

2.4.3.4 Corinthian Repentance and Future Judgment. Like Paul, the repentant Corinthians have been saved through judgment. Some were grieved by the harsh letter Paul sent, and that grief resulted from the condemnation and judgment communicated by that letter (2 Cor. 7:8). This grief produced a godly repentance

[68]Hafemann writes, "Paul contended in II Cor. 2:14–16a that his suffering was the vehicle through which the knowledge and glory of the crucified Christ was now effecting salvation and judgment in the world" (*Suffering and Ministry in the Spirit*, 84).

that leads to salvation (7:9–10). The Corinthians responded with a zeal that comforted and rejoiced Paul to the glory of God (7:11–13).

For those Corinthians who remain unrepentant, Paul explains that though Christ may seem weak by worldly standards, he has been raised by God's power (2 Cor. 13:3–4). Similarly, Paul may seem weak, but he too lives by God's power and will deal with the unrepentant in that power (13:4b). This is a threat of judgment through which Paul intends to bring the unrepentant Corinthians to salvation for God's glory.[69]

The glory of God in salvation through judgment is the center of Paul's theology. The central event in human history, the cross of Christ, informs Paul's understanding of what is happening in his own life in and through his suffering; it is his message and by it he interprets the results of his ministry; and it shapes his expectation of what must take place in the lives of others. God will be glorified in salvation through judgment.

2.5 *Galatians*

Paul's letter to the Galatians begins with a theologically loaded greeting (Gal. 1:1–5) and Paul's assessment of the problem at Galatia—they are in danger of abandoning the gospel (1:6–10). From there Paul explains that he received the gospel not from man but from God (1:11–2:21). Paul then defends the gospel on the basis of what the Galatians experienced and what the Scriptures teach (3:1–4:11), before calling them to live in the freedom for which God set them free (4:12–6:10). The letter closes with a summary and restatement of Paul's case (6:11–18).[70] The message that courses through this letter is the glory of God in the salvation through judgment he accomplished in the gospel. In this letter, Paul explains how the implications of the center of his theology impinge upon the Galatians themselves and the false teachers troubling them.

2.5.1 *Deliverance in Christ for God's Glory (Gal. 1:1–5)*

Before Paul directly addresses the way that the false teaching in Galatia detracts from God's glory in the gospel and threatens to cut the Galatians off from Christ, he opens with a celebration of what God has done in Christ (Gal. 1:1–5). He will argue that his gospel came from God, not man (1:11–2:21), and his declaration that he is an apostle not from or through man but through Jesus Christ and God the Father lays the foundation for that argument (1:1). The gospel Paul preaches results in glory to God alone because it is God who saves by judging Jesus in place of sinners. Thus, Paul offers grace and peace to the Galatians from God

---

[69]Some four decades later the Corinthian church was called to repentance again by the letter to them from the church in Rome attributed to Clement. *First Clement* pronounces judgment on the divisive and disruptive in the church in an effort to restore harmony and love: through judgment Clement seeks the salvation of the whole church (see, e.g., the examples of Lot and Rahab who were saved from judgment, in *1 Clement* 11–12, followed by the exhortation to appropriate behavior in *1 Clement* 13; cf. *1 Clem*. 34:1–3).

[70]Following the outline in Thomas R. Schreiner, *Galatians*, ZECNT (Grand Rapids: Zondervan, forthcoming).

and Christ, because Christ "gave himself for our sins" (1:3–4a). The sacrifice of Christ was a judgment that accomplished deliverance, "that he might deliver us from the present evil age" (1:4b).[71] Having been judged, Jesus himself was vindicated in his resurrection from the dead (1:1), and in response to this Paul ascribes glory to God forever (1:5). This salutation celebrates the glory of God in the salvation he accomplished through the judgment of Jesus and his resurrection from the dead.

2.5.2 The Problem in Galatia (Gal. 1:6–10)

There are competing messages in Galatia coming from competing teachers. Paul wants to convince the Galatians to believe him and embrace the gospel he preaches. He condemns the message that competes against his gospel as a different gospel (Gal. 1:6) that is in fact a non-gospel (1:7)—it is not good news that the Galatians must do certain things to attain salvation. Not only does Paul pronounce judgment on the message, but he twice anathematizes the messengers (1:8, 9). Through these judgments Paul wants the Galatians to be saved, which will mean their continuance in the grace of God (1:6), in the gospel of Christ (1:7). Paul asserts that he seeks to please God, not man, as he serves Christ (1:10), and this is pertinent because the heralds of the non-gospel are trying to convince the Galatians that they must live up to man-made standards by man-made power for man-made approval (cf. 3:3; 4:17, 23; 5:3; 6:12–13). Paul's message is that God deserves glory because he has saved the Galatians through the judgment of Jesus (e.g., 1:3–5; 3:13), and it is as though Paul now seeks to preserve them in that salvation through the judgment he renders against those teaching the non-gospel (cf., e.g., 4:19–20).

2.5.3 Paul's Gospel from God, Not Man (Gal. 1:11–2:21)

Paul asserts that in contrast to the false teachers, he is an apostle from God (Gal. 1:1) with a message that came from God, not man (1:11). Paul cites his former way of life in Judaism, with his violent persecution of the church (1:13–14), as evidence that God revealed himself to him (1:12, 15–22). The way that Paul was converted, having all his assumptions condemned by God's revelation of Jesus Christ to him (1:16), resulted in people glorifying God (1:24).

Another revelation occasioned Paul's second (cf. Gal. 1:18–19) meeting with the apostles in Jerusalem (2:1–10).[72] The salvation of the Galatians through the judgment of the false teachers that Paul seeks to accomplish in this letter was

[71]Todd Wilson argues that "at several points in [Galatians] Paul appears to juxtapose (1) a description of the Christ-event in terms reminiscent of the Exodus with (2) a rebuke of or warning against apostasy in terms reminiscent of the Israelites' own wilderness defection" (Todd A. Wilson, "Wilderness Apostasy and Paul's Portrayal of the Crisis in Galatians," *NTS* 50 [2004]: 552).

[72]I take the view that Galatians was written before the Jerusalem Council described in Acts 15 and would align Paul's first two visits to Jerusalem as described in Galatians and Acts as follows: first visit, Acts 9:26–30 and Gal. 1:18–19; second visit, Acts 11:29–30 and Gal. 2:1–10.

established in that meeting with the apostles, and Paul relates how he did not yield to the slave makers, so that the gospel would be preserved for the Gentiles in Galatia (2:4–5). With this the Jerusalem apostles agreed, for Paul laid his gospel before them (2:1–2), and they did not insist on the circumcision of Titus (2:3) but gave Paul the right hand of fellowship (2:6–10).

Paul then relates a confrontational experience of the church at Antioch as an instance of how his gospel accomplished salvation through judgment. On that occasion Peter behaved in a way that was consistent with what the false teachers apparently advocated in Galatia, separating himself from Gentiles on the basis of Mosaic prescriptions regarding clean and unclean table fellowship. Paul's verdict was clear: he opposed Peter to his face, for Peter stood condemned (Gal. 2:11–13). Behavior such as Peter's is not required by God; it is hypocrisy (2:13) and out of step with the gospel (2:14a). Paul exposed Peter's blameworthy behavior, and Peter apparently repented unto salvation through the experience of judgment (cf. Acts 15:10–11).

When Paul indicted Peter for living like a Gentile and not like a Jew (Gal. 2:14b), he had in view Peter's abandonment of total adherence to the Mosaic law (cf. Acts 10:9–15).[73] This also explains Paul's reference to requiring Gentiles to live like Jews (Gal. 2:14c). The idea is that *on certain points* the Gentiles were required to adhere to the demands of the law of Moses.[74] Paul's implicit objections to the "man-made" requirements of the non-gospel preached by the false teachers, then, are not indications that Paul views the law of Moses as man-made. Rather, in Paul's view the selection of certain Mosaic requirements as necessary for salvation is man-made. For Paul, now that Christ has come, those who would be saved through the law of Moses must attain perfect obedience to the whole law (3:10–12; 5:3).[75]

No one is justified by doing what the law requires (Gal. 2:16), because not even those born Jewish, like Paul and Peter (2:15), perfectly keep the whole law (cf. Acts 13:38–39; 15:10). Thus, the only way of salvation is faith in Christ (Gal. 2:16). Jews who are justified by faith in Christ alone are "found to be sinners" (2:17) in the sense that they live like "Gentile sinners" (2:15). This does

[73]The constant theme of justification by faith rather than by works of law (Gal. 2:15–21, esp. 2:16), the focused explanation of the relationship between the law of Moses and the promise to Abraham (3:1–29, esp. 3:15–18), and the explicit identification of the opponents with Mount Sinai (Gal. 4:24–25), point toward the problem in Galatia mainly involving the Mosaic law. Since Paul never explicitly mentions the Roman Imperial Cult in his letters, I am not persuaded that the issues Paul addressed in Galatians arose from the church's attempts to navigate their civic status as it related to the Imperial Cult (*pace* Justin K. Hardin, *Galatians and the Imperial Cult: A Critical Analysis of the First-Century Social Context of Paul's Letter*, WUNT 2.237 [Tübingen: Mohr Siebeck, 2008]). The explicit issue in Galatians is the question of how one can be justified before God: by works of law as the opponents would have it, or by faith as Paul teaches?

[74]Rightly Thomas R. Schreiner, "The Commands of God," in *Central Themes in Biblical Theology: Mapping Unity in Diversity*, ed. Scott J. Hafemann and Paul R. House (Grand Rapids: Baker, 2007), 68: "In most instances in the New Testament the law refers specifically to what is demanded in the Mosaic covenant." See further Thomas R. Schreiner, *The Law and Its Fulfillment: A Pauline Theology of Law* (Grand Rapids: Baker, 1993).

[75]Thomas R. Schreiner, "'Works of Law' in Paul," *Novum Testamentum* 33 (1991): 239–244.

not mean that Christ causes more sin to be committed (2:17), because living like a Gentile is "sinful" only if one demands obedience to the law of Moses, which Paul shockingly says that he has torn down (2:18). Only if Paul were to rebuild the demand to obey the law of Moses would Christ be "a minister of sin" (2:17–18). But rather than rebuilding the demand to obey Moses, Paul explains that the law judged him, so that through that judgment Christ could save him: "For through the law to the law I died, in order that I might live to God. With Christ I have been crucified, and I no longer live, but Christ lives in me. The life I now live in the flesh, I live by faith in the son of God, who loved me and gave himself for me" (2:19–20). Paul was condemned by the law of Moses (2:19). His statement that he was crucified with Christ both explains how the law killed him and treats the death of Christ on the cross as a result of the condemnation stemming from the law of Moses (cf. also 3:13). By faith, when Christ died on the cross, Paul died there with him (2:19–20), with the result that by faith, the life Paul now lives is no longer him living but Christ living in him. Paul was saved through judgment. This undercuts the teaching of the anathematized non-gospel preachers in Galatia because if one could be righteous by obeying the law, Christ did not need to die on the cross to accomplish salvation (2:21).

2.5.4 Paul's Gospel Proved by Experience and Scripture (Gal. 3:1–4:11)

Paul's understanding of the Old Testament and the outworking of redemptive history comes to the fore in this section of his letter to the Galatians. His assertion that Jesus Christ was publicly portrayed as crucified before their eyes (Gal. 3:1) establishes that God has accomplished salvation in Christ, which in turn affirms that righteousness does not come from the law (2:21). His question about the reception of the Spirit (3:2) assumes the Old Testament's teaching about when the Spirit would be poured out—after exile. At the restoration of Israel (e.g., Isa. 32:15), when the punishment for breaking the covenant was paid in full (40:2), in the latter days, the Spirit would be poured out (Joel 3:1–5, ET 2:28–32). Paul's question in Galatians 3:2 ("Did you receive the Spirit by works of law or by hearing with faith?") assumes that the Galatians have experienced the outpouring of the Spirit, and it also assumes that Paul has taught them when the Old Testament indicated such a blessing would be enjoyed—in the latter days.[76] This statement contributes to the argument Paul will move to and develop more fully, that the time in which the Mosaic law was operative has come to an end (see 3:15–4:11).

Paul is essentially condemning the Galatians for being tempted to abandon the gospel—he calls them foolish and asks who has bewitched them (Gal. 3:1). The evidence of their experience of the Spirit (3:2–3, 5) and their partaking in

[76]Rightly Schreiner, *New Testament Theology*, 99–100; N. T. Wright, *The Climax of the Covenant: Christ and the Law in Pauline Theology* (Minneapolis: Fortress, 1992), 154.

suffering—perhaps the suffering of the messianic woes (3:4, cf. table 6.2 below)—prove that the last days have been inaugurated. The law of Moses is no longer the regulative standard for the people of God. Further, they experience the Spirit apart from the law, so they are like Abraham, who was reckoned righteous by faith, not works (3:5–6). In addition to citing Genesis 15:6 against his opponents (Gal. 3:6), Paul cites Genesis 12:3 (Gal. 3:8, 14).

Paul is opposing those who would constrain the Gentiles to obey aspects of the law of Moses, and he opposes their argument by explaining the relationship between the covenant God made with Abraham and the covenant God made with Moses. Having thus shown what the Scripture said to Abraham about justification and the Gentiles (Gal. 3:6–9), Paul turns to what the law of Moses says.

As we consider Paul's comments here, it is important to note that Paul is not explaining the function of the law of Moses in the lives of those who lived before the coming of Christ (see Gal. 3:14, 17, 19, 23–25; 4:1–7). That is, Paul is writing to *Christians* who are being wrongly encouraged to pursue justification by means of obedience to certain parts of the law of Moses. So when Paul speaks of those "who rely on works of the law" (3:10 ESV), he is referring not to faithful members of the old covenant remnant but to those who mistakenly think they must adhere to certain parts of the old covenant to partake of the new. The old covenant cannot be selectively obeyed (cf. 5:3), and deciding to pursue God through the old covenant *now that Christ has come* cuts one off from Christ (5:3). This is why "all who rely on works of the law are under a curse" (3:10a ESV).

The law of Moses placed a curse on those who broke the covenant, and Paul's citation of Deuteronomy 27:26 in Galatians 3:10 shows that the curse in view is the curse of the Mosaic covenant, the curse that included exile from the land. Paul next asserts that Habakkuk 2:4, "the righteous by faith shall live" (Gal. 3:11b), demonstrates the clarity of the point that "no one will be justified by the law before God" (3:11a; cf. 2:16). When Paul quotes Leviticus 18:5 in Galatians 3:12, "But the law is not of faith, rather 'The one who does them shall live by them,'" again, he is not saying that Moses taught a works-based legalism, nor is he claiming that faith was unnecessary for old covenant Israelites who sought to keep the law. Paul is not explaining Leviticus 18:5 in the context of Leviticus, when the law of Moses was the norm of life for the nation of Israel.[77] Rather, Paul is explaining to the Galatians what they must achieve if they decide to pursue justification by means of obedience to the law of Moses now that Christ

[77] *Contra* Mark A. Seifrid, *Christ, Our Righteousness: Paul's Theology of Justification*, NSBT (Downers Grove, IL: InterVarsity, 2000), 105, see the quote in chap. 2 n. 99, and *contra* Francis Watson, *Paul and the Hermeneutics of Faith* (New York: T&T Clark, 2004), 67, who quotes this line from Seifrid approvingly in n. 75.

has come.[78] Now that Christ has come, there are two possibilities: either trust him for justification and be saved, or rely on works of the law, fail as all sinful humans will, and be damned.[79]

Paul explains in Galatians 3:13–14 how Christ has completed Israel's story, fulfilled the law, and made the blessings promised to Abraham available. When Paul states in 3:13, "Messiah redeemed us from the curse of the law," he has the same curse in view that he wrote of in Galatians 3:10.[80] This means that Paul sees the covenant curses, supremely encapsulated in the exile of the people from God's presence, as being exhausted when Christ died on the cross: "Messiah redeemed us from the curse of the law, having become a curse for us, because it has been written, 'Cursed is everyone who is hanged on a tree'" (3:13).[81]

Christ became a curse, was hanged on a tree, and thereby redeemed his people from the curse. Thus, what Isaiah prophesied about the sins of the people being pardoned because they had been punished (Isa. 40:2), has at last been realized. That statement of Isaiah is recognizably set in a context in which he deals with Israel's glorious eschatological restoration that will come through and after judgment, after exile. There is a sense, then, in which the exile finds its fullest realization in Christ's death on the cross. The curse was poured out in full. This kind of fulfillment of the payment for sin prophesied by Isaiah (40:2) is also in keeping with what Isaiah said about the one who would bear the sins of the people (52:13–53:12, esp. 53:4–6, 8). Isaiah even said the servant's work would benefit "many nations" (52:15; cf. Gen. 12:3), that he would "see his seed" (Isa. 53:10; cf. Gen. 22:17–18), who would be "justified" because he bore their sins (Isa. 53:11). Isaiah made it clear that the judgment he announced against Israel arose from their failure to keep the covenant (cf., e.g., Deut. 4:26, where heaven and earth are the witnesses to the covenant, and Isa. 1:2, where Isaiah calls on the witnesses to the covenant), and so the servant in Isaiah 53 is bearing

---

[78]See further James M. Hamilton Jr., "The One Who Does Them Shall Live By Them: Leviticus 18:5 in Galatians 3:12," *Gospel Witness*, August 2005, 10–14.

[79]Preston M. Sprinkle (*Law and Life: The Interpretation of Leviticus 18:5 in Early Judaism and in Paul*, WUNT 2.241 [Tübingen: Mohr Siebeck, 2008], 164) writes: "Paul understands Lev 18:5 to be a merely human way to attain eschatological life . . . . For Paul in Gal 3:12, Lev 18:5 is unduly optimistic about humanity's ability to rescue itself from the plight of the curse of the law (3:10)." Against this, Paul is not objecting to the meaning of Lev. 18:5 in its Old Testament context but stating what the text means for the Galatians *now that Christ has come*. I would argue that Paul understood Lev. 18:5 in its Old Testament context to mean what I argued the text means in chap. 2, §4, on Leviticus above: Yahweh commands that Israel do certain things to deal with their uncleanness so that they can remain in his presence "lest they die" (e.g., Lev. 10:7; 15:31; 22:9) as Nadab and Abihu did (10:1–2). The one who *believes* that Yahweh really is in the midst of Israel, really is holy, and really has given instructions that must be kept or death results, that kind of person will live by doing what Yahweh has commanded (18:5). But Paul is not addressing members of the old covenant remnant who can go to the tabernacle or temple to offer the sacrifice for their cleansing. Rather, Paul writes *after Christ has come* and put an end to sacrifice. Now that Christ has come and put an end to sacrifice, the whole law must be kept if one wants to be justified by law, which is what Paul means when he quotes Lev. 18:5 to Christians being urged to add law keeping to their trust in Christ (Gal. 3:12).

[80]See Todd A. Wilson, "'Under Law' in Galatians: A Pauline Theological Abbreviation," *JTS* 56 (2005): 362–92.

[81]So also Wright, *The Climax of the Covenant*, 146, 151, 156.

the punishment the people deserve for having broken the Mosaic covenant. In Galatians 3:13–14, Paul is arguing that Jesus has taken the punishment incurred from the failure to keep the Mosaic covenant, with the result that the blessings promised to Abraham can be enjoyed by the Gentiles: "Messiah redeemed us from the curse of the law, having become a curse for us, . . . in order that the blessing of Abraham might come to the Gentiles in messiah Jesus, that we might receive the promise of the Spirit through faith" (3:13–14). The exile is over. The restoration has begun, and the age in which the Spirit is poured out has dawned (cf. 3:2).

Isaiah and the other Old Testament prophets proclaimed an eschatological future for Israel that would come through and after the judgment of the exile, and one key characteristic of that future was the outpouring of the Holy Spirit. From what Paul says here in Galatians 3:13–14, we see that Paul understands Isaiah and the prophets to be pointing to the day when the blessing of Abraham would be realized. Isaiah's own references to the *nations* being blessed by the work of the servant (e.g., Isa. 52:15; cf. Gen. 12:3) and the servant seeing his *seed* (Isa. 53:10; cf. Gen. 22:17–18) employ key concepts from the blessings promised to Abraham, demonstrating that Paul rightly understands Isaiah's eschatological promises to point to the fulfillment of what was promised to Abraham (Gen. 12:1–3).

In all this Paul seeks to convince the Galatians that they do not need to add obedience to the law of Moses to their faith in Christ in order to be justified.[82] The next step in his argument is his explanation that the promise was given to Abraham and to his singular seed, who is Christ, and then 430 years later the law was given. The law was not given as a means to attain the inheritance; rather, the inheritance was given as a promise (Gal. 3:15–18). If the law was not the means whereby the inheritance would be received, why was it given? Having raised the question, Paul explains that the law "was added because of transgressions, until the seed came to whom the promise was made" (3:19a). The law being added "because of transgression" appears to mean that the law was given to increase transgression,[83] but Paul clearly sees the law being in force until the coming of the seed of Abraham, to whom the promises were made (cf. 3:16). Paul goes on to explain that the law is not contrary to God's promises, but neither can it give life (3:21). The law was given to set the stage for salvation by faith in Christ, imprisoning everything in sin so that those who believe in Jesus would be saved by faith and not by works (3:22).

[82]For my take on the way Paul contrasts righteousness based on the law and righteousness based on Spirit-initiated reliance arising from hearing and believing, see Hamilton, "N. T. Wright and Saul's Moral Bootstraps," 152–55.

[83]For this conclusion and discussion of other options, which include the law being given to restrain, define, or deal with sin, see Schreiner, *Galatians*, forthcoming.

Paul explains that the law was a "custodian"[84] to conduct people to justification by faith (Gal. 3:23–24). This custodian was in force "before faith came" (3:23)—which does not mean that the old covenant remnant was saved apart from faith, for even then it was those of faith who were blessed with Abraham (cf. 3:6–9). These references to the time before "faith" came use "faith" as a shorthand reference to the period of time before the messiah came and justification by faith in Jesus was revealed (cf. 2:16).[85] This can be seen from the way that both this statement at the beginning of Galatians 3:23 and another later in the verse, "until the coming faith would be revealed," have as their point of reference the phrase in 3:24, "until messiah came."

In view of the purpose clause at the end of Galatians 3:24, "in order that we might be justified by faith," it seems that the law "was added because of transgressions" (3:19) and served as a "custodian" (3:24) for the same purpose: to show human inability to be justified by works and thereby to lead people to the only available way to be justified, through faith in messiah Jesus. Thus, the Galatians to whom Paul writes do not need to add law keeping to their faith in Christ. That, Paul explains, is not why the law was given. The law was given to lead people to possess what the Galatians already have and are being tempted to abandon: justification by faith. Those who believe no longer need the custodian (3:25), for through faith they are those who will receive the promised inheritance, sons of God (3:26). This means that the teachers who set themselves up as being closer to God by keeping the law of Moses are mistaken. Moreover, by faith the Galatian Christians have been baptized into Christ and are united to him (3:27), with the result that neither ethnicity nor social status nor gender positions one person closer than another to being justified by faith (3:28). Since they are united to Christ by faith, they are also united to one another, and being united to Christ joins them to the singular seed of Abraham to whom the promise was made (3:29; cf. 3:16).

Paul continues this line of argumentation in Galatians 4:1–11. As surprising as Paul's language may be, the point he is making is clear: before the coming of messiah Jesus, humanity was "enslaved to the elementary principles of the world" (4:3b). Whatever Paul means when he refers to "elementary principles," from the wider context it is clear that this time of enslavement is the same time in which the Mosaic law was in force.[86] Then when the time was ripe, God sent his Son,

---

[84]For this translation, see ibid.

[85]I am grateful for conversations with Todd Wilson at Tyndale House, Cambridge, where he brought this to my attention. See his suggested criteria for discerning the use of rhetorical shorthand: "First, a shorthand expression obviously must be *shorter* or more condensed than its longhand equivalent. Secondly, a shorthand expression must have some *discernable verbal connection* to its longhand equivalent. . . . Thirdly, a shorthand expression must have the *same referent* as its longhand equivalent" (Wilson, "'Under Law' in Galatians," 364).

[86]See the discussion in Schreiner, *Galatians*.

who was born of woman under law (4:4), and he redeemed those under law and made adoption possible (4:5). The proof that the Galatians have been adopted is again their reception of the eschatological gift of the Spirit (4:6; cf. 3:2–5, 14). Therefore, the Galatians should not turn back to the Mosaic law (4:7–11).

What Paul has done through this section renders judgment on the ideas of the false teachers. By disproving the tenets of their views, Paul seeks to bring the Galatians through the judgment of those false perspectives to the salvation of a right understanding of justification. He wants the Galatians to join him in boasting only in the cross (Gal. 6:14), glorifying God alone and giving no credit to the works they do in obedience to the law.

2.5.5 Call to Freedom in the Spirit (Gal. 4:12–6:10)

Paul calls the Galatians to become as he is, for he has become as they are (Gal. 4:12). Apparently he means that he now lives apart from the Mosaic law, like a Gentile, and he wants the Gentile Christians in Galatia to resist the false teachers who demand obedience to the law.

He then assures them of his genuine ministry and concern for them (Gal. 4:13–20), and employs an "allegory" designed to enable the Galatians to understand their place in salvation history and how they should conduct themselves (4:21–31). Paul calls this an "allegory" (4:24), but his interpretation looks more like typology than like the allegorical interpretations of Philo, Origen, and others.[87] Paul likens the child born by natural means from Abraham's union with Hagar to those wrongly encouraging the Galatians to keep the law of Moses. Ishmael was born because of what is possible by human power, and he was born precisely because Abraham and Sarah doubted that God would keep the promise he made to them and tried to achieve the promise on their own. The false teachers are doing the same thing. They are identified with Hagar and Mount Sinai because they are seeking to compel the Galatians to accomplish their justification by human power rather than by the power of God's word and Spirit accomplishing justification through the instrument of faith. The Galatian Christians, by contrast, are identified with Isaac, who was born by the miraculous power of God in the face of all human norms and expectations. God promised a child, and in spite of the human inability of Abraham and Sarah, God kept his promise. The slave makers who want to constrain obedience to the law of Moses are identified with Hagar, who was a slave (4:22), and those who identify

[87]Similarly K. J. Woollcombe, "The Biblical Origins and Patristic Development of Typology," in *Essays on Typology*, ed. G. W. H. Lampe and K. J. Woollcombe, Studies in Biblical Theology (Naperville, IL: Allenson, 1957), 53: "In the Pauline interpretation, *the historical pattern* of the story of Sarah and Hagar is used as a parable of the historical pattern of God's dealings with the Old and the New Israel. In the Philonic interpretation, however, the historical pattern of the story plays no part at all." On allegorical interpretation, see Gerald Bray, *Biblical Interpretation: Past and Present* (Downers Grove, IL: InterVarsity, 1996), 99–103. *Pace* Jason C. Meyer (*The End of the Law: Mosaic Covenant in Pauline Theology*, NACSBT [Nashville: Broadman & Holman, 2000], 116–19) who argues that this is allegory rather than typology.

with the false teachers become enslaved to their requirements (4:24–25; cf. 4:17). Those who are justified by faith in God's promise are identified with Isaac, the child of the promise (4:28).

Paul's quotation of Isaiah 54:1 in Galatians 4:27 is explosive: that text follows hard on the heels of Isaiah 53, which describes the sin-bearing, justifying work of the servant, through which the exile would be fulfilled (cf. Gal. 3:13–14). The words of the text speak of a barren woman giving birth to children, which recalls Sarah, and the barrenness giving way to fruitfulness evokes images of return from exile and the blooming of the desert. Paul is evoking these themes because the Galatian Christians have been justified by faith in the redemption wrought by the servant (3:13; 4:5), which brought the exile to an end and initiated the new exodus and return from exile. As with barren Sarah, who gave birth to Isaac, God has kept his promises and blessed the nations through the seed of Abraham even though that was not possible by the power of what human flesh could accomplish. Just as Ishmael mocked Isaac, the non-gospel preachers want to constrain the Galatian Christians to obey the law (4:28). Just as Abraham and Sarah drove Hagar and Ishmael away, so the Galatian Christians should reject the false teachers and send them away (4:30), for those who believe are born of faith in God's promise, not of works (4:31).

Law keeping will not help the Galatians but they should work out their faith through love (Gal. 5:6), not submit to slavery (5:1), which would cut them off from Christ (5:2) and obligate them to keeping the whole law perfectly (5:3). By announcing this judgment, Paul means to preserve the Galatians in the salvation that comes "through the Spirit by faith" as they await the "hope of righteousness" (5:5). Paul also announces the penalty faced by those who trouble the Galatians with this non-gospel (5:9), and he urges his readers to fulfill the law by loving one another (5:13–14). As the Galatians walk by the Spirit, the glory of God will be seen in their lives (5:22–25). The law of Christ (6:2) calls them to bear the burdens of others, just as Christ bore the burdens of his people. What is sown will be reaped (6:7–10).

2.5.6 Boasting Only in the Cross (Gal. 6:11–18)

Paul's letter to the Galatians is about the glory of God in salvation through judgment. Jesus has been judged, and thereby the exile is over and the eschatological age of salvation, in which the Spirit is poured out, has begun. Salvation has come through the judgment of Jesus, and the desert has begun to bloom. The Galatians should not follow those "who want to make a good showing in the flesh" (Gal. 6:12), who establish their own glory by doing (parts of) the law of Moses. Rather than giving these who seek their own glory cause for boasting about what they accomplish in the flesh of the Galatian Christians (6:13), the Galatian Christians are to join Paul in boasting in the cross of Christ alone (6:14).

God is glorified in the salvation through judgment he accomplished in Christ, and Paul seeks to preserve the Galatians in this salvation through the judgment of the false teachers. The new creation (Gal. 6:15) will be radiant with the glory of God, in which the barren will rejoice (cf. Isa. 54:1 in Gal. 4:27).

2.6 *Ephesians*

Paul's letter to the Ephesians celebrates the glory of God in salvation through judgment demonstrated in "the mystery of Christ, which was not made known to the sons of men in other generations as it has now been revealed to the holy apostles and prophets in the Spirit, for the Gentiles to be co-heirs and co-bodied and co-partakers of the promise in messiah Jesus through the gospel" (Eph. 3:4b–6). It is this radical assertion that Paul explains in the first two chapters of Ephesians, and then he makes it explicit in Ephesians 3 before addressing the life that corresponds to this gospel in Ephesians 4–6. Are the Gentiles on equal footing with the Jews in God's plan? Paul's radical answer to that question is yes, and in Ephesians he explains how God's glory in salvation through judgment is displayed in making this to be so.

The profound statements in Ephesians 1 are thus not abstract declarations of theological truth but revolutionary applications of what was revealed to Paul about the Gentiles (Eph. 3:3). If any selection from Paul's writings makes the case for the centrality of God's glory in his theology, Ephesians 1 does. Paul begins by blessing God "who has blessed us with every spiritual blessing in the heavenlies in messiah" (1:3), and then it seems that he enumerates the blessings he has in mind. The first blessing is that of election (1:4). The Jews were God's chosen people (e.g., Deut. 7:6–8), and now Paul asserts that just as God chose Israel to be a holy nation, "he chose us in him before the foundation of the world, for us to be holy and blameless before him" (Eph. 1:4). The "us" here has Jews and Gentiles in view,[88] and this is "the administration of the mystery which has been kept hidden from the ages in God, who created all things" (3:9). The election of Jews *and Gentiles* is the "eternal purpose which he worked in messiah Jesus our Lord" (3:11), and this was "in order that he might now make known to the rulers and to the authorities in the heavenlies the manifold wisdom of God through the church" (3:10). So God chose Gentiles from eternity past (1:4, 3:11), then he kept the plan hidden for ages and generations (3:5, 9), then accomplished salvation in Christ and united Gentiles and Jews in the church to show his multifaceted wisdom to demonic rulers and authorities (3:10). By triumphing over racism and alienation, uniting bitterly divided people, God

[88]See the discussion of the inclusive "we" in Wallace, *Greek Grammar*, 397–98.

judges and condemns the powers at work in those who differentiate themselves from others (2:1–3), and through the judgment of the demonic forces at work in racial segregation, God accomplishes salvation that unifies people in Christ, demonstrating his glory.

The Gentiles are coheirs with the Jews (Eph. 3:6) precisely because of the second blessing Paul states that God blessed "us" with (1:3): "In love he predestined us to adoption through Jesus the messiah for himself, according to the good pleasure of his will" (1:5). God is the initiator here: God chose, God loved, God predestined, God adopted, and God did all this according to the pleasure of his will (1:3–4). God did not do this for the Jews or the Gentiles because either group had earned it, because either group had sought it, or because either group would respond rightly to it. God did this "for himself, according to the pleasure of his will" (1:5). He did it because *he* wanted to, and Paul gives the ultimate reason he did it in Ephesians 1:6: "for the praise of the glory of his grace, with which he graced us in the beloved." God wanted his grace to be praised, so he stunned cognizant beings in the heavens and on earth (3:10, 20–21) by including the Gentiles in Christ. The Gentiles did not earn this. God graced them in his beloved Son (1:6).

In the mystery of his will (Eph. 3:4–6), God made Israel his special possession, and he allotted the Gentiles to other gods (cf. Deut. 4:19; 29:26). What about the claim that Zeus and his demonic cohorts (cf. 1 Cor. 10:20) have on these people? Not that Satan or Zeus have any right to people that God created, but the power of sin does keep people walking "according to the ruler of the authority of the air" (Eph. 2:2), and their sin creates a massive debt to God. Paul addresses these problems in the third blessing with which God "blessed us" (1:3), saying in Ephesians 1:7, "In him we have the redemption through his blood, the forgiveness of trespasses, according to the wealth of his grace." God chose and predestined Jews and Gentiles for adoption for the praise of his grace (1:4–6), and he redeemed them according to the wealth of his grace (1:7). But it does not stop there.

God was pleased to make known his marvelous plans by revealing the mystery to Paul (Eph. 3:3). Paul considers this a spiritual blessing (1:3), an expression of the wealth of God's grace (1:8), "which he lavished upon us in all wisdom and insight, having made known to us the mystery of his will according to his good pleasure which he purposed in him as an administration for the fullness of the times, to sum up everything in Christ, things in the heavens and things on the earth in him" (1:8–10). The mystery of God's will that he purposed in Christ in 1:9 is the same mystery Paul elaborates on in 3:2–13, and Paul seems to refer back to statements already made in the letter when he says in 3:3, "as I wrote previously in part."

As noted above, under the old covenant Israel was God's inheritance, his special portion, and the nations were allotted to other gods (Deut. 4:19–20). But now in Christ, Paul explains, "in him also we are made his inheritance, having been predestined according to the purpose of the one who works all things according to the counsel of his will, that we who have already hoped in Christ should be to the praise of his glory" (Eph. 1:11–12).[89] God has brought Jews and Gentiles together as his heritage for the praise of his glory. He accomplished this through the proclamation of the gospel, which the elect believed,[90] and to ensure their preservation God sealed them with the Spirit as a down payment of "our inheritance, for the redemption of the possession, for the praise of his glory" (1:13–14). God chose and predestined for adoption Jews and Gentiles for his glory (1:4–6). God redeemed and lavished grace by revealing his plan to consummate everything in Christ, making Jews and Gentiles his heritage, for the praise of his glory (1:7–12). And God sent the good news and sealed those who believed with the down payment of the Spirit for the praise of his glory (1:13–14).

Paul's response to all that God has done for the Ephesian Christians is to give thanks to God for them (Eph. 1:15–16). He also prays that God, "the Father of glory," would give them "the Spirit of wisdom and revelation in the knowledge of him" (1:17). Paul then enumerates the three particular things he prays God will reveal to them: the hope of their calling, the wealth of the glory of God's inheritance in the saints (1:18), and the surpassing greatness of God's resurrection power toward believers (1:19). These are all related. God has called Jews and Gentiles together (the hope of their calling) to be his inheritance as a display of his glory, and he has accomplished this by the same power that raised Christ from the dead and enthroned him above all his enemies, putting everything under his feet and making him Head of the church, which is his body (1:20–23). God has triumphed, then, over death, over hostile demonic powers, and over divisive forces in humanity. The racial unity of the church is the demonstration of God's glory. Paul prays that God would reveal all this to the Ephesians (1:17–19) just as God revealed it to him (3:3–6).

Paul explains what the unification of Jew and Gentile in the church looks like in individual and corporate terms in Ephesians 2. Individually, Gentiles and

[89]For discussion of this translation, see Harold W. Hoehner, *Ephesians: An Exegetical Commentary* (Grand Rapids: Baker, 2002), 226–27, 231–34.

[90]Ben Witherington claims, "Election for Paul is corporate" (*1 and 2 Thessalonians: A Socio-Rhetorical Commentary* [Grand Rapids: Eerdmans, 2006], 65). But groups of people, corporate entities, are made up of individuals, and it is impossible to choose a group of people without choosing the individuals that make up that group. If I. Howard Marshall (*New Testament Theology: Many Witnesses, One Gospel* [Downers Grove, IL: InterVarsity, 2004], 241) were correct that "the term *elect* is always applied to those who have actually become members of God's people rather than to those whom God has predestined to salvation before they have actually received it," then the *electing* is done by people rather than God. Against Marshall's claim, see 2 Tim. 2:10. For further discussion, see Thomas R. Schreiner, "Corporate and Individual Election in Romans 9: A Response to Brian Abasciano," *JETS* 49 (2006): 351–71.

Jews were dead in trespasses and sins (Eph. 2:1–3, 5). Paul explains that deadness in sin means "doing the desires of the flesh and of the mind" (2:3). So the problem is not the lack of willpower when one is dead in sin; rather, willpower that is dead to God is the problem (cf. 4:17–19). God's response to individual Gentiles and Jews who were dead in sin and enslaved to the dark lord (2:2) was to love them mercifully by making them alive, saving them by grace (2:4–5). God united them to Christ by faith (2:8), with the result that they are made alive with Christ, raised with him, and seated with him on his triumphant throne over all enemy powers in the heavenlies (2:5–6; cf. 1:20–23). This is the power at work in believers (1:19), a power that saves through the judgment of evil, triumphs over death, and preserves to the end. God does this "in order to demonstrate in the ages to come the surpassing riches of his grace in kindness toward us in messiah Jesus" (2:7). In short, God does it to display his glory. God saves through judgment for his own glory. By grace, through faith, the gift of God, not from works, no one can boast, and it issues in good works (2:8–10).

At the corporate level Paul calls the Gentiles to remember how things were for them before God showed them mercy (Eph. 2:11–12). Those who formerly were far off have been brought near in Christ by his blood (2:13). Jesus is our peace, who made the two groups—Jew and Gentile—one by destroying the divisions between them through his death on the cross (2:14). The law has been nullified by Christ's death, and the two have been made into one new man in Christ (2:15). Christ has reconciled Jew and Gentile to God in his body through the cross (2:16), and the message is preached to both Jew and Gentile (2:17). Through Christ Jew and Gentile have access in the one Spirit to the Father (2:18). The Gentiles are no longer strangers and aliens but are fellow citizens with the saints and members of God's household, being part of the temple that God is building on the foundation of the apostles and prophets, of which Christ is the cornerstone (2:19–22).

Ephesians 3 is not a digression in thought. Rather, this chapter simply makes more explicit everything Paul has said to this point. Paul is a prisoner on behalf of the nations (Eph. 3:1). He is imprisoned because of his work to proclaim the good news of what God has done in Christ—this mystery of including Gentile and Jew, making one new man in Christ by the gospel. This is the stewardship of God's grace given to Paul (3:2), what God revealed to him that he has written about a little in this letter (3:3). God gave this message to Paul to proclaim (3:8) so that Paul could speak truth to the powers for God's glory (3:10).[91] Paul's afflictions glorify the significance of what God has done in the Ephesians (3:13).

[91]Similarly Timothy Gombis, "Ephesians 3:2–13: Pointless Digression, or Epitome of the Triumph of God in Christ?" *WTJ* 66 (2004): 313–23.

That is, as Paul suffers, his message is authenticated, and Paul's suffering for the message demonstrates the value of the message.

Just as Paul recounted all that God had done in Ephesians 1:3–14, then prayed that the Ephesians would understand it in 1:15–22, so he has retold the story of what God has done from different perspectives in 2:1–3:13, and again prays that God would enable the Ephesians to understand it in 3:14–19. Notably, he wants God to strengthen them with power according to the wealth of his glory for messiah to dwell in their hearts by faith, so they can be rooted and founded on love, that they might know the unknowable love of messiah (3:16–19). And here we meet again the concept of the fullness of God (3:19; cf. 1:23), which seems to point to God's glory filling the dry lands as the waters cover the sea when the church loves the way Christ has loved.[92] If any in the audience of the letter are inclined to think this impossible, Paul answers with a doxology: "Now to the one who is able to do abundantly more than all we ask or imagine according to the power at work in us [cf. 1:19–20], to him be glory in the church and in messiah Jesus unto all generations forever and ever, amen" (3:20–21).

The remainder of Paul's letter to the Ephesians is intensely practical: Paul tells the Ephesians what living out the love of Christ for the glory of God looks like. Their unity (Eph. 4:1–7) flows from Christ's conquest and distribution of the "spoils" of war as he gave gifts to the church (4:8).[93] These gifts are the ministers who will lead the church to build itself up in love for the display of God's glory in the world (4:9–16). Paul calls the Ephesians to put off the old man and put on the new man of Christlike self-sacrificial love for others (4:17–32, esp. 22, 24). He calls them to imitate God and walk in love now that they are in the light (5:1–17), to be filled with the Spirit and reflect Christ in their marriages (5:18–33),[94] as they relate to their children (6:1–4), and in their dealings as slaves

[92]In support of this understanding I would appeal to the theme that begins in Eden, from which point Adam was to rule over the earth and bring it into subjection, so that God's glory would fill the earth (cf. Gen. 1:29; Num. 14:21). Adam was expelled from Eden, and God continued to pursue the same goal in Israel, where his glory was to emanate out from the tabernacle and later the temple until it covered the dry lands as the waters cover the sea (cf. Hab. 2:14). God is now pursuing this same agenda, filling the world with his glory, through the church, his new temple (Eph. 2:20–22). See appendix 2 (§6) to chap. 3, "All the Earth Filled with the Knowledge of Yahweh's Glory." Cf. also Timothy G. Gombis, "Being the Fullness of God in Christ by the Spirit: Ephesians 5:18 in Its Epistolary Setting," *TynBul* 53 (2002): 259–71.

[93]See Timothy Gombis, "Cosmic Lordship and Divine Gift-Giving: Psalm 68 in Ephesians 4:8," *NovT* 47 (2005): 367–80, esp. 375: "He is not simply quoting one verse—Ps. 68:19 in abstraction from the remainder of the psalm—but rather appropriating the narrative movement of the entire psalm. In this manner, the author [*sic*] portrays Christ as the victorious Divine Warrior who has the right to give gifts to his people because of his triumphs."

[94]For my attempt to exposit this passage, see James M. Hamilton Jr., "The Mystery of Marriage," in *For the Fame of God's Name: Essays in Honor of John Piper*, ed. Sam Storms and Justin Taylor (Wheaton, IL: Crossway, 2010), 263–69 (253–71). Cf. Timothy Gombis ("A Radically New Humanity: The Function of the *Haustafel* in Ephesians," *JETS* 48 [2005]: 324), who explains that Paul's words are "aimed at counteracting the devastating effects of the powers upon human relationships and in transforming relationships within appropriate hierarchical structures."

and masters (6:5–9), and these instructions can be applied to all structures of authority whether one is slave or free.[95]

God's glory can clearly be seen as the center of Paul's theology in Ephesians, but is this glory mainly seen in salvation through judgment? I contend that it is because it is through the judgment that fell on Christ at the cross that God has saved Jews and Gentiles and united them as a display of his glory (esp. Eph. 2:14–16; 3:10, 21). Moreover, Paul is explicit on the point that Christ's death and resurrection mean the judgment of and triumph over hostile spiritual powers and principalities (1:21; 2:2, 7; 3:10; 4:8).[96] God shows his glory by saving the church through the judgment that fell on Christ, and the death and resurrection of Jesus mean judgment and defeat for Satan and his forces. Paul concludes the letter to the Ephesians by calling the one new man in Christ, the church, to arm himself for the spiritual warfare of standing firm in true beliefs, right actions, proclamation of the gospel,[97] believing God's promises, helmeted by salvation, and wielding the word of God (6:10–17). God will get glory in the church (Eph. 3:21) as the church triumphs over and serves as evidence of God's judgment against the cosmic powers of darkness and spiritual forces of evil in heavenly places (6:12) by faith in Christ (2:8) and a life of good deeds (2:10) that are worthy of their calling (4:1) in imitation of God himself (5:1). Ephesians demonstrates that the glory of God in salvation through judgment is the center of Paul's theology.

2.7 *Philippians*

The cruciform shape of the values Paul articulates in Philippians is not only at variance with the values of ancient Roman Philippi; it is at variance with the tendencies and inclinations of the fleshly impulses of all humans anytime and everywhere.[98] Paul's cruciformed instructions spring from the center of his theology—God's glory in salvation through judgment—and Paul teaches that those who live by the values he advocates become a demonstration of the coming salvation through judgment for God's glory on the day of Christ (Phil. 1:28; 3:17–21). The cruciform lifestyle Paul advocates in Philippians has the imitation of Christ at its heart: he was judged on behalf of others that they might be saved, so that God's glory might be displayed (2:5–11). In his letter to the Philippians, Paul operates from cruciform convictions in the ways he prays (1:3–11), reports his circumstances (1:12–26), calls the Philippians to live (1:27–2:18), speaks of

[95]What Gombis ("A Radically New Humanity," 319) writes of the household code is, in my opinion, applicable to the whole of Ephesians 4–6: Paul "is laying out a manifesto for the New Humanity, painting in broad strokes a vision for how believers ought to conduct themselves in new creation communities, thus epitomizing the triumph of God in Christ."

[96]See further Timothy G. Gombis, "Ephesians 2 as a Narrative of Divine Warfare," *JSNT* 26 (2004): 403–18.

[97]See the discussion in Plummer, *Paul's Understanding of the Church's Mission*, 77–80.

[98]My thinking on the topic of conformity to Christ, especially imitating the way he took up the cross for others, has been stimulated by Gorman, *Apostle of the Crucified Lord*, 118–19, 120–24.

Timothy and Epaphroditus (2:19–30), warns of those who are not conformed to Christ (3:1–3), relates how Christ is being formed in his own person (3:4–14), calls the Philippians to imitate him (3:15–4:9), and thanks them for their support (4:10–20). This examination of Paul's theology in Philippians aims to highlight the way Paul patterns his own life after the example of Christ, explains the way of Jesus, holds forth others who have joined him in following that example, and calls the Philippians to the same lifestyle. This pattern of life reflects, demonstrates, and looks forward to the glory of God in salvation through judgment.

When Paul wrote to the Philippians, he was imprisoned, apparently in Rome (Phil. 1:13; 4:22). Rather than being concerned about his safety, his reputation, and his freedom, he was thanking God for the Philippians, praying for them, and demonstrating his concern for them by writing the letter under discussion here (cf. 1:3–8). In this concern for others at the expense of himself Paul is following the example of Jesus.

The concern for others continues as Paul relates how he prays for the Philippians: he wants their *love* to abound in knowledge and discernment (Phil. 1:9). Specifically, he wants them to be able "to test the things that are superior" (1:10a), and from what he says in the rest of the letter we know what he has in mind. Paul wants them to join him in cruciformity—to follow the one who laid down his life for the spiritual benefit of others by likewise laying down their lives for the spiritual benefit of others. This is a love that rejoices in what is best for others, as Paul clearly takes his joy from the spiritual health of the Philippians and wants them to rejoice in him (cf. 1:3–8, 24–26; 2:16–18; 4:1–3, 10–18). This kind of love will not result in selfish behavior that sinfully exploits others but produces "sincerity and blamelessness for the day of Christ" (1:10b). This kind of love will fill the Philippians "with the fruit of the righteousness that is through Jesus the messiah, for the glory and praise of God" (1:11). God will be glorified when the Philippians live this way because mercy and love condemn selfishness and hate, salvation coming through discerning judgment for God's glory.

Rather than being upset that he has been unjustly imprisoned, Paul rejoices because of the benefit his imprisonment brings to others (Phil. 1:12–18). He rejoices because at his expense other people are hearing the gospel. Even as those trying to make things worse for him "proclaim Christ" (1:17), he is glad for any proclamation of the glory of God in salvation through judgment (1:18). Paul explains his confidence of deliverance—whether release to continue to proclaim Christ or release to depart and be with him (i.e., death)—either way Christ will be honored (1:19–20). When he says "to live is Christ" (1:21a), he means that he is following in the footsteps of Jesus by laying down his life for others. This will mean fruitful labor (1:22a) that will benefit the Philippians (1:24–25), and they will glory in Christ Jesus (1:26). This salvation, which comes for the glory of Christ, comes through the condemnation of the world and its values: so Paul considers death "gain" (1:21b) because it would be better to be with Christ than to continue in this world (1:23), and he only continues so that he can live out Christ by pursuing joy and progress in the faith for other people (1:25). For Paul, life and death are about salvation through judgment for God's glory in Christ.

This cruciformity is precisely what it means to live a life worthy of the gospel of Christ (Phil. 1:27a). Paul wants the Philippians to strive for the gospel (1:27b) by adopting his perspective and doing what he is doing. If they will embrace this cruciform pattern, they will agree that "to live is Christ" (1:21a), and they will suffer for Christ (1:29b) and join Paul in the self-sacrificing struggle for the souls of others (1:30). They will also agree that death is gain (1:21b), which will make them fearless before their opponents (1:28a). Living this way on the basis of the glory of God in the salvation through judgment he accomplished by Christ's death on the cross will enact salvation through judgment in their own experience: the Philippian Christians will become living demonstrations that God will destroy the wicked and save his people (1:28b). The life worthy of the gospel is based on and lives out God's glory in salvation through judgment.

Paul then enumerates the specifics of the glory of God in the lives of believers—the encouragement they have in Christ, the comfort from love, participation in the Spirit, affection, and sympathy (Phil. 2:1); and he calls the Philippians to give him joy by their unity (2:2), again evidencing his love for them through the joy he derives from their experience of God's glory. They are to leave off rivalry and conceit in favor of humble service in the interests of others (2:3–4), and to illustrate this Paul gives them the supreme example of Jesus (2:5–11). Jesus had advantages, but he surrendered them to serve others (2:6–7a).[99] The outrageous thought of a powerful God becoming a weak human (2:7b) is augmented by the humble obedience of Jesus even unto death, and his death was the most humiliating way to die, crucifixion (2:8). Paul is giving Jesus as an example of looking not to one's own interests but to the interests of others (2:4), and Jesus died on behalf of others. Jesus was judged so that others could be saved. This resulted in his exaltation and God's glory: because Jesus served others, God gave him the name above all names (2:9). Every knee will bow to him (2:10), every tongue confess him Lord, and this is to the glory of the Father (2:11). The life that Paul calls the Philippians to live is based on the glory of God in salvation through judgment accomplished in Christ's death on the cross. Gorman writes, "Paul desires that the hymnic story (2:6–11) that he and the Philippians use to proclaim the exalted crucified Jesus as Lord is also the story of their lives as

[99]See especially Denny Burk, "On the Articular Infinitive in Philippians 2:6: A Grammatical Note with Christological Implications," *TynBul* 55 (2004): 253–74; and Burk, *Articular Infinitives*, 137–39.

citizens . . . . As such, that story they sing must constantly form and re-form their common life."[100]

Paul explains that the Philippians living this way will display God's glory as they shine like stars in the midst of a crooked and depraved generation (Phil. 2:15). God is working in them to do it, so they should live this way to work out their salvation (2:12–13). The symptoms of the life worthy of the gospel include a peculiar rejection of grumbling and questioning (2:14), and those who live this way enact God's glory as they experience the joys of salvation through the condemnation of sinful ways in their transformed lifestyles (2:12–18).[101]

Then come positive and negative examples. Timothy is genuinely concerned for the welfare of the Philippians and seeks the interests of Jesus (Phil. 2:19–24). Similarly, though Epaphroditus was so sick he was near death, his concern was for how others would be distressed by his illness. He put his life on the line for Christ's sake (2:25–30). The negative examples are those who insist on circumcision and boast in the advantages of their ancestry or accomplishments (3:1–6). Here Paul describes his own cruciformity. Like Jesus, Paul has claims to unparalleled standing (3:4–6), but also like Jesus, Paul has abandoned whatever stature these things would give him so that he can benefit other people. He considers his accomplishments and advantages loss for Christ's sake (3:7), explaining that knowing Jesus is so much better than his reasons for fleshly confidence that such confidence becomes rubbish (3:8).[102] However confidence in the flesh might stand one before men, it would not give Paul righteousness. The only way he can get that is through faith in Christ (3:9).[103] Paul recognizes that before God the fleshly confidence style of righteousness that would count in the eyes of men will only lead to condemnation. Through his perception of that judgment he sees his need for the righteousness that comes from God through faith in Christ and he is saved (3:9),[104] and his preference for God and Christ over any glory he might get from men exalts and glorifies the God of his salvation. He is conforming himself to the death of Jesus for the benefit of others (3:10), so that, like Jesus, he can be raised from the dead (3:11).

Paul calls the mature to think this way (Phil. 3:15), and he calls the Philippians to imitate him and others who are already imitating him (3:17). This exalts

[100] Gorman, *Apostle of the Crucified Lord*, 449–50.

[101] Plummer, *Paul's Understanding of the Church's Mission*, 74–77, shows that this also entails "an offering of the gospel to those who do not presently adhere to it—a proclamation of the gospel by the Philippian church."

[102] Cf. Seifrid, *Christ, Our Righteousness*, 17: "Paul's conversion involved two dimensions. . . . He came to understand that God's judgment rests on the entire human race . . . . Concomitantly, the mercy of God thereby became the mercy of *God* for Paul."

[103] Cf. Schreiner, *Paul*, 200: "Philippians 3:9 refers to 'the righteousness from God' . . . . The contrast between 'the righteousness from God' and 'my own righteousness' in this verse—and Paul's contrast between his devotion to the law and his newfound allegiance to Christ—indicates that 'the righteousness from God' here is a divine gift. It is a righteousness that comes *from* God and is accessed by faith."

[104] Similarly Vickers, *Jesus' Blood and Righteousness*, 205–11.

not Paul but Christ, for Paul himself is imitating Jesus (cf. 1 Cor. 11:1). Those who do not give their lives to benefit others spiritually "walk as enemies of the cross of Christ. Their end is destruction" (Phil. 3:18b–19a ESV). But those who follow Paul as he follows Christ await "a Savior, the Lord Jesus Christ, who will transform our lowly body to be like his glorious body, by the power that enables him to subject all things to himself" (3:20b–21 ESV). On that day, salvation will come through judgment for God's glory in Christ. Paul calls the Philippians to unite (4:1–5), to pray with gratitude (4:6), to be guarded by the peace of God (4:7), with minds set on the specifics of God's glory (4:8), as they imitate Paul's own cruciformity (4:9). Like Paul, they will know the one who meets every need from his riches in glory in Christ (4:10–19). They will thereby join Paul in ascribing glory to the Father forever (4:20) by the grace of the Lord Jesus (4:23).

2.8 Colossians

Either the church at Colossae was threatened by false teachers, or Paul sought to equip them against what he suspected would threaten them.[105] Paul had not been to the church himself (Col. 2:1) but had learned of the fruitfulness and growth of the gospel in Colossae from Epaphras, who took the gospel to them and told Paul of its success (1:6–7). Paul warns the Christians in Colossae against the deception of plausible arguments (2:4), against the captivity that could result from "philosophy and empty deceit according to the tradition of men, according to the elements of the world and not according to Christ" (2:8). Paul also warns the church against those who would judge them or disqualify them on the basis of their adherence to aspects of the Mosaic law (2:16) and what appears to be Jewish mysticism (2:18–19). Paul's question in Colossians 2:20 may indicate that these false teachings have already crept into the church. Whatever the precise nature of this Colossian heresy, we have Paul's strategic response to it.

Paul's encouragement to the embattled church at Colossae is laser-like in its focus on exalting Christ. Paul combats the opponents of the gospel in Colossians by proclaiming the glory of God in Christ, and at the center of his proclamation is the glory of Christ as the agent of God's salvation through judgment. The density of this letter may never be fully unpacked, but my purpose here can be accomplished by summarizing Paul's focus on the glory of Christ, on the Colossians' participation in Christ by faith, and on the salvation God has accomplished through judgment in Christ.

---

[105]For discussion of what can be known of the false teaching, see Douglas J. Moo, *The Letters to the Colossians and to Philemon*, Pillar New Testament Commentary (Grand Rapids: Eerdmans, 2008), 46–60; and Peter T. O'Brien, *Colossians, Philemon*, WBC (Waco, TX: Thomas Nelson, 1982), xxx–xli.

2.8.1 The Glory of Christ in Colossians

Paul evidently thought his announcement of the glory of Jesus the best way to expose and disarm the paltry deception being peddled to the church in Colossae. Having thanked God for the faith, hope, and love with which the Colossians responded to the gospel (Col. 1:3–8), Paul tells them how he prays for them. It seems that Paul first reports what he prays (1:9–12), then seeks to be used of the Lord as part of the answer to that prayer (1:13–20).

Paul prays that the Colossians will "be filled with the knowledge of [God's] will in all wisdom and spiritual insight" (Col. 1:9), so they will walk in a way worthy of God and please him by the good works they do as they grow in the knowledge of God (1:10), being strengthened according to the might of God's glory for perseverance and patience (1:11), giving thanks with joy because of what God has done for them (1:12). Paul then sets out to fill them with exactly what he told them he was asking God to put in them: the knowledge of God's will in all spiritual wisdom and understanding (1:9). Paul seeks to be the answer to his own prayer by extolling the redemption God accomplished in Christ (1:13–14), and then heightening their appreciation of this redemption by raising Christ in their esteem (1:15–20).

Paul heralds Jesus as the "image of the invisible God, the firstborn over all creation" (Col. 1:15), then explains that this is so because all things were created by him—in heaven and on earth, visible and invisible, thrones, powers, rulers, or authorities—"all things were created by him and for him" (1:16). Paul sings that Christ "is before all things, and all things in him hold together, and he is the head of the body, the church; he is the beginning, the firstborn from the dead, that in everything he might have preeminence" (1:17–18). Thus, Christ is the image of the invisible God, and he stands before God the way a firstborn stood before his father in the ancient world—in first place, with inheritance rights.[106] Moreover, Christ is the Creator, through whom and for whom everything exists. He holds the universe together; he is the beginning of creation and of new creation as the Firstborn from the dead. But Paul is not finished yet: he grounds the preeminence of Christ in the fact that "in him all the fullness was pleased to dwell" (1:19). Through Christ, who lacked nothing of deity, God reconciled "all things to himself, making peace through the blood of his cross" (1:20). This hymn praises Christ as the image of the invisible God, the agent of creation for whom all is, the preeminent Head of the church and ruler of the world, the instigator of the new creation as Firstborn from the dead, the one who is fully God, and through whom God accomplished reconciliation. From creation to new creation, from church

[106] For further discussion, see Moo, *Letters to the Colossians and to Philemon*, 119.

to world, from humanity to deity, from reconciliation to peace, Christ is preeminent in all.

God has reconciled his enemies to himself in Christ (Col. 1:21). The Colossians' hope of glory is that Christ is in them (1:27). All the treasures of wisdom and knowledge are hidden in Christ (2:3). "All the fullness of deity" dwells "bodily" in Christ (2:9), the Colossians have been filled in him, and he is "the head of all rule and authority" (2:10). Christ is the substance of which the requirements of the Mosaic law were but a shadow (2:16–17). The body, the church, grows because of its vital union with the Head, Christ (2:19). Christ is seated at the right hand of God (3:1). The life of the Colossians is hidden in Christ, who is their life (3:3–4).[107] Among those being renewed in his image (3:9), "Christ is all in all" (3:10). Christ is so great, Paul instructs the Colossian Christians to do everything in his name (3:17), for him and not man (3:23), for in all they do they serve Christ (3:24). The glory of Christ is such that by extolling it, Paul expects its reality to eclipse all other concerns, including those that come from people pushing plausible arguments (2:4, 8) or legalistic accomplishments (2:18, 21–23). Paul answers deceitful philosophy (2:8) and self-made religion (2:23) with the glory of Christ.

2.8.2 The Colossians "in Christ" by Faith

Everything the Colossians need comes from Christ, to whom they are united by faith (Col. 1:4, 22; 2:5, 7, 12). The believers in Colossae were dead in their sins and in their spiritually uncircumcised state (2:13a). They also had a rap sheet, a list of transgressions standing against them (2:14a). At that time they were alive to the world (2:20b), and their home was the domain of darkness (1:13). Then through faith (2:12) God made them alive and forgave their transgressions (2:13b), the legal demands of which were nailed to the cross (2:14b). As they were made alive with Christ, they simultaneously died to the world (2:20a; 3:3). This death to the world and resurrection life in Christ is symbolized in baptism, whereby the Colossian Christians were buried with Christ and raised with him *through faith* (2:12).[108] The problem of their uncircumcision was answered by their regeneration: "You, who were dead in your trespasses and the uncircumcision of your flesh, God made alive together with him" (2:13 ESV). Thus, the circumcision they experienced, which was not made with hands, by which they put off the body of flesh, this "circumcision of Christ" (2:11) is not baptism but regeneration. Baptism is a symbol of what has happened to them by faith. By faith they have been united with Christ in his death and resurrection, and their death to the world and resurrection to life in Christ is symbolized in baptism

[107]For wider discussion of the theme, see M. A. Seifrid, "In Christ," *DPL*, 433–36.

[108]See the studies in Thomas R. Schreiner and Shawn D. Wright, eds., *Believer's Baptism: Sign of the New Covenant in Christ*, NACSBT (Nashville: Broadman & Holman, 2006).

(2:12). No ritual washing accomplishes union with Christ; only faith does that. Baptism, then, is a picture of what has happened to those who are united to Christ by faith.

Table 6.1. "In Christ" in Colossians

1:14	in whom we have redemption
1:16	in him all things were created
1:19	in him all the fullness of God was pleased to dwell
1:22	reconciled in his body of flesh
2:3	in whom are hidden all the treasures of wisdom and knowledge
2:6	walk in him
2:7	rooted and built up in him
2:9	in him all the fullness of deity dwells bodily
2:10	and you have been filled in him
2:11	you were circumcised in him
2:12	in him you were raised up
2:15	triumphing over them in him
3:20	pleasing in the Lord
4:7	fellow servant in the Lord
4:17	the ministry that you have received in the Lord

2.8.3 God Accomplished Salvation through Judgment in the Glorious Christ

The redemption God accomplished in Christ was his triumph over "the authority of darkness" so that he "rescued us . . . and transferred us to the Kingdom of the Son of his love" (Col. 1:13). Paul explains that this redemption entails the forgiveness of sins (1:14), and both aspects of this redemption—triumph over the authority of darkness and forgiveness of sins—entail salvation through judgment, as Paul details later in the letter.

God has nullified the demands for justice that stood against believers by the death of Christ (Col. 2:13–14). The debts are paid. God's justice is satisfied. His former enemies are reconciled and made holy by the death of Jesus (1:21–22). Through the judgment that resulted in the death of Christ God saved believers that they might live "in the name of the Lord Jesus" (3:17).

Through the judgment that resulted in the death of Jesus God also "disarmed the rulers and authorities and put them to open shame, by triumphing over them in him" (Col. 2:15 ESV). This means that the judgment that fell on Jesus resulted in a judgment against the kingdom and agents of darkness, so that believers are redeemed from that kingdom and their sins are forgiven. Salvation comes through judgment for God's glory.

Yet another aspect of salvation through judgment for God's glory in Colossians comes in the condemnation of worldly wisdom. The Colossian Christians are not to evaluate arguments by human standards but are to measure all things by Christ (Col. 2:8; 3:15–16).

Paul's household code goes in this direction of rejecting the flesh and the world in favor of Christlike wisdom. The call for wives to submit to their husbands (Col. 3:18a) not only stands counter to twenty-first-century culture; it stands counter to all human cultures because all human cultures are under the curse of Genesis 3:16. Women are cursed with a desire to control their husbands the way sin wanted to control Cain—to set his agenda and dictate his actions (Gen. 4:7). Paul calls women to reject the impulse of the flesh and submit to their husbands, for this is the appropriate way for people "in Christ" to live (Col. 3:18b). So also the curse of Genesis 3:16 says that husbands will "rule over" their wives the way Cain was called to "master" sin with a take-no-prisoners kind of intolerance toward evil inclinations (Gen. 4:7). That is the way the flesh leads husbands to treat their wives, but Paul calls husbands to love their wives and not treat them harshly (Col. 3:19). A child's flesh leads him to disregard his parents, but children who would please the Lord must obey their parents (3:20). The fleshly tendency of fathers to exasperate their children is to be checked by a fatherly concern not to discourage his children (3:21). With slaves and masters, slaves are to think not of themselves but of the Lord, and masters are to treat their slaves with justice and fairness, for the Lord will judge them (3:22–4:1). As worldliness is rejected and Christlikeness embraced, salvation through judgment for God's glory is displayed in the condemnation of the "wisdom" that comes from the flesh and the world and the corresponding enactment of behavior that pleases the Lord and displays his justice and mercy, goodness and kindness, truth and love.

Paul also lives out the glory of God in salvation through judgment as he rejoices in his sufferings for the sake of the Colossians (Col. 1:24a). The statement about "filling up what is lacking in Christ's afflictions for the sake of his body, that is, the church" (1:24b) is to be understood as Paul's embrace of his portion of the "messianic woes" (see table 6.2).[109] Paul indicates here and elsewhere that sufferings are necessary before the consummation of the age to come when the kingdom will be inherited, and this is in keeping with Old Testament precursors and other New Testament teaching (see also §3.4.2 in this chapter, below).

[109]See especially O'Brien, *Colossians, Philemon*, 78–80. *Pace* Plummer, *Paul's Understanding of the Church's Mission*, 131–32, who rejects this understanding because "the apostle is writing to a Gentile congregation that he has apparently never visited or written to in the past (Col 1:3–8)." The same could be said of Paul's comments to the Thessalonians and Peter's to the churches he addresses in his first letter. In both cases, the churches are called to a Christlikeness similar to what Paul describes here, which in my view establishes the "messianic woes" interpretation as the most likely. I should also note that I do not think the "messianic woes" view and the view Plummer adopts, which is that Paul's suffering gives a visible copy of Christ's (132) are mutually exclusive. In fact I think they work together: Jesus sets the pattern followed by his disciples, who participate in the messianic woes as they follow their Lord.

Table 6.2. The Messianic Woes in the Old and New Testaments

Persecution of Saints	Judgment on Persecutor	Kingdom of God
Dan. 7:25: Horn persecutes the saints	Dan. 7:26: Judgment on the horn	7:27: Kingdom of God
Dan. 8:9–13: Little horn persecutes saints		Dan. 8:14: Restoration
Dan. 9:26b–27a: Abominations and desolations	Dan. 9:27b: Judgment on the desolator	Dan. 9:24: (After the seventy weeks) everlasting righteousness
Dan. 11:31: Abomination of desolation; 11:33–35, people of God endure.	Dan. 11:45: Persecutor comes to an end.	Dan. 12:1–3: Deliverance of God's people
Matt. 24:8–9: Believers hated and persecuted; 24:13: perseverance leads to salvation.	Matt. 24:27–30: Judgment and glory	Matt. 24:30–31: Glory and salvation
Mark 13:5–8: Birth pangs	Mark 13:19–23: The Lord cuts short the tribulation.	Mark 13:24–27: Son of Man in glory to save
Luke 21:5–24: Desolation and distress through the times of the Gentiles	Luke 21:25–27: Son of Man coming with power and glory	Luke 21:28: Redemption draws near for the people of Jesus.
John 16:33: "In the world you will have tribulation, but be courageous: I have overcome the world."		
Acts 14:22: "Through many tribulations we must enter the kingdom of God."		
Rom. 8:18: "The sufferings of the present time are not worthy to be compared to the coming glory to be revealed in us."		
2 Cor. 4:17: "For our momentary, light affliction works for us an eternal weight of glory beyond all comparison."		
Col. 1:24: "I fill up in my flesh what is lacking in the afflictions of the messiah for the sake of his body."		
1 Thess. 3:3–4: "For you yourselves know that we were appointed for [these tribulations]; for even when we were with you, we were telling you beforehand that we were about to be in tribulation, just as it also happened and you know it."		
2 Thess. 2:3–4: The rebellion—the lawless son of destruction proclaims himself God.	2 Thess. 2:8: Jesus will kill him with the sword of his mouth.	2 Thess. 2:13–14: Salvation and glory
1 Tim. 4:1–3: False teaching from deceitful spirits and demon doctrines in the last times, hypocrisy of liars with seared consciences forbidding marriage and demanding abstinence from foods		
2 Tim. 1:8–12: "Join in suffering for the gospel . . . I was appointed . . . for which reason I also suffer these things. . . . he is able to guard my deposit for that day."		
2 Tim. 2:3, 8–10: "Share in suffering as a good soldier of messiah Jesus. . . . according to my gospel, for which I suffer . . . on account of this I endure everything . . ."		
Heb. 10:32–38: "You endured great trial with sufferings . . . tribulation . . . . endurance . . . . the one who comes will come and he will not delay . . ."		
James 1:2: "Consider it all joy, my brothers, when you fall into various trials."		
1 Peter (see table 6.6: "Suffering and Exaltation in 1 Peter")		
Rev. 1:9: "I John, your brother and partner in the tribulation and kingdom and endurance in Jesus . . ."		
Rev. 2:10: "For ten days you will have tribulation."		
Rev. 6:11: ". . . until the full number of their fellow servants and brothers who are about to be killed as they were was filled."		
Rev. 7:14: "These are the ones who come from the great tribulation."		
Rev. 11:4–11: Two witnesses prophesy, are killed, then are resurrected.		
Cf. *1 En.* 47:1–4; 99:4; *2 Bar.* 30:1–2; 48:30–37; 70:2; *Sib. Or.* 2:154–74		

It is necessary for believers to pass through these woes and then enter glory, just as it was "necessary that the Christ should suffer . . . and enter into his glory" (Luke 24:26 ESV). The church, then, is following in the footsteps of the messiah (1 Pet. 2:21), passing through appointed afflictions (1 Thess. 3:3–4). In this pattern, seen in Israel's prophets, in the messiah, and in the church, there is a suffering of judgment: the prophets, the messiah, and the church are all judged and condemned by their contemporaries. Faithfully enduring this false judgment unexpectedly exposes God's true judgment, which is that those the world has condemned are approved by God, while those condemning the approved are under God's justice. In their faithfulness, the faithful who are judged by the world condemn the world (cf. Heb. 11:7). Through all this judgment salvation comes to those who believe. In spite of the world's condemnation, they trust God, and because of God's triumph in the death and resurrection of Jesus, they are saved by faith. This means that God has worked salvation in the messiah through judgment for his glory—glory seen in the wisdom, in the justice, and in the mercy. The Old Testament believers and the believing new covenant church also participate in this pattern of salvation through judgment, as their faithfulness to God and his anointed brings them under the condemnation of the world, through which the world is condemned and they are saved. God is glorified as his people trust him through the messianic woes, and he will save them through these judgments.

2.9 First Thessalonians

Luke's account of Paul's visit to Thessalonica (Acts 17:1–9) shows Paul explaining from the Old Testament the necessity of the suffering and rising of the messiah, which Paul sees fulfilled in Jesus (17:3), Jewish opposition that resulted in mob violence (17:5), and false charges designed to be politically damaging to Christians (17:6–8). The city authorities, however, only took money as security from a Christian named Jason; after that the Christians were released (17:6, 8–9). Having been there for some three Sabbaths (17:2), Paul was sent on by the new believers (17:10), apparently to get him out of harm's way.

This background fits with and informs what we see in Paul's letters to the Thessalonians. The opposition to the Christians in Thessalonica evidently continued after Paul left, and Paul was concerned that "the tempter" might render his labor vain (1 Thess. 3:5). In this statement, Paul is aligning the forces at work against the Thessalonian Christians with the one who repeatedly hindered his attempts to get back to Thessalonica: Satan (2:18). The statements Paul makes to the Thessalonians reflect his perspective, which is that there are two kingdoms at war in a cosmic, spiritual conflict. The rebels are led by Satan (2:18), the tempter (3:5), with human allies from Jews and Gentiles.

Satan's Gentile allies are the countrymen of the Thessalonian Christians who afflict the Christians (1 Thess. 2:14). Satan's Jewish allies are those "who killed both the Lord Jesus and the prophets, and drove us out, and displease God and oppose all mankind by hindering us from speaking to the Gentiles that they might be saved" (2:15–16a ESV). The rebel strategy is one of deception, persecution, defilement, opposition, and affliction (1:6, 9; 2:3, 14–16, 18; 3:3–4; 4:5–6; 5:3, 7). The fact that Satan's allies are both Jews and Gentiles demonstrates that this is not an issue of ethnicity but one of allegiance. Paul's comments are neither anti-Semitic nor anti-Gentile, but they are anti-Satan and his seed.[110]

Paul's statements on this conflict demonstrate the centrality of the glory of God in salvation through judgment in his theology, and this is reflected in 1 Thessalonians. God has made salvation from Satan and his rebel forces available through Jesus (1 Thess. 5:9), "who died for us" that "we might live with him" (5:10; cf. 4:14). Paul's references to "our gospel" (1:5; 2:2, 4, 8, 9) and "the word of the Lord" (1:8; 2:13 [2x]; cf. 4:15) that the Thessalonians "believed" (1:3, 8; 2:13; 3:5, 6; 5:8) in 1 Thessalonians indicate that though he does not go into more detail on it in this letter, this is the same gospel he has explained in other letters (e.g., Rom. 3:21–26).[111] This is the gospel whereby God has demonstrated his glory in salvation through judgment. God's judgment is satisfied by Christ's death on the cross, so that those who confess him as Lord and believe he was raised will be saved (cf. Rom. 10:9–10). Salvation comes through judgment, and simultaneously, God triumphs over Satan and his forces through the salvation through judgment at the cross (cf. Col. 2:14–15).

In 1 Thessalonians it is as though Satan has been thrown down by Christ, the seed of the woman, has realized that his time is short, and viciously makes war on the rest of the woman's seed (cf. Rev. 12:1–17). In spite of the opposition he encounters from Satan and his seed, Paul goes about proclaiming the gospel (cf. 1 Thess. 1:5; 2:2–13; 4:14–15; 5:9–10). As he does this, Paul is imitating Jesus, who gave himself for others. Paul boldly proclaims the gospel at the expense of his ease and safety for the benefit of other people (e.g., 2:2, 8).

Those who believe Paul's proclamation exercise salvation through judgment for God's glory in the present and then become testimonies to its future realities. They exercise it in the present as they judge idols to be worthless, turn from them, and through the condemnation and rejection of idolatry are saved to enjoy the

[110]Bell (*The Irrevocable Call of God*, 61) fails to understand this and wrongly concludes that "the views expressed in 1 Thes. 2.13–16 on the Jews cannot be reconciled with Romans 9–11."

[111]At the conclusion of a discussion of "Salvation as Deliverance from the Wrath of God through Christ's Atoning Death," Seyoon Kim writes, "Therefore, 1 Thess 1:10; 4:14; 5:9–10, 23 contain basically the same thought as the classical expression in Rom 3:24–26 of Paul's gospel of justification by faith in Christ's atoning death" (*Paul and the New Perspective*, 88; cf. 86–88). See also the explanation of "word" as "gospel" in Michael W. Pahl, *Discerning the "Word of the Lord": The "Word of the Lord" in 1 Thessalonians 4:15*, LNTS (New York: T&T Clark, 2009), 125–39. Pahl concludes that "the most probable referent of the phrase ἐν λόγῳ κυρίου [1 Thess. 4:15] is the salvific message about Jesus centred on his death and resurrection" (139).

living God (1 Thess. 1:9). They become testimonies to the future, apocalyptic[112] glory of God in salvation through judgment as they imitate those who have gone before them. These who have gone before are the seed of the woman who have suffered at the hands of the seed of the serpent: the prophets and Jesus (2:15a), Paul (2:15b), and the churches in Judea (2:14). Thus Paul tells the Thessalonians that they have become "imitators of us and of the Lord, for you received the word in much affliction, with the joy of the Holy Spirit" (1:6 ESV). They have followed in the footsteps of Jesus (cf. 1 Pet. 2:21). Paul follows Christ in this and calls others to follow him in this same pattern, or *type*, of discipleship (cf. 1 Cor. 11:1). This is a pattern of faithfulness to God in faith, hope, and love in the face of satanic opposition. The Thessalonians have followed the example set for them by Jesus and Paul, and in doing so they have become a *type*, or example, for "all the believers in Macedonia and Achaia" (1 Thess. 1:7). Like Peter (1 Pet. 2:21), Paul believes that those who follow Christ are "destined for this" (1 Thess. 3:3; 5:18), and he warns the Thessalonians that it is coming (3:4).

As the seed of the serpent makes war on the seed of the woman (cf. 1 Thess. 2:14–16), the response of the seed of the woman testifies to the past, present, and future realities of the glory of God in salvation through judgment. The past reality is the triumph of God in Christ, on which the faith of the Thessalonians is based (1:3; 3:5–6). What God has done in Christ frees the Thessalonians to live by faith and enact the present reality of God's glory in salvation through judgment, which is evident in their love for one another and even for their persecutors (1:3; 2:12; 3:6; 4:2–8, 9–12, 13–18; 5:8, 12–28). This love exposes and overcomes the hatred and brutality and shameful conduct of Satan and his seed. The future reality of the glory of God in salvation through judgment is focused on the future visitation of God's wrath (1:10). The rebel seed of the serpent are filling up the full measure of their iniquity for that great day of God's wrath (2:16). Jesus will execute this wrath on "the day of the Lord" (5:2), when he will bring sudden destruction on his enemies who have troubled his people (5:3), simultaneously—at his coming—delivering those who believe the gospel and imitate his patient endurance in faithfulness to God (1:10; 2:19; 4:13, 16–17; 5:9, 23).[113]

The faith, love, and hope of the Thessalonian believers is grounded in and enacting the manifestation of the glory of God in salvation through judgment at the cross, and in their endurance of persecution and affliction they are looking forward to vindication at the coming of Christ. This causes God's glory to be "sounded forth" from them (1 Thess. 1:8),[114] and it makes them Paul's joy as he

[112]Gorman provides a definition: "Apocalyptic may be defined as a worldview about the meaning and goal of history, understood as a cosmic battle between God and the forces of evil, that is communicated through visions and other forms of unusual revelations" (*Apostle of the Crucified Lord*, 22).

[113]Similarly Marshall, *New Testament Theology*, 244.

[114]For the light this text sheds on the role of the Thessalonians in spreading the gospel message, see Plummer, *Paul's Understanding of the Church's Mission*, 60–63.

rejoices in their steadfastness and claims the Thessalonians as his glory (2:19–20; 3:8–9). This is not a glory that is somehow selfish or increases his standing in the eyes of men (2:3–6), but rather the Thessalonians are Paul's glory precisely in their display of God's glory. He takes his joy and standing from their progress in the faith. Paul concludes this letter with what amounts to an announcement of his recognition of the scriptural status of what he has written to the Thessalonians: "I put you under oath before the Lord to have this letter read to all the brothers" (5:27).

2.10 Second Thessalonians

Paul's second letter to the church at Thessalonica again shows him ministering from the center of his theology: the glory of God in salvation through judgment. Paul first assures the Thessalonians that God will show his glory in salvation through judgment (2 Thessalonians 1). Paul then gives them evidence that history has not yet reached the climactic moment of salvation through judgment for God's glory (2 Thessalonians 2). Finally, he instructs the church how to live as that day approaches (2 Thessalonians 3).

Paul agrees with the teaching of John that Christians are "in" God and Christ (2 Thess. 1:1; cf. John 14:20; 15:1–11; 17:21, 26).[115] He wants them to experience grace from God and Christ (2 Thess. 1:2), and he thanks God for the way their confidence in God's reliability (faith) is increasing, as is their conformity to the way God treats others (love), and these qualities are verified by the steadfastness of the Thessalonian believers through the messianic woes of persecution and affliction (1:3–4).

Paul states that the steadfast faith of the Thessalonians, even though they are suffering (2 Thess. 1:4; cf. table 6.2), gives "evidence of the righteous judgment of God" (1:5 ESV). He explains what he means by saying that God will

> repay the ones afflicting you with affliction and you the ones being afflicted with rest, with us, at the revelation of the Lord Jesus from heaven with the angels of his power in a fire of flame, giving vengeance to the ones who do not know God and who do not obey the gospel of our Lord Jesus; these will undergo the penalty as everlasting destruction away from the presence of the Lord and from the glory of his might, when he comes to be glorified among his holy ones and to be marveled at among all those who have believed. (1:6b–10b)

Paul here encourages the afflicted Thessalonians with the truth that God is going to be glorified when he saves them through judgment. They have already been saved through the judgment that fell on Christ for God's glory (cf. 2 Thess. 1:3, 10b, 14a), and when Jesus comes (1:7b) they will be saved through the judg-

[115]Cf. Ellis, *Christ and the Future in New Testament History*, 86.

ment he brings on their enemies (1:8). The justice that Jesus visits on that day will be an awesome display of God's glory and power: it will be God's repaying afflicters with affliction (1:6) and Jesus revealed with the angels of his power (1:7), with flaming fire inflicting vengeance on rebels (1:8), and their punishment will never end (1:9). At the same time, this will be the moment when God shows his glory in Christ by his manifest power to deliver afflicted and persecuted believers: their afflicters will be repaid (1:6), they will be granted relief (1:7), and they will enjoy the presence of the Lord and the glory of his might (1:9b), glorifying Jesus and marveling at him (1:10). This display of the glory of God in Christ in the salvation of his people through the judgment of their enemies is what Paul has in mind when he speaks of "the righteous judgment of God" (1:5). Paul knows the Thessalonians will be those who glorify Jesus and marvel at him (1:10a–b) "because our testimony was believed by you" (1:10c). Paul prays for the Thessalonians so that they will experience this glory (1:11a), and his prayer is that God will make them worthy of this calling and fulfill their desires to do good (1:11b), that Jesus might be glorified in them, and that they might experience that glory, by the grace of God and Christ (1:12).

Evidently the Thessalonians have been troubled by false information regarding "the day of the Lord" (2 Thess. 2:2c), which Paul equates with the Lord's "coming" (2:1a), when the decisive moment of salvation through judgment for God's glory described in 2 Thessalonians 1:7b–10b will take place. Paul does not want the Thessalonians to be alarmed or shaken by a false spirit, a false message, or even a letter that seems to come from him. It should be noted that the apostle here recognizes that letters forged in his name are a possibility, and he equips his churches with ways to discern between what is authentic and what is not. Therefore, if any forgery were accepted as a genuine Pauline letter, we would have to conclude that the churches failed to practice discernment. In addition, it would seem that Paul's emphatic signings of his name are also intended to guard Christians against deception (cf. 1 Cor. 16:21; 2 Cor. 10:1; Gal. 5:2; 6:11; Eph. 3:1; Col. 1:23; 4:18; 1 Thess. 2:18; 2 Thess. 3:17; Philem. 1:19).[116] Paul wants the churches to be guarded against deceptive ideas regarding messages that come to

[116]*Contra* Karl Paul Donfried, *Paul, Thessalonica, and Early Christianity* (Grand Rapids: Eerdmans, 2002), 46–47: "2 Thessalonians is not from the hand of Paul . . . . We understand 2 Thessalonians to be non-Pauline in the technical sense." Donfried's contorted explanation that 2 Thess. 2:2 refers to a misunderstanding of 1 Thessalonians fails to account for the word ὡς in the phrase referring to a "letter, as though from us" (NRSV) (54–55). No more successful is his appeal to "corporate personality" as a legitimating rationale for the forger who, in his view, added the Pauline autograph in 2 Thess. 3:17 (55). Donfried acknowledges the illegitimacy of the deception this would involve when he writes, "Certainly a letter from Timothy alone would not carry the same weight or be as effective in refuting distortions directed primarily at Paul" (56). Donfried's views amount to an uncritical rejection of primary source data in favor of an explanation (Paul did not write 2 Thessalonians) that is nothing more than a scholarly fad in the modern West. Maarten J. J. Menken's argument for pseudonymity is no more convincing that Donfried's (*2 Thessalonians: Facing the End with Sobriety* [New York: Routledge, 1994], 27–43). Which will it be? An explanation that fits the primary sources, or an explanation that fits the guild's "critical" orthodoxy?

them, and his concern in this instance is to protect them against false messages concerning the day of the Lord (2 Thess. 2:1–2).

Paul tells the Thessalonians that "the rebellion" and "revelation" of the "man of lawlessness, the son of destruction" will precede "that day" (2 Thess. 2:3). In 2 Thessalonians 2:3–8 Paul seems to interpret Daniel 11:36–45 and other biblical passages (cf. Dan. 7:24b–27; 8:9–14; 9:26b–27; 12:1–3, 11–12) to point toward a final enemy, "whom the Lord Jesus will destroy by the breath of his mouth and will nullify by the manifestation of his coming" (2 Thess. 2:8b). Paul then explains the roles that Satan and God play in ensuring that there will be objects of wrath on whom God will display his justice (2:9–12). Just as the declaration of the judgment Jesus will bring (2 Thess. 1:6–10) was accompanied by the deliverance of his people in the first chapter, so also salvation follows the description of judgment in the second: again Paul thanks God for choosing the Thessalonians for salvation (2:13; cf. 1:3). They were called to salvation through the gospel that they might experience the glory of Christ (2:14). Their final salvation will come through the judgment of the man of lawlessness and those who do his will, and when Jesus accomplishes this, he will be glorified (2:3–14).[117] On the basis of these truths, Paul evidences his convictions regarding the reality of both human responsibility and divine sovereignty, calling the Thessalonians to stand firm and praying that God would enable them to do just that (2:15–17).

At this point we can see that the moment when Jesus comes to judge his enemies and deliver his people is the burden of these first two chapters of 2 Thessalonians. Paul describes this future moment when God will be glorified in salvation through judgment accomplished by Jesus in 2 Thessalonians 1, then assures the Thessalonians that it has not happened by showing them what must precede it in 2 Thessalonians 2.

Paul concludes this letter to the Thessalonians by telling them how they should respond to the truth that God is going to be glorified in the salvation through judgment he will accomplish at the coming of Jesus. They should pray for Paul so that the Lord's word will make swift progress and be glorified (2 Thess. 3:1), so that he will be delivered from opponents in the present (3:2). Paul extols the Lord's faithfulness (3:3), tells the Thessalonians he is confident that the Lord will enable them to obey (3:4), and prays that their hearts will be directed to the love of God and the endurance of Christ (3:5). Paul has heard that some of the Thessalonians are lazy (3:11), so having urged separation from those who are unrepentant in their laziness (3:6), having given himself and his coworkers as an

[117] Cf. the early Christian interpretation of the events of the end in *Did.* 16:3–8, where "the world-deceiver will appear as the Son of God, and he will do signs and wonders, and the earth will be given over into his hand, and he will do disgusting things which have never been done before" (16:4). There is a test on humanity in 16:5, and many fall away. Three signs appear in 16:6: heaven opens, the trumpet sounds, and the dead are raised. *Did.* 16:7 says the same thing as Rev. 20:4, asserting that not all the dead are raised but only the saints. Then *Did.* 16:8 says the Lord will come on the clouds of heaven, in fulfillment of Dan. 7:13.

example of hardworking diligence (3:7–10a), and having reminded them of his rule that those who do not work do not eat (3:10b), he encourages all to work quietly and earn their own keep (3:12). With final instructions regarding church discipline (3:13–15) and his closing authentic greeting (3:16–18), Paul concludes this letter that centers on the glory of God in salvation through judgment that the messiah has accomplished on the cross and will accomplish again on the day of the Lord.

2.11 First Timothy

Paul wrote what we know as 1 Timothy[118] so that if he was delayed in getting to Ephesus, Timothy would "know how it is necessary to conduct oneself in the house of God, which is the church of the living God, the pillar and buttress of the truth" (1 Tim. 3:14–15). Paul begins by addressing the problem of false teaching that Timothy faces, and Paul counters the false teaching with the gospel (1 Timothy 1). From there Paul gives specific instructions about living out the gospel as people of different genders, ages, and life stations in relationship to one another in church. Paul first addresses men (2:1–8) and women in general (2:9–15).[119] He then turns to the leadership of the church: first male overseers (3:1–7), then men (3:8–10) and women (3:11) deacons (3:8–13),[120] basing his instructions about how church life is to go (3:14–15) on what God has done in Christ (3:16). Paul explains the inevitability of false teaching and counters it with God's truth (4:1–4), then mandates that Timothy teach the things Paul is saying in this letter (4:5–16; cf. "these things" in 4:6, 11, 15; 5:7 [cf. 21]; 6:2). Paul tells Timothy how to relate to older and younger men and women (5:1–2), then gives instructions for the church's care for widows (5:3–16). Paul instructs Timothy on how he is to deal with elders who do well (5:17–18) and those who

[118]Marshall, *New Testament Theology*, 398 n. 4, writes: "I use the term *pseudonymous* to refer to documents that were intended to deceive their recipients . . . and the term *allonymous* to refer to documents composed by somebody other than the purported author . . . but in a way that was transparent and not intended to deceive the readers." This statement is astonishing. These letters are so personal that to claim that it is transparent that Paul did not write them is nothing short of preposterous. Discussing "The Deceptive Character of Apostolic Pseudepigrapha," Earle Ellis notes that "the early Christians knew how to transmit the teachings of an authority figure without engaging in pseudepigrapha" (citing Mark's Gospel and the *Didache*). Having cataloged the many ways that "the assumed pseudo-Pauline and pseudo-Petrine authors did not merely create a title but engaged in an elaborate and complex deception to transmit their own ideas under apostolic color," Ellis concludes, "Scholars cannot have it both ways" (*History and Interpretation in New Testament Perspective*, 25–29). Cf. also William D. Mounce, *Pastoral Epistles*, WBC (Nashville: Thomas Nelson, 2000), cxxvi: "On the one hand, the forger is so versed in Paul and so clever at writing that he fooled the church for 1800 years. . . . Yet, on the other hand, the forger makes such obvious blunders that to modern scholarship it is inconceivable that Paul could have been the author." Cf. also Luke Timothy Johnson, *The First and Second Letters to Timothy*, AB (New York: Doubleday, 2001), 55: "It should be remembered that highly intelligent and by no means uncritical scholars read the Pastorals from within an exact opposite construal for six times the period in which the current paradigm has reigned."

[119]See especially Thomas R. Schreiner and Andreas J. Köstenberger, eds., *Women in the Church: An Analysis and Application of 1 Timothy 2:9–15*, 2nd ed. (Grand Rapids: Baker, 2005).

[120]Cf. the "references to deaconesses prior to the third century" in Mounce, *Pastoral Epistles*, 210–12. He cites a letter of Pliny to Trajan (*Ep.* 10.96), Clement of Alexandria, Origen, the *Didascalia Apostolorum*, and the fourth century *Apostolic Constitutions*.

sin and are even unrepentant (5:19–25). He gives directions for slaves and masters (6:1–2), and again explicitly connects his teaching on how people are to live to the truth of the gospel (6:2b–5), warning against the desire to be rich (6:6–10). Paul places a solemn and binding charge on Timothy to do what he, Paul, says for God's glory (6:11–16), gives instructions for the rich (6:17–19), and again calls Timothy to "guard the deposit" by the power of grace (6:20–21).

Paul begins this letter, in which he instructs Timothy on how he is to teach and act in the church, with a call to command some not to propound heterodox teaching (1 Tim. 1:3). Such teaching apparently focused on myths and genealogies, promoting speculation about fantastic supernatural explanations and predictions rather than trust in God and Christ (1:4). The goal of Paul's command to Timothy on this point is not some kind of power-hungry desire for control but "love from a pure heart and a good conscience and a sincere faith" (1:5). Paul evidently believes that the myths would lead to disputes and speculations (1:4), but they would not promote confidence that, because of Christ's death and resurrection, believers have a clear conscience by faith and are freed to love as Christ has loved them (1:5). Similarly, the interest in "endless genealogies" (1:4) probably sought to establish some kind of birthright to God's favor, excluding those not connected to the right ancestors and nullifying the good news that sinners can be made right with God by faith in Christ. True love for people results in a desire to see them liberated from sin and shame and fear by faith in Christ, freed to love others by following his powerful example of self-giving sacrifice to benefit those whom he loved. Those teaching these other doctrines have turned from Christian truth to vain babbling (1:6), and they fail to understand the law (1:7). Their teaching probably included a requirement to keep aspects of the law (cf. 4:1–3), prompting Paul to explain that the law was not given for those made righteous by faith (1:8–9a) but rather to convict sinners of their need to be made right with God (1:9b–10), "in accordance with the good news of the glory of the blessed God, with which [Paul] was entrusted" (1:11). Paul's gospel is a gospel of salvation through judgment for God's glory, and his gospel is the "good news of the glory of the blessed God" (1:11). This glory of God is a glory in which justice is meant to lead people to mercy (1:8–11), mercy and justice highlighting each other and coming together to display the character of the blessed God.

Paul offers himself as exhibit A for the case of the true gospel that glorifies God (1 Tim. 1:12–17). He thanks God for deciding that he would be faithful and appointing him to service (1:12). The statement in 1 Timothy 1:12 that God judged Paul faithful cannot mean that God saw that Paul was one of the good guys and decided he needed to pick him for his team. It cannot mean this because of what Paul goes on to say, explaining that he was "a blasphemer, persecutor, and insolent opponent" (1:13a ESV). Those are not characteristics that mark the good guys. God judged Paul faithful and appointed him to service *in spite of*, not because of, what he was. When Paul says in 1 Timothy 1:13, "But I received mercy because I had acted ignorantly in unbelief" (ESV), he is not saying that his ignorance and unbelief were mitigating factors that prompted God to show him mercy. No, elsewhere Paul is clear that people are condemned for unbelief (e.g., Rom. 11:20), and zeal for God without knowledge does not help his kinsmen (Rom. 10:2). Paul cites his ignorance and unbelief to show that he did not get what he deserved but that he was shown mercy. He is proving that what he got was mercy rather than what he deserved, and his proof is the ignorance and unbelief in which he acted.[121] This fits with what Paul says next in verse 14 about the Lord's grace overflowing with the faith and love that are in Jesus, with the "trustworthy saying" in verse 15 that Christ Jesus came to save sinners, and with his description of himself as the foremost sinner in verse 16. Paul says, in fact, that he got mercy precisely because he was the foremost sinner so that God could demonstrate his "perfect patience," making Paul a kind of paradigm for salvation (1 Tim. 1:16). That is, God saves people no one would expect him to save, and God saves people who do not deserve to be saved. Paul clearly thought that he was doing the right thing as he made his way toward Damascus, but God brought all that under judgment. God saved Paul through judgment, and he saved him so that Paul could say what he says in 1 Timothy 1:17: "To the King of ages, immortal, invisible, the only God, be honor and glory forever and ever. Amen" (ESV).

Paul calls Timothy to fight the good fight for faith and the good conscience it brings (1 Tim. 1:18–19), and he states plainly that to turn from the faith is a shipwreck, incurring damage and loss (1:19). Paul names the names of those who endanger the church, and he states plainly that he has exercised church discipline on them for the sake of their own souls (1:20).

Paul, then, was saved through judgment by God's grace through faith in Jesus for God's glory, and he wants Timothy to teach that message (1 Tim. 1:3–19). Paul also pronounces judgment on Hymenaeus and Alexander so that they will be saved (1:20). In the rest of the letter Paul condemns and commends: he condemns wicked behavior as he commends righteous ways for people of different gender, age, and station to relate to one another.

This begins with men. By calling for men in all churches (1 Tim. 2:8) to pray for everyone, including leaders, that the gospel might advance in peace (2:1–2), Paul condemns selfish unconcern for others. He condemns the view that salvation is the exclusive preserve of an inner circle who have private access to esoteric and secret truth derived from myths or handed down from ancestors, accessed perhaps by those who know to keep the certain essential laws that must be

[121]So also Johnson, *The First and Second Letters to Timothy*, 178–79.

obeyed in order for the elite to be saved. No, God wants everyone to be saved and come to the knowledge of the truth, not just some secret council of Essenes or Gnostics (2:3–4). Moreover, there is no other God, nor is there any other way of salvation with some other mediator and some other promised renewal of all things. Rather, "there is one God, and there is one mediator between God and man, the man Christ Jesus" (2:5–6). Jesus gave himself as a ransom for all (2:7), not just the elite few. He is the only ransom available to humanity, and the only way to be saved is to believe the good news Paul was appointed to proclaim (2:7). This call for men to pray (2:1–2), with its theological justification (2:3–7), announces judgment against all the stale nonsense that makes people self-righteous and unloving, which appears to be what those false teachers were peddling. Paul concludes with a plain statement for men to pray, not fight with each other (2:8).

Paul next addresses the behavior of women "in every place"—the "likewise" at the beginning of 1 Timothy 2:9 (ESV) continues the statement of what Paul wants men to do "in every place" in 2:8. Women are to adorn themselves in ways that befit godliness (2:9–10), and they are to *learn* with *submissiveness* (2:11). The things Paul says women are to do, *learning* and *submitting*, match the things he says women are not to do in 2:12, *teaching men* or *exercising authority over men*. Paul gives two reasons for this: first, Adam was created first, then Eve; and second, the woman was deceived, not Adam (2:13–14). Women whose faith is actualized in the glad acceptance of the gender identity God has assigned to them will be saved (2:15).[122]

Consider the behaviors condemned by Paul's instructions: he condemns immodest, ungodly ways women adorn themselves (1 Tim. 2:9–10); he condemns the refusal of men to allow women to learn, and/or the refusal of women to learn (2:11); he condemns the reversal of assigned gender roles—so women are not to be unsubmissive (2:11), nor are they to teach men or exercise authority over men (2:12). The reasons Paul gives for these ways to practice godliness, these ways of applying the gospel to relations between people of different genders, have to do with the created order, not the situation in Ephesus.[123] Paul bases his instructions not on the fact that women were teaching false doctrine in Ephesus, nor on the fact that women were teaching in ways that inappropriately subverted authority or took too much authority,[124] nor on any other situation-specific circumstance

[122]For patient and compelling answers to the creative arguments of egalitarians, see Thomas R. Schreiner, "An Interpretation of 1 Timothy 2:9–15: A Dialogue with Scholarship," in Köstenberger and Schreiner, *Women in the Church*, 85–120; Schreiner, "William J. Webb's *Slaves, Women and Homosexuals*: A Review Article," *SBJT* 6, no. 1 (2002): 46–64; Schreiner, "A Review of Scot McKnight, *The Blue Parakeet*," *JBMW* 14 (2009): 60–67; and Schreiner, "Philip Payne on Familiar Ground: A Review of Philip B. Payne, *Man and Woman, One in Christ*," *JBMW* 15, no. 1 (2010): 33–46.

[123]*Contra* Marshall, *New Testament Theology*, 402 n. 7.

[124]Andreas J. Köstenberger, "A Complex Sentence: The Syntax of 1 Timothy 2:12," in Köstenberger and Schreiner, *Women in the Church*, 53–84.

presenting a problem in Ephesus.[125] Rather, Paul gives the order of creation and the events of the fall as his reasons for saying what he does. This means, too, that Paul's appeal is based not on post-fall realities but on the pre-fall creation order.[126]

Paul's meaning is clear. We may conclude that he is wrong, as Richard B. Hays[127] and Luke Timothy Johnson[128] do, but we cannot make his words mean the opposite of what they actually say. Those who would install women as regular teachers of men in churches, and those who would make women pastors, are openly rejecting Paul's teaching. As Hays writes, Paul's "arguments may appear unpersuasive and objectionable to modern readers, but there is no point in attempting to explain away what Paul actually wrote."[129] The better course, in my view, is to embrace the reality that the Bible teaches many things that are out of step with the culture and the spirit of the age. Those who follow Jesus will never be able to remove themselves from the inevitable reproach of the cross (cf. Gal. 5:11), and we should not want to do so. When the Bible shocks our sensibilities, we should pray that God would conform our sensibilities to his word, asking for grace to stand with the now silent generations that have gone before us, believing the Bible and seeking to practice everything it teaches.

Paul means to enable people to work out their salvation, whether male or female, through the judgment of inappropriate behaviors typical to males and females. Males tend to be argumentative and excessively exclusive, and so they are to pray for all people without quarreling (1 Tim. 2:1–8). Women tend not to realize how their immodesty affects men, they tend to speak when they should not, and they tend toward unsubmissive, authoritarian behavior, and so Paul urges women to modesty and submission, and he forbids them teaching or exercising authority over men (2:9–12). He bases his argument not on aberrant behaviors in Ephesus but on the way God has created things to be and on the events of the fall (2:13–15).

Turning to the leadership of the church, Paul gives the qualifications for "overseers," a term that is used interchangeably with "elders" and "pastors" (cf. Acts 20:17, 28; Titus 1:5, 7; 1 Pet. 5:1–2). It is clear from what Paul says here and elsewhere that only men are to be elders/overseers/pastors. Paul forbids women from teaching or exercising authority over men (1 Tim. 2:12), and teaching and ruling in the church are the two activities for which good elders

---

[125]*Contra* Linda L. Belleville, "Teaching and Usurping Authority: 1 Timothy 2:11–15," in *Discovering Biblical Equality: Complementarity without Hierarchy*, ed. Ronald W. Pierce and Rebecca Merrill Groothuis (Downers Grove, IL: InterVarsity, 2004), 205–23.

[126]Paul's instructions here fit with what he says in 1 Cor. 11:3–16; 1 Cor. 14:32–36; Eph. 5:21–33; and Col. 3:17–19, matching also what Peter teaches in 1 Pet. 3:1–7. For my synthesis of these issues, see Hamilton, "What Women Can Do in Ministry."

[127]Richard B. Hays, *First Corinthians*, Interpretation (Louisville: Westminster John Knox, 1997), 190–92.

[128]Johnson, *The First and Second Letters to Timothy*, 208–11.

[129]Hays, *First Corinthians*, 187.

are to be commended (5:17). Elders/overseers/pastors must have character that is above reproach (3:1–2a, 3). They must be able to teach (3:2b). They must manage their homes and families well (3:4–5). And they must neither be recent converts (3:6) nor be poorly thought of by non-Christians (3:7). The affirmation of these qualities condemns elders who do not understand what they try to teach (1:7), who make shipwreck of the truth of the gospel (1:19), who are not convicted when they sin (4:2) and teach false, demonic doctrines (4:1–3, 7), which stir up unnecessary strife (6:4), arising from greed (6:5), and who all the while seek to take advantage of women in immoral, destructive ways (2 Tim. 3:1–7; cf. 1 Tim. 5:11–15).

Paul then describes the qualifications for deacons, who must be blameless and orthodox (1 Tim. 3:8–10). The first three things named about male deacons—that they are to be (1) dignified, (2) not double-tongued, and (3) not drunkards—are repeated after the phrase "women likewise" in 1 Timothy 3:11: (1) dignified, (2) not slanderers, and (3) sober-minded. Then just as the males must hold the faith with a clear conscience (3:9), the females must be "faithful in all things" (3:11). The instructions for male deacons in 3:12 have counterparts for women that are obvious and do not need to be restated. Thus it appears that Paul is describing female deacons rather than the wives of male deacons (cf. also Rom. 16:1). Further, why would Paul list qualifications for the wives of deacons when he has not listed qualifications for the wives of elders? Would not the wives of elders be as significant as the wives of deacons? It seems preferable, then, to see that whereas only men can be elders, both men and women can be deacons. Elders teach and lead, which Paul explicitly forbids women from doing in relationship to men. Deacons must be blameless and orthodox, but they mainly serve. There is no requirement that they be able to teach, while there is such a requirement for elders (1 Tim. 3:2).

Having described the problem in Ephesus (1 Tim. 1:3–11), given his own testimony as a verification of the true gospel (1:12–17), and charged Timothy to fight the good fight defending the gospel (1:18–21), Paul has addressed men in general (2:1–8), women in general (2:9–15), male elders (3:1–7), and male and female deacons (3:8–13). He now explains to Timothy that he is writing so that in case he is delayed in getting to Ephesus, Timothy will know how one ought to behave in the church so that the truth is upheld (3:14–15). Paul then bases these instructions about godliness on the way that Jesus embodied godliness in relationship to his humanity, the Holy Spirit, the angels, the nations, the world, and his reception into glory (3:16).[130] It seems, then, that there is a connection between the godliness exemplified by the members of the church as they relate in

[130]Similarly Mounce, *Pastoral Epistles*, 224, who notes that 1 Tim. 3:16 gives the reasons 1 Timothy 2–3 are to be obeyed.

appropriate ways to God and each other, and the godliness of the Lord Jesus.[131] The church is called to image forth a godliness that communicates the glory of Christ. The relational arrangements that Paul describes in this letter are the church's way of displaying the godliness inherent in whose body she is.

Paul returns to the subject of the false teachers in 1 Timothy 4:1–3a, having already warned the Ephesian elders about false teachers rising from their midst in Acts 20:29–30. He counters the views of the false teachers in 1 Timothy 4:3b–5, then charges Timothy to teach what he, Paul, has said in the letter for Timothy's own benefit in 4:6–10, as well as the benefit of others in 4:11–16. Doing so will ensure the salvation of both Timothy and the church (4:16).

Having instructed Timothy on older and younger males and females (1 Tim. 5:1–2) and widows (5:3–16), Paul addresses good and bad elders (5:17–25). The good are worthy of double honor (5:17–18). Charges against the bad must be confirmed by multiple witnesses (5:19), and "those who persist in sin" are to be rebuked publicly as a warning to others (5:20). Paul solemnly charges Timothy to show no partiality (5:21), not to make elders too quickly, and to keep himself pure (5:22). The word about drinking wine (5:23), coming as it does in the discussion about elders, may be related to the way the false teachers were requiring abstinence from foods (4:3a). Timothy may have avoided wine he needed out of deference to sensibilities ultimately deriving from the false teachers, who may themselves have come from among the elders of the church in Ephesus. This may explain why Paul inserts this comment on Timothy taking wine for his stomach in 1 Timothy 5:23, only to return to the way that good or bad deeds will be conspicuous (5:24–25), which probably relates to the activities of the elders and the false teachers.

By fighting the good fight of faith (1 Tim. 6:12), Timothy will proclaim and live out the salvation through judgment God accomplished in Christ on the cross. It is this message of Christ crucified and risen, because of which justification by grace through faith is possible, that will be preached from love that begets pure hearts, clear consciences, and sincere faith (cf. 1:5). And the godliness that matches this gospel will enact judgment against all deviant and variant ways of living. Through the living out of such godliness the church will give evidence of its salvation and bring glory to God.[132] Then will come the appearing of Jesus, "the blessed and only Sovereign, the King of kings and Lord of lords, who alone has immortality, who dwells in unapproachable light, whom no one has ever seen or can see. To him be honor and eternal dominion. Amen" (6:14–16 ESV).

[131]See BDAG s.v. εὐσέβεια, 412–13.
[132]Similarly Frank Thielman, *Theology of the New Testament: A Canonical and Synthetic Approach* (Grand Rapids: Zondervan, 2005), 420.

2.12 Second Timothy

Knowing that his end is near (2 Tim. 4:6–7), Paul writes to Timothy urging him to fan the gift of God into flame and join Paul in unashamed suffering for the gospel (cf. 1:6, 8, 12; 2:3, 9–10, 15; 3:10–11; 4:5).[133] Though Paul has suffered famously because of the gospel, and though it has resulted in much that is shameful by worldly standards, Paul is not ashamed (1 Tim. 1:12; cf. Rom. 1:16).[134] He is not ashamed because he is confident that the message he proclaims has eternal roots. From eternity past God granted grace in Christ Jesus to the elect, not because of what they would do (or how they would respond to the proclamation of the gospel) but because of his own purpose and grace (2 Tim. 1:9). This grace has been made manifest at the turning point of the ages, in the salvation through judgment accomplished by Jesus for the glory of God. Jesus judged and abolished death, and through that judgment he brought life and immortality to light (1:10).

Paul urges Timothy to be strengthened in the grace that is in Christ Jesus (2 Tim. 2:1). Since the previous reference to the grace in Christ Jesus was to the grace granted "before the times of the ages" (1:9), it appears that Paul wants Timothy to be strengthened by the fact that before time began, God granted Timothy grace in Christ Jesus. The eternal roots of this grace prepare Timothy to stand and face whatever he might suffer for the cause of the gospel. Nothing will uproot that grace. Nothing can sever Timothy from it. Nothing can reach back before it. If Timothy does not belong to Jesus, he will deny Jesus and be denied by him (2:12). If Timothy belongs to Jesus, though he die, he will die with Jesus and also live after death with him (2:11). If Timothy belongs to Jesus, even if he is faithless and stumbles, Jesus will not deny him, for he cannot deny himself (2:13). Thinking on this eternal gift of grace will make Timothy strong indeed.

From eternity past God planned to destroy death. From eternity past God purposed to visit judgment on Jesus so that he could show mercy to the elect. From eternity past God planned for his ministers to suffer as they proclaim the gospel in the face of hostile opposition from Satan, sin, death, and hell. Cer-

---

[133]For the situation and date of 2 Timothy, see Ellis, *History and Interpretation in New Testament Perspective*, 74.

[134]Cf. Brian Rapske's summary (*The Book of Acts and Paul in Roman Custody*, The Book of Acts in Its First Century Setting [Grand Rapids: Eerdmans, 1994], 283): "Ancient literary sources link prison with dishonor. The process of being conducted there, particularly while bound, and even the wearing of chains when one was not imprisoned or prison-bound, was perceived (as was intended) to be degrading. Public exposure, irrespective of innocence or guilt, resulted in a shame that could be life-long. Because prisoners no longer possessed their former dignity there was great social pressure to withdraw from or abandon the prisoner. This pressure was felt most keenly by close friends, associates and family members. Christians too felt it despite calls for solidarity and loving care. . . . The higher a prisoner's status and the more severe the form of custody . . . the greater the sense of shame. The record of Paul's imprisonments reveals that he recognizes the shame and fears the negative effects. The reader is left by the last verse of Acts, however, with the conviction that, far from being overcome by the shame of his circumstances, Paul overcame them" (italics and paragraph breaks removed).

tain of all this, Paul is not ashamed of what looks shameful—suffering for the gospel—and he calls Timothy to join him. Moreover, Paul knows that there are people whom God has chosen who have yet to hear the gospel, and he knows that part of what will convince them of its truth is the attestation that comes from his own suffering for it. Thus he endures "for the sake of the elect, that they also may obtain the salvation that is in Christ Jesus with eternal glory" (2 Tim. 2:10 ESV).

The world's false verdict is that the proclamation of the gospel deserves the kind of shameful treatment Paul has endured (2 Tim. 3:10–12) and is enduring (4:16–18). But God is a just Judge who will render a true verdict (4:8).

Satan's cunning strategy is to deceive through false teachers (2 Tim. 2:16–18, 23; 3:1–8, 13; 4:3, 14–15). In the face of such opposition, Paul urges Timothy to hold closely to "the example of sound words" he has heard from Paul (1:13). Apparently Paul wants Timothy to proclaim the gospel in the same words, and, at least in some instances, in the same sequences of those words, that he himself has proclaimed.[135] Part of this is no doubt restated in 2 Timothy 1:8–10 and 2:9, and Timothy was surely aware of other formulations that have come down to us in Paul's letters.

Jesus has defeated Satan, accomplishing salvation through judgment for God's glory. Satan's opposition to the gospel will win the same kinds of victories that Satan won at the cross. He may seem to overcome, but unexpectedly, out of defeat, God triumphs in life from death. No one will ever defeat God, and though the opponents of the gospel seem to have overcome the preachers, apostles, and teachers of the gospel, their victories will unexpectedly become their defeats. Onesimus may have died for the gospel (2 Tim. 1:16–18, note how Paul speaks of him in the past tense), and Phygelus and Hermogenes may seem to have made the right choice, the choice by which they kept their lives and avoided shameful treatment (1:15). But on "that Day" (1:18) there will be only justice and no mercy for those who turn away from the gospel. The talk of those who swerve from the truth may spread—like a disease—but "God's firm foundation stands, bearing this seal: 'The Lord knows those who are his' . . ." (2:17–19 ESV). Jannes and Jambres seemed impressive for a while against Moses, but they met the end that awaits all those who oppose God and the gospel (3:8–9). Paul might be in chains, but the word of God is not bound (2:9). All abandoned Paul at his first defense, but the Lord stood by him to strengthen him, that he might proclaim the gospel, that the Gentiles might hear of the justice and mercy of God (4:16–17). Through the judgment of their enemies, God saves his people for his glory.

[135]See the discussion of "Implications of Preformed Traditions for Pauline Christology," in Ellis, *History and Interpretation in New Testament Perspective*, 144–50.

2.13 Titus

In his letter to Titus, Paul celebrates God's glory in the salvation through judgment he accomplished in Christ, and Paul calls Titus to apply justice against the false teachers, that the church might be saved. After the opening (Titus 1:1–4), Paul states the requirements for church leaders (1:5–9), which are necessary because of the false teachers (1:10–15). Paul then tells Titus what he must teach, and the gist is that the true gospel produces virtuous living (2:1–3:15).

Paul insists that the truth accords with godliness probably because the false teachers have been peddling a message that accommodates ungodliness (Titus 1:1), and he asserts that God never lies probably because he regards the false teachers to be doing just that (1:2; cf. "deceivers," 1:10, "Cretans are always liars," 1:12). Paul left Titus in Crete to appoint elders in every place (1:5), and these elders are to be men whose character is above reproach (1:6–8). Character, however, is not all that is necessary to qualify a man as an elder/overseer. Paul also declares, "He must hold firm to the trustworthy word as taught, so that he may be able to give instruction in sound doctrine and also to rebuke those who contradict it" (1:9 ESV). At the very least, we can say that "the trustworthy word as taught" includes all that Paul teaches in his letters, and if we add the things taught by Paul's traveling companions Mark and Luke, and those who gave him the right hand of fellowship, Peter, James, and John, we approximate the whole of New Testament teaching. Paul clearly expects elders/overseers to be firm in the apostolic faith, to communicate it to new disciples, and to defend it against attackers.

It seems that the false teachers were promoting interest in Jewish myths and that their commands were tied up with the advocacy of circumcision as a necessity for uncircumcised converts to Christianity (Titus 1:10, 14; cf. Gal. 2:3). Paul wants these rebellious, empty-talking deceivers silenced (Titus 1:10–11), not because he is afraid of debate but because they are wrong. Further, he wants them and the Christians they are leading astray rebuked, that they might be sound in faith (1:13). In short, Paul wants them saved through the judgment of their false ideas.

Paul then begins to instruct Titus regarding what he should teach. He begins with behavioral instructions (Titus 2:1–10),[136] then explains that this behavior is necessary because of the saving grace of God in Christ (2:11–15).[137] Jesus gave himself to redeem people from sin and purify them (2:14). He saved them by taking the judgment against their sin and breaking its power. And this Jesus, the "great God and Savior," will appear in *glory* (2:13).

---

[136]Cf. *1 Clem.* 1:3 and Titus 2:4–5.

[137]Plummer, *Paul's Understanding of the Church's Mission*, 99–105, shows that "the various segments of the Christian community are to live praiseworthy lives—not simply for the sake of obeying God, but also because their behavior will commend or detract from the gospel" (104–5).

Paul returns to this gospel after giving more specifics about the godliness that accords with the truth (Titus 3:1–2; cf. 1:1). However much modern scholars want to make Paul into their own image as a revolutionary against imperialism, Paul calls Titus to teach people to be submissive and obedient to rulers and authorities (3:1; cf. Rom. 13:1–7). He wants the knowledge Christians have of the miry pit of sinfulness they were hauled out of (Titus 3:3) to keep them from being rude to those wallowing in that hole (3:2). God saves Christians not because they have been righteous but because he is merciful (3:4–5a). God saves Christians not because they are already spiritually alive but by the regeneration of the Spirit, not because they are clean but through the washing and renewal of the Spirit (3:5b). This means that any commands given by the false teachers are unnecessary and will not stand people closer to God's salvation—God saves those who are justified by grace through faith, not works (3:6–8). Those who continue to reject the true gospel are to be excluded from the fellowship of the church (3:8–11), and through the judgment of the unrepentant the repentant will be saved, protected from wolves.

2.14 Philemon

The subversive power of Paul's letter to Philemon comes in its application of the glory of God in salvation through judgment to the relationships between human beings. In order to grasp this, consider the realities of this letter from a worldly perspective: Paul is an old man (Philem. 1:9), probably 50–56 years old,[138] and he is in prison, in Roman custody either in Caesarea or Rome (1:1, 9, 13). By the standards of the empire, Paul has nothing to offer Philemon, and Philemon's standing in society will not be helped by association with Paul. To the worldly, Paul seems to be delusional (cf. Acts 26:24), considering himself imprisoned on behalf of a man executed by the state (Philem.1:1, 9), and referring to the message that has landed him in prison as "good news" (1:13). This old prisoner Paul is, by Roman standards, useless to Philemon. Apparently one of Philemon's slaves, Onesimus (whose name means "useful") has somehow found his way to Paul, probably not with Philemon's permission, and Paul is sending him back to his master with this letter.

The intercession Paul makes for Onesimus in his letter to Philemon indicates that Onesimus is likely facing what could be regarded as just retribution from Philemon on his arrival. Paul does not even mention the mitigation of the punishment of Onesimus, calling instead for behavior that would be inexplicable to the mindset of a Roman slaveholder. Paul first has the audacity to associate himself with Philemon as though they are "fellow workers" and "fellow soldiers" in an "assembly [church]" meeting in Philemon's house (Philem. 1:1–2).

[138] Cf. BDAG, s.v., πρεσβύτης ("old man, aged man"), 863.

Evidently Paul does not expect Philemon to be offended by these presumptions. Nor, apparently, does Paul fear any shame he might bring on Philemon or the "assembly" by associating himself, a prisoner, with them. Does Paul know who Philemon is? He is dealing with a slaveholding man whose house is large enough for the church to gather there. Has Paul no consideration for what is appropriate Roman etiquette?

Paul then offers grace and peace from God and the Lord Christ, thanking God for what he hears of Philemon's behavior, which is anything but commendable by Roman standards. Philemon has not been concerning himself with his advancement in society,[139] nor is he seeking to improve Rome's estimation of his city. Instead, Philemon is living out the teaching of one who was humiliated and whose cause was stopped when he was executed by the state. Philemon, Paul says, is loving and trusting Jesus, and loving the saints (1:4–5). Rather than admonishing Philemon to be a better Roman, Paul prays that "the participation of your faith might become active in the knowledge of every good thing which is in us for the sake of Christ" (1:6). Paul then speaks of what is "required" of Philemon (1:8), but he clearly does not mean what a Roman would think to be required for a runaway slave who is being sent home.[140] Paul has a different requirement in mind, but he does not make it mandatory, preferring to allow Philemon to choose to do the right thing for himself (1:8–9).

Paul then discloses that he has become Onesimus's father (Philem. 1:10), apparently assuming that Philemon will understand that through Paul's testimony to this "good news" that has done so much for Paul, Onesimus has been "born again." Onesimus was evidently not a good servant to Philemon before he found his way to Paul, for Paul openly states that formerly he was useless (1:11a). Paul also claims that now Onesimus will live up to his name and be useful to both Philemon and Paul (1:11b).

The statements that follow from Paul seem to assume a notion he expresses elsewhere: the unity of believers with Christ and one another. Thus he refers to Onesimus as "my very heart" (Philem. 1:12 ESV) and tells Philemon to "receive him as you would receive me" (1:17 ESV). This may have implications for the guest room that Paul instructs Philemon to prepare for his coming (1:22). It may be that the "even more" that Paul knows Philemon will do (1:21) includes affording to Onesimus the hospitality he would afford to Paul (cf. 1:17).

---

[139]Cf. Robert Louis Wilken, *The Christians as the Romans Saw Them* (New Haven, CT: Yale University Press, 1984), 6–7. Explaining a statement made by Pliny the Younger, Wilkin writes, "His comment sounds vain and self-serving, but the sensibilities of the Romans were different from ours. They openly praised their own accomplishments and were not embarrassed to seek glory."

[140]Joseph A. Fitzmyer (*The Letter to Philemon: A New Translation with Introduction and Commentary*, AB [New York: Doubleday, 2000], 28) writes, "Severe penalties were permitted by law to be carried out against a runaway slave: . . . he could be scourged, branded, mutilated, or fitted with a metal collar, perhaps even be crucified, thrown to beasts, or killed."

Where does this audacity come from? How can Paul expect a slaveholder to treat a returned slave this way? The expectations that enable Paul to speak with such temerity arise from the glory of God in salvation through judgment. Paul knows that Philemon has felt the crushing weight of the holiness of God standing over his sin, judging and condemning him. Apparently Paul fathered Philemon just as he fathered Onesimus (Philem. 1:10, 19). Paul knows that the justice of God against Philemon's sin led him to the mercy of God available because God did justice through Christ's death on the cross. Paul then embodies the sacrifice of Christ for believers in his offer to pay whatever Onesimus owes (1:18), just as Christ paid everything believers owed. What we have in this letter from Paul to Philemon, then, is an application of the center of Paul's theology to the specific question of a runaway slave who has become a Christian and is being restored to his former master. Now the slave is a brother in Christ, beloved, no less (1:16). God's glory renders judgment against the norms of Roman society, and through that judgment salvation comes to those who know the glory of God's justice and mercy.

2.15 The Center of Paul's Theology

Is there a theme that dominates Paul's thought? Is there a big idea that organizes all the other themes and ideas that are so powerfully and flexibly deployed in pursuit of the Great Commission task of making disciples by building churches? With so many unique situations addressed by these letters from the apostle, does the theology reflected in these letters have a center?

Is there an organized relationship between the apocalyptic triumph of God in Christ, justification by faith, new creation, reconciliation, salvation history, and union with Christ?[141] Do these themes have a common termination point? Is there one massive sun in the center of this cosmos holding everything in orbit by its planetary force? Ralph Martin writes that we press forward to answer these questions in spite of the difficulties, "unless we are prepared to abandon the quest and treat Paul's theology as fragmentary responses delivered ad hoc."[142] Frank Thielman observes that "even scholars who are unhappy with talk of a 'center' or 'core' for Paul's thought often find themselves eventually speaking of a basic principle around which Paul's theology is organized."[143]

Martin, Plevnik, and Schreiner have suggested criteria that help us establish the center of Paul's theology. Plevnik writes, "Anything that is derived from something else in Pauline theology is not the center."[144] Schreiner's charge against the proposals set forth above stands: "Every proposed center suppresses part of the

[141] For documentation of who proposed these centers and where, see Schreiner, *Paul*, 17–18.
[142] R. P. Martin, "Center of Paul's Theology," *DPL*, 93.
[143] Thielman, *Theology of the New Testament*, 231.
[144] Joseph Plevnik, "The Center of Pauline Theology," *CBQ* 51 (1989): 466.

Pauline gospel."[145] Martin writes, "The 'center' is thus the primal reality from which he draws his entire theology."[146] For a proposal to be compelling, then, it must be primal, or underived, and holding it up as central cannot suppress other significant themes. I am in basic agreement with Schreiner's proposal that God's glory in Christ is central to Paul's theology.[147] As will be clear from my analysis of Paul's letters, it seems to me that at the very heart of God's glory in Christ, the big muscle that pumps the blood through the living body of his thought, is the manifestation of the mercy and justice of God, with mercy magnified by justice.[148]

Consider how the glory of God in salvation through judgment functions in the indicatives of Paul's theology (i.e., statements of what God has done in Christ by the Spirit): this reality fulfills Israel's history because the exile prophesied in the Torah, narrated in the Prophets, and sung in the Writings is fulfilled and terminated in Christ's death on the cross. Simultaneously the new exodus and return from exile begin with the resurrection of Jesus from the dead. In the display of mercy and justice at the cross,[149] God accomplishes redemption and reconciliation. God's glory in salvation through judgment is existentially experienced in and served by the individual's experience of being justified by faith.

The glory of God in salvation through judgment also empowers the imperatives of Paul's theology: it is enacted when Christians heed Paul's injunctions to reject false gods, repent of their sins, and trust in Christ. It is displayed when believers obey Paul's imperatives and live out the very implications of the gospel of Christ by the power of the Spirit and in union with Christ himself by faith. And the living out of the gospel's implications is motivated by a yet future display of God's glory in salvation through judgment accomplished by Jesus the messiah, when he will come in blazing glory to avenge himself on his enemies and deliver all those who trust him.

God's glory in salvation through judgment is on display in the community that was bought with the price of Christ's death on the cross, the church. The church exists because of that display of God's character in the death of Christ, and the church lives out a pattern of Christlikeness as believers lay down their lives for others as Christ did for them. The church also enacts the justice and mercy of God as the gospel is proclaimed, as believers are baptized into the display of God's judgment and mercy in Christ's death on the cross and raised to live a new life with him, as the Lord's Supper is celebrated, as the body of Christ conforms

[145]Schreiner, *Paul*, 18.
[146]Martin, "Center of Paul's Theology," 93.
[147]Schreiner, *Paul*, 15–35.
[148]I find this more satisfying than Thielman's proposal: "God's graciousness toward his weak and sinful creatures" (*Theology of the New Testament*, 232, italics removed).
[149]Cf. Seifrid, *Christ, Our Righteousness*, 171: "God's saving righteousness and his righteous wrath stand in a synthetic relation, rather than a strictly antithetical one."

to the character of her Lord, and as the church disciplines the unrepentant to call them back to submission to the lordship of Jesus. All through the church God's glory shines in salvation through judgment as the truth is grounded in and upheld by these realities (cf. 1 Tim. 3:15).

Nothing is more primal or ultimate. God's glory in salvation through judgment in Christ is not derived from anything else, and as all else serves to display God's glory and terminates in its expression, nothing is suppressed by holding it up as central. The center of Paul's theology is God's glory in salvation through judgment.

3. Catholic Epistles

The obvious similarities between Jude and 2 Peter point to a high level of theological resonance between Peter and Jude. As for John and James and the author of Hebrews, we will see as we survey their brief writings that, like Peter and Jude, these authors present Jesus as Lord, the servant who suffered for his people, brought resolution to Israel's story, and made the church the new people of God. Jesus is the fulfiller of the exile and the realizer of the promises of a new exodus and return from exile. He is the great shepherd who is leading his flock, the church, through the wilderness to the Promised Land. God has accomplished salvation through judgment for glory in him at the cross. Under his leadership the church is experiencing and enacting that salvation through judgment on the way to the final climactic display when the elements melt with intense heat, and the king will be the centerpiece of praise.

Do these authors evidence a theology that has a unified center? Obviously these short letters do not provide a full account of everything they believed. Still, I will seek to show that the evidence we have supports the thesis being argued in this book. For instance, Hebrews ascribes glory to Christ for the blood of the eternal covenant. James calls people to a living faith that asks God for his wisdom and lives according to it rather than the world's wisdom. Peter describes the joy inexpressible and full of glory that the redeemed feel even as they suffer for a little while. John articulates what the little children experience as perfect love that has driven out all fear. And Jude celebrates the eternal glory, majesty, dominion, and authority of the one who is able to keep his people from stumbling and present them before himself blameless with great joy. At the center of the theology reflected in the Catholic Epistles is the glory of God in salvation through judgment.

3.1 Other Letters Book by Book

Hebrews teaches the glory of God in the salvation through judgment accomplished in Christ Jesus, whose revelation of God is superior to what came through angels at Sinai, who fulfills the roles of Moses and Aaron, who has taken up the role of everlasting Melchizedekian High Priest, and through whom salvation is available, while those who forsake him face certain judgment. James calls believers to speak and act not according to the standards of this world but in ways that correspond to the faith believers have in the Lord of glory. First Peter addresses the sojourners and aliens who have been redeemed by the spotless Lamb and are being built into a spiritual temple; Peter summons his readers to rejoice in Christ with joy unspeakable and full of glory. Second Peter affirms the reality of the things to which Peter himself was an eyewitness; it exhorts its audience to grow in virtue and reject false teachers and their lascivious ways, for the end will surely come. First John rejects the notions that Christ did not come in the flesh and that sin does not need to be confessed or renounced; it celebrates fellowship with God and believers in truth and light. Second John warns that deceivers are not to be shown hospitality. Third John calls for the support of those who have gone out for the sake of the name. And Jude contends for the faith against false teachers, whose judgment is typologically foreshadowed by various Old Testament manifestations of God's wrath; Jude simultaneously calls believers to build themselves up in the confidence that the God of glory can keep them and present them blameless with great joy.

3.2 Hebrews

Hebrews teaches that God has shown his glory by accomplishing salvation through the judgment that fell on Christ. The author seeks to save his audience through judgment for God's glory. He teaches what God has done in Jesus to accomplish salvation, and he rehearses the judgment that unbelieving Israelites experienced. He announces certain judgment for those who fall away, and he speaks of future judgment. Through these words of judgment, the author means to bring his audience safely to salvation. This is not an evangelizing letter calling for conversion but a discipling letter calling for perseverance, growth in holiness, and deeper perception of what God has done in Christ. We will look first at the centrality of God's glory in Christ in the prologue to the letter, then at the narrative substructure evidenced in the epistle. From there we will look at salvation through judgment for God's glory in Hebrews.

3.2.1 The Glory of God in Christ in the Opening Lines of Hebrews

The glory of God in Christ is clearly the gravitational center of the theology of Hebrews (cf. Heb. 1:3a). The centrality of Christ's glory can be seen in the chiastic structure of Hebrews 1:1–4 (table 6.3).[150]

[150] Daniel J. Ebert, "The Chiastic Structure of the Prologue to Hebrews," *TJ* 13 (1992): 168.

Table 6.3. Chiastic Structure in Hebrews 1:1–4

1:1–2a, The Son contrasted with the prophets
  1:2b, The Son as messianic heir
    1:2c, The Son's creative work
      1:3a–b, The Son: radiance of God's glory and ruler
    1:3c, The Son's redemptive work
  1:3d, The Son as messianic king
1:4, The Son contrasted with angels

Following this celebration of Christ and his work, the author of Hebrews cites seven Old Testament passages that demonstrate the superiority of Christ over angels. Significantly, the citations begin and end with texts that herald the triumph of God and his messiah: Psalm 2:7 and 110:1 (Heb. 1:5–13).

3.2.2 The Narrative Substructure of Hebrews

We can begin to get at the substructure of the author's thought[151] by pursuing the following question: Why does the author address the topics he does? Why does he begin with angels (Heb. 1:5–2:18), through whom the law was given at Sinai (2:1–4)? Why does he then go to Moses (3:1–6) and warn against being like the wilderness generation while holding out the promise of entering rest (3:5–4:13)? Why does he move from there to the subject of the high priesthood of Jesus, who in contrast to Aaron (4:14–5:4) has been appointed as the Davidic-Melchizedekian High Priest (5:5–7:28)? Why does he address the new covenant (8:1–13), rehearsing the furnishings of the old covenant tabernacle to set up the better place and benefits of the sacrifice of Christ (9:1–10:39)? Why does he tell his audience about those who died in faith, not receiving the promises but seeking a homeland (11:1–40, cf. 13–14)? What is this "race set before us," on the path of which believers are being disciplined as sons (12:1–17)? What is the significance of this mountain to which we have come (12:18–27), and what is this kingdom that will not be shaken (12:28–29)? In giving his concluding instructions (13:1–25), why does the author speak as though Christians are encamped together (13:10–15)?

The preceding paragraph of questions seeks to highlight the narrative undercurrent that runs through the Epistle to the Hebrews. That narrative undercurrent may even be present in the title to the letter: to *the Hebrews*. The recipients of the letter may indeed be exclusively Jewish, but do we have evidence from the

[151]Here I am considering what lies beneath the statements made by the author of Hebrews and seeking to elucidate the theological worldview from which he writes. For excellent studies of the structure of his epistle, see George H. Guthrie, *The Structure of Hebrews: A Text-Linguistic Analysis* (Grand Rapids: Baker, 1998); and Barry C. Joslin, "Can Hebrews Be Structured? An Assessment of Eight Approaches," *Currents in Biblical Research* 6 (2007): 99–129.

first century of Christian churches composed *only* of Jews? Could it be that the author is addressing a typical church of Jews and Gentiles (and perhaps intends to address churches everywhere), and he calls them *Hebrews* to begin the process of reshaping their identity?[152] Even if that is not the case and the author is addressing a church composed only of those who are physically descended from Abraham—Hebrews—the author is reshaping their identity, and he is using people, events, and institutions from the Old Testament to do so.

It seems that the topics the author has chosen all point to the fulfillment of the Old Testament. The death of Jesus inaugurates the new exodus. As Paul says in 1 Corinthians 5:7, Jesus is the slain Passover Lamb. With the new exodus has come a new Sinai experience. In fulfillment of the law of Moses given by angels at Sinai (a law that itself followed previous revelation to the fathers), God has spoken in his Son (cf. Heb. 1:1–3; 2:1–4).

In fulfillment of the role played by the faithful servant Moses, who led the people through the wilderness, Jesus is faithful as a Son (Heb. 3:1–6). Moreover, Christians are now passing through the wilderness, sojourning toward the Promised Land, the city that is to come (cf. 11:10, 16, 40; 13:14), and they are warned not to harden their hearts as the nation of Israel did when they came out of Egypt (3:7–19). The author exhorts his audience to strive to enter the rest by faith (4:1–13).

Jesus is not only a new and greater Moses, but he is also a new Aaron, greater than the priest who served with Moses (Heb. 4:14–5:4). The priesthood of Jesus not only fulfills the priestly ministry of Aaron and his sons, however; it also fulfills the Mechizedekian type that was granted to the Davidic messiah in Psalm 110 (Heb. 5:5–7:28), in fulfillment of the promises to Abraham (6:13–20).

Just as Israel entered into a covenant with God at Sinai, the church has entered into a new covenant (Heb. 8:1–13), which has a better tabernacle (9:1–28) and a better sacrifice (10:1–39). Christians are like the faithful of the Old Testament, who believed God's promises as they made their way to the Promised Land (11:1–40). Christians must persevere through the race to the city, receiving God's discipline, for they have been to Mount Zion, where the new covenant was inaugurated (12:1–29). God is with them as he was with Israel (13:5), and just as Jesus suffered outside the camp, so Christians must embrace the reproach of the cross as they sojourn toward the city with foundations (13:11–15; 11:10).

[152]The notion that the author of Hebrews writes to Jewish converts to Christianity who are tempted to return to Judaism is a pervasive commonplace in writings about this New Testament epistle. I wonder, though, whether it is necessary to hold that these Jewish believers in Jesus were tempted to return to Judaism? Could it be that the author of the epistle is merely warning the congregation(s) he addresses (cf. 13:22) in view of the intense struggle facing them (cf. 10:32–35)? And as for the many comparisons to Old Testament realities such as angels, Moses, the old covenant priests, and the old covenant itself, could the author be simply teaching his congregation? And what more effective way to exalt Christ is open to him than the demonstration of the superiority of Christ as compared with the old covenant, the high priest, Moses, and the angels?

All this builds to the suggestion that the people, events, and institutions in the narratives of the Law and the Prophets are the narrative substructure of the letter to the Hebrews. The author addresses his audience as though they are living out the fulfillment of the story of the Old Testament, and this fulfillment recapitulates the story and offers opportunities to succeed where Israel failed. That offer of success is based on the finished work of Christ, and on his ongoing role as a sympathetic High Priest who gives help in time of need. The drama described by the author of Hebrews has a plot that turns on and culminates in the glory of God in salvation through judgment.

3.2.3 Salvation through Judgment for God's Glory in Hebrews

The narrative substructure of Hebrews centers on the glory of God in salvation through judgment supremely accomplished in Christ, as the concluding doxology demonstrates (Heb. 13:20–21). The rehearsal of the judgment that fell on the Israelites who came out of Egypt and did not believe (cf. 2:2; 3:7–11, 16–19; 4:2, 6, 11; 10:28; 12:25) also contributes to the theme of salvation through judgment. The author cites these examples of judgment to encourage his audience to do everything they can to avoid a similar, though worse, judgment (cf. 2:3; 3:12–15; 4:1, 3, 6, 11; 10:29; 12:25). In other words, the author of Hebrews means to save his audience through these reminders of past judgment. The exhortations, however, are not only negative. The positive side of the exhortation comes in the author's jubilant expressions of the greatness of what God has done in Christ.

Inevitable judgment awaits those who side with those who put Christ to death and crucify for themselves the Lord of glory (Heb. 6:6). That is, those who fall away have rejected Jesus and are not believers, however exposed to gospel truth they may have been (cf. 6:4–5). The point of this passage is not to teach that genuine believers can lose their salvation but to urge genuine believers not to fall away.[153] The author expresses his confidence that his teaching will have its intended affect (6:10). Through the announcement of judgment on those who fall away, the author intends to save his audience from that fate.

There are also references to a future judgment in Hebrews (cf., e.g., Heb. 9:27; 10:37–39; 12:26–27), and the author announces this coming judgment so that his audience will be saved through their knowledge that they must trust Christ to stand on that day. The author also renders his judgment that the old covenant is now obsolete (8:13) precisely so that his audience will flee to the forgiveness found in the new covenant (e.g., 8:10–12).[154] God's glory in salvation through

[153]Thomas R. Schreiner and Ardel B. Caneday, *The Race Set Before Us: A Biblical Theology of Perseverance and Assurance* (Downers Grove, IL: InterVarsity, 2001), 193–213.

[154]For an argument that Christ has transformed and fulfilled the law, see Barry C. Joslin, *Hebrews, Christ and the Law: The Theology of the Mosaic Law in Hebrews 7:1–10:18*, Paternoster Biblical Monographs (Milton Keynes: Paternoster, 2008); summarized in Joslin, "Hebrews 7–10 and the Transformation of the Law," in *A*

judgment is central in Hebrews, first and foremost in the salvation through judgment that comes through the better sacrifice of Jesus, which results in a clean conscience for those who believe (9:14). And on the basis of that, the author uses judgment as a tool to spur his audience to hold fast their confession and draw near to God.

3.3 James

The first chapter of the letter of James functions like a table of contents for chapters 2–5,[155] and the burden of the epistle is to condemn worldliness and a worldly approach to the faith. Through that condemnation James seeks to bring the audience of his letter safely to salvation for God's glory.[156] James teaches that those who have been brought forth by the word of truth (James 1:18) have a set of values that reverses worldly norms and expectations.[157]

Those who embrace the friendship of the world (James 4:4) have their standards of measure condemned, and through that judgment James preserves his people, who are in the "dispersion" (1:1) waiting for the return from exile at the coming of the Lord (5:8). Thus, the worldly enjoyment of trial-free life is countered by the call to consider trials joy for the perseverance they produce (1:2–4). The unworldly perspective James advocates is the essence of the wisdom people should pray in faith to receive (1:5–8). The worldly appreciation of wealth is reversed in the call for the poor to boast in their exaltation, while the rich are warned that their day in the sun will soon cause their flower to wither (1:9–11).

The rest of James's letter clarifies that the humiliated rich, whose flower will fade (James 1:10–11), are not pious people of wealth but those who oppose the church. These are the rich who oppress Christians and drag them into court (2:6), who blaspheme the name of Christ (2:7); these are the rich who have defrauded those who work for them (5:1–5) and who are guilty of the murder of the righteous one (5:6).[158] James has no condemnation for Christians to whom God

Cloud of Witnesses: The Theology of Hebrews in Its Ancient Contexts, ed. Richard Bauckham et al., LNTS (New York: T&T Clark, 2008), 100–17.

[155]Mark E. Taylor and George H. Guthrie, "The Structure of James," *CBQ* 68 (2006): 682–83. My reading of James is heavily influenced by this essay. Cf. also Mark E. Taylor, "Recent Scholarship on the Structure of James," *Currents in Biblical Research* 3 (2004): 86–115.

[156]Andrew Chester writes, "The themes of judgment, testing, and threat are set over, and within, the work as a whole, but so also are those of hope for the messianic age and final reward, and the immediate, urgent implications of this for the way life should be lived in the present" (Andrew Chester and Ralph P. Martin, *The Theology of the Letters of James, Peter, and Jude*, New Testament Theology [New York: Cambridge University Press, 1994], 20).

[157]Similarly Luke Timothy Johnson, *The Letter of James*, AB (New York: Doubleday, 1995), 14: "An important organizing (and selecting) principle in James is a central set of convictions concerning the absolute incompatibility of two construals of reality and two modes of behavior following from such diverse understandings. This 'deep structure' of polar opposition between 'friendship with the world' and 'friendship with God' undergirds the inclusion and shaping of James' material."

[158]For the view that the righteous one is not Jesus, see Craig L. Blomberg and Mariam J. Kamell, *James*, ZECNT (Grand Rapids: Zondervan, 2008), 224–25; and Johnson, *The Letter of James*, 305. Several texts in Acts speak

has entrusted much in the way of financial resources, but he does condemn the worldly wealthy who are opposed to God and the gospel.

Through this condemnation, James means to bring his audience to the saving perspective that those who have the gospel, though they might be poor in terms of monetary resources and worldly approval, are exalted (James 1:9). They will face trials, but contrary to all worldly ways of assessing things, James teaches that those who endure trials are those who are blessed rather than those who face no trials. Their reward is the crown of life God has promised to those who love him (1:12). God cannot be tempted by evil, nor does he tempt people to it, but people are tempted because of their own desire for evil, which results in sin (1:13–14).

The call not to be deceived in James 1:16 applies to all the topics James addresses: do not be deceived into discouragement by trials, but count them joy (1:2–4); do not be deceived into unbelief, but ask God for wisdom in faith (1:5–8); do not be deceived by the appearance of worldly wealth, but rejoice in the true wealth of knowing the gospel (1:9–11); do not be deceived by the appearance of ease, but know that those who persevere to the end are blessed (1:12); and do not be deceived into thinking that God is responsible for human sin, but know that he is not tempted by evil and does not tempt to it (1:13–15). The good and perfect gifts, including the heavenly wisdom necessary for right understanding of life (cf. 3:13–18) come from God above (1:17), who caused believers to be born again by the word of truth (1:18).

Having brought his audience through this judgment on worldly thinking, James focuses his attention on speaking and acting.[159] Often he juxtaposes right speaking with right acting, as table 6.4 shows.

James pronounces judgment on speaking too quickly and becoming rashly angry, and through that judgment he seeks to deliver his audience to a posture of humble reception of God's word (James 1:19–21). From there he condemns the mere hearing of the word, and through that judgment he seeks to deliver his audience to the blessing of doing the word (1:22–25). Nor does James leave worthless religion uncondemned, but in keeping with his focus on unworldly values, he commends the pure and undefiled religion—unstained by the world—of helping those who can neither help themselves nor offer help in return: orphans and widows (1:26–27).

In the first chapter James introduces his set of topics, then he returns to them to give specific, practical applications. Christians are to apply their unworldly values regarding wealth and poverty (James 1:9–11) when rich and poor people come to church (2:1–13). Christians are to be doers of the word, not merely

of the "Righteous One" being murdered (cf. esp. Acts 3:14; 7:52; 22:14), so it may be that in James 5:6 there is a reference to *the* righteous one in whose steps Christians follow.

[159]Taylor and Guthrie, "The Structure of James," 694–97.

Table 6.4. Juxtaposition of Speaking and Acting in James[1]

Speaking	Acting
1:5: "ask God"	
1:9–10: "Let the lowly brother boast . . . and the rich . . ."	1:12: "Blessed is the man who remains steadfast under trial."
1:13: "Let no one say when he is tempted . . ."	
1:19: "be . . . slow to speak"	1:19: "be quick to hear . . . slow to anger"
	1:21–25: "put away . . . receive . . . . be doers of the word . . ."
1:26: "If anyone . . . does not bridle his tongue . . ."	1:27: "visit orphans and widows . . . keep oneself unstained from the world"
2:3, 7: "If you . . . say . . . while you say . . . . are they not the ones who blaspheme . . . ?"	2:1–11: "show no partiality . . . . fulfill the royal law"
2:12: "so speak . . ."	2:12: ". . . and so act . . ."
2:14–26: "someone says he has faith . . ."	2:14–26: "I will show you my faith by my works."
3:1–12: the danger of the tongue	
3:14: "do not boast"	3:13–18: "By his good conduct let him show his works in the meekness of wisdom."
4:1–6: "quarrels . . . you do not ask. You ask . . ."	4:1–6: "fights . . . . murder. . . . covet . . . . friendship with the world"
4:11: "Do not speak evil . . ."	4:7–10: "Submit . . . . Resist . . . . Draw near . . . . Cleanse . . . . Be wretched . . . . Humble yourselves . . ."
4:13–16: "you who say . . . . you ought to say . . . . you boast"	4:17: "Whoever knows the right thing to do and fails to do it, for him it is sin."
5:1: "weep and howl"	
5:4: "The wages . . . are crying out against you, and the cries of the harvesters have reached the ears of the Lord of hosts."	5:3–6: "You have laid up treasure . . . . You have lived . . . You have fattened . . . . you have . . . murdered"
5:9: "Do not grumble . . ."	5:7–8: "Be patient . . . . Establish your hearts."
5:10: "the prophets who spoke"	
5:12–20: "do not swear . . . let your "yes" . . . and your "no" . . . . Let him pray. . . . sing praise. . . . call for the elders . . . let them pray . . . . the prayer . . . . confess your sins . . . pray for one another . . . . he prayed , . . . brings him back . . ."	

[1]All texts here are from the ESV.

hearers (1:22), and their deeds are to give evidence that they have living faith (2:14–26). Christians are to be quick to listen and slow to speak (1:19), and not many should become teachers (3:1). Those whose religion is worthless do not bridle their tongues (1:26), and the one who can bridle his tongue can bridle his whole body (3:2–8). Those who speak as they should, counting trials joy (1:2–4), praying in faith (1:5–8), boasting in the exaltation of having nothing and possessing everything (1:9–11), speaking rightly of God and temptation (1:12–15), they show what kind of spring their hearts are, what kind of tree they are, blessing God and not cursing people (3:9–12). Those who have earthly, unspiritual, demonic "wisdom" will not do these things (3:14–16), but those who pray in faith for wisdom and heed the salvation through judgment James teaches will have the wisdom (cf. 1:5) from above (3:13–18).

The evil desires for which God cannot be blamed (James 1:13–15) resurface when James addresses the quarrels and fights among Christians (4:1–2). These desires reflect a passion for worldly things loved by God's enemies (4:3–5). James calls the Christians to humble themselves, resist the Devil, cleanse themselves from faithless worldly pleasures, and mourn over their sin (4:6–9). Humbling themselves in response to the judgment James pronounces will result in exaltation (4:10).

James again urges his hearers to be doers of the law (James 4:11–12; cf. 1:22). Again he calls for humility with respect to things financial (4:13–17; cf. 1:9–11). And then James directly confronts the sin of the rich (5:1–6). Here he pronounces the judgment that is coming upon them, and through the announcement of condemnation he hopes to bring them through to repentance. James closes his letter with a call for patient endurance of trials (5:7–11; cf. 1:12) and right speaking in various situations (5:13–18; cf. 1:26). His final words exhort the believers he addresses to seek to save others through judgment in the way that he has, announcing their multitude of sins and the certain death that awaits those who will not turn back (5:19–20). James wants people to realize the guilt of their sin, and through that judgment confess sin and be healed (5:16). The letter of James is about the glory of God in Christ (2:1; 3:9, 18; 5:7, 9) in salvation through judgment, with judgment setting the stage for the triumph of mercy (2:13).

3.4 First Peter

Peter's first letter turns on the two instances of "Beloved" at 2:11 and 4:12.[160] From 1:1 through 2:10, Peter blesses God for the great mercy he has shown (1:1–12) and calls the sojourners he addresses to be holy as God is holy (1:13–2:10). This section is dominated by new-exodus imagery. Peter's Old Testament quotations strategically declare the significance of what God has done in Christ. From the new exodus Peter moves to the wilderness sojourn in 2:11–4:11, teaching the redeemed how to sojourn toward the Promised Land.[161] This portion of the letter

[160] Similarly Ralph P. Martin in Chester and Martin, *The Theology of the Letters of James, Peter, and Jude*, 101.

[161] As instances of typology in 1 Peter, note the sojourning and exile of Israel and the identification of Christians as sojourners and exiles (1 Pet. 1:1, 17; 2:11); the old covenant tabernacle and temple fulfilled in the new covenant temple—the believers and the church (2:5); Israel's role in the world ("kingdom of priests") is fulfilled by the church's role in the world (2:9–10); Christ's suffering is "filled up" (cf. Col. 1:24) as Christians follow his

deals with submission and suffering. The sojourners are to submit to governing authorities (2:13–17), slaves are to submit to their masters (2:18–25), and wives to their husbands (3:1–7). The sojourners are also called to suffer for doing good, not for doing evil (3:8–4:11). In the final section of the letter (4:12–5:14), Peter calls the churches to recognize that it is through much tribulation that they will enter the kingdom (4:12–19), calls the elders to shepherd the flock faithfully through the wilderness of the messianic woes (5:1–5), and prepares them for struggle through which they will enter into glory (5:6–14).

In all this, the glory of God is seen in many ways, as reflected in table 6.5.

Table 6.5. The Glory of God and Christ in 1 Peter[1]

1:3	"Blessed be the God and Father of our Lord Jesus Christ!"
1:7	"to result in praise and glory and honor at the revelation of Jesus Christ"
1:8	"and rejoice with joy that is inexpressible and filled with glory"
1:21	"who raised him from the dead and gave him glory"
2:9	"that you may proclaim the excellencies of him who called you"
2:12	"that they may . . . glorify God on the day of visitation"
4:11	". . . that in everything God may be glorified through Jesus Christ. To him belong glory and dominion forever and ever. Amen."
4:13	"when his glory is revealed"
4:14	"the Spirit of glory and of God rests upon you"
4:16	"let him glorify God in that name"
5:1	"the glory that is going to be revealed"
5:4	"you will receive the unfading crown of glory"
5:10	"who has called you to his eternal glory in Christ"
5:11	"To him be the dominion forever and ever. Amen."

[1]All texts here are from the ESV.

3.4.1 The New Exodus: Praise God and Be Ye Holy (1 Pet. 1:1–2:10)

Peter opens his letter by addressing the "chosen sojourners" dispersed abroad (1 Pet. 1:1). Like Old Testament Israel, they are chosen. Like Old Testament Israel, they are sojourning toward the Promised Land. Unlike Old Testament Israel, they know the names and ministries of all three members of the Trinity (1:2).

Peter goes on to bless God for his mercy to these sojourners in Pontus, Galatia, Cappadocia, Asia, and Bithynia.[162] Through the resurrection of Jesus they have been born again to a living hope (1 Pet. 1:3), to an imperishable inheritance (1:4), and by God's power they are kept through faith for the salvation that will

example through the messianic woes (2:12–23; 4:1, 12–19); the conduct of the holy women and Sarah sets the pattern for Christian wives to fulfill (3:5–6); and the salvation through judgment at the flood is a type of the salvation through judgment enacted in Christian baptism (3:21).

[162]Karen H. Jobes (*1 Peter*, BECNT [Grand Rapids: Baker, 2005], 79) entitles her discussion of 1 Pet. 1:3–12, "Doxology as the Basis for the Christian Life."

be revealed (1:5). The new life of the new birth (1:3) evokes the resurrection promised in the return to the land (Ezek. 37:14), and an "inheritance" may also point to the fulfillment of the promise of land that Israel was to inherit. Peter's chosen sojourners have been saved through the triumph of Jesus over the judgment that fell on him (1 Pet. 1:3); they rejoice in the mercy of God they have received (1:6); and their endurance through trial will bring glory to Jesus (1:6–7). Their joy in Christ is unspeakable and saturated with glory (1:8). This salvation (1:9) is precious: Old Testament prophets foretold it by the Spirit of Christ in them, and angels would love to examine it more carefully (1:10–12). Schreiner points out that "the salvation given in Jesus Christ is the new exodus, to which the Egyptian liberation pointed (cf. 1 Pet 1:10–12)."[163]

Having celebrated redemption, Peter urges the churches to which he writes to focus on the hope they have, the full revelation of Jesus Christ (1 Pet. 1:13). They are called to be holy as the Father is holy (1:14–16) because as Israel was redeemed from Egypt by the Passover lamb, they have been redeemed by the blood of *the* Lamb, Christ (1:17–21). Peter's citation of Leviticus 19:2 (LXX; cf. also 11:44; 20:7–8; 20:26) in 1 Peter 1:16 is strategically placed. Just as Israel was called to be holy in Leviticus after the exodus from Egypt, so Peter calls this new Israel to be holy after the new exodus he has just described. The call to "gird up the loins of your mind" in 1 Peter 1:13 may be intended to prepare the churches for their sojourn through the wilderness to the Promised Land.

Having announced that they were redeemed by the fulfillment of the Passover Lamb, Christ (1 Pet. 1:18–19), who was slain to accomplish the new and greater exodus, and having called them to gird up the loins of their minds and be holy (1:13–16), Peter heralds an Isaianic return-from-exile text. Now that the redeemed are on their way to the Promised Land, they must purify themselves (1:22)—not outwardly but in terms of their behavior. They are to love, because they have been born again (1:23a; cf. Ezek. 37:14). The agent of their new birth was the word of God (1 Pet. 1:23b), and here Peter quotes from Isaiah 40:6 and 8. In Isaiah these verses follow the announcement of comfort because warfare resulting in exile is over, iniquity is pardoned, and Yahweh has visited his justice (Isa. 40:1–2). The voice has cried out that the way is to be made straight for Yahweh's return to Zion (40:3–4). Yahweh's glory will be seen by all flesh (40:5), because Yahweh has given his word and it will stand forever (40:6–8). Hard on the heels of the announcement of redemption in Christ, the unblemished Lamb (1 Pet. 1:18–21; cf. Isa. 40:2), then, this quotation of Isaiah 40:6 and 8 amounts to an assertion that just as God has accomplished the new exodus in Christ's death and resurrection, so he will accomplish the return from exile. His word will stand forever (1 Pet. 1:25). Therefore Peter's audience must purify itself

[163]Schreiner, *New Testament Theology*, 156.

for life in the land, the new heavens and the new earth (1:22–25). When Peter asserts that "this is the word that was gospelled to you" in 1 Peter 1:25, his use of the word "gospel" or "good news" (εὐαγγελίζω) is undoubtedly influenced by Isaiah's use of that language (cf. LXX Isa. 40:9; 52:7; 60:6; 61:1).

The new exodus has taken place, the return from exile has begun, and just as Israel built the tabernacle in the wilderness, so Peter tells the churches they are "like living stones, being built into a spiritual house, as a holy priesthood, to offer spiritual sacrifices acceptable to God through Jesus the messiah" (1 Pet. 2:5). The new Passover Lamb has been slain. The new Israel has been called to be holy. The new exodus and return from exile have been announced. And in 1 Peter 2:4–5 Peter tells the churches that they are the new temple that is being built. Borrowing the language of Exodus 19:6, Peter tells his churches that they are the people of God: "a chosen race, a royal priesthood, a holy nation, a people for his possession, that you might declare the virtues of the one who called you out of darkness into his marvelous light" (1 Pet. 2:9). Peter then borrows language from Hosea, language that in its original context referred to God's mercy to his people after the discipline of exile (1 Pet. 2:10; cf. Hos. 1:6, 9–10; 2:23). A new people of God has been formed through a new exodus, and they are the new temple as they set out on a new sojourn to a new land, the new heaven and earth.

3.4.2 Submitting and Suffering Sojourners (1 Pet. 2:11–4:11)

Given their locations (cf. 1 Pet. 1:1), the churches to whom Peter wrote were at least partly, if not predominantly, Gentile. This makes Peter's call to these new sojourners (2:11) to abstain from warring passions and to keep their conduct honorable "among the Gentiles" (2:11b–12) all the more striking. This new (Gentile) people of God is, theologically speaking, no longer Gentile. It is difficult to see how the church here is anything other than the new Israel.

This new Israel, however, is neither an empire nor explicitly subversive of empires. However much contemporary scholars enjoy the topic of "anti-imperialism in the New Testament," like the apostle Paul (cf. Rom. 13:1–7), the apostle Peter calls for submission to the empire, not subversion of it (1 Pet. 2:13–17). Of course, Christianity does subvert God-dishonoring, Christ-rejecting ideas, as well as all the expressions of those ideas in acts of human pride and wickedness and self-seeking. But this kind of subversion applies as much, if not more, to the political agendas of tenured theologians as it does to government officials and politicians.

So Peter calls the sojourners to submit to the government over them (1 Pet. 2:13–17), and, if they are slaves, to submit to their masters (2:18–25). Christians have been called to suffer unjustly because they are called to follow in the footsteps of Christ (2:21), who bore our sins in his body on the tree (2:24), through which judgment we are saved.[164]

It is shocking how controversial these sections of 1 Peter are today. What Peter teaches here is openly rejected by the elite, professional academic custodians of Bible and theology. Try telling a tenured Bible scholar or theologian at Yale, Princeton, Duke, or Fuller (to say nothing of German, British, or French universities), that the Bible commands Christians to submit to the governing authorities (1 Pet. 2:13–17), slaves to be subject to their masters (2:18–25), and wives to be subject to their husbands (3:1–7). The same incredulity and amazement that would greet an argument for slaves to submit greets any suggestion that the emperor deserves honor (2:17) or that wives should adorn themselves with gentle and quiet spirits (3:4).[165] Of course we must account for societal differences between Peter's day and ours, but only worldly wisdom can remove the authority structures enjoined upon Christians. We should also observe that whereas the Bible teaches that God instituted marriage in the garden of Eden (Gen. 2:18–25), the Bible's instructions on slavery regulate a wicked human practice that, unlike marriage, was not instituted by God in Eden. Peter's instructions to slaves have in view the advancement of the gospel. Many contemporaries would be shocked that Peter would value the gospel more than he would social justice, but these instructions indicate that he did. The salvation offered in the gospel is eternal. For the gospel, Christians must submit to the governing authorities, as well as to their employers and other figures of authority in socio-economic settings, and wives must submit to their husbands.[166]

Peter calls these sojourners to the good life, the life that will guarantee inheritance of the land and its enjoyment (1 Pet. 3:8–12). If they are to suffer, it must be for doing good (3:13–17). Having accomplished salvation through judgment, Christ proclaimed his victory to the sinning angels from Noah's day (3:18–20; cf. Gen. 6:1–4).[167] Just as Noah was saved through the judgment of the flood, those who are baptized into Christ by faith are saved through the judgment that fell on Jesus (1 Pet. 3:21). By following in the footsteps of Christ in humbly suffering for what is good, Christians will advance the gospel (4:1–11).

---

[164]Cf. 1 Pet. 2:22 and Isa. 53:9; 1 Pet. 2:24 and Isa. 53:5; and 1 Pet. 2:25 and Isa. 53:6. Clement seems to have learned from Peter and other New Testament authors to interpret the atoning death of Jesus through Isaiah 53 while simultaneously offering the conduct of Jesus, as prophesied in Isaiah 53, as a pattern for Christians to follow. See *1 Clem.* 15:1–16:14, 17.

[165]See, e.g., the summary of feminist scholarship in Margaret Y. MacDonald, "Women in Early Christianity: The Challenge to a New Testament Theology," in *The Nature of New Testament Theology: Essays in Honour of Robert Morgan*, ed. Christopher Rowland and Christopher Tuckett (Oxford: Blackwell, 2006), 135–57.

[166]See further Thomas R. Schreiner, *1, 2 Peter, Jude*, NAC (Nashville: Broadman & Holman, 2003), 136; and Jobes, *1 Peter*, 211.

[167]See John Dennis, "Cosmology in the Petrine Literature and Jude," in Pennington and McDonough, *Cosmology and New Testament Theology*, 165.

3.4.3 Shepherded through Messianic Woes to Glory (1 Pet. 4:12–5:14)

The Old Testament gave rise to a widespread expectation that the people of God would experience intense suffering before the coming of the kingdom of God, an expectation nourished in the Intertestamental literature and widely attested in the New Testament as well (cf., e.g., Isa. 26:17–19, and see the other Old Testament, Intertestamental, and New Testament texts in table 6.2 above).[168] This probably informs what Peter says about the "fiery trial" and the sharing in Christ's sufferings that his audience will pass through on their way to his glory (1 Pet. 4:12–13). Peter calls them to reconfigure their thinking, so that they regard themselves as blessed to suffer for the glory of Christ (4:14–19). An aspect of this, as Schreiner points out, is "the threat that they will be judged if they turn away from the gospel" (cf., e.g., 4:17). Schreiner explains, "The promise and threat are corollaries in the letter, for the threat of final judgment also spurs the readers to set their hope entirely on the promise. They realize that the future reward is also matched by future judgment and that hoping in God is not trivial but momentous."[169] The threat of judgment is meant to ensure salvation. This also informs Peter's call to elders to set willing examples for the flocks they serve in order to gain the crown of unfading glory (5:1–5). God will bring them through to the end (5:6–14).

The pattern of moving through judgment to salvation is seen often in 1 Peter, as table 6.6 demonstrates.

Through the judgment that fell on Christ, Christians are saved to the glory of God. And as they sojourn toward the Promised Land, Christians experience the messianic woes, the birth pains through which new life will come, and the threat of judgment spurs them to set their hope on the salvation to be revealed. So in the new exodus of Christ's death and resurrection, in the moment of conversion, and in the experience of Christian life enduring the messianic woes, there is a consistent pattern: through judgment salvation comes to God's glory.

John Elliott discusses the theology of Peter under four headings: "God, Christ and salvation, eschatology, and ecclesiology and ethics." I would argue that the hub of these four spokes, the center that binds them together, is God's glory in salvation through judgment. Elliott seems to agree:

> For Christians at odds with their environment and pressured to conform and assimilate, honor and shame are theologically redefined in this letter and reckoned according to a calculus of divine reversal, preeminently expressed in God's honor-

[168]For discussion, see Dale C. Allison, *The End of the Ages Has Come: An Early Interpretation of the Passion and Resurrection of Jesus* (Philadelphia: Fortress, 1985).
[169]Schreiner, *1, 2 Peter, Jude*, 46.

Table 6.6. Suffering and Exaltation in 1 Peter

Text[1]	Suffering	Exaltation
1:6–9	"grieved by various trials . . . tested genuineness . . . refined"	"the outcome of your faith, the salvation of your souls"
2:18–20	"also to the unjust. . . . sorrows while suffering unjustly. . . . do good and suffer for it"	"This is a gracious thing in the sight of God."
3:1	"be subject . . . even if some do not obey the word"	". . . they may be won without a word."
3:13–22	"suffer for righteousness' sake . . . when you are slandered, those who revile . . . . suffer for doing good"	"you will be blessed. . . . that he might bring us to God . . . . Baptism . . . now saves you . . . an appeal to God for a good conscience"
4:1–5	"Since . . . Christ suffered . . . arm yourselves with the same way of thinking . . . they malign you"	". . . they will give an account."
4:12–19	"fiery trial . . . to test you . . . . you share Christ's sufferings . . . . insulted for the name of Christ . . . . if anyone suffers as a Christian . . . . let those who suffer according to God's will"	"that you may also rejoice and be glad when his glory is revealed. . . . you are blessed . . . . let him glorify God in that name."
5:9–10	"The same kinds of suffering are being experienced by your brotherhood throughout the world."	"The God of all grace, who has called you to his eternal glory in Christ, will himself restore, confirm, strengthen, and establish you."

[1]All texts here are from the ESV.

> ing of the shamed Messiah and honoring of those who share both his innocent suffering and his glorious vindication.[170]

In other words, on the basis of the salvation through judgment accomplished at the cross, God has condemned the world's notions of honor (glory) and reshaped how the people of God are to regard honor and shame around what he accomplished in Christ. Through judgment, God saves to his glory. This is the center of the theology of 1 Peter.[171]

3.5 Second Peter

In his second letter (2 Pet. 3:1), Peter celebrates the saving power of the knowledge of God and Christ (1:2–3). Peter closes the letter with another reference to

[170]John H. Elliott, *1 Peter: A New Translation with Introduction and Commentary*, AB (New York: Doubleday, 2000), 109–18, quotes on 109 and 118.

[171]Martin identifies "hope in Christ" as the "central motif" of 1 Peter (in Chester and Martin, *The Theology of the Letters of James, Peter, and Jude*, 132). I think this stops one step short, for the hope is specifically hope that Christ will soon bring the judgment through which salvation will come to the glory of God.

the knowledge of the Lord Jesus (3:18), forming an *inclusio*.[172] There is also a "glory" *inclusio* in the references to the glory of God and Christ in 1:3 and 3:18. Peter assures his audience of the truth he has taught them (2 Peter 1), exposes the true nature of false teachers (2 Peter 2), and warns of the coming day of the Lord (2 Peter 3).

By his power, glory, and virtue, Christ called believers (2 Pet. 1:3) and promised rare and magnificent things to them (1:4a). Such promises expose sinful pleasures as cheap nothings, enabling believers (1:1) to escape the corruption of the world (1:4b). Through judgment on false pleasure believers are saved by and for God's glory in Christ.

The privilege of being saved by the righteous glory of Jesus entails the responsibility to grow in virtue and godliness (2 Pet. 1:5–11). Humbled to have received faith (1:1), Peter is committed to serving the churches by reminding them of the truth he has taught them (1:12–15).

Peter then appears to counter the claims of false teachers by asserting the reliability of his eyewitness testimony to the majesty of the Lord Jesus (1:16). It is worth pointing out here that if, as many scholars believe, Peter did not write this letter, the argument here is worthless.[173] The whole point depends on the apostle Peter being the author, an eyewitness of Jesus' receiving honor and glory from God the Father (1:17). Peter asserts that he heard it (1:18). Following this account of his experience of the majestic glory of the Father giving honor and glory to Christ in majesty (1:16–18), Peter directs his people to the Bible, which was inspired by the Holy Spirit (1:19–20).

Having reminded his readers of the glory of God in their salvation and called them to hold fast to apostolic testimony and the Scriptures in chapter 1, Peter begins to interpret the Old Testament for the benefit of his audience in chapter 2. Old Testament Israel was redeemed from Egypt, and then false prophets arose among the people. This type[174] means that false teachers will arise in the churches, and just as those false prophets in Israel incurred the wrath of and were destroyed by the one who redeemed them, so the Redeemer will swiftly destroy the false teachers (2 Pet. 2:1–3). Proof of their certain destruction is provided from God's judgment on the offending angels (2:4; cf. Gen. 6:1–4), his salvation of Noah through the judgment of the flood (2 Pet. 2:5), and his salvation of Lot through the judgment of Sodom and Gomorrah (2:6–8), each of which proves

[172]Schreiner, *1, 2 Peter, Jude*, 283.

[173]For a compelling argument that Peter wrote 2 Peter, see Schreiner, *1, 2 Peter, Jude*, 253–76.

[174]The types in 2 Peter include: the false prophets and Balaam, who portend the greedy false teachers (2 Pet. 2:1–3, 15–16); the judgment of the angels, which guarantees the judgment of the wicked (2:4, 9–10); the flood, which guarantees the judgment of the wicked (2:5, 9–10); the salvation of Noah, which promises the salvation of the godly (2:5, 9); the judgment on Sodom and Gomorrah, which guarantees the judgment of the wicked (2:6, 9–10); and the salvation of Lot, which guarantees the salvation of the godly (2:8–9).

that the Lord knows how to save the righteous and judge the wicked (2:9–10).[175] The clear implication here is that God will save the church through the judgment of the false teachers that have and will come.

Peter then describes the lusting madness (2 Pet. 2:10b–16) and the fruitless deception (2:17–19) of the false teachers. This announcement of condemnation against them is meant to liberate the churches from their influence. Peter means to save the churches by announcing the certain judgment that awaits the false teachers. The false teachers themselves seemed to have been delivered through the knowledge of Christ, but their return to sin makes their last state worse than their first, showing also that they are pigs and dogs who were never redeemed to begin with (2:20–22).[176]

In 2 Peter 3, Peter again reminds the churches of the teaching of the Scriptures and the apostles (2 Pet. 3:1–2; cf. 1:12–13, 16–21). Mockers, perhaps the false teachers themselves, may cast doubt on the certainty of the coming of the Lord to save and judge on the great day (3:3–4), but the teaching of the Old Testament shows that God saves through judgment. Peter asserts that the mockers willfully fail to notice the way God saved through judgment at the flood (3:5–6), and he teaches that God will again save through judgment, this time with fire (3:7–10). On the basis of the coming judgment, Peter calls the churches to lives of holiness, expecting and hastening the day of the Lord, looking forward to the new heavens and the new earth (3:11–14).[177] He means to deliver his audience to the glory of God through the announcement of coming judgment. Peter teaches that God's patience is for all the elect to be saved (3:9, 15). He also claims that his teaching is the same as Paul's (3:15–16), whose writings are Scripture (3:16).

Knowing all this, Peter's audience is called to avoid the false teachers and grow in the knowledge of Jesus (2 Pet. 3:17–18a). Peter closes with a doxology ascribing glory to Jesus now and forever (3:18b). The whole of 2 Peter announces judgment on wicked false teachers for the purpose of wooing those who will be saved to the enjoyment of knowing God in Christ. The center of Peter's theology is thus the glory of God in Christ in salvation that comes through judgment.

---

[175]Dennis ("Cosmology in the Petrine Literature and Jude," 176) speaks of "2 Peter's view (consistent with Jewish and Christian eschatology) that cosmic destruction is a *final* judgement which brings about *the final* renewal of the cosmos."

[176]Schreiner, *1, 2 Peter, Jude*, 330–31, 363–65.

[177]Similarly Dennis, "Cosmology in the Petrine Literature and Jude," 177: "Cosmogony and cosmology, here in 2 Peter as well as 1 Peter and Jude, serve the main concerns of theology and ethical formation and transformation."

3.6 First John

Since the structure of 1 John is disputed,[178] rather than attempt to walk through the literary structure of the letter, I will highlight the center of John's[179] theology as it is reflected in his first letter. I will seek to demonstrate that the center of the theology of 1 John is the glory of God in salvation through judgment by culling statements from the letter that reflect John's views of

- the state of the world,
- apostates who were drawn to the church but returned to their true home, the world,
- God's work to save,
- how that work of salvation is applied to worldlings who become children of God,
- how the glory of God is reflected in the new life he gives to his children, as truth triumphs over lies and love overcomes hatred.

3.6.1 The World

What can we know about the world from 1 John? The whole world has sins that need to be propitiated (1 John 2:1). Those who love the world do not love God the Father (2:15), for the world is characterized by things that do not come from the Father—lust of the flesh, lust of the eyes, and the pride of life (2:16). This world will not last; it is passing away (2:17). The world does not recognize its God, nor does it recognize the children of God (3:1) but hates them (3:13). This hatred marks worldlings as those who are "of the evil one" (3:12), but this Evil One, for all his false prophets (4:1), though he is "in the world," is not greater than God (4:4). The worldlings are "from the world." They speak from the world, and so the world listens to them (4:5). We will see below that the world will be overcome (5:4–5), but here we close with John's assertion that "the whole world is laid in the power of the evil one" (5:19).

3.6.2 Apostates

First John is addressed to churches. From what John says in the letter, these churches have been confronted with the claims of people who deny that Jesus has come in the flesh (cf. 1 John 1:1–4), that he is the messiah, and that sin is sinful; and some of these deniers seem to have been in the church but have gone out from it. It is striking how contemporary this ancient letter seems. Much of 1 John seeks to differentiate between those who truly belong to the world and

[178]Cf. Robert W. Yarbrough, *1–3 John*, BECNT (Grand Rapids: Baker, 2008), 21, who "simply follows the inner marginal numbers of NA[27], which in turn reflect the divisions that came to be standard among scribal copyists through the centuries." See also Marshall, *New Testament Theology*, 532.

[179]For a ringing, refreshing, sane defense of the idea that John the son of Zebedee wrote 1–3 John, see Yarbrough, *1–3 John*, 5–15.

those who are children of God. John has not a little to say about how to discern the difference between the two.

Writing in the first person plural, including himself and his hearers ("we"), John says that those who claim fellowship with God while walking in darkness are liars (1 John 1:6). Again in the first-person plural ("we"), John says that those who deny that they have sin deceive themselves and the truth is not in them (1:8). In yet another first-person plural ("we"), John says that those who say they have not sinned are making God into a liar (1:10). This clearly means that God says humans are sinful, and so people who deny that are either self-deceived or declaring God to be a liar. They show themselves to be liars by claiming to love God while hating their brothers (4:20).

Those who claim to be believers but do not keep God's commandments are denounced by John as truthless liars (1 John 2:4). In fact, those who continue in unrepentant sin are lawless (3:4). Those who keep on sinning have neither seen nor known God (3:6). They are of the Devil (3:8), and they prove it by refusing to practice righteousness and love their brothers (3:10).[180] Not loving the brothers, they remain in death (3:14), they are murderers, and they do not have eternal life (3:15; 5:12). Those who do not love do not know God (4:8).

Those who claim to be in the light but hate their brothers identify themselves as remaining in darkness (2:9). Such people are blinded by the darkness, and do not know where they are going (2:11). Those who love the world do not know the love of the Father (2:15).

Perhaps some of these people were formerly associated with the church, only to reject the idea that Jesus is the messiah and to leave the church. This would explain why John says that liars and antichrists deny that Jesus is the Christ (1 John 2:22), that "they went out from us, but they were not of us" (2:19), and that many antichrists have come (2:18). These people may have claimed to be right with God, but John declares that one cannot have the Father apart from the Son (2:23). Not only do they make God a liar by denying their sin (1:10), but since God has borne witness concerning Jesus, by denying Jesus they make God a liar on that point too (5:10). This reality prompts John's call to test the spirits

[180]Cf. John 8:44, where Jesus tells the Jews, "You are of your father the devil, and your will is to do your father's desires. He was a murderer from the beginning, and has nothing to do with the truth, because there is no truth in him" (ESV). John seems to be thinking in categories he learned from Jesus when he writes in 1 John 3:8, "Whoever makes a practice of sinning is of the devil, for the devil has been sinning from the beginning" (ESV). John speaks of the "children of the devil" in 3:10, then apparently identifies the Devil's activity as "a murderer from the beginning" (John 8:44) with Cain's murder of Abel in 1 John 3:12: "We should not be like Cain, who was of the evil one and murdered his brother." Early Christians appear to have learned this way of identifying true believers as "seed of the woman" and the enemies of the church as "seed of the serpent" from John who learned it from Jesus. *First Clement* 3–7 deals with the jealous uprising of some in the church at Corinth who have rejected the church's rightful leadership. As Clement addresses this problem, he likens the jealousy of the divisive in Corinth to Israel's discontent in Deut. 32:15 (*1 Clem.* 3:1–4), then retells the story of Cain and Abel (*1 Clem.* 4:1–7). He is identifying the disruptive usurpers in the Corinthian church with Cain, just as Jesus and John identified their opponents with Cain. This all builds to the call to repentance in *1 Clement* 7.

(4:1). The spirit that does not confess Jesus is not from God but is the spirit of the antichrist (4:3). Such spirits are from the world, they speak like it, and the world loves their message (4:5). The other side of this coin is that they refuse to listen to the message John and the other children of God proclaim (4:6).

I would suggest that refusing to acknowledge one's sin (1 John 1:10), refusing to believe God's testimony concerning Jesus (5:10), and thus refusing the one who made propitiation (2:1–2) is to commit the sin that leads to death (5:16). Thus, it seems that the sin unto death is the refusal to repent of sin and believe the gospel, choosing instead to remain in the world, under the power of the Evil One (5:19).

3.6.3 God Works Salvation in Christ

Salvation is described in a number of ways in 1 John. One of the ways is as eternal life (1:2; 2:25; 5:11). John proclaims Jesus, who is eternal life, to his audience (1:2). The children of God have this eternal life abiding in them (3:15). God gave this eternal life to his children, and this eternal life is in Jesus (5:11). Those who have Jesus have it, and those who do not have Jesus, do not have it (5:12). Those who believe in Jesus have eternal life (5:13). Jesus is this eternal life (5:20).

Another description of salvation in 1 John is the idea of fellowship, fellowship with the Father and the Son, as well as other Christians (1 John 1:3). John explains that he testifies to Jesus so that people will have this fellowship (1:3). To walk in the light is to enjoy this fellowship (1:7), but it is not possible to walk in darkness and have it (1:6).

Salvation is impossible unless God forgives sin and cleanses sinners. Fellowship is not possible for those who walk in darkness (1 John 1:6), because sin separates people from God. The salvation that God has accomplished in Jesus makes eternal life and fellowship between God and people possible because Jesus made propitiation for sin (2:1–2). Jesus did no sin and appeared to take away sin (3:5). God showed his love by sending Jesus to make propitiation for our sins (4:10).[181] Apart from the sending of the Son, life through him would not be possible (4:9). The result of the Son's work is that those who confess their sins are *forgiven* and *cleansed* (1:9). To fellowship with God and believers is to have cleansing from sin by the blood of Jesus (1:7). Salvation explicitly comes through judgment for God's glory. The death of Jesus on the cross is the judgment through which believers are saved, and this is for God's glory. John writes that believers have their sins forgiven "for his name's sake" (2:12).

---

[181]Cf. Schreiner, *New Testament Theology*, 160: "God sent Jesus in love to appease his wrath. . . . What we have here is a complex understanding of God. He is both loving and angry. His anger is rooted in his goodness and holiness . . . . We must be careful to preserve the mystery of God's person here, for we have no human analogies to one who has anger that is completely righteous and whose love satisfies his own anger. No neat equations or formulas adequately explain the reality portrayed."

The Father's remarkable love is seen in that the Son is sent not to those who are favorably disposed to the Father, but to the world in need of the Savior (1 John 4:14)—the world in rebellion against God. How can God save the world, which is under the power of the Evil One (5:19)? He saves it through judgment: the Father sent the Son "to destroy the works of the devil" (3:8 ESV). How that salvation gets applied to worldlings is the subject of the next section.

3.6.4 The Application of Salvation to Worldlings

Those who are saved were dead and are now alive—they "passed out of death into life" (1 John 3:14 ESV). This passage from death to life takes place when worldlings are "born of God" (3:9; 4:7; 5:1, 4, 18). Those who are born of God know God (4:7), believe that Jesus is the messiah (5:1), and stop sinning—they are unable to continue in it (3:9; 5:18). They love the children of God (4:7; 5:1), and they overcome the world by faith (5:4). The one who believes in Jesus overcomes the world (5:5). How do they live the rest of their lives?

3.6.5 The New Life

In all this, the worldlings who are "born of God" come to love others and do precisely the opposite of what they formerly did. Where formerly they denied Jesus, they confess him. Where formerly they hated and murdered, they love. Where formerly they deceived themselves, lied, and made God a liar, they now confess sin, abide in the truth, know the true God (1 John 5:20), and believe his testimony (5:9–10).

This new life reflects the glory of God in salvation through judgment, and it points forward to the glory that will be revealed when the children of God see Christ as he is (1 John 3:2).[182] God's glory is seen in his ability to destroy the works of Satan through Christ (3:8), to make propitiation in Christ (2:2; 4:10), to forgive sin and cleanse sinners (1:7, 9; 2:12), to protect his children because he is greater than their enemy (4:4; 5:18), to enable them to overcome the Evil One (2:14), and to transform their behavior such that they have confidence for his appearing (2:28).

The glory of God is also seen in the way that God loves people such that they come to love the way he does (1 John 4:19). God loved sinners by sending Jesus to reconcile them to himself (4:10, 14). The love of God is then "perfected" in sinners who love others the way God has loved them (4:11–12, 16; 5:1). God's glory is seen in those who know God (2:13–14; 4:6), who abide in God by confessing and believing in Jesus (4:15), remembering the truth they have heard (2:24), attending to the apostolic teaching (4:6), and loving the chil-

[182]Marshall (*New Testament Theology*, 537) holds that "the central theme [of 1 John] is encouragement to the readers to persist in truth and love on the basis of their spiritual union with God." I would preface this as follows: John's main application of the center of his theology, which is the glory of God in salvation through judgment, is to encourage his readers to persist.

dren of God (2:10). They abide in God (2:24; 4:15–16), and the Father (3:24; 4:12–13, 15–16), Son (3:9), and Spirit (2:20, 27; 3:24) abide in them.[183] Robert Yarbrough concludes:

> Finally, if 1–3 John leave the disciple who studies them with any single lasting impression, it is the grandeur and centrality of God (here linking John's thought with Paul's, if Schreiner 2001 is correct). Part of this is the sheer volume of references to him. There is hardly a verse or even clause anywhere that does not name a person of the Godhead (Trinity), a divine attribute, or a divine work (like a command that has come from God). . . . No OT psalmist is any more God saturated in awareness than the writer of these letters.[184]

3.7 *Second John*

In his second letter John declares judgment on the deceivers who deny the coming of Jesus the messiah in the flesh (2 John 1:7). Through this declaration he means to save the church, the noble "lady" (1:5), from the deceivers and antichrists (1:7) who deny her Lord. Such people do not have God (1:9). The faithful should exercise judgment on them by refusing to receive them and house them, for whoever welcomes them advances their wicked works (1:10–11; cf. Rev. 2:2). Those who belong to God, who are saved through the judgment that fell on Jesus (2 John 1:3, 7, 10), walk in the truth as commanded (1:4), keeping the new commandment that was from the beginning (1:5). By pronouncing judgment against the deceivers (1:7), John means to bring his audience through judgment to salvation—the full reward (1:8). The truth (1:1–4) and love (1:1, 3, 5–6) are God's, and those brought through the condemnation of falsehood and lovelessness to the salvation of knowing God glorify God as they walk in truth and love.

3.8 *Third John*

In his third letter John announces judgment on those who oppose him and the gospel—imagine the folly of Diotrephes, who refused to acknowledge the beloved disciple himself (3 John 1:9)! John promises to take action against him in judgment if he comes (1:10), and John warns the faithful not to imitate this adversary's negative example (1:11). On the other side of things, those who have been saved through the judgment that fell on Jesus walk in the truth (1:3–4) and receive and send missionaries in a God-honoring way (1:5–6). These missionaries go out for the glory of Christ (1:7), and the good example of Demetrius is commended (1:12). As missionaries go out "for the sake of the name" (1:7), God is glorified in salvation through judgment in 3 John.

---

[183]See further Christopher D. Bass, *That You May Know: Assurance of Salvation in 1 John*, NACSBT (Nashville: Broadman & Holman, 2008).
[184]Yarbrough, *1–3 John*, 27–28.

3.9 Jude

Jude's letter is centered on God's glory in salvation through judgment. After the salutation (Jude 1:1–2), Jude urges his audience to contend for the faith (1:3) against false teachers (1:4). Jude reminds his audience of the wicked who were judged in the Old Testament (1:5–7) because they typify the judgment awaiting the false teachers (1:8–16). He calls his audience to faith in apostolic teaching and reliance on the Spirit in prayer (1:17–21), while at the same time they should actively seek to deliver those in need of mercy (1:22–23).

The faithful to whom Jude writes are those who are saved through the judgment that fell on Jesus (1:3–4),[185] and they are those who will be saved through the warning that God has judged in the past and will do so again (1:5–7)—those judged in the past are an example (1:7). Similarly, the woe on the ungodly (1:11), and the promise that the Lord will come and judge (1:14–16) guarantee justice to the wicked. Ideally, this promise of justice will prompt repentance, and if so, the false teachers will be saved through the announcement of judgment. The judgment is God's justice, and the salvation is by God's power, so he gets the glory for the salvation and preservation he accomplishes through judgment (1:24–25).

3.10 The Center of the Theology of the Catholic Epistles

What is remarkable about these letters is not diversity but complex unity.[186] They are agreed that the God of glory has demonstrated his justice and his mercy through the death and resurrection of Jesus, by which the salvation of those who believe has been accomplished. They are agreed that what God has done in Jesus is the "new exodus" act of salvation prophesied in the Old Testament. They are agreed that believers experience a new birth that brings them into the family of God. They are agreed that what God has done in Christ and is now doing in the church represents the fulfillment of the promises to Abraham, of the law of Moses, of the promises made to David, and of what the prophets from Isaiah to Malachi foretold. They are agreed that the church is the typological fulfillment of the people of God, redeemed from slavery and now sojourning toward the Land of Promise, the new heavens and new earth, the city whose architect and builder is God. They are agreed on the function of the threat of judgment—it is used to preserve believers and to enable them to persevere to the end. They are agreed on the unique ethic propounded by Christianity, an ethic that calls for love of neighbor and enemy. They advocate clearly defined gender roles and a sexual morality that was as radical in the first century as it is in the

[185]Quoting Richard Bauckham (*Jude and the Relatives of Jesus in the Early Church* [Edinburgh: T&T Clark, 1990], 312–13), Schreiner (*New Testament Theology*, 411 n. 96) writes, "According to Jude, 'Jesus is the eschatological agent of God's salvation and judgment,' and he is the Messiah."

[186]Cf. Frank J. Matera, "The Diverse Unity of New Testament Theology," in *New Testament Theology: Exploring Diversity and Unity* (Louisville: Westminster John Knox, 2007), 423–80, esp. 425, where he cites the six statements in which Peter Stuhlmacher "summarizes the central message of the New Testament."

twenty-first. They are agreed in their affirmation of the oneness of God, and at the same time in their affirmation of the personal nature of Father, Son, and Holy Spirit, who are together uniquely divine. That is, these authors teach what has come to be regarded as orthodox trinitarianism. They agree that justification is by faith alone in Christ alone by grace alone to the glory of God alone. They point their audience to the Scriptures alone, never quoting extracanonical writings as Scripture. They agree that people stand guilty before God and need the righteousness of Christ and his atoning work. They agree that God is glorified in salvation through judgment, in mercy and justice, with justice highlighting mercy, and that everything exists to display the glory of this God's holiness and loving-kindness.

4. The Center of the Theology of the New Testament Letters

The authors of these twenty-one letters are radically united in the proclamation of bizarre ideas. To see this, let us engage in a bit of contrastive analysis, contemplating what these authors did *not* do and what their letters do *not* advocate.

Rome was not their kingdom, and they were not trying to make it home. They sought the city that is to come. Not one of these authors gave his life to address the systemic injustice of the Roman Empire by means of political reform. Not one of these authors went the way of Josephus and sought to cozy up to the emperor, though Paul seems to have had opportunities to seek such "influence" with some high-ranking officials. Not one of these authors did or said anything about trying to stop Rome from fighting its wars. Not one of them championed the idea that the government should take money from the rich and redistribute it equally to the poor, nor did they leave the ministry to advocate a government of greater fiscal responsibility, lowered taxes, and increased national security. Not one of these authors taught that the way to change the world is by initiating a universal, government-funded education program. Not one of these authors was out to make as much money as he possibly could. Not one of these authors embraced one of the popular philosophies of the day, nor did they seek to synthesize the message of Jesus with the spirit of their age. None of them advocated higher moral standards in society at large (outside the church), nor did they lobby for universal health care or a revised definition of marriage that would legitimate same-sex unions.[187] None of them seem to have cared whether anyone reading their letters would be perceived by the broader culture as hip, savvy, chic, or cool. They had a different program.

These authors believed that the decisive event in the story of the world had taken place. God loved the world by sending his Son, condemned sin in the

[187]For my view of how these realities should influence what believers should do today, along with chap. 9 below, see James M. Hamilton Jr., "The Church Militant and Her Warfare: We Are Not Another Interest Group," *SBJT* 11, no. 4 (2007): 70–80.

flesh of Jesus, poured out all his wrath on Jesus at the cross, and accomplished salvation through that ultimate display of justice. God raised Jesus from the dead, and Jesus commissioned his followers to make disciples by proclaiming the good news.

How did they go about carrying out this commission? They all basically did the same thing. None appears to have sought to carry out the commission through political or educational institutions. According to the book of Acts, they simply told people, whether groups or individuals, who God is, what he had accomplished in Jesus, and what this implied for them. God accomplished salvation through judgment in Jesus, and the implication for every auditor of the message is that they would either believe and be saved or disobey (be unpersuaded by) the gospel and be judged. Through the announcement of judgment, the saved rejoiced in and glorified God. The converts, those who believed the message, were gathered into congregations, churches. Paul, Peter, and James all refer to elders who led these churches.

The authors of the letters studied in this chapter wrote what they did to form, instruct, and protect the churches. Their message is that God has glorified himself by working salvation through judgment in fulfillment of the Old Testament in the death and resurrection of Jesus. Their message is that there is a way of life that evidences belief in that message, and a way of life that does not. Their message is that God has sent the Spirit, who has given new life to those who believe; and the Spirit will keep them to the end, so that on the last day, when Christ comes to save through judgment, they will be those who glorify God for his mercy. The center of the theology of the letters of the New Testament is the glory of God in salvation through judgment.

5. Appendix

Table 6.7. Doxologies in the New Testament[1]

Luke 1:68	"Blessed be the Lord God of Israel."
Rom. 1:25	". . . the Creator, who is blessed forever! Amen."
Rom. 9:5	". . . the Christ who is God over all, blessed forever. Amen."
Rom. 11:33–36	"Oh, the depth of the riches and wisdom and knowledge of God! How unsearchable are his judgments and how inscrutable his ways! 'For who has known the mind of the Lord, or who has been his counselor?' 'Or who has given a gift to him that he might be repaid?' For from him and through him and to him are all things. To him be glory forever. Amen."

Rom. 16:25–27	"Now to him who is able to strengthen you according to my gospel and the preaching of Jesus Christ, according to the revelation of the mystery that was kept secret for long ages but has now been disclosed and through the prophetic writings has been made known to all nations, according to the command of the eternal God, to bring about the obedience of faith—to the only wise God be glory forevermore through Jesus Christ! Amen."
2 Cor. 1:3	"Blessed be the God and Father of our Lord Jesus Christ."
2 Cor. 11:31	"The God and Father of the Lord Jesus, he who is blessed forever . . ."
Gal. 1:4–5	". . . our God and Father, to whom be the glory forever and ever. Amen."
Eph. 1:3	"Blessed be the God and Father of our Lord Jesus Christ."
Eph. 3:20–21	"Now to him who is able to do far more abundantly than all that we ask or think, according to the power at work within us, to him be glory in the church and in Christ Jesus throughout all generations, forever and ever. Amen."
Phil. 4:20	"To our God and Father be glory forever and ever. Amen."
1 Tim. 1:17	"To the King of ages, immortal, invisible, the only God, be honor and glory forever and ever. Amen."
1 Tim. 6:15–16	". . . he who is the blessed and only Sovereign, the King of kings and Lord of lords, who alone has immortality, who dwells in unapproachable light, whom no one has ever seen or can see. To him be honor and eternal dominion. Amen."
2 Tim. 4:18	"The Lord will rescue me from every evil deed and bring me safely into his heavenly kingdom. To him be the glory forever and ever. Amen."
Heb. 13:20–21	"Now may the God of peace who brought again from the dead our Lord Jesus, the great shepherd of the sheep, by the blood of the eternal covenant, equip you with everything good that you may do his will, working in us that which is pleasing in his sight, through Jesus Christ, to whom be glory forever and ever. Amen."
1 Pet. 1:3	"Blessed be the God and Father of our Lord Jesus Christ!"
1 Pet. 4:11	"To him belong glory and dominion forever and ever. Amen."
1 Pet. 5:11	"To him be the dominion forever and ever. Amen."
2 Pet. 3:18	". . . our Lord and Savior Jesus Christ. To him be the glory both now and to the day of eternity. Amen."
Jude 1:24–25	"Now to him who is able to keep you from stumbling and to present you blameless before the presence of his glory with great joy, to the only God, our Savior, through Jesus Christ our Lord, be glory, majesty, dominion, and authority, before all time and now and forever. Amen."
Rev. 1:5–6	"To him who loves us and has freed us from our sins by his blood and made us a kingdom, priests to his God and Father, to him be glory and dominion forever and ever. Amen."

[1]All texts quoted are from the ESV. Cf. *1 Clem*. 20:11–12; 34:6; 38:4; 43:6; 45:7; 50:7; 58:2; 61:3; 64; 65:2; *Diogn*. 12:9

Ten thousand times ten thousand in sparkling raiment bright,
The armies of the ransomed saints throng up the steeps of light;
'Tis finished, all is finished, their fight with death and sin;
Fling open wide the golden gates, and let the victors in.

What rush of alleluias fills all the earth and sky!
What ringing of a thousand harps bespeaks the triumph nigh!
O day, for which creation and all its tribes were made;
O joy, for all its former woes a thousandfold repaid!

O then what raptured greetings on Canaan's happy shore;
What knitting severed friendships up, where partings are no more!
Then eyes with joy shall sparkle, that brimmed with tears of late;
Orphans no longer fatherless, nor widows desolate.

Bring near Thy great salvation, Thou Lamb for sinners slain;
Fill up the roll of Thine elect, then take Thy power, and reign;
Appear, Desire of nations, Thine exiles long for home;
Show in the heaven Thy promised sign; Thou Prince and Savior, come.

—Henry Alford, 1867

Chapter 7

God's Glory in Salvation through Judgment IN REVELATION

1. Introduction

The Apocalypse of John is like an exclamation point at the end of the long sentence that is the Bible. John writes as the last prophet who is consciously taking up all the threads of prophecy that precede him and tying everything together. Richard Bauckham states:

> John's great oracle against Babylon (18:1–19:8) echoes every one of the oracles against Babylon in the Old Testament prophets, as well as the two major oracles against Tyre. It seems that John not only writes in the tradition of the Old Testament prophets, but understands himself to be writing at the climax of the tradition, when all the eschatological oracles of the prophets are about to be finally fulfilled, and so he interprets and gathers them up in his own prophetic revelation.[1]

My aim here is to show that the center of the theology of Revelation is the glory of God in salvation through judgment. The Apocalypse of John has an opening that identifies what kind of book he has written[2] (Rev. 1:1–8) and a closing to match

[1]Richard Bauckham, *The Theology of the Book of Revelation*, New Testament Theology (New York: Cambridge University Press, 1993), 5.

[2]On "The Nature of Apocalyptic" literature, see Roger Beckwith, *The Old Testament Canon of the New Testament Church and Its Background in Early Judaism* (Grand Rapids: Eerdmans, 1985), 344–45. Cf. Bauckham, *The Theology of the Book of Revelation*, 2, where he states that the book of Revelation is "an apocalyptic prophecy in the form of a circular letter."

(22:10–21).[3] Between the opening and the closing, John relates the vision he had on the Lord's Day (1:9–22:9). John has marked the turning points in his vision by, among other things, four key uses of the phrase "in the Spirit." This phrase occurs only at Revelation 1:10; 4:2; 17:3; and 21:10.[4] The vision thus breaks down into three parts, which I'll call Jesus and the Letters (1:9–3:22), The Throne and the Judgments (4:1–16:21), and The Harlot, the King, and the Bride (17:1–22:9). Here I will first overview the contents of Revelation, then discuss the book's chiastic structure,[5] before concluding with observations on the ways that Revelation presents the fulfillment of the exodus and the return from the exile from Eden.[6]

2. An Overview of the Contents of Revelation

The first part of the body of the vision can be labeled Jesus and the Letters because it is dominated by Jesus, who speaks the seven letters to John. John is "in the Spirit on the Lord's day" (Rev. 1:10) and has an overwhelming vision of the risen Christ in glory (1:9–20). Jesus begins to speak to John in that vision (1:11, 17–20) and continues speaking to him, dictating the letters to the seven churches recorded in Revelation 2–3.

The second section of the vision, The Throne and the Judgments in chapters 4–16, is marked by features that tie the judgments of chapters 6–16 directly back to the throne-room vision of chapters 4–5. Perhaps the most obvious of these are the heavenly figures who carry out the judgments (such as the four living creatures who are at the throne in 4:6 and then speak at the opening of the first four seals in Revelation 6) and the cosmic disturbances that John sees issuing from the throne: "flashes of lightning, and rumblings and peals of thunder" (4:5 ESV), which recur elsewhere in Revelation only after the seventh seal (8:5), after the seventh trumpet (11:19), and after the seventh bowl (16:18). These features tie the judgments directly to God—the judgments issue from the throne.[7]

The third section of the vision, The Harlot, the King, and the Bride, is structured by John's repetition of key phrases at the beginning and end of the sections on the harlot and the bride.[8] These key phrases are set forth in tables 7.1 and 7.2.

[3]Rev. 22:6–9 is a transitional passage, so in some cases I will refer to a division at 22:10, and in other cases I will refer to a break at 22:7. The overlapping character of these verses will be obvious to anyone who examines them closely. My understanding of Revelation's structure is heavily influenced by Richard Bauckham, *The Climax of Prophecy: Studies on the Book of Revelation* (Edinburgh: T&T Clark, 1993); and Bauckham, *The Theology of the Book of Revelation*.

[4]Bauckham, *The Climax of Prophecy*, 3.

[5]See the alternative proposals for a chiastic structure of Revelation in G. K. Beale, *The Book of Revelation: A Commentary on the Greek Text*, NIGTC (Grand Rapids: Eerdmans, 1999), 130–32. I offer this proposal in full awareness of the cautions voiced by David A. deSilva, "X Marks the Spot? A Critique of the Use of Chiasmus in Macro-Structural Analyses of Revelation," *JSNT* 30 (2008): 343–71.

[6]For my attempt at further exposition of the Apocalypse of John, see James M. Hamilton Jr., *Revelation*, Preaching the Word (Wheaton, IL: Crossway, forthcoming).

[7]Bauckham, *The Theology of the Book of Revelation*, 41–42.

[8]Bauckham, *The Climax of Prophecy*, 4.

Table 7.1. Matching Language Opening the Sections on the Harlot and the Bride

Revelation 17:1, 3	Revelation 21:9–10
"Then one of the seven angels who had the seven bowls came and said to me, 'Come, I will show you . . .' And he carried me away in the Spirit . . ." (ESV).	"Then came one of the seven angels who had the seven bowls . . . and spoke to me, saying, 'Come, I will show you . . .' And he carried me away in the Spirit . . ." (ESV).

Table 7.2. Matching Language Ending the Sections on the Harlot and the Bride

Revelation 19:9–10	Revelation 22:6, 8–9
"And he said to me, 'These are the true words of God.' Then I fell down at his feet to worship him, but he said to me, 'You must not do that! I am a fellow servant with you and your brothers who hold to the testimony of Jesus. Worship God'" (ESV).	"And he said to me, 'These words are trustworthy and true.' . . . I fell down to worship at the feet of the angel who showed them to me, but he said to me, 'You must not do that! I am a fellow servant with you and your brothers the prophets, and with those who keep the words of this book. Worship God'" (ESV).

Between the end of the section on the harlot (Rev. 19:9–10) and the beginning of the section on the bride (21:9–10) is the section on the King, Jesus, who comes and sets up his kingdom in 19:11–21:8.

3. The Chiastic Structure of Revelation

Why does the proclamation that the kingdom of the world has become the kingdom of our God and of his Christ come at the middle of the book rather than at its end? I would suggest that the reason for this is that John has placed this announcement, which follows the seventh trumpet blast, at the very center of his book, and then he has structured everything else around the worship of God at the announcement of kingdom come.

The chiastic shape I am proposing for Revelation can be seen in table 7.3.

Before walking through the stair-step chiasm that surrounds the announcement of the kingdom come, for the purposes of the thesis of this book I would observe the following: that announcement in Revelation 11:15–19 is surrounded by salvation through judgment. God is saving his people through judgment on the world.[9]

On either side of the announcement that the kingdom of the world is now the kingdom of God and Christ are pictures of the church being persecuted. Before the announcement, in Revelation 11:1–14, the two witnesses prophesy for 1,260

[9]So also Bauckham, *The Theology of the Book of Revelation*, 67: "The role of Christ in Revelation is to establish God's kingdom on earth: in the words of 11:15, to turn 'the kingdom of the world' (currently ruled by evil) into 'the kingdom of our Lord and his Messiah.' This is a work of both salvation and judgment. As we shall see, salvation and judgment are inevitably the two sides of a single coin."

Table 7.3. The Chiastic Structure of Revelation

- 1:1–8: Letter opening: revelation of Jesus and the things that must soon take place
  - 1:9–3:22: Letters to the seven churches: the church in the world
    - 4:1–6:17: Throne room vision, Christ conquers and opens the scroll
      - 7:1–9:21: The sealing of the saints and the trumpets announcing plagues
        - 10:1–11: The angel and John (true prophet)
          - 11:1–14: The church: two witnesses prophesy for 1,260 days, then opposition from the beast
            - 11:15–19: Seventh trumpet: "The kingdom of the world has become the kingdom of our Lord and of his Christ, and he shall reign forever and ever."
          - 12:1–13:10: The church: The woman nourished for 1,260 days, then opposition from the dragon and the second beast
        - 13:11–18: The deceiving beast (false prophet)
      - 14:1–19:10: The redemption of the saints and the bowls of wrath
    - 19:11–20:15: Return of Christ, he conquers, sets up his thousand-year kingdom, and opens the scrolls
  - 21:1–22:7: New heavens and new earth: the church in glory
- 22:8–21: Letter closing: Jesus is coming soon

days (11:3). After the announcement, in Revelation 12:1–13:10, the woman is nourished by God in the wilderness for 1,260 days (12:6), a period of time that is also designated "a time, and times, and half a time" (12:14). The period of time that the two witnesses will prophesy in chapter 11 seems to be equated with the period of time that the woman will be nourished in chapter 12,[10] so it seems that both the two witnesses and the woman symbolize the people of God.[11] The two witnesses point to the church's role of bearing prophetic witness to the culture, and the woman nourished in the wilderness points to God's provision for and protection of his people (cf. Elijah). Though Satan is making war on the woman and her seed (11:5; 12:12–17), God will empower the church to proclaim the gospel for the entirety of the appointed time. Once the gospel has been fully proclaimed, the two witnesses will be slain by the beast (11:7), whom God allows to kill the saints (13:7).

At the middle is the proclamation that the kingdom is God's (Rev. 11:15–19), which is framed by the pictures of the gospel-preaching (11:1–14), God-protected church (12:1–13:10). These two pictures of the church are likewise framed by two prophets: John is identified as a true prophet by means of the Ezekiel-like

[10]So also Beale, *The Book of Revelation*, 642.

[11]So also Bauckham, *The Theology of the Book of Revelation*, 85, 128.

experience he has of eating the scroll (cf. 10:1–11 and Ezek. 2:8–3:4); the true prophet before the two pictures of the church is matched by the false prophet on the other side in Revelation 13:11–18.

The next matching sections are wider, but the two sections proceed in similar order. Revelation 7–9 consists of a picture of the 144,000 sealed saints (Revelation 7), followed by the first six trumpet blasts (Revelation 8–9). This is matched on the other side by another picture of the 144,000 sealed saints (Revelation 14), followed by the seven bowls and their repercussions (Rev. 15:1–19:10).[12]

Preceding and following these sections on the 144,000 (Revelation 7, 14) and the trumpets (Revelation 8–9) and bowls (Revelation 15–19) are sections that deal with thrones (Revelation 4, 20), conquests (Revelation 5, 19), and the opening of seals (Revelation 6, 20). The throne of God in Revelation 4 (4:2)[13] is matched by the great white throne in Revelation 20 (20:11). The conquest of Christ that enabled him to take the scroll in Revelation 5 (5:5) is matched by the way he conquers his enemies in Revelation 19 (19:11–19).[14] And Christ's opening the seals on the scroll in Revelation 6 (6:1–17) is matched by the opening of the scrolls by which all are judged in Revelation 20 (20:12, 15).

Before and after the sections that deal with thrones, conquest, and seals (Revelation 4–6 and 19:11–20:15) are pictures of the church. The letters to the seven churches in Revelation 2–3 show the church in the world, struggling to proclaim the gospel while avoiding idolatry and sexual immorality. This is matched by the picture of the church in glory, the pure bride of the Lamb, in the new heaven and new earth in Revelation 21:1–22:7.

The apocalyptic prophecy in the form of a circular letter has a blessing in the opening, along with the epistolary greeting and doxology (Rev. 1:1–8). This is matched by the blessing in the closing, which also has an epistolary closing in the grace (22:10–21).[15]

I should observe at this point that even if this proposal for a chiastic structure of Revelation is rejected, it is still manifestly clear that Revelation is pervaded with

---

[12]It may be objected that Rev. 17:1–19:10 does not fit in this chiastic arrangement and I am forcing it into the section on the bowls to make the chiasm work. I would respond that the "judgment of the great prostitute" (17:1) and the announcement of the repercussions of the fall of Babylon (18:1–19:10) are intimately related to the outpouring of the seven bowls that complete God's wrath (Revelation 16). As a consequence of this relationship, it is as though these passages (17:1–19:10) are the reverberations of the shock produced by the seven bowls of wrath. Grant Osborne also makes the pertinent observation, "No single structural scheme for the book will suffice because the sections relate at more than one level" (Grant R. Osborne, *Revelation*, BECNT [Grand Rapids: Baker, 2002], 29). Bauckham also treats Revelation 15–19 as a unit (*The Theology of the Book of Revelation*, 101–102).

[13]Cf. Beale, *The Book of Revelation*, 369: "The above analysis [of the Old Testament Background of Revelation 4–5] shows that the goal of God in everything is to glorify himself, to enjoy that glory, and to have his creation enjoy glorifying him forever."

[14]See especially David Andrew Thomas, *Revelation 19 in Historical and Mythological Context*, Studies in Biblical Literature 118 (New York: Peter Lang, 2008).

[15]See further the discussion of the "number of literary ways in which the prologue and the epilogue correspond," in Bauckham, *The Theology of the Book of Revelation*, 57.

the reality of God glorifying himself by saving his people through the judgment of his and their enemies. I submit this chiastic structure because of the ways in which it highlights this theme, with God and Christ taking the kingdom at the center of the book in Revelation 11:15–19.

The kingdom belongs to God and Christ (Rev. 11:15–19). The church will be protected by God to proclaim the gospel until the times are fulfilled (11:1–14; 12:1–13:10). John is a true prophet (10:1–11), and Satan deceives by means of a false prophet (13:11–18). God's people are sealed (Revelation 7) and will be delivered to stand with the Lamb on Mount Zion (Revelation 14) through a new exodus of plague-like judgments in the trumpets (Revelation 7–8) and bowls (Revelation 15–19). Christ has conquered through his death and resurrection (5:5–6), and he will come again to conquer on a white horse with a sharp two-edged sword coming from his mouth (19:11–21). The church in the world is called to overcome (Revelation 2–3), that she might be the bride of Christ in glory in the new heaven and new earth (Revelation 21–22).

God's power to protect his people by sealing them brings him glory. God's power to judge the seemingly unconquerable world brings him glory. God's justice on all wickedness brings him glory,[16] and the glory of the justice heightens the glory of the mercy he shows to those freed from their sins by the blood of the Lamb (Rev. 1:5).

4. The New Exodus and Return from Exile in Revelation

Jesus is the Lamb slain (Rev. 1:5; 5:6). His death has inaugurated the new exodus, and that new exodus will be consummated by the two sets of seven plagues that accompany the trumpets (Revelation 8–9) and the outpouring of the bowls of God's wrath (Revelation 16).[17] Just as the people of Israel cried out to God under their harsh bondage in Egypt (Ex. 2:23–25), so now in Revelation the prayers of God's people rise before him (Rev. 8:3–4). Just as God delivered Israel from slavery through judgment on Egypt, so God will deliver his people from bondage to corruption through judgment on the world of rebellion. Just as God used plagues on Egypt to deliver his people, so God will use the plague judgments of the trumpets and the bowls to save his people in the final exodus. John communicates this to his audience by showing correspondences between the plagues on Egypt and the judgments of the trumpets and bowls, as can be seen in tables 7.4 (trumpets) and 7.5 (bowls).

[16]Cf. ibid., 42: "God's holiness is manifested in judgment on evil."
[17]See the similar discussions in Beale, *The Book of Revelation*, 465–67; and Bauckham, *The Theology of the Book of Revelation*, 70–72.

Table 7.4. The Exodus Plagues and Revelation's Trumpets

Trumpets in Revelation	Plagues in Exodus
1. Rev. 8:7, hail, fire	7th, Ex. 9:23–25, hail, fire
2. Rev. 8:8–9, sea to blood; one-third of living creatures die	1st, Ex. 7:20–21, Nile to blood; fish died
3. Rev. 8:10–11, rivers and springs made bitter	1st, Ex. 7:19, rivers, canals
4. Rev. 8:12, one-third of sun, moon, and stars darkened	9th, Ex. 10:21–29, three days of darkness
5. Rev. 9:1–11, darkness, locusts like scorpions	9th and 8th, Ex. 10:21–29, darkness; Ex. 10:12–20, locusts
6. Rev. 9:12–19, angels released; mounted troops, fire, smoke, and sulfur kill one-third of humanity	10th? Ex. 11:1–10; 12:29–32, death angel?
7. Rev. 10:1, angel wrapped in a cloud with legs like pillars of fire	Israel led out of Egypt by the pillar of cloud by day and fire by night

The judgments of the trumpets are worse than the plagues on Egypt, killing one-third of the living creatures in the sea (Rev. 8:8–9) and darkening one-third of the lights of heaven (8:12). The judgments of the bowls are comprehensive, killing all living things in the sea (16:3).

Table 7.5. The Exodus Plagues and Revelation's Bowls

Bowls in Revelation	Plagues in Exodus
1. Rev. 16:2, sores	6th, Ex. 9:10, boils/sores
2. Rev. 16:3, sea to blood; all living things die	1st, Ex. 7:17–21, Nile to blood; fish die
3. Rev. 16:4–7, rivers and springs to blood	1st, Ex. 7:17–21, rivers and springs to blood
4. Rev. 16:8–9, sun burns people	
5. Rev. 16:10–11, darkness	9th, Ex. 10:21–29, darkness
6. Rev. 16:12–15, Euphrates dried up and the demons prepared for battle	10th? Ex. 11:1–10; 12:29–32, death angel? Ex. 14, Red Sea parted
7. Rev. 16:17–21, air, earthquake, hail	7th, Ex. 9:13–35, hail

After the exodus from Egypt, God's people lived in tents, or booths, throughout the time of their wilderness sojourn. They were instructed to celebrate God's provision for them in the wilderness at the Feast of Booths, and they were to celebrate with palm branches (Lev. 23:40). The innumerable multitude that John sees from every tribe and nation and people and language stands before the throne and the Lamb, and they have palm branches in their hands (Rev. 7:9). They celebrate the fulfillment of the new exodus and God's provision for them through their wilderness wandering now that they have finally returned from exile. Similarly, just as God bore Israel to himself at Sinai on the wings of an eagle (Ex. 19:4) and promised a new exodus and a return from exile in which those who hoped in him would mount up with wings as eagles (Isa. 40:31), so God gives the woman the two wings of an eagle that she might escape from the serpent (Rev. 12:14).[18]

At the exodus from Egypt, after God brought Israel through the Red Sea and used those same waters to bring judgment on the armies of Pharaoh, Israel sang the song of Moses in praise of the way God saved them through the judgment of Egypt (Ex. 15:1–21). So also after God brings his people out through the judgments on the world in Revelation, the redeemed "sing the song of Moses . . . and the song of the Lamb" (Rev. 15:3–4).[19] Just as Israel came out of Egypt, built the tabernacle, and God took up residence in it, filling it with a cloud so that none could enter (Ex. 40:34–38), so also as God prepares his new dwelling place (the new heaven and earth) "the sanctuary was filled with smoke from the glory of God and from his power, and no one could enter the sanctuary until the seven plagues of the seven angels were finished" (Rev. 15:8 ESV).

God inaugurates the new exodus with the death and resurrection of Jesus, and he consummates it with the plagues of the trumpets and bowls in Revelation. There is also a fulfillment of the return from exile and a new conquest of the land. It was the fall of Babylon that brought Cyrus the Persian to the throne, with the result that he issued the decree that the Israelites could return to the land (cf. Dan. 5:30; 6:28; 2 Chron. 36:22–23). The fall of Babylon thus opened the way to return from exile, and this is also the way the fall of "Babylon" functions in the book of Revelation (cf. Rev. 14:8; 16:19; 18:2). The fall of Babylon means return from exile, and the prophetic calls for Israel to come out of Babylon (e.g., Isa. 48:20) are fulfilled in the call for God's people to come out of Babylon in Revelation 18:4.

The exodus was followed by the conquest of Canaan (see the book of Joshua), and some texts in the Prophets point to a new conquest after the return from exile (e.g., Hos. 2:15; Amos 9:11–15; Obad. 1:18–21, etc.). The hope of a new conquest of the land is fulfilled in Revelation 19 when Jesus comes as a conquering new Joshua. He defeats his enemies (Rev. 19:11–21), sets up his kingdom (20:1–6),[20]

---

[18]For other Old Testament allusions and relevant extrabiblical literature, see Beale, *The Book of Revelation*, 643–45.

[19]See the discussion of God's glory in salvation through judgment in Bauckham, *The Theology of the Book of Revelation*, 99.

[20]Cf. ibid., 108: "John has taken from the Jewish apocalyptic tradition the notion of a temporary messianic reign on earth before the last judgment and the new creation (cf. 2 Bar. 40:3; 4 Ezra 7:28–9; b.Sanh. 99a), but he has characteristically made something different of it. He has used it to depict an essential aspect of his concept of the victory of the martyrs over the beast. He has given the image of the millennium a very specific function." Bauckham goes on to suggest that the image should not be taken literally, but he cites no evidence from Revelation for this view. He only raises questions John does not address. Though John does not answer all the questions his teaching raises, he does teach that there will be a millennium.

puts down a final rebellion (20:7–10), enacts the final judgment (20:11–15), and rules with God in the new heaven and new earth (Revelation 21–22). This new heaven and earth is a new and better Eden. The return from the exile from Eden has finally been fulfilled. Salvation has come through judgment for God's glory. God's people worship him for his mercy and justice forever (19:1–3; cf. Isa. 66:21–24).

5. The Center of the Theology of Revelation

Major commentators are in agreement about the center of the theology of the Apocalypse. G. K. Beale writes, "The main idea of the entire book may be roughly formulated as follows: *The sovereignty of God and Christ in redeeming and judging brings them glory, which is intended to motivate saints to worship God and reflect his glorious attributes through obedience to his word.*"[21] Grant Osborne writes, "It seems clear that the primary theme of the book is the sovereignty of God . . . . The heavenly scenes typify worship, joy, peace, and triumph, while the earthly scenes typify troubles, chaos, apostasy, and judgment."[22] Bauckham asserts that "John's apocalypse . . . is exclusively concerned with eschatology: with eschatological judgment and salvation, and with the impact of these on the present situation in which he writes." He later adds, "With the words 'Worship God!' the angel directs John back to the central theme of all prophecy and certainly of the revelation that is to be the theme of John's prophecy."[23] In other words, the book of Revelation is about the glory of God in salvation through judgment.

6. The Center of New Testament and Biblical Theology

God intends to fill the earth with the knowledge of his glory.[24] He created the world as a cosmic temple, a theater for the display of his glory in justice and mercy. When he declares his name to Moses, showing him his glory and goodness, he identifies himself and his glory with his justice and his mercy.[25]

He saved Noah through judgment at the flood and then saved Israel through the judgment of Egypt at the exodus, and later through judgment on the people of the land in which Israel took up residence, a new Eden. The story of the Old Testament from Leviticus forward revolves around the salvation through judgment the nation will experience when they are exiled from that new Eden, through which judgment will come salvation—the prophesied second exodus and return

---

[21]Beale, *The Book of Revelation*, 151.
[22]Osborne, *Revelation*, 31–32.
[23]Bauckham, *The Theology of the Book of Revelation*, 6, 121. Bauckham later writes that "the New Testament's central theme [is] salvation in Christ" (164), to which I would only add that this salvation comes through judgment and is for the glory of God.
[24]See appendix 2 (§6) to chap. 3, "All the Earth Filled with the Knowledge of Yahweh's Glory."
[25]See the appendix (§8) to chap. 2, which catalogs Ex. 34:6–7 in the Law, Prophets, and Writings.

from exile. The old covenant remnant understood that God's supreme concern was for his glory, and they joined him in pursuing his glory.[26]

The authors of the New Testament interpret the salvation God accomplished through the judgment that fell on Jesus as the fulfillment of the hoped for new exodus and the inauguration of the return from exile. They praise God for what he accomplished in Jesus.[27] The Bible's apocalyptic statements, prominent in Isaiah 24–27, Daniel, Zechariah, and Revelation, look forward to a climactic display of salvation through judgment for the glory of God. The apocalyptic consummation of all things will fulfill the hopes for a final exodus from bondage to corruption and a return from the exile from Eden. In the descriptions of the new heaven and earth, God's people worship him for the justice he continues to uphold against his enemies, which magnifies the mercy they have received.

Thus, the story of the Bible is the story of God's glory in salvation through judgment. This central theme is exposited as salvation history unfolds. It is served by Creation, when God built the matrix for the display of his glory. In election God freely chose the recipients of his mercy. God reveals himself to those he has chosen, declaring his name to them. What he reveals and declares is his own glory in salvation through judgment. When God makes covenants with his people, he promises that he will be true to his just and merciful character.

The supreme display of God's judgment through which salvation comes, when the marvelous glory amazes all creation, is the remarkable moment when Jesus dies on the cross. God's commitment to his righteousness warrants the extreme measure of the death of his Son. What could more effectively communicate God's holiness? Simultaneously, God acts from unsearchable depths of love and mercy. Wrath and mercy come together in a paradoxical display of holiness and loving-kindness. The Father shows his love by sending Jesus to uphold justice. Jesus shows his righteousness by obeying the Father, by which also he loves his Father and his people to the end. God is glorified in salvation through judgment in Christ's death on the cross. Selah.

The elect then experience God's glory in salvation through judgment when they are justified by faith. God's righteousness condemns every attempt to be justified by works. Through that judgment salvation comes to those who believe, and God is glorified. The life of faith is a life that enacts God's glory in salvation through judgment, as every God-dishonoring behavior is judged and avoided because of the fear of God and the knowledge that he will judge each thought and word. Through judgment salvation comes to God's glory.

The Son of Man will come on the clouds of heaven with all his holy ones. All the tribes of the earth will wail on account of him. They face judgment. For

---

[26]See the appendix (§7) to chap. 4, table 4.9, "Old Testament Prayers Appealing to God's Concern for His Own Glory."

[27]See the Appendix (§5) to chap. 6, table 6.7, "Doxologies in the New Testament."

the objects of mercy, redemption draws nigh. Jesus will come to save through judgment for the glory of God. He is worthy of trust. Every human should trust him, even now.

The center of biblical theology is the glory of God in salvation through judgment, as can be seen in creation and covenant, salvation history and story line, exodus and exile, new exodus and return to Eden, warning and repentance, fear of God and wrath to come. He will save and judge, and there will be no need of sun or moon, for the glory of God and the Lamb will shine forever.

> Soon comes the King, in splendor laden light;
> Awed, we shall sing and praise his glorious might.
> Together we wait for the coming Lord,
> In green pastures grazing, fed by the Word,
>
> Redeemed by the Lamb, who stands as though slain,
> Known by the Father, and bearing his name,
> Alive by the Spirit, who quickens hearts.
> Faith is our shield against all Satan's darts
>
> That fly against us on this pilgrim way,
> And if our paths part until that great day,
> Hold fast the Word, which is able to save,
> And he'll gather us home beyond the grave,
>
> When together again our Lord we'll praise.
> Standing before him and seeing his face.
>
> —June 22, 2008, on the occasion of our farewell
> to the saints at Baptist Church of the Redeemer
> in Houston, TX.

Chapter 8

God's Glory in Salvation through Judgment

AND OBJECTIONS TO ITS CENTRALITY

[God] had respect to himself, as the last and highest end, in this work; because he is worthy in himself to be so, being infinitely the greatest and best of beings. All things else, with regard to worthiness, importance, and excellence, are perfectly as nothing in comparison of him.

—Jonathan Edwards, *The End for Which God Created the World*

1. Introduction

This chapter aims to address objections to the thesis I have set forth in this book.[1] I am under no illusions. The fact that I respond to objections does not mean that those who raise them will be satisfied. But at least they will not have to guess what my response to their objections would be.

There will be disagreements at the methodological level, at the level of the interpretation of particular texts, and at broader theological levels. Discussions are advanced when points of disagreement are clearly understood, when reasons

[1]In addition to substantive objections to interpretations and arguments, one sometimes sees (particularly in book reviews) suggestions that basically amount to a reviewer saying that an author should have written a different book altogether. This book has primarily engaged the biblical text. No doubt some readers would like for me to have given more space to discussion of other approaches to biblical theology or other arguments for its center. The scope of this project did not permit that kind of interaction, nor was that kind of interaction the purpose of this book. Some books read like a collection of smaller book reviews: they first summarize the arguments of other scholars, then engage those arguments with the biblical text and the arguments of still other scholars, repeating the process throughout the book. These can be valuable discussions, but here I have tried to allow the biblical text to set the agenda for the contents of this book. Those who wish to see my interaction with other scholars may be interested in the list of published book reviews on the "Book Reviews" page of my blog, For His Renown, http://jimhamilton.wordpress.com.

for disagreement are fairly represented, and when, so far as possible, logical and rhetorical fallacies are cleared away so that the real contours of the disagreement can be examined.

There are real disagreements. I would like to persuade those who disagree with me to see things as I do, but if I cannot do that, perhaps the least that can be achieved is a fair and charitable clarification of the disagreement itself. This chapter will be driven not by my attempt to anticipate objections to what I have argued but by actual responses from two prominent scholars: I. Howard Marshall[2] and Ben Witherington. Professor Witherington responded not to me directly but to another presentation arguing that God's glory in Christ by the Spirit is the center of New Testament theology.[3] I have grouped the concerns these two respected scholars raise under three headings: Method and Biblical Theology, Particular Texts and Biblical Theology, and Theology Proper and Biblical Theology.

2. Method and Biblical Theology

Three issues call for attention here: (1) the question of the nature of the Bible as progressive revelation; (2) what is meant by the metaphor of a "center"; and (3) the question as to whether my definition of the center of biblical theology has illegitimately colored my conclusions.

2.1 Progressive Revelation?

I. Howard Marshall asks: "What kind of coherence does the Bible display as a record of progressive revelation?"

My argument in this book has been in keeping with the evangelical understanding of the role of both the divine and human authors of Scripture. At the human level, later biblical authors learned from earlier ones. The earliest

---

[2]In the summer of 2004 it was my privilege to present the thesis of this book in seed form to the Biblical Theology Study Group of the Tyndale Fellowship that met in Nantwich, England (later published as "The Glory of God in Salvation Through Judgment: The Centre of Biblical Theology?" *TynBul* 57 [2006]: 57–84). On that occasion Professor I. Howard Marshall was the respondent to my presentation. He printed and distributed his remarks, and I have excerpted his main concerns and quoted them in the discussion below (I. Howard Marshall, "Response to James Hamilton" presented at the Triennial Conference of the Tyndale Fellowship: Biblical Theology Study Group, Nantwich, England, 2004). As I prepared this chapter, Professor Marshall graciously interacted with me on these issues again, granting permission to use his earlier response and even reading a first draft of this chapter. His comments have pushed me to clarify my thinking, for which I am deeply grateful.

[3]In November of 2007 Professor Ben Witherington posted an entry on his Weblog in response to Thomas R. Schreiner's *New Testament Theology: Magnifying God in Christ*. Witherington does not name Schreiner, but he says that he was "reading through the proofs of a new book on New Testament Theology, and it was stated that the most basic theme or thesis of NT theology is—'God magnifying himself through Jesus Christ by means of the Holy Spirit.'" Since there is a blurb on the back cover of Schreiner's book from Witherington (which means he had the page proofs), and since the thesis Witherington cites is Schreiner's, it is clear that Witherington's post was in response to Schreiner's book. See Ben Witherington, "'For God So Loved Himself?' Is God a Narcissist?" Ben Witherington Blog, posted November 20, 2007, http://benwitherington.blogspot.com/2007/11/for-god-so-loved-himself-is-god.html. Witherington's 680-word post, which was less than two pages, generated over 100 comments that amount to more than 20,000 words and over 40 pages of text. John Piper also responded to the post, "God's Loving Self-Exaltation: A Response to Ben Witherington," desiringGod Blog, posted November 24, 2007, http://www.desiringgod.org/Blog/931_gods_loving_selfexaltation_a_response_to_ben_witherington/.

biblical author on record, Moses, related a profound experience of God's glory (Ex. 33:18–34:7) where God declared his own name, showing Moses his glory, and announcing that he is a God who shows mercy and justice. Naturally, this experience made a massive impact on the theology of Moses, an impact reflected in the Pentateuch. Later authors learned from Moses that Yahweh shows his glory by showing justice in ways intended to create a context for spotlighting his mercy. Simultaneously, the Holy Spirit so worked in the biblical authors that they understood what God meant them to know and enabled them to communicate what God wanted them to say.

2.2 The Metaphor of a Center?

In response to my statement that the "centre of the Bible's theology acts as the centre of gravity for all of its other themes, it undergirds biblical wisdom, and it presents itself as the apex of the purposes of the God who speaks and acts,"[4] Marshall cautions: "My worry here is the juxtaposition of three rather different metaphors, and I should want to ask what each of them is meant to convey. How do we define what we mean by a 'centre'?"

Just as the Bible itself does not use the word *Trinity* or *inerrancy* while teaching the realities signified by that theological shorthand, so also, I would suggest, the Bible does not use the phrase "center of biblical theology" while nevertheless showing the centrality of the glory of God in salvation through judgment. The concept of "center" is simply a metaphor meant to communicate that this idea is the theme that holds all others in orbit, the hub of the wheel; it is the theme out of which all others flow, the theme all others exposit and feed back into. I have no problem using other metaphors to communicate the significance of God's glory in salvation through judgment, and I know of no binding rules against the use of other metaphors. The aim is simply to capture and convey the significance of this theme. So when I say that this theme undergirds biblical wisdom, I simply mean that the fear of God, so central to the Wisdom Literature, is a fear of God's judgment that is meant to curb people's behavior and lead them to salvation for God's glory. When I say that this theme is the apex of God's purposes, I mean that the biblical texts indicate that God intends to show his glory by upholding justice so that mercy will be seen in all its unconstrained beauty. John Piper has observed that "Daniel Fuller draws out the implication from Edwards, that all the attributes of God find exercise in the eternal life of the Trinity except mercy, or grace."[5]

My argument is that God's glory in salvation through judgment is the center of biblical theology because it reflects God's ultimate purpose. Other metaphors

---

[4]Hamilton, "The Centre of Biblical Theology," 59.

[5]John Piper, *God's Passion for His Glory: Living the Vision of Jonathan Edwards, with the Complete Text of* The End for Which God Created the World (Wheaton, IL: Crossway, 1998), 147 n. 23.

can be used, some of which have appeared in the pages of this book. We could say that God's glory in salvation through judgment is the *heart* of the Bible, the idea being that it is the muscle that pumps life-giving blood to the whole body. We could say it is the Bible's chief idea, with the connotation that it reigns over the others and controls them. We could say that it is the main, being the largest, central line that runs through the whole. We could say it is the Bible's foundation, everything else being built upon it. We could say that this theme is the *fundus*, the base of the organ out of which the rest of the tissue grows. Or we could simply call it the Bible's big idea. No metaphor or figure of speech will be perfect. That is the nature of analogous language. Our words bend against the burdens they carry. The bottom line is this: the Bible teaches that to know God is to perceive his worship-inspiring holiness and love, severity and kindness, righteousness and mercy. To know God is to see his glory, which is displayed as he upholds truth and somehow, astonishingly, makes ways to be both just and merciful.

2.3 Persuasive Definition?

Marshall writes regarding my presentation:

> The essay is going to go on to argue that the glory of God is the ultimate reason for all that he does. But what is the basis for this definition that simply *states* that the centre of biblical theology is the ultimate reason for what God does? So far as I can see, this definition is merely stated without any attempt at justification of it; but once you have accepted the definition, then it is arguable that the identification of the centre of biblical theology follows automatically.

My response to this is to ask if there is a better way to get at the center of biblical theology?[6] I would also point out what Ralph Martin says:

> There is here the obvious danger of a hermeneutical circle since the criteria are drawn from the same body of data that hypothetically contains the organizing principle; so, it may well be objected that we are selecting criteria which we know in advance will serve the interests of our proposed term. There seems to be no way to escape this dilemma unless we are prepared to abandon the quest.[7]

Rather than abandon the quest, let us consider some criteria that others have set forth. Plevnik writes that the center of Paul's thought cannot be derived from something else, and Martin says that the center of Paul's thought will be the

[6]See further the examination of God's ultimate purposes by Jonathan Edwards in *The End for Which God Created the World*, in Piper, *God's Passion for His Glory*, 185–91. Edwards's whole treatise could be cited in answer to the question at issue here.

[7]R. P. Martin, "Center of Paul's Theology," *DPL*, 93.

"primal reality from which he draws his entire theology."[8] My definition of the center of biblical theology simply applies what Martin and Plevnik say about Paul to all the biblical authors. This comes down to the simple idea that God is more important to the biblical authors than anything else, and whatever is most important to God is most important to the biblical authors.[9]

A friend and former colleague, Professor Ben Phillips,[10] set this forth in the form of a syllogism as follows:

> Living faith[11] in God entails sharing God's priorities.
> The biblical authors had living faith in God.
> Therefore the biblical authors shared God's priorities.

It may be objected that no one shares God's priorities as they should. Acknowledging that everyone acts in ways that deny God's priorities, it would seem that the inspiration of the Holy Spirit ensured that as the biblical authors wrote, their priorities reflected God's will. We can link the above to the following:

> The biblical authors shared God's priorities.
> God himself is top priority.
> Therefore the biblical authors had God as their top priority.

I have argued in this book that the biblical authors present God "acting for his own sake" because they understand God to be ultimate, underived, primal, central. See, for instance, the texts demonstrating the significance of Exodus 34:6–7 in the Law, Prophets, and Writings in the appendix (§8) to chapter 2; the texts asserting God's intention to fill the earth with the knowledge of his glory in appendix 2 (§6) to chapter 3; the catalog of Old Testament prayers appealing to God's concern for his own glory in table 4.9 in the appendix (§7) to chapter 4; and the doxologies in the New Testament in table 6.7 in the appendix (§5) to chapter 6.

I regard this evidence as sufficient warrant for defining the center of biblical theology as the ultimate purpose the biblical authors ascribe to God. Moreover, in their prayers and praises and assertions that God's glory will fill the earth, all of which reflect God's own declaration of his name (see again the texts alluded to in the previous paragraph), the biblical authors declare the glory

---

[8] Joseph Plevnik, "The Center of Pauline Theology," *CBQ* 51 (1989): 466; Martin, "Center of Paul's Theology," 93.

[9] I wish to thank Andy Naselli for this precise formulation.

[10] I wish to thank Ben Phillips for interacting with me on this issue and providing such clearly reasoned help. What follows quotes and summarizes his logical missive.

[11] I have changed the simpler "Belief" to "Living faith" because Andy Naselli pointed out to me that Satan and his demons believe but do not share God's priorities (cf. James 2:17–19).

of God in salvation through judgment to be ultimate. The evidence analyzed here also demonstrates that God's glory in salvation through judgment passes the four validation tests for proposed centers of biblical theology outlined by G. K. Beale:

> First, the proposed centre needs to be shown to be more overarching than other centres, with the others logically sub-categories of it . . . . Second, the proposed centre needs to be related to the various major themes of the New Testament documents to see if it adequately comprehends the diversity present throughout the New Testament . . . . Third, any viable centre must be integrally related to major Old Testament themes, be undergirded by a broad story-line which expresses a theological world-view or belief system about God's relationship with humanity, and be anchored in Christ's death and resurrection. Fourth, each competing centre needs to be analysed in turn for its comprehensiveness to see if it might not be the most overarching.[12]

God saves through judgment to show the glory of his character at the fall, at the flood, at the exodus from Egypt, at Israel's exile from the land, at the cross, and at the existential point of conversion for everyone who repents of sin and believes unto salvation; and God will show his glory by saving through judgment when all things are consummated at the return of Christ.[13] Beale himself seems to agree:

> The most comprehensive centre of New Testament theology is: Christ's life, and especially *his death and resurrection* through the Spirit, is the "already and not yet" end-time new creation *for God's glory*. The *glory of God* is the *primary goal* even within this centre, since every aspect of the consummated new creation is designed *to display the divine glory* completely in contrast to the partial manifestation of it on earth during pre-consummation history.[14]

2.4 The Discussion Continues

This book will not be the last word in biblical theology. The Bible's teaching cannot be exhausted. This section seeks to move toward methodological clarity, and this study as a whole seeks to swing the pendulum back toward an appreciation of the Bible's unity centered on God's glory in salvation through judgment.

---

[12]G. K. Beale, "The Eschatological Conception of New Testament Theology," in *Eschatology in the Bible and Theology: Evangelical Essays at the Dawn of a New Millennium*, ed. Kent E. Brower and Mark W. Elliott (Downers Grove, IL: InterVarsity, 1997), 45–46, from the "Appendix: Methodological issues for a single-centre biblical theology," 45–52.

[13]See also Edwards's summary of the biblical evidence in his *The End for Which God Created the World*, in Piper, *God's Passion for His Glory*, 191–241.

[14]Beale, "Eschatological Conception," 51–52, italics removed and emphasis added.

3. Particular Texts and Biblical Theology

3.1 God's Purpose and the Biblical Authors

I am grateful that Marshall has pushed me to justify my identification of the center of biblical theology as God's ultimate purpose, and as I move to his next concern, it is as though he has anticipated how I would answer. He writes:

> The correct identification of the ultimate *purpose of God* might not be the same thing as the *main interest* that drives the *biblical writers*. Suppose that the ultimate purpose is the glory of God; it might nevertheless be the case that the centre of interest of the writers is not so much the ultimate purpose in itself as rather the ways in which this purpose is attained . . . . So, for example, if I take the Gospel of Mark, there is no doubt of course that the glory of God and of Christ is mentioned occasionally . . . but what is interesting is that this element can scarcely be described as *thematic*; it is almost taken for granted. Mark knows that God is glorious and that the Son of Man will share that glory, but that is not really what the Gospel is about. The bulk of it is not concerned with that glory. It is more concerned to present a message of good news from God for needy humanity and of judgment upon human sinfulness. And it is the newness of this good news that really grips Mark.

I will work backward through this statement, from end to beginning. Marshall concludes by saying that the good news is concerned with judgment and salvation, and with this I am in obvious agreement. Prior to that he says that the glory of God and Christ "can scarcely be described as *thematic*." At the level of the use of words like *glory* and *glorify*, he is of course correct. The Greek word δόξα, "glory," occurs only three times in Mark (8:38; 10:37; 13:26), and the verb δοξάζω, "glorify," only once (2:12). But biblical theology is more than word studies, and I would argue that while Mark may only rarely *say* that Jesus is glorious, he everywhere *shows him to be glorious*. In response to an earlier draft of this chapter, Marshall asks, "If you asked Mark about each pericope 'Was your conscious, deliberate purpose in writing this paragraph to show that Jesus is glorious?' Would he say yes?"[15] I think Mark would say that yes, his ultimate purpose in every word was to show the glory of Christ, consciously and deliberately.

And this brings us to the point of contact between God's purpose and the main interest of the biblical writers. Isaiah and Ezekiel make explicit statements about God's acting for his own sake (e.g., Isa. 48:9–11; Ezek. 36:22). Mark may not speak this way, but he shows Jesus breaking down the doors of the strong man's house, binding him, and plundering his possessions. But that house does not belong to the strong man. The strong man is like Tobiah the Ammonite

[15] Personal communication, December 2009, for which I again express my gratitude.

who took up residence in the chambers of God's temple (Neh. 13:4–5). He has no business there. That place was not built as his dwelling. He has dispossessed God, in whose house he is but a squatter. So when Jesus barnstorms the land, driving out demons, healing the sick, and teaching the truth, he is taking back from Satan what rightly belongs to him as God's Son. Mark may not use the word *glory* to describe what Jesus is doing, but he is showing the glory of Christ without using the word. The same could be said about the cross in Mark's Gospel. Jesus is judged so that those who trust him can be saved to the glory of God. We have a diversity of *expression* in the Bible between Ezekiel and Mark, but they are unified in the message they communicate. I have argued in this book that God's ultimate purpose is the main concern of the biblical authors, even when they are describing the subordinate ends on the way to the chief end.

3.2 One-Sided Expressions?

At one point in his response, Marshall raised the concern that "the concept of God saving his people 'by judging those who afflict them' is one-sided." There may be points in this book where readers have felt similar concerns. Here I simply want to point out that I agree that the judgment of those who afflict the people of God is not the whole story. Still, there are places, such as 2 Thessalonians 1:6 (the passage in question), where Paul is content to describe the glory of God and Christ in the salvation of believers through the judgment of those who afflict them. Anyone who has read to this point in this book will know that that is not the only referent I assign to the word *judgment*. We cannot tell the whole story in every utterance, and I am content to be as one-sided in my statements as the biblical authors are. I hope that I have not gone beyond them.

3.3 Learning from the Biblical Authors

The biblical authors not only tell us particular truths, but they also model for us how to interpret the Bible and how to communicate God's truth. We will never exhaust what the Bible has to teach us on these three fronts.

4. Theology Proper and Biblical Theology

4.1 God's Love and His Pursuit of His Glory

Howard Marshall writes:

> . . . this could make his love for sinners ultimately a means of self-glorification, and the emotion and action of love on his part would cease to be truly the kind of love that is concerned for the good of those who are loved rather than arising because to show that kind of care will be for his own good reputation. . . . The love must be prior and the good reputation is a by-product. . . . There is at least a danger here that love may not get its proper place.

Ben Witherington has a similar concern:

> There were various nuances and amplifications to the discussion, but the more one read, the more it appeared clear that God was being presented as a self-centered, self-referential being, whose basic motivation for what he does, including his motivation for saving people, is so that he might receive more glory. Even the sending of the Son and the work of the Spirit is said to be but a means to an end of God's self-adulation and praise.[16]

In these statements Marshall and Witherington are not distinguishing between what happens when God seeks his own glory and what happens when fallen humans seek their own glory. Witherington makes this explicit when he writes:

> If we go back to the Garden of Eden story, one immediately notices that it is the Fall and sin which turned Adam and Eve into self-aware, self-centered, self-protecting beings. This is not how God had created them. Rather, he had created them in the divine image, and that divine image involves other directed, other centered love and relating. It follows from this that not the fallen narcissistic tendencies we manifest reflect what God is really like, but rather other directed, self-giving loving tendency.[17]

No one who celebrates the idea that God seeks his own glory means to communicate that God operates according to "the fallen narcissistic tendencies we manifest." It is somewhat difficult to understand how or why someone as gifted and learned as Ben Witherington could imagine that anyone would think that. We who celebrate the idea that God seeks his own glory mean to communicate exactly what Witherington and Marshall celebrate about God's love. God's glory is shown when he gives himself for others, and there is nothing better that he could give to others than himself. This is not narcissistic because it is true. What better could God give us than himself? If there is nothing better than God, and God gives us something other than himself (supremely manifested in his glory), then God has not given us what is best but what is lesser. So in giving us himself he is loving us by seeking what is best for us. He is loving us *by* seeking his own glory, and he is seeking his own glory and acting according to his nature *by* loving us. As Jonathan Edwards wrote long ago, "God acting for *himself*, or making himself his last end, and his acting for *their* sake, are not to be set in opposition; they are rather to be considered as coinciding one with the other, and implied one in the other."[18]

---

[16] Witherington, "Is God a Narcissist?" Paragraph break removed.
[17] Ibid.
[18] Edwards, *The End for Which God Created the World*, in Piper, *God's Passion for His Glory*, 156.

To summarize: it is evil and sinful for fallen human beings to seek their own glory. The reason this is evil is that fallen humans do not deserve glory, and if they were to attain their own glory, it would not be what is best for others. By contrast, it is *neither* evil *nor* sinful for God to seek his own glory. In fact, it is righteous for God to seek his own glory. He is God and has no other gods before himself. He deserves glory. Humans were created to see and savor his glory. There is nothing better that God could give to humans than his glory—which consists in his display of self-giving love and truth-maintaining justice.

4.2 The Justice of God

Marshall writes, "There is something of a difference between judgment as the retribution that comes upon unrepentant sinners and the judgment borne by God himself in the person of the Son through which sinners can be saved. These seem to be two rather different things, and I think that the formula of 'salvation through judgment' does not adequately recognise the difference."

We may be on the cusp of a real disagreement here, or perhaps Marshall is thinking of something that is not clear to me. But I disagree with his statement. I believe the Bible teaches that the wrath of God that Jesus propitiated on the cross (Rom. 3:24–26) is the same wrath from which those who trust in Jesus and are justified by faith (5:1) are saved (5:9–11). So I see no difference between the judgment that will be visited "as the retribution that comes upon unrepentant sinners and the judgment borne by God himself in the person of the Son through which sinners can be saved." Believers are saved because Jesus paid their penalty, and unbelievers suffer the wrath Jesus bore. They refused God, so they pay their own penalty.

4.3 Can There Be More than One Ultimate Purpose?

Marshall states, "I think that it is an ultimate purpose of God, perhaps not the only one, and certainly not the one that the Bible produces every time in an overt manner."

The word *ultimate* means last, final result, not subsidiary, best, greatest, not to be improved upon or surpassed. So if the glory of God in salvation through judgment is *an* ultimate purpose of God, there must be *other* purposes on level with it. In that case the word "ultimate" in Marshall's statement should be replaced with something like "*pen*ultimate." It also follows that there would be something beyond that *pen*ultimate level, something that God exalts over himself. I do not mean *pen*ultimate, however, but ultimate, for I think there is nothing beyond the glory of God in salvation through judgment, nothing that surpasses it, nothing to which it is subsidiary. God's glory, chiefly displayed in the manifestation of his justice and mercy, is, I believe, the ultimate reason God creates, judges, and redeems.

5. Conclusion

In the end, Marshall disagrees with the way that I have defined the center of biblical theology and with the conclusion at which I arrive. He writes:

> If there is a centre of biblical theology it is not the ultimate aim of God but rather the actual organizing centre or centres of the biblical writers whose teaching seems to me to be much more focused on the mighty actions of God to overcome sin and bring sinners to salvation. Granted that one ultimate aim of God is desire that all should glorify him, the actual centre of biblical theology is to be found in the nature and actions of God in creating and re-creating his people.

It will be obvious here that I think God's ultimate aim *is* the actual organizing center of what the biblical authors focus on as they recount "the mighty actions of God to overcome sin and bring sinners to repentance," at the same time he judges those who do not believe in Jesus, to *the ultimate end* that God is glorified in Christ by the power of the Spirit because of the ways in which he has shown his unfaltering, unquestionable justice to set the stage for the display of his stunning mercy.

The four living creatures cry, "Holy, holy, holy," day and night forever. The twenty-four elders fall down and worship. And all the redeemed see the smoke from the judgment on the harlot Babylon and shout, "Hallelujah, salvation and glory and honor be to our God, world without end. Amen."

Chapter 9

God's Glory in Salvation through Judgment

IN MINISTRY TODAY

For it is not in one place nor in a small plot that the glory of God rests, but on all the ends of the inhabited earth his grace has been poured out, and here the almighty God has tabernacled through Messiah Jesus; to whom be glory forever. Amen.

—Melito of Sardis, *Peri Pascha*

1. Introduction

So what? Why bother with the question of the center of biblical theology? To quote the institutional motto of Southern Seminary: "For the truth. For the church. For the world. For the glory of God." This book has been written that God might be glorified in the church and in Christ Jesus by the power of the Spirit (Eph. 3:21, cf. 14–20). It is an effort "to equip the saints for the work of ministry, for building up the body of Christ" (4:12 ESV).

D. A. Carson has written, "While considerable thought has been devoted in recent years to the move from exegesis to biblical theology, relatively little has been devoted to the move from biblical theology to systematic theology and to pastoral theology."[1] This chapter seeks to take some initial steps in the direction of applying the center of biblical theology to pastoral theology and the Christian life. These thoughts are but starting points. Here I will briefly consider evangelism, discipleship, and corrective church discipline in the context of local church ministry, then Bible reading and prayer as personal spiritual disciplines.

[1]D. A. Carson, "Current Issues in Biblical Theology: A New Testament Perspective," *BBR* 5 (1995): 36.

2. Church Ministry

Jesus promised that he would build his church (Matt. 16:18). He commissioned his disciples to make other disciples (28:16–20). And he told them how to deal with those in the church who stopped acting like disciples by refusing to repent of sin (18:15–18). In the book of Acts we find an unbroken apostolic pattern: everywhere the disciples went and everything they did was aimed at obeying Jesus in the Great Commission task he gave them. They all went about that task in the same way, proclaiming the good news of what God had done in Christ by the power of the Spirit, baptizing those who believed the message, and gathering the new converts into churches. Then they taught those churches the Bible, and they modeled how to live out the teachings of the Bible in conformity to the character of Jesus the messiah, who loved and served others for their spiritual benefit.

Does this have anything to do with the glory of God in salvation through judgment? I would suggest that the center of biblical theology has specific application to announcing what God has done and persuading people to believe in Jesus (evangelism), to teaching all that Jesus commanded (discipleship), and to pursuing the purity of the bride of Christ (corrective church discipline).

2.1 Evangelism

When we lived in the Houston area, one of our neighbors was attending Joel Osteen's Lakewood Church. As I was once conversing with this neighbor, he offered me a conclusion that I could see was a reaction to what he was hearing at Lakewood. He said, "The Bible is a book of good news, but there's bad news in there, too." The Bible's bad news is not to be glossed over, hidden away, or avoided. Without the Bible's bad news, its good news will have no meaning. The center of biblical theology is nonnegotiable for evangelism precisely because God saves people through judgment for his glory. If a man does not perceive that God is holy, righteous, just, and personally offended by transgressions, he will sense no need for Jesus.[2]

God is holy, righteous, just, and personally offended by the sins we commit, and the more clearly we see this, the more deeply we will feel our desperate need for Jesus. God's wrath makes his mercy beautiful. Without his wrath, his mercy has no meaning and no one has any need for it.

Seeing that the glory of God in salvation through judgment is the center of biblical theology will liberate us to announce the bad news so that the gospel will be seen as good news. Our culture tells so many lies about what it means to do evangelism that we need huge doses of the Bible to counteract the world's

[2]For my response to a recent argument for inclusivism, see James M. Hamilton Jr., "Who Can Be Saved? A Review Article," *TJ* 28 (2007): 89–112.

poison.[3] We must love God and know him in all his judging and saving glory so that we will have boldness to tell the truth.

2.2 Discipleship

Look at the word *discipleship*. There within it is the word *disciple*, which is obviously related to the word *discipline*. In view of the next section on corrective church discipline, I would point out that discipleship is the other side of the coin—it is formative church discipline. These words, *discipleship/discipline/disciple,* all connote ideas of training, and all training sometimes feels like punishment (cf. Heb. 12:7–11). The training in view here involves being taught to obey everything Jesus commanded. The commands of Jesus[4] often go against our instincts, impulses, inclinations, and desires. Sometimes they seem to make no sense. Embracing the center of biblical theology as a disciple of Jesus means recognizing that we are on a lifelong pilgrimage whose starting point was a moment of salvation through judgment for God's glory, and the pattern of growth will be the same. We will be saved through the judgment of our pride for God's glory. We will be saved through the judgment of our fleshly desires that we might walk in holiness to honor God. We will be saved through the judgment of our selfishness so that we can be selfless like Jesus so that God will be glorified. We will be saved through the judgment of our greed, of our trust in money, of our self-reliance, of our sloth, of our anger, of our gluttony, and of our envy, all so that we can know God's abundant provision so that he will be glorified as the one who can supply every need, who can avenge every wrong, who can satisfy our longings, and who is worthy of full devotion. God will be glorified in salvation through judgment as disciples of Jesus continue on the pilgrim pathway.

2.3 Corrective Church Discipline

God is holy. He really is. Jesus gave instructions for putting people out of the church (Matt. 18:15–18). He really did. The early church followed those instructions (1 Cor. 5:1–13; 2 Cor. 2:6–7; 1 Thess. 5:14; 2 Thess. 3:6–15; Titus 3:10–11; 2 John 1:7–10; 3 John 1:9–12). They obeyed Jesus and enacted God's holiness. Corrective church discipline is enacted against unrepentant people because people who have been born again repent of their sin. Those who refuse to repent show that they have never been born again. Only those who have been born again are united to Christ by faith and truly members of his body, the church; so when it becomes evident that someone has not been born again (by their refusal to repent), they are to be removed from church membership. This action is for the salvation of those who are expelled from the church (cf. 1 Cor. 5:5; 1 Tim. 1:20). The church is telling the unrepentant that they need the gospel; they need to

---

[3]See especially Mark Dever, *The Gospel and Personal Evangelism* (Wheaton, IL: Crossway, 2007).

[4]For a full treatment, see John Piper, *What Jesus Demands from the World* (Wheaton, IL: Crossway, 2006).

believe in Jesus. The church is hoping that they will trust in Christ, repent of their sin, and be reconciled to God.

Churches full of people who do not understand the center of biblical theology will not practice corrective church discipline. They will not understand how the church is to apply God's holiness to their lives. They will be impure churches, and their membership will include unbelievers. Those unbelievers will be surprised to hear Jesus tell them he never knew them (Matt. 7:21–23). Those churches will have blood on their hands (Ezek. 3:18, 20), and their pastors will give an account (Heb. 13:17).

Churches full of people who understand and embrace the glory of God in salvation through judgment will want to see God's holiness displayed in their congregation so that God's mercy will have meaning. Members of such churches will take God and his holiness more seriously when they see his holiness applied to the unrepentant. They will live in fear of God and in gratitude for his mercy, and they will press on to holiness, without which no one will see the Lord (Heb. 12:14). God is glorified in salvation through judgment in individual lives in evangelism and discipleship, and he is glorified in salvation through judgment in the lives of churches that obey Jesus and practice church discipline.[5]

3. Personal Spiritual Discipline

In moving to consider personal spiritual discipline, I do not intend this discussion to be a move away from the ministry of the local church. God's word in the Bible creates his people as faith comes by hearing the word of Christ (Rom. 10:17), and in turn, God's people gathered in a local church is to become a community of the Book (Acts 20:32). A community where what is "normal" is what the Bible says.

The Bible is to believers what universities, movies, sitcoms, and the media are to godless culture. The Bible must be our metanarrative that forms our identity, creates our community, provides our shared fund of language, builds our common network of assumptions, and dictates our responses to international, local, and personal events. The community context God has given for making the Bible function this way in the lives of believers is the local church. The church spurs people to read the Bible, and believers read the Bible for the church. This symbiotic relationship will also spur people to pray the Bible for themselves, for those with whom they are in covenant in a local church, and for the advance of God's kingdom in the world. Thus, personal Bible reading and private prayer can only be associated with the individualism of the modern West if these disciplines are dissociated from a strong local church.

[5]See also my argument in James M. Hamilton Jr., "The Church Militant and Her Warfare: We Are Not Another Interest Group" *SBJT* 11, no. 4 (2007): 70–80.

The best thing a man can do for his personal Bible reading is join a strong local church where the Bible is preached and the gospel is clear.

Likewise, the best thing a man can do for his personal *prayer life* is join a strong local church where the Bible is preached and the gospel is clear.[6]

3.1 Bible Reading

We do not read the Bible as an end in itself. We read the Bible to know God. God reveals himself in the Bible in awesome justice and almost incomprehensible mercy. To see his justice and mercy is to perceive his severity and his kindness. When the Spirit gives us eyes to see the glory of God in Christ, we begin to be transformed into the image of Christ (cf. 2 Cor. 3:18). Being conformed to the image of Christ results from seeing Christ in the Scriptures. When this happens, we begin to care for God the way that Jesus cared for God. We care for God's truth and righteousness the way that God cares for his truth and righteousness. We make progress in being set apart for God, just as God is holy. Similarly, having been shown such startling mercy, those who know God by reading the Bible become people who are able to forgive because they have been forgiven.

None of this is useless. Daniel 11:32 states, "The people who know their God shall stand firm and take action." People who know God are able to stand firm and take action because they know that God and his truth and his kingdom are more important than their own lives continuing. God and his gospel are more important than money, success, image, approval from the world, and even life itself. This abandonment to God and his glory in justice and mercy does not take away life but rather makes it abundant.

Knowing the center of biblical theology keeps Bible reading from being a random, disconnected exercise. Understanding the story's plot and purpose enriches our reading and our living. The glory of God in salvation through judgment is the main theme and end goal of the Bible, and understanding this opens up the contents of the Bible, which in turn summons our hearts to worship God for the glory he reveals in Christ through the Spirit-inspired word.

3.2 Prayer

Prayer is motivated by the knowledge of God. If we know God as he is, we will cry out to him. If we know him to be holy, we will cry out to him for justice. If we know him to be forgiving because of Christ's death and resurrection, we will cry out to him for mercy. If we know that he delights to glorify himself by giving victory to the weak and humble while defeating the proud and strong, we will rejoice in our weakness as we cry out to him for deliverance. We will expect

[6]See, too, James M. Hamilton Jr. and Jonathan Leeman, "A Biblical Theology of Corporate Prayer," *9Marks eJournal* 5, no. 1 (2008): 10–12, http://filemanager.silaspartners.com/dox/9marks/9news/jan-feb08ejournal.pdf.

him to act as he always has and exalt the lowly while humbling the proud. We will pray for him to do so, and we will rejoice that only he can take credit for his triumphs. We will pray for him to triumph, and we will ascribe glory to him when he does.

When we know God in his justice and his mercy, we will not shrink from praying the imprecatory psalms against those who are enemies of God and the gospel. We can pray that God would be glorified in salvation that comes through judgment. We can pray that God would either save his enemies or do whatever necessary to thwart their efforts to stop the advance of the gospel. We should pray that God would either convert those who purvey smut or destroy all their efforts to ruin lives, destroy families, exploit women, ensnare the young, and enslave the souls they lure into filth. We should pray that God would save them through judgment for his glory as they hear the gospel and repent, and we should pray that if they are not going to repent, his judgment would fall swiftly on them and stop their program of defilement.

God is glorified when we pray, and the godly in the Bible often appeal to God's concern for his own glory.[7] So should we. We should pray to God because his name is at stake in our churches. His gospel is at stake in our marriages. His reputation is at stake in the purity of our pastors. His renown is on the line when we open the Bible and seek to explain it. We should call on him to act for the sake of his name—to visit us with such an outpouring of his Spirit that we might see a great awakening in our day to the glory of his justice and mercy in Christ. May the Lord fill our churches and raise up a great testimony to his name.

4. Conclusion

The center of biblical theology has application in the church, in Bible study, and in the prayer closet. More significantly, it has application on the great day. When God arises to judge the earth, he will display the glory of his justice and his mercy. Those who have trusted in Jesus will be astonished at the mercy shown to them, and that mercy will be all the more precious in view of the everlasting display of justice God will visit on the objects of his wrath.

From creation to new creation, at the fall and at the flood, in the exodus and the exile, in the new exodus and the return from exile accomplished in the death and resurrection of Jesus, in the church's pilgrimage through the world, and on the last day: God gets glory in salvation through judgment. His praise endures forever.

[7]See the appendix (§7) to chap. 4, table 4.9, "Old Testament Prayers Appealing to God's Concern for His Own Glory."

Thy mercy, my God, is the theme of my song,
The joy of my heart, and the boast of my tongue;
Thy free grace alone, from the first to the last,
Hath won my affections, and bound my soul fast.

Without Thy sweet mercy I could not live here;
Sin would reduce me to utter despair;
But through Thy free goodness my spirits revive,
And He that first made me still keeps me alive.

Thy mercy is more than a match for my heart,
Which wonders to feel its own hardness depart;
Dissolved by Thy goodness, I fall to the ground,
And weep to the praise of the mercy I've found.

Great Father of mercies, Thy goodness I own,
And the covenant love of Thy crucified Son;
All praise to the Spirit, Whose whisper divine
Seals mercy, and pardon, and righteousness mine.

—John Stocker, 1776

SELECTED BIBLIOGRAPHY

1. Primary Sources and Translations

Charlesworth, J. H., ed. *The Old Testament Pseudepigrapha*. 2 vols. New York: Doubleday, 1983, 1985.

Cross, F. M., D. W. Parry, R. J. Saley, and E. Ulrich, eds. *Qumran Cave 4.XXI: 1–2 Samuel*. Discoveries in the Judaean Desert 17. Oxford: Clarendon, 2005.

Elliger, K., and W. Rudolph, eds. *Biblia Hebraica Stuttgartensia*. Stuttgart: Deutsche Bibelgesellschaft, 1969/77, 1997.

Eusebius, *Historia Ecclesiastica*. Translated by K. Lake and J. E. L. Oulton. 2 vols. Loeb Classical Library. Cambridge, MA: Harvard University Press, 1926, 1932.

García Martínez, Florentino. *The Dead Sea Scrolls Translated*. 2nd ed. Grand Rapids: Eerdmans, 1996.

Hallo, William W., ed. *The Context of Scripture: Canonical Compositions from the Biblical World*. 3 vols. Boston: Brill, 2003.

Hesiod, *The Homeric Hymns and Homerica*. Translated by Hugh G. Evelyn-White. Loeb Classical Library. Cambridge: Harvard University Press, 1914.

Homer, *The Iliad: Books 13–24*. Translated by A. T. Murray, revised by William F. Wyatt. 2nd ed. Loeb Classical Library. Cambridge: Harvard University Press, 1999.

Holmes, Michael W., ed. *The Apostolic Fathers: Greek Texts and English Translations*. 3rd ed. Grand Rapids: Baker, 2007.

Josephus. 10 vols. Loeb Classical Library. Cambridge, MA: Harvard University Press, 1926–1965.

Melito of Sardis. *On Pascha and Fragments*. Edited by Stuart George Hall. Oxford: Clarendon Press, 1979.

Nestle, Eberhard, Barbara Aland, Kurt Aland, Johannes Karavidopoulos, Carlo M. Martini, and Bruce M. Metzger, eds. *Novum Testamentum Graece*. 27th ed. Stuttgart: Deutsche Bibelgesellschaft, 1993.

Rahlfs, Alfred. *Septuaginta, Id est Vetus Testamentum graece iuxta LXX interpretes*. Stuttgart: Württembergische Bibelanstalt, 1935.

Schneemelcher, Wilhelm. *New Testament Apocrypha*. Rev. ed. English translation edited by R. McL. Wilson. 2 vols. Louisville: Westminster John Knox, 1991, 1992.

Tov, Emanuel. With the collaboration of R. A. Kraft and a contribution by P. J. Parsons. *The Greek Minor Prophets Scroll from Naḥal Ḥever (8HevXIIgr)*. Discoveries in the Judaean Desert 8. Oxford: Clarendon, 1990.

Ulrich, Eugene, Frank Moore Cross, Russell E. Fuller, Judith E. Sanderson, Patrick W. Skehan, and Emanuel Tov. With the collaboration of Catherin M. Murphy and Curt Niccum. *Qumran Cave 4.X: The Prophets*. Discoveries in the Judaean Desert 15. Oxford: Clarendon, 1997.

Wevers, John William, ed. *Deuteronomium*. 2nd ed. Septuaginta Vetus Testamentum Graecum 3. Göttingen: Vandenhoeck and Ruprecht, 2006.

———, ed. *Exodus*. Septuaginta Vetus Testamentum Graecum 2. Göttingen: Vandenhoeck and Ruprecht, 1991.

Ziegler, Joseph, ed. *Ieremias, Baruch, Threni, Epistula Ieremiae*. 3rd ed. Septuaginta Vetus Testamentum Graecum 15. Göttingen: Vandenhoeck and Ruprecht, 2006.

2. Concordances, Grammars, and Lexicons

Abbott, Edwin A. *Johannine Grammar*. London: Black, 1905.

Bauer, Walter. *A Greek-English Lexicon of the New Testament and Other Early Christian Literature*. Translated by W. F. Arndt and F. W. Gingrich. Revised and edited by Frederick William Danker. 3rd ed. Chicago: University of Chicago Press, 2000.

Blass, F., and A. Debrunner. *A Greek Grammar of the New Testament and Other Early Christian Literature*. Edited and translated by R. W. Funk. 9th–10th ed. Chicago: University of Chicago Press, 1961.

Even-Shoshan, Abraham, ed. *A New Concordance of the Old Testament*. 2nd ed. Jerusalem: Kiryat-Sefer, 1997.

Gesenius, W., and E. Kautzsch. *Gesenius' Hebrew Grammar*. 28th ed. Translated by A. E. Cowley. 2nd English ed. Oxford: Clarendon, 1910.

Hatch, Edwin, and Henry A. Redpath. *A Concordance to the Septuagint and the Other Greek Versions of the Old Testament (Including the Apocryphal Books)*. Oxford: Clarendon, 1897–1906. Reprint, Grand Rapids: Baker, 1983.

Joüon, P. *A Grammar of Biblical Hebrew*. Translated and revised by T. Muraoka. 2 vols. Subsidia biblica 14. Rome: Pontificio Istituto Biblico, 1991.

Koehler, Ludwig, and Walter Baumgartner. *The Hebrew and Aramaic Lexicon of the Old Testament*. Study edition. Revised by W. Baumgartner and J. J. Stamm. Translated and edited by M. E. J. Richardson. 2 vols. Boston: Brill, 2001.

Kohlenberger, John R., III, Edward W. Goodrick, and James A. Swanson. *The Exhaustive Concordance to the Greek New Testament*. Grand Rapids: Zondervan, 1995.

Liddell, H. G., and R. Scott. *A Greek-English Lexicon*. 9th ed. revised by H. S. Jones with a revised supplement by P. G. W. Glare. Oxford, 1996.

Moulton, James Hope, and George Milligan. *The Vocabulary of the Greek New Testament Illustrated from the Papyri and Other Non-Literary Sources*. London: Hodder and Stoughton, 1930. Reprint, Grand Rapids: Eerdmans, 1974.

Robertson, A. T. *A Grammar of the Greek New Testament in the Light of Historical Research*. Nashville: Broadman, 1934.

Wallace, Daniel B. *Greek Grammar beyond the Basics: An Exegetical Syntax of the New Testament*. Grand Rapids: Zondervan, 1996.

Waltke, Bruce K., and M. O'Connor. *An Introduction to Biblical Hebrew Syntax*. Winona Lake, IN: Eisenbrauns, 1990.

3. Secondary Literature

Alexander, T. Desmond. *From Paradise to the Promised Land: An Introduction to the Main Themes of the Pentateuch*. Grand Rapids: Baker, 1995.

———. "Genealogies, Seed and the Compositional Unity of Genesis." *Tyndale Bulletin* 44 (1993): 255–70.

———. *The Servant King: The Bible's Portrait of the Messiah*. Leicester: Inter-Varsity, 1998.

Allison, Dale C. *The End of the Ages Has Come: An Early Interpretation of the Passion and Resurrection of Jesus*. Philadelphia: Fortress, 1985.

Avemarie, Freidrich. "Erwählung und Vergeltung." *New Testament Studies* 45 (1999): 108–26.

———. *Tora und Leben: Untersuchungen zur Heilsbedeutung der Tora in der frühen rabbinischen Literatur*. Texte und Studien zum antiken Judentum. Tübingen: J.C.B. Mohr, 1996.

Baird, William. *History of New Testament Research: From Jonathan Edwards to Rudolf Bultmann*. Minneapolis: Fortress, 2003.

Bass, Christopher D. *That You May Know: Assurance of Salvation in 1 John*. NAC Studies in Bible and Theology. Nashville: Broadman & Holman, 2008.

Bauckham, Richard. *The Climax of Prophecy: Studies on the Book of Revelation*. Edinburgh: T&T Clark, 1993.

———. *Jude and the Relatives of Jesus in the Early Church*. Edinburgh: T&T Clark, 1990.

———. "Reading Scripture as a Coherent Story." In *The Art of Reading Scripture*, edited by Ellen F. Davis and Richard B. Hays, 38–53. Grand Rapids: Eerdmans, 2003.

———. *The Testimony of the Beloved Disciple: Narrative, History, and Theology in the Gospel of John*. Grand Rapids: Baker, 2007.

———. *The Theology of the Book of Revelation*. New Testament Theology. New York: Cambridge University Press, 1993.

Beale, G. K. *The Book of Revelation: A Commentary on the Greek Text*. New International Greek Testament Commentary. Grand Rapids: Eerdmans, 1999.

———. "Did Jesus and the Apostles Preach the Right Doctrine from the Wrong Texts? Revisiting the Debate Seventeen Years Later in the Light of Peter Enns' Book, *Inspiration and Incarnation*." *Themelios* 32 (2006): 18–43.

———. "Myth, History, and Inspiration: A Review Article of *Inspiration and Incarnation* by Peter Enns." *Journal of the Evangelical Theological Society* 49 (2006): 287–312.

———. ed. *The Right Doctrine from the Wrong Texts? Essays on the Use of the Old Testament in the New*. Grand Rapids: Baker, 1994.

———. *The Temple and the Church's Mission: A Biblical Theology of the Dwelling Place of God*. New Studies in Biblical Theology. Downers Grove, IL: InterVarsity, 2004.

———. *We Become What We Worship: A Biblical Theology of Idolatry*. Downers Grove, IL: InterVarsity, 2008.

Beale, G. K., and D. A. Carson, eds. *Commentary on the New Testament Use of the Old Testament*. Grand Rapids: Baker, 2007.

Beckwith, Roger. "The Early History of the Psalter." *Tyndale Bulletin* 46 (1995): 1–27.

———. "Early Traces of the Book of Daniel." *Tyndale Bulletin* 53 (2002): 75–82.

———. *The Old Testament Canon of the New Testament Church and Its Background in Early Judaism*. Grand Rapids: Eerdmans, 1985.

Beckwith Roger T., and Martin J. Selman, eds. *Sacrifice in the Bible*. Grand Rapids: Baker, 1995.

Bell, Richard H. *The Irrevocable Call of God: An Inquiry into Paul's Theology of Israel*, Wissenschaftliche Untersuchungen zum Neuen Testament 184. Tübingen: Mohr Siebeck, 2005.

Blomberg, Craig L., and Mariam J. Kamell. *James*. Zondervan Exegetical Commentary on the New Testament. Grand Rapids: Zondervan, 2008.

Bolt, Peter G. *The Cross from a Distance: Atonement in Mark's Gospel*. New Studies in Biblical Theology. Downers Grove, IL: InterVarsity, 2004.

Bray, Gerald. *Biblical Interpretation: Past and Present*. Downers Grove, IL: InterVarsity, 1996.

———. "The Church Fathers and Biblical Theology." In *Out of Egypt: Biblical Theology and Biblical Interpretation*, edited by C. Bartholomew, M. Healy, K. Möller, and R. Parry, 23–40. Scripture and Hermeneutics 5. Grand Rapids: Zondervan, 2004.

Brueggemann, Walter. *An Introduction to the Old Testament: The Canon and Christian Imagination*. Louisville: Westminster John Knox, 2003.

———. *Theology of the Old Testament: Testimony, Dispute, Advocacy*. Minneapolis: Fortress, 1997.

Bryan, Steven M. *Jesus and Israel's Traditions of Judgment and Restoration*. Society for New Testament Studies Monograph Series. Cambridge: Cambridge University Press, 2002.

Bultmann, Rudolf. *Theology of the New Testament*. Translated by Kendrick Grobel. 2 vols. New York: Scribners, 1951, 1955.

Burk, Denny. *Articular Infinitives in the Greek of the New Testament: On the Exegetical Benefit of Grammatical Precision*. New Testament Monographs 14. Sheffield: Sheffield Phoenix, 2006.

———. "Discerning Corinthian Slogans through Paul's Use of the Diatribe in 1 Corinthians 6:12–20." *Bulletin for Biblical Research* 18 (2008): 99–121.

———. "Is Paul's Gospel Counterimperial? Evaluating the Prospects of the "Fresh Perspective" for Evangelical Theology." *Journal of the Evangelical Theological Society* 51 (2008): 309–37.

———. "On the Articular Infinitive in Philippians 2:6: A Grammatical Note with Christological Implications." *Tyndale Bulletin* 55 (2004): 253–74.

Carson, D. A. *The Cross and Christian Ministry: An Exposition of Passages from 1 Corinthians*. Grand Rapids: Baker, 1993.

———. "Current Issues in Biblical Theology: A New Testament Perspective." *Bulletin for Biblical Research* 5 (1995): 17–41.

———. *Divine Sovereignty and Human Responsibility: Biblical Perspectives in Tension*. Grand Rapids: Baker, 1994. Reprint, Eugene: Wipf and Stock, 2002.

Carson, D. A., and Douglas J. Moo. *An Introduction to the New Testament*. 2nd ed. Grand Rapids: Zondervan, 2005.

Chester, Andrew. *Messiah and Exaltation: Jewish Messianic and Visionary Traditions and New Testament Christology*, Wissenschaftliche Untersuchungen zum Neuen Testament 207. Tübingen: Mohr Siebeck, 2007.

Chester, Andrew, and Ralph P. Martin. *The Theology of the Letters of James, Peter, and Jude*. New Testament Theology. New York: Cambridge University Press, 1994.

Ciampa, Roy E. "The History of Redemption." In *Central Themes in Biblical Theology: Mapping Unity in Diversity*, edited by Scott J. Hafemann and Paul R. House, 254–308. Grand Rapids: Baker, 2007.

Clines, David J. A. *The Theme of the Pentateuch*. 2nd ed. Sheffield: JSOT, 1997.

Collins, Jack. "A Syntactical Note (Genesis 3:15): Is the Woman's Seed Singular or Plural?" *Tyndale Bulletin* 48 (1997): 139–48.

Curtis, Byron G. *Up the Steep and Stony Road: The Book of Zechariah in Social Location Trajectory Analysis*. Academia Biblica. Atlanta: Society of Biblical Literature, 2006.

Dempster, Stephen. *Dominion and Dynasty: A Theology of the Hebrew Bible*, New Studies in Biblical Theology. Downers Grove, IL: InterVarsity, 2003.

———. "An 'Extraordinary Fact': *Torah and Temple* and the Contours of the Hebrew Canon: Parts 1 and 2." *Tyndale Bulletin* 48 (1997): 23–56, 191–218.

———. "The Servant of the Lord." In *Central Themes in Biblical Theology: Mapping Unity in Diversity*, edited by Scott J. Hafemann and Paul R. House, 128–78. Grand Rapids: Baker, 2007.

Dumbrell, William J. *The Faith of Israel: A Theological Survey of the Old Testament*. 2nd ed. Grand Rapids: Baker, 2002.

Edwards, Jonathan. "The End for Which God Created the World." In *God's Passion for His Glory*, by John Piper, 125–251. Wheaton, IL: Crossway, 1998.

Eichrodt, Walther. *Theology of the Old Testament*. Translated by J. A. Baker. 2 vols. Philadelphia: Westminster, 1961, 1967.

Ellis, E. Earle. *Christ and the Future in New Testament History*. Boston: Brill, 2000.

———. *History and Interpretation in New Testament Perspective*. Biblical Interpretation Series. Boston: Brill, 2001.

———. *The Making of the New Testament Documents*. Boston: Brill, 1999.

Firth, David, and Philip S. Johnston, eds. *Interpreting the Psalms: Issues and Approaches*. Downers Grove, IL: InterVarsity, 2005.

Fishbane, Michael. *Biblical Interpretation in Ancient Israel*. Oxford: Clarendon, 1985.

Freedman, David N. "The Symmetry of the Hebrew Bible." *Studia Theologica* 46 (1992): 83–108.

———. *The Unity of the Hebrew Bible*. Ann Arbor: University of Michigan Press, 1991.

Frei, Hans W. *The Eclipse of Biblical Narrative: A Study in Eighteenth and Nineteenth Century Hermeneutics*. New Haven, CT: Yale University Press, 1974.

Fuller, Russell T. "Exodus 21:22–23: The Miscarriage Interpretation and the Personhood of the Fetus." *Journal of the Evangelical Theological Society* 37 (1994): 169–84.

———. "Ezra: The Teacher of God's Word and Agent of Revival." *The Southern Baptist Journal of Theology* 9, no. 3 (2005): 52–61.

Fyall, Robert S. *Now My Eyes Have Seen You: Images of Creation and Evil in the Book of Job*. New Studies in Biblical Theology. Downers Grove, IL: InterVarsity, 2002.

Garrett, Duane A. *Proverbs, Ecclesiastes, Song of Songs*. New American Commentary. Nashville: Broadman, 1993.

Gathercole, Simon. "Jesus' Eschatological Vision of the Fall of Satan: Luke 10.18 Reconsidered." *Zeitschrift für die neutestamentliche Wissenschaft* 94 (2003): 143–63.

———. *The Preexistent Son: Recovering the Christologies of Matthew, Mark, and Luke*. Grand Rapids: Eerdmans, 2006.

———. "The Son of Man in Mark's Gospel." *Expository Times* 115, no. 11 (2004): 366–72.

———. *Where Is Boasting? Early Jewish Soteriology and Paul's Response in Romans 1–5*. Grand Rapids: Eerdmans, 2002.

Gentry, Peter J. "Kingdom through Covenant: Humanity as the Divine Image." *The Southern Baptist Journal of Theology* 12, no. 1 (2008): 16–42.

———. "Nehemiah 12: Restoring the City of God or How to Preach a List of Names." *The Southern Baptist Journal of Theology* 9, no. 3 (2005): 28–37.

———. "Rethinking the 'Sure Mercies of David' in Isaiah 55:3." *Westminster Theological Journal* 69 (2007): 279–304.

———. "The Septuagint and the Text of the Old Testament." *Bulletin for Biblical Research* 16 (2006): 193–218.

Gombis, Timothy. "Being the Fullness of God in Christ by the Spirit: Ephesians 5:18 in Its Epistolary Setting." *Tyndale Bulletin* 53 (2002): 259–71.

———. "Cosmic Lordship and Divine Gift-Giving: Psalm 68 in Ephesians 4:8." *Novum Testamentum* 47 (2005): 367–80.

———. "Ephesians 2 as a Narrative of Divine Warfare." *Journal for the Study of the New Testament* 26 (2004): 403–18.

———. "Ephesians 3:2–13: Pointless Digression, or Epitome of the Triumph of God in Christ?" *Westminster Theological Journal* 66 (2004): 313–23.

Gorman, Michael J. *Apostle of the Crucified Lord: A Theological Introduction to Paul and His Letters*. Grand Rapids: Eerdmans, 2004.

Grant, Jamie A. *The King as Exemplar: The Function of Deuteronomy's Kingship Law in the Shaping of the Book of Psalms*. SBL Academia Biblica. Atlanta: SBL, 2004.

Gurtner, Daniel M. *The Torn Veil: Matthew's Exposition of the Death of Jesus*. Society for New Testament Studies Monograph Series. New York: Cambridge University Press, 2007.

Hafemann, Scott J., ed. *Biblical Theology: Retrospect and Prospect*. Downers Grove, IL: InterVarsity, 2002.

———. "The Covenant Relationship." In *Central Themes in Biblical Theology: Mapping Unity in Diversity*, edited by Scott J. Hafemann and Paul R. House, 20–65. Grand Rapids: Baker, 2007.

———. *Suffering and Ministry in the Spirit: Paul's Defense of His Ministry in II Corinthians 2:14–3:3*. Grand Rapids: Eerdmans, 1990.

Halton, Charles. "Allusions to the Stream of Tradition in the Neo-Assyrian Oracles." *Ancient Near Eastern Studies* 46 (2009): 50–61.

———. "Samson's Last Laugh: The *Ś/ŠḤQ* Pun in Judges 16:25–27." *Journal of Biblical Literature* 128 (2009): 61–64.

Hamilton, James M., Jr. "Biblical Theology and Preaching." In *Text-Driven Preaching: God's Word at the Heart of Every Sermon*, edited by Daniel L. Akin, David Allen, and Ned L. Mathews, 193–218. Nashville: Broadman & Holman, 2010.

———. "The Center of Biblical Theology in Acts: Deliverance and Damnation Display the Divine." *Themelios* 33 (2008): 34–47.

———. "The Church Militant and Her Warfare: We Are Not Another Interest Group." *The Southern Baptist Journal of Theology* 11, no. 4 (2007): 70–80.

———. "Gender Roles and the Glory of God: A Sermon on 1 Corinthians 11:2–12." *Journal for Biblical Manhood and Womanhood* 9 (2004): 35–39.

———. "The Glory of God in Salvation through Judgment: The Centre of Biblical Theology?" *Tyndale Bulletin* 57 (2006): 57–84.

———. "God with Men in the Prophets and the Writings: An Examination of the Nature of God's Presence." *Scottish Bulletin of Evangelical Theology* 23 (2005): 166–93.

———. "God with Men in the Torah." *Westminster Theological Journal* 65 (2003): 113–33.

———. *God's Indwelling Presence*. NAC Studies in Bible and Theology. Nashville: Broadman & Holman, 2006.

———. "The Lord's Supper in Paul: An Identity Shaping Proclamation of the Gospel." In *The Lord's Supper*, edited by Thomas R. Schreiner and Matt Crawford. NAC Studies in Bible and Theology. Nashville: Broadman & Holman, forthcoming.

———. "The Messianic Music of the Song of Songs: A Non-Allegorical Interpretation." *Westminster Theological Journal* 68 (2006): 331–45.

———. "N. T. Wright and Saul's Moral Bootstraps: Newer Light on 'The New Perspective,'" 25 (2004): 139–55.

———. "The One Who Does Them Shall Live by Them: Leviticus 18:5 in Galatians 3:12." *Gospel Witness*, August 2005, 10–14.

———. "The Seed of the Woman and the Blessing of Abraham." *Tyndale Bulletin* 58 (2007): 253–73.

———. "The Skull Crushing Seed of the Woman: Inner-Biblical Interpretation of Genesis 3:15." *The Southern Baptist Journal of Theology* 10, no. 2 (2006): 30–54.

———. "Still *Sola Scriptura*: An Evangelical View of Scripture." In *The Sacred Text: Excavating the Texts, Exploring the Interpretations, and Engaging the Theologies of the Christian Scriptures*, edited by Michael Bird and Michael Pahl, 215–40. Piscataway, NJ: Gorgias, 2010.

———. "The Typology of David's Rise to Power." A Julius Brown Gay Lecture presented at The Southern Baptist Theological Seminary on March 13, 2008. Available online in audio or PDF.

———. "The Virgin Will Conceive: Typological Fulfillment in Matthew 1:18–23." In *Built upon the Rock: Studies in the Gospel of Matthew*, edited by John Nolland and Dan Gurtner, 228–47. Grand Rapids: Eerdmans, 2008.

———. "Was Joseph a Type of the Messiah? Tracing the Typological Identification between Joseph, David, and Jesus." *The Southern Baptist Journal of Theology* 12, no. 4 (2008): 52–77.

———. "Were Old Covenant Believers Indwelt by the Holy Spirit?" *Themelios* 30 (2004): 12–22.

———. "What Women Can Do in Ministry: Full Participation within Biblical Boundaries." In *Women, Ministry and the Gospel: Exploring New Paradigms*, edited by Mark Husbands and Timothy Larsen, 32–52. Downers Grove, IL: InterVarsity, 2007.

———. "*Who Can Be Saved?* by Terrance L. Thiessen: A Review Essay." *Trinity Journal* 28 (2007): 89–112.

Harrison, Roland Kenneth. *Introduction to the Old Testament*. Grand Rapids: Eerdmans, 1969. Reprint, Peabody, MA: Prince Press, 1999.

Hasel, G. F. *New Testament Theology: Basic Issues in the Current Debate*. Grand Rapids: Eerdmans, 1978.

———. *Old Testament Theology: Basic Issues in the Current Debate*. 4th ed. Grand Rapids: Eerdmans, 1991.

Hays, Richard B. *The Conversion of the Imagination: Paul as Interpreter of Israel's Scripture*. Grand Rapids: Eerdmans, 2005.

Hengel, Martin. *The Four Gospels and the One Gospel of Jesus Christ: An Investigation of the Collection and Origin of the Canonical Gospels*. Translated by John Bowden. Harrisburg, PA: Trinity Press International, 2000.

Hoskins, Paul M. *Jesus as the Fulfillment of the Temple in the Gospel of John*. Paternoster Biblical Monographs. Waynesboro, GA: Paternoster, 2006.

House, Paul R. *Old Testament Theology*. Downers Grove, IL: InterVarsity, 1998.

———. *The Unity of the Twelve*, JSOT Supplement. Sheffield: Almond, 1990.

Howard, David M., Jr. *The Structure of Psalms 93–100*. Biblical and Judaic Studies from the University of California, San Diego. Winona Lake, IN: Eisenbrauns, 1997.

Hurtado, Larry W. *The Earliest Christian Artifacts: Manuscripts and Christian Origins*. Grand Rapids: Eerdmans, 2006.

Jeffery, Steve, Michael Ovey, and Andrew Sach. *Pierced for Our Transgressions: Rediscovering the Glory of Penal Substitution*. Wheaton, IL, Crossway: 2007.

Jensen, Joseph. "Yahweh's Plan in Isaiah and in the Rest of the Old Testament." *Catholic Biblical Quarterly* 48 (1986): 443–55.

Jobes, Karen H., and Moisés Silva, *Invitation to the Septuagint*. Grand Rapids: Baker, 2000.

Joslin, Barry C. "Can Hebrews Be Structured? An Assessment of Eight Approaches." *Currents in Biblical Research* 6 (2007): 99–129.

———. *Hebrews, Christ and the Law: The Theology of the Mosaic Law in Hebrews 7:1–10:18*. Paternoster Biblical Monographs. Milton Keynes: Paternoster, 2008.

———. "Hebrews 7–10 and the Transformation of the Law." In *A Cloud of Witnesses: The Theology of Hebrews in Its Ancient Contexts*, edited by Richard Bauckham, Trevor Hart, Nathan Macdonald, and Daniel Driver, 100–17. Library of New Testament Studies. New York: T&T Clark, 2008.

Kaiser, Walter C., Jr. *The Promise-Plan of God: A Biblical Theology of the Old and New Testaments*. Grand Rapids: Zondervan, 2008.

Kennedy, Joel. *The Recapitulation of Israel: Use of Israel's History in Matthew 1:1–4:11*. Wissenschaftliche Untersuchungen zum Neuen Testament 2.257. Tübingen: Mohr Siebeck, 2008.

Kim, Seyoon. *Paul and the New Perspective: Second Thoughts on the Origin of Paul's Gospel*. Grand Rapids: Eerdmans, 2002.

Köstenberger, Andreas J. "A Complex Sentence: The Syntax of 1 Timothy 2:12." In *Women in the Church: An Analysis and Application of 1 Timothy 2:9–15*, edited by Andreas J. Köstenberger and Thomas R. Schreiner. 2nd ed., 53–84. Grand Rapids: Baker, 2005.

———. "Diversity and Unity in the New Testament." In *Biblical Theology: Retrospect and Prospect*, edited by Scott J. Hafemann, 144–58. Downers Grove, IL: InterVarsity, 2002.

———. *A Theology of John's Gospel and Letters: The Word, the Christ, the Son of God*. Biblical Theology of the New Testament. Grand Rapids: Zondervan, 2009.

Ladd, George Eldon. *A Theology of the New Testament*. Rev. ed. Grand Rapids: Eerdmans, 1993.

Lamarche, Paul. *Zacharie IX-XIV: Structure littéraire et messianisme*. Paris: Gabalda, 1961.

Leithart, Peter J. *A Son to Me: An Exposition of 1 and 2 Samuel*. Moscow, ID: Canon, 2003.

Lemke, Werner E. "Theology (OT)." In *The Anchor Bible Dictionary,* vol. 6, edited by David Noel Freedman, 449–73. New York: Doubleday, 1992.

Levenson, Jon D. *Sinai and Zion: An Entry into the Jewish Bible*. San Francisco: Harper and Row, 1985.

Lohfink, Norbert. "The Song of Victory at the Red Sea." In *The Inerrancy of Scripture and Other Essays*, translated by R. A. Wilson, 67–86. Berkeley: Bibal, 1992. Reprint of *The Christian Meaning of the Old Testament*, 1968.

Lohfink, Norbert, and Erich Zenger. *The God of Israel and the Nations: Studies in Isaiah and the Psalms*. Translated by Everett R. Kalin. Collegeville: Liturgical, 2000.

Lövestam, Evald. *Jesus and "This Generation": A New Testament Study*. Translated by Moira Linnarud. Coniectanea Biblica. Stockholm: Almqvist and Wiksell, 1995.

Marcos, Natalio Fernández. *The Septuagint in Context: Introduction to the Greek Versions of the Bible*. Boston: Brill, 2000.

Marshall, I. Howard. *New Testament Theology: Many Witnesses, One Gospel*. Downers Grove, IL: InterVarsity, 2004.

Martens, Elmer A. *Old Testament Theology*. IBR Bibliographies 13. Grand Rapids: Baker, 1997.

———. "Old Testament Theology Since Walter C. Kaiser, Jr." *Journal of the Evangelical Theological Society* 50 (2007): 673–91.

McConville, J. G. "Ezra–Nehemiah and the Fulfillment of Prophecy." *Vetus Testamentum* 36 (1986): 205–24.

———. *Grace in the End: A Study in Deuteronomic Theology*. Grand Rapids: Zondervan, 1993.

———. *Judgment and Promise: An Interpretation of the Book of Jeremiah*. Winona Lake, IN: Eisenbrauns, 1993.

Merrill, Eugene H. *Everlasting Dominion: A Theology of the Old Testament*. Nashville: Broadman & Holman, 2006.

———. *Kingdom of Priests: A History of Old Testament Israel*. Grand Rapids: Baker, 1987, 1996.

———. "Royal Priesthood: An Old Testament Motif." *Bibliotheca Sacra* 150 (1993): 50–61.

Meyer, Jason C. *The End of the Law: Mosaic Covenant in Pauline Theology*. NAC Studies in Bible and Theology. Nashville: Broadman & Holman, 2000.

Millar, J. Gary. *Now Choose Life: Theology and Ethics in Deuteronomy*. New Studies in Biblical Theology. Downers Grove, IL: InterVarsity, 1998.

Miller, Patrick D. *The Way of the Lord: Essays in Old Testament Theology*. Grand Rapids: Eerdmans, 2007.

Moberly, R. W. L. "How May We Speak of God? A Reconsideration of the Nature of Biblical Theology." *Tyndale Bulletin* 53 (2002): 177–202.

Moo, Douglas J. *The Letters to the Colossians and to Philemon*. Pillar New Testament Commentary. Grand Rapids: Eerdmans, 2008.

———. *The Old Testament in the Gospel Passion Narratives*. Sheffield: Almond, 1983.

Morgan, Robert. "Theology (NT)." In *The Anchor Bible Dictionary*, vol. 6, edited by David Noel Freedman, 473–83. New York: Doubleday, 1992.

Mounce, William D. *Pastoral Epistles*. Word Biblical Commentary. Nashville: Nelson, 2000.

Naselli, Andrew David. "Paul's Use of Isaiah 40:13 and Job 41:3a (Eng. 41:11a) in Romans 11:34–35." PhD diss., Trinity Evangelical Divinity School, 2010.

Neill, Stephen, and Tom Wright. *The Interpretation of the New Testament, 1861–1986*. 2nd ed. Oxford: Oxford University Press, 1988.

Niehaus, Jeffrey J. "An Argument against Theologically Constructed Covenants." *Journal of the Evangelical Theological Society* 50 (2007): 259–73.

———. *Ancient Near Eastern Themes in Biblical Theology*. Grand Rapids: Kregel, 2008.

Olmstead, Wesley G. *Matthew's Trilogy of Parables: The Nation, the Nations and the Reader in Matthew 21.28–22.14*. Society for New Testament Studies Monograph Series. New York: Cambridge University Press, 2003.

Ortlund, Raymond C., Jr. *God's Unfaithful Wife: A Biblical Theology of Spiritual Adultery*. New Studies in Biblical Theology. Downers Grove, IL: InterVarsity, 1996.

Oswalt, John N. "The Book of Isaiah: A Short Course on Biblical Theology." *Calvin Theological Journal* 39 (2004): 54–71.

Pahl, Michael W. *Discerning the "Word of the Lord": The "Word of the Lord" in 1 Thessalonians 4:15*. Library of New Testament Studies 389. New York: T&T Clark, 2009.

Pao, David W. *Acts and the Isaianic New Exodus*. Grand Rapids: Baker, 2002.

Pennington, Jonathan T. *Heaven and Earth in the Gospel of Matthew*. Leiden: Brill, 2007.

———. "The Kingdom of Heaven in the Gospel of Matthew." *The Southern Baptist Journal of Theology* 12, no. 1 (2008): 44–51.

Perrin, Nicholas. "Messianism in the Narrative Frame of Ecclesiastes?" *Revue Biblique* 108 (2001): 37–60.

Peterson, David, ed. *Where Wrath and Mercy Meet: Proclaiming the Atonement Today*. Carlisle, PA: Paternoster, 2001.

Pietersma, Albert. "Kyrios or Tetragram: A Renewed Quest for the Original Septuagint." In *De Septuaginta*, edited by Albert Pietersma and Claude Cox, 85–101. Mississauga, ON: Benben, 1984.

———. "Septuagintal Exegesis and the Superscriptions of the Greek Psalter." In *The Book of Psalms: Composition and Reception*, edited by Peter W. Flint and Patrick D. Miller, 443–75. Leiden: Brill, 2005.

Piper, John. *The Future of Justification: A Response to N. T. Wright*. Wheaton, IL: Crossway, 2007.

———. *The Justification of God: An Exegetical and Theological Study of Romans 9:1–23*. 2nd ed. Grand Rapids: Baker, 1993.

Plevnik, Joseph. "The Center of Pauline Theology." *Catholic Biblical Quarterly* 51 (1989): 461–78.

Plummer, Robert L. *Paul's Understanding of the Church's Mission: Did the Apostle Paul Expect the Early Christian Communities to Evangelize?* Paternoster Biblical Monographs. Waynesboro, GA: Paternoster, 2006.

Polhill, John B. *Paul and His Letters*. Nashville: Broadman & Holman, 1999.

Poythress, Vern Sheridan. "Kinds of Biblical Theology." *Westminster Theological Journal* 70 (2008): 129–42.

Rapske, Brian. *The Book of Acts and Paul in Roman Custody*. The Book of Acts in Its First Century Setting 3. Grand Rapids: Eerdmans, 1994.

Redditt, Paul L. and Aaron Schart, *Thematic Threads in the Book of the Twelve*, Beihefte zur Zeitschrift für die alttestamentliche Wissenschaft. New York: Walter de Gruyter, 2003.

Reimer, David J. *The Oracles Against Babylon in Jeremiah 50–51: A Horror Among the Nations*. San Francisco: Mellen Research University Press, 1993.

Rendtorff, Rolf. *The Canonical Hebrew Bible: A Theology of the Old Testament*. Translated by David E. Orton. Tools for Biblical Study. Leiden: Deo, 2005.

Reventlow, Henning Graf. *Problems of Biblical Theology in the Twentieth Century*. Translated by John Bowden. Philadelphia: Fortress, 1986.

———. "Theology (Biblical), History of." In *The Anchor Bible Dictionary*, vol. 6, edited by David Noel Freedman, 483–505. New York: Doubleday, 1992.

Rezetko, Robert, Timothy H. Lim, and W. Brian Aucker, eds. *Reflection and Refraction: Studies in Biblical Historiography in Honour of A. Graeme Auld*. Supplements to *Vetus Testamentum*. Boston: Brill, 2007.

Richter, Sandra L. *The Deuteronomistic History and the Name Theology: lešakkēn šemô šām in the Bible and the Ancient Near East*. Beihefte zur Zeitschrift für die alttestamentliche Wissenschaft. New York: Walter de Gruyter, 2002.

Roberts, J. J. M. "Isaiah in Old Testament Theology." *Interpretation* 36 (1982): 130–43.

Robertson, O. Palmer. *The Christ of the Prophets*. Phillipsburg, NJ: P&R, 2004.

Ross, Allen P. *Recalling the Hope of Glory: Biblical Worship from the Garden to the New Creation*. Grand Rapids: Kregel, 2006.

Routledge, Robin. "Is There a Narrative Substructure Underlying the Book of Isaiah?" *Tyndale Bulletin* 55 (2004): 183–204.

———. *Old Testament Theology: A Thematic Approach*. Downers Grove, IL: InterVarsity, 2008.

Rowe, C. Kavin. *Early Narrative Christology: The Lord in the Gospel of Luke*. Grand Rapids: Baker, 2009.

Sailhamer, John H. "Creation, Genesis 1–11, and the Canon." *Bulletin for Biblical Research* 10 (2000): 89–106.

———. *Introduction to Old Testament Theology: A Canonical Approach*. Grand Rapids: Zondervan, 1995.

———. *The Meaning of the Pentateuch: Revelation, Composition and Interpretation*. Downers Grove, IL: InterVarsity, 2009.

———. "The Messiah in the Hebrew Bible." *Journal of the Evangelical Theological Society* 44 (2001): 5–23.

———. *The Pentateuch as Narrative: A Biblical-Theological Commentary*. Grand Rapids: Zondervan, 1992.

Sandys-Wunsch, John, and Laurence Eldredge, "J. P. Gabler and the Distinction between Biblical and Dogmatic Theology." *Scottish Journal of Theology* 33 (1980): 133–58.

Schlatter, Adolf. "The Theology of the New Testament and Dogmatics." In *The Nature of New Testament Theology*, edited by R. Morgan, 117–66. 1909. Reprint, Naperville, IL: Allenson, 1973.

Schnabel, Eckhard. *Early Christian Mission*. 2 vols. Downers Grove, IL: InterVarsity, 2004.

Schreiner, Thomas R. "The Commands of God." In *Central Themes in Biblical Theology: Mapping Unity in Diversity*, edited by Scott J. Hafemann and Paul R. House, 66–101. Grand Rapids: Baker, 2007.

———. "Corporate and Individual Election in Romans 9: A Response to Brian Abasciano." *Journal of the Evangelical Theological Society* 49 (2006): 351–71.

———. *1, 2 Peter, Jude*. New American Commentary. Nashville: Broadman & Holman, 2003.

———. *Galatians*. Zondervan Exegetical Commentary on the New Testament. Grand Rapids: Zondervan, 2010.

———. "Head Coverings, Prophecies and the Trinity: 1 Corinthians 11:2–16." In *Recovering Biblical Manhood and Womanhood: A Response to Evangelical Feminism*, edited by John Piper and Wayne Grudem, 124–39, 485–87. Wheaton, IL: Crossway, 1991.

———. "An Interpretation of 1 Timothy 2:9–15: A Dialogue with Scholarship." In *Women in the Church: An Analysis and Application of 1 Timothy 2:9–15*, edited by Andreas J. Köstenberger and Thomas R. Schreiner, 2nd ed., 85–120. Grand Rapids: Baker, 2005.

———. *The Law and Its Fulfillment: A Pauline Theology of Law*. Grand Rapids: Baker, 1993.

———. *New Testament Theology: Magnifying God in Christ*. Grand Rapids: Baker, 2008.

———. *Paul, Apostle of God's Glory in Christ: A Pauline Theology*. Downers Grove, IL: InterVarsity, 2001.

———. "Philip Payne on Familiar Ground: A Review of Philip B. Payne, *Man and Woman, One in Christ*." *Journal of Biblical Manhood and Womanhood* 15, no 1 (2010): 33–46.

———. "'Praying and Prophesying in the Assemblies: I Corinthians 11:2–16' (Ch 8) by Gordon D. Fee." *Journal for Biblical Manhood and Womanhood* 10 (2005): 17–21.

———. "A Review of Scot McKnight, *The Blue Parakeet*." *Journal for Biblical Manhood and Womanhood* 14 (2009): 60–67.

———. *Romans*. Baker Exegetical Commentary on the New Testament. Grand Rapids: Baker, 1998.

———. "William J. Webb's *Slaves, Women and Homosexuals*: A Review Article." *The Southern Baptist Journal of Theology* 6, no. 1 (2002): 46–64.

———. "'Works of Law' in Paul." *Novum Testamentum* 33 (1991): 217–44.

Schreiner, Thomas R., and Ardel B. Caneday. *The Race Set Before Us: A Biblical Theology of Perseverance and Assurance*. Downers Grove, IL: InterVarsity, 2001.

Schreiner, Thomas R., and Shawn D. Wright, eds. *Believer's Baptism: Sign of the New Covenant in Christ*. NAC Studies in Bible and Theology. Nashville: Broadman & Holman, 2006.

Schürer, Emil. *The History of the Jewish People in the Age of Jesus Christ (175 B.C.–A.D. 135)*. Edited by Geza Vermes, Fergus Millar, and Matthew Black. 4 vols. Edinburgh: T&T Clark, 1973.

Scobie, C. H. H. *The Ways of Our God: An Approach to Biblical Theology*. Grand Rapids: Eerdmans, 2003.

Seifrid, Mark A. *Christ, Our Righteousness: Paul's Theology of Justification*. New Studies in Biblical Theology. Downers Grove, IL: InterVarsity, 2000.

———. "Righteousness Language in the Hebrew Scriptures and Early Judaism." In *Justification and Variegated Nomism: A Fresh Appraisal of Paul and Second Temple Judaism*. Vol. 1, *The Complexities of Second Temple Judaism*, edited by D. A. Carson, Peter T. O'Brien, and Mark A. Seifrid, 415–42. Grand Rapids: Baker, 2001.

———. "Unrighteous by Faith: Apostolic Proclamation in Romans 1:18–3:20." In *Justification and Variegated Nomism: A Fresh Appraisal of Paul and Second Temple Judaism*. Vol. 2, *The Paradoxes of Paul*, edited by D. A. Carson, Peter T. O'Brien, and Mark A. Seifrid, 105–45. Grand Rapids: Baker, 2004.

Seitz, Christopher. "Canon, Narrative, and the Old Testament's Literal Sense: A Response to John Goldingay, 'Canon and Old Testament Theology,'" *Tyndale Bulletin* 59 (2008): 27–34.

Smith, Jay E. "1 Corinthians." In *The Bible Knowledge Word Study: Acts–Ephesians*, edited by Darrell L. Bock, 205–326. Colorado Springs: Victor, 2006.

———. "The Roots of a Libertine Slogan in 1 Corinthians 6:18." *Journal of Theological Studies* 59 (2008): 63–95.

Spieckermann, Hermann. "God's Steadfast Love: Towards a New Conception of Old Testament Theology." *Biblica* 81 (2000): 305–27.

Sprinkle, Preston M. *Law and Life: The Interpretation of Leviticus 18:5 in Early Judaism and in Paul*. Wissenschaftliche Untersuchungen zum Neuen Testament 2.241. Tübingen: Mohr Siebeck, 2008.

Steinmetz, David C. "Uncovering a Second Narrative: Detective Fiction and the Construction of Historical Method." In *The Art of Reading Scripture*, edited by Ellen F. Davis and Richard B. Hays, 54–65. Grand Rapids: Eerdmans, 2003.

Strauss, Mark L. *Four Portraits, One Jesus: An Introduction to Jesus and the Gospels*. Grand Rapids: Zondervan, 2007.

Strazicich, John. *Joel's Use of Scripture and the Scripture's Use of Joel: Appropriation and Resignification in Second Temple Judaism and Early Christianity*. Biblical Interpretation Series. Boston: Brill, 2007.

Taylor, John W. "From Faith to Faith: Romans 1.17 in the Light of Greek Idiom." *New Testament Studies* 50 (2004): 337–48.

Taylor, Mark E. "Recent Scholarship on the Structure of James." *Currents in Biblical Research* 3 (2004): 86–115.

Taylor, Mark E., and George H. Guthrie. "The Structure of James." *Catholic Biblical Quarterly* 68 (2006): 681–705.

Thielman, Frank. "The Atonement." In *Central Themes in Biblical Theology: Mapping Unity in Diversity*, edited by Scott J. Hafemann and Paul R. House, 102–27. Grand Rapids: Baker, 2007.

———. *Theology of the New Testament: A Canonical and Synthetic Approach*. Grand Rapids: Zondervan, 2005.

Thigpen, J. Michael. "Lord of All the Earth: Yahweh and Baal in Joshua 3." *Trinity Journal* 27 (2006): 245–54.

Thomas, David Andrew. *Revelation 19 in Historical and Mythological Context*. Studies in Biblical Literature 118. New York: Peter Lang, 2008.

Tigay, Jeffrey. *Deuteronomy*, JPS Torah Commentary. Philadelphia: Jewish Publication Society, 1996.

Treier, Daniel J. "Biblical Theology and/or Theological Interpretation of Scripture?" *Scottish Journal of Theology* 61 (2008): 16–31.

Vanhoozer, Kevin J. *Is There a Meaning in This Text? The Bible, the Reader, and the Morality of Literary Knowledge*. Grand Rapids: Zondervan, 1998.

Vickers, Brian. *Jesus' Blood and Righteousness: Paul's Theology of Imputation*. Wheaton, IL: Crossway, 2006.

———. "Mark's Good News of the Kingdom of God." *The Southern Baptist Journal of Theology* 8, no. 3 (2004): 12–35.

Vogt, Peter T. *Deuteronomic Theology and the Significance of* Torah*: A Reappraisal*. Winona Lake, IN: Eisenbrauns, 2006.

Vos, Geerhardus. *Biblical Theology: Old and New Testaments*. Grand Rapids: Eerdmans, 1948.

Wagner, J. Ross. *Heralds of the Good News: Isaiah and Paul in Concert in the Letter to the Romans*. Supplements to Novum Testamentum. Boston: Brill, 2003.

Waltke, Bruce. *An Old Testament Theology: An Exegetical, Canonical, and Thematic Approach*. Grand Rapids: Zondervan, 2007.

Walton, John H. "The Imagery of the Substitute King Ritual in Isaiah's Fourth Servant Song." *Journal of Biblical Literature* 122 (2003): 734–43.

Watson, Francis. *Paul and the Hermeneutics of Faith*. New York: T&T Clark, 2004.

———. *Text and Truth: Redefining Biblical Theology*. Edinburgh: T&T Clark, 1997.

Watts, Rikki E. *Isaiah's New Exodus in Mark*. Grand Rapids: Baker, 2000.

Webb, Barry G. *Five Festal Garments: Christian Reflections on the Song of Songs, Ruth, Lamentations, Ecclesiastes, and Esther*. New Studies in Biblical Theology. Downers Grove, IL: InterVarsity, 2000.

———. *The Message of Zechariah*. The Bible Speaks Today. Downers Grove, IL: InterVarsity, 2003.

Wells, David. *God in the Wasteland: The Reality of Truth in a World of Fading Dreams*. Grand Rapids: Eerdmans, 1994.

———. *Losing Our Virtue: Why the Church Must Recover Its Moral Vision*. Grand Rapids: Eerdmans, 1998.

———. *No Place for Truth, or, Whatever Happened to Evangelical Theology?* Grand Rapids: Eerdmans, 1993.

Wenham, David. *Paul: Follower of Jesus or Founder of Christianity?* Grand Rapids: Eerdmans, 1995.

———. "Unity and Diversity in the New Testament." In George Eldon Ladd, *A Theology of the New Testament*, revised and edited by Donald A. Hagner, 684–719. Grand Rapids: Eerdmans, 1993.

Wenham, Gordon J. *The Book of Leviticus*. New International Commentary on the Old Testament. Grand Rapids: Eerdmans, 1979.

———. "Sanctuary Symbolism in the Garden of Eden Story." In *I Studied Inscriptions from before the Flood*, edited by R. S. Hess and D. T. Tsumara, 399–404. Winona Lake, IN: Eisenbrauns, 1994.

———. "Towards a Canonical Reading of the Psalms." In *Canon and Biblical Interpretation*, edited by C. G. Bartholomew, S. Hahn, R. Parry, C. Seitz, A. Wolters, 333–51. Scripture and Hermeneutics Series 7. Grand Rapids: Zondervan, 2006.

Wevers, John William. "The Rendering of the Tetragram in the Psalter and Pentateuch: A Comparative Study." In *The Old Greek Psalter: Studies in Honor of Albert Pietersma*, edited by Robert J. V. Hiebert, Claude E. Cox, and Peter J. Gentry. Journal for the Study of the Old Testament Supplement Series 332. Sheffield: Sheffield Academic, 2001.

Wilken, Robert Louis. *The Christians as the Romans Saw Them*. New Haven, CT: Yale University Press, 1984.

Williamson, Paul R. *Sealed with an Oath: Covenant in God's Unfolding Purpose*. New Studies in Biblical Theology. Downers Grove, IL: InterVarsity, 2007.

Wilson, Gerald H. "The Structure of the Psalter." In *Interpreting the Psalms: Issues and Approaches*, edited by David Firth and Philip S. Johnston, 229–40. Downers Grove, IL: InterVarsity, 2005.

———. "The Use of Royal Psalms at the 'Seams' of the Hebrew Psalter." *Journal for the Study of the Old Testament* 35 (1986): 85–94.

Wilson, Todd A. "'Under Law' in Galatians: A Pauline Theological Abbreviation." *Journal of Theological Studies* 56 (2005): 362–92.

———. "Wilderness Apostasy and Paul's Portrayal of the Crisis in Galatians." *New Testament Studies* 50 (2004): 550–71.

Wong, Gregory T. K. *Compositional Strategy of the Book of Judges: An Inductive, Rhetorical Study*. Supplements to *Vetus Testamentum*. Boston: Brill, 2006.

Woollcombe, K. J. "The Biblical Origins and Patristic Development of Typology." In *Essays on Typology*, edited by G. W. H. Lampe and K. J. Woollcombe, 39–75. Studies in Biblical Theology. Naperville, IL: Allenson, 1957.

Wright, Addison G. "Additional Numerical Patterns in Qoheleth." *Catholic Biblical Quarterly* 45 (1983): 32–43.

———. "The Riddle of the Sphinx: The Structure of the Book of Qoheleth." *Catholic Biblical Quarterly* 30 (1968): 313–34.

———. "The Riddle of the Sphinx Revisited: Numerical Patterns in the Book of Qoheleth." *Catholic Biblical Quarterly* 42 (1980): 38–51.

Wright, N. T. *The Climax of the Covenant: Christ and the Law in Pauline Theology*. Minneapolis: Fortress, 1992.

———. *Jesus and the Victory of God*. Christian Origins and the Question of God 2. Minneapolis: Fortress, 1996.

———. *The New Testament and the People of God*. Christian Origins and the Question of God 1. Minneapolis: Fortress, 1992.

———. *The Resurrection of the Son of God*. Christian Origins and the Question of God 3. Minneapolis: Fortress, 2003.

Yarbrough, Robert W. *1–3 John*. Baker Exegetical Commentary on the New Testament. Grand Rapids: Baker, 2008.

———. "The Last and Next Christendom: Implications for Interpreting the Bible." *Themelios* 29 (2003): 30–37.

Zimmerli, Walther. *The Fiery Throne: The Prophets and Old Testament Theology*. Minneapolis: Fortress, 2003.

GENERAL INDEX

Aaron, 100, 101, 103, 115, 117
Abdon, 155
Abel, 81, 82, 83, 85, 87, 176, 320n84
abiding in God, 535
abiding in Jesus, 417
Abijah, 345
Abimelech, 83, 87, 155, 281
Abner, 171
abomination of desolation, 325n95, 377, 389
Abraham
  blessing of, 68, 79, 80–82, 83, 87, 207
  and Moses, 113n104
  promises to, 89, 90, 102–3, 118, 172, 207, 255, 356, 363, 475, 536
Abrahamic covenant, 338, 473
Absalom, 143, 158, 160, 168, 173–74, 176, 281, 283, 284
Achan, 149, 150–51
Acts, 361, 419–39
Adam
  exile of, 193
  called to expand borders of Eden, 73, 171, 255, 356
  failure of, 356
  and Jesus, 396–97
  shifts blame, 103
  temptation of, 152
Adam and Eve, 50, 68, 75–80, 307
Adonijah, 177, 178–79, 180
adoption, 477, 480–81
adultery, 176, 187, 294
Aeneas, 439
affliction, 495, 496, 497, 498
  in Ecclesiastes, 316
  in Job, 301
  in Lamentations, 306
  in Psalms, 283, 284
Agabus, 437
age to come, 241, 377, 492
Agrippa, 435–36, 438
Agur, 291, 300
Ahab, 181, 182, 184, 248, 348–49, 437n167
Ahasuerus, 321–22
Ahaz, 184, 194–95, 201
Ahaziah, 181, 184
Ahithophel, 160, 284
Ai, 149, 150–51
Alexander, T. Desmond, 74, 95, 99n66, 502
Alexander the Great, 331
Alford, Henry, 540
alienation, 75, 78, 182, 307, 479
allegory
  of modern scholarship, 100
  in Paul, 477
already/not yet, 323, 357n5, 447, 558
Amalekites, 97
Amasai, 341
Amaziah, 184
Amelakites, 168, 421
Ammonites, 221, 253, 346
Amnon, 168, 173, 176
Amos, 188, 189, 229–30, 241–45, 266
analogous language, 556
Ananias and Sapphira, 421, 424, 427
ancient Near East
  mythology of, 70, 104, 125
  treaties of, 242
  wisdom literature of, 291
Ancient of Days, 330, 333
Anderson, Francis I., 247–48
angel of Yahweh, 156
angels, 148n14, 516
  judgment of, 529

anointing, of king, 161–62, 164–65
antichrist(s), 335, 532, 535
Antioch, 431, 444, 471
Antiochus Epiphanes, 325n95, 331, 335
antitheses, in Matthew, 369
antithetical statements, in Proverbs, 297–98
Apocalypse, of Isaiah, 198–99
apocalyptic, 335, 496n112, 550
Apollo, 439
apostasy, 129
apostates, 531–33
Apostolic Constitutions, 500n120
apostolic teaching, 374, 509, 529, 534, 536
Araunah, 175
ark of the covenant, 101, 115, 160, 163, 341–42
aroma of Christ, 463, 464
Asa, 182, 345–46, 347
Ashton, John, 355n1
Assyria, 143, 184–85, 191, 194–97, 199, 200, 201, 215, 230, 253, 266, 267, 366
Athaliah, 184
Athens, 436
atonement, 68, 103, 118, 225
Auld, Graeme, 146n10
Avemarie, Friedrich, 447n17
Azariah, 326–27

Baal, 183, 184, 234–35, 236, 237
Baasha, 181, 182
Babel, 90, 253, 425
Babylon, 186, 220, 223, 228–29, 252, 266, 267, 336, 357
  destruction of, 197–98, 221–22, 230, 548
  mythology of, 70, 72
Babylonian captivity, 351. *See also* exile
bad news, 566
Baird, William, 48n63
Balaam, 69, 118, 119, 142, 148, 529n174
ban, on Canaanites, 141–42, 149
baptism, 359, 368, 440, 441, 490–91, 523n161
Baptist General Convention of Texas, 43n37
Barabbas, 390, 418
Barnabas, 434, 444, 445
barrenness, 80–81, 85, 86, 87, 159
Barth, Karl, 44
Bartimaeus, 389
Barton, John, 47n58, 186, 240n58, 241, 351
Bathsheba, 168, 173, 176, 179, 281, 284, 339, 421
Bauckham, Richard, 328n98, 541, 543n9, 546n185, 548n20, 549n23
Beale, G. K., 50, 70n1, 74, 97n61, 190n105, 203n133, 327n96, 545n13, 549, 558
beatitudes, 369
beauty, irreligiously esteemed, 193
Beckwith, Roger, 276n11, 281n27, 323n92
Behemoth, 304
Belial, 159, 162
Bell, Richard H., 87n48, 112n101
Belshazzar, 326, 329
Ben-hadad, 184
Benjamin, tribe of, 158, 164–65
Beowulf, 81n40, 355
Berlin, Adele, 253n255
Berlioz, Hector, 186
Bethlehem, 249
Bible
  authority of, 46
  center of, 40–41
  coherence of, 39
  divine and human authors of, 554–55
  inspiration of, 529
  metanarrative of, 49, 58, 64, 355, 568
  unity of, 40–41
Bible reading, 568–69
biblical theology, 38, 41–47, 355
  as academic discipline, 41–43
  approaches to, 64n113
  in believing community, 41–43
  as "bridge discipline," 47
  center of, 38–41, 52, 190, 549–51, 563
  and method, 554–58
  and particular texts, 559–60
  and pastoral theology, 565–70
  and systematic theology, 46–47
  and theology proper, 560–62
  and wisdom literature, 272–73, 299
Bildad, 302–3
Blenkinsopp, Joseph, 191n107, 196n119, 199n124, 339n115
blessedness
  follows obedience, 125, 127–29
  of keeping Torah, 273
  of Psalms, 282
blindness, 389, 412
Block, Daniel I., 223n181
Blomberg, Craig L., 394
blood of Jesus, 390, 403
blood of the lamb, 224, 378, 524
boasting, in the cross, 478–79
Boaz, 305–6, 309
Boda, Mark J., 257n260, 259n267
body of Christ, 390
Bolt, Peter G., 371n32, 388n77, 390n85
Book of Consolation (Jeremiah), 211, 219–21
Book of Glory (John), 415–18
Book of Immanuel (Isaiah), 191, 194–97, 200
Book of Signs (John), 407–15
Book of the Twelve, 188, 229–34, 254, 266, 267
Book of Truth, 60, 61, 272, 275–76
born of God, 406, 534

Bostrom, N. E. L., 235
bowls of God's wrath, 545, 546, 547
Bozrah, 211
Branch, 192, 196, 259, 366
Bray, Gerald, 477n87
Bread of Life, 410, 411, 412
Bride, 542–43
Bright, John, 64n113
broken cisterns, 215, 222
bronze serpent, 118, 410
brood of vipers, as seed of the serpent, 367, 372, 377
Brueggemann, Walter, 38, 40, 41, 42n32, 43n37, 44–45, 48n65, 99n64, 235
Bryan, Steven M., 357n3, 384n71
Bultmann, Rudolf, 46
burden/oracle, in Nahum, 250–51
burdens, 257–58
Burk, Denny, 41, 446n14
burning bush, 148

Caesar, 435
Cain, 81, 82, 83, 87, 176, 532n180
Caird, G. B., 445n7
Caleb, 121
Canaanites, 141–42, 145, 153, 154
canonical approach, to biblical theology, 63, 64
Carson, D. A., 52, 64n113, 565
Catholic Epistles, 514–15, 536–37
census, 69, 114, 118
center, as metaphor, 355, 555–56
Chaldeans, 220–21
Chebar, 190
cherubim, 74, 101, 108, 148
Chester, Andrew, 148n14, 231, 453n32, 519n156
Chesterton, G. K., 145n9, 383–84
Chicago Manuel of Style, 77
Chicago Statement on Biblical Inerrancy, 333n102
child, Isaiah's prophecy of, 195–96
childbearing, difficulty of, 79, 80, 85, 86, 87, 88–89, 305
Childs, B. S, 64n113
Christian life, 416, 452, 454, 527, 565
Christlikeness, 460, 483, 492
christology, of Mark, 387, 392
Chronicles, 323, 324, 339–50
  genealogies of, 363
  purpose of, 339, 345
  as a theology of the Old Testament, 324
church, 513, 536
  growth of, 421, 423, 440
  as new Israel, 525
  as new temple, 467, 525
  sojourn in wilderness, 467
  schisms in, 457–58
  triumphs over powers of darkness, 484
  vigilance of, 456–57
  in the world, 522n161, 545, 546
church discipline, 500, 514, 566, 567–68
church membership, 567, 569
circumcision, 361, 487, 509
  and conquest, 148, 149n17
  and exodus, 148, 149n17
circumcision of Christ, 490
circumcision of the heart, 124–25, 127, 129, 130, 131, 166, 220n173, 221, 243
cities of refuge, 128
clean and unclean, 68, 107, 108
cleansing, 192, 212, 533, 534
Clement of Alexandria, 212n150, 500n120
Clement of Rome, 469n69, 526n164
Clements, Ronald E., 146n10
Clendenen, E. Ray, 264n280
Clines, David J. A., 37
Cogan, Mordechai, 176n75
Coleridge, Samuel Taylor, 67
Collins, Jack, 76n26
Colossians, 488–94
comfort, 202, 207
concursus, 336, 340, 345. *See also* divine sovereignty and human responsibility
conquest, 69, 114, 115, 147–48, 149–52, 176, 253, 267, 548
  and exodus, 148–49
  failure to complete, 154–55
  justice of, 141–42
conscience, 501, 502, 505
consolation of Israel, 396
consuming fire, 100, 107, 117, 120, 123, 126, 151, 201, 243, 292, 293
consummation, 49, 57, 64, 358, 492, 550
contradictions, in New Testament, 446
conversion, 527
Corinthians
  First, 448, 457–61
  Second, 448, 462–69
Cornelius, 361, 431
cornerstone, 200
courage, 145
covenant, 49, 55–56, 99n63, 256
  breaking of, 129–30, 132, 224, 231
  curses of, 213, 229, 239, 473–74
  inaugurated with blood, 100
  as marriage with Yahweh, 214, 234, 356
  as organizing center, 48n65
  renewal of, 151, 153, 324, 338
  stipulations of, 127–29
covenant infidelity, 214
cowardice, 166
Cranfield, C. E. B., 454

created order, and gender roles, 503–4
creation, 49, 70, 71–73
as formless and void, 72, 216
in prologue to Gospel of John, 361
as temple, 203n133, 356
as theater, 53
Cretans, 509
cross, 57, 370, 469, 474, 513
boasting in, 478–79
at center of theology of Gospels, 400
glorification at, 413–14, 416, 458
as new exodus, 358
patterns Christian life, 416
in Paul, 466
taking up of, 371–72, 374, 386–88
weakness of, 457
crucifixion, 424, 486
cruciformity, 484–88
cup of judgment, 208, 219, 360
cup of Yahweh's wrath, 219
curse
answered by blessing, 80–82
of ground, 79–80, 85, 88, 305, 308, 309
removal of, 88, 148, 197, 211
on Saul, 167–68
Curtis, Byron, 254–55, 258n266, 259n267, 261n270, 263
Cush, 281
Cushan, 253
Cyrus, 206, 219n70, 323, 336, 350, 357, 548

Dagon, 163
Dahl, Nils, 392n97
daily bread, 234
Damascus, 198, 221
Daniel, 187, 190, 210, 323–24, 325–35, 350, 357–58, 377, 389, 425
Danites, 158
Darius, 219n170, 329–30
darkness, 53, 370
at death of Jesus, 379
of exile, 195, 200
forces of, 403, 439, 491
walking in, 533
David, 158, 168–76, 267
anointed king, 171
in Chronicles, 340–42, 347n123
defeats Philistines, 173
in genealogy of Matthew, 363–64
and Goliath, 143, 160, 168–69
house of, 172, 177, 200, 282
instruction to Solomon, 177–78
lament for Saul, 175
as new Adam, 173, 176
promises to, 339, 536
rise through afflictions, 275
sin of, 141, 143, 160, 168, 173–74, 175, 176, 179, 187, 275, 281, 284, 339, 421
studied Torah, 341
as type, 170, 372
Davidic covenant, 209, 221, 224
Davidic king, 196, 209, 221, 264, 275, 395
Davidic psalms, 277–79, 281–84, 287–88
Davies, Philip R., 309n67
Day of Atonement, 111
day of the Lord, 240, 243, 253, 254, 265, 266, 367, 496, 498–99, 508, 530
deaconesses, 500n120, 505
deacons, 424, 500, 505
death, 76, 78–79, 80
as "gain," 486
Deborah, 155
deceivers, 515, 535
de-creation, 216
De Jong, Stephan, 313n71
Delitzsch, F., 230n196, 307n60
deliverance, 308, 485
through Christ, 469–70
in Daniel, 326
of judges, 155
in Psalms, 275, 289
Demetrius, 535
demons, casting out, 360, 382, 383, 386, 397, 439
Dempster, Stephen, 59–60, 62, 63–64, 65, 148n15, 153n25, 184n92, 188n101, 190, 218n165, 220n173, 357n3
Dennis, John, 530n175, 530n177
desire, 307–8
desire of all the nations, 257
Deuteronomist, 100, 146, 172n70, 186
Deuteronomy, 69, 119–32, 146, 190
as heart of Old Testament, 274
and Proverbs, 291–93
Didascalia Apostolorum, 500n120
Dinah, rape of, 83, 85
Diotrephes, 535
discernment, 485
disciples, 398–99, 401, 417, 418
discipleship, 375, 385, 496, 566, 567
discipline, 107, 212
in Judges, 156
in wilderness, 126
disobedience, and cursing, 127–29
divine sovereignty and human responsibility, 121–22, 131, 162–63, 210, 296, 297, 340, 447, 454, 499
divine warrior, 175, 210, 483n93
divorce, 128, 388
Doeg the Edomite, 281
dominion and dynasty, 65n115

Donfried, Karl Paul, 498n116
Dostoevsky, Fyodor, 78n32, 443
doxologies, of New Testament, 538–39
dragon, 198–99, 211
drought, 242
Dumbrell, William J., 56n87, 64n113, 115, 211n145, 218n167, 222n180, 229, 235, 250

Eaton, Michael A., 315n77
Ecclesiastes, 180n85, 299, 306, 313–20
Eden, 68, 73–74, 81, 101, 156, 207, 307–8, 357n3
Edom, 173, 221, 229, 245–46, 264, 266
Edwards, Jonathan, 48–49, 553, 561
egalitarians, 503n122
Egypt, 191, 198, 199, 201, 356, 366. *See also* exodus
  Israel's reliance on, 215
  judgment against, 106, 221
  mythology of, 70–71, 72
Ehud, 155, 156, 158
Eichrodt, Walther, 46, 48n65, 55–56, 64n113, 70n1, 99, 186
Elam, 221
elders, 500, 504–5, 506, 509, 538
Eleazar, 340
election, 264, 450, 452, 454–55, 479–80, 481n90
elementary principles, 476
Eli, sons of, 142, 159, 160, 162–63
Elihu, 303
Elijah, 177, 181–83, 184, 188, 374, 397, 398
  appeals to God, 183
  coming of, 265, 394
  prepares the way, 408
  prepares way for Messiah, 229
  at transfiguration, 374, 388, 400–401
Eliphaz, 302–3
Elisha, 177, 181, 188, 397
Elliott, John, 527–28
Elliott, Mark Adam, 447n17
Ellis, E. Earle, 97n61, 392n96, 396nn104–5, 399, 403n119, 445n6, 500n118
Ellis, P. F., 64n113
Elon, 155
Elymas the magician, 433
enmity, between seeds, 79–80, 197
ends, subordinate and ultimate, 48–49
endurance, of trials, 499, 520, 522
Enlightenment, 42–43
Enoch, 110
Enuma Elish, 70
Epaphras, 488
Epaphroditus, 485, 487
Ephesians, 448, 479–84
Ephesus, 436–37, 500, 503–4, 505
Ephraim, 194–95
Esau, 83, 88, 264
eschatological triumph, in Psalms, 288
eschaton, 447
Essenes, 503
Esther, 306, 320–22
eternal life, 411, 433, 533
Ethan the Ezrahite, 286
Ethiopia, 198, 253, 345–46
Ethiopian eunuch, 431
Eutychus, 436
evangelicalism, 39
evangelism, 566
Eve, temptation of, 178
evil, 199, 205, 304
exaltation, in 1 Peter, 528
exegesis, and systematic theology, 47
exile, 49, 125, 176–77, 186, 188, 190, 200, 238, 322, 350, 356
  blessing in, 210
  of Daniel, 325, 326–27
  darkness of, 195
  as de-creation, 216
  displays Yahweh's justice, 256
  end of, 130, 202, 233, 333, 334–35, 378, 398, 400
  follows covenant breaking, 129
  fulfillment of, 419
  in John, 409
  and Prophets, 140, 144
  in the Psalms, 275, 279, 286–87
  salvation through, 212, 350
exodus, 68, 106, 122, 144, 214, 253, 337, 338, 351, 356, 378, 403–4, 549
  and conquest, 148–49
  remembrance of, 238
Exodus (book), 68, 90–107, 146, 273–74
exorcisms, 370n30. *See also* demons, casting out
Ezekiel, 188, 190, 222–29, 267, 410, 467, 559
Ezra, 62–63, 323, 324, 335–39, 350

faith, 497
  in exile, 286–87
  of Joshua, 150
  and Levitical system, 110, 111–14
  as living, 514
faithfulness, 126, 494, 496, 499
faithlessness, 380
fall, 49, 50, 75–80
falling away, 518
false apostles, 465–66
false gods, 341. *See also* idolatry
false gospel, 465–66
false messages, 498–99
false prophets, 128, 225, 349, 378, 529, 545, 546

false teachers, 371, 452, 457, 465, 470–71, 477, 479, 488, 500, 506, 508, 509–10, 515, 529–30, 536
false worship, 131
famine, 85–86, 88, 174, 182, 242, 305, 308, 309
fasting, 260
fate, 102n76
fear of God, 100, 151, 272, 300, 319, 320, 346, 555
  in Proverbs, 290, 291–93, 295, 297–99
Feast of Booths, 547
Feast of Tabernacles, 411
Feinberg, Charles L., 215n160
Felix, 438
fellowship with God and believers, 515, 533
female deacons, 500n120, 505
feminism, 79
fertility cult, 237
Festus, 435–36, 438
fideism, 44
fiery furnace, 324, 328
fiery serpents, 117–18
figs, 219
fig tree, 376, 378, 389
final judgment, 549
fire, 403
Firstborn from the dead, 489
Fishbane, Michael, 99n65, 147n13
fishing, 368, 397, 418
Fitzmyer, Joseph A., 511n139
flaming sword, at Eden, 74, 101, 148
flood, 68, 216, 523n161, 526, 529, 549
folly, 294, 298, 299
forgiveness, 344, 360–61, 397, 431, 491, 518, 533, 534
Former Prophets, 60, 61, 140, 141–43, 187–88, 254, 271, 350
forsaking Yahweh, 213, 214, 221, 222
fortress, 213, 214, 217
Fox, Michael V., 291n48
fragrance of knowledge of Christ, 468
Freedman, David Noel, 61–63, 187n99, 188n101, 247–48
freedom, 107, 469, 477
Frei, Hans, 42
fulfillment, in Matthew, 364–67, 369, 379
Fuller, Daniel, 555
Fuller, Russell E., 188n100
Fyall, Robert, 301, 304

Gabriel, 330, 332–33, 394
Gad, 175
Galatians, 437n168, 448, 469–79
garden-temple, 50, 178
Garrett, Duane, 241, 272, 320n84
Gath, 248
Gathercole, Simon, 359n10, 368n25, 372n34, 378n47, 382n63, 390, 401n114
Gehazi, 184
gender relations and roles, 85–87, 305, 307, 309, 321, 460, 492, 503, 536
genealogies
  in Chronicles, 339–40
  in Luke, 396
  in Mark, 380
  in Matthew, 363–64
generosity, 465
Genesis, 65, 67–68, 70–89, 273, 320n84
genocide, 141n3
Gentiles, 245, 260, 525
  adoption of, 480–81
  election of, 479–80
  full number of, 359
  gospel to, 431–32
  and Mosaic law, 471–72, 473, 475–78
  and promise to Abraham, 475
  as righteous by faith, 450–51
  saved through judgment, 151
Gentry, Peter J., 56n87, 209, 212n148
geography and genealogy, 65n115
Geshurites, 152
Gibeah, 158
Gibeon, 149
Gibeonites, 151–52, 174–75
Gideon, 155, 156–57, 158, 195
Gillingham, S. E., 282n30
giving, 465
glory, of the cross, 413–14, 416, 458
glory-cloud, 115
glory of Christ
  in Colossians, 488–90
  in First Peter, 523
  in Hebrews, 515–16
glory of God, 39, 41, 123, 199, 206, 558
  in Acts, 422–23
  through anointed king, 162
  in Book of the Twelve, 233
  as center of biblical theology, 53–56
  in conquest, 123, 149–52, 153, 154
  consummation of, 467
  covers dry land, 73, 116, 255–56, 267, 268–69, 323, 339, 343, 356, 483
  in creation, 70
  in Deuteronomy, 132
  in Ezekiel, 222–23, 229
  filled tabernacle, 106, 107
  filled temple, 343
  in First Peter, 523
  in Genesis, 89
  in Isaiah, 193
  in John, 405

in Levitical system, 110
in Luke, 392–93
in Mark, 559–60
as metanarrative, 359
in Old Testament prayers, 352–53
in Psalms, 289–90
in Romans, 451–57
in salvation through judgment, 56–59, 132–33
glory of man, 411, 415
Gnostics, 503
God. *See also* glory of God
anger of, 150, 155
authority of, 127
called to remember, 286
as Creator, 204
disciplines Israel, 163
dwells in tabernacle, 108
faithfulness of, 145, 186, 311, 338, 351
goodness of, 103–5, 205, 238
holiness of, 53–54, 103, 108, 110, 145, 151, 194, 212, 226–27, 242, 311–12, 341, 512
incomparability of, 201–6
as lion, 229, 238, 242, 266
love of, 54, 55, 63, 102, 104, 244, 351, 534, 537, 560–62
name of, 103–4, 226–28
nature of, 77–78
presence among Israel, 101, 106
promises of, 187–88
reveals identity in Egypt, 94–96
righteousness of, 104, 332
self-revelation of, 53
sovereignty of, 130, 160, 162, 196, 205, 243, 273, 298, 347–49, 433, 434
transcendence of, 343
as witness against Israel, 248
godliness, 505–6, 510, 529
golden calf, 97, 102, 116, 126, 338
golden calves, 248, 345
Goldingay, John, 46, 64n113,
Goliath, 143, 158, 160, 168–69, 327
Gombis, Timothy G., 483n93, 484n95
good life, 526
good news, 203, 525, 566
Good Shepherd, 261, 262–63, 412–13
good works, 489
Gorman, Michael J., 446n13, 486, 496n112
gospel, 495, 525
advance of, 358, 361, 432, 526
glorifies Christ, 501
in Romans, 453
governing authorities, 523, 525–26, 537
grace, 507, 511
Grant, Jamie, 279–81, 282n31
Great Commission, 445, 566
Greece, 334
greed, 300
Greek gods, 71, 72, 104, 125, 439
Grudem, Wayne, 437n167

Habakkuk, 189, 229–30, 231, 252–53, 266
Hadley, Judith M., 234n208
Hafemann, Scott, 56, 464n62, 467n66, 468n68
Hagar, 477–78
Haggai, 229–30, 254–57
hallel psalms, 290
hallelujah, 277, 279
Halton, Charles, 77, 157n35
Haman, 306, 322
Hamath, 173
Hanani, 346
Hananiah (Daniel), 326–27
Hananiah (Jeremiah), 220
Hannah, 142, 158, 159–62, 164, 170, 175, 395
hardening
of kings of land at conquest, 149
of Israel, 373, 359, 415
of Pharaoh, 92–95, 121, 149
Harlot, 542–43
Hasel, Gerhard, 52, 211n146
Hays, Richard B., 81n40, 504
Hazael, 181, 184
headship, 460
healing ministry of Jesus, 360, 370, 373, 376, 382, 383, 398, 399
hearing, in Micah, 247, 249
heart, 123–25, 129, 130, 132
as metaphor, 556
heart of flesh, 225
heaven and earth, as witnesses to covenant, 131, 248, 474
heavens and earth, shaking of, 255–57, 267
Hebrews, 444, 514–19
Heman the Ezrahite, 286
hermeneutical circle, 556
Hermes, 439
Hermogenes, 508
Herod, 395, 431
Herodotus, 234n208
Hesiod, 71, 72, 75
Hezekiah, 185, 191, 201, 346–47
Hilkiah, 212
Hill, Andrew E., 264n279
Hiram, 343
historical critical scholarship, 42, 445n7
Hoehner, Harold W., 333n104
holiness, 55, 68, 101, 108, 320, 530, 568
Holy of Holies, 108, 115, 405
Holy Spirit, 417
and authors of Scripture, 529, 555

outpouring of, 201, 398, 408, 421, 426, 475, 478
holy war, reversal of in exile, 218
Homer, 102n76
hope, 191, 192, 194, 366, 450, 523
beyond judgment, 130, 200, 218–20
in Lamentations, 311–13
in Luke, 395–96
in prophets, 231
in Psalms, 286–87
Hophni and Phineas, 162, 163
Hopkins, Gerard Manley, 38, 60n93
Hosea, 188, 189, 229–30, 234–39, 365–66, 525
Hoskins, Paul, 64
House, Paul, 64n113, 110, 118, 156n30, 178, 183n91, 184n93, 234, 235n210, 240, 247n242, 265, 292, 308n61, 309n66
household code, 484n95, 492
Howard, David, 287
human wisdom, 187, 199, 457–58
humility, 166, 320, 375, 395, 522
Hurtado, Larry W., 447n15
husbands and wives, 492, 523, 526
Hyginus, 71
Hymenaeus, 502

I Am, Jesus as, 361, 411–12
Ibzan, 155
idolatry, 118, 178, 184–85, 203–4, 210, 212, 224, 328, 438–39, 459, 495, 545
of Canaanites, 142, 145, 149
corruption of, 181–82
of Israel, 155, 163
Ignatius, 437n168
Iliad, 102n76
image of God, 101, 356, 561
imitation of Christ, 484–85, 488, 496
Immanuel, 194–95
Imperial Cult, 471n73
imprecatory psalms, 288–89, 570
inaugurated eschatology, in Old Testament, 323
"in Christ," 490–91, 492
indicatives and imperatives, in Paul, 513
individualism, 568
inheritance, 481, 524, 526
integrity, 320
intermarriage, 180, 324
interpretation, 38–39
intertestamental literature, 527
Isaac, 81, 85, 87–88, 89, 153, 477–78
Isaiah, 188, 189, 190, 191–211, 267, 356–57, 467, 474–75, 559
in John, 414–15
in Luke, 398
in Mark, 382, 392
in Matthew, 365
Ish-bosheth, 171
Ishmael, 83, 87, 478
Israel
appeal for king, 163–65
Canaanization of, 267
as choice vine, 214n157
confession of fidelity, 153
disobedience of, 126, 154
division of kingdom, 176–77, 180–85, 267
election of, 55, 125, 454–55
failure of, 50–51
as firstborn son, 214n157
fruitful and multiplied, 90
as great nation, 68, 82
grumbling in wilderness, 96–97, 115–19
heart problem of, 123–25
idolatry of, 155, 163
as light to the nations, 246
progressive deterioration of, 158
rebellion in wilderness, 69
rejection of messiah, 450–51
saved through judgment, 106–7, 115
temptation in land, 152
as vineyard, 193
as whoring wife, 235–37
wickedness of, 114, 248, 250
Israel (northern kingdom). *See* northern kingdom

Jabesh Gilead, 167
Jacob, 83–84, 85, 88, 89,
blessing of Judah, 118, 119
Jael, 156
Jahaziel, 346
Jair, 155
Jambres, 508
James, 437, 444, 445, 515
James (letter of), 446, 519–22
Jannes, 508
Jebusites, 152, 340
Jedidiah, 176
Jehoahaz, 184
Jehoiachin, 187, 213, 254
Jehoida, 184
Jehoram, 184
Jehoshaphat, 183, 346, 347, 348
Jehovah, 54n83
Jehu, 181, 184
Jephthah, 155, 156, 157, 158
Jeremiah, 188, 189, 190, 211–22, 267, 323, 335, 336, 374
cited by Matthew, 366–67
and Ezekiel, 228
Jericho, 149–50
Jeroboam, 143, 180–82, 184, 186, 241, 345, 347
Jerome, 212n150, 324n93

Jerusalem, 168, 171, 253, 307
destruction of, 190, 212, 221, 223–25, 254, 285, 376–77
exaltation of, 192, 194, 264, 323
Jesus enters, 375–77, 389–90, 401–3, 405, 413
Paul goes to, 437
Jerusalem Council, 433, 434, 437, 470–71
Jesse, 208, 306, 309
Jesus Christ
ascension of, 424–25, 426
authority of, 370, 382, 386, 387, 397
baptism of, 367–68
birth of, 394–96
blood of, 379
as Bridegroom, 371, 398, 410
brings end to exile, 372, 373
as Creator, 489
crucifixion of, 446
became curse, 474
death and resurrection of, 49–50, 360, 378, 381, 388, 390–92, 399–400, 404, 409, 418, 419, 424, 439, 448, 464, 467, 484, 494
death of, 486, 491
as end of the law for righteousness, 112
faithfulness of, 517
as fulfillment of new exodus, 550
glorified in Acts, 422–23
godliness of, 505–6
as Head of the church, 489, 490
as life, 406
"lifted up," 411, 412, 414
as light, 406, 410, 412
as messiah, 407, 408
as new Moses, 400–401, 517
obedience of, 486
as Passover Lamb, 359, 517
rejection of, 406
relives history of Israel, 359–60, 362, 363–67, 439, 474
resurrection of, 446
became sin, 466
suffering of, 374, 494, 527
as temple, 361, 379
temptation in wilderness, 368, 369, 396–97
transfiguration of, 374, 388, 400–401
weakness of, 466
Jewish feasts, in John, 408–9, 418
Jewish mysticism, 488
Jews and Gentiles, unity of, 481–84
Jezebel, 183
Joab, 171, 175, 178
Joash, 184
Job, 275–76, 301–5, 350
Jobes, Karen H., 192n109, 523n162
Joel, 239–41
John, 445
First John, 515, 531–35
Gospel of, 361, 405–19, 444
Second John, 515, 535
Third John, 515, 535
as true prophet, 544–45, 546
Johnson, Luke Timothy, 500n118, 504, 519n157
John the Baptist, 357, 358, 367, 372, 373, 374, 376, 380–81, 384, 394, 396, 397, 398, 403, 406, 407
Jonah, 229–30, 246–47, 266, 362
Jonathan, 158, 167–68, 169, 170, 421
Joosten, Jan, 239n218
Jordan River, 144, 147, 367–68
Joseph, 83–84, 88, 89, 357–58, 428–29
Josephus, 157n34, 331n99, 537
Joshua, 121, 132, 141–42, 259, 356, 548
address of, 153
appeals to Yahweh, 150, 162–63
conquest under, 267
faith of, 150
as new Moses, 144, 148–49
Joshua (book), 139, 141–42, 144–54, 187, 274
Joshua (high priest), 255, 259
Josiah, 186, 212, 338n112, 347
Joüon, P. A., 123n127
joy, 486
Jubilee, 199, 332
Judah (southern kingdom), 143, 185–86, 262, 267, 345–49
Judah (tribe), 89, 107n81, 114, 119, 177, 309
Judas, 415, 421, 425
Jude, 444–45, 515, 536
judges, 141, 154–58, 167, 267, 338
Judges (book), 142, 154–58, 274
judgment, 56–59, 377–78
in Book of the Twelve, 232
brought by Jesus, 389, 403, 498, 499
on enemies in Chronicles, 345–46
ensures salvation, 527
falls on Jesus, 209, 404, 408, 413, 439, 484, 491, 507, 538
of false teachers, 509, 530
in Jeremiah, 216
on Jerusalem, 376–77
as penultimate, 235
and prayer, 162–63
preserves believers, 126, 536
in Proverbs, 296–97
in Psalms, 286
as purging, 231
as purifying, 265, 341–42
and salvation, 126
in Second Corinthians, 469
on serpent, 76–78

on those who crucified Jesus, 424
from throne, 542
in wilderness, 115–19, 121
judgment day, 285, 436
justice, 78–79, 84–86, 244, 491, 555, 562
of conquest, 141–42, 149
in Egypt, 92, 95
in Proverbs, 300
justice and mercy, 86, 87, 116, 501
in Job, 302, 305
in the wilderness, 103–5
justification by faith, 344, 449–50, 471–72, 513, 537, 550
justification by works, 550
Justin Martyr, 70n1

Kedar and Hazor, 221
Keil, C. F., 157n34, 212n150
Ketuvim. *See* Writings
Kim, Jinkyu, 288n40
Kim, Seyoon, 495n111
king, kingship, 157–58, 280, 345–49
as agent of salvation through judgment, 298
after God's own heart, 168, 172n69
like all the nations, 141, 163–64, 187
restraint of, 163, 165
kingdom of God, 329, 330, 339, 374, 380, 391, 546
in Matthew, 369–70
parables of, 363, 373, 399
and repentance, 368, 382
kingdom of priests, 163, 522n161
kingdoms, in Daniel, 326, 327, 330–34
Kings (books), 143, 176–87
Kiuchi, Nobuyoshi, 109n92, 110, 111, 114
Klein, Ralph W., 161n44
Kline, M. G., 259n267
knowledge, 485
knowledge of God, 237, 238, 292–93, 299–300, 489
knowledge of Jesus, 529, 530
Knowles, Michael, 366n21, 368n26, 378n49
Koorevaar, H. J., 144n6
Korah, 117
Köstenberger, Andreas, 52

Laato, Antti, 202n130
Ladd, George Eldon, 367n23, 392n93
Lady Wisdom, 293–96
Lady Zion, 306, 310–11
Lamarche, Paul, 261n271
Lamb of God, 408, 409
Lamech (father of Noah), 88, 152
Lamentations, 306, 310–13, 350
land promise, 81–82
Latter Prophets, 60, 61, 140, 188–91, 212, 214, 254, 266–67, 271, 443
law. *See also* Mosaic law; Torah
as custodian, 476
Stephen on, 427–30
written on hearts, 208
Law and the Prophets, 377, 518
fulfilled by Jesus, 374, 377, 388, 400–401
lawlessness, 532
law of Christ, 359
lawsuits, in the church, 458
Lazarus, 412
laziness, 499–500
leadership in the church, 500
legalism, 473
Leithart, Peter J., 321n89
Lemuel, 291, 300, 301
lepers, 109
leprosy, 183–84
letter to exiles (Jeremiah), 220, 228–29
letters to seven churches, 542, 545
Levi, house of, 107
Leviathan, 198–99, 285, 304
Levine, Lee I., 336n108, 338n112
Levinskaya, Irina, 431n157
levirate marriage, 128
Levites, 114–15
Levite's concubine, 158
Levitical system, 105, 409
and faith, 110, 111–14
Leviticus, 68–69, 107–14, 225, 274
liars, 532
life worthy of the gospel, 486–87
lion, Yahweh as, 229, 238, 242, 266
lion's den, 324, 326, 329–30
literary approach to biblical theology, 64n113
living hope, 523
living water, 97, 411
locust plague, 229, 239, 241, 242, 266
Lohfink, Norbert, 96n58
Longman, Tremper, III, 272n4, 313n71
Lord (title), 54n83, 401
Lord of the Sabbath, 372, 382, 398
Lord's Supper, 359, 404, 459, 460, 513
lost sheep of house of Israel, 371
Lot, 83, 85, 89, 529
love, 416–17, 419, 460, 485, 497, 499, 501, 524
and obedience, 125, 127, 132
lovelessness, 466
Lövestam, Evald, 378n48
Luke, Gospel of, 360–61, 392–404, 444
and Samuel, 393, 420–21
Lundbom, Jack R., 211n147, 213n151

Maacathites, 152
Machen, J. Gresham, 39

Madame Folly, 293–96
magic, 436
Maher-shalal-hashbaz, 195
Malachi, 229, 231, 263–66
Maly, Eugene H., 238
Manasseh (king), 185–86, 347
Manasseh (tribe), 152
manna, 96, 115, 126, 411
man of God, 164, 181, 186
marital intimacy, 305, 307
Mark, Gospel of, 360, 380–92, 444, 559–60
marriage, 128, 296, 459, 483, 526
  between Yahweh and Israel, 235–37
Marshall, I. Howard, 380, 392n94, 392n99, 406n128, 418n142, 481n90, 500n118, 534n182, 554–63
Martens, Elmer, 52, 64n113, 65
Martin, Ralph, 512–13, 528n171, 556–57
Mary, 394, 395
Masoretes, 333
Massah, 97
Matera, Frank J., 536n186
Matthew, Gospel of, 359–60, 362–80, 444
  and Pentateuch, 392
Mattingly, Gerald, 234
Mays, James Luther, 276, 281–82
McCarter, Kyle, Jr., 167
McComiskey, Douglas S., 373n37
McConville, J. G., 212n149, 215n159, 216n163, 218, 339n113
Medes, 197, 221
meditation, on word of Yahweh, 139
Megilloth, 60, 61, 272, 305–6
Melchizedek, 515, 516, 517
Mendenhall, George, 99n64
Menken, Maarten J. J., 498n116
Mephibosheth, 173
mercy, 78, 84, 216, 237, 238, 240
  and justice, 86, 116, 501
  to David, 172
  to Mary, 395
  in Passover, 95
  Paul on, 451
  in Proverbs, 300
  in return from exile, 256
  in Romans, 455–56
  and sacrifices, 114
  in the wilderness, 103
mercy seat, 101
Meribah, 97
Merrill, Eugene H., 157n36
messiah, 57, 285, 390
  in Daniel, 334
  Jesus as, 407, 408
  judgment on, 413
  in Psalms, 279, 280–83
  in Romans, 453n32
  suffering of, 467
"Messianic Secret," 386n73
messianic wisdom, in Ecclesiastes, 315
messianic woes, 369, 467, 492–94, 497, 523, 527
metaphors, 555–56
Micah, 189, 229–30, 231, 247–50, 266
Micah of Ephraim, 157
Micah of Moresheth, 220
Micaiah, 348–49
Michal, 169
Midianites, 195, 253
mighty works, 329, 363, 370–71, 397, 427, 439
Millar, J. Gary, 120n118, 123n127, 124n130, 128n139
millennium, 548n20
miracles. *See* mighty works
Miriam, 115
Mishael, 326–27
Moab, Moabites, 173, 198, 221, 253, 305, 309, 346
mockers, 530
modesty, 504
Moo, Douglas J., 403n118
Mordecai, 306, 321–22
Moriah, 87
Mosaic covenant, 101, 107, 231, 473
Mosaic law, 111–13, 242, 338, 468, 471–77, 488, 536
Moses, 63, 356, 358, 388
  and Abraham, 113n104
  appeals to Yahweh, 102–3, 116, 117, 126, 150, 162–63
  authorship of Pentateuch, 44, 555
  as builder of tabernacle, 342
  and burning bush, 148
  death of, 132, 144
  fulfilled by Jesus, 374, 375
  judgment against, 117, 119, 122
  last will and testament, 129–32
  and Paul, 462, 464
  prophet like, 132n143, 207, 218n165, 369, 375, 400
  psalm of, 286
  recounts history in Deuteronomy, 120–21
  on Sinai, 98–101
  Stephen on, 427–30
  strikes rock, 117
  at transfiguration, 374, 388, 400–401
Motyer, J. Alec, 192n110
Mounce, William D., 500n118, 500n120
murder, 176, 187
mysterious working of God, 318, 320
mystery, of God's will, 480
myths, 501, 509

Naaman, 183–84
Nabal, 160
Nadab and Abihu, 100, 108, 272
Nahum, 189, 229–30, 231, 250–51, 266
name of Jesus, 401n114, 421n149
name of Yahweh, 54, 63
Name Theology, 172n70
Naomi, 309
narcissism, 561
narrative theology, 64n113
Nathan, 173
nations
  bring justice against God's people, 221–22
  judgment against, 190, 197–98
  streaming to Zion, 192
Nazirites, 157, 242, 312, 394
Nebuchadnezzar, 220, 326, 327–29, 332
Nehemiah, 62–63, 323, 324, 335–39, 350
Neviim. *See* Prophets
new Aaron, 517
new Adam, 322
  David as, 176
  Israel as, 267
  Solomon as, 143, 179
new birth, 124, 406–7, 524, 536
new commandment, 416, 535
new conquest, 257, 548
new covenant, 209, 220, 222n180, 236–37, 256, 257, 322–23, 369, 400, 403, 408, 462, 464, 516, 517, 518
  gives life, 468
  inauguration of, 359, 404
new creation, 51, 479, 489
new David, 190, 218–19, 233, 257, 267, 279, 322–23, 339, 357, 369, 404
new Eden, 211, 322, 549
  Promised Land as, 255–56, 267, 356
  tabernacle as, 108
  under David, 172, 173, 176
new Elijah, 367, 373–74
new exodus, 49, 322–23, 369, 378, 400, 404, 410, 412, 419, 513, 522, 523–25, 536
  fulfilled in Jesus, 357, 550
  inauguration of, 391, 398, 418, 517
  kingdom as, 368
  and Passover meal, 390
  and resurrection of Jesus, 379, 381
  as return from exile, 195, 197, 208, 218–19, 249, 256, 257, 337, 356–57, 366–67, 467
  Revelation as, 546–48
new heart, 225
new heavens and new earth, 357, 525, 530, 536, 545, 549
New Humanity, 484n95
new Israel, 369
New Jerusalem, 211, 358
new Joshua, 548
new life, 410, 513, 524, 527, 534
new man, 483, 484
new Moses, 369
new Sinai, 369
new temple, 190, 409
New Testament
  diversity of theology of, 445–46
  shape of, 63–64
Nicodemus, 410
Niehaus, Jeffrey J., 146n10, 171n67
Nineveh, 229, 246–47, 250, 251, 266
Noah, 68, 88, 378, 526, 529, 549
Nogalski, James, 231n200
Nolland, John, 369
northern kingdom, 143, 177, 180–85, 194, 195, 199, 248, 267, 365–66
Noth, Martin, 146nn10–11, 186
Numbers, 69, 114–19, 274

Obadiah, 229–30, 245–46, 266
Obed, 309
obedience, 99–100, 117, 122–27, 132, 157, 273
  and blessing, 127–29
  in Ecclesiastes, 320
  in Proverbs, 290–91, 292, 301
O'Connor, M., 244n236
O'Dowd, Ryan P., 272n4
Og, 118, 122, 146
old covenant, 57, 105, 462, 481
  as ministry of death, 468
  obsolescence of, 518
  remnant in, 125
old man, 483
Old Testament
  canon of, 63
  as forward-looking, 351
  fulfillment of, 517–18, 537
  sequence of, 59–63
  theology of, 351–52
Olivet Discourse, 377–78
Olmstead, Wesley G., 376n43, 377, 379nn51–52
Olson, Dennis, 292
Omri, 181
Onesimus, 508, 510–12
opposition
  to Jesus, 372, 414
  to early church, 424, 427, 433
  to the gospel, 435, 439, 440, 495, 508
oracles, against the nations, 197–98, 212, 221–22, 245–46, 251
Origen, 324n93, 477, 500n120
orphans, 520
Ortlund, Raymond C., 235n210

Osborne, Grant, 545n12, 549
Osteen, Joel, 566
Oswalt, John N., 196n119, 210, 211n146
Other Sacred Writings, 60, 61, 272, 322–24
Othniel, 155
overseers, 504–5, 509

Pahl, Michael W., 495n111
pain and sorrow, 317
painful toil, work as, 88
Pao, David W., 419n145
parables, 363, 373, 378, 383, 399
parents, instruction of children, 274, 294, 492
Passover, 359, 409
 Jesus' celebration of, 378, 390, 403–4
Passover lamb, 95, 110, 418, 517, 524, 525
pastoral theology, 565–70
pastors, 504–5
patriarchs, 88, 144
Paul, 361, 419, 443–44, 446
 center of theology, 512–14
 conversion of, 487n102, 501–2
 imprisonment of, 482, 485
 letters of, 447–49
 missionary journeys of, 432–37
 on Mosaic law, 111–13, 471–77
 and Moses, 462, 464
 opponents of, 462–66
 and Peter, 444–45, 471
 goes to Rome, 438
 salvation of, 464
 suffering of, 421, 462, 466, 467–68, 492, 507, 508
peace, 490
penal substitution, 114, 209
Peninnah, 158, 159, 160
Pennington, Jonathan, 380
Pentateuch, 67, 180n86. *See also* Torah
Pentecost, 421, 424, 425, 432
Perrin, Nicholas, 315n76
persecution, 361, 377, 427, 495, 496, 497
perseverance, 519, 536
Persia, 321, 334
Peter, 361, 397, 431, 432, 445, 515
 confession of, 281, 385, 386, 399
 First Peter, 426, 515, 522–28
 and Paul, 444–45, 471
 Pentecost sermon, 425–26
 Second Peter, 515, 528–30
Pharaoh, 91–96, 121, 144, 149
Pharisees, 372, 373, 376, 377, 382, 384, 386, 398, 412
Philemon, 448, 510–12
Philip, 417
Philippians, 448, 484–88
Philistia, 198, 221
Philistines, 83, 96, 160, 163, 170, 173, 245, 253, 281, 340–41, 346
Phillips, Ben, 557
Philo, 477
Phinehas, 118
Phygelus, 508
physical death, 78–79
pilgrimage, Christian life as, 567
pillar of fire and cloud, 115, 131, 256
Piper, John, 52n82, 449n22, 450n27, 455, 555
Pisidian Antioch, 432, 433
plagues
 in Amos, 242
 of Egypt, 91, 95–96, 253, 356, 358, 546, 547
 in Revelation, 546
pleasure, 316, 320
Plevnik, Joseph, 512, 556–57
Pliny the Younger, 511n139
Plummer, Robert L., 487n101, 492n109, 509n137
poetic commentary, 60–61, 62, 140, 271, 320, 322–23, 350, 358, 443
pornography, 204n135
Potiphar's wife, 85
potter and clay, 200
power, through weakness, 461, 463–66
Poythress, Vern, 43, 47n60
praise, in Psalms, 277, 279, 284, 289
prayer, 503, 568, 569–70
 appealing to God's concern for his glory, 352–53
 of Jeremiah, 220
 and judgment, 162–63
 in Luke, 402
 Yahweh answers, 183
preeminence of Christ, 489–90
presuppositions, 47
pride, 142, 160, 244, 245, 395
principalities and powers, 386, 439, 484
progressive revelation, 554–55
Prometheus, 71, 72
promise and fulfillment, 55, 57, 68
Promised Land, 121, 125, 126, 153, 255, 308, 356, 359, 411, 522, 523
 as new Eden, 81–82, 322
prophet like Moses, 132n143, 207, 218n165, 369, 375, 400
Prophets, 59–60, 61, 139–40, 188, 338. *See also* Former Prophets; Latter Prophets
 announce new exodus, 357
 and Mosaic covenant, 231
 like Moses, 132n143, 207, 218n165, 369, 375, 400
 rejection of, 374, 428–29
 theology of, 267
 true and false, 222, 544–45, 546

propitiation, 453–54, 533, 534, 562
prosperity, 139, 245, 282
prostitutes, 458
Provan, Iain, 176
Proverbs, 272–73, 275, 290–301
providence, 205
Psalms, 274, 275, 276–90
Purim, 321n86
purpose, ultimate and penultimate, 562

Queen of Sheba, 179, 345

Rachel, 87
racism, 479
Rad, von, Gerhard, 64n113, 186
Rahab, 96, 144, 145–46, 149, 150, 151
rain, 234, 237
ransom, 388–89, 503
Rapske, Brian, 507n134
Rebekah, 87, 88
reconciliation, 489–90, 491, 534
  of Jews and Gentiles, 482
  of nations, 247
Redditt, Paul, 229n195
redemption, 49, 212, 491, 524
"redemption of Jerusalem," 396
redemptive history, goal of, 58
Red Sea, 95–96
regeneration, 166, 243, 407, 490
Rehoboam, 180, 345, 347, 348
Reimer, David, 212n148, 220n172, 222
remnant, 82, 125, 181, 196, 202, 225, 249, 263, 337–38, 357, 550
Rendtorff, Rolf, 64n113, 77n29, 221, 227n191
repentance, 162–63, 167n59, 168n60, 224, 424, 431, 440
  in Amos, 243–44
  in Chronicles, 347–49
  in Corinthian church, 465, 468–69
  of Daniel, 331–32
  of David, 174
  in Isaiah, 193
  John the Baptist on, 396
  in Jeremiah, 190, 215–16
  Jesus on, 362, 375
  in Joel, 240–41
  in Matthew, 367–68
  prophets on, 231, 267
  in Zephaniah, 253
rest
  of David, 171
  in Joshua, 152, 154
  in Judges, 156
restoration, 49, 130, 219–21, 323
  eschatological, 474–75
  in Hosea, 236–37
  inauguration of, 324
  Jeremiah on, 220
  of nation, 195, 197
  as new exodus, 218–19
resurrection, 286, 335, 460–61, 490
  of Jonah, 246
retribution, 562
return from exile, 202–3, 206, 208, 256, 257, 262, 400, 407–12, 419, 467, 513, 524–25
  fulfilled by Christ, 357, 391
  as new exodus, 356–57, 366–67
  Revelation as, 546–48
Revelation (book), 358, 425, 541–49
Reventlow, Henning Graf, 47
reversals, in Samuel, 158–59, 160, 175
revival, 265, 324
Richter, Sandra L., 146n11
righteousness, 238
righteousness of God, 449, 453–54, 487n103
righteousness through faith, 252, 473, 487
road to Damascus, 438, 442, 502
road to Emmaus, 404
Roberts, J. J. M., 211n146
rock, 374n40
Roman Empire, 435–36, 537
Romans (letter), 448, 449–57
Rome, 432, 438
Rooker, Mark, 236
Rose, Wolter H., 259n267
Rosner, Brian S., 421n148
Ross, Allen P., 343n122
Routledge, Robin, 54n84, 211n145
Rowe, Kavin, 392n97
Ruth, 305–6, 308–9, 350

Sabbath, 372, 382, 398, 410
sacred prostitution, 234
sacrifices, 100, 103, 105, 107, 108, 110–14, 332, 409, 418
Sadducees, 377, 389, 427
Sailhammer, John H., 64n113, 80, 98n62, 107n83, 113n104, 132n143, 133, 350n128
salvation
  in Book of the Twelve, 232–34
  through exile, 350
  in First John, 533
  in intimate terms, 237
  in Old Testament, 344
  in Psalms, 289
salvation history, 439n170
salvation through judgment, 53, 54, 56–59, 76–80, 126, 570
Samaria, 248, 431–32
Samaritan woman, 410, 411

Samson, 155, 156, 157, 158, 167
Samuel, 142, 158, 159–64, 165–66, 167
Samuel (books), 142–43, 158–76, 187, 274, 392
Sanders, E. P., 447n17
Sanhedrin, 438
Sarah, 80–81, 85, 87, 477–78
Satan, 499
  deception of, 508, 546
  falls like lightning, 402, 404
  Jewish and Gentile allies, 494–95
  and Job, 301, 304
Saul, 142–43, 158, 164–68, 267, 281
  in Chronicles, 340, 347n123
  David's lament for, 175
  death of, 160, 168, 248, 421
  judgment of, 141, 164, 166–68, 187
  pursues David, 169–70
  rejection of, 168
  replaced by David, 160
Saul (Paul), persecution of church, 421, 431
Savran, George, 177n77
scepter and star, arising out of Jacob, 118, 119, 142, 283
Schlatter, Adolf, 38, 43
Schreiner, Thomas R., 38, 40, 45n45, 52–53n82, 194n117, 380, 404, 414n135, 423n150, 449n22, 453n35, 467n65, 471n74, 487n103, 512–13, 524, 528, 533n181, 536n185, 554n3
Schultz, Richard L., 262n274
Schürer, Emil, 369n29
Scobie, Charles, 52
scribes, 372, 377, 382
sea, 199
seals, 545
second exodus, 549–50. *See also* new exodus
second temple, 256
secret things, belong to Yahweh, 130, 131
seed conflict in Genesis, 82–84
seed of Abraham, 81–82
seed of the serpent, 81, 82–83, 84, 87, 89, 91, 496, 532n180
  brood of vipers as, 367, 372, 377
  crushing head of, 118, 119, 199
  Goliath as, 169
  and sons of Belial, 159, 162
seed of the woman, 76, 79, 81, 82–83, 84, 86, 87, 89, 349, 532n180
  crushes head of serpent, 305, 308, 321–22, 327
  David as, 169
  in Egypt, 91
  from house of Levi, 107
seeking Yahweh, 347
Seifrid, Mark A., 451n29, 453n34, 487n102, 513n149
Seitz, Christopher, 61
self-glorification, as narcissistic, 560–62
selfishness, 372, 380, 466
Sennacherib, 185, 346–47
sensus plenior, 196n119
Seow, C. L., 320n82
seraphim, 193–94, 197
Sermon on the Mount, 362, 369–70
sermons, in Acts, 420
serpent, 75–80
  as Adonijah, 178–79, 180
  strikes heal of seed of woman, 161
servanthood, 376
servant of Yahweh, 205, 206–9, 211, 397. *See also* suffering servant
servant songs, 385n72
Seth, 82, 88
seven plagues (Revelation), 546
seventy weeks, 332–34
seventy years, of exile, 331, 335, 336, 357
sexual immorality, 294, 300, 458–59, 545
sexuality, 128
shame, 171, 209
Shamgar, 155, 156
Shechem, 153
Shemaiah, 348
shepherd, 315, 319
Shimei, 178
showbread, 101
Shunammite woman, 184
Sidon, 227
Sienkiewicz, Henryk, 271
signs, 414
Sihon, 118, 121–22
silence, 320
Silva, Moisés, 192n109
Simeon and Anna, 396, 397
sin, 109–10, 114
  deadness in, 482
  unto death, 533
  disabling of, 217
  folly of, 203, 222
Sinai, 68, 97–101, 107, 123, 153, 155, 186, 256, 356, 359
sin-judgment-salvation cycle in Judges, 154–55
sin offering, 101
slaves and masters, 492, 501, 512, 523, 525–26
Smith, Gary, 242
Smith, Ralph, 251n250, 253n254
social justice, 526
Sodom, 83, 89
Sodom and Gomorrah, 198, 529
sojourners, 515, 522–25, 536

Solomon, 176
  anointing of, 177
  authorship of Ecclesiastes, 314–15
  and building of temple, 141, 178, 267, 339, 342–43
  in Chronicles, 342–45
  instruction of son, 275
  as new Adam, 143, 179
  prayer of, 331, 343–44
  and Proverbs, 290–91
  psalm of, 278n19, 284, 285
  repentance of, 180n85
  sin of, 141, 179–80, 267, 339
  wisdom of, 176
Solomonic king, 307
song of Moses, 96n58, 131, 548
Song of Songs, 305, 306–8, 350
song of the Lamb, 548
Son of David, 389
son of God, 196n119, 322, 366, 390
Son of Man, 330, 358, 378, 382n65, 390, 408, 413, 425, 550
sons of Belial, 159, 162, 167, 345
sons of Eli, 176
Sons of Korah, 283–84
speaking and acting, in James, 520–21
speech-act philosophy, 39
spies, 116, 120, 121, 122, 144, 145, 147
spiritual adultery, 214, 215, 229, 235, 238, 356
spiritual discipline, 568–70
spiritual gifts, 460
spiritual warfare, 484
Sprinkle, Preston M., 474n79
steadfastness, 497
Stein, Robert H., 391
stem of Jesse, 196
Stephen, 424, 427–30
stewardship, 296
Stocker, John, 571
Strauss, Mark L., 362n12, 391, 419n143
Strazicich, John, 239n220, 240n223
"striving after wind," 316–17
strong, made weak, 245
Stuhlmacher, Peter, 536n186
submission, 503–4
  to governing authorities, 510, 523, 525–26
  to husbands, 492, 523, 526
substitution, 95, 105, 110, 114
suffering, 486, 492–94, 508, 514, 525–26, 527–28
suffering servant, 374, 414, 418, 419
super-apostles, 466
superscriptions
  of Gospels, 381n58
  of Psalms, 276n11, 277–79, 284
superstition, 436
Swanson, Dwight D., 276n11
Sweeney, Marvin A., 253
Synoptic Gospels, 401n114
Synoptic problem, 444n5
Syria, 173, 194–95
systematic theology, 565
  and biblical theology, 46–47
  disdain for, 41
  and glory of God, 53n82

tabernacle, 73, 74, 97–98, 100–101, 106, 109, 114–15, 359, 525
  as new Eden, 68, 101, 108
Tamar, 85, 87, 168, 173, 176
Tammuz, 225
Taylor, Justin, 39
Taylor, Richard, 255
temple, 168, 171–73
  abomination of, 224
  body of Jesus as, 379, 409
  building of, 175, 342–43
  church as, 467
  cleansing of, 376, 379, 409
  destroyed as servant dies on cross, 419
  destruction of, 109, 177, 216, 225, 285, 360, 379, 409, 413
  Eden as, 73–74
  eschatological, 223, 228
  filled with glory of God, 343
  Jesus as fulfillment of, 418
  as new garden, 143
  rebuilding of, 229, 255, 256, 258, 259, 260, 266, 332, 337–38, 339, 350
  of the Spirit, 359, 361
  Stephen on, 427–30
  trust in, 224–25, 229
temptation, 375
Ten Commandments, 69, 99, 123, 127–28, 153, 238, 256, 273, 292
Tertullian, 224n186
theodicy, in Old Testament, 351
Theodotion, 333
theological interpretation of Scripture, 64n113
theophanic glory, 248
Theophilus, 394
Thessalonians
  First, 448, 494–97
  Second, 448, 497–500
Thessalonica, 494
Thielman, Frank, 42n32, 383n68, 439n170, 512, 513n148
thirty sayings of the wise, 291, 299
Thomas, 417, 418
Thompson, J. A., 212n149, 213n151, 215n160
thrones, 542, 545

thunder and lightning, 99, 542
Tigay, Jeffrey H., 54n83, 120n121, 124n129
Timothy, 434, 485, 487, 500, 501, 506, 507
    First Timothy, 448, 500–506
    Second Timothy, 448, 507–8
tithes and offerings, 128
Titus, 509–10
Tola, 155
toledoths, 65, 363
Torah, 59–60, 61, 67–69, 122, 128–29, 180, 271, 273
    delighting in, 281–82
    proclaims glory of God, 132–33
    in Proverbs, 275
    written on hearts, 220
Tov, Emanuel, 61–62, 192n109
transfiguration, 400–401
transgressions, 109–10
transgressors, path of, 239
tree of life, 78
tree of the knowledge of good and evil, 76
Treier, Daniel J., 64n113
trials, 520, 522, 527
tribes of Israel, 114, 132, 141
tribulation, 377–78, 390
Troas, 436
Troxel, Ronald L., 192n109
trumpets, 199, 545, 546, 547
trusting Yahweh, 187–88, 194–95, 210, 215, 252, 288, 299
truth, 39, 535
Tuckett, Christopher, 76n26
Twelve. *See* Book of the Twelve
twelve memorial stones, 144, 147
typology, 42, 64n113, 147n13, 365–65, 477n87

unbelief, 502
uncircumcised ears, 217, 222
uncircumcised hearts, 217, 222
uncleanness, 109, 114
ungodliness, 509
union with Christ, 440, 476, 490–91, 513
unity
    of believers, 511
    of church, 481–84
    between Jesus and Father, 417
unrighteousness, 210
Upper Room Discourse, 419
Uriah, 173, 176
Uzzah, 341–42, 347n123
Uzziah, 241, 346

Vanhoozer, Kevin, 38–39
vanity of life, 306, 315–16, 320
Vashti, 321–22
vessels of wrath, 455
Vickers, Brian J., 391–92n93, 454n36
vineyard, 199
violence, 296
virtue, 529
virtuous wife, 300, 301
visions
    of Amos, 244
    of Daniel, 326, 330–35
    of prophets, 272–73
    of Zechariah, 258
Vogt, Peter, 120, 122, 123n127, 128
Vos, Geerhardus, 43, 193

Wagner, J. Ross, 56, 450n27
walls of Jerusalem, rebuilding of, 324, 337–38
Waltke, Bruce K., 52n82, 75n21, 145n8, 149n17, 156n29, 158n40, 177n77, 244n236, 291n48
warfare, 128
warnings, in Book of the Twelve, 232
water, from rock, 117
waters of judgment, Red Sea as, 96
Watson, Francis, 40–41, 266n282
Watts, Rikki, 251n250, 381n62, 389n80, 391n90, 392
way of wisdom, 295–96
weak and strong, 158–59, 160–61, 306
weaker consciences, 459
weakness and folly, of God as world thinks, 457–58
wealth, 296, 300, 388, 519–20, 522
Webb, Barry, 192, 258, 310
wedding, imagery, 214n157, 408
Wells, David F., 37–40, 449
Wenham, Gordon, 73n16, 74, 110–11, 277
White, Joel, 450n26, 461n56
Whitley, C. F., 315n76
wicked, 301, 303
wickedness, 90, 297, 299
widow of Zarephath, 182
widows, 506, 520
wilderness, 96, 107, 115–19, 126, 338, 368, 547–58
    of the church, 359, 366, 522, 523–25
wilderness generation, 69, 114, 116, 119, 121, 141, 148
Wilken, Robert Louis, 511n139
Williams, P. J., 349n127
Williamson, H. G. M., 48n65, 324n93
Wilson, Gerald, 289n42, 290
Wilson, Todd, 470n71, 476n85
wings of an eagle, 548
wisdom, 239, 292–93, 294, 295, 298, 299, 522
    in Ecclesiastes, 316–17

wisdom literature, and biblical theology, 272–73, 299
witch of Endor, 170
Witherington, Ben, 481n90, 554, 561
witnesses, 419–20
woes, against scribes and Pharisees, 377
Wolff, H. W., 186, 236n214
woman, creation of, 72–73
women, in the church, 500, 503–4
Wong, Gregory T. K., 155n28, 158
Woollcombe, K. J., 477n87
word counts, 187n99, 188n101
Word of Yahweh, as standard of judgment, 139
word-study fallacy, 77
work, 79
"working and keeping," 73, 79
works of the law, 471n73, 473–74
world, 531
worldliness, 376, 380, 492
worldly wisdom, 157, 461, 492, 514, 526
worship, 99, 100, 128, 198, 459–60, 549
  Isaiah on, 211
  purified by judgment, 341–42
wrath and mercy, 550
wrath of God, 58, 89, 111, 129, 196, 198, 222, 223, 240, 341, 453, 454–55, 515
  in exile, 219
  against Israel, 174–75, 339, 415
  on Jesus, 416
  against Jonah, 246
  in Kings, 182, 186
  and need for mercy, 566
  as retribution, 562
  against Zion, 312–13
Wright, Addison G., 313n71, 314n75
Wright, N. T., 112n101, 357n3, 358n7, 390n81, 404, 409–10, 419n144, 435, 436n166, 447n17
Writings, 59–60, 61, 271, 273–75, 350–51, 358, 443

Yahweh, 54. *See also* God
Yarbrough, Robert W., 531n178, 535
Yeats, William Butler, 35, 37, 40, 237

zeal, for God's glory, 338
Zechariah, 203n131, 229–30, 231, 257–63, 335, 390, 413
Zechariah (father of John the Baptist), 394, 395
Zedekiah, 220
Zenger, Erich, 286, 288
Zephaniah, 189, 229–30, 253–54, 266
Zerah the Ethiopian, 345–46
Zerubbabel, 255, 257, 259
Zeus, 72–73, 439
Zimmerli, Walther, 228
Zion, 194, 198, 200, 211, 266, 307, 310–11, 517
  nations streaming toward, 264, 323
  restoration of, 207–8
  Yahweh's jealousy for, 260–61
Ziphites, 281
Zobah, 173
Zophar, 302–3

SCRIPTURE INDEX
WITH EXTRABIBLICAL LITERATURE

References are according to the versification of English translations.

Genesis

1—70, 71, 73, 146
1–3—320n84
1–11—69, 80, 154
1:1—204n136
1:2—216
1:3—139, 216
1:6—139
1:9—139
1:11—139
1:14—139
1:20—139
1:24—139
1:26—139, 327n96
1:26–28—52n75
1:27—99
1:28—73, 79, 90, 139, 142, 142n4, 327n96
1:29—139, 483n92
1:30—236
1:31—72
2—70, 72, 73
2:2–3—152
2:4—65, 363
2:8–10—81, 82
2:9—74
2:10–14—74
2:11–12—74
2:15—73, 74
2:16–17—76
2:18—73, 79, 316
2:18–25—526
2:20—73
2:23–24—99
2:23–25—79
2:25—75, 307
3—65, 79, 80, 82, 85, 114, 118n114, 202, 309, 357
3:1–5—75
3:1–7—178
3:6–8—75
3:7—78, 307
3:8—74, 78, 81, 108
3:9—76
3:10–13—76, 78
3:12–13—307
3:14—76, 207, 250
3:14–15—284
3:14–19—86, 207, 321, 356
3:15—57, 76, 77, 82, 119, 161, 184n92, 197, 199, 250, 253, 283, 288, 308, 323, 327, 456
3:15–17—308
3:16—80, 81, 82, 85, 88, 307, 308, 309, 321, 322, 395, 492
3:16a—79
3:16b—79
3:17—79, 85, 88, 308
3:17–19—79, 82, 85, 199
3:19—286
3:20—79
3:22—78
3:24—74, 148
3:24–25—78
4:1—85, 88
4:1–16—84
4:4—87
4:7—79n33, 492
4:25—82, 88
4:26—89
5—80
5:1—65
5:2—363
5:5—78
5:24—89, 110
5:29—88, 89, 152
6:1–4—526
6:5—105, 123
6:9—65
7:19—85
7:21—85
7:21–23—96
7:22—85
8:17—90
8:21—105
9:1—90
9:6—99
9:7—90
10:1—65
11—80, 253, 425
11:10—65
11:27—65
11:30—80, 82, 85, 86
12—68, 80, 82, 118n114
12–50—69, 80, 154
12:1—146
12:1–2—82
12:1–3—80, 83, 119, 207, 356, 475
12:2—81, 82, 90, 102
12:3—81, 82, 118, 215, 284, 309, 473, 474, 475
12:7—81, 82, 83, 86, 88
12:10—85
12:10–20—84, 85, 86
12:16—88
13:6—88
13:14–19—77, 80
13:15–16—83
13:16—118
13:18—145
14:13–24—84
14:14–16—83
14:22–24—83
15:1—283
15:4—81
15:5—83
15:6—473
15:7—146
15:12–17—96n57
15:13–14—356
15:13–16—96n57
15:14—96n57
15:18—83
16:1–4—86
16:1–5—81
16:3–4—85, 86
16:5—85, 86
16:6—85
16:12—83

17:1–9—83
17:6—142, 163
17:7—87
17:16—82
17:19—81, 83
18:18—83
18:22–33—216
19:5—85, 86
19:8—85, 86
19:16—89
19:30–38—85, 86
20:1–13—85, 86
20:3—87
20:6–7—87
21—56n87, 65
21:1—87
21:8–9—83, 84
21:22—88
21:22–34—83, 84
21:27—84
22—95
22:3—88
22:5—88
22:8—88
22:10—88
22:14—88
22:17—90
22:17–18—83, 474, 475
22:18—81, 82
24—87
24:12—87
24:14—87
24:21—87
24:26–27—87
24:35—88
24:44—87
24:48—87
24:60—83
24:67—85, 87
25:12—65
25:19—65
25:21—85, 86, 87
25:23—83
25:34—83
26:1—85
26:2–5—83
26:4—81, 82
26:6–11—85
26:8–9—87
26:12–14—88
26:14–16—83, 84
26:22—90
26:24—83, 90
27—118n114
27:27–29—83
27:39–40—83
27:41—83, 84
28:2–4—83
28:3–4—90
28:13–15—83
29:18—87
29:31—85, 86, 87
30:1—85, 86
30:1–2—85, 86
30:14—86
30:22—85, 86, 87
31:5–9—88
33:11—88
34:1–29—84
34:2—85, 86
34:30—84
35:1—90
35:9–12—83
35:11—90
35:16–20—86
35:22—86
36:1—64
36:9—65
37–44—84
37:1–28—84
37:2—65
37:4–5—83, 84
37:18—84
37:18–19—83
38:1–30—87
38:6–14—85
38:8–9—86
38:11–18—86
38:14—86
38:15–18—85
38:27–30—87
39:7—85
39:7–18—86
39:10–18—85
39:19–20—85
41:38—428n154
41:54—85
41:57—88
42:1–5—85
42:1–22—429
44:16—430
44:18–34—430
45:1–15—84
45:9—430
46:2–4—83
47:1–2—430
47:27—90
48:4—90
48:14–20—83
48:16—90
49—118n114
49:8–12—83, 164
49:9—118
49:9–11—142, 163
49:10—119, 283, 309
49:24—107n81
50:15–18—430
50:20—88, 430
50:24–25—154

Exodus

1–14—96
1–15—69, 154
1:7—90, 195
1:12—90
1:15–17—91
1:22—91
2:1–10—91
2:2–25—546
2:14—430
3:12—96n60
3:13–15—55
3:14—94
4:11—94
4:16—430
4:21—91, 92, 93
4:22–23—99, 366
5:2—93
5:3—96n60
5:17—96n60
6:2—94
6:6—94
6:7—91, 94, 94n54, 96, 102
6:8—94
6:29—94
7:3—92, 93
7:5—94, 94n54
7:13—92
7:16—96n60
7:17—94, 94n54
7:17–21—547
7:19—547
7:20–21—547
7:22—92
8:1—96n60
8:8—93, 96n60
8:10—94
8:15—92, 93
8:19—92
8:20—96n60
8:20–22—91
8:22—94, 94n54
8:27—96n60
8:28—93
8:32—92, 93
9:1—96n60
9:7—92
9:10—547
9:12—92
9:13—96n60
9:13–35—547
9:14—94
9:14–16—91
9:16—91, 92, 95, 146
9:16a—91
9:16b—91
9:23–25—547
9:27—93
9:27–28—93
9:29—91, 94
9:34—92
9:35—92
9:35–10:1—93
10:1—92
10:1–2—93
10:2—91, 94, 94n54
10:3—96n60
10:7—96n60
10:11—96n60
10:12–20—547
10:16–17—93
10:20—92, 93
10:21–29—547
10:24—93
10:27—92, 93
11:1–10—547
11:4–5—91
11:7—94
11:10—92
12:1–13—95
12:12—95
12:29–32—547
12:31–32—93
12:46—418
13:19—154
14—146, 547
14:4—92, 94, 94n54, 95, 430
14:4–5—93
14:5—92, 166n54
14:8—92, 93
14:17—92, 93, 95
14:18—94, 94n54
14:20—261n270
15—59
15:1—257
15:1–18—96, 192n109
15:1–21—548
15:3—101
15:6—77
15:17—178n80
15:18—101
15:22–25—183
15:24—96
15:25—96
15:26—94, 96
16–18—69
16:2–3—96
16:3—123n128
16:4–5—96
16:6—96
16:10—96
16:12—94n54, 96
16:19–20—96
16:27—96
16:28–29—96
16:30—96
16:35—96
17:1–7—97
17:2—96

17:6—97
17:8–13—97
17:14—97
17:15–16—97
18:1–8—97
18:9–12—97
19—97, 98, 98n62, 155
19–24—97
19:1—69
19:4—548
19:5—98
19:6—98, 163, 203, 247
19:7–9—98
19:10–15—98
19:12—98n62
19:12–13—98
19:13—98n62
19:16—98
19:17—98
19:18—98
19:20–21—98
19:22—98
19:24—98
19:25—98
20—98n62
20:1—102, 107, 146
20:2—99, 99n65
20:5–6—104n
20:5–7—134
20:6—119
20:9—236
20:13—292n51
20:15—292n51
20:17—292n51
20:18–19—99
20:20—100, 292
21–23—99
21:12—173
23:20–21—100
24:1–2—100
24:4—100
24:5–8—100
24:9–11—100
24:13–16—100
24:17—100
25–31—97, 100, 101
25:7—74
25:8—101
25:9—101
25:10–22—74
25:11—74
25:16—101
25:17–21—101
25:22—101
25:30—74, 101
25:31–40—74, 101
25:40—101
26:1—74
26:30—101
27:8—101
28:1–3—101
28:3—101
28:35—101
28:41—161n45
28:43—101
29:14—101
29:43—101
29:45—101
29:46—94n54, 101
31:1–6—101
31:13—94n54
32–34—97, 101
32:1—101
32:1–4—103
32:4—102n74
32:5—102
32:7—102
32:9–10—102
32:10—102
32:11—102
32:11–13—103
32:11–14—162, 430
32:12—102, 183, 352
32:13—102
32:14—102
32:22–24—103
32:25—103
32:26–28—103
32:30—103
32:31—103
32:31–34—430
32:32—103
32:33–35—103
33:1–7—103
33:7—103, 106
33:18—63, 103, 455
33:18–19—227, 274
33:18–34:7—58, 103, 205, 555
33:18–34:8—63
33:19—58n92, 63, 104n, 136, 150, 455, 455n41
33:19a—103
33:19b—104, 105
34:6–7—55n, 57, 58n92, 63, 104, 104n, 116, 116n112, 126, 126n135, 133, 134, 135, 136, 149, 220n175, 227, 230, 237, 240, 242n33, 246, 250, 251, 264, 274, 287, 430, 455, 549n25
34:6b–7a—56
34:7—182, 246
34:7b—57
34:8—63, 105
34:10—105
35–40—97, 101
35:21–22—10
36:4–7—106
39:1—39:5
39:6—106
39:21—106
39:26—106
39:29—106
39:31—106
39:32—106
39:42—106
39:43—106
40—98
40:16—106
40:17—114
40:19—106
40:21—106
40:23—106
40:25—106
40:26—106
40:27—106
40:29—106
40:32—106
40:34–38—106, 548
40:38—261n270

Leviticus

1–7—108, 110
1:4—111
4:2—109
8–10—108
10—272
10:1–2—474n79
10:1–3—53
10:1–11—108
10:7—474n79
10:10—53, 225
11:44—108, 524
11:44–45—119n117
12—109
13—109
13:45–46—109
15:31—110, 474n79
16—111
16:21—111
17–24—108
17:11—111
18—111, 112
18:2—119n117
18:4—119n117
18:5—110, 112, 113, 119n117, 225, 243, 473, 474n79
18:6—119n117
18:8—242
18:15—242
18:21—119n117
18:30—119n117
19:2—108, 524
19:3—119n117
19:4—119n117
19:10—119n117
19:12—119n117
19:14—119n117
19:18—119n117
19:25—119n117
19:28—119n117
19:30—119n117
19:31—119n117
19:32—119n117
19:34—119n117
20:7–8—524
20:24—111
20:26—524
22:9—110, 474n79
23:40—547
24:15–16—54n83
24:17—173
25:8–12—199
26—155, 213, 292
26:11–12—81
26:11–13—74, 108
26:14–45—331
26:33—331
26:40—331
26:40–42—331
26:42—331

Numbers

1—114
1:1—114
1:47–54—114
1:51—114
1:53—109
2–11—114
2:1–9—114
2:1–31—109
2:10–16—114
2:18–24—114
2:25–31—114
3:1–9—115
3:7–8—73n16, 74
3:10—115
3:11–13—115
3:13—115
3:38—74, 109
4–9—115
4:6–7—341
4:15—341
4:19–20—341
8:26—73n16, 74
9:12—418
10—97
10–13—121
10:10—69
10:11–12—114
10:11–13—115
10:11–36:13—69
10:35–36—115
11:1–2—115

11:4–5—115
11:6—115
11:10—115
11:10–15—115
11:20—115
11:29—123n128
12–25—114
12:1–6—115
12:1–8—428n154
13—116
13:28—122
13:33—145
14:1–23—430
14:3—116
14:11—116
14:11–24—274
14:12—116
14:13–19—183, 352
14:13–20—430
14:14—116
14:17—116
14:17–19—116
14:18—104n, 116, 134
14:19—116
14:20—116
14:21—50, 53, 73, 116, 154, 197, 268, 430, 483n92
14:22–23—116
14:29—116
14:33—116
15:27–31—109
16:1–3—117
16:11—117
16:19—117
16:20–22—117
16:30—117
16:31–33—117
16:35—117
16:41—117
17—117
18:5–6—73n16, 74, 117
20—117
20:1—117
20:2–5—117
20:6–8—117
20:11—117
20:12—117
20:13—117
21—146
21:5—117
21:6—117
21:7—118
21:8–9—118
21:9—410
21:21–35—118
22–24—119
22:2–6—118
22:22–35—148
23:8—118
23:10—118
23:19—99, 118
23:20—118
23:22—118
23:23—118
23:24—118
24:5–6—81
24:6—82, 148
24:7—77, 163
24:8—77
24:9—118
24:17—118, 142, 368
25:1–2—118
25:3—118
25:4–5—118
25:6–8—118
25:13—118
26—114, 118
27–36—114, 118
31:15–16—118
35:30—173

Deuteronomy

1–3—120, 130, 132
1:1—120n118
1:1–5—120n118
1:2—120n118
1:3—120, 120n118
1:4—120n118
1:5—120, 120n118
1:5–8—120
1:9–18—120
1:19–28—120
1:19–2:1—120n118
1:29–31—120–21
1:32—121
1:36—121
1:38—121
1:41–45—121, 122
2:1–8—121
2:8–13—121
2:14–16—121
2:16—430
2:17–23—121
2:24–25—121
2:24–3:11—120n118
2:25—145, 146
2:30—91n51, 121
2:31—121
2:33—122
3:1–11—122
3:21–22—122
3:23–28—122
3:24—122
3:27—122
4—122, 132
4–11—120, 122, 129, 130
4:1–14—122
4:5–8—122
4:9–24—122
4:11—292n54
4:12—292
4:15—292
4:19—234, 480
4:19–20—481
4:20—234
4:23–24—292
4:24—292
4:25–31—122, 127, 231, 313, 322, 331
4:26—192, 215, 474
4:29—156, 220
4:29–30—220n172
4:29–31—331
4:31—104n, 136
4:32–40—122, 214
4:33—292
4:35—122
4:36—292
4:39—122
4:40—122
4:44—120n118
5—123, 127, 132
5:1–6:9—123n127
5:4—123, 292n54
5:5—123
5:6—123
5:7–21—123
5:9–10—104n
5:9–11—134
5:10—125n132
5:16—112
5:17—292n51
5:19—292n51
5:21—292n51
5:22—292n54
5:24—123, 292n54
5:24–27—153
5:25—123, 292n54
5:26—123n128, 292, 292n54
5:27—123, 236
5:28—123
5:28–29—153
5:29—123, 123n128
6—274, 290n46, 319, 320
6–11—128, 132
6–25—127
6:1–3—125
6:4—124
6:4–5—293
6:4–6—125
6:4–9—291
6:5—125n132
6:6—208
6:6–8—274
6:6–9—127
6:7—125
6:8—125
6:9—125
6:10–13—125
6:14–15—125
6:16–19—125
6:20–24—125
6:25—125
7:1–5—286
7:3–4—180
7:6–7—125
7:6–8—264
7:7—55, 150
7:7–8—150
7:8—125
7:9—125n132
7:9–10—55, 104n, 126, 134
7:11–16—126
7:16—286
7:17–26—126
8–10—126
8:2—126
8:3—126
8:5—126
8:7–9—126
8:11–14—126
8:15–16—126
8:17–20—126
9:1–3—126
9:3—292n54
9:4–5—126
9:4–6—125
9:5—149
9:6—126
9:7—126
9:8–21—126
9:10—292n54
9:15—292n54
9:22–24—126
9:25–29—126, 352
9:26—126
9:27—126
9:28—126
9:29—126
10:1–5—126
10:4—292n54
10:6—126
10:7—126
10:8–9—126
10:10–11—126
10:12—125n132
10:12–13—126, 293
10:12–22—126
10:14—127
10:15—127
10:16—124, 127
10:17—127
10:18–19—127
10:20—127
10:21–22—127
11:1—125n132, 127
11:2–7—127

11:8–15—127
11:13—125n132
11:14–15—234
11:16–17—127, 234
11:18–25—127
11:22—125n132
11:26–32—127
12—128
12–13—128
12–26—120n118, 127, 129, 292
12–28—120, 122, 130, 132
12:1—120n118
12:1–5—128n139
12:5—418n140
12:6–14—418n140
13—128
13–14—128
13:3—125n132
14–15—128
14–16—128
16–17—128
16:18–18:22—128
17—161n45, 275, 282, 290, 290n46, 291, 319, 320, 368
17:14–20—142, 163, 177, 180, 280, 282n31
17:18–19—274
17:18–20—157, 291
18:15—400n
18:15–18—132n142, 369, 375, 429
18:15–19—207, 222
18:15–20—132n142
18:16—292n54
18:18—218n165
18:21–22—222
19—128
19–22—128
19:9—125n132
19:11–13—173
20–21—128
20:16–18—149
22—128
22–23—128
22:25–29—173
23—128
23–25—128
23:3–4—309
23:14—74, 81, 112
24–25—128
25—128
26—128
27–28—129
27:26—473
28—155, 213, 239, 240, 292
28:13—310
28:15—239
28:15–68—183
28:38—239
28:44—310
28:49–68—240
28:63—129
28:64—129
29—130
29–34—120
29:1—120n118
29:4—112, 113, 124, 124n129, 129, 130, 131, 132, 153
29:5—94n54
29:5–9—129
29:10–15—129
29:16–17—129
29:18–30:10—231
29:18–19—129
29:20—129
29:21–28—129
29:24—129
29:25–26—129
29:26—286, 480
29:28—129
29:29—129, 130, 131, 132
30—111, 112, 130
30:1—132
30:1–3—130
30:1–10—127
30:2—156
30:2–10—132
30:4—130
30:5—125, 130
30:6—124, 125, 125n132, 132, 166n55
30:6a—130
30:6b—130
30:11–14—112, 113, 153
30:11–18—131
30:14—113, 130
30:16—125n132
30:19—131, 215
30:19–20—131
30:20—125n132
31:1–8—145
31:3—131
31:6—131, 145
31:9—100n71
31:16–21—130, 155
31:16–32:42—132
31:17—286
31:17–18—131
31:19—131
31:24—100n71
31:27–29—130
32—286
32:1—131, 192, 215
32:3—131
32:4—131, 286
32:5—131
32:6–14—131
32:15–18—131
32:17—286
32:27—131
32:28–33—131
32:34—131, 132
32:35—131
32:36—131, 156
32:37–38—131
32:39—99, 131
32:40–42—131
32:43—131, 132
32:46—131
32:48–51—132
33—132
33:1—120n118
33:4—100n71
33:26—132
34:1–5—132
34:1–10—132n143
34:6—132
34:8—132
34:9—132, 151
34:10—132n142
34:10–12—132

Joshua

1—144, 145
1–5—144, 144n6
1–11—141, 143
1:1–9—144
1:2—144
1:3—145
1:5—145
1:6–9—145, 177
1:7—100n71
1:8—100n71, 139
1:9—145
1:17—145
1:31—100n71
2—144, 147
2:9–10—96
2:9–11—145, 149
2:24—147
3–4—144
3:5—147
3:10—147, 149
3:13–17—147
4:1–9—147
4:6—147
4:21—147
4:23—147, 148
4:24—148, 149
5—144
5:1—148, 150
5:2–8—148
5:6—148
5:9—148
5:13—148
5:13–15—148
5:13–16—148
5:14—148
5:15—148
6—149
6–12—144, 144n6
6:1–5—150
6:6–16—150
6:17—150
6:20—150
6:22–23—150
6:25—150
7–8—149
7:1—150
7:2–5—150
7:5—150
7:6–9—162
7:9—150, 183, 352
7:12—150
7:19–20—151
7:21—151
7:25–26—150
8:1–29—151
8:30–35—151, 155
8:34—151
9—149
9:1–2—151
9:9—151
9:14—151
9:15—151
9:23—151
9:24—151
9:27—151
10—149
10:1–2—152
10:3–5—152
10:6—152
10:8—152
10:10—152
10:10–14—200
10:11—152
10:12–14—152
10:24—77, 152
10:28–43—152
11—149
11:1–5—152
11:6–15—152
11:16–23—152
11:18—149
11:20—91n51, 149
12—149
12–24—141, 143
13–21—144, 144n6
13–22—152
13:13—152
15:63—152, 152n21
16:10—152
17:11–13—152
18:1—142, 142n4

21:43—152
21:44—152
21:45—153
22—153
22–24—144, 144n6
23—153
23:2—153
23:3—153
23:8—153
23:5—153
23:6—153
23:6–8—100n71
23:7—152
23:11—153
23:12—152
23:13—153
23:14—152
24—42, 153, 167
24:2—87
24:2–3—153
24:3–13—153
24:14–15—153
24:16–18—153
24:19—153
24:21—153
24:22—153
24:31—154

Judges

1—142, 155n28
1–2—143
1:1–19—154
1:1–2:5—155n27
1:1–3:6—154
1:7–16:31—154
1:21—154
1:27–36—154
2:1—154, 155
2:1–3—154
2:3—154
2:6–19—155
2:11—155
2:11–3:6—154
2:12—155
2:14–15—155
2:16—155
2:17—155
2:18—155
2:19—155
3–16—143
3:7—155
3:7–11—155
3:8—156
3:9—156
3:10—156
3:11—156
3:12—155, 156
3:12–30—155, 158
3:15—156
3:30—156
3:31—155
4:1—155
4:1–5:31—155
4:3—156
4:4–9—156
4:21—77, 156
5—59
5:26—77, 156
5:31—156
6–8—143
6:1—155, 156
6:1–8:35—155
6:6–7—156
6:11—156
6:11–12—156
6:13—156
6:17–21—156
6:27—156
6:34—156
7—195
7:2—157
7:4—157
7:8—157
7:12—157
7:16–21—157
7:22—157, 257
8—157
8:7–19—158
8:23—163
8:30—156
9:1–57—155
9:8—161n45
9:53—77
10:1–2—155
10:3–4—155
10:6—155
10:6–12:7—155
10:7—156
10:10–16—156
11–12—143
11:1—157
11:29–40—158
12:1–6—158
12:8–9—155
12:11–12—155
12:13–15—155
13–16—143, 158
13:1—155, 156
13:1–16:31—155
13:3–23—156
13:6—167
13:19—166
13:25—156
14:1–7—158
14:6—156
14:19—156
15:1–8—158
15:14—156
16:25–27—157n35
17–18—157, 158
17–21—143, 155, 155n27
17:1–21:25—154
17:4—155
17:6—157
18:1—155, 157
18:1–31—158
19–20—166
19:1—155, 157
19:1–20:7—158
19:29—167
20:12–16—158
20:29–48—158
21:1–25—158
21:25—155, 157

Ruth

1:1—308
1:2–5—309
1:6—309
1:20–21—309
2:3—309
2:20—309
4:13—309
4:18–22—87
4:21—309

1 Samuel

1—159
1–2—160
1–8—143, 158
1:2—159
1:5—159
1:5–6—395
1:6—159
1:16—162n46
1:19–20—159, 395
2:1—159
2:1–10—158, 159, 170, 172
2:1–11—159
2:2—159
2:3—159
2:4–5—159, 160
2:6—159, 160
2:7—99, 160n42
2:7–8—160
2:9—161
2:10—77, 161, 161n44, 164
2:10a—161n44
2:12–17—160, 162
2:12–36—159
2:13–16—162
2:21—160
2:25—160, 162
2:27–36—162
2:30—162
2:34—162
2:34–35—160
3:1–21—159
3:10–18a—162
3:11–14—162
3:12–13—162
3:13—162
3:18—162
3:19–4:1—160
4:1–7:2—159
4:11—160, 163
5:1–3—160
5:2—163
5:3—163
5:4—160, 163
5:6—163
5:6–6:1—160
5:8–9—163
5:10–11—163
6:5—163
6:19–20—160
7:2—159
7:3–17—159, 163
7:10—161, 163
8—102n73, 165
8:1–22—159
8:5—163
8:7—163, 166
8:8—163
8:9—163n50
8:10–18—163, 165n52
8:11—163n50
8:13—163n50
8:14—163n50
8:15—163n50
8:16—164n50
8:17—164n59
8:18—164
8:19—164
8:20—163
8:20–22—164
9—165
9–15—143, 158
9:1–5—164
9:2—164, 168
9:6—164
9:7—164
9:8—164
9:9–14—164
9:15—164
9:16—165
9:16–17—164, 165n52
9:19—165
9:20—165, 257, 257n260
9:21—165
9:22–24—165
9:27—165
10:1—165
10:1b—165
10:2—165
10:2–8—165

10:3–4—166
10:5–6—166
10:6—166, 167
10:7—166
10:9a—166
10:16—166
10:17–21—166
10:19—166
10:22—166
10:26—166
10:27—166, 167
11—164, 167n59
11:1–11—166, 167
11:12—167
11:13—167
12—167
12:6–12—167
12:13–15—167
12:18—167
12:22—167
13–16—158
13:1–14—167
13:8–14—166
13:14—168, 172n69
14:6—167, 345
14:7—172n69
14:24—168
14:24–30—167
14:30—168
14:31—166
14:31–33—168
14:31–35—165n52
14:36–44—167
14:45—168
14:47—166
15:1–9—166, 168
15:10–35—168
15:12—102n73, 168
15:23—168
15:26—168
15:28—168
15:30—168n60
16—143, 158
16:1–12—168
16:11–13—168
17:36—169
17:37—169
17:45—169
17:45–47—169
17:46—169
17:47—169
17:49—77, 169
18:3–4—169
18:20—169
18:21—169
19:11–17—169
21:1–6—169
21:8–9—169
21:10–15—169
22:2—170
22:6–9—170
22:20–22—170
23:1–13—170
23:14—169
24:10—169
25:38—160
26:10—160
27:1–6—170
27:8–12—170
28—170
28:19—160
29—170
29:4—170
30:1–5—170
30:4—160
30:6–29—170
30:26–31—170
31—170
31:4—169
31:9—248

2 Samuel

1—421
1:17–27—170
1:19–27—158, 159
1:20—248
2—169, 421
2–4—421
2:1–7—171
2:1–10—395
2:8–11—171
2:12–3:6—171
2:14–16—83n46
3–5—421
3:7–8—171
3:9—171
3:26–30—171
3:31–39—171
4:1—96n59
4:1–8—171
4:7–8—96
4:9–12—171
5—169
5:1–5—171
5:6–9—171
5:6–10—152n22
5:10—171
5:17–25—171
5:20—200
6—284, 421
6:1–23—171
6:3—341
6:5—342
6:6—96
6:7—160, 341
6:8–9—341
7—172, 177, 179n82, 283, 284, 286n37, 307, 315, 421
7–10—284, 421
7:1—171
7:1–16—172
7:2—171, 172
7:4–17—172
7:6–7—74, 171
7:11—282
7:12—282
7:12–16—177, 328
7:13—282
7:14—196n119, 282, 394
7:18–29—712
7:20–22—172
7:21—172, 172n69
7:22—173
7:23—172
7:26—172, 183, 352
7:27—172
8—173
8–10—172, 284, 421
8:1—73
8:2—173
8:3–8—173
8:6—173
8:9–10—173
8:11–12—173
8:13–14—173
8:14—173
8:15–18—173n72
8:18—179
9—173
9–10—173n72
10—173
11—421
11–12—284
11–20—173n72
11:1–27—173
12—421
12:7—421
12:9—173
12:10—173
12:11—173
12:13—174
12:14—173
12:16—174
12:18—173
12:20—174
12:25—176
13–20—284
13–24—421
13:14—173
13:28–29—173
15–17—284
15:1–6—160
15:10–14—174
15:16—173, 174
16:22—174
18:14–15—174
19:1—123n128
19:18–23—167n59
20:1–2—174
20:23–26—173n72
21–24—174
21:1—174
21:1–14—174
21:2–3—174
21:4–6—174
21:14—174
21:15–22—174, 175
22—174
22:1–7—175
22:1–23:7—158, 159, 174
22:8–16—175
22:17–46—175
22:39—77
22:43—77
22:47–51—175
23:8–39—174, 175
24—158, 175
24:1—175
24:1–25—174
24:3–4—175
24:14—175
24:15—160, 175
24:16—176

1 Kings

1–2—143, 176, 177n
1:1–11:25—177n
1:9–10—177
1:12—178
1:18–19—177
1:25–26—177
1:32–35—177
1:38–40—177
1:43–46—177
1:47–48—177
2–11—143
2:2–4—177
2:3—100n71, 177
2:4—178
2:5–6—178
2:7—178
2:8–9—178
2:13–25—178
2:17–20—178
2:19—178
2:22—178
2:23–25—178
2:25—178
2:28–34—178
2:36–46—178
3–11—176, 177n
3:4–14—314
3:12—291
4:21—178
4:24—178
4:25—178, 232
4:29—179
4:29–31—291
4:29–34—314

4:32—291
4:33—179
5:7—179
6–7—179
6:1—96n59
7:29—74
7:48—74
8—179n82
8:5—179
8:10–11—179
8:15–21—179
8:22–52—240n223
8:22–60—179
8:27—428
8:43—179, 183
8:46–53—179, 331
8:49–50—331
8:56–58—179
8:60—179, 183, 352
8:62–63—179
10:1—179
10:9—179
10:14–11:8—180
11:26–14:31—177n
11:29–39—180
12—143, 177, 177n
12:15—180
12:22–24—180
12:26–27—180
12:28–33—180, 181
13—180, 186
13:9—181
13:10–19—181
13:18—181
13:23–25—181
13:33–34—181
13:34—181
14:11—181
14:11–13—181
14:16—180
14:17—181
14:21—180
14:31—180
15:1–16:22—177n
15:16–19—182
15:20–21—182
15:25–26—180
15:30—180, 181
15:34—180
16:2—180, 181
16:4—181
16:7—181
16:13—181
16:23—177n
16:26—181
16:33—181, 182
17—143
17:1—182
17:2–7—182
17:8–16—182
17:17–23—182
17:23—398n109
17:24—183
18:21—182
18:23–29—183
18:30–38—183
18:36–37—182, 183, 352
18:38–39—183
19:2—183
19:15–16—181
19:17—181
19:18—181
20:13—94n54, 182
20:28—94n54, 182
21:2–19—248
21:19—437n167
21:20–27—181
21:22—181
21:24—181, 437n167
21:25—182
21:28–29—182
22:34–37—437n167
22:37—437n167
22:53—181

2 Kings

1:8—367
2:14—183
2:19–22—183
2:23–24—183
3:11—184
3:11–25—183
4:1–7—183
4:14–37—183
4:38–41—183
4:42–44—183
5:1–19—183
5:8—184
5:12—183
5:17–19—183n91
5:19—183
5:20–27—184
6:1–6—184
6:8–17—184
6:24–33—184
7:1–20—184
8:1–6—184
8:7–15—184
8:16–24—184
8:25–9:29—184
9:30–37—184
10:1–11—184
10:10—184
10:12–14—184
10:15–17—184
10:17—184
10:18–28—184
10:28–36—184
11:1–21—184
12—177n
12:1–21—184
13—143
13–16—177n
13:1–9—184
13:2—180
13:14–25—184
13:20–21—184n93
14:1–22—184
14:6—100n71
14:23–15:38—184
14:25—189
14:25–27—246
15:28—180
16:1–20—184
16:5–9—194
16:10–18—194
17—143, 177, 177n
17:1–6—184
17:7–23—184
17:24–26—185
17:27–41—185
17:37—100n71
18–19—185
18–20—201
18–25—143, 177, 177n
19:15—185
19:16—185
19:19—185, 352
19:20–34—185
19:34—185
19:35–37—185
20:1–6—185
20:6—185
21:1–9—185
21:6—185
21:10–15—186
21:12—186
21:15—186
22—217
22:5—186
22:8—212n150
22:8–11—186
22:14–23:14—186
22:15–16—186
23:26—186
25—310
25:4–7—225
25:8—260n
25:25—260n
25:27–30—187

1 Chronicles

1–9—339, 340
4:22—340
5:2—83, 107n81
6:13—212n150
6:31–33—283–84
6:31–39—278n19
6:37—284
6:39—284
8:33—171
10—340
10:4—340
10:13—340
10:14—340
11–29—340
11:4–5—340
11:9—340
11:13–14—340, 340n118
12:16—341
12:17—341
12:18—341
13:7—341
13:8—342
13:10—341
13:11–12—341
14:11—341
14:12—341
15:2—341
15:13—341
15:15—341, 342
15:16–24—342
15:26—342
15:27–29—342
16:1–7—342
16:8–13—342
16:14–22—342
16:23–30—342
16:33—342
16:34—342
16:35–36—342
16:40—100n71
17—323, 339
17:19—353
17:21—353
17:24—353
21:1—175
23:2–32—340
28:15—74

2 Chronicles

1–9—342
1:1—342
1:8—342
2–7—339
2:1—343
2:4—343
2:5—343
2:6—343
2:11–12—343
3–4—343
5:13—343
5:13–14—343
5:14—343
6:1–15—343
6:16–17—343
6:18—343
6:22–23—344
6:24—343

6:26—343
6:28—343
6:29—344
6:29–30—344
6:31—344
6:32–33—344–45, 353
6:37—344
6:39—344
7:1—343
7:1–3—343
7:2—343
7:3—343
9—345
9:23—345
10–36—345
10:13–14—347n
10:15—345, 348
11:4—345, 348
11:14–16—347
12:5–8—345
12:14—347
13:3—347n
13:5—345
13:6—345
13:8—345
13:10–12—345
13:13—345
13:14–17—345
13:18—345
13:20—345
14—345
14:4—347
14:7—347
14:8—345
14:9—345
14:11—346, 353
14:12–13—346
14:14—346
15:2—347
15:4—347
15:12—338n
15:12–13—347
15:13—347n
15:15—347
16:1–6—346
16:7–10—346
16:9—346
16:10–11—347n
16:12—347
17:3–4—347
17:9—100n71
18:4—347, 348
18:6—348
18:7—347, 348
18:10–11—348
18:13–14—348
18:16—348
18:17—348
18:18–22—348–49
18:31—346
18:33–34—349
19:3—347
20:1—346
20:3–4—347
20:5–8—346
20:9—346, 353
20:12—346
20:14—346
20:15—346
20:17—346
20:18–19—346
20:20—346
20:21—346
20:22–23—346
20:24—346
20:25—346
20:26—346
21:20—165n53
22:9—347
22:19—347n
23:16—338n
23:18—100n71
25:20—345
26:7—346
29:10—338n
29:36—347
30:9—104n, 136
30:10—348
30:12—348
31:3—100n71
31:21—347
32:7–8—346
32:9–12—346
32:13–16—346
32:17–19—346
32:20–22—346–47
32:24—347
33:1—347
33:12–13—347
34:3—347
34:21—347
34:26—347
34:31—338n
35:26—100n71
36:22–23—350, 548

Ezra

1:1—335
1:1–2—335, 336
1:7—337
3:2—100n71
3:10–11—337
3:10–13—337
4:4—337
6:14–17—337
6:21—347n
7:6—61
7:10—347n
7:27–28—337
8:22—338, 347n
8:31—337, 338
9:4—337
9:5–7—337
9:8—337
9:9—337
9:13—337
9:15—337
10:1–44—337
10:3—337, 338n

Nehemiah

1:3–11—337
1:5—104n, 137
2:17–18—338
4:1–3—337
4:4–5—337
4:5—337
4:14—338
4:15—338
4:20—338
5:13—337
5:19—338
6:5–9—338
6:14—337
6:15—337
6:16—338
8:5–6—337
8:12—337
9—338
9:3–38—337
9:7–8—338
9:9–12—338
9:10—338
9:13–14—338
9:15–17—338
9:17—104n
9:18–21—338
9:22—338
9:23—338
9:28—338
9:30—338
9:31–32—104n, 136, 338
9:32–38—338
9:33—338
9:34–35—338
12:31–43—337
12:31–47—337
13:4–5—560
13:7–9—337
13:14—338
13:22—338
13:23–31—338
13:29—337
13:31—338

Esther

1:3–4—321
1:5—321
1:12—321
1:19—321
2:8—321
2:15—322
2:17–18—322
2:20—321
4:13–5:3—321
4:16—322
7–8—322

Job

1–2—301
1:5—304
1:7–12—301
1:22—301, 304
2:1–6—301
2:10—301
3—301
3:1–10—301
3:11–19—301
3:20–26—301
4–5—302
4–14—302
4–25—301
4:7—302
4:17—302
6–7—302
6:29–30—302
8—302
8:3–6—302
8:20—302
9–10—302
9:8—384, 384n70
9:15—302
9:21—302
9:32–35—302, 304
11—302
11:14—302
12–14—302
13:15—302, 304
15—302
15–21—302
15:6—302
16–17—302
16:2–3—302
16:5–21—302
16:18–21—304
16:19—302
16:21—302
18—302
19—302
19:25—302, 304, 304n
19:26—302
20—302
20:5—303
20:29—303
21—302
21:7—303
22—302
22–25—302
22:5–9—303

23—303
23–24—302
24—303
25—302
25:4—303
26–31—302, 303
26:12–13—77
26:13—303
28:28—303
31:1–4—303
31:33—303
31:38–40—303
32–37—303
33:6—303
33:32—303
34:10–11—303
34:22–25—77
35:6–7—303
36:4—303
36:5–10—303
37:22–24—303
38–41—304, 305
38–42—303
38:1—304
38:4–38—304
38:39–39:30—304
40:4—304
40:4–5—304
40:6–14—304
40:15–24—304
40:25–41:26—77
41:1–34—304
42:1–6—304
42:2—305
42:6—305
42:7—301, 305
42:7–8—301, 304
42:7–10—303
42:9—304
42:10–17—304

Psalms

1—177, 239, 277, 280, 281, 282, 283, 289, 368
1–14—280
1–41—277, 279, 280
1:1–2—282, 427
1:2—139, 274, 282, 283
1:3—139, 282
1:4—282
1:5—282
1:6—282, 290
2—278, 280, 281, 282, 283, 289, 414, 432
2:1–2—283
2:1–3—151
2:1–4—282
2:1–12—50
2:4–9—283
2:5–7—282
2:7—282, 516
2:8—173, 256, 282
2:9—77, 282, 283
3—278, 281n27, 283
3ff.—278n21
3:3—283
3:7—283
4:8—237
7—278, 281
7:6–8—290
7:12—109
8:2—305, 376
9—278
10—278
12:6—25
15—280
15–24—280
16—280, 425, 426, 432
16:10–11—283
16:11—99
17—280
18—59, 175, 278, 280, 281
18–21—280
18:7–15—289
18:38—77
19—280
19:1—53
19:7—25
20–21—280
22—280, 283
23—280
23:3—289
24—280
25–41—280
25:11—289, 352
27:4—289
29:2—54
30—278
31:3—289, 352
32—275
34—278, 281
34:20—418
41:9—415
41:13—289
42–49—278n19, 283
42–72—277, 283
44—301
44:5—77
44:19—77
50—278n19, 284
51—275, 278, 281
52—278, 281, 284
54—278, 281
55:12–14—284
55:20–21—284
55:22–23—284
56—278, 281
56–64—284
57—278, 281
58—456
58:4—76
58:4–6—77, 456
58:6—76
58:10—76, 77, 456
59—278, 281
59:1—289
60—278
60:12—77
63—278, 281
65:2—284
65:7—383n
66—278n19
66:5—284
66:20—284
67—278n19, 284
68—284
68:19—483n93
68:21–23—77
69–71—284
71—278n19
72—277, 278, 278n19, 278n21, 284, 285
72:1–3—284
72:4—77, 284
72:8—284
72:9—77, 284
72:17—284
72:19—53, 269, 289
72:20—278, 284
73—285, 301
73–89—277, 285
74—278, 285
74:3–8—278
74:10—285
74:12–14—77
74:13–14—285
75—285
77—285
77:21—286
78—97, 285
78:15–20—97
78:18—104n
78:35—97
78:38—137
78:67–68—107n81
78:67–69—83
79—278, 285
79:1—278
79:1–13—290
79:9—285, 289, 352
80—285
80:3—285
80:7—285
80:14–15—286
80:19—285
81—276n13, 285
82—285
83—285
83:14–18—285
84—285
85:10—105, 285, 352, 419
85:10–11—55
86—286
86:5—104n, 137
86:11—348
86:15—104n, 136
87—286
88—285, 286
89—209n142, 277, 278, 278n21, 285, 286n36
89:3–4—286
89:9—383n
89:10—77, 285
89:14—55
89:19–37—286
89:23—77
89:38–49—286
89:38–51—285
89:39–40—286
89:49—287
89:50—286
89:50–51—286
89:51—286
89:52—289
90—278, 286
90–92—286, 287
90–106—277, 286
90:1—286
90:3—286
91—286
91:9—286
91:11–13—77
91:12–13—161
91:13—76
92—278, 286
92:15—286
93–100—286, 287
99:6—286
99:8—104n, 137
100—278
101—278, 287
101:1—287
102—278, 287
103—278, 287
103:3—287
103:8—104n, 136, 287
104–6—287
104:2–30—287
105:7–11—287
105:16–25—287
105:17—356
105:25—166n54
105:26—286
105:26–45—287
106—286
106:7—137
106:8—287
106:9–12—287

106:13–27—287
106:16—286
106:23—286
106:28–31—287
106:31—286
106:32–33—287
106:34–39—287
106:40–46—287
106:45—137, 287
106:47—287
106:48—289
107—288
107–50—277, 287, 323
107:1—287
107:2–3—287
107:23–30—383, 383n
108–10—279, 288
108:13—76, 77
109:21—289, 353
110—279, 286, 323, 426
110:1—152, 516
110:6—77, 279
111–12—288
111–13—279
111:4—104n, 136
112:4—104n, 137
113–18—288
115:1—54
116:5—104n, 137
118—279, 413
118:19–26—279
118:22—427
118:25–26—413n
119—125, 279, 288
119:97—25
119:89—25
120–34—279
120–37—288
127:3—26
128:3—214n157
132:7–8—108
135—279
136—279
137—279, 288
137:8–9—279, 288
137:9—77
138–44—288
138–45—279
138:2—25
142—278
145—288
145:8—104n, 136
145:21—290
146–50—279, 290
150:1–6—289

Proverbs

1–9—291, 293, 294
1:1—290
1:1–7—291
1:4—295
1:7—292, 293, 295
1:8—273, 291n49, 294, 295
1:8–19—292n51, 293
1:9–19—273
1:10—291n49, 292n51
1:11—273
1:12—292n51
1:13—273, 292n51
1:15—291n49
1:18—294
1:19—273, 292n51
1:20–21—294
1:20–33—293
1:23—295
1:24—294
1:32—294
2:1—291n49, 294
2:1–22—293
2:7–8—295
2:10—295
2:12—295
2:16—273, 294, 295
2:19—294
2:20–21—295
2:22—294
3:1—291n49, 294
3:1–21—293
3:1–4:27—293
3:2—295
3:4—295
3:5–6—150, 295
3:6—273
3:11—291n49
3:11–12—295
3:14–15—295
3:16—295
3:18—295
3:19—295
3:19–20—294
3:21—294
3:22—295
3:27–35—293
3:32–33—294
3:33—295
4:1—291n49, 294
4:1–27—293
4:11—294
4:18—296
4:20—291n49, 294
5:1—291n49, 294
5:1–4—296
5:1–23—293
5:1–6:35—293
5:4–5—294
5:7—294
5:15–19—296
5:21—273, 294, 296
6:1—291n49, 294
6:1–5—294
6:1–9—293
6:6–11—294, 296
6:12–19—294, 296
6:16—294
6:16–19—273
6:20—291n49, 294
6:20–22—274
6:20–35—293
6:27–35—294
7:1—291n49, 294
7:1–27—293
7:5–9—294
7:24—294
7:26–27—294
8:1–3—294
8:1–36—293
8:4–21—296
8:13—273, 295
8:22–31—294, 296
8:30—294
8:32–35—296
8:36—294
9—296
9:1–18—293
9:3—294
9:10—292, 293, 295
9:17–18—295
10–15—296, 297, 298
10:1—273, 290, 291n49, 296
10:1–22:16—290, 296, 298
10:2—296
10:3—297
10:4—296
10:5—296
10:6–7—296
10:8—296
10:9–12—296
10:29—296
11:21—297
12:2—297
13:1—291n49
14:2—297
14:27—297
15:3—293
15:20—291n49
16:1–22:16—296, 297, 298
16:4—273, 298
16:5—297
16:6—297
16:9—298
16:10—298
16:10–15—298
16:12—298
16:13—298
16:14—298
16:15—298
16:20—297
16:33—298
17:5—297
17:7—298
18:10—273, 297
18:22—25
19:12—298
19:13—291n49
19:14—298
19:21—298
19:23—298
19:26—291n49
19:27—291n49
20:2—298
20:3—298
20:8—298
20:10—297
20:23—297
20:24—298
20:26—298
21:1—298, 336
21:12—297
21:30–31—298
22:4—298
22:17–24:22—291, 299
22:19—299
22:20—291
22:22–23—299
22:26–28—299
22:29—299
23:1–3—299
23:13–14—299
23:15—291n49
23:19—291n49
23:22–25—299
23:24—291n49
23:26—291n49
24:13—291n49
24:17–18—299
24:21—291n49, 299
24:23–34—299
24:24–26—299
24:27—299
24:30–34—299
25–29—299
25:1—291, 299
27:11—291n49
28:5—299
28:7—291n49
28:13—300, 344
28:25—300
29:18—272, 273
30—300
30:1—291, 300
30:3—300
30:4—300
30:5—25, 300
30:9—273
30:32—300
31—300
31:1—291, 300
31:2—291n49

31:2–9—300
31:10–31—300
31:28–31—301

Ecclesiastes

1:1—314, 314n75, 315, 319, 320
1:1–6:9—313
1:2—314, 314nn74–75
1:2–11—315, 319
1:12—314, 314n75
1:12–18—316
1:12–6:9—315, 316, 319
1:15—316, 317
1:16—314, 320
1:17—320
1:18—316, 317
2:1–11—316
2:3b—316
2:4—320
2:4–9—314
2:5—320
2:6—320
2:7—320
2:8—320
2:11—316
2:12–17—316
2:17—316
2:18—316n79
2:18–23—320
2:18–26—316
2:19—316n79
2:20—316n79
2:21—316n79
2:22—316n79
2:24—316n79
2:24–25—317
2:26—316, 317, 318, 319
3:1–8—319
3:1–4:6—316
3:9—316n79
3:12–13—317
3:13—316n79
3:14—319
3:17—320
3:22—317
4:1–4—320
4:4—316n79
4:4–6—316
4:6—316n79
4:7–8—320
4:7–16—316
4:8—316n79
4:9—316n79
4:13–16—320
4:16—316
5:1–2—320
5:1–6:9—316
5:3—320
5:4—320
5:5–6—320
5:7—320
5:10–17—320
5:15—316n79
5:16—316n79
5:18—316n79, 319
5:18–19—317
5:19—316n79
5:19–20—320
6:1–6—320
6:2—317
6:7—315n79
6:9—316
6:10–11:6—315, 317, 319
6:10–12:14—313
6:12—317, 318
7:1–8:17—317
7:13–14—320n82
7:14—317
7:24—317
7:28–29—317
8:15—318
8:17—317, 320n82
9:1—318
9:1–11:6—318
9:5—318
9:7—318
9:9—314n73, 318
9:10—318
9:12—318
10:14—318
10:15—318
11:2—318
11:5—320n82
11:5–6—318
11:7–12:8—315, 319
11:9—315, 320
12:1—315, 320
12:2–7—315
12:8—314n74
12:9—314n75, 319
12:9–14—315, 319
12:11—315, 319, 320
12:12—314n75, 319
12:13—319, 320
12:13–14—320
12:14—319, 320

Song of Songs

1–2—307
1:1—306
1:4—307
1:5—306, 307
1:6—308
1:8—307
1:8–10—308
1:12—307
1:12–14—308
1:15—308
1:16–2:1—308
2:7—307
2:8–17—308
2:9—308
2:12–13—307
3:1–3—308
3:1–6—307
3:4—308
3:5—307
3:6–11—307, 308
3:7—307
3:9—307
3:10—307
3:11—307
4:1–15—307
4:7—307
4:12—307
4:16–5:1—307
5:2–3—308
5:2–8—307
5:5—308
5:8—307
5:9–6:3—307
5:10—307
5:16—307
6:2—307
6:4—307
6:4–10—307
6:8–9—307
6:11—307
6:11–13—307
6:12—307
7:1–8:14—307
7:5—307
7:10—308
8:4—307
8:11—307
8:12—307

Isaiah

1–5—191, 192, 197
1–11—197
1–39—191n107, 194
1:1—272n5
1:2—192, 215, 474
1:4—192
1:4–5—77
1:18—192
1:24—192
1:25—192
1:26—192
1:27—192, 454
1:28—192
2—211, 236, 237, 247
2:1–4—203
2:1–5—50, 192, 194, 208, 249
2:2–4—211n145
2:3—260
2:4—237
2:10–11—193
2:12—232n
2:16—165n53
2:17—193
2:19—193
2:21—193
3:8—193
3:18–23—193
4—211
4:2—192, 192n110, 196
4:2–6—192, 203
4:3—192
4:4—192
4:5—193, 194
4:6—193
5—193
5:1–7—193, 199
5:1–11—417
5:8–30—193
5:16—193
5:24—193
6—191, 193, 200, 415, 415n136
6:1—194
6:3—53, 73, 193, 268
6:3b—197
6:4—193
6:5—193, 194
6:5–10—213n152
6:8—194
6:9–10—124n129, 194, 200, 205, 217, 358, 359
6:9–11—217
6:9–13—365, 373
6:10—414, 415
6:11—365
6:11–12—194
6:11–13—196, 206, 415
6:13—417
7—194n117
7–12—191, 194, 200
7:1—413n
7:1–9—194
7:3—201
7:4—194, 201
7:7–9—194
7:8—194
7:8–9—77
7:10–11—194
7:11—201
7:13—194
7:14—194, 195, 364, 365
7:15—194
7:15–16—365
7:15–25—195

7:16—194
7:17—194
8:1–10—195
8:4—195
8:8—195, 200
8:18—195
8:22—195
9—200, 395
9:1—195
9:1–2—195, 195n, 368
9:3—195
9:3–5—195
9:6—196n119
9:6–7—195
9:8–10:4—196
9:12—196, 197
9:17—196, 197
9:19—196
9:21—196, 197
10—201
10:4—196, 197
10:5–6—196
10:5–9—201
10:5–15—196
10:5–19—311
10:7–11—196
10:12–15—196
10:16–34—196
10:19—196
10:20–23—196
10:22—200
11—211, 236, 237, 323, 356, 366, 367
11:1—192, 194, 196, 208, 417
11:1–5—196
11:2—196
11:3—192n109, 196
11:4—196
11:5—196
11:6–7—197
11:6–8—237
11:8—323
11:18—197
11:9—50, 268
11:9b—197
11:15—197
11:16—197
12—197
12:1—197
13–23—191, 197
13:1—197, 251
13:6—232n
13:9—232n
13:17—197, 221–22
13:19—198
14:4—197n122
14:25—77, 197n122
14:28—251
14:28–32—198
14:30—237
15:1—251
15:1–16:14—198
16:5—200
17:1—251
17:1–4—198
18:1–19:25—198
19:1—251
19:20—200
20:1–6—198
21:1—251
21:1–17—198
22:1–25—198
21:11—251
21:13—251
22:1—251
22:5—232
22:22–25—200
23:1—251
23:1–18—198
24—198
24–27—191, 198, 550
24:14–16—198
24:16—198
24:17–23—198
24:19—198
24:23—198
25:1—198
25:3—198
25:4—198
25:5—198
25:6—198
25:7–8—198
25:9–12—198
26—198
26:17–19—526
26:19—335n106
27—198, 211
27:1—77, 198, 199
27:2—199
27:4—199
27:13—199
28—199
28–35—191, 199
28:1—199n124
28:1–4—199
28:1–29—199
28:1–29:24—199
28:2—200
28:3—77
28:5—199
28:7–9—199
28:11—199
28:14—199, 200
28:15—200
28:16—200
28:17—200
28:17–18—200
28:18—200
28:18b—200
28:21—200
29:1—199n124
29:1–10—200
29:1–24—199
29:10—124n129
29:11—200
29:14—200
29:15—199n124, 200
29:16—200
29:17—201
29:18—200
29:19—200
29:23—200
30:1—199n124
30:1–31:9—199, 201
30:6—251
30:18—201n126
30:27—192n109
31:1—199n124
32:1—201
32:1–20—199
32:3–4—201
32:14—201
32:15—201, 381, 408, 472
33—201
33:1—199, 199n124, 201
33:14—107, 201
33:17—192n109
33:22—206
34—199, 211
34:8—232
34:11—216
35—199, 211
36–39—201
36:2—201
37:6—201
37:20—352
37:30—201
39:5–8—202
40—202, 211
40–48—191, 201, 202, 203, 205
40–53—202n
40–55—202, 202n
40–66—194, 201, 202
40:1—207
40:1–2—202, 524
40:1–11—258
40:2—55, 209, 332, 397, 472, 474, 524
40:3—202, 357, 358, 367, 381, 381n62
40:3–4—524
40:3–5—202
40:3–8—202n
40:4—202
40:5—202, 524
40:6—192n109, 524
40:6–8—202, 524
40:8—524
40:9—202, 203, 525
40:10—381n62
40:10–11—203
40:12—203
40:13–14—203
40:17—203
40:18—203
40:18–20—203
40:19–20—203
40:21—203
40:22—204
40:25—203
40:26—203, 204
40:31—206, 548
41—204n134
41:2—206n
41:2–4—204n134, 206
41:5—205
41:5–7—203, 204n134
41:8–9—205
41:8–20—205
41:16—206
41:18–20—204n134
41:20—204
41:21–24—204n134
41:22—204, 205
41:23a—204
41:24—204
41:25—206n
41:25–29—204n134, 206
41:28—203, 205
41:29—204
42:1–4—205
42:5—204
42:6—205, 206
42:7—205
42:8—206
42:9—205
42:10–13—206
42:14–15—206
42:14–17—202n
42:16—205
42:18–19—205
42:19—205
42:21—206
42:23—205
42:24–25—205
43:1–28—205
43:5–6—206
43:7—206
43:8—205
43:9—205
43:10—205
43:11—205
43:13—205
43:14–20—206
43:21—206
43:24—205
43:25—206
44:1—205
44:4—204

44:6—205
44:7—205
44:8—205
44:9–20—204
44:18—205
44:21—205
44:22—205
44:23—206
44:24—335
44:28–45:1—206
44:28–45:4—357
44:28—335
45:3—94n54, 206
45:4—205
45:4–5—336
45:5–7—204
45:6—205, 206
45:7—205
45:11—205
45:14—206
45:16—205
45:17—205
45:18—204, 205, 206
45:21—205
45:21–22—205
45:23—206
45:25—206
46:1—206
46:2—206
46:4—205
46:5—203
46:6–7—204
46:9—205
46:10—205
46:11—206
46:12–13—205
47:1–15—206
48:3–8—205
48:9—104n, 136, 206
48:9–11—559
48:11—206, 387, 387n75
48:12—205
48:13—204
48:14—206
48:15—206
48:20—548
48:20–21—206
48:20–22—202
49–55—191, 202, 206, 209
49:3—206, 207
49:5—207
49:6—207, 419n145
49:9—207
49:10—207
49:12—207
49:13—207
49:14–26—207
49:16—207
49:23—77, 94n54, 207
49:26—94n54, 207
50—207
50:1–3—207
50:4–5—207
50:6—207
50:7–9—207
50:10—207
50:11—207
51—207, 211
51:3—207, 323
51:4—208
51:4–6—208
51:5—208
51:7–8—208
51:9—77, 199, 381n62
51:9–16—208
51:17—208
51:18–21—208
51:22–23—208
52—208
52:1–2—208
52:3–10—208
52:5b–6—208
52:7—251, 452, 525
52:10—208, 381n62
52:11–12—208, 209
52:12—208
52:13–53:12—205, 208, 413, 414, 474
52:13—206, 208, 413, 414
52:14—192n109, 208
52:15–53:1—208
52:15—208, 413, 414, 474, 475
53—208, 209, 211, 376n42, 388n77, 403n120, 408, 413, 414, 415, 415n136, 431, 474, 478, 526n164
53:1—381n62, 414, 415
53:2—192n109, 417
53:2a—208
53:2b–3a—208
53:3b—208
53:3c—208
53:4—209, 415
53:4–6—474
53:5—209, 526n164
53:6—209, 526n164
53:7—209, 415
53:8—474
53:8–9—209
53:9—418, 526n164
53:10—209, 474, 475
53:11–12—209
53:12—403n120
54:1—209, 478, 479
54:2–3—209
54:5—209
54:7–8—104n, 137, 209
55—209
55–66—191
55:1—210
55:1–3—209
55:1–5—209n142
55:1–8—210
55:3—243
55:4–5—209
55:10–11—202
55:12–13—202
56–66—210
56:1—210
56:3–8—210
56:9–59:15a—210
59:15b–21—210
59:16ff.—381n62
60–62—210
60:6—525
60:16—94n54
61:1—525
61:1–4—199
63—211
63:1–6—210
63:2–3—310
63:3—77
63:5—381n62
63:7–66:17—210
63:7—104n, 135
65:17—205, 357, 467
66—211
66:1–2—428
66:18–24—210
66:20–24—58
66:22—467

Jeremiah

1—211, 212
1:1–3—213
1:5—213
1:6—213
1:6–7—213n151
1:7—218n165
1:8—213
1:8–9—213
1:10—213
1:9—218n165
1:11–12—213
1:13–15—213
1:16—213, 213n154, 214
1:17–18—213
1:17–19—214
1:18–19—217
1:19—213
2—215n159
2–6—211, 212, 214
2:1—214
2:2—214
2:4–5—214
2:5—213n154
2:7—214
2:9—214
2:10–11—215
2:12—215
2:13—213n154, 215
2:14–17—215
2:17—213n154
2:18—215
2:19—213n154, 215
2:20—214n157
2:21—214n157
2:22—215, 217
2:23—215
2:23–25—215
2:26–28—215
2:27—213n154
2:32—214
2:36—215
3–4—215
3:1—215, 408
3:10–11—215
3:11–13—215
3:12—408
3:13—215
3:14–17—215
3:16–18—218
3:19—214n157
3:20—214n157
3:22–25—215
4:1–2—215
4:2—215
4:4—215, 217, 220n173
4:5—215
4:5–9—215
4:8—215
4:10—216
4:20—216
4:23—216
4:23–36—216
4:24—216
4:25—215
4:26—216
5:1—216
5:7—213n154
5:9—216, 216n163
5:14—216
5:18—216
5:19—213n154
5:21—217
5:29—216, 216n163
6:10—124, 166n55, 217, 243
6:14—217
6:16—216
6:20–37—214
6:27—214
6:27–29—217

7—229
7–20—211, 217
7:1—214n155
7:16—217
7:23—212
7:27—217
8:9—217
9:9—216, 216n163
9:13—217
9:22–23—161n44
9:23–24—161n44, 218
9:24—94n54
9:25–26—220n173
9:26—217
10:6–10—218
10:23—217
11:1—214n155
11:4—212
11:14—217
11:18–19—218
11:20—218
11:21–23—218
12:17—213n153
13:14—77
13:23—217
14:1—214n155
14:7—218, 352
14:7–9—218
14:11—217
14:14—272n5
14:20–22—218
14:21—218, 352
15:1—217
15:6—213n154
15:15—104n, 137
15:16—217
15:20–21—214n156
16:1—214n156
16:1–4—218
16:11—213n154
16:13—368
16:14–15—368, 368n26
16:16—218, 368, 368n26
17:1—217
17:9—217
17:13—213n154, 215
17:14–18—211n147
17:19—214n155
17:24–26—218
18:1—214n155
18:1–11—162
18:1–17—218n167
18:5–10—219
18:5–11—218
18:7—213n153
18:18—218
19:4—213n154
20:11–13—211n147
21–24—211, 218
21:1—214n155, 218, 218n168
21:3—218
21:7—218
21:10—218
21:11–12—218
22:1–7—218
22:9—213n154
22:11—218
22:18—218
22:24—218
22:24–30—221
22:28–30—218
23—366
23:5—192n110, 229, 367
23:5–6—219, 221
23:7–8—219
23:16—272n5
23:19—77
23:29—77
24—219
24:1—214n155, 218
24:1–2—219
24:4–6—219
24:6—213n153
24:7—94n54, 212, 219
24:8—214n155, 218
24:8–10—219
24:12—214n155
25—219
25–33—211, 219
25:1—214n155, 218n168, 219
25:9—219
25:11—219
25:11–12—336
25:12—219, 331, 357
25:13—212n148
25:15–29—219
25:30–38—219
26—219
26:1–3—219
26:3—219
26:8—220
26:12–13—219
26:16—220
26:17–19—220
26:24—212n150
27—229
27–28—220
27:1—214n155
27:1–11—220
27:6—220
27:12—220
27:17—220
28:1–11—220
28:12–16—220
28:17—220
29:1–32—220
29:10—220
29:10–14—336
29:11—218
29:11–14—220
30–33—211, 219
30:1—214n155
30:8—220
30:22—212
30:23—77
31—229
31:1—212
31:2—366
31:3—220
31:10—366
31:14—220
31:15—364, 366
31:16—366
31:28—213n153, 220
31:31—220
31:31–34—408
31:33—124, 212, 220
31:34—220
31:40—213n153
32:1—214n155
32:1–5—220
32:6–15—220
32:16–23—220
32:17—220
32:18—104n, 135, 220
32:19—220
32:20—220
32:21—220
32:22—220
32:23—220
32:24–25—220
32:26–35—220
32:29—125
32:36–44—220
32:38—212
32:39—123, 123n128
33—214n155
33:1—214n155
33:1–5—221
33:6–13—221
33:9—221
33:15—192n110
33:15–16—221
33:17—221
33:19—214n155
33:19–26—221
33:23—214n155
34—221
34–37—221
34–45—212, 221
35—221
35:1—214n155
35:12—214n155
36—221
36:1—214n155
37—221
38—221
39—221
39–45—221
39:1–10—212
39:2–7—225
40–44—221
41:1–3—260n
45—221
46—212
46–51—212n148, 221
46:10—232n
47—221
48—221
48:4—77
49:1–6—221
49:7–22—221
49:23–27—221
49:28–33—221
49:34–39—221
50–51—214n157, 222
50:4–5—220n172
50:18–20—222n178
50:31—251n249
51–52—221
51:11—197, 221
51:20–23—77
51:25—251n249
51:28—197, 221
52—212, 222, 310
52:31–34—212, 213

Lamentations

1—311
1–2—311
1:1—310
1:2—310
1:5—310
1:9—310, 311
1:11—311
1:12—232n
1:16–17—310
1:17—310
1:18—310
1:20—166n54, 311
1:20–22—311
1:21—310
2—310, 311
2:1—311
2:6—311
2:7–9—311
2:9—272n5
2:16—311
2:17—311
2:20—311, 312
2:20–22—311
2:21c–22b—311
2:22—232n
3—310, 311
3:1–20—311
3:21—311
3:21–26—311–12
3:22—119

3:23—313
3:37–38—312
3:39–42—312
3:50—312
3:55–66—311
4—312
4:1—312
4:2—312
4:3–4—312
4:5—312
4:6—312
4:7–8—312
4:9—312
4:10—312
4:12—312
4:22—313
5:1–22—313
5:11—313
5:12—313
5:19—313
5:21—313
5:21–22—339n114
5:22—313

Ezekiel

1—226
1–3—223
1:1–2:8—223
1:3—225
1:4–28—224
1:28—222
2:9–3:2—223
3:12—223
3:17—224
3:18—224, 568
3:19—224
3:20—224, 568
3:21—224
4–7—225
4–24—223
5:8—224
5:13—94n54, 223n182
6:3–5—224
6:7—94n54, 223n182
6:9—224
6:10—94n54, 223n182, 224
6:13—94n54, 223n182
6:14—94n54, 223n182
7:4—94n54, 223n182
7:9—94n54, 223n182
7:27—94n54, 223n182
8–11—223, 225, 226, 229
8:1–3—224
8:7–10—224
8:11–12—224
8:13–14—224
8:15–16—224
9:1–11—224
9:4—224
10:1–22—224
11:10—94n54, 223n182, 225
11:12—94n54, 223n182, 225
11:16—225
11:19—225
11:20—225
12–24—225
12:1–14—225
12:15—94n54, 223n182
12:15–16—225
12:16—94n54, 223n182
12:20—94n54, 223n182
12:21–14:11—225
13:5—232n
13:14—94n54, 223n182
13:21—94n54, 223n182
13:23—94n54, 223n182
14:8—94n54, 223n182
14:12–21—225
14:14—190
14:20—190
14:22—225
14:23—225
15:7—94n54, 223n182
16:60—225
16:61—225
16:62—94n54, 223n182, 225
16:63—225
17:21—94n54, 223n182
17:24—94n54, 223n182
18:9—225
20—226
20:9—226
20:11—225
20:12—94n54, 223n182
20:13—225
20:14—226
20:20—94n54, 223n182
20:21—225
20:22—226
20:38—94n54, 223n182
20:41—226
20:42—94n54, 223n182
20:43—226
20:44—94n54, 223n182, 226
20:48—94n54, 223n182
21:5—94n54, 223n182
22:16—94n54, 223n182
22:22—94n54, 223n182
22:26—225
24:27—94n54, 223n182
25–32—223
25:5—94n54, 223n182
25:7—94n54, 223n182
25:11—94n54, 223n182
25:17—94n54, 223n182
26:6—94n54, 223n182
26:12—165n53
26:14—94n54, 223n182
28:22—94n54, 223n182, 227
28:23—94n54, 223n182
28:26—94n54, 223n182
29:6—94n54, 223n182
29:9—94n54, 223n182
29:21—94n54, 223n182
30:3—232n
30:8—94n54, 223n182
30:19—94n54, 223n182
30:25—94n54, 223n182
30:26—94n54, 223n182
32:15—94n54, 223n182
33–48—223
33:29—94n54, 223n182
34:1–10—412
34:23–24—412
34:27—94n54, 223n182
34:30—94n54, 223n182
35:4—94n54, 223n182
35:9—94n54, 223n182
35:12—94n54, 223n182
35:15—94n54, 22n182
36—229
36:11—94n54, 223n182
36:21–23—227
36:22—559
36:23—94n54, 223n182
36:25—367, 407
36:25–27—410
36:26—123, 123n128, 125
36:27—381, 408
36:32—227
36:36—94n54, 223n182
36:38—94n54, 223n182
37—412
37:1–4—410
37:1–13—412
37:6—94n54, 223n182
37:11–14—398
37:13—94n54, 223n182
37:13–14—467
37:14—94n54, 223n182, 381, 412, 524
37:24—229, 367, 412
37:28—94n54, 223n182
38:16—227
38:23—94n54, 223n182, 227
39:6—94n54, 223n182
39:7—94n54, 223n182, 228
39:13—228
39:21—228
39:22—94n54, 223n182
39:25—228
39:27—228
40–48—223, 226, 228, 229
44:23—225
47:1—74
48:35—228

Daniel

1—325, 326
1:2—326
1:6—326
1:9—327
1:17—327
1:20—327
2—325, 326, 327, 330, 332, 333, 334
2–7—325
2:1–3—327
2:12–13—327
2:17—327
2:19–23—327
2:20—327

2:21a—327
2:21b–22—327
2:23—327
2:30—327
2:31–35—327
2:34–35—77
2:36–45—327
2:37–38—328
2:44—327
2:47—328
3—325, 326, 328
3:1–6—328
3:7–12—328
3:22—328
3:25—328
3:27—328
3:29—328
4—325, 326, 328, 329, 330
4–5—326
4:1–3—328
4:10–12—383
4:17—328, 329
4:20–22—383
4:22—329
4:25—328, 329
4:26—328
4:29—329
4:30—328
4:31—328
4:32—328, 329
4:34—329
4:35—329
4:37—329
5—325, 326, 329
5:1–4—329
5:2–3—337
5:5—329
5:6—329
5:18—329
5:21—329
5:23—329
5:26—329
5:27—329
5:28—329
5:30—329, 548
5:30–31—219
6—325, 326, 329
6:16—329
6:17—329
6:20—329
6:22–23—329
6:24—330
6:25–27—330
6:28—219n170, 548
7—325, 330, 332, 333, 334, 382n65, 388n77, 413, 415n136
7–9—325, 326, 330
7:1–14—330
7:6—331
7:10–12—330
7:13—330, 413, 414, 425, 499n
7:14—330, 425
7:18—330
7:24b–27—499
7:25—493
7:26—493
7:26–27—425
7:27—330, 493
7:27b—493
8—330, 334
8–9—325
8:1—272n5
8:5–8a—331
8:8b—331
8:9–12—331
8:9–13—493
8:9–14—499
8:14—493
8:16—331
8:17—330
8:21—331
8:22—331
8:23–26—331
9—331, 334
9:2—331, 332, 357
9:3–19—331
9:4—104n, 137, 331
9:4–6—331
9:7—326, 331
9:9—331
9:11—100n71
9:12—331
9:13—100n71, 331
9:14—331
9:16—332
9:16–19—353
9:17—332
9:18b—332
9:19—332
9:21—332
9:24—332, 493
9:25—333
9:26—408
9:26b—334
9:26b–27—499
9:26b–27a—493
9:27—425
10—334
10–12—325, 326, 334
10:5—334
10:16—334
10:21—334
11—325n95
11–12—334
11:2—334
11:2–45—334
11:8—165n53
11:27—335
11:29—335
11:31—325n95, 493
11:32—569
11:32b–33a—334
11:33–35—493
11:35—335
11:36—335
11:36–45—499
11:40—335
11:45—335, 493
12—325n95
12:1—335, 369n29
12:1–3—425, 493, 499
12:2—335, 335n106
12:2–3—334
12:3—335
12:4—335, 350
12:8—335
12:9—335, 350
12:11–12—499

Hosea

1—235
1–3—235, 235n210
1:2—235
1:6—525
1:7—233
1:8—232
1:9–10—525
1:10–2:1—235
1:11—232
2—235, 237
2:2—214
2:2–7—235
2:5—235
2:6–7—235
2:7—235, 236
2:8—236
2:8–10—236
2:8–15—235
2:11—236
2:12—232, 236
2:13—236
2:14–15—236
2:14–23—235
2:15—233, 548
2:15–16—214
2:16–17—236
2:16–20—408
2:17—236
2:18—236, 237
2:19–20—135, 237, 238
2:20—233, 236
2:21–22—237
2:21–23—237
2:22—371n
2:23—233, 525
3—238
3:1—238
3:5—232, 233, 235, 238, 367
4–14—235, 235n210
4:1—232, 233
4:2—238
4:3–10—238
4:13—235
4:14—235
4:15—235
4:18—235
5:4—233
5:14—181, 232, 238
5:14–6:3—238
5:15—233, 238
6:1—232
6:1–2—238
6:3—233, 238
6:6—110, 233
6:28—548
7:7—233
7:10—233
7:14—233
8:2—233
8:4—181n87
8:12—100n71
8:14—233
9:1—232, 235
10:3—233
10:12—233, 238
10:15—238
10:15–11:1—413n
11:1—232, 238n217, 364, 366
11:1–2—366
11:1–4—365
11:1–11—238
11:5–6—366
11:8—166n54
11:9—233
11:10—232
11:10–11—233, 235
12:5—233
12:6—232
12:9—233
12:11—272n5
13:1–2—235
13:4—233
13:7—233
13:7–8—232
13:8—183
13:9—233
13:10—232
13:13—369n26
14:2—230n196
14:2–3—232
14:5–9—235
14:7—230
14:9—239

Joel

1—239
1:1–20—239
1:2—230
1:2–4—242
1:4—232
1:5—230
1:7—230, 232
1:12—232
1:15—232, 232n, 240
2:1—232, 232n
2:1–2—240
2:1–11—239
2:2—232
2:6—232
2:10—232
2:11—232, 232n, 240
2:12—230n196, 240
2:12–13—232
2:12–17—239
2:13—135, 240, 244
2:14—232, 240
2:15–17—240
2:17—240
2:18—240
2:18–27—239
2:20—240
2:21—233
2:22—232
2:23—233
2:25—232, 241
2:26—233
2:27—233
2:28–32—239, 241, 381, 408, 472
2:31—232
2:32—232, 233
3—230, 241
3:1—241
3:1–3—239
3:2—232, 240
3:4—232, 232n, 240
3:4–14—239
3:7—232
3:8—232
3:10—241
3:12—240
3:13—104n
3:14—232
3:15–21—239
3:16—181, 230, 232, 233, 241
3:17—94n54, 233, 241
3:18—74, 232, 241
3:19—240
3:21—241
4:14—232n
4:16—230n196
4:17—232

Amos

1–2—241, 242
1:1—232, 241
1:2—181, 230, 230n196, 232, 233, 241, 242
1:3–2:16—230, 241
2:4—242
2:7—233, 242
2:9—242
2:9–11—233
2:10—242
2:11—242
2:12—242
2:13–16—242
3–6—241, 242
3:1—241
3:4—242
3:8—232, 233, 242
3:12—242
3:13—241
4—242
4:1—241
4:2—233, 242
4:6—242
4:8—242
4:9—232, 242
4:10—242
4:11—232, 242
4:12—242n233
4:12–13—242–43, 242n233
4:13—232, 233, 242n233, 243, 244, 266
5:1—241
5:4—243
5:5—242
5:6—243
5:8—232, 233, 243, 244
5:8–9—233, 242n233, 243, 244n237
5:9—266
5:13—232
5:15—232
5:15a—244
5:15b—244
5:17—243
5:18—232, 232n, 241, 243
5:19—183, 242
5:20—232, 232n, 243
5:24—244
5:25–27—428
5:27—242, 243, 266
6:1—241
6:7—242
6:8—233, 244
7–9—241, 242
7:1—232, 241, 241n230
7:2—244n236
7:2–3—244
7:4—241, 241n230
7:5—244n236
7:5–6—244
7:7—241
7:8—241n230, 243
7:11—242
7:16—232
8:1—241
8:2—243
8:9—232, 243
8:11—232
9:1—241, 241n230
9:1–4—244
9:4—242, 244, 244n237
9:4b–6—244–45
9:5–6—233, 242n233, 244, 244n237
9:6—233, 243, 266
9:7—232, 244n237, 245
9:7–9—244n237
9:9—245
9:11—245, 367
9:11–15—232, 242, 548
9:12—230, 230n196, 233, 245
9:13—232, 245
9:14—245
9:15—245

Obadiah

1:1—230, 230n196, 272n5
1:1–9—245
1:3—245
1:3–4—245
1:5–6—245
1:7—245
1:8–9—245
1:10—245
1:10–14—245
1:11—230
1:11–13—245
1:12–14—230
1:14—245
1:15—232, 232n
1:15–16—245
1:17—232
1:17–21—245, 246
1:18—232, 246
1:18–21—548
1:19—230n196
1:19–20—246
1:21—246

Jonah

1:2—230
1:3—246
1:3–16—246
1:6—230, 232, 233
1:7—230
1:9—233
1:13—233
1:14—233
1:16—233
1:17—246
2:1–2—233
2:2—246
2:3—246
2:5–9—233
2:6—246
2:7—233
2:9—233, 246
3:2—246
3:3–10—246
3:8—232
3:9—232, 244
4:2—104n, 135, 230, 230n196, 233
4:3–11—246
4:5—230

Micah

1:1—250
1:2—247, 248, 249
1:2b–2:11—247
1:3—248
1:3–4—232, 233
1:4—248
1:5—248
1:7—232
1:10—248
2:1–2—248
2:3—232
2:3–5—248
2:6—232
2:6–11—249
2:12—249
2:12–13—233, 247
2:13—232, 249
3:1—247, 249
3:1a—247n232
3:1–3—249
3:1–12—247
3:4–7—249
3:6—232
3:8—249
3:9—247n242
3:9a—247n232
3:9–11—249
3:12—249
3:23—232n
4—247
4–5—247

4:1–2—232
4:1–5—249
4:1–5:14—233
4:2—260
4:4—232
4:5—233
4:7—232
4:8–13—249
4:12—233
5:1—249
5:2—249
5:2–4—367
5:3—249
5:3–5a—249
5:4—233
5:5–6—249
5:7–15—249
6:1—247, 247n232, 249
6:1–2—249
6:1–7:6—247, 249
6:2—232, 247n242
6:3–4—249
6:5—233, 250
6:6–8—110
6:7—232
6:8—250
6:9–16—250
7:1–6—250
7:7—233, 250
7:7–20—247
7:8—250
7:9—250
7:10—250
7:10–17—233
7:11–17—250
7:17—77
7:18—104n, 135, 250
7:18–19—230, 230n196, 233
7:19–20—250

Nahum

1:1—230n196, 232, 250, 272n5
1:2–3—104n, 135, 230, 230n196
1:2–8—233, 251n248
1:3—251
1:3b—251
1:4—251
1:5—232, 251
1:6—232, 251
1:7—251
1:15—452
2:2—251
2:10—232
2:13—251
3:7—230
3:15–17—232
3:18—230
3:19—251

Habakkuk

1:1—230n196, 232, 250
1:2–4—252
1:3—232
1:5–11—252
1:5–2:20—311
1:12–2:1—252
1:16—230
2:2—272n5
2:2–3—252
2:2–20—252
2:3—272n5
2:4—252, 473
2:5–13—252
2:14—50, 53, 73, 233, 252, 265, 268–69, 483n92
2:20—230, 230n196, 233, 252
3:1–9—252
3:1–19—252
3:2—252
3:3—233, 253
3:5—253
3:5–6—232
3:6—253
3:8–9—253
3:10—232, 253
3:12–13—253
3:13—77, 232
3:14–15—233
3:16—233
3:16a—252
3:17—232
3:17–19—233, 252

Zephaniah

1:1—253
1:2–6—253
1:7—230, 230n196, 232, 233
1:7–18—253
1:14–16—232
1:15—232
2:1–3—253
2:3—232, 253
2:4–7—253
2:4–3:7—253
2:8–11—253
2:11—233
2:12—253
2:13–15—253
3:1–7—253
3:8—232, 253
3:8–13—253
3:9—233, 253
3:10—253
3:11—253
3:12–13—254
3:14—254
3:14–15—233
3:15—254, 413n
3:17—254
3:18–20—254
3:20—230

Haggai

1:1—255
1:1–11—255
1:2—230
1:4—230, 255
1:5–6—255
1:8—233, 256
1:12—233
1:12–15—255
1:14–15—255
2:1–9—255
2:3—256
2:4–5—256
2:6–7—232
2:6–9—256, 257n260
2:7—233, 256
2:8—257
2:9—233
2:10—255
2:10–19—255
2:18—255
2:19—232
2:20—230
2:20–23—255
2:21—232, 257
2:22—257
2:23—232, 257

Zechariah

1–6—260
1:1—230, 257
1:1–6—255, 258
1:3—258
1:3–4—232
1:7—257
1:7–17—258
1:7–6:8—255, 257
1:12—357
1:13–17—258
1:18–21—258
2:1–4—258
2:1–13—258
2:5—233, 261
2:5–17—259
2:10—233, 262n274
2:12—233
3:1–10—258, 259
3:2—232
3:8—192n110
3:10—232
4:1–14—258, 259
4:6—233, 260
4:6–7—230
5:1–4—258, 259
5:5–11—258
6—366
6:1—232
6:1–8—258
6:9–15—257, 259
6:12—192n110, 259, 366
6:13—233, 259
6:15—259
7–8—259, 260
7:1—257
7:1–3—259, 260
7:1–14—255
7:2—260
7:3—260
7:4–7—259, 260
7:4–8:23—258
7:8–10—259, 260
7:11–14—259, 260
8—231n198
8:1–6—259, 260
8:2— 260
8:3—232, 260
8:4–5—260
8:6—260
8:7–14—260
8:7–15—259
8:16–17—259, 260
8:18–19—259, 260
8:19—260
8:20–23—259
8:21–22—233
8:22—260
8:23—260
9–14—231n198, 261, 262, 262n273
9:1—232, 250, 257
9:1–5—262
9:1–17—261
9:1–11:17—258, 261
9:6–7—262
9:8—262
9:9—233, 262, 413
9:9–10—262, 262n274, 390n84
9:10—262, 284
9:12–13—262
9:13—262
9:15—262
9:14–16—262
9:14–17—233
9:17—262
9:17–10:1—262
10:1–12—261
10:2—262

10:3—262
10:4—262
10:5—77
10:6—233, 262
10:6–7—262
10:7—262
10:8—262
10:9–10—262
10:10—262
10:11–12—262
10:12—233, 262
11—413
11:1–3—262
11:1–17—261
11:4–14—262
11:12–13—390n84
11:15–17—262
12:1—232, 250, 257
12:1–14—261
12:1–14:21—258, 261
12:2–9—262
12:6—262
12:8—262
12:10—51, 232, 262, 263, 390n84, 408, 418
12:10–14—262
12:14—262
13:1—262, 283
13:1–9—261
13:2—262
13:7—262, 390n84, 408, 413
13:9—233, 262
14:1—232, 232n
14:1–9—262
14:1–21—261
14:2—232
14:3–4—233
14:4—232
14:8—74, 262
14:9—233
14:10–11—262
14:12–16—262
14:15—232
14:16—263
14:16–19—262
14:20–21—230, 262

Malachi

1:1—232, 250, 263
1:2—263, 264
1:2–3—264
1:2–5—263, 264
1:3–4—264
1:4—230
1:5—233
1:6—233
1:6–7—263
1:6–2:16—263, 264
1:11—233, 265
1:14—233, 265
2:2—233, 265
2:4–6—265
2:5—233
2:17—263
2:17–3:5—263, 265
3:1—233, 381
3:2—232
3:5—233
3:6—233
3:6–12—263, 265
3:7—232
3:7–8—263
3:13—263
3:13–15—263, 265
3:16—233
3:16–18—264, 265
4:1–6—264, 265
4:2—233
4:2–3—77
4:5—232, 373

Matthew

1–2—362, 363, 364
1:1–17—363
1:17—364
1:21—365
1:22–23—194n117, 364, 365
1:25—365
2—365, 366
2:2—368
2:5–6—249, 364
2:9–10—368
2:13–15—366
2:14—366
2:15—238n217, 364, 366, 368, 413n134
2:16–17—366
2:17–18—364
2:23—364, 366
3–4—362, 367
3:1—441
3:3—367
3:4—367
3:6—441
3:7—367
3:11—367, 441
3:11–12—367
3:13—441
3:13–17—367
3:14—441
3:16—441
4:1–11—366, 370
4:6—161
4:10—368
4:12—372
4:12–16—195n118
4:13—368
4:14–16—368
4:17—362, 368
4:19—218, 368
4:23—370
4:23–25—369
4:24—369
5–7—362, 363, 369, 370
5:3–10—369
5:5—369
5:9—196n119
5:11—387
5:11–12—369
5:13–16—369
5:17—370
5:17–20—369
5:21–26—369
5:21–48—369
5:27–30—369
5:31–32—369
5:33–37—369
5:38–42—369
5:43–48—369
5:46–47—375
6:1–4—369
6:5–15—370
6:14–15—375
6:16–18—370
6:19–24—370
6:25–34—370
7:1–6—370
7:7–11—370
7:12—370
7:13–14—370
7:15—371
7:15–20—370
7:21–23—370, 568
7:24–27—370
7:28—363
7:28–29—370
8–9—363, 370
8:1–4—370
8:5–13—370
8:14–17—370
8:17—370, 371
8:18–22—371
8:23–27—370
8:27—371
8:34—371
9:1–8—370
9:3—371
9:6—370
9:7—371
9:9–13—371
9:14–17—371
9:18–26—370
9:26—371
9:27–31—370
9:31—370
9:32–34—370
9:33—371
9:34—371
9:35—370
10—363, 371
10:1—371
10:6—371
10:7–8—371
10:16—371, 456
10:18—371, 387
10:22—371
10:28—371
10:32—371
10:37—371
10:38—371
10:39—372, 387
11–12—363, 372
11:1—363
11:2–6—372
11:7–15—372
11:10—367
11:11—441
11:12—441
11:14—367
11:16–19—372
11:19—399n111
11:20–24—372
11:25–27—372, 373, 374
11:27—373
11:28–30—372
12:1–2—372
12:3–6—372
12:6—372
12:8—372
12:9–13—372
12:14—372
12:15—372
12:22—372
12:23—372
12:28—372
12:31–32—372
12:34—372
12:38–42—373
13—363, 373
13:10–17—373n37
13:14–15—373
13:16—272
13:35—373
13:38—373
13:42—373
13:43—373
13:44–46—373
13:53—363
14–17—363, 373
14:1–12—373
14:2—441
14:8—441
14:13–21—373
14:22–25—373
14:26—373
14:27—373
14:33—373

15:1–20—373
15:21–25—373
15:26–28—373
15:29–31—373
16:13–14—374
16:14—441
16:16—374
16:18—374n40, 380, 566
16:21—362, 368, 374, 375, 379
16:22—374
16:23—374
16:24–26—374
16:25—387
16:27—374
17:1—374
17:2–4—374
17:5—375
17:9—375
17:13—441
17:22–23—379
17:23—375
18—363, 375
18:1–4—375
18:5–6—375
18:7–9—375
18:10–14—375
18:15–18—566, 567
18:15–20—375
18:21—375
18:23–35—375
19–23—363, 375
19:1—363
19:1–12—375
19:13–15—375
19:16–22—375
19:23–30—376
19:29—376
19:30—376
20:1–15—376
20:15—376
20:16—376
20:17–19—376, 379
20:20–25—376
20:26—376
20:27—376
20:28—376, 376n42
20:29–34—376
21—376
21:1–11—376
21:12–13—376
21:14–17—376
21:18–20—376
21:21–22—376
21:23–27—376
21:25—441
21:28–32—376
21:33–42—377
21:38—377
21:43–44—377
21:45–46—377
22:1–4—377
22:15–22—377
22:22—377
22:23–33—377
22:33—377
22:34–40—377
22:41–45—377
22:45–46—377
23–24—379
23:1–36—377
23:29–36—377
23:33—377
23:37–39—377
23:39—377
24–25—363, 377
24:1–2—377
24:3—377
24:4–14—377
24:8—369n29
24:8–9—493
24:14—358
24:15—325n95, 377
24:15–28—377
24:21—377
24:24—378
24:27—377
24:27–30—493
24:29—377
24:29–30—378
24:30–31—493
24:31—378
24:32–35—378
24:34—378n48
24:36–39—378
24:40–44—378
24:45–47—378
24:48–51—378
25:1–13—378
25:14–30—378
25:31—378
25:31–40—378
25:32—378
25:41–46—378
26–28—363, 378
26:1—363
26:26–28—378
26:28—379
26:53—379
26:54–56—379
26:61—379, 428
26:64—379, 425
27:9—379
27:40—379
27:45—379, 428
27:51—379
27:52–53—379
28:16–20—379n51, 566
28:17—379
28:17b—391n88
28:18—379
28:18–20—391n88, 445
28:19—379n52, 441
28:19–20—380

Mark

1:1–13—381
1:1–8:26—392
1:4—441
1:5—441
1:8—381, 441
1:9—441
1:14–8:30—381
1:15—382, 391
1:16–21—382
1:22—382
1:25—382, 386
1:26—382
1:27—382
1:28—382
1:29–34—382
1:34—386
1:39—382
1:40–44—382
1:44—386
1:45—382
2:2—382
2:5—382
2:10—382
2:12—382, 559
2:13—382
2:16—382
2:19–20—382
2:25–26—382
2:28—382
3:1–5—382
3:6—382
3:12—386
3:13–19—382
3:17—445
3:20–21—382
3:22—382
3:23–27—382
3:28–30—382
3:31–35—382
4:10–12—373n37, 386
4:11—382
4:13–20—383
4:30–32—383
4:34—386
4:35–41—196n119
4:35–5:43—381n62
4:39—383
4:40—383
5:19—383
5:20—383
5:21–23—383
5:25–34—383
5:29—383
5:35–36—383
5:37–40—383
5:41–43—383
5:43—386
6:1–6—384
6:7–13—384
6:14—441
6:14–29—384
6:24—441
6:25—441
6:30–43—384
6:34–44—381n62
6:45–52—381n62, 384
6:53–56—384
7:1–13—384
7:4—441
7:14–23—384
7:17—386
7:24—386
7:24–30—384
7:31–35—384
7:32–37—381n62
7:36—386
7:36–37—384
8–10—385
8:1–10—381n62, 384
8:11–12—384
8:13–21—385
8:22–26—385
8:24—385
8:26—386
8:27–30—381
8:27–10:52—392
8:28—441
8:29—385
8:30—386
8:31—385, 386
8:31–10:52—381, 386
8:32—385
8:32–34—386
8:33–9:1—385
8:34—386
8:35—386, 387
8:36–37—387
8:38—388, 559
9:1–5—388
9:2–8—388n76
9:6–7—388
9:9—386
9:9–13—388
9:10—446n14
9:23—388
9:30—386
9:30–31—385
9:30–32—388
9:32—385
9:33–37—388
9:33–50—385
9:37—391n88
9:38–41—388
10:1–12—388

10:13–16—388
10:17–31—388
10:29—387
10:32–34—388
10:33–34—385
10:35–37—385
10:35–45—388
10:37—559
10:38—441
10:38–45—385
10:39—441
10:45—376n42, 388
10:46–52—389
10:47–48—389
10:52—389
11:1–11—389
11:1–13—381
11:1–16:8—381, 389, 392
11:12–14—389
11:14—389
11:15–19—389
11:20–21—389
11:22–25—389
11:27–33—389
11:30—441
12:1–2—389
12:9—389
12:11—389
12:13–17—389
12:18–27—389
12:28–34—389
12:35–37—389
12:38–40—389
12:41–44—389
13:2—389
13:5–8—493
13:6—389
13:8—369n29
13:9—387
13:10—389
13:12—389
13:14–27—390
13:19—390
13:19–23—493
13:24–27—493
13:26—559
13:26–27—390
14:1–2—390
14:3–9—390
14:10–11—390
14:12–16—390
14:17–21—390
14:22–24—390
14:25—390
14:26–31—390
14:32–42—390
14:43–50—390
14:58—390, 428
14:62—390, 425
15:2—390
15:6–15—390
15:29—390, 428
15:33—390
15:38—390
16:1–8—391
16:9—391n88
16:9–20—391n88
16:10—391n88
16:11—391n88
16:12–13—391n88
16:14—391n88
16:15–16—391n88
16:16—391n88, 441
16:17—391n88
16:17–18—391n88
16:18—391n88
16:19—391n88
16:20—391n88

Luke

1–3—393, 394
1:1–4—394
1:3—394
1:4—394
1:5—395
1:10—402
1:12—393
1:13—394, 402
1:14—393
1:15—394
1:16–17—394
1:20—395
1:29—393
1:30–31—394
1:32—196n119, 394
1:32–33—395
1:34–38—395
1:46—393
1:46–55—395, 402
1:47—393
1:50—393
1:51–53—395
1:54—395
1:55—395
1:57—395
1:58—393
1:64—393, 395
1:65—393
1:66—396
1:67–79—402
1:68—393, 538
1:68–69—395
1:68–79—395
1:70–71—395
1:72—393, 395
1:73—395
1:74—395
1:74–75—395
1:77—395
1:78—393
1:78–79—395
2:1–20—395
2:9—393
2:13—393, 402
2:14—393, 396
2:18—393
2:19—393, 396
2:20—393, 402
2:22–24—396
2:25—396
2:27—396
2:28—393, 396
2:28–32—402
2:32—393
2:34—396
2:37—393
2:37–38—396, 402
2:38—393, 396
2:39—396
2:47—393
2:48—393
2:50—393, 401
2:51—396
3:1–9—396
3:3—441
3:7—441
3:10–17—396
3:12—441
3:16—441
3:16–17—398
3:21—402, 441
3:23–38—396
3:38—396
4—393, 396, 432
4:1—396
4:2—396, 397
4:3–13—397
4:10–11—161
4:14—393
4:15—393
4:16–21—397
4:22—393
4:23—393
4:24–27—397
4:28–29—397
4:30—397
4:31–37—432
4:31–41—397
4:32—393
4:36—393
4:37—393
4:42–44—397
5–9—393, 397
5:4–6—397
5:5—397
5:8—393, 397
5:9—393
5:10—393, 397
5:11—397
5:12—393
5:12–14—397
5:15—393, 397
5:16—397, 402
5:17–24—397
5:24—397
5:25—393
5:25–26—398
5:26—393
5:27—398
5:27–32—398
5:33—402
5:33–39—398
5:36—393
5:36–39—398
6:1–5—398
6:6–11—398, 432
6:12—402
6:12–16—398
6:17–49—398
6:28—402
7:1–10—398
7:9—398
7:11–17—432
7:13—393
7:15—398n108
7:15–17—398
7:16—393
7:17—393
7:18–19—398
7:20—441
7:22—398
7:23–24—398
7:29—441
7:29–30—399
7:30—441
7:33—441
7:35—398, 399, 399n111
7:36–50—399
7:41–50—399
7:50—399
8:1–3—399
8:2—391n88
8:4–15—399
8:9–10—373n37
8:10—393, 401
8:13—393
8:16—393
8:19–20—399
8:21—399
8:22–25—399
8:25—393, 399
8:26–39—399
8:28—393
8:35—393
8:38—393
8:39—393, 399
8:40–56—399
8:42–48—432
8:56—393
9:1–6—399
9:7–9—399

9:10—399
9:11–17—399
9:18—402
9:19—441
9:22—400, 430
9:23—400
9:24—387, 393, 400
9:25—400
9:26—393, 400
9:27–36—400
9:28–36—402
9:29—393
9:31—50, 359, 401, 403
9:32—393
9:34—393
9:35—400, 400n113
9:37–43—401
9:43—393, 401
9:44—400, 401
9:45—393, 401
9:46–48—401
9:48—393
9:49—393
9:49–50—401
9:51–19:27—393, 401
9:54—445
10:1—393
10:2—402
10:17—393
10:18—402
10:19—391n88, 402
10:21—393
10:21–22—393, 401, 402
11:1–4—402
11:2—393
11:5–13—402
11:14—393
11:14–23—403
11:28—403
11:38—441
11:49–51—429
12:5—393
12:8–9—393
12:13–21—403
12:40—393
12:49—403, 403n118
12:50—400, 403, 441
13:1–9—403
13:13—393
13:17—393, 403
13:32–33—400
13:35—393
14:11—403
15:6—393
15:9–10—393
15:17–19—403
15:21—403
17:13—403
17:15—393
17:16—393
17:18—393
17:19—403
17:24—393
17:25—400
17:30—393
18:1—402
18:8—393, 403
18:9–14—402
18:13—403
18:32–33—400
18:33—430
18:34—393, 401
18:37—403
18:39—403
18:42—403
18:43—393
19:6—393
19:28–24:53—393, 403
19:29—393
19:37—393
19:37–40—403
19:38—393
19:41–44—403
19:45–48—403
19:46—402
20:9–18—403
20:19–26—403
20:26—393
20:27–40—403
20:40—441
20:47—402
21:5–24—493
21:5–36—403
21:8—393
21:12—393
21:25–27—493
21:27—393
21:28—493
21:34–36—393
21:36—402
22:6—404
22:14–20—403
22:17—393
22:19—393
22:32—402, 430
23:34—430
22:37—302, 403n120, 404
23:40—393, 402
22:41—402
23:43—396n105
22:44—402
22:45–46—402
22:68—425
22:69—393
23:47—393
24—432
24–Acts 1—394
24:6–7—400
24:7—430
24:11—391n88
24:12—393, 404
24:13–17—404
24:13–35—391n88
24:14—391n88
24:16—393, 401, 404
24:25–26—400
24:25–27—429
24:26—393, 425, 430, 494
24:31—393, 404
24:31–32—401
24:32—393
24:37—393
24:41—391n88
24:44—60, 61
24:44–46—404, 429
24:45—393, 401
24:46—400, 430
24:46–47—431n155
24:47—393
24:47–53—404
24:50–53—391n88
24:52—393
24:53—393

John

1–12—415
1:1—380–81, 406, 419
1:1–2—406
1:1–5—405
1:1–18—405
1:4—406
1:4–5—406
1:5—406n126
1:6–8—405, 406
1:9—405, 406, 410
1:10–11—405, 406, 407
1:12—406n128
1:12–13—405, 406, 406n128
1:13—406n128, 407
1:14—405, 406, 410, 418n140
1:15—405
1:16–18—405, 406
1:17—104n78, 406
1:18—406
1:19—408
1:19–12:50—405, 407
1:20—408
1:21—408
1:23—407
1:25—407, 408, 441
1:26—441
1:28—441
1:29—409, 415
1:31—441
1:32–33—418n140
1:33—408, 441
1:36—408
1:38—408
1:41—408
1:45—408
1:49—408
1:51—408, 418n140
2—408, 410, 415
2:3—408
2:6—408
2:7—408
2:8–9—408
2:10—408
2:11—406
2:13—409
2:13–25—408
2:14–16—409
2:17—409
2:17–21—428
2:19—50, 379, 409, 418n140
2:20—409
2:21—409
2:22—409
2:23—409
3—410
3:1–12—406
3:3—407
3:3–8—406n128
3:5—407
3:6—407
3:7—407
3:8—407, 410
3:14—410
3:16–17—410
3:17–18—391n88
3:18—410
3:19–20—410
3:19–21—406
3:21—410
3:22—441
3:23—441
3:26—441
3:29—410
3:36—58, 406
4—410
4:1—441
4:2—441
4:10–14—97, 411
4:46–54—410
4:50—410
4:53—410
5—415
5:1—409, 410
5:2–19—410
5:19–47—411
5:22–23—410
5:23—411
5:24—407
5:25—411
5:25–29—406

5:26—411
5:27—411
5:29—406, 411
5:30—411
5:31–32—411
5:33–35—411
5:36—411
5:37–38—411
5:39—411, 429
5:44—411, 415, 429
5:45–46—411
5:46—429
6—410, 415
6:1–14—412
6:1–15—411
6:4—409
6:16–21—411
6:20—412
6:29—411
6:32–33—411
6:35—411, 412
6:37—411
6:39—411
6:40—407, 411
6:44—407, 411
6:47—411
6:48—412
6:50—411
6:51—411, 412
6:53–57—411
6:54—411
6:58—411
6:60—407
6:63—407, 411
6:65—407, 411
7–8—411
7:1—411
7:2—409
7:6—411
7:7—411
7:8—411
7:18—412
7:19—411
7:20—411
7:25—411
7:30—411
7:32—411
7:37–39—97, 411
7:39—406, 418n140
7:44—411
7:53–8:11—411n133
8:12—406, 411, 412
8:14—418
8:19—411
8:20—411
8:23—411
8:24—412
8:28—412
8:29—412
8:34—411
8:37—411
8:38—411
8:40—411
8:43—407, 411
8:44—81, 81n40, 83, 406, 411, 532n180
8:45—411
8:47—411
8:51—407
8:52—412
8:54—406, 412
8:58—412
8:59—411
9:3—412
9:5—412
9:24—412
9:40—412
9:41—412
10—412, 413
10:7—412
10:9—412
10:11—412, 418n140
10:14—412
10:17–18—418n140
10:22—409
10:35—25
10:40—441
11—412, 415
11:4—406, 412
11:25—412
11:25–26—406
11:26—412
11:40—412
11:43–44—412
11:49–52—418n140
11:50—418
11:51–52—196n119
11:55—409
12—413, 419
12:1—409
12:13—413, 413n134
12:14–15—413
12:15—413
12:16—406, 413
12:20–23—413
12:23—413
12:24—413
12:25—413
12:27—413
12:28—414
12:31—57, 414, 414n135
12:32—414
12:33—414
12:34—414
12:35–36—414
12:37–38—414
12:39—407, 414
12:39–40—415
12:40—414
12:41—414
12:42–43—415
12:43—411
13—419
13–17—415n137
13–18:27—415
13–20—405, 415
13:1–11—415
13:1–35—415n137
13:12–17—415
13:18—415
13:26—415
13:27–30—415
13:31—406
13:32—406, 416, 416n138
13:34—417
13:34–35—416
13:36–38—415n137
14:1–4—417
14:1–14—415n137
14:5–11—417
14:6—412
14:12—391n88
14:12–31—417
14:15–17—428
14:15–26—415n137
14:17—407, 418n140
14:20—497
14:27–31—415n137
15:1—412
15:1–6—417
15:1–11—497
15:1–17—415n137
15:7—417
15:8—417
15:9—417
15:11—417
15:12–17—417
15:18–25—417, 430
15:26–27—417
16—417
16:1–4—417
16:5–15—415n137, 417
16:7—418n140, 428
16:14—406
16:16–28—415n137
16:29–33—415n137
16:33—417, 493
17—417, 419
17:1—406, 417
17:1–26—415n137
17:4–5—417
17:5—406
17:6—417
17:8—417
17:9—417
17:10—406
17:10–13—417
17:11—417
17:14—417
17:17—25, 417
17:19—417
17:20—417
17:21—417, 497
17:21–23—417
17:22—417
17:23—417
17:24—417
17:26—417, 497
18:1–14—418
18:5—412
18:14—418
18:19–24—418
18:28–38—418
18:28–19:42—415
18:39–40—418
19:30—418n140
19:34—97
19:38–42—418
20:1–10—418
20:1–29—415
20:11–18—391n88, 418
20:19—391n88
20:19–23—419
20:21–23—428
20:22—418n140
20:23—418n140
20:24–29—419
20:26—391n88
20:30–31—419
20:31—407
21—405, 418
21:1–14—418
21:15–23—418
21:24–25—418

Acts

1—4
1–3—424
1–7—419, 420, 424, 432
1:1—403
1:1–11—421
1:1–31—431
1:2—391n88
1:3—424
1:5—441
1:6—424
1:7–8—424
1:8—358, 419, 419n145, 420
1:9—424
1:10—424
1:11—391n88, 424
1:12–14—424
1:12–26—421
1:15—423
1:16–20—425
1:22—391n88, 424, 441

2—424
2–3—432
2–28—391n88
2:1–4—425
2:1–12—421, 425
2:3–4—391n88
2:5–11—425
2:11—422
2:14–21—425
2:14–26—420
2:14–47—421
2:16–21—425
2:22—425
2:23—425, 430, 434
2:23–24—425, 425n151
2:24—425, 426, 430
2:24–31—283
2:24–32—432
2:29—425
2:30a—425
2:30b—425
2:31a—425
2:31b—425
2:32—426
2:33—422
2:34–35—426
2:36—422, 426
2:37—426
2:38—401, 420n147, 426, 431n155, 441
2:39—434
2:40—426
2:41—423, 426, 434, 441
2:42–47—424
2:43—421n149
2:47—422, 423, 426, 434
3—426
3–4—424
3:1–10—421, 426, 432
3:1–26—421
3:6—401, 420n147
3:11–26—420
3:13—422
3:14—520n138
3:14–15—426
3:15—425n151, 430
3:16—401, 420n14, 426, 434
3:18—426, 434
3:19—431n155
3:20—426
3:21—426
3:21–24—426
3:22—429
4—426
4–5—421
4–7—424
4:1–7—426
4:4—423
4:7—401, 420n147
4:8–12—427
4:10—401, 420n147, 425n151, 430
4:11—427
4:12—401, 420n147, 426, 431n155
4:13–20—427
4:17—401, 420n14
4:19–20—435
4:21—427
4:21–22—422
4:23–28—427
4:25–26—432
4:27–28—425, 434
4:29—427
4:30—401, 420n147, 421n149, 427
4:31—427
4:31–35—424
5—421, 424
5:1–2—427
5:1–11—421
5:3–10—427
5:5—421n149
5:11—421n14, 427
5:12—421n149
5:12–16—424, 427
5:14—423, 434
5:15—432
5:16—432
5:16–18—432
5:17–18—427
5:28—401, 420n147
5:29—427, 435
5:30—425n151, 427, 430
5:31—422, 427, 431n155, 434
5:39—426
5:40—401, 420n147
5:41—401, 420n147, 424, 427
6—424
6–12—421
6:1—423, 427
6:2–6—427
6:7—423, 424, 427, 431n156
6:9—427
6:11—427, 428
6:13–14—427, 429
6:14—428
7—424
7–8—421
7:1–53—420
7:2—422, 427
7:9—427, 428
7:9–10—428
7:12–15—429
7:17—427
7:23–29—428–29
7:27—428
7:30—427
7:33—427
7:35—429
7:36—429
7:37—429
7:39—429
7:47–48—428
7:48–50—428
7:51—428
7:51–53—428
7:52—520n138
7:53—428
7:54–60—430
7:55–56—391n88, 422
7:60—430
8—432
8–12—419, 420, 431
8:1–4—431
8:4–7—422
8:5–25—431
8:8—422
8:12—401, 420n147, 441
8:13—441
8:16—401, 420n147, 441
8:26–40—431
8:35—422
8:36—441
8:38—441
8:39—422
9—421
9:14—401, 420n147
9:15—401, 419, 420, 420n147
9:16—401, 420n147, 421
9:18—441
9:21—401, 420n147
9:26–30—470n72
9:27—420n147
9:27–28—401
9:28—420n147
9:31—421n149, 423
9:32—439
9:35—423
9:36–43—432
9:42—423
10—432
10:1–48—431
10:9–15—471
10:34–43—420
10:37—441
10:39—430
10:39–40—425n151
10:40—430
10:43—401, 420n147, 431n155
10:46—391n88, 422
10:47—441
10:48—401, 420n147, 441
11—432
11:1–18—431
11:16—441
11:18—422, 434
11:19–30—431
11:21—423
11:24—423, 434
11:29–30—470n72
12:1–5—431
12:6–19—431
12:20–25—431
12:23—422
12:24—423, 431n156
13—432, 444
13–14—420, 433
13–28—419, 420, 421, 432
13:1–4—433n161
13:9–11—433
13:12—433
13:16–47—420
13:24—441
13:28—430
13:28–30—425
13:29–30—433
13:30—430
13:33—432
13:35—283
13:35–37—432
13:37—433
13:38—431n155
13:38–39—433, 434, 471
13:40—433
13:40–41—433
13:45–46—433
13:47—359
13:48—422, 423, 433, 434
13:49—431n156
13:50—433
14:1—423, 433
14:2—433
14:3—421n149
14:4–5—433
14:8–10—432
14:8–18—433
14:12—439
14:15—439
14:19—433
14:20—433
14:22—434, 493
14:23—434
14:27—434
15—420, 432, 433, 434, 470n72
15:2—433n161

15:8–9—434
15:9—434
15:10—471
15:10–11—471
15:11—434
15:17—401, 420n147
15:35–36—433n161
15:36–39—445
16–18—432, 434
16–20—420
16:1–5—434
16:3—435
16:5—423
16:14—434
16:15—441
16:16–18—432
16:18—401, 420n14, 435
16:19–24—435
16:25–34—435
16:33—441
16:34—435
16:35–40—435, 435n164
17—432, 435
17:1–9—494
17:2—494
17:2–3—429
17:3—494
17:4—423
17:5—435, 494
17:6—494
17:6–8—494
17:7—435, 436n166
17:8–9—435n164, 494
17:10—494
17:12—423
17:34—423
17:22–31—420
17:29–31—439
17:31—436
17:32–34—436
18:8—423, 441
18:10—436
18:12–17—435, 435n164
18:18—437
18:22—433n161
18:22–23—433n161
18:24–28—439
18:25—441
18:27—434
19–21—433, 436
19:1–10—436
19:3—441
19:4—441
19:5—401, 420n147, 441
19:6—39n88
19:10—436
19:11–12—432
19:11–20—436
19:13—401, 420n147
19:15—435
19:17—401, 420n147, 422, 436
19:19—436
19:20—436
19:21–41—436
19:35–40—435n164
20—436
20:4—439
20:7–12—432, 436
20:17—504
20:17–38—436
20:18–35—420
20:19—436
20:21—436
20:22—437
20:23—437
20:24—437
20:27—436
20:28—436, 504
20:29–30—506
20:32—436, 568
20:35—436
20:36–38—437
21–23—420
21:4—437
21:11—437, 437n167
21:12—437
21:13—401, 420n147
21:14—437
21:17—433n161
21:17–26—437, 444
21:20—422, 423
21:23–24—437
21:25—437
21:27–36—437n167
22–28—432, 438
22:1–21—420, 438
22:11—422
22:14—520n138
22:16—401, 420n147, 441
22:22–23—438
22:24–29—438
22:25–29—435n164
23:1–10—438
23:11—438
23:12–35—438
23:13–16—438
23:29—435n164
24–26—420
24:1–21—438
24:10–21—420
24:22–27—435n164, 438
24:25—438
25:1–10—435
25:1–12—438
25:8—435
25:9—435n164
25:11—435, 435n164
25:13–26:32—438
25:19—435
25:25–27—436
25:26–27—435n164
26:1–29—420
26:12–18—438
26:22–23—438
26:24—510
26:32—435n164, 436, 438
27–28—420
27:10–11—438
27:21—438
27:23–26—238
27:27–44—438
27:31—438
27:33–36—438
28—420
28:1–6—438
28:3–4—391n88
28:7–10—438
28:11–16—438
28:14—438
28:17–31—438
28:24—423
28:25–27—359
28:28—359

Romans

1–4—449
1–11—451
1:1—452
1:1–4—453n32
1:1–7—449, 451, 452
1:3—452
1:4—452
1:5—452, 453
1:8–15—449
1:16—453, 507
1:16–17—449, 451, 453
1:16b–15:13—454
1:17—453
1:18—453
1:18–20—242
1:18–32—292, 453
1:18–3:20—449, 453
1:18–3:26—453
1:18–4:25—452
1:21—95, 150, 452
1:22—292
1:24—349
1:25—463, 538
1:26—349
1:28—292, 349
2:1–3:18—453
2:4—235
2:12–15—242
2:24—452
2:29—243
3:4—155
3:16–17—453n34
3:19—453
3:19–20—453
3:20—111n99, 453
3:21–22—113
3:21–26—449, 452, 453, 495
3:23—95, 452, 453
3:24—453
3:24–25—453
3:24–26—57, 105, 562
3:25—453
3:25–26—448, 454
3:26—453n34, 454
3:26a—454
3:26b—454
3:27—111n99
3:27–31—449
4:1–25—449
4:5—453, 454
4:17—71
4:20—340, 452
4:20–21—147
5–8—448, 449, 450
5:1—562
5:1–11—450
5:2—452
5:9–11—562
5:12–21—450
5:12ff.—396n105
6:1–14—450, 452, 454
6:2—452, 454
6:3—441, 454
6:4—441, 454
6:6—454
6:7—454
6:11—454
6:15–7:6—450
6:17—454
7:7–12—450
7:13–15—446
7:13–25—450
7:25—452
8:1–11—450
8:3—55
8:12–17—450
8:17—452
8:18—450n26, 493
8:18–25—450
8:20—322
8:21—450n26
8:26–30—450
8:28–30—450n26
8:31–38—450
8:34—391n88
8:35—450
8:39—450

9–11—449, 450, 495n110
9:1–5—450
9:5—452, 538
9:6—450
9:6–13—450
9:7–8—83n47
9:8–13—83n47
9:14–18—92, 450, 454
9:15—455
9:18—454
9:19—454
9:19–23—92
9:19–29—450
9:20–21—454
9:22—289n42, 455
9:22–23—452, 454, 455
9:23—452, 455
9:29—83n47
9:30–10:4—450
10—111, 113, 452
10:2—113, 502
10:3—113
10:4—112, 113
10:5—111n99, 112
10:5–8—111, 113
10:5–13—450
10:6—112
10:9—58
10:9–10—113, 495
10:13—54
10:14–21—450
10:17—568
11—448
11:1–6—450
11:5—125
11:7–10—451
11:8—124n129
11:11–24—451
11:20—502
11:25—377
11:25–27—359
11:25–32—451
11:32—452, 456
11:32–36—452
11:33–36—451, 456, 538
11:36—53, 452
12–15—448, 449, 456
12:1—452
12:1–2—451
12:3–8—451
12:9–13—451
12:14–21—451
13—452
13:1–6—451
13:1–7—510, 525
13:7–10—451
13:11–14—451
14:1–6—451
14:1–15:13—451
14:6–9—452
14:7–12—451
14:13–23—451
15:1–6—451
15:7–13—451
15:8–9—452
15:14–16—451
15:17–21—451
15:22–29—451
15:30–33—451
16—449
16:1—505
16:1–23—451
16:17—456
16:17–20—451, 452
16:18—456
16:19—456
16:20—76, 84, 456
16:21—392n96
16:25–27—451, 457, 539
16:27—452

1 Corinthians

1–4—457, 458, 461
1:10—458
1:11—457
1:12–13—458
1:13—441
1:14—441
1:15—441
1:16—441
1:17—441
1:18–25—391n90, 458
1:19—458
1:25—458
1:26–28—458
1:29—458
1:30—458
1:31—458
2:7–13—458
2:14—124
3:4–9—458
3:16—359, 428
3:19—458
4:7—458
4:9—464
4:9–13—458
4:9–16—45
4:16—458
5–7—457, 458
5:1—457
5:1–13—458, 567
5:4—458
5:5—567
5:6–8—458
5:7—359, 458, 517
5:9—461n57
6:1–11—458
6:11—458
6:12–20—459
6:15—458
6:19—35, 428
6:20—35, 459
7:1—457
7:1–40—459
7:23—459
7:25—457
7:28—85
8–10—457, 459
8:1—457
8:4–6—459
8:7–8—459
8:7–13—459
9:1–27—459
9:5—459
9:18—459
9:20—437
9:21—359
10:1–4—356
10:1–6—359
10:1–13—459
10:2—441
10:14–22—459
10:20—480
10:20–21—459
10:23–33—459
10:31—459
11–14—457, 459
11:1—459, 488, 496
11:2–16—460
11:3—460
11:3–16—504n126
11:7—460
11:17–34—460
11:18—457, 460
11:19—460
11:20—460
11:21—460
11:22—460
11:23–26—460
11:26—460
11:33—460
11:34—460
12–14—460
12:1—457
12:13—441
12:21–26—460
12:28—391n88
13:1–13—460
14:3–5—460
14:32–36—504n126
15—457, 460
15:1–11—461
15:7—444
15:12—457
15:12–19—461
15:20–28—461
15:28—449, 461n56
15:29—441
15:29–34—461
15:33—461
15:35–36—445n7
15:35–49—461
15:45—396n105
15:50–58—461
15:58—461
16—457, 461
16:1—457
16:1–4—461
16:5–11—461
16:12—457, 461
16:13–18—461
16:21—498

2 Corinthians

1–7—461, 465
1:3—463, 467, 539
1:3–11—463
1:3–2:13—464
1:4—463
1:4–6—467
1:5—467
1:8–9—467
1:9—463
1:9–10—467
1:11—467
1:12—462
1:12–14—463
1:12–2:13—463
1:13—461
1:15–24—463
1:17—462
2:1–4—463
2:3–4—461n57
2:5–11—464
2:6–7—567
2:12–13—464
2:14—464, 468
2:14–15—462
2:14–16—464n62
2:14–16a—468n68
2:14–17—463, 464, 465, 468
2:15—464, 471
2:15–16—39, 464, 468
2:15–21—471n73
2:16—471, 471n73, 473, 476
2:17—462, 464, 465, 471, 472
2:17–18—472
2:18—472
2:19—472
2:19–20—472
2:21—472
3—467
3:1—462, 464, 472
3:1–18—464
3:1–29—471n73

3:1–4:11—472
3:1–7:16—462
3:2—472, 475
3:2–3—472
3:2–5—477
3:4—473
3:5—472
3:5–6—473
3:6—468, 473
3:6–9—473, 476
3:7—468
3:7–13—462
3:8—473
3:9—468
3:10—473, 474, 474n79
3:10a—473
3:11a—473
3:11b—473
3:12—473, 474n79
3:13—472, 474, 478
3:13–14—477, 478
3:15–18—471n73, 475
3:15–4:11—472
3:16—475, 476
3:17—473
3:18—468, 569
3:18–4:6—39
3:19—473, 476
3:19a—475
3:21—475
3:22—475
3:23—476
3:23–24—476
3:23–25—473
3:24—476
3:25—476
3:26—476
3:27—476
3:28—476
3:29—476
4:1—468
4:1–7—473
4:1–11—476
4:1–18—464
4:2—462
4:3–4—462
4:3b—476
4:4—477
4:5—477, 478
4:6—468, 477
4:7–11—477
4:7–12—462
4:10a—468
4:10b—468
4:11a—468
4:11b—468
4:12—477
4:12a—468
4:12b—468
4:12–6:10—477
4:13–20—477
4:14—468
4:15—468
4:16–18—462
4:17—468, 478, 493
4:21–31—477
4:22—477
4:24—477
4:24–25—471n73, 478
4:27—478, 479
4:28—478
4:30—478
4:31—478
5:1—478
5:1–21—464
5:2—478
5:3—473, 478
5:5—478
5:6—478
5:9—478
5:12—462
5:13–14—478
5:14—466
5:14–15—466
5:15—466, 467
5:16—462
5:17—467
5:19—466
5:19b—466
5:20—467
5:21—465, 466, 467, 467n65
5:22–25—478
6:1–18—465
6:2—478
6:4—462
6:4–10—462
6:7–10—478
6:11–18—478
6:12—478
6:13—478
6:14—477, 479
6:14–7:1—46
6:15—479
7:1–7—465
7:8—468
7:8–12—465
7:9–10—469
7:11—462
7:11–13—469
7:13–16—465
8–9—461, 465
8:1–5—465
8:1–9:15—463
8:4—465
8:6–8—465
8:9—465, 467n66
8:16–24—465
9:1–4—465
9:5–15—465
10–13—461
10:1—462, 465, 498
10:1–6—465
10:1–13:13—463
10:2–3—462
10:7–11—465
10:9–11—462
10:12—462
10:12–18—465
10:18—462
11:1–4—465
11:4—461, 463
11:5–15—465
11:14–15—463
11:16–33—462, 465
11:30—465
11:31—463, 539
12:1–6—465
12:7–10—465
12:9—465
12:9–10—467
12:11—462, 465, 466
12:11–18—465
12:19–21—465
13:1–5—466
13:3–4—467n66, 469
13:4—465
13:4b—469
13:14—463

Galatians

1:1—469, 470
1:1–5—469
1:3–4a—470
1:3–5—470
1:4b—470
1:4–5—539
1:5—470
1:6—470
1:6–10—469, 470
1:7—470
1:8—470
1:8–9—446
1:9—470
1:10—470
1:11—470
1:11–2:21—469, 470
1:12—470
1:13–14—470
1:15–22—470
1:16—470
1:18—444
1:18–19—470, 471n72
1:19—444
1:24—470
2:1–2—471
2:1–10—470, 470n72
2:3—471, 509
2:4–5—471
2:6–10—471
2:9—444
2:11—445
2:11–13—471
2:13—471
2:14a—471
2:14b—471
2:14c—471
2:15—471
2:16—471
3—111
3:1–4:11—469
3:3—470
3:10–12—471
3:10–14—111n100
3:12—111nn99–100
3:13—470
3:14—81
3:15–4:7—112
3:16—84, 456
3:26–29—456
3:27—441
4:12–6:10—469
4:17—470
4:19–20—470
4:23—470
5:2—498
5:2–3—113
5:3—470, 471
5:11—504
6:11—498
6:11–18—469
6:12–13—470

Ephesians

1—479
1:3—463, 479, 480, 539
1:3–4—480
1:3–14—483
1:4—479
1:4–6—480
1:5—480
1:6—480
1:7—480
1:7–12—481
1:8–10—480
1:9—480
1:11–12—481
1:13–14—481
1:15–16—481
1:15–22—482
1:17—481
1:17–19—481
1:18—481
1:19—481, 482
1:19–20—483
1:20—391n88
1:20–23—481, 482
1:21—484
1:23—483
2—481

2:1–3—480, 482
2:1–3:13—483
2:2—480, 484
2:3—482
2:4–5—482
2:5—482
2:5–6—482
2:7—482, 484
2:8—482, 484
2:8–10—482
2:10—484
2:11–12—482
2:13—482
2:14—482
2:14–16—484
2:15—482
2:16—482
2:17—482
2:18—482
2:19–22—51, 482
2:20—374n40
2:20–22—483n92
3—479, 482
3:1—482, 498
3:2—482
3:2–13—480
3:3—479, 480, 482
3:3–6—481
3:4–6—480
3:4b–6—479
3:5—479
3:6—480
3:8—482
3:9—479
3:10—479, 480, 482, 484
3:11—479
3:13—482
3:14–19—482
3:14–20—565
3:16–19—482
3:19—482
3:20–21—480, 483, 539
3:21—484, 565
4–6—479
4:1—484
4:1–7—483
4:5—441
4:8—483, 483n93, 484
4:9–16—483
4:10—444
4:12—565
4:17–19—482
4:17–32—483
4:22—483
4:24—483
5:1—484
5:1–17—483
5:18—483n92
5:21–33—504n126
6:1–4—483
6:5–9—484
6:10–17—484
6:10–18—391n88
6:12—484

Philippians

1:3–8—485
1:3–11—484
1:9—485
1:10a—485
1:10b—485
1:11—485
1:12–18—485
1:12–26—484
1:13—485
1:17—485
1:18—485
1:19–20—485
1:21a—485
1:21b—486
1:22a—485
1:23—486
1:24–25—485
1:24–26—485
1:25—486
1:26—485
1:27a—486
1:27b—486
1:27–2:18—484
1:28—484
1:28a—486
1:28b—486
1:29b—486
1:30—486
2:1—486
2:2—486
2:3–4—486
2:4—486
2:5–11—484, 486
2:6–7a—486
2:6–11—486
2:7b—486
2:8—486
2:9—486
2:10—486
2:11—486
2:12–13—487
2:12–18—487
2:14—487
2:15—487
2:16–18—485
2:19–24—487
2:19–30—485
2:25–30—485
3:1–3—485
3:1–6—487
3:4–6—487
3:4–14—485
3:7—487
3:8—487
3:9—487
3:10—487
3:11—487
3:15—487
3:15–4:9—485
3:18b–19a—488
3:17—487
3:17–21—484
3:18–19—456
3:20b–21—488
4:1–3—485
4:1–5—488
4:6—488
4:7—488
4:8—488
4:9—488
4:10–18—485
4:10–19—488
4:20—488, 539
4:22—485
4:23—488

Colossians

1:3–8—489, 492n109
1:4—490
1:6–7—488
1:9—489
1:9–12—489
1:10—489
1:11—489
1:12—489
1:13—490, 491
1:13–14—489
1:13–20—489
1:14—491
1:15—489
1:15–20—489
1:16—489, 491
1:17–18—489
1:19—489, 491
1:20—489
1:21—490
1:21–22—491
1:22—490, 491
1:23—498
1:24—493, 522n161
1:24a—492
1:24b—492
1:27—490
2:1—488
2:3—490, 491
2:4—488, 490
2:5—490
2:6—491
2:7—490, 491
2:8—488, 490, 492
2:9—490, 491
2:10—490, 491
2:11—490, 491
2:11–13—243
2:12—441, 490, 491
2:13—490
2:13–14—491
2:13a—490
2:13b—490
2:14a—490
2:14b—490
2:14–15—495
2:15—456, 491
2:16—488
2:16–17—490
2:18—490
2:18–19—488
2:19—490
2:20—488
2:20a—490
2:20b—490
2:21–23—490
2:23—490
3:1—391n88, 490
3:3—490
3:3–4—490
3:9—490
3:10—490
3:15–16—492
3:17—490, 491
3:17–19—504n126
3:18a—492
3:18b—492
3:19—492
3:20—491, 492
3:21—492
3:22–4:1—492
3:23—490
3:24—490
4:7—491
4:17—491
4:18—498

1 Thessalonians

1:3—495, 496
1:5—495
1:6—495, 496
1:7—496
1:8—495, 496
1:9—495, 496
1:10—495n111, 496
2:2—495
2:2–13—495
2:3—495
2:3–6—497
2:4—495
2:8—495
2:9—495
2:12—496
2:13—495
2:13–16—495n110
2:14—495, 496
2:14–16—495, 496

2:15a—496
2:15b—496
2:15–16a—495
2:16—496
2:18—494, 495, 498
2:19—496
2:19–20—497
3:3—496
3:3–4—493, 494, 495
3:4—496
3:5—494, 495
3:5–6—496
3:6—495, 496
3:8–9—497
4:2–8—496
4:5–6—495
4:9–12—496
4:13—496
4:13–18—496
4:14—495, 495n111
4:14–15—495
4:15—495, 495n111
4:16–17—496
5:2—496
5:3—495, 496
5:7—495
5:8—495, 496
5:9—495, 496
5:9–10—495, 495n111
5:10—495
5:12–28—496
5:14—567
5:18—496
5:23—495n111, 496
5:27—497

2 Thessalonians

1—497, 499
1:1—497
1:3—497, 499
1:3–4—497
1:4—497
1:5—497, 498
1:5–10—425
1:6—57, 498, 560
1:6–10—57, 499
1:6b–10b—497
1:7—498
1:7b—497
1:7b–10b—498
1:8—498
1:9—498
1:10—498
1:10a–b—498
1:10b—499
1:10c—498
1:11a—498
1:11b—498
1:12—498
1:14a—497
2—497, 499
2:1a—498
2:1–2—499
2:2—498n116
2:2c—498
2:3—499
2:3–4—493
2:3–8—499
2:3–14—499
2:8—493
2:8b—499
2:9–12—499
2:10–12—349
2:13—499
2:13–14—493
2:14—499
2:15–17—499
3—497
3:1—499
3:3—499
3:4—499
3:5—499
3:6—499
3:6–15—567
3:7–10a—500
3:10b—500
3:11—499
3:12—500
3:13–15—500
3:16–18—500
3:17—498, 498n116

1 Timothy

1—500
1:3—501
1:3–11—505
1:3–19—502
1:4—501
1:5—501, 506
1:6—501
1:7—501, 505
1:8–9a—501
1:8–11—501
1:9b–10—501
1:11—501
1:12—501, 507
1:12–17—501, 505
1:13—502
1:13a—501
1:14—502
1:15—501
1:16—502
1:17—502, 539
1:18–19—502
1:18–21—505
1:19—502, 505
1:20—502, 567
2–3—505n130
2:1–2—503
2:1–8—500, 504, 505
2:3–4—503
2:3–7—503
2:5–6—503
2:7—503
2:8—502, 503
2:9—503
2:9–10—503
2:9–12—504
2:9–15—500, 503n122, 505
2:11—503
2:12—503, 504
2:13–14—503
2:13–15—504
2:15—503
3:1–2a—505
3:1–7—500, 505
3:2—505
3:2b—505
3:3—505
3:4–5—505
3:6—505
3:7—505
3:8–10—500, 505
3:8–13—500, 505
3:9—505
3:11—500, 505
3:12—505
3:14–15—500, 505
3:15—514
3:16—391n8, 500, 505, 505n130
4:1—456
4:1–2—456
4:1–3—493, 501, 505
4:1–3a—506
4:1–4—500
4:2—505
4:3a—506
4:3b–5—506
4:5–16—500
4:6—500
4:6–10—506
4:7—505
4:11—500
4:11–16—506
4:15—500
4:16—506
5:1–2—500, 506
5:3–16—500, 506
5:7—500
5:11–15—505
5:17—505
5:17–18—500, 506
5:17–25—506
5:19—506
5:19–25—501
5:20—506
5:21—500, 506
5:22—506
5:23—506
5:24–25—506
6:1–2—501
6:2—500
6:2b–5—501
6:4—505
6:5—505
6:6–10—501
6:11–16—501
6:12—506
6:14–16—506
6:15–16—463, 539
6:17–19—501
6:20–21—501

2 Timothy

1:6—507
1:8—507
1:8–10—508
1:8–12—493
1:9—507
1:10—507
1:12—507
1:13—508
1:15—508
1:16–18—508
1:18—508
2:1—507
2:3—493, 507
2:8–10—493
2:9—508
2:9–10—507
2:10—481n90, 508
2:11—507
2:12—507
2:13—507
2:15—507
2:16–18—508
2:17–19—508
2:23—508
3:1–8—508
3:2–6—456
3:8–9—508
3:10–11—507
3:10–12—508
3:13—508
3:15—273n7
4:3—508
4:5—507
4:6–7—507
4:8—508, 539
4:11—444
4:14–15—508
4:16–17—508
4:16–18—508

Titus

1:1—509, 510
1:1–4—509
1:2—509

1:5—504, 509
1:5–9—509
1:6–8—509
1:7—504
1:9—509
1:10—509
1:10–11—509
1:10–15—509
1:12—509
1:13—509
1:14—509
2:1–10—509
2:1–3:15—509
2:4–5—509n136
2:11–15—509
2:13—509
2:14—509
3:1—510
3:1–2—510
3:2—510
3:3—510
3:4–5a—510
3:5—391n88
3:5b—510
3:6–8—510
3:8–11—510
3:10–11—567

Philemon

1:1—510
1:1–2—510
1:4–5—511
1:6—511
1:8—511
1:8–9—511
1:9—510
1:10—511, 512
1:11a—510
1:11b—510
1:12—510
1:13—510
1:16—512
1:17—511
1:18—512
1:19—498, 512
1:21—511
1:22—511

Hebrews

1:1–2a—516
1:1–3—517
1:1–4—515, 516
1:2b—516
1:2c—516
1:3—391n88
1:3a—515
1:3a–b—516
1:3c—516
1:3d—516
1:4—516
1:5–13—516
1:5–2:18—516
2:1–4—516, 517
2:2—518
2:3—444, 518
2:3–4—391n88
2:6ff.—396n105
2:10—40
3:1–6—516, 517
3:5–4:13—516
3:7–11—518
3:7–19—517
3:12–15—518
3:16–19—518
4:1—518
4:1–13—517
4:2—518
4:3—518
4:6—518
4:11—518
4:14–5:4—516, 517
5:5–7:28—516, 517
6:2—441
6:4–5—518
6:6—518
6:10—518
6:13–20—517
8:1—391n88
8:1–13—516, 517
8:10–12—518
8:13—518
9:1–28—517
9:1–10:39—516
9:10—441
9:14—519
9:27—518
10:1–39—517
10:12—391n88
10:24–25—444
10:26—112
10:28—518
10:29—518
10:32–35—517n152
10:32–38—493
10:37–39—518
11:1–40—516, 517
11:3—71
11:10—517
11:13–16—122
11:16—517
11:17—494
11:17–19—88
11:23–28—113n104
11:25—203
11:26—356
11:40—517
12:1–17—516
12:1–29—517
12:2—391n88
12:7–11—567
12:14—568
12:18–27—516
12:25—518
12:26–27—518
12:28–29—516
13:1–25—516
13:5—517
13:10–15—516
13:11–15—517
13:14—517
13:17—568
13:20–21—518, 539
13:22—517n152

James

1:1—519
1:2—493
1:2–4—519, 520, 521
1:5—521, 522
1:5–8—519, 520, 522
1:9—520
1:9–10—521
1:9–11—519, 520, 522
1:10–11—519
1:12—520, 521, 522
1:12–15—522
1:13—175, 521
1:13–14—520
1:13–15—520, 522
1:16—520
1:17—72, 520
1:18—519, 520
1:19—521
1:19–21—520
1:21–25—521
1:22—521, 522
1:22–25—520
1:26—521, 522
1:26–27—520
1:27—521
2–5—519
2:1—522
2:1–11—521
2:1–13—520
2:3—521
2:6—519
2:7—519, 521
2:10—113
2:12—521
2:13—522
2:14–26—521
2:17–19—557n11
3:1—521
3:1–12—521
3:2–8—521
3:9—522
3:9–12—522
3:13–18—520, 521, 522
3:14—512
3:14–16—522
3:18—522
4:1–2—522
4:1–6—521
4:3–5—522
4:4—519
4:6–9—522
4:7–10—521
4:10—522
4:11—521
4:11–12—522
4:13–16—521
4:13–17—522
4:17—521
5:1—521
5:1–5—519
5:1–6—445, 522
5:3–6—521
5:4—521
5:6—519
5:7—522
5:7–8—521
5:7–11—522
5:8—519
5:9—521, 522
5:10—521
5:11—104n78, 301
5:12–20—521
5:13–16—391n88
5:13–18—522
5:16—522
5:19–20—522

1 Peter

1:1—522n161, 523, 525
1:1–12—522
1:1–2:10—522, 523
1:2—523
1:3—523, 524, 539
1:3–12—523n162
1:4—534
1:5—524
1:6—524
1:6–7—524
1:6–9—528
1:7—523
1:8—523, 524
1:9—524
1:10–12—426, 524
1:13—524
1:13–16—524
1:13–2:10—522
1:14–16—524
1:16—524
1:17—522n161
1:17–21—524
1:18–19—524
1:18–21—524
1:20—426

1:21—426, 523
1:22—524
1:22–25—525
1:23a—524
1:23b—524
1:25—524, 525
2:4–5—51, 525
2:5—522n161, 525
2:9—523, 525
2:9–10—522n161
2:10—525
2:11—522, 522n161, 525
2:11b–12—525
2:11–4:11—522, 525
2:12—523
2:12–23—523n161
2:13–17—523, 525, 526
2:17—526
2:18–20—528
2:18–25—523, 525, 526
2:21—496, 526
2:22—526n164
2:24—526, 526n164
2:25—526n164
3:1–7—504n12, 523, 526
3:4—526
3:5–6—523n161
3:8–12—526
3:8–4:11—523
3:13–17—526
3:13–22—528
3:18–20—526
3:21—391n88, 441, 523n161, 526
3:22—391n88
4:1—523n161
4:1–5—528
4:1–11—526
4:11—523, 539
4:12—522
4:12–13—527
4:12–19—523, 523n161, 528
4:12–5:14—523, 527
4:13—523
4:14—523
4:14–19—527
4:16—523
4:17—527
5:1—523
5:1–2—504
5:1–5—523, 527
5:4—523
5:6–14—523, 527
5:9–10—528
5:10—523
5:11—523, 539

2 Peter

1—529
1:1—529
1:2–3—528
1:3—529
1:4a—529
1:4b—529
1:5–11—529
1:12–13—530
1:12–15—529
1:16—529
1:16–18—529
1:16–21—530
1:17—529
1:18—529
1:19–20—529
2—529
2:1–3—529, 529n174
2:4—529
2:5—529, 529n174
2:6—529n174
2:6–8—529
2:8–9—529n174
2:9—529n174
2:9–10—529n174, 530
2:10b–16—230
2:15–16—529n174
2:17–19—530
2:20–2:22—530
2:21—496
3—529, 530
3:1—528
3:1–2—530
3:3–4—530
3:5–6—530
3:7–10—530
3:9—530
3:11–14—530
3:15—530
3:15–16—444, 530
3:16—530
3:17–18a—530
3:18—529
3:18b—530

1 John

1:1–4—531
1:2—533
1:3—533
1:6—532, 533
1:7—533, 534
1:8—532
1:8–10—446
1:9—533, 534
1:10—532, 533
2:1—531
2:1–2—533
2:2—534
2:3—446
2:4—532
2:9—532
2:10—535
2:11—532
2:12—533, 534
2:14—534
2:15—531, 532
2:16—531
2:17—531
2:18—532
2:19—532
2:20—535
2:22—532
2:23—532
2:24—534, 535
2:25—533
2:27—535
2:28—534
3:1—531
3:2—534
3:4—532
3:5—533
3:6—532
3:8—532, 532n180, 534
3:8–15—81, 81n40
3:9—534, 535
3:10—83, 532
3:12—83, 531, 532n180
3:13—531
3:14—532, 534
3:15—532, 533
3:24—535
4:1—531, 533
4:3—533
4:4—531, 534
4:5—531, 533
4:6—533, 534
4:7—534
4:8—532
4:9—533
4:10—533, 534
4:11–12—534
4:12–13—535
4:14—534
4:15—534
4:15–16—535
4:16—534
4:19—534
4:20—532
5:1—534
5:4—534
5:4–5—531
5:5—534
5:9–10—534
5:10—532, 533
5:11—533
5:12—352, 533
5:13—533
5:16—533
5:18—534
5:19—531, 533, 534
5:20—533, 534

2 John

1:1—535
1:1–4—535
1:3—535
1:4—535
1:5—535
1:5–6—535
1:7—535
1:7–10—567
1:8—535
1:9—535
1:10—535
1:10–11—535

3 John

1:3–4—535
1:5–6—535
1:7—535
1:9—535
1:9–12—567
1:10—535
1:11—535
1:12—535

Jude

1:1—444
1:1–2—536
1:3—536
1:3–4—536
1:4—536
1:5–7—536
1:7—536
1:8–16—536
1:11—536
1:14–16—536
1:17–21—536
1:22–23—536
1:24–25—536, 539

Revelation

1:1—43n37
1:1–8—541, 544, 545
1:5—546
1:5–6—539
1:7—51
1:9—493
1:9–3:22—542, 544
1:9–20—542
1:9–22:9—542
1:10—542
1:11—542
1:17–20—542
2–3—542, 545, 546

2:1–7—436
2:2—535
2:10—493
3:21—391n88
4—545
4–5—542
4–6—545
4–16—542
4:1–6:17—544
4:1–16:21—542
4:2—542, 545
4:4—198
4:5—542
4:6—542
4:11—53
5—545
5:5—545
5:5–6—546
5:6—546
6—542, 545
6–16—542
6:1–17—545
6:11—493
7—545, 546
7–8—546
7:1–9:21—544
7:9—547
8–9—545, 546
8:3–4—546
8:5—542
8:7—547
8:8–9—547
8:10–11—547
8:12—547
9:1–11—547
9:12–19—547
10:1—547
10:1–11—544, 545, 546
11—544
11:1–14—543, 544, 546
11:3—544
11:5—544
11:7—544
11:15—543n9
11:15–19—543, 544, 546
11:17–18—59
11:19—542
12—544
12:1–6—321n85
12:1–17—456, 495
12:1–13:10—544, 546
12:6—544
12:12–17—544
12:13–16—84
12:13–17—321n85
12:14—544, 548
12:17—84
13:7—544
13:11–18—544, 545, 546
14—545, 546
14:1–19:10—544
14:6–7—57
14:8—548
15–19—545, 545n12, 546
15:1–19:10—545
15:3–4—548
15:8—548
16—545n12
16:2—547
16:3—547
16:4–7—547
16:8–9—547
16:10–11—547
16:12–15—547
16:17–21—547
16:18—542
16:19—548
17:1—543, 545n12
17:1–19:10—545n12
17:1–22:9—542
17:3—542, 543
17:17—175
18:1–19:8—541
18:1–19:10—545n12
18:2—548
18:4—548
19—545, 548
19–20—51
19:1–3—549
19:1–8—58
19:9–10—543
19:11–19—545
19:11–20:15—544, 545
19:11–21—425, 546, 548
19:11–21:8—543
20—545
20:1–6—548
20:4—499n117
20:7–10—549
20:11—545
20:11–15—549
20:12—545
20:15—545
21–22—51, 546, 549
21:1–22:7—544, 545
21:9–10—543
21:10—542
21:22—51
21:23–24—51
22:6—543
22:8–9—543
22:8–21—544
22:6–9—542n3
22:7—542n3
22:10—542n3
22:10–21—542, 545

Apocrypha

2 Esdras

14:44–45—229n195

Additions to Esther

1:1d–j—321n85
10:3a–i—321n85

1 Maccabees

14:41—396n104

Sirach

2:11—104n
5:4–7—104n
49:10—229n195

Pseudepigrapha

2 Baruch

40:3—548n20

4 Ezra

7:28–29—548n20

Jubilees

1:20—162n46
15:33—162n46
20:1—162n46

Mart. Isa.

1:8—162n46
2:4—162n46
4:2—162n46

Test. Zebulun

9:8—397n106

Qumran

CD

16:5—162n46

1QM

13:31—162n46

Talmud

b.Sanhedrin

99a—548n20